2002

COLLEGE & UNIVERSITY ALMANAC

PETERSON'S
THOMSON LEARNING™

Australia • Canada • Mexico • Singapore • Spain • United Kingdom • United States

PETERSON'S
THOMSON LEARNING

About Peterson's

Founded in 1966, Peterson's, a division of Thomson Learning, is the nation's largest and most respected provider of lifelong learning online resources, software, reference guides, and books. The Education Supersite℠ at petersons.com—the Web's most heavily traveled education resource—has searchable databases and interactive tools for contacting U.S.-accredited institutions and programs. CollegeQuest® (CollegeQuest.com) offers a complete solution for every step of the college decision-making process. GradAdvantage™ (GradAdvantage.org), developed with Educational Testing Service, is the only electronic admissions service capable of sending official graduate test score reports with a candidate's online application. Peterson's serves more than 55 million education consumers annually.

Thomson Learning is among the world's leading providers of lifelong learning, serving the needs of individuals, learning institutions, and corporations with products and services for both traditional classrooms and for online learning. For more information about the products and services offered by Thomson Learning, please visit www.thomsonlearning.com. Headquartered in Stamford, Connecticut, with offices worldwide, Thomson Learning is part of The Thomson Corporation (www.thomson.com), a leading e-information and solutions company in the business, professional, and education marketplaces. The Corporation's common shares are listed on the Toronto and London stock exchanges.

For more information, contact Peterson's, 2000 Lenox Drive, Lawrenceville, NJ 08648; 800-338-3282; or find us on the World Wide Web at: www.petersons.com/about

ISSN 1523-9128
ISBN 0-7689-0558-3

Printed in Canada

10 9 8 7 6 5 4 3 2 03 02 01

Contents

A Guide to Good Four-Year Colleges

by Ernest L. Boyer, edited by Paul Boyer

When you think of college, you probably imagine the cliché or Hollywood image: a campus filled with ivy-covered buildings, students socializing in the academic quad, and the faint sounds of a professor's voice coming from an open window. Despite this stereotypical picture of what college might look like on the surface, there is no single model of a "good college." Missions and circumstances vary greatly from one campus to another. Each four-year college and university has something different to offer its students. And with college costs rising, you want to be assured that you will get the best value out of the college investment. This makes choosing the right college even more difficult. It may help to know that despite all of the differences among colleges, there are characteristics commonly shared by reputable schools that you should consider in your search.

Although these standards can be used to evaluate any college, you should narrow your list prior to the "test of quality" and put these questions to the schools on your final list. First, consider other facts that may be important to you, such as location or size. As you work through the list, you will find that a great deal of this information can be uncovered by reading this book, as well as by reading literature from individual colleges. In order to come up with the most complete review of a particular school, though, you will need to discuss these items with your guidance counselor, representatives from the colleges, and other advisers.

Some Common Measures of Quality

Every college should be guided by a clear and vital mission. It should understand its unique role in higher education and present itself honestly to prospective students through its literature and other information outlets. An institution cannot be all things to all people, so choices must be made and priorities assigned. What shows the strength of an institution is whether it has clearly defined its focus and, beyond that, whether it has successfully turned those goals into a living purpose for the campus. Of course, you also need to determine if the college's mission matches up with your own goals and values. At the very least, you need to know that you will be comfortable at a college and that it will deliver the type of educational experience you are seeking.

The quality of the undergraduate college is measured largely by the extent of its cooperation with high schools and by its willingness to smooth the transition of students into college. The way you are recruited by a college helps to shape your expectations of that college. A good college conducts its recruitment and selection with the best interests of the student in mind and should, therefore, try to learn more about you than simply your test scores and class rank.

Beyond the admissions process, it is important for a college to continue to demonstrate commitment to you by taking steps to make you feel at home. The first few weeks on campus are a major rite of passage and may have a significant influence on your entire undergraduate experience. In short, you will want to determine whether the freshman year is viewed as something special and whether the college has a well-planned orientation program that addresses the particular concerns of the new student.

Since students need guidance throughout their entire education, a college of quality has a year-round program of academic advising and personal counseling, structured to serve all undergraduates, including part-time and commuting students. You will want to find out if faculty members are available to freshmen to talk about their disciplines and whether or not faculty members give guidance to young students who are considering career choices. A college worthy of commendation works as hard at holding students as it does at getting them to the campus in the first place. You may wish to investigate a college's retention rate over the past five years and find out whether or not it offers guidance programs for students who are having trouble. These are all measures of a college's dedication to its students.

A Planned, Yet Flexible, Curriculum

At a good college, the academic major will broaden rather than restrict the student's perspective, presenting, in effect, an enriched major. An enriched major will answer three essential questions: What are the history and traditions of the field to be examined? What are the social and economic implications to be pursued? What are the ethical and moral issues within the specialty that need to be confronted? Rather than dividing the undergraduate experience into separate camps—general versus specialized education—the curriculum at a college of high quality will bring the two together. Therefore, it is important to determine if the college has a coherent general education sequence—an integrated core—rather than a more loosely connected distribution arrangement. This core academic program should provide not only for an integration of the separate academic principles but also for their application and relationship to life. All colleges impose requirements for graduation, including a set number of credits and some predetermined courses within a major. But within this set of general expectations, there is also room for flexibility. Increasingly, innovative colleges are recognizing the needs and skills of older students, encouraging individual learning, giving credit for experience, and helping students craft their own unique majors. Students should not have to march on to graduation in four years if they have interests, skills, and needs that are not acknowledged by a traditional degree program. New types of students are enrolling, and the location of learning has moved beyond the campus—to the home, the workplace, and around the world. In recognition of this trend, an effective college designs programs that meet new patterns and creates ways to both extend and encourage diversity on the campus.

The Classroom Climate

The undergraduate experience, at its best, encourages students to be active rather than passive learners. In measuring the quality of a college, students should ask if the institution has a climate that encourages independent, self-directed study, where teaching is perceived as more than just lecturing. If a college encourages small discussion sessions in which students work together on group assignments, it may indicate dedication to the undergraduate curriculum. In addition, if undergraduate courses are taught by the most respected and most gifted teachers on campus, it speaks further to this commitment.

Indeed, the strength of the faculty plays a leading role in determining the quality of the undergraduate experience. Students and parents have become increasingly concerned with the balance of time that faculty members spend on research and publishing requirements versus lecturing or advising. To uncover how an institution views this balance, you should ask if good teaching is valued equally with research and if it is an important criterion for tenure and promotion. It is important to know if the college recognizes that some faculty members are great teachers, others great researchers, and still others a blend of both. The central qualities that make for successful teaching are the ones that can be simply stated: command of the material to be taught; a contagious enthusiasm for the play of ideas; optimism about the potential of one's students; and sensitivity, integrity, and warmth as a human being. At a good college, this combination is present in the classroom.

Devoting Resources to Learning

An institution of high quality is one that supports its mission of learning both financially and philosophically. In doing so, a college should allot ample funds to its library and other educational resources. In terms of its use, one should determine if the library is more than just a study hall and if students are encouraged to spend at least as much time with library resources as they spend in classes. These resources should primarily serve the interests of undergraduate research and not be dominated by narrow scholarly interests of faculty members or graduate students. In addition, computers offer great potential for learning on campus. Some colleges now require that you purchase a computer before coming to campus. Others make terminals available to all students in common areas. Particularly if you are looking to advance in computer-related fields, or if you are inclined toward furthering your computer skills, you will want to know if campus terminals are linked to wider networks (including the Internet) and if the college connects technology, the library, and the classroom, letting each resource do what it does best and encouraging students to engage in creative, independent learning.

The Campus Culture

A college campus is also a community. A high-quality college will work to make the time spent outside of the classroom as meaningful as the time spent in class. The high-quality college sees academic and nonacademic functions as related and arranges events ranging from lecture series and concerts to sports and student organizations to reinforce the curriculum. These campuswide activities, intended for both faculty members and students, should encourage community, sustain college traditions, and stimulate both social and cultural interaction. Because much learning occurs outside the classroom, it is important to know how accessible faculty members are to their students—not only through office hours, but also elsewhere on the campus, at social or extracurricular functions. In this setting, the academic campus transcends the classroom and is viewed as a place for learning. Beyond the structured programs, the campus culture extends into the residence halls and other social areas on campus. Residential living can be one of the most chaotic parts of campus life, yet it has the potential of being one of the most rewarding. It is a good idea to find out if residence halls also promote a sense of community through organized activities and informal learning.

A Final Word of Advice

In the end, a high-quality college is concerned about outcomes. It asks questions about student development that go beyond the evaluation of skill. But a good college will avoid measuring that which matters least and will focus on the need for students to think clearly, to be well informed, to integrate their knowledge, and to apply what they have learned.

The impact of college extends beyond graduation, and a college of quality will provide placement guidance to its students and follow their careers. These students will be well equipped to put their work in context and adequately prepared to move from one intellectual challenge to another. The undergraduate experience will also have prepared students to see beyond the narrow boundaries of their own interests and discover global connections. The college succeeds as its graduates are inspired by a larger vision, using their newfound knowledge to form values and advance the common good.

When you make your college contacts and campus visits, you now know what questions to ask and what to look for in order to make an informed decision. In doing so, however, you should always take into account your specific goals and you'll find that some colleges will immediately fall from your list. In the end, the important thing to remember is that a college of high quality is one that will prepare you for a productive career, but will also offer you values and principles that you can apply *beyond* graduation day.

Using This Book

In the preceding article, "A Guide to Good Four-Year Colleges," you were presented with several points to consider when evaluating the quality of a particular college. There are other factors to consider, in addition, that do not necessarily point to the overall quality of the education you might receive, but that heavily influence your final choice. Among the many criteria you might use are the location, size, cost, entrance selectivity, or diversity of an institution. Rather than flipping through the hundreds of pages in this guide to find the perfect college, you might first consider other means of narrowing your search. By answering some of the following types of questions, you will be able to develop a personalized list of criteria. What part of the country do you want to be in? Do you prefer an urban or rural setting? Are you looking for a small, intimate environment or a college with a large student body? By compiling that list of questions and answers, you will soon arrive at a list of things you will need to research for each college under consideration.

This guide's easy-to-use college profiles are designed to provide you with the data you will need to single out colleges for "the final list." In addition to using resources such as this one, do not underestimate the guidance of your parents, high school guidance counselor, friends, and alumni of the institutions you are considering. Be sure to carefully review the college's viewbook and recruiting literature and make use of the campus visit, especially as a screening tool for your narrowed list.

Considering Your Options

If you have a very specific idea of what you want out of a college education, you will have an easier time compiling your list of prospective colleges. By considering some of the following criteria, you will soon find that your initial list of perhaps fifty colleges has been narrowed to a more reasonable number.

1. **Location**. For some students, staying close to home might be a priority. Or, venturing all the way across the country might be something you have always wanted to do and college seems like the perfect time to do it. Likewise, you may know that city life is not for you; therefore, you will need to limit your search to suburban or even

rural colleges. Whatever the reason, the location of a college often plays a key role in the college selection process.

2. **Entrance Difficulty**. Many students will look to a college's entrance difficulty as an indication of whether or not they will be admitted. For instance, if you have an excellent academic record, you might wish to primarily consider highly selective colleges. Although entrance difficulty does not necessarily translate into quality of education, it does often indicate whether a college is highly sought-after.
3. **Education Costs**. As the price tag for higher education continues to rise, cost becomes an increasingly important factor when selecting a college. Certainly it is necessary to consider your family's resources when choosing a list of schools to which you might apply. On the other hand, avoid eliminating colleges that you might otherwise consider based solely on cost. You may be able to obtain the necessary financial aid to allow you to enroll in your higher-priced college of choice.
4. **Most Frequently Chosen Baccalaureate Fields**. Despite all of the other factors that might influence your selection, one of the most important is whether a college offers a program in your academic area of interest. Or, conversely, if you have not selected a program at the onset, you will want to find a college with a broad enough selection to satisfy your eventual choice.

Beyond these major factors, you will undoubtedly uncover other criteria that will strongly influence your choice of where to attend college. Questions about a particular institution's size, the diversity of its student body, or special academic programs or services may weigh heavily in the decision process. The straightforward format of the College Profiles makes it easy to gather the facts on all of these points and more, providing you with the answers you need to make the most informed choice. The following paragraph describes in detail the data that is contained within these features.

How Hard Is It to Get In?

The five levels of entrance difficulty, as defined below, are based on the percentage of applicants who were accepted for fall 2000 freshman admission (or, in the case of upper-level schools, for entering-class admission) and on the high school class rank and standardized test scores of the accepted freshmen who actually enrolled in fall 2000. The colleges were asked to select the level that most closely corresponds to their entrance difficulty, according to the guidelines below, to assist prospective students in assessing their chances for admission.

The five levels of entrance difficulty are as follows:

1. **Most difficult:** More than 75% of the freshmen were in the top 10% of their high school class and scored 1250 or higher on the SAT I (verbal and mathematical combined) or 29 or higher on the ACT (composite); about 30% or fewer of the applicants were accepted.
2. **Very difficult:** More than 50% of the freshmen were in the top 10% of their high school class and scored 1150 or higher on the SAT I or 26 or higher on the ACT; about 60% or fewer of the applicants were accepted.
3. **Moderately difficult:** More than 75% of the freshmen were in the top half of their high school class and scored 900 or higher on the SAT I or 18 or higher on the ACT; about 85% or fewer of the applicants were accepted.
4. **Minimally difficult:** Most freshmen were not in the top half of their high school class and scored somewhat below 900 on the SAT I or below 19 on the ACT; up to 95% of the applicants were accepted.
5. **Noncompetitive:** Virtually all applicants were accepted regardless of high school rank or test scores.

Profile Highlights

Setting: Designated as urban (located within a major city), suburban (a residential area within commuting distance of a major city), small town (a small but compactly settled area not within commuting distance of a major city), or rural (a remote and sparsely populated area).

Total enrollment: The number of matriculated undergraduate and (if applicable) graduate students, both full-time and part-time, as of fall 2000.

Student/faculty ratio: The school's estimate of the ratio of matriculated undergraduate students to faculty members teaching undergraduate courses.

Application Deadline: Deadlines and dates for notification of acceptance or rejection are given either as specific dates or as rolling and continuous. Rolling means that applications are processed as they are received, and qualified students are accepted as long as there are openings. Continuous notification means that applicants are notified of acceptance or rejection as applications are processed up until the date indicated or the actual beginning of classes.

Freshmen: Figures are given for the percentage of applicants who were accepted.

Housing: Indicates whether or not on-campus housing is available.

Expenses: *Tuition* is the average basic tuition for an academic year presented as a dollar amount. *Room & board* is the average yearly room and board cost presented as a dollar amount.

Undergraduates: Percentages of undergraduates who are women, part-time students, 25 years or older, Native American (Indian, Eskimo, Polynesian), Hispanic, African American, and Asian American are given.

Most frequently chosen baccalaureate fields: The most popular majors of the 1999 graduating class.

Average class size: The average class size for required undergraduate courses.

Advanced placement: Credit toward a degree awarded for acceptable scores on some or all College Board Advanced Placement tests.

Accelerated degree program: Students may earn a bachelor's degree in three academic years.

Self-designed majors: Students may design their own program of study based on individual interests.

Honors program: Unusually challenging academic program for superior students.

Summer session for credit: Summer courses through which students may make up degree work or accelerate their program.

Part-time degree programs: Students may earn a degree without having to attend classes full-time; part-time degree programs may be offered for students attending regular-session classes (daytime) or evening, weekend, or summer classes.

External degree programs: Students may earn a degree through a program that (1) requires no more than 25% of the degree credit to be earned through campus-located instruction, (2) grants credit for documented extra-institutional and experiential learning, and (3) emphasizes off-campus self-directed study.

Adult/continuing education programs: Courses offered for nontraditional students who are currently working or are returning to formal education.

Cooperative (co-op) education programs: Formal arrangement with off-campus employers allowing students to combine work and study in order to gain degree-related experience, usually extending the time required to complete a degree.

Internships: College-arranged work experience for which students earn academic credit.

Contact: The name, title, mailing address, and telephone number of the person to contact for further information are given at the end of the profile. Toll-free telephone numbers may also be included. The admission office fax number, e-mail address, and Web site may be provided.

The Colleges and Universities in This Guide

The profiles of the colleges and universities include all four-year colleges in the United States that appear in *Peterson's Guide to Four-Year Colleges 2002.* The term "four-year college" is the commonly used designation for institutions that grant the baccalaureate, since four years is the normal duration of the traditional undergraduate curriculum. However, some bachelor's programs may be completed in three years, others require five years, and, of course, part-time programs may take a considerably longer period. Also included are upper-level institutions that award the baccalaureate but require that entering students have at least two years of previous college-level credit and, thus, normally require an additional two years to complete a degree program.

Accreditation

To be included in this guide, an institution must have full accreditation or candidate-for-accreditation (preaccreditation) status granted by an institutional or specialized accrediting body recognized by the U.S. Department of Education or the Council on Postsecondary Accreditation. Recognized institutional accrediting bodies, which consider each institution as a whole, are the following: the six regional associations of schools and colleges (Middle States, New England, North Central, Northwest, Southern, and Western), each of which is responsible for a specified portion of the United States and its territories; the Accrediting Association of Bible Colleges (AABC); the Accrediting Council for Independent Colleges and Schools (ACICS); the Accrediting Commission of Career Schools/Colleges of Technology (ACCSCT); The Distance Education and Training Council (DETC); and the Transnational Association of Christian Schools (TRACS). Program registration by the New York State Board of Regents is considered to be the equivalent of institutional accreditation, since the Board requires that all programs offered by an institution meet its standards before recognition is granted. A Canadian institution must be chartered and authorized to grant degrees by the provincial government, affiliated with a chartered institution, or accredited by a recognized U.S. accrediting body. This guide also includes institutions outside the United States, the U.S. territories, and Canada that are accredited by recognized U.S. accrediting bodies. There are recognized specialized accrediting bodies in more than forty different fields, each of which is authorized to accredit specific programs in its particular field. This can serve as the equivalent of institutional accreditation for specialized institutions that offer programs in one field only (schools of art, music, optometry, theology, etc.). For a full explanation of the accrediting process and complete information on recognized accrediting bodies, refer to *Peterson's Directory of College and University Administrators.*

Research Procedures

The data contained in the college indexes and college profiles was collected between fall 2000 and spring 2001 through Peterson's Annual Survey of Undergraduate Institutions. Surveys were sent to the colleges and universities that meet the criteria for inclusion outlined above. All data that appears in this edition has been submitted by officials (usually admission and financial aid officers, registrars, or institutional research personnel) at the schools themselves. In addition, the great majority of institutions that submitted data were contacted directly by Peterson's editorial and research staff to verify unusual figures, resolve discrepancies, and obtain additional data. All usable information received in time for publication has been included. The omission of any particular item from an index or profile listing signifies that the item is either not applicable to that institution or that data was not available. Because of the comprehensive editorial review that takes place in our offices and because all material comes directly from college officials, we have every reason to believe that the information presented in this guide is accurate. However, students should check with a specific college or university at the time of application to verify such figures as tuition and fees, which may have changed since the publication of this volume.

For Further Information

If you would like in-depth information about the colleges of your choice, refer to Peterson's Web site at http://www.CollegeQuest.com.

A Guide to Financing a College Education

by Don M. Betterton, Director of Undergraduate Aid,
Princeton University

Given the lifelong benefit of a college degree (college graduates are projected to earn in a lifetime an average of $800,000 to $1 million more than those with only a high school diploma), higher education is a very worthwhile investment. However, it is also an expensive one made even harder to manage by cost increases that have outpaced both inflation and gains in family income. This reality of higher education economics means that parental concern about how to pay college costs is a dilemma that shows no sign of getting easier.

Because of the high cost involved (even the most inexpensive four-year education at a public institution costs about $10,000 a year), good information about college budgets and strategies for reducing the "sticker price" is essential. In the following chapter, you will learn valuable information about the four main sources of aid—federal, state, college, and private. Before you learn about the various programs, however, it will be helpful if you have an overview of how the college financial aid system operates and what long-range financing strategies are available.

Financial Aid

Financial aid refers to money that is awarded to a student, usually in a "package" that consists of gift aid (commonly called a scholarship or grant), a student loan, and a campus job.

College Costs and Qualifying for Need-Based Aid

The starting point for organizing a plan to pay for your college education is to make a good estimate of the yearly cost of attendance. The profiles give you an estimate of tuition, but there are other costs to consider. *Peterson's College Money Handbook* is an excellent resource to make this first step of determining total costs easy for you.

The next step is to evaluate whether or not you are likely to qualify for financial aid based on need. This step is critical, since more than 90 percent of the yearly total of $65 billion in student aid is awarded only after a determination is made that the family lacks sufficient financial resources to pay the full cost of college on their own. To judge your chance of receiving need-based aid, it is necessary to estimate an

Expected Family Contribution (EFC) according to a government formula known as the Federal Methodology, also found in the *College Money Handbook*.

Applying for Need-Based Aid

Because the federal government provides about 75 percent of all aid awarded, the application and need evaluation process is controlled by Congress and the U.S. Department of Education. The application used is called the Free Application for Federal Student Aid, or FAFSA. The FAFSA is your "passport" to receiving your share of the billions of dollars awarded annually in need-based aid. If you think you might qualify for aid, pick up a FAFSA from your high school guidance office after mid-November 2001. The form will ask for 2001 financial data, and it should be filed after January 1, 2002, in time to meet the earliest college or state scholarship deadline. Within two to four weeks after you submit the form, you will receive a summary of the FAFSA information, called the Student Aid Report, or SAR. The SAR will give you the EFC and will also allow you to make corrections to the data you submitted.

Students can apply for federal student aid over the Internet using FAFSA on the Web. FAFSA on the Web can be accessed at http://www.fafsa.ed.gov.

Many colleges feel that the federal aid system (FAFSA) does not collect or evaluate information thoroughly enough to be used to award their institutional funds. These colleges have made an arrangement with the College Scholarship Service, a branch of the College Board, to establish a separate application system to meet their needs. The application is called PROFILE, and the need formula is the Institutional Methodology. (When used, PROFILE is always in addition to the FAFSA; it does not replace it.) If you apply for financial aid at one of the approximately 400 colleges that uses PROFILE, the admission material will state that PROFILE is required in addition to the FAFSA. You should read the information carefully and file PROFILE to meet the earliest college deadline. Before you can receive PROFILE, however, you must register, providing enough basic information so the PROFILE package can be designed specifically for you. The FAFSA is free, but there is a charge for PROFILE.

Many colleges provide the option to apply for early decision admission. If you apply for this before January 1, which is prior to when FAFSA can be used, follow the college's instructions. Many colleges use either PROFILE or their own application form for early decision candidates.

Awarding Aid

About the same time you receive the SAR, the colleges you list will receive the FAFSA information so they can calculate a financial aid award in a package that typically includes aid from at least one of the major sources—federal, state, college, or private. In addition, the award will probably consist of a combination of a scholarship or grant, a loan, and a campus job. These last two pieces—loan and job—are called self-help aid because they require effort on the part of the student. Scholarships or grants are outright gifts that have no such obligation.

When you receive an award letter from a college, it is important that you understand each part of the package. For example: How much is gift aid? What are the interest rate and repayment terms of the student loan? How many hours per week does the campus job require? There should be an enclosure with the award letter that answers these kinds of questions. If not, make a list of your questions and call or visit the financial aid office.

Once you understand the terms of each item in the award letter, you should turn your attention to the "bottom line"—how much you will have to pay for each college to which you are admitted. In addition to understanding the aid award, you must have a good estimate of the college budget so that you can accurately calculate how much you and your family will have to contribute (often an aid package does not cover the entire need). If you think that what the college expects you and your family to pay is too high, you should contact the college's financial aid office and ask whether additional aid is available. Many colleges, private high-cost colleges in particular, are enrollment oriented—they are willing to work with families to help make attendance at their colleges possible. If there is still a gap between the expected contribution and what you feel you can pay from income and savings, you are left with two choices. One option is to attend a college where paying your share of the bill will not be a problem. (This assumes that an affordable option was included on the original list of colleges, a wise admission application strategy.) The second is to look into an alternate method of financing, including loans and tuition payment plans. A loan can bring the yearly cost down to a manageable level by spreading payments over a number of years. A tuition payment plan is essentially a short-term loan and allows you to pay the cost over ten to twelve months. It is an option for families who have the resources available but need help with managing their cash flow.

Aid Not Based on Need

Whether or not you qualify for a need-based award, it is always worthwhile to look into merit, or non-need, scholarships from sources such as foundations, agencies, religious groups, and service organizations. If you are not eligible for need-based aid, merit scholarships are the only form of gift aid available. If you later qualify for a need-based award, a merit scholarship can be quite helpful in providing additional resources when the aid does not fully cover the costs. Even if the college meets 100 percent of need, a merit scholarship can benefit the student by reducing the self-help (loan and job) portion of an award.

In searching for outside merit-based scholarships, keep in mind that there are relatively few awards (compared to those that are need-based), and most of them are highly competitive. Use the following checklist when investigating merit scholarships:

- Take advantage of any scholarships for which you are automatically eligible based on employer benefits, military service, association or church membership, other affiliations, or student or parent attributes (ethnic background, nationality, etc.). Company or union tuition remissions are the most common examples of these awards.
- Look for other awards for which you might be eligible based on the characteristics and affiliations indicated above, but where there is a selection process and an application required. Computerized searches are available on the Internet. Scholarship directories, such as *Peterson's Scholarships, Grants & Prizes* which details some 2,000 scholarship programs, are useful resources and can be found in bookstores, high school guidance offices, and public libraries.
- Look into national scholarship competitions. High school guidance counselors usually know about these scholarships. Examples of these awards are the National Merit Scholarship, Coca Cola Scholarship, Aid Association for Lutherans, Westinghouse Science Talent Search, and the U.S. Senate Youth Program. *Winning Money for College* (Peterson's, 4th ed., 1997) provides detailed profiles of fifty of the most lucrative and prestigious competitions open to high school students.
- ROTC (Reserve Officers' Training Corps) scholarships are offered by the Army, Navy, Air Force, and Marine Corps. A full ROTC scholarship covers tuition, fees, and textbook costs. Acceptance of an ROTC scholarship entails a commitment to take military science courses and to serve for a specific number of years as an officer in the sponsoring branch of the service. Competition is heavy, and preference may be given to students in certain fields of study such as engineering or science. Contact an armed services recruiter or a high school guidance counselor for further information.
- Investigate community scholarships. The high school guidance counselor usually has a list of these awards, and announcements are

published in the town newspaper. Most common are awards given by such service organizations as the American Legion, Rotary International, and the local women's club.

- If you are strong academically (for example, a National Merit Commended Scholar or better) or are very talented in fields such as athletics or performing/creative arts, you may want to consider colleges that offer their own merit awards to gifted students they wish to enroll.

In addition to merit scholarships, there are loan and job opportunities for students who do not qualify for need-based aid. Some of the organizations that sponsor scholarships—for example, the Air Force Aid Society—also provide loans.

Work opportunities during the academic year are another type of assistance that are not restricted to aid recipients. Many colleges, after assigning jobs to students on aid, will open campus positions to all students looking for work. In addition, there are usually off-campus employment opportunities available to everyone.

Tuition Tax Credits

Tuition tax credits allow families to reduce their tax bill by the amount of out-of-pocket college tuition expenses. Unlike a tax deduction, which is modified according to your tax bracket, a tax credit is a dollar-for-dollar reduction in taxes paid.

There are two programs: the HOPE Scholarship tax credit and the Lifetime Learning tax credit. As is true of many federal programs, there are many rules and restrictions that apply. You should check with your tax preparer or financial adviser for information about your own particular situation.

HOPE Scholarship

The HOPE Scholarship is a tax credit that applies for the first two years of college. A student must be a dependent and enrolled in at least a half-time program. The party paying the tuition may deduct the net tuition paid after January 1, 2001, from his or her 2001 federal income tax. The credit equals the first $1000 of qualifying expenses and 50 percent of the next $1000, to a limit of $1500 per eligible student. There is no restriction on how many family members may be eligible for the credit.

Lifetime Learning Tax Credit

The Lifetime Learning tax credit is similar to the HOPE Scholarship, except that it applies to postsecondary education after the first two years of college and to graduate school education as well as training to improve job skills. The maximum credit is 20 percent of the out-of-pocket tuition expense up to $5000. The Lifetime Learning tax credit is limited to one $1000 credit per tax return. (The HOPE Scholarship can be multiplied by the number of eligible students.)

Other Restrictions

There are income limitations for these credits. Joint filers with an Adjusted Gross Income (AGI) of $100,000 or more and single filers with an AGI of $50,000 or more may not claim either tax credit. The credits are scaled down for joint filers with an AGI of more than $80,000 and for single filers with an AGI of $40,000 or more. The credit may not exceed the tax amount. Colleges are responsible for notifying families of the yearly charges against which the tax credit may be applied.

Financing Your College Education

In this section, "financing" means putting together resources to pay the balance due to the college over and above payments from the primary sources of aid—scholarships, student loans, and jobs. Financing strategies are important because the high cost of a college education today often requires you, whether you receive aid or not, to think about stretching the college payment beyond the four-year period of enrollment. For high-cost colleges, it is not unreasonable to think about a 10-4-10 plan: ten years of saving; four years of paying college bills out of current income, savings, and borrowing; and ten years to repay a loan.

Savings

Although saving for college is always a good idea, many families are unclear about its advantages. Families do not save for two reasons. First, after expenses have been covered, many families do not have much money to set aside. An affordable but regular savings plan through a payroll deduction is usually the answer to the problem of spending your entire paycheck every month.

The second reason that saving for college is not a high priority is the belief that the financial aid system penalizes a family by lowering aid eligibility. The Federal Methodology of need determination is very kind to savers. In fact, savings are ignored completely for those who earn less than $50,000.

A sensible savings plan is important because of the financial advantage of saving compared to borrowing. The amount of money students borrow for college is now greater than the amount they receive in grants and scholarships. With loans becoming so widespread, savings should be carefully considered as an alternative to borrowing. Your incentive for saving is that a dollar saved is a dollar not borrowed.

Borrowing

Once you've calculated your "bottom-line" parental contribution and determined that the amount is not affordable out of your current income and assets, the most likely alternative is borrowing. First determine if you are eligible for a subsidized Stafford or Direct loan. Because no interest is due while a student attends college, these are the most favorable loans. If you are not eligible, look into the unsubsidized Stafford or Direct loan, which does not require a needs test but where the interest is due each year. The freshman year limit (either subsidized or unsubsidized) is $2625.

After you have taken out the maximum amount of student loans, the next step is to look into parental loans. The federal government's parent loan program is called PLUS and is the standard against which other loans should be judged. A local bank that participates in PLUS can give you a schedule of monthly repayments per $1000 borrowed. Use this repayment figure to compare other parental loans available through commercial lenders (including home equity loans), state programs, or colleges themselves. Choose the one that offers the best terms after all up-front costs, tax advantages, and the amount of monthly payments are considered.

Creditworthiness

If you will be borrowing to pay for your college education, making sure you qualify for a loan is critical. For the most part, that means your credit record must be free of default or delinquency. You can check your credit history with a credit bureau and clean up any adverse information that appears.

Making Financial Aid Work for You

This overview is intended to provide you with a road map to help you think about financing strategies and navigate through the complexities of the financial aid process. For further information about the process, consult *Peterson's College Money Handbook*. Use the parental contribution tables in conjunction with the college cost worksheet to estimate need eligibility. If there is any chance you will qualify for aid, complete the FAFSA (and PROFILE if required). At the same time, look into merit scholarships. Finally, check out the terms of PLUS and other parental loan options. The key is to understand the financial aid system and to follow the best path for you. The result of good information and good planning should be that you will receive your fair share of the billions of dollars of financial aid available each year and that the cost of college will not prevent you from attending.

Federal Financial Aid Programs

There are a number of sources of financial aid available to students: federal and state governments, private agencies, and colleges themselves. In addition, there are three different forms of aid: grants, work, and loans.

The federal government is the single largest source of financial aid for students. The U.S. Department of Education's student financial aid programs will make more than $46 billion available to about 8.8 million students. There are two federal grant programs—the Federal Pell Grant and the Federal Supplemental Educational Opportunity Grant (FSEOG); three loan programs—the Federal Perkins loan and the Stafford and Direct loans; and a program that helps colleges provide jobs for students, the Federal Work-Study (FWS).

The two grants, Federal Work-Study, Federal Perkins loan, and two subsidized loan programs—Direct and Stafford—are awarded to students with demonstrated financial need. Interest on the loans is paid by the government during the time the student is in school. For the unsubsidized Direct loan and unsubsidized Stafford loan, the interest begins to accrue as soon as the money is received. There is also a parental loan (PLUS) available.

Federal Pell Grant

The Federal Pell Grant is the largest grant program; almost 4 million students receive awards annually. This grant is intended to be the starting point of assistance for lower-income families. Eligibility for a Federal Pell Grant depends on the Expected Family Contribution (EFC). The amount you receive will depend on your EFC and the cost of education at the college you will attend. The highest award depends on how much the program is funded. The maximum for 2001-2002 is $3750.

Federal Supplemental Educational Opportunity Grant (FSEOG)

As its name implies, the Federal Supplemental Educational Opportunity Grant provides additional need-based federal grant money to supplement the Federal Pell Grant. Each participating college is given funds to award to especially needy students. The maximum award is $4000 per year, but the amount you receive depends on the college's policy, the availability of FSEOG funds, the total cost of education, and the amount of other aid awarded.

Federal Work-Study (FWS)

This program provides jobs for students who demonstrate need. Salaries are paid by funds from the federal government as well as the college. You work on an hourly basis in jobs on or off campus and must be paid at least the federal minimum wage. You may earn only up to the amount awarded in the financial aid package.

Federal Perkins Loan

This loan is a low-interest (5 percent) loan for students with exceptional financial need. Federal Perkins loans are made through the college's financial aid office with the college as the lender. Students may borrow a maximum of $4000 per year for up to five years of undergraduate study. They may take up to ten years to repay the loan, beginning nine months after they graduate, leave school, or drop below half-time status. No interest accrues while they are in school, and, under certain conditions (e.g., they teach in low-income areas, work in law enforcement, are full-time nurses or medical technicians, serve as Peace Corps or VISTA volunteers, etc.), some or all of the loan can be canceled or payments deferred.

Stafford/Direct Loans

Stafford and Direct loans have the same interest rates, loan maximums, deferments, and cancellation benefits. A Stafford loan may be borrowed from a commercial lender such as a bank or credit union. A Direct loan is borrowed directly from the U.S. Department of Education.

The interest rate varies annually (there is a maximum of 8.25 percent); the rate for 2001–2002 is 5.99 percent during repayment and 5.39 percent while students attend college. If you qualify for a need-based subsidized Stafford loan, the interest is paid by the federal government while you are enrolled in college. There is also an unsubsidized Stafford loan that is not based on need for which you are eligible regardless of your family income.

The maximum amount dependent students may borrow in any one year is $2625 for freshmen, $3500 for sophomores, and $5500 for juniors and seniors, with a maximum of $23,000 for the total undergraduate program. The maximum amount independent students can borrow is $6625 for freshmen (no more than $2625 can be in subsidized loans),

$7500 for sophomores (no more than $3500 can be in subsidized loans), and $10,500 for juniors and seniors (no more than $5500 can be in subsidized loans). Borrowers must pay a 3 percent fee, which is deducted from the loan proceeds.

To apply for a Stafford loan, you must first complete a FAFSA to determine eligibility for a subsidized loan and then complete a separate loan application that is submitted to a lender. The financial aid office can help in selecting a lender. The lender will send a promissory note where you agree to repay the loan. The proceeds of the loan, less the origination fee, will be sent to your college to be either credited to your account or released to you.

If you qualify for a subsidized Stafford loan, you do not have to pay interest while in school. For an unsubsidized Stafford loan, you will be responsible for paying the interest from the time the loan is established. However, some lenders will permit borrowers to delay making payments and will add the interest to the loan. Once the repayment period starts, borrowers of both subsidized and unsubsidized Stafford loans will have to pay a combination of interest and principal monthly for up to a ten-year period.

PLUS Loans

PLUS is for parents of dependent students to help families with cash-flow problems. There is no needs test to qualify. The loan has a variable interest rate that cannot exceed 9 percent (the rate for 2001-2002 is 6.79 percent). There is no yearly limit; parents can borrow up to the cost of their child's education, less other financial aid received. Repayment begins sixty days after the money is advanced. A 3 or 4 percent fee is subtracted from the proceeds. Parent borrowers must generally have a good credit record to qualify.

PLUS loans may be processed under either the Direct or Stafford system, depending on the type of loan program for which the college has contracted.

AmeriCorps

AmeriCorps is a program for students. Participants work in a public or private nonprofit agency providing service to the community in one of four priority areas: education, human services, the environment, or public safety. In exchange, they earn a stipend between $7400 and $14,800 a year for living expenses and $4725 per year for up to two years to apply toward college expenses. Students can work either before, during, or after they go to college and can use the funds to pay either current educational expenses or repay federal student loans. Speak to a college financial aid officer for more details about this program.

Returning to School: A Guide for Adult Students

by Sandra Cook, Ph.D., Director, University Advising Center, San Diego State University

Many adults think about returning to school for a long time without taking any action. One purpose of this article is to help the "thinkers" finally make some decisions by examining what is keeping them from action. Another purpose is to describe not only some of the difficulties and obstacles that adult students may face when returning to school but also tactics for coping with them.

If you have been thinking about going back to college, and believing that you are the only person your age contemplating college, you should know that approximately 7 million adult students are currently enrolled in higher education institutions. This number represents 50 percent of total higher education enrollments. The majority of adult students are enrolled at two-year colleges.

There are many reasons why adult students choose to attend a two-year college. Studies have shown that the three most important criteria that adult students consider when choosing a college are location, cost, and availability of the major or program desired. Most two-year colleges are public institutions that serve a geographic district, making them readily accessible to the community. Costs at most two-year colleges are far less than at other types of higher education institutions. For many students who plan to pursue a bachelor's degree, completing their first two years of college at a community college is an affordable means to that end. If you are interested in an academic program that will transfer to a four-year institution, most two-year colleges offer the "general education" courses that comprise most freshman and sophomore years. If you are interested in a vocational or technical program, two-year colleges excel in providing this type of training.

Uncertainty, Choice, and Support

There are three different "stages" in the process of adults returning to school. The first stage is uncertainty. Do I really want to go back to school? What will my friends or family think? Can I compete with those 18-year-old whiz kids? Am I too old? The second stage is choice. Once the decision to return has been made, you must choose where you will attend. There are many criteria to use in making this decision. The third stage is support. You have just added another role to your already-too-busy life. There are, however, strategies that will help you accomplish your goals—perhaps not without struggle, but with grace and humor. Let's look at each of these stages.

Uncertainty

Why are you thinking about returning to school? Is it to:

- fulfill a dream that had to be delayed?
- become more educationally well rounded?
- fill an intellectual void in your life?

These reasons focus on *personal growth*.
If you are returning to school to:

- meet people and make friends
- attain and enjoy higher social status and prestige among friends, relatives, and associates
- understand/study a cultural heritage, or
- have a medium in which to exchange ideas,

you are interested in *social and cultural opportunities*.
If you are like most adult students, you want to:

- qualify for a new occupation
- enter or reenter the job market
- increase earnings potential, or
- qualify for a more challenging position in the same field of work.

You are seeking *career growth*.

Understanding the reasons why you want to go back to school is an important step in setting your educational goals and will help you to establish some criteria for selecting a college. However, don't delay your decision because you have not been able to clearly define your motives. Many times, these aren't clear until you have already begun the process, and they may change as you move through your college experience.

Assuming that you agree that additional education will be of benefit to you, what is it that keeps you from returning to school? You may have a litany of excuses running through your mind:

- I don't have time.
- I can't afford it.
- I'm too old to learn.
- My friends will think I'm crazy.
- The teachers will be younger than me.

- My family can't survive without me to take care of them every minute.
- I'll be X years old when I finish.
- I'm afraid.
- I don't know what to expect.

And that is just what these are—excuses. You can make school, like anything else in your life, a priority or not. If you really want to return, you can. The more you understand your motivation for returning to school and the more you understand what excuses are keeping you from taking action, the easier your task will be.

If you think you don't have time: The best way to decide how attending class and studying can fit into your schedule is to keep track of what you do with your time each day for several weeks. Completing a standard time-management grid (each day is plotted out by the half hour) is helpful for visualizing how your time is spent. For each 3-credit-hour class you take, you will need to find 3 hours for class plus 6 to 9 hours for reading-studying-library time. This study time should be spaced evenly throughout the week, not loaded up on one day. It is not possible to learn or retain the material that way. When you examine your grid, see where there are activities that could be replaced with school and study time. You may decide to give up your bowling league or some time in front of the TV. Try not to give up sleeping, and don't cut out every moment of free time. There are also a number of smaller ways to divert time to school. Here are some suggestions that have come from adults who have returned to school:

- Enroll in a time-management workshop. It helps you rethink how you use your time.
- Don't think you have to take more than one course at a time. You may eventually want to work up to taking more, but consider starting with one. (It is more than you are taking now!)
- If you have a family, start assigning those household chores that you usually do to them—and don't redo what they do.
- Use your lunch hour or commuting time for reading.

If you think you can not afford it: As mentioned earlier, two-year colleges are extremely affordable. If you cannot afford the tuition, look into the various financial aid options. Most federal and state funds are available to full- and part-time students. Loans are also available. While many people prefer not to accumulate a debt for school, these same people will think nothing of taking out a loan to buy a car. After five or six years, which is the better investment? Adult students who work should look into whether their company has a tuitionreimbursement policy. There are also an increasing number of private scholarships, available through foundations, service organizations, and clubs, that are focused on adult learners. Your public library and a college financial aid adviser are two excellent sources for reference materials regarding financial aid.

If you think you are too old to learn: This is pure myth. A number of studies have shown that adult learners perform as well as or better than traditional-age students.

If you are afraid your friends will think you're crazy: Who cares? Maybe they will, maybe they won't. Usually, they will admire your courage and be just a little jealous of your ambition (although they'll never tell you that). Follow your dreams, not theirs.

If you are concerned because the teachers or students will be younger than you: Don't be. The age differences that may be apparent in other settings evaporate in the classroom. If anything, an adult in the classroom strikes fear into the hearts of some 18-year-olds because adults have been known to be prepared, ask questions, be truly motivated, and be there to learn!

If you think your family will have a difficult time surviving while you are in school: If you have done everything for them up to now, they might struggle. Consider this an opportunity to help them become independent and self-sufficient. Your family can only make you feel guilty if you let them. You are not abandoning them; you are becoming an educational role model. When you are happy and working toward your goals, everyone benefits. Admittedly, it sometimes takes time for them to realize this. For single parents, there are schools that have begun to offer support groups, child care, and cooperative babysitting.

If you're appalled at the thought of being X years old when you graduate in Y years: How old will you be in Y years if you don't go back to school?

If you are afraid or don't know what to expect: Know that these are natural feelings when one encounters any new situation. Adult students find that their fears usually dissipate once they begin classes. Fear of trying is usually the biggest roadblock to the reentry process.

No doubt you have dreamed up a few more reasons for not making the decision to return to school. Keep in mind that what you are doing is making up excuses, and you are using these excuses to release you from the obligation to make a decision about your life. The thought of returning to college can be scary. Anytime anyone ventures into unknown territory, there is a risk, but taking risks is a necessary component of personal and professional growth. It is your life, and you alone are responsible for making the decisions that determine its course. Education is an investment in your future.

Choice

Once you have decided to go back to school, your next task is to decide where to go. If your educational goals are well defined (e.g., you want to pursue a degree in order to change careers), then your task is a bit easier. But even if your educational goals are still evolving, do not deter your return. Many students who enter higher education with a specific major in mind change that major at least once.

Most students who attend a public two-year college choose the community college in the district in which they live. This is generally the closest and least expensive option if the school offers the programs you want. If you are planning to begin your education at a two-year college and then transfer to a four-year school, there are distinct advantages to choosing your four-year school early. Many community and four-year colleges have "articulation" agreements that designate what credits from the two-year school will transfer to the four-year college and how. Some four-year institutions accept an associate degree as equivalent to the freshman and sophomore years, regardless of the courses you have taken. Some four-year schools accept two-year college work only on a course-by-course basis. If you can identify which school you will transfer to, you can know in advance exactly how your two-year credits will apply. This can prevent an unexpected loss of credit or time. You can use the strategies outlined below not only to help you choose your two-year college but also to help you identify early which four-year school you will transfer to.

Each institution of higher education is distinctive. Your goal in choosing a college is to come up with the best student-institution fit—matching your needs with the offerings and characteristics of the school. The first step in choosing a college is to determine what criteria are most important to you in attaining your educational goals. Location, cost, and program availability are the three main factors that influence an adult student's college choice. In considering location, don't forget that some colleges have conveniently located branch campuses. In considering cost, remember to explore your financial aid options before ruling out an institution because of its tuition. Program availability should include not only the major in which you are interested, but also whether or not classes in that major are available when you can take them.

Some additional considerations beyond location, cost, and programs are:

- Does the school have a commitment to adult students and offer appropriate services, such as child care, tutoring, and advising?
- Are classes offered at times when you can take them?
- Are there academic options for adults, such as credit for life or work experience, credit by examination (including CLEP and PEP), credit for military service, or accelerated programs?
- Is the faculty sensitive to the needs of adult learners?

Once you determine which criteria are vital in your choice of an institution, you can begin to narrow your choices. There are myriad ways for you to locate the information you desire. This guide and others, including *Peterson's Guide to Four-Year Colleges,* are excellent sources of information. Many urban newspapers publish a "School Guide" several times a year in which colleges and universities advertise to an adult student market. In addition, schools themselves publish catalogs, class schedules, and promotional materials that contain much of the information you need, and they are yours for the asking. Many colleges sponsor information sessions and open houses that allow you to visit the campus and ask questions. An appointment with an adviser is a good way to assess the fit between you and the institution. Be sure to bring your questions with you to your interview.

Support

Once you have made the decision to return to school and have chosen the institution that best meets your needs, take some additional steps to ensure your success during your crucial first semester. Take advantage of institutional support and build some social support systems of your own. Here are some ways of doing just that:

- Plan to participate in any orientation programs. These serve the threefold purpose of providing you with a great deal of important information, familiarizing you with the campus and its facilities, and giving you the opportunity to meet and begin networking with other students.
- Take steps to deal with any academic weaknesses. Take mathematics and writing placement tests if you have reason to believe you may need some extra help in these areas. It is not uncommon for adult students to need a math refresher course or a program to help alleviate math anxiety. Ignoring a weakness won't make it go away.

- Look into adult reentry programs. Many institutions offer adults workshops focusing on ways to improve study skills, textbook reading, test-taking, and time-management skills.
- Build new support networks by joining an adult student organization, making a point of meeting other adult students through workshops, or actively seeking out a "study buddy" in each class—that invaluable friend who shares and understands your experience.
- You can incorporate your new status as "student" into your family life. Doing your homework with your children at a designated "homework time" is a valuable family activity and reinforces the importance of education.
- Make sure you take a reasonable course load in your first semester. It is far better to have some extra time on your hands and to succeed magnificently than to spend the entire semester on the brink of a breakdown. Also, whenever possible, try to focus your first courses not only on requirements, but also in areas of personal interest.
- Faculty members, advisers, and student affairs personnel are there to help you during difficult times—let them assist you as often as necessary.

After completing your first semester, you will probably look back in wonder at why you thought going back to school was so imposing. Certainly, it's not without its occasional exasperations. But, as with life, keeping things in perspective and maintaining your sense of humor make the difference between just coping and succeeding brilliantly.

PROFILES

This section contains quick-reference profiles of colleges and universities, covering such items as background information, entrance difficulty, academic programs, and contact information. The data in each of these profiles, collected from fall 2000 to spring 2001, comes solely from Peterson's Annual Survey of Undergraduate Institutions, which was sent to deans or admissions officers at each institution. The profiles are organized first by region and then by state and arranged alphabetically within those sections by the official names of the institutions.

ALABAMA

ALABAMA AGRICULTURAL AND MECHANICAL UNIVERSITY
NORMAL, ALABAMA

General State-supported, university, coed **Entrance** Minimally difficult **Setting** 2,001-acre suburban campus **Total enrollment** 5,523 **Student/faculty ratio** 21:1 **Application deadline** Rolling (freshmen), rolling (transfer) **Freshmen** 24% were admitted **Housing** Yes **Expenses** Tuition $2820; Room & Board $4500 **Undergraduates** 52% women, 8% part-time, 9% 25 or older, 0.3% Native American, 0.3% Hispanic American, 91% African American, 0.3% Asian American/Pacific Islander **The most frequently chosen baccalaureate fields are** business/marketing, biological/life sciences, education **Academic program** Advanced placement, honors program, summer session, adult/continuing education programs **Contact** Mr. Antonio Boyle, Director of Admissions, Alabama Agricultural and Mechanical University, PO Box 908, Normal, AL 35762. Telephone: 256-851-5245 or toll-free 800-553-0816. Fax: 256-851-9747. E-mail: jheyward@asnaam.aamu.edu. Web site: http://www.aamu.edu/.

ALABAMA STATE UNIVERSITY
MONTGOMERY, ALABAMA

General State-supported, comprehensive, coed **Entrance** Minimally difficult **Setting** 114-acre urban campus **Total enrollment** 5,269 **Student/faculty ratio** 18:1 **Application deadline** 7/30 (freshmen), 7/30 (transfer) **Freshmen** 62% were admitted **Housing** Yes **Undergraduates** 58% women, 17% part-time, 0.05% Native American, 0.3% Hispanic American, 92% African American, 0.2% Asian American/Pacific Islander **The most frequently chosen baccalaureate fields are** business/marketing, biological/life sciences, education **Academic program** Advanced placement, honors program, summer session, adult/continuing education programs, internships **Contact** Mrs. Danielle Kennedy-Lamar, Director of Admissions and Recruitment, Alabama State University, PO Box 271, Montgomery, AL 36101-0271. Telephone: 334-229-4291 or toll-free 800-253-5037. Fax: 334-229-4984. E-mail: dlamar@asunet.alasu.edu. Web site: http://www.alasu.edu/.

AMERICAN COLLEGE OF COMPUTER & INFORMATION SCIENCES
BIRMINGHAM, ALABAMA

General Proprietary, comprehensive, coed **Entrance** Moderately difficult **Total enrollment** 9,000 **Application deadline** Rolling (freshmen), rolling (transfer) **Academic program** Advanced placement, accelerated degree program, honors program, adult/continuing education programs **Contact** Ms. Natalie Nixon, Director of Admissions, American College of Computer & Information Sciences, 2101 Magnolia Avenue, Birmingham, AL 35205. Telephone: 205-323-6191 or toll-free 800-767-AICS. Fax: 205-328-2229. E-mail: admiss@accis.edu. Web site: http://www.accis.edu/.

ANDREW JACKSON UNIVERSITY
BIRMINGHAM, ALABAMA

Contact Andrew Jackson University, 10 Old Montgomery Highway, Birmingham, AL 35209. Web site: http://www.aju.edu/.

ATHENS STATE UNIVERSITY
ATHENS, ALABAMA

General State-supported, upper-level, coed **Entrance** Noncompetitive **Setting** 45-acre small-town campus **Total enrollment** 2,662 **Student/faculty ratio** 17:1 **Application deadline** Rolling (transfer) **First-Year Students** 80% were admitted **Housing** Yes **Expenses** Tuition $2370; Room only $840 **Undergraduates** 67% women, 60% part-time, 62% 25 or older, 2% Native American, 0.4% Hispanic American, 12% African American, 1% Asian American/Pacific Islander **The most frequently chosen baccalaureate fields are** business/marketing, education, protective services/public administration **Academic program** Advanced placement, summer session, adult/continuing education programs, internships **Contact** Ms. Necedah Henderson, Coordinator of Admissions, Athens State University, 300 North Beaty Street, Athens, AL 35611-1902. Telephone: 256-233-8217 or toll-free 800-522-0272. Fax: 256-233-6565. E-mail: henden@athens.edu. Web site: http://www.athens.edu/.

AUBURN UNIVERSITY
AUBURN, ALABAMA

General State-supported, university, coed **Entrance** Moderately difficult **Setting** 1,875-acre small-town campus **Total enrollment** 21,136 **Student/faculty ratio** 16:1 **Application deadline** 8/1 (freshmen), 8/1 (transfer) **Freshmen** 85% were admitted **Housing** Yes **Expenses** Tuition $3154; Room & Board $4640 **Undergraduates** 48% women, 11% part-time, 6% 25 or older, 0.5% Native American, 1% Hispanic American, 7% African American, 1% Asian American/Pacific Islander **The most frequently chosen baccalaureate fields are** business/marketing, education, engineering/engineering technologies **Academic program** English as a second language, advanced placement, accelerated degree program, honors program, summer session, adult/continuing education programs, internships **Contact** Dr. John Fletcher, Acting Assistant Vice President of Enrollment Management, Auburn University, 202 Mary Martin Hall, Auburn University, AL 36849-0001. Telephone: 334-844-4080 or toll-free 800-AUBURN9. E-mail: fletcjt@mail.auburn.edu. Web site: http://www.auburn.edu/.

AUBURN UNIVERSITY MONTGOMERY
MONTGOMERY, ALABAMA

General State-supported, comprehensive, coed **Entrance** Moderately difficult **Setting** 500-acre sub-

Auburn University Montgomery *(continued)*

urban campus **Total enrollment** 4,900 **Student/faculty ratio** 18:1 **Housing** Yes **Expenses** Tuition $3000; Room only $2060 **Undergraduates** 63% women, 36% part-time, 29% 25 or older, 0.4% Native American, 1% Hispanic American, 32% African American, 2% Asian American/Pacific Islander **The most frequently chosen baccalaureate fields are** business/marketing, biological/life sciences, education **Academic program** English as a second language, advanced placement, accelerated degree program, self-designed majors, honors program, summer session, adult/continuing education programs, internships **Contact** Ms. Valerie Samuel, Assistant Director, Admissions, Auburn University Montgomery, PO Box 244023, Montgomery, AL 36124-4023. Telephone: 334-244-3667 or toll-free 800-227-2649 (in-state). Fax: 334-244-3795. E-mail: auminfo@mickey.aum.edu. Web site: http://www.aum.edu/.

BIRMINGHAM-SOUTHERN COLLEGE
BIRMINGHAM, ALABAMA

General Independent Methodist, comprehensive, coed **Entrance** Moderately difficult **Setting** 196-acre urban campus **Total enrollment** 1,477 **Student/faculty ratio** 13:1 **Application deadline** Rolling (freshmen), rolling (transfer) **Freshmen** 98% were admitted **Housing** Yes **Expenses** Tuition 16,269; Room & Board 5652 **Undergraduates** 59% women, 5% part-time, 1% 25 or older, 1% Native American, 1% Hispanic American, 10% African American, 4% Asian American/Pacific Islander **The most frequently chosen baccalaureate fields are** business/marketing, English, interdisciplinary studies **Academic program** Advanced placement, accelerated degree program, self-designed majors, honors program, summer session, adult/continuing education programs, internships **Contact** Ms. DeeDee Barnes Bruns, Dean of Admission and Financial Aid, Birmingham-Southern College, Box 549008, Birmingham, AL 35254. Telephone: 205-226-4696 or toll-free 800-523-5793. Fax: 205-226-3074. E-mail: admissions@bsc.edu. Web site: http://www.bsc.edu/.

COLUMBIA SOUTHERN UNIVERSITY
ORANGE BEACH, ALABAMA

General Proprietary, comprehensive, coed **Entrance** Noncompetitive **Total enrollment** 2,050 **Student/faculty ratio** 58:1 **Application deadline** Rolling (freshmen), rolling (transfer) **Academic program** Adult/continuing education programs **Contact** Mr. Poche Waguespack, Dean of Students, Columbia Southern University, 24847 Commercial Avenue, Orange Beach, AL 36561. Telephone: 334-981-3771 Ext. 110 or toll-free 800-977-8449. E-mail: tommy@columbiasouthern.edu. Web site: http://www.colsouth.edu/.

CONCORDIA COLLEGE
SELMA, ALABAMA

Contact Ms. Gwendolyn Moore, Director of Admissions, Concordia College, 1804 Green Street, PO Box 1329, Selma, AL 36701. Telephone: 334-874-7143. Fax: 334-874-3728.

EDUCATION AMERICA, SOUTHEAST COLLEGE OF TECHNOLOGY, MOBILE CAMPUS
MOBILE, ALABAMA

General Independent, 4-year **Contact** Mr. Randall Olsen, Director of Recruitment, Education America, Southeast College of Technology, Mobile Campus, 828 Downtowner Loop West, Mobile, AL 36609-5404. Telephone: 334-343-8200 Ext. 221.

FAULKNER UNIVERSITY
MONTGOMERY, ALABAMA

General Independent, comprehensive, coed, affiliated with Church of Christ **Entrance** Minimally difficult **Setting** 75-acre urban campus **Total enrollment** 2,660 **Student/faculty ratio** 20:1 **Application deadline** Rolling (freshmen), rolling (transfer) **Freshmen** 68% were admitted **Housing** Yes **Expenses** Tuition $7800; Room & Board $3950 **Undergraduates** 59% women, 26% part-time, 53% 25 or older, 1% Hispanic American, 38% African American, 0.4% Asian American/Pacific Islander **The most frequently chosen baccalaureate fields are** business/marketing, education, law/legal studies **Academic program** Advanced placement, accelerated degree program, summer session, adult/continuing education programs, internships **Contact** Mr. Keith Mock, Director of Admissions, Faulkner University, 5345 Atlanta Highway, Montgomery, AL 36109. Telephone: 334-386-7200 or toll-free 800-879-9816. Fax: 334-386-7137. E-mail: admissions@faulkner.edu. Web site: http://www.faulkner.edu/.

HUNTINGDON COLLEGE
MONTGOMERY, ALABAMA

General Independent United Methodist, 4-year, coed **Entrance** Moderately difficult **Setting** 58-acre suburban campus **Total enrollment** 705 **Student/faculty ratio** 12:1 **Application deadline** Rolling (freshmen), rolling (transfer) **Freshmen** 73% were admitted **Housing** Yes **Expenses** Tuition $11,910; Room & Board $5740 **Undergraduates** 62% women, 12% part-time, 10% 25 or older, 1% Native American, 0.3% Hispanic American, 7% African American, 2% Asian American/Pacific Islander **The most frequently chosen baccalaureate fields are** business/marketing, English, visual/performing arts **Academic program** Advanced placement, accelerated degree program, self-designed majors, honors program, summer session, adult/continuing education programs, internships **Contact** Mrs. Laura Duncan, Director of Admissions, Huntingdon College, 1500 East Fairview Avenue, Montgomery, AL 36106. Telephone: 334-

833-4496 or toll-free 800-763-0313. Fax: 334-833-4347. E-mail: admiss@huntingdon.edu. Web site: http://www.huntingdon.edu/.

INTERNATIONAL BIBLE COLLEGE
FLORENCE, ALABAMA

General Independent, 4-year, coed, affiliated with Church of Christ **Entrance** Noncompetitive **Setting** 43-acre small-town campus **Total enrollment** 203 **Application deadline** Rolling (freshmen), rolling (transfer) **Freshmen** 85% were admitted **Housing** Yes **Expenses** Tuition $5744; Room only $1200 **Undergraduates** 65% 25 or older **The most frequently chosen baccalaureate field is** philosophy, religion, and theology **Academic program** Accelerated degree program, summer session, adult/continuing education programs, internships **Contact** Mr. Scott Lovelace, Director of Enrollment Services, International Bible College, PO Box IBC, Florence, AL 35630-0050. Telephone: 256-766-6610 Ext. 26 or toll-free 800-367-3565. Web site: http://www.i-b-c.edu/.

JACKSONVILLE STATE UNIVERSITY
JACKSONVILLE, ALABAMA

General State-supported, comprehensive, coed **Entrance** Minimally difficult **Setting** 345-acre small-town campus **Total enrollment** 8,002 **Student/faculty ratio** 22:1 **Application deadline** Rolling (freshmen), rolling (transfer) **Freshmen** 50% were admitted **Housing** Yes **Expenses** Tuition $2640; Room & Board $3080 **Undergraduates** 56% women, 22% part-time, 25% 25 or older, 1% Native American, 1% Hispanic American, 19% African American, 1% Asian American/Pacific Islander **The most frequently chosen baccalaureate fields are** business/marketing, education, protective services/public administration **Academic program** English as a second language, advanced placement, accelerated degree program, honors program, summer session, adult/continuing education programs, internships **Contact** Ms. Martha Mitchell, Freshman Admission and Recruiting, Jacksonville State University, 700 Pelham Road North, Jacksonville, AL 36265. Telephone: 256-782-5363 or toll-free 800-231-5291. Fax: 256-782-5291. E-mail: jsmith@jsucc.edu. Web site: http://www.jsu.edu/.

JUDSON COLLEGE
MARION, ALABAMA

General Independent Baptist, 4-year, women only **Entrance** Moderately difficult **Setting** 80-acre rural campus **Total enrollment** 321 **Student/faculty ratio** 10:1 **Application deadline** Rolling (freshmen), rolling (transfer) **Freshmen** 81% were admitted **Housing** Yes **Expenses** Tuition $7640; Room & Board $4600 **Undergraduates** 17% part-time, 23% 25 or older, 0% Native American, 0% Hispanic American, 13% African American, 1% Asian American/Pacific Islander **The most frequently chosen baccalaureate fields are** business/marketing, education, psychology **Academic program** Advanced placement, accelerated degree program, self-designed majors, honors program, summer session, adult/continuing education programs, internships **Contact** Mrs. Charlotte Clements, Director of Admissions, Judson College, PO Box 120, Marion, AL 36756. Telephone: 334-683-5110 Ext. 110 or toll-free 800-447-9472. Fax: 334-683-5158. E-mail: admissions@future.judson.edu. Web site: http://home.judson.edu/.

MILES COLLEGE
BIRMINGHAM, ALABAMA

Contact Mr. Cornell Howard, Interim Director of Admissions and Recruitment, Miles College, PO Box 3800, Birmingham, AL 35208. Telephone: 205-929-1657.

OAKWOOD COLLEGE
HUNTSVILLE, ALABAMA

General Independent Seventh-day Adventist, 4-year, coed **Entrance** Minimally difficult **Setting** 1,200-acre campus **Total enrollment** 1,767 **Student/faculty ratio** 17:1 **Application deadline** Rolling (freshmen), rolling (transfer) **Freshmen** 46% were admitted **Housing** Yes **Expenses** Tuition $9058; Room & Board $2646 **Undergraduates** 57% women, 10% part-time, 13% 25 or older, 0.2% Native American, 1% Hispanic American, 80% African American, 0.2% Asian American/Pacific Islander **The most frequently chosen baccalaureate fields are** biological/life sciences, business/marketing, education **Academic program** Advanced placement, honors program, internships **Contact** Mr. Fred Pullins, Director of Enrollment Management, Oakwood College, 7000 Adventist Boulevard, NW, Huntsville, AL 35896. Telephone: 256-726-7354 or toll-free 800-358-3978 (in-state). Fax: 256-726-7154. E-mail: admission@oakwood.edu. Web site: http://www.oakwood.edu/.

SAMFORD UNIVERSITY
BIRMINGHAM, ALABAMA

General Independent Baptist, university, coed **Entrance** Moderately difficult **Setting** 180-acre suburban campus **Total enrollment** 4,379 **Student/faculty ratio** 13:1 **Application deadline** Rolling (transfer) **Freshmen** 88% were admitted **Housing** Yes **Expenses** Tuition 10,738; Room & Board 4720 **Undergraduates** 62% women, 7% part-time, 2% 25 or older, 0.4% Native American, 1% Hispanic American, 6% African American, 1% Asian American/Pacific Islander **The most frequently chosen baccalaureate fields are** business/marketing, education, health professions and related sciences **Academic program** Advanced placement, accelerated degree program, self-designed majors, honors program, summer session, adult/continuing education programs, internships **Contact** Dr. Phil Kimrey, Dean of Admissions and Financial Aid, Samford University, 800 Lakeshore Drive, Samford Hall, Birmingham, AL 35229-0002. Telephone: 205-726-3673 or toll-free

Samford University *(continued)*

800-888-7218. Fax: 205-726-2171. E-mail: seberry@vm.samford.edu. Web site: http://www.samford.edu/.

SOUTHEASTERN BIBLE COLLEGE
BIRMINGHAM, ALABAMA

General Independent nondenominational, 4-year, coed **Entrance** Moderately difficult **Setting** 10-acre suburban campus **Total enrollment** 217 **Application deadline** Rolling (freshmen), rolling (transfer) **Freshmen** 52% were admitted **Housing** Yes **Expenses** Tuition $6300; Room & Board $3440 **Undergraduates** 38% 25 or older **Academic program** Advanced placement, summer session, adult/continuing education programs, internships **Contact** Mrs. Monie Ingram, Registrar, Southeastern Bible College, 3001 Highway 280 East, Birmingham, AL 35243. Telephone: 205-970-9208. Fax: 205-970-9207. E-mail: ningram@sebc.edu. Web site: http://www.sebc.edu.

SOUTHERN CHRISTIAN UNIVERSITY
MONTGOMERY, ALABAMA

General Independent, comprehensive, coed, affiliated with Church of Christ **Entrance** Minimally difficult **Setting** 9-acre urban campus **Total enrollment** 332 **Student/faculty ratio** 14:1 **Application deadline** Rolling (freshmen), rolling (transfer) **Housing** No **Expenses** Tuition 11,550 **Undergraduates** 25% women, 1% part-time, 90% 25 or older, 0% Native American, 1% Hispanic American, 25% African American, 1% Asian American/Pacific Islander **Academic program** Advanced placement, accelerated degree program, summer session, adult/continuing education programs, internships **Contact** Ms. Becky Bagwell, Admissions Officer, Southern Christian University, 1200 Taylor Road, Montgomery, AL 36117. Telephone: 334-387-3877 Ext. 224 or toll-free 800-351-4040 Ext. 224. E-mail: admissions@southernchristian.edu. Web site: http://www.southernchristian.edu/.

SPRING HILL COLLEGE
MOBILE, ALABAMA

General Independent Roman Catholic (Jesuit), comprehensive, coed **Entrance** Moderately difficult **Setting** 500-acre suburban campus **Total enrollment** 1,484 **Student/faculty ratio** 13:1 **Application deadline** 7/1 (freshmen), 8/1 (transfer) **Freshmen** 89% were admitted **Housing** Yes **Expenses** Tuition $17,230; Room & Board $6020 **Undergraduates** 62% women, 18% part-time, 18% 25 or older, 1% Native American, 3% Hispanic American, 13% African American, 1% Asian American/Pacific Islander **The most frequently chosen baccalaureate fields are** business/marketing, communications/communication technologies, psychology **Academic program** English as a second language, advanced placement, accelerated degree program, self-designed majors, honors program, summer session, adult/continuing education programs, internships **Contact** Mr. Steve Pochard, Dean of Enrollment Management, Spring Hill College, 4000 Dauphin Street, Mobile, AL 36608-1791. Telephone: 334-380-3030 or toll-free 800-SHC-6704. Fax: 334-460-2186. E-mail: admit@shc.edu. Web site: http://www.shc.edu/.

STILLMAN COLLEGE
TUSCALOOSA, ALABAMA

General Independent, 4-year, coed, affiliated with Presbyterian Church (U.S.A.) **Contact** Mr. Mason Bonner, Director of Admissions, Stillman College, P.O. Box 1430, 3600 Stillman Boulevard, Tuscaloosa, AL 35403. Telephone: 205-366-8817 or toll-free 800-841-5722. Web site: http://www.stillman.edu/.

TALLADEGA COLLEGE
TALLADEGA, ALABAMA

General Independent, 4-year, coed **Entrance** Minimally difficult **Setting** 130-acre small-town campus **Total enrollment** 460 **Student/faculty ratio** 9:1 **Application deadline** 4/1 (freshmen), rolling (transfer) **Freshmen** 22% were admitted **Housing** Yes **Expenses** Tuition $6752; Room & Board $3260 **Undergraduates** 13% 25 or older **The most frequently chosen baccalaureate fields are** biological/life sciences, business/marketing, social sciences and history **Academic program** Adult/continuing education programs, internships **Contact** Ms. Muaco Wilson, Acting Director of Admissions, Talladega College, 627 West Battle Street, Talladega, AL 35160. Telephone: 256-761-6359 or toll-free 800-762-2168 (in-state); 800-633-2440 (out-of-state). Fax: 256-362-2268. E-mail: be21long@talladega.edu. Web site: http://www.talladega.edu/.

TROY STATE UNIVERSITY
TROY, ALABAMA

General State-supported, comprehensive, coed **Entrance** Moderately difficult **Setting** 577-acre small-town campus **Total enrollment** 6,299 **Student/faculty ratio** 23:1 **Application deadline** Rolling (freshmen), rolling (transfer) **Freshmen** 64% were admitted **Housing** Yes **Expenses** Tuition 3126; Room & Board 4274 **Undergraduates** 60% women, 18% part-time, 26% 25 or older, 1% Native American, 1% Hispanic American, 24% African American, 1% Asian American/Pacific Islander **The most frequently chosen baccalaureate fields are** business/marketing, education, protective services/public administration **Academic program** English as a second language, advanced placement, accelerated degree program, self-designed majors, honors program, summer session, adult/continuing education programs, internships **Contact** Mr. Buddy Starling, Dean of Enrollment Services, Troy State University, Adams Administration Building, Room 134, Troy, AL 36082. Telephone: 334-670-3179 or toll-free 800-551-9716 (in-state). Fax: 334-670-3733. E-mail: bstar@trojan.troyst.edu. Web site: http://www.troyst.edu/.

TROY STATE UNIVERSITY DOTHAN
DOTHAN, ALABAMA

General State-supported, comprehensive, coed **Entrance** Minimally difficult **Setting** 250-acre small-town campus **Total enrollment** 1,958 **Student/faculty ratio** 17:1 **Application deadline** Rolling (freshmen), rolling (transfer) **Freshmen** 76% were admitted **Housing** No **Expenses** Tuition 3084 **Undergraduates** 63% women, 45% part-time, 61% 25 or older, 1% Native American, 2% Hispanic American, 17% African American, 1% Asian American/Pacific Islander **Academic program** Advanced placement, accelerated degree program, summer session, internships **Contact** Mr. Bob Willis, Director of Enrollment Services, Troy State University Dothan, PO Box 8368, Dothan, AL 36304-0368. Telephone: 334-983-6556 Ext. 205. Fax: 334-983-6322. E-mail: bwillis@asntsu.asn.net. Web site: http://www.tsud.edu/.

TROY STATE UNIVERSITY MONTGOMERY
MONTGOMERY, ALABAMA

General State-supported, comprehensive, coed **Entrance** Noncompetitive **Setting** 6-acre urban campus **Total enrollment** 3,090 **Application deadline** Rolling (freshmen), rolling (transfer) **Housing** No **Expenses** Tuition $2760 **Undergraduates** 64% women, 67% part-time, 58% 25 or older, 1% Native American, 2% Hispanic American, 43% African American, 2% Asian American/Pacific Islander **Academic program** Advanced placement, accelerated degree program, self-designed majors, honors program, summer session, adult/continuing education programs **Contact** Mr. Frank Hrabe, Director of Enrollment Management, Troy State University Montgomery, PO Drawer 4419, Montgomery, AL 36103-4419. Telephone: 334-241-9506 or toll-free 800-355-TSUM. E-mail: admit@tsum.edu. Web site: http://www.tsum.edu/.

TUSKEGEE UNIVERSITY
TUSKEGEE, ALABAMA

General Independent, comprehensive, coed **Entrance** Moderately difficult **Setting** 4,390-acre small-town campus **Total enrollment** 2,826 **Student/faculty ratio** 13:1 **Application deadline** 4/15 (freshmen), 4/15 (transfer) **Freshmen** 71% were admitted **Housing** Yes **Expenses** Tuition $10,084; Room & Board $5328 **Undergraduates** 58% women, 4% part-time, 5% 25 or older, 0% Native American, 0.04% Hispanic American, 97% African American, 0% Asian American/Pacific Islander **The most frequently chosen baccalaureate fields are** business/marketing, engineering/engineering technologies, health professions and related sciences **Academic program** English as a second language, honors program, summer session, internships **Contact** Mr. William E. Mathis, Admissions, Tuskegee University, 102 Old Administration Building, Tuskegee, AL 36088. Telephone: 334-727-8500 or toll-free 800-622-6531. Web site: http://www.tusk.edu/.

THE UNIVERSITY OF ALABAMA
TUSCALOOSA, ALABAMA

General State-supported, university, coed **Entrance** Moderately difficult **Setting** 1,000-acre suburban campus **Total enrollment** 19,277 **Student/faculty ratio** 18:1 **Application deadline** 7/1 (freshmen), rolling (transfer) **Freshmen** 86% were admitted **Housing** Yes **Expenses** Tuition $3014; Room & Board $3800 **Undergraduates** 52% women, 10% part-time, 16% 25 or older, 1% Native American, 1% Hispanic American, 15% African American, 1% Asian American/Pacific Islander **The most frequently chosen baccalaureate fields are** business/marketing, communications/communication technologies, education **Academic program** English as a second language, advanced placement, accelerated degree program, self-designed majors, honors program, summer session, adult/continuing education programs, internships **Contact** Dr. Lisa B. Harris, Assistant Vice President for Undergraduate Admissions and Financial Aid, The University of Alabama, Box 870132, Tuscaloosa, AL 35487-0132. Telephone: 205-348-5666 or toll-free 800-933-BAMA. Fax: 205-348-9046. E-mail: uaadmit@ua1vm.ua.edu. Web site: http://www.ua.edu/.

THE UNIVERSITY OF ALABAMA AT BIRMINGHAM
BIRMINGHAM, ALABAMA

General State-supported, university, coed **Entrance** Moderately difficult **Setting** 265-acre urban campus **Total enrollment** 14,951 **Student/faculty ratio** 18:1 **Application deadline** 8/1 (freshmen), 8/31 (transfer) **Freshmen** 90% were admitted **Housing** Yes **Expenses** Tuition 3363; Room & Board 6471 **Undergraduates** 59% women, 32% part-time, 33% 25 or older, 0.3% Native American, 1% Hispanic American, 29% African American, 3% Asian American/Pacific Islander **The most frequently chosen baccalaureate fields are** business/marketing, education, health professions and related sciences **Academic program** Advanced placement, self-designed majors, honors program, summer session, adult/continuing education programs, internships **Contact** Ms. Chenise Ryan, Director of Undergraduate Admissions, The University of Alabama at Birmingham, Office of Undergraduate Admissions, 260 HUC, 1530 3rd Avenue south, Birmingham, AL 35294-1150. Telephone: 205-934-8221 or toll-free 800-421-8743 (in-state). Fax: 205-975-7114. E-mail: uabadmit@uabdpo.dpo.uab.edu. Web site: http://www.uab.edu.

THE UNIVERSITY OF ALABAMA IN HUNTSVILLE
HUNTSVILLE, ALABAMA

General State-supported, university, coed **Entrance** Moderately difficult **Setting** 376-acre suburban campus **Total enrollment** 6,563 **Student/faculty ratio** 14:1 **Application deadline** 8/15 (freshmen), 8/15 (transfer) **Freshmen** 92% were admitted **Housing** Yes **Expenses** Tuition 3284; Room & Board 4300 **Undergraduates** 51% women, 39% part-time, 36%

The University of Alabama in Huntsville *(continued)*

25 or older, 2% Native American, 2% Hispanic American, 15% African American, 4% Asian American/Pacific Islander **The most frequently chosen baccalaureate fields are** engineering/engineering technologies, business/marketing, health professions and related sciences **Academic program** English as a second language, advanced placement, accelerated degree program, honors program, summer session, adult/continuing education programs, internships **Contact** Ms. Sabrina Williams, Associate Director of Admissions, The University of Alabama in Huntsville, 301 Sparkman Drive, Huntsville, AL 35899. Telephone: 256-824-6070 or toll-free 800-UAH-CALL. Fax: 256-824-6073. E-mail: admitme@email.uah.edu. Web site: http://www.uah.edu/.

UNIVERSITY OF MOBILE
MOBILE, ALABAMA

General Independent Southern Baptist, comprehensive, coed **Entrance** Moderately difficult **Setting** 830-acre suburban campus **Total enrollment** 1,918 **Student/faculty ratio** 15:1 **Application deadline** Rolling (freshmen), rolling (transfer) **Freshmen** 98% were admitted **Housing** Yes **Expenses** Tuition $8300; Room & Board $2550 **Undergraduates** 68% women, 20% part-time, 22% 25 or older, 1% Native American, 1% Hispanic American, 21% African American, 1% Asian American/Pacific Islander **The most frequently chosen baccalaureate fields are** business/marketing, education, health professions and related sciences **Academic program** English as a second language, advanced placement, accelerated degree program, honors program, summer session, adult/continuing education programs, internships **Contact** Mr. Brian Boyle, Director of Admissions, University of Mobile, PO Box 13220, Mobile, AL 36663-0220. Telephone: 334-442-2287 or toll-free 800-946-7267. Fax: 334-442-2498. E-mail: adminfo@umoblie.edu. Web site: http://www.umobile.edu/.

UNIVERSITY OF MONTEVALLO
MONTEVALLO, ALABAMA

General State-supported, comprehensive, coed **Entrance** Moderately difficult **Setting** 106-acre small-town campus **Total enrollment** 3,014 **Application deadline** 8/1 (freshmen), rolling (transfer) **Freshmen** 77% were admitted **Housing** Yes **Expenses** Tuition $3480; Room & Board $3390 **Undergraduates** 68% women, 11% part-time, 11% 25 or older, 1% Native American, 1% Hispanic American, 14% African American, 1% Asian American/Pacific Islander **Academic program** Advanced placement, accelerated degree program, honors program, summer session, internships **Contact** Mr. William C. Cannon, Director of Admissions, University of Montevallo, Station #6030, Montevallo, AL 35115-6030. Telephone: 205-665-6030 or toll-free 800-292-4349. Fax: 205-665-6032. E-mail: admissions@um.montevallo.edu. Web site: http://www.montevallo.edu/.

UNIVERSITY OF NORTH ALABAMA
FLORENCE, ALABAMA

General State-supported, comprehensive, coed **Entrance** Minimally difficult **Setting** 125-acre urban campus **Total enrollment** 5,601 **Student/faculty ratio** 21:1 **Application deadline** Rolling (freshmen), rolling (transfer) **Freshmen** 83% were admitted **Housing** Yes **Expenses** Tuition $2915; Room & Board $3506 **Undergraduates** 59% women, 16% part-time, 21% 25 or older, 2% Native American, 1% Hispanic American, 10% African American, 1% Asian American/Pacific Islander **The most frequently chosen baccalaureate fields are** business/marketing, education, health professions and related sciences **Academic program** English as a second language, advanced placement, accelerated degree program, summer session, adult/continuing education programs, internships **Contact** Mrs. Kim O. Mauldin, Director of Admissions, University of North Alabama, Office of Admissions, Box 5011, Florence, AL 35632-0001. Telephone: 256-765-4680 or toll-free 800-TALKUNA. Fax: 256-765-4329. E-mail: admis1@unanov.una.edu. Web site: http://www.una.edu/.

UNIVERSITY OF SOUTH ALABAMA
MOBILE, ALABAMA

General State-supported, university, coed **Entrance** Moderately difficult **Setting** 1,215-acre suburban campus **Total enrollment** 11,673 **Student/faculty ratio** 22:1 **Application deadline** 8/10 (freshmen), 8/10 (transfer) **Freshmen** 94% were admitted **Housing** Yes **Expenses** Tuition $3230; Room & Board $3543 **Undergraduates** 58% women, 37% part-time, 29% 25 or older, 1% Native American, 1% Hispanic American, 15% African American, 3% Asian American/Pacific Islander **The most frequently chosen baccalaureate fields are** business/marketing, education, health professions and related sciences **Academic program** English as a second language, advanced placement, accelerated degree program, self-designed majors, summer session, adult/continuing education programs, internships **Contact** Ms. Melissa Jones, Director, University of South Alabama, 307 University Boulevard, Mobile, AL 36688-0002. Telephone: 334-460-6141 or toll-free 800-872-5247. E-mail: admiss@jaguarl.usouthal.edu. Web site: http://www.southalabama.edu.

THE UNIVERSITY OF WEST ALABAMA
LIVINGSTON, ALABAMA

General State-supported, comprehensive, coed **Entrance** Minimally difficult **Setting** 595-acre small-town campus **Total enrollment** 1,924 **Student/faculty ratio** 18:1 **Application deadline** Rolling (freshmen), rolling (transfer) **Freshmen** 69% were admitted **Housing** Yes **Expenses** Tuition $2894; Room & Board $2822 **Undergraduates** 55% women, 9% part-time, 11% 25 or older, 0.4% Native American, 0.4% Hispanic American, 40% African American, 0.2% Asian American/Pacific Islander **The most frequently chosen baccalaureate fields are** business/

marketing, education, social sciences and history **Academic program** Advanced placement, accelerated degree program, honors program, summer session, internships **Contact** Mr. Richard Hester, Vice President for Student Affairs, The University of West Alabama, Station 4, Livingston, AL 35470. Telephone: 205-652-3400 Ext. 3578 or toll-free 800-621-7742 (in-state); 800-621-8044 (out-of-state). Fax: 205-652-3522. E-mail: rhester@uwa.edu. Web site: http://www.uwa.edu/.

VIRGINIA COLLEGE AT BIRMINGHAM
BIRMINGHAM, ALABAMA

General Proprietary, 4-year, coed **Entrance** Moderately difficult **Setting** 1-acre urban campus **Total enrollment** 1,143 **Application deadline** Rolling (freshmen) **Housing** No **Expenses** Tuition $8000 **Undergraduates** 75% 25 or older **Contact** Ms. Bibbie J. McLaughlin, Director of Admissions, Virginia College at Birmingham, 65 Bagby Drive, PO Box 19249, Birmingham, AL 35209. Telephone: 205-802-1200 Ext. 207. Fax: 205-802-7045. E-mail: bibbie@vc.edu. Web site: http://www.vc.edu/.

ALASKA

ALASKA BIBLE COLLEGE
GLENNALLEN, ALASKA

General Independent nondenominational, 4-year, coed **Entrance** Minimally difficult **Setting** 80-acre rural campus **Total enrollment** 44 **Student/faculty ratio** 6:1 **Application deadline** 7/1 (freshmen), 7/1 (transfer) **Freshmen** 96% were admitted **Housing** Yes **Expenses** Tuition 4800; Room & Board 4000 **Undergraduates** 30% women, 30% part-time, 69% 25 or older, 15% Native American, 0% Hispanic American, 0% African American, 3% Asian American/Pacific Islander **The most frequently chosen baccalaureate field is** philosophy, religion, and theology **Academic program** Advanced placement, self-designed majors, internships **Contact** Ms. Jackie Colwell, Admissions Officer, Alaska Bible College, Box 289, Glennallen, AK 99588-0289. Telephone: 907-822-3201 or toll-free 800-478-7884. Fax: 907-822-5027. E-mail: akbibcol@alaska.net. Web site: http://www.akbible.edu/.

ALASKA PACIFIC UNIVERSITY
ANCHORAGE, ALASKA

General Independent, comprehensive, coed **Entrance** Moderately difficult **Setting** 170-acre suburban campus **Total enrollment** 688 **Student/faculty ratio** 7:1 **Application deadline** 2/1 (freshmen), 2/1 (transfer) **Freshmen** 80% were admitted **Housing** Yes **Expenses** Tuition $14,480; Room & Board $5450 **Undergraduates** 63% women, 38% part-time, 26% 25 or older, 16% Native American, 4% Hispanic American, 6% African American, 5% Asian American/Pacific Islander **The most frequently chosen baccalaureate fields are** business/marketing, education, parks and recreation **Academic program** Advanced placement, accelerated degree program, self-designed majors, summer session, adult/continuing education programs, internships **Contact** Mr. Dale Montague, Director of Admissions, Alaska Pacific University, 4101 University Drive, Anchorage, AK 99508-4672. Telephone: 907-564-8248 or toll-free 800-252-7528. Fax: 907-564-8317. E-mail: apu@corecom.net. Web site: http://www.alaskapacific.edu/.

SHELDON JACKSON COLLEGE
SITKA, ALASKA

General Independent, 4-year, coed, affiliated with Presbyterian Church (U.S.A.) **Entrance** Noncompetitive **Setting** 320-acre small-town campus **Total enrollment** 94 **Application deadline** 7/15 (freshmen), 7/15 (transfer) **Freshmen** 100% were admitted **Housing** Yes **Expenses** Tuition 7220; Room & Board 5150 **Undergraduates** 68% 25 or older **The most frequently chosen baccalaureate fields are** education, liberal arts/general studies, natural resources/environmental science **Academic program** Advanced placement, self-designed majors, internships **Contact** Ms. Elizabeth Lower, Chief Admissions Officer, Sheldon Jackson College, 801 Lincoln Street, Sitka, AK 99835. Telephone: 907-747-5208 or toll-free 800-478-5220 (in-state); 800-949-5220 (out-of-state). Fax: 907-747-6366. E-mail: elower@sj-alaska.edu. Web site: http://www.sj-alaska.edu/.

UNIVERSITY OF ALASKA ANCHORAGE
ANCHORAGE, ALASKA

General State-supported, comprehensive, coed **Entrance** Noncompetitive **Setting** 428-acre urban campus **Total enrollment** 14,765 **Application deadline** Rolling (freshmen), rolling (transfer) **Housing** Yes **Expenses** Tuition $1800 **Undergraduates** 62% 25 or older **Academic program** Advanced placement, self-designed majors, summer session, adult/continuing education programs, internships **Contact** Ms. Cecile Mitchell, Director of Enrollment Services, University of Alaska Anchorage, Administration Building, Room 176, Anchorage, AK 99508-8060. Telephone: 907-786-1558. Fax: 907-786-4888. Web site: http://www.uaa.alaska.edu/.

UNIVERSITY OF ALASKA FAIRBANKS
FAIRBANKS, ALASKA

General State-supported, university, coed **Entrance** Moderately difficult **Setting** 2,250-acre small-town campus **Total enrollment** 7,131 **Application deadline** 8/1 (freshmen), 8/1 (transfer) **Freshmen** 86% were admitted **Housing** Yes **Expenses** Tuition $3510; Room & Board $4610 **Undergraduates** 60% women, 51% part-time, 37% 25 or older, 17% Native American, 3% Hispanic American, 4% African American, 3% Asian American/Pacific Islander **The most frequently chosen baccalaureate fields are** education, engineering/engineering technologies, protective services/

University of Alaska Fairbanks *(continued)*

public administration **Academic program** Advanced placement, accelerated degree program, self-designed majors, honors program, summer session, adult/continuing education programs, internships **Contact** Ms. Nancy Dix, Interim Director, University of Alaska Fairbanks, PO Box 757480, Fairbanks, AK 99775-7480. Telephone: 907-474-7500 or toll-free 800-478-1823 (out-of-state). Fax: 907-474-5379. E-mail: fyapply@aurora.alaska.edu. Web site: http://www.uaf.edu/.

UNIVERSITY OF ALASKA SOUTHEAST

JUNEAU, ALASKA

General State-supported, comprehensive, coed **Entrance** Noncompetitive **Setting** 198-acre small-town campus **Total enrollment** 2,799 **Application deadline** Rolling (freshmen), rolling (transfer) **Housing** Yes **Expenses** Tuition $2602 **Undergraduates** 56% 25 or older **Academic program** Advanced placement, self-designed majors, summer session, adult/continuing education programs, internships **Contact** Mr. Greg Wagner, Director of Admissions, University of Alaska Southeast, 11120 Glacier Highway, Juneau, AK 99801. Telephone: 907-465-6239. Fax: 907-465-6365. E-mail: jyuas@acadi.alaska.edu. Web site: http://www.jun.alaska.edu/.

AL COLLINS GRAPHIC DESIGN SCHOOL

See Collins College: A School of Design and Technology

ARIZONA

AMERICAN INDIAN COLLEGE OF THE ASSEMBLIES OF GOD, INC.

PHOENIX, ARIZONA

General Independent, 4-year, coed, affiliated with Assemblies of God **Entrance** Minimally difficult **Setting** 10-acre urban campus **Total enrollment** 76 **Student/faculty ratio** 3:1 **Application deadline** 8/15 (freshmen), 8/15 (transfer) **Freshmen** 46% were admitted **Housing** Yes **Expenses** Tuition $4330; Room & Board $3310 **Undergraduates** 59% women, 17% part-time, 42% 25 or older, 78% Native American, 8% Hispanic American, 0% African American, 3% Asian American/Pacific Islander **The most frequently chosen baccalaureate fields are** education, philosophy, religion, and theology **Academic program** Internships **Contact** Ms. Sandy Ticeahkie, Admissions Coordinator, American Indian College of the Assemblies of God, Inc., 10020 North 15th Avenue, Phoenix, AZ 85021. Telephone: 602-944-3335 Ext. 227 or toll-free 800-933-3828. Fax: 602-943-8299. E-mail: aicadm@juno.com.

ARIZONA STATE UNIVERSITY

TEMPE, ARIZONA

General State-supported, university, coed **Entrance** Moderately difficult **Setting** 814-acre suburban campus **Total enrollment** 44,126 **Student/faculty ratio** 20:1 **Application deadline** Rolling (freshmen), rolling (transfer) **Freshmen** 77% were admitted **Housing** Yes **Expenses** Tuition $2346; Room & Board $5240 **Undergraduates** 52% women, 21% part-time, 20% 25 or older, 2% Native American, 11% Hispanic American, 3% African American, 5% Asian American/Pacific Islander **The most frequently chosen baccalaureate fields are** business/marketing, communications/communication technologies, social sciences and history **Academic program** Advanced placement, accelerated degree program, honors program, summer session, adult/continuing education programs, internships **Contact** Mr. Timothy J. Desch, Director of Undergraduate Admissions, Arizona State University, Box 870112, Tempe, AZ 85287-0112. Telephone: 480-965-7788. Fax: 480-965-3610. E-mail: ugradadm@asuvm.inre.asu.edu. Web site: http://www.asu.edu/.

ARIZONA STATE UNIVERSITY EAST

MESA, ARIZONA

General State-supported, comprehensive, coed **Entrance** Moderately difficult **Setting** 600-acre suburban campus **Total enrollment** 1,939 **Student/faculty ratio** 14:1 **Application deadline** Rolling (freshmen), rolling (transfer) **Freshmen** 83% were admitted **Housing** Yes **Expenses** Tuition $2296; Room & Board $4540 **Undergraduates** 49% women, 71% part-time, 36% 25 or older, 2% Native American, 10% Hispanic American, 2% African American, 5% Asian American/Pacific Islander **The most frequently chosen baccalaureate fields are** agriculture, engineering/engineering technologies **Academic program** Advanced placement, accelerated degree program, self-designed majors, honors program, summer session, internships **Contact** Ms. Carmen Prado, Student Recruitment/Retention Specialist, Arizona State University East, Undergraduate Admissions, Arizona State University, PO Box 870112, Tempe, AZ 85287-0112. Telephone: 480-727-1165 or toll-free 480-965-7788 (in-state). Fax: 480-727-1008. Web site: http://www.east.asu.edu/.

ARIZONA STATE UNIVERSITY WEST

PHOENIX, ARIZONA

General State-supported, upper-level, coed **Entrance** Moderately difficult **Setting** 300-acre urban campus **Total enrollment** 5,325 **Student/faculty ratio** 18:1 **Application deadline** Rolling (transfer) **First-Year Students** 100% were admitted **Housing** No **Expenses** Tuition $2345 **Undergraduates** 71% women, 52% part-time, 57% 25 or older, 2% Native American, 15% Hispanic American, 2% African American, 4% Asian American/Pacific Islander **The most frequently chosen baccalaureate fields are** business/marketing, education, social sciences and history

Academic program Self-designed majors, honors program, summer session, adult/continuing education programs, internships **Contact** Ms. B.J. Hart, Coordinator of Admissions, Arizona State University West, 4701 West Thunderbird Road, PO Box 37100, Phoenix, AZ 85069-7100. Telephone: 602-543-9378. Web site: http://www.west.asu.edu/.

THE ART INSTITUTE OF PHOENIX
PHOENIX, ARIZONA

General Proprietary, 4-year, coed, primarily men **Entrance** Minimally difficult **Setting** suburban campus **Total enrollment** 1,000 **Student/faculty ratio** 20:1 **Application deadline** Rolling (freshmen) **Freshmen** 100% were admitted **Housing** Yes **Expenses** Tuition 13,632; Room only 4302 **Undergraduates** 25% 25 or older **Academic program** Advanced placement, honors program, internships **Contact** Mr. Timothy J. Dengler, Director of Admissions, The Art Institute of Phoenix, 2233 West Dunlap Avenue, Phoenix, AZ 85021-2859. Telephone: 602-678-4300 Ext. 102 or toll-free 800-474-2479 Ext. 102 (in-state). Fax: 602-216-0439. E-mail: sweeneys@aii.edu. Web site: http://www.aipx.edu/.

COLLINS COLLEGE: A SCHOOL OF DESIGN AND TECHNOLOGY
TEMPE, ARIZONA

General Proprietary, 4-year, coed **Contact** Mr. Jeff Marcus, Vice President of Marketing, Collins College: A School of Design and Technology, 1140 South Priest, Tempe, AZ 85281. Telephone: 480-966-3000 Ext. 121 or toll-free 800-876-7070 (out-of-state). Fax: 480-966-2599. E-mail: jen@alcollins.com. Web site: http://www.collinscollege.edu/.

DEVRY INSTITUTE OF TECHNOLOGY
PHOENIX, ARIZONA

General Proprietary, 4-year, coed **Entrance** Minimally difficult **Setting** 18-acre urban campus **Total enrollment** 3,705 **Student/faculty ratio** 32:1 **Application deadline** Rolling (freshmen), rolling (transfer) **Freshmen** 62% were admitted **Housing** No **Expenses** Tuition 8805 **Undergraduates** 25% women, 24% part-time, 44% 25 or older, 4% Native American, 14% Hispanic American, 6% African American, 6% Asian American/Pacific Islander **The most frequently chosen baccalaureate fields are** computer/information sciences, business/marketing, engineering/engineering technologies **Academic program** Advanced placement, accelerated degree program, summer session, adult/continuing education programs **Contact** Raymond Toledo, Director of Admissions, DeVry Institute of Technology, 2149 West Dunlap, Phoenix, AZ 85021-2995. Telephone: 602-870-9201 Ext. 451 or toll-free 800-528-0250 (out-of-state). E-mail: webadmin@devry phx.edu. Web site: http://www.devry-phx.edu/.

EDUCATION AMERICA, TEMPE CAMPUS
TEMPE, ARIZONA

Contact Education America, Tempe Campus, 875 West Elliot Road, Suite 216, Tempe, AZ 85284. Telephone: or toll-free 800-395-4322. Web site: http://educationamerica.com/.

EMBRY-RIDDLE AERONAUTICAL UNIVERSITY
PRESCOTT, ARIZONA

General Independent, 4-year, coed, primarily men **Entrance** Moderately difficult **Setting** 547-acre small-town campus **Total enrollment** 1,689 **Student/faculty ratio** 16:1 **Application deadline** Rolling (freshmen), rolling (transfer) **Freshmen** 73% were admitted **Housing** Yes **Expenses** Tuition $11,700; Room & Board $4320 **Undergraduates** 15% women, 10% part-time, 12% 25 or older, 1% Native American, 4% Hispanic American, 1% African American, 6% Asian American/Pacific Islander **The most frequently chosen baccalaureate fields are** engineering/engineering technologies, computer/information sciences, trade and industry **Academic program** English as a second language, advanced placement, summer session, adult/continuing education programs, internships **Contact** Bill Thompson, Director of Admissions, Embry-Riddle Aeronautical University, 3200 Willow Creek Road, Prescott, AZ 86301. Telephone: 520-708-6692 or toll-free 800-888-3728. Fax: 520-708-6606. E-mail: admit@pr.erau.edu. Web site: http://www.embryriddle.edu/.

GRAND CANYON UNIVERSITY
PHOENIX, ARIZONA

General Independent Southern Baptist, comprehensive, coed **Entrance** Moderately difficult **Setting** 90-acre suburban campus **Total enrollment** 3,615 **Student/faculty ratio** 16:1 **Application deadline** Rolling (freshmen), rolling (transfer) **Freshmen** 76% were admitted **Housing** Yes **Expenses** Tuition 9660; Room & Board 4286 **Undergraduates** 64% women, 17% part-time, 27% 25 or older, 2% Native American, 8% Hispanic American, 5% African American, 2% Asian American/Pacific Islander **The most frequently chosen baccalaureate fields are** biological/life sciences, education, psychology **Academic program** English as a second language, advanced placement, accelerated degree program, honors program, summer session, adult/continuing education programs, internships **Contact** April Chapman, Director of Admissions, Grand Canyon University, 3300 West Camelback Road, PO Box 11097, Phoenix, AZ 86017-3030. Telephone: 602-589-2855 Ext. 2811 or toll-free 800-800-9776 (in-state). Fax: 602-589-2580. E-mail: smarch@enet.net. Web site: http://www.grand-canyon.edu/.

INTERNATIONAL BAPTIST COLLEGE
TEMPE, ARIZONA

General Independent Baptist, comprehensive, coed **Entrance** Minimally difficult **Setting** 12-acre subur-

International Baptist College *(continued)*

ban campus **Total enrollment** 65 **Application deadline** Rolling (freshmen), rolling (transfer) **Housing** Yes **Expenses** Tuition $4350; Room & Board $3000 **Undergraduates** 0% Native American, 8% Hispanic American, 6% African American, 4% Asian American/Pacific Islander **Contact** Dr. Stanley Bushey, Administrative Services Director, International Baptist College, 2150 East Southern Avenue, Tempe, AZ 85282. Telephone: 480-838-7070 or toll-free 800-422-4858. Fax: 480-838-1533.

METROPOLITAN COLLEGE OF COURT REPORTING
PHOENIX, ARIZONA

General Proprietary, 4-year, coed, primarily women **Setting** 1-acre suburban campus **Total enrollment** 118 **Student/faculty ratio** 12:1 **Freshmen** 100% were admitted **Housing** No **Expenses** Tuition $5990 **Undergraduates** 97% women, 85% 25 or older **Academic program** Accelerated degree program, summer session, adult/continuing education programs, internships **Contact** Ms. Shannon Buchanan, Admissions, Metropolitan College of Court Reporting, 4640 East Elwood Street, Suite 12, Phoenix, AZ 85040. Telephone: 480-955-5900. Fax: 480-894-8999. Web site: http://www.metropolitancollege.edu/.

NORTHERN ARIZONA UNIVERSITY
FLAGSTAFF, ARIZONA

General State-supported, university, coed **Entrance** Moderately difficult **Setting** 730-acre small-town campus **Total enrollment** 19,964 **Student/faculty ratio** 18:1 **Application deadline** Rolling (freshmen), rolling (transfer) **Freshmen** 81% were admitted **Housing** Yes **Expenses** Tuition $2346; Room & Board $4391 **Undergraduates** 59% women, 16% part-time, 21% 25 or older, 8% Native American, 9% Hispanic American, 2% African American, 2% Asian American/Pacific Islander **The most frequently chosen baccalaureate fields are** business/marketing, education, liberal arts/general studies **Academic program** English as a second language, advanced placement, accelerated degree program, honors program, summer session, internships **Contact** Ms. Pamela Van Wyck, Assistant Director, Northern Arizona University, PO Box 4084, Flagstaff, AZ 86011. Telephone: 520-523-6008 or toll-free 888-MORE-NAU. Fax: 520-523-6023. E-mail: ugrad@nau.edu. Web site: http://www.nau.edu/.

PRESCOTT COLLEGE
PRESCOTT, ARIZONA

General Independent, comprehensive, coed **Entrance** Moderately difficult **Setting** small-town campus **Total enrollment** 904 **Application deadline** 2/1 (freshmen), 2/1 (transfer) **Housing** No **Expenses** Tuition $13,589; Room & Board $9866 **Undergraduates** 59% women, 12% part-time, 14% 25 or older, 6% Native American, 2% Hispanic American, 0.1% African American, 0.4% Asian American/Pacific Islander **Academic program** Advanced placement, accelerated degree program, self-designed majors, summer session, adult/continuing education programs, internships **Contact** Ms. Shari Sterling, Director of Admissions, Prescott College, 220 Grove Avenue, Prescott, AZ 86301-2990. Telephone: 520-778-2090 Ext. 2101 or toll-free 800-628-6364 (out-of-state). Fax: 520-776-5137. E-mail: applypc@aztec.asu.edu. Web site: http://www.prescott.edu/.

SOUTHWESTERN COLLEGE
PHOENIX, ARIZONA

General Independent Conservative Baptist, 4-year, coed **Entrance** Minimally difficult **Setting** 19-acre urban campus **Total enrollment** 257 **Student/faculty ratio** 16:1 **Application deadline** 8/15 (freshmen), 8/15 (transfer) **Freshmen** 59% were admitted **Housing** Yes **Expenses** Tuition $8250; Room & Board $3170 **Undergraduates** 43% women, 10% part-time, 32% 25 or older, 1% Native American, 7% Hispanic American, 4% African American, 2% Asian American/Pacific Islander **Academic program** Advanced placement, accelerated degree program, summer session, adult/continuing education programs, internships **Contact** Mrs. Karen Lokken, Admissions Coordinator, Southwestern College, 2625 East Cactus Road, Phoenix, AZ 85032-7042. Telephone: 602-992-6101 Ext. 108 or toll-free 800-247-2697 (out-of-state). Fax: 602-404-2159. E-mail: admissions@southwesterncollege.edu. Web site: http://www.southwesterncollege.edu/.

UNIVERSITY OF ADVANCING COMPUTER TECHNOLOGY
TEMPE, ARIZONA

General Proprietary, comprehensive, coed **Setting** urban campus **Total enrollment** 1,055 **Application deadline** Rolling (freshmen) **Housing** No **Expenses** Tuition 11,484 **Undergraduates** 19% women, 2% Native American, 13% Hispanic American, 3% African American, 3% Asian American/Pacific Islander **Academic program** Accelerated degree program **Contact** Mr. Dominic Pistillo, President, University of Advancing Computer Technology, 2625 West Baseline Road, Tempe, AZ 85283-1042. Telephone: 602-383-8228 or toll-free 602-383-8228 (in-state); 800-658-5744 (out-of-state). Fax: 602-383-8222. E-mail: admissions@uact.edu. Web site: http://www.uact.edu/.

THE UNIVERSITY OF ARIZONA
TUCSON, ARIZONA

General State-supported, university, coed **Entrance** Moderately difficult **Setting** 351-acre urban campus **Total enrollment** 34,560 **Student/faculty ratio** 18:1 **Application deadline** 4/1 (freshmen), 5/1 (transfer) **Freshmen** 84% were admitted **Housing** Yes **Expenses** Tuition 2348; Room & Board 5888 **Undergraduates** 53% women, 18% part-time, 16% 25 or older, 2% Native American, 14% Hispanic American, 3% African American, 5% Asian American/Pacific Islander

The most frequently chosen baccalaureate fields are business/marketing, biological/life sciences, social sciences and history **Academic program** English as a second language, advanced placement, honors program, summer session, adult/continuing education programs, internships **Contact** Ms. Lori Goldman, Director of Admissions, The University of Arizona, PO Box 210040, Tucson, AZ 85721-0040. Telephone: 520-621-3237. Fax: 520-621-9799. E-mail: appinfo@arizona.edu. Web site: http://www.arizona.edu/.

UNIVERSITY OF PHOENIX–PHOENIX CAMPUS
PHOENIX, ARIZONA

General Proprietary, comprehensive, coed **Entrance** Noncompetitive **Setting** urban campus **Total enrollment** 66,534 **Student/faculty ratio** 13:1 **Application deadline** Rolling (freshmen), rolling (transfer) **Housing** No **Expenses** Tuition $7740 **Undergraduates** 56% women, 86% 25 or older, 2% Native American, 18% Hispanic American, 13% African American, 6% Asian American/Pacific Islander **The most frequently chosen baccalaureate fields are** business/marketing, health professions and related sciences **Academic program** Advanced placement, accelerated degree program, adult/continuing education programs **Contact** Ms. Beth Barilla, Director of Admissions, University of Phoenix–Phoenix Campus, 4615 East Elwood Street, Phoenix, AZ 85040-1948. Telephone: 480-927-0099 Ext. 1216 or toll-free 800-776-4867 (in-state); 800-228-7240 (out-of-state). Fax: 480-894-1758. E-mail: babarill@oramail@apollogrp.edu. Web site: http://www.phoenix.edu/.

UNIVERSITY OF PHOENIX–SOUTHERN ARIZONA CAMPUS
TUCSON, ARIZONA

General Proprietary, comprehensive, coed **Entrance** Noncompetitive **Total enrollment** 66,534 **Student/faculty ratio** 13:1 **Application deadline** Rolling (freshmen), rolling (transfer) **Expenses** Tuition $7740 **Undergraduates** 56% women, 86% 25 or older, 2% Native American, 18% Hispanic American, 13% African American, 6% Asian American/Pacific Islander **Academic program** Advanced placement, accelerated degree program, adult/continuing education programs **Contact** Ms. Beth Barilla, Director of Admissions, University of Phoenix–Southern Arizona Campus, 4615 East Elwood Street, Phoenix, AZ 85040-1948. Telephone: 480-927-0099 Ext. 1218 or toll-free 800-228-7240. Fax: 480-594-1758. E-mail: beth.barilla@apollogrp.edu. Web site: http://www.phoenix.edu/.

WESTERN INTERNATIONAL UNIVERSITY
PHOENIX, ARIZONA

General Proprietary, comprehensive, coed **Entrance** Moderately difficult **Setting** 4-acre urban campus **Total enrollment** 2,690 **Application deadline** Rolling (freshmen), rolling (transfer) **Housing** No **Expenses** Tuition $7920 **Undergraduates** 42% women, 54% part-time, 90% 25 or older, 1% Native American, 7% Hispanic American, 4% African American, 2% Asian American/Pacific Islander **Academic program** English as a second language, advanced placement, accelerated degree program, honors program, summer session, adult/continuing education programs **Contact** Ms. Jo Arney, Director of Student Services, Western International University, 9215 North Black Canyon Highway, Phoenix, AZ 85021-2718. Telephone: 602-943-2311 Ext. 139. Web site: http://www.wintu.edu/.

ARKANSAS

ARKANSAS BAPTIST COLLEGE
LITTLE ROCK, ARKANSAS

General Independent Baptist, 4-year, coed **Entrance** Noncompetitive **Setting** urban campus **Total enrollment** 201 **Application deadline** Rolling (freshmen) **Housing** Yes **Expenses** Tuition 2200 **Academic program** Accelerated degree program, summer session, adult/continuing education programs **Contact** Mrs. Annie Hightower, Registrar, Arkansas Baptist College, 1600 Bishop Street, Little Rock, AR 72202-6067. Telephone: 501-374-7856 Ext. 19.

ARKANSAS STATE UNIVERSITY
JONESBORO, ARKANSAS

General State-supported, comprehensive, coed **Entrance** Moderately difficult **Setting** 900-acre small-town campus **Total enrollment** 10,429 **Student/faculty ratio** 18:1 **Freshmen** 65% were admitted **Housing** Yes **Expenses** Tuition $3160; Room & Board $3071 **Undergraduates** 58% women, 21% part-time, 21% 25 or older, 0.2% Native American, 1% Hispanic American, 13% African American, 1% Asian American/Pacific Islander **The most frequently chosen baccalaureate fields are** business/marketing, education, health professions and related sciences **Academic program** English as a second language, advanced placement, accelerated degree program, honors program, summer session, internships **Contact** Ms. Paula James, Director of Admissions, Arkansas State University, PO Box 1630, State University, AR 72467. Telephone: 870-972-3024 or toll-free 800-382-3030 (in-state); 800-643-0080 (out-of-state). Fax: 870-910-8094. E-mail: admissions@chickasaw.astate.edu. Web site: http://www.astate.edu/.

ARKANSAS TECH UNIVERSITY
RUSSELLVILLE, ARKANSAS

General State-supported, comprehensive, coed **Entrance** Minimally difficult **Setting** 517-acre small-town campus **Total enrollment** 5,172 **Student/faculty ratio** 18:1 **Freshmen** 54% were admitted **Housing** Yes **Expenses** Tuition $2768; Room & Board $3336 **Undergraduates** 53% women, 17% part-time, 27% 25 or older, 1% Native American, 2% Hispanic American, 4% African American, 1% Asian

Arkansas Tech University *(continued)*

American/Pacific Islander **The most frequently chosen baccalaureate fields are** business/marketing, education, health professions and related sciences **Academic program** English as a second language, advanced placement, accelerated degree program, honors program, summer session, adult/continuing education programs, internships **Contact** Ms. Shauna Donnell, Director of Enrollment Management, Arkansas Tech University, L.L. "DOC" Bryan Student Services Building, Suite 141, Russellville, AR 72801-2222. Telephone: 501-968-0404 or toll-free 800-582-6953 (in-state). Fax: 501-964-0522. E-mail: adrf@atuvm.atu.edu. Web site: http://www.atu.edu/.

CENTRAL BAPTIST COLLEGE
CONWAY, ARKANSAS

General Independent Baptist, 4-year, coed **Entrance** Minimally difficult **Setting** 11-acre small-town campus **Total enrollment** 381 **Student/faculty ratio** 17:1 **Application deadline** 8/15 (freshmen), 8/15 (transfer) **Freshmen** 87% were admitted **Housing** Yes **Expenses** Tuition $6058; Room & Board $3816 **Undergraduates** 48% women, 11% part-time, 19% 25 or older, 0.3% Native American, 0.3% Hispanic American, 5% African American, 1% Asian American/Pacific Islander **The most frequently chosen baccalaureate field is** philosophy, religion, and theology **Academic program** Advanced placement, summer session, adult/continuing education programs, internships **Contact** Mr. Cory Calhoun, Admissions Counselor, Central Baptist College, 1501 College Avenue, Conway, AR 72032-6470. Telephone: 501-329-6872 Ext. 167 or toll-free 800-205-6872. Fax: 501-329-2941. E-mail: cjackson@cbc.edu. Web site: http://www.cbc.edu/.

HARDING UNIVERSITY
SEARCY, ARKANSAS

General Independent, comprehensive, coed, affiliated with Church of Christ **Entrance** Moderately difficult **Setting** 200-acre small-town campus **Total enrollment** 4,337 **Student/faculty ratio** 16:1 **Application deadline** 7/1 (freshmen), 7/1 (transfer) **Freshmen** 81% were admitted **Housing** Yes **Expenses** Tuition 8425; Room & Board 4336 **Undergraduates** 55% women, 10% part-time, 8% 25 or older, 1% Native American, 1% Hispanic American, 4% African American, 0.4% Asian American/Pacific Islander **The most frequently chosen baccalaureate fields are** business/marketing, education, health professions and related sciences **Academic program** English as a second language, advanced placement, accelerated degree program, self-designed majors, honors program, summer session, adult/continuing education programs, internships **Contact** Mr. Mike Williams, Assistant Vice President of Admissions, Harding University, Box 11255, Searcy, AR 72149-0001. Telephone: 501-279-4407 or toll-free 800-477-4407. Fax: 501-279-4865. E-mail: admissions@harding.edu. Web site: http://www.harding.edu/.

HENDERSON STATE UNIVERSITY
ARKADELPHIA, ARKANSAS

General State-supported, comprehensive, coed **Entrance** Moderately difficult **Setting** 135-acre small-town campus **Total enrollment** 3,430 **Student/faculty ratio** 16:1 **Application deadline** 7/15 (freshmen), rolling (transfer) **Freshmen** 67% were admitted **Housing** Yes **Expenses** Tuition $2795; Room & Board $3152 **Undergraduates** 55% women, 11% part-time, 17% 25 or older, 1% Native American, 1% Hispanic American, 15% African American, 1% Asian American/Pacific Islander **The most frequently chosen baccalaureate fields are** business/marketing, education, social sciences and history **Academic program** Advanced placement, honors program, summer session, internships **Contact** Ms. Vikita Hardwrick, Director of University Relations/Admissions, Henderson State University, 1100 Henderson Street, PO Box 7560, Arkadelphia, AR 71999-0001. Telephone: 870-230-5028 or toll-free 800-228-7333. Fax: 870-230-5066. E-mail: hardwrv@oaks.hsu.edu. Web site: http://www.hsu.edu/.

HENDRIX COLLEGE
CONWAY, ARKANSAS

General Independent United Methodist, 4-year, coed **Entrance** Very difficult **Setting** 158-acre suburban campus **Total enrollment** 1,137 **Student/faculty ratio** 13:1 **Application deadline** Rolling (freshmen), rolling (transfer) **Freshmen** 87% were admitted **Housing** Yes **Expenses** Tuition 12,665; Room & Board 4625 **Undergraduates** 54% women, 1% part-time, 1% 25 or older, 1% Native American, 2% Hispanic American, 5% African American, 2% Asian American/Pacific Islander **The most frequently chosen baccalaureate fields are** biological/life sciences, psychology, social sciences and history **Academic program** Advanced placement, self-designed majors, internships **Contact** Mr. Rock Jones, Vice President for Enrollment, Hendrix College, 1600 Washington Avenue, Conway, AR 72032. Telephone: 501-450-1362 or toll-free 800-277-9017. Fax: 501-450-3843. E-mail: adm@hendrix.edu. Web site: http://www.hendrix.edu/.

JOHN BROWN UNIVERSITY
SILOAM SPRINGS, ARKANSAS

General Independent interdenominational, comprehensive, coed **Entrance** Moderately difficult **Setting** 200-acre small-town campus **Total enrollment** 1,517 **Student/faculty ratio** 16:1 **Application deadline** 3/1 (freshmen), 3/1 (transfer) **Freshmen** 80% were admitted **Housing** Yes **Expenses** Tuition $11,492; Room & Board $4478 **Undergraduates** 52% women, 7% part-time, 24% 25 or older, 1% Native American, 2% Hispanic American, 1% African American, 1% Asian American/Pacific Islander **The most frequently chosen baccalaureate fields are** business/marketing, education, philosophy, religion, and theology **Academic program** English as a second language, advanced placement, honors program, adult/

continuing education programs, internships **Contact** Ms. Karyn Byrne, Application Coordinator, John Brown University, 200 West University Street, Siloam Springs, AR 72761-2121. Telephone: 501-524-7454 or toll-free 877-JBU-INFO. Fax: 501-524-4196. E-mail: jbuinfo@acc.jbu.edu. Web site: http://www.jbu.edu/.

LYON COLLEGE
BATESVILLE, ARKANSAS

General Independent Presbyterian, 4-year, coed **Entrance** Very difficult **Setting** 136-acre small-town campus **Total enrollment** 476 **Student/faculty ratio** 10:1 **Application deadline** Rolling (freshmen), rolling (transfer) **Freshmen** 85% were admitted **Housing** Yes **Expenses** Tuition $11,375; Room & Board $5125 **Undergraduates** 57% women, 7% part-time, 7% 25 or older, 1% Native American, 1% Hispanic American, 3% African American, 1% Asian American/Pacific Islander **The most frequently chosen baccalaureate fields are** biological/life sciences, English, social sciences and history **Academic program** Advanced placement, self-designed majors, summer session, internships **Contact** Mr. David Wilkey, Vice President for Enrollment Services, Lyon College, PO Box 2317, 2300 Highland Road, Batesville, AR 72503-2317. Telephone: 870-698-4250 or toll-free 800-423-2542. Fax: 870-793-1291. E-mail: admissions@lyon.edu. Web site: http://www.lyon.edu/.

OUACHITA BAPTIST UNIVERSITY
ARKADELPHIA, ARKANSAS

General Independent Baptist, 4-year, coed **Entrance** Moderately difficult **Setting** 84-acre small-town campus **Total enrollment** 1,714 **Student/faculty ratio** 13:1 **Application deadline** 8/15 (freshmen), 8/15 (transfer) **Freshmen** 83% were admitted **Housing** Yes **Expenses** Tuition 10,000; Room & Board 4100 **Undergraduates** 54% women, 5% part-time, 3% 25 or older, 0.4% Native American, 1% Hispanic American, 4% African American, 1% Asian American/Pacific Islander **The most frequently chosen baccalaureate fields are** education, business/marketing, philosophy, religion, and theology **Academic program** English as a second language, advanced placement, accelerated degree program, honors program, summer session, internships **Contact** Mrs. Rebecca Jones, Director of Admissions Counseling, Ouachita Baptist University, 410 Ouachita Street, Arkadelphia, AR 71998-0001. Telephone: 870-245-5110 or toll-free 800-342-5628 (in-state). Fax: 870-245-5500. E-mail: jonesj@sigma.obu.edu. Web site: http://www.obu.edu/.

PHILANDER SMITH COLLEGE
LITTLE ROCK, ARKANSAS

General Independent United Methodist, 4-year, coed **Contact** Mrs. Arnella Hayes, Admission Officer, Philander Smith College, 812 West 13th Street, Little Rock, AR 72202-3718. Telephone: 501-370-5310 or toll-free 800-446-6772. Fax: 501-370-5225. E-mail: admvonda@philander.edu. Web site: http://www.philander.edu/.

SOUTHERN ARKANSAS UNIVERSITY–MAGNOLIA
MAGNOLIA, ARKANSAS

General State-supported, comprehensive, coed **Entrance** Moderately difficult **Setting** 781-acre small-town campus **Total enrollment** 2,977 **Student/faculty ratio** 16:1 **Application deadline** 8/15 (freshmen), 8/15 (transfer) **Freshmen** 92% were admitted **Housing** Yes **Expenses** Tuition $2454; Room & Board $2930 **Undergraduates** 57% women, 13% part-time, 25% 25 or older, 1% Native American, 1% Hispanic American, 23% African American, 0.3% Asian American/Pacific Islander **The most frequently chosen baccalaureate fields are** business/marketing, education, psychology **Academic program** Advanced placement, accelerated degree program, summer session, adult/continuing education programs, internships **Contact** Mr. James E. Whittington, Director of Admissions, Southern Arkansas University–Magnolia, PO Box 9382, 100 East University, Magnolia, AR 71754-9382. Telephone: 870-235-4040. Fax: 870-235-5005. E-mail: adsonny@saumag.edu. Web site: http://www.saumag.edu/.

UNIVERSITY OF ARKANSAS
FAYETTEVILLE, ARKANSAS

General State-supported, university, coed **Entrance** Moderately difficult **Setting** 445-acre suburban campus **Total enrollment** 15,346 **Student/faculty ratio** 16:1 **Application deadline** 2/15 (freshmen), 8/15 (transfer) **Freshmen** 90% were admitted **Housing** Yes **Expenses** Tuition 3880; Room & Board 4454 **Undergraduates** 49% women, 15% part-time, 13% 25 or older, 2% Native American, 1% Hispanic American, 6% African American, 3% Asian American/Pacific Islander **The most frequently chosen baccalaureate fields are** business/marketing, engineering/engineering technologies, trade and industry **Academic program** English as a second language, advanced placement, honors program, summer session, internships **Contact** Ms. Maribeth Lynes, Director of Undergraduate Recruitment, University of Arkansas, 200 Silas H. Hunt Hall, Fayetteville, AR 72701-1201. Telephone: 501-575-5346 or toll-free 800-377-8632. Fax: 501-575-7515. E-mail: uafadmis@comp.uark.edu. Web site: http://www.uark.edu/.

UNIVERSITY OF ARKANSAS AT LITTLE ROCK
LITTLE ROCK, ARKANSAS

General State-supported, university, coed **Entrance** Minimally difficult **Setting** 150-acre urban campus **Total enrollment** 10,541 **Application deadline** Rolling (freshmen), rolling (transfer) **Freshmen** 62% were admitted **Housing** Yes **Expenses** Tuition $2996; Room only $2600 **Undergraduates** 35% 25 or older **Academic program** English as a second language,

University of Arkansas at Little Rock *(continued)*

advanced placement, accelerated degree program, self-designed majors, honors program, summer session, adult/continuing education programs, internships **Contact** Office of Admissions and Records, University of Arkansas at Little Rock, 2801 South University Avenue, Little Rock, AR 72204-1099. Telephone: 501-569-3127 or toll-free 800-482-8892 (in-state). Fax: 501-569-8915. Web site: http://www.ualr.edu/.

UNIVERSITY OF ARKANSAS AT MONTICELLO

MONTICELLO, ARKANSAS

General State-supported, comprehensive, coed **Entrance** Noncompetitive **Setting** 400-acre small-town campus **Total enrollment** 2,323 **Student/faculty ratio** 17:1 **Application deadline** 8/1 (freshmen), 8/1 (transfer) **Housing** Yes **Expenses** Tuition 2670; Room & Board 2780 **Undergraduates** 57% women, 13% part-time, 22% 25 or older, 1% Native American, 1% Hispanic American, 22% African American, 1% Asian American/Pacific Islander **The most frequently chosen baccalaureate fields are** business/marketing, agriculture, education **Academic program** Advanced placement, accelerated degree program, summer session **Contact** Mary Whiting, Director of Admissions, University of Arkansas at Monticello, PO Box 3600, Monticello, AR 71656. Telephone: 870-460-1026 or toll-free 800-844-1826 (in-state). Fax: 870-460-1321. E-mail: admissions@uamont.edu. Web site: http://www.uamont.edu/.

UNIVERSITY OF ARKANSAS AT PINE BLUFF

PINE BLUFF, ARKANSAS

General State-supported, comprehensive, coed **Entrance** Minimally difficult **Setting** 327-acre urban campus **Total enrollment** 3,042 **Student/faculty ratio** 18:1 **Application deadline** 8/1 (freshmen) **Freshmen** 71% were admitted **Housing** Yes **Expenses** Tuition 3090; Room & Board 4100 **Undergraduates** 55% women, 10% part-time, 16% 25 or older, 0% Native American, 0.2% Hispanic American, 95% African American, 0.2% Asian American/Pacific Islander **The most frequently chosen baccalaureate fields are** business/marketing, education, protective services/public administration **Academic program** Advanced placement, accelerated degree program, honors program, summer session, adult/continuing education programs, internships **Contact** Ms. Kwurly M. Floyd-Tate, Director of Admissions and Academic Records, University of Arkansas at Pine Bluff, UAPB Box 17, 1200 University Drive, Pine Bluff, AR 71601-2799. Telephone: 870-575-8487 or toll-free 800-264-6585 (in-state). Fax: 870-543-2021.

UNIVERSITY OF ARKANSAS FOR MEDICAL SCIENCES

LITTLE ROCK, ARKANSAS

General State-supported, upper-level, coed **Contact** Mr. Paul Carter, Assistant to the Vice Chancellor for Academic Affairs, University of Arkansas for Medical Sciences, 4301 West Markham-Slot 601, Little Rock, AR 72205-7199. Telephone: 501-686-5454. Web site: http://www.uams.edu/.

UNIVERSITY OF CENTRAL ARKANSAS

CONWAY, ARKANSAS

General State-supported, comprehensive, coed **Entrance** Moderately difficult **Setting** 365-acre small-town campus **Total enrollment** 8,481 **Student/faculty ratio** 18:1 **Application deadline** Rolling (freshmen), rolling (transfer) **Freshmen** 62% were admitted **Housing** Yes **Expenses** Tuition $3402; Room & Board $3290 **Undergraduates** 14% 25 or older **The most frequently chosen baccalaureate fields are** business/marketing, education, health professions and related sciences **Academic program** English as a second language, advanced placement, accelerated degree program, honors program, summer session, internships **Contact** Ms. Penny Hatfield, Director of Admissions, University of Central Arkansas, 201 Donaghey Avenue, Conway, AR 72035-0001. Telephone: 501-450-5145 or toll-free 800-243-8245 (in-state). Fax: 501-450-5228. E-mail: admisson@ecom.uca.edu. Web site: http://www.uca.edu/.

UNIVERSITY OF THE OZARKS

CLARKSVILLE, ARKANSAS

General Independent Presbyterian, 4-year, coed **Entrance** Moderately difficult **Setting** 56-acre small-town campus **Total enrollment** 622 **Student/faculty ratio** 11:1 **Application deadline** Rolling (freshmen), 8/15 (transfer) **Freshmen** 74% were admitted **Housing** Yes **Expenses** Tuition 9105; Room & Board 4080 **Undergraduates** 52% women, 7% part-time, 6% 25 or older, 2% Native American, 2% Hispanic American, 2% African American, 1% Asian American/Pacific Islander **The most frequently chosen baccalaureate fields are** biological/life sciences, education, liberal arts/general studies **Academic program** English as a second language, advanced placement, summer session, internships **Contact** Mr. James D. Decker, Director of Admissions, University of the Ozarks, 415 North College Avenue, Clarksville, AR 72830-2880. Telephone: 501-979-1209 or toll-free 800-264-8636. Fax: 501-979-1355. E-mail: admiss@ozarks.edu. Web site: http://www.ozarks.edu/.

WILLIAMS BAPTIST COLLEGE

WALNUT RIDGE, ARKANSAS

General Independent Southern Baptist, 4-year, coed **Entrance** Minimally difficult **Setting** 186-acre rural campus **Total enrollment** 660 **Student/faculty ratio** 16:1 **Application deadline** Rolling (freshmen), rolling (transfer) **Freshmen** 75% were admitted **Hous-**

ing Yes **Expenses** Tuition $7250; Room & Board $3400 **Undergraduates** 60% women, 28% part-time, 13% 25 or older, 1% Native American, 1% Hispanic American, 4% African American, 0% Asian American/Pacific Islander **The most frequently chosen baccalaureate fields are** education, philosophy, religion, and theology, psychology **Academic program** Advanced placement, self-designed majors, honors program, summer session, adult/continuing education programs, internships **Contact** Angela Flippo, Director of Admissions, Williams Baptist College, PO Box 3665, Walnut Ridge, AR 72476. Telephone: 870-886-6741 Ext. 127 or toll-free 800-722-4434. Fax: 870-886-3924. E-mail: admissions@wbclab.wbcoll.edu. Web site: http://wbcoll.edu/.

CALIFORNIA

ACADEMY OF ART COLLEGE
SAN FRANCISCO, CALIFORNIA

General Proprietary, comprehensive, coed **Entrance** Noncompetitive **Setting** 3-acre urban campus **Total enrollment** 5,995 **Student/faculty ratio** 15:1 **Application deadline** Rolling (freshmen), rolling (transfer) **Freshmen** 45% were admitted **Housing** Yes **Expenses** Tuition $12,060; Room only $7600 **Undergraduates** 43% women, 42% part-time, 20% 25 or older, 1% Native American, 8% Hispanic American, 3% African American, 15% Asian American/Pacific Islander **The most frequently chosen baccalaureate field is** visual/performing arts **Academic program** English as a second language, summer session, adult/continuing education programs, internships **Contact** Ms. Sandra Weber, Vice President-Admissions, Academy of Art College, 79 New Montgomery Street, San Francisco, CA 94105. Telephone: 415-263-2084 Ext. 2084 or toll-free 800-544-ARTS. Fax: 415-263-4130. E-mail: info@academyart.edu. Web site: http://www.academyart.edu/.

THE AMERICAN COLLEGE
See American InterContinental University

AMERICAN INTERCONTINENTAL UNIVERSITY
LOS ANGELES, CALIFORNIA

General Proprietary, comprehensive, coed **Contact** Mr. Eric Thompson, Director of Admissions, American InterContinental University, 12655 West Jefferson Boulevard, Los Angeles, CA 90066. Telephone: 310-302-2482. Fax: 310-302-2001. Web site: http://www.aiuniv.edu/.

ANTIOCH UNIVERSITY LOS ANGELES
MARINA DEL REY, CALIFORNIA

General Independent, upper-level, coed **Entrance** Moderately difficult **Setting** 1-acre urban campus **Total enrollment** 499 **Student/faculty ratio** 21:1 **Application deadline** 8/1 (transfer) **Housing** No **Expenses** Tuition $13,600 **Undergraduates** 74% women, 70% part-time, 0% Native American, 8% Hispanic American, 21% African American, 3% Asian American/Pacific Islander **Academic program** Advanced placement, accelerated degree program, self-designed majors, summer session, adult/continuing education programs, internships **Contact** Ms. Chloe Reid, Executive Dean, Antioch University Los Angeles, 13274 Fiji Way, Marina del Rey, CA 90292-7090. Telephone: 310-578-1080 Ext. 244 or toll-free 800-7ANTIOCH. Fax: 310-822-4824. E-mail: mehee_hyun@antiochla.edu. Web site: http://www.antiochla.edu/.

ANTIOCH UNIVERSITY SANTA BARBARA
SANTA BARBARA, CALIFORNIA

General Independent, upper-level, coed **Entrance** Minimally difficult **Setting** small-town campus **Total enrollment** 271 **Student/faculty ratio** 15:1 **Application deadline** Rolling (transfer) **Housing** No **Expenses** Tuition 10,200 **The most frequently chosen baccalaureate field is** liberal arts/general studies **Academic program** Accelerated degree program, self-designed majors, summer session, adult/continuing education programs, internships **Contact** Mrs. Carol Flores, Director of Admissions, Antioch University Santa Barbara, 801 Garden Street, Santa Barbara, CA 93101-1580. Telephone: 805-962-8179 Ext. 113. Fax: 805-962-4786. E-mail: linda_ferro@antiochsb.edu. Web site: http://www.antiochsb.edu/.

ARMSTRONG UNIVERSITY
OAKLAND, CALIFORNIA

General Independent, comprehensive, coed **Entrance** Moderately difficult **Setting** urban campus **Total enrollment** 103 **Application deadline** Rolling (freshmen), rolling (transfer) **Housing** No **Expenses** Tuition 6192 **Undergraduates** 45% 25 or older **Academic program** English as a second language, advanced placement, accelerated degree program, summer session **Contact** Ms. Sarah Hofberg, Director of Admission, Armstrong University, 1608 Webster Street, Oakland, CA 94612. Telephone: 510-835-7900 Ext. 10. Fax: 510-835-8935. E-mail: admin@armstrongu.edu. Web site: http://www.armstrong-u.edu/.

ART CENTER COLLEGE OF DESIGN
PASADENA, CALIFORNIA

General Independent, comprehensive, coed **Entrance** Very difficult **Setting** 175-acre suburban campus **Total enrollment** 1,459 **Student/faculty ratio** 9:1 **Application deadline** Rolling (freshmen), rolling (transfer) **Freshmen** 63% were admitted **Housing** No **Expenses** Tuition 19,900 **Undergraduates** 39% women, 66% 25 or older, 1% Native American, 9% Hispanic American, 1% African American, 30% Asian American/Pacific Islander **The most frequently chosen baccalaureate field is** visual/performing arts **Academic program** Advanced placement, accelerated degree program, summer session, adult/

Art Center College of Design *(continued)*

continuing education programs, internships **Contact** Ms. Kit Baron, Vice President, Student Services, Art Center College of Design, 1700 Lida Street, Pasadena, CA 91103-1999. Telephone: 626-396-2373. Fax: 626-795-0578. E-mail: admissions@artcenter.edu. Web site: http://www.artcenter.edu/.

THE ART INSTITUTE OF CALIFORNIA
SAN DIEGO, CALIFORNIA

General Proprietary, 4-year, coed **Entrance** Minimally difficult **Setting** urban campus **Total enrollment** 450 **Student/faculty ratio** 28:1 **Application deadline** Rolling (freshmen), rolling (transfer) **Freshmen** 85% were admitted **Housing** No **Expenses** Tuition $10,790 **Undergraduates** 47% women, 10% 25 or older **Academic program** Summer session, internships **Contact** Ms. Tracy Myers, Vice President and Director of Admissions, The Art Institute of California, 10025 Mesa Rim Road, San Diego, CA 92121. Telephone: 858-546-0602. E-mail: info.@taac.edu. Web site: http://www.taac.edu/.

ART INSTITUTE OF SOUTHERN CALIFORNIA
LAGUNA BEACH, CALIFORNIA

General Independent, 4-year, coed **Entrance** Moderately difficult **Setting** 9-acre small-town campus **Total enrollment** 280 **Student/faculty ratio** 10:1 **Application deadline** 3/2 (freshmen), 4/2 (transfer) **Freshmen** 93% were admitted **Housing** No **Expenses** Tuition $13,320 **Undergraduates** 46% women, 26% 25 or older **Academic program** English as a second language, advanced placement, summer session, adult/continuing education programs, internships **Contact** Mr. Anthony Padilla, Dean of Admissions, Art Institute of Southern California, 2222 Laguna Canyon Road, Laguna Beach, CA 92651-1136. Telephone: 949-376-6000 Ext. 232 or toll-free 800-255-0762. Fax: 949-376-6009 Ext. 232. E-mail: admissions@aisc.edu. Web site: http://www.aisc.edu/.

ART INSTITUTES INTERNATIONAL AT SAN FRANCISCO
SAN FRANCISCO, CALIFORNIA

General Independent, 4-year, coed **Contact** Ms. Donna Scott, Acting Director of Admissions, Art Institutes International at San Francisco, 1170 Market Street, San Francisco, CA 94102-4908. Telephone: 415-865-0198 or toll-free 888-493-3261. Web site: http://www.aisf.artinstitutes.edu/.

AZUSA PACIFIC UNIVERSITY
AZUSA, CALIFORNIA

General Independent nondenominational, comprehensive, coed **Entrance** Moderately difficult **Setting** 60-acre small-town campus **Total enrollment** 6,497 **Student/faculty ratio** 15:1 **Application deadline** 7/1 (freshmen), 7/1 (transfer) **Freshmen** 73% were admitted **Housing** Yes **Expenses** Tuition 15,210; Room & Board 4962 **Undergraduates** 64% women, 3% part-time, 10% 25 or older, 1% Native American, 13% Hispanic American, 3% African American, 6% Asian American/Pacific Islander **The most frequently chosen baccalaureate fields are** business/marketing, health professions and related sciences, liberal arts/general studies **Academic program** English as a second language, advanced placement, accelerated degree program, honors program, summer session, adult/continuing education programs, internships **Contact** Mrs. Deana Porterfield, Dean of Enrollment, Azusa Pacific University, 901 East Alosta Avenue, PO Box 7000, Azusa, CA 91720-7000. Telephone: 626-812-3016 or toll-free 800-TALK-APU. E-mail: admissions@apu.edu. Web site: http://www.apu.edu/.

BETHANY COLLEGE OF THE ASSEMBLIES OF GOD
SCOTTS VALLEY, CALIFORNIA

General Independent, comprehensive, coed, affiliated with Assemblies of God **Entrance** Minimally difficult **Setting** 40-acre small-town campus **Total enrollment** 577 **Application deadline** 7/1 (freshmen), 7/1 (transfer) **Freshmen** 71% were admitted **Housing** Yes **Expenses** Tuition $11,375; Room & Board $4928 **Undergraduates** 48% 25 or older, 0.4% Native American, 13% Hispanic American, 10% African American, 4% Asian American/Pacific Islander **Academic program** Advanced placement, accelerated degree program, summer session, adult/continuing education programs, internships **Contact** Ms. Deborah Sain, Director of Admissions, Bethany College of the Assemblies of God, 800 Bethany Drive, Scotts Valley, CA 95066-2820. Telephone: 831-438-3800 Ext. 1400 or toll-free 800-843-9410. Fax: 831-438-4517. E-mail: info@bethany.edu. Web site: http://www.bethany.edu/.

BETHESDA CHRISTIAN UNIVERSITY
ANAHEIM, CALIFORNIA

General Independent, comprehensive, affiliated with Full Gospel World Mission **Entrance** Moderately difficult **Total enrollment** 235 **Student/faculty ratio** 15:1 **Application deadline** 8/10 (freshmen), 8/10 (transfer) **Freshmen** 91% were admitted **Housing** No **Expenses** Tuition $3180 **Undergraduates** 70% women, 34% part-time, 70% 25 or older, 0% Native American, 0% Hispanic American, 0% African American, 30% Asian American/Pacific Islander **The most frequently chosen baccalaureate fields are** education, philosophy, religion, and theology **Academic program** English as a second language, accelerated degree program, summer session, adult/continuing education programs, internships **Contact** Ms. Haein Hong, Admissions & Registrar, Bethesda Christian University, 730 N. Euclid Street, Anaheim, CA 92801. Telephone: 714-517-1945. Fax: 714-517-1948. E-mail: admin@bcu.edu. Web site: http://www.bcu.edu/.

BIOLA UNIVERSITY
LA MIRADA, CALIFORNIA

General Independent interdenominational, university, coed **Entrance** Moderately difficult **Setting** 95-acre suburban campus **Total enrollment** 3,928 **Student/faculty ratio** 18:1 **Application deadline** 6/1 (freshmen), 6/1 (transfer) **Freshmen** 82% were admitted **Housing** Yes **Expenses** Tuition 16,630; Room & Board 5272 **Undergraduates** 63% women, 4% part-time, 19% 25 or older, 1% Native American, 7% Hispanic American, 2% African American, 9% Asian American/Pacific Islander **The most frequently chosen baccalaureate fields are** business/marketing, communications/communication technologies, philosophy, religion, and theology **Academic program** English as a second language, advanced placement, accelerated degree program, honors program, summer session, adult/continuing education programs, internships **Contact** Mr. André Stephens, Director of Admissions, Biola University, 13800 Biola Avenue, La Mirada, CA 90639. Telephone: 562-903-4752 or toll-free 800-652-4652. Fax: 562-903-4709. E-mail: admissions@biola.edu. Web site: http://www.biola.edu/.

BROOKS INSTITUTE OF PHOTOGRAPHY
SANTA BARBARA, CALIFORNIA

General Proprietary, comprehensive, coed **Contact** Ms. Inge B. Kautzmann, Director of Admissions, Brooks Institute of Photography, 801 Alston Road, Santa Barbara, CA 93108-2399. Telephone: 805-966-3888 Ext. 4601. Fax: 805-564-1475. E-mail: admissions@brooks.edu. Web site: http://www.brooks.edu/.

CALIFORNIA BAPTIST UNIVERSITY
RIVERSIDE, CALIFORNIA

General Independent Southern Baptist, comprehensive, coed **Entrance** Minimally difficult **Setting** 75-acre suburban campus **Total enrollment** 2,043 **Student/faculty ratio** 19:1 **Application deadline** 8/1 (freshmen), 8/1 (transfer) **Freshmen** 80% were admitted **Housing** Yes **Expenses** Tuition 11,240; Room & Board 4966 **Undergraduates** 63% women, 18% part-time, 28% 25 or older, 1% Native American, 11% Hispanic American, 4% African American, 3% Asian American/Pacific Islander **The most frequently chosen baccalaureate fields are** education, liberal arts/general studies, psychology **Academic program** Advanced placement, accelerated degree program, summer session, adult/continuing education programs, internships **Contact** Mr. Doug Wible, Dean of Admissions, California Baptist University, Office of Admissions, 8432 Magnolia Avenue, Riverside, CA 92504-3297. Telephone: 909-343-4212 or toll-free 877-228-8866. Fax: 909-343-4525. E-mail: admissions@calbaptist.edu. Web site: http://www.calbaptist.edu/.

CALIFORNIA CHRISTIAN COLLEGE
FRESNO, CALIFORNIA

General Independent religious, 4-year, coed **Entrance** Noncompetitive **Total enrollment** 90 **Student/faculty ratio** 8:1 **Application deadline** Rolling (freshmen), rolling (transfer) **Freshmen** 100% were admitted **Housing** Yes **Expenses** Tuition 3940; Room & Board 2760 **Undergraduates** 34% women, 22% part-time, 59% 25 or older, 0% Native American, 8% Hispanic American, 16% African American, 0% Asian American/Pacific Islander **The most frequently chosen baccalaureate field is** philosophy, religion, and theology **Academic program** Accelerated degree program, summer session **Contact** Mrs. Marjorie James, Registrar, California Christian College, 4881 East University Avenue, Fresno, CA 93703. Telephone: 559-251-4215 Ext. 5565. Fax: 559-251-4231. E-mail: cccfresno@aol.com. Web site: http://www.calchristiancollege.org/.

CALIFORNIA COLLEGE FOR HEALTH SCIENCES
NATIONAL CITY, CALIFORNIA

General Proprietary, comprehensive, coed **Entrance** Noncompetitive **Setting** 2-acre urban campus **Total enrollment** 5,742 **Application deadline** Rolling (freshmen), rolling (transfer) **Housing** No **Undergraduates** 85% 25 or older **Contact** Ms. Marita Gubbe, Director of Student Affairs, California College for Health Sciences, 2423 Hoover Avenue, National City, CA 91950. Telephone: 619-477-4800 Ext. 320 or toll-free 800-221-7374 (out-of-state). Fax: 619-477-4360. E-mail: admissns@cchs.edu. Web site: http://www.cchs.edu/.

CALIFORNIA COLLEGE OF ARTS AND CRAFTS
SAN FRANCISCO, CALIFORNIA

General Independent, comprehensive, coed **Entrance** Moderately difficult **Setting** 4-acre urban campus **Total enrollment** 1,213 **Student/faculty ratio** 10:1 **Application deadline** Rolling (freshmen), rolling (transfer) **Freshmen** 72% were admitted **Housing** Yes **Expenses** Tuition $19,460; Room & Board $6051 **Undergraduates** 59% women, 13% part-time, 46% 25 or older, 1% Native American, 7% Hispanic American, 3% African American, 13% Asian American/Pacific Islander **The most frequently chosen baccalaureate fields are** architecture, visual/performing arts **Academic program** Advanced placement, self-designed majors, summer session, internships **Contact** Molly Ryan, Director of Admissions, California College of Arts and Crafts, 1111 Eighth Street at 16th and Wisconsin, San Francisco, CA 94107. Telephone: 415-703-9523 Ext. 9532 or toll-free 800-447-1ART. Fax: 415-703-9539. E-mail: enroll@ccac-art.edu. Web site: http://www.ccac-art.edu/.

▶ **For more information, see page 392.**

CALIFORNIA INSTITUTE OF INTEGRAL STUDIES
SAN FRANCISCO, CALIFORNIA

General Independent, upper level, coed **Student/faculty ratio** 19:1 **Expenses** Tuition $14,542 **Aca-**

California Institute of Integral Studies *(continued)*

demic program Adult/continuing education programs **Contact** Mr. Henry B. Villareal, Dean of Enrollment Management, California Institute of Integral Studies, 1453 Mission Street, San Francisco, CA 94103. Telephone: 415-575-6156. Fax: 415-575-1268. E-mail: info@ciis.edu. Web site: http://www.ciis.edu/.

CALIFORNIA INSTITUTE OF TECHNOLOGY
PASADENA, CALIFORNIA

General Independent, university, coed **Entrance** Most difficult **Setting** 124-acre suburban campus **Total enrollment** 1,968 **Student/faculty ratio** 3:1 **Application deadline** 1/1 (freshmen), 3/1 (transfer) **Freshmen** 13% were admitted **Housing** Yes **Expenses** Tuition $21,120; Room & Board $6543 **Undergraduates** 32% women, 0% 25 or older, 0.3% Native American, 6% Hispanic American, 1% African American, 25% Asian American/Pacific Islander **The most frequently chosen baccalaureate fields are** engineering/engineering technologies, biological/life sciences, physical sciences **Academic program** Self-designed majors, internships **Contact** Ms. Charlene Liebau, Director of Admissions, California Institute of Technology, 1200 East California Boulevard, Pasadena, CA 91125-0001. Telephone: 626-395-6341 or toll-free 800-568-8324. Fax: 626-683-3026. E-mail: ugadmissions@caltech.edu. Web site: http://www.caltech.edu/.

CALIFORNIA INSTITUTE OF THE ARTS
VALENCIA, CALIFORNIA

General Independent, comprehensive, coed **Entrance** Very difficult **Setting** 60-acre suburban campus **Total enrollment** 1,224 **Student/faculty ratio** 7:1 **Application deadline** Rolling (freshmen), rolling (transfer) **Freshmen** 40% were admitted **Housing** Yes **Expenses** Tuition $20,930; Room only $2850 **Undergraduates** 44% women, 2% part-time, 18% 25 or older, 2% Native American, 9% Hispanic American, 5% African American, 9% Asian American/Pacific Islander **The most frequently chosen baccalaureate field is** visual/performing arts **Academic program** Advanced placement, self-designed majors, internships **Contact** Mr. Kenneth Young, Director of Admissions, California Institute of the Arts, 24700 McBean Parkway, Valencia, CA 91355-2340. Telephone: 661-253-7863 or toll-free 800-292-ARTS (in-state); 800-545-ARTS (out-of-state). E-mail: admiss@muse.calarts.edu. Web site: http://www.calarts.edu/.

CALIFORNIA LUTHERAN UNIVERSITY
THOUSAND OAKS, CALIFORNIA

General Independent Lutheran, comprehensive, coed **Entrance** Moderately difficult **Setting** 290-acre suburban campus **Total enrollment** 2,766 **Student/faculty ratio** 15:1 **Application deadline** 6/1 (freshmen), 6/1 (transfer) **Freshmen** 79% were admitted **Housing** Yes **Expenses** Tuition 17,000; Room & Board 6460 **Undergraduates** 56% women, 13% part-time, 7% 25 or older, 1% Native American, 12% Hispanic American, 2% African American, 5% Asian American/Pacific Islander **Academic program** Advanced placement, accelerated degree program, self-designed majors, summer session, adult/continuing education programs, internships **Contact** Mr. Marc D. Meredith, Director of Admission, California Lutheran University, Office of Admission, #1350, Thousand Oaks, CA 91360. Telephone: 805-493-3135 or toll-free 877-258-3678. Fax: 805-493-3114. E-mail: cluadm@callutheran.edu. Web site: http://www.clunet.edu/.

CALIFORNIA MARITIME ACADEMY
VALLEJO, CALIFORNIA

General State-supported, 4-year, coed, primarily men **Entrance** Moderately difficult **Setting** 67-acre suburban campus **Total enrollment** 583 **Student/faculty ratio** 17:1 **Application deadline** 3/2 (freshmen), 3/2 (transfer) **Freshmen** 76% were admitted **Housing** Yes **Expenses** Tuition $2206; Room & Board $5900 **Undergraduates** 17% women, 17% 25 or older, 1% Native American, 4% Hispanic American, 3% African American, 13% Asian American/Pacific Islander **Academic program** Advanced placement, summer session, internships **Contact** Ms. Patricia Beitter, Admissions Counselor, California Maritime Academy, PO Box 1392, Vallejo, CA 94590-0644. Telephone: 707-654-1333 or toll-free 800-561-1945. Fax: 707-654-1336. E-mail: enroll@prop.csum.edu.

CALIFORNIA NATIONAL UNIVERSITY FOR ADVANCED STUDIES
NORTH HILLS, CALIFORNIA

Contact California National University for Advanced Studies, 16909 Parthenia Street, North Hills, CA 91343. Web site: http://www.cnuas.edu/.

CALIFORNIA POLYTECHNIC STATE UNIVERSITY, SAN LUIS OBISPO
SAN LUIS OBISPO, CALIFORNIA

General State-supported, comprehensive, coed **Entrance** Moderately difficult **Setting** 6,000-acre small-town campus **Total enrollment** 16,877 **Student/faculty ratio** 20:1 **Application deadline** 11/30 (freshmen), 11/30 (transfer) **Freshmen** 45% were admitted **Housing** Yes **Expenses** Tuition 2135; Room & Board 6246 **Undergraduates** 44% women, 7% part-time, 10% 25 or older, 1% Native American, 11% Hispanic American, 1% African American, 11% Asian American/Pacific Islander **The most frequently chosen baccalaureate fields are** agriculture, business/marketing, engineering/engineering technologies **Academic program** English as a second language, advanced placement, honors program, summer session, internships **Contact** Mr. James Maraviglia, Director of Admissions and Evaluations, California Polytechnic State University, San Luis Obispo, San Luis Obispo, CA 93407. Telephone: 805-756-2311. Fax: 805-756-5400. E-mail: dp141@oasis.calpoly.edu. Web site: http://www.calpoly.edu/.

CALIFORNIA STATE POLYTECHNIC UNIVERSITY, POMONA
POMONA, CALIFORNIA

General State-supported, comprehensive, coed **Entrance** Moderately difficult **Setting** 1,400-acre urban campus **Total enrollment** 18,424 **Student/faculty ratio** 19:1 **Application deadline** 4/1 (freshmen), 5/1 (transfer) **Freshmen** 70% were admitted **Housing** Yes **Expenses** Tuition $1772; Room & Board $6113 **Undergraduates** 44% women, 21% part-time, 22% 25 or older, 1% Native American, 23% Hispanic American, 3% African American, 35% Asian American/Pacific Islander **The most frequently chosen baccalaureate fields are** business/marketing, computer/information sciences, engineering/engineering technologies **Academic program** English as a second language, advanced placement, summer session, adult/continuing education programs, internships **Contact** Ms. Dena Bennett, Assistant Director of Admissions, California State Polytechnic University, Pomona, 3801 West Temple Avenue, Pomona, CA 91768. Telephone: 909-869-2991. Fax: 909-869-4529. E-mail: cppadmit@csupomona.edu. Web site: http://www.csupomona.edu/.

▶ **For more information, see page 393.**

CALIFORNIA STATE UNIVERSITY, BAKERSFIELD
BAKERSFIELD, CALIFORNIA

Contact Dr. Homer S. Montalvo, Associate Dean of Admissions and Records, California State University, Bakersfield, 9001 Stockdale Highway, Bakersfield, CA 93311-1099. Telephone: 805-664-2160 or toll-free 800-788-2782 (in-state). Web site: http://www.csubak.edu/.

CALIFORNIA STATE UNIVERSITY, CHICO
CHICO, CALIFORNIA

General State-supported, comprehensive, coed **Entrance** Moderately difficult **Setting** 119-acre small-town campus **Total enrollment** 15,909 **Student/faculty ratio** 20:1 **Application deadline** 11/30 (freshmen) **Freshmen** 91% were admitted **Housing** Yes **Expenses** Tuition $2030; Room & Board $6216 **Undergraduates** 53% women, 10% part-time, 19% 25 or older, 1% Native American, 9% Hispanic American, 2% African American, 4% Asian American/Pacific Islander **The most frequently chosen baccalaureate fields are** business/marketing, liberal arts/general studies, social sciences and history **Academic program** English as a second language, advanced placement, self-designed majors, honors program, summer session, adult/continuing education programs, internships **Contact** California State University, Chico, 400 West First Street, Chico, CA 95929-0722. Telephone: or toll-free 800-542-4426. Fax: 530-898-6456. E-mail: info@oavax.csuchico.edu. Web site: http://www.csuchico.edu/.

CALIFORNIA STATE UNIVERSITY, DOMINGUEZ HILLS
CARSON, CALIFORNIA

General State-supported, comprehensive, coed **Entrance** Moderately difficult **Setting** 350-acre urban campus **Total enrollment** 12,848 **Student/faculty ratio** 21:1 **Application deadline** Rolling (freshmen), rolling (transfer) **Freshmen** 77% were admitted **Housing** Yes **Expenses** Room only $3436 **Undergraduates** 70% women, 40% part-time, 56% 25 or older, 1% Native American, 32% Hispanic American, 28% African American, 10% Asian American/Pacific Islander **The most frequently chosen baccalaureate fields are** business/marketing, health professions and related sciences, liberal arts/general studies **Academic program** English as a second language, advanced placement, self-designed majors, honors program, summer session, adult/continuing education programs, internships **Contact** Information Center, California State University, Dominguez Hills, 1000 East Victoria Street, Carson, CA 90747-0001. Telephone: 310-243-3696. Web site: http://www.csudh.edu/.

CALIFORNIA STATE UNIVERSITY, FRESNO
FRESNO, CALIFORNIA

General State-supported, comprehensive, coed **Entrance** Moderately difficult **Setting** 1,410-acre urban campus **Total enrollment** 19,114 **Student/faculty ratio** 18:1 **Application deadline** 7/28 (freshmen), 7/28 (transfer) **Freshmen** 67% were admitted **Housing** Yes **Expenses** Tuition 1746; Room & Board 5876 **Undergraduates** 56% women, 20% part-time, 24% 25 or older, 1% Native American, 28% Hispanic American, 5% African American, 14% Asian American/Pacific Islander **The most frequently chosen baccalaureate fields are** business/marketing, health professions and related sciences, liberal arts/general studies **Academic program** English as a second language, advanced placement, accelerated degree program, self-designed majors, honors program, summer session, adult/continuing education programs, internships **Contact** Ms. Vivian Franco, Director, California State University, Fresno, 5150 North Maple Avenue, M/S JA 57, Fresno, CA 93740-8026. Telephone: 559-278-2261. Fax: 559-278-4812. E-mail: donna_mills@csufresno.edu. Web site: http://www.csufresno.edu/.

CALIFORNIA STATE UNIVERSITY, FULLERTON
FULLERTON, CALIFORNIA

General State-supported, comprehensive, coed **Entrance** Moderately difficult **Setting** 225-acre suburban campus **Total enrollment** 28,381 **Student/faculty ratio** 22:1 **Application deadline** Rolling (freshmen), rolling (transfer) **Freshmen** 72% were admitted **Housing** Yes **Expenses** Tuition 1810; Room only 2782 **Undergraduates** 59% women, 30% part-time, 26% 25 or older, 1% Native American, 23%

California State University, Fullerton *(continued)*

Hispanic American, 3% African American, 24% Asian American/Pacific Islander **The most frequently chosen baccalaureate fields are** business/marketing, home economics/vocational home economics, social sciences and history **Academic program** English as a second language, advanced placement, self-designed majors, honors program, summer session, adult/continuing education programs, internships **Contact** Ms. Nancy J. Dority, Admissions Director, California State University, Fullerton, Office of Admissions and Records, PO Box 6900, Fullerton, CA 92834-6900. Telephone: 714-278-2370. Web site: http://www.fullerton.edu/.

CALIFORNIA STATE UNIVERSITY, HAYWARD
HAYWARD, CALIFORNIA

General State-supported, comprehensive, coed **Entrance** Moderately difficult **Setting** 343-acre suburban campus **Total enrollment** 12,705 **Student/faculty ratio** 21:1 **Application deadline** 9/7 (freshmen), 9/7 (transfer) **Freshmen** 62% were admitted **Housing** Yes **Expenses** Room only $3200 **Undergraduates** 64% women, 26% part-time, 35% 25 or older, 1% Native American, 13% Hispanic American, 12% African American, 27% Asian American/Pacific Islander **The most frequently chosen baccalaureate fields are** business/marketing, liberal arts/general studies, social sciences and history **Academic program** English as a second language, advanced placement, accelerated degree program, self-designed majors, honors program, summer session, adult/continuing education programs, internships **Contact** Ms. Susan Lakis, Associate Director of Admissions, California State University, Hayward, 25800 Carlos Bee Boulevard, Hayward, CA 94542-3035. Telephone: 510-885-3248. Fax: 510-885-3816. E-mail: adminfo@csuhayward.edu. Web site: http://www.csuhayward.edu/.

CALIFORNIA STATE UNIVERSITY, LONG BEACH
LONG BEACH, CALIFORNIA

General State-supported, comprehensive, coed **Entrance** Moderately difficult **Setting** 320-acre suburban campus **Total enrollment** 30,918 **Student/faculty ratio** 20:1 **Application deadline** 11/30 (freshmen) **Freshmen** 86% were admitted **Housing** Yes **Expenses** Room & Board $5800 **Undergraduates** 58% women, 23% part-time, 27% 25 or older, 1% Native American, 22% Hispanic American, 7% African American, 22% Asian American/Pacific Islander **The most frequently chosen baccalaureate fields are** business/marketing, psychology, social sciences and history **Academic program** English as a second language, advanced placement, accelerated degree program, self-designed majors, honors program, summer session, adult/continuing education programs, internships **Contact** Mr. Thomas Enders, Director of Enrollment Services, California State University, Long Beach, Brotman Hall, 1250 Bellflower Boulevard, Long Beach, CA 90840. Telephone: 562-985-4641. Web site: http://www.csulb.edu/.

CALIFORNIA STATE UNIVERSITY, LOS ANGELES
LOS ANGELES, CALIFORNIA

General State-supported, comprehensive, coed **Entrance** Moderately difficult **Setting** 173-acre urban campus **Total enrollment** 19,593 **Student/faculty ratio** 20:1 **Application deadline** 6/15 (freshmen), 6/15 (transfer) **Freshmen** 50% were admitted **Housing** Yes **Expenses** Tuition $1722; Room & Board $6201 **Undergraduates** 61% women, 29% part-time, 0.4% Native American, 49% Hispanic American, 8% African American, 20% Asian American/Pacific Islander **The most frequently chosen baccalaureate fields are** business/marketing, education, protective services/public administration **Academic program** English as a second language, advanced placement, accelerated degree program, self-designed majors, honors program, summer session, adult/continuing education programs, internships **Contact** Mr. Vince Lopez, Director of Outreach and Recruitment, California State University, Los Angeles, 5151 State University Drive, Los Angeles, CA 90032-8530. Telephone: 323-343-3195. E-mail: jslanin@calstatela.edu. Web site: http://www.calstatela.edu/.

CALIFORNIA STATE UNIVERSITY, MONTEREY BAY
SEASIDE, CALIFORNIA

General State-supported, comprehensive, coed **Contact** Ms. Beth Appenzeller, Director of Admissions and Records, California State University, Monterey Bay, 100 Campus Center, Seaside, CA 93955-8001. Telephone: 831-582-3518. Fax: 831-582-3087. E-mail: student.info@monterey.edu. Web site: http://www.monterey.edu/.

CALIFORNIA STATE UNIVERSITY, NORTHRIDGE
NORTHRIDGE, CALIFORNIA

General State-supported, comprehensive, coed **Entrance** Moderately difficult **Setting** 353-acre urban campus **Total enrollment** 29,066 **Application deadline** 11/30 (freshmen), rolling (transfer) **Freshmen** 78% were admitted **Housing** Yes **Expenses** Room & Board 6400 **Undergraduates** 58% women, 25% part-time, 1% Native American, 25% Hispanic American, 9% African American, 14% Asian American/Pacific Islander **Academic program** English as a second language, advanced placement, accelerated degree program, self-designed majors, honors program, summer session, adult/continuing education programs **Contact** Ms. Mary Baxton, Associate Director of Admissions and Records, California State University, Northridge, 18111 Nordhoff Street, Northridge, CA 91330-8207. Telephone: 818-677-3777. Fax: 818-

677-3766. E-mail: outreach.recruitment@csun.edu. Web site: http://www.csun.edu/.

CALIFORNIA STATE UNIVERSITY, SACRAMENTO

SACRAMENTO, CALIFORNIA

General State-supported, comprehensive, coed **Entrance** Moderately difficult **Setting** 288-acre urban campus **Total enrollment** 24,530 **Student/faculty ratio** 21:1 **Application deadline** Rolling (freshmen), 8/1 (transfer) **Freshmen** 41% were admitted **Housing** Yes **Expenses** Tuition $1867; Room & Board $5510 **Undergraduates** 56% women, 25% part-time, 32% 25 or older, 1% Native American, 13% Hispanic American, 7% African American, 18% Asian American/Pacific Islander **The most frequently chosen baccalaureate fields are** business/marketing, protective services/public administration, social sciences and history **Academic program** English as a second language, advanced placement, self-designed majors, summer session, internships **Contact** Mr. Emiliano Diaz, Director of University Outreach Services, California State University, Sacramento, 6000 J Street, Lassen Hall, Sacramento, CA 95819-6048. Telephone: 916-278-7362. Fax: 916-278-5603. E-mail: glasmirel@csus.edu. Web site: http://www.csus.edu/.

CALIFORNIA STATE UNIVERSITY, SAN BERNARDINO

SAN BERNARDINO, CALIFORNIA

General State-supported, comprehensive, coed **Entrance** Moderately difficult **Setting** 430-acre suburban campus **Total enrollment** 14,909 **Application deadline** Rolling (freshmen), rolling (transfer) **Housing** Yes **Undergraduates** 38% 25 or older **Academic program** English as a second language, advanced placement, self-designed majors, honors program, summer session, adult/continuing education programs **Contact** Ms. Cynthia Shum, Admissions Counselor, California State University, San Bernardino, 5500 University Parkway, San Bernardino, CA 92407-2397. Telephone: 909-880-5212. Web site: http://www.csusb.edu/.

CALIFORNIA STATE UNIVERSITY, SAN MARCOS

SAN MARCOS, CALIFORNIA

General State-supported, comprehensive, coed **Entrance** Moderately difficult **Setting** 302-acre suburban campus **Total enrollment** 5,500 **Application deadline** Rolling (freshmen), rolling (transfer) **Freshmen** 66% were admitted **Housing** Yes **Expenses** Tuition $1706 **Undergraduates** 62% women, 33% part-time, 38% 25 or older, 1% Native American, 19% Hispanic American, 3% African American, 9% Asian American/Pacific Islander **Academic program** English as a second language, advanced placement, self-designed majors, summer session, adult/continuing education programs, internships **Contact** Ms. Cherine Heckman, Director of Admissions, California State University, San Marcos, San Marcos, CA 92096-0001. Telephone: 760-750-4848. Fax: 760-750-3285. E-mail: apply@csusm.edu. Web site: http://ww2.csusm.edu/.

CALIFORNIA STATE UNIVERSITY, STANISLAUS

TURLOCK, CALIFORNIA

General State-supported, comprehensive, coed **Entrance** Moderately difficult **Setting** 220-acre small-town campus **Total enrollment** 7,062 **Student/faculty ratio** 19:1 **Application deadline** 6/30 (freshmen), 6/30 (transfer) **Freshmen** 73% were admitted **Housing** Yes **Expenses** Room & Board $6480 **Undergraduates** 65% women, 31% part-time, 35% 25 or older, 1% Native American, 25% Hispanic American, 3% African American, 8% Asian American/Pacific Islander **The most frequently chosen baccalaureate fields are** business/marketing, liberal arts/general studies, social sciences and history **Academic program** English as a second language, advanced placement, self-designed majors, honors program, summer session, adult/continuing education programs, internships **Contact** Admissions Office, California State University, Stanislaus, Enrollment Services, 801 West Monte Vista Avenue, Turlock, CA 95382. Telephone: 209-667-3070 or toll-free 800-300-7420 (in-state). Fax: 209-667-3788. E-mail: outreach@toto.csustan.edu. Web site: http://www.csustan.edu/.

CHAPMAN UNIVERSITY

ORANGE, CALIFORNIA

General Independent, comprehensive, coed, affiliated with Christian Church (Disciples of Christ) **Entrance** Moderately difficult **Setting** 42-acre suburban campus **Total enrollment** 4,341 **Student/faculty ratio** 13:1 **Application deadline** 1/31 (freshmen), 3/15 (transfer) **Freshmen** 63% were admitted **Housing** Yes **Expenses** Tuition 21,314; Room & Board 7246 **Undergraduates** 55% women, 7% part-time, 17% 25 or older, 1% Native American, 11% Hispanic American, 3% African American, 9% Asian American/Pacific Islander **Academic program** English as a second language, advanced placement, accelerated degree program, honors program, summer session, adult/continuing education programs, internships **Contact** Mr. Michael O. Drummy, Associate Dean for Enrollment Services and Chief Admission Officer, Chapman University, One University Drive, Orange, CA 92866. Telephone: 714-997-6711 or toll-free 888-CUAPPLY. Fax: 714-997-6713. E-mail: low@chapman.edu. Web site: http://www.chapman.edu/.

CHARLES R. DREW UNIVERSITY OF MEDICINE AND SCIENCE

LOS ANGELES, CALIFORNIA

General Independent, comprehensive, coed **Entrance** Moderately difficult **Total enrollment** 626 **Application deadline** 4/30 (freshmen), 4/30 (transfer) **Freshmen** 25% were admitted **Housing** No **Academic program** Internships **Contact** Ms. Mala Sharma,

Charles R. Drew University of Medicine and Science *(continued)*

Director of Enrollment Services, Charles R. Drew University of Medicine and Science, 1731 East 120th Street, Los Angeles, CA 90059. Telephone: 323-563-4832. Web site: http://www.cdrewu.edu/.

CHRISTIAN HERITAGE COLLEGE
EL CAJON, CALIFORNIA

General Independent nondenominational, 4-year, coed **Entrance** Moderately difficult **Setting** 32-acre suburban campus **Total enrollment** 675 **Application deadline** 8/1 (freshmen), 8/1 (transfer) **Freshmen** 79% were admitted **Housing** Yes **Expenses** Tuition 12,550; Room & Board 5330 **Undergraduates** 52% 25 or older, 1% Native American, 12% Hispanic American, 9% African American, 2% Asian American/Pacific Islander **Academic program** English as a second language, advanced placement, self-designed majors, summer session, adult/continuing education programs, internships **Contact** Mr. Paul Berry, Vice President of Enrollment Management/Registrar, Christian Heritage College, 2100 Greenfield Drive, El Cajon, CA 92019-1157. Telephone: 619-441-2200 or toll-free 800-676-2242. Fax: 619-440-0209. E-mail: chcinfo@isat.com. Web site: http://www.christianheritage.edu/.

CLAREMONT MCKENNA COLLEGE
CLAREMONT, CALIFORNIA

General Independent, 4-year, coed **Entrance** Very difficult **Setting** 50-acre small-town campus **Total enrollment** 1,002 **Student/faculty ratio** 7:1 **Application deadline** 1/1 (freshmen), 4/1 (transfer) **Freshmen** 28% were admitted **Housing** Yes **Expenses** Tuition 22,390; Room & Board 7420 **Undergraduates** 43% women, 1% 25 or older, 0.4% Native American, 11% Hispanic American, 5% African American, 17% Asian American/Pacific Islander **The most frequently chosen baccalaureate fields are** interdisciplinary studies, psychology, social sciences and history **Academic program** Advanced placement, accelerated degree program, self-designed majors, honors program, internships **Contact** Mr. Richard C. Vos, Vice President/Dean of Admission and Financial Aid, Claremont McKenna College, 890 Columbia Avenue, Claremont, CA 91711. Telephone: 909-621-8088. E-mail: admission@mckenna.edu. Web site: http://www.claremontmckenna.edu.

▶ **For more information, see page 400.**

CLEVELAND CHIROPRACTIC COLLEGE OF LOS ANGELES
LOS ANGELES, CALIFORNIA

Contact Cleveland Chiropractic College of Los Angeles, 590 North Vermont Avenue, Los Angeles, CA 90004-2196. Telephone: or toll-free 800-446-CCLA. Web site: http://www.clevelandchiropractic.edu/.

COGSWELL POLYTECHNICAL COLLEGE
SUNNYVALE, CALIFORNIA

General Independent, 4-year, coed **Entrance** Moderately difficult **Setting** 2-acre suburban campus **Total enrollment** 500 **Application deadline** 6/1 (freshmen), 6/1 (transfer) **Freshmen** 85% were admitted **Housing** Yes **Undergraduates** 50% 25 or older, 1% Native American, 5% Hispanic American, 2% African American, 17% Asian American/Pacific Islander **Academic program** Advanced placement, summer session, adult/continuing education programs **Contact** Mr. Paul A. Schreivogel, Dean of Recruitment and Marketing, Cogswell Polytechnical College, 1175 Bordeaux Drive, Sunnyvale, CA 94089. Telephone: 408-541-0100 Ext. 112 or toll-free 800-264-7955. Fax: 408-747-0764. E-mail: admin@cogswell.edu. Web site: http://www.cogswell.edu/.

COLEMAN COLLEGE
LA MESA, CALIFORNIA

General Independent, comprehensive, coed **Contact** Admissions Department, Coleman College, 7380 Parkway Drive, La Mesa, CA 91942-1532. Telephone: 619-465-3990. Fax: 619-465-0162. E-mail: jschafer@cts.com. Web site: http://www.coleman.edu/.

COLLEGE OF NOTRE DAME
BELMONT, CALIFORNIA

General Independent Roman Catholic, comprehensive, coed **Entrance** Moderately difficult **Setting** 80-acre suburban campus **Total enrollment** 1,670 **Student/faculty ratio** 15:1 **Application deadline** Rolling (freshmen), rolling (transfer) **Freshmen** 79% were admitted **Housing** Yes **Expenses** Tuition 17,095; Room & Board 8476 **Undergraduates** 46% 25 or older, 0.4% Native American, 15% Hispanic American, 5% African American, 12% Asian American/Pacific Islander **Academic program** English as a second language, advanced placement, accelerated degree program, summer session, adult/continuing education programs, internships **Contact** Martin Bednarek, Director of Undergraduate Admission, College of Notre Dame, 1500 Ralston Avenue, Belmont, CA 94002-1997. Telephone: 650-508-3534 or toll-free 800-263-0545 (in-state). Fax: 650-508-3426. E-mail: admiss@cnd.edu.

COLUMBIA COLLEGE–HOLLYWOOD
TARZANA, CALIFORNIA

General Independent, 4-year, coed **Entrance** Minimally difficult **Setting** 1-acre urban campus **Total enrollment** 100 **Application deadline** Rolling (freshmen) **Freshmen** 88% were admitted **Housing** No **Expenses** Tuition $10,725 **Undergraduates** 35% 25 or older **Academic program** Accelerated degree program, summer session, adult/continuing education programs **Contact** Ms. Jacqueline Rossman, Admissions Director, Columbia College–Hollywood, 18618 Oxnard Street, Tarzana, CA 91356. Telephone: 818-345-8414. Fax: 818-345-9053. E-mail:

cchadfin@columbiacollege.edu. Web site: http://www.columbiacollege.edu/.

CONCORDIA UNIVERSITY
IRVINE, CALIFORNIA

General Independent, comprehensive, coed, affiliated with Lutheran Church–Missouri Synod **Entrance** Moderately difficult **Setting** 70-acre suburban campus **Total enrollment** 1,334 **Student/faculty ratio** 18:1 **Application deadline** Rolling (freshmen), rolling (transfer) **Freshmen** 31% were admitted **Housing** Yes **Expenses** Tuition $15,700; Room & Board $5600 **Undergraduates** 69% women, 18% part-time, 5% 25 or older, 0.5% Native American, 9% Hispanic American, 3% African American, 7% Asian American/Pacific Islander **The most frequently chosen baccalaureate fields are** business/marketing, education, social sciences and history **Academic program** English as a second language, advanced placement, self-designed majors, honors program, summer session, adult/continuing education programs, internships **Contact** Mr. Gary R. McDaniel, Vice President of Enrollment Services, Concordia University, 153 Concordia West, Irvine, CA 92612-3299. Telephone: 949-854-8002 Ext. 1108 or toll-free 800-229-1200. Fax: 949-854-6894. E-mail: admission@cui.edu. Web site: http://www.cui.edu/.

DESIGN INSTITUTE OF SAN DIEGO
SAN DIEGO, CALIFORNIA

General Proprietary, 4-year, coed **Entrance** Noncompetitive **Setting** urban campus **Total enrollment** 350 **Application deadline** Rolling (freshmen), rolling (transfer) **Housing** No **Expenses** Tuition $10,200 **Undergraduates** 70% 25 or older **Academic program** Internships **Contact** Ms. Paula Parrish, Director of Admissions, Design Institute of San Diego, 8555 Commerce Avenue, San Diego, CA 92121-2685. Telephone: 619-566-1200 or toll-free 800-619-4DESIGN (out-of-state). Fax: 619-566-2711. E-mail: marydisd@aol.com.

DEVRY INSTITUTE OF TECHNOLOGY
FREMONT, CALIFORNIA

General Proprietary, 4-year, coed **Entrance** Minimally difficult **Setting** 17-acre suburban campus **Total enrollment** 2,149 **Student/faculty ratio** 29:1 **Application deadline** Rolling (freshmen), rolling (transfer) **Freshmen** 60% were admitted **Housing** No **Expenses** Tuition $9865 **Undergraduates** 23% women, 22% part-time, 30% 25 or older, 1% Native American, 14% Hispanic American, 5% African American, 37% Asian American/Pacific Islander **Academic program** Advanced placement, accelerated degree program, summer session, adult/continuing education programs **Contact** Ms. Jade Muranka, Director of Admissions, DeVry Institute of Technology, 6600 Dumbarton Circle, Fremont, CA 94555. Telephone: 510-574-1100 or toll-free 888-393-3879 (out-of-state). Web site: http://www.fre.devry.edu/.

DEVRY INSTITUTE OF TECHNOLOGY
LONG BEACH, CALIFORNIA

General Proprietary, 4-year, coed **Entrance** Minimally difficult **Setting** 23-acre urban campus **Total enrollment** 2,877 **Student/faculty ratio** 22:1 **Application deadline** Rolling (freshmen), rolling (transfer) **Freshmen** 65% were admitted **Housing** No **Expenses** Tuition $9205 **Undergraduates** 29% women, 30% part-time, 50% 25 or older, 1% Native American, 25% Hispanic American, 15% African American, 31% Asian American/Pacific Islander **The most frequently chosen baccalaureate fields are** business/marketing, computer/information sciences, engineering/engineering technologies **Academic program** Advanced placement, summer session, adult/continuing education programs **Contact** Ms. Lisa Flores, New Student Coordinator, DeVry Institute of Technology, 3880 Kilroy Airport, Long Beach, CA 90806. Telephone: 562-427-0861 or toll-free 800-597-0444 (out-of-state). Web site: http://www.lb.devry.edu/.

DEVRY INSTITUTE OF TECHNOLOGY
POMONA, CALIFORNIA

General Proprietary, 4-year, coed **Entrance** Minimally difficult **Setting** 15-acre urban campus **Total enrollment** 3,674 **Student/faculty ratio** 24:1 **Application deadline** Rolling (freshmen), rolling (transfer) **Freshmen** 68% were admitted **Housing** No **Expenses** Tuition $9205 **Undergraduates** 27% women, 30% part-time, 42% 25 or older, 0.5% Native American, 28% Hispanic American, 7% African American, 36% Asian American/Pacific Islander **The most frequently chosen baccalaureate fields are** business/marketing, computer/information sciences, engineering/engineering technologies **Academic program** Advanced placement, accelerated degree program, summer session, adult/continuing education programs **Contact** Mr. Byron Chung, Director of Admissions, DeVry Institute of Technology, 901 Corporate Center Drive, Pomona, CA 91768-2642. Telephone: 909-622-9800 or toll-free 800-243-3660. Web site: http://www.pom.devry.edu/.

DEVRY INSTITUTE OF TECHNOLOGY
WEST HILLS, CALIFORNIA

General Proprietary, 4-year, coed **Entrance** Minimally difficult **Total enrollment** 886 **Student/faculty ratio** 22:1 **Application deadline** Rolling (freshmen), rolling (transfer) **Freshmen** 58% were admitted **Expenses** Tuition 9205 **Undergraduates** 23% women, 36% part-time, 43% 25 or older, 0.5% Native American, 22% Hispanic American, 6% African American, 31% Asian American/Pacific Islander **Academic program** Advanced placement, summer session, adult/continuing education programs **Contact** Ms. Kathy Courtney, New Student Coordinator, DeVry Institute of Technology, 22801 Roscoe Boulevard, West Hills, CA 91304. Telephone: 818-932-3001. Fax: 818-713-8118. Web site: http://www.wh.devry.edu/.

DOMINICAN SCHOOL OF PHILOSOPHY AND THEOLOGY
BERKELEY, CALIFORNIA

General Independent Roman Catholic, upper-level, coed **Entrance** Moderately difficult **Setting** urban campus **Total enrollment** 90 **Student/faculty ratio** 6:1 **Application deadline** Rolling (transfer) **First-Year Students** 100% were admitted **Housing** Yes **Expenses** Tuition $8210 **Undergraduates** 83% 25 or older, 25% Hispanic American, 25% Asian American/Pacific Islander **Contact** Ms. Susan McGinnis Hardie, Admissions Director, Dominican School of Philosophy and Theology, 2401 Ridge Road, Berkeley, CA 94709-1295. Telephone: 510-883-2073. Fax: 510-849-1372. E-mail: susanmcginnis@compuserve.com. Web site: http://www.dspt.edu/.

DOMINICAN UNIVERSITY OF CALIFORNIA
SAN RAFAEL, CALIFORNIA

General Independent, comprehensive, coed, affiliated with Roman Catholic Church **Entrance** Moderately difficult **Setting** 80-acre suburban campus **Total enrollment** 1,369 **Student/faculty ratio** 12:1 **Application deadline** Rolling (freshmen), rolling (transfer) **Freshmen** 73% were admitted **Housing** Yes **Expenses** Tuition $17,606; Room & Board $8440 **Undergraduates** 80% women, 31% part-time, 45% 25 or older, 1% Native American, 10% Hispanic American, 7% African American, 12% Asian American/Pacific Islander **The most frequently chosen baccalaureate fields are** business/marketing, health professions and related sciences, psychology **Academic program** English as a second language, advanced placement, self-designed majors, honors program, summer session, adult/continuing education programs, internships **Contact** Ms. Kris Thornton, Director of Admissions, Dominican University of California, 50 Acacia Avenue, San Rafael, CA 94901-2298. Telephone: 415-257-1338 or toll-free 888-323-6763. Fax: 415-385-3214. E-mail: enroll@dominican.edu. Web site: http://www.dominican.edu/.

EDUCATION AMERICA UNIVERSITY
SAN DIEGO, CALIFORNIA

Contact Education America University, 123 Camino de la Reina, North Building, Suite 100, San Diego, CA 92108. Telephone: or toll-free 800-214-7001.

EMMANUEL BIBLE COLLEGE
PASADENA, CALIFORNIA

General Independent, 4-year, affiliated with Church of the Nazarene **Total enrollment** 20 **Student/faculty ratio** 10:1 **Application deadline** 9/15 (freshmen) **Freshmen** 100% were admitted **Housing** No **Expenses** Tuition 48,000; Room & Board 4800 **Undergraduates** 20% women, 70% part-time, 100% 25 or older, 35% Hispanic American, 5% Asian American/Pacific Islander **The most frequently chosen baccalaureate field is** philosophy, religion, and theology **Academic program** Adult/continuing education programs, internships **Contact** Mr. Yeghia Babikian, President, Emmanuel Bible College, 1605 East Elizabeth Street, 1536 East Howard Street, Pasadena, CA 91104. Telephone: 626-791-2575. Fax: 626-398-2424. Web site: http://www.emmanuelbiblecollege.edu.

FRESNO PACIFIC UNIVERSITY
FRESNO, CALIFORNIA

General Independent, comprehensive, coed, affiliated with Mennonite Brethren Church **Entrance** Moderately difficult **Setting** 42-acre suburban campus **Total enrollment** 1,686 **Student/faculty ratio** 16:1 **Application deadline** Rolling (freshmen), rolling (transfer) **Freshmen** 72% were admitted **Housing** Yes **Expenses** Tuition 15,310; Room & Board 4680 **Undergraduates** 67% women, 10% part-time, 1% Native American, 19% Hispanic American, 3% African American, 4% Asian American/Pacific Islander **The most frequently chosen baccalaureate fields are** business/marketing, education, philosophy, religion, and theology **Academic program** English as a second language, advanced placement, accelerated degree program, self-designed majors, summer session, adult/continuing education programs, internships **Contact** Cary Templeton, Assistant Dean of Enrollment Services, Fresno Pacific University, 1717 South Chestnut Avenue, Fresno, CA 93702-4709. Telephone: 559-453-2000 or toll-free 800-660-6089 (in-state). Fax: 559-453-2007. E-mail: cwtemple@fresno.edu. Web site: http://www.fresno.edu/.

GOLDEN GATE UNIVERSITY
SAN FRANCISCO, CALIFORNIA

General Independent, university, coed **Entrance** Moderately difficult **Setting** urban campus **Total enrollment** 5,379 **Application deadline** Rolling (freshmen), rolling (transfer) **Freshmen** 97% were admitted **Housing** No **Expenses** Tuition 8832 **Undergraduates** 58% women, 74% part-time, 80% 25 or older, 0.2% Native American, 9% Hispanic American, 10% African American, 14% Asian American/Pacific Islander **The most frequently chosen baccalaureate fields are** business/marketing, computer/information sciences, trade and industry **Academic program** English as a second language, advanced placement, accelerated degree program, summer session, adult/continuing education programs, internships **Contact** Enrollment Services, Golden Gate University, 536 Mission Street, San Francisco, CA 94105-2968. Telephone: 415-442-7800 or toll-free 800-448-4968. Fax: 415-442-7807. E-mail: info@ggu.edu. Web site: http://www.ggu.edu/.

HARVEY MUDD COLLEGE
CLAREMONT, CALIFORNIA

General Independent, comprehensive, coed **Entrance** Most difficult **Setting** 33-acre suburban campus **Total enrollment** 719 **Student/faculty ratio** 9:1 **Application deadline** 1/15 (freshmen), 5/1 (transfer) **Fresh-**

men 35% were admitted **Housing** Yes **Expenses** Tuition 23,187; Room & Board 8418 **Undergraduates** 29% women, 0.4% part-time, 1% 25 or older, 0.3% Native American, 4% Hispanic American, 0.4% African American, 22% Asian American/Pacific Islander **The most frequently chosen baccalaureate fields are** engineering/engineering technologies, computer/information sciences, protective services/ public administration **Academic program** Advanced placement, self-designed majors, internships **Contact** Mr. Deren Finks, Vice President, Dean of Admissions and Financial Aid, Harvey Mudd College, 301 East 12th Street, Claremont, CA 91711. Telephone: 909-621-8011. Fax: 909-607-7046. E-mail: admission@hmc.edu. Web site: http://www.hmc.edu/.

HOLY NAMES COLLEGE
OAKLAND, CALIFORNIA

General Independent Roman Catholic, comprehensive, coed, primarily women **Entrance** Moderately difficult **Setting** 60-acre urban campus **Total enrollment** 945 **Student/faculty ratio** 12:1 **Application deadline** 8/1 (freshmen), 8/1 (transfer) **Freshmen** 71% were admitted **Housing** Yes **Expenses** Tuition $16,620; Room & Board $6600 **Undergraduates** 81% women, 53% part-time, 67% 25 or older, 0.3% Native American, 14% Hispanic American, 30% African American, 10% Asian American/Pacific Islander **The most frequently chosen baccalaureate fields are** business/marketing, health professions and related sciences, liberal arts/general studies **Academic program** English as a second language, advanced placement, accelerated degree program, self-designed majors, honors program, summer session, adult/ continuing education programs, internships **Contact** Mr. Jeffrey D. Miller, Vice President for Enrollment Management, Holy Names College, Admission Office, Oakland, CA 94619. Telephone: 510-436-1321 or toll-free 800-430-1321. Fax: 510-436-1325. E-mail: admissions@admin.hnc.edu. Web site: http://www.hnc.edu/.

HOPE INTERNATIONAL UNIVERSITY
FULLERTON, CALIFORNIA

General Independent, comprehensive, coed, affiliated with Christian Churches and Churches of Christ **Entrance** Moderately difficult **Setting** 16-acre suburban campus **Total enrollment** 916 **Student/faculty ratio** 15:1 **Application deadline** 5/1 (freshmen), 5/1 (transfer) **Freshmen** 42% were admitted **Housing** Yes **Expenses** Tuition $12,140; Room & Board $4424 **Undergraduates** 53% women, 18% part-time, 37% 25 or older, 0.2% Native American, 14% Hispanic American, 4% African American, 4% Asian American/ Pacific Islander **Academic program** English as a second language, advanced placement, accelerated degree program, self-designed majors, honors program, summer session, adult/continuing education programs, internships **Contact** Ms. Midge Madden, Assistant Director, Admissions, Hope International University, 2500 East Nutwood Avenue, Fullerton, CA 92831-3138. Telephone: 714-879-3901 Ext. 2235 or toll-free 800-762-1294 Ext. 2235. Fax: 714-526-0231 Ext. 2235. E-mail: mfmadden@hiu.edu. Web site: http://www.hiu.edu/.

HUMBOLDT STATE UNIVERSITY
ARCATA, CALIFORNIA

General State-supported, comprehensive, coed **Entrance** Moderately difficult **Setting** 161-acre rural campus **Total enrollment** 7,433 **Student/faculty ratio** 18:1 **Application deadline** Rolling (freshmen), 11/30 (transfer) **Freshmen** 73% were admitted **Housing** Yes **Expenses** Room & Board $6092 **Undergraduates** 54% women, 11% part-time, 26% 25 or older, 3% Native American, 8% Hispanic American, 2% African American, 3% Asian American/Pacific Islander **The most frequently chosen baccalaureate fields are** interdisciplinary studies, natural resources/ environmental science, social sciences and history **Academic program** English as a second language, advanced placement, self-designed majors, honors program, summer session, adult/continuing education programs, internships **Contact** Mr. Jeffery Savage, Office of Admissions and School Relations, Humboldt State University, 1 Harpst Street, Arcata, CA 95521-8299. Telephone: 707-826-4402. Fax: 707-826-6194. E-mail: hsuinfo@laurel.humboldt.edu. Web site: http://www.humboldt.edu/.

HUMPHREYS COLLEGE
STOCKTON, CALIFORNIA

General Independent, comprehensive, coed **Contact** Ms. Wilma Okamoto Vaughn, Dean of Administration, Humphreys College, 6650 Inglewood Avenue, Stockton, CA 95207-3896. Telephone: 209-478-0800. Fax: 209-478-8721. Web site: http://www.humphreys.edu/.

INSTITUTE OF COMPUTER TECHNOLOGY
LOS ANGELES, CALIFORNIA

General Proprietary, 4-year, coed **Entrance** Noncompetitive **Setting** urban campus **Total enrollment** 264 **Housing** No **Expenses** Tuition 8775 **Undergraduates** 30% women, 94% 25 or older **Academic program** Advanced placement, internships **Contact** Mr. Phil Singer, Director of Admissions, Institute of Computer Technology, 3200 Wilshire Boulevard, # 400, Los Angeles, CA 90010-1308. Telephone: 213-838-8300. Web site: http://www.ictcollege.edu/.

INTERIOR DESIGNERS INSTITUTE
NEWPORT BEACH, CALIFORNIA

Contact Interior Designers Institute, 1061 Camelback Road, Newport Beach, CA 92660.

INTERNATIONAL TECHNOLOGICAL UNIVERSITY
SANTA CLARA, CALIFORNIA

Contact International Technological University, 1650 Warburton Avenue, Santa Clara, CA 95050. Web site: http://www.itu.edu/.

JOHN F. KENNEDY UNIVERSITY
ORINDA, CALIFORNIA

General Independent, comprehensive, coed **Entrance** Noncompetitive **Setting** 14-acre suburban campus **Total enrollment** 1,567 **Student/faculty ratio** 12:1 **Application deadline** Rolling (transfer) **Housing** No **Expenses** Tuition 10,746 **Undergraduates** 81% women, 90% part-time, 93% 25 or older **The most frequently chosen baccalaureate fields are** business/marketing, liberal arts/general studies, psychology **Academic program** Advanced placement, self-designed majors, summer session, adult/continuing education programs **Contact** Ms. Ellena Bloedorn, Director of Admissions and Records, John F. Kennedy University, 12 Altarinda Road, Orinda, CA 94563-2689. Telephone: 925-258-2213. Fax: 925-254-6964. E-mail: proginfo@jfku.edu. Web site: http://www.jfku.edu/.

LA SIERRA UNIVERSITY
RIVERSIDE, CALIFORNIA

General Independent Seventh-day Adventist, comprehensive, coed **Contact** Dr. Tom Smith, Vice President for Enrollment Services, La Sierra University, 4700 Pierce Street, Riverside, CA 92515-8247. Telephone: 909-785-2432 or toll-free 800-874-5587. Fax: 909-785-2901. E-mail: ivy@polaris.lasierra.edu. Web site: http://www.lasierra.edu/.

LEE COLLEGE AT THE UNIVERSITY OF JUDAISM
See University of Judaism

LIFE BIBLE COLLEGE
SAN DIMAS, CALIFORNIA

General Independent, 4-year, coed, affiliated with International Church of the Foursquare Gospel **Entrance** Moderately difficult **Setting** 9-acre suburban campus **Total enrollment** 488 **Student/faculty ratio** 6:1 **Application deadline** 7/1 (freshmen), 7/1 (transfer) **Freshmen** 94% were admitted **Housing** Yes **Expenses** Tuition $5800; Room & Board $3200 **Undergraduates** 48% women, 20% part-time, 20% 25 or older, 1% Native American, 12% Hispanic American, 5% African American, 5% Asian American/Pacific Islander **The most frequently chosen baccalaureate field is** philosophy, religion, and theology **Academic program** Advanced placement, summer session, adult/continuing education programs, internships **Contact** Mrs. Linda Hibdon, Admissions Director, LIFE Bible College, 1100 Covina Boulevard, San Dimas, CA 91773-3298. Telephone: 909-599-5433 Ext. 343 or toll-free 877-886-5433. Fax: 909-599-6690. E-mail: lifebibl@tstonramp.com. Web site: http://www.lifebible.edu/.

LINCOLN UNIVERSITY
OAKLAND, CALIFORNIA

General Independent, comprehensive, coed **Contact** Ms. Vivian Xu, Admissions Officer, Lincoln University, 401 15th Street, Oakland, CA 94612. Telephone: 415-221-1212 Ext. 115. Fax: 415-387-9730. E-mail: admissions@lincolnuca.edu. Web site: http://www.lincolnuca.edu/.

LOMA LINDA UNIVERSITY
LOMA LINDA, CALIFORNIA

General Independent Seventh-day Adventist, university, coed **Setting** small-town campus **Total enrollment** 3,110 **Housing** Yes **Expenses** Tuition 14,220; Room & Board 8370 **Undergraduates** 75% women, 24% part-time, 53% 25 or older, 1% Native American, 16% Hispanic American, 8% African American, 25% Asian American/Pacific Islander **Academic program** English as a second language **Contact** Dr. Cyril Connelly, Director of Marketing, Loma Linda University, Loma Linda, CA 92350. Telephone: 909-824-4792. Web site: http://www.llu.edu/.

LOUISE SALINGER ACADEMY OF FASHION
See Art Institutes International at San Francisco

LOYOLA MARYMOUNT UNIVERSITY
LOS ANGELES, CALIFORNIA

General Independent Roman Catholic, comprehensive, coed **Entrance** Very difficult **Setting** 128-acre suburban campus **Total enrollment** 7,515 **Student/faculty ratio** 13:1 **Application deadline** 2/1 (freshmen), 7/1 (transfer) **Freshmen** 62% were admitted **Housing** Yes **Expenses** Tuition $20,834; Room & Board $7100 **Undergraduates** 57% women, 6% part-time, 7% 25 or older, 1% Native American, 18% Hispanic American, 6% African American, 12% Asian American/Pacific Islander **Academic program** Advanced placement, accelerated degree program, self-designed majors, honors program, summer session, adult/continuing education programs, internships **Contact** Mr. Matthew X. Fissinger, Director of Admissions, Loyola Marymount University, 7900 Loyola Boulevard, Los Angeles, CA 90045-8366. Telephone: 310-338-2750 or toll-free 800-LMU-INFO. E-mail: admissns@lmumail.lmu.edu. Web site: http://www.lmu.edu/.

▶ **For more information, see page 439.**

THE MASTER'S COLLEGE AND SEMINARY
SANTA CLARITA, CALIFORNIA

General Independent nondenominational, comprehensive, coed **Entrance** Moderately difficult **Setting** 110-acre suburban campus **Total enrollment** 1,435 **Student/faculty ratio** 19:1 **Application deadline** 3/2 (freshmen), 3/2 (transfer) **Freshmen** 79% were admitted **Housing** Yes **Expenses** Tuition $14,300; Room & Board $5800 **Undergraduates** 52% women, 7% part-time, 12% 25 or older, 1% Native American, 6% Hispanic American, 1% African American, 4% Asian American/Pacific Islander **Academic program** Advanced placement, accelerated degree program, summer session, adult/continuing education programs, internships **Contact** Mr. Yaphet Peterson, Director of Enrollment, The Master's College and Seminary, 21726 Placerita Canyon Road, Santa Clarita, CA 91321. Telephone: 661-259-3540 Ext. 3365 or toll-free 800-568-6248. Fax: 661-288-1037. E-mail: enrollment@masters.edu. Web site: http://www.masters.edu/.

MENLO COLLEGE
ATHERTON, CALIFORNIA

General Independent, 4-year, coed **Entrance** Minimally difficult **Setting** 45-acre small-town campus **Total enrollment** 662 **Student/faculty ratio** 16:1 **Application deadline** Rolling (freshmen), rolling (transfer) **Freshmen** 73% were admitted **Housing** Yes **Expenses** Tuition $18,400; Room & Board $6800 **Undergraduates** 43% women, 16% part-time, 22% 25 or older, 0.3% Native American, 10% Hispanic American, 7% African American, 15% Asian American/Pacific Islander **Academic program** English as a second language, advanced placement, accelerated degree program, self-designed majors, honors program, summer session, adult/continuing education programs, internships **Contact** Dr. Greg Smith, Director of Admissions, Menlo College, 1000 El Camino Real, Atherton, CA 94027. Telephone: 650-543-3910 or toll-free 800-556-3656. Fax: 650-617-2395. E-mail: admissions@menlo.edu. Web site: http://www.menlo.edu/.

MILLS COLLEGE
OAKLAND, CALIFORNIA

General Independent, comprehensive, women only **Entrance** Moderately difficult **Setting** 135-acre urban campus **Total enrollment** 1,070 **Student/faculty ratio** 11:1 **Application deadline** 2/15 (freshmen), 3/2 (transfer) **Freshmen** 75% were admitted **Housing** Yes **Expenses** Tuition $19,056; Room & Board $7588 **The most frequently chosen baccalaureate fields are** interdisciplinary studies, social sciences and history, visual/performing arts **Academic program** Advanced placement, self-designed majors, adult/continuing education programs, internships **Contact** Avis Hinkson, Dean of Admission, Mills College, 5000 MacArthur Boulevard, Oakland, CA 94613-1000. Telephone: 510-430-2135 or toll-free 800-87-MILLS. Fax: 510-430-3314. E-mail: admission@mills.edu. Web site: http://www.mills.edu/.

▶ **For more information, see page 449.**

MOUNT ST. MARY'S COLLEGE
LOS ANGELES, CALIFORNIA

General Independent Roman Catholic, comprehensive, coed, primarily women **Entrance** Moderately difficult **Setting** 71-acre suburban campus **Total enrollment** 1,973 **Student/faculty ratio** 16:1 **Application deadline** Rolling (freshmen), 3/15 (transfer) **Freshmen** 54% were admitted **Housing** Yes **Expenses** Tuition 17,666; Room & Board 7070 **Undergraduates** 95% women, 29% part-time, 31% 25 or older, 0.4% Native American, 43% Hispanic American, 13% African American, 17% Asian American/Pacific Islander **The most frequently chosen baccalaureate fields are** health professions and related sciences, biological/life sciences, liberal arts/general studies **Academic program** Advanced placement, accelerated degree program, self-designed majors, honors program, summer session, adult/continuing education programs, internships **Contact** Ms. Katy Murphy, Executive Director of Admissions and Financial Aid, Mount St. Mary's College, 12001 Chalon Road, Los Angeles, CA 90049-1599. Telephone: 310-954-4252 or toll-free 800-999-9893. E-mail: admmsmc@aol.com. Web site: http://www.msmc.la.edu/.

MT. SIERRA COLLEGE
MONROVIA, CALIFORNIA

General Proprietary, 4-year **Entrance** Moderately difficult **Total enrollment** 1,222 **Student/faculty ratio** 20:1 **Freshmen** 73% were admitted **Expenses** Tuition $9552 **Undergraduates** 34% women, 1% part-time, 60% 25 or older **Academic program** Accelerated degree program, summer session, adult/continuing education programs, internships **Contact** Mr. Eric Thompson, Director of Admissions, Mt. Sierra College, 101 E. Huntington Drive, Monrovia, CA 91016. Telephone: 626-873-2113 or toll-free 888-MtSierra (in-state). Fax: 626-359-5528. Web site: http://www.mtsierra.edu/.

MUSICIANS INSTITUTE
HOLLYWOOD, CALIFORNIA

Contact Mr. Steve Lunn, Admissions Representative, Musicians Institute, 1655 North McCadden Place, Hollywood, CA 90028. Telephone: 323-462-1384 Ext. 156 or toll-free 800-255-PLAY.

THE NATIONAL HISPANIC UNIVERSITY
SAN JOSE, CALIFORNIA

General Independent, 4-year, coed **Entrance** Minimally difficult **Setting** 1-acre urban campus **Total enrollment** 450 **Application deadline** 8/15 (freshmen), 8/15 (transfer) **Freshmen** 82% were admitted **Housing** No **Expenses** Tuition 3100 **Undergraduates** 40% 25 or older **Academic program** English as a second language, advanced placement, accelerated degree program, summer session, adult/continuing education programs, internships **Contact** Office of Admissions, The National Hispanic University, 14271 Story Road, San Jose, CA 95127-3823. Telephone: 408-254-6900.

NATIONAL UNIVERSITY
LA JOLLA, CALIFORNIA

General Independent, comprehensive, coed **Entrance** Noncompetitive **Setting** 15-acre urban campus **Total enrollment** 22,858 **Student/faculty ratio** 10:1 **Application deadline** Rolling (freshmen), rolling (transfer) **Freshmen** 100% were admitted **Housing** No **Expenses** Tuition $7755 **Undergraduates** 55% women, 14% part-time, 81% 25 or older, 1% Native American, 19% Hispanic American, 14% African

National University *(continued)*

American, 9% Asian American/Pacific Islander **The most frequently chosen baccalaureate fields are** business/marketing, interdisciplinary studies, psychology **Academic program** English as a second language, advanced placement, accelerated degree program, summer session, adult/continuing education programs, internships **Contact** Ms. Nancy Rohland, Director of Enrollment Management, National University, 11255 North Torrey Pines Road, La Jolla, CA 92037. Telephone: 858-642-8180 or toll-free 800-628-8648. Fax: 858-642-8710. E-mail: nrohland@nu.edu. Web site: http://www.nu.edu/.

NEW COLLEGE OF CALIFORNIA
SAN FRANCISCO, CALIFORNIA

General Independent, comprehensive, coed **Entrance** Noncompetitive **Setting** urban campus **Total enrollment** 1,088 **Application deadline** Rolling (freshmen), rolling (transfer) **Housing** No **Expenses** Tuition 9240 **Undergraduates** 50% 25 or older **Academic program** English as a second language, advanced placement, accelerated degree program, self-designed majors, internships **Contact** Ms. Jean Lee, Admissions Inquiry Office, New College of California, 50 Fell Street, San Francisco, CA 94102-5206. Telephone: 415-437-3429 or toll-free 888-437-3460. Fax: 415-865-2636. E-mail: jeanlee@ncgate.newcollege.edu. Web site: http://www.newcollege.edu/.

NEWSCHOOL OF ARCHITECTURE & DESIGN
SAN DIEGO, CALIFORNIA

General Proprietary, comprehensive, coed, primarily men **Entrance** Moderately difficult **Setting** urban campus **Total enrollment** 143 **Student/faculty ratio** 5:1 **Application deadline** 8/15 (freshmen), 8/15 (transfer) **Freshmen** 100% were admitted **Housing** Yes **Expenses** Tuition $13,659 **Undergraduates** 22% women, 33% part-time, 65% 25 or older, 0% Native American, 33% Hispanic American, 11% African American, 0% Asian American/Pacific Islander **Academic program** English as a second language, advanced placement, summer session, adult/continuing education programs, internships **Contact** Mr. Victor Parga, Director of Admissions, Newschool of Architecture & Design, 1249 F Street, San Diego, CA 92101-6634. Telephone: 619-235-4100 Ext. 104. E-mail: nsa1249@aol.com. Web site: http://www.newschoolarch.edu/.

NORTHWESTERN POLYTECHNIC UNIVERSITY
FREMONT, CALIFORNIA

General Independent, comprehensive, coed **Contact** Dr. Dan Chang, Associate Dean of Academic Affairs and Admissions, Northwestern Polytechnic University, 117 Fourier Avenue, Fremont, CA 94539-7482. Telephone: 510-657-5985. Fax: 510-657-8975. E-mail: npuadm@npu.edu. Web site: http://www.npu.edu/.

OCCIDENTAL COLLEGE
LOS ANGELES, CALIFORNIA

General Independent, comprehensive, coed **Entrance** Very difficult **Setting** 120-acre urban campus **Total enrollment** 1,726 **Student/faculty ratio** 12:1 **Application deadline** 1/15 (freshmen), 3/15 (transfer) **Freshmen** 57% were admitted **Housing** Yes **Expenses** Tuition $23,828; Room & Board $6820 **Undergraduates** 58% women, 1% part-time, 2% 25 or older, 1% Native American, 14% Hispanic American, 6% African American, 18% Asian American/Pacific Islander **The most frequently chosen baccalaureate fields are** biological/life sciences, social sciences and history, visual/performing arts **Academic program** Advanced placement, accelerated degree program, self-designed majors, honors program, summer session, internships **Contact** Mr. Mark Hatch, Director of Admission, Occidental College, 1600 Campus Road, Los Angeles, CA 90041-3314. Telephone: 323-259-2700 or toll-free 800-825-5262. Fax: 323-341-4875. E-mail: admission@oxy.edu. Web site: http://www.oxy.edu/.

OTIS COLLEGE OF ART AND DESIGN
LOS ANGELES, CALIFORNIA

General Independent, comprehensive, coed **Entrance** Moderately difficult **Setting** 5-acre urban campus **Total enrollment** 924 **Student/faculty ratio** 11:1 **Application deadline** Rolling (freshmen), rolling (transfer) **Freshmen** 61% were admitted **Housing** No **Expenses** Tuition $19,294 **Undergraduates** 62% women, 2% part-time, 22% 25 or older, 0.4% Native American, 12% Hispanic American, 3% African American, 29% Asian American/Pacific Islander **The most frequently chosen baccalaureate fields are** architecture, visual/performing arts **Academic program** English as a second language, advanced placement, honors program, summer session, adult/continuing education programs, internships **Contact** Mr. Marc Meredith, Dean of Admissions, Otis College of Art and Design, 9045 Lincoln Boulevard, Los Angeles, CA 90045-9785. Telephone: 310-665-6800 Ext. 6815 or toll-free 800-527-OTIS. Fax: 310-665-6821. E-mail: otisart@otisart.edu. Web site: http://www.otisart.edu/.

PACIFIC OAKS COLLEGE
PASADENA, CALIFORNIA

General Independent, upper-level, coed, primarily women **Setting** 2-acre small-town campus **Total enrollment** 824 **Student/faculty ratio** 7:1 **Application deadline** 6/1 (transfer) **Housing** No **Expenses** Tuition $12,660 **Undergraduates** 94% women, 95% part-time, 86% 25 or older, 3% Native American, 23% Hispanic American, 13% African American, 6% Asian American/Pacific Islander **The most frequently chosen baccalaureate field is** social sciences and history **Academic program** Summer session, adult/continuing education programs, internships **Contact** Ms. Marsha Franker, Director of Admissions, Pacific Oaks College, Admissions Office,

Pacific Oaks College, 5 Westmoreland Place, Pasadena, CA 91103. Telephone: 626-397-1349 or toll-free 800-684-0900. Fax: 626-577-6144. E-mail: admissions@pacificoaks.edu. Web site: http://www.pacificoaks.edu/.

PACIFIC STATES UNIVERSITY
LOS ANGELES, CALIFORNIA

General Independent, comprehensive, coed **Entrance** Minimally difficult **Setting** 1-acre urban campus **Total enrollment** 91 **Application deadline** 6/15 (freshmen) **Housing** No **Expenses** Tuition $10,560; Room & Board $9000 **Undergraduates** 24% women, 80% 25 or older, 100% Asian American/Pacific Islander **Academic program** English as a second language, accelerated degree program, self-designed majors, summer session, adult/continuing education programs **Contact** Mr. Seth Ozen, Admissions Officer, Pacific States University, 1516 South Western Avenue, Los Angeles, CA 90006. Telephone: 323-731-2383 or toll-free 888-200-0383. E-mail: admission@psuca.edu. Web site: http://www.psuca.edu/.

PACIFIC UNION COLLEGE
ANGWIN, CALIFORNIA

General Independent Seventh-day Adventist, comprehensive, coed **Entrance** Moderately difficult **Setting** 200-acre rural campus **Total enrollment** 1,456 **Student/faculty ratio** 12:1 **Application deadline** Rolling (freshmen), rolling (transfer) **Housing** Yes **Expenses** Tuition $15,075; Room & Board $4530 **Undergraduates** 56% women, 9% part-time, 0.3% Native American, 10% Hispanic American, 6% African American, 19% Asian American/Pacific Islander **The most frequently chosen baccalaureate fields are** business/marketing, engineering/engineering technologies, health professions and related sciences **Academic program** English as a second language, advanced placement, accelerated degree program, self-designed majors, honors program, summer session, adult/continuing education programs, internships **Contact** Mr. Sean Kootsey, Director of Enrollment Services, Pacific Union College, Enrollment Services, Angwin, CA 94508-9707. Telephone: 707-965-6425 or toll-free 800-862-7080. Fax: 707-965-6432. E-mail: enroll@puc.edu. Web site: http://www.puc.edu/.

PATTEN COLLEGE
OAKLAND, CALIFORNIA

General Independent interdenominational, comprehensive, coed **Entrance** Noncompetitive **Setting** 5-acre urban campus **Total enrollment** 635 **Student/faculty ratio** 16:1 **Application deadline** 7/31 (freshmen), rolling (transfer) **Freshmen** 68% were admitted **Housing** Yes **Expenses** Tuition $8400; Room & Board $4800 **Undergraduates** 39% women, 55% part-time, 59% 25 or older, 0% Native American, 12% Hispanic American, 22% African American, 23% Asian American/Pacific Islander **The most frequently chosen baccalaureate fields are** business/marketing, liberal arts/general studies, philosophy, religion, and theology **Academic program** Advanced placement, accelerated degree program, honors program, summer session, adult/continuing education programs, internships **Contact** Ms. Inez Bailey, Director of Admissions, Patten College, 2433 Coolidge Avenue, Oakland, CA 94601. Telephone: 510-261-8500. Fax: 510-534-4344. Web site: http://www.diac.com/~patten/.

PEPPERDINE UNIVERSITY
MALIBU, CALIFORNIA

General Independent, university, coed, affiliated with Church of Christ **Entrance** Very difficult **Setting** 830-acre small-town campus **Total enrollment** 6,317 **Student/faculty ratio** 13:1 **Application deadline** 1/15 (freshmen), 1/15 (transfer) **Freshmen** 35% were admitted **Housing** Yes **Expenses** Tuition 24,050; Room & Board 7290 **Undergraduates** 91% women, 7% part-time, 3% 25 or older, 1% Native American, 9% Hispanic American, 6% African American, 6% Asian American/Pacific Islander **The most frequently chosen baccalaureate fields are** business/marketing, communications/communication technologies, liberal arts/general studies **Academic program** Advanced placement, accelerated degree program, self-designed majors, honors program, summer session, internships **Contact** Mr. Paul A. Long, Dean of Admission, Pepperdine University, 24255 Pacific Coast Highway, Malibu, CA 90263-0002. Telephone: 310-456-4392. Fax: 310-456-4861. E-mail: admission-seaver@pepperdine.edu. Web site: http://www.pepperdine.edu/.

PITZER COLLEGE
CLAREMONT, CALIFORNIA

General Independent, 4-year, coed **Entrance** Moderately difficult **Setting** 35-acre suburban campus **Total enrollment** 924 **Student/faculty ratio** 12:1 **Application deadline** 2/1 (freshmen), 4/15 (transfer) **Freshmen** 56% were admitted **Housing** Yes **Expenses** Tuition 25,238; Room & Board 6458 **Undergraduates** 62% women, 14% part-time, 9% 25 or older, 1% Native American, 14% Hispanic American, 5% African American, 11% Asian American/Pacific Islander **The most frequently chosen baccalaureate fields are** psychology, social sciences and history, visual/performing arts **Academic program** English as a second language, advanced placement, self-designed majors, honors program, adult/continuing education programs, internships **Contact** Dr. Arnaldo Rodriguez, Vice President for Admission and Financial Aid, Pitzer College, 1050 North Mills Avenue, Claremont, CA 91711-6101. Telephone: 909-621-8129 or toll-free 800-748-9371. Fax: 909-621-8770. E-mail: admission@email.pitzer.edu. Web site: http://www.pitzer.edu/.

POINT LOMA NAZARENE UNIVERSITY
SAN DIEGO, CALIFORNIA

General Independent Nazarene, comprehensive, coed **Entrance** Moderately difficult **Setting** 88-acre sub-

Point Loma Nazarene University *(continued)*

urban campus **Total enrollment** 2,741 **Student/faculty ratio** 16:1 **Application deadline** 3/1 (freshmen), rolling (transfer) **Freshmen** 75% were admitted **Housing** Yes **Expenses** Tuition 14,340; Room & Board 5990 **Undergraduates** 59% women, 4% part-time, 5% 25 or older, 1% Native American, 7% Hispanic American, 2% African American, 4% Asian American/Pacific Islander **The most frequently chosen baccalaureate fields are** business/marketing, education, liberal arts/general studies **Academic program** English as a second language, advanced placement, summer session, internships **Contact** Mr. Scott Shoemaker, Director of Admissions, Point Loma Nazarene University, 3900 Lomaland Drive, San Diego, CA 92106-2899. Telephone: 619-849-2225 or toll-free 800-733-7770 (out-of-state). Fax: 619-849-2601. E-mail: cnlsr3ad@ptloma.edu. Web site: http://www.ptloma.edu/.

POMONA COLLEGE
CLAREMONT, CALIFORNIA

General Independent, 4-year, coed **Entrance** Most difficult **Setting** 140-acre suburban campus **Total enrollment** 1,565 **Student/faculty ratio** 9:1 **Application deadline** 1/2 (freshmen), 3/15 (transfer) **Freshmen** 30% were admitted **Housing** Yes **Expenses** Tuition 24,170; Room & Board 8170 **Undergraduates** 49% women, 1% part-time, 1% 25 or older, 1% Native American, 9% Hispanic American, 4% African American, 16% Asian American/Pacific Islander **The most frequently chosen baccalaureate fields are** biological/life sciences, physical sciences, social sciences and history **Academic program** Advanced placement, self-designed majors, internships **Contact** Mr. Bruce Poch, Vice President and Dean of Admissions, Pomona College, 333 North College Way, Claremont, CA 91711. Telephone: 909-621-8134. Fax: 909-621-8403. E-mail: admissions@pomona.edu. Web site: http://www.pomona.edu/.

ST. JOHN'S SEMINARY COLLEGE
CAMARILLO, CALIFORNIA

General Independent Roman Catholic, 4-year, men only **Entrance** Moderately difficult **Setting** 100-acre suburban campus **Total enrollment** 95 **Student/faculty ratio** 4:1 **Application deadline** 6/21 (freshmen), 6/21 (transfer) **Freshmen** 75% were admitted **Housing** Yes **Expenses** Tuition $7600; Room & Board $5000 **Undergraduates** 5% part-time, 39% 25 or older, 49% Hispanic American, 32% Asian American/Pacific Islander **The most frequently chosen baccalaureate fields are** English, foreign language/literature, philosophy, religion, and theology **Academic program** English as a second language, advanced placement, honors program, adult/continuing education programs **Contact** Ms. Therese Esposito, Director of Admissions, St. John's Seminary College, 5118 Seminary Road, Camarillo, CA 93012-2599. Telephone: 805-482-2755 Ext. 2032. Fax: 805-987-5097. Web site: http://www.west.net/~sjsc.

SAINT MARY'S COLLEGE OF CALIFORNIA
MORAGA, CALIFORNIA

General Independent Roman Catholic, comprehensive, coed **Entrance** Moderately difficult **Setting** 420-acre suburban campus **Total enrollment** 4,142 **Student/faculty ratio** 13:1 **Application deadline** 2/1 (freshmen), 7/1 (transfer) **Freshmen** 76% were admitted **Housing** Yes **Expenses** Tuition 19,525; Room & Board 8050 **Undergraduates** 61% women, 19% part-time, 3% 25 or older, 1% Native American, 15% Hispanic American, 6% African American, 9% Asian American/Pacific Islander **The most frequently chosen baccalaureate fields are** business/marketing, health professions and related sciences, social sciences and history **Academic program** Advanced placement, self-designed majors, honors program, adult/continuing education programs, internships **Contact** Ms. Dorothy Benjamin, Dean of Admissions, Saint Mary's College of California, PO Box 4800, Moraga, CA 94556-4800. Telephone: 925-631-4224 or toll-free 800-800-4SMC. Fax: 925-376-7193. E-mail: smcadmit@stmarys-ca.edu. Web site: http://www.stmarys-ca.edu/.

SAMUEL MERRITT COLLEGE
OAKLAND, CALIFORNIA

General Independent, comprehensive, coed, primarily women **Entrance** Moderately difficult **Setting** 1-acre urban campus **Total enrollment** 714 **Application deadline** 3/1 (freshmen), 3/1 (transfer) **Freshmen** 71% were admitted **Housing** Yes **Expenses** Tuition $16,425; Room only $3510 **Undergraduates** 92% women, 8% part-time, 56% 25 or older, 3% Native American, 10% Hispanic American, 12% African American, 20% Asian American/Pacific Islander **Academic program** Advanced placement, summer session, internships **Contact** Mr. John Garten-Shuman, Director of Admissions, Samuel Merritt College, 370 Hawthorne Avenue, Oakland, CA 94609-3108. Telephone: 510-869-6727 or toll-free 800-607-MERRITT. Fax: 510-869-6525. E-mail: jgartenshuman@compuserve.com. Web site: http://www.samuelmerritt.edu/.

SAN DIEGO STATE UNIVERSITY
SAN DIEGO, CALIFORNIA

General State-supported, university, coed **Entrance** Moderately difficult **Setting** 300-acre urban campus **Total enrollment** 31,609 **Student/faculty ratio** 17:1 **Application deadline** 11/30 (freshmen) **Freshmen** 65% were admitted **Housing** Yes **Expenses** Tuition $1776; Room & Board $7110 **Undergraduates** 57% women, 25% part-time, 20% 25 or older, 1% Native American, 21% Hispanic American, 5% African American, 14% Asian American/Pacific Islander **The most frequently chosen baccalaureate fields are** business/marketing, psychology, social sciences and history **Academic program** English as a second language, advanced placement, self-designed majors, honors program, summer session, internships **Contact** Prospective Student Center, San Diego State

University, 5500 Campanile Drive, San Diego, CA 92182-7455. Telephone: 619-594-6886. E-mail: admissions@sdsu.edu. Web site: http://www.sdsu.edu/.

SAN FRANCISCO ART INSTITUTE
SAN FRANCISCO, CALIFORNIA

General Independent, comprehensive, coed **Entrance** Moderately difficult **Setting** 3-acre urban campus **Total enrollment** 618 **Student/faculty ratio** 8:1 **Application deadline** 8/27 (freshmen), rolling (transfer) **Freshmen** 61% were admitted **Housing** No **Expenses** Tuition $20,200 **Undergraduates** 51% women, 16% part-time, 44% 25 or older, 1% Native American, 10% Hispanic American, 3% African American, 7% Asian American/Pacific Islander **The most frequently chosen baccalaureate field is** visual/performing arts **Academic program** English as a second language, advanced placement, accelerated degree program, summer session, adult/continuing education programs, internships **Contact** Mark Takiguchi, Director of Admissions, San Francisco Art Institute, 800 Chestnut Street, San Francisco, CA 94133. Telephone: 415-749-4500 or toll-free 800-345-SFAI. E-mail: admissions@sfai.edu. Web site: http://www.sfai.edu/.

SAN FRANCISCO CONSERVATORY OF MUSIC
SAN FRANCISCO, CALIFORNIA

General Independent, comprehensive, coed **Entrance** Moderately difficult **Setting** 2-acre urban campus **Total enrollment** 263 **Student/faculty ratio** 7:1 **Application deadline** 2/15 (freshmen), 2/15 (transfer) **Freshmen** 64% were admitted **Housing** No **Expenses** Tuition 19,580 **Undergraduates** 55% women, 3% part-time, 10% 25 or older, 1% Native American, 7% Hispanic American, 5% African American, 16% Asian American/Pacific Islander **The most frequently chosen baccalaureate field is** visual/performing arts **Academic program** Advanced placement **Contact** Susan Dean, Director of Admissions, San Francisco Conservatory of Music, 1201 Ortega Street, San Francisco, CA 94122-4411. Telephone: 415-759-3431. Fax: 415-759-3499. E-mail: jgordan@sirius.com. Web site: http://www.sfcm.edu/.

SAN FRANCISCO STATE UNIVERSITY
SAN FRANCISCO, CALIFORNIA

General State-supported, comprehensive, coed **Entrance** Moderately difficult **Setting** 90-acre urban campus **Total enrollment** 26,826 **Student/faculty ratio** 20:1 **Application deadline** 8/1 (freshmen) **Freshmen** 67% were admitted **Housing** Yes **Expenses** Tuition 1826; Room & Board 6930 **Undergraduates** 60% women, 28% part-time, 30% 25 or older, 1% Native American, 13% Hispanic American, 6% African American, 33% Asian American/Pacific Islander **The most frequently chosen baccalaureate fields are** business/marketing, social sciences and history, visual/performing arts **Academic program** English as a second language, advanced placement, accelerated degree program, self-designed majors, honors program, summer session, adult/continuing education programs, internships **Contact** Ms. Patricia Wade, Admissions Officer, San Francisco State University, 1600 Holloway Avenue, Administration 154, San Francisco, CA 94132. Telephone: 415-338-2037. Fax: 415-338-7196. E-mail: ugadmit@apollo.sfsu.edu. Web site: http://www.sfsu.edu/.

SAN JOSE CHRISTIAN COLLEGE
SAN JOSE, CALIFORNIA

General Independent nondenominational, 4-year, coed **Entrance** Noncompetitive **Setting** 9-acre urban campus **Total enrollment** 400 **Student/faculty ratio** 12:1 **Application deadline** 8/1 (freshmen), 8/1 (transfer) **Freshmen** 42% were admitted **Housing** Yes **Expenses** Tuition $10,340; Room & Board $5109 **Undergraduates** 63% 25 or older, 1% Native American, 10% Hispanic American, 8% African American, 13% Asian American/Pacific Islander **The most frequently chosen baccalaureate field is** philosophy, religion, and theology **Academic program** English as a second language, advanced placement, accelerated degree program, summer session, internships **Contact** Ms. Stephani Haskins, Admissions Counselor, San Jose Christian College, 790 South Twelfth Street, San Jose, CA 95112-2381. Telephone: 408-278-4333 or toll-free 800-355-7522. Fax: 408-293-7352. E-mail: rjones@sjchristian.edu. Web site: http://www.sjchristiancol.edu/.

SAN JOSE STATE UNIVERSITY
SAN JOSE, CALIFORNIA

General State-supported, comprehensive, coed **Entrance** Moderately difficult **Setting** 104-acre urban campus **Total enrollment** 26,698 **Application deadline** Rolling (freshmen), rolling (transfer) **Freshmen** 72% were admitted **Housing** Yes **Expenses** Tuition $1939; Room & Board $6248 **Undergraduates** 51% women, 30% part-time, 33% 25 or older, 1% Native American, 15% Hispanic American, 4% African American, 40% Asian American/Pacific Islander **Academic program** English as a second language, advanced placement, accelerated degree program, self-designed majors, honors program, summer session, adult/continuing education programs, internships **Contact** Mr. John Bradbury, Interim Director of Admissions, San Jose State University, One Washington Square, San Jose, CA 95192-0001. Telephone: 408-924-2000. Fax: 408-924-2050. E-mail: contact@sjsu.edu. Web site: http://www.sjsu.edu/.

SANTA CLARA UNIVERSITY
SANTA CLARA, CALIFORNIA

General Independent Roman Catholic (Jesuit), university, coed **Entrance** Moderately difficult **Setting** 104-acre suburban campus **Total enrollment** 7,356 **Student/faculty ratio** 13:1 **Application deadline** 1/15 (freshmen), 5/15 (transfer) **Freshmen** 62% were admitted **Housing** Yes **Expenses** Tuition 20,577; Room & Board 8034 **Undergraduates** 54% women,

Santa Clara University *(continued)*

3% part-time, 3% 25 or older, 1% Native American, 14% Hispanic American, 2% African American, 19% Asian American/Pacific Islander **The most frequently chosen baccalaureate fields are** business/marketing, engineering/engineering technologies, social sciences and history **Academic program** Advanced placement, self-designed majors, honors program, summer session, internships **Contact** Ms. Sandra Hayes, Dean of Undergraduate Admissions, Santa Clara University, 500 El Camino Real, Santa Clara, CA 95053. Telephone: 408-554-4700. Fax: 408-554-5255. E-mail: ugadmissions@scu.edu. Web site: http://www.scu.edu/.

SCRIPPS COLLEGE
CLAREMONT, CALIFORNIA

General Independent, 4-year, women only **Entrance** Very difficult **Setting** 30-acre suburban campus **Total enrollment** 800 **Student/faculty ratio** 12:1 **Application deadline** 2/1 (freshmen), 4/1 (transfer) **Freshmen** 68% were admitted **Housing** Yes **Expenses** Tuition $22,600; Room & Board $7800 **Undergraduates** 1% part-time, 1% 25 or older, 1% Native American, 5% Hispanic American, 3% African American, 14% Asian American/Pacific Islander **The most frequently chosen baccalaureate fields are** social sciences and history, interdisciplinary studies, visual/performing arts **Academic program** Advanced placement, accelerated degree program, self-designed majors, honors program, internships **Contact** Ms. Patricia F. Goldsmith, Dean of Admission and Financial Aid, Scripps College, 1030 Columbia Avenue, Claremont, CA 91711-3948. Telephone: 909-621-8149 or toll-free 800-770-1333. Fax: 909-607-7508. E-mail: admofc@ad.scrippscol.edu. Web site: http://www.scrippscollege.edu/.

SHASTA BIBLE COLLEGE
REDDING, CALIFORNIA

General Independent nondenominational, 4-year, coed **Entrance** Noncompetitive **Setting** 25-acre small-town campus **Total enrollment** 317 **Student/faculty ratio** 14:1 **Freshmen** 100% were admitted **Housing** Yes **Expenses** Tuition $5825; Room & Board $3576 **Undergraduates** 67% women, 84% part-time, 50% 25 or older, 2% Native American, 2% Hispanic American, 1% African American, 1% Asian American/Pacific Islander **Academic program** Adult/continuing education programs **Contact** Ms. Dawn Rodriguez, Registrar, Shasta Bible College, 2980 Hartnell Avenue, Redding, CA 96002. Telephone: 530-221-4275 or toll-free 800-800-45BC (in-state); 800-800-6929 (out-of-state). Fax: 530-221-6929. E-mail: ggunn@shasta.edu. Web site: http://www.shasta.edu/.

SIMPSON COLLEGE AND GRADUATE SCHOOL
REDDING, CALIFORNIA

General Independent, comprehensive, coed, affiliated with The Christian and Missionary Alliance **Contact** Mrs. Beth Spencer, Administrative Assistant to Vice President for Enrollment, Simpson College and Graduate School, 2211 College View Drive, Redding, CA 96003-8606. Telephone: 530-224-5606 Ext. 2602 or toll-free 800-598-2493. Fax: 530-224-5627. E-mail: admissions@simpsonca.edu. Web site: http://www.simpsonca.edu/.

SONOMA STATE UNIVERSITY
ROHNERT PARK, CALIFORNIA

General State-supported, comprehensive, coed **Entrance** Moderately difficult **Setting** 220-acre small-town campus **Total enrollment** 7,402 **Student/faculty ratio** 20:1 **Application deadline** 12/31 (freshmen), 1/31 (transfer) **Freshmen** 92% were admitted **Housing** Yes **Expenses** Tuition $2002; Room & Board $6471 **Undergraduates** 65% women, 16% part-time, 23% 25 or older, 1% Native American, 10% Hispanic American, 2% African American, 5% Asian American/Pacific Islander **The most frequently chosen baccalaureate fields are** business/marketing, psychology, social sciences and history **Academic program** English as a second language, advanced placement, accelerated degree program, self-designed majors, honors program, summer session, adult/continuing education programs, internships **Contact** Mr. Louis Naranjo, Director, New Student Programs, Sonoma State University, 1801 East Cotati Avenue, Rohnert Park, CA 94928. Telephone: 707-664-3032. Fax: 707-664-2060. E-mail: admitme@sonoma.edu. Web site: http://www.sonoma.edu/.

SOUTHERN CALIFORNIA BIBLE COLLEGE & SEMINARY
EL CAJON, CALIFORNIA

Contact Southern California Bible College & Seminary, 2075 East Madison Avenue, El Cajon, CA 92019. Web site: http://www.scbcs.edu/.

SOUTHERN CALIFORNIA COLLEGE
See Vanguard University of Southern California

SOUTHERN CALIFORNIA INSTITUTE OF ARCHITECTURE
LOS ANGELES, CALIFORNIA

General Independent, comprehensive, coed **Entrance** Moderately difficult **Setting** urban campus **Total enrollment** 430 **Application deadline** Rolling (freshmen), rolling (transfer) **Housing** No **Expenses** Tuition 16,061 **Undergraduates** 42% 25 or older **Academic program** English as a second language, advanced placement, summer session, internships **Contact** Ms. Debra Abel, Director of Admissions, Southern California Institute of Architecture, Freight Yard, 960 East 3rd Street, Los Angeles, CA 90013. Telephone: 213-613-2200 Ext. 320. Fax: 213-613-2260. E-mail: admissions@sciarc.edu. Web site: http://www.sciarc.edu/.

STANFORD UNIVERSITY
STANFORD, CALIFORNIA

General Independent, university, coed **Entrance** Most difficult **Setting** 8,180-acre suburban campus **Total enrollment** 18,549 **Student/faculty ratio** 7:1 **Application deadline** 12/15 (freshmen), 3/15 (transfer) **Freshmen** 13% were admitted **Housing** Yes **Expenses** Tuition 24,441; Room & Board 8030 **Undergraduates** 52% women, 20% part-time, 1% 25 or older, 2% Native American, 10% Hispanic American, 9% African American, 25% Asian American/Pacific Islander **The most frequently chosen baccalaureate fields are** engineering/engineering technologies, interdisciplinary studies, social sciences and history **Academic program** Advanced placement, self-designed majors, honors program, summer session, internships **Contact** Ms. Robin G. Mamlet, Dean of Undergraduate Admissions and Financial Aid, Stanford University, Old Union 232, Old Union, 520 Lasuen Mall, Stanford, CA 94305. Telephone: 650-723-2091. Fax: 650-723-6050. E-mail: undergrad.admissions@forsythe.stanford.e. Web site: http://www.stanford.edu/.

THOMAS AQUINAS COLLEGE
SANTA PAULA, CALIFORNIA

General Independent Roman Catholic, 4-year, coed **Entrance** Very difficult **Setting** 170-acre rural campus **Total enrollment** 277 **Student/faculty ratio** 11:1 **Application deadline** Rolling (freshmen) **Freshmen** 77% were admitted **Housing** Yes **Expenses** Tuition $15,400; Room & Board $4400 **Undergraduates** 47% women, 7% 25 or older, 0.4% Native American, 6% Hispanic American, 0.4% African American, 4% Asian American/Pacific Islander **The most frequently chosen baccalaureate field is** liberal arts/general studies **Contact** Mr. Thomas J. Susanka Jr., Director of Admissions, Thomas Aquinas College, 10000 North Ojai Road, Santa Paula, CA 93060-9980. Telephone: 805-525-4417 Ext. 361 or toll-free 800-634-9797. Fax: 805-525-9342. E-mail: greatbooks@freemark.com. Web site: http://www.thomasaquinas.edu/.

TOURO UNIVERSITY INTERNATIONAL
LOS ALAMITOS, CALIFORNIA

General Independent, comprehensive, coed **Entrance** Minimally difficult **Total enrollment** 650 **Student/faculty ratio** 45:1 **Freshmen** 64% were admitted **Expenses** Tuition $5760 **Undergraduates** 31% women, 13% part-time, 60% 25 or older **Academic program** Summer session, adult/continuing education programs **Contact** Dr. Robert Koester, Academic Dean of Administration, Touro University International, 10542 Calle Lee, Los Alamitos, CA 90720. Telephone: 714-816-0366 or toll-free 714-816-0366. Fax: 714-816-0367. E-mail: rkoester@tourou.edu. Web site: http://www.tourouniversity.edu/.

UNITED STATES INTERNATIONAL UNIVERSITY
SAN DIEGO, CALIFORNIA

General Independent, university, coed **Entrance** Moderately difficult **Setting** 200-acre suburban campus **Total enrollment** 1,335 **Student/faculty ratio** 19:1 **Application deadline** Rolling (freshmen), rolling (transfer) **Freshmen** 62% were admitted **Housing** Yes **Expenses** Tuition $14,340; Room & Board $6180 **Undergraduates** 56% women, 7% part-time, 21% 25 or older, 1% Native American, 21% Hispanic American, 9% African American, 6% Asian American/Pacific Islander **The most frequently chosen baccalaureate fields are** business/marketing, liberal arts/general studies, social sciences and history **Academic program** English as a second language, advanced placement, honors program, summer session, adult/continuing education programs, internships **Contact** Ms. Susan Topham, Director of Admissions, United States International University, 10455 Pomerado Road, San Diego, CA 92131-1799. Telephone: 858-635-4772. Fax: 858-635-4739. E-mail: usiu_adm@sanac.usiu.edu. Web site: http://www.usiu.edu/.

UNIVERSITY OF CALIFORNIA, BERKELEY
BERKELEY, CALIFORNIA

General State-supported, university, coed **Entrance** Very difficult **Setting** 1,232-acre urban campus **Total enrollment** 31,347 **Student/faculty ratio** 17:1 **Application deadline** 11/30 (freshmen), 11/30 (transfer) **Freshmen** 27% were admitted **Housing** Yes **Expenses** Tuition 4047; Room & Board 8670 **Undergraduates** 51% women, 7% part-time, 11% 25 or older, 1% Native American, 10% Hispanic American, 5% African American, 39% Asian American/Pacific Islander **Academic program** English as a second language, advanced placement, accelerated degree program, self-designed majors, honors program, summer session, adult/continuing education programs, internships **Contact** Pre-Admission Advising, Office of Undergraduate Admission and Relations With Schools, University of California, Berkeley, Berkeley, CA 94720. Telephone: 510-642-3175. Fax: 510-642-7333. E-mail: ouars@uclink.berkeley.edu. Web site: http://www.berkeley.edu/.

UNIVERSITY OF CALIFORNIA, DAVIS
DAVIS, CALIFORNIA

General State-supported, university, coed **Entrance** Very difficult **Setting** 5,993-acre suburban campus **Total enrollment** 26,121 **Student/faculty ratio** 19:1 **Application deadline** 11/30 (freshmen), 11/30 (transfer) **Freshmen** 63% were admitted **Housing** Yes **Expenses** Tuition $4087; Room & Board $6800 **Undergraduates** 56% women, 12% part-time, 6% 25 or older, 1% Native American, 10% Hispanic American, 3% African American, 34% Asian American/Pacific Islander **The most frequently chosen baccalaureate fields are** biological/life sciences, psychology, social sciences and history **Academic program** English as a second language, advanced placement,

University of California, Davis *(continued)*

self-designed majors, honors program, summer session, adult/continuing education programs, internships **Contact** Dr. Gary Tudor, Director of Undergraduate Admissions, University of California, Davis, Undergraduate Admission and Outreach Services, 175 Mrak Hall, Davis, CA 95616. Telephone: 530-752-2971. Fax: 530-752-1280. E-mail: thinkucd@ucdavis.edu. Web site: http://www.ucdavis.edu/.

UNIVERSITY OF CALIFORNIA, IRVINE
IRVINE, CALIFORNIA

General State-supported, university, coed **Entrance** Moderately difficult **Setting** 1,489-acre suburban campus **Total enrollment** 20,211 **Student/faculty ratio** 18:1 **Application deadline** 11/30 (freshmen), 11/30 (transfer) **Freshmen** 57% were admitted **Housing** Yes **Expenses** Tuition 4556; Room & Board 7098 **Undergraduates** 52% women, 4% part-time, 5% 25 or older, 0.4% Native American, 11% Hispanic American, 2% African American, 54% Asian American/Pacific Islander **The most frequently chosen baccalaureate fields are** biological/life sciences, interdisciplinary studies, social sciences and history **Academic program** English as a second language, advanced placement, honors program, summer session, adult/continuing education programs, internships **Contact** Dr. Susan Wilbur, Director of Admissions, University of California, Irvine, 204 Administration, Irvine, CA 92697-1075. Telephone: 949-824-6701. Web site: http://www.uci.edu/.

UNIVERSITY OF CALIFORNIA, LOS ANGELES
LOS ANGELES, CALIFORNIA

General State-supported, university, coed **Entrance** Very difficult **Setting** 419-acre urban campus **Total enrollment** 36,890 **Student/faculty ratio** 18:1 **Application deadline** 11/30 (freshmen), 11/30 (transfer) **Freshmen** 29% were admitted **Housing** Yes **Expenses** Tuition $3698; Room & Board $8565 **Undergraduates** 55% women, 5% part-time, 8% 25 or older, 1% Native American, 14% Hispanic American, 4% African American, 37% Asian American/Pacific Islander **The most frequently chosen baccalaureate fields are** psychology, biological/life sciences, social sciences and history **Academic program** English as a second language, advanced placement, self-designed majors, honors program, summer session, adult/continuing education programs, internships **Contact** Dr. Rae Lee Siporin, Director of Undergraduate Admissions, University of California, Los Angeles, 405 Hilgard Avenue, Los Angeles, CA 90095. Telephone: 310-825-3101. E-mail: ugadm@saonet.ucla.edu. Web site: http://www.ucla.edu/.

UNIVERSITY OF CALIFORNIA, RIVERSIDE
RIVERSIDE, CALIFORNIA

General State-supported, university, coed **Entrance** Very difficult **Setting** 1,200-acre urban campus **Total enrollment** 13,063 **Student/faculty ratio** 19:1 **Application deadline** 11/30 (freshmen), rolling (transfer) **Freshmen** 85% were admitted **Housing** Yes **Expenses** Tuition 3862; Room & Board 7200 **Undergraduates** 54% women, 4% part-time, 8% 25 or older, 0.4% Native American, 21% Hispanic American, 6% African American, 41% Asian American/Pacific Islander **The most frequently chosen baccalaureate fields are** business/marketing, biological/life sciences, social sciences and history **Academic program** Advanced placement, accelerated degree program, self-designed majors, honors program, summer session, adult/continuing education programs, internships **Contact** Ms. Laurie Nelson, Director of Undergraduate Admission, University of California, Riverside, 1138 Hinderaker Hall, Riverside, CA 92521. Telephone: 909-787-3411. Fax: 909-787-6344. E-mail: hsro@ucrac1.ucr.edu. Web site: http://www.ucr.edu/.

UNIVERSITY OF CALIFORNIA, SAN DIEGO
LA JOLLA, CALIFORNIA

General State-supported, university, coed **Entrance** Very difficult **Setting** 1,976-acre suburban campus **Total enrollment** 20,212 **Student/faculty ratio** 19:1 **Application deadline** 11/30 (freshmen), 11/30 (transfer) **Freshmen** 38% were admitted **Housing** Yes **Expenses** Tuition 3848; Room & Board 7425 **Undergraduates** 52% women, 5% 25 or older, 1% Native American, 10% Hispanic American, 1% African American, 35% Asian American/Pacific Islander **Academic program** English as a second language, accelerated degree program, self-designed majors, honors program, summer session, internships **Contact** Associate Director of Admissions and Outreach, University of California, San Diego, 9500 Gilman Drive, 0337, La Jolla, CA 92093-0337. Telephone: 858-534-4831. E-mail: admissionsinfo@ucsd.edu. Web site: http://www.ucsd.edu/.

UNIVERSITY OF CALIFORNIA, SANTA BARBARA
SANTA BARBARA, CALIFORNIA

General State-supported, university, coed **Entrance** Very difficult **Setting** 989-acre suburban campus **Total enrollment** 19,962 **Student/faculty ratio** 20:1 **Application deadline** 11/30 (freshmen), 11/30 (transfer) **Freshmen** 65% were admitted **Housing** Yes **Expenses** Tuition $3836; Room & Board $7577 **Undergraduates** 54% women, 4% part-time, 5% 25 or older, 1% Native American, 14% Hispanic American, 3% African American, 14% Asian American/Pacific Islander **The most frequently chosen baccalaureate fields are** business/marketing, biological/life sciences, social sciences and history **Academic program** Advanced placement, accelerated degree program, self-designed majors, honors program, summer session, internships **Contact** Mr. William Villa, Director of Admissions/Relations with Schools, University of California, Santa Barbara, Santa Barbara, CA 93106. Telephone: 805-893-2485. Fax: 805-893-2676. E-mail: appinfo@sa.ucsb.edu. Web site: http://www.ucsb.edu/.

UNIVERSITY OF CALIFORNIA, SANTA CRUZ
SANTA CRUZ, CALIFORNIA

General State-supported, university, coed **Entrance** Very difficult **Setting** 2,000-acre small-town campus **Total enrollment** 12,685 **Student/faculty ratio** 20:1 **Application deadline** 11/30 (freshmen), 11/30 (transfer) **Freshmen** 80% were admitted **Housing** Yes **Expenses** Room & Board 8106 **Undergraduates** 57% women, 5% part-time, 1% Native American, 13% Hispanic American, 2% African American, 16% Asian American/Pacific Islander **Academic program** English as a second language, advanced placement, self-designed majors, honors program, summer session, adult/continuing education programs, internships **Contact** Mr. J. Michael Thompson, Associate Vice Chancellor, Outreach, Admissions, and Student Academic Services, University of California, Santa Cruz, Admissions Office, Cook House, Santa Cruz, CA95064. Telephone: 831-459-4008. E-mail: admissions@cats.ucsc.edu. Web site: http://www.ucsc.edu/.

UNIVERSITY OF JUDAISM
BEL AIR, CALIFORNIA

General Independent Jewish, comprehensive, coed **Entrance** Moderately difficult **Setting** 28-acre suburban campus **Total enrollment** 213 **Student/faculty ratio** 6:1 **Application deadline** 1/31 (freshmen), 4/15 (transfer) **Freshmen** 100% were admitted **Housing** Yes **Expenses** Tuition 15,530; Room & Board 8100 **Undergraduates** 67% women, 7% part-time, 13% 25 or older, 0% Native American, 6% Hispanic American, 2% African American, 0% Asian American/Pacific Islander **The most frequently chosen baccalaureate fields are** area/ethnic studies, biological/life sciences, English **Academic program** Advanced placement, accelerated degree program, self-designed majors, honors program, adult/continuing education programs, internships **Contact** Mr. Richard Scaffidi, Dean of Admissions, University of Judaism, 15600 Mulholland Drive, Bel Air, CA 90077. Telephone: 310-476-9777 Ext. 250 or toll-free 888-853-6763. Fax: 310-471-3657. E-mail: admissions@uj.edu. Web site: http://www.uj.edu/.

UNIVERSITY OF LA VERNE
LA VERNE, CALIFORNIA

General Independent, university, coed **Entrance** Moderately difficult **Setting** 26-acre suburban campus **Total enrollment** 3,004 **Student/faculty ratio** 11:1 **Application deadline** Rolling (freshmen), rolling (transfer) **Freshmen** 74% were admitted **Housing** Yes **Expenses** Tuition 18,000; Room & Board 6280 **Undergraduates** 58% women, 4% part-time, 5% 25 or older, 1% Native American, 33% Hispanic American, 10% African American, 7% Asian American/Pacific Islander **The most frequently chosen baccalaureate fields are** business/marketing, education, social sciences and history **Academic program** English as a second language, advanced placement, accelerated degree program, self-designed majors, honors program, summer session, adult/continuing education programs, internships **Contact** Ms. Lisa Meyer, Director of Admissions, University of La Verne, 1950 Third Street, La Verne, CA 91750-4443. Telephone: 800-876-4858 or toll-free 800-876-4858. Fax: 909-392-2714. E-mail: laup@ulavacs.ulaverne.edu. Web site: http://www.ulv.edu/.

UNIVERSITY OF PHOENIX–NORTHERN CALIFORNIA CAMPUS
PLEASANTON, CALIFORNIA

General Proprietary, comprehensive, coed **Entrance** Noncompetitive **Total enrollment** 66,534 **Student/faculty ratio** 13:1 **Application deadline** Rolling (freshmen), rolling (transfer) **Expenses** Tuition $7740 **Undergraduates** 56% women, 86% 25 or older, 2% Native American, 18% Hispanic American, 13% African American, 6% Asian American/Pacific Islander **Academic program** Advanced placement, accelerated degree program, adult/continuing education programs **Contact** Ms. Beth Barilla, Director of Admissions, University of Phoenix–Northern California Campus, 4615 East Elwood Street, Phoenix, AZ 85040-1948. Telephone: 480-927-0099 Ext. 1218 or toll-free 800-228-7240. Fax: 480-594-1758. E-mail: beth.barilla@apollogrp.edu. Web site: http://www.phoenix.edu/.

UNIVERSITY OF PHOENIX–SACRAMENTO CAMPUS
SACRAMENTO, CALIFORNIA

General Proprietary, comprehensive, coed **Entrance** Noncompetitive **Total enrollment** 66,534 **Student/faculty ratio** 13:1 **Application deadline** Rolling (freshmen), rolling (transfer) **Expenses** Tuition $7740 **Undergraduates** 56% women, 86% 25 or older, 2% Native American, 18% Hispanic American, 13% African American, 6% Asian American/Pacific Islander **Academic program** Advanced placement, accelerated degree program, adult/continuing education programs **Contact** Ms. Beth Barilla, Director of Admissions, University of Phoenix–Sacramento Campus, 4615 East Elwood Street, Phoenix, AZ 85040-1948. Telephone: 480-927-0099 Ext. 1218. Fax: 480-594-1758. E-mail: beth.barilla@apollo.grp.edu. Web site: http://www.phoenix.edu/.

UNIVERSITY OF PHOENIX–SAN DIEGO CAMPUS
SAN DIEGO, CALIFORNIA

General Proprietary, comprehensive, coed **Entrance** Noncompetitive **Total enrollment** 66,534 **Student/faculty ratio** 15:1 **Application deadline** Rolling (freshmen), rolling (transfer) **Expenses** Tuition $7740 **Undergraduates** 56% women, 86% 25 or older, 2% Native American, 18% Hispanic American, 13% African American, 6% Asian American/Pacific Islander **Academic program** Advanced placement, accelerated degree program, adult/continuing education programs **Contact** Ms. Beth Barilla, Director of Admis-

University of Phoenix–San Diego Campus *(continued)*

sions, University of Phoenix–San Diego Campus, 4615 East Elwood Street, Phoenix, AZ 85040-1948. Telephone: 480-927-0099 Ext. 1218. Fax: 480-594-1758. E-mail: beth.barilla@apollogrp.edu.

UNIVERSITY OF PHOENIX–SOUTHERN CALIFORNIA CAMPUS

FOUNTAIN VALLEY, CALIFORNIA

General Proprietary, comprehensive, coed **Entrance** Noncompetitive **Total enrollment** 66,534 **Student/faculty ratio** 13:1 **Application deadline** Rolling (freshmen), rolling (transfer) **Expenses** Tuition $7740 **Undergraduates** 56% women, 86% 25 or older, 2% Native American, 18% Hispanic American, 13% African American, 6% Asian American/Pacific Islander **Academic program** Advanced placement, accelerated degree program, adult/continuing education programs **Contact** Ms. Beth B arilla, Director of Admissions, University of Phoenix–Southern California Campus, 10540 Talbert Avenue, West Building, Suite 100, Fountain Valley, CA 92708. Telephone: 480-927-0099 Ext. 1218. Web site: http://www.phoenix.edu/.

UNIVERSITY OF REDLANDS

REDLANDS, CALIFORNIA

General Independent, comprehensive, coed **Entrance** Moderately difficult **Setting** 140-acre small-town campus **Total enrollment** 1,803 **Student/faculty ratio** 12:1 **Application deadline** 2/1 (freshmen), rolling (transfer) **Freshmen** 78% were admitted **Housing** Yes **Expenses** Tuition 20,836; Room & Board 7590 **Undergraduates** 56% women, 2% part-time, 3% 25 or older, 1% Native American, 12% Hispanic American, 3% African American, 6% Asian American/Pacific Islander **The most frequently chosen baccalaureate fields are** business/marketing, interdisciplinary studies, social sciences and history **Academic program** Advanced placement, self-designed majors, honors program, adult/continuing education programs, internships **Contact** Mr. Paul Driscoll, Dean of Admissions, University of Redlands, PO Box 3080, Redlands, CA 92373-0999. Telephone: 909-335-4074 or toll-free 800-455-5064. Fax: 909-335-4089. E-mail: adkwolf@ultrix.uor.edu. Web site: http://www.redlands.edu/.

UNIVERSITY OF SAN DIEGO

SAN DIEGO, CALIFORNIA

General Independent Roman Catholic, university, coed **Entrance** Moderately difficult **Setting** 180-acre urban campus **Total enrollment** 6,943 **Student/faculty ratio** 18:1 **Application deadline** 1/5 (freshmen), 3/1 (transfer) **Freshmen** 50% were admitted **Housing** Yes **Expenses** Tuition $19,128; Room & Board $8440 **Undergraduates** 59% women, 4% part-time, 11% 25 or older, 1% Native American, 13% Hispanic American, 2% African American, 7% Asian American/Pacific Islander **Academic program** Advanced placement, honors program, summer session, adult/continuing education programs, internships **Contact** Mr. Stephen Pultz, Director of Undergraduate Admissions, University of San Diego, 5998 Alcala Park, San Diego, CA 92110. Telephone: 619-260-4506 or toll-free 800-248-4873 Ext. 4506. Fax: 619-260-6836. E-mail: vmuller@acusd.edu. Web site: http://www.sandiego.edu/.

UNIVERSITY OF SAN FRANCISCO

SAN FRANCISCO, CALIFORNIA

General Independent Roman Catholic (Jesuit), university, coed **Entrance** Moderately difficult **Setting** 55-acre urban campus **Total enrollment** 6,207 **Student/faculty ratio** 13:1 **Application deadline** 2/1 (freshmen), rolling (transfer) **Housing** Yes **Expenses** Tuition $19,060; Room & Board $8242 **Undergraduates** 9% 25 or older, 1% Native American, 10% Hispanic American, 5% African American, 22% Asian American/Pacific Islander **The most frequently chosen baccalaureate fields are** business/marketing, health professions and related sciences, interdisciplinary studies **Academic program** English as a second language, advanced placement, accelerated degree program, self-designed majors, honors program, summer session, adult/continuing education programs, internships **Contact** Mr. William Henley, Director of Admissions, University of San Francisco, Office of Admissions, 2130 Fulton Street, San Francisco, CA 94117-1080. Telephone: 415-422-6563 or toll-free 800-CALL USF (out-of-state). Fax: 415-422-2217. E-mail: admissions@usfca.edu. Web site: http://www.usfca.edu/.

UNIVERSITY OF SARASOTA, CALIFORNIA CAMPUS

ORANGE, CALIFORNIA

Contact University of Sarasota, California Campus, 3745 Chapman Avenue, Suite 100, Orange, CA 92868. Telephone: or toll-free 800-716-9598. Web site: http://www.sarasota.edu/.

UNIVERSITY OF SOUTHERN CALIFORNIA

LOS ANGELES, CALIFORNIA

General Independent, university, coed **Entrance** Very difficult **Setting** 155-acre urban campus **Total enrollment** 29,194 **Student/faculty ratio** 11:1 **Application deadline** 1/10 (freshmen), 3/1 (transfer) **Freshmen** 34% were admitted **Housing** Yes **Expenses** Tuition 24,124; Room & Board 7610 **Undergraduates** 50% women, 4% part-time, 7% 25 or older, 1% Native American, 14% Hispanic American, 6% African American, 23% Asian American/Pacific Islander **Academic program** English as a second language, advanced placement, accelerated degree program, self-designed majors, honors program, summer session, internships **Contact** Mr. Joseph Allen, Vice Provost for Enrollment, University of Southern California, University Park Campus, Los Angeles, CA 90089. Telephone: 213-740-1111. Fax: 213-740-6364. E-mail: admapp@enroll1.usc.edu. Web site: http://www.usc.edu/.

UNIVERSITY OF THE PACIFIC
STOCKTON, CALIFORNIA

General Independent, university, coed **Entrance** Moderately difficult **Setting** 175-acre suburban campus **Total enrollment** 5,609 **Student/faculty ratio** 14:1 **Application deadline** 2/15 (freshmen), 2/15 (transfer) **Freshmen** 76% were admitted **Housing** Yes **Expenses** Tuition $21,525; Room & Board $6700 **Undergraduates** 58% women, 3% part-time, 8% 25 or older, 1% Native American, 9% Hispanic American, 3% African American, 26% Asian American/ Pacific Islander **The most frequently chosen baccalaureate fields are** biological/life sciences, business/ marketing, social sciences and history **Academic program** English as a second language, advanced placement, accelerated degree program, self-designed majors, honors program, summer session, adult/ continuing education programs, internships **Contact** Mr. Marc McGee, Director of Admissions, University of the Pacific, 3601 Pacific Avenue, Stockton, CA 95211-0197. Telephone: 209-946-2211 or toll-free 800-959-2867. Fax: 209-946-2413. E-mail: admissions@uop.edu. Web site: http://www.uop.edu/.

UNIVERSITY OF WEST LOS ANGELES
INGLEWOOD, CALIFORNIA

General Independent, upper-level, coed **Entrance** Minimally difficult **Setting** 2-acre suburban campus **Total enrollment** 248 **Student/faculty ratio** 10:1 **Application deadline** Rolling (transfer) **Housing** No **Expenses** Tuition $6435 **Undergraduates** 73% women, 97% part-time, 90% 25 or older, 0% Native American, 24% Hispanic American, 49% African American, 0% Asian American/Pacific Islander **The most frequently chosen baccalaureate field is** law/ legal studies **Academic program** Adult/continuing education programs, internships **Contact** Ms. Yvonne Alwag, Admissions Counselor, University of West Los Angeles, School of Paralegal Studies, 1155 West Arbor Vitae Street, Inglewood, CA 90301-2902. Telephone: 310-342-5287. Fax: 310-342-5296. E-mail: paralegaladmissions@uwla.edu. Web site: http:// www.uwla.edu/.

VANGUARD UNIVERSITY OF SOUTHERN CALIFORNIA
COSTA MESA, CALIFORNIA

General Independent, comprehensive, coed, affiliated with Assemblies of God **Entrance** Moderately difficult **Setting** 38-acre suburban campus **Total enrollment** 1,660 **Student/faculty ratio** 16:1 **Application deadline** Rolling (freshmen), rolling (transfer) **Freshmen** 88% were admitted **Housing** Yes **Expenses** Tuition $14,584; Room & Board $2634 **Undergraduates** 61% women, 25% part-time, 27% 25 or older, 1% Native American, 10% Hispanic American, 4% African American, 3% Asian American/ Pacific Islander **The most frequently chosen baccalaureate fields are** business/marketing, liberal arts/ general studies, philosophy, religion, and theology **Academic program** Advanced placement, accelerated degree program, summer session, adult/ continuing education programs, internships **Contact** Ms. Jessica Mireles, Director of Admissions, Vanguard University of Southern California, 55 Fair Drive, Costa Mesa, CA 92626. Telephone: 714-556-3610 Ext. 327 or toll-free 800-722-6279. Fax: 714-966-5471. E-mail: admissions@sccu.edu. Web site: http://www.vanguard.edu/.

WESTMONT COLLEGE
SANTA BARBARA, CALIFORNIA

General Independent nondenominational, 4-year, coed **Entrance** Moderately difficult **Setting** 133-acre suburban campus **Total enrollment** 1,278 **Student/faculty ratio** 13:1 **Application deadline** 2/15 (freshmen), 3/1 (transfer) **Freshmen** 70% were admitted **Housing** Yes **Expenses** Tuition $22,256; Room & Board $7492 **Undergraduates** 62% women, 0.4% part-time, 1% 25 or older, 1% Native American, 8% Hispanic American, 1% African American, 4% Asian American/Pacific Islander **The most frequently chosen baccalaureate fields are** biological/ life sciences, liberal arts/general studies, social sciences and history **Academic program** Advanced placement, accelerated degree program, self-designed majors, honors program, summer session, internships **Contact** Mrs. Joyce Luy, Director of Admissions, Westmont College, 955 La Paz Road, Santa Barbara, CA 93108. Telephone: 805-565-6200 Ext. 6005 or toll-free 800-777-9011. Fax: 805-565-6234. E-mail: admissions@westmont.edu. Web site: http:// www.westmont.edu/.

WESTWOOD COLLEGE OF AVIATION TECHNOLOGY–LOS ANGELES
INGLEWOOD, CALIFORNIA

Contact Mr. Bill Robinson, Director of Admissions, Westwood College of Aviation Technology–Los Angeles, 8911 Aviation Boulevard, Inglewood, CA 90301-2904. Telephone: 310-337-4444 or toll-free 800-597-8690.

WHITTIER COLLEGE
WHITTIER, CALIFORNIA

General Independent, comprehensive, coed **Entrance** Moderately difficult **Setting** 95-acre suburban campus **Total enrollment** 2,203 **Student/faculty ratio** 12:1 **Application deadline** Rolling (freshmen), rolling (transfer) **Freshmen** 89% were admitted **Housing** Yes **Expenses** Tuition 20,724; Room & Board 6736 **Undergraduates** 56% women, 2% part-time, 7% 25 or older, 1% Native American, 26% Hispanic American, 5% African American, 8% Asian American/ Pacific Islander **The most frequently chosen baccalaureate fields are** business/marketing, biological/ life sciences, interdisciplinary studies **Academic program** Advanced placement, accelerated degree program, self-designed majors, summer session, adult/ continuing education programs, internships **Contact** Ms. Urmi Kar, Dean of Enrollment, Whittier College, 13406 E Philadelphia Street, PO Box 634, Whittier,

Whittier College *(continued)*

CA 90608-0634. Telephone: 562-907-4238. Fax: 562-907-4870. E-mail: admission@whittier.edu. Web site: http://www.whittier.edu/.

WOODBURY UNIVERSITY
BURBANK, CALIFORNIA

General Independent, comprehensive, coed **Entrance** Moderately difficult **Setting** 23-acre suburban campus **Total enrollment** 1,342 **Student/faculty ratio** 12:1 **Application deadline** Rolling (freshmen), rolling (transfer) **Freshmen** 85% were admitted **Housing** Yes **Expenses** Tuition $17,458; Room & Board $6756 **Undergraduates** 55% women, 24% part-time, 37% 25 or older, 0.4% Native American, 29% Hispanic American, 7% African American, 17% Asian American/Pacific Islander **The most frequently chosen baccalaureate fields are** architecture, business/marketing, visual/performing arts **Academic program** Advanced placement, accelerated degree program, summer session, adult/continuing education programs, internships **Contact** Mr. Don St. Clair, Vice-President of Enrollment Planning, Woodbury University, 7500 Glenoaks Boulevard, Burbank, CA 91504-1099. Telephone: 818-767-0888 or toll-free 800-784-WOOD. Fax: 818-767-7520. E-mail: admissions@vaxb.woodbury.edu. Web site: http://www.woodbury.edu/.

► **For more information, see page 494.**

YESHIVA OHR ELCHONON CHABAD/ WEST COAST TALMUDICAL SEMINARY
LOS ANGELES, CALIFORNIA

General Independent Jewish, 4-year, men only **Entrance** Moderately difficult **Setting** 4-acre urban campus **Total enrollment** 62 **Application deadline** Rolling (freshmen), rolling (transfer) **Housing** Yes **Expenses** Tuition $7900; Room & Board $4500 **Undergraduates** 0% 25 or older, 0% Native American, 0% Hispanic American, 0% African American, 3% Asian American/Pacific Islander **The most frequently chosen baccalaureate field is** philosophy, religion, and theology **Academic program** Honors program, summer session, adult/continuing education programs, internships **Contact** Rabbi Ezra Binyomin Schochet, Dean, Yeshiva Ohr Elchonon Chabad/West Coast Talmudical Seminary, 7215 Waring Avenue, Los Angeles, CA 90046-7660. Telephone: 213-937-3763.

COLORADO

ADAMS STATE COLLEGE
ALAMOSA, COLORADO

General State-supported, comprehensive, coed **Entrance** Moderately difficult **Setting** 90-acre small-town campus **Total enrollment** 6,948 **Student/faculty ratio** 15:1 **Application deadline** 8/1 (freshmen), 8/1 (transfer) **Freshmen** 96% were admitted **Housing** Yes **Expenses** Tuition 2396; Room & Board 5185 **Undergraduates** 57% women, 20% part-time, 29% 25 or older, 2% Native American, 27% Hispanic American, 4% African American, 1% Asian American/Pacific Islander **The most frequently chosen baccalaureate fields are** business/marketing, liberal arts/general studies, social sciences and history **Academic program** Advanced placement, accelerated degree program, self-designed majors, summer session, adult/continuing education programs, internships **Contact** Mr. Matt Gallegas, Director of Admissions, Adams State College, 208 Edgemont Boulevard, Alamosa, CO 81102. Telephone: 719-587-7712 or toll-free 800-824-6494. Fax: 719-587-7522. E-mail: gpierson@adams.edu. Web site: http://www.adams.edu/.

THE ART INSTITUTE OF COLORADO
DENVER, COLORADO

General Proprietary, 4-year, coed **Entrance** Minimally difficult **Setting** urban campus **Total enrollment** 2,090 **Student/faculty ratio** 20:1 **Application deadline** Rolling (freshmen), rolling (transfer) **Freshmen** 74% were admitted **Housing** Yes **Expenses** Tuition $13,824; Room & Board $5994 **Undergraduates** 44% women, 32% part-time, 41% 25 or older, 1% Native American, 5% Hispanic American, 3% African American, 4% Asian American/Pacific Islander **Academic program** Advanced placement, adult/continuing education programs, internships **Contact** Ms. Barbara Browning, Vice President and Director of Admissions, The Art Institute of Colorado, 1200 Lincoln Street, Denver, CO 80203. Telephone: 303-837-0825 Ext. 4729 or toll-free 800-275-2420. Fax: 303-860-8520. E-mail: aicinfo@aii.edu. Web site: http://www.aic.artinstitutes.edu/.

COLORADO CHRISTIAN UNIVERSITY
LAKEWOOD, COLORADO

General Independent interdenominational, comprehensive, coed **Entrance** Moderately difficult **Setting** 26-acre suburban campus **Total enrollment** 2,082 **Student/faculty ratio** 12:1 **Application deadline** 3/1 (freshmen) **Freshmen** 75% were admitted **Housing** Yes **Expenses** Tuition $10,400; Room & Board $5330 **Undergraduates** 54% women, 40% part-time, 50% 25 or older, 1% Native American, 5% Hispanic American, 7% African American, 1% Asian American/Pacific Islander **The most frequently chosen baccalaureate fields are** business/marketing, education, philosophy, religion, and theology **Academic program** Advanced placement, accelerated degree program, self-designed majors, honors program, summer session, adult/continuing education programs, internships **Contact** Ms. Kim Myrick, Director of Admissions, Colorado Christian University, 180 South Garrison Street, Lakewood, CO 80226-7499. Telephone: 303-963-3203 or toll-free 800-44-FAITH. Fax: 303-963-3201. E-mail: admissions@ccu.edu. Web site: http://www.ccu.edu/.

THE COLORADO COLLEGE
COLORADO SPRINGS, COLORADO

General Independent, comprehensive, coed **Entrance** Very difficult **Setting** 90-acre urban campus **Total enrollment** 1,942 **Student/faculty ratio** 10:1 **Application deadline** 1/15 (freshmen), 4/1 (transfer) **Freshmen** 62% were admitted **Housing** Yes **Expenses** Tuition 24,528; Room & Board 6064 **Undergraduates** 54% women, 1% part-time, 0.01% 25 or older, 1% Native American, 6% Hispanic American, 2% African American, 4% Asian American/Pacific Islander **The most frequently chosen baccalaureate fields are** biological/life sciences, English, social sciences and history **Academic program** English as a second language, advanced placement, self-designed majors, honors program, summer session **Contact** Mr. Terrance K. Swenson, Dean of Admission and Financial Aid, The Colorado College, 14 East Cache la Poudre, 900 Block North Cascade, West, Colorado Springs, CO 80903-3294. Telephone: 719-389-6344 or toll-free 800-542-7214. Fax: 719-389-6816. E-mail: admission@cc.colorado.edu. Web site: http://www.coloradocollege.edu/.

COLORADO SCHOOL OF MINES
GOLDEN, COLORADO

General State-supported, university, coed **Entrance** Very difficult **Setting** 373-acre small-town campus **Total enrollment** 3,211 **Student/faculty ratio** 11:1 **Application deadline** 5/1 (freshmen), 5/1 (transfer) **Freshmen** 81% were admitted **Housing** Yes **Expenses** Tuition 5412; Room & Board 4900 **Undergraduates** 25% women, 4% part-time, 2% 25 or older, 1% Native American, 7% Hispanic American, 1% African American, 5% Asian American/Pacific Islander **The most frequently chosen baccalaureate fields are** engineering/engineering technologies, mathematics, physical sciences **Academic program** English as a second language, advanced placement, accelerated degree program, honors program, summer session, internships **Contact** Ms. Tricia Douthit, Assistant Director of Enrollment Management, Colorado School of Mines, Weaver Towers-1811 Elm Street, Golden, CO 80401-1842. Telephone: 303-273-3224 or toll-free 800-446-9488 (out-of-state). Fax: 303-273-3509. E-mail: admit@mines.edu. Web site: http://www.mines.edu/.

COLORADO STATE UNIVERSITY
FORT COLLINS, COLORADO

General State-supported, university, coed **Entrance** Moderately difficult **Setting** 666-acre urban campus **Total enrollment** 23,098 **Student/faculty ratio** 20:1 **Application deadline** 7/1 (freshmen), 7/1 (transfer) **Freshmen** 78% were admitted **Housing** Yes **Expenses** Tuition $3858; Room & Board $5280 **Undergraduates** 52% women, 11% part-time, 12% 25 or older, 1% Native American, 6% Hispanic American, 2% African American, 3% Asian American/Pacific Islander **The most frequently chosen baccalaureate fields are** business/marketing, agriculture, engineering/engineering technologies **Academic program** English as a second language, advanced placement, accelerated degree program, self-designed majors, honors program, summer session, adult/continuing education programs, internships **Contact** Ms. Mary Ontiveros, Director of Admissions, Colorado State University, Spruce Hall, Fort Collins, CO 80523-0015. Telephone: 970-491-6909. E-mail: admissions@vines.colostate.edu. Web site: http://www.colostate.edu/.

COLORADO TECHNICAL UNIVERSITY
COLORADO SPRINGS, COLORADO

General Proprietary, comprehensive, coed **Entrance** Minimally difficult **Setting** 14-acre suburban campus **Total enrollment** 1,851 **Student/faculty ratio** 20:1 **Application deadline** Rolling (freshmen), rolling (transfer) **Freshmen** 93% were admitted **Housing** No **Expenses** Tuition 8043 **Undergraduates** 27% women, 80% part-time, 76% 25 or older, 0.4% Native American, 6% Hispanic American, 9% African American, 3% Asian American/Pacific Islander **The most frequently chosen baccalaureate fields are** computer/information sciences, engineering/engineering technologies **Academic program** Advanced placement, accelerated degree program, summer session, adult/continuing education programs, internships **Contact** Ms. Terri Johnson, Director of Admissions, Colorado Technical University, 4435 North Chestnut Street, Colorado Springs, CO 80907-3896. Telephone: 719-598-0200. Fax: 719-598-3740. E-mail: tjohnson@cos.coloradotech.edu. Web site: http://www.coloradotech.edu.

COLORADO TECHNICAL UNIVERSITY DENVER CAMPUS
GREENWOOD VILLAGE, COLORADO

General Proprietary, comprehensive, coed **Entrance** Minimally difficult **Setting** 1-acre urban campus **Total enrollment** 341 **Student/faculty ratio** 14:1 **Application deadline** 10/2 (freshmen), rolling (transfer) **Freshmen** 65% were admitted **Housing** No **Expenses** Tuition $8505 **Undergraduates** 28% women, 83% part-time, 60% 25 or older, 0.5% Native American, 7% Hispanic American, 11% African American, 7% Asian American/Pacific Islander **Academic program** Advanced placement, honors program, adult/continuing education programs **Contact** Ms. Terri Johnson, Director of Admissions, Colorado Technical University Denver Campus, 5775 DTC Boulevard, Suite 100, Greenwood Village, CO 80111. Telephone: 303-694-6600. Fax: 303-694-6673. E-mail: ctudenver@coloradotech.edu. Web site: http://www.coloradotech.edu/.

COMMONWEALTH INTERNATIONAL UNIVERSITY

See Education America, Denver Campus

DENVER INSTITUTE OF TECHNOLOGY

See Westwood College of Technology Denver North

DENVER TECHNICAL COLLEGE
DENVER, COLORADO

General Proprietary, 4-year, coed, primarily men **Entrance** Moderately difficult **Setting** 1-acre urban campus **Total enrollment** 864 **Application deadline** Rolling (freshmen), rolling (transfer) **Housing** No **Undergraduates** 31% women, 64% part-time, 90% 25 or older, 0.1% Native American, 6% Hispanic American, 9% African American, 4% Asian American/ Pacific Islander **Academic program** Accelerated degree program, honors program, summer session, adult/continuing education programs **Contact** Mr. Rick Rodman, Directors of Admissions, Denver Technical College, 925 South Niagara Street, Denver, CO 80224-1658. Telephone: 303-329-3000. Web site: http://www.dtc.edu/.

DENVER TECHNICAL COLLEGE AT COLORADO SPRINGS
COLORADO SPRINGS, COLORADO

General Proprietary, 4-year, coed **Entrance** Noncompetitive **Setting** 3-acre urban campus **Total enrollment** 450 **Application deadline** 9/15 (freshmen), 9/15 (transfer) **Freshmen** 97% were admitted **Housing** No **Undergraduates** 74% 25 or older **Academic program** Summer session, adult/continuing education programs, internships **Contact** Mr. Rick Modman, Director of Admissions, Denver Technical College at Colorado Springs, 225 South Union Boulevard, Colorado Springs, CO 80910. Telephone: 719-632-3000 Ext. 8133. Fax: 719-632-1909. Web site: http://www.dtc.edu/.

EDUCATION AMERICA, COLORADO SPRINGS CAMPUS
COLORADO SPRINGS, COLORADO

Contact Education America, Colorado Springs Campus, 6050 Erin Park Drive, #250, Colorado Springs, CO 80918. Telephone: or toll-free 719-264-1234 (out-of-state).

EDUCATION AMERICA, DENVER CAMPUS
LAKEWOOD, COLORADO

Contact Admissions Office, Education America, Denver Campus, 11011 West 6th Avenue, Lakewood, CO 80215-0090. Telephone: 303-426-1000 or toll-free 800-999-5181.

FORT LEWIS COLLEGE
DURANGO, COLORADO

General State-supported, 4-year, coed **Entrance** Moderately difficult **Setting** 350-acre small-town campus **Total enrollment** 4,289 **Student/faculty ratio** 19:1 **Application deadline** 8/2 (freshmen), 7/15 (transfer) **Freshmen** 88% were admitted **Housing** Yes **Expenses** Tuition $2330; Room & Board $5172 **Undergraduates** 47% women, 14% part-time, 16% 25 or older, 17% Native American, 5% Hispanic American, 1% African American, 1% Asian American/Pacific Islander **The most frequently chosen baccalaureate fields are** business/marketing, English, social sciences and history **Academic program** English as a second language, advanced placement, accelerated degree program, self-designed majors, honors program, summer session, adult/ continuing education programs, internships **Contact** Mr. Harlan Steinle, Vice President of Admission, Fort Lewis College, 1000 Rim Drive, Durango, CO 81301. Telephone: 970-247-7184. Fax: 970-247-7179. E-mail: steinle_h@fortlewis.edu. Web site: http://www.fortlewis.edu/.

INTERNATIONAL UNIVERSITY
See Jones International University

JOHNSON & WALES UNIVERSITY
DENVER, COLORADO

General Independent, 4-year, coed **Entrance** Minimally difficult **Setting** small-town campus **Total enrollment** 325 **Student/faculty ratio** 18:1 **Application deadline** Rolling (freshmen), rolling (transfer) **Freshmen** 81% were admitted **Housing** Yes **Expenses** Tuition $16,893; Room & Board $7506 **Undergraduates** 43% women, 8% part-time, 0% Native American, 11% Hispanic American, 4% African American, 3% Asian American/Pacific Islander **Academic program** Summer session, adult/ continuing education programs, internships **Contact** Mr. Dave McKlveen, Director of Admissions, Johnson & Wales University, 7150 Montview Boulevard, Denver, CO 80220. Telephone: 303-256-9300 or toll-free 877-598-3368. Fax: 303-256-9333. E-mail: admissions@jwu.edu. Web site: http://www.jwu.edu.

JONES INTERNATIONAL UNIVERSITY
ENGLEWOOD, COLORADO

General Independent, upper-level, coed **Entrance** Noncompetitive **Total enrollment** 1,796 **Application deadline** Rolling (transfer) **Housing** No **Expenses** Tuition $4290 **Undergraduates** 100% 25 or older, 11% African American **The most frequently chosen baccalaureate field is** business/ marketing **Academic program** Accelerated degree program, summer session, adult/continuing education programs **Contact** Ms. Candice Morrisey, Assistant Director of Admissions, Jones International University, 9697 East Mineral Avenue, Englewood, CO 80112. Telephone: 303-784-8247 or toll-free 800-811-5663. Fax: 303-784-8547. E-mail: info@international.edu. Web site: http://www.jonesinternational.edu/.

MESA STATE COLLEGE
GRAND JUNCTION, COLORADO

General State-supported, comprehensive, coed **Contact** Mr. Mike Poll, Associate Director, Admissions and Recruitment, Mesa State College, PO Box 2647, Grand Junction, CO 81502-2647. Telephone: 970-248-1875 or toll-free 800-982-MESA. Fax: 970-248-

1973. E-mail: pjones@mesa5.mesa.colorado.edu. Web site: http://www2.mesastate.edu/.

METROPOLITAN STATE COLLEGE OF DENVER
DENVER, COLORADO

General State-supported, 4-year, coed **Entrance** Minimally difficult **Setting** 175-acre urban campus **Total enrollment** 17,688 **Student/faculty ratio** 20:1 **Application deadline** 8/1 (freshmen), rolling (transfer) **Freshmen** 84% were admitted **Housing** No **Expenses** Tuition $2975 **Undergraduates** 57% women, 45% part-time, 42% 25 or older, 1% Native American, 13% Hispanic American, 6% African American, 4% Asian American/Pacific Islander **The most frequently chosen baccalaureate fields are** business/marketing, protective services/public administration, social sciences and history **Academic program** Advanced placement, accelerated degree program, self-designed majors, honors program, summer session, adult/continuing education programs, internships **Contact** Ms. Miriam Tapia, Assistant Director, Metropolitan State College of Denver, PO Box 173362, Campus Box 16, Denver, CO 80217-3362. Telephone: 303-556-2615. Fax: 303-556-6345. Web site: http://www.mscd.edu/.

NAROPA UNIVERSITY
BOULDER, COLORADO

General Independent, comprehensive, coed **Entrance** Moderately difficult **Setting** 4-acre urban campus **Total enrollment** 1,037 **Student/faculty ratio** 10:1 **Application deadline** Rolling (freshmen), rolling (transfer) **Freshmen** 93% were admitted **Housing** Yes **Expenses** Tuition $14,096; Room only $4000 **Undergraduates** 68% women, 20% part-time, 33% 25 or older, 2% Native American, 4% Hispanic American, 0.5% African American, 1% Asian American/ Pacific Islander **The most frequently chosen baccalaureate fields are** psychology, natural resources/ environmental science, visual/performing arts **Academic program** Advanced placement, self-designed majors, summer session, adult/continuing education programs, internships **Contact** Ms. Sally Forester, Admissions Counselor, Naropa University, 2130 Arapahoe Avenue, Boulder, CO 80302-6697. Telephone: 303-546-5285 or toll-free 800-772-0410 (out-of-state). Fax: 303-546-3583. E-mail: tracy@naropa.edu. Web site: http://www.naropa.edu/.

NATIONAL AMERICAN UNIVERSITY
COLORADO SPRINGS, COLORADO

General Proprietary, 4-year, coed **Entrance** Noncompetitive **Setting** 1-acre suburban campus **Total enrollment** 325 **Application deadline** Rolling (freshmen), rolling (transfer) **Housing** No **Expenses** Tuition $9360 **Undergraduates** 98% 25 or older **Academic program** English as a second language, accelerated degree program, summer session, adult/continuing education programs, internships **Contact** Ms. Dawn Collins, Director of Admissions, National American University, 5125 North Academy Boulevard, Colorado Springs, CO 80918. Telephone: 719-277-0588 or toll-free 888-471-4781. Fax: 719-471-4751. E-mail: nau@clsp.uswest.net.

NATIONAL AMERICAN UNIVERSITY
DENVER, COLORADO

General Proprietary, 4-year, coed **Entrance** Noncompetitive **Setting** urban campus **Total enrollment** 380 **Application deadline** Rolling (freshmen), rolling (transfer) **Housing** No **Expenses** Tuition $9360 **Undergraduates** 85% 25 or older **Academic program** English as a second language, advanced placement, accelerated degree program, summer session, adult/continuing education programs **Contact** Mr. Tom De Felice, Director of Admissions, National American University, 1325 South Colorado Blvd, Suite 100, Denver, CO 80222. Telephone: 303-758-6700. Fax: 303-758-6810.

NAZARENE BIBLE COLLEGE
COLORADO SPRINGS, COLORADO

General Independent, 4-year, coed, affiliated with Church of the Nazarene **Entrance** Noncompetitive **Setting** 64-acre urban campus **Total enrollment** 473 **Student/faculty ratio** 14:1 **Application deadline** 8/31 (freshmen), 8/31 (transfer) **Freshmen** 60% were admitted **Housing** No **Expenses** Tuition $5826 **Undergraduates** 30% women, 59% part-time, 89% 25 or older, 2% Native American, 1% Hispanic American, 3% African American, 2% Asian American/ Pacific Islander **The most frequently chosen baccalaureate field is** philosophy, religion, and theology **Academic program** Summer session, internships **Contact** Dr. David Phillips, Director of Admissions/ Public Relations, Nazarene Bible College, 1111 Academy Park Loop, Colorado Springs, CO 80910-3704. Telephone: 719-884-5031 or toll-free 800-873-3873 (out-of-state). Fax: 719-884-5199. Web site: http:// www.nbc.edu/.

REGIS UNIVERSITY
DENVER, COLORADO

General Independent Roman Catholic (Jesuit), comprehensive, coed **Entrance** Moderately difficult **Setting** 90-acre suburban campus **Total enrollment** 11,000 **Application deadline** 8/15 (freshmen), 8/15 (transfer) **Freshmen** 84% were admitted **Housing** Yes **Expenses** Tuition 17,570; Room & Board 6700 **Undergraduates** 7% 25 or older, 0.5% Native American, 8% Hispanic American, 2% African American, 3% Asian American/Pacific Islander **Academic program** Advanced placement, accelerated degree program, self-designed majors, honors program, summer session, adult/continuing education programs, internships **Contact** Mr. Vic Davolt, Director of Admissions, Regis University, 3333 Regis Boulevard, Denver, CO 80221-1099. Telephone: 303-458-4905 or toll-free 800-388-2366 Ext. 4900. Fax: 303-964-5534. E-mail: regisadm@regis.edu. Web site: http:// www.regis.edu/.

ROCKY MOUNTAIN COLLEGE OF ART & DESIGN
DENVER, COLORADO

General Proprietary, 4-year, coed **Entrance** Moderately difficult **Setting** 1-acre urban campus **Total enrollment** 410 **Student/faculty ratio** 15:1 **Application deadline** Rolling (freshmen), rolling (transfer) **Housing** No **Expenses** Tuition $17,238 **Undergraduates** 52% women, 22% part-time, 26% 25 or older, 0.5% Native American, 6% Hispanic American, 2% African American, 2% Asian American/ Pacific Islander **Academic program** Advanced placement, accelerated degree program, summer session, internships **Contact** Ms. Amy Williams, Assistant Director of Admissions, Rocky Mountain College of Art & Design, 6875 East Evans Avenue, Denver, CO 80224-2329. Telephone: 303-753-6046 or toll-free 800-888-ARTS. Fax: 303-759-4970. E-mail: admit@rmcad.edu. Web site: http://www.rmcad.edu/.

TEIKYO LORETTO HEIGHTS UNIVERSITY
DENVER, COLORADO

Contact Teikyo Loretto Heights University, 3001 South Federal Boulevard, Denver, CO 80236-2711.

UNITED STATES AIR FORCE ACADEMY
COLORADO SPRINGS, COLORADO

General Federally supported, 4-year, coed, primarily men **Entrance** Most difficult **Setting** 18,000-acre suburban campus **Total enrollment** 4,319 **Student/ faculty ratio** 8:1 **Application deadline** 1/31 (freshmen), 1/31 (transfer) **Freshmen** 18% were admitted **Housing** Yes **Expenses** Tuition $0 **Undergraduates** 15% women, 1% Native American, 7% Hispanic American, 5% African American, 4% Asian American/ Pacific Islander **The most frequently chosen baccalaureate fields are** engineering/engineering technologies, business/marketing, social sciences and history **Academic program** English as a second language, advanced placement, self-designed majors, summer session, internships **Contact** Mr. Rolland Stoneman, Associate Director of Admissions/ Selections, United States Air Force Academy, HQ USAFA/RR 2304 Cadet Drive, Suite 200, USAF Academy, CO 80840-5025. Telephone: 719-333-2520 or toll-free 800-443-9266. Fax: 719-333-3012. E-mail: wilsoncm.rr@usafa.af.mil. Web site: http://www.usafa.edu/rr.

UNIVERSITY OF COLORADO AT BOULDER
BOULDER, COLORADO

General State-supported, university, coed **Entrance** Moderately difficult **Setting** 600-acre suburban campus **Total enrollment** 28,910 **Student/faculty ratio** 14:1 **Application deadline** 2/15 (freshmen), 4/1 (transfer) **Freshmen** 86% were admitted **Housing** Yes **Expenses** Tuition 3188; Room & Board 5538 **Undergraduates** 48% women, 11% part-time, 8% 25 or older, 1% Native American, 5% Hispanic American, 2% African American, 6% Asian American/ Pacific Islander **The most frequently chosen baccalaureate fields are** business/marketing, communications/ communication technologies, social sciences and history **Academic program** English as a second language, advanced placement, accelerated degree program, self-designed majors, honors program, summer session, adult/continuing education programs, internships **Contact** Admission Counselor, University of Colorado at Boulder, Campus Box 30, Boulder, CO 80309-0030. Telephone: 303-492-6301. Fax: 303-492-7115. E-mail: apply@colorado.edu. Web site: http://www.colorado.edu/.

UNIVERSITY OF COLORADO AT COLORADO SPRINGS
COLORADO SPRINGS, COLORADO

General State-supported, comprehensive, coed **Entrance** Moderately difficult **Setting** 400-acre suburban campus **Total enrollment** 6,588 **Student/ faculty ratio** 16:1 **Application deadline** 7/1 (freshmen), 7/1 (transfer) **Freshmen** 75% were admitted **Housing** Yes **Expenses** Tuition $2743; Room & Board $5893 **Undergraduates** 61% women, 26% part-time, 1% Native American, 8% Hispanic American, 4% African American, 5% Asian American/ Pacific Islander **The most frequently chosen baccalaureate fields are** business/marketing, communications/ communication technologies, psychology **Academic program** Advanced placement, accelerated degree program, summer session, adult/continuing education programs, internships **Contact** Mr. James Tidwell, Assistant Admissions Director, University of Colorado at Colorado Springs, PO Box 7150, Colorado Springs, CO 80933-7150. Telephone: 719-262-3383 or toll-free 800-990-8227 Ext. 3383. E-mail: admrec@mail.uccs.edu. Web site: http://www.uccs.edu/.

UNIVERSITY OF COLORADO AT DENVER
DENVER, COLORADO

General State-supported, university, coed **Entrance** Moderately difficult **Setting** 171-acre urban campus **Total enrollment** 14,113 **Student/faculty ratio** 14:1 **Application deadline** 7/22 (freshmen), 7/22 (transfer) **Freshmen** 73% were admitted **Housing** No **Expenses** Tuition $2723 **Undergraduates** 56% women, 46% part-time, 40% 25 or older, 1% Native American, 11% Hispanic American, 5% African American, 10% Asian American/Pacific Islander **The most frequently chosen baccalaureate fields are** business/marketing, psychology, social sciences and history **Academic program** Advanced placement, self-designed majors, honors program, summer session, adult/continuing education programs, internships **Contact** Associate Director of Admissions, University of Colorado at Denver, PO Box 173364, Campus Box 167, Denver, CO 80217-3364. Telephone: 303-556-2400. Fax: 303-556-4838. E-mail: admissions@castle.cudenver.edu. Web site: http://www.cudenver.edu/.

UNIVERSITY OF COLORADO HEALTH SCIENCES CENTER
DENVER, COLORADO

General State-supported, upper-level, coed **Entrance** Moderately difficult **Setting** 40-acre urban campus **Total enrollment** 2,059 **Application deadline** 10/1 (transfer) **First-Year Students** 46% were admitted **Housing** No **Expenses** Tuition $8304 **Undergraduates** 85% women, 2% Native American, 8% Hispanic American, 4% African American, 13% Asian American/ Pacific Islander **The most frequently chosen baccalaureate field is** health professions and related sciences **Academic program** Advanced placement, summer session, adult/continuing education programs, internships **Contact** Dr. David P. Sorenson, Director of Admissions, University of Colorado Health Sciences Center, 4200 East Ninth Avenue, Denver, CO 80262. Telephone: 303-315-7676. Fax: 303-315-3358. E-mail: stuserv@mongo.uchsc.edu. Web site: http://www.uchsc.edu/.

UNIVERSITY OF DENVER
DENVER, COLORADO

General Independent, university, coed **Entrance** Moderately difficult **Setting** 125-acre suburban campus **Total enrollment** 9,444 **Student/faculty ratio** 13:1 **Application deadline** Rolling (freshmen), rolling (transfer) **Freshmen** 78% were admitted **Housing** Yes **Expenses** Tuition 20,556; Room & Board 6438 **Undergraduates** 57% women, 14% part-time, 16% 25 or older, 1% Native American, 6% Hispanic American, 4% African American, 5% Asian American/ Pacific Islander **The most frequently chosen baccalaureate fields are** business/marketing, communications/ communication technologies, social sciences and history **Academic program** English as a second language, advanced placement, accelerated degree program, self-designed majors, honors program, summer session, adult/continuing education programs, internships **Contact** Mr. Morris Price, Dean of Admission, University of Denver, University Park, Denver, CO 80208. Telephone: 303-871-3373 or toll-free 800-525-9495 (out-of-state). Fax: 303-871-3301. E-mail: admission@du.edu. Web site: http://www.du.edu/.

UNIVERSITY OF NORTHERN COLORADO
GREELEY, COLORADO

General State-supported, university, coed **Entrance** Moderately difficult **Setting** 240-acre suburban campus **Total enrollment** 12,163 **Application deadline** Rolling (freshmen), rolling (transfer) **Freshmen** 79% were admitted **Housing** Yes **Expenses** Tuition $2783; Room & Board $4996 **Undergraduates** 60% women, 11% part-time, 8% 25 or older, 1% Native American, 8% Hispanic American, 2% African American, 5% Asian American/Pacific Islander **The most frequently chosen baccalaureate fields are** business/ marketing, parks and recreation, social sciences and history **Academic program** English as a second language, advanced placement, self-designed majors, honors program, summer session, adult/continuing education programs, internships **Contact** Mr. Gary O. Gullickson, Director of Admissions, University of Northern Colorado, Greeley, CO 80639. Telephone: 970-351-2881. E-mail: unc@mail.univnorthco.edu. Web site: http://www.unco.edu/.

UNIVERSITY OF PHOENIX–COLORADO CAMPUS
LONE TREE, COLORADO

General Proprietary, comprehensive, coed **Entrance** Noncompetitive **Total enrollment** 66,534 **Student/ faculty ratio** 13:1 **Application deadline** Rolling (freshmen), rolling (transfer) **Expenses** Tuition $7740 **Undergraduates** 56% women, 86% 25 or older, 2% Native American, 18% Hispanic American, 13% African American, 6% Asian American/Pacific Islander **Academic program** Advanced placement, accelerated degree program, adult/continuing education programs **Contact** Ms. Beth Barilla, Director of Admissions, University of Phoenix–Colorado Campus, 4615 East Elwood Street, Phoenix, AZ 85040-1948. Telephone: 480-927-0099 Ext. 1218 or toll-free 800-228-7240. Fax: 480-594-1758. E-mail: beth.barilla@ apollogrp.edu. Web site: http://www.phoenix.edu/.

UNIVERSITY OF PHOENIX–SOUTHERN COLORADO CAMPUS
COLORADO SPRINGS, COLORADO

General Proprietary, comprehensive, coed **Entrance** Noncompetitive **Total enrollment** 66,534 **Student/ faculty ratio** 13:1 **Application deadline** Rolling (freshmen), rolling (transfer) **Expenses** Tuition $7740 **Undergraduates** 56% women, 2% Native American, 18% Hispanic American, 13% African American, 6% Asian American/Pacific Islander **Academic program** Advanced placement, accelerated degree program, adult/continuing education programs **Contact** Ms. Beth Barilla, Director of Admissions, University of Phoenix–Southern Colorado Campus, 4615 East Elwood Street, Phoenix, AZ 85040-1948. Telephone: 480-927-0099 Ext. 1218 or toll-free 800-228-7240. Fax: 480-894-1758. E-mail: beth.barilla@apollogrp.edu.

UNIVERSITY OF SOUTHERN COLORADO
PUEBLO, COLORADO

General State-supported, comprehensive, coed **Entrance** Moderately difficult **Setting** 275-acre suburban campus **Total enrollment** 5,791 **Student/ faculty ratio** 17:1 **Application deadline** Rolling (freshmen), rolling (transfer) **Freshmen** 81% were admitted **Housing** Yes **Expenses** Tuition $2369; Room & Board $5164 **Undergraduates** 57% women, 34% part-time, 35% 25 or older, 1% Native American, 26% Hispanic American, 4% African American, 2% Asian American/Pacific Islander **The most frequently chosen baccalaureate fields are** business/ marketing, engineering/engineering technologies, social sciences and history **Academic program** English as a second language, advanced placement, accelerated degree program, honors program, sum-

University of Southern Colorado *(continued)*

mer session, adult/continuing education programs, internships **Contact** Ms. Pamela L. Anastassiou, Director of Admissions and Records, University of Southern Colorado, 2200 Bonforte Boulevard, Pueblo, CO 81001. Telephone: 719-549-2461 or toll-free 877-872-9653. Fax: 719-549-2419. E-mail: kidd@starburst.uscolo.edu. Web site: http://www.uscolo.edu/.

WESTERN STATE COLLEGE OF COLORADO
GUNNISON, COLORADO

General State-supported, 4-year, coed **Entrance** Moderately difficult **Setting** 381-acre small-town campus **Total enrollment** 2,366 **Student/faculty ratio** 18:1 **Application deadline** Rolling (freshmen), rolling (transfer) **Freshmen** 66% were admitted **Housing** Yes **Expenses** Tuition $2980; Room & Board $5652 **Undergraduates** 42% women, 11% part-time, 12% 25 or older, 1% Native American, 4% Hispanic American, 1% African American, 1% Asian American/Pacific Islander **The most frequently chosen baccalaureate fields are** business/marketing, parks and recreation, social sciences and history **Academic program** Advanced placement, accelerated degree program, self-designed majors, honors program, summer session, adult/continuing education programs, internships **Contact** Mr. Timothy L. Albers, Director of Admissions, Western State College of Colorado, 600 North Adams Street, Gunnison, CO 81231. Telephone: 970-943-2119 or toll-free 800-876-5309. Fax: 970-943-2212. E-mail: saxelson@western.edu. Web site: http://www.western.edu/.

WESTWOOD COLLEGE OF TECHNOLOGY–DENVER NORTH
DENVER, COLORADO

General Proprietary, 4-year, coed **Contact** Ms. Louisa Duley, New Student Coordinator, Westwood College of Technology–Denver North, 7350 North Broadway, Denver, CO 80221-3653. Telephone: 303-650-5050 Ext. 329 or toll-free 800-992-5050. Web site: http://www.westwood.edu/.

YESHIVA TORAS CHAIM TALMUDICAL SEMINARY
DENVER, COLORADO

Contact Rabbi Israel Kagan, Dean, Yeshiva Toras Chaim Talmudical Seminary, 1400 Quitman Street, Denver, CO 80204-1415. Telephone: 303-629-8200. Fax: 303-623-5949.

CONNECTICUT

ALBERTUS MAGNUS COLLEGE
NEW HAVEN, CONNECTICUT

General Independent Roman Catholic, comprehensive, coed **Entrance** Moderately difficult **Setting** 55-acre suburban campus **Total enrollment** 2,105 **Application deadline** Rolling (freshmen), rolling (transfer) **Freshmen** 89% were admitted **Housing** Yes **Expenses** Tuition $14,785; Room & Board $6708 **Undergraduates** 66% women, 11% part-time, 71% 25 or older, 1% Native American, 7% Hispanic American, 19% African American, 1% Asian American/Pacific Islander **Academic program** English as a second language, advanced placement, accelerated degree program, self-designed majors, honors program, summer session, adult/continuing education programs, internships **Contact** Ms. Rebecca George, Associate Dean of Admissions, Albertus Magnus College, 700 Prospect Street, New Haven, CT 06511-1189. Telephone: 203-773-8501 or toll-free 800-578-9160. Fax: 203-773-5248. E-mail: admissions@albertus.edu. Web site: http://www.albertus.edu/.

BETH BENJAMIN ACADEMY OF CONNECTICUT
STAMFORD, CONNECTICUT

Contact Rabbi David Mayer, Director of Admissions, Beth Benjamin Academy of Connecticut, 132 Prospect Street, Stamford, CT 06901-1202. Telephone: 203-325-4351.

CENTRAL CONNECTICUT STATE UNIVERSITY
NEW BRITAIN, CONNECTICUT

General State-supported, comprehensive, coed **Entrance** Moderately difficult **Setting** 294-acre suburban campus **Total enrollment** 12,252 **Student/faculty ratio** 16:1 **Application deadline** 5/1 (freshmen), 5/1 (transfer) **Freshmen** 67% were admitted **Housing** Yes **Expenses** Tuition $3972; Room & Board $5824 **Undergraduates** 51% women, 32% part-time, 25% 25 or older, 0.4% Native American, 6% Hispanic American, 8% African American, 3% Asian American/Pacific Islander **The most frequently chosen baccalaureate fields are** business/marketing, psychology, social sciences and history **Academic program** English as a second language, advanced placement, self-designed majors, honors program, summer session, adult/continuing education programs, internships **Contact** Ms. Myrna Garcia-Bowen, Director of Admissions, Central Connecticut State University, 1615 Stanley Street, New Britain, CT 06050-4010. Telephone: 860-832-2285 or toll-free 800-755-2278 (out-of-state). Fax: 860-832-2522. E-mail: admissions@ccsu.edu. Web site: http://www.ccsu.edu/.

CHARTER OAK STATE COLLEGE
NEW BRITAIN, CONNECTICUT

General State-supported, 4-year, coed **Entrance** Noncompetitive **Setting** small-town campus **Total enrollment** 1,453 **Application deadline** Rolling (transfer) **Housing** No **Undergraduates** 52% women, 100% part-time, 98% 25 or older, 1% Native American, 4% Hispanic American, 8% African American, 2% Asian American/Pacific Islander **The most frequently cho-**

sen baccalaureate field is liberal arts/general studies **Academic program** Advanced placement, accelerated degree program, self-designed majors, adult/continuing education programs **Contact** Mr. Harry White, Dean of Enrollment Management, Charter Oak State College, 55 Paul Manafort Drive, New Britain, CT 06053-2142. Telephone: 860-832-3855. Fax: 860-832-3855. E-mail: pmorganti@commnet.edu. Web site: http://www.cosc.edu/.

CONNECTICUT COLLEGE
NEW LONDON, CONNECTICUT

General Independent, comprehensive, coed **Entrance** Very difficult **Setting** 702-acre suburban campus **Total enrollment** 1,856 **Student/faculty ratio** 11:1 **Application deadline** 1/15 (freshmen), 4/1 (transfer) **Freshmen** 32% were admitted **Housing** Yes **Expenses** Tuition 31,985 **Undergraduates** 57% women, 6% part-time, 1% 25 or older, 0.3% Native American, 3% Hispanic American, 3% African American, 3% Asian American/Pacific Islander **Academic program** Advanced placement, accelerated degree program, self-designed majors, honors program, summer session, adult/continuing education programs, internships **Contact** Mr. Lee A. Coffin, Dean of Admissions, Connecticut College, 270 Mohegan Avenue, New London, CT 06320-4196. Telephone: 860-439-2202. Fax: 860-439-4301. E-mail: admit@conncoll.edu. Web site: http://www.camel.conncoll.edu/.

EASTERN CONNECTICUT STATE UNIVERSITY
WILLIMANTIC, CONNECTICUT

General State-supported, comprehensive, coed **Entrance** Moderately difficult **Setting** 178-acre small-town campus **Total enrollment** 5,145 **Student/faculty ratio** 16:1 **Application deadline** Rolling (transfer) **Freshmen** 64% were admitted **Housing** Yes **Expenses** Tuition $4146; Room & Board $5850 **Undergraduates** 57% women, 28% part-time, 22% 25 or older, 1% Native American, 4% Hispanic American, 8% African American, 2% Asian American/Pacific Islander **The most frequently chosen baccalaureate fields are** psychology, business/marketing, social sciences and history **Academic program** Advanced placement, self-designed majors, honors program, summer session, adult/continuing education programs, internships **Contact** Ms. Kimberly Crone, Director of Admissions and Enrollment Management, Eastern Connecticut State University, 83 Windham street, Willimantic, CT 06336. Telephone: 860-465-5286 or toll-free 877-353-3278. Fax: 860-465-5544. E-mail: admissions@ecsu.ctstateu.edu. Web site: http://www.easternct.edu.

FAIRFIELD UNIVERSITY
FAIRFIELD, CONNECTICUT

General Independent Roman Catholic (Jesuit), comprehensive, coed **Entrance** Moderately difficult **Setting** 200-acre suburban campus **Total enrollment** 5,188 **Student/faculty ratio** 13:1 **Application deadline** 2/1 (freshmen), 6/1 (transfer) **Freshmen** 63% were admitted **Housing** Yes **Expenses** Tuition 21,435; Room & Board 7630 **Undergraduates** 55% women, 18% part-time, 1% 25 or older, 0.2% Native American, 4% Hispanic American, 2% African American, 2% Asian American/Pacific Islander **The most frequently chosen baccalaureate fields are** business/marketing, English, social sciences and history **Academic program** Advanced placement, honors program, summer session, adult/continuing education programs, internships **Contact** Ms. Judy Dobai, Director of Admission (Acting), Fairfield University, 1073 North Benson Road, Fairfield, CT 06430-5195. Telephone: 203-254-4100. Fax: 203-254-4199. E-mail: admis@fair1.fairfield.edu. Web site: http://www.fairfield.edu/.

HARTFORD COLLEGE FOR WOMEN
HARTFORD, CONNECTICUT

General Independent, 4-year, women only **Entrance** Moderately difficult **Setting** 13-acre suburban campus **Total enrollment** 178 **Student/faculty ratio** 12:1 **Application deadline** Rolling (freshmen), rolling (transfer) **Freshmen** 64% were admitted **Undergraduates** 90% part-time, 44% 25 or older, 1% Native American, 11% Hispanic American, 20% African American, 1% Asian American/Pacific Islander **Academic program** Advanced placement, accelerated degree program, summer session, adult/continuing education programs, internships **Contact** Ms. Annette Rogers, Admissions Director, Hartford College for Women, 1265 Asylum Avenue, Hartford, CT 06105-2299. Telephone: 860-768-5646 or toll-free 800-582-6118. Fax: 860-768-5693. E-mail: ggardner@uhavax.hartford.edu.

HOLY APOSTLES COLLEGE AND SEMINARY
CROMWELL, CONNECTICUT

General Independent Roman Catholic, comprehensive, coed **Entrance** Noncompetitive **Setting** small-town campus **Total enrollment** 150 **Application deadline** Rolling (freshmen), rolling (transfer) **Housing** Yes **Undergraduates** 95% 25 or older, 0% Native American, 0% Hispanic American, 0% African American, 0% Asian American/Pacific Islander **Academic program** English as a second language, accelerated degree program, adult/continuing education programs, internships **Contact** Rev. Raymond Halliwell MSA, Director of Admissions, Holy Apostles College and Seminary, 33 Prospect Hill Road, Cromwell, CT 06416-2005. Telephone: 860-632-3030 or toll-free 800-330-7272. Fax: 860-632-3075. E-mail: holy_apostles@msn.com. Web site: http://www.holy-apostles.org/.

LYME ACADEMY OF FINE ARTS
OLD LYME, CONNECTICUT

General Independent, 4-year, coed **Entrance** Moderately difficult **Setting** 3-acre small-town campus **Total enrollment** 191 **Student/faculty ratio** 8:1

Lyme Academy of Fine Arts *(continued)*

Application deadline Rolling (freshmen), rolling (transfer) **Freshmen** 97% were admitted **Housing** No **Expenses** Tuition $11,300 **Undergraduates** 63% women, 70% part-time, 52% 25 or older, 1% Native American, 9% Hispanic American, 1% African American, 3% Asian American/Pacific Islander **The most frequently chosen baccalaureate field is** visual/performing arts **Academic program** Summer session **Contact** Christophers Rose, Associate Dean of Enrollment Management, Lyme Academy of Fine Arts, 84 Lyme Street, Old Lyme, CT 06371. Telephone: 860-434-5232 Ext. 122. Fax: 860-434-8725. E-mail: admissions@lymeacademy.edu. Web site: http://www.lymeacademy.edu/.

PAIER COLLEGE OF ART, INC.
HAMDEN, CONNECTICUT

General Proprietary, 4-year, coed **Entrance** Minimally difficult **Setting** 3-acre suburban campus **Total enrollment** 282 **Student/faculty ratio** 6:1 **Application deadline** Rolling (freshmen), rolling (transfer) **Freshmen** 78% were admitted **Housing** No **Expenses** Tuition $11,235 **Undergraduates** 58% women, 44% part-time, 12% 25 or older, 0% Native American, 4% Hispanic American, 3% African American, 1% Asian American/Pacific Islander **The most frequently chosen baccalaureate field is** visual/performing arts **Academic program** Advanced placement, summer session **Contact** Ms. Lynn Pascale, Secretary to Admissions, Paier College of Art, Inc., 20 Gorham Avenue, Hamden, CT 06514-3902. Telephone: 203-287-3031. Fax: 203-287-3021. E-mail: info@paierart.com. Web site: http://www.paierart.com/.

QUINNIPIAC UNIVERSITY
HAMDEN, CONNECTICUT

General Independent, comprehensive, coed **Entrance** Moderately difficult **Setting** 300-acre suburban campus **Total enrollment** 6,477 **Student/faculty ratio** 16:1 **Application deadline** 2/15 (freshmen), rolling (transfer) **Freshmen** 75% were admitted **Housing** Yes **Expenses** Tuition $17,780; Room & Board $8170 **Undergraduates** 64% women, 9% part-time, 10% 25 or older, 0.3% Native American, 3% Hispanic American, 2% African American, 2% Asian American/Pacific Islander **The most frequently chosen baccalaureate fields are** business/marketing, health professions and related sciences, liberal arts/general studies **Academic program** Advanced placement, self-designed majors, honors program, summer session, adult/continuing education programs, internships **Contact** Ms. Joan Isaac-Mohr, Vice President and Dean of Admissions, Quinnipiac University, 275 Mount Carmel Avenue, Hamden, CT 06518-1940. Telephone: 203-582-8600 or toll-free 800-462-1944 (out-of-state). Fax: 203-582-8906. E-mail: admissions@quinnipiac.edu. Web site: http://www.quinnipiac.edu/.

SACRED HEART UNIVERSITY
FAIRFIELD, CONNECTICUT

General Independent Roman Catholic, comprehensive, coed **Entrance** Moderately difficult **Setting** 56-acre suburban campus **Total enrollment** 5,684 **Student/faculty ratio** 14:1 **Application deadline** Rolling (freshmen), rolling (transfer) **Freshmen** 74% were admitted **Housing** Yes **Expenses** Tuition $15,464; Room & Board $7614 **Undergraduates** 62% women, 34% part-time, 1% 25 or older, 0.1% Native American, 6% Hispanic American, 7% African American, 2% Asian American/Pacific Islander **The most frequently chosen baccalaureate fields are** business/marketing, protective services/public administration, psychology **Academic program** English as a second language, advanced placement, accelerated degree program, self-designed majors, honors program, summer session, adult/continuing education programs, internships **Contact** Ms. Karen N. Guastelle, Dean of Undergraduate Admissions, Sacred Heart University, 5151 Park Avenue, Fairfield, CT 06432-1000. Telephone: 203-371-7880. Fax: 203-365-7607. E-mail: enroll@sacredheart.edu. Web site: http://www.sacredheart.edu/.

SAINT JOSEPH COLLEGE
WEST HARTFORD, CONNECTICUT

General Independent Roman Catholic, comprehensive, women only **Entrance** Moderately difficult **Setting** 84-acre suburban campus **Total enrollment** 1,823 **Student/faculty ratio** 11:1 **Application deadline** 5/1 (freshmen), 7/1 (transfer) **Freshmen** 83% were admitted **Housing** Yes **Expenses** Tuition $17,430; Room & Board $7140 **Undergraduates** 44% part-time, 26% 25 or older, 0.2% Native American, 4% Hispanic American, 9% African American, 2% Asian American/Pacific Islander **The most frequently chosen baccalaureate fields are** health professions and related sciences, education, protective services/public administration **Academic program** English as a second language, advanced placement, accelerated degree program, self-designed majors, honors program, summer session, adult/continuing education programs, internships **Contact** Ms. Kelly Crowley, Director of Admissions, Saint Joseph College, 1678 Asylum Avenue, West Hartford, CT 06117-2700. Telephone: 860-231-5216 or toll-free 800-285-6565. Fax: 860-233-5695. E-mail: admissions@mercy.sjc.edu. Web site: http://www.sjc.edu/.

SOUTHERN CONNECTICUT STATE UNIVERSITY
NEW HAVEN, CONNECTICUT

General State-supported, comprehensive, coed **Entrance** Moderately difficult **Setting** 168-acre urban campus **Total enrollment** 12,127 **Application deadline** 7/1 (freshmen), 7/1 (transfer) **Freshmen** 71% were admitted **Housing** Yes **Expenses** Tuition $3850; Room & Board $6011 **Undergraduates** 59% women, 26% part-time, 23% 25 or older, 0.3% Native American, 5% Hispanic American, 12% African American,

2% Asian American/Pacific Islander **Academic program** Advanced placement, accelerated degree program, self-designed majors, honors program, summer session, adult/continuing education programs, internships **Contact** Ms. Paula Kennedy, Associate Director of Admissions, Southern Connecticut State University, Admissions House, New Haven, CT 06515-1202. Telephone: 203-392-5651. Fax: 203-392-5727. E-mail: adminfo@scsu.ctstateu.edu. Web site: http://www.southernct.edu/.

▶ **For more information, see page 469.**

TEIKYO POST UNIVERSITY

WATERBURY, CONNECTICUT

General Independent, 4-year, coed **Entrance** Minimally difficult **Setting** 70-acre suburban campus **Total enrollment** 1,356 **Student/faculty ratio** 15:1 **Application deadline** Rolling (freshmen), rolling (transfer) **Freshmen** 71% were admitted **Housing** Yes **Expenses** Tuition $14,125; Room & Board $6300 **Undergraduates** 64% women, 52% part-time, 48% 25 or older, 0.4% Native American, 6% Hispanic American, 13% African American, 4% Asian American/Pacific Islander **The most frequently chosen baccalaureate fields are** business/marketing, liberal arts/general studies, psychology **Academic program** English as a second language, advanced placement, accelerated degree program, summer session, adult/continuing education programs, internships **Contact** Mr. William Johnson, Senior Assistant Director of Admissions, Teikyo Post University, PO Box 2540, Waterbury, CT 06723. Telephone: 203-596-4520 or toll-free 800-345-2562. Fax: 203-756-5810. E-mail: tpuadmiss@teikyopost.edu. Web site: http://teikyopost.edu/.

TRINITY COLLEGE

HARTFORD, CONNECTICUT

General Independent, comprehensive, coed **Entrance** Very difficult **Setting** 100-acre urban campus **Total enrollment** 2,246 **Student/faculty ratio** 10:1 **Application deadline** 1/15 (freshmen), 4/1 (transfer) **Freshmen** 30% were admitted **Housing** Yes **Expenses** Tuition 25,440; Room & Board 7160 **Undergraduates** 50% women, 8% part-time, 7% 25 or older, 0.2% Native American, 5% Hispanic American, 6% African American, 5% Asian American/Pacific Islander **The most frequently chosen baccalaureate fields are** biological/life sciences, English, social sciences and history **Academic program** Advanced placement, accelerated degree program, self-designed majors, honors program, summer session, adult/continuing education programs, internships **Contact** Mr. Larry Dow, Dean of Admissions and Financial Aid, Trinity College, 300 Summit Street, Hartford, CT 06106-3100. Telephone: 860-297-2180. Fax: 860-297-2287. E-mail: admissions.office@mail.trincoll.edu. Web site: http://www.trincoll.edu/.

UNITED STATES COAST GUARD ACADEMY

NEW LONDON, CONNECTICUT

General Federally supported, 4-year, coed **Entrance** Very difficult **Setting** 110-acre suburban campus **Total enrollment** 879 **Student/faculty ratio** 7:1 **Application deadline** 12/15 (freshmen) **Freshmen** 6% were admitted **Housing** Yes **Undergraduates** 26% women, 0% 25 or older, 1% Native American, 6% Hispanic American, 6% African American, 5% Asian American/Pacific Islander **The most frequently chosen baccalaureate fields are** engineering/engineering technologies, business/marketing, law/legal studies **Academic program** English as a second language, summer session, internships **Contact** Capt. R. W. Thorne, Director of Admissions, United States Coast Guard Academy, 31 Mohegan Avenue, New London, CT 06320-4195. Telephone: 860-444-8500 or toll-free 800-883-8724. Fax: 860-701-6700. E-mail: uscgatr@dcseq.uscga.edu. Web site: http://www.cga.edu/.

UNIVERSITY OF BRIDGEPORT

BRIDGEPORT, CONNECTICUT

General Independent, comprehensive, coed **Entrance** Moderately difficult **Setting** 86-acre urban campus **Total enrollment** 2,686 **Student/faculty ratio** 12:1 **Application deadline** 4/1 (freshmen), rolling (transfer) **Freshmen** 78% were admitted **Housing** Yes **Expenses** Tuition 15,012; Room & Board 7070 **Undergraduates** 53% women, 22% part-time, 29% 25 or older, 0.2% Native American, 8% Hispanic American, 17% African American, 5% Asian American/Pacific Islander **The most frequently chosen baccalaureate fields are** business/marketing, home economics/vocational home economics, protective services/public administration **Academic program** English as a second language, advanced placement, accelerated degree program, self-designed majors, honors program, summer session, adult/continuing education programs, internships **Contact** Joseph Marrone, Director of Undergraduate Admissions, University of Bridgeport, 380 University Avenue, Bridgeport, CT 06601. Telephone: 203-576-4552 or toll-free 800-EXCEL-UB (in-state); 800-243-9496 (out-of-state). Fax: 203-576-4941. E-mail: admit@cse.bridgeport.edu. Web site: http://www.bridgeport.edu/.

UNIVERSITY OF CONNECTICUT

STORRS, CONNECTICUT

General State-supported, university, coed **Entrance** Moderately difficult **Setting** 4,178-acre rural campus **Total enrollment** 19,393 **Student/faculty ratio** 15:1 **Application deadline** 3/1 (freshmen), 5/1 (transfer) **Freshmen** 67% were admitted **Housing** Yes **Expenses** Tuition 5596; Room & Board 6062 **Undergraduates** 52% women, 7% part-time, 6% 25 or older, 0.3% Native American, 4% Hispanic American, 5% African American, 6% Asian American/Pacific Islander **The most frequently chosen baccalaureate fields are** business/marketing, health professions and related sciences, social sciences and history **Academic pro-**

University of Connecticut *(continued)*

gram English as a second language, advanced placement, accelerated degree program, self-designed majors, honors program, summer session, adult/continuing education programs, internships **Contact** Mr. Brian Usher, Associate Director of Admissions, University of Connecticut, 2131 Hillside Road, U-88, Storrs, CT 06269-3088. Telephone: 860-486-3137. Fax: 860-486-1476. E-mail: beahusky@uconnvm.uconn.edu. Web site: http://www.uconn.edu/.

UNIVERSITY OF HARTFORD
WEST HARTFORD, CONNECTICUT

General Independent, comprehensive, coed **Entrance** Moderately difficult **Setting** 320-acre suburban campus **Total enrollment** 6,897 **Student/faculty ratio** 13:1 **Application deadline** Rolling (freshmen), rolling (transfer) **Freshmen** 71% were admitted **Housing** Yes **Expenses** Tuition 20,810; Room & Board 8074 **Undergraduates** 52% women, 22% part-time, 14% 25 or older, 0.1% Native American, 5% Hispanic American, 8% African American, 2% Asian American/Pacific Islander **The most frequently chosen baccalaureate fields are** health professions and related sciences, business/marketing, visual/performing arts **Academic program** English as a second language, advanced placement, self-designed majors, honors program, summer session, adult/continuing education programs, internships **Contact** Mr. Richard Zeiser, Dean of Admissions, University of Hartford, 200 Bloomfield Avenue, West Hartford, CT 06117-1599. Telephone: 860-768-4296 or toll-free 800-947-4303. Fax: 860-768-4961. E-mail: admission@uhavax.hartford.edu. Web site: http://www.hartford.edu/.

UNIVERSITY OF NEW HAVEN
WEST HAVEN, CONNECTICUT

General Independent, university, coed **Entrance** Moderately difficult **Setting** 78-acre suburban campus **Total enrollment** 4,348 **Student/faculty ratio** 10:1 **Application deadline** Rolling (freshmen), rolling (transfer) **Freshmen** 82% were admitted **Housing** Yes **Expenses** Tuition $16,562; Room & Board $7370 **Undergraduates** 40% women, 37% part-time, 31% 25 or older, 0.4% Native American, 6% Hispanic American, 11% African American, 1% Asian American/Pacific Islander **The most frequently chosen baccalaureate fields are** business/marketing, engineering/engineering technologies, protective services/public administration **Academic program** English as a second language, advanced placement, accelerated degree program, self-designed majors, honors program, summer session, adult/continuing education programs, internships **Contact** Ms. Jane C. Sangeloty, Director of Undergraduate Admissions and Financial Aid, University of New Haven, Bayer Hall, 300 Orange Avenue, West Haven, CT 06516. Telephone: 203-932-7319 or toll-free 800-DIAL-UNH. Fax: 203-931-6093. E-mail: adminfo@charger.newhaven.edu. Web site: http://www.newhaven.edu/.

WESLEYAN UNIVERSITY
MIDDLETOWN, CONNECTICUT

General Independent, university, coed **Entrance** Most difficult **Setting** 120-acre small-town campus **Total enrollment** 3,158 **Student/faculty ratio** 10:1 **Application deadline** 1/1 (freshmen), 3/15 (transfer) **Freshmen** 27% were admitted **Housing** Yes **Expenses** Tuition $26,180; Room & Board $6630 **Undergraduates** 52% women, 1% part-time, 0% 25 or older, 0.2% Native American, 6% Hispanic American, 9% African American, 8% Asian American/Pacific Islander **The most frequently chosen baccalaureate fields are** psychology, English, social sciences and history **Academic program** English as a second language, advanced placement, accelerated degree program, self-designed majors, summer session, adult/continuing education programs, internships **Contact** Mrs. Nancy Hargrave Meislahn, Dean of Admissions and Financial Aid, Wesleyan University, Stewart M Reid House, Middletown, CT 06459-0265. Telephone: 860-685-3000. Fax: 860-685-3001. E-mail: admissions@wesleyan.edu. Web site: http://www.wesleyan.edu/.

WESTERN CONNECTICUT STATE UNIVERSITY
DANBURY, CONNECTICUT

General State-supported, comprehensive, coed **Entrance** Moderately difficult **Setting** 340-acre urban campus **Total enrollment** 5,806 **Student/faculty ratio** 15:1 **Application deadline** 5/1 (freshmen), 7/1 (transfer) **Freshmen** 69% were admitted **Housing** Yes **Expenses** Tuition $3910; Room & Board $5668 **Undergraduates** 55% women, 32% part-time, 21% 25 or older, 0.3% Native American, 6% Hispanic American, 6% African American, 3% Asian American/Pacific Islander **The most frequently chosen baccalaureate fields are** business/marketing, education, protective services/public administration **Academic program** English as a second language, advanced placement, accelerated degree program, self-designed majors, honors program, summer session, adult/continuing education programs, internships **Contact** Mr. William Hawkins, Enrollment Management Officer, Western Connecticut State University, Undergraduate Admissions Office, 181 White Street, Danbury, CT 06810. Telephone: 203-837-9000 or toll-free 877-837-9278. Fax: 203-837-8338. E-mail: weasil@wcsu.edu. Web site: http://www.wcsu.edu/.

YALE UNIVERSITY
NEW HAVEN, CONNECTICUT

General Independent, university, coed **Entrance** Most difficult **Setting** 200-acre urban campus **Total enrollment** 11,032 **Application deadline** 12/31 (freshmen), 3/1 (transfer) **Freshmen** 16% were admitted **Housing** Yes **Expenses** Tuition 25,220; Room & Board 7660 **Undergraduates** 50% women, 1% part-time, 1% 25 or older, 1% Native American, 6% Hispanic American, 7% African American, 16% Asian American/Pacific Islander **Academic program** English as a second language, advanced placement, accelerated degree program, self-designed majors, honors program, summer session **Contact** Admissions Director, Yale University, PO Box 208234, New Haven, CT 06520-8324. Telephone: 203-432-9300. Fax: 203-432-9392. E-mail: undergraduate.admissions@yale.edu. Web site: http://www.yale.edu/.

DELAWARE

DELAWARE STATE UNIVERSITY
DOVER, DELAWARE

General State-supported, comprehensive, coed **Entrance** Moderately difficult **Setting** 400-acre small-town campus **Total enrollment** 3,103 **Student/faculty ratio** 15:1 **Application deadline** 4/1 (freshmen), 4/1 (transfer) **Freshmen** 74% were admitted **Housing** Yes **Expenses** Tuition $3650; Room & Board $5710 **Undergraduates** 58% women, 21% part-time, 17% 25 or older, 0.4% Native American, 2% Hispanic American, 78% African American, 1% Asian American/Pacific Islander **The most frequently chosen baccalaureate fields are** business/marketing, education, protective services/public administration **Academic program** English as a second language, advanced placement, accelerated degree program, self-designed majors, honors program, summer session, adult/continuing education programs, internships **Contact** Mr. Jethro C. Williams, Director of Admissions, Delaware State University, 1200 North Dupont Highway, Dover, DE 19901. Telephone: 302-857-6353. Fax: 302-857-6352. E-mail: dadmiss@dsc.edu. Web site: http://www.dsc.edu/.

GOLDEY-BEACOM COLLEGE
WILMINGTON, DELAWARE

General Independent, comprehensive, coed **Entrance** Moderately difficult **Setting** 27-acre suburban campus **Total enrollment** 1,400 **Student/faculty ratio** 28:1 **Application deadline** Rolling (freshmen), rolling (transfer) **Freshmen** 84% were admitted **Housing** Yes **Expenses** Tuition $9398; Room only $3490 **Undergraduates** 43% 25 or older **Academic program** Advanced placement, accelerated degree program, honors program, summer session, internships **Contact** Mr. Kevin M. McIntyre, Dean of Admissions, Goldey-Beacom College, 4701 Limestone Road, Wilmington, DE 19808-1999. Telephone: 302-998-8814 Ext. 266 or toll-free 800-833-4877. Fax: 302-996-5408. E-mail: mcintyrk@goldey.gbc.edu. Web site: http://goldey.gbc.edu/.

UNITED STATES OPEN UNIVERSITY
WILMINGTON, DELAWARE

Contact United States Open University, 6 Denny Road, Suite 301, Wilmington, DE 19809. Telephone: or toll-free 800-232-7705. Web site: http://www.open.edu/.

UNIVERSITY OF DELAWARE
NEWARK, DELAWARE

General State-related, university, coed **Entrance** Moderately difficult **Setting** 1,000-acre small-town campus **Total enrollment** 20,276 **Student/faculty ratio** 13:1 **Application deadline** 2/15 (freshmen), 5/1 (transfer) **Freshmen** 49% were admitted **Housing** Yes **Expenses** Tuition 4993; Room & Board 5312 **Undergraduates** 59% women, 17% part-time, 7% 25 or older, 0.3% Native American, 3% Hispanic American, 6% African American, 3% Asian American/Pacific Islander **The most frequently chosen baccalaureate fields are** business/marketing, education, social sciences and history **Academic program** English as a second language, advanced placement, accelerated degree program, self-designed majors, honors program, summer session, adult/continuing education programs, internships **Contact** Mr. Larry Griffith, Director of Admissions, University of Delaware, 116 Hullihen Hall, Newark, DE 19716. Telephone: 302-831-8123. Fax: 302-831-6905. E-mail: ask.admissions@mvs.udel.edu. Web site: http://www.udel.edu/.

WESLEY COLLEGE
DOVER, DELAWARE

General Independent United Methodist, comprehensive, coed **Entrance** Moderately difficult **Setting** 20-acre small-town campus **Total enrollment** 1,490 **Student/faculty ratio** 19:1 **Application deadline** Rolling (freshmen), rolling (transfer) **Freshmen** 72% were admitted **Housing** Yes **Expenses** Tuition $11,719; Room & Board $5266 **Undergraduates** 54% women, 24% part-time, 4% 25 or older, 0% Native American, 2% Hispanic American, 16% African American, 1% Asian American/Pacific Islander **The most frequently chosen baccalaureate fields are** business/marketing, education, psychology **Academic program** English as a second language, advanced placement, accelerated degree program, summer session, adult/continuing education programs, internships **Contact** Mr. Art Jacobs, Director of Admissions, Wesley College, 120 North State Street, Dover, DE 19901-3875. Telephone: 302-736-2400 or toll-free 800-937-5398 (out-of-state). Fax: 302-736-2301. E-mail: admissions@mail.wesley.edu. Web site: http://www.wesley.edu/.

WILMINGTON COLLEGE
NEW CASTLE, DELAWARE

General Independent, comprehensive, coed **Entrance** Noncompetitive **Setting** 17-acre suburban campus **Total enrollment** 7,000 **Student/faculty ratio** 18:1 **Application deadline** Rolling (freshmen), rolling (transfer) **Freshmen** 99% were admitted **Housing** No **Expenses** Tuition 6290 **Undergraduates** 51% 25 or older **Academic program** Accelerated degree program, summer session, adult/continuing education programs, internships **Contact** Dr. JoAnn Ciuffetelli, Assistant Director of Admissions, Wilmington College, 320 DuPont Highway, New Castle, DE

Wilmington College *(continued)*

19720-6491. Telephone: 302-328-9407 Ext. 104 or toll-free 877-967-5464. Fax: 302-328-5902. E-mail: jciuf@wilm.coll.edu. Web site: http://www.wilmcoll.edu/.

DISTRICT OF COLUMBIA

AMERICAN UNIVERSITY
WASHINGTON, DISTRICT OF COLUMBIA

General Independent Methodist, university, coed **Entrance** Moderately difficult **Setting** 77-acre suburban campus **Total enrollment** 10,778 **Student/faculty ratio** 14:1 **Application deadline** 2/1 (freshmen), 7/1 (transfer) **Freshmen** 72% were admitted **Housing** Yes **Expenses** Tuition $21,399; Room & Board $8372 **Undergraduates** 61% women, 11% part-time, 6% 25 or older, 0.4% Native American, 5% Hispanic American, 7% African American, 4% Asian American/Pacific Islander **The most frequently chosen baccalaureate fields are** business/marketing, communications/communication technologies, social sciences and history **Academic program** English as a second language, advanced placement, accelerated degree program, self-designed majors, honors program, summer session, adult/continuing education programs, internships **Contact** Dr. Sharon Alston, Director of Admissions, American University, 4400 Massachusetts Avenue, NW, Washington, DC 20016-8001. Telephone: 202-885-6000. Fax: 202-885-1025. E-mail: afa@american.edu. Web site: http://www.american.edu/.

THE CATHOLIC UNIVERSITY OF AMERICA
WASHINGTON, DISTRICT OF COLUMBIA

General Independent, university, coed, affiliated with Roman Catholic Church **Entrance** Moderately difficult **Setting** 144-acre urban campus **Total enrollment** 5,493 **Student/faculty ratio** 10:1 **Application deadline** 2/15 (freshmen), 5/1 (transfer) **Freshmen** 87% were admitted **Housing** Yes **Expenses** Tuition 19,930; Room & Board 8073 **Undergraduates** 54% women, 9% part-time, 10% 25 or older, 0.2% Native American, 4% Hispanic American, 7% African American, 4% Asian American/Pacific Islander **The most frequently chosen baccalaureate fields are** architecture, engineering/engineering technologies, social sciences and history **Academic program** English as a second language, advanced placement, accelerated degree program, self-designed majors, honors program, summer session, adult/continuing education programs, internships **Contact** Ms. Michelle D. Petro-Siraj, Executive Director of Undergraduate Admission, The Catholic University of America, 102 McMahon Hall, Washington, DC 20064. Telephone: 202-319-5305 or toll-free 800-673-2772 (out-of-state). Fax: 202-319-6533. E-mail: cua-admissions@cua.edu. Web site: http://www.cua.edu/.

▶ **For more information, see page 396.**

CORCORAN COLLEGE OF ART AND DESIGN
WASHINGTON, DISTRICT OF COLUMBIA

General Independent, 4-year, coed **Entrance** Moderately difficult **Setting** 7-acre urban campus **Total enrollment** 341 **Student/faculty ratio** 8:1 **Application deadline** Rolling (freshmen), rolling (transfer) **Freshmen** 58% were admitted **Housing** No **Expenses** Tuition 15,550 **Undergraduates** 24% 25 or older, 0.3% Native American, 7% Hispanic American, 8% African American, 8% Asian American/Pacific Islander **The most frequently chosen baccalaureate field is** visual/performing arts **Academic program** English as a second language, advanced placement, summer session, adult/continuing education programs, internships **Contact** Ms. Anne E. Bowman, Director of Admissions, Corcoran College of Art and Design, 500 17th Street, NW, Washington, DC 20006-4804. Telephone: 202-639-1814 or toll-free 888-CORCORAN (out-of-state). Fax: 202-639-1830. E-mail: admofc@aol.com. Web site: http://www.corcoran.edu/.

GALLAUDET UNIVERSITY
WASHINGTON, DISTRICT OF COLUMBIA

General Independent, university, coed **Entrance** Moderately difficult **Setting** 99-acre urban campus **Total enrollment** 1,661 **Student/faculty ratio** 7:1 **Application deadline** 8/1 (freshmen), 5/15 (transfer) **Freshmen** 67% were admitted **Housing** Yes **Expenses** Tuition 8420; Room & Board 7340 **Undergraduates** 54% women, 16% part-time, 29% 25 or older, 1% Native American, 6% Hispanic American, 11% African American, 5% Asian American/Pacific Islander **The most frequently chosen baccalaureate fields are** biological/life sciences, education, protective services/public administration **Academic program** English as a second language, advanced placement, accelerated degree program, self-designed majors, honors program, summer session, adult/continuing education programs, internships **Contact** Ms. Deborah E. DeStefano, Director of Admissions, Gallaudet University, 800 Florida Avenue, NE, Washington, DC 20002-3625. Telephone: 202-651-5750 or toll-free 800-995-0550 (out-of-state). Fax: 202-651-5774. E-mail: admissions@gallua.gallaudet.edu. Web site: http://www.gallaudet.edu/.

GEORGETOWN UNIVERSITY
WASHINGTON, DISTRICT OF COLUMBIA

General Independent Roman Catholic (Jesuit), university, coed **Entrance** Most difficult **Setting** 110-acre urban campus **Total enrollment** 12,427 **Student/faculty ratio** 10:1 **Application deadline** 1/10 (freshmen), 3/1 (transfer) **Freshmen** 22% were admitted **Housing** Yes **Expenses** Tuition 24,168; Room & Board 9103 **Undergraduates** 54% women, 3% part-time, 4% 25 or older, 0.3% Native American, 5% Hispanic

American, 6% African American, 9% Asian American/Pacific Islander **The most frequently chosen baccalaureate fields are** business/marketing, English, social sciences and history **Academic program** English as a second language, advanced placement, self-designed majors, honors program, summer session, adult/continuing education programs, internships **Contact** Mr. Charles A. Deacon, Dean of Undergraduate Admissions, Georgetown University, 37th and O Street, NW, Washington, DC 20057. Telephone: 202-687-3600. Fax: 202-687-6660. E-mail: guadmiss@gunet.georgetown.edu. Web site: http://www.georgetown.edu/.

THE GEORGE WASHINGTON UNIVERSITY
WASHINGTON, DISTRICT OF COLUMBIA

General Independent, university, coed **Entrance** Very difficult **Setting** 36-acre urban campus **Total enrollment** 20,527 **Student/faculty ratio** 13:1 **Application deadline** 1/15 (freshmen), 6/1 (transfer) **Freshmen** 49% were admitted **Housing** Yes **Expenses** Tuition 25,040; Room & Board 8538 **Undergraduates** 57% women, 12% part-time, 4% 25 or older, 0.3% Native American, 5% Hispanic American, 6% African American, 10% Asian American/Pacific Islander **The most frequently chosen baccalaureate fields are** business/marketing, psychology, social sciences and history **Academic program** English as a second language, advanced placement, accelerated degree program, self-designed majors, honors program, summer session, adult/continuing education programs, internships **Contact** Dr. Kathryn M. Napper, Director of Admission, The George Washington University, 2121 Eye Street, NW, Washington, DC 20052. Telephone: 202-994-6040 or toll-free 800-447-3765. Fax: 202-944-0325. E-mail: gwadm@gwis2.circ.gwu.edu. Web site: http://www.gwu.edu/.

HOWARD UNIVERSITY
WASHINGTON, DISTRICT OF COLUMBIA

General Independent, university, coed **Entrance** Moderately difficult **Setting** 242-acre urban campus **Total enrollment** 10,700 **Application deadline** 4/1 (freshmen), 4/1 (transfer) **Freshmen** 56% were admitted **Housing** Yes **Expenses** Tuition 10,220; Room & Board 5000 **Undergraduates** 33% 25 or older **The most frequently chosen baccalaureate fields are** business/marketing, biological/life sciences, health professions and related sciences **Academic program** Advanced placement, accelerated degree program, self-designed majors, honors program, summer session, adult/continuing education programs, internships **Contact** Ms. Linda Sanders-Hawkins, Interim Director of Admissions, Howard University, 2400 Sixth Street, NW, Washington, DC 20059-0002. Telephone: 202-806-2700 or toll-free 800-HOWARD-U (out-of-state). Fax: 202-806-4465. E-mail: admissions@howard.edu. Web site: http://www.howard.edu/.

MOUNT VERNON COLLEGE
See The George Washington University

POTOMAC COLLEGE
WASHINGTON, DISTRICT OF COLUMBIA

Contact Mr. Charles Dresser, Office of Admissions, Potomac College, 4000 Chesapeake Street, NW, Washington, DC 20016. Telephone: 202-686-0876 or toll-free 888-686-0876. Fax: 202-686-0818. E-mail: cdresser@potomac.edu. Web site: http://www.potomac.edu/.

SOUTHEASTERN UNIVERSITY
WASHINGTON, DISTRICT OF COLUMBIA

General Independent, comprehensive, coed **Entrance** Noncompetitive **Setting** 1-acre urban campus **Total enrollment** 1,057 **Student/faculty ratio** 14:1 **Application deadline** Rolling (freshmen), rolling (transfer) **Freshmen** 66% were admitted **Housing** No **Expenses** Tuition $8265 **Undergraduates** 68% women, 75% part-time, 58% 25 or older, 0% Native American, 1% Hispanic American, 75% African American, 4% Asian American/Pacific Islander **Academic program** English as a second language, advanced placement, accelerated degree program, honors program, summer session, adult/continuing education programs, internships **Contact** Mr. Jack Flinter, Director of Admissions, Southeastern University, 501 I Street, SW, Washington, DC 20024-2788. Telephone: 202-265-5343 Ext. 211. Fax: 202-488-8162. E-mail: jackf@admin.seu.com.edu. Web site: http://www.seu.edu/.

STRAYER UNIVERSITY
WASHINGTON, DISTRICT OF COLUMBIA

General Proprietary, comprehensive, coed **Entrance** Minimally difficult **Setting** urban campus **Total enrollment** 12,096 **Student/faculty ratio** 24:1 **Application deadline** Rolling (freshmen), rolling (transfer) **Housing** No **Expenses** Tuition 8505 **Undergraduates** 57% women, 78% part-time, 82% 25 or older, 0.3% Native American, 4% Hispanic American, 42% African American, 5% Asian American/Pacific Islander **Academic program** Advanced placement, accelerated degree program, summer session, adult/continuing education programs, internships **Contact** Ms. Betty Shuford, Administrative Dean, Region I, Strayer University, 1025 Fifteenth Street, NW, Washington, DC 20005. Telephone: 202-408-2400 or toll-free 888-4-STRAYER. Fax: 202-289-1831. E-mail: mw@net.strayer.edu. Web site: http://www.strayer.edu/.

TRINITY COLLEGE
WASHINGTON, DISTRICT OF COLUMBIA

General Independent Roman Catholic, comprehensive, women only **Entrance** Moderately difficult **Setting** 26-acre urban campus **Total enrollment** 1,325 **Student/faculty ratio** 12:1 **Application deadline** 2/1 (freshmen), rolling (transfer) **Freshmen** 73% were admitted **Housing** Yes **Expenses** Tuition $14,440; Room & Board $6700 **Undergraduates** 44% part-time, 49% 25 or older, 0.1% Native American, 8%

Trinity College *(continued)*

Hispanic American, 65% African American, 2% Asian American/Pacific Islander **Academic program** English as a second language, advanced placement, accelerated degree program, self-designed majors, honors program, summer session, adult/continuing education programs, internships **Contact** Ms. Wendy Kares, Director of Admissions, Trinity College, 125 Michigan Avenue, NE, Washington, DC 20017-1094. Telephone: 202-884-9400. Fax: 202-884-9229. Web site: http://www.trinitydc.edu/.

UNIVERSITY OF THE DISTRICT OF COLUMBIA

WASHINGTON, DISTRICT OF COLUMBIA

General District-supported, comprehensive, coed **Entrance** Noncompetitive **Setting** 28-acre urban campus **Total enrollment** 5,358 **Student/faculty ratio** 13:1 **Application deadline** 8/1 (freshmen), 8/1 (transfer) **Freshmen** 86% were admitted **Housing** No **Expenses** Tuition $2070 **Undergraduates** 63% women, 66% part-time, 48% 25 or older, 0.2% Native American, 5% Hispanic American, 75% African American, 2% Asian American/Pacific Islander **The most frequently chosen baccalaureate fields are** business/marketing, computer/information sciences, protective services/public administration **Academic program** English as a second language, accelerated degree program, honors program, summer session, adult/continuing education programs, internships **Contact** Mr. LaHugh Bankston, Registrar, University of the District of Columbia, 4200 Connecticut Avenue NW, Building 39 - A-Level, Washington, DC 20008. Telephone: 202-274-6200. Fax: 202-274-6067. Web site: http://www.udc.edu/.

FLORIDA

AMERICAN COLLEGE OF PREHOSPITAL MEDICINE

NAVARRE, FLORIDA

General Proprietary, 4-year, coed **Entrance** Moderately difficult **Total enrollment** 200 **Application deadline** Rolling (freshmen), rolling (transfer) **Freshmen** 100% were admitted **Housing** No **Undergraduates** 90% 25 or older **The most frequently chosen baccalaureate field is** health professions and related sciences **Contact** Dr. Richard A. Clinchy, Chairman/CEO, American College of Prehospital Medicine, 7552 Navarre Parkway, Suite 1, Navarre, FL 32566-7312. Telephone: 850-939-0840 or toll-free 800-735-2276. Fax: 800-350-3870. E-mail: acpmceo@aol.com. Web site: http://www.acpm.edu/.

AMERICAN INTERCONTINENTAL UNIVERSITY

PLANTATION, FLORIDA

General Proprietary, comprehensive **Total enrollment** 601 **Expenses** Tuition 8022 **Contact** Ms. Ramona Harper, Vice President of Admissions, American InterContinental University, 8151 West Peters Road, Suite 1000, Plantation, FL 33324. Telephone: 954-835-0939. Web site: http://www.aiuniv.edu/.

THE BAPTIST COLLEGE OF FLORIDA

GRACEVILLE, FLORIDA

General Independent Southern Baptist, 4-year, coed **Entrance** Noncompetitive **Setting** 165-acre small-town campus **Total enrollment** 583 **Student/faculty ratio** 24:1 **Application deadline** Rolling (freshmen), rolling (transfer) **Freshmen** 96% were admitted **Housing** Yes **Expenses** Tuition $5160; Room & Board $3150 **Undergraduates** 36% women, 17% part-time, 48% 25 or older, 1% Native American, 4% Hispanic American, 6% African American, 1% Asian American/Pacific Islander **The most frequently chosen baccalaureate fields are** education, philosophy, religion, and theology, visual/performing arts **Academic program** Advanced placement, accelerated degree program, summer session, adult/continuing education programs, internships **Contact** Mr. O. Lavan Wilson, Director of Admissions, The Baptist College of Florida, 5400 College Drive, Graceville, FL 32440-1898. Telephone: 850-263-3261 Ext. 460 or toll-free 800-328-2660 Ext. 460. Fax: 850-263-7506. E-mail: admissions@baptistcollege.edu. Web site: http://www.baptistcollege.edu/.

BARRY UNIVERSITY

MIAMI SHORES, FLORIDA

General Independent Roman Catholic, university, coed **Entrance** Moderately difficult **Setting** 122-acre suburban campus **Total enrollment** 8,650 **Student/faculty ratio** 13:1 **Application deadline** Rolling (freshmen), rolling (transfer) **Freshmen** 72% were admitted **Housing** Yes **Expenses** Tuition $16,600; Room & Board $6400 **Undergraduates** 65% women, 54% part-time, 62% 25 or older, 0.2% Native American, 32% Hispanic American, 18% African American, 1% Asian American/Pacific Islander **The most frequently chosen baccalaureate fields are** health professions and related sciences, education, liberal arts/general studies **Academic program** English as a second language, advanced placement, accelerated degree program, honors program, summer session, adult/continuing education programs, internships **Contact** Ms. Tracey Fontaine, Director of Admissions, Barry University, Kelly Youse, 11300 Northeast Second Avenue, Miami Shores, FL 33161. Telephone: 308-699-3127 or toll-free 800-695-2279. Fax: 305-899-2971. E-mail: admissions@pcsa01.barry.edu. Web site: http://www.barry.edu/.

BETHUNE-COOKMAN COLLEGE

DAYTONA BEACH, FLORIDA

General Independent Methodist, 4-year, coed **Entrance** Minimally difficult **Setting** 60-acre urban campus **Total enrollment** 2,745 **Student/faculty ratio** 17:1 **Application deadline** 7/30 (freshmen), 7/30 (transfer) **Freshmen** 74% were admitted **Hous-**

ing Yes **Expenses** Tuition $8988; Room & Board $5782 **Undergraduates** 57% women, 6% part-time, 10% 25 or older, 0% Native American, 1% Hispanic American, 89% African American, 0.3% Asian American/Pacific Islander **The most frequently chosen baccalaureate fields are** business/marketing, education, protective services/public administration **Academic program** Advanced placement, accelerated degree program, honors program, summer session, adult/continuing education programs, internships **Contact** Mr. William A. T. Byrd, Assistant Vice President for Enrollment Management, Bethune-Cookman College, 640 Dr. Mary McLeod Bethune Boulevard, Daytona Beach, FL 32114-3099. Telephone: 904-255-1401 Ext. 358 or toll-free 800-448-0228. Fax: 904-257-5338. E-mail: byrdw@cookman.edu. Web site: http://www.bethune.cookman.edu/.

CARLOS ALBIZU UNIVERSITY, MIAMI CAMPUS

MIAMI, FLORIDA

General Independent, upper-level, coed, primarily women **Setting** 2-acre urban campus **Total enrollment** 596 **Student/faculty ratio** 10:1 **Application deadline** Rolling (transfer) **First-Year Students** 60% were admitted **Housing** No **Expenses** Tuition $7419 **Undergraduates** 72% women, 59% part-time, 87% 25 or older, 0% Native American, 84% Hispanic American, 9% African American, 0% Asian American/Pacific Islander **The most frequently chosen baccalaureate field is** psychology **Academic program** Advanced placement, summer session, adult/continuing education programs, internships **Contact** Mr. Gustavo B. Marin JD, Director of Admissions, Recruitment and Outreach, Carlos Albizu University, Miami Campus, Carlos Albizu University Miami Campus, Recruitment and Outreach, 2173 NW 99th Av, Recruitment and Outreach, 8180 Northwest 36th Street, Miami, FL 33172. Telephone: 305-593-1223 Ext. 136 or toll-free 800-672-3246. Fax: 305-593-1854. E-mail: gmarin@albizu.edu. Web site: http://www.albizu.edu/.

CLEARWATER CHRISTIAN COLLEGE

CLEARWATER, FLORIDA

General Independent nondenominational, 4-year, coed **Entrance** Minimally difficult **Setting** 50-acre suburban campus **Total enrollment** 652 **Student/faculty ratio** 15:1 **Application deadline** 7/15 (freshmen), 7/15 (transfer) **Freshmen** 86% were admitted **Housing** Yes **Expenses** Tuition 8950; Room & Board 4050 **Academic program** Advanced placement, summer session, internships **Contact** Mr. Benjamin J. Puckett, Dean of Enrollment Services, Clearwater Christian College, 3400 Gulf-to-Bay Boulevard, Clearwater, FL 33759-4595. Telephone: 727-726-1153 or toll-free 800-348-4463. Fax: 813-726-8597. E-mail: admissions@clearwater.edu. Web site: http://www.clearwater.edu/.

DEVRY INSTITUTE OF TECHNOLOGY

ORLANDO, FLORIDA

Contact Jody Wasmer, Dean of Admissions, DeVry Institute of Technology, 4000 Millenia Boulevard, Orlando, FL 32839. Telephone: 407-355-4860 or toll-free 800-fl-devry (in-state). Web site: http://www.or.devry.edu/.

ECKERD COLLEGE

ST. PETERSBURG, FLORIDA

General Independent Presbyterian, 4-year, coed **Entrance** Moderately difficult **Setting** 267-acre suburban campus **Total enrollment** 1,572 **Student/faculty ratio** 14:1 **Application deadline** Rolling (freshmen), rolling (transfer) **Freshmen** 73% were admitted **Housing** Yes **Expenses** Tuition 18,785; Room & Board 5110 **Undergraduates** 55% women, 1% part-time, 3% 25 or older, 0% Native American, 4% Hispanic American, 2% African American, 2% Asian American/Pacific Islander **The most frequently chosen baccalaureate fields are** biological/life sciences, business/marketing, social sciences and history **Academic program** English as a second language, advanced placement, accelerated degree program, self-designed majors, honors program, summer session, adult/continuing education programs, internships **Contact** Dr. Richard R. Hallin, Dean of Admissions, Eckerd College, 4200 54th Avenue South, St. Petersburg, FL 33711. Telephone: 727-864-8331 or toll-free 800-456-9009. Fax: 727-866-2304. E-mail: admissions@eckerd.edu. Web site: http://www.eckerd.edu/.

EDWARD WATERS COLLEGE

JACKSONVILLE, FLORIDA

Contact Mr. Richard F. Pride, Director of Admissions, Edward Waters College, 1658 Kings Road, Jacksonville, FL 32209-6199. Telephone: 904-366-2715.

EMBRY-RIDDLE AERONAUTICAL UNIVERSITY

DAYTONA BEACH, FLORIDA

General Independent, comprehensive, coed, primarily men **Entrance** Moderately difficult **Setting** 178-acre urban campus **Total enrollment** 4,803 **Student/faculty ratio** 18:1 **Application deadline** 7/1 (freshmen), 7/1 (transfer) **Freshmen** 74% were admitted **Housing** Yes **Expenses** Tuition $11,690; Room & Board $5390 **Undergraduates** 15% women, 11% part-time, 11% 25 or older, 1% Native American, 5% Hispanic American, 5% African American, 3% Asian American/Pacific Islander **The most frequently chosen baccalaureate fields are** engineering/engineering technologies, business/marketing, trade and industry **Academic program** English as a second language, advanced placement, summer session, adult/continuing education programs, internships **Contact** Ms. Carol Hogan, Director of Admissions, Embry-Riddle Aeronautical University, 600 South Clyde Morris Boulevard, Daytona Beach, FL 32114-3900.

Embry-Riddle Aeronautical University *(continued)*

Telephone: 904-226-6112 or toll-free 800-862-2416. Fax: 904-226-7070. E-mail: admit@db.erau.edu. Web site: http://www.embryriddle.edu/.

▶ **For more information, see page 413.**

EMBRY-RIDDLE AERONAUTICAL UNIVERSITY, EXTENDED CAMPUS
DAYTONA BEACH, FLORIDA

General Independent, comprehensive, coed, primarily men **Entrance** Minimally difficult **Total enrollment** 8,044 **Student/faculty ratio** 3:1 **Application deadline** Rolling (freshmen), rolling (transfer) **Housing** No **Expenses** Tuition $2064 **Undergraduates** 10% women, 98% part-time, 1% Native American, 6% Hispanic American, 7% African American, 3% Asian American/Pacific Islander **The most frequently chosen baccalaureate fields are** business/marketing, trade and industry **Academic program** Advanced placement, adult/continuing education programs **Contact** Mrs. Pam Thomas, Director of Admissions, Records and Registration, Embry-Riddle Aeronautical University, Extended Campus, 600 South Clyde Morris Boulevard, Daytona Beach, FL 32114-3900. Telephone: 904-226-7610 or toll-free 800-862-2416 (out-of-state). Fax: 904-226-6984. E-mail: ecinfo@ec.db.erau.edu. Web site: http://www.embryriddle.edu/.

EVERGLADES COLLEGE
FT. LAUDERDALE, FLORIDA

Contact Everglades College, 1500 NW 49th Street, Suite 600, Ft. Lauderdale, FL 33309. Web site: http://www.evergladescollege.edu/.

FLAGLER COLLEGE
ST. AUGUSTINE, FLORIDA

General Independent, 4-year, coed **Entrance** Moderately difficult **Setting** 36-acre small-town campus **Total enrollment** 1,830 **Student/faculty ratio** 19:1 **Application deadline** 3/1 (freshmen), 3/1 (transfer) **Freshmen** 41% were admitted **Housing** Yes **Expenses** Tuition $6320; Room & Board $3910 **Undergraduates** 63% women, 2% part-time, 5% 25 or older, 0.1% Native American, 2% Hispanic American, 1% African American, 1% Asian American/Pacific Islander **The most frequently chosen baccalaureate fields are** business/marketing, communications/communication technologies, education **Academic program** Advanced placement, summer session, internships **Contact** Mr. Marc G. Williar, Director of Admissions, Flagler College, PO Box 1027, St. Augustine, FL 32085-1027. Telephone: 904-829-6481 Ext. 220 or toll-free 800-304-4208. E-mail: admiss@flagler.edu. Web site: http://www.flagler.edu/.

FLORIDA AGRICULTURAL AND MECHANICAL UNIVERSITY
TALLAHASSEE, FLORIDA

General State-supported, university, coed **Entrance** Moderately difficult **Setting** 419-acre urban campus **Total enrollment** 12,126 **Application deadline** 5/1 (freshmen), 5/1 (transfer) **Freshmen** 65% were admitted **Housing** Yes **Expenses** Tuition $2269; Room & Board $4214 **Undergraduates** 57% women, 14% part-time, 20% 25 or older, 0.04% Native American, 1% Hispanic American, 95% African American, 0.4% Asian American/Pacific Islander **The most frequently chosen baccalaureate fields are** education, engineering/engineering technologies, health professions and related sciences **Academic program** Advanced placement, accelerated degree program, honors program, summer session, adult/continuing education programs, internships **Contact** Ms. Barbara R. Cox, Director of Admissions, Florida Agricultural and Mechanical University, Office of Admissions, Tallahassee, FL 32307. Telephone: 850-599-3796. Fax: 850-599-3069. E-mail: bcox@ns1.famu.edu. Web site: http://www.famu.edu/.

FLORIDA ATLANTIC UNIVERSITY
BOCA RATON, FLORIDA

General State-supported, university, coed **Entrance** Moderately difficult **Setting** 850-acre suburban campus **Total enrollment** 21,229 **Student/faculty ratio** 15:1 **Application deadline** Rolling (freshmen), rolling (transfer) **Freshmen** 72% were admitted **Housing** Yes **Expenses** Tuition $2396; Room & Board $4993 **Undergraduates** 61% women, 49% part-time, 40% 25 or older, 0.4% Native American, 12% Hispanic American, 15% African American, 4% Asian American/Pacific Islander **The most frequently chosen baccalaureate fields are** business/marketing, education, health professions and related sciences **Academic program** English as a second language, advanced placement, accelerated degree program, self-designed majors, honors program, summer session, adult/continuing education programs, internships **Contact** Coordinator, Freshmen Recruitment, Florida Atlantic University, 777 Glades Road, PO Box 3091, Boca Raton, FL 33431-0991. Telephone: 561-297-2458 or toll-free 800-299-4FAU. Fax: 561-297-2758. Web site: http://www.fau.edu/.

FLORIDA BAPTIST THEOLOGICAL COLLEGE
See The Baptist College of Florida

FLORIDA CHRISTIAN COLLEGE
KISSIMMEE, FLORIDA

General Independent, 4-year, coed, affiliated with Christian Churches and Churches of Christ **Entrance** Minimally difficult **Setting** 40-acre small-town campus **Total enrollment** 223 **Student/faculty ratio** 16:1 **Application deadline** 7/15 (freshmen), 7/15 (transfer) **Freshmen** 66% were admitted **Housing** Yes **Expenses** Tuition $5870; Room only $1680

Undergraduates 48% women, 17% part-time, 31% 25 or older, 0% Native American, 4% Hispanic American, 5% African American, 2% Asian American/ Pacific Islander **Academic program** Advanced placement, summer session, adult/continuing education programs, internships **Contact** Mr. Terry Davis, Admissions Director, Florida Christian College, 1011 Bill Beck Boulevard, Kissimmee, FL 34744-5301. Telephone: 407-847-8966 Ext. 305. Web site: http:// www.fcc.edu/.

FLORIDA COLLEGE
TEMPLE TERRACE, FLORIDA

General Independent, 4-year, coed **Entrance** Moderately difficult **Setting** 95-acre small-town campus **Total enrollment** 555 **Student/faculty ratio** 16:1 **Application deadline** 8/1 (freshmen), 8/1 (transfer) **Freshmen** 91% were admitted **Housing** Yes **Expenses** Tuition $7700; Room & Board $5660 **Undergraduates** 52% women, 3% part-time, 1% 25 or older, 0.4% Native American, 4% Hispanic American, 1% African American, 0.2% Asian American/Pacific Islander **The most frequently chosen baccalaureate field is** philosophy, religion, and theology **Academic program** Advanced placement **Contact** Mrs. Mari Smith, Assistant Director of Admissions, Florida College, 119 North Glen Arven Avenue, Temple Terrace, FL 33617. Telephone: 813-988-5131 Ext. 6716 or toll-free 800-326-7655. Fax: 813-899-6772. E-mail: admissions@flcoll.edu. Web site: http:// www.flcoll.edu/.

FLORIDA GULF COAST UNIVERSITY
FORT MYERS, FLORIDA

General State-supported, comprehensive, coed **Entrance** Moderately difficult **Setting** 760-acre suburban campus **Total enrollment** 3,664 **Student/ faculty ratio** 15:1 **Application deadline** 8/15 (freshmen), rolling (transfer) **Freshmen** 72% were admitted **Housing** Yes **Expenses** Tuition 2201; Room & Board 7000 **Undergraduates** 65% women, 48% part-time, 0.3% 25 or older **The most frequently chosen baccalaureate fields are** education, health professions and related sciences, protective services/public administration **Academic program** Advanced placement, accelerated degree program, honors program, summer session, internships **Contact** Ms. Michele Yovanovich, Director of Admissions, Florida Gulf Coast University, 10501 FGCU Boulevard South, Fort Myers, FL 33965-6565. Telephone: 941-590-7878 or toll-free 800-590-3428. Fax: 941-590-7894. E-mail: oar@fgcu.edu. Web site: http://www.fgcu.edu/.

FLORIDA INSTITUTE OF TECHNOLOGY
MELBOURNE, FLORIDA

General Independent, university, coed **Entrance** Moderately difficult **Setting** 130-acre small-town campus **Total enrollment** 4,248 **Student/faculty ratio** 11:1 **Application deadline** Rolling (freshmen), rolling (transfer) **Freshmen** 80% were admitted **Housing** Yes **Expenses** Tuition 18,450; Room & Board 5590 **Undergraduates** 30% women, 6% part-time, 9% 25 or older, 0.2% Native American, 5% Hispanic American, 4% African American, 3% Asian American/ Pacific Islander **The most frequently chosen baccalaureate fields are** biological/life sciences, engineering/ engineering technologies, trade and industry **Academic program** English as a second language, advanced placement, accelerated degree program, summer session, adult/continuing education programs, internships **Contact** Director of Undergraduate Admissions, Florida Institute of Technology, 150 West University Boulevard, Melbourne, FL 32901-6975. Telephone: 321-674-8030 or toll-free 800-348-4636 (in-state); 800-888-4348 (out-of-state). Fax: 321-723-9468. E-mail: admissions@fit.edu. Web site: http://www.fit.edu/.

FLORIDA INTERNATIONAL UNIVERSITY
MIAMI, FLORIDA

General State-supported, university, coed **Entrance** Moderately difficult **Setting** 573-acre urban campus **Total enrollment** 31,945 **Student/faculty ratio** 14:1 **Application deadline** Rolling (freshmen), rolling (transfer) **Freshmen** 54% were admitted **Housing** Yes **Expenses** Tuition 2410; Room only 4230 **Undergraduates** 56% women, 44% part-time, 30% 25 or older, 0.2% Native American, 55% Hispanic American, 14% African American, 4% Asian American/ Pacific Islander **The most frequently chosen baccalaureate fields are** business/marketing, education, health professions and related sciences **Academic program** English as a second language, advanced placement, accelerated degree program, honors program, summer session, adult/continuing education programs, internships **Contact** Ms. Carmen Brown, Director of Admissions, Florida International University, University Park, Miami, FL 33199. Telephone: 305-348-3675. Fax: 305-348-3648. E-mail: admiss@ servms.fiu.edu. Web site: http://www.fiu.edu/ ~wellness.

FLORIDA MEMORIAL COLLEGE
MIAMI-DADE, FLORIDA

Contact Mrs. Peggy Murray Martin, Director of Admissions and International Student Advisor, Florida Memorial College, 15800 NW 42nd Avenue, Miami-Dade, FL 33054. Telephone: 305-626-3147 or toll-free 800-822-1362. Web site: http://www.fmc.edu/ main.cfm.

FLORIDA METROPOLITAN UNIVERSITY–BRANDON CAMPUS
TAMPA, FLORIDA

General Proprietary, comprehensive, coed **Entrance** Minimally difficult **Setting** 5-acre urban campus **Total enrollment** 739 **Student/faculty ratio** 14:1 **Application deadline** Rolling (freshmen), rolling (transfer) **Housing** No **Expenses** Tuition 6735 **Undergraduates** 47% 25 or older, 1% Native American, 11% Hispanic American, 33% African American, 2% Asian American/Pacific Islander **The most fre-**

Florida Metropolitan University–Brandon Campus *(continued)*

quently chosen baccalaureate fields are business/marketing, computer/information sciences, protective services/public administration **Academic program** Accelerated degree program, honors program, summer session, adult/continuing education programs, internships **Contact** Mrs. Dee McKee, Director of Admissions, Florida Metropolitan University–Brandon Campus, 3924 Coconut Palm Drive, Tampa, FL 33619. Telephone: 813-621-0041 Ext. 45. Fax: 813-623-5769. E-mail: dpearson@cci.edu. Web site: http://135.145.62.96/realdefault.html.

FLORIDA METROPOLITAN UNIVERSITY–FORT LAUDERDALE COLLEGE

FORT LAUDERDALE, FLORIDA

General Proprietary, comprehensive, coed **Entrance** Minimally difficult **Setting** suburban campus **Total enrollment** 954 **Student/faculty ratio** 17:1 **Application deadline** Rolling (freshmen), rolling (transfer) **Freshmen** 84% were admitted **Housing** No **Expenses** Tuition $6810 **Undergraduates** 54% women, 25% part-time, 25% 25 or older, 1% Native American, 11% Hispanic American, 37% African American, 8% Asian American/Pacific Islander **Academic program** English as a second language, advanced placement, accelerated degree program, summer session, adult/continuing education programs, internships **Contact** Mr. Tony Wallace, Director of Admissions, Florida Metropolitan University–Fort Lauderdale College, 1040 Bayview Drive, Fort Lauderdale, FL 33304-2522. Telephone: 954-568-1600 or toll-free 800-468-0168. Fax: 305-568-2008. Web site: http://www.fmu.edu.

FLORIDA METROPOLITAN UNIVERSITY–MELBOURNE CAMPUS

MELBOURNE, FLORIDA

General Proprietary, comprehensive, coed **Entrance** Noncompetitive **Setting** 5-acre small-town campus **Total enrollment** 580 **Student/faculty ratio** 13:1 **Application deadline** Rolling (freshmen), rolling (transfer) **Freshmen** 68% were admitted **Housing** No **Expenses** Tuition $9942 **Undergraduates** 68% women, 1% Native American, 7% Hispanic American, 21% African American, 3% Asian American/Pacific Islander **Academic program** Advanced placement, accelerated degree program, summer session, internships **Contact** Ms. Teresa Stinson-Kumar, Director of Admissions, Florida Metropolitan University–Melbourne Campus, 2401 North Harbor City Boulevard, Melbourne, FL 32935-6657. Telephone: 407-253-2929 Ext. 11.

FLORIDA METROPOLITAN UNIVERSITY–ORLANDO COLLEGE, NORTH

ORLANDO, FLORIDA

General Proprietary, comprehensive, coed **Entrance** Minimally difficult **Setting** 1-acre urban campus **Total enrollment** 867 **Student/faculty ratio** 15:1 **Application deadline** Rolling (freshmen), rolling (transfer) **Housing** No **Expenses** Tuition 7350 **Undergraduates** 66% women, 43% part-time, 32% 25 or older, 0.5% Native American, 18% Hispanic American, 32% African American, 4% Asian American/Pacific Islander **Academic program** Advanced placement, summer session, internships **Contact** Ms. Charlene Donnelly, Director of Admissions, Florida Metropolitan University–Orlando College, North, 5421 Diplomat Circle, Orlando, FL 32810-5674. Telephone: 407-628-5870 Ext. 108 or toll-free 800-628-5870.

FLORIDA METROPOLITAN UNIVERSITY–ORLANDO COLLEGE, SOUTH

ORLANDO, FLORIDA

General Proprietary, comprehensive, coed **Entrance** Minimally difficult **Total enrollment** 1,500 **Housing** No **Expenses** Tuition 6338 **Academic program** Accelerated degree program, internships **Contact** Ms. Annette Cloin, Director of Admissions, Florida Metropolitan University–Orlando College, South, 2411 Sand Lake Road, Orlando, FL 32809. Telephone: 407-851-2525 Ext. 30. Fax: 407-851-1477.

FLORIDA METROPOLITAN UNIVERSITY–PINELLAS CAMPUS

CLEARWATER, FLORIDA

Contact Mr. Wayne Childers, Director of Admissions, Florida Metropolitan University–Pinellas Campus, 2471 McMullen Booth Road, Suite 200, Clearwater, FL 33759. Telephone: 727-725-2688 Ext. 702 or toll-free 800-353-FMUS. Fax: 727-796-3722. E-mail: tcpinellas2@juno.com.

FLORIDA METROPOLITAN UNIVERSITY–TAMPA COLLEGE

TAMPA, FLORIDA

General Proprietary, comprehensive, coed **Entrance** Minimally difficult **Setting** 4-acre urban campus **Total enrollment** 1,218 **Student/faculty ratio** 15:1 **Application deadline** Rolling (freshmen), rolling (transfer) **Housing** No **Expenses** Tuition $7206 **Undergraduates** 61% women, 38% part-time, 46% 25 or older, 0.4% Native American, 23% Hispanic American, 24% African American, 3% Asian American/Pacific Islander **Academic program** English as a second language, advanced placement, accelerated degree program, self-designed majors, summer session, adult/continuing education programs, internships **Contact** Ms. Georjia Fantazia, Director of Admissions, Florida Metropolitan University–Tampa College, 3319 W. Hillsborough Avenue, Tampa, FL 33614. Telephone: 813-879-6000 Ext. 129. Fax: 813-871-2483. Web site: http://www.cci.edu/.

FLORIDA METROPOLITAN UNIVERSITY–TAMPA COLLEGE, LAKELAND
LAKELAND, FLORIDA

General Proprietary, comprehensive, coed **Entrance** Minimally difficult **Setting** suburban campus **Total enrollment** 724 **Student/faculty ratio** 16:1 **Freshmen** 91% were admitted **Housing** No **Expenses** Tuition $6555 **Undergraduates** 56% 25 or older **Academic program** Advanced placement, summer session, adult/continuing education programs, internships **Contact** Joe Rostkowski, Director of Admissions, Florida Metropolitan University–Tampa College, Lakeland, 995 East Memorial Boulevard, Suite 110, Lakeland, FL 33801. Telephone: 863-686-1444. Fax: 863-686-1727. E-mail: dsimmons@cci.edu. Web site: http://www.cci.edu/.

FLORIDA SOUTHERN COLLEGE
LAKELAND, FLORIDA

General Independent, comprehensive, coed, affiliated with United Methodist Church **Entrance** Moderately difficult **Setting** 100-acre suburban campus **Total enrollment** 1,803 **Student/faculty ratio** 17:1 **Application deadline** Rolling (transfer) **Freshmen** 80% were admitted **Housing** Yes **Expenses** Tuition $13,930; Room & Board $5600 **Undergraduates** 61% women, 5% part-time, 6% 25 or older, 1% Native American, 4% Hispanic American, 5% African American, 1% Asian American/Pacific Islander **The most frequently chosen baccalaureate fields are** business/marketing, education, health professions and related sciences **Academic program** Advanced placement, honors program, summer session, adult/continuing education programs, internships **Contact** Mr. Robert Palmer, Vice President of Enrollment Management, Florida Southern College, 111 Lake Hollingsworth Drive, Lakeland, FL 33801-5698. Telephone: 863-680-6212 or toll-free 800-274-4131. Fax: 863-680-4120. E-mail: fscadm@flsouthern.edu. Web site: http://www.flsouthern.edu/.

FLORIDA STATE UNIVERSITY
TALLAHASSEE, FLORIDA

General State-supported, university, coed **Entrance** Very difficult **Setting** 456-acre suburban campus **Total enrollment** 33,951 **Application deadline** 3/1 (freshmen), 7/13 (transfer) **Freshmen** 54% were admitted **Housing** Yes **Expenses** Tuition 2379; Room & Board 5150 **Undergraduates** 56% women, 14% part-time, 9% 25 or older, 0.4% Native American, 8% Hispanic American, 12% African American, 3% Asian American/Pacific Islander **The most frequently chosen baccalaureate fields are** business/marketing, education, social sciences and history **Academic program** English as a second language, advanced placement, accelerated degree program, honors program, summer session, adult/continuing education programs, internships **Contact** Office of Admissions, Florida State University, A2500 University Center, Tallahassee, FL 32306-2400. Telephone: 850-644-6200. Fax: 850-644-0197. E-mail: admissions@admin.fsu.edu. Web site: http://www.fsu.edu/.

HOBE SOUND BIBLE COLLEGE
HOBE SOUND, FLORIDA

General Independent nondenominational, 4-year, coed **Entrance** Noncompetitive **Setting** 84-acre small-town campus **Total enrollment** 151 **Student/faculty ratio** 8:1 **Application deadline** Rolling (freshmen), rolling (transfer) **Freshmen** 91% were admitted **Housing** Yes **Expenses** Tuition $4080; Room & Board $3005 **Undergraduates** 48% women, 32% part-time, 24% 25 or older, 0% Native American, 4% Hispanic American, 11% African American, 2% Asian American/Pacific Islander **Academic program** English as a second language, advanced placement, summer session, internships **Contact** Mrs. Ann French, Director of Admissions, Hobe Sound Bible College, PO Box 1065, Hobe Sound, FL 33475-1065. Telephone: 561-546-5534 Ext. 415 or toll-free 800-881-5534. Fax: 561-545-1422. E-mail: hsbcuwin@aol.com.

INTERNATIONAL ACADEMY OF DESIGN & TECHNOLOGY
TAMPA, FLORIDA

General Proprietary, 4-year, coed **Entrance** Noncompetitive **Setting** 1-acre urban campus **Total enrollment** 1,359 **Student/faculty ratio** 13:1 **Application deadline** Rolling (freshmen), rolling (transfer) **Housing** No **Expenses** Tuition $10,620 **Undergraduates** 59% women, 20% part-time, 41% 25 or older, 2% Native American, 15% Hispanic American, 13% African American, 3% Asian American/Pacific Islander **The most frequently chosen baccalaureate fields are** business/marketing, visual/performing arts **Academic program** Advanced placement, accelerated degree program, summer session, adult/continuing education programs, internships **Contact** Mr. Sean Kuhn, Director of Admissions, International Academy of Design & Technology, 5225 Memorial Highway, Tampa, FL 33634-7350. Telephone: 813-881-0007 or toll-free 800-ACADEMY. Fax: 813-881-0008. E-mail: mpage@academy.edu. Web site: http://www.academy.edu/.

INTERNATIONAL COLLEGE
NAPLES, FLORIDA

General Independent, comprehensive, coed **Entrance** Minimally difficult **Setting** suburban campus **Total enrollment** 1,026 **Student/faculty ratio** 31:1 **Application deadline** Rolling (freshmen), rolling (transfer) **Freshmen** 87% were admitted **Housing** No **Expenses** Tuition $7230 **Undergraduates** 63% women, 23% part-time, 94% 25 or older, 1% Native American, 12% Hispanic American, 10% African American, 1% Asian American/Pacific Islander **The most frequently chosen baccalaureate fields are** business/marketing, law/legal studies **Academic program** English as a second language, advanced placement, accelerated degree program, summer session, adult/continuing education programs, internships

International College *(continued)*

Contact Ms. Rita Lampus, Director of Admissions, International College, 2655 Northbrooke Drive, Naples, FL 34119. Telephone: 941-513-1122 Ext. 104 or toll-free 800-466-8017. E-mail: admit@naples.net. Web site: http://www.internationalcollege.edu/.

INTERNATIONAL FINE ARTS COLLEGE
MIAMI, FLORIDA

General Proprietary, comprehensive, coed **Entrance** Moderately difficult **Setting** 4-acre urban campus **Total enrollment** 1,100 **Student/faculty ratio** 18:1 **Application deadline** Rolling (freshmen), rolling (transfer) **Housing** Yes **Expenses** Tuition $13,025 **Undergraduates** 22% 25 or older **Academic program** English as a second language, summer session, internships **Contact** Ms. Elsia Suarez, Director of Admissions, International Fine Arts College, 1737 North Bayshore Drive, Miami, FL 33132-1121. Telephone: 305-373-4684 or toll-free 800-225-9023. Web site: http://www.ifac.edu/.

JACKSONVILLE UNIVERSITY
JACKSONVILLE, FLORIDA

General Independent, comprehensive, coed **Entrance** Moderately difficult **Setting** 260-acre suburban campus **Total enrollment** 2,052 **Student/faculty ratio** 14:1 **Application deadline** Rolling (freshmen), rolling (transfer) **Freshmen** 72% were admitted **Housing** Yes **Expenses** Tuition $15,990; Room & Board $5680 **Undergraduates** 51% women, 14% part-time, 15% 25 or older, 1% Native American, 5% Hispanic American, 14% African American, 3% Asian American/Pacific Islander **The most frequently chosen baccalaureate fields are** business/marketing, computer/information sciences, health professions and related sciences **Academic program** English as a second language, advanced placement, accelerated degree program, self-designed majors, honors program, summer session, adult/continuing education programs, internships **Contact** Mr. David L. Lesesne, Director of Admissions, Jacksonville University, 2800 University Boulevard North, Jacksonville, FL 32211. Telephone: 904-745-7000 or toll-free 800-225-2027. Fax: 904-745-7012. E-mail: admissions@junix.ju.edu. Web site: http://www.ju.edu/.

JOHNSON & WALES UNIVERSITY
NORTH MIAMI, FLORIDA

Contact Mr. Jeff Greenip, Director of Admissions, Johnson & Wales University, 1701 Northeast 127th Street, North Miami, FL 33181. Telephone: 305-892-7002 or toll-free 800-232-2433. Fax: 305-892-7020. E-mail: admissions@jwu.edu. Web site: http://www.jwu.edu/.

JONES COLLEGE
JACKSONVILLE, FLORIDA

General Independent, 4-year, coed **Entrance** Noncompetitive **Setting** 5-acre urban campus **Total enrollment** 654 **Student/faculty ratio** 14:1 **Application deadline** Rolling (freshmen), rolling (transfer) **Housing** No **Undergraduates** 73% women, 77% part-time, 65% 25 or older, 0.3% Native American, 3% Hispanic American, 46% African American, 4% Asian American/Pacific Islander **The most frequently chosen baccalaureate field is** business/marketing **Academic program** Advanced placement, accelerated degree program, self-designed majors, summer session, adult/continuing education programs, internships **Contact** Mr. Barry Darden, Director of Admissions, Jones College, 5355 Arlington Expressway, Jacksonville, FL 32211. Telephone: 904-743-1122 Ext. 115. Fax: 904-743-4446. E-mail: bdarden@jones.edu. Web site: http://www.jones.edu/.

LYNN UNIVERSITY
BOCA RATON, FLORIDA

General Independent, comprehensive, coed **Entrance** Minimally difficult **Setting** 123-acre suburban campus **Total enrollment** 2,037 **Student/faculty ratio** 19:1 **Application deadline** 8/15 (freshmen), 8/15 (transfer) **Freshmen** 81% were admitted **Housing** Yes **Expenses** Tuition $20,250; Room & Board $7200 **Undergraduates** 24% 25 or older **Academic program** English as a second language, advanced placement, honors program, summer session, adult/continuing education programs, internships **Contact** Mr. James P. Sullivan, Director of Admissions, Lynn University, 3601 North Military Trail, Boca Raton, FL 33431-5598. Telephone: 561-237-7837 or toll-free 800-888-LYNN (in-state); 800-544-8035 (out-of-state). Fax: 561-237-7100. E-mail: admission@lynn.edu. Web site: http://www.lynn.edu/.

▶ **For more information, see page 443.**

NEW COLLEGE OF THE UNIVERSITY OF SOUTH FLORIDA
SARASOTA, FLORIDA

General State-supported, 4-year, coed **Entrance** Very difficult **Setting** 140-acre suburban campus **Total enrollment** 649 **Student/faculty ratio** 11:1 **Application deadline** 5/1 (freshmen), rolling (transfer) **Freshmen** 70% were admitted **Housing** Yes **Expenses** Tuition 2663; Room & Board 4877 **Undergraduates** 63% women, 3% 25 or older, 0% Native American, 6% Hispanic American, 3% African American, 3% Asian American/Pacific Islander **The most frequently chosen baccalaureate field is** liberal arts/general studies **Academic program** Accelerated degree program, self-designed majors, honors program, internships **Contact** Mr. Joel Bauman, Acting Director, Admission and Campus Financial Aid, New College of the University of South Florida, 5700 North Tamiami Trail, Sarasota, FL 34243-2197. Telephone: 941-359-4269. Fax: 941-359-4435. E-mail: ncadmissions@virtu.sar.usf.edu. Web site: http://www.newcollege.usf.edu/.

NEW WORLD SCHOOL OF THE ARTS
MIAMI, FLORIDA

General State-supported, 4-year, coed **Entrance** Minimally difficult **Setting** 5-acre urban campus **Total enrollment** 339 **Student/faculty ratio** 4:1 **Freshmen** 62% were admitted **Housing** No **Expenses** Tuition $1638 **Undergraduates** 53% women, 10% 25 or older, 49% Hispanic American, 13% African American, 4% Asian American/Pacific Islander **Academic program** English as a second language, advanced placement, honors program, summer session, internships **Contact** Ms. Pamela Neumann, Recruitment and Admissions Coordinator, New World School of the Arts, 300 NE Second Avenue, Miami, FL 33132. Telephone: 305-237-7007. Fax: 305-237-3794. E-mail: nwsapost.robs@mdcc.edu. Web site: http://www.mdcc.edu/nwsa/.

NORTHWOOD UNIVERSITY, FLORIDA CAMPUS
WEST PALM BEACH, FLORIDA

General Independent, 4-year, coed **Entrance** Moderately difficult **Setting** 90-acre suburban campus **Total enrollment** 969 **Application deadline** Rolling (freshmen), rolling (transfer) **Freshmen** 69% were admitted **Housing** Yes **Expenses** Tuition 12,063; Room & Board 6216 **Undergraduates** 47% women, 22% part-time, 7% 25 or older, 0% Native American, 7% Hispanic American, 12% African American, 1% Asian American/Pacific Islander **The most frequently chosen baccalaureate fields are** business/marketing, computer/information sciences **Academic program** English as a second language, advanced placement, accelerated degree program, honors program, summer session, adult/continuing education programs, internships **Contact** Mr. John M. Letvinchuck, Director of Admissions, Northwood University, Florida Campus, 2600 North Military Trail, West Palm Beach, FL 33409-2911. Telephone: 561-478-5500 or toll-free 800-458-8325. Fax: 561-640-3328. E-mail: fladmit@northwood.edu. Web site: http://www.northwood.edu/.

NOVA SOUTHEASTERN UNIVERSITY
FORT LAUDERDALE, FLORIDA

General Independent, university, coed **Entrance** Moderately difficult **Setting** 232-acre suburban campus **Total enrollment** 18,587 **Application deadline** 7/1 (freshmen), rolling (transfer) **Freshmen** 74% were admitted **Housing** Yes **Expenses** Tuition $13,570; Room & Board $6800 **Undergraduates** 74% women, 37% part-time, 61% 25 or older, 0.3% Native American, 22% Hispanic American, 23% African American, 3% Asian American/Pacific Islander **The most frequently chosen baccalaureate fields are** business/marketing, education, health professions and related sciences **Academic program** Advanced placement, accelerated degree program, summer session, adult/continuing education programs, internships **Contact** Lynne Cawley, Acting Director of Undergraduate Admissions, Nova Southeastern University, 3301 College Avenue, Ft. Lauderdale, FL 33314. Telephone: 954-262-8000 or toll-free 800-541-6682 Ext. 8000. E-mail: ncsinfo@polaris.acast.nova.edu. Web site: http://www.nova.edu/.

PALM BEACH ATLANTIC COLLEGE
WEST PALM BEACH, FLORIDA

General Independent nondenominational, comprehensive, coed **Entrance** Moderately difficult **Setting** 25-acre urban campus **Total enrollment** 2,456 **Student/faculty ratio** 19:1 **Application deadline** Rolling (freshmen), rolling (transfer) **Freshmen** 63% were admitted **Housing** Yes **Expenses** Tuition $11,670; Room & Board $4950 **Undergraduates** 64% women, 12% part-time, 24% 25 or older, 0.1% Native American, 8% Hispanic American, 11% African American, 1% Asian American/Pacific Islander **The most frequently chosen baccalaureate fields are** business/marketing, education, psychology **Academic program** English as a second language, advanced placement, self-designed majors, honors program, summer session, adult/continuing education programs, internships **Contact** Mr. Buck James, Dean of Enrollment Services, Palm Beach Atlantic College, 901 South Flagler Dr, PO Box 24708, West Palm Beach, FL 33416-4708. Telephone: 561-803-2100 or toll-free 800-238-3998. Fax: 561-803-2115. E-mail: admit@pbac.edu. Web site: http://www.pbac.edu/.

RINGLING SCHOOL OF ART AND DESIGN
SARASOTA, FLORIDA

General Independent, 4-year, coed **Entrance** Moderately difficult **Setting** 35-acre urban campus **Total enrollment** 958 **Student/faculty ratio** 19:1 **Application deadline** Rolling (freshmen), rolling (transfer) **Freshmen** 43% were admitted **Housing** Yes **Expenses** Tuition $16,430; Room & Board $7844 **Undergraduates** 45% women, 3% part-time, 18% 25 or older, 1% Native American, 7% Hispanic American, 2% African American, 3% Asian American/Pacific Islander **The most frequently chosen baccalaureate field is** visual/performing arts **Academic program** Advanced placement, summer session, internships **Contact** Mr. James Dean, Dean of Admissions, Ringling School of Art and Design, 2700 North Tamiami Trail, Sarasota, FL 34234. Telephone: 941-351-5100 Ext. 7525 or toll-free 800-255-7695. Fax: 941-359-7517. E-mail: admissions@rsad.edu. Web site: http://www.rsad.edu/.

ROLLINS COLLEGE
WINTER PARK, FLORIDA

General Independent, comprehensive, coed **Entrance** Very difficult **Setting** 67-acre suburban campus **Total enrollment** 2,320 **Student/faculty ratio** 12:1 **Application deadline** 2/15 (freshmen), 4/15 (transfer) **Freshmen** 68% were admitted **Housing** Yes **Expenses** Tuition $23,882; Room & Board $7341 **Undergraduates** 60% women, 0.2% part-time, 2% 25 or older, 1% Native American, 7% Hispanic American, 3% African American, 3% Asian American/Pacific Islander

Rollins College *(continued)*

The most frequently chosen baccalaureate fields are psychology, social sciences and history, visual/performing arts **Academic program** Advanced placement, accelerated degree program, self-designed majors, honors program, adult/continuing education programs, internships **Contact** Mr. David Erdmann, Dean of Admissions and Student Financial Planning, Rollins College, 1000 Holt Avenue, Winter Park, FL 32789-4499. Telephone: 407-646-2161. Fax: 407-646-1502. E-mail: admission@rollins.edu. Web site: http://www.rollins.edu/.

ST. JOHN VIANNEY COLLEGE SEMINARY

MIAMI, FLORIDA

Contact Br. Edward Van Merrienboer, Academic Dean, St. John Vianney College Seminary, 2900 Southwest 87th Avenue, Miami, FL 33165-3244. Telephone: 305-223-4561 Ext. 13. E-mail: academic@sjvcs.edu.

SAINT LEO UNIVERSITY

SAINT LEO, FLORIDA

General Independent Roman Catholic, comprehensive, coed **Entrance** Moderately difficult **Setting** 170-acre rural campus **Total enrollment** 1,624 **Student/faculty ratio** 15:1 **Application deadline** 8/1 (freshmen), 8/1 (transfer) **Freshmen** 71% were admitted **Housing** Yes **Expenses** Tuition $12,090; Room & Board $6300 **Undergraduates** 57% women, 30% part-time, 56% 25 or older, 1% Native American, 8% Hispanic American, 7% African American, 1% Asian American/Pacific Islander **The most frequently chosen baccalaureate fields are** business/marketing, protective services/public administration, social sciences and history **Academic program** English as a second language, advanced placement, accelerated degree program, honors program, summer session, adult/continuing education programs, internships **Contact** Dr. Susan Hallenbeck, Director of Undergraduate Admission, Saint Leo University, MC 2008, PO Box 6665, Saint Leo, FL 33574-6665. Telephone: 352-588-8283 or toll-free 800-334-5532. Fax: 352-588-8257. E-mail: admissns@saintleo.edu. Web site: http://www.saintleo.edu/.

ST. THOMAS UNIVERSITY

MIAMI, FLORIDA

General Independent Roman Catholic, comprehensive, coed **Entrance** Moderately difficult **Setting** 140-acre suburban campus **Total enrollment** 2,231 **Student/faculty ratio** 13:1 **Application deadline** Rolling (freshmen), rolling (transfer) **Freshmen** 75% were admitted **Housing** Yes **Expenses** Tuition $19,850; Room & Board $4400 **Undergraduates** 55% women, 26% part-time, 36% 25 or older, 0.2% Native American, 52% Hispanic American, 19% African American, 1% Asian American/Pacific Islander **Academic program** English as a second language, advanced placement, honors program, summer session, adult/continuing education programs, internships **Contact** Mr. Andre Lightbourne, Associate Director of Admissions, St. Thomas University, 16400 Northwest 32nd Avenue, Miami, FL 33054-6459. Telephone: 305-628-6546 or toll-free 800-367-9006 (in-state); 800-367-9010 (out-of-state). Fax: 305-628-6591. E-mail: signup@stu.edu. Web site: http://www.stu.edu/.

SCHILLER INTERNATIONAL UNIVERSITY

DUNEDIN, FLORIDA

General Independent, comprehensive, coed **Entrance** Noncompetitive **Setting** suburban campus **Total enrollment** 243 **Application deadline** Rolling (freshmen), rolling (transfer) **Housing** Yes **Expenses** Tuition 13,790; Room & Board 5700 **Undergraduates** 13% 25 or older **Academic program** English as a second language, advanced placement, accelerated degree program, self-designed majors, summer session, adult/continuing education programs, internships **Contact** Markus Leibrecht, Director of Admissions, Schiller International University, 453 Edgewater Drive, Dunedin, FL 34698-7532. Telephone: 727-736-5082 or toll-free 800-336-4133. Fax: 727-734-0359. E-mail: admissions@schiller.edu. Web site: http://www.schiller.edu/.

SOUTHEASTERN COLLEGE OF THE ASSEMBLIES OF GOD

LAKELAND, FLORIDA

General Independent, 4-year, coed, affiliated with Assemblies of God **Entrance** Minimally difficult **Setting** 62-acre small-town campus **Total enrollment** 1,232 **Student/faculty ratio** 19:1 **Application deadline** 8/1 (freshmen), 8/1 (transfer) **Freshmen** 68% were admitted **Housing** Yes **Expenses** Tuition $6563; Room & Board $3850 **Undergraduates** 53% women, 4% part-time, 15% 25 or older, 1% Native American, 9% Hispanic American, 5% African American, 1% Asian American/Pacific Islander **The most frequently chosen baccalaureate fields are** education, philosophy, religion, and theology, psychology **Academic program** Advanced placement, accelerated degree program, summer session, internships **Contact** Ms. Rachel Bowen, Admission Secretary, Southeastern College of the Assemblies of God, 1000 Longfellow Boulevard, Lakeland, FL 33801-6099. Telephone: 863-667-5018 or toll-free 800-500-8760 (out-of-state). Fax: 941-667-5200. E-mail: rmshelto@secollege.edu. Web site: http://www.secollege.edu/.

STETSON UNIVERSITY

DELAND, FLORIDA

General Independent, comprehensive, coed **Entrance** Moderately difficult **Setting** 162-acre small-town campus **Total enrollment** 3,199 **Student/faculty ratio** 10:1 **Application deadline** 3/15 (freshmen), rolling (transfer) **Freshmen** 75% were admitted **Housing** Yes **Expenses** Tuition $19,310; Room & Board $6330 **Undergraduates** 57% women, 4% part-time, 7% 25 or older, 0.5% Native American, 5% Hispanic American, 4% African American, 2% Asian American/Pacific Islander **The most frequently chosen baccalaureate fields are** business/marketing, education, social sciences and history **Academic program** Advanced placement, accelerated degree program, self-designed majors, honors program, summer session, adult/continuing education programs, internships **Contact** Dean of Admissions, Stetson University, Unit 8378, DeLand, FL 32720-3781. Telephone: 386-822-7100 or toll-free 800-688-0101. Fax: 386-822-8832. E-mail: admissions@.stetson.edu. Web site: http://www.stetson.edu/.

TALMUDIC COLLEGE OF FLORIDA
MIAMI BEACH, FLORIDA

Contact Ira Hill, Administrator, FAL, Talmudic College of Florida, 4014 Chase Avenue, Miami Beach, FL 33139. Telephone: 305-534-7050.

TRINITY BAPTIST COLLEGE
JACKSONVILLE, FLORIDA

General Independent Baptist, 4-year, coed **Entrance** Moderately difficult **Setting** 148-acre urban campus **Total enrollment** 362 **Student/faculty ratio** 10:1 **Application deadline** Rolling (freshmen), rolling (transfer) **Freshmen** 83% were admitted **Housing** Yes **Expenses** Tuition $4290; Room & Board $3200 **Undergraduates** 46% women, 14% part-time, 29% 25 or older, 0% Native American, 1% Hispanic American, 4% African American, 2% Asian American/Pacific Islander **The most frequently chosen baccalaureate fields are** education, philosophy, religion, and theology **Academic program** Advanced placement, accelerated degree program, summer session, adult/continuing education programs, internships **Contact** Mr. Larry Appleby, Administrative Dean, Trinity Baptist College, 800 Hammond Boulevard, Jacksonville, FL 32221. Telephone: 904-596-2538 or toll-free 800-786-2206 (out-of-state). Fax: 904-596-2531. E-mail: trinity@tbc.edu. Web site: http://www.tbc.edu/.

TRINITY COLLEGE OF FLORIDA
NEW PORT RICHEY, FLORIDA

General Independent nondenominational, 4-year, coed **Entrance** Minimally difficult **Setting** 20-acre small-town campus **Total enrollment** 157 **Student/faculty ratio** 14:1 **Application deadline** Rolling (freshmen), rolling (transfer) **Freshmen** 77% were admitted **Housing** Yes **Expenses** Tuition $5048; Room & Board $2920 **Undergraduates** 47% women, 28% part-time, 50% 25 or older, 1% Native American, 4% Hispanic American, 6% African American, 3% Asian American/Pacific Islander **The most frequently chosen baccalaureate field is** philosophy, religion, and theology **Academic program** Advanced placement, summer session, adult/continuing education programs, internships **Contact** Mr. Paul Heier, Director of Admissions, Trinity College of Florida, 2430 Welbilt Boulevard, New Port Richey, FL 34655. Telephone: 727-376-6911 Ext. 1120 or toll-free 888-776-4999. Fax: 727-376-0781. E-mail: admissions@trinitycollege.edu. Web site: http://www.trinitycollege.edu/.

UNIVERSITY OF CENTRAL FLORIDA
ORLANDO, FLORIDA

General State-supported, university, coed **Entrance** Moderately difficult **Setting** 1,445-acre suburban campus **Total enrollment** 33,713 **Student/faculty ratio** 21:1 **Application deadline** 5/15 (freshmen), 5/15 (transfer) **Freshmen** 63% were admitted **Housing** Yes **Expenses** Tuition 2385; Room & Board 5436 **Undergraduates** 55% women, 28% part-time, 22% 25 or older, 1% Native American, 11% Hispanic American, 8% African American, 5% Asian American/Pacific Islander **The most frequently chosen baccalaureate fields are** business/marketing, education, health professions and related sciences **Academic program** English as a second language, advanced placement, accelerated degree program, honors program, summer session, adult/continuing education programs, internships **Contact** Undergraduate Admissions Office, University of Central Florida, PO Box 160111, Orlando, FL 32816. Telephone: 407-823-2000. Fax: 407-823-5625. E-mail: kcornett@pegasus.cc.ucf.edu. Web site: http://www.ucf.edu/.

UNIVERSITY OF FLORIDA
GAINESVILLE, FLORIDA

General State-supported, university, coed **Entrance** Very difficult **Setting** 2,000-acre suburban campus **Total enrollment** 45,114 **Student/faculty ratio** 20:1 **Application deadline** 1/16 (freshmen), 1/30 (transfer) **Freshmen** 62% were admitted **Housing** Yes **Expenses** Tuition $2256; Room & Board $5440 **Undergraduates** 53% women, 10% part-time, 6% 25 or older, 1% Native American, 11% Hispanic American, 8% African American, 7% Asian American/Pacific Islander **The most frequently chosen baccalaureate fields are** business/marketing, engineering/engineering technologies, social sciences and history **Academic program** English as a second language, advanced placement, accelerated degree program, self-designed majors, honors program, summer session, adult/continuing education programs, internships **Contact** Office of Admissions, University of Florida, PO Box 114000, Gainesville, FL 32611-4000. Telephone: 352-392-1365. E-mail: freshmen@ufl.edu. Web site: http://www.ufl.edu/.

UNIVERSITY OF MIAMI
CORAL GABLES, FLORIDA

General Independent, university, coed **Entrance** Moderately difficult **Setting** 260-acre suburban campus **Total enrollment** 13,963 **Student/faculty ratio** 13:1 **Application deadline** 3/1 (freshmen), 3/1 (transfer) **Freshmen** 53% were admitted **Housing** Yes **Expenses** Tuition 22,528; Room & Board 7934 **Undergraduates** 55% women, 9% part-time, 8% 25 or older, 0.3% Native American, 27% Hispanic American, 10% African American, 5% Asian American/Pacific Islander **The most frequently chosen baccalaureate fields are** business/marketing, health professions and related sciences, visual/performing arts **Academic program** English as a second lan-

University of Miami *(continued)*

guage, advanced placement, accelerated degree program, self-designed majors, honors program, summer session, adult/continuing education programs, internships **Contact** Mr. Edward M. Gillis, Associate Dean of Enrollment and Director of Admission, University of Miami, PO Box 248025, Ashe Building Room 132, 1252 Memorial Drive, Coral Gables, FL 33146-4616. Telephone: 305-284-4323. Fax: 305-284-2507. E-mail: admission@admiss.msmail.miami.edu. Web site: http://www.miami.edu/.

UNIVERSITY OF NORTH FLORIDA
JACKSONVILLE, FLORIDA

General State-supported, comprehensive, coed **Entrance** Very difficult **Setting** 1,300-acre urban campus **Total enrollment** 12,550 **Student/faculty ratio** 19:1 **Application deadline** 7/3 (freshmen), 7/2 (transfer) **Freshmen** 72% were admitted **Housing** Yes **Expenses** Tuition $1941; Room & Board $4990 **Undergraduates** 58% women, 38% part-time, 25% 25 or older, 0.4% Native American, 4% Hispanic American, 10% African American, 6% Asian American/Pacific Islander **The most frequently chosen baccalaureate fields are** business/marketing, education, health professions and related sciences **Academic program** Advanced placement, accelerated degree program, honors program, summer session, adult/continuing education programs, internships **Contact** Ms. Deborah M. Kaye, Executive Director of Enrollment Services, University of North Florida, 4567 St. Johns Bluff Road South, Jacksonville, FL 32224. Telephone: 904-620-2624. Fax: 904-620-2414. E-mail: osprey@unfivm.unf.edu. Web site: http://www.unf.edu/.

UNIVERSITY OF PHOENIX–FORT LAUDERDALE CAMPUS
PLANTATION, FLORIDA

General Proprietary, comprehensive, coed **Entrance** Noncompetitive **Total enrollment** 66,534 **Student/faculty ratio** 13:1 **Application deadline** Rolling (freshmen), rolling (transfer) **Expenses** Tuition $7740 **Undergraduates** 56% women, 86% 25 or older, 2% Native American, 18% Hispanic American, 13% African American, 6% Asian American/Pacific Islander **Academic program** Advanced placement, accelerated degree program, adult/continuing education programs **Contact** Ms. Beth Barilla, Director of Admissions, University of Phoenix–Fort Lauderdale Campus, 4615 East Elwood Street, Phoenix, AZ 85040-1948. Telephone: 480-927-0099 Ext. 1218 or toll-free 800-228-7240. Fax: 480-594-1758. E-mail: beth.barilla@apollogrp.edu. Web site: http://www.phoenix.edu/.

UNIVERSITY OF PHOENIX–JACKSONVILLE CAMPUS
JACKSONVILLE, FLORIDA

General Proprietary, comprehensive, coed **Entrance** Noncompetitive **Total enrollment** 66,534 **Student/faculty ratio** 13:1 **Application deadline** Rolling (freshmen), rolling (transfer) **Expenses** Tuition $7740 **Undergraduates** 56% women, 86% 25 or older, 2% Native American, 18% Hispanic American, 13% African American, 6% Asian American/Pacific Islander **Academic program** Advanced placement, accelerated degree program, adult/continuing education programs **Contact** Ms. Beth Barilla, Director of Admissions, University of Phoenix–Jacksonville Campus, 4615 East Elwood Street, Phoenix, AZ 85040-1948. Telephone: 480-927-0099 Ext. 1218 or toll-free 800-228-7240. Fax: 480-594-1758. E-mail: beth.barilla@apollogrp.edu. Web site: http://www.phoenix.edu/.

UNIVERSITY OF PHOENIX–ORLANDO CAMPUS
MAITLAND, FLORIDA

General Proprietary, comprehensive, coed **Entrance** Noncompetitive **Total enrollment** 66,534 **Student/faculty ratio** 13:1 **Application deadline** Rolling (freshmen), rolling (transfer) **Expenses** Tuition $7740 **Undergraduates** 56% women, 86% 25 or older, 2% Native American, 18% Hispanic American, 13% African American, 6% Asian American/Pacific Islander **Academic program** Advanced placement, accelerated degree program, adult/continuing education programs **Contact** Ms. Beth Barilla, Director of Admissions, University of Phoenix–Orlando Campus, 4615 East Elwood Street, Phoenix, AZ 85040-1948. Telephone: 480-927-0099 Ext. 1218 or toll-free 800-228-7240. Fax: 480-594-1758. E-mail: beth.barilla@apollogrp.edu. Web site: http://www.phoenix.edu/.

UNIVERSITY OF PHOENIX–TAMPA CAMPUS
TAMPA, FLORIDA

General Proprietary, comprehensive, coed **Entrance** Noncompetitive **Total enrollment** 66,534 **Student/faculty ratio** 13:1 **Application deadline** Rolling (freshmen), rolling (transfer) **Expenses** Tuition $7740 **Undergraduates** 56% women, 86% 25 or older, 2% Native American, 18% Hispanic American, 13% African American, 6% Asian American/Pacific Islander **Academic program** Advanced placement, accelerated degree program, adult/continuing education programs **Contact** Ms. Beth Barilla, Director of Admissions, University of Phoenix–Tampa Campus, 4615 East Elwood Street, Phoenix, AZ 85040-1948. Telephone: 480-927-0099 Ext. 1218 or toll-free 800-228-7240. Fax: 480-594-1758. E-mail: beth.barilla@apollogrp.edu. Web site: http://www.phoenix.edu/.

UNIVERSITY OF SARASOTA
SARASOTA, FLORIDA

Contact University of Sarasota, 5250 17th Street, Sarasota, FL 34235-8246. Web site: http://www.sarasota.edu/.

UNIVERSITY OF SOUTH FLORIDA
TAMPA, FLORIDA

General State-supported, university, coed **Entrance** Moderately difficult **Setting** 1,913-acre urban campus **Total enrollment** 35,561 **Student/faculty ratio** 18:1 **Freshmen** 58% were admitted **Housing** Yes **Expenses** Tuition $2388; Room & Board $4494 **Undergraduates** 59% women, 38% part-time, 30% 25 or older, 0.4% Native American, 10% Hispanic American, 11% African American, 6% Asian American/Pacific Islander **The most frequently chosen baccalaureate fields are** business/marketing, education, social sciences and history **Academic program** Advanced placement, accelerated degree program, self-designed majors, honors program, summer session, adult/continuing education programs, internships **Contact** Ms. Cecelia Leslie, Director of Admissions, University of South Florida, 4202 East Fowler Avenue, SVC 1036, Tampa, FL 33620-9951. Telephone: 813-974-3350. Fax: 813-974-9689. E-mail: bullseye@admin.usf.edu. Web site: http://www.usf.edu/.

UNIVERSITY OF SOUTH FLORIDA, NEW COLLEGE

See New College of the University of South Florida

THE UNIVERSITY OF TAMPA
TAMPA, FLORIDA

General Independent, comprehensive, coed **Entrance** Moderately difficult **Setting** 75-acre urban campus **Total enrollment** 3,560 **Student/faculty ratio** 16:1 **Application deadline** Rolling (freshmen), rolling (transfer) **Freshmen** 76% were admitted **Housing** Yes **Expenses** Tuition 16,102; Room & Board 5418 **Undergraduates** 61% women, 16% part-time, 21% 25 or older, 1% Native American, 9% Hispanic American, 7% African American, 2% Asian American/Pacific Islander **The most frequently chosen baccalaureate fields are** biological/life sciences, business/marketing, communications/communication technologies **Academic program** English as a second language, advanced placement, honors program, summer session, adult/continuing education programs, internships **Contact** Ms. Barbara P. Strickler, Vice President for Enrollment, The University of Tampa, 401 West Kennedy Boulevard, Tampa, FL 33606-1480. Telephone: 813-253-6211 or toll-free 800-733-4773. Fax: 813-254-4955. E-mail: bstrickler@alpha.utampa.edu. Web site: http://www.utampa.edu/.

UNIVERSITY OF WEST FLORIDA
PENSACOLA, FLORIDA

General State-supported, comprehensive, coed **Entrance** Moderately difficult **Setting** 1,600-acre suburban campus **Total enrollment** 8,479 **Student/faculty ratio** 20:1 **Application deadline** 6/30 (freshmen), 6/30 (transfer) **Freshmen** 82% were admitted **Housing** Yes **Expenses** Tuition $2398; Room & Board $4668 **Undergraduates** 58% women, 34% part-time, 36% 25 or older, 1% Native American, 4% Hispanic American, 9% African American, 5% Asian American/Pacific Islander **The most frequently chosen baccalaureate fields are** business/marketing, education, psychology **Academic program** English as a second language, advanced placement, honors program, summer session, internships **Contact** Ms. Susie Neeley, Director of Admissions, University of West Florida, 11000 University Parkway, Pensacola, FL 32514-5750. Telephone: 850-474-2230. E-mail: sneeley@uwf.edu. Web site: http://uwf.edu/.

WARNER SOUTHERN COLLEGE
LAKE WALES, FLORIDA

General Independent, 4-year, coed, affiliated with Church of God **Entrance** Minimally difficult **Setting** 320-acre rural campus **Total enrollment** 999 **Student/faculty ratio** 14:1 **Application deadline** Rolling (freshmen), rolling (transfer) **Freshmen** 54% were admitted **Housing** Yes **Expenses** Tuition $9480; Room & Board $4640 **Undergraduates** 59% women, 12% part-time, 55% 25 or older, 1% Native American, 7% Hispanic American, 15% African American, 0.2% Asian American/Pacific Islander **The most frequently chosen baccalaureate fields are** business/marketing, education, philosophy, religion, and theology **Academic program** Advanced placement, summer session, adult/continuing education programs, internships **Contact** Mr. Jason Roe, Director of Admissions, Warner Southern College, Warner Southern Center, Lake Wales, FL 33853. Telephone: 863-638-7212 Ext. 7213 or toll-free 800-949-7248 (in-state). Fax: 863-638-1472. E-mail: admissions@warner.edu. Web site: http://www.warner.edu/.

WEBBER COLLEGE
BABSON PARK, FLORIDA

General Independent, comprehensive, coed **Entrance** Moderately difficult **Setting** 110-acre small-town campus **Total enrollment** 457 **Student/faculty ratio** 20:1 **Application deadline** Rolling (freshmen), rolling (transfer) **Freshmen** 52% were admitted **Housing** Yes **Expenses** Tuition $10,300; Room & Board $3740 **Undergraduates** 50% women, 15% part-time, 24% 25 or older, 0% Native American, 6% Hispanic American, 6% African American, 1% Asian American/Pacific Islander **The most frequently chosen baccalaureate fields are** business/marketing, parks and recreation **Academic program** Advanced placement, accelerated degree program, summer session, adult/continuing education programs, internships **Contact** Dr. Deborah Milliken, Executive Vice President, Webber College, 1201 Scenic Highway, South, Babson Park, FL 33827-0096. Telephone: 941-638-2910 or toll-free 800-741-1844. Fax: 941-638-2823. E-mail: warriors@interserv.com. Web site: http://www.webber.edu/.

▶ **For more information, see page 487.**

GEORGIA

AGNES SCOTT COLLEGE
DECATUR, GEORGIA

General Independent, comprehensive, women only, affiliated with Presbyterian Church (U.S.A.) **Entrance**

Agnes Scott College *(continued)*

Very difficult **Setting** 100-acre urban campus **Total enrollment** 901 **Student/faculty ratio** 10:1 **Application deadline** 3/1 (freshmen), 3/1 (transfer) **Freshmen** 72% were admitted **Housing** Yes **Expenses** Tuition 16,745; Room & Board 6900 **Undergraduates** 5% part-time, 7% 25 or older, 0.1% Native American, 4% Hispanic American, 20% African American, 5% Asian American/Pacific Islander **The most frequently chosen baccalaureate fields are** biological/life sciences, English, social sciences and history **Academic program** Advanced placement, accelerated degree program, self-designed majors, summer session, adult/continuing education programs, internships **Contact** Ms. Stephanie Balmer, Associate Vice President for Enrollment and Director of Admission, Agnes Scott College, 141 East College Avenue, Atlanta/Decatur, GA 30030-3797. Telephone: 404-471-6285 or toll-free 800-868-8602. Fax: 404-471-6414. E-mail: admission@asc.agnesscott.edu. Web site: http://www.agnesscott.edu/.

ALBANY STATE UNIVERSITY
ALBANY, GEORGIA

General State-supported, comprehensive, coed **Entrance** Minimally difficult **Setting** 144-acre urban campus **Total enrollment** 3,525 **Student/faculty ratio** 20:1 **Application deadline** 7/15 (freshmen), 7/15 (transfer) **Freshmen** 29% were admitted **Housing** Yes **Undergraduates** 67% women, 18% part-time, 0.1% Native American, 0.4% Hispanic American, 95% African American, 0.1% Asian American/ Pacific Islander **The most frequently chosen baccalaureate fields are** health professions and related sciences, protective services/public administration, social sciences and history **Academic program** Advanced placement, honors program, summer session, adult/continuing education programs, internships **Contact** Mrs. Patricia Price, Director of Recruitment Admissions, Albany State University, 504 College Drive, Albany, GA 31705. Telephone: 229-430-4645 or toll-free 800-822-RAMS (in-state). Fax: 229-430-3936. Web site: http://asuweb.asurams.edu/asu/.

THE AMERICAN COLLEGE
See American InterContinental University

AMERICAN INTERCONTINENTAL UNIVERSITY
ATLANTA, GEORGIA

General Proprietary, 4-year, coed **Entrance** Noncompetitive **Setting** urban campus **Total enrollment** 860 **Student/faculty ratio** 13:1 **Application deadline** 10/15 (freshmen), rolling (transfer) **Housing** Yes **Expenses** Tuition $12,600; Room only $4605 **Undergraduates** 60% women, 40% part-time, 33% 25 or older, 0% Native American, 4% Hispanic American, 41% African American, 5% Asian American/Pacific Islander **Academic program** English as a second language, accelerated degree program, summer session, adult/continuing education programs, internships **Contact** Ms. Janice Davidson, Director of Admissions, American InterContinental University, 3330 Peachtree Road, NE, Atlanta, GA 30326-1016. Telephone: 404-965-5700 or toll-free 888-999-4248 (out-of-state). Fax: 404-965-5701. E-mail: acatl@ix.netcom.com. Web site: http://www.aiuniv.edu/.

AMERICAN INTERCONTINENTAL UNIVERSITY
ATLANTA, GEORGIA

General Proprietary, comprehensive, coed **Total enrollment** 450 **Student/faculty ratio** 20:1 **Housing** No **Undergraduates** 42% women, 17% part-time, 92% 25 or older, 0% Native American, 2% Hispanic American, 42% African American, 4% Asian American/ Pacific Islander **Contact** Mr. Jeff Bostick, Director of Admissions, American InterContinental University, 6600 Peachtree-Dunwoody Road, 500 Embassy Row, Atlanta, GA 30328. Telephone: 404-965-8050 or toll-free 800-255-6839. Web site: http://www.aiuniv.edu/.

ARMSTRONG ATLANTIC STATE UNIVERSITY
SAVANNAH, GEORGIA

General State-supported, comprehensive, coed **Entrance** Minimally difficult **Setting** 250-acre suburban campus **Total enrollment** 5,496 **Student/faculty ratio** 15:1 **Application deadline** 7/1 (freshmen), 7/1 (transfer) **Housing** Yes **Expenses** Tuition $2242; Room & Board $4582 **Undergraduates** 69% women, 43% part-time, 21% 25 or older, 0.4% Native American, 3% Hispanic American, 21% African American, 3% Asian American/Pacific Islander **The most frequently chosen baccalaureate fields are** education, health professions and related sciences, liberal arts/general studies **Academic program** Advanced placement, honors program, summer session, adult/continuing education programs, internships **Contact** Ms. Melanie Mirande, Assistant Director of Recruitment, Armstrong Atlantic State University, 11935 Abercorn Street, Savannah, GA 31419. Telephone: 912-925-5275 or toll-free 800-633-2349. Fax: 912-921-5462. E-mail: cynthia_buskey@mailgate.armstrong.edu. Web site: http://www.armstrong.edu/.

ATLANTA CHRISTIAN COLLEGE
EAST POINT, GEORGIA

General Independent Christian, 4-year, coed **Entrance** Moderately difficult **Setting** 52-acre suburban campus **Total enrollment** 385 **Student/faculty ratio** 16:1 **Application deadline** Rolling (freshmen), rolling (transfer) **Freshmen** 73% were admitted **Housing** Yes **Expenses** Tuition $9648; Room & Board $3790 **Undergraduates** 51% women, 17% part-time, 30% 25 or older, 1% Hispanic American, 18% African American, 1% Asian American/Pacific Islander **Academic program** Advanced placement, summer session, internships **Contact** Mr. Keith Wagner, Director of Admissions, Atlanta Christian College, 2605

Ben Hill Road, East Point, GA 30344-1999. Telephone: 404-761-8861 or toll-free 800-776-1ACC. Fax: 404-669-2024. E-mail: chargers777@juno.com. Web site: http://www.acc.edu/.

ATLANTA COLLEGE OF ART
ATLANTA, GEORGIA

General Independent, 4-year, coed **Entrance** Moderately difficult **Setting** 6-acre urban campus **Total enrollment** 379 **Student/faculty ratio** 12:1 **Application deadline** Rolling (freshmen), rolling (transfer) **Freshmen** 62% were admitted **Housing** Yes **Expenses** Tuition $15,000; Room only $4400 **Undergraduates** 16% 25 or older, 63% Native American, 3% Hispanic American, 21% African American, 5% Asian American/Pacific Islander **The most frequently chosen baccalaureate field is** visual/performing arts **Academic program** Advanced placement, self-designed majors, summer session, internships **Contact** Ms. Lucy Leusch, Vice President of Enrollment Management, Atlanta College of Art, 1280 Peachtree Street, NE, Atlanta, GA 30309-3582. Telephone: 404-733-5101 or toll-free 800-832-2104. Fax: 404-733-5107. E-mail: acainfo@woodruff-arts.org. Web site: http://www.aca.edu/.

▶ **For more information, see page 386.**

AUGUSTA STATE UNIVERSITY
AUGUSTA, GEORGIA

General State-supported, comprehensive, coed **Entrance** Minimally difficult **Setting** 72-acre urban campus **Total enrollment** 5,070 **Student/faculty ratio** 17:1 **Application deadline** 7/21 (freshmen), rolling (transfer) **Freshmen** 72% were admitted **Housing** No **Expenses** Tuition $2222 **Undergraduates** 63% women, 38% part-time, 31% 25 or older, 0.4% Native American, 2% Hispanic American, 24% African American, 3% Asian American/Pacific Islander **The most frequently chosen baccalaureate fields are** business/marketing, education, social sciences and history **Academic program** English as a second language, advanced placement, honors program, summer session, adult/continuing education programs, internships **Contact** Catherine R. Tuthill, Augusta State University, 2500 Walton Way, Augusta, GA 30904-2200. Telephone: 706-737-1400. Fax: 706-667-4355. E-mail: admissions@ac.edu. Web site: http://www.aug.edu/.

BEACON COLLEGE
COLUMBUS, GEORGIA

General Independent religious, comprehensive, coed **Total enrollment** 57 **Student/faculty ratio** 5:1 **Application deadline** 9/1 (freshmen), 9/1 (transfer) **Freshmen** 96% were admitted **Housing** No **Expenses** Tuition $2855 **Undergraduates** 39% women, 56% part-time, 53% 25 or older, 4% Hispanic American, 32% African American **The most frequently chosen baccalaureate field is** philosophy, religion, and theology **Academic program** Advanced placement, accelerated degree program, summer session, adult/continuing education programs **Contact** Ms. Donna M. Smith, Director of Admissions and Student Records, Beacon College, 6003 Veterans Parkway, Columbus, GA 31909. Telephone: 706-323-5364 Ext. 201. Fax: 706-323-5891. E-mail: registrar@beacon.edu. Web site: http://www.beacon.edu/.

BERRY COLLEGE
MOUNT BERRY, GEORGIA

General Independent interdenominational, comprehensive, coed **Entrance** Moderately difficult **Setting** 28,000-acre small-town campus **Total enrollment** 2,033 **Student/faculty ratio** 12:1 **Application deadline** 7/28 (freshmen), 7/28 (transfer) **Freshmen** 79% were admitted **Housing** Yes **Expenses** Tuition 12,500; Room & Board 5488 **Undergraduates** 4% 25 or older **Academic program** Advanced placement, accelerated degree program, self-designed majors, honors program, summer session, adult/continuing education programs, internships **Contact** Mr. George Gaddie, Dean of Admissions, Berry College, PO Box 490159, Mount Berry, GA 30149-0159. Telephone: 706-236-2215 or toll-free 800-237-7942. Fax: 706-290-2178. E-mail: admissions@berry.edu. Web site: http://www.berry.edu/.

BEULAH HEIGHTS BIBLE COLLEGE
ATLANTA, GEORGIA

General Independent Pentecostal, 4-year, coed **Entrance** Noncompetitive **Setting** 10-acre urban campus **Total enrollment** 585 **Student/faculty ratio** 17:1 **Application deadline** Rolling (freshmen), rolling (transfer) **Freshmen** 90% were admitted **Housing** Yes **Expenses** Tuition $3680; Room only $1500 **Undergraduates** 90% 25 or older, 0% Native American, 0.2% Hispanic American, 75% African American, 0.3% Asian American/Pacific Islander **The most frequently chosen baccalaureate field is** philosophy, religion, and theology **Academic program** Advanced placement, accelerated degree program, summer session, adult/continuing education programs, internships **Contact** Ms. Dama Riles, Director of Admissions, Beulah Heights Bible College, 892 Berne Street, SE, PO Box 18145, Atlanta, GA 30316. Telephone: 404-627-2681 Ext. 114 or toll-free 888-777-BHBC. Fax: 404-627-0702. E-mail: cjkjr@aol.com. Web site: http://www.beulah.org/.

BRENAU UNIVERSITY
GAINESVILLE, GEORGIA

General Independent, comprehensive, women only **Entrance** Moderately difficult **Setting** 57-acre small-town campus **Total enrollment** 644 **Student/faculty ratio** 7:1 **Application deadline** Rolling (freshmen), rolling (transfer) **Freshmen** 85% were admitted **Housing** Yes **Expenses** Tuition 12,180; Room & Board 7170 **Undergraduates** 11% part-time, 17% 25 or older, 0.5% Native American, 2% Hispanic American, 11% African American, 2% Asian American/Pacific Islander **The most frequently chosen baccalaureate fields are** education, business/marketing,

Brenau University *(continued)*

health professions and related sciences **Academic program** Advanced placement, honors program, summer session, internships **Contact** Ms. Christina Cochran, Coordinator of Women's College Admissions, Brenau University, Admissions, 1 Centennial Circle, Gainesville, GA 30501. Telephone: 770-534-6100 or toll-free 800-252-5119 (out-of-state). Fax: 770-538-4306. E-mail: wcadmissions@lib.brenau.edu. Web site: http://www.brenau.edu/.

BREWTON-PARKER COLLEGE
MT. VERNON, GEORGIA

Contact Mr. James E. Beall, Director of Admissions, Brewton-Parker College, Highway 280, Mt. Vernon, GA 30445-0197. Telephone: 912-583-3268 Ext. 268 or toll-free 800-342-1087. Fax: 912-583-4498. Web site: http://www.bpc.edu/.

CLARK ATLANTA UNIVERSITY
ATLANTA, GEORGIA

General Independent United Methodist, university, coed **Entrance** Moderately difficult **Setting** 113-acre urban campus **Total enrollment** 5,010 **Application deadline** 3/1 (freshmen), 3/1 (transfer) **Freshmen** 72% were admitted **Housing** Yes **Expenses** Tuition $11,120; Room & Board $5974 **Undergraduates** 72% women, 4% part-time, 6% 25 or older, 0% Native American, 0% Hispanic American, 99% African American, 0.02% Asian American/Pacific Islander **Academic program** English as a second language, advanced placement, accelerated degree program, honors program, summer session, adult/continuing education programs, internships **Contact** Office of Admissions, Clark Atlanta University, 223 James P. Brawley Drive, SW, Atlanta, GA 30314. Telephone: 404-880-8784 Ext. 6650 or toll-free 800-688-3228. Fax: 404-880-6174. Web site: http://www.cau.edu/.

CLAYTON COLLEGE & STATE UNIVERSITY
MORROW, GEORGIA

General State-supported, 4-year, coed **Entrance** Minimally difficult **Setting** 163-acre suburban campus **Total enrollment** 4,455 **Student/faculty ratio** 14:1 **Application deadline** 7/17 (freshmen) **Freshmen** 61% were admitted **Housing** No **Expenses** Tuition $2770 **Undergraduates** 64% women, 57% part-time, 51% 25 or older, 1% Native American, 2% Hispanic American, 37% African American, 3% Asian American/Pacific Islander **The most frequently chosen baccalaureate fields are** business/marketing, education, health professions and related sciences **Academic program** Advanced placement, self-designed majors, honors program, summer session, adult/continuing education programs, internships **Contact** Ms. Carol S. Montgomery, Admissions, Clayton College & State University, 5900 North Lee Street, Morrow, GA 30260-0285. Telephone: 770-961-3500. Fax: 770-961-3752. E-mail: csc-info@ce.clayton.peachnet.edu. Web site: http://www.clayton.edu/.

COLUMBUS STATE UNIVERSITY
COLUMBUS, GEORGIA

General State-supported, comprehensive, coed **Entrance** Minimally difficult **Setting** 132-acre suburban campus **Total enrollment** 5,191 **Student/faculty ratio** 18:1 **Application deadline** 8/2 (freshmen), 8/2 (transfer) **Freshmen** 69% were admitted **Housing** Yes **Expenses** Tuition $3040; Room & Board $4560 **Undergraduates** 62% women, 36% part-time, 30% 25 or older, 1% Native American, 3% Hispanic American, 27% African American, 2% Asian American/Pacific Islander **The most frequently chosen baccalaureate fields are** business/marketing, education, protective services/public administration **Academic program** Advanced placement, honors program, summer session, adult/continuing education programs, internships **Contact** Ms. Susan Lovell, Admission Counselor, Columbus State University, 4225 University Avenue, Columbus, GA 31907-5645. Telephone: 706-568-2035. Fax: 706-568-2462. Web site: http://www.colstate.edu/.

COVENANT COLLEGE
LOOKOUT MOUNTAIN, GEORGIA

General Independent, comprehensive, coed, affiliated with Presbyterian Church in America **Entrance** Moderately difficult **Setting** 250-acre suburban campus **Total enrollment** 1,158 **Student/faculty ratio** 14:1 **Application deadline** Rolling (freshmen), rolling (transfer) **Freshmen** 98% were admitted **Housing** Yes **Expenses** Tuition $17,070; Room & Board $5000 **Undergraduates** 58% women, 3% part-time, 0.4% Native American, 2% Hispanic American, 4% African American, 1% Asian American/Pacific Islander **The most frequently chosen baccalaureate fields are** business/marketing, education, social sciences and history **Academic program** Advanced placement, self-designed majors, summer session, adult/continuing education programs, internships **Contact** Ms. Leda Goodman, Regional Director, Covenant College, 14049 Scenic Highway, Lookout Mountain, GA 30750. Telephone: 706-820-1560 Ext. 1644 or toll-free 888-451-2683 (in-state). Fax: 706-820-0893. E-mail: admissions@covenant.edu. Web site: http://www.covenant.edu/.

DALTON STATE COLLEGE
DALTON, GEORGIA

General State-supported, 4-year, coed **Entrance** Noncompetitive **Setting** 141-acre small-town campus **Total enrollment** 3,139 **Student/faculty ratio** 25:1 **Application deadline** Rolling (freshmen), rolling (transfer) **Freshmen** 67% were admitted **Housing** No **Expenses** Tuition $1508 **Undergraduates** 39% 25 or older, 0.3% Native American, 3% Hispanic American, 2% African American, 1% Asian American/Pacific Islander **Academic program** English as a second language, advanced placement, summer session, adult/continuing education programs, internships **Contact** Dr. Angela Harris, Assistant Director of Admissions, Dalton State College, 213 North

College Drive, Dalton, GA 30720-3797. Telephone: 706-272-4476 or toll-free 800-829-4436. Fax: 706-272-2530. E-mail: aharris@em.daltonstate.edu. Web site: http://www.daltonstate.edu/.

DEVRY INSTITUTE OF TECHNOLOGY
ALPHARETTA, GEORGIA

General Proprietary, 4-year, coed **Entrance** Minimally difficult **Setting** 9-acre suburban campus **Total enrollment** 1,513 **Student/faculty ratio** 22:1 **Application deadline** Rolling (freshmen), rolling (transfer) **Freshmen** 62% were admitted **Housing** No **Expenses** Tuition $8805 **Undergraduates** 32% women, 28% part-time, 54% 25 or older, 0.4% Native American, 2% Hispanic American, 31% African American, 5% Asian American/Pacific Islander **The most frequently chosen baccalaureate fields are** business/marketing, computer/information sciences **Academic program** Advanced placement, accelerated degree program, summer session, adult/continuing education programs **Contact** Mr. Gerry Purcell, Director of Admissions, DeVry Institute of Technology, 2555 Northwinds Parkway, Alpharetta, GA 30004. Telephone: 770-664-9520. Fax: 770-664-8824. Web site: http://www.atl.devry.edu/alpharetta/.

DEVRY INSTITUTE OF TECHNOLOGY
DECATUR, GEORGIA

General Proprietary, 4-year, coed **Entrance** Minimally difficult **Setting** 21-acre suburban campus **Total enrollment** 2,916 **Student/faculty ratio** 24:1 **Application deadline** Rolling (freshmen), rolling (transfer) **Freshmen** 51% were admitted **Housing** No **Expenses** Tuition $8805 **Undergraduates** 42% women, 24% part-time, 48% 25 or older, 0.2% Native American, 1% Hispanic American, 77% African American, 2% Asian American/Pacific Islander **The most frequently chosen baccalaureate fields are** business/marketing, computer/information sciences, engineering/engineering technologies **Academic program** Advanced placement, accelerated degree program, summer session, adult/continuing education programs **Contact** George Ollennu, Director of Admissions, DeVry Institute of Technology, 250 North Arcadia Avenue, Decatur, GA 30030. Telephone: 404-292-2645 Ext. 430 or toll-free 800-221-4771 (out-of-state). E-mail: dwalters@admin.atl.devry.edu. Web site: http://www.atl.devry.edu/.

EMMANUEL COLLEGE
FRANKLIN SPRINGS, GEORGIA

General Independent, 4-year, coed, affiliated with Pentecostal Holiness Church **Entrance** Minimally difficult **Setting** 90-acre rural campus **Total enrollment** 782 **Student/faculty ratio** 14:1 **Application deadline** 8/1 (freshmen), 8/1 (transfer) **Freshmen** 51% were admitted **Housing** Yes **Expenses** Tuition $7861; Room & Board $3776 **Undergraduates** 55% women, 9% part-time, 10% 25 or older, 0.1% Native American, 1% Hispanic American, 13% African American, 1% Asian American/Pacific Islander **The most frequently chosen baccalaureate fields are** business/marketing, education, philosophy, religion, and theology **Academic program** English as a second language, advanced placement, summer session, internships **Contact** Mr. Barry Wood, Director of Admissions, Emmanuel College, PO Box 129, 181 Spring Street, Franklin Springs, GA 30639-0129. Telephone: 706-245-7226 Ext. 2871 or toll-free 800-860-8800 (in-state). Fax: 706-245-4424. E-mail: admissions@emmanuel-college.edu. Web site: http://www.emmanuel-college.edu/.

EMORY UNIVERSITY
ATLANTA, GEORGIA

General Independent Methodist, university, coed **Entrance** Most difficult **Setting** 631-acre suburban campus **Total enrollment** 11,294 **Student/faculty ratio** 7:1 **Application deadline** 1/15 (freshmen), 6/1 (transfer) **Freshmen** 45% were admitted **Housing** Yes **Expenses** Tuition $24,532; Room & Board $7868 **Undergraduates** 55% women, 3% part-time, 0% 25 or older, 0.2% Native American, 3% Hispanic American, 10% African American, 15% Asian American/Pacific Islander **The most frequently chosen baccalaureate fields are** business/marketing, biological/life sciences, psychology **Academic program** Advanced placement, accelerated degree program, honors program, summer session, internships **Contact** Mr. Daniel C. Walls, Dean of Admission, Emory University, Boisfeuillet Jones Center–Office of Admissions, Atlanta, GA 30322-1100. Telephone: 404-727-6036 or toll-free 800-727-6036. E-mail: admiss@unix.cc.emory.edu. Web site: http://www.emory.edu/.

FORT VALLEY STATE UNIVERSITY
FORT VALLEY, GEORGIA

General State-supported, comprehensive, coed **Entrance** Moderately difficult **Setting** 1,307-acre small-town campus **Total enrollment** 2,561 **Student/faculty ratio** 19:1 **Application deadline** 8/1 (freshmen), 8/1 (transfer) **Freshmen** 49% were admitted **Housing** Yes **Expenses** Tuition $1742; Room & Board $1801 **Undergraduates** 57% women, 12% part-time, 0.05% Native American, 1% Hispanic American, 94% African American, 0.2% Asian American/Pacific Islander **The most frequently chosen baccalaureate fields are** business/marketing, biological/life sciences, education **Academic program** Advanced placement, honors program, summer session, adult/continuing education programs, internships **Contact** Mrs. Debra McGhee, Admissions Coordinator, Fort Valley State University, 1005 State University Drive, Fort Valley, GA 31030. Telephone: 912-825-6307 or toll-free 800-248-7343. Fax: 912-825-6169. E-mail: admissap@mail.fusu.edu. Web site: http://www.fvsu.edu/.

GEORGIA BAPTIST COLLEGE OF NURSING OF MERCER UNIVERSITY
ATLANTA, GEORGIA

General Independent Baptist, 4-year, coed, primarily women **Entrance** Moderately difficult **Setting** 20-acre

Georgia Baptist College of Nursing of Mercer University *(continued)*

urban campus **Total enrollment** 312 **Student/faculty ratio** 9:1 **Application deadline** 5/15 (freshmen), 5/15 (transfer) **Freshmen** 46% were admitted **Housing** Yes **Expenses** Tuition $10,589; Room only $940 **Undergraduates** 97% women, 20% part-time, 32% 25 or older, 0.4% Native American, 3% Hispanic American, 27% African American, 2% Asian American/Pacific Islander **The most frequently chosen baccalaureate field is** health professions and related sciences **Academic program** Advanced placement, summer session **Contact** Ms. Kim W. Hays, Associate Director of Admissions, Georgia Baptist College of Nursing of Mercer University, 274 Boulevard, NE, Atlanta, GA 30312. Telephone: 673-547-6702 or toll-free 800-551-8835. Fax: 673-547-6811. E-mail: gbcnadm@mindspring.com. Web site: http://www.nursing.mercer.edu/.

GEORGIA COLLEGE AND STATE UNIVERSITY

MILLEDGEVILLE, GEORGIA

General State-supported, comprehensive, coed **Entrance** Moderately difficult **Setting** 666-acre small-town campus **Total enrollment** 5,076 **Student/faculty ratio** 15:1 **Application deadline** 7/15 (freshmen), 7/15 (transfer) **Freshmen** 74% were admitted **Housing** Yes **Expenses** Tuition $2358; Room & Board $4312 **Undergraduates** 62% women, 22% part-time, 17% 25 or older, 0.1% Native American, 1% Hispanic American, 14% African American, 1% Asian American/Pacific Islander **The most frequently chosen baccalaureate fields are** business/marketing, education, health professions and related sciences **Academic program** Advanced placement, accelerated degree program, self-designed majors, honors program, summer session, internships **Contact** Ms. Maryllis Wolfgang, Director of Admissions, Georgia College and State University, CPO Box 023, Milledgeville, GA 31061. Telephone: 912-445-6285 or toll-free 800-342-0471 (in-state). Fax: 912-445-1914. E-mail: gcsu@mail.gac.peachnet.edu. Web site: http://www.gcsu.edu/.

GEORGIA INSTITUTE OF TECHNOLOGY

ATLANTA, GEORGIA

General State-supported, university, coed **Entrance** Very difficult **Setting** 360-acre urban campus **Total enrollment** 14,804 **Student/faculty ratio** 15:1 **Application deadline** 1/15 (freshmen), 5/1 (transfer) **Freshmen** 57% were admitted **Housing** Yes **Expenses** Tuition 3308; Room & Board 5234 **Undergraduates** 29% women, 8% part-time, 5% 25 or older, 0.2% Native American, 3% Hispanic American, 8% African American, 13% Asian American/Pacific Islander **The most frequently chosen baccalaureate fields are** business/marketing, computer/information sciences, engineering/engineering technologies **Academic program** English as a second language, advanced placement, accelerated degree program, self-designed majors, honors program, summer session, internships **Contact** Ms. Deborah Smith, Director of Admissions, Georgia Institute of Technology, 225 North Avenue, NW, Atlanta, GA 30332-0320. Telephone: 404-894-4154. Fax: 404-894-9511. E-mail: admissions@success.gatech.edu. Web site: http://www.gatech.edu/.

GEORGIA SOUTHERN UNIVERSITY

STATESBORO, GEORGIA

General State-supported, comprehensive, coed **Entrance** Moderately difficult **Setting** 601-acre small-town campus **Total enrollment** 14,184 **Student/faculty ratio** 19:1 **Application deadline** 7/1 (freshmen), rolling (transfer) **Freshmen** 79% were admitted **Housing** Yes **Expenses** Tuition $2500; Room & Board $4154 **Undergraduates** 53% women, 10% part-time, 7% 25 or older **The most frequently chosen baccalaureate fields are** business/marketing, education, parks and recreation **Academic program** English as a second language, advanced placement, self-designed majors, honors program, summer session, adult/continuing education programs, internships **Contact** Dr. Irene Prue, Assistant Director of Admissions, Georgia Southern University, GSU PO Box 8024, Statesboro, GA 30460. Telephone: 912-681-5977. Fax: 912-681-5635. E-mail: admissions@gasou.edu. Web site: http://www.gasou.edu/.

GEORGIA SOUTHWESTERN STATE UNIVERSITY

AMERICUS, GEORGIA

General State-supported, comprehensive, coed **Entrance** Moderately difficult **Setting** 255-acre small-town campus **Total enrollment** 2,622 **Student/faculty ratio** 16:1 **Application deadline** Rolling (freshmen), rolling (transfer) **Freshmen** 65% were admitted **Housing** Yes **Expenses** Tuition 2398; Room & Board 3690 **Undergraduates** 64% women, 27% part-time, 5% 25 or older, 0.2% Native American, 1% Hispanic American, 28% African American, 1% Asian American/Pacific Islander **The most frequently chosen baccalaureate fields are** business/marketing, education, social sciences and history **Academic program** English as a second language, advanced placement, honors program, summer session, adult/continuing education programs, internships **Contact** Mr. Gary Fallis, Director of Admissions, Georgia Southwestern State University, 800 Wheatley Street, Americus, GA 31709-4693. Telephone: 229-928-1273 or toll-free 800-338-0082. Fax: 229-931-2983. E-mail: gswadm@gsw1500.gsw.peachnet.edu. Web site: http://www.gsw.edu/.

GEORGIA STATE UNIVERSITY

ATLANTA, GEORGIA

General State-supported, university, coed **Entrance** Moderately difficult **Setting** 24-acre urban campus **Total enrollment** 23,619 **Student/faculty ratio** 15:1 **Application deadline** 5/1 (freshmen), 6/1 (transfer) **Freshmen** 59% were admitted **Housing** Yes **Expenses** Tuition 3132; Room only 4190 **Undergraduates**

62% women, 40% part-time, 21% 25 or older, 0.3% Native American, 0.1% Hispanic American, 33% African American, 8% Asian American/Pacific Islander **The most frequently chosen baccalaureate fields are** business/marketing, computer/information sciences, social sciences and history **Academic program** English as a second language, self-designed majors, honors program, summer session, adult/continuing education programs, internships **Contact** Mr. Rob Sheinkopf, Dean of Admissions and Acting Dean for Enrollment Services, Georgia State University, PO Box 4009, Atlanta, GA 30302-4009. Telephone: 404-651-2365 or toll-free 404-651-2365 (in-state). Fax: 404-651-4811. Web site: http://www.gsu.edu/.

KENNESAW STATE UNIVERSITY
KENNESAW, GEORGIA

General State-supported, comprehensive, coed **Entrance** Moderately difficult **Setting** 185-acre suburban campus **Total enrollment** 13,392 **Student/faculty ratio** 24:1 **Application deadline** 7/21 (freshmen), 7/21 (transfer) **Freshmen** 73% were admitted **Housing** No **Expenses** Tuition $2306 **Undergraduates** 45% 25 or older, 0.3% Native American, 3% Hispanic American, 10% African American, 3% Asian American/Pacific Islander **The most frequently chosen baccalaureate fields are** business/marketing, education, health professions and related sciences **Academic program** English as a second language, advanced placement, honors program, summer session, adult/continuing education programs, internships **Contact** Mr. Joe F. Head, Director of Admissions and Dean of Enrollment Services, Kennesaw State University, 1000 Chastain Road, Kennesaw, GA 30144. Telephone: 770-423-6300. Fax: 770-420-4435. E-mail: ksuadmit@ksumail.kennesaw.edu. Web site: http://www.kennesaw.edu/.

LAGRANGE COLLEGE
LAGRANGE, GEORGIA

General Independent United Methodist, comprehensive, coed **Entrance** Moderately difficult **Setting** 120-acre small-town campus **Total enrollment** 916 **Student/faculty ratio** 12:1 **Application deadline** 8/15 (freshmen), 8/15 (transfer) **Freshmen** 83% were admitted **Housing** Yes **Expenses** Tuition 11,660; Room & Board 4846 **Undergraduates** 64% women, 14% part-time, 13% 25 or older, 0.3% Native American, 1% Hispanic American, 15% African American, 1% Asian American/Pacific Islander **The most frequently chosen baccalaureate fields are** business/marketing, education, protective services/public administration **Academic program** English as a second language, advanced placement, summer session, adult/continuing education programs, internships **Contact** Mr. Andy Geeter, Director of Admission, LaGrange College, 601 Broad Street, LaGrange, GA 30240-2999. Telephone: 706-880-8253 or toll-free 800-593-2885. Fax: 706-880-8010. E-mail: p.dodson@mentor.lgc.peachnet.edu. Web site: http://www.lgc.edu/.

► **For more information, see page 437.**

LIFE UNIVERSITY
MARIETTA, GEORGIA

Contact Office of Admissions, Life University, 1269 Barclay Circle, Marietta, GA 30060-2903. Telephone: 800-543-3202. Web site: http://www.life.edu/.

LUTHER RICE BIBLE COLLEGE AND SEMINARY
LITHONIA, GEORGIA

General Independent Baptist, comprehensive, coed **Entrance** Noncompetitive **Setting** 5-acre urban campus **Total enrollment** 1,300 **Application deadline** Rolling (freshmen), rolling (transfer) **Housing** No **Expenses** Tuition $2592 **Undergraduates** 88% 25 or older **Academic program** Adult/continuing education programs **Contact** Dr. Dennis Dieringer, Director of Admissions and Records, Luther Rice Bible College and Seminary, 3038 Evans Mill Road, Lithonia, GA 30038-2454. Telephone: 770-484-1204 or toll-free 800-442-1577. E-mail: 70420.1270@compuserve.com. Web site: http://www.lrs.edu/.

MACON STATE COLLEGE
MACON, GEORGIA

General State-supported, 4-year, coed **Entrance** Minimally difficult **Setting** 167-acre urban campus **Total enrollment** 4,118 **Student/faculty ratio** 17:1 **Application deadline** Rolling (freshmen), rolling (transfer) **Housing** No **Expenses** Tuition 1438 **Undergraduates** 66% women, 63% part-time, 49% 25 or older **Academic program** Advanced placement, honors program, summer session, adult/continuing education programs, internships **Contact** Mr. Terrell Mitchell, Director of Admissions, Macon State College, 100 College Station Drive, Macon, GA 31206. Telephone: 912-471-2800 Ext. 2854 or toll-free 800-272-7619. E-mail: mcinfo@cennet.mc.peachnet.edu. Web site: http://www.maconstate.edu/.

MEDICAL COLLEGE OF GEORGIA
AUGUSTA, GEORGIA

General State-supported, upper-level, coed **Entrance** Moderately difficult **Setting** 100-acre urban campus **Total enrollment** 1,930 **Application deadline** Rolling (transfer) **Housing** Yes **Expenses** Tuition 2974; Room only 1302 **Undergraduates** 86% women, 8% part-time, 36% 25 or older, 0.3% Native American, 1% Hispanic American, 14% African American, 4% Asian American/Pacific Islander **The most frequently chosen baccalaureate field is** health professions and related sciences **Academic program** Summer session **Contact** Ms. Carol S. Nobles, Director of Student Recruitment and Admissions, Medical College of Georgia, AA-170 Administration-Kelly Building, Augusta, GA 30912. Telephone: 706-721-2725. Fax: 706-721-7279. E-mail: underadm@mail.mcg.edu. Web site: http://www.mcg.edu/.

MERCER UNIVERSITY
MACON, GEORGIA

General Independent Baptist, comprehensive, coed **Entrance** Moderately difficult **Setting** 130-acre suburban campus **Total enrollment** 6,908 **Student/faculty ratio** 15:1 **Application deadline** 7/1 (freshmen), rolling (transfer) **Freshmen** 73% were admitted **Housing** Yes **Expenses** Tuition 17,028; Room & Board 5378 **Undergraduates** 64% women, 17% part-time, 7% 25 or older, 1% Native American, 1% Hispanic American, 27% African American, 3% Asian American/Pacific Islander **The most frequently chosen baccalaureate fields are** business/marketing, engineering/engineering technologies, social sciences and history **Academic program** English as a second language, advanced placement, accelerated degree program, self-designed majors, honors program, summer session, adult/continuing education programs, internships **Contact** Mr. Allen S. London, Assistant Vice President for Admissions and Freshman Recruitment, Mercer University, 1400 Coleman Avenue, Macon, GA 31207-0003. Telephone: 478-301-2650 or toll-free 800-840-8577. Fax: 478-301-2828. E-mail: admissions@mercer.edu. Web site: http://www.mercer.edu/.

MOREHOUSE COLLEGE
ATLANTA, GEORGIA

General Independent, 4-year, men only **Entrance** Moderately difficult **Setting** 61-acre urban campus **Total enrollment** 2,970 **Student/faculty ratio** 13:1 **Application deadline** 2/15 (freshmen), 2/15 (transfer) **Freshmen** 75% were admitted **Housing** Yes **Expenses** Tuition 12,432; Room & Board 7382 **Undergraduates** 6% part-time, 5% 25 or older, 0% Native American, 0.3% Hispanic American, 93% African American, 0.1% Asian American/Pacific Islander **The most frequently chosen baccalaureate fields are** business/marketing, psychology, social sciences and history **Academic program** Advanced placement, honors program, summer session, internships **Contact** Mr. Terrance Dixon, Director of Admissions, Morehouse College, 830 Westview Drive, SW, Atlanta, GA 30314. Telephone: 404-215-2632 or toll-free 800-851-1254. Fax: 404-524-5635. E-mail: admissions@morehouse.edu. Web site: http://www.morehouse.edu/.

MORRIS BROWN COLLEGE
ATLANTA, GEORGIA

General Independent, 4-year, coed, affiliated with African Methodist Episcopal Church **Entrance** Minimally difficult **Setting** 21-acre urban campus **Total enrollment** 2,787 **Student/faculty ratio** 20:1 **Application deadline** Rolling (freshmen), rolling (transfer) **Freshmen** 58% were admitted **Housing** Yes **Expenses** Tuition $10,426; Room & Board $5262 **Undergraduates** 58% women, 5% part-time, 9% 25 or older, 0.04% Native American, 0.1% Hispanic American, 97% African American, 0.1% Asian American/Pacific Islander **Academic program** English as a second language, accelerated degree program, honors program, adult/continuing education programs, internships **Contact** Ms. Karla Heyward, Interim Director, Morris Brown College, 643 Martin Luther King Jr. Drive, NW, Atlanta, GA 30314. Telephone: 404-739-1560. Fax: 404-739-1565. E-mail: admissions@morrisbrown.edu. Web site: http://www.morrisbrown.edu/.

NORTH GEORGIA COLLEGE & STATE UNIVERSITY
DAHLONEGA, GEORGIA

General State-supported, comprehensive, coed **Entrance** Moderately difficult **Setting** 140-acre small-town campus **Total enrollment** 3,525 **Student/faculty ratio** 17:1 **Application deadline** 7/15 (freshmen), 7/1 (transfer) **Freshmen** 47% were admitted **Housing** Yes **Expenses** Tuition $2354; Room & Board $3612 **Undergraduates** 64% women, 17% part-time, 15% 25 or older, 0.4% Native American, 1% Hispanic American, 2% African American, 1% Asian American/Pacific Islander **The most frequently chosen baccalaureate fields are** business/marketing, biological/life sciences, education **Academic program** Advanced placement, honors program, summer session, internships **Contact** Robert J. LaVerriere, Director of Admissions and Recruitment, North Georgia College & State University, Admissions Center, 32 College Circle, Dahlonega, GA 30597. Telephone: 706-864-1800 or toll-free 800-498-9581. Fax: 706-864-1478. E-mail: tdavis@nugget.ngc.peachnet.edu. Web site: http://www.ngcsu.edu/.

► **For more information, see page 455.**

OGLETHORPE UNIVERSITY
ATLANTA, GEORGIA

General Independent, comprehensive, coed **Entrance** Very difficult **Setting** 118-acre suburban campus **Total enrollment** 1,267 **Student/faculty ratio** 13:1 **Application deadline** Rolling (freshmen), rolling (transfer) **Freshmen** 70% were admitted **Housing** Yes **Expenses** Tuition $18,390; Room & Board $5560 **Undergraduates** 67% women, 19% part-time, 5% 25 or older, 0.1% Native American, 2% Hispanic American, 18% African American, 4% Asian American/Pacific Islander **The most frequently chosen baccalaureate fields are** business/marketing, psychology, social sciences and history **Academic program** Advanced placement, accelerated degree program, self-designed majors, honors program, summer session, adult/continuing education programs, internships **Contact** Mr. Dennis T. Matthews, Associate Dean for Enrollment Management, Oglethorpe University, 4484 Peachtree Road, NE, Atlanta, GA 30319-2797. Telephone: 404-364-8307 or toll-free 800-428-4484. Fax: 404-364-8500. E-mail: dtmou@mindspring.com. Web site: http://www.oglethorpe.edu/.

PAINE COLLEGE
AUGUSTA, GEORGIA

General Independent Methodist, 4-year, coed **Entrance** Minimally difficult **Setting** 54-acre urban campus **Total enrollment** 858 **Student/faculty ratio** 12:1 **Application deadline** 8/1 (freshmen), 8/1 (transfer) **Freshmen** 54% were admitted **Housing** Yes **Expenses** Tuition 7848; Room & Board 3432 **Undergraduates** 70% women, 15% part-time, 19% 25 or older, 0% Native American, 0.2% Hispanic American, 99% African American, 0% Asian American/Pacific Islander **The most frequently chosen baccalaureate fields are** business/marketing, education, psychology **Academic program** Advanced placement, accelerated degree program, honors program, summer session, internships **Contact** Mr. Joseph Tinsley, Director of Admissions, Paine College, 1235 15th Street, Augusta, GA 30901-3182. Telephone: 706-821-8320 or toll-free 800-476-7703. Fax: 706-821-8691. E-mail: ek@mail.paine.edu. Web site: http://www.paine.edu/.

PIEDMONT COLLEGE
DEMOREST, GEORGIA

General Independent, comprehensive, coed, affiliated with Congregational Christian Church **Entrance** Moderately difficult **Setting** 115-acre rural campus **Total enrollment** 1,728 **Student/faculty ratio** 12:1 **Application deadline** Rolling (freshmen), rolling (transfer) **Freshmen** 72% were admitted **Housing** Yes **Expenses** Tuition 10,500; Room & Board 4400 **Undergraduates** 63% women, 17% part-time, 31% 25 or older, 0.1% Native American, 1% Hispanic American, 8% African American, 1% Asian American/Pacific Islander **The most frequently chosen baccalaureate fields are** business/marketing, education, social sciences and history **Academic program** Advanced placement, accelerated degree program, self-designed majors, honors program, summer session, adult/continuing education programs, internships **Contact** Ms. Kathy Edwards, Director of Undergraduate Admissions, Piedmont College, PO Box 10, Demorest, GA 30535-0010. Telephone: 706-776-0103 Ext. 1299 or toll-free 800-277-7020. Fax: 706-776-6635. E-mail: jem.clement@gateway.piedmont.edu. Web site: http://www.piedmont.edu/.

REINHARDT COLLEGE
WALESKA, GEORGIA

General Independent, 4-year, coed, affiliated with United Methodist Church **Entrance** Moderately difficult **Setting** 600-acre rural campus **Total enrollment** 1,078 **Student/faculty ratio** 11:1 **Application deadline** Rolling (freshmen), rolling (transfer) **Freshmen** 89% were admitted **Housing** Yes **Expenses** Tuition $8800; Room & Board $4716 **Undergraduates** 63% women, 16% part-time, 25% 25 or older, 1% Native American, 1% Hispanic American, 3% African American, 1% Asian American/Pacific Islander **The most frequently chosen baccalaureate fields are** business/marketing, communications/communication technologies, liberal arts/general studies **Academic program** Advanced placement, honors program, summer session, adult/continuing education programs, internships **Contact** Ms. Kathryn Smith, Director of Admissions, Reinhardt College, 7300 Reinhardt College Circle, Waleska, GA 30183-0128. Telephone: 770-720-5526 or toll-free 87-REINHARDT. Fax: 770-720-5602. E-mail: admissions@mail.reinhardt.edu. Web site: http://www.reinhardt.edu/.

SAVANNAH COLLEGE OF ART AND DESIGN
SAVANNAH, GEORGIA

General Independent, comprehensive, coed **Entrance** Moderately difficult **Setting** urban campus **Total enrollment** 4,923 **Student/faculty ratio** 18:1 **Application deadline** Rolling (freshmen), rolling (transfer) **Freshmen** 84% were admitted **Housing** Yes **Expenses** Tuition $17,325; Room & Board $7250 **Undergraduates** 43% women, 11% part-time, 8% 25 or older, 0.3% Native American, 3% Hispanic American, 5% African American, 2% Asian American/Pacific Islander **The most frequently chosen baccalaureate fields are** architecture, visual/performing arts **Academic program** English as a second language, advanced placement, summer session, internships **Contact** Ms. Pamela Afifi, Vice President for Admission, Savannah College of Art and Design, 342 Bull Street, PO Box 3146, Savannah, GA 31402-3146. Telephone: 912-525-5100 or toll-free 800-869-7223. Fax: 912-525-5983. E-mail: admissions@scad.edu. Web site: http://www.scad.edu/.

► **For more information, see page 465.**

SAVANNAH STATE UNIVERSITY
SAVANNAH, GEORGIA

General State-supported, comprehensive, coed **Entrance** Minimally difficult **Setting** 165-acre suburban campus **Total enrollment** 2,500 **Student/faculty ratio** 16:1 **Application deadline** 6/1 (freshmen), 6/1 (transfer) **Housing** Yes **Expenses** Tuition $2494; Room & Board $4144 **Undergraduates** 0.1% Native American, 1% Hispanic American, 92% African American, 0.2% Asian American/Pacific Islander **Academic program** Advanced placement, accelerated degree program, summer session, adult/continuing education programs, internships **Contact** Mrs. Gwendolyn J. Moore, Associate Director of Admissions, Savannah State University, PO Box 20209, Savannah, GA 31404. Telephone: 912-356-2181 or toll-free 800-788-0478. Fax: 912-356-2566. Web site: http://www.savstate.edu/.

SHORTER COLLEGE
ROME, GEORGIA

General Independent Baptist, comprehensive, coed **Entrance** Moderately difficult **Setting** 155-acre small-town campus **Total enrollment** 1,925 **Student/faculty ratio** 17:1 **Application deadline** Rolling (freshmen), rolling (transfer) **Freshmen** 87% were admitted **Housing** Yes **Expenses** Tuition $9470; Room & Board $4900 **Undergraduates** 65% women, 2% part-time, 8% 25 or older, 1% Native American, 1% Hispanic American, 20% African American, 0.2% Asian American/Pacific Islander **The most frequently chosen baccalaureate fields are** business/

Shorter College *(continued)*

marketing, education, visual/performing arts **Academic program** Advanced placement, accelerated degree program, self-designed majors, honors program, summer session, adult/continuing education programs, internships **Contact** Ms. Wendy Sutton, Director of Admissions, Shorter College, 315 Shorter Avenue, Rome, GA 30165. Telephone: 706-233-7342 or toll-free 800-868-6980. Fax: 706-236-7224. E-mail: admissions@shorter.edu. Web site: http://www.shorter.edu/.

SOUTH COLLEGE
SAVANNAH, GEORGIA

General Proprietary, 4-year, coed **Entrance** Minimally difficult **Setting** 6-acre suburban campus **Total enrollment** 483 **Application deadline** Rolling (freshmen), rolling (transfer) **Housing** No **Expenses** Tuition 10,396 **Undergraduates** 75% women, 20% part-time, 53% 25 or older, 0% Native American, 3% Hispanic American, 33% African American, 1% Asian American/Pacific Islander **Academic program** Accelerated degree program, summer session, adult/continuing education programs, internships **Contact** Ms. Deborah Welsh, Director of Admissions, South College, 709 Mall Boulevard, Savannah, GA 31406-4881. Telephone: 912-691-6000. Fax: 912-691-6070. E-mail: southcollege@sava.gulfnet.com. Web site: http://www.southcollege.edu/.

SOUTHERN POLYTECHNIC STATE UNIVERSITY
MARIETTA, GEORGIA

General State-supported, comprehensive, coed **Entrance** Moderately difficult **Setting** 200-acre suburban campus **Total enrollment** 3,397 **Student/faculty ratio** 17:1 **Application deadline** 8/1 (freshmen), 8/1 (transfer) **Freshmen** 64% were admitted **Housing** Yes **Expenses** Tuition $2210; Room & Board $4308 **Undergraduates** 17% women, 40% part-time, 37% 25 or older, 0.2% Native American, 3% Hispanic American, 19% African American, 6% Asian American/Pacific Islander **The most frequently chosen baccalaureate fields are** computer/information sciences, architecture, engineering/engineering technologies **Academic program** Advanced placement, summer session, adult/continuing education programs, internships **Contact** Ms. Virginia A. Head, Director of Admissions, Southern Polytechnic State University, 1100 South Marietta Parkway, Marietta, GA 30060-2896. Telephone: 770-528-7281 or toll-free 800-635-3204. Fax: 770-528-7292. E-mail: vhead@sct.edu. Web site: http://www.spsu.edu/.

SPELMAN COLLEGE
ATLANTA, GEORGIA

General Independent, 4-year, women only **Entrance** Very difficult **Setting** 32-acre urban campus **Total enrollment** 1,897 **Student/faculty ratio** 14:1 **Application deadline** 2/1 (freshmen), 2/1 (transfer) **Freshmen** 53% were admitted **Housing** Yes **Expenses** Tuition $11,135; Room & Board $6880 **Undergraduates** 4% 25 or older **Academic program** Advanced placement, self-designed majors, honors program, adult/continuing education programs, internships **Contact** Ms. Theodora Riley, Interim Director of Admissions and Orientation Services, Spelman College, 350 Spelman Lane, SW, Atlanta, GA 30314-4399. Telephone: 404-681-3643 Ext. 2585 or toll-free 800-982-2411 (out-of-state). Fax: 404-215-7788. E-mail: admiss@spelman.edu. Web site: http://www.spelman.edu/.

STATE UNIVERSITY OF WEST GEORGIA
CARROLLTON, GEORGIA

General State-supported, comprehensive, coed **Entrance** Minimally difficult **Setting** 400-acre small-town campus **Total enrollment** 8,959 **Student/faculty ratio** 19:1 **Application deadline** 7/31 (freshmen), 6/15 (transfer) **Freshmen** 73% were admitted **Housing** Yes **Expenses** Tuition $2394; Room & Board $3854 **Undergraduates** 61% women, 18% part-time, 14% 25 or older, 0.2% Native American, 1% Hispanic American, 22% African American, 1% Asian American/Pacific Islander **The most frequently chosen baccalaureate fields are** business/marketing, education, psychology **Academic program** Advanced placement, accelerated degree program, honors program, summer session, adult/continuing education programs, internships **Contact** Dr. Robert Johnson, Director of Admissions, State University of West Georgia, 1600 Maple Street, Carrollton, GA 30118. Telephone: 770-836-6416. Fax: 770-836-4659. E-mail: rjohnson@westga.edu. Web site: http://www.westga.edu/.

THOMAS UNIVERSITY
THOMASVILLE, GEORGIA

General Independent, comprehensive, coed **Entrance** Noncompetitive **Setting** 24-acre small-town campus **Total enrollment** 591 **Student/faculty ratio** 10:1 **Application deadline** Rolling (freshmen), rolling (transfer) **Freshmen** 100% were admitted **Housing** No **Expenses** Tuition $7870; Room only $2000 **Undergraduates** 66% women, 27% part-time, 50% 25 or older, 0.2% Native American, 1% Hispanic American, 24% African American, 1% Asian American/Pacific Islander **The most frequently chosen baccalaureate fields are** education, health professions and related sciences, protective services/public administration **Academic program** Advanced placement, accelerated degree program, summer session, adult/continuing education programs, internships **Contact** Director of Student Affairs, Thomas University, 1501 Millpond Road, Thomasville, GA 31792-7499. Telephone: 229-226-1621 Ext. 122 or toll-free 800-538-9784. Fax: 229-227-1653. Web site: http://www.thomasu.edu/.

TOCCOA FALLS COLLEGE
TOCCOA FALLS, GEORGIA

General Independent interdenominational, comprehensive, coed **Entrance** Moderately difficult **Setting**

1,100-acre small-town campus **Total enrollment** 958 **Student/faculty ratio** 15:1 **Application deadline** Rolling (freshmen), rolling (transfer) **Freshmen** 64% were admitted **Housing** Yes **Expenses** Tuition $9700; Room & Board $4170 **Undergraduates** 56% women, 7% part-time, 5% 25 or older, 0.1% Native American, 2% Hispanic American, 1% African American, 4% Asian American/Pacific Islander **The most frequently chosen baccalaureate fields are** education, philosophy, religion, and theology, psychology **Academic program** Advanced placement, accelerated degree program, summer session, internships **Contact** Director of Admissions, Toccoa Falls College, Office of Admissions, PO Box 899, Toccoa Falls, GA 30598-1000. Telephone: 706-886-6831 or toll-free 800-868-3257. Fax: 706-886-6412 Ext. 5380. E-mail: admissio@toccoafalls.edu. Web site: http://www.toccoafalls.edu/.

UNIVERSITY OF GEORGIA
ATHENS, GEORGIA

General State-supported, university, coed **Entrance** Moderately difficult **Setting** 1,289-acre suburban campus **Total enrollment** 31,288 **Student/faculty ratio** 12:1 **Application deadline** 1/15 (freshmen), 6/1 (transfer) **Freshmen** 62% were admitted **Housing** Yes **Expenses** Tuition $3276; Room & Board $5080 **Undergraduates** 6% 25 or older, 0.2% Native American, 1% Hispanic American, 6% African American, 3% Asian American/Pacific Islander **The most frequently chosen baccalaureate fields are** business/marketing, education, social sciences and history **Academic program** English as a second language, advanced placement, accelerated degree program, self-designed majors, honors program, summer session, adult/continuing education programs, internships **Contact** Dr. John Albright, Associate Director of Admissions, University of Georgia, Athens, GA 30602. Telephone: 706-542-3000. E-mail: undergrad@admissions.uga.edu. Web site: http://www.uga.edu/.

VALDOSTA STATE UNIVERSITY
VALDOSTA, GEORGIA

General State-supported, university, coed **Entrance** Moderately difficult **Setting** 200-acre small-town campus **Total enrollment** 8,687 **Student/faculty ratio** 16:1 **Application deadline** 8/1 (freshmen), 8/1 (transfer) **Freshmen** 65% were admitted **Housing** Yes **Expenses** Tuition 2992; Room & Board 4214 **Undergraduates** 60% women, 24% part-time, 21% 25 or older, 0.3% Native American, 1% Hispanic American, 23% African American, 2% Asian American/Pacific Islander **The most frequently chosen baccalaureate fields are** business/marketing, education, social sciences and history **Academic program** English as a second language, advanced placement, accelerated degree program, honors program, summer session, adult/continuing education programs, internships **Contact** Mr. Walter Peacock, Director of Admissions, Valdosta State University, 1500 North Patterson Street, Valdosta, GA 31698. Telephone: 912-333-5791 or toll-free 800-618-1878 Ext. 1. Fax: 912-333-5482. E-mail: btillman@grits.valdosta.peachnet.edu. Web site: http://www.valdosta.edu/.

WESLEYAN COLLEGE
MACON, GEORGIA

General Independent United Methodist, comprehensive, women only **Entrance** Moderately difficult **Setting** 200-acre suburban campus **Total enrollment** 599 **Student/faculty ratio** 11:1 **Application deadline** 3/1 (freshmen), rolling (transfer) **Freshmen** 78% were admitted **Housing** Yes **Expenses** Tuition $16,300; Room & Board $7150 **Undergraduates** 25% part-time, 29% 25 or older, 1% Native American, 3% Hispanic American, 33% African American, 3% Asian American/Pacific Islander **The most frequently chosen baccalaureate fields are** education, business/marketing, psychology **Academic program** Advanced placement, accelerated degree program, self-designed majors, honors program, summer session, adult/continuing education programs, internships **Contact** Mr. Jonathan Stroud, Vice-President for Enrollment and Marketing, Wesleyan College, 4760 Forsyth Road, Macon, GA 31210-4462. Telephone: 478-757-5206 or toll-free 800-447-6610. Fax: 478-757-4030. E-mail: admissions@post.wesleyan-college.edu. Web site: http://www.wesleyancollege.edu/.

HAWAII

BRIGHAM YOUNG UNIVERSITY–HAWAII CAMPUS
LAIE, HAWAII

General Independent Latter-day Saints, 4-year, coed **Entrance** Moderately difficult **Setting** 60-acre small-town campus **Total enrollment** 2,358 **Student/faculty ratio** 21:1 **Application deadline** 2/15 (freshmen), 3/15 (transfer) **Freshmen** 55% were admitted **Housing** Yes **Expenses** Tuition $3113; Room & Board $5500 **Undergraduates** 60% women, 6% part-time, 23% 25 or older, 0.3% Native American, 1% Hispanic American, 0.3% African American, 15% Asian American/Pacific Islander **The most frequently chosen baccalaureate fields are** business/marketing, computer/information sciences, education **Academic program** English as a second language, advanced placement, accelerated degree program, honors program, summer session, adult/continuing education programs, internships **Contact** Dr. Bruce A. Bowen, Dean for Admissions and Records, Brigham Young University–Hawaii Campus, 55-220 Kulanui Street, Laie, Oahu, HI 96762. Telephone: 808-293-3738. Web site: http://www.byuh.edu/.

CHAMINADE UNIVERSITY OF HONOLULU
HONOLULU, HAWAII

General Independent Roman Catholic, comprehensive, coed **Entrance** Moderately difficult **Setting**

Chaminade University of Honolulu *(continued)*

62-acre urban campus **Total enrollment** 2,489 **Student/faculty ratio** 16:1 **Application deadline** Rolling (freshmen), rolling (transfer) **Freshmen** 69% were admitted **Housing** Yes **Expenses** Tuition 12,590; Room & Board 5580 **Undergraduates** 58% women, 43% part-time, 40% 25 or older, 2% Native American, 8% Hispanic American, 14% African American, 32% Asian American/Pacific Islander **The most frequently chosen baccalaureate fields are** protective services/public administration, business/marketing, social sciences and history **Academic program** Advanced placement, accelerated degree program, self-designed majors, summer session, adult/continuing education programs, internships **Contact** Office of Admissions, Chaminade University of Honolulu, 3140 Waialae Avenue, Honolulu, HI 96816-1578. Telephone: 808-735-4735 or toll-free 800-735-3733 (out-of-state). Fax: 808-739-4647. E-mail: cuhadmin@lava.net. Web site: http://www.chaminade.edu/.

▶ **For more information, see page 398.**

EDUCATION AMERICA, HONOLULU CAMPUS
HONOLULU, HAWAII

Contact Education America, Honolulu Campus, 1111 Bishop Street, Suite 400, Honolulu, HI 96813.

HAWAII PACIFIC UNIVERSITY
HONOLULU, HAWAII

General Independent, comprehensive, coed **Entrance** Moderately difficult **Setting** 140-acre urban campus **Total enrollment** 8,228 **Student/faculty ratio** 15:1 **Application deadline** Rolling (freshmen), rolling (transfer) **Freshmen** 84% were admitted **Housing** Yes **Expenses** Tuition 8920; Room & Board 8350 **Undergraduates** 52% women, 31% part-time, 35% 25 or older, 1% Native American, 6% Hispanic American, 7% African American, 28% Asian American/Pacific Islander **The most frequently chosen baccalaureate fields are** business/marketing, computer/information sciences, health professions and related sciences **Academic program** English as a second language, advanced placement, accelerated degree program, self-designed majors, honors program, summer session, adult/continuing education programs, internships **Contact** Mr. Scott Stensrud, Director of Admissions, Hawaii Pacific University, 1164 Bishop Street, Honolulu, HI 96813-2785. Telephone: 808-544-0238 or toll-free 800-669-4724 (out-of-state). Fax: 808-544-1136. E-mail: admissions@hpu.edu. Web site: http://www.hpu.edu/.

▶ **For more information, see page 430.**

INTERNATIONAL COLLEGE AND GRADUATE SCHOOL
HONOLULU, HAWAII

General Independent interdenominational, upper-level, coed **Total enrollment** 31 **Student/faculty ratio** 1:1 **Application deadline** Rolling (transfer) **Housing** No **Expenses** Tuition 4580 **Undergraduates** 27% women, 73% part-time, 4% 25 or older, 0% Native American, 0% Hispanic American, 0% African American, 50% Asian American/Pacific Islander **Academic program** Advanced placement, summer session, adult/continuing education programs, internships **Contact** Mr. Jon Rawlings, Director of Admissions, International College and Graduate School, 20 Dowsett Avenue, Honolulu, HI 96817. Telephone: 808-595-4247. Fax: 808-595-4779. E-mail: lcgs@pixie.com. Web site: http://home.hawaii.rr.com/international/icgs.html.

UNIVERSITY OF HAWAII AT HILO
HILO, HAWAII

General State-supported, 4-year, coed **Entrance** Moderately difficult **Setting** 115-acre small-town campus **Total enrollment** 2,874 **Application deadline** 7/1 (freshmen), 7/1 (transfer) **Freshmen** 63% were admitted **Housing** Yes **Expenses** Tuition $1466; Room & Board $4989 **Undergraduates** 60% women, 20% part-time, 31% 25 or older, 1% Native American, 2% Hispanic American, 1% African American, 50% Asian American/Pacific Islander **Academic program** English as a second language, advanced placement, self-designed majors, honors program, summer session, internships **Contact** Mr. James Cromwell, UH Student Services Specialist III, University of Hawaii at Hilo, 200 West Kawili Street, Hilo, HI 96720-4091. Telephone: 808-974-7414 or toll-free 808-974-7414 (in-state); 800-897-4456 (out-of-state). E-mail: uhhao@uhhadc.uhh.hawaii.edu. Web site: http://www.uhh.hawaii.edu/.

UNIVERSITY OF HAWAII AT MANOA
HONOLULU, HAWAII

General State-supported, university, coed **Entrance** Moderately difficult **Setting** 300-acre urban campus **Total enrollment** 17,263 **Student/faculty ratio** 12:1 **Application deadline** 6/1 (freshmen), 6/1 (transfer) **Freshmen** 71% were admitted **Housing** Yes **Expenses** Tuition $3157; Room & Board $4933 **Undergraduates** 55% women, 17% part-time, 19% 25 or older, 0.2% Native American, 1% Hispanic American, 1% African American, 75% Asian American/Pacific Islander **The most frequently chosen baccalaureate fields are** business/marketing, education, social sciences and history **Academic program** English as a second language, advanced placement, accelerated degree program, self-designed majors, honors program, summer session, adult/continuing education programs, internships **Contact** Dr. David Robb, Director of Admissions and Records, University of Hawaii at Manoa, 2600 Campus Road, Room 001, Honolulu, HI 96822. Telephone: 808-956-8975 or toll-free 800-823-9771. Fax: 808-956-4148. E-mail: ar-info@hawaii.edu. Web site: http://www.uhm.hawaii.edu/.

UNIVERSITY OF HAWAII–WEST OAHU
PEARL CITY, HAWAII

General State-supported, upper-level, coed **Entrance** Moderately difficult **Setting** small-town campus **Total**

enrollment 685 **Student/faculty ratio** 20:1 **Application deadline** 8/1 (transfer) **First-Year Students** 75% were admitted **Housing** No **Expenses** Tuition $1978 **Undergraduates** 68% women, 50% part-time, 76% 25 or older, 0.1% Native American, 2% Hispanic American, 1% African American, 59% Asian American/Pacific Islander **Academic program** Summer session, internships **Contact** Mr. Dan Cormany, Dean of Student Services, University of Hawaii–West Oahu, 96-043 Ala Ike, Pearl City, HI 96782. Telephone: 808-453-6565. Fax: 805-453-6076. E-mail: danc@uhwoa.uhwo.hawaii.edu.

UNIVERSITY OF PHOENIX–HAWAII CAMPUS
HONOLULU, HAWAII

General Proprietary, comprehensive, coed **Entrance** Noncompetitive **Total enrollment** 66,534 **Student/faculty ratio** 13:1 **Application deadline** Rolling (freshmen), rolling (transfer) **Expenses** Tuition $7740 **Undergraduates** 56% women, 86% 25 or older, 2% Native American, 18% Hispanic American, 13% African American, 6% Asian American/Pacific Islander **Academic program** Advanced placement, accelerated degree program, adult/continuing education programs **Contact** Ms. Beth Barilla, Director of Admissions, University of Phoenix–Hawaii Campus, 4615 East Elwood Street, Phoenix, AZ 85040-1948. Telephone: 480-927-0099 Ext. 1218 or toll-free 800-228-7240 (out-of-state). Fax: 480-594-1758. E-mail: beth.barilla@apollogrp.edu. Web site: http://www.phoenix.edu/.

IDAHO

ALBERTSON COLLEGE OF IDAHO
CALDWELL, IDAHO

General Independent, 4-year, coed **Entrance** Moderately difficult **Setting** 43-acre small-town campus **Total enrollment** 812 **Student/faculty ratio** 13:1 **Application deadline** 6/1 (freshmen), 8/1 (transfer) **Freshmen** 97% were admitted **Housing** Yes **Expenses** Tuition 16,600; Room & Board 4400 **Undergraduates** 53% women, 8% part-time, 3% 25 or older, 1% Native American, 5% Hispanic American, 1% African American, 4% Asian American/Pacific Islander **The most frequently chosen baccalaureate fields are** biological/life sciences, business/marketing, social sciences and history **Academic program** English as a second language, advanced placement, self-designed majors, honors program, internships **Contact** Mr. Dennis P. Bergvall, Dean of Admissions, Albertson College of Idaho, 2112 Cleveland Boulevard, Caldwell, ID 83605-4494. Telephone: 208-459-5305 or toll-free 800-AC-IDAHO. Fax: 208-459-5757. E-mail: admissio@stimpy.acofi.edu. Web site: http://www.albertson.edu/.

BOISE BIBLE COLLEGE
BOISE, IDAHO

General Independent nondenominational, 4-year, coed **Contact** Mr. Ross Knudsen, Director of Admissions, Boise Bible College, 8695 Marigold Street, Boise, ID 83704. Telephone: 208-376-7731 or toll-free 800-893-7755. Fax: 208-376-7743. E-mail: boibible@micron.net.

BOISE STATE UNIVERSITY
BOISE, IDAHO

General State-supported, comprehensive, coed **Entrance** Minimally difficult **Setting** 130-acre urban campus **Total enrollment** 16,282 **Student/faculty ratio** 17:1 **Application deadline** 7/18 (freshmen), 7/18 (transfer) **Freshmen** 86% were admitted **Housing** Yes **Expenses** Tuition 2451; Room & Board 3570 **Undergraduates** 55% women, 40% part-time, 44% 25 or older, 1% Native American, 5% Hispanic American, 1% African American, 2% Asian American/Pacific Islander **The most frequently chosen baccalaureate fields are** business/marketing, education, health professions and related sciences **Academic program** English as a second language, advanced placement, self-designed majors, honors program, summer session, adult/continuing education programs, internships **Contact** Mr. Mark Wheeler, Dean of Enrollment Services, Boise State University, Enrollment Services, 1910 University Drive, Boise, ID 83725. Telephone: 208-426-1177 or toll-free 800-632-6586 (in-state); 800-824-7017 (out-of-state). E-mail: mwheeler@bsu.idbsu.edu. Web site: http://www.boisestate.edu/.

IDAHO STATE UNIVERSITY
POCATELLO, IDAHO

General State-supported, university, coed **Entrance** Minimally difficult **Setting** 735-acre small-town campus **Total enrollment** 13,045 **Application deadline** 8/1 (freshmen), 8/1 (transfer) **Freshmen** 75% were admitted **Housing** Yes **Expenses** Room & Board $3920 **Undergraduates** 35% 25 or older, 2% Native American, 3% Hispanic American, 1% African American, 1% Asian American/Pacific Islander **The most frequently chosen baccalaureate fields are** business/marketing, education, health professions and related sciences **Academic program** English as a second language, advanced placement, self-designed majors, honors program, summer session, adult/continuing education programs, internships **Contact** Mr. Guy Hollingsworth, Director of Recruitment, Idaho State University, Campus Box 8270, Pocatello, ID 83209. Telephone: 208-282-3279. Fax: 208-236-4231. E-mail: echamike@isu.edu.

► **For more information, see page 433.**

LEWIS-CLARK STATE COLLEGE
LEWISTON, IDAHO

General State-supported, 4-year, coed **Entrance** Minimally difficult **Setting** 44-acre small-town cam-

Lewis-Clark State College *(continued)*

pus **Total enrollment** 2,702 **Student/faculty ratio** 15:1 **Application deadline** Rolling (freshmen), rolling (transfer) **Freshmen** 62% were admitted **Housing** Yes **Expenses** Tuition 4720; Room & Board 3050 **Undergraduates** 62% women, 29% part-time, 7% Native American, 2% Hispanic American, 0.2% African American, 1% Asian American/Pacific Islander **The most frequently chosen baccalaureate fields are** business/marketing, education, health professions and related sciences **Academic program** English as a second language, advanced placement, accelerated degree program, self-designed majors, honors program, summer session, adult/continuing education programs, internships **Contact** Ms. Rosanne English, Office Specialist II, Lewis-Clark State College, 500 8th Avenue, Lewiston, ID 83501. Telephone: 208-792-2210 or toll-free 800-933-LCSC Ext. 2210. Fax: 208-792-2876. E-mail: sbussoli@lcsc.edu. Web site: http://www.lcsc.edu/.

NORTHWEST NAZARENE UNIVERSITY
NAMPA, IDAHO

General Independent, comprehensive, coed, affiliated with Church of the Nazarene **Entrance** Moderately difficult **Setting** 85-acre small-town campus **Total enrollment** 1,316 **Student/faculty ratio** 13:1 **Application deadline** 9/1 (freshmen), 9/1 (transfer) **Freshmen** 73% were admitted **Housing** Yes **Expenses** Tuition $14,240; Room & Board $4140 **Undergraduates** 55% women, 9% part-time, 7% 25 or older, 1% Native American, 2% Hispanic American, 1% African American, 1% Asian American/Pacific Islander **The most frequently chosen baccalaureate fields are** education, business/marketing, philosophy, religion, and theology **Academic program** Advanced placement, accelerated degree program, self-designed majors, honors program, summer session, internships **Contact** Ms. Stacey Berggren, Director of Admissions, Northwest Nazarene University, 623 Holly Street, Nampa, ID 83686. Telephone: 208-467-8648 or toll-free 877-NNU-4YOU. Fax: 208-467-8645. E-mail: admissions@nnu.edu. Web site: http://www.nnu.edu/.

UNIVERSITY OF IDAHO
MOSCOW, IDAHO

General State-supported, university, coed **Entrance** Moderately difficult **Setting** 1,450-acre small-town campus **Total enrollment** 11,635 **Student/faculty ratio** 17:1 **Application deadline** 8/1 (freshmen), rolling (transfer) **Freshmen** 83% were admitted **Housing** Yes **Expenses** Tuition $2476; Room & Board $4064 **Undergraduates** 46% women, 14% part-time, 15% 25 or older, 1% Native American, 3% Hispanic American, 1% African American, 1% Asian American/Pacific Islander **The most frequently chosen baccalaureate fields are** business/marketing, education, engineering/engineering technologies **Academic program** Advanced placement, accelerated degree program, self-designed majors, honors program, summer session, adult/continuing education programs, internships **Contact** Mr. Dan Davenport, Director of Admissions, University of Idaho, Admissions Office, PO Box 444264, Moscow, ID 83844-4264. Telephone: 208-885-6326 or toll-free 888-884-3246 (out-of-state). Fax: 208-885-9119. E-mail: admappl@uidaho.edu. Web site: http://www.uidaho.edu/.

ILLINOIS

AMERICAN ACADEMY OF ART
CHICAGO, ILLINOIS

General Proprietary, 4-year, coed **Entrance** Moderately difficult **Setting** urban campus **Total enrollment** 398 **Student/faculty ratio** 11:1 **Application deadline** Rolling (freshmen), rolling (transfer) **Freshmen** 100% were admitted **Housing** No **Expenses** Tuition 15,080 **Undergraduates** 32% women, 24% part-time, 27% 25 or older, 0% Native American, 23% Hispanic American, 10% African American, 5% Asian American/Pacific Islander **The most frequently chosen baccalaureate field is** visual/performing arts **Academic program** Accelerated degree program, summer session, adult/continuing education programs, internships **Contact** Ms. Ione Fitzgerald, Director of Admissions, American Academy of Art, 332 South Michigan Ave, Suite 300, Chicago, IL 60604-4302. Telephone: 312-461-0600 Ext. 143. Web site: http://www.aaart.edu/.

AMERICAN INTERCONTINENTAL UNIVERSITY ONLINE
HOFFMAN ESTATES, ILLINOIS

Contact American InterContinental University Online, 2895 Greenspoint Parkway, Suite 400, Hoffman Estates, IL 60195. Telephone: or toll-free 877-221-5800 Ext. 2604 (in-state); 877-701-3800 (out-of-state). Web site: http://www.aiu-online.com/.

AUGUSTANA COLLEGE
ROCK ISLAND, ILLINOIS

General Independent, 4-year, coed, affiliated with Evangelical Lutheran Church in America **Entrance** Moderately difficult **Setting** 115-acre suburban campus **Total enrollment** 2,261 **Student/faculty ratio** 12:1 **Application deadline** Rolling (freshmen), rolling (transfer) **Freshmen** 72% were admitted **Housing** Yes **Expenses** Tuition 17,913; Room & Board 5214 **Undergraduates** 57% women, 1% part-time, 1% 25 or older, 0.2% Native American, 3% Hispanic American, 3% African American, 2% Asian American/Pacific Islander **The most frequently chosen baccalaureate fields are** biological/life sciences, business/marketing, health professions and related sciences **Academic program** Advanced placement, accelerated degree program, honors program, summer session, internships **Contact** Mr. Martin Sauer, Director of Admissions, Augustana College, 639 38th Street, Rock Island, IL 61201-2296. Telephone: 309-794-

7341 or toll-free 800-798-8100. Fax: 309-794-7431. E-mail: admissions@augustana.edu. Web site: http://www.augustana.edu/.

AURORA UNIVERSITY
AURORA, ILLINOIS

General Independent, comprehensive, coed **Entrance** Moderately difficult **Setting** 26-acre suburban campus **Total enrollment** 2,391 **Student/faculty ratio** 15:1 **Application deadline** Rolling (freshmen), rolling (transfer) **Freshmen** 62% were admitted **Housing** Yes **Expenses** Tuition $13,368; Room & Board $5133 **Undergraduates** 59% women, 28% part-time, 35% 25 or older, 1% Native American, 9% Hispanic American, 15% African American, 2% Asian American/Pacific Islander **Academic program** Advanced placement, self-designed majors, summer session, adult/continuing education programs, internships **Contact** Mr. James Lancaster, Freshman Recruitment Coordinator, Aurora University, 347 South Gladstone Avenue, Aurora, IL 60506-4892. Telephone: 630-844-5533 or toll-free 800-742-5281. Fax: 630-844-5535. E-mail: admissions@admin.aurora.edu. Web site: http://www.aurora.edu/.

BARAT COLLEGE
LAKE FOREST, ILLINOIS

General Independent Roman Catholic, comprehensive, coed **Entrance** Moderately difficult **Setting** 30-acre suburban campus **Total enrollment** 799 **Student/faculty ratio** 12:1 **Application deadline** Rolling (freshmen), rolling (transfer) **Freshmen** 62% were admitted **Housing** Yes **Expenses** Tuition $13,950; Room & Board $5500 **Undergraduates** 73% women, 28% part-time, 27% 25 or older, 0.4% Native American, 9% Hispanic American, 11% African American, 4% Asian American/Pacific Islander **The most frequently chosen baccalaureate fields are** social sciences and history, health professions and related sciences, visual/performing arts **Academic program** English as a second language, advanced placement, accelerated degree program, self-designed majors, honors program, summer session, adult/continuing education programs, internships **Contact** Ms. Mary Kay Farrell, Assistant Vice President for Admissions, Barat College, 700 East Westleigh Road, Lake Forest, IL 60045. Telephone: 847-615-5678 or toll-free 877-OKBARAT (in-state). Fax: 847-604-6300. E-mail: admissions@barat.edu. Web site: http://www.barat.edu/.

BENEDICTINE UNIVERSITY
LISLE, ILLINOIS

General Independent Roman Catholic, comprehensive, coed **Entrance** Moderately difficult **Setting** 108-acre suburban campus **Total enrollment** 2,868 **Student/faculty ratio** 14:1 **Application deadline** Rolling (freshmen), rolling (transfer) **Freshmen** 81% were admitted **Housing** Yes **Expenses** Tuition $14,880; Room & Board $5500 **Undergraduates** 59% women, 30% part-time, 21% 25 or older, 0.1% Native American, 7% Hispanic American, 3% African American, 13% Asian American/Pacific Islander **The most frequently chosen baccalaureate fields are** biological/life sciences, business/marketing, health professions and related sciences **Academic program** English as a second language, advanced placement, accelerated degree program, honors program, summer session, adult/continuing education programs, internships **Contact** Amy Graham, Benedictine University, 5700 College Road, Lisle, IL 60532-0900. Telephone: 630-829-6300 or toll-free 888-829-6363 (out-of-state). Fax: 630-960-1126. E-mail: admit@eagle.ibc.edu. Web site: http://www.ben.edu/.

► **For more information, see page 388.**

BLACKBURN COLLEGE
CARLINVILLE, ILLINOIS

General Independent Presbyterian, 4-year, coed **Entrance** Moderately difficult **Setting** 80-acre small-town campus **Total enrollment** 540 **Student/faculty ratio** 15:1 **Application deadline** Rolling (freshmen), rolling (transfer) **Freshmen** 72% were admitted **Housing** Yes **Expenses** Tuition 8720; Room & Board 3990 **Undergraduates** 6% 25 or older **Academic program** Advanced placement, accelerated degree program, self-designed majors, honors program, internships **Contact** Mr. John Malin, Director of Admissions, Blackburn College, 700 College Avenue, Carlinville, IL 62626-1498. Telephone: 217-854-3231 Ext. 4252 or toll-free 800-233-3550. Fax: 217-854-3713. E-mail: jmali@mail.blackburn.edu.

BLESSING-RIEMAN COLLEGE OF NURSING
QUINCY, ILLINOIS

General Independent, 4-year, coed, primarily women **Entrance** Moderately difficult **Setting** 1-acre small-town campus **Total enrollment** 126 **Student/faculty ratio** 8:1 **Application deadline** Rolling (freshmen), rolling (transfer) **Freshmen** 100% were admitted **Housing** Yes **Expenses** Tuition $10,950; Room & Board $4570 **Undergraduates** 94% women, 13% part-time, 27% 25 or older, 2% Native American, 1% Hispanic American, 4% African American, 1% Asian American/Pacific Islander **The most frequently chosen baccalaureate field is** health professions and related sciences **Academic program** Advanced placement, honors program, summer session, adult/continuing education programs, internships **Contact** Ms. Linda Cornwell, Director of Support Services/Registrar, Blessing-Rieman College of Nursing, Broadway at 11th, Quincy, IL 62305-7005. Telephone: 217-228-5520 Ext. 6992 or toll-free 800-877-9140. Fax: 217-223-4661. E-mail: bradmiss@moses.culver.edu. Web site: http://www.brcn.edu/.

BRADLEY UNIVERSITY
PEORIA, ILLINOIS

General Independent, comprehensive, coed **Entrance** Moderately difficult **Setting** 65-acre urban campus **Total enrollment** 5,951 **Student/faculty ratio** 14:1 **Application deadline** Rolling (freshmen), rolling

Bradley University *(continued)*

(transfer) **Freshmen** 79% were admitted **Housing** Yes **Expenses** Tuition 14,580; Room & Board 5460 **Undergraduates** 54% women, 9% part-time, 9% 25 or older, 0.3% Native American, 2% Hispanic American, 5% African American, 2% Asian American/Pacific Islander **The most frequently chosen baccalaureate fields are** business/marketing, communications/communication technologies, engineering/engineering technologies **Academic program** Advanced placement, accelerated degree program, self-designed majors, honors program, summer session, adult/continuing education programs, internships **Contact** Ms. Nickie Roberson, Director of Admissions, Bradley University, 1501 West Bradley Avenue, 100 Swords Hall, Peoria, IL 61625-0002. Telephone: 309-677-1000 or toll-free 800-447-6460. E-mail: admissions@bradley.edu. Web site: http://www.bradley.edu/.

CHICAGO STATE UNIVERSITY
CHICAGO, ILLINOIS

General State-supported, comprehensive, coed **Contact** Ms. Addie Epps, Director of Admissions, Chicago State University, 95th Street at King Drive, ADM 200, Chicago, IL 60628. Telephone: 773-995-2513. E-mail: ug-admissions@csu.edu. Web site: http://www.csu.edu/.

CHRISTIAN LIFE COLLEGE
MOUNT PROSPECT, ILLINOIS

Contact Christian Life College, 400 East Gregory Street, Mount Prospect, IL 60056.

COLLEGE OF ST. FRANCIS
See University of St. Francis

COLUMBIA COLLEGE CHICAGO
CHICAGO, ILLINOIS

General Independent, comprehensive, coed **Entrance** Noncompetitive **Setting** urban campus **Total enrollment** 9,056 **Student/faculty ratio** 13:1 **Application deadline** 8/15 (freshmen), 8/15 (transfer) **Freshmen** 90% were admitted **Housing** Yes **Expenses** Tuition $11,780; Room only $5525 **Undergraduates** 50% women, 21% part-time, 22% 25 or older, 1% Native American, 11% Hispanic American, 18% African American, 4% Asian American/Pacific Islander **Academic program** English as a second language, advanced placement, self-designed majors, summer session, internships **Contact** Ms. Susan Greenwald, Director of Admissions and Recruitment, Columbia College Chicago, 600 South Michigan Avenue, Chicago, IL 60605-1996. Telephone: 312-663-1600 Ext. 7133. E-mail: admissions@mail.colum.edu. Web site: http://www.colum.edu/.

CONCORDIA UNIVERSITY
RIVER FOREST, ILLINOIS

General Independent, comprehensive, coed, affiliated with Lutheran Church–Missouri Synod **Entrance** Moderately difficult **Setting** 40-acre suburban campus **Total enrollment** 1,900 **Student/faculty ratio** 10:1 **Application deadline** Rolling (freshmen), rolling (transfer) **Freshmen** 30% were admitted **Housing** Yes **Expenses** Tuition $13,843; Room & Board $5365 **Undergraduates** 68% women, 24% part-time, 22% 25 or older, 0.1% Native American, 5% Hispanic American, 9% African American, 2% Asian American/Pacific Islander **Academic program** Advanced placement, accelerated degree program, honors program, summer session, adult/continuing education programs, internships **Contact** Ms. Deborah A. Ness, Dean of Enrollment Services, Concordia University, 7400 Augusta Street, River Forest, IL 60305. Telephone: 708-209-3100 or toll-free 800-285-2668. Fax: 708-209-3473. E-mail: crfadmis@crf.cuis.edu. Web site: http://www.curf.edu/.

DEPAUL UNIVERSITY
CHICAGO, ILLINOIS

General Independent Roman Catholic, university, coed **Entrance** Moderately difficult **Setting** 36-acre urban campus **Total enrollment** 20,548 **Student/faculty ratio** 16:1 **Application deadline** Rolling (freshmen), rolling (transfer) **Freshmen** 73% were admitted **Housing** Yes **Expenses** Tuition $15,420; Room & Board $6675 **Undergraduates** 59% women, 31% part-time, 30% 25 or older, 0.3% Native American, 13% Hispanic American, 12% African American, 9% Asian American/Pacific Islander **The most frequently chosen baccalaureate fields are** business/marketing, liberal arts/general studies, social sciences and history **Academic program** English as a second language, advanced placement, accelerated degree program, honors program, summer session, adult/continuing education programs, internships **Contact** Mr. Paul Roberts, Director of University Admission, DePaul University, 1 East Jackson Boulevard, Chicago, IL 60604. Telephone: 312-362-8300 or toll-free 800-4DE-PAUL (out-of-state). E-mail: admitdpu@wppost.depaul.edu. Web site: http://www.depaul.edu/.

DEVRY INSTITUTE OF TECHNOLOGY
ADDISON, ILLINOIS

General Proprietary, 4-year, coed **Entrance** Minimally difficult **Setting** 14-acre suburban campus **Total enrollment** 4,006 **Student/faculty ratio** 21:1 **Application deadline** Rolling (freshmen), rolling (transfer) **Freshmen** 65% were admitted **Housing** No **Expenses** Tuition 8740 **Undergraduates** 23% women, 38% part-time, 45% 25 or older, 0.3% Native American, 8% Hispanic American, 10% African American, 15% Asian American/Pacific Islander **The most frequently chosen baccalaureate fields are** business/marketing, computer/information sciences, engineering/engineering technologies **Academic program** Advanced placement, accelerated degree program, summer session, adult/continuing education programs **Contact** Sandra Stack, Director of Admissions, DeVry Institute of Technology, 18624 W. Creek Drive, Tinley Park, IL 60477. Telephone: 630-953-

1300 or toll-free 800-346-5420 (out-of-state). Fax: 630-953-1236. Web site: http://www.dpg.devry.edu.

DEVRY INSTITUTE OF TECHNOLOGY
CHICAGO, ILLINOIS

General Proprietary, 4-year, coed **Entrance** Minimally difficult **Setting** 17-acre urban campus **Total enrollment** 4,095 **Student/faculty ratio** 28:1 **Application deadline** Rolling (freshmen), rolling (transfer) **Freshmen** 66% were admitted **Housing** No **Expenses** Tuition $8805 **Undergraduates** 36% women, 36% part-time, 43% 25 or older, 0.4% Native American, 24% Hispanic American, 33% African American, 15% Asian American/Pacific Islander **The most frequently chosen baccalaureate fields are** business/marketing, computer/information sciences, engineering/engineering technologies **Academic program** English as a second language, advanced placement, accelerated degree program, summer session, adult/continuing education programs **Contact** Christine Hierl, Director of Admissions, DeVry Institute of Technology, 3300 North Campbell Avenue, Chicago, IL 60618-5994. Telephone: 773-929-6550 or toll-free 800-383-3879 (out-of-state). Fax: 773-929-8093. E-mail: gkroepel@chi.devry.edu. Web site: http://www.chi.devry.edu/.

DEVRY INSTITUTE OF TECHNOLOGY
TINLEY PARK, ILLINOIS

Contact Mr. Bruce Jones, Director of Admissions, DeVry Institute of Technology, 18624 West Creek Drive, Tinley Park, IL 60477. Telephone: 708-342-3300 or toll-free 877-305-8184 (out-of-state). Web site: http://www.tp.devry.edu/.

DR. WILLIAM M. SCHOLL COLLEGE OF PODIATRIC MEDICINE
CHICAGO, ILLINOIS

General Independent, upper-level, coed **Entrance** Moderately difficult **Setting** urban campus **Total enrollment** 271 **Student/faculty ratio** 7:1 **Application deadline** 4/1 (transfer) **Housing** No **Expenses** Tuition 21,475 **Undergraduates** 64% 25 or older **Academic program** Accelerated degree program, honors program, adult/continuing education programs **Contact** Mr. Thomas C. Taylor, Associate Dean for Student Affairs, Dr. William M. Scholl College of Podiatric Medicine, Office of Student Affairs, 1001 North Dearborn Street, Chicago, IL 60610. Telephone: 312-280-2940 or toll-free 800-843-3059 (out-of-state). Fax: 312-280-2997. E-mail: admiss@scholl.edu. Web site: http://www.scholl.edu/.

DOMINICAN UNIVERSITY
RIVER FOREST, ILLINOIS

General Independent Roman Catholic, comprehensive, coed **Entrance** Moderately difficult **Setting** 30-acre suburban campus **Total enrollment** 2,317 **Student/faculty ratio** 13:1 **Application deadline** Rolling (freshmen), rolling (transfer) **Freshmen** 79% were admitted **Housing** Yes **Expenses** Tuition $15,700; Room & Board $5630 **Undergraduates** 69% women, 23% part-time, 23% 25 or older, 0.1% Native American, 14% Hispanic American, 5% African American, 1% Asian American/Pacific Islander **The most frequently chosen baccalaureate fields are** business/marketing, psychology, social sciences and history **Academic program** English as a second language, advanced placement, accelerated degree program, self-designed majors, honors program, summer session, adult/continuing education programs, internships **Contact** Ms. Hildegarde Schmidt, Dean of Admissions and Financial Aid, Dominican University, 7900 West Division Street, River Forest, IL 60305-1099. Telephone: 708-524-6800 or toll-free 800-828-8475. Fax: 708-366-5360. E-mail: domadmis@email.dominuniv.edu. Web site: http://www.dom.edu/.

EASTERN ILLINOIS UNIVERSITY
CHARLESTON, ILLINOIS

General State-supported, comprehensive, coed **Entrance** Moderately difficult **Setting** 320-acre small-town campus **Total enrollment** 10,635 **Student/faculty ratio** 16:1 **Application deadline** Rolling (freshmen), rolling (transfer) **Freshmen** 73% were admitted **Housing** Yes **Expenses** Tuition $3688; Room & Board $5400 **Undergraduates** 58% women, 10% part-time, 10% 25 or older, 0.2% Native American, 2% Hispanic American, 6% African American, 1% Asian American/Pacific Islander **The most frequently chosen baccalaureate fields are** business/marketing, education, English **Academic program** English as a second language, advanced placement, honors program, summer session, adult/continuing education programs, internships **Contact** Mr. Dale W. Wolf, Director of Admissions, Eastern Illinois University, 600 Lincoln Avenue, Charleston, IL 61920-3099. Telephone: 217-581-2223 or toll-free 800-252-5711. Fax: 217-581-7060. E-mail: cdadmit@eiu.edu. Web site: http://www.eiu.edu/.

EAST-WEST UNIVERSITY
CHICAGO, ILLINOIS

Contact Mr. Michael Gray, Director of Admissions, East-West University, 816 South Michigan Avenue, Chicago, IL 60605-2103. Telephone: 312-939-0111. Fax: 312-939-0083.

ELMHURST COLLEGE
ELMHURST, ILLINOIS

General Independent, comprehensive, coed, affiliated with United Church of Christ **Entrance** Moderately difficult **Setting** 38-acre suburban campus **Total enrollment** 2,611 **Student/faculty ratio** 14:1 **Application deadline** 7/15 (freshmen), 8/1 (transfer) **Freshmen** 71% were admitted **Housing** Yes **Expenses** Tuition $15,000; Room & Board $5500 **Undergraduates** 64% women, 23% part-time, 36% 25 or older, 0.4% Native American, 6% Hispanic American, 5% African American, 3% Asian American/Pacific Islander **The most frequently chosen baccalaureate fields**

Elmhurst College *(continued)*

are business/marketing, education, social sciences and history **Academic program** Advanced placement, accelerated degree program, honors program, summer session, adult/continuing education programs, internships **Contact** Mr. Darryl Calkins, Associate Dean of Admission, Elmhurst College, 190 Prospect Avenue, Elmhurst, IL 60126-3296. Telephone: 630-617-3400 Ext. 3068 or toll-free 800-697-1871 (out-of-state). Fax: 630-617-5501. E-mail: admit@elmhurst.edu. Web site: http://www.elmhurst.edu/.

EUREKA COLLEGE
EUREKA, ILLINOIS

General Independent, 4-year, coed, affiliated with Christian Church (Disciples of Christ) **Entrance** Moderately difficult **Setting** 112-acre small-town campus **Total enrollment** 441 **Student/faculty ratio** 14:1 **Application deadline** Rolling (freshmen), rolling (transfer) **Freshmen** 78% were admitted **Housing** Yes **Expenses** Tuition 16,100; Room & Board 5100 **Undergraduates** 6% 25 or older, 0% Native American, 1% Hispanic American, 3% African American, 0% Asian American/Pacific Islander **Academic program** Advanced placement, self-designed majors, honors program, internships **Contact** Mr. John R. Clayton, Dean of Admissions and Financial Aid, Eureka College, 300 East College Avenue, Eureka, IL 61530-0128. Telephone: 309-467-6350 or toll-free 888-4-EUREKA. Fax: 309-467-6576. E-mail: admissions@eureka.edu. Web site: http://www.eureka.edu/.

FINCH UNIVERSITY OF HEALTH SCIENCES/THE CHICAGO MEDICAL SCHOOL
NORTH CHICAGO, ILLINOIS

General Independent, upper-level, coed **Entrance** Minimally difficult **Setting** 50-acre suburban campus **Total enrollment** 1,372 **Application deadline** 8/15 (transfer) **Housing** No **Expenses** Tuition $34,533 **Undergraduates** 100% women, 18% part-time, 93% 25 or older, 0% Native American, 0% Hispanic American, 4% African American, 7% Asian American/Pacific Islander **The most frequently chosen baccalaureate field is** health professions and related sciences **Academic program** Advanced placement, summer session, adult/continuing education programs **Contact** Ms. Kristine A. Jones, Director of Admissions and Records, Finch University of Health Sciences/The Chicago Medical School, Undergraduate Admissions, 3333 Green Bay Road, North Chicago, IL 60064. Telephone: 847-578-3204. Fax: 847-578-3284. E-mail: admissions@finchcms.edu. Web site: http://www.finchcms.edu/.

GOVERNORS STATE UNIVERSITY
UNIVERSITY PARK, ILLINOIS

General State-supported, upper-level, coed **Entrance** Minimally difficult **Setting** 750-acre suburban campus **Total enrollment** 6,116 **Student/faculty ratio** 16:1 **Application deadline** 7/15 (transfer) **First-Year Students** 66% were admitted **Housing** No **Expenses** Tuition $2520 **Undergraduates** 68% women, 70% part-time, 54% 25 or older, 0.2% Native American, 5% Hispanic American, 28% African American, 1% Asian American/Pacific Islander **The most frequently chosen baccalaureate fields are** business/marketing, computer/information sciences, education **Academic program** Advanced placement, self-designed majors, honors program, summer session, adult/continuing education programs, internships **Contact** Executive Director of Enrollment Services, Governors State University, One University Parkway, University Park, IL 60466. Telephone: 708-534-4490. Fax: 708-534-1640. Web site: http://www.govst.edu/.

GREENVILLE COLLEGE
GREENVILLE, ILLINOIS

General Independent Free Methodist, comprehensive, coed **Entrance** Moderately difficult **Setting** 12-acre small-town campus **Total enrollment** 1,179 **Student/faculty ratio** 16:1 **Application deadline** Rolling (freshmen), rolling (transfer) **Freshmen** 97% were admitted **Housing** Yes **Expenses** Tuition $12,974; Room & Board $4994 **Undergraduates** 50% women, 5% part-time, 21% 25 or older, 1% Native American, 2% Hispanic American, 7% African American, 1% Asian American/Pacific Islander **The most frequently chosen baccalaureate fields are** business/marketing, biological/life sciences, education **Academic program** English as a second language, advanced placement, accelerated degree program, self-designed majors, honors program, summer session, adult/continuing education programs, internships **Contact** Mr. Randy Comfort, Dean of Admissions, Greenville College, 315 East College, PO Box 159, Greenville, IL 62246-0159. Telephone: 618-664-7100 or toll-free 800-248-2288 (in-state); 800-345-4440 (out-of-state). Fax: 618-664-9841. E-mail: admissions@greenville.edu. Web site: http://www.greenville.edu/.

HARRINGTON INSTITUTE OF INTERIOR DESIGN
CHICAGO, ILLINOIS

General Proprietary, 4-year, coed, primarily women **Entrance** Noncompetitive **Setting** urban campus **Total enrollment** 643 **Student/faculty ratio** 15:1 **Application deadline** Rolling (freshmen) **Freshmen** 73% were admitted **Housing** No **Expenses** Tuition $12,804 **Undergraduates** 87% women, 54% part-time, 53% 25 or older, 0% Native American, 8% Hispanic American, 10% African American, 5% Asian American/Pacific Islander **The most frequently chosen baccalaureate field is** visual/performing arts **Academic program** Adult/continuing education programs, internships **Contact** Ms. Wendi Franczyk, Director of Admissions, Harrington Institute of Interior Design, 410 South Michigan Avenue, Chicago, IL 60605-1496. Telephone: 877-939-4975 or toll-free 877-939-4975 (out-of-state). Fax: 312-939-8005.

E-mail: harringtoninstitute@interiordesign.edu. Web site: http://www.interiordesign.edu/.

HEBREW THEOLOGICAL COLLEGE
SKOKIE, ILLINOIS

General Independent Jewish, comprehensive, men only, coordinate institution with Anne M. Blitstein Teachers Institute of the Hebrew Theological College **Contact** Office of Admissions, Hebrew Theological College, 7135 North Carpenter Road, Skokie, IL 60077-3263. Telephone: 847-982-2500. Web site: http://www.htcnet.edu/.

ILLINOIS COLLEGE
JACKSONVILLE, ILLINOIS

General Independent interdenominational, 4-year, coed **Entrance** Moderately difficult **Setting** 62-acre small-town campus **Total enrollment** 909 **Student/faculty ratio** 14:1 **Application deadline** 8/15 (freshmen), 8/15 (transfer) **Freshmen** 74% were admitted **Housing** Yes **Expenses** Tuition 10,735; Room & Board 4725 **Undergraduates** 55% women, 3% part-time, 3% 25 or older, 1% Native American, 1% Hispanic American, 3% African American, 0.5% Asian American/Pacific Islander **Academic program** Advanced placement, accelerated degree program, summer session, internships **Contact** Randall S Beachy, Executive Director of Recruitment and Marketing, Illinois College, 1101 West College Avenue, Jacksonville, IL 62650-2299. Telephone: 217-245-3030 or toll-free 888-595-3030. E-mail: admissions@hilltop.ic.edu. Web site: http://www.ic.edu/.

THE ILLINOIS INSTITUTE OF ART
CHICAGO, ILLINOIS

General Proprietary, 4-year, coed **Entrance** Minimally difficult **Setting** urban campus **Total enrollment** 1,250 **Application deadline** Rolling (freshmen), rolling (transfer) **Housing** No **Expenses** Tuition 12,780 **Undergraduates** 30% 25 or older **Academic program** Advanced placement, accelerated degree program, summer session, adult/continuing education programs, internships **Contact** Ms. Janis Anton, Director of Admissions, The Illinois Institute of Art, 350 North Orleans, Chicago, IL 60654. Telephone: 312-280-3500 Ext. 132 or toll-free 800-351-3450. Fax: 312-280-8562. E-mail: antonj@aii.edu. Web site: http://www.ilia.aii.edu/.

THE ILLINOIS INSTITUTE OF ART-SCHAUMBURG
SCHAUMBURG, ILLINOIS

General Proprietary, 4-year, coed **Total enrollment** 850 **Student/faculty ratio** 16:1 **Freshmen** 100% were admitted **Housing** Yes **Expenses** Tuition $12,436 **Undergraduates** 28% 25 or older, 0% Native American, 7% Hispanic American, 3% African American, 9% Asian American/Pacific Islander **Contact** Ms. Stephanie Schweihofer, Director of Admissions, The Illinois Institute of Art-Schaumburg, 1000 Plaza Drive, Schaumburg, IL 60173. Telephone: 847-619-3450 Ext. 116 or toll-free 800-314-3450. Web site: http://www.ilis.artinstitutes.edu.

ILLINOIS INSTITUTE OF TECHNOLOGY
CHICAGO, ILLINOIS

General Independent, university, coed **Entrance** Very difficult **Setting** 128-acre urban campus **Total enrollment** 6,003 **Student/faculty ratio** 11:1 **Application deadline** Rolling (freshmen), 7/1 (transfer) **Freshmen** 65% were admitted **Housing** Yes **Expenses** Tuition 18,100; Room & Board 5428 **Undergraduates** 25% women, 19% part-time, 20% 25 or older, 0.5% Native American, 7% Hispanic American, 7% African American, 15% Asian American/Pacific Islander **The most frequently chosen baccalaureate fields are** architecture, computer/information sciences, engineering/engineering technologies **Academic program** English as a second language, advanced placement, accelerated degree program, summer session, internships **Contact** Mr. Terry Miller, Dean of Undergraduate Admission, Illinois Institute of Technology, 10 West 33rd Street PH101, Chicago, IL 60616-3793. Telephone: 312-567-3025 or toll-free 800-448-2329 (out-of-state). Fax: 312-567-6939. E-mail: admission@vax1.ais.iit.edu. Web site: http://www.iit.edu/.

ILLINOIS STATE UNIVERSITY
NORMAL, ILLINOIS

General State-supported, university, coed **Entrance** Moderately difficult **Setting** 850-acre urban campus **Total enrollment** 20,755 **Student/faculty ratio** 19:1 **Application deadline** 4/1 (freshmen), 6/30 (transfer) **Freshmen** 76% were admitted **Housing** Yes **Expenses** Tuition $4482; Room & Board $4544 **Undergraduates** 58% women, 8% part-time, 16% 25 or older, 0.3% Native American, 2% Hispanic American, 7% African American, 2% Asian American/Pacific Islander **The most frequently chosen baccalaureate fields are** business/marketing, education, social sciences and history **Academic program** English as a second language, advanced placement, accelerated degree program, self-designed majors, honors program, summer session, adult/continuing education programs, internships **Contact** Mr. Steve Adams, Director of Admissions, Illinois State University, Campus Box 2200, Normal, IL 61790-2200. Telephone: 309-438-2181 or toll-free 800-366-2478 (in-state). Fax: 309-438-3932. E-mail: pawutz@rs6000.cmp.ilstu.edu. Web site: http://www.ilstu.edu/.

ILLINOIS WESLEYAN UNIVERSITY
BLOOMINGTON, ILLINOIS

General Independent, 4-year, coed **Entrance** Very difficult **Setting** 70-acre suburban campus **Total enrollment** 2,102 **Student/faculty ratio** 13:1 **Application deadline** 3/1 (freshmen), rolling (transfer) **Freshmen** 60% were admitted **Housing** Yes **Expenses** Tuition 21,640; Room & Board 5330 **Undergradu-**

Illinois Wesleyan University *(continued)*

ates 57% women, 1% part-time, 0.05% Native American, 2% Hispanic American, 3% African American, 3% Asian American/Pacific Islander **The most frequently chosen baccalaureate fields are** business/marketing, social sciences and history, visual/performing arts **Academic program** Advanced placement, self-designed majors, honors program, summer session, internships **Contact** Mr. James R. Ruoti, Dean of Admissions, Illinois Wesleyan University, PO Box 2900, Bloomington, IL 61702-2900. Telephone: 309-556-3031 or toll-free 800-332-2498. Fax: 309-556-3411. E-mail: iwuadmit@titan.iwu.edu. Web site: http://www.iwu.edu/.

INTERNATIONAL ACADEMY OF DESIGN & TECHNOLOGY
CHICAGO, ILLINOIS

General Proprietary, 4-year, coed **Entrance** Minimally difficult **Setting** urban campus **Total enrollment** 1,739 **Student/faculty ratio** 23:1 **Application deadline** Rolling (freshmen), rolling (transfer) **Freshmen** 68% were admitted **Housing** No **Expenses** Tuition 10,890 **Undergraduates** 65% women, 7% part-time, 25% 25 or older, 0.2% Native American, 21% Hispanic American, 30% African American, 6% Asian American/Pacific Islander **Academic program** Advanced placement, summer session, adult/continuing education programs, internships **Contact** Ms. Robyn Palmersheim, Director of Admissions, International Academy of Design & Technology, One North State Street, Suite 400, Chicago, IL 60602. Telephone: 312-541-3900 or toll-free 877-ACADEMY (out-of-state). Fax: 312-541-3929. E-mail: academy@iamd.edu. Web site: http://www.iamd.edu/.

JUDSON COLLEGE
ELGIN, ILLINOIS

General Independent Baptist, 4-year, coed **Entrance** Moderately difficult **Setting** 80-acre suburban campus **Total enrollment** 1,111 **Student/faculty ratio** 15:1 **Application deadline** Rolling (freshmen), rolling (transfer) **Freshmen** 76% were admitted **Housing** Yes **Expenses** Tuition $14,422; Room & Board $5570 **Undergraduates** 58% women, 25% part-time, 28% 25 or older **Academic program** Advanced placement, accelerated degree program, self-designed majors, honors program, adult/continuing education programs, internships **Contact** Mr. Billy Dean, Director of Admissions, Judson College, 1151 North State Street, Elgin, IL 60123-1498. Telephone: 847-695-2500 Ext. 2322 or toll-free 800-879-5376. Fax: 847-695-0216. E-mail: admission@judson-il.edu. Web site: http://www.judson-il.edu/.

KENDALL COLLEGE
EVANSTON, ILLINOIS

General Independent United Methodist, 4-year, coed **Entrance** Minimally difficult **Setting** 1-acre suburban campus **Total enrollment** 600 **Student/faculty ratio** 15:1 **Application deadline** Rolling (freshmen), rolling (transfer) **Freshmen** 83% were admitted **Housing** Yes **Expenses** Tuition $13,065; Room & Board $5529 **Undergraduates** 45% 25 or older, 0.2% Native American, 9% Hispanic American, 18% African American, 4% Asian American/Pacific Islander **Academic program** English as a second language, advanced placement, accelerated degree program, self-designed majors, summer session, adult/continuing education programs, internships **Contact** Carl Goodmonson, Assistant Director of Admissions, Kendall College, 2408 Orrington Avenue, Evanston, IL 60201-2899. Telephone: 847-866-1300 Ext. 1307 or toll-free 877-588-8860 (in-state). Fax: 847-866-1320. E-mail: admissions@kendall.edu. Web site: http://www.kendall.edu/.

KNOX COLLEGE
GALESBURG, ILLINOIS

General Independent, 4-year, coed **Entrance** Very difficult **Setting** 82-acre small-town campus **Total enrollment** 1,199 **Student/faculty ratio** 11:1 **Application deadline** 2/1 (freshmen), 4/1 (transfer) **Freshmen** 72% were admitted **Housing** Yes **Expenses** Tuition 22,620; Room & Board 5610 **Undergraduates** 57% women, 2% part-time, 2% 25 or older, 0.4% Native American, 3% Hispanic American, 4% African American, 5% Asian American/Pacific Islander **The most frequently chosen baccalaureate fields are** biological/life sciences, social sciences and history, visual/performing arts **Academic program** English as a second language, advanced placement, self-designed majors, honors program, internships **Contact** Paul Steenis, Director of Admissions, Knox College, Admission Office, Box K-148, Galesburg, IL 61401. Telephone: 309-341-7100 or toll-free 800-678-KNOX. Fax: 309-341-7070. E-mail: admission@knox.edu. Web site: http://www.knox.edu/.

LAKE FOREST COLLEGE
LAKE FOREST, ILLINOIS

General Independent, comprehensive, coed **Entrance** Very difficult **Setting** 110-acre suburban campus **Total enrollment** 1,270 **Student/faculty ratio** 13:1 **Application deadline** 3/1 (freshmen), rolling (transfer) **Freshmen** 71% were admitted **Housing** Yes **Expenses** Tuition $22,206; Room & Board $5254 **Undergraduates** 60% women, 2% part-time, 2% 25 or older, 0.2% Native American, 3% Hispanic American, 6% African American, 5% Asian American/Pacific Islander **The most frequently chosen baccalaureate fields are** business/marketing, interdisciplinary studies, social sciences and history **Academic program** Advanced placement, accelerated degree program, self-designed majors, honors program, summer session, adult/continuing education programs, internships **Contact** Mr. William G. Motzer Jr., Director of Admissions, Lake Forest College, 555 North Sheridan Road, Lake Forest, IL 60045-2399. Telephone: 847-735-5000 or toll-free 800-828-4751. Fax: 847-735-6271. E-mail: motzer@lfc.edu. Web site: http://www.lakeforest.edu/.

LAKEVIEW COLLEGE OF NURSING
DANVILLE, ILLINOIS

General Independent, upper-level, coed, primarily women **Entrance** Moderately difficult **Setting** small-town campus **Total enrollment** 56 **Student/faculty ratio** 5:1 **Application deadline** Rolling (transfer) **Housing** No **Expenses** Tuition 7750 **Undergraduates** 71% 25 or older, 0% Native American, 3% Hispanic American, 6% African American, 3% Asian American/Pacific Islander **The most frequently chosen baccalaureate field is** health professions and related sciences **Academic program** Summer session **Contact** Ms. Kelly Holden, Registrar, Lakeview College of Nursing, 903 North Logan Avenue, Danville, IL 61832. Telephone: 217-443-5385. Fax: 217-442-2279. E-mail: kholden@lakeviewcol.edu.

LEWIS UNIVERSITY
ROMEOVILLE, ILLINOIS

General Independent, comprehensive, coed, affiliated with Roman Catholic Church **Entrance** Moderately difficult **Setting** 600-acre small-town campus **Total enrollment** 4,304 **Student/faculty ratio** 15:1 **Application deadline** Rolling (freshmen), rolling (transfer) **Freshmen** 70% were admitted **Housing** Yes **Expenses** Tuition $13,320; Room & Board $6000 **Undergraduates** 56% women, 37% part-time, 43% 25 or older, 0.2% Native American, 7% Hispanic American, 16% African American, 2% Asian American/Pacific Islander **The most frequently chosen baccalaureate fields are** business/marketing, health professions and related sciences, protective services/public administration **Academic program** English as a second language, advanced placement, accelerated degree program, self-designed majors, honors program, summer session, adult/continuing education programs, internships **Contact** Ms. Karen Calloway, Assistant Director of Admissions, Lewis University, Box 297, One University Parkway, Romeoville, IL 60446. Telephone: 815-838-0500 Ext. 5237 or toll-free 800-897-9000. Fax: 815-836-5002. E-mail: admissions@lewisu.edu. Web site: http://www.lewisu.edu/.

LINCOLN CHRISTIAN COLLEGE
LINCOLN, ILLINOIS

General Independent, 4-year, coed, affiliated with Christian Churches and Churches of Christ **Entrance** Moderately difficult **Setting** 227-acre small-town campus **Total enrollment** 653 **Student/faculty ratio** 13:1 **Application deadline** Rolling (freshmen), rolling (transfer) **Freshmen** 81% were admitted **Housing** Yes **Expenses** Tuition $8128; Room & Board $4100 **Undergraduates** 52% women, 22% part-time, 21% 25 or older, 0.3% Native American, 1% Hispanic American, 2% African American, 2% Asian American/Pacific Islander **Academic program** English as a second language, advanced placement, summer session, adult/continuing education programs, internships **Contact** Mrs. Mary K. Davis, Assistant Director of Admissions, Lincoln Christian College, 1100 Campus View Drive, Lincoln, IL 62656. Telephone: 217-732-3168 Ext. 2251 or toll-free 888-522-5228. Fax: 217-732-5914. E-mail: lccs-college@prairienet.org. Web site: http://www.lccs.edu/.

LOYOLA UNIVERSITY CHICAGO
CHICAGO, ILLINOIS

General Independent Roman Catholic (Jesuit), university, coed **Entrance** Moderately difficult **Setting** 105-acre urban campus **Total enrollment** 12,605 **Student/faculty ratio** 13:1 **Application deadline** 4/1 (freshmen), 7/9 (transfer) **Freshmen** 80% were admitted **Housing** Yes **Expenses** Tuition $18,726; Room & Board $7266 **Undergraduates** 64% women, 30% part-time, 6% 25 or older, 0.1% Native American, 9% Hispanic American, 9% African American, 12% Asian American/Pacific Islander **The most frequently chosen baccalaureate fields are** business/marketing, psychology, social sciences and history **Academic program** English as a second language, advanced placement, accelerated degree program, honors program, summer session, adult/continuing education programs, internships **Contact** Mr. Aaron Meis, Acting Director of Admissions, Loyola University Chicago, 820 North Michigan Avenue, Suite 613, Chicago, IL 60611. Telephone: 312-915-6500 or toll-free 800-262-2373. Fax: 312-915-7216. E-mail: admission@luc.edu. Web site: http://www.luc.edu/.

► **For more information, see page 440.**

MACMURRAY COLLEGE
JACKSONVILLE, ILLINOIS

General Independent United Methodist, 4-year, coed **Entrance** Moderately difficult **Setting** 60-acre small-town campus **Total enrollment** 727 **Student/faculty ratio** 13:1 **Application deadline** Rolling (freshmen), rolling (transfer) **Freshmen** 69% were admitted **Housing** Yes **Expenses** Tuition $13,140; Room & Board $4650 **Undergraduates** 51% women, 6% part-time, 13% 25 or older, 0.3% Native American, 6% Hispanic American, 11% African American, 1% Asian American/Pacific Islander **The most frequently chosen baccalaureate fields are** education, protective services/public administration, psychology **Academic program** Advanced placement, honors program, summer session, internships **Contact** Mr. Tom McGinnis, Dean of Enrollment, MacMurray College, 447 East College Avenue, Jacksonville, IL 62650. Telephone: 217-479-7056 or toll-free 800-252-7485 (in-state); 217-479-7056 (out-of-state). Fax: 217-291-0702. E-mail: admiss@mac.edu. Web site: http://www.mac.edu/.

MCKENDREE COLLEGE
LEBANON, ILLINOIS

General Independent, 4-year, coed, affiliated with United Methodist Church **Entrance** Moderately difficult **Setting** 80-acre small-town campus **Total enrollment** 1,993 **Student/faculty ratio** 16:1 **Application deadline** Rolling (freshmen), rolling (transfer) **Freshmen** 69% were admitted **Housing** Yes

McKendree College *(continued)*

Expenses Tuition $13,350; Room & Board $4935 **Undergraduates** 62% women, 25% part-time, 34% 25 or older, 1% Native American, 2% Hispanic American, 10% African American, 1% Asian American/ Pacific Islander **The most frequently chosen baccalaureate fields are** business/marketing, education, health professions and related sciences **Academic program** Advanced placement, accelerated degree program, self-designed majors, honors program, summer session, internships **Contact** Sue MacGregor, Dean of Admissions and Financial Aid, McKendree College, 701 College Road, Lebanon, IL 62254. Telephone: 618-537-4481 Ext. 6831 or toll-free 800-232-7228 Ext. 6835. Fax: 618-537-6496. E-mail: suemac@atlas.mckendree.edu. Web site: http://www.mckendree.edu/.

MENNONITE COLLEGE OF NURSING

See Illinois State University

MILLIKIN UNIVERSITY

DECATUR, ILLINOIS

General Independent, 4-year, coed, affiliated with Presbyterian Church (U.S.A.) **Entrance** Moderately difficult **Setting** 70-acre suburban campus **Total enrollment** 2,307 **Student/faculty ratio** 13:1 **Application deadline** Rolling (freshmen), rolling (transfer) **Freshmen** 99% were admitted **Housing** Yes **Expenses** Tuition $17,359; Room & Board $5594 **Undergraduates** 58% women, 4% part-time, 5% 25 or older, 0.3% Native American, 2% Hispanic American, 7% African American, 1% Asian American/ Pacific Islander **The most frequently chosen baccalaureate fields are** business/marketing, education, visual/performing arts **Academic program** Advanced placement, self-designed majors, honors program, summer session, internships **Contact** Mr. Lin Stoner, Dean of Admission, Millikin University, 1184 West Main Street, Decatur, IL 62522-2084. Telephone: 217-424-6210 or toll-free 800-373-7733 Ext. # 5. Fax: 217-425-4669. E-mail: admis@mail.millikin.edu. Web site: http://www.millikin.edu/.

MONMOUTH COLLEGE

MONMOUTH, ILLINOIS

General Independent, 4-year, coed, affiliated with Presbyterian Church **Entrance** Moderately difficult **Setting** 40-acre small-town campus **Total enrollment** 1,069 **Student/faculty ratio** 14:1 **Application deadline** Rolling (freshmen), rolling (transfer) **Freshmen** 78% were admitted **Housing** Yes **Expenses** Tuition 16,380; Room & Board 4500 **Undergraduates** 57% women, 1% part-time, 2% 25 or older, 0.3% Native American, 2% Hispanic American, 5% African American, 1% Asian American/Pacific Islander **The most frequently chosen baccalaureate fields are** business/marketing, education, social sciences and history **Academic program** Advanced placement, self-designed majors, honors program, internships **Contact** Mrs. Marybeth Kemp, Vice President for Admissions, Monmouth College, 700 East Broadway, Monmouth, IL 61462-1998. Telephone: 309-457-2131 or toll-free 800-747-2687. Fax: 309-457-2141. E-mail: admit@monm.edu. Web site: http://www.monm.edu/.

MOODY BIBLE INSTITUTE

CHICAGO, ILLINOIS

General Independent nondenominational, comprehensive, coed **Entrance** Moderately difficult **Setting** 25-acre urban campus **Total enrollment** 1,470 **Student/faculty ratio** 18:1 **Application deadline** 3/1 (freshmen), 3/1 (transfer) **Freshmen** 41% were admitted **Housing** Yes **Expenses** Tuition $1225; Room & Board $5500 **Undergraduates** 46% women, 5% part-time, 7% 25 or older, 1% Native American, 4% Hispanic American, 2% African American, 3% Asian American/Pacific Islander **The most frequently chosen baccalaureate fields are** communications/ communication technologies, foreign language/ literature, philosophy, religion, and theology **Academic program** English as a second language, advanced placement, summer session, adult/ continuing education programs, internships **Contact** Mrs. Marthe Campa, Application Coordinator, Moody Bible Institute, 820 North LaSalle Boulevard, Chicago, IL 60610. Telephone: 312-329-4266 or toll-free 800-967-4MBI. Fax: 312-329-8987. E-mail: admissions@moody.edu. Web site: http://www.moody.edu/.

NAES COLLEGE

CHICAGO, ILLINOIS

General Independent, 4-year, coed **Contact** Ms. Christine Redcloud, Registrar, NAES College, 2838 West Peterson Avenue, Chicago, IL 60659-3813. Telephone: 773-761-5000. Fax: 773-761-3808.

NATIONAL-LOUIS UNIVERSITY

EVANSTON, ILLINOIS

General Independent, university, coed **Entrance** Minimally difficult **Setting** 12-acre campus **Total enrollment** 4,183 **Student/faculty ratio** 13:1 **Application deadline** Rolling (freshmen), rolling (transfer) **Freshmen** 77% were admitted **Housing** Yes **Expenses** Tuition 13,095; Room & Board 5519 **Undergraduates** 1% Native American, 9% Hispanic American, 29% African American, 3% Asian American/ Pacific Islander **Academic program** English as a second language, advanced placement, accelerated degree program, honors program, summer session, adult/continuing education programs, internships **Contact** Ms. Pat Petillo, Director of Admissions, National-Louis University, 2840 Sheridan Road, Evanston, IL 60201-1796. Telephone: 888-NLU-TODAY or toll-free 888-NLU-TODAY Ext. 5151 (in-state); 800-443-5522 Ext. 5151 (out-of-state). Web site: http://www.nl.edu/.

NORTH CENTRAL COLLEGE

NAPERVILLE, ILLINOIS

General Independent United Methodist, comprehensive, coed **Entrance** Moderately difficult **Setting**

56-acre suburban campus **Total enrollment** 2,532 **Student/faculty ratio** 14:1 **Application deadline** Rolling (freshmen), rolling (transfer) **Freshmen** 76% were admitted **Housing** Yes **Expenses** Tuition 16,095; Room & Board 5472 **Undergraduates** 58% women, 17% part-time, 25% 25 or older, 0.3% Native American, 3% Hispanic American, 4% African American, 2% Asian American/Pacific Islander **The most frequently chosen baccalaureate fields are** business/marketing, communications/communication technologies, education **Academic program** English as a second language, advanced placement, accelerated degree program, self-designed majors, honors program, summer session, adult/continuing education programs, internships **Contact** Mr. Stephen Potts, Coordinator of Freshman Admission, North Central College, 30 North Brainard Street, PO Box 3063, Naperville, IL 60566-7063. Telephone: 630-637-5815 or toll-free 800-411-1861. Fax: 630-637-5819. E-mail: ncadm@noctrl.edu. Web site: http://www.noctrl.edu/.

NORTHEASTERN ILLINOIS UNIVERSITY
CHICAGO, ILLINOIS

General State-supported, comprehensive, coed **Entrance** Minimally difficult **Setting** 67-acre urban campus **Total enrollment** 10,941 **Student/faculty ratio** 18:1 **Application deadline** 7/1 (freshmen), 7/1 (transfer) **Freshmen** 70% were admitted **Housing** No **Expenses** Tuition $2664 **Undergraduates** 62% women, 43% part-time, 43% 25 or older, 0.2% Native American, 27% Hispanic American, 13% African American, 14% Asian American/Pacific Islander **The most frequently chosen baccalaureate fields are** education, business/marketing, liberal arts/general studies **Academic program** English as a second language, advanced placement, honors program, summer session, adult/continuing education programs, internships **Contact** Ms. Kay D. Gulli, Administrative Assistant, Northeastern Illinois University, 500 North St. Louis Avenue, Chicago, IL 60625. Telephone: 773-442-4000. Fax: 773-794-6243. E-mail: admrec@neiu.edu. Web site: http://www.neiu.edu/.

NORTHERN ILLINOIS UNIVERSITY
DE KALB, ILLINOIS

General State-supported, university, coed **Entrance** Moderately difficult **Setting** 589-acre small-town campus **Total enrollment** 23,248 **Student/faculty ratio** 17:1 **Application deadline** 8/1 (freshmen), 8/1 (transfer) **Freshmen** 65% were admitted **Housing** Yes **Expenses** Tuition $4275; Room & Board $5036 **Undergraduates** 53% women, 11% part-time, 13% 25 or older, 0.3% Native American, 5% Hispanic American, 12% African American, 7% Asian American/Pacific Islander **The most frequently chosen baccalaureate fields are** business/marketing, education, English **Academic program** Advanced placement, accelerated degree program, self-designed majors, honors program, summer session, adult/continuing education programs, internships **Contact** Dr. Robert Burk, Director of Admissions, Northern Illinois University, DeKalb, IL 60113-2857. Telephone: 815-753-0446 or toll-free 800-892-3050 (in-state). E-mail: admission-info@niu.edu. Web site: http://www.niu.edu/.

NORTH PARK UNIVERSITY
CHICAGO, ILLINOIS

General Independent, comprehensive, coed, affiliated with Evangelical Covenant Church **Entrance** Moderately difficult **Setting** 30-acre urban campus **Total enrollment** 2,387 **Student/faculty ratio** 16:1 **Application deadline** Rolling (freshmen), rolling (transfer) **Freshmen** 74% were admitted **Housing** Yes **Expenses** Tuition $16,910; Room & Board $5870 **Undergraduates** 62% women, 31% part-time, 20% 25 or older, 1% Native American, 9% Hispanic American, 11% African American, 5% Asian American/Pacific Islander **The most frequently chosen baccalaureate fields are** health professions and related sciences, business/marketing, social sciences and history **Academic program** English as a second language, advanced placement, accelerated degree program, self-designed majors, honors program, summer session, adult/continuing education programs, internships **Contact** Office of Admissions, North Park University, 3225 West Foster Avenue, Chicago, IL 60625-4895. Telephone: 773-244-5500 or toll-free 800-888-NPC8. Fax: 773-583-0858. E-mail: afao@northpark.edu. Web site: http://www.northpark.edu/.

NORTHWESTERN UNIVERSITY
EVANSTON, ILLINOIS

General Independent, university, coed **Entrance** Most difficult **Setting** 250-acre suburban campus **Total enrollment** 15,663 **Student/faculty ratio** 7:1 **Application deadline** 1/1 (freshmen), 6/1 (transfer) **Freshmen** 33% were admitted **Housing** Yes **Expenses** Tuition 24,648; Room & Board 7471 **Undergraduates** 52% women, 2% part-time, 1% 25 or older, 0.2% Native American, 4% Hispanic American, 7% African American, 17% Asian American/Pacific Islander **The most frequently chosen baccalaureate fields are** engineering/engineering technologies, English, social sciences and history **Academic program** Advanced placement, accelerated degree program, self-designed majors, honors program, summer session, adult/continuing education programs, internships **Contact** Ms. Carol Lunkenheimer, Director of Admissions, Northwestern University, PO Box 3060, Evanston, IL 60204-3060. Telephone: 847-491-7271. E-mail: ug-admission@nwu.edu. Web site: http://www.northwestern.edu/.

OLIVET NAZARENE UNIVERSITY
BOURBONNAIS, ILLINOIS

General Independent, comprehensive, coed, affiliated with Church of the Nazarene **Entrance** Moderately difficult **Setting** 168-acre small-town campus **Total enrollment** 2,859 **Student/faculty ratio** 18:1 **Application deadline** Rolling (freshmen), rolling (transfer) **Freshmen** 83% were admitted **Housing** Yes **Expenses** Tuition $13,464; Room & Board $4980

Olivet Nazarene University *(continued)*

Undergraduates 59% women, 13% part-time, 18% 25 or older, 0.2% Native American, 2% Hispanic American, 8% African American, 1% Asian American/ Pacific Islander **The most frequently chosen baccalaureate fields are** business/marketing, biological/ life sciences, health professions and related sciences **Academic program** Advanced placement, summer session, adult/continuing education programs, internships **Contact** Mr. Brian Parker, Director of Admissions, Olivet Nazarene University, One University Avenue, Bourbonnais, IL 60914. Telephone: 815-939-5203 or toll-free 800-648-1463. Fax: 815-935-4998. E-mail: admissions@olivet.edu. Web site: http://www.olivet.edu/.

PRINCIPIA COLLEGE
ELSAH, ILLINOIS

General Independent Christian Science, 4-year, coed **Entrance** Moderately difficult **Setting** 2,600-acre rural campus **Total enrollment** 560 **Student/faculty ratio** 9:1 **Application deadline** 3/1 (freshmen), 3/1 (transfer) **Freshmen** 86% were admitted **Housing** Yes **Expenses** Tuition 16,840; Room & Board 5790 **Undergraduates** 54% women, 4% part-time, 3% 25 or older, 0.2% Native American, 1% Hispanic American, 2% African American, 1% Asian American/ Pacific Islander **The most frequently chosen baccalaureate fields are** business/marketing, social sciences and history, visual/performing arts **Academic program** English as a second language, advanced placement, accelerated degree program, self-designed majors, honors program, adult/ continuing education programs, internships **Contact** Martha Green Quirk, Dean of Admissions, Principia College, Office of Admissions and Enrollment, Elsah, IL 62028. Telephone: 618-374-5180 or toll-free 800-277-4648 Ext. 2802. Fax: 618-374-4000. E-mail: collegeadmissions@prin.edu. Web site: http://www.prin.edu/college.

QUINCY UNIVERSITY
QUINCY, ILLINOIS

General Independent Roman Catholic, comprehensive, coed **Entrance** Moderately difficult **Setting** 75-acre small-town campus **Total enrollment** 1,188 **Student/faculty ratio** 15:1 **Application deadline** Rolling (freshmen), rolling (transfer) **Freshmen** 98% were admitted **Housing** Yes **Expenses** Tuition $14,700; Room & Board $4780 **Undergraduates** 56% women, 7% part-time, 10% 25 or older, 0.1% Native American, 2% Hispanic American, 7% African American, 1% Asian American/Pacific Islander **The most frequently chosen baccalaureate fields are** business/ marketing, education, social sciences and history **Academic program** English as a second language, advanced placement, accelerated degree program, self-designed majors, honors program, summer session, adult/continuing education programs, internships **Contact** Mr. Kevin A. Brown, Director of Admissions, Quincy University, 1800 College Avenue, Quincy, IL 62301-2699. Telephone: 217-222-8020 Ext. 5215 or toll-free 800-688-4295. E-mail: admissions@quincy.edu. Web site: http://www.quincy.edu/.

ROBERT MORRIS COLLEGE
CHICAGO, ILLINOIS

General Independent, 4-year, coed **Entrance** Minimally difficult **Setting** urban campus **Total enrollment** 4,938 **Student/faculty ratio** 23:1 **Application deadline** Rolling (freshmen), rolling (transfer) **Freshmen** 71% were admitted **Housing** No **Expenses** Tuition $12,150 **Undergraduates** 67% women, 11% part-time, 37% 25 or older, 0.5% Native American, 25% Hispanic American, 39% African American, 4% Asian American/Pacific Islander **The most frequently chosen baccalaureate field is** business/ marketing **Academic program** Advanced placement, accelerated degree program, honors program, summer session, adult/continuing education programs, internships **Contact** Ms. Mablene Krueger, Senior Vice President of Advancement, Robert Morris College, 401 South State Street, Chicago, IL 60605. Telephone: 312-935-6645 Ext. 6645 or toll-free 800-225-1520. Fax: 312-935-6819. E-mail: enroll@rmcil.edu. Web site: http://www.rmcil.edu/.

ROCKFORD COLLEGE
ROCKFORD, ILLINOIS

General Independent, comprehensive, coed **Entrance** Moderately difficult **Setting** 130-acre suburban campus **Total enrollment** 1,315 **Student/faculty ratio** 10:1 **Application deadline** Rolling (freshmen), rolling (transfer) **Freshmen** 63% were admitted **Housing** Yes **Expenses** Tuition 17,450; Room & Board 5630 **Undergraduates** 65% women, 22% part-time, 32% 25 or older, 1% Native American, 4% Hispanic American, 7% African American, 2% Asian American/ Pacific Islander **The most frequently chosen baccalaureate fields are** business/marketing, education, health professions and related sciences **Academic program** English as a second language, advanced placement, self-designed majors, honors program, summer session, adult/continuing education programs, internships **Contact** Mr. William Laffey, Director of Admission, Rockford College, Nelson Hall, Rockford, IL 61108-2393. Telephone: 815-226-4050 Ext. 4149 or toll-free 800-892-2984. Fax: 815-226-2822. E-mail: admission@rockford.edu. Web site: http://www.rockford.edu/.

ROOSEVELT UNIVERSITY
CHICAGO, ILLINOIS

General Independent, comprehensive, coed **Entrance** Moderately difficult **Setting** urban campus **Total enrollment** 7,359 **Student/faculty ratio** 16:1 **Application deadline** 8/15 (freshmen), 8/15 (transfer) **Freshmen** 51% were admitted **Housing** Yes **Expenses** Tuition $13,070; Room & Board $6040 **Undergraduates** 62% women, 62% part-time, 63% 25 or older, 0.2% Native American, 11% Hispanic American, 27% African American, 4% Asian American/Pacific Islander **Academic program** English as a second language, advanced placement, accelerated degree program, self-designed majors, honors program, summer session, adult/continuing education programs, internships **Contact** Mr. Larry Polselli, Director of Admission, Roosevelt University, Office of Admissions, Chicago, IL 60605-1394. Telephone: 312-341-2101 or toll-free 877-APPLYRU. Fax: 312-341-3523. E-mail: dessimm@admvsbk.roosevelt.edu. Web site: http://www.roosevelt.edu/.

RUSH UNIVERSITY
CHICAGO, ILLINOIS

General Independent, upper-level, coed **Entrance** Moderately difficult **Setting** 35-acre urban campus **Total enrollment** 1,882 **Application deadline** Rolling (transfer) **First-Year Students** 72% were admitted **Housing** Yes **Expenses** Tuition $13,500; Room only $7560 **Undergraduates** 89% women, 8% part-time, 43% 25 or older, 1% Native American, 11% Hispanic American, 13% African American, 11% Asian American/Pacific Islander **The most frequently chosen baccalaureate field is** health professions and related sciences **Contact** Ms. Hicela Castruita, Director of College Admission Services, Rush University, 600 S. Paulina - Suite 440, College Admissions Services, Chicago, IL 60612-3878. Telephone: 312-942-7100. Fax: 312-942-2219. E-mail: ruadmissions@rushu.rush.edu. Web site: http://www.rushu.rush.edu/.

SAINT ANTHONY COLLEGE OF NURSING
ROCKFORD, ILLINOIS

General Independent Roman Catholic, upper-level, coed, primarily women **Entrance** Moderately difficult **Setting** 17-acre urban campus **Total enrollment** 71 **Student/faculty ratio** 6:1 **Application deadline** Rolling (transfer) **Housing** No **Expenses** Tuition 22,090 **Undergraduates** 92% women, 21% part-time, 50% 25 or older, 0% Native American, 3% Hispanic American, 2% African American, 3% Asian American/Pacific Islander **The most frequently chosen baccalaureate field is** health professions and related sciences **Academic program** Advanced placement, summer session **Contact** Financial Aid Officer, Saint Anthony College of Nursing, 5658 East State Street, Rockford, IL 61108-2468. Telephone: 815-395-5091. Fax: 815-395 Ext. 2275. E-mail: nancysanders@sacn.edu. Web site: http://www.sacn.edu/.

ST. AUGUSTINE COLLEGE
CHICAGO, ILLINOIS

General Independent, 4-year, coed **Entrance** Noncompetitive **Setting** 4-acre urban campus **Total enrollment** 1,543 **Student/faculty ratio** 13:1 **Application deadline** Rolling (freshmen), rolling (transfer) **Housing** No **Expenses** Tuition $6740 **Undergraduates** 79% women, 24% part-time, 59% 25 or older, 0.1% Native American, 84% Hispanic American, 10% African American, 4% Asian American/Pacific Islander **Academic program** English as a second language, summer session, internships **Contact** Ms. Soledad Ruiz, Director of Admissions, St. Augustine College, 1333-1345 West Argyle, Chicago, IL 60640-3501. Telephone: 773-878-8756 Ext. 243. Web site: http://www.staugustinecollege.edu/.

SAINT FRANCIS MEDICAL CENTER COLLEGE OF NURSING
PEORIA, ILLINOIS

General Independent Roman Catholic, upper-level, coed, primarily women **Entrance** Moderately difficult **Setting** urban campus **Total enrollment** 134 **Student/faculty ratio** 8:1 **Application deadline** Rolling (transfer) **First-Year Students** 80% were admitted **Housing** Yes **Expenses** Tuition $9372; Room only $1680 **Undergraduates** 93% women, 13% part-time, 47% 25 or older, 0% Native American, 1% Hispanic American, 4% African American, 2% Asian American/Pacific Islander **The most frequently chosen baccalaureate field is** health professions and related sciences **Academic program** Advanced placement, summer session **Contact** Mrs. Janice Farquharson, Director of Admissions and Registrar, Saint Francis Medical Center College of Nursing, 511 Greenleaf Street, Peoria, IL 61603-3783. Telephone: 309-655-2596. Fax: 309-624-8973. E-mail: janice.farquharson@osfhealthcare.org. Web site: http://www.sfmccon.edu/.

ST. JOHN'S COLLEGE
SPRINGFIELD, ILLINOIS

General Independent Roman Catholic, upper-level, coed, primarily women **Entrance** Moderately difficult **Setting** urban campus **Total enrollment** 60 **Student/faculty ratio** 6:1 **First-Year Students** 97% were admitted **Housing** No **Expenses** Tuition $7952 **Undergraduates** 95% women, 3% part-time, 28% 25 or older, 0% Native American, 5% Hispanic American, 8% African American, 0% Asian American/Pacific Islander **The most frequently chosen baccalaureate field is** health professions and related sciences **Contact** Ms. Beth Beasley, Student Development Officer, St. John's College, 421 North Ninth Street, Springfield, IL 62702-5317. Telephone: 217-525-5628 Ext. 45468. Web site: http://www.st-johns.org/collegeofnursing/.

SAINT JOSEPH COLLEGE OF NURSING
See University of St. Francis

SAINT XAVIER UNIVERSITY
CHICAGO, ILLINOIS

General Independent Roman Catholic, comprehensive, coed **Entrance** Moderately difficult **Setting** 55-acre urban campus **Total enrollment** 4,602 **Student/faculty ratio** 15:1 **Application deadline** 8/15 (freshmen), 8/15 (transfer) **Freshmen** 73% were admitted **Housing** Yes **Expenses** Tuition $14,530; Room & Board $5744 **Undergraduates** 73% women, 31% part-time, 32% 25 or older, 0.4% Native American, 12% Hispanic American, 16% African American, 2% Asian American/Pacific Islander **The most**

Saint Xavier University *(continued)*

frequently chosen baccalaureate fields are business/marketing, education, health professions and related sciences **Academic program** English as a second language, advanced placement, accelerated degree program, self-designed majors, honors program, summer session, adult/continuing education programs, internships **Contact** Elizabeth A. Gierach, Director of Enrollment Services, Saint Xavier University, 3700 West 103rd Street, Chicago, IL 60655-3105. Telephone: 773-298-3063 or toll-free 800-462-9288. Fax: 773-298-3076 Ext. 3050. E-mail: admissions@sxu.edu. Web site: http://www.sxu.edu/.

SCHOOL OF THE ART INSTITUTE OF CHICAGO
CHICAGO, ILLINOIS

General Independent, comprehensive, coed **Entrance** Moderately difficult **Setting** 1-acre urban campus **Total enrollment** 2,578 **Student/faculty ratio** 13:1 **Application deadline** 8/15 (freshmen), 8/15 (transfer) **Freshmen** 76% were admitted **Housing** Yes **Expenses** Tuition $21,300; Room only $6500 **Undergraduates** 63% women, 24% part-time, 1% Native American, 6% Hispanic American, 3% African American, 9% Asian American/Pacific Islander **Academic program** English as a second language, advanced placement, self-designed majors, summer session, internships **Contact** Kendra E. Dane, Executive Director of Admissions and Marketing, School of the Art Institute of Chicago, 37 South Wabash, Chicago, IL 60603. Telephone: 312-899-5219 or toll-free 800-232-SAIC. E-mail: admiss@artic.edu. Web site: http://www.artic.edu/saic/.

SHIMER COLLEGE
WAUKEGAN, ILLINOIS

General Independent, 4-year, coed **Entrance** Moderately difficult **Setting** 3-acre suburban campus **Total enrollment** 114 **Student/faculty ratio** 10:1 **Application deadline** 8/30 (freshmen), 8/30 (transfer) **Freshmen** 96% were admitted **Housing** Yes **Expenses** Tuition $15,110; Room only $2300 **Undergraduates** 51% women, 12% part-time, 46% 25 or older, 2% Native American, 4% Hispanic American, 8% African American, 1% Asian American/Pacific Islander **The most frequently chosen baccalaureate fields are** library science, social sciences and history **Academic program** Accelerated degree program, self-designed majors, summer session, adult/continuing education programs **Contact** Mr. David Buchanan, Admissions Counselor, Shimer College, PO Box 500, Waukegan, IL 60079-0500. Telephone: 847-249-7174 or toll-free 800-215-7173. Fax: 847-249-7171. E-mail: admissions@shimer.edu. Web site: http://www.shimer.edu/.

SOUTHERN ILLINOIS UNIVERSITY CARBONDALE
CARBONDALE, ILLINOIS

General State-supported, university, coed **Entrance** Moderately difficult **Setting** 1,128-acre small-town campus **Total enrollment** 22,552 **Student/faculty ratio** 19:1 **Application deadline** Rolling (freshmen), rolling (transfer) **Freshmen** 71% were admitted **Housing** Yes **Expenses** Tuition 4113; Room & Board 4104 **Undergraduates** 43% women, 11% part-time, 26% 25 or older, 0.3% Native American, 3% Hispanic American, 14% African American, 1% Asian American/Pacific Islander **The most frequently chosen baccalaureate fields are** education, business/marketing, engineering/engineering technologies **Academic program** English as a second language, advanced placement, accelerated degree program, honors program, summer session, adult/continuing education programs, internships **Contact** Mr. Walker Allen, Director of Admissions, Southern Illinois University Carbondale, Mail Code 4710, Carbondale, IL 62901-4710. Telephone: 618-536-4405. Fax: 618-453-3250. E-mail: admrec@siu.edu. Web site: http://www.siu.edu/siuc/.

SOUTHERN ILLINOIS UNIVERSITY EDWARDSVILLE
EDWARDSVILLE, ILLINOIS

General State-supported, comprehensive, coed **Entrance** Moderately difficult **Setting** 2,660-acre suburban campus **Total enrollment** 12,193 **Student/faculty ratio** 16:1 **Application deadline** 7/31 (freshmen), 7/31 (transfer) **Freshmen** 86% were admitted **Housing** Yes **Expenses** Tuition $3285; Room & Board $4870 **Undergraduates** 58% women, 19% part-time, 22% 25 or older, 0.4% Native American, 1% Hispanic American, 12% African American, 1% Asian American/Pacific Islander **The most frequently chosen baccalaureate fields are** business/marketing, education, health professions and related sciences **Academic program** English as a second language, advanced placement, accelerated degree program, self-designed majors, honors program, summer session, adult/continuing education programs, internships **Contact** Mr. Boyd Bradshaw, Director of Admissions, Southern Illinois University Edwardsville, Box 1600, Edwardsville, IL 62026-0001. Telephone: 618-650-3705 or toll-free 800-447-SIUE. Fax: 618-650-5013. E-mail: admis@siue.edu. Web site: http://www.siue.edu/.

TELSHE YESHIVA–CHICAGO
CHICAGO, ILLINOIS

Contact Rosh Hayeshiva, Telshe Yeshiva–Chicago, 3535 West Foster Avenue, Chicago, IL 60625-5598. Telephone: 773-463-7738.

TRINITY CHRISTIAN COLLEGE
PALOS HEIGHTS, ILLINOIS

General Independent interdenominational, 4-year, coed **Entrance** Moderately difficult **Setting** 53-acre suburban campus **Total enrollment** 854 **Student/faculty ratio** 13:1 **Application deadline** Rolling (freshmen), rolling (transfer) **Freshmen** 99% were admitted **Housing** Yes **Expenses** Tuition $13,240; Room & Board $5190 **Undergraduates** 63% women,

13% part-time, 6% 25 or older, 0.4% Native American, 3% Hispanic American, 5% African American, 2% Asian American/Pacific Islander **The most frequently chosen baccalaureate fields are** education, business/marketing, health professions and related sciences **Academic program** Advanced placement, honors program, adult/continuing education programs, internships **Contact** Mr. Pete Hamstra, Dean of Admissions, Trinity Christian College, 6601 West College Drive, Palos Heights, IL 60463-0929. Telephone: 708-239-4709 or toll-free 800-748-0085. Fax: 708-239-4826. E-mail: admissions@trnty.edu. Web site: http://www.trnty.edu/.

TRINITY COLLEGE OF NURSING AND SCHOOLS OF ALLIED HEALTH
MOLINE, ILLINOIS

General Independent, 4-year, coed, primarily women **Entrance** Most difficult **Setting** 1-acre urban campus **Total enrollment** 200 **Student/faculty ratio** 16:1 **Application deadline** 6/1 (freshmen), 6/1 (transfer) **Freshmen** 60% were admitted **Housing** Yes **Expenses** Tuition 8275 **Undergraduates** 35% 25 or older **Academic program** Honors program, summer session, adult/continuing education programs **Contact** Cara A. Banks, Assistant Director of Student Services, Trinity College of Nursing and Schools of Allied Health, 555 6th Street, Suite 300, Moline, IL 61265-1216. Telephone: 309-779-7704. Fax: 309-757-2194. E-mail: carterc@trinityqc.com. Web site: http://www.trinityqc.com/college/default.htm.

TRINITY INTERNATIONAL UNIVERSITY
DEERFIELD, ILLINOIS

General Independent, university, coed, affiliated with Evangelical Free Church of America **Entrance** Moderately difficult **Setting** 108-acre suburban campus **Total enrollment** 2,152 **Student/faculty ratio** 17:1 **Application deadline** Rolling (freshmen), rolling (transfer) **Freshmen** 86% were admitted **Housing** Yes **Expenses** Tuition 15,350; Room & Board 5290 **Undergraduates** 57% women, 11% part-time, 36% 25 or older, 1% Native American, 4% Hispanic American, 12% African American, 3% Asian American/Pacific Islander **Academic program** Advanced placement, honors program, adult/continuing education programs, internships **Contact** Mr. Matt Yoder, Director of Undergraduate Admissions, Trinity International University, 2065 Half Day Road, Peterson Wing, McLennan Building, Deerfield, IL 60015-1284. Telephone: 847-317-7000 or toll-free 800-822-3225 (out-of-state). Fax: 847-317-7081. E-mail: tcoadm@trin.edu. Web site: http://www.tiu.edu/.

UNIVERSITY OF CHICAGO
CHICAGO, ILLINOIS

General Independent, university, coed **Entrance** Most difficult **Setting** 203-acre urban campus **Total enrollment** 12,531 **Student/faculty ratio** 4:1 **Application deadline** 1/1 (freshmen), 4/15 (transfer) **Freshmen** 44% were admitted **Housing** Yes **Expenses** Tuition $25,239; Room & Board $8070 **Undergraduates** 49% women, 2% part-time, 1% 25 or older, 0.3% Native American, 7% Hispanic American, 4% African American, 18% Asian American/Pacific Islander **The most frequently chosen baccalaureate fields are** biological/life sciences, interdisciplinary studies, social sciences and history **Academic program** Advanced placement, accelerated degree program, self-designed majors, summer session, adult/continuing education programs, internships **Contact** Mr. Theodore O'Neill, Dean of Admissions, University of Chicago, 1116 East 59th Street, Chicago, IL 60637-1513. Telephone: 773-702-8650. Fax: 773-702-4199. E-mail: college-admissions@uchicago.edu. Web site: http://www.uchicago.edu/.

UNIVERSITY OF ILLINOIS AT CHICAGO
CHICAGO, ILLINOIS

General State-supported, university, coed **Entrance** Moderately difficult **Setting** 216-acre urban campus **Total enrollment** 24,541 **Student/faculty ratio** 14:1 **Application deadline** 2/28 (freshmen), 6/1 (transfer) **Freshmen** 60% were admitted **Housing** Yes **Expenses** Tuition $4944; Room & Board $6026 **Undergraduates** 55% women, 13% part-time, 15% 25 or older, 0.3% Native American, 17% Hispanic American, 10% African American, 23% Asian American/Pacific Islander **The most frequently chosen baccalaureate fields are** business/marketing, engineering/engineering technologies, psychology **Academic program** English as a second language, advanced placement, accelerated degree program, self-designed majors, honors program, summer session, internships **Contact** Ms. Stacey Neil, Associate Director for Undergraduate Admissions, University of Illinois at Chicago, Box 5220, Chicago, IL 60680-5220. Telephone: 312-996-4350. Fax: 312-413-7628. E-mail: cqadmit@uicvmc.aiss.uic.edu. Web site: http://www.uic.edu/grad.

UNIVERSITY OF ILLINOIS AT SPRINGFIELD
SPRINGFIELD, ILLINOIS

General State-supported, upper-level, coed **Entrance** Minimally difficult **Setting** 746-acre suburban campus **Total enrollment** 3,942 **Student/faculty ratio** 12:1 **Application deadline** Rolling (transfer) **Housing** Yes **Expenses** Tuition 3715; Room only 3060 **Undergraduates** 64% women, 49% part-time, 59% 25 or older **The most frequently chosen baccalaureate fields are** business/marketing, protective services/public administration, psychology **Academic program** Self-designed majors, summer session, adult/continuing education programs, internships **Contact** Office of Enrollment Services, University of Illinois at Springfield, Building SAB, Springfield, IL 62794-9243. Telephone: 217-206-6626 or toll-free 800-252-8533 (in state). Fax: 217-206-6620. Web site: http://www.uis.edu/.

UNIVERSITY OF ILLINOIS AT URBANA–CHAMPAIGN
URBANA, ILLINOIS

General State-supported, university, coed **Entrance** Very difficult **Setting** 1,470-acre small-town campus **Total enrollment** 37,965 **Student/faculty ratio** 20:1 **Application deadline** 1/1 (freshmen), 3/15 (transfer) **Freshmen** 64% were admitted **Housing** Yes **Expenses** Tuition $5028; Room & Board $5844 **Undergraduates** 49% women, 4% part-time, 2% 25 or older, 0.2% Native American, 6% Hispanic American, 7% African American, 13% Asian American/Pacific Islander **The most frequently chosen baccalaureate fields are** business/marketing, engineering/engineering technologies, social sciences and history **Academic program** Advanced placement, accelerated degree program, self-designed majors, honors program, summer session, internships **Contact** Ms. Tammy Bouseman, Assistant Director of Admissions, University of Illinois at Urbana–Champaign, 901 West Illinois, Urbana, IL 61801. Telephone: 217-333-0302. E-mail: admssion@uiuc.edu. Web site: http://www.uiuc.edu/.

UNIVERSITY OF ST. FRANCIS
JOLIET, ILLINOIS

General Independent Roman Catholic, comprehensive, coed **Entrance** Moderately difficult **Setting** 16-acre suburban campus **Total enrollment** 2,742 **Student/faculty ratio** 12:1 **Application deadline** Rolling (freshmen), rolling (transfer) **Freshmen** 71% were admitted **Housing** Yes **Expenses** Tuition $14,290; Room & Board $5350 **Undergraduates** 69% women, 28% part-time, 37% 25 or older, 0.2% Native American, 4% Hispanic American, 6% African American, 1% Asian American/Pacific Islander **The most frequently chosen baccalaureate fields are** health professions and related sciences, business/marketing, interdisciplinary studies **Academic program** Advanced placement, accelerated degree program, self-designed majors, summer session, adult/continuing education programs, internships **Contact** Mr. Mike Rodewald, Director of Freshman Admission, University of St. Francis, 500 North Wilcox Street, Joliet, IL 60435-6188. Telephone: 815-740-3400 or toll-free 800-735-7500. Fax: 815-740-4285. E-mail: csfinfo@vax.colsf.edu. Web site: http://www.stfrancis.edu/.

VANDERCOOK COLLEGE OF MUSIC
CHICAGO, ILLINOIS

General Independent, comprehensive, coed **Entrance** Moderately difficult **Setting** 1-acre urban campus **Total enrollment** 265 **Student/faculty ratio** 9:1 **Application deadline** Rolling (freshmen), rolling (transfer) **Freshmen** 59% were admitted **Housing** Yes **Expenses** Tuition $13,810; Room & Board $5600 **Undergraduates** 16% 25 or older **Academic program** Advanced placement, summer session, adult/continuing education programs, internships **Contact** Mr. James Malley, Director of Undergraduate Admission, VanderCook College of Music, 3140 South Federal Street, Chicago, IL 60616-3731. Telephone: 800-448-2655 Ext. 241 or toll-free 800-448-2655. Fax: 312-225-5211. E-mail: vcmusic@mcs.com. Web site: http://www.vandercook.edu/.

WESTERN ILLINOIS UNIVERSITY
MACOMB, ILLINOIS

General State-supported, comprehensive, coed **Entrance** Moderately difficult **Setting** 1,050-acre small-town campus **Total enrollment** 13,093 **Student/faculty ratio** 16:1 **Application deadline** 8/1 (freshmen), rolling (transfer) **Freshmen** 65% were admitted **Housing** Yes **Expenses** Tuition $4206; Room & Board $5022 **Undergraduates** 51% women, 14% part-time, 7% 25 or older, 0.2% Native American, 3% Hispanic American, 7% African American, 1% Asian American/Pacific Islander **The most frequently chosen baccalaureate fields are** education, liberal arts/general studies, protective services/public administration **Academic program** English as a second language, advanced placement, self-designed majors, honors program, summer session, adult/continuing education programs, internships **Contact** Ms. Karen Helmers, Director of Admissions, Western Illinois University, 1 University Circle, 115 Sherman Hall, Macomb, IL 61455-1390. Telephone: 309-298-3157. Fax: 309-298-3111. E-mail: karen_helmers@uniu.edu. Web site: http://www.wiu.edu/.

▶ **For more information, see page 490.**

WEST SUBURBAN COLLEGE OF NURSING
OAK PARK, ILLINOIS

Contact Mr. Edward Pryor, Director of Admission, West Suburban College of Nursing, 3 Erie Court, Oak Park, IL 60302. Telephone: 708-763-6530. Fax: 708-763-1531.

WHEATON COLLEGE
WHEATON, ILLINOIS

General Independent nondenominational, comprehensive, coed **Entrance** Very difficult **Setting** 80-acre suburban campus **Total enrollment** 2,827 **Student/faculty ratio** 13:1 **Application deadline** 1/15 (freshmen), 3/1 (transfer) **Freshmen** 58% were admitted **Housing** Yes **Expenses** Tuition 15,540; Room & Board 5260 **Undergraduates** 53% women, 2% part-time, 1% 25 or older, 0.2% Native American, 3% Hispanic American, 2% African American, 4% Asian American/Pacific Islander **The most frequently chosen baccalaureate fields are** English, philosophy, religion, and theology, social sciences and history **Academic program** Advanced placement, self-designed majors, summer session, internships **Contact** Ms. Shawn Leftwich, Director of Admissions, Wheaton College, 501 College Avenue, Wheaton, IL 60187-5593. Telephone: 630-752-5011 or toll-free 800-222-2419 (out-of-state). Fax: 630-752-5285. E-mail: admissions@wheaton.edu. Web site: http://www.wheaton.edu/.

INDIANA

ANDERSON UNIVERSITY
ANDERSON, INDIANA

General Independent, comprehensive, coed, affiliated with Church of God **Entrance** Moderately difficult **Setting** 100-acre suburban campus **Total enrollment** 2,381 **Student/faculty ratio** 14:1 **Application deadline** 7/1 (freshmen), 8/25 (transfer) **Freshmen** 76% were admitted **Housing** Yes **Expenses** Tuition $14,680; Room & Board $4750 **Undergraduates** 57% women, 8% part-time, 9% 25 or older, 0.3% Native American, 1% Hispanic American, 4% African American, 0.4% Asian American/Pacific Islander **The most frequently chosen baccalaureate fields are** business/marketing, education, philosophy, religion, and theology **Academic program** Advanced placement, accelerated degree program, self-designed majors, honors program, summer session, adult/continuing education programs, internships **Contact** Mr. Jim King, Director of Admissions, Anderson University, 1100 East 5th Street, Anderson, IN 46012-3495. Telephone: 765-641-4080 or toll-free 800-421-3014 (in-state); 800-428-6414 (out-of-state). Fax: 765-641-3851. E-mail: info@anderson.edu. Web site: http://www.anderson.edu/.

BALL STATE UNIVERSITY
MUNCIE, INDIANA

General State-supported, university, coed **Entrance** Moderately difficult **Setting** 955-acre suburban campus **Total enrollment** 19,004 **Student/faculty ratio** 18:1 **Application deadline** Rolling (freshmen), rolling (transfer) **Freshmen** 79% were admitted **Housing** Yes **Expenses** Tuition $3830; Room & Board $4830 **Undergraduates** 53% women, 10% part-time, 9% 25 or older, 0.3% Native American, 1% Hispanic American, 6% African American, 1% Asian American/Pacific Islander **The most frequently chosen baccalaureate fields are** business/marketing, communications/communication technologies, education **Academic program** English as a second language, advanced placement, honors program, summer session, adult/continuing education programs, internships **Contact** Dr. Lawrence Waters, Dean of Admissions and Financial Aid, Ball State University, 2000 University Avenue, Muncie, IN 47306. Telephone: 765-285-8300 or toll-free 800-482-4BSU. Fax: 765-285-1632. E-mail: askus@wp.bsu.edu. Web site: http://www.bsu.edu/.

BETHEL COLLEGE
MISHAWAKA, INDIANA

General Independent, comprehensive, coed, affiliated with Missionary Church **Entrance** Moderately difficult **Setting** 70-acre suburban campus **Total enrollment** 1,647 **Student/faculty ratio** 18:1 **Application deadline** 8/1 (freshmen), 8/1 (transfer) **Freshmen** 68% were admitted **Housing** Yes **Expenses** Tuition $12,650; Room & Board $4150 **Undergraduates** 65% women, 25% part-time, 37% 25 or older, 0.3% Native American, 1% Hispanic American, 8% African American, 1% Asian American/Pacific Islander **Academic program** Advanced placement, accelerated degree program, honors program, summer session, adult/continuing education programs, internships **Contact** Ms. Andrea M. Helmuth, Director of Admissions, Bethel College, 1001 West McKinley Avenue, Mishawaka, IN 46545-5591. Telephone: 219-257-3319 or toll-free 800-422-4101. Fax: 219-257-3335. E-mail: helmuta@bethel-in.edu. Web site: http://www.bethel-in.edu/.

BUTLER UNIVERSITY
INDIANAPOLIS, INDIANA

General Independent, comprehensive, coed **Entrance** Moderately difficult **Setting** 290-acre urban campus **Total enrollment** 4,166 **Student/faculty ratio** 11:1 **Application deadline** 8/15 (freshmen), 8/15 (transfer) **Freshmen** 84% were admitted **Housing** Yes **Expenses** Tuition 18,230; Room & Board 6140 **Undergraduates** 63% women, 3% part-time, 4% 25 or older, 0.2% Native American, 1% Hispanic American, 4% African American, 2% Asian American/Pacific Islander **The most frequently chosen baccalaureate fields are** business/marketing, education, health professions and related sciences **Academic program** English as a second language, advanced placement, accelerated degree program, honors program, summer session, adult/continuing education programs, internships **Contact** Mr. William Preble, Dean of Admissions, Butler University, 4600 Sunset Avenue, Indianapolis, IN 46208-3485. Telephone: 317-940-8100 Ext. 8124 or toll-free 888-940-8100. Fax: 317-940-8150. E-mail: admission@butler.edu. Web site: http://www.butler.edu/.

CALUMET COLLEGE OF SAINT JOSEPH
WHITING, INDIANA

General Independent Roman Catholic, 4-year, coed **Contact** Mr. Thomas A. Clark, Vice President for Enrollment Management, Calumet College of Saint Joseph, 2400 New York Avenue, Whiting, IN 46394-2195. Telephone: 219-473-4215 or toll-free 877-700-9100. Fax: 219-473-4259. Web site: http://www.ccsj.edu/.

CROSSROADS BIBLE COLLEGE
INDIANAPOLIS, INDIANA

Contact Crossroads Bible College, 601 North Shortridge Road, Indianapolis, IN 46219. Telephone: or toll-free 800-273-2224.

DEPAUW UNIVERSITY
GREENCASTLE, INDIANA

General Independent, 4-year, coed, affiliated with United Methodist Church **Entrance** Moderately difficult **Setting** 175-acre small-town campus **Total enrollment** 2,225 **Student/faculty ratio** 10:1 **Application deadline** 2/1 (freshmen), 3/1 (transfer) **Fresh-**

DePauw University *(continued)*

men 61% were admitted **Housing** Yes **Expenses** Tuition 20,510; Room & Board 6324 **Undergraduates** 56% women, 2% part-time, 1% 25 or older, 0.3% Native American, 2% Hispanic American, 6% African American, 1% Asian American/Pacific Islander **The most frequently chosen baccalaureate fields are** communications/communication technologies, English, social sciences and history **Academic program** Advanced placement, self-designed majors, honors program, internships **Contact** Director of Admission, DePauw University, 101 East Seminary Street, Greencastle, IN 46135-0037. Telephone: 765-658-4006 or toll-free 800-447-2495. Fax: 765-658-4007. E-mail: admission@depauw.edu. Web site: http://www.depauw.edu/.

EARLHAM COLLEGE
RICHMOND, INDIANA

General Independent, 4-year, coed, affiliated with Society of Friends **Entrance** Moderately difficult **Setting** 800-acre small-town campus **Total enrollment** 1,104 **Student/faculty ratio** 12:1 **Application deadline** 2/15 (freshmen), 4/1 (transfer) **Freshmen** 85% were admitted **Housing** Yes **Expenses** Tuition 21,070; Room & Board 4936 **Undergraduates** 56% women, 2% part-time, 2% 25 or older, 0.3% Native American, 2% Hispanic American, 9% African American, 2% Asian American/Pacific Islander **The most frequently chosen baccalaureate fields are** biological/life sciences, interdisciplinary studies, social sciences and history **Academic program** Advanced placement, accelerated degree program, self-designed majors, internships **Contact** Director of Admissions, Earlham College, 801 National Road West, Richmond, IN 47374. Telephone: 765-983-1200 or toll-free 800-327-5426. Fax: 765-983-1560. E-mail: admission@earlham.edu. Web site: http://www.earlham.edu/.

▶ **For more information, see page 409.**

FRANKLIN COLLEGE OF INDIANA
FRANKLIN, INDIANA

General Independent, 4-year, coed, affiliated with American Baptist Churches in the U.S.A. **Entrance** Moderately difficult **Setting** 74-acre small-town campus **Total enrollment** 1,020 **Student/faculty ratio** 12:1 **Application deadline** Rolling (freshmen), rolling (transfer) **Freshmen** 77% were admitted **Housing** Yes **Expenses** Tuition $14,245; Room & Board $4590 **Undergraduates** 51% women, 5% part-time, 3% 25 or older, 0% Native American, 1% Hispanic American, 2% African American, 0.4% Asian American/Pacific Islander **The most frequently chosen baccalaureate fields are** business/marketing, biological/life sciences, education **Academic program** Advanced placement, summer session, internships **Contact** Mr. Bruce Stephen Richards, Dean of Admissions and Financial Aid, Franklin College of Indiana, 501 East Monroe Street, Franklin, IN 46131. Telephone: 317-738-8062 or toll-free 800-852-0232. Fax: 317-738-8062. E-mail: admissions@franklincoll.edu. Web site: http://www.franklincoll.edu/.

GOSHEN COLLEGE
GOSHEN, INDIANA

General Independent Mennonite, 4-year, coed **Entrance** Moderately difficult **Setting** 135-acre small-town campus **Total enrollment** 1,084 **Student/faculty ratio** 12:1 **Application deadline** 8/15 (freshmen), 8/15 (transfer) **Freshmen** 68% were admitted **Housing** Yes **Expenses** Tuition $13,140; Room & Board $4640 **Undergraduates** 57% women, 9% part-time, 11% 25 or older, 0% Native American, 3% Hispanic American, 2% African American, 1% Asian American/Pacific Islander **The most frequently chosen baccalaureate fields are** business/marketing, education, health professions and related sciences **Academic program** English as a second language, advanced placement, accelerated degree program, self-designed majors, honors program, summer session, adult/continuing education programs, internships **Contact** Ms. Marty Kelley, Director of Admissions, Goshen College, 1700 South Main Street, Goshen, IN 46526-4794. Telephone: 219-535-7535 or toll-free 800-348-7422. Fax: 219-535-7609. E-mail: admissions@goshen.edu. Web site: http://www.goshen.edu/.

GRACE COLLEGE
WINONA LAKE, INDIANA

General Independent, comprehensive, coed, affiliated with Fellowship of Grace Brethren Churches **Entrance** Moderately difficult **Setting** 160-acre small-town campus **Total enrollment** 1,059 **Student/faculty ratio** 19:1 **Application deadline** 8/1 (freshmen), 8/1 (transfer) **Freshmen** 88% were admitted **Housing** Yes **Expenses** Tuition 10,998; Room & Board 4685 **Undergraduates** 58% women, 9% part-time, 5% 25 or older, 0.2% Native American, 1% Hispanic American, 4% African American, 0.2% Asian American/Pacific Islander **The most frequently chosen baccalaureate fields are** business/marketing, education, psychology **Academic program** Advanced placement, accelerated degree program, summer session, internships **Contact** Mr. Ron Henry, Dean of Admissions, Grace College, 200 Seminary Drive, Winona Lake, IN 46590-1294. Telephone: 219-372-5100 Ext. 6006 or toll-free 800-54-GRACE (in-state); 800-54 GRACE (out-of-state). E-mail: rhenry@grace.edu. Web site: http://www.grace.edu/.

▶ **For more information, see page 427.**

HANOVER COLLEGE
HANOVER, INDIANA

General Independent Presbyterian, 4-year, coed **Entrance** Moderately difficult **Setting** 630-acre rural campus **Total enrollment** 1,142 **Student/faculty ratio** 12:1 **Application deadline** 3/1 (freshmen), 3/1 (transfer) **Freshmen** 83% were admitted **Housing** Yes **Expenses** Tuition 11,770; Room & Board 4930 **Undergraduates** 55% women, 1% part-time, 1% 25 or older, 0.2% Native American, 1% Hispanic American, 1% African American, 2% Asian American/Pacific Islander **The most frequently chosen baccalaureate fields are** business/marketing, communications/communication technologies, social sciences and history **Academic program** Advanced placement, accelerated degree program, honors program, internships **Contact** Mr. Kenneth Moyer Jr., Dean of Admissions, Hanover College, Box 108, Hanover, IN 47243-0108. Telephone: 812-866-7021 or toll-free 800-213-2178. Fax: 812-866-7098. E-mail: admissions@hanover.edu. Web site: http://www.hanover.edu/.

HUNTINGTON COLLEGE
HUNTINGTON, INDIANA

General Independent, comprehensive, coed, affiliated with Church of the United Brethren in Christ **Entrance** Moderately difficult **Setting** 200-acre small-town campus **Total enrollment** 904 **Application deadline** 8/1 (freshmen), rolling (transfer) **Freshmen** 93% were admitted **Housing** Yes **Expenses** Tuition $15,030; Room & Board $5450 **Undergraduates** 62% women, 8% part-time, 10% 25 or older, 0% Native American, 1% Hispanic American, 0.2% African American, 1% Asian American/Pacific Islander **The most frequently chosen baccalaureate fields are** business/marketing, education, philosophy, religion, and theology **Academic program** English as a second language, advanced placement, summer session, adult/continuing education programs **Contact** Mr. Jeff Berggren, Dean of Enrollment, Huntington College, 2303 College Avenue, Huntington, IN 46750-1299. Telephone: 219-359-4000 Ext. 4016 or toll-free 800-642-6493. Fax: 219-356-9448. E-mail: kjohnson@huntcol.edu. Web site: http://www.huntington.edu/.

INDIANA INSTITUTE OF TECHNOLOGY
FORT WAYNE, INDIANA

General Independent, comprehensive, coed **Entrance** Moderately difficult **Setting** 25-acre urban campus **Total enrollment** 2,167 **Student/faculty ratio** 22:1 **Application deadline** 9/1 (freshmen) **Freshmen** 14% were admitted **Housing** Yes **Expenses** Tuition $12,300; Room & Board $4996 **Undergraduates** 51% women, 54% part-time, 39% 25 or older, 0.3% Native American, 1% Hispanic American, 6% African American, 0.3% Asian American/Pacific Islander **The most frequently chosen baccalaureate fields are** business/marketing, computer/information sciences, engineering/engineering technologies **Academic program** English as a second language, advanced placement, accelerated degree program, self-designed majors, summer session, adult/continuing education programs, internships **Contact** Mrs. Andrea James, Registrar, Indiana Institute of Technology, 1600 East Washington Boulevard, Fort Wayne, IN 46803-1297. Telephone: 219-422-5561 Ext. 2231 or toll-free 800-937-2448 (in-state); 888-666-TECH (out-of-state). Fax: 219-422-7696. E-mail: lange@indtech.edu. Web site: http://www.indtech.edu/.

INDIANA STATE UNIVERSITY
TERRE HAUTE, INDIANA

General State-supported, university, coed **Entrance** Moderately difficult **Setting** 91-acre suburban campus **Total enrollment** 11,051 **Student/faculty ratio** 15:1 **Application deadline** 8/15 (freshmen), rolling (transfer) **Freshmen** 83% were admitted **Housing** Yes **Expenses** Tuition $3564; Room & Board $4604 **Undergraduates** 52% women, 15% part-time, 19% 25 or older, 0.3% Native American, 1% Hispanic American, 10% African American, 1% Asian American/Pacific Islander **The most frequently chosen baccalaureate fields are** business/marketing, education, social sciences and history **Academic program** English as a second language, advanced placement, accelerated degree program, honors program, summer session, adult/continuing education programs, internships **Contact** Mr. Ronald Brown, Director of Admissions, Indiana State University, 210 North Seventh Street, Terre Haute, IN 47809-1401. Telephone: 812-237-2121 or toll-free 800-742-0891. Fax: 812-237-8023. E-mail: admisu@amber.indstate.edu. Web site: http://web.indstate.edu/.

INDIANA UNIVERSITY BLOOMINGTON
BLOOMINGTON, INDIANA

General State-supported, university, coed **Entrance** Moderately difficult **Setting** 1,931-acre small-town campus **Total enrollment** 37,076 **Student/faculty ratio** 20:1 **Application deadline** 2/1 (freshmen), rolling (transfer) **Freshmen** 82% were admitted **Housing** Yes **Expenses** Tuition 4405; Room & Board 5608 **Undergraduates** 53% women, 8% part-time, 6% 25 or older, 0.3% Native American, 2% Hispanic American, 4% African American, 3% Asian American/Pacific Islander **The most frequently chosen baccalaureate fields are** business/marketing, education, protective services/public administration **Academic program** English as a second language, advanced placement, accelerated degree program, self-designed majors, honors program, summer session, adult/continuing education programs, internships **Contact** Mr. Don Hossler, Vice Chancellor for Enrollment Services, Indiana University Bloomington, 300 North Jordan Avenue, Bloomington, IN 47405-1106. Telephone: 812-855-0661. Fax: 812-855-5102. E-mail: iuadmit@indiana.edu. Web site: http://www.iub.edu/.

INDIANA UNIVERSITY EAST
RICHMOND, INDIANA

General State-supported, 4-year, coed **Entrance** Moderately difficult **Setting** 194-acre small-town campus **Total enrollment** 2,335 **Student/faculty ratio** 14:1 **Application deadline** Rolling (freshmen), rolling (transfer) **Freshmen** 64% were admitted **Housing** No **Expenses** Tuition 3206 **Undergraduates** 69% women, 56% part-time, 43% 25 or older, 0.4% Native American, 1% Hispanic American, 5% African American, 1% Asian American/Pacific Islander **The most frequently chosen baccalaureate fields are** business/marketing, education, health profes-

Indiana University East *(continued)*

sions and related sciences **Academic program** Advanced placement, summer session, adult/continuing education programs, internships **Contact** Ms. Susanna Tanner, Admissions Counselor, Indiana University East, 2325 Chester Boulevard, WZ 116, Richmond, IN 47374-1289. Telephone: 765-973-8415 or toll-free 800-959-EAST. Fax: 765-973-8288. E-mail: eaadmit@indiana.edu. Web site: http://www.indiana.edu/.

INDIANA UNIVERSITY KOKOMO

KOKOMO, INDIANA

General State-supported, comprehensive, coed **Entrance** Minimally difficult **Setting** 51-acre small-town campus **Total enrollment** 2,682 **Student/faculty ratio** 15:1 **Application deadline** 8/3 (freshmen), 8/3 (transfer) **Freshmen** 91% were admitted **Housing** No **Expenses** Tuition $3212 **Undergraduates** 70% women, 54% part-time, 39% 25 or older, 0.5% Native American, 1% Hispanic American, 3% African American, 1% Asian American/Pacific Islander **The most frequently chosen baccalaureate fields are** education, business/marketing, health professions and related sciences **Academic program** Advanced placement, honors program, summer session, adult/continuing education programs, internships **Contact** Mr. Darren Bush, Admissions Director, Indiana University Kokomo, PO Box 9003, Kelley Student Center 230A, Kokomo, IN 46904-9003. Telephone: 765-455-9217 or toll-free 888-875-4485. Fax: 765-455-9537. E-mail: iukadmis@iukfs1.indiana.edu. Web site: http://www.indiana.edu.

INDIANA UNIVERSITY NORTHWEST

GARY, INDIANA

General State-supported, comprehensive, coed **Entrance** Minimally difficult **Setting** 38-acre urban campus **Total enrollment** 4,649 **Student/faculty ratio** 13:1 **Application deadline** 8/1 (freshmen) **Freshmen** 75% were admitted **Housing** No **Expenses** Tuition 3237 **Undergraduates** 70% women, 46% part-time, 42% 25 or older, 0.3% Native American, 10% Hispanic American, 25% African American, 1% Asian American/Pacific Islander **The most frequently chosen baccalaureate fields are** business/marketing, education, health professions and related sciences **Academic program** Advanced placement, accelerated degree program, self-designed majors, honors program, summer session, adult/continuing education programs, internships **Contact** Mr. William Lee, Director of Admissions, Indiana University Northwest, Hawthorne 100, 3400 Broadway, Gary, IN 46408-1197. Telephone: 219-980-6991 or toll-free 800-968-7486. Fax: 219-981-4219. E-mail: wlee@unhaw1.iun.indiana.edu. Web site: http://www.indiana.edu/.

INDIANA UNIVERSITY–PURDUE UNIVERSITY FORT WAYNE

FORT WAYNE, INDIANA

General State-supported, comprehensive, coed **Entrance** Minimally difficult **Setting** 565-acre urban campus **Total enrollment** 10,532 **Student/faculty ratio** 16:1 **Application deadline** 8/1 (freshmen), 8/1 (transfer) **Freshmen** 94% were admitted **Housing** No **Expenses** Tuition $2946 **Undergraduates** 57% women, 46% part-time, 35% 25 or older, 0.3% Native American, 2% Hispanic American, 5% African American, 3% Asian American/Pacific Islander **The most frequently chosen baccalaureate fields are** business/marketing, education, engineering/engineering technologies **Academic program** English as a second language, advanced placement, accelerated degree program, self-designed majors, honors program, summer session, adult/continuing education programs, internships **Contact** Ms. Carol Isaacs, Director of Admissions, Indiana University–Purdue University Fort Wayne, Admissions Office, 2101 East Coliseum Boulevard, Fort Wayne, IN 46805-1499. Telephone: 219-481-6812. Fax: 219-481-6880. E-mail: ipfwadms@ipfw.edu. Web site: http://www.ipfw.edu/.

INDIANA UNIVERSITY–PURDUE UNIVERSITY INDIANAPOLIS

INDIANAPOLIS, INDIANA

General State-supported, university, coed **Entrance** Moderately difficult **Setting** 511-acre urban campus **Total enrollment** 27,525 **Student/faculty ratio** 18:1 **Application deadline** Rolling (freshmen), rolling (transfer) **Freshmen** 80% were admitted **Housing** Yes **Expenses** Tuition 3881; Room & Board 5098 **Undergraduates** 59% women, 42% part-time, 38% 25 or older, 0.3% Native American, 2% Hispanic American, 11% African American, 2% Asian American/Pacific Islander **The most frequently chosen baccalaureate fields are** business/marketing, education, health professions and related sciences **Academic program** English as a second language, advanced placement, honors program, summer session, adult/continuing education programs, internships **Contact** Dr. Alan Crist, Executive Director for Enrollment Services, Indiana University–Purdue University Indianapolis, 425 N. University Boulevard, Cavanaugh Hall Room 129, Indianapolis, IN 46202-5143. Telephone: 317-274-4591. Fax: 317-278-1862. E-mail: apply@ses.iupui.edu. Web site: http://www.indiana.edu/.

INDIANA UNIVERSITY SOUTH BEND

SOUTH BEND, INDIANA

General State-supported, comprehensive, coed **Entrance** Moderately difficult **Setting** 73-acre suburban campus **Total enrollment** 7,252 **Student/faculty ratio** 14:1 **Application deadline** 7/1 (freshmen), 6/1 (transfer) **Freshmen** 84% were admitted **Housing** No **Expenses** Tuition 3300 **Undergraduates** 64% women, 50% part-time, 37% 25 or older, 0.4% Native American, 2% Hispanic American, 6% African American, 1% Asian American/Pacific Islander

The most frequently chosen baccalaureate fields are business/marketing, education, liberal arts/general studies **Academic program** English as a second language, accelerated degree program, honors program, summer session, adult/continuing education programs, internships **Contact** Mr. Peter J. Biegel, Director of Enrollment Management Systems, Indiana University South Bend, 1700 Mishawaka Avenue, Administration Building, Room 169, PO Box 7111, South Bend, IN 46634-7111. Telephone: 219-237-4839. Fax: 219-237-4834. E-mail: admissions@iusb.edu. Web site: http://www.indiana.edu/.

INDIANA UNIVERSITY SOUTHEAST
NEW ALBANY, INDIANA

General State-supported, comprehensive, coed **Entrance** Minimally difficult **Setting** 177-acre suburban campus **Total enrollment** 6,427 **Student/faculty ratio** 17:1 **Application deadline** 7/15 (freshmen), 7/1 (transfer) **Freshmen** 91% were admitted **Housing** No **Expenses** Tuition 3248 **Undergraduates** 62% women, 47% part-time, 37% 25 or older, 0.2% Native American, 1% Hispanic American, 3% African American, 0.4% Asian American/Pacific Islander **The most frequently chosen baccalaureate fields are** business/marketing, education, health professions and related sciences **Academic program** Advanced placement, accelerated degree program, summer session, adult/continuing education programs, internships **Contact** Mr. David B. Campbell, Director of Admissions, Indiana University Southeast, University Center Building, Room 100, 4201 Grant Line Road, New Albany, IN 47150. Telephone: 812-941-2212 or toll-free 800-852-8835 (in-state). Fax: 812-941-2595. E-mail: admissions@ius.indiana.edu. Web site: http://www.indiana.edu/.

INDIANA WESLEYAN UNIVERSITY
MARION, INDIANA

General Independent Wesleyan, comprehensive, coed **Entrance** Moderately difficult **Setting** 132-acre small-town campus **Total enrollment** 6,969 **Student/faculty ratio** 17:1 **Application deadline** Rolling (freshmen), rolling (transfer) **Freshmen** 78% were admitted **Housing** Yes **Expenses** Tuition $12,740; Room & Board $4940 **Undergraduates** 63% women, 8% part-time, 59% 25 or older, 1% Native American, 1% Hispanic American, 10% African American, 1% Asian American/Pacific Islander **The most frequently chosen baccalaureate fields are** business/marketing, education, health professions and related sciences **Academic program** Advanced placement, accelerated degree program, self-designed majors, honors program, summer session, adult/continuing education programs, internships **Contact** Ms. Gaytha Holloway, Director of Admissions, Indiana Wesleyan University, 4201 South Washington Street, 4216 South Nebraska, Marion, IN 46953. Telephone: 765-677-2138 or toll-free 800-332-6901. Fax: 765-677-2333. E-mail: ghollaway@indwes.edu. Web site: http://www.indwes.edu/.

LUTHERAN COLLEGE OF HEALTH PROFESSIONS
See University of Saint Francis

MANCHESTER COLLEGE
NORTH MANCHESTER, INDIANA

General Independent, comprehensive, coed, affiliated with Church of the Brethren **Entrance** Moderately difficult **Setting** 125-acre small-town campus **Total enrollment** 1,106 **Student/faculty ratio** 14:1 **Application deadline** Rolling (freshmen), rolling (transfer) **Freshmen** 81% were admitted **Housing** Yes **Expenses** Tuition $15,440; Room & Board $5630 **Undergraduates** 55% women, 2% part-time, 3% 25 or older, 0.5% Native American, 2% Hispanic American, 4% African American, 1% Asian American/Pacific Islander **The most frequently chosen baccalaureate fields are** business/marketing, communications/communication technologies, education **Academic program** Advanced placement, self-designed majors, honors program, summer session, adult/continuing education programs, internships **Contact** Ms. Jolane Rohr, Director of Admissions, Manchester College, 604 East College Avenue, North Manchester, IN 46962-1225. Telephone: 219-982-5055 or toll-free 800-852-3648. Fax: 219-982-5043. E-mail: admissionsinfo@manchester.edu. Web site: http://www.manchester.edu/.

MARIAN COLLEGE
INDIANAPOLIS, INDIANA

General Independent Roman Catholic, 4-year, coed **Entrance** Moderately difficult **Setting** 114-acre urban campus **Total enrollment** 1,411 **Student/faculty ratio** 10:1 **Application deadline** 8/15 (freshmen), 8/1 (transfer) **Freshmen** 89% were admitted **Housing** Yes **Expenses** Tuition $14,836; Room & Board $5046 **Undergraduates** 75% women, 37% part-time, 39% 25 or older, 0.3% Native American, 2% Hispanic American, 15% African American, 1% Asian American/Pacific Islander **The most frequently chosen baccalaureate fields are** business/marketing, education, health professions and related sciences **Academic program** Advanced placement, accelerated degree program, honors program, summer session, adult/continuing education programs, internships **Contact** Ms. Karen Kist, Director of Admission, Marian College, 3200 Cold Spring Road, Indianapolis, IN 46222-1997. Telephone: 317-955-6300 or toll-free 800-772-7264 (in-state). Web site: http://www.marian.edu/.

MARTIN UNIVERSITY
INDIANAPOLIS, INDIANA

General Independent, comprehensive, coed **Entrance** Noncompetitive **Setting** 5-acre urban campus **Total enrollment** 556 **Application deadline** Rolling (freshmen), rolling (transfer) **Housing** No **Undergraduates** 73% women, 46% part-time, 80% 25 or older **Academic program** Advanced placement, accelerated degree program, self-designed majors, honors program, summer session, adult/continuing educa-

Martin University *(continued)*

tion programs, internships **Contact** Ms. Brenda Shaheed, Director of Enrollment Management, Martin University, 2171 Avondale Place, PO Box 18567, Indianapolis, IN 46218-3867. Telephone: 317-543-3237. Fax: 317-543-4790.

OAKLAND CITY UNIVERSITY
OAKLAND CITY, INDIANA

General Independent General Baptist, comprehensive, coed **Entrance** Minimally difficult **Setting** 20-acre rural campus **Total enrollment** 1,789 **Student/faculty ratio** 36:1 **Application deadline** Rolling (freshmen) **Freshmen** 100% were admitted **Housing** Yes **Expenses** Tuition $11,266; Room & Board $4100 **Undergraduates** 51% women, 22% part-time, 40% 25 or older, 0.3% Native American, 2% Hispanic American, 12% African American, 0.4% Asian American/Pacific Islander **The most frequently chosen baccalaureate fields are** business/marketing, education, philosophy, religion, and theology **Academic program** Advanced placement, accelerated degree program, summer session, adult/continuing education programs **Contact** Jeff Main, Director of Admissions, Oakland City University, 143 North Lucretia Street, Oakland City, IN 47660-1099. Telephone: 812-749-1222 or toll-free 800-737-5125. Web site: http://www.oak.edu/.

PURDUE UNIVERSITY
WEST LAFAYETTE, INDIANA

General State-supported, university, coed **Entrance** Moderately difficult **Setting** 1,579-acre suburban campus **Total enrollment** 37,871 **Application deadline** Rolling (freshmen), rolling (transfer) **Freshmen** 78% were admitted **Housing** Yes **Expenses** Tuition $3872; Room & Board $5800 **Undergraduates** 43% women, 7% part-time, 6% 25 or older, 0.4% Native American, 2% Hispanic American, 3% African American, 4% Asian American/Pacific Islander **The most frequently chosen baccalaureate fields are** business/marketing, education, engineering/engineering technologies **Academic program** Advanced placement, accelerated degree program, self-designed majors, honors program, summer session, adult/continuing education programs, internships **Contact** Director of Admissions, Purdue University, Schleman Hall, West Lafayette, IN 47907-1080. Telephone: 765-494-4600. E-mail: admissions@adms.purdue.edu. Web site: http://www.purdue.edu/.

PURDUE UNIVERSITY CALUMET
HAMMOND, INDIANA

General State-supported, comprehensive, coed **Entrance** Minimally difficult **Setting** 167-acre urban campus **Total enrollment** 7,784 **Application deadline** Rolling (freshmen), rolling (transfer) **Freshmen** 99% were admitted **Housing** No **Expenses** Tuition $7419 **Undergraduates** 56% women, 42% part-time, 47% 25 or older, 0.4% Native American, 14% Hispanic American, 12% African American, 2% Asian American/Pacific Islander **Academic program** Advanced placement, honors program, summer session, adult/continuing education programs, internships **Contact** Paul McGuinness, Director of Admissions, Purdue University Calumet, 173rd and Woodmar Avenue, Hammond, IN 46323-2094. Telephone: 219-989-2213 or toll-free 800-447-8738 (in-state). E-mail: williamf@calumet.purdue.edu. Web site: http://www.calumet.purdue.edu/.

PURDUE UNIVERSITY NORTH CENTRAL
WESTVILLE, INDIANA

General State-supported, comprehensive, coed **Entrance** Noncompetitive **Setting** 264-acre rural campus **Total enrollment** 3,459 **Student/faculty ratio** 17:1 **Application deadline** 8/6 (freshmen), 8/1 (transfer) **Freshmen** 98% were admitted **Housing** No **Expenses** Tuition $3338 **Undergraduates** 60% women, 46% part-time, 58% 25 or older, 1% Native American, 3% Hispanic American, 4% African American, 1% Asian American/Pacific Islander **The most frequently chosen baccalaureate fields are** business/marketing, education, liberal arts/general studies **Academic program** Advanced placement, self-designed majors, honors program, summer session, adult/continuing education programs, internships **Contact** Ms. Cathy Buckman, Director of Admissions, Purdue University North Central, 1401 South U.S. Highway 421, Westville, IN 46391. Telephone: 219-785-5458 or toll-free 800-872-1231 (in-state). E-mail: cbuckman@purduenc.edu. Web site: http://www.purduenc.edu/.

ROSE-HULMAN INSTITUTE OF TECHNOLOGY
TERRE HAUTE, INDIANA

General Independent, comprehensive, coed, primarily men **Entrance** Very difficult **Setting** 130-acre rural campus **Total enrollment** 1,725 **Student/faculty ratio** 15:1 **Application deadline** 3/1 (freshmen), 6/15 (transfer) **Freshmen** 77% were admitted **Housing** Yes **Expenses** Tuition $22,545; Room & Board $6100 **Undergraduates** 17% women, 1% part-time, 1% 25 or older, 0.1% Native American, 1% Hispanic American, 1% African American, 3% Asian American/Pacific Islander **The most frequently chosen baccalaureate fields are** computer/information sciences, engineering/engineering technologies, physical sciences **Academic program** Advanced placement, honors program, summer session, adult/continuing education programs, internships **Contact** Mr. Charles G. Howard, Dean of Admissions/Vice President, Rose-Hulman Institute of Technology, 5500 Wabash Avenue, Terre Haute, IN 47803-3920. Telephone: 812-877-8213 or toll-free 800-552-0725 (in-state); 800-248-7448 (out-of-state). Fax: 812-877-8941. E-mail: admis.ofc@rose-hulman.edu. Web site: http://www.rose-hulman.edu/.

SAINT FRANCIS COLLEGE
See University of Saint Francis

SAINT JOSEPH'S COLLEGE
RENSSELAER, INDIANA

General Independent Roman Catholic, comprehensive, coed **Entrance** Moderately difficult **Setting** 340-acre small-town campus **Total enrollment** 935 **Student/faculty ratio** 14:1 **Application deadline** Rolling (freshmen), rolling (transfer) **Freshmen** 74% were admitted **Housing** Yes **Expenses** Tuition $15,080; Room & Board $5380 **Undergraduates** 56% women, 12% part-time, 7% 25 or older, 0.3% Native American, 3% Hispanic American, 5% African American, 1% Asian American/Pacific Islander **The most frequently chosen baccalaureate fields are** business/marketing, biological/life sciences, education **Academic program** Advanced placement, accelerated degree program, self-designed majors, honors program, summer session, internships **Contact** Mr. Frank P. Bevec, Director of Admissions, Saint Joseph's College, PO Box 815, Rensselaer, IN 47978-0850. Telephone: 219-866-6170 or toll-free 800-447-8781 (out-of-state). Fax: 219-866-6122. E-mail: admissions@saintjoe.edu. Web site: http://www.saintjoe.edu/.

SAINT MARY-OF-THE-WOODS COLLEGE
SAINT MARY-OF-THE-WOODS, INDIANA

General Independent Roman Catholic, comprehensive, women only **Entrance** Moderately difficult **Setting** 67-acre rural campus **Total enrollment** 1,470 **Student/faculty ratio** 12:1 **Application deadline** 8/15 (freshmen), 8/15 (transfer) **Freshmen** 88% were admitted **Housing** Yes **Expenses** Tuition $14,840; Room & Board $5540 **Undergraduates** 72% part-time, 50% 25 or older, 1% Native American, 1% Hispanic American, 3% African American, 0.4% Asian American/Pacific Islander **The most frequently chosen baccalaureate fields are** business/marketing, education, social sciences and history **Academic program** Advanced placement, accelerated degree program, self-designed majors, summer session, adult/continuing education programs, internships **Contact** Ms. Patty R. Young, Director of Admission, Saint Mary-of-the-Woods College, Guerin Hall, Saint Mary-of-the-Woods, IN 47876. Telephone: 812-535-5106 or toll-free 800-926-SMWC. Fax: 812-535-4900. E-mail: adms@woods.smwc.edu. Web site: http://www.smwc.edu/.

SAINT MARY'S COLLEGE
NOTRE DAME, INDIANA

General Independent Roman Catholic, 4-year, women only **Entrance** Moderately difficult **Setting** 275-acre suburban campus **Total enrollment** 1,455 **Student/faculty ratio** 11:1 **Application deadline** 3/1 (freshmen), rolling (transfer) **Freshmen** 83% were admitted **Housing** Yes **Expenses** Tuition $18,300; Room & Board $6174 **Undergraduates** 3% part-time, 1% 25 or older, 0.3% Native American, 4% Hispanic American, 1% African American, 1% Asian American/Pacific Islander **The most frequently chosen baccalaureate fields are** business/marketing, education, social sciences and history **Academic program** Advanced placement, accelerated degree program, self-designed majors, internships **Contact** Ms. Mary Pat Nolan, Director of Admissions, Saint Mary's College, Notre Dame, IN 46556. Telephone: 219-284-4587 or toll-free 800-551-7621 (in-state); 219-284-4716 (out-of-state). E-mail: admission@saintmarys.edu. Web site: http://www.saintmarys.edu/.

TAYLOR UNIVERSITY
UPLAND, INDIANA

General Independent interdenominational, 4-year, coed **Entrance** Very difficult **Setting** 250-acre rural campus **Total enrollment** 1,886 **Student/faculty ratio** 16:1 **Application deadline** Rolling (freshmen), rolling (transfer) **Freshmen** 67% were admitted **Housing** Yes **Expenses** Tuition $15,820; Room & Board $4740 **Undergraduates** 2% 25 or older, 0.5% Native American, 2% Hispanic American, 1% African American, 2% Asian American/Pacific Islander **The most frequently chosen baccalaureate fields are** business/marketing, education, psychology **Academic program** Advanced placement, accelerated degree program, self-designed majors, honors program, summer session, internships **Contact** Mr. Stephen R. Mortland, Director of Admissions, Taylor University, 236 West Reade Avenue, Upland, IN 46989-1001. Telephone: 765-998-5134 or toll-free 800-882-3456. Fax: 765-998-4925. E-mail: admissions_u@tayloru.edu. Web site: http://www.tayloru.edu/.

TAYLOR UNIVERSITY, FORT WAYNE CAMPUS
FORT WAYNE, INDIANA

General Independent interdenominational, 4-year, coed **Entrance** Moderately difficult **Setting** 32-acre suburban campus **Total enrollment** 477 **Student/faculty ratio** 14:1 **Application deadline** Rolling (freshmen), rolling (transfer) **Freshmen** 84% were admitted **Housing** Yes **Expenses** Tuition $13,366; Room & Board $4366 **Undergraduates** 56% women, 25% part-time, 8% 25 or older, 0.2% Native American, 1% Hispanic American, 6% African American, 1% Asian American/Pacific Islander **The most frequently chosen baccalaureate fields are** education, law/legal studies, philosophy, religion, and theology **Academic program** Advanced placement, accelerated degree program, self-designed majors, summer session, internships **Contact** Mr. Leo Gonot, Director of Admissions, Taylor University, Fort Wayne Campus, 1025 West Rudisill Boulevard, Fort Wayne, IN 46807-2197. Telephone: 219-744-8689 or toll-free 800-233-3922. Fax: 219-744-8660. E-mail: admissions_f@tayloru.edu. Web site: http://www.tayloru.edu/fw.

TRI-STATE UNIVERSITY
ANGOLA, INDIANA

General Independent, 4-year, coed **Entrance** Moderately difficult **Setting** 400-acre small-town campus **Total enrollment** 1,267 **Student/faculty ratio** 17:1 **Application deadline** 6/1 (freshmen), 8/15 (transfer)

Tri-State University *(continued)*

Freshmen 81% were admitted **Housing** Yes **Expenses** Tuition $13,700; Room & Board $4950 **Undergraduates** 31% women, 11% part-time, 6% 25 or older, 0.2% Native American, 0.5% Hispanic American, 2% African American, 0.4% Asian American/Pacific Islander **The most frequently chosen baccalaureate fields are** business/marketing, education, engineering/engineering technologies **Academic program** Advanced placement, summer session, adult/continuing education programs, internships **Contact** Pat Dean, Admissions Officer, Tri-State University, 1 University Avenue, Angola, IN 46703. Telephone: 219-665-4132 or toll-free 800-347-4TSU. Fax: 219-665-4578. E-mail: admit@alpha.tristate.edu. Web site: http://www.tristate.edu/.

UNIVERSITY OF EVANSVILLE
EVANSVILLE, INDIANA

General Independent, 4-year, coed, affiliated with United Methodist Church **Entrance** Moderately difficult **Setting** 75-acre suburban campus **Total enrollment** 2,797 **Student/faculty ratio** 13:1 **Application deadline** 2/15 (freshmen), 7/1 (transfer) **Freshmen** 91% were admitted **Housing** Yes **Expenses** Tuition $16,404; Room & Board $5270 **Undergraduates** 60% women, 11% part-time, 5% 25 or older, 0.2% Native American, 1% Hispanic American, 2% African American, 1% Asian American/Pacific Islander **The most frequently chosen baccalaureate fields are** business/marketing, engineering/engineering technologies, health professions and related sciences **Academic program** English as a second language, advanced placement, honors program, summer session, adult/continuing education programs, internships **Contact** Mr. Scot Schaeffer, Dean of Admission, University of Evansville, 1800 Lincoln Avenue, Evansville, IN 47722-0002. Telephone: 812-479-2468 or toll-free 800-992-5877 (in-state); 800-423-8633 (out-of-state). Fax: 812-474-4076. E-mail: admission@evansville.edu. Web site: http://www.evansville.edu/.

UNIVERSITY OF INDIANAPOLIS
INDIANAPOLIS, INDIANA

General Independent, comprehensive, coed, affiliated with United Methodist Church **Entrance** Moderately difficult **Setting** 60-acre suburban campus **Total enrollment** 3,601 **Student/faculty ratio** 14:1 **Application deadline** Rolling (freshmen), rolling (transfer) **Freshmen** 82% were admitted **Housing** Yes **Expenses** Tuition $14,630; Room & Board $5225 **Undergraduates** 66% women, 31% part-time, 28% 25 or older, 0.4% Native American, 1% Hispanic American, 7% African American, 1% Asian American/Pacific Islander **The most frequently chosen baccalaureate fields are** business/marketing, biological/life sciences, education **Academic program** English as a second language, advanced placement, accelerated degree program, self-designed majors, honors program, summer session, adult/continuing education programs, internships **Contact** Mr. Ronald Wilks, Director of Admissions, University of Indianapolis, 1400 East Hanna Avenue, Indianapolis, IN 46227-3697. Telephone: 317-788-3216 or toll-free 800-232-8634 Ext. 3216. Fax: 317-778-3300. E-mail: admissions@gandlf.uindy.edu. Web site: http://www.uindy.edu/.

UNIVERSITY OF NOTRE DAME
NOTRE DAME, INDIANA

General Independent Roman Catholic, university, coed **Entrance** Most difficult **Setting** 1,250-acre suburban campus **Total enrollment** 10,800 **Application deadline** 1/9 (freshmen), 4/15 (transfer) **Freshmen** 34% were admitted **Housing** Yes **Expenses** Tuition 23,357; Room & Board 5920 **Undergraduates** 46% women, 0.3% part-time, 0% 25 or older, 0.5% Native American, 7% Hispanic American, 3% African American, 4% Asian American/Pacific Islander **The most frequently chosen baccalaureate fields are** business/marketing, engineering/engineering technologies, social sciences and history **Academic program** English as a second language, advanced placement, self-designed majors, honors program, summer session, internships **Contact** Mr. Daniel J. Saracino, Assistant Provost for Enrollment, University of Notre Dame, 220 Main Building, Notre Dame, IN 46556-5612. Telephone: 219-631-7505. Fax: 219-631-8865. E-mail: admissions.admissio.1@nd.edu. Web site: http://www.nd.edu/.

UNIVERSITY OF SAINT FRANCIS
FORT WAYNE, INDIANA

General Independent Roman Catholic, comprehensive, coed **Entrance** Moderately difficult **Setting** 73-acre suburban campus **Total enrollment** 1,587 **Student/faculty ratio** 11:1 **Application deadline** Rolling (freshmen), rolling (transfer) **Freshmen** 83% were admitted **Housing** Yes **Expenses** Tuition $13,570; Room & Board $5000 **Undergraduates** 67% women, 28% part-time, 32% 25 or older, 0.2% Native American, 2% Hispanic American, 7% African American, 1% Asian American/Pacific Islander **Academic program** Advanced placement, honors program, summer session, adult/continuing education programs, internships **Contact** Mr. David McMahan, Director of Admissions, University of Saint Francis, 2701 Spring Street, Fort Wayne, IN 46808. Telephone: 219-434-3279 or toll-free 800-729-4732. E-mail: admiss@sfc.edu. Web site: http://www.sf.edu/.

UNIVERSITY OF SOUTHERN INDIANA
EVANSVILLE, INDIANA

General State-supported, comprehensive, coed **Entrance** Noncompetitive **Setting** 300-acre suburban campus **Total enrollment** 9,012 **Student/faculty ratio** 19:1 **Application deadline** 8/15 (freshmen), 8/15 (transfer) **Freshmen** 95% were admitted **Housing** Yes **Expenses** Tuition $3075; Room & Board $5182 **Undergraduates** 60% women, 25% part-time, 18% 25 or older, 0.1% Native American, 1% Hispanic American, 3% African American, 1% Asian American/Pacific Islander **The most frequently cho-**

sen baccalaureate fields are business/marketing, education, health professions and related sciences **Academic program** Advanced placement, honors program, summer session, adult/continuing education programs, internships **Contact** Mr. Eric Otto, Director of Admission, University of Southern Indiana, 8600 University Boulevard, Evansville, IN 47712-3590. Telephone: 812-464-1765 or toll-free 800-467-1965. Fax: 812-465-7154. E-mail: enroll@usi.edu. Web site: http://www.usi.edu/.

VALPARAISO UNIVERSITY
VALPARAISO, INDIANA

General Independent, comprehensive, coed, affiliated with Lutheran Church **Entrance** Moderately difficult **Setting** 310-acre small-town campus **Total enrollment** 3,654 **Student/faculty ratio** 13:1 **Application deadline** Rolling (freshmen), rolling (transfer) **Freshmen** 81% were admitted **Housing** Yes **Expenses** Tuition $17,636; Room & Board $4660 **Undergraduates** 54% women, 7% part-time, 6% 25 or older, 0.4% Native American, 2% Hispanic American, 3% African American, 2% Asian American/Pacific Islander **The most frequently chosen baccalaureate fields are** business/marketing, health professions and related sciences, trade and industry **Academic program** Advanced placement, accelerated degree program, self-designed majors, honors program, summer session, adult/continuing education programs, internships **Contact** Ms. Karen Foust, Director of Admissions, Valparaiso University, 651 South College Avenue, Valparaiso, IN 46383-6493. Telephone: 219-464-5011 or toll-free 888-GO-VALPO (out-of-state). Fax: 219-464-6898. E-mail: undergrad_admissions@valpo.edu. Web site: http://www.valpo.edu/.

▶ **For more information, see page 483.**

WABASH COLLEGE
CRAWFORDSVILLE, INDIANA

General Independent, 4-year, men only **Entrance** Moderately difficult **Setting** 50-acre small-town campus **Total enrollment** 852 **Student/faculty ratio** 10:1 **Application deadline** 3/15 (freshmen), 3/15 (transfer) **Freshmen** 65% were admitted **Housing** Yes **Expenses** Tuition 18,294; Room & Board 5761 **Undergraduates** 0.1% part-time, 0.01% 25 or older, 0.4% Native American, 5% Hispanic American, 5% African American, 3% Asian American/Pacific Islander **Academic program** Advanced placement, accelerated degree program, internships **Contact** Mr. Steve Klein, Director of Admissions, Wabash College, PO Box 362, Crawfordsville, IN 47933-0352. Telephone: 765-361-6225 or toll-free 800-345-5385. Fax: 765-361-6437. E-mail: admissions@wabash.edu. Web site: http://www.wabash.edu/.

IOWA

ALLEN COLLEGE
WATERLOO, IOWA

General Independent, comprehensive, coed, primarily women **Entrance** Moderately difficult **Setting** 20-acre suburban campus **Total enrollment** 271 **Student/faculty ratio** 11:1 **Application deadline** 8/1 (freshmen), 8/1 (transfer) **Freshmen** 53% were admitted **Housing** No **Expenses** Tuition 9030 **Undergraduates** 93% women, 25% part-time, 32% 25 or older, 1% Native American, 1% Hispanic American, 2% African American, 0.4% Asian American/Pacific Islander **The most frequently chosen baccalaureate field is** health professions and related sciences **Academic program** Advanced placement **Contact** Ms. Lois Hagedorn, Student Services, Allen College, Barrett Forum, 1825 Logan Avenue, Waterloo, IA 50703. Telephone: 319-226-2000. Fax: 319-226-2051. E-mail: hagedole@ihs.org. Web site: http://www.allencollege.edu/.

BRIAR CLIFF COLLEGE
SIOUX CITY, IOWA

General Independent Roman Catholic, 4-year, coed **Entrance** Moderately difficult **Setting** 70-acre suburban campus **Total enrollment** 917 **Student/faculty ratio** 12:1 **Application deadline** Rolling (freshmen), rolling (transfer) **Freshmen** 80% were admitted **Housing** Yes **Expenses** Tuition $13,890; Room & Board $4767 **Undergraduates** 65% women, 27% part-time, 30% 25 or older, 1% Native American, 2% Hispanic American, 2% African American, 2% Asian American/Pacific Islander **Academic program** English as a second language, advanced placement, accelerated degree program, self-designed majors, summer session, adult/continuing education programs, internships **Contact** Ms. Sharisue Wilcoxon, Vice President for Enrollment Management, Briar Cliff College, 3303 Rebecca Street, Sioux City, IA 51106. Telephone: 712-279-5200 Ext. 1628 or toll-free 800-662-3303. Fax: 712-279-5410. E-mail: admissions@briarcliff.edu. Web site: http://www.briarcliff.edu/.

BUENA VISTA UNIVERSITY
STORM LAKE, IOWA

General Independent, comprehensive, coed, affiliated with Presbyterian Church (U.S.A.) **Entrance** Moderately difficult **Setting** 60-acre small-town campus **Total enrollment** 1,381 **Student/faculty ratio** 15:1 **Application deadline** 6/1 (freshmen), 6/1 (transfer) **Freshmen** 86% were admitted **Housing** Yes **Expenses** Tuition 17,176; Room & Board 4795 **Undergraduates** 51% women, 2% part-time, 2% 25 or older, 0.2% Native American, 1% Hispanic American, 1% African American, 1% Asian American/Pacific Islander **The most frequently chosen baccalaureate fields are** business/marketing, education, protective services/public administration **Academic program** English as a second language, advanced

Buena Vista University *(continued)*

placement, self-designed majors, honors program, summer session, adult/continuing education programs, internships **Contact** Ms. Louise Cummings-Simmons, Director of Admissions, Buena Vista University, 610 West Fourth Street, Storm Lake, IA 50588. Telephone: 712-749-2351 or toll-free 800-383-9600. E-mail: admissions@bvu.edu. Web site: http://www.bvu.edu/.

CENTRAL COLLEGE
PELLA, IOWA

General Independent, 4-year, coed, affiliated with Reformed Church in America **Entrance** Moderately difficult **Setting** 133-acre small-town campus **Total enrollment** 1,336 **Student/faculty ratio** 13:1 **Application deadline** Rolling (freshmen), rolling (transfer) **Freshmen** 88% were admitted **Housing** Yes **Expenses** Tuition $14,754; Room & Board $5242 **Undergraduates** 57% women, 4% part-time, 1% 25 or older, 0.2% Native American, 1% Hispanic American, 0.5% African American, 1% Asian American/Pacific Islander **The most frequently chosen baccalaureate fields are** business/marketing, communications/communication technologies, English **Academic program** English as a second language, advanced placement, self-designed majors, honors program, summer session, internships **Contact** John Olsen, Vice President of Admission and Student Enrollment Services, Central College, 812 University Street, Pella, IA 50219-1999. Telephone: 641-628-7600 or toll-free 800-458-5503. Fax: 641-628-5316. E-mail: admissions@central.edu. Web site: http://www.central.edu/.

CLARKE COLLEGE
DUBUQUE, IOWA

General Independent Roman Catholic, comprehensive, coed **Entrance** Moderately difficult **Setting** 55-acre urban campus **Total enrollment** 1,118 **Student/faculty ratio** 9:1 **Application deadline** Rolling (freshmen), rolling (transfer) **Freshmen** 73% were admitted **Housing** Yes **Expenses** Tuition $14,136; Room & Board $5172 **Undergraduates** 67% women, 20% part-time, 31% 25 or older, 0.2% Native American, 3% Hispanic American, 1% African American, 0.4% Asian American/Pacific Islander **The most frequently chosen baccalaureate fields are** business/marketing, computer/information sciences, health professions and related sciences **Academic program** English as a second language, advanced placement, self-designed majors, honors program, summer session, adult/continuing education programs, internships **Contact** Mr. Omar G. Correa, Executive Director of Admissions and Financial Aid, Clarke College, 1550 Clarke Drive, Dubuque, IA 52001-3198. Telephone: 319-588-6316 or toll-free 800-383-2345. Fax: 319-588-6789. E-mail: admissions@keller.clarke.edu. Web site: http://www.clarke.edu/.

COE COLLEGE
CEDAR RAPIDS, IOWA

General Independent, comprehensive, coed, affiliated with Presbyterian Church **Entrance** Moderately difficult **Setting** 55-acre urban campus **Total enrollment** 1,301 **Student/faculty ratio** 11:1 **Application deadline** 3/1 (freshmen), rolling (transfer) **Freshmen** 81% were admitted **Housing** Yes **Expenses** Tuition 18,415; Room & Board 5200 **Undergraduates** 55% women, 9% part-time, 3% 25 or older, 0.1% Native American, 1% Hispanic American, 2% African American, 1% Asian American/Pacific Islander **The most frequently chosen baccalaureate fields are** business/marketing, social sciences and history, visual/performing arts **Academic program** English as a second language, advanced placement, accelerated degree program, self-designed majors, honors program, summer session, adult/continuing education programs, internships **Contact** Mr. Dennis Trotter, Vice President of Admission and Financial Aid, Coe College, 1220 1st Avenue, NE, Cedar Rapids, IA 52402-5070. Telephone: 319-399-8500 or toll-free 877-225-5263. Fax: 319-399-8816. E-mail: admission@coe.edu. Web site: http://www.coe.edu/.

CORNELL COLLEGE
MOUNT VERNON, IOWA

General Independent Methodist, 4-year, coed **Entrance** Moderately difficult **Setting** 129-acre small-town campus **Total enrollment** 987 **Student/faculty ratio** 12:1 **Application deadline** 2/1 (freshmen), 2/1 (transfer) **Freshmen** 74% were admitted **Housing** Yes **Expenses** Tuition 19,570; Room & Board 5410 **Undergraduates** 59% women, 1% part-time, 1% 25 or older, 1% Native American, 2% Hispanic American, 3% African American, 1% Asian American/Pacific Islander **The most frequently chosen baccalaureate fields are** biological/life sciences, psychology, social sciences and history **Academic program** English as a second language, advanced placement, self-designed majors, adult/continuing education programs, internships **Contact** Ms. Florence W. Hines, Dean of Admission and Financial Assistance, Cornell College, 600 First Street West, Mount Vernon, IA 52314-1098. Telephone: 319-895-4477 or toll-free 800-747-1112. Fax: 319-895-4451. E-mail: admissions@cornell-iowa.edu. Web site: http://www.cornell-iowa.edu/.

DES MOINES UNIVERSITY OSTEOPATHIC MEDICAL CENTER
DES MOINES, IOWA

General Independent, upper-level, coed **Contact** Dr. Dennis Bates, Director of Admissions, Des Moines University Osteopathic Medical Center, Des Moines University, Des Moines, IA 50312. Telephone: 515-271-1450. Fax: 515-271-1578. E-mail: pchamber@uomhs.edu. Web site: http://www.dsmu.edu/.

DIVINE WORD COLLEGE
EPWORTH, IOWA

Contact Br. Dennis Newton SVD, Vice President of Recruitment/Director of Admissions, Divine Word College, 102 Jacoby Drive SW, Epworth, IA 52045-0380. Telephone: 319-876-3332 or toll-free 800-553-3321. Fax: 319-876-3407.

DORDT COLLEGE
SIOUX CENTER, IOWA

General Independent Christian Reformed, comprehensive, coed **Entrance** Moderately difficult **Setting** 65-acre small-town campus **Total enrollment** 1,420 **Student/faculty ratio** 15:1 **Application deadline** 8/1 (freshmen), 8/1 (transfer) **Freshmen** 95% were admitted **Housing** Yes **Expenses** Tuition $13,350; Room & Board $3800 **Undergraduates** 56% women, 3% part-time, 10% 25 or older, 0.2% Hispanic American, 1% African American, 1% Asian American/Pacific Islander **The most frequently chosen baccalaureate fields are** business/marketing, education, engineering/engineering technologies **Academic program** English as a second language, advanced placement, self-designed majors, internships **Contact** Mr. Quentin Van Essen, Executive Director of Admissions, Dordt College, 498 4th Avenue, NE, Sioux Center, IA 51250-1697. Telephone: 712-722-6080 or toll-free 800-343-6738. Fax: 712-722-1967. E-mail: admissions@dordt.edu. Web site: http://www.dordt.edu/.

DRAKE UNIVERSITY
DES MOINES, IOWA

General Independent, university, coed **Entrance** Moderately difficult **Setting** 120-acre suburban campus **Total enrollment** 5,126 **Student/faculty ratio** 13:1 **Application deadline** Rolling (freshmen), rolling (transfer) **Freshmen** 87% were admitted **Housing** Yes **Expenses** Tuition 17,090; Room & Board 4870 **Undergraduates** 61% women, 8% part-time, 4% 25 or older, 1% Native American, 1% Hispanic American, 3% African American, 4% Asian American/Pacific Islander **The most frequently chosen baccalaureate fields are** business/marketing, communications/communication technologies, health professions and related sciences **Academic program** English as a second language, advanced placement, self-designed majors, honors program, summer session, internships **Contact** Mr. Thomas F. Willoughby, Dean of Admission, Drake University, 2507 University Avenue, Des Moines, IA 50311-4516. Telephone: 515-271-3181 or toll-free 800-44DRAKE. Fax: 515-271-2831. E-mail: admitinfo@acad.drake.edu. Web site: http://www.drake.edu/.

EMMAUS BIBLE COLLEGE
DUBUQUE, IOWA

General Independent nondenominational, 4-year, coed **Entrance** Noncompetitive **Setting** 22-acre small-town campus **Total enrollment** 293 **Student/faculty ratio** 15:1 **Application deadline** 8/1 (freshmen), 8/1 (transfer) **Freshmen** 100% were admitted **Housing** Yes **Expenses** Tuition $5720; Room & Board $2920 **Undergraduates** 53% women, 6% part-time, 14% 25 or older, 1% Native American, 3% Hispanic American, 2% African American, 1% Asian American/Pacific Islander **The most frequently chosen baccalaureate fields are** education, philosophy, religion, and theology **Academic program** Advanced placement, internships **Contact** Mr. Mark Stevenson, Registrar, Emmaus Bible College, 2570 Asbury Road, Dubuque, IA 52001-3097. Telephone: 319-588-8000 Ext. 1103 or toll-free 800-397-2425. Fax: 319-588-1216. E-mail: registrar@emmausl.edu. Web site: http://www.emmaus.edu/.

FAITH BAPTIST BIBLE COLLEGE AND THEOLOGICAL SEMINARY
ANKENY, IOWA

General Independent, comprehensive, coed, affiliated with General Association of Regular Baptist Churches **Entrance** Minimally difficult **Setting** 52-acre small-town campus **Total enrollment** 494 **Student/faculty ratio** 20:1 **Application deadline** 8/1 (freshmen), 8/1 (transfer) **Freshmen** 65% were admitted **Housing** Yes **Expenses** Tuition $8542; Room & Board $3200 **Undergraduates** 55% women, 9% part-time, 4% 25 or older, 0% Native American, 1% Hispanic American, 1% African American, 2% Asian American/Pacific Islander **The most frequently chosen baccalaureate fields are** education, philosophy, religion, and theology **Academic program** Advanced placement, summer session, adult/continuing education programs, internships **Contact** Miss Michelle McWilliams, Admissions Office Secretary, Faith Baptist Bible College and Theological Seminary, 1900 NW 4th Street, Ankeny, IA 50021. Telephone: 515-964-0601 Ext. 233 or toll-free 888-FAITH 4U. Fax: 515-964-1638. E-mail: fbblenroll@aol.com. Web site: http://www.faith.edu/.

GRACELAND UNIVERSITY
LAMONI, IOWA

General Independent Reorganized Latter Day Saints, comprehensive, coed **Entrance** Moderately difficult **Setting** 169-acre small-town campus **Total enrollment** 3,192 **Student/faculty ratio** 16:1 **Application deadline** Rolling (freshmen), rolling (transfer) **Freshmen** 69% were admitted **Housing** Yes **Expenses** Tuition 13,145; Room & Board 4305 **Undergraduates** 75% women, 58% part-time, 6% 25 or older, 1% Native American, 2% Hispanic American, 5% African American, 3% Asian American/Pacific Islander **The most frequently chosen baccalaureate fields are** business/marketing, health professions and related sciences, liberal arts/general studies **Academic program** English as a second language, advanced placement, accelerated degree program, self-designed majors, honors program, summer session, adult/continuing education programs, internships **Contact** Ms. Bonita A. Booth, Vice Provost and Dean of Admissions, Graceland University, 1 University Place, Lamoni, IA 50140. Telephone: 641-784-5118 or toll-

Graceland University *(continued)*

free 888-472-235263 (in-state); 800-472-235263 (out-of-state). Fax: 641-784-5480. E-mail: admissions@graceland.edu. Web site: http://www2.graceland.edu/.

GRAND VIEW COLLEGE
DES MOINES, IOWA

General Independent, 4-year, coed, affiliated with Evangelical Lutheran Church in America **Entrance** Noncompetitive **Setting** 25-acre urban campus **Total enrollment** 1,380 **Student/faculty ratio** 13:1 **Application deadline** Rolling (freshmen), rolling (transfer) **Freshmen** 63% were admitted **Housing** Yes **Expenses** Tuition $12,886; Room & Board $4166 **Undergraduates** 65% women, 33% part-time, 32% 25 or older, 0.4% Native American, 1% Hispanic American, 3% African American, 2% Asian American/Pacific Islander **The most frequently chosen baccalaureate fields are** business/marketing, education, health professions and related sciences **Academic program** Advanced placement, accelerated degree program, self-designed majors, honors program, summer session, internships **Contact** Ms. Debbie Barger, Vice President, Enrollment Management, Grand View College, 1200 Grandview Avenue, Des Moines, IA 50316-1599. Telephone: 515-263-6012 or toll-free 800-444-6083. Fax: 515-263-2974. E-mail: admiss@gvc.edu. Web site: http://www.gvc.edu/.

GRINNELL COLLEGE
GRINNELL, IOWA

General Independent, 4-year, coed **Entrance** Very difficult **Setting** 95-acre small-town campus **Total enrollment** 1,344 **Student/faculty ratio** 10:1 **Application deadline** 1/20 (freshmen), 5/1 (transfer) **Freshmen** 64% were admitted **Housing** Yes **Expenses** Tuition 20,500; Room & Board 5820 **Undergraduates** 56% women, 3% part-time, 0.4% Native American, 4% Hispanic American, 3% African American, 5% Asian American/Pacific Islander **The most frequently chosen baccalaureate fields are** biological/life sciences, English, social sciences and history **Academic program** Advanced placement, accelerated degree program, self-designed majors, internships **Contact** Mr. James Sumner, Dean for Admission and Financial Aid, Grinnell College, Grinnell, IA 50112-1690. Telephone: 641-269-3600 or toll-free 800-247-0113. Fax: 641-269-4800. E-mail: askgrin@admin.grin.edu. Web site: http://www.grinnell.edu/.

HAMILTON TECHNICAL COLLEGE
DAVENPORT, IOWA

General Proprietary, 4-year, coed **Entrance** Noncompetitive **Setting** urban campus **Total enrollment** 380 **Application deadline** Rolling (freshmen), rolling (transfer) **Housing** No **Expenses** Tuition 6300 **The most frequently chosen baccalaureate field is** trade and industry **Academic program** Accelerated degree program **Contact** Mr. Robert Hoffmann, Director of Admissions, Hamilton Technical College, 1011 East 53rd Street, Davenport, IA 52807. Telephone: 319-386-3570. Fax: 319-386-6756.

IOWA STATE UNIVERSITY OF SCIENCE AND TECHNOLOGY
AMES, IOWA

General State-supported, university, coed **Entrance** Moderately difficult **Setting** 1,788-acre suburban campus **Total enrollment** 26,845 **Student/faculty ratio** 14:1 **Application deadline** 8/21 (freshmen), rolling (transfer) **Freshmen** 91% were admitted **Housing** Yes **Expenses** Tuition $3132; Room & Board $4432 **Undergraduates** 45% women, 8% part-time, 9% 25 or older, 0.4% Native American, 2% Hispanic American, 2% African American, 2% Asian American/Pacific Islander **The most frequently chosen baccalaureate fields are** business/marketing, agriculture, engineering/engineering technologies **Academic program** English as a second language, advanced placement, accelerated degree program, self-designed majors, honors program, summer session, adult/continuing education programs, internships **Contact** Mr. Phil Caffrey, Associate Director for Freshman Admissions, Iowa State University of Science and Technology, 100 Alumni Hall, Ames, IA 50011-2010. Telephone: 515-294-5836 or toll-free 800-262-3810. Fax: 515-294-2592. E-mail: admissions@iastate.edu. Web site: http://www.iastate.edu/.

IOWA WESLEYAN COLLEGE
MOUNT PLEASANT, IOWA

General Independent United Methodist, 4-year, coed **Entrance** Moderately difficult **Setting** 60-acre small-town campus **Total enrollment** 777 **Student/faculty ratio** 11:1 **Application deadline** 8/15 (freshmen), 8/15 (transfer) **Freshmen** 82% were admitted **Housing** Yes **Expenses** Tuition $13,200; Room & Board $4250 **Undergraduates** 60% women, 38% part-time, 40% 25 or older, 0.1% Native American, 4% Hispanic American, 9% African American, 1% Asian American/Pacific Islander **The most frequently chosen baccalaureate fields are** business/marketing, education, psychology **Academic program** English as a second language, advanced placement, self-designed majors, summer session, adult/continuing education programs, internships **Contact** James Lynes, Director of Admissions, Iowa Wesleyan College, 601 North Main Street, Mount Pleasant, IA 52641-1398. Telephone: 319-385-6230 or toll-free 800-582-2383. Fax: 319-385-6296. E-mail: admitrwl@iwc.edu. Web site: http://www.iwc.edu/.

LORAS COLLEGE
DUBUQUE, IOWA

General Independent Roman Catholic, comprehensive, coed **Entrance** Moderately difficult **Setting** 60-acre suburban campus **Total enrollment** 1,725 **Student/faculty ratio** 12:1 **Application deadline** Rolling (freshmen), rolling (transfer) **Freshmen** 79% were admitted **Housing** Yes **Expenses** Tuition 15,329; Room & Board 5475 **Undergraduates** 53% women,

6% part-time, 6% 25 or older, 0.1% Native American, 2% Hispanic American, 2% African American, 0.2% Asian American/Pacific Islander **The most frequently chosen baccalaureate fields are** business/marketing, biological/life sciences, education **Academic program** English as a second language, advanced placement, self-designed majors, honors program, summer session, adult/continuing education programs, internships **Contact** Mr. Tim Hauber, Director of Admissions, Loras College, 1450 Alta Vista, Dubuque, IA 52004-0178. Telephone: 319-588-7829 or toll-free 800-245-6727. Fax: 319-588-7119. E-mail: adms@lora.edu. Web site: http://www.loras.edu/.

LUTHER COLLEGE
DECORAH, IOWA

General Independent, 4-year, coed, affiliated with Evangelical Lutheran Church in America **Entrance** Moderately difficult **Setting** 800-acre small-town campus **Total enrollment** 2,621 **Student/faculty ratio** 13:1 **Freshmen** 84% were admitted **Housing** Yes **Expenses** Tuition 18,080; Room & Board 3914 **Undergraduates** 60% women, 3% part-time, 3% 25 or older, 0.1% Native American, 1% Hispanic American, 1% African American, 1% Asian American/Pacific Islander **The most frequently chosen baccalaureate fields are** biological/life sciences, business/marketing, visual/performing arts **Academic program** Advanced placement, self-designed majors, honors program, summer session, internships **Contact** Mr. Jon Lund, Vice President for Enrollment and Marketing, Luther College, 700 College Drive, Decorah, IA 52101-1045. Telephone: 319-387-1287 or toll-free 800-458-8437. Fax: 319-387-2159. E-mail: admissions@luther.edu. Web site: http://www.luther.edu/.

▶ **For more information, see page 442.**

MAHARISHI UNIVERSITY OF MANAGEMENT
FAIRFIELD, IOWA

General Independent, university, coed **Entrance** Moderately difficult **Setting** 262-acre small-town campus **Total enrollment** 678 **Student/faculty ratio** 12:1 **Application deadline** 8/1 (freshmen), 8/1 (transfer) **Housing** Yes **Expenses** Tuition $15,660; Room & Board $5200 **Undergraduates** 50% women, 10% part-time, 26% 25 or older **The most frequently chosen baccalaureate fields are** business/marketing, computer/information sciences, visual/performing arts **Academic program** English as a second language, advanced placement, self-designed majors, honors program, adult/continuing education programs, internships **Contact** Mr. Brad Mylett, Director of Admissions, Maharishi University of Management, 1000 North 4th Street, Fairfield, IA 52557. Telephone: 641-472-1110. Fax. 641-472-1179. E-mail: admissions@miu.edu. Web site: http://www.mum.edu/.

MARYCREST INTERNATIONAL UNIVERSITY
DAVENPORT, IOWA

General Independent, comprehensive, coed **Entrance** Moderately difficult **Setting** 30-acre urban campus **Total enrollment** 730 **Student/faculty ratio** 13:1 **Application deadline** Rolling (freshmen), rolling (transfer) **Freshmen** 68% were admitted **Housing** Yes **Expenses** Tuition $13,280; Room & Board $4840 **Undergraduates** 53% women, 19% part-time, 51% 25 or older, 0.3% Native American, 5% Hispanic American, 9% African American, 3% Asian American/Pacific Islander **The most frequently chosen baccalaureate fields are** business/marketing, computer/information sciences, health professions and related sciences **Academic program** English as a second language, accelerated degree program, self-designed majors, summer session, adult/continuing education programs, internships **Contact** Meg Farber, Director of Admission, Marycrest International University, 1607 West 12th Street, Davenport, IA 52804. Telephone: 319-327-9609 or toll-free 800-728-9705 Ext. 2225. Fax: 319-327-9620. E-mail: tmcdonough@acc.mcrest.edu. Web site: http://www.mcrest.edu/.

MERCY COLLEGE OF HEALTH SCIENCES
DES MOINES, IOWA

General Independent, 4-year, coed, primarily women, affiliated with Roman Catholic Church **Total enrollment** 409 **Application deadline** Rolling (freshmen) **Freshmen** 25% were admitted **Expenses** Tuition $3900 **Undergraduates** 92% women **Contact** Mr. Ron Askland, Admissions Representative, Mercy College of Health Sciences, 928 Sixth Avenue, Des Moines, IA 50309-1239. Telephone: 515-643-6604 or toll-free 800-637-2994. Web site: http://www.mchs.edu/.

MORNINGSIDE COLLEGE
SIOUX CITY, IOWA

General Independent United Methodist, comprehensive, coed **Entrance** Moderately difficult **Setting** 41-acre suburban campus **Total enrollment** 1,049 **Student/faculty ratio** 11:1 **Application deadline** Rolling (freshmen), rolling (transfer) **Freshmen** 77% were admitted **Housing** Yes **Expenses** Tuition $13,606; Room & Board $4794 **Undergraduates** 64% women, 13% part-time, 7% 25 or older, 1% Native American, 2% Hispanic American, 3% African American, 1% Asian American/Pacific Islander **The most frequently chosen baccalaureate fields are** business/marketing, biological/life sciences, education **Academic program** English as a second language, advanced placement, accelerated degree program, self-designed majors, honors program, summer session, adult/continuing education programs, internships **Contact** Joel Weyand, Director of Admissions, Morningside College, 1501 Morningside Avenue, Sioux City, IA 51106-1751. Telephone: 712-274-5111 or toll-free 800-831-0806. E-mail: mscadm@alpha.morningside.edu. Web site: http://www.morningside.edu/.

MOUNT MERCY COLLEGE
CEDAR RAPIDS, IOWA

General Independent Roman Catholic, 4-year, coed **Entrance** Moderately difficult **Setting** 36-acre suburban campus **Total enrollment** 1,363 **Student/faculty ratio** 13:1 **Application deadline** 8/30 (freshmen), 8/30 (transfer) **Freshmen** 90% were admitted **Housing** Yes **Expenses** Tuition $13,850; Room & Board $4600 **Undergraduates** 68% women, 35% part-time, 44% 25 or older, 0.4% Native American, 2% Hispanic American, 2% African American, 1% Asian American/Pacific Islander **The most frequently chosen baccalaureate fields are** business/marketing, education, protective services/public administration **Academic program** Advanced placement, accelerated degree program, self-designed majors, honors program, summer session, adult/continuing education programs, internships **Contact** Dr. Alex Popovics, Vice President for Enrollment Management, Mount Mercy College, 1330 Elmhurst Drive, NE, Cedar Rapids, IA 52402. Telephone: 319-368-6460 or toll-free 800-248-4504. Fax: 319-363-5270. E-mail: admission@mmc.mtmercy.edu. Web site: http://www.mtmercy.edu/.

MOUNT ST. CLARE COLLEGE
CLINTON, IOWA

General Independent Roman Catholic, 4-year, coed **Entrance** Minimally difficult **Setting** 24-acre small-town campus **Total enrollment** 618 **Student/faculty ratio** 13:1 **Application deadline** 8/15 (freshmen), rolling (transfer) **Freshmen** 78% were admitted **Housing** Yes **Expenses** Tuition $13,420; Room & Board $4630 **Undergraduates** 55% women, 21% part-time, 35% 25 or older, 0% Native American, 3% Hispanic American, 6% African American, 1% Asian American/Pacific Islander **The most frequently chosen baccalaureate fields are** business/marketing, education, liberal arts/general studies **Academic program** English as a second language, advanced placement, self-designed majors, honors program, summer session, adult/continuing education programs, internships **Contact** Ms. Waunita M. Sullivan, Director of Enrollment, Mount St. Clare College, 400 North Bluff Boulevard, PO Box 2967, Clinton, IA 52733-2967. Telephone: 319-242-4023 Ext. 3401 or toll-free 800-242-4153 Ext. 3400. Fax: 319-243-6102. E-mail: admiffnf@clare.edu. Web site: http://www.clare.edu/.

NORTHWESTERN COLLEGE
ORANGE CITY, IOWA

General Independent, 4-year, coed, affiliated with Reformed Church in America **Entrance** Moderately difficult **Setting** 45-acre rural campus **Total enrollment** 1,243 **Student/faculty ratio** 16:1 **Application deadline** Rolling (freshmen), rolling (transfer) **Freshmen** 88% were admitted **Housing** Yes **Expenses** Tuition $13,000; Room & Board $3650 **Undergraduates** 61% women, 5% part-time, 3% 25 or older, 0.3% Native American, 0.5% Hispanic American, 0.3% African American, 0.3% Asian American/Pacific Islander **The most frequently chosen baccalaureate fields are** business/marketing, biological/life sciences, education **Academic program** English as a second language, advanced placement, accelerated degree program, self-designed majors, honors program, summer session, internships **Contact** Mr. Ronald K. DeJong, Director of Admissions, Northwestern College, 101 College Lane, Orange City, IA 51041-1996. Telephone: 712-737-7130 or toll-free 800-747-4757. Fax: 712-737-7164. E-mail: markb@nwciowa.edu. Web site: http://www.nwciowa.edu/.

PALMER COLLEGE OF CHIROPRACTIC
DAVENPORT, IOWA

General Independent, comprehensive, coed **Entrance** Moderately difficult **Setting** 3-acre urban campus **Total enrollment** 1,731 **Application deadline** Rolling (freshmen) **Freshmen** 100% were admitted **Housing** No **Expenses** Tuition $16,290 **Undergraduates** 78% women, 15% part-time **The most frequently chosen baccalaureate field is** interdisciplinary studies **Academic program** Summer session, internships **Contact** Dr. David Anderson, Director of Admissions, Palmer College of Chiropractic, 1000 Brady Street, Davenport, IA 52803-5287. Telephone: 319-884-5656 or toll-free 800-722-3648. Fax: 319-884-5414. E-mail: pcadmit@palmer.edu. Web site: http://www.palmer.edu/.

ST. AMBROSE UNIVERSITY
DAVENPORT, IOWA

General Independent Roman Catholic, comprehensive, coed **Entrance** Moderately difficult **Setting** 11-acre urban campus **Total enrollment** 3,011 **Student/faculty ratio** 15:1 **Application deadline** Rolling (freshmen), rolling (transfer) **Freshmen** 86% were admitted **Housing** Yes **Expenses** Tuition 14,654; Room & Board 5340 **Undergraduates** 60% women, 25% part-time, 31% 25 or older, 0.5% Native American, 4% Hispanic American, 3% African American, 1% Asian American/Pacific Islander **Academic program** Advanced placement, accelerated degree program, self-designed majors, summer session, adult/continuing education programs, internships **Contact** Ms. Meg Flaherty, Director of Admissions, St. Ambrose University, 518 West Locust, Davenport, IA 52803-2898. Telephone: 563-333-6300 Ext. 6311 or toll-free 800-383-2627. Fax: 563-333-6297. E-mail: mflaherty@sau.edu. Web site: http://www.sau.edu/.

▶ **For more information, see page 472.**

SIMPSON COLLEGE
INDIANOLA, IOWA

General Independent United Methodist, 4-year, coed **Entrance** Moderately difficult **Setting** 68-acre small-town campus **Total enrollment** 1,912 **Student/faculty ratio** 16:1 **Application deadline** 8/15 (freshmen), 8/15 (transfer) **Freshmen** 86% were admitted **Housing** Yes **Expenses** Tuition 15,150; Room & Board 5040 **Undergraduates** 57% women, 29%

part-time, 25% 25 or older, 1% Native American, 1% Hispanic American, 1% African American, 1% Asian American/Pacific Islander **The most frequently chosen baccalaureate fields are** business/marketing, communications/communication technologies, education **Academic program** Advanced placement, accelerated degree program, self-designed majors, honors program, summer session, adult/continuing education programs, internships **Contact** Mr. John Kellogg, Vice President for Enrollment, Simpson College, 701 North C Street, Indianola, IA 50125-1297. Telephone: 515-961-1624 or toll-free 800-362-2454. Fax: 515-961-1870. E-mail: admiss@simpson.edu. Web site: http://www.simpson.edu/.

► **For more information, see page 468.**

UNIVERSITY OF DUBUQUE
DUBUQUE, IOWA

General Independent Presbyterian, comprehensive, coed **Entrance** Moderately difficult **Setting** 56-acre suburban campus **Total enrollment** 955 **Student/faculty ratio** 15:1 **Application deadline** Rolling (freshmen), rolling (transfer) **Freshmen** 82% were admitted **Housing** Yes **Expenses** Tuition $14,130; Room & Board $4820 **Undergraduates** 41% women, 9% part-time, 8% 25 or older, 0.3% Native American, 2% Hispanic American, 5% African American, 1% Asian American/Pacific Islander **The most frequently chosen baccalaureate fields are** education, social sciences and history, trade and industry **Academic program** English as a second language, advanced placement, accelerated degree program, self-designed majors, summer session, adult/continuing education programs, internships **Contact** Mr. Jesse James, Director of Admissions and Records, University of Dubuque, 2000 University Avenue, Dubuque, IA 52001-5099. Telephone: 319-589-3214 or toll-free 800-722-5583 (in-state). Fax: 319-589-3690. E-mail: admssns@dbq.edu. Web site: http://www.dbq.edu/.

THE UNIVERSITY OF IOWA
IOWA CITY, IOWA

General State-supported, university, coed **Entrance** Moderately difficult **Setting** 1,900-acre small-town campus **Total enrollment** 28,311 **Student/faculty ratio** 14:1 **Application deadline** 5/15 (freshmen), 5/15 (transfer) **Freshmen** 83% were admitted **Housing** Yes **Expenses** Tuition 3522; Room & Board 4870 **Undergraduates** 54% women, 12% part-time, 10% 25 or older, 0.5% Native American, 2% Hispanic American, 2% African American, 3% Asian American/Pacific Islander **The most frequently chosen baccalaureate fields are** business/marketing, education, social sciences and history **Academic program** English as a second language, advanced placement, accelerated degree program, self-designed majors, honors program, summer session, adult/continuing education programs, internships **Contact** Mr. Michael Barron, Director of Admissions, The University of Iowa, 107 Calvin Hall, Iowa City, IA 52242. Telephone: 319-335-3847 or toll-free 800-553-4692. Fax: 319-335-1535. E-mail: admissions@uiowa.edu. Web site: http://www.uiowa.edu/.

UNIVERSITY OF NORTHERN IOWA
CEDAR FALLS, IOWA

General State-supported, comprehensive, coed **Entrance** Moderately difficult **Setting** 940-acre small-town campus **Total enrollment** 14,106 **Student/faculty ratio** 16:1 **Application deadline** 8/15 (freshmen), 8/15 (transfer) **Freshmen** 82% were admitted **Housing** Yes **Expenses** Tuition $3130; Room & Board $4149 **Undergraduates** 58% women, 12% part-time, 9% 25 or older, 0.3% Native American, 1% Hispanic American, 2% African American, 1% Asian American/Pacific Islander **The most frequently chosen baccalaureate fields are** business/marketing, education, social sciences and history **Academic program** English as a second language, advanced placement, accelerated degree program, self-designed majors, honors program, summer session, adult/continuing education programs, internships **Contact** Mr. Clark Elmer, Director of Enrollment Management and Admissions, University of Northern Iowa, 120 Gilchrist Hall, Cedar Falls, IA 50614-0018. Telephone: 319-273-2281 or toll-free 800-772-2037. Fax: 319-273-2885. E-mail: admissions@uni.edu. Web site: http://www.uni.edu/.

UPPER IOWA UNIVERSITY
FAYETTE, IOWA

General Independent, comprehensive, coed **Entrance** Moderately difficult **Setting** 80-acre rural campus **Total enrollment** 697 **Student/faculty ratio** 16:1 **Application deadline** Rolling (freshmen), rolling (transfer) **Freshmen** 75% were admitted **Housing** Yes **Expenses** Tuition $11,290; Room & Board $4364 **Undergraduates** 39% women, 4% part-time, 0.4% Native American, 5% Hispanic American, 12% African American, 4% Asian American/Pacific Islander **The most frequently chosen baccalaureate fields are** business/marketing, education, psychology **Academic program** Advanced placement, accelerated degree program, self-designed majors, summer session, adult/continuing education programs, internships **Contact** Mr. Kent McElvania, Director of Admissions, Upper Iowa University, Box 1859, Fayette, IA 52142-1857. Telephone: 319-425-5281 Ext. 5279 or toll-free 800-553-4150. Fax: 319-425-5277. E-mail: admission@uiu.edu. Web site: http://www.uiu.edu/.

WARTBURG COLLEGE
WAVERLY, IOWA

General Independent Lutheran, 4-year, coed **Entrance** Moderately difficult **Setting** 118-acre small-town campus **Total enrollment** 1,600 **Student/faculty ratio** 14:1 **Application deadline** 5/1 (freshmen) **Freshmen** 89% were admitted **Housing** Yes **Expenses** Tuition $16,565; Room & Board $4600 **Undergraduates** 57% women, 5% part-time, 2% 25 or older, 0.2% Native American, 0.4% Hispanic

Wartburg College *(continued)*

American, 3% African American, 1% Asian American/ Pacific Islander **The most frequently chosen baccalaureate fields are** business/marketing, biological/ life sciences, education **Academic program** English as a second language, advanced placement, accelerated degree program, self-designed majors, honors program, summer session, internships **Contact** Doug Bowman, Director of Admissions, Wartburg College, 222 Ninth Street, NW, PO Box 1003, Waverly, IA 50677-0903. Telephone: 319-352-8264 or toll-free 800-772-2085. Fax: 319-352-8579. E-mail: admissions@wartburg.edu. Web site: http://www.wartburg.edu/.

WILLIAM PENN UNIVERSITY
OSKALOOSA, IOWA

General Independent, 4-year, coed, affiliated with Society of Friends **Entrance** Moderately difficult **Setting** 40-acre rural campus **Total enrollment** 1,353 **Student/faculty ratio** 15:1 **Freshmen** 76% were admitted **Housing** Yes **Expenses** Tuition $12,770; Room & Board $4140 **Undergraduates** 42% women, 5% part-time, 24% 25 or older, 2% Native American, 3% Hispanic American, 9% African American, 2% Asian American/Pacific Islander **The most frequently chosen baccalaureate fields are** business/ marketing, education, engineering/engineering technologies **Academic program** English as a second language, advanced placement, accelerated degree program, self-designed majors, summer session, adult/ continuing education programs, internships **Contact** Mrs. Mary Boyd, Director of Admissions, William Penn University, 201 Trueblood Avenue, Oskaloosa, IA 52577. Telephone: 641-673-1012 Ext. 1015 or toll-free 800-779-7366. Fax: 641-673-1396. E-mail: ottoe@wmpenn.edu. Web site: http://www.wmpenn.edu/.

KANSAS

BAKER UNIVERSITY
BALDWIN CITY, KANSAS

General Independent United Methodist, comprehensive, coed **Entrance** Moderately difficult **Setting** 26-acre small-town campus **Total enrollment** 2,817 **Student/faculty ratio** 12:1 **Application deadline** Rolling (freshmen), rolling (transfer) **Freshmen** 81% were admitted **Housing** Yes **Expenses** Tuition 12,300; Room & Board 4750 **Undergraduates** 58% women, 4% part-time, 49% 25 or older, 1% Native American, 2% Hispanic American, 4% African American, 1% Asian American/Pacific Islander **The most frequently chosen baccalaureate fields are** business/ marketing, education, health professions and related sciences **Academic program** English as a second language, advanced placement, self-designed majors, honors program, summer session, internships **Contact** Ms. Paige Illum, Director of Admission, Baker University, PO Box 65, Baldwin City, KS 66006-0065. Telephone: 785-594-6451 Ext. 458 or toll-free 800-873-4282. Fax: 785-594-8372. E-mail: adm_constant@george.bakeru.edu. Web site: http://www.bakeru.edu/.

BARCLAY COLLEGE
HAVILAND, KANSAS

General Independent, 4-year, coed, affiliated with Society of Friends **Entrance** Minimally difficult **Setting** 13-acre rural campus **Total enrollment** 193 **Student/faculty ratio** 10:1 **Application deadline** 9/1 (freshmen), 9/1 (transfer) **Freshmen** 42% were admitted **Housing** Yes **Expenses** Tuition $7450; Room & Board $3750 **Undergraduates** 53% women, 11% part-time, 53% 25 or older, 2% Native American, 4% Hispanic American, 4% African American, 3% Asian American/Pacific Islander **The most frequently chosen baccalaureate fields are** business/ marketing, philosophy, religion, and theology, psychology **Academic program** Advanced placement, accelerated degree program, self-designed majors, adult/continuing education programs, internships **Contact** Ryan Haase, Director of Admissions, Barclay College, 607 North Kingman, Haviland, KS 67059. Telephone: 316-862-5252 Ext. 41 or toll-free 800-862-0226. Fax: 316-862-5242. E-mail: admissions@barclaycollege.edu. Web site: http://www.barclaycollege.edu/.

BENEDICTINE COLLEGE
ATCHISON, KANSAS

General Independent Roman Catholic, comprehensive, coed **Entrance** Moderately difficult **Setting** 225-acre small-town campus **Total enrollment** 1,369 **Student/faculty ratio** 15:1 **Freshmen** 92% were admitted **Housing** Yes **Expenses** Tuition $12,630; Room & Board $4790 **Undergraduates** 56% women, 37% part-time, 6% 25 or older, 0.5% Native American, 5% Hispanic American, 5% African American, 1% Asian American/Pacific Islander **The most frequently chosen baccalaureate fields are** education, biological/life sciences, social sciences and history **Academic program** English as a second language, advanced placement, self-designed majors, summer session, internships **Contact** Ms. Kelly Vowels, Dean of Enrollment Management, Benedictine College, 1020 N. 2nd Street, Atchison, KS 66002. Telephone: 913-367-5340 Ext. 2476 or toll-free 800-467-5340. Fax: 913-367-5462. E-mail: mail@benedictine.edu. Web site: http://www.benedictine.edu/.

BETHANY COLLEGE
LINDSBORG, KANSAS

General Independent Lutheran, 4-year, coed **Entrance** Moderately difficult **Setting** 80-acre small-town campus **Total enrollment** 611 **Student/faculty ratio** 12:1 **Application deadline** 7/1 (freshmen), rolling (transfer) **Freshmen** 63% were admitted **Housing** Yes **Expenses** Tuition $12,664; Room & Board $3641 **Undergraduates** 46% women, 10% part-time, 31% 25 or older, 1% Native American, 4% Hispanic American, 4% African American, 1% Asian American/Pacific Islander **The most frequently cho-**

sen baccalaureate fields are business/marketing, education, protective services/public administration **Academic program** Advanced placement, accelerated degree program, self-designed majors, summer session, internships **Contact** Daniel McKinney, Dean of Admissions and Financial Aid, Bethany College, 421 North First Street, Lindsborg, KS 67456-1897. Telephone: 785-227-3311 Ext. 8108 or toll-free 800-826-2281. Fax: 785-227-2004. E-mail: admissions@bethany.bethanylb.edu. Web site: http://www.bethanylb.edu/.

BETHEL COLLEGE
NORTH NEWTON, KANSAS

General Independent, 4-year, coed, affiliated with General Conference Mennonite Church **Entrance** Moderately difficult **Setting** 60-acre small-town campus **Total enrollment** 502 **Student/faculty ratio** 10:1 **Application deadline** 8/15 (freshmen), 8/15 (transfer) **Freshmen** 79% were admitted **Housing** Yes **Expenses** Tuition 12,300; Room & Board 5150 **Undergraduates** 52% women, 9% part-time, 9% 25 or older, 1% Native American, 6% Hispanic American, 5% African American, 2% Asian American/Pacific Islander **The most frequently chosen baccalaureate fields are** business/marketing, health professions and related sciences, visual/performing arts **Academic program** Advanced placement, summer session, internships **Contact** Dr. Shirley King, Dean of Enrollment Services, Bethel College, 300 East 27th Street, North Newton, KS 67117. Telephone: 316-283-2500 Ext. 230 or toll-free 800-522-1887. Fax: 316-284-5870. E-mail: admissions@bethelks.edu. Web site: http://www.bethelks.edu/.

EMPORIA STATE UNIVERSITY
EMPORIA, KANSAS

General State-supported, comprehensive, coed **Entrance** Noncompetitive **Setting** 207-acre small-town campus **Total enrollment** 5,614 **Student/faculty ratio** 18:1 **Application deadline** Rolling (freshmen), rolling (transfer) **Freshmen** 100% were admitted **Housing** Yes **Expenses** Tuition $2744; Room & Board $3774 **Undergraduates** 59% women, 13% part-time, 15% 25 or older, 1% Native American, 4% Hispanic American, 4% African American, 1% Asian American/Pacific Islander **The most frequently chosen baccalaureate fields are** business/marketing, education, social sciences and history **Academic program** English as a second language, advanced placement, accelerated degree program, self-designed majors, honors program, summer session, adult/continuing education programs, internships **Contact** Ms. Susan Brinkman, Interim Director of Admissions, Emporia State University, 1200 Commercial, Emporia, KS 66801-5087. Telephone: 316-341-5465 or toll-free 877-GOTOESU (in-state); 877-468-6378 (out-of-state). Fax: 316 341-5599. E-mail: ugadmiss@esumail.emporia.edu. Web site: http://www.emporia.edu/.

FORT HAYS STATE UNIVERSITY
HAYS, KANSAS

General State-supported, comprehensive, coed **Entrance** Noncompetitive **Setting** 200-acre small-town campus **Total enrollment** 5,506 **Application deadline** Rolling (freshmen), rolling (transfer) **Freshmen** 99% were admitted **Housing** Yes **Expenses** Tuition $2178; Room & Board $2375 **Undergraduates** 54% women, 16% part-time, 1% Native American, 3% Hispanic American, 1% African American, 1% Asian American/Pacific Islander **The most frequently chosen baccalaureate fields are** business/marketing, education, health professions and related sciences **Academic program** English as a second language, advanced placement, summer session, adult/continuing education programs, internships **Contact** Mr. Joey Linn, Director of Admissions, Fort Hays State University, 600 Park Street, Hays, KS 67601-4099. Telephone: 785-628-5666 or toll-free 800-628-FHSU. Fax: 785-628-4187. E-mail: tigers@fhsuvm.fhsu.edu. Web site: http://www.fhsu.edu/.

FRIENDS UNIVERSITY
WICHITA, KANSAS

General Independent, comprehensive, coed **Entrance** Moderately difficult **Setting** 45-acre urban campus **Total enrollment** 3,247 **Application deadline** Rolling (freshmen), rolling (transfer) **Freshmen** 93% were admitted **Housing** Yes **Expenses** Tuition 11,660; Room & Board 3540 **Undergraduates** 0.3% 25 or older **Academic program** Advanced placement, accelerated degree program, self-designed majors, honors program, summer session, adult/continuing education programs, internships **Contact** Mr. Tony Meyers, Director of Admissions, Friends University, 2100 West University Street, Wichita, KS 67213. Telephone: 316-295-5100 or toll-free 800-577-2233. Fax: 316-262-5027. E-mail: tonym@friends.edu. Web site: http://www.friends.edu/.

HASKELL INDIAN NATIONS UNIVERSITY
LAWRENCE, KANSAS

General Federally supported, 4-year, coed **Entrance** Minimally difficult **Setting** 320-acre suburban campus **Total enrollment** 915 **Student/faculty ratio** 15:1 **Application deadline** 7/15 (freshmen), 7/15 (transfer) **Housing** Yes **Undergraduates** 1% 25 or older, 100% Native American **Academic program** Advanced placement, self-designed majors, summer session **Contact** Ms. Patty Grant, Recruitment Officer, Haskell Indian Nations University, 155 Indian Avenue, #5031, Lawrence, KS 66046-4800. Telephone: 785-749-8437 Ext. 437. Fax: 785-749-8429.

KANSAS NEWMAN COLLEGE
See Newman University

KANSAS STATE UNIVERSITY
MANHATTAN, KANSAS

General State-supported, university, coed **Entrance** Noncompetitive **Setting** 668-acre suburban campus

Kansas State University *(continued)*

Total enrollment 21,929 **Student/faculty ratio** 15:1 **Application deadline** Rolling (freshmen), rolling (transfer) **Freshmen** 61% were admitted **Housing** Yes **Expenses** Tuition $2333; Room & Board $4240 **Undergraduates** 47% women, 14% part-time, 11% 25 or older, 1% Native American, 2% Hispanic American, 3% African American, 1% Asian American/Pacific Islander **The most frequently chosen baccalaureate fields are** agriculture, business/marketing, education **Academic program** English as a second language, advanced placement, accelerated degree program, honors program, summer session, adult/continuing education programs, internships **Contact** Mr. Larry Moeder, Interim Director of Admissions, Kansas State University, 119 Anderson Hall, Manhattan, KS 66506. Telephone: 785-532-6250 or toll-free 800-432-8270 (in-state). Fax: 785-532-6393. E-mail: kstate@ksu.edu. Web site: http://www.ksu.edu/.

KANSAS WESLEYAN UNIVERSITY

SALINA, KANSAS

General Independent United Methodist, comprehensive, coed **Entrance** Moderately difficult **Setting** 28-acre urban campus **Total enrollment** 747 **Student/faculty ratio** 14:1 **Application deadline** Rolling (freshmen), rolling (transfer) **Freshmen** 70% were admitted **Housing** Yes **Expenses** Tuition $12,600; Room & Board $4400 **Undergraduates** 30% 25 or older **Academic program** English as a second language, advanced placement, self-designed majors, summer session, adult/continuing education programs, internships **Contact** Mr. Jeffery D. Miller, Director of Admissions, Kansas Wesleyan University, 100 East Claflin, Salina, KS 67401-6196. Telephone: 785-827-5541 Ext. 1283 or toll-free 800-874-1154 Ext. 1285. Fax: 785-827-0927. E-mail: admissions@diamond.kwu.edu. Web site: http://www.kwu.edu/.

MANHATTAN CHRISTIAN COLLEGE

MANHATTAN, KANSAS

General Independent, 4-year, coed, affiliated with Christian Churches and Churches of Christ **Contact** Mr. John W. Poulson, Vice President of Admissions, Manhattan Christian College, 1415 Anderson, Manhattan, KS 66502-4081. Telephone: 785-539-3571 Ext. 30 or toll-free 877-246-4622. Fax: 785-539-0832. Web site: http://www.mccks.edu/.

MCPHERSON COLLEGE

MCPHERSON, KANSAS

General Independent, 4-year, coed, affiliated with Church of the Brethren **Entrance** Moderately difficult **Setting** 26-acre small-town campus **Total enrollment** 463 **Student/faculty ratio** 10:1 **Application deadline** Rolling (freshmen), rolling (transfer) **Freshmen** 69% were admitted **Housing** Yes **Expenses** Tuition $12,720; Room & Board $4990 **Undergraduates** 51% women, 11% part-time, 12% 25 or older, 1% Native American, 7% Hispanic American, 8% African American, 2% Asian American/Pacific Islander **The most frequently chosen baccalaureate fields are** business/marketing, biological/life sciences, education **Academic program** English as a second language, advanced placement, self-designed majors, summer session, adult/continuing education programs, internships **Contact** Mr. Fred Schmidt, Director of Admission and Financial Aid, McPherson College, 1600 East Euclid, PO Box 1402, McPherson, KS 67460-1402. Telephone: 316-241-0731 Ext. 1270 or toll-free 800-365-7402 Ext. 1270. Fax: 316-241-8443 Ext. 1270. E-mail: madm@acck.edu. Web site: http://www.mcpherson.edu/.

MIDAMERICA NAZARENE UNIVERSITY

OLATHE, KANSAS

General Independent, comprehensive, coed, affiliated with Church of the Nazarene **Entrance** Minimally difficult **Setting** 112-acre suburban campus **Total enrollment** 1,714 **Student/faculty ratio** 19:1 **Application deadline** 8/1 (freshmen), 8/1 (transfer) **Freshmen** 58% were admitted **Housing** Yes **Expenses** Tuition $11,066; Room & Board $5074 **Undergraduates** 52% women, 8% part-time, 42% 25 or older, 1% Native American, 2% Hispanic American, 8% African American, 1% Asian American/Pacific Islander **The most frequently chosen baccalaureate fields are** communications/communication technologies, engineering/engineering technologies, home economics/vocational home economics **Academic program** Advanced placement, accelerated degree program, summer session, adult/continuing education programs, internships **Contact** Mr. Mike Redwine, Vice President for Enrollment Development, MidAmerica Nazarene University, 2030 East College Way, Olathe, KS 66062-1899. Telephone: 913-791-3380 Ext. 481 or toll-free 800-800-8887. Fax: 913-791-3481. E-mail: admissions@manc.edu. Web site: http://www.mnu.edu/.

NEWMAN UNIVERSITY

WICHITA, KANSAS

General Independent Roman Catholic, comprehensive, coed **Entrance** Minimally difficult **Setting** 53-acre urban campus **Total enrollment** 1,967 **Student/faculty ratio** 11:1 **Application deadline** Rolling (freshmen), rolling (transfer) **Freshmen** 98% were admitted **Housing** Yes **Expenses** Tuition $10,298; Room & Board $3950 **Undergraduates** 65% women, 41% part-time, 46% 25 or older, 1% Native American, 3% Hispanic American, 7% African American, 1% Asian American/Pacific Islander **The most frequently chosen baccalaureate fields are** education, business/marketing, home economics/vocational home economics **Academic program** Advanced placement, accelerated degree program, summer session, adult/continuing education programs, internships **Contact** Ms. Marla McClure, Director of Admissions and Financial Aid, Newman University, 3100 McCormick Avenue, Wichita, KS 67213-2097. Telephone: 316-942-4291 Ext. 133 or toll-free 877-NEWMANU. Fax: 316-942-4483. E-mail: admissions@newmanu.edu. Web site: http://www.newmanu.edu/.

OTTAWA UNIVERSITY
OTTAWA, KANSAS

General Independent American Baptist, comprehensive, coed **Entrance** Moderately difficult **Setting** 60-acre small-town campus **Total enrollment** 433 **Student/faculty ratio** 14:1 **Application deadline** Rolling (freshmen), rolling (transfer) **Freshmen** 68% were admitted **Housing** Yes **Expenses** Tuition $11,000; Room & Board $4642 **Undergraduates** 45% women, 6% part-time, 9% 25 or older, 2% Native American, 4% Hispanic American, 11% African American, 0.5% Asian American/Pacific Islander **The most frequently chosen baccalaureate fields are** education, communications/communication technologies, social sciences and history **Academic program** English as a second language, advanced placement, self-designed majors, summer session, internships **Contact** Ms. Lanette Stineman, Director of Admissions, Ottawa University, 1001 South Cedar, Ottawa, KS 66067-3399. Telephone: 785-242-5200 Ext. 1051 or toll-free 800-755-5200. Fax: 785-242-7429. E-mail: wwwadmiss@ott.edu. Web site: http://www.ottawa.edu/.

PITTSBURG STATE UNIVERSITY
PITTSBURG, KANSAS

General State-supported, comprehensive, coed **Entrance** Noncompetitive **Setting** 233-acre small-town campus **Total enrollment** 6,418 **Student/faculty ratio** 23:1 **Application deadline** Rolling (freshmen), rolling (transfer) **Housing** Yes **Expenses** Tuition $2260; Room & Board $3990 **Undergraduates** 48% women, 10% part-time, 19% 25 or older, 1% Native American, 2% Hispanic American, 2% African American, 1% Asian American/Pacific Islander **Academic program** English as a second language, advanced placement, self-designed majors, honors program, summer session, adult/continuing education programs, internships **Contact** Ms. Ange Peterson, Director of Admission and Retention, Pittsburg State University, 1701 South Broadway, Pittsburg, KS 66762. Telephone: 316-235-4251 or toll-free 800-854-7488 Ext. 1. Fax: 316-235-6003. E-mail: psuadmit@pittstate.edu. Web site: http://www.pittstate.edu/.

SAINT MARY COLLEGE
LEAVENWORTH, KANSAS

General Independent Roman Catholic, comprehensive, coed **Entrance** Moderately difficult **Setting** 240-acre small-town campus **Total enrollment** 777 **Student/faculty ratio** 10:1 **Application deadline** Rolling (freshmen), rolling (transfer) **Freshmen** 83% were admitted **Housing** Yes **Expenses** Tuition $12,070; Room & Board $4880 **Undergraduates** 65% women, 34% part-time, 11% 25 or older, 1% Native American, 4% Hispanic American, 11% African American, 2% Asian American/Pacific Islander **The most frequently chosen baccalaureate fields are** education, psychology, social sciences and history **Academic program** Advanced placement, self-designed majors, honors program, summer session, adult/continuing education programs, internships **Contact** Mr. Todd Moore, Enrollment Services, Directors, Saint Mary College, 4100 South Fourth Street, Leavenworth, KS 66048. Telephone: 913-682-5151 Ext. 6118 or toll-free 800-758-6140 (out-of-state). E-mail: admiss@hub.smcks.edu. Web site: http://www.smcks.edu/.

SOUTHWESTERN COLLEGE
WINFIELD, KANSAS

General Independent United Methodist, comprehensive, coed **Entrance** Moderately difficult **Setting** 70-acre small-town campus **Total enrollment** 1,143 **Student/faculty ratio** 13:1 **Application deadline** 8/1 (freshmen), 8/1 (transfer) **Freshmen** 96% were admitted **Housing** Yes **Expenses** Tuition $13,076; Room & Board $4580 **Undergraduates** 51% women, 41% part-time, 17% 25 or older, 2% Native American, 3% Hispanic American, 5% African American, 1% Asian American/Pacific Islander **The most frequently chosen baccalaureate fields are** business/marketing, biological/life sciences, health professions and related sciences **Academic program** Advanced placement, self-designed majors, honors program, summer session, adult/continuing education programs, internships **Contact** Ms. Brenda D. Hicks, Director of Admission, Southwestern College, 100 College Street, Winfield, KS 67156-2499. Telephone: 620-229-6236 or toll-free 800-846-1543. Fax: 620-229-6344. E-mail: scadmit@jinx.sckans.edu. Web site: http://www.sckans.edu/.

STERLING COLLEGE
STERLING, KANSAS

General Independent Presbyterian, 4-year, coed **Entrance** Minimally difficult **Setting** 46-acre small-town campus **Total enrollment** 439 **Student/faculty ratio** 12:1 **Application deadline** Rolling (freshmen), rolling (transfer) **Freshmen** 66% were admitted **Housing** Yes **Expenses** Tuition $11,582; Room & Board $4788 **Undergraduates** 51% women, 7% part-time, 1% 25 or older, 1% Native American, 4% Hispanic American, 3% African American, 1% Asian American/Pacific Islander **The most frequently chosen baccalaureate fields are** biological/life sciences, business/marketing, education **Academic program** Advanced placement, self-designed majors, honors program, internships **Contact** Susan Sankey, Vice President for Enrollment Services, Sterling College, PO Box 98, Sterling, KS 67579-0098. Telephone: 316-278-4364 Ext. 364 or toll-free 800-346-1017. Fax: 316-278-3690. E-mail: admissions@sterling.edu. Web site: http://www.sterling.edu/.

TABOR COLLEGE
HILLSBORO, KANSAS

General Independent Mennonite Brethren, comprehensive, coed **Entrance** Moderately difficult **Setting** 26-acre small-town campus **Total enrollment** 586 **Student/faculty ratio** 14:1 **Application deadline** 8/1 (freshmen), 8/1 (transfer) **Freshmen** 68% were admitted **Housing** Yes **Expenses** Tuition $12,410, Room & Board $4480 **Undergraduates** 47% women,

Tabor College *(continued)*

26% part-time, 21% 25 or older, 1% Native American, 2% Hispanic American, 4% African American, 1% Asian American/Pacific Islander **The most frequently chosen baccalaureate fields are** business/marketing, education, philosophy, religion, and theology **Academic program** Advanced placement, accelerated degree program, self-designed majors, honors program, summer session, adult/continuing education programs, internships **Contact** Glenn Lygrisse, Vice President for Enrollment Management, Tabor College, 400 South Jefferson, Hillsboro, KS 67063. Telephone: 316-947-3121 Ext. 1723 or toll-free 800-822-6799. Fax: 316-947-2607. E-mail: glenl@tcnet.tabor.edu. Web site: http://www.tabor.edu/.

UNIVERSITY OF KANSAS
LAWRENCE, KANSAS

General State-supported, university, coed **Entrance** Moderately difficult **Setting** 1,000-acre suburban campus **Total enrollment** 28,329 **Student/faculty ratio** 14:1 **Application deadline** 4/1 (freshmen), rolling (transfer) **Freshmen** 76% were admitted **Housing** Yes **Expenses** Tuition 2791; Room & Board 4348 **Undergraduates** 53% women, 10% part-time, 8% 25 or older, 1% Native American, 2% Hispanic American, 3% African American, 3% Asian American/Pacific Islander **The most frequently chosen baccalaureate fields are** business/marketing, health professions and related sciences, social sciences and history **Academic program** English as a second language, advanced placement, accelerated degree program, self-designed majors, honors program, summer session, adult/continuing education programs, internships **Contact** Mr. Alan Cerveny, Director of Admissions and Scholarships, University of Kansas, KU Visitor Center, 1502 Iowa Street, Lawrence, KS 66045-1910. Telephone: 785-864-3911 or toll-free 888-686-7323 (in-state). Fax: 785-864-5006. E-mail: be.a.jayhawk@st37.eds.ukans.edu. Web site: http://www.ku.edu.

WASHBURN UNIVERSITY OF TOPEKA
TOPEKA, KANSAS

General City-supported, comprehensive, coed **Entrance** Noncompetitive **Setting** 160-acre urban campus **Total enrollment** 5,917 **Student/faculty ratio** 15:1 **Application deadline** 8/1 (freshmen), 8/1 (transfer) **Freshmen** 100% were admitted **Housing** Yes **Expenses** Tuition $3052; Room & Board $3410 **Undergraduates** 62% women, 41% part-time, 50% 25 or older, 2% Native American, 4% Hispanic American, 6% African American, 2% Asian American/Pacific Islander **Academic program** English as a second language, advanced placement, self-designed majors, honors program, summer session, adult/continuing education programs, internships **Contact** Ms. April Hansen, Director of Admission, Washburn University of Topeka, 1700 SW College Avenue, Topeka, KS 66621. Telephone: 785-231-1010 Ext. 1293 or toll-free 800-332-0291 (in-state). Fax: 785-231-1089. E-mail: zzgomez@acc.wacc.edu. Web site: http://www.washburn.edu/.

WICHITA STATE UNIVERSITY
WICHITA, KANSAS

General State-supported, university, coed **Entrance** Noncompetitive **Setting** 335-acre urban campus **Total enrollment** 14,810 **Student/faculty ratio** 17:1 **Application deadline** Rolling (freshmen), rolling (transfer) **Freshmen** 75% were admitted **Housing** Yes **Expenses** Tuition $2757; Room & Board $4120 **Undergraduates** 56% women, 42% part-time, 32% 25 or older, 1% Native American, 4% Hispanic American, 7% African American, 7% Asian American/Pacific Islander **The most frequently chosen baccalaureate fields are** business/marketing, education, health professions and related sciences **Academic program** English as a second language, advanced placement, accelerated degree program, self-designed majors, honors program, summer session, internships **Contact** Ms. Christine Schneikart-Luebbe, Director of Admissions, Wichita State University, 1845 North Fairmount, Wichita, KS 67260. Telephone: 316-978-3085 or toll-free 800-362-2594. Fax: 316-978-3174. E-mail: crabtree@twsuvm.uc.twsu.edu. Web site: http://www.wichita.edu/.

KENTUCKY

ALICE LLOYD COLLEGE
PIPPA PASSES, KENTUCKY

General Independent, 4-year, coed **Entrance** Moderately difficult **Setting** 175-acre rural campus **Total enrollment** 558 **Application deadline** 8/1 (freshmen), rolling (transfer) **Freshmen** 66% were admitted **Housing** Yes **Expenses** Tuition $360 **Undergraduates** 10% 25 or older, 0.2% Native American, 0.4% Hispanic American, 0.2% African American, 1% Asian American/Pacific Islander **The most frequently chosen baccalaureate fields are** biological/life sciences, business/marketing, education **Academic program** Advanced placement **Contact** John Mills, Director of Admissions, Alice Lloyd College, 100 Purpose Road, Pippa Passes, KY 41844. Telephone: 606-368-2101 Ext. 6134. Fax: 606-368-2125. Web site: http://www.alc.edu/.

ASBURY COLLEGE
WILMORE, KENTUCKY

General Independent nondenominational, comprehensive, coed **Entrance** Moderately difficult **Setting** 400-acre small-town campus **Total enrollment** 1,357 **Student/faculty ratio** 12:1 **Application deadline** Rolling (freshmen), rolling (transfer) **Freshmen** 82% were admitted **Housing** Yes **Expenses** Tuition $13,884; Room & Board $3566 **Undergraduates** 59% women, 4% part-time, 4% 25 or older, 0.2% Native American, 1% Hispanic American, 1% African American, 1%

Asian American/Pacific Islander **The most frequently chosen baccalaureate fields are** education, English, philosophy, religion, and theology **Academic program** Advanced placement, summer session, internships **Contact** Mr. Stan F. Wiggam, Dean of Admissions, Asbury College, 1 Macklem Drive, Wilmore, KY 40390. Telephone: 859-858-3511 Ext. 2142 or toll-free 800-888-1818. Fax: 859-858-3921. E-mail: admissions@asbury.edu. Web site: http://www.asbury.edu/.

BELLARMINE UNIVERSITY
LOUISVILLE, KENTUCKY

General Independent Roman Catholic, comprehensive, coed **Entrance** Moderately difficult **Setting** 120-acre suburban campus **Total enrollment** 2,175 **Student/faculty ratio** 14:1 **Application deadline** 8/15 (freshmen), 8/15 (transfer) **Freshmen** 95% were admitted **Housing** Yes **Expenses** Tuition $13,760; Room & Board $4160 **Undergraduates** 23% 25 or older, 0.2% Native American, 1% Hispanic American, 3% African American, 1% Asian American/Pacific Islander **The most frequently chosen baccalaureate fields are** business/marketing, health professions and related sciences, social sciences and history **Academic program** Advanced placement, accelerated degree program, self-designed majors, honors program, summer session, adult/continuing education programs, internships **Contact** Mr. Timothy A., Dean of Admission, Bellarmine University, 2001 Newburg Road, Louisville, KY 40205-0671. Telephone: 502-452-8131 or toll-free 800-274-4723 Ext. 8131. Fax: 502-452-8002. E-mail: admissions@bellarmine.edu. Web site: http://www.bellarmine.edu/.

BEREA COLLEGE
BEREA, KENTUCKY

General Independent, 4-year, coed **Entrance** Very difficult **Setting** 140-acre small-town campus **Total enrollment** 1,590 **Student/faculty ratio** 11:1 **Application deadline** Rolling (transfer) **Freshmen** 34% were admitted **Housing** Yes **Expenses** Tuition 205; Room & Board 4099 **Undergraduates** 58% women, 3% part-time, 5% 25 or older, 1% Native American, 1% Hispanic American, 13% African American, 1% Asian American/Pacific Islander **The most frequently chosen baccalaureate fields are** business/marketing, home economics/vocational home economics, social sciences and history **Academic program** Advanced placement, self-designed majors, honors program, summer session, internships **Contact** Mr. Joseph Bagnoli, Director of Admissions, Berea College, CPO 2220, Berea, KY 40404. Telephone: 859-985-3500 or toll-free 800-326-5948. Fax: 859-985-3512. E-mail: admissions@berea.edu. Web site: http://www.berea.edu/.

BRESCIA UNIVERSITY
OWENSBORO, KENTUCKY

General Independent Roman Catholic, comprehensive, coed **Entrance** Moderately difficult **Setting** 6-acre urban campus **Total enrollment** 729 **Student/faculty ratio** 13:1 **Application deadline** Rolling (freshmen), rolling (transfer) **Housing** Yes **Expenses** Tuition $9545; Room & Board $4240 **Undergraduates** 61% women, 30% part-time, 36% 25 or older, 0.2% Native American, 1% Hispanic American, 4% African American, 1% Asian American/Pacific Islander **The most frequently chosen baccalaureate fields are** business/marketing, health professions and related sciences, protective services/public administration **Academic program** English as a second language, advanced placement, self-designed majors, honors program, summer session, adult/continuing education programs, internships **Contact** Sr. Mary Austin Blank, Director of Admissions, Brescia University, 717 Frederica Street, Owensboro, KY 42301-3023. Telephone: 270-686-4241 Ext. 241 or toll-free 877-BRESCIA. Fax: 270-686-4201. E-mail: mcnair@brescia.edu. Web site: http://www.brescia.edu/.

CAMPBELLSVILLE UNIVERSITY
CAMPBELLSVILLE, KENTUCKY

General Independent, comprehensive, coed, affiliated with Kentucky Baptist Convention **Entrance** Moderately difficult **Setting** 70-acre small-town campus **Total enrollment** 1,601 **Student/faculty ratio** 16:1 **Application deadline** Rolling (freshmen), rolling (transfer) **Freshmen** 84% were admitted **Housing** Yes **Expenses** Tuition $9050; Room & Board $4320 **Undergraduates** 60% women, 26% part-time, 18% 25 or older, 0.5% Native American, 1% Hispanic American, 5% African American, 0.1% Asian American/Pacific Islander **Academic program** English as a second language, advanced placement, accelerated degree program, honors program, summer session, adult/continuing education programs, internships **Contact** Mr. R. Trent Argo, Director of Admissions, Campbellsville University, 1 University Drive, Campbellsville, KY 42718-2799. Telephone: 270-789-5552 or toll-free 800-264-6014. Fax: 270-789-5071. E-mail: targo@unix.campbellsvil.edu. Web site: http://www.campbellsvil.edu/.

CENTRE COLLEGE
DANVILLE, KENTUCKY

General Independent, 4-year, coed, affiliated with Presbyterian Church (U.S.A.) **Entrance** Very difficult **Setting** 100-acre small-town campus **Total enrollment** 1,057 **Student/faculty ratio** 11:1 **Application deadline** 2/1 (freshmen), 6/1 (transfer) **Freshmen** 88% were admitted **Housing** Yes **Expenses** Tuition 22,450 **Undergraduates** 53% women, 1% part-time, 1% 25 or older, 0.2% Native American, 0.4% Hispanic American, 3% African American, 1% Asian American/Pacific Islander **The most frequently chosen baccalaureate fields are** English, biological/life sciences, social sciences and history **Academic program** Advanced placement, self-designed majors, internships **Contact** Mr. J. Carey Thompson, Dean of Admission and Financial Aid, Centre College, 600 West Walnut Street, Danville, KY 40422-1394. Telephone: 859-238-5350 or toll-

Centre College *(continued)*

free 800-423-6236. Fax: 859-238-5373. E-mail: admission@centre.edu. Web site: http://www.centre.edu/.

CLEAR CREEK BAPTIST BIBLE COLLEGE
PINEVILLE, KENTUCKY

General Independent Southern Baptist, 4-year, coed, primarily men **Entrance** Noncompetitive **Setting** 700-acre rural campus **Total enrollment** 190 **Application deadline** 7/15 (freshmen), 7/15 (transfer) **Freshmen** 83% were admitted **Housing** Yes **Expenses** Tuition $3870; Room & Board $2740 **Undergraduates** 15% women, 13% part-time, 90% 25 or older **Academic program** Summer session **Contact** Mr. Donnie Fox, Director of Admissions, Clear Creek Baptist Bible College, 300 Clear Creek Road, Pineville, KY 40977-9754. Telephone: 606-337-3196 Ext. 103. Fax: 606-337-2372. E-mail: ccbbc@ccbbc.edu. Web site: http://www.ccbbc.edu/.

CUMBERLAND COLLEGE
WILLIAMSBURG, KENTUCKY

General Independent Kentucky Baptist, comprehensive, coed **Entrance** Moderately difficult **Setting** 30-acre rural campus **Total enrollment** 1,702 **Student/faculty ratio** 17:1 **Application deadline** Rolling (freshmen), rolling (transfer) **Freshmen** 68% were admitted **Housing** Yes **Expenses** Tuition $10,388; Room & Board $4476 **Undergraduates** 53% women, 16% part-time, 0.1% Native American, 1% Hispanic American, 3% African American, 0.2% Asian American/Pacific Islander **The most frequently chosen baccalaureate fields are** business/marketing, education, psychology **Academic program** English as a second language, advanced placement, accelerated degree program, self-designed majors, honors program, summer session, adult/continuing education programs, internships **Contact** Mrs. Erica Harris, Coordinator of Admissions, Cumberland College, 6178 College Station Drive, Williamsburg, KY 40769. Telephone: 606-539-4241 or toll-free 800-343-1609. Fax: 606-539-4303. E-mail: admiss@cc.cumber.edu. Web site: http://cc.cumber.edu/.

EASTERN KENTUCKY UNIVERSITY
RICHMOND, KENTUCKY

General State-supported, comprehensive, coed **Entrance** Noncompetitive **Setting** 500-acre small-town campus **Total enrollment** 14,428 **Student/faculty ratio** 16:1 **Application deadline** Rolling (freshmen), rolling (transfer) **Freshmen** 71% were admitted **Housing** Yes **Expenses** Tuition $2542; Room & Board $3796 **Undergraduates** 58% women, 23% part-time, 27% 25 or older, 0.3% Native American, 0.5% Hispanic American, 5% African American, 0.5% Asian American/Pacific Islander **The most frequently chosen baccalaureate fields are** education, health professions and related sciences, protective services/public administration **Academic program** English as a second language, advanced placement, accelerated degree program, self-designed majors, honors program, summer session, adult/continuing education programs, internships **Contact** Stephen A. Byrn, Director of Admissions, Eastern Kentucky University, Coates 2A, 521 Lancaster Avenue, Richmond, KY 40475-3102. Telephone: 859-622-2106 or toll-free 800-465-9191 (in-state). Web site: http://www.eku.edu/.

GEORGETOWN COLLEGE
GEORGETOWN, KENTUCKY

General Independent, comprehensive, coed, affiliated with Baptist Church **Entrance** Moderately difficult **Setting** 110-acre suburban campus **Total enrollment** 1,736 **Student/faculty ratio** 12:1 **Application deadline** 7/1 (freshmen), rolling (transfer) **Freshmen** 97% were admitted **Housing** Yes **Expenses** Tuition $13,580; Room & Board $4820 **Undergraduates** 58% women, 4% part-time, 2% 25 or older, 0% Native American, 1% Hispanic American, 2% African American, 0.1% Asian American/Pacific Islander **The most frequently chosen baccalaureate fields are** biological/life sciences, business/marketing, psychology **Academic program** Advanced placement, accelerated degree program, self-designed majors, summer session, internships **Contact** Mr. Brian Taylor, Director of Admissions, Georgetown College, 400 East College Street, Georgetown, KY 40324-1696. Telephone: 502-863-8009 or toll-free 800-788-9985. E-mail: admissions@gtc.georgetown.ky.us. Web site: http://www.georgetowncollege.edu/.

KENTUCKY CHRISTIAN COLLEGE
GRAYSON, KENTUCKY

General Independent, 4-year, coed, affiliated with Christian Churches and Churches of Christ **Entrance** Moderately difficult **Setting** 124-acre rural campus **Total enrollment** 587 **Student/faculty ratio** 18:1 **Application deadline** Rolling (freshmen), rolling (transfer) **Freshmen** 90% were admitted **Housing** Yes **Expenses** Tuition $7360; Room & Board $4070 **Undergraduates** 55% women, 5% part-time, 7% 25 or older, 0.4% Native American, 0.4% Hispanic American, 1% African American, 0.2% Asian American/Pacific Islander **The most frequently chosen baccalaureate fields are** education, business/marketing, philosophy, religion, and theology **Academic program** Advanced placement, accelerated degree program, summer session, internships **Contact** Sandra Deakins, Director of Admissions, Kentucky Christian College, 100 Academic Parkway, Grayson, KY 41143-2205. Telephone: 606-474-3266 or toll-free 800-522-3181. Fax: 606-474-3155. E-mail: admiss@kcc.edu. Web site: http://www.kcc.edu/.

KENTUCKY MOUNTAIN BIBLE COLLEGE
VANCLEVE, KENTUCKY

General Independent interdenominational, 4-year, coed **Entrance** Moderately difficult **Setting** 35-acre rural campus **Total enrollment** 90 **Student/faculty ratio** 5:1 **Application deadline** Rolling (freshmen), rolling (transfer) **Freshmen** 52% were admitted **Hous-**

ing Yes **Expenses** Tuition $4170; Room & Board $2800 **Undergraduates** 43% women, 16% part-time, 21% 25 or older, 0% Native American, 0% Hispanic American, 1% African American, 1% Asian American/Pacific Islander **The most frequently chosen baccalaureate field is** philosophy, religion, and theology **Academic program** Advanced placement, adult/continuing education programs, internships **Contact** Mr. James Nelson, Director of Recruiting, Kentucky Mountain Bible College, PO Box 10, Vancleve, KY 41385-0010. Telephone: 606-666-5000 Ext. 130 or toll-free 800-879-KMBC. Fax: 606-666-7744. E-mail: jnelson@kmbc.edu. Web site: http://www.kmbc.edu/.

KENTUCKY STATE UNIVERSITY
FRANKFORT, KENTUCKY

General State-related, comprehensive, coed **Entrance** Minimally difficult **Setting** 485-acre small-town campus **Total enrollment** 2,254 **Student/faculty ratio** 15:1 **Application deadline** Rolling (freshmen), rolling (transfer) **Freshmen** 45% were admitted **Housing** Yes **Expenses** Tuition $2440; Room & Board $3740 **Undergraduates** 56% women, 29% part-time, 26% 25 or older **The most frequently chosen baccalaureate fields are** education, business/marketing, protective services/public administration **Academic program** English as a second language, advanced placement, accelerated degree program, self-designed majors, honors program, summer session, adult/continuing education programs, internships **Contact** Mr. Vory Billaps, Director of Records, Registration, and Admission, Kentucky State University, 400 East Main, Frankfort, KY 40601. Telephone: 502-597-6340 or toll-free 800-633-9415 (in-state); 800-325-1716 (out-of-state). Fax: 502-597-6239. E-mail: jburrell@qwmail.kysu.edu. Web site: http://www.kysu.edu/.

KENTUCKY WESLEYAN COLLEGE
OWENSBORO, KENTUCKY

General Independent Methodist, 4-year, coed **Entrance** Moderately difficult **Setting** 52-acre suburban campus **Total enrollment** 680 **Student/faculty ratio** 14:1 **Application deadline** 9/1 (freshmen), 9/1 (transfer) **Freshmen** 79% were admitted **Housing** Yes **Expenses** Tuition $10,070; Room & Board $4830 **Undergraduates** 54% women, 7% part-time, 5% African American **The most frequently chosen baccalaureate fields are** business/marketing, education, health professions and related sciences **Academic program** Advanced placement, self-designed majors, summer session, internships **Contact** Mr. Chris Houk, Interim Dean of Admission, Kentucky Wesleyan College, 3000 Frederica Street, PO Box 1039, Owensboro, KY 42302-1039. Telephone: 270-926-3111 Ext. 5145 or toll-free 800-999-0592 (in-state); 270-999-0592 (out-of-state). Fax: 502-926-3196. E-mail: admission@kwc.edu. Web site: http://www.kwc.edu/.

▶ **For more information, see page 435.**

LINDSEY WILSON COLLEGE
COLUMBIA, KENTUCKY

General Independent United Methodist, comprehensive, coed **Entrance** Minimally difficult **Setting** 40-acre rural campus **Total enrollment** 1,415 **Student/faculty ratio** 20:1 **Application deadline** Rolling (freshmen), rolling (transfer) **Freshmen** 83% were admitted **Housing** Yes **Expenses** Tuition $9798; Room & Board $4680 **Undergraduates** 63% women, 10% part-time, 29% 25 or older, 0.3% Native American, 1% Hispanic American, 7% African American, 1% Asian American/Pacific Islander **Academic program** English as a second language, advanced placement, accelerated degree program, self-designed majors, summer session, adult/continuing education programs, internships **Contact** Mr. Claude Bacon, Director of Admissions, Lindsey Wilson College, 210 Lindsey Wilson Street, Columbia, KY 42728-1298. Telephone: 270-384-8100 Ext. 8008 or toll-free 800-264-0138. Fax: 270-384-8200. E-mail: baconc@lindsey.edu. Web site: http://www.lindsey.edu/.

MID-CONTINENT COLLEGE
MAYFIELD, KENTUCKY

General Independent Southern Baptist, 4-year, coed **Entrance** Minimally difficult **Setting** 60-acre small-town campus **Total enrollment** 455 **Student/faculty ratio** 10:1 **Application deadline** Rolling (freshmen), rolling (transfer) **Freshmen** 65% were admitted **Housing** Yes **Expenses** Tuition $6880; Room & Board $4200 **Undergraduates** 46% women, 10% part-time, 37% 25 or older, 0.4% Native American, 7% African American, 1% Asian American/Pacific Islander **The most frequently chosen baccalaureate field is** philosophy, religion, and theology **Academic program** English as a second language, advanced placement, accelerated degree program, summer session **Contact** Ms. Darla Zakowicz, Director of Enrollment and Retention, Mid-Continent College, 99 Powell Road East, Mayfield, KY 42066. Telephone: 270-247-8521. Fax: 270-247-3115. E-mail: mcollege@apex.net. Web site: http://www.midcontinent.edu.

MIDWAY COLLEGE
MIDWAY, KENTUCKY

General Independent, 4-year, women only, affiliated with Christian Church (Disciples of Christ) **Entrance** Minimally difficult **Setting** 105-acre small-town campus **Total enrollment** 834 **Student/faculty ratio** 12:1 **Application deadline** Rolling (freshmen), rolling (transfer) **Freshmen** 92% were admitted **Housing** Yes **Expenses** Tuition 9666; Room & Board 4850 **Undergraduates** 33% part-time, 54% 25 or older, 1% Native American, 0.5% Hispanic American, 4% African American, 0% Asian American/Pacific Islander **The most frequently chosen baccalaureate fields are** business/marketing, education, health professions and related sciences **Academic program** Advanced placement, honors program, summer session, adult/continuing education programs, internships **Contact** Mr. K. Bryan, Director of Admissions,

Midway College *(continued)*

Midway College, 512 East Stephens Street, Pinkerton Building, Midway, KY 40347-1120. Telephone: 859-846-5346 or toll-free 800-755-0031. Fax: 859-846-5823. E-mail: admissions@midway.edu. Web site: http://www.midway.edu/.

MOREHEAD STATE UNIVERSITY
MOREHEAD, KENTUCKY

General State-supported, comprehensive, coed **Entrance** Minimally difficult **Setting** 809-acre small-town campus **Total enrollment** 8,322 **Student/faculty ratio** 18:1 **Application deadline** Rolling (freshmen), rolling (transfer) **Freshmen** 74% were admitted **Housing** Yes **Expenses** Tuition 2710; Room & Board 3800 **Undergraduates** 60% women, 15% part-time, 0.4% Native American, 0.4% Hispanic American, 4% African American, 0.3% Asian American/Pacific Islander **The most frequently chosen baccalaureate fields are** business/marketing, education, social sciences and history **Academic program** English as a second language, advanced placement, accelerated degree program, self-designed majors, honors program, summer session, adult/continuing education programs, internships **Contact** Mr. Tim Rhodes, Assistant Vice President of Admissions, Financial Aid and Housing, Morehead State University, Howell McDowell 301, Morehead, KY 40351. Telephone: 606-783-2000 or toll-free 800-585-6781. Fax: 606-783-5038. E-mail: d.cornett@morehead-st.edu. Web site: http://www.moreheadstate.edu/.

MURRAY STATE UNIVERSITY
MURRAY, KENTUCKY

General State-supported, comprehensive, coed **Entrance** Moderately difficult **Setting** 238-acre small-town campus **Total enrollment** 9,136 **Student/faculty ratio** 17:1 **Application deadline** Rolling (freshmen), rolling (transfer) **Freshmen** 87% were admitted **Housing** Yes **Expenses** Tuition 2754; Room & Board 4250 **Undergraduates** 58% women, 15% part-time, 22% 25 or older, 0.3% Native American, 1% Hispanic American, 6% African American, 1% Asian American/Pacific Islander **The most frequently chosen baccalaureate fields are** business/marketing, education, health professions and related sciences **Academic program** English as a second language, advanced placement, accelerated degree program, honors program, summer session, adult/continuing education programs, internships **Contact** Mrs. Stacy Bell, Admission Clerk, Murray State University, PO Box 9, Murray, KY 42071-0009. Telephone: 270-762-3035 or toll-free 800-272-4678. Fax: 270-762-3050. E-mail: pbryan@msumusik.mursuky.edu. Web site: http://www.murraystate.edu/.

NORTHERN KENTUCKY UNIVERSITY
HIGHLAND HEIGHTS, KENTUCKY

General State-supported, comprehensive, coed **Entrance** Noncompetitive **Setting** 300-acre suburban campus **Total enrollment** 12,080 **Student/faculty ratio** 17:1 **Application deadline** 8/21 (freshmen), 8/1 (transfer) **Freshmen** 98% were admitted **Housing** Yes **Expenses** Tuition $2754; Room & Board $4172 **Undergraduates** 59% women, 28% part-time, 26% 25 or older, 0.3% Native American, 0.5% Hispanic American, 4% African American, 1% Asian American/Pacific Islander **The most frequently chosen baccalaureate fields are** business/marketing, education, social sciences and history **Academic program** Advanced placement, honors program, summer session, adult/continuing education programs, internships **Contact** Mrs. Debbie Poweleit, Associate Director of Admissions, Northern Kentucky University, Administrative Center 400, Highland Heights, KY 41099-7010. Telephone: 606-572-5220 Ext. 5154 or toll-free 800-637-9948 (out-of-state). Fax: 859-572-6665. E-mail: admitnku@nku.edu. Web site: http://www.nku.edu/.

▶ **For more information, see page 457.**

PIKEVILLE COLLEGE
PIKEVILLE, KENTUCKY

General Independent, comprehensive, coed, affiliated with Presbyterian Church (U.S.A.) **Entrance** Noncompetitive **Setting** 25-acre small-town campus **Total enrollment** 1,156 **Student/faculty ratio** 15:1 **Application deadline** 8/24 (freshmen), 8/24 (transfer) **Freshmen** 100% were admitted **Housing** Yes **Expenses** Tuition $7800; Room & Board $3340 **Undergraduates** 59% women, 6% part-time, 14% 25 or older, 0% Native American, 1% Hispanic American, 6% African American, 0.3% Asian American/Pacific Islander **The most frequently chosen baccalaureate fields are** business/marketing, education, psychology **Academic program** Advanced placement, summer session, internships **Contact** Ms. Melinda Lynch, Director of Admissions, Pikeville College, 147 Sycamore Street, Pikeville, KY 41501. Telephone: 606-218-5251. Fax: 606-218-5269. Web site: http://www.pc.edu/.

SOUTHERN BAPTIST THEOLOGICAL SEMINARY
LOUISVILLE, KENTUCKY

Contact Southern Baptist Theological Seminary, 2825 Lexington Road, Louisville, KY 40280-0004. Web site: http://www.sbts.edu/.

SPALDING UNIVERSITY
LOUISVILLE, KENTUCKY

General Independent, comprehensive, coed, affiliated with Roman Catholic Church **Entrance** Moderately difficult **Setting** 5-acre urban campus **Total enrollment** 1,481 **Student/faculty ratio** 16:1 **Application deadline** 8/1 (freshmen), 8/1 (transfer) **Freshmen** 71% were admitted **Housing** Yes **Expenses** Tuition $11,496; Room & Board $2930 **Undergraduates** 77% women, 40% part-time, 53% 25 or older, 0.2% Native American, 1% Hispanic American, 15% African American, 1% Asian American/Pacific Islander

Academic program Advanced placement, accelerated degree program, summer session, adult/continuing education programs, internships **Contact** Ms. Kathleen C. Hodapp, Director of Admission, Spalding University, 851 South Fourth Street, Louisville, KY 40203. Telephone: 502-585-7111 Ext. 2226 or toll-free 800-896-8941 Ext. 2111. Fax: 502-992-2148. E-mail: admissions@spalding30.win.net. Web site: http://www.spalding.edu/.

SULLIVAN UNIVERSITY

LOUISVILLE, KENTUCKY

General Proprietary, comprehensive, coed **Entrance** Minimally difficult **Setting** 10-acre suburban campus **Total enrollment** 4,000 **Student/faculty ratio** 18:1 **Application deadline** Rolling (freshmen), rolling (transfer) **Housing** Yes **Expenses** Tuition 10,080; Room only 2970 **Undergraduates** 50% 25 or older, 1% Native American, 0.3% Hispanic American, 21% African American **Academic program** Advanced placement, accelerated degree program, summer session, adult/continuing education programs **Contact** Mr. Greg Cawthon, Director of Admissions, Sullivan University, 3101 Bardstown Road, Louisville, KY 40205. Telephone: 502-456-6504 Ext. 330 or toll-free 800-844-1354 (in-state). Fax: 502-454-4880. E-mail: tfd@corp.sullivan.edu. Web site: http://www.sullivan.edu/.

THOMAS MORE COLLEGE

CRESTVIEW HILLS, KENTUCKY

General Independent Roman Catholic, comprehensive, coed **Entrance** Moderately difficult **Setting** 100-acre suburban campus **Total enrollment** 1,417 **Student/faculty ratio** 12:1 **Application deadline** 8/15 (freshmen), 8/15 (transfer) **Freshmen** 79% were admitted **Housing** Yes **Expenses** Tuition $12,580; Room & Board $3756 **Undergraduates** 55% women, 35% part-time, 36% 25 or older, 1% Native American, 1% Hispanic American, 4% African American, 0.4% Asian American/Pacific Islander **The most frequently chosen baccalaureate fields are** biological/life sciences, business/marketing, liberal arts/general studies **Academic program** Advanced placement, accelerated degree program, self-designed majors, honors program, summer session, adult/continuing education programs, internships **Contact** Mr. Robert A. McDermott, Director of Admissions, Thomas More College, 333 Thomas More Parkway, Crestview Hills, KY 41017. Telephone: 606-344-3332 or toll-free 800-825-4557. Fax: 606-344-3444. E-mail: cantralk@thomasmore.edu. Web site: http://www.thomasmore.edu/.

TRANSYLVANIA UNIVERSITY

LEXINGTON, KENTUCKY

General Independent, 4-year, coed, affiliated with Christian Church (Disciples of Christ) **Entrance** Very difficult **Setting** 35-acre urban campus **Total enrollment** 1,083 **Student/faculty ratio** 13:1 **Application deadline** 2/1 (freshmen), rolling (transfer) **Freshmen** 91% were admitted **Housing** Yes **Expenses** Tuition 15,270; Room & Board 5530 **Undergraduates** 58% women, 1% part-time, 1% 25 or older, 0.3% Native American, 1% Hispanic American, 3% African American, 3% Asian American/Pacific Islander **The most frequently chosen baccalaureate fields are** biological/life sciences, business/marketing, social sciences and history **Academic program** Advanced placement, self-designed majors, summer session, internships **Contact** Ms. Sarah Coen, Director of Admissions, Transylvania University, 300 North Broadway, Lexington, KY 40508-1797. Telephone: 859-233-8242 or toll-free 800-872-6798. Fax: 859-233-8797. E-mail: admsapp@music.transy.edu. Web site: http://www.transy.edu/.

UNION COLLEGE

BARBOURVILLE, KENTUCKY

General Independent United Methodist, comprehensive, coed **Entrance** Moderately difficult **Setting** 110-acre small-town campus **Total enrollment** 908 **Student/faculty ratio** 12:1 **Application deadline** 8/1 (freshmen), 8/31 (transfer) **Freshmen** 75% were admitted **Housing** Yes **Expenses** Tuition $11,295; Room & Board $3650 **Undergraduates** 48% women, 9% part-time, 19% 25 or older, 0.3% Native American, 2% Hispanic American, 10% African American, 1% Asian American/Pacific Islander **Academic program** Advanced placement, accelerated degree program, honors program, summer session, internships **Contact** Joretta Nelson, Vice President for Enrollment and Recruitment, Union College, 310 College Street, Barbourville, KY 40906-1499. Telephone: 606-546-1220 or toll-free 800-489-8646. Fax: 606-546-1667. E-mail: enroll@unionky.edu. Web site: http://www.unionky.edu/.

UNIVERSITY OF KENTUCKY

LEXINGTON, KENTUCKY

General State-supported, university, coed **Entrance** Moderately difficult **Setting** 685-acre urban campus **Total enrollment** 23,114 **Student/faculty ratio** 16:1 **Application deadline** 2/15 (freshmen), 8/1 (transfer) **Freshmen** 61% were admitted **Housing** Yes **Expenses** Tuition 3706 **Undergraduates** 52% women, 11% part-time, 12% 25 or older, 0.2% Native American, 1% Hispanic American, 6% African American, 2% Asian American/Pacific Islander **The most frequently chosen baccalaureate fields are** business/marketing, engineering/engineering technologies, health professions and related sciences **Academic program** English as a second language, advanced placement, accelerated degree program, self-designed majors, honors program, summer session, adult/continuing education programs, internships **Contact** Mr. Don Byars, Associate Director of Admissions, University of Kentucky, 100 W.D. Funkhouser Building, Lexington, KY 40506-0054. Telephone: 859-257-2000 or toll-free 800-432-0967 (in-state). E-mail: admissio@pop.uky.edu. Web site: http://www.uky.edu/.

University of Kentucky *(continued)*

UNIVERSITY OF LOUISVILLE
LOUISVILLE, KENTUCKY

General State-supported, university, coed **Entrance** Moderately difficult **Setting** 169-acre urban campus **Total enrollment** 19,771 **Application deadline** Rolling (freshmen), rolling (transfer) **Freshmen** 89% were admitted **Housing** Yes **Expenses** Tuition 3447; Room & Board 3500 **Undergraduates** 54% women, 32% part-time, 31% 25 or older, 0.3% Native American, 1% Hispanic American, 13% African American, 3% Asian American/Pacific Islander **The most frequently chosen baccalaureate fields are** business/marketing, engineering/engineering technologies, social sciences and history **Academic program** English as a second language, advanced placement, accelerated degree program, self-designed majors, honors program, summer session, adult/continuing education programs, internships **Contact** Ms. Jenny Sawyer, Executive Director for Admissions, University of Louisville, 2211 South Brook, Louisville, KY 40292. Telephone: 502-852-6531 or toll-free 502-852-6531 (in-state); 800-334-8635 (out-of-state). Fax: 502-852-4776 Ext. 6531. E-mail: admitme@ulkyvm.louisville.edu. Web site: http://www.louisville.edu/.

WESTERN KENTUCKY UNIVERSITY
BOWLING GREEN, KENTUCKY

General State-supported, comprehensive, coed **Entrance** Moderately difficult **Setting** 223-acre suburban campus **Total enrollment** 15,479 **Student/faculty ratio** 19:1 **Application deadline** 8/1 (freshmen), 8/1 (transfer) **Freshmen** 87% were admitted **Housing** Yes **Expenses** Tuition $2534; Room & Board $3813 **Undergraduates** 58% women, 20% part-time, 24% 25 or older, 0.3% Native American, 1% Hispanic American, 8% African American, 1% Asian American/Pacific Islander **The most frequently chosen baccalaureate fields are** business/marketing, communications/communication technologies, education **Academic program** English as a second language, advanced placement, accelerated degree program, self-designed majors, honors program, summer session, adult/continuing education programs, internships **Contact** Ms. Sharon Dyrsen, Director of Admissions and Academic Services, Western Kentucky University, Potter Hall 117, 1 Big Red Way, Bowling Green, KY 42101-3576. Telephone: 270-745-4241 or toll-free 800-495-8463 (in-state). Fax: 270-745-6133. E-mail: admission@wku.edu. Web site: http://www.wku.edu/.

LOUISIANA

CENTENARY COLLEGE OF LOUISIANA
SHREVEPORT, LOUISIANA

General Independent United Methodist, comprehensive, coed **Entrance** Moderately difficult **Setting** 65-acre suburban campus **Total enrollment** 1,035 **Student/faculty ratio** 12:1 **Application deadline** 2/15 (freshmen), 8/1 (transfer) **Freshmen** 89% were admitted **Housing** Yes **Expenses** Tuition 14,600; Room & Board 4500 **Undergraduates** 61% women, 3% part-time, 1% 25 or older, 1% Native American, 3% Hispanic American, 6% African American, 1% Asian American/Pacific Islander **The most frequently chosen baccalaureate fields are** business/marketing, biological/life sciences, social sciences and history **Academic program** Advanced placement, self-designed majors, honors program, summer session, adult/continuing education programs, internships **Contact** Dr. Eugene Gregory, Vice President of College Relations, Centenary College of Louisiana, 2911 Centenary Blvd, PO Box 41188, Shreveport, LA 71134-1188. Telephone: 318-869-5131 or toll-free 800-234-4448. Fax: 318-869-5005. E-mail: tcrowley@beta.centenary.edu. Web site: http://www.centenary.edu/.

DILLARD UNIVERSITY
NEW ORLEANS, LOUISIANA

General Independent interdenominational, 4-year, coed **Entrance** Moderately difficult **Setting** 46-acre urban campus **Total enrollment** 1,953 **Student/faculty ratio** 13:1 **Application deadline** 7/1 (freshmen), 7/1 (transfer) **Freshmen** 72% were admitted **Housing** Yes **Expenses** Tuition $9200; Room & Board $5350 **Undergraduates** 78% women, 11% part-time, 10% 25 or older, 0% Native American, 0.3% Hispanic American, 99% African American, 0.1% Asian American/Pacific Islander **The most frequently chosen baccalaureate fields are** business/marketing, health professions and related sciences, protective services/public administration **Academic program** Advanced placement, honors program, summer session, internships **Contact** Mr. Darrin Q. Rankin, Assistant Vice President, Enrollment Management, Dillard University, 2601 Gentilly Boulevard, New Orleans, LA 70122. Telephone: 504-286-4670. Fax: 504-286-4895.

GRAMBLING STATE UNIVERSITY
GRAMBLING, LOUISIANA

Contact Mr. Martin Lemelle, Head Recruiter/Admission Officer, Grambling State University, PO Box 607, Grambling, LA 71245. Telephone: 318-274-3395. E-mail: bingamann@medgar.gram.edu.

GRANTHAM COLLEGE OF ENGINEERING
SLIDELL, LOUISIANA

General Proprietary, 4-year, coed, primarily men **Entrance** Noncompetitive **Setting** small-town campus **Total enrollment** 967 **Application deadline** Rolling (freshmen), rolling (transfer) **Housing** No **Expenses** Tuition $5250 **Undergraduates** 96% 25 or older **Academic program** Advanced placement, accelerated degree program, honors program, adult/continuing education programs **Contact** Mrs. Maria Adcock, Student Services Manager, Grantham College of Engineering, PO Box 5700, Slidell, LA 70460-6815. Telephone: 504-649-4191 or toll-free 800-955-2527. Fax: 504-649-4183. E-mail: gogce@aol.com. Web site: http://www.grantham.edu/.

LOUISIANA COLLEGE
PINEVILLE, LOUISIANA

General Independent Southern Baptist, 4-year, coed **Contact** Mr. Byron McGee, Director of Admissions, Louisiana College, Box 560, Pineville, LA 71359-0001. Telephone: 318-487-7259 Ext. 7301 or toll-free 800-487-1906. Fax: 318-487-7550. E-mail: admissions@andria.lacollege.edu. Web site: http://www.lacollege.edu/.

LOUISIANA STATE UNIVERSITY AND AGRICULTURAL AND MECHANICAL COLLEGE
BATON ROUGE, LOUISIANA

General State-supported, university, coed **Entrance** Moderately difficult **Setting** 2,000-acre urban campus **Total enrollment** 30,861 **Student/faculty ratio** 21:1 **Application deadline** 5/1 (freshmen), 5/1 (transfer) **Freshmen** 78% were admitted **Housing** Yes **Expenses** Tuition $3395; Room & Board $4270 **Undergraduates** 53% women, 11% part-time, 11% 25 or older, 0.4% Native American, 2% Hispanic American, 10% African American, 4% Asian American/Pacific Islander **The most frequently chosen baccalaureate fields are** business/marketing, education, engineering/engineering technologies **Academic program** English as a second language, advanced placement, accelerated degree program, self-designed majors, honors program, summer session, adult/continuing education programs, internships **Contact** Cleve Brooks, Interim Director of Admissions, Louisiana State University and Agricultural and Mechanical College, 110 Thomas Boyd Hall, Baton Rouge, LA 70803. Telephone: 225-578-1175. Fax: 225-578-4433. E-mail: admit@unix1.sncc.lsu.edu. Web site: http://www.lsu.edu/.

LOUISIANA STATE UNIVERSITY HEALTH SCIENCES CENTER
NEW ORLEANS, LOUISIANA

General State-supported, university, coed **Setting** urban campus **Total enrollment** 2,720 **Application deadline** 3/1 (transfer) **Housing** Yes **Expenses** Tuition $3659; Room only $1750 **Undergraduates** 24% 25 or older, 0.3% Native American, 2% Hispanic American, 9% African American, 6% Asian American/Pacific Islander **The most frequently chosen baccalaureate field is** health professions and related sciences **Academic program** Advanced placement, summer session, internships **Contact** Mr. Edmund A. Vidacovich, Registrar, Louisiana State University Health Sciences Center, 433 Bolivar Street, New Orleans, LA 70112-2223. Telephone: 504-568-4829. Web site: http://www.lsumc.edu/.

LOUISIANA STATE UNIVERSITY IN SHREVEPORT
SHREVEPORT, LOUISIANA

General State-supported, comprehensive, coed **Entrance** Noncompetitive **Setting** 200-acre urban campus **Total enrollment** 4,108 **Student/faculty ratio** 18:1 **Application deadline** 8/5 (freshmen), 8/5 (transfer) **Freshmen** 100% were admitted **Housing** Yes **Expenses** Tuition $2550 **Undergraduates** 61% women, 34% part-time, 37% 25 or older, 1% Native American, 2% Hispanic American, 19% African American, 2% Asian American/Pacific Islander **The most frequently chosen baccalaureate fields are** business/marketing, education, liberal arts/general studies **Academic program** Advanced placement, accelerated degree program, self-designed majors, honors program, summer session, adult/continuing education programs, internships **Contact** Ms. Julie Wilkins, Assistant Director of Admissions and Records, Louisiana State University in Shreveport, One University Place, Shreveport, LA 71115-2399. Telephone: 318-797-5057 or toll-free 800-229-5957 (in-state). Fax: 318-797-5286. E-mail: admissions@pilot.lsus.edu. Web site: http://www.lsus.edu/.

LOUISIANA TECH UNIVERSITY
RUSTON, LOUISIANA

General State-supported, university, coed **Entrance** Moderately difficult **Setting** 247-acre small-town campus **Total enrollment** 10,363 **Student/faculty ratio** 23:1 **Application deadline** 7/3 (freshmen), rolling (transfer) **Freshmen** 93% were admitted **Housing** Yes **Expenses** Tuition $2748; Room & Board $3195 **Undergraduates** 48% women, 18% part-time, 17% 25 or older, 0.5% Native American, 1% Hispanic American, 14% African American, 1% Asian American/Pacific Islander **Academic program** English as a second language, advanced placement, honors program, summer session, adult/continuing education programs, internships **Contact** Mrs. Jan B. Albritton, Director of Admissions, Louisiana Tech University, PO Box 3178, Ruston, LA 71272. Telephone: 318-257-3036 or toll-free 800-528-3241. Fax: 318-257-2499. E-mail: usjba@latech.edu. Web site: http://www.latech.edu/.

LOYOLA UNIVERSITY NEW ORLEANS
NEW ORLEANS, LOUISIANA

General Independent Roman Catholic (Jesuit), comprehensive, coed **Entrance** Moderately difficult **Setting** 26-acre urban campus **Total enrollment** 5,279 **Student/faculty ratio** 12:1 **Application deadline** Rolling (freshmen), rolling (transfer) **Freshmen** 74% were admitted **Housing** Yes **Expenses** Tuition $16,700; Room & Board $6806 **Undergraduates** 64% women, 16% part-time, 8% 25 or older, 0.5% Native American, 9% Hispanic American, 11% African American, 4% Asian American/Pacific Islander **The most frequently chosen baccalaureate fields are** business/marketing, communications/communication technologies, social sciences and history **Academic program**

Loyola University New Orleans *(continued)*

English as a second language, advanced placement, accelerated degree program, self-designed majors, honors program, summer session, adult/continuing education programs, internships **Contact** Ms. Debbie Stieffel, Director of Admission and Enrollment Management, Loyola University New Orleans, 6363 Saint Charles Avenue, Box 18, New Orleans, LA 70118-6195. Telephone: 504-865-3240 or toll-free 800-4-LOYOLA. Fax: 504-865-3383. E-mail: admit@loyno.edu. Web site: http://www.loyno.edu/.

► **For more information, see page 441.**

MCNEESE STATE UNIVERSITY
LAKE CHARLES, LOUISIANA

General State-supported, comprehensive, coed **Entrance** Moderately difficult **Setting** 580-acre suburban campus **Total enrollment** 7,603 **Student/faculty ratio** 20:1 **Application deadline** Rolling (freshmen), rolling (transfer) **Freshmen** 72% were admitted **Housing** Yes **Expenses** Tuition 2471; Room & Board 2620 **Undergraduates** 59% women, 18% part-time, 22% 25 or older, 1% Native American, 1% Hispanic American, 17% African American, 1% Asian American/Pacific Islander **The most frequently chosen baccalaureate fields are** business/marketing, education, social sciences and history **Academic program** English as a second language, advanced placement, accelerated degree program, honors program, summer session, adult/continuing education programs, internships **Contact** Ms. Tammie Pettis, Director of Admissions, McNeese State University, PO Box 92495, Kaufman Hall, 4100 Ryan Street, Lake Charles, LA 70609-2495. Telephone: 337-475-5148 or toll-free 800-622-3352. Fax: 337-475-5189. E-mail: kbond@mcneese.edu.

NEW ORLEANS BAPTIST THEOLOGICAL SEMINARY
NEW ORLEANS, LOUISIANA

Contact Dr. Paul E. Gregoire Jr., Registrar/Director of Admissions, New Orleans Baptist Theological Seminary, 3939 Gentilly Boulevard, New Orleans, LA 70126-4858. Telephone: 504-282-4455 Ext. 3632 or toll-free 800-662-8701. Web site: http://www.nobts.edu/.

NICHOLLS STATE UNIVERSITY
THIBODAUX, LOUISIANA

General State-supported, comprehensive, coed **Entrance** Noncompetitive **Setting** 210-acre small-town campus **Total enrollment** 7,326 **Student/faculty ratio** 23:1 **Application deadline** Rolling (freshmen), rolling (transfer) **Freshmen** 93% were admitted **Housing** Yes **Expenses** Tuition $2368; Room & Board $3002 **Undergraduates** 62% women, 17% part-time, 21% 25 or older, 2% Native American, 1% Hispanic American, 15% African American, 1% Asian American/Pacific Islander **The most frequently chosen baccalaureate fields are** education, business/marketing, liberal arts/general studies **Academic program** English as a second language, advanced placement, accelerated degree program, honors program, summer session, adult/continuing education programs, internships **Contact** Mrs. Becky L. Durocher, Director of Admissions, Nicholls State University, PO Box 2004-NSU, Thibodaux, LA 70310. Telephone: 504-448-4507 or toll-free 877-NICHOLLS. Fax: 504-448-4929. E-mail: nicholls@nich-nsunet.nich.edu. Web site: http://www.nicholls.edu.

NORTHEAST LOUISIANA UNIVERSITY
See University of Louisiana at Monroe

NORTHWESTERN STATE UNIVERSITY OF LOUISIANA
NATCHITOCHES, LOUISIANA

General State-supported, comprehensive, coed **Entrance** Noncompetitive **Setting** 1,000-acre small-town campus **Total enrollment** 9,011 **Student/faculty ratio** 24:1 **Application deadline** Rolling (freshmen), rolling (transfer) **Freshmen** 98% were admitted **Housing** Yes **Expenses** Tuition $2493; Room & Board $2896 **Undergraduates** 62% women, 25% part-time, 33% 25 or older, 2% Native American, 2% Hispanic American, 25% African American, 1% Asian American/Pacific Islander **The most frequently chosen baccalaureate fields are** education, health professions and related sciences, liberal arts/general studies **Academic program** Advanced placement, honors program, summer session, adult/continuing education programs, internships **Contact** Ms. Jana Lucky, Director of Recruiting and Admissions, Northwestern State University of Louisiana, Roy Hall, Room 101, Natchitoches, LA 71497. Telephone: 318-357-4503 or toll-free 800-426-3754 (in-state); 800-327-1903 (out-of-state). E-mail: admissions@alpha.nsula.edu. Web site: http://www.nsula.edu/.

OUR LADY OF HOLY CROSS COLLEGE
NEW ORLEANS, LOUISIANA

General Independent Roman Catholic, comprehensive, coed **Entrance** Minimally difficult **Setting** 40-acre suburban campus **Total enrollment** 1,233 **Student/faculty ratio** 21:1 **Application deadline** Rolling (freshmen), rolling (transfer) **Freshmen** 45% were admitted **Housing** No **Expenses** Tuition $6090 **Undergraduates** 76% women, 46% part-time, 35% 25 or older, 1% Native American, 5% Hispanic American, 12% African American, 3% Asian American/Pacific Islander **The most frequently chosen baccalaureate fields are** education, business/marketing, health professions and related sciences **Academic program** Advanced placement, summer session, adult/continuing education programs, internships **Contact** Ms. Kristine Hatfield Kopecky, Director of Student Affairs and Admissions, Our Lady of Holy Cross College, 4123 Woodland Drive, New Orleans, LA 70131-7399. Telephone: 504-394-7744 Ext. 185 or toll-free 800-259-7744 Ext. 175. Fax: 504-391-2421. Web site: http://www.olhcc.edu/.

SAINT JOSEPH SEMINARY COLLEGE
SAINT BENEDICT, LOUISIANA

Contact Mr. Thomas A. Siegrist, Registrar/Director of Admissions, Saint Joseph Seminary College, Saint Benedict, LA 70457. Telephone: 504-892-1800 Ext. 29. Web site: http://www.stjosephabbey.org.

SOUTHEASTERN LOUISIANA UNIVERSITY
HAMMOND, LOUISIANA

General State-supported, comprehensive, coed **Entrance** Minimally difficult **Setting** 375-acre small-town campus **Total enrollment** 14,525 **Student/faculty ratio** 27:1 **Application deadline** 7/15 (freshmen), rolling (transfer) **Freshmen** 77% were admitted **Housing** Yes **Expenses** Tuition $2490; Room & Board $3006 **Undergraduates** 63% women, 16% part-time, 24% 25 or older, 1% Native American, 2% Hispanic American, 14% African American, 0.4% Asian American/Pacific Islander **The most frequently chosen baccalaureate fields are** business/marketing, education, health professions and related sciences **Academic program** Advanced placement, honors program, summer session, adult/continuing education programs, internships **Contact** Ms. Pat Duplessis, University Admissions Analyst, Southeastern Louisiana University, SLU 10752, North Campus-Building B, Hammond, LA 70402. Telephone: 504-549-2066 or toll-free 800-222-7358. Fax: 504-549-5632. E-mail: ssoutullo@selu.edu. Web site: http://www.selu.edu/.

SOUTHERN UNIVERSITY AND AGRICULTURAL AND MECHANICAL COLLEGE
BATON ROUGE, LOUISIANA

General State-supported, comprehensive, coed **Entrance** Noncompetitive **Setting** 964-acre suburban campus **Total enrollment** 9,449 **Student/faculty ratio** 17:1 **Application deadline** 6/1 (freshmen), 6/1 (transfer) **Housing** Yes **Expenses** Tuition $2286; Room & Board $3410 **Undergraduates** 57% women, 10% part-time, 14% 25 or older, 0% Native American, 0.1% Hispanic American, 97% African American, 0.4% Asian American/Pacific Islander **Academic program** Advanced placement, honors program, summer session, adult/continuing education programs, internships **Contact** Ms. Velva Thomas, Director of Admissions, Southern University and Agricultural and Mechanical College, PO Box 9901, Baton Rouge, LA 70813. Telephone: 225-771-2430 or toll-free 800-256-1531 (in-state). Fax: 225-771-2500. Web site: http://www.subr.edu/.

SOUTHERN UNIVERSITY AT NEW ORLEANS
NEW ORLEANS, LOUISIANA

Contact Registrar/Director of Admissions, Southern University at New Orleans, 6400 Press Drive, New Orleans, LA 70126-1009. Telephone: 504-286-5314. Web site: http://www.gnofn.org/~zaire/suno4.htm.

TULANE UNIVERSITY
NEW ORLEANS, LOUISIANA

General Independent, university, coed **Entrance** Very difficult **Setting** 110-acre urban campus **Total enrollment** 12,160 **Student/faculty ratio** 9:1 **Application deadline** 1/15 (freshmen), 6/1 (transfer) **Freshmen** 73% were admitted **Housing** Yes **Expenses** Tuition 25,390; Room & Board 6908 **Undergraduates** 53% women, 23% part-time, 15% 25 or older, 0.3% Native American, 4% Hispanic American, 7% African American, 5% Asian American/Pacific Islander **The most frequently chosen baccalaureate fields are** business/marketing, engineering/engineering technologies, social sciences and history **Academic program** English as a second language, advanced placement, accelerated degree program, self-designed majors, honors program, summer session, adult/continuing education programs, internships **Contact** Mr. Richard Whiteside, Vice President of Enrollment Management and Institutional Research, Tulane University, 6823 St Charles Avenue, New Orleans, LA 70118-5669. Telephone: 504-865-5731 or toll-free 800-873-9283. Fax: 504-862-8715. E-mail: undergrad.admission@tulane.edu. Web site: http://www.tulane.edu/.

► **For more information, see page 477.**

UNIVERSITY OF LOUISIANA AT LAFAYETTE
LAFAYETTE, LOUISIANA

General State-supported, university, coed **Entrance** Minimally difficult **Setting** 1,375-acre urban campus **Total enrollment** 15,742 **Student/faculty ratio** 23:1 **Application deadline** Rolling (freshmen), rolling (transfer) **Freshmen** 78% were admitted **Housing** Yes **Expenses** Tuition $2275; Room & Board $2726 **Undergraduates** 56% women, 18% part-time, 23% 25 or older, 0.5% Native American, 1% Hispanic American, 18% African American, 2% Asian American/Pacific Islander **The most frequently chosen baccalaureate fields are** business/marketing, education, liberal arts/general studies **Academic program** Advanced placement, honors program, summer session, adult/continuing education programs, internships **Contact** Mr. Leroy Broussard Jr., Director of Admissions, University of Louisiana at Lafayette, PO Drawer 41210, Lafayette, LA 70504. Telephone: 337-482-6473 or toll-free 800-752-6553 (in-state). Fax: 337-482-6195. E-mail: admissions@louisiana.edu. Web site: http://www.louisiana.edu/.

UNIVERSITY OF LOUISIANA AT MONROE
MONROE, LOUISIANA

General State-supported, comprehensive, coed **Entrance** Noncompetitive **Setting** 238-acre urban campus **Total enrollment** 9,400 **Application deadline** Rolling (freshmen), rolling (transfer) **Freshmen** 95% were admitted **Housing** Yes **Expenses** Tuition 2719; Room & Board 3660 **Undergraduates** 62%

University of Louisiana at Monroe *(continued)*

women, 18% part-time, 28% 25 or older, 0.3% Native American, 1% Hispanic American, 29% African American, 2% Asian American/Pacific Islander **Academic program** English as a second language, advanced placement, accelerated degree program, honors program, summer session, internships **Contact** Ms. Carlette Browder, Associate Director of Admissions, University of Louisiana at Monroe, 700 University Avenue, Monroe, LA 71209-1115. Telephone: 318-362-4661 or toll-free 800-372-5127. Fax: 318-342-5274. E-mail: reweems@alpha.nlu.edu. Web site: http://www.nlu.edu/.

UNIVERSITY OF NEW ORLEANS
NEW ORLEANS, LOUISIANA

General State-supported, university, coed **Entrance** Moderately difficult **Setting** 345-acre urban campus **Total enrollment** 16,218 **Student/faculty ratio** 19:1 **Application deadline** Rolling (freshmen), rolling (transfer) **Freshmen** 83% were admitted **Housing** Yes **Expenses** Tuition $2882; Room & Board $3300 **Undergraduates** 57% women, 28% part-time, 28% 25 or older, 0.5% Native American, 6% Hispanic American, 22% African American, 5% Asian American/ Pacific Islander **The most frequently chosen baccalaureate fields are** business/marketing, education, liberal arts/general studies **Academic program** English as a second language, advanced placement, self-designed majors, honors program, summer session, adult/continuing education programs, internships **Contact** Ms. Roslyn S. Sheley, Director of Admissions, University of New Orleans, Lake Front, New Orleans, LA 70145. Telephone: 504-280-6595 or toll-free 888-514-4275. Fax: 504-280-5522. E-mail: ehs@uno.edu. Web site: http://www.uno.edu/.

UNIVERSITY OF PHOENIX-LOUISIANA CAMPUS
METAIRIE, LOUISIANA

General Proprietary, comprehensive, coed **Entrance** Noncompetitive **Total enrollment** 66,534 **Student/ faculty ratio** 13:1 **Application deadline** Rolling (freshmen), rolling (transfer) **Expenses** Tuition $7740 **Undergraduates** 56% women, 86% 25 or older, 2% Native American, 18% Hispanic American, 13% African American, 6% Asian American/Pacific Islander **Academic program** Advanced placement, accelerated degree program, adult/continuing education programs **Contact** Ms. Beth Barilla, Director of Admissions, University of Phoenix-Louisiana Campus, 4615 East Elwood Street, Phoenix, AZ 85040-1948. Telephone: 480-927-0099 Ext. 1218 or toll-free 800-228-7240. Fax: 480-594-1758. E-mail: beth.barilla@apollogrp.edu. Web site: http://www.phoenix.edu/.

UNIVERSITY OF SOUTHWESTERN LOUISIANA
See University of Louisiana at Lafayette

XAVIER UNIVERSITY OF LOUISIANA
NEW ORLEANS, LOUISIANA

General Independent Roman Catholic, comprehensive, coed **Entrance** Moderately difficult **Setting** 23-acre urban campus **Total enrollment** 3,797 **Student/faculty ratio** 16:1 **Application deadline** 3/1 (freshmen), 6/1 (transfer) **Freshmen** 84% were admitted **Housing** Yes **Expenses** Tuition $10,100; Room & Board $5400 **Undergraduates** 73% women, 5% part-time, 10% 25 or older, 0.03% Native American, 0.3% Hispanic American, 96% African American, 2% Asian American/Pacific Islander **The most frequently chosen baccalaureate fields are** biological/ life sciences, physical sciences, psychology **Academic program** Advanced placement, accelerated degree program, honors program, summer session, adult/continuing education programs, internships **Contact** Mr. Winston Brown, Dean of Admissions, Xavier University of Louisiana, 1 Drexel Drive, New Orleans, LA 70125. Telephone: 504-483-7388. E-mail: apply@xula.edu. Web site: http://www.xula.edu/.

MAINE

BATES COLLEGE
LEWISTON, MAINE

General Independent, 4-year, coed **Entrance** Most difficult **Setting** 109-acre suburban campus **Total enrollment** 1,694 **Student/faculty ratio** 10:1 **Application deadline** 1/15 (freshmen), 3/1 (transfer) **Freshmen** 29% were admitted **Housing** Yes **Expenses** Tuition 32,650 **Undergraduates** 52% women, 1% 25 or older, 0.1% Native American, 1% Hispanic American, 2% African American, 4% Asian American/ Pacific Islander **The most frequently chosen baccalaureate fields are** biological/life sciences, psychology, social sciences and history **Academic program** Advanced placement, accelerated degree program, self-designed majors, honors program, internships **Contact** Mr. Wylie L. Mitchell, Dean of Admissions, Bates College, 23 Campus Avenue, Lewiston, ME 04240-6028. Telephone: 207-786-6000. Fax: 207-786-6025. E-mail: admissions@bates.edu. Web site: http://www.bates.edu/.

BOWDOIN COLLEGE
BRUNSWICK, MAINE

General Independent, 4-year, coed **Entrance** Most difficult **Setting** 110-acre small-town campus **Total enrollment** 1,609 **Student/faculty ratio** 10:1 **Application deadline** 1/1 (freshmen), 3/1 (transfer) **Freshmen** 28% were admitted **Housing** Yes **Expenses** Tuition $25,890; Room & Board $6760 **Undergraduates** 51% women, 0.4% part-time, 1% 25 or older, 0.4% Native American, 3% Hispanic American, 2% African American, 7% Asian American/Pacific Islander **The most frequently chosen baccalaureate fields are** biological/life sciences, foreign language/

literature, social sciences and history **Academic program** Advanced placement, accelerated degree program, self-designed majors **Contact** Cheri Bernier, Receptionist, Bowdoin College, 5000 College Station, Brunswick, ME 04011-8441. Telephone: 207-725-3958. Fax: 207-725-3101. E-mail: admissions-lit@polar.bowdoin.edu. Web site: http://www.bowdoin.edu/.

COLBY COLLEGE
WATERVILLE, MAINE

General Independent, 4-year, coed **Entrance** Most difficult **Setting** 714-acre small-town campus **Total enrollment** 1,814 **Student/faculty ratio** 10:1 **Application deadline** 1/15 (freshmen), 3/1 (transfer) **Freshmen** 37% were admitted **Housing** Yes **Expenses** Tuition 32,750 **Undergraduates** 54% women, 4% 25 or older, 0.3% Native American, 2% Hispanic American, 3% African American, 5% Asian American/Pacific Islander **The most frequently chosen baccalaureate fields are** biological/life sciences, English, social sciences and history **Academic program** English as a second language, advanced placement, self-designed majors, honors program, internships **Contact** Dean of Admissions and Financial Aid, Colby College, Office of Admissions and Financial Aid, 4800 Mayflower Hill, Waterville, ME 04901-8848. Telephone: 207-872-3168 or toll-free 800-723-3032. Fax: 207-872-3474. E-mail: admissions@colby.edu. Web site: http://www.colby.edu/.

COLLEGE OF THE ATLANTIC
BAR HARBOR, MAINE

General Independent, comprehensive, coed **Entrance** Very difficult **Setting** 25-acre small-town campus **Total enrollment** 280 **Student/faculty ratio** 10:1 **Application deadline** 3/1 (freshmen), 4/1 (transfer) **Freshmen** 80% were admitted **Housing** Yes **Expenses** Tuition 20,361; Room & Board 5343 **Undergraduates** 64% women, 5% part-time, 0.4% Native American, 0.4% Hispanic American, 0.4% African American, 0.4% Asian American/Pacific Islander **The most frequently chosen baccalaureate field is** liberal arts/general studies **Academic program** Advanced placement, accelerated degree program, self-designed majors, internships **Contact** Ms. Donna L McFarland, Director of Admission, College of the Atlantic, 105 Eden Street, Bar Harbor, ME 04609-1198. Telephone: 207-288-5015 Ext. 233 or toll-free 800-528-0025. Fax: 207-288-4126. E-mail: inquiry@ecology.coa.edu. Web site: http://www.coa.edu/.

HUSSON COLLEGE
BANGOR, MAINE

General Independent, comprehensive, coed **Entrance** Moderately difficult **Setting** 170-acre suburban campus **Total enrollment** 1,892 **Student/faculty ratio** 19:1 **Application deadline** 9/1 (freshmen), 9/1 (transfer) **Freshmen** 97% were admitted **Housing** Yes **Expenses** Tuition $9580; Room & Board $5150 **Undergraduates** 66% women, 44% part-time, 20% 25 or older, 1% Native American, 1% Hispanic American, 2% African American, 4% Asian American/Pacific Islander **The most frequently chosen baccalaureate fields are** business/marketing, computer/information sciences, health professions and related sciences **Academic program** English as a second language, advanced placement, self-designed majors, summer session, adult/continuing education programs, internships **Contact** Mrs. Jane Goodwin, Director of Admissions, Husson College, One College Circle, Bangor, ME 04401-2999. Telephone: 207-941-7100 or toll-free 800-4-HUSSON. Fax: 207-941-7935. E-mail: admit@husson.husson.edu. Web site: http://www.husson.edu/.

MAINE COLLEGE OF ART
PORTLAND, MAINE

General Independent, comprehensive, coed **Entrance** Moderately difficult **Setting** urban campus **Total enrollment** 442 **Student/faculty ratio** 10:1 **Application deadline** Rolling (freshmen), rolling (transfer) **Freshmen** 87% were admitted **Housing** Yes **Expenses** Tuition 17,780; Room & Board 6556 **Undergraduates** 60% women, 14% part-time, 23% 25 or older, 0.5% Native American, 0.5% Hispanic American, 1% African American, 2% Asian American/Pacific Islander **The most frequently chosen baccalaureate field is** visual/performing arts **Academic program** Advanced placement, self-designed majors, adult/continuing education programs, internships **Contact** Kathryn Quin-Easter, Admissions Assistant, Maine College of Art, 97 Spring Street, Portland, ME 04101-3987. Telephone: 207-775-3052 Ext. 226 or toll-free 800-639-4808. Fax: 207-772-5069. E-mail: admsns@meca.edu. Web site: http://www.meca.edu/.

MAINE MARITIME ACADEMY
CASTINE, MAINE

General State-supported, comprehensive, coed **Entrance** Moderately difficult **Setting** 35-acre small-town campus **Total enrollment** 748 **Student/faculty ratio** 12:1 **Application deadline** 7/1 (freshmen), 7/1 (transfer) **Freshmen** 81% were admitted **Housing** Yes **Expenses** Tuition 5590; Room & Board 5327 **Undergraduates** 15% women, 2% part-time, 15% 25 or older **The most frequently chosen baccalaureate fields are** engineering/engineering technologies, biological/life sciences, trade and industry **Academic program** Advanced placement, adult/continuing education programs, internships **Contact** Mr. Jeffrey C. Wright, Director of Admissions, Maine Maritime Academy, 67 Pleasant Street, Castine, ME 04420. Telephone: 207-326-2215 or toll-free 800-464-6565 (in-state); 800-227-8465 (out-of-state). Fax: 207-326-2515. E-mail: admissions@bell.mma.edu. Web site: http://www.mainemaritime.edu/.

NEW ENGLAND SCHOOL OF COMMUNICATIONS
BANGOR, MAINE

General Private, 4-year, coed **Entrance** Noncompetitive **Total enrollment** 135 **Student/faculty ratio**

New England School of Communications *(continued)*

12:1 **Application deadline** Rolling (freshmen) **Freshmen** 41% were admitted **Housing** Yes **Expenses** Tuition $8745; Room & Board $5440 **Undergraduates** 28% women, 4% part-time, 17% 25 or older, 1% Native American, 1% Hispanic American, 1% African American, 3% Asian American/Pacific Islander **Academic program** English as a second language, advanced placement, self-designed majors, adult/continuing education programs, internships **Contact** Ms. Louise G. Grant, Director of Admissions, New England School of Communications, 1 College Circle, Bangor, ME 04401. Telephone: 207-941-7176 Ext. 1093 or toll-free 888-877-1876. Fax: 207-947-3987. Web site: http://www.nescom.org/.

SAINT JOSEPH'S COLLEGE
STANDISH, MAINE

General Independent, comprehensive, coed, affiliated with Roman Catholic Church **Entrance** Moderately difficult **Setting** 330-acre small-town campus **Total enrollment** 832 **Student/faculty ratio** 16:1 **Application deadline** Rolling (freshmen), rolling (transfer) **Freshmen** 84% were admitted **Housing** Yes **Expenses** Tuition 14,415; Room & Board 6250 **Undergraduates** 67% women, 3% part-time, 65% 25 or older, 0.2% Native American, 1% Hispanic American, 1% African American, 1% Asian American/Pacific Islander **The most frequently chosen baccalaureate fields are** education, business/marketing, health professions and related sciences **Academic program** Advanced placement, accelerated degree program, honors program, summer session, adult/continuing education programs, internships **Contact** Mr. William Dunfey, Dean of Enrollment Management, Saint Joseph's College, 278 Whites Bridge Road, Standish, ME 04084-5263. Telephone: 207-893-7746 Ext. 7741 or toll-free 800-338-7057. Fax: 207-893-7862. E-mail: fstone@sjcme.edu. Web site: http://www.sjcme.edu/.

THOMAS COLLEGE
WATERVILLE, MAINE

General Independent, comprehensive, coed **Entrance** Minimally difficult **Setting** 70-acre small-town campus **Total enrollment** 786 **Student/faculty ratio** 13:1 **Application deadline** Rolling (freshmen), rolling (transfer) **Freshmen** 96% were admitted **Housing** Yes **Expenses** Tuition $13,290; Room & Board $5885 **Undergraduates** 56% women, 30% part-time, 34% 25 or older, 0.2% Native American, 0% Hispanic American, 1% African American, 1% Asian American/Pacific Islander **The most frequently chosen baccalaureate fields are** business/marketing, computer/information sciences, parks and recreation **Academic program** Advanced placement, summer session, adult/continuing education programs, internships **Contact** Mr. Robert Callahan, Director of Admissions, Thomas College, 180 West River Road, Waterville, ME 04901. Telephone: 207-859-1101 or toll-free 800-339-7001. Fax: 207-859-1114. E-mail: admiss@host2.thomas.edu. Web site: http://www.thomas.edu/.

UNITY COLLEGE
UNITY, MAINE

General Independent, 4-year, coed **Entrance** Moderately difficult **Setting** 205-acre rural campus **Total enrollment** 512 **Student/faculty ratio** 16:1 **Application deadline** Rolling (freshmen), rolling (transfer) **Freshmen** 69% were admitted **Housing** Yes **Expenses** Tuition $13,730; Room & Board $5500 **Undergraduates** 34% women, 4% part-time, 8% 25 or older, 0% Native American, 0.2% Hispanic American, 0.4% African American **The most frequently chosen baccalaureate fields are** natural resources/environmental science, liberal arts/general studies, parks and recreation **Academic program** English as a second language, advanced placement, accelerated degree program, self-designed majors, honors program, summer session, internships **Contact** Dr. John M. B. Craig, Vice President and Dean for Admissions, Unity College, PO Box 532, Unity, ME 04988-0532. Telephone: 207-948-3131 Ext. 222. Fax: 207-948-6277. Web site: http://www.unity.edu/.

UNIVERSITY OF MAINE
ORONO, MAINE

General State-supported, university, coed **Entrance** Moderately difficult **Setting** 3,298-acre small-town campus **Total enrollment** 10,282 **Student/faculty ratio** 15:1 **Application deadline** Rolling (freshmen), rolling (transfer) **Freshmen** 83% were admitted **Housing** Yes **Expenses** Tuition $4764; Room & Board $5360 **Undergraduates** 52% women, 20% part-time, 12% 25 or older, 2% Native American, 1% Hispanic American, 1% African American, 1% Asian American/Pacific Islander **The most frequently chosen baccalaureate fields are** education, business/marketing, engineering/engineering technologies **Academic program** English as a second language, advanced placement, self-designed majors, honors program, summer session, adult/continuing education programs, internships **Contact** Mr. Jonathan H. Henry, Director, University of Maine, 5713 Chadbourne Hall, Orono, ME 04469-5713. Telephone: 207-581-1561 or toll-free 877-486-2364. Fax: 207-581-1213. E-mail: um_admit@maine.maine.edu. Web site: http://www.umaine.edu/.

THE UNIVERSITY OF MAINE AT AUGUSTA
AUGUSTA, MAINE

General State-supported, 4-year, coed **Entrance** Noncompetitive **Setting** 165-acre small-town campus **Total enrollment** 5,617 **Student/faculty ratio** 20:1 **Application deadline** Rolling (freshmen), rolling (transfer) **Freshmen** 67% were admitted **Housing** No **Expenses** Tuition $3575 **Undergraduates** 60% 25 or older, 3% Native American, 1% Hispanic American, 1% African American, 0.5% Asian American/

Pacific Islander **The most frequently chosen baccalaureate fields are** business/marketing, liberal arts/general studies, protective services/public administration **Academic program** Advanced placement, self-designed majors, honors program, summer session, adult/continuing education programs, internships **Contact** Mr. William Clark Ketcham, Director of Enrollment Services, The University of Maine at Augusta, 46 University Drive, Augusta, ME 04330-9410. Telephone: 207-621-3185 or toll-free 800-696-6000 Ext. 3185 (in-state). Fax: 207-621-3116. E-mail: umaar@maine.maine.edu. Web site: http://www.uma.maine.edu/.

UNIVERSITY OF MAINE AT FARMINGTON

FARMINGTON, MAINE

General State-supported, 4-year, coed **Entrance** Moderately difficult **Setting** 50-acre small-town campus **Total enrollment** 2,413 **Student/faculty ratio** 16:1 **Application deadline** 4/15 (freshmen), 5/1 (transfer) **Freshmen** 66% were admitted **Housing** Yes **Expenses** Tuition $3996; Room & Board $4614 **Undergraduates** 68% women, 13% part-time, 10% 25 or older, 1% Native American, 0.5% Hispanic American, 0.2% African American, 0.5% Asian American/Pacific Islander **The most frequently chosen baccalaureate fields are** education, interdisciplinary studies, psychology **Academic program** Advanced placement, accelerated degree program, self-designed majors, honors program, summer session, internships **Contact** Mr. James G. Collins, Associate Director of Admissions, University of Maine at Farmington, 246 Main Street, Farmington, ME 04938-1994. Telephone: 207-778-7050. Fax: 207-778-8182. E-mail: umfadmit@maine.maine.edu. Web site: http://www.umf.maine.edu/.

UNIVERSITY OF MAINE AT FORT KENT

FORT KENT, MAINE

General State-supported, 4-year, coed **Entrance** Moderately difficult **Setting** 52-acre rural campus **Total enrollment** 886 **Student/faculty ratio** 15:1 **Application deadline** Rolling (freshmen), rolling (transfer) **Freshmen** 85% were admitted **Housing** Yes **Expenses** Tuition $3404; Room & Board $4100 **Undergraduates** 63% women, 28% part-time, 7% 25 or older, 1% Native American, 0.5% African American, 1% Asian American/Pacific Islander **The most frequently chosen baccalaureate fields are** business/marketing, education, psychology **Academic program** English as a second language, advanced placement, self-designed majors, honors program, summer session, internships **Contact** Mr. John L. Martin, Director of Enrollment Management, University of Maine at Fort Kent, 25 Pleasant Street, Fort Kent, ME 04743-1292. Telephone: 207-834-7600 Ext. 568 or toll-free 888-TRY-UMFK. Fax: 207-834-7609. E-mail: umfkadm@maine.maine.edu. Web site: http://www.umfk.maine.edu/.

UNIVERSITY OF MAINE AT MACHIAS

MACHIAS, MAINE

General State-supported, 4-year, coed **Entrance** Moderately difficult **Setting** 42-acre rural campus **Total enrollment** 927 **Student/faculty ratio** 13:1 **Application deadline** Rolling (freshmen), rolling (transfer) **Freshmen** 87% were admitted **Housing** Yes **Expenses** Tuition $3575; Room & Board $4490 **Undergraduates** 67% women, 46% part-time, 64% 25 or older, 3% Native American, 0.2% Hispanic American, 0.4% African American, 1% Asian American/Pacific Islander **The most frequently chosen baccalaureate fields are** education, business/marketing, natural resources/environmental science **Academic program** Advanced placement, accelerated degree program, self-designed majors, summer session, adult/continuing education programs, internships **Contact** Mr. David Baldwin, Director of Admissions, University of Maine at Machias, 9 O'Brien Avenue, Machias, ME 04654. Telephone: 207-255-1318 or toll-free 888-GOTOUMM. Fax: 207-255-1363. E-mail: admissions@acad.umm.maine.edu. Web site: http://www.umm.maine.edu/.

UNIVERSITY OF MAINE AT PRESQUE ISLE

PRESQUE ISLE, MAINE

General State-supported, 4-year, coed **Entrance** Minimally difficult **Setting** 150-acre small-town campus **Total enrollment** 1,427 **Student/faculty ratio** 14:1 **Application deadline** Rolling (freshmen), rolling (transfer) **Freshmen** 88% were admitted **Housing** Yes **Expenses** Tuition $3520; Room & Board $4140 **Undergraduates** 63% women, 29% part-time, 31% 25 or older, 3% Native American, 1% Hispanic American, 1% African American, 1% Asian American/Pacific Islander **The most frequently chosen baccalaureate fields are** education, interdisciplinary studies, liberal arts/general studies **Academic program** Advanced placement, accelerated degree program, self-designed majors, honors program, summer session, adult/continuing education programs, internships **Contact** Mr. Michael Sullivan, Admissions Representative, University of Maine at Presque Isle, 181 Main Street, Presque Isle, ME 04769. Telephone: 207-768-9534. Fax: 207-768-9608. E-mail: infoumpi@paris.umpi.maine.edu. Web site: http://www.umpi.maine.edu/.

UNIVERSITY OF NEW ENGLAND

BIDDEFORD, MAINE

General Independent, comprehensive, coed **Entrance** Moderately difficult **Setting** 410-acre small-town campus **Total enrollment** 3,323 **Application deadline** Rolling (freshmen), rolling (transfer) **Freshmen** 72% were admitted **Housing** Yes **Expenses** Tuition $16,250; Room & Board $6420 **Undergraduates** 81% women, 27% part-time, 10% 25 or older, 0% Native American, 0.2% Hispanic American, 0.5% African American, 0.5% Asian American/Pacific Islander **The most frequently chosen baccalaure-**

University of New England *(continued)*

ate fields are biological/life sciences, business/marketing, health professions and related sciences **Academic program** English as a second language, advanced placement, accelerated degree program, self-designed majors, honors program, summer session, adult/continuing education programs, internships **Contact** Ms. Patricia Cribby, Dean of Admissions, University of New England, Hills Beach Road, Biddeford, ME 04005-9526. Telephone: 207-283-0170 Ext. 2240 or toll-free 800-477-4UNE. E-mail: msinkowicz@mailbox.une.edu. Web site: http://www.une.edu/.

UNIVERSITY OF SOUTHERN MAINE
PORTLAND, MAINE

General State-supported, comprehensive, coed **Entrance** Moderately difficult **Setting** 144-acre suburban campus **Total enrollment** 10,820 **Student/faculty ratio** 13:1 **Application deadline** 2/1 (freshmen), 2/1 (transfer) **Freshmen** 78% were admitted **Housing** Yes **Expenses** Tuition $4309; Room & Board $5202 **Undergraduates** 60% women, 52% part-time, 40% 25 or older, 1% Native American, 1% Hispanic American, 1% African American, 1% Asian American/Pacific Islander **The most frequently chosen baccalaureate fields are** health professions and related sciences, business/marketing, social sciences and history **Academic program** English as a second language, advanced placement, self-designed majors, honors program, summer session, adult/continuing education programs, internships **Contact** Mr. David M. Pirani, Director of Admission, University of Southern Maine, 37 College Avenue, Gorham, ME 04038. Telephone: 207-780-5670 or toll-free 800-800-4USM Ext. 5670. Fax: 207-780-5640. E-mail: usmadm@maine.maine.edu. Web site: http://www.usm.maine.edu/.

WESTBROOK COLLEGE
See University of New England

MARYLAND

BALTIMORE HEBREW UNIVERSITY
BALTIMORE, MARYLAND

Contact Dr. George Berlin, Dean, Baltimore Hebrew University, 5800 Park Heights Avenue, Baltimore, MD 21215-3996. Telephone: 410-578-6912 or toll-free 888-248-7420. Fax: 410-578-6940. E-mail: bhu@bhu.edu. Web site: http://www.bhu.edu/.

BALTIMORE INTERNATIONAL COLLEGE
BALTIMORE, MARYLAND

General Independent, 4-year, coed **Entrance** Minimally difficult **Setting** 6-acre urban campus **Total enrollment** 456 **Student/faculty ratio** 21:1 **Application deadline** Rolling (freshmen), rolling (transfer) **Freshmen** 49% were admitted **Housing** Yes **Expenses** Tuition $14,003; Room & Board $5182 **Undergraduates** 46% women, 5% part-time, 32% 25 or older, 0.2% Native American, 5% Hispanic American, 44% African American, 1% Asian American/Pacific Islander **Academic program** Advanced placement, accelerated degree program, honors program, adult/continuing education programs, internships **Contact** Ms. Lori Makowski, Director of Admissions, Baltimore International College, Commerce Exchange, 17 Commerce Street, Baltimore, MD 21202-3230. Telephone: 410-752-4710 Ext. 125 or toll-free 800-624-9926 Ext. 120 (out-of-state). Fax: 410-752-3730. E-mail: admissions@bic.edu. Web site: http://www.bic.edu/.

BOWIE STATE UNIVERSITY
BOWIE, MARYLAND

General State-supported, comprehensive, coed **Entrance** Minimally difficult **Setting** 312-acre small-town campus **Total enrollment** 4,700 **Student/faculty ratio** 14:1 **Application deadline** 4/1 (freshmen), 4/1 (transfer) **Freshmen** 44% were admitted **Housing** Yes **Expenses** Tuition $3778; Room & Board $4744 **Undergraduates** 60% women, 28% part-time, 33% 25 or older, 0.4% Native American, 1% Hispanic American, 88% African American, 2% Asian American/Pacific Islander **The most frequently chosen baccalaureate fields are** business/marketing, psychology, social sciences and history **Academic program** Advanced placement, accelerated degree program, honors program, summer session, adult/continuing education programs, internships **Contact** Shingiral Chanaiwa, Coordinator of Undergraduate Enrollment, Bowie State University, 14000 Jericho Park Road, Bowie, MD 20715-9465. Telephone: 301-860-3425 or toll-free 877-772-6943. Fax: 301-60-3438. E-mail: hope.ransome@bowiestate.edu. Web site: http://www.bowiestate.edu/.

▶ **For more information, see page 390.**

CAPITOL COLLEGE
LAUREL, MARYLAND

General Independent, comprehensive, coed **Entrance** Minimally difficult **Setting** 52-acre suburban campus **Total enrollment** 787 **Student/faculty ratio** 17:1 **Application deadline** Rolling (freshmen), rolling (transfer) **Freshmen** 80% were admitted **Housing** Yes **Expenses** Tuition 13,750; Room only 3340 **Undergraduates** 27% women, 49% part-time, 0.3% Native American, 1% Hispanic American, 38% African American, 8% Asian American/Pacific Islander **The most frequently chosen baccalaureate field is** engineering/engineering technologies **Academic program** English as a second language, advanced placement, accelerated degree program, summer session, adult/continuing education programs **Contact** Director of Admissions, Capitol College, 11301 Springfield Road, Laurel, MD 20708-9759. Telephone: 301-953-3200 or toll-free 800-950-1992. E-mail: admissions@capitol-college.edu. Web site: http://www.capitol-college.edu/.

COLLEGE OF NOTRE DAME OF MARYLAND
BALTIMORE, MARYLAND

General Independent Roman Catholic, comprehensive, women only **Entrance** Moderately difficult **Setting** 58-acre suburban campus **Total enrollment** 3,178 **Student/faculty ratio** 12:1 **Application deadline** Rolling (freshmen), rolling (transfer) **Freshmen** 80% were admitted **Housing** Yes **Expenses** Tuition $16,900; Room & Board $7200 **Undergraduates** 65% part-time, 0.3% Native American, 2% Hispanic American, 21% African American, 2% Asian American/Pacific Islander **The most frequently chosen baccalaureate fields are** business/marketing, education, health professions and related sciences **Academic program** English as a second language, advanced placement, accelerated degree program, self-designed majors, honors program, summer session, adult/continuing education programs, internships **Contact** Mrs. Karen Stakem Hornig, Vice President for Enrollment Management, College of Notre Dame of Maryland, 4701 North Charles Street, Baltimore, MD 21210. Telephone: 410-532-5330 or toll-free 800-435-0200 (in-state); 800-435-0300 (out-of-state). Fax: 410-532-6287. E-mail: admiss@ndm.edu. Web site: http://www.ndm.edu/.

COLUMBIA UNION COLLEGE
TAKOMA PARK, MARYLAND

General Independent Seventh-day Adventist, comprehensive, coed **Entrance** Minimally difficult **Setting** 19-acre suburban campus **Total enrollment** 1,030 **Student/faculty ratio** 14:1 **Application deadline** Rolling (freshmen), rolling (transfer) **Freshmen** 54% were admitted **Housing** Yes **Expenses** Tuition $13,305; Room & Board $4619 **Undergraduates** 59% women, 38% part-time, 0.1% Native American, 9% Hispanic American, 45% African American, 7% Asian American/Pacific Islander **The most frequently chosen baccalaureate fields are** business/marketing, health professions and related sciences, psychology **Academic program** Advanced placement, accelerated degree program, self-designed majors, honors program, summer session, adult/continuing education programs, internships **Contact** Mr. Emil John, Director of Admissions, Columbia Union College, 7600 Flower Avenue, Takoma Park, MD 20912. Telephone: 301-891-4080 or toll-free 800-835-4212. Fax: 301-891-4230. E-mail: enroll@cuc.edu. Web site: http://www.cuc.edu/.

COPPIN STATE COLLEGE
BALTIMORE, MARYLAND

General State-supported, comprehensive, coed **Contact** Ms. Michelle Gross, Director of Admissions, Coppin State College, 2500 West North Avenue, Baltimore, MD 21216. Telephone: 410-383-5990 or toll-free 800-635-3674. E-mail: amosley@coe.coppin.umd.edu. Web site: http://www.coppin.edu/.

FROSTBURG STATE UNIVERSITY
FROSTBURG, MARYLAND

General State-supported, comprehensive, coed **Entrance** Moderately difficult **Setting** 260-acre small-town campus **Total enrollment** 5,348 **Student/faculty ratio** 17:1 **Application deadline** Rolling (freshmen), rolling (transfer) **Freshmen** 73% were admitted **Housing** Yes **Expenses** Tuition 4256; Room & Board 5266 **Undergraduates** 53% women, 8% part-time, 9% 25 or older, 0.4% Native American, 2% Hispanic American, 12% African American, 2% Asian American/Pacific Islander **The most frequently chosen baccalaureate fields are** business/marketing, education, social sciences and history **Academic program** Advanced placement, honors program, summer session, adult/continuing education programs, internships **Contact** Dr. Stuart Tennant, Vice President for Enrollment Management, Frostburg State University, 101 Braddock Road, Frostburg, MD 21532-1099. Telephone: 301-687-4201. Fax: 301-687-7074. E-mail: fsuadmissions@frostburg.edu. Web site: http://www.frostburg.edu/.

GOUCHER COLLEGE
BALTIMORE, MARYLAND

General Independent, comprehensive, coed **Entrance** Moderately difficult **Setting** 287-acre suburban campus **Total enrollment** 1,973 **Student/faculty ratio** 10:1 **Application deadline** 2/1 (freshmen), 4/1 (transfer) **Freshmen** 82% were admitted **Housing** Yes **Expenses** Tuition 21,290; Room & Board 7650 **Undergraduates** 73% women, 6% part-time, 4% 25 or older, 1% Native American, 3% Hispanic American, 8% African American, 3% Asian American/Pacific Islander **The most frequently chosen baccalaureate fields are** biological/life sciences, English, visual/performing arts **Academic program** Advanced placement, accelerated degree program, self-designed majors, honors program, adult/continuing education programs, internships **Contact** Mr. Carlton E. Surbeck III, Director of Admissions, Goucher College, 1021 Dulaney Valley Road, Baltimore, MD 21204-2794. Telephone: 410-337-6100 or toll-free 800-GOUCHER. Fax: 410-337-6354. E-mail: admission@goucher.edu. Web site: http://www.goucher.edu/.

▶ **For more information, see page 426.**

GRIGGS UNIVERSITY
SILVER SPRING, MARYLAND

General Independent Seventh-day Adventist, 4-year, coed, primarily men **Entrance** Minimally difficult **Setting** suburban campus **Total enrollment** 322 **Application deadline** Rolling (freshmen), rolling (transfer) **Housing** No **Expenses** Tuition $5460 **The most frequently chosen baccalaureate fields are** business/marketing, philosophy, religion, and theology **Academic program** Advanced placement, accelerated degree program, summer session, adult/continuing education programs **Contact** Ms. Eva Michel, Enrollment Officer, Griggs University, PO Box 4437, Silver Spring, MD 20914-4437. Tele-

Griggs University *(continued)*

phone: 301-680-6593 or toll-free 800-782-4769 (in-state). Fax: 301-680-6577. E-mail: 74617.74@compuserve.com. Web site: http://www.griggs.edu/.

HOOD COLLEGE
FREDERICK, MARYLAND

General Independent, comprehensive, women only **Entrance** Moderately difficult **Setting** 50-acre suburban campus **Total enrollment** 1,708 **Student/faculty ratio** 9:1 **Application deadline** 2/15 (freshmen), rolling (transfer) **Freshmen** 77% were admitted **Housing** Yes **Expenses** Tuition $18,620; Room & Board $6900 **Undergraduates** 25% part-time, 26% 25 or older, 0.2% Native American, 3% Hispanic American, 13% African American, 2% Asian American/Pacific Islander **The most frequently chosen baccalaureate fields are** psychology, biological/life sciences, social sciences and history **Academic program** English as a second language, advanced placement, accelerated degree program, self-designed majors, honors program, summer session, adult/continuing education programs, internships **Contact** Ms. Mauree Donahue, Director of Admissions, Hood College, 401 Rosemont Avenue, Frederick, MD 21701. Telephone: 301-696-3400 or toll-free 800-922-1599. Fax: 301-696-3819. E-mail: admissions@nimue.hood.edu. Web site: http://www.hood.edu/.

JOHNS HOPKINS UNIVERSITY
BALTIMORE, MARYLAND

General Independent, university, coed **Entrance** Most difficult **Setting** 140-acre urban campus **Total enrollment** 5,285 **Student/faculty ratio** 10:1 **Application deadline** 1/1 (freshmen), 3/15 (transfer) **Freshmen** 32% were admitted **Housing** Yes **Expenses** Tuition $24,930; Room & Board $8185 **Undergraduates** 42% women, 1% part-time, 0% 25 or older, 0.2% Native American, 2% Hispanic American, 6% African American, 19% Asian American/Pacific Islander **Academic program** English as a second language, advanced placement, accelerated degree program, self-designed majors, honors program, summer session, adult/continuing education programs, internships **Contact** Mr. Samuel McNair, Interim Director of Undergraduate Admissions, Johns Hopkins University, 140 Garland Hall, 3400 North Charles Street, Baltimore, MD 21218-2699. Telephone: 410-516-8341. Fax: 410-516-6025. E-mail: gotojhu@jhu.edu. Web site: http://www.jhu.edu/.

LOYOLA COLLEGE IN MARYLAND
BALTIMORE, MARYLAND

General Independent Roman Catholic (Jesuit), comprehensive, coed **Entrance** Moderately difficult **Setting** 89-acre urban campus **Total enrollment** 6,073 **Student/faculty ratio** 14:1 **Application deadline** 1/15 (freshmen) **Freshmen** 61% were admitted **Housing** Yes **Expenses** Tuition $21,515; Room & Board $6040 **Undergraduates** 56% women, 2% part-time, 1% 25 or older, 0.03% Native American, 2% Hispanic American, 5% African American, 2% Asian American/Pacific Islander **Academic program** Advanced placement, accelerated degree program, honors program, summer session, internships **Contact** Mr. William Bossemeyer, Dean of Admissions, Loyola College in Maryland, 4501 North Charles Street, Baltimore, MD 21210. Telephone: 410-617-2000 Ext. 2252 or toll-free 800-221-9107 Ext. 2252 (in-state). Fax: 410-617-2176. Web site: http://www.loyola.edu/.

MAPLE SPRINGS BAPTIST BIBLE COLLEGE AND SEMINARY
CAPITOL HEIGHTS, MARYLAND

Contact Ms. Mazie Murphy, Assistant Director of Admissions and Records, Maple Springs Baptist Bible College and Seminary, 4130 Belt Road, Capitol Heights, MD 20743. Telephone: 301-736-3631. Fax: 301-735-6507.

MARYLAND INSTITUTE, COLLEGE OF ART
BALTIMORE, MARYLAND

General Independent, comprehensive, coed **Entrance** Very difficult **Setting** 12-acre urban campus **Total enrollment** 1,302 **Student/faculty ratio** 10:1 **Application deadline** 1/15 (freshmen), 3/15 (transfer) **Freshmen** 45% were admitted **Housing** Yes **Expenses** Tuition 20,080; Room only 4500 **Undergraduates** 58% women, 1% part-time, 5% 25 or older, 0.4% Native American, 4% Hispanic American, 4% African American, 6% Asian American/Pacific Islander **The most frequently chosen baccalaureate field is** visual/performing arts **Academic program** Advanced placement, accelerated degree program, self-designed majors, summer session, adult/continuing education programs, internships **Contact** Mr. Hans Ever, Director of Undergraduate Admission, Maryland Institute, College of Art, 1300 Mount Royal Avenue, Baltimore, MD 21217-4191. Telephone: 410-225-2222. Fax: 410-225-2337. E-mail: admissions@mica.edu. Web site: http://www.mica.edu/.

MORGAN STATE UNIVERSITY
BALTIMORE, MARYLAND

General State-supported, university, coed **Entrance** Moderately difficult **Setting** 140-acre urban campus **Total enrollment** 6,269 **Student/faculty ratio** 18:1 **Application deadline** Rolling (freshmen), rolling (transfer) **Housing** Yes **Expenses** Tuition $4388; Room & Board $5780 **Undergraduates** 59% women, 15% part-time, 27% 25 or older, 0.2% Native American, 0.5% Hispanic American, 92% African American, 0.3% Asian American/Pacific Islander **Academic program** Advanced placement, accelerated degree program, honors program, summer session, adult/continuing education programs, internships **Contact** Mr. Edwin T. Johnson, Director of Admissions and Recruitment, Morgan State University, 1700 East Cold Spring Lane, Baltimore, MD 21251. Telephone:

443-885-3000 or toll-free 800-332-6674. E-mail: tjenness@moac.morgan.edu. Web site: http://www.morgan.edu/.

MOUNT SAINT MARY'S COLLEGE AND SEMINARY
EMMITSBURG, MARYLAND

General Independent Roman Catholic, comprehensive, coed **Entrance** Moderately difficult **Setting** 1,400-acre rural campus **Total enrollment** 1,859 **Student/faculty ratio** 14:1 **Application deadline** 3/1 (freshmen), 6/1 (transfer) **Freshmen** 87% were admitted **Housing** Yes **Expenses** Tuition $17,400; Room & Board $6860 **Undergraduates** 59% women, 13% part-time, 13% 25 or older, 0.1% Native American, 3% Hispanic American, 5% African American, 2% Asian American/Pacific Islander **The most frequently chosen baccalaureate fields are** business/marketing, education, social sciences and history **Academic program** English as a second language, advanced placement, accelerated degree program, self-designed majors, honors program, summer session, adult/continuing education programs, internships **Contact** Mr. Stephen Neitz, Executive Director of Admissions and Financial Aid, Mount Saint Mary's College and Seminary, 16300 Old Emmitsburg Road, Emmitsburg, MD 21727-7799. Telephone: 301-447-5214 or toll-free 800-448-4347. Fax: 301-447-5860. E-mail: admissions@msmary.edu. Web site: http://www.msmary.edu/.

NER ISRAEL RABBINICAL COLLEGE
BALTIMORE, MARYLAND

Contact Rabbi Berel Weisbord, Dean of Admissions, Ner Israel Rabbinical College, Mount Wilson Lane, Baltimore, MD 21208. Telephone: 410-484-7200.

PEABODY CONSERVATORY OF MUSIC OF THE JOHNS HOPKINS UNIVERSITY
BALTIMORE, MARYLAND

General Independent, comprehensive, coed **Entrance** Very difficult **Setting** urban campus **Total enrollment** 650 **Student/faculty ratio** 7:1 **Application deadline** 12/15 (freshmen), 12/15 (transfer) **Freshmen** 42% were admitted **Housing** Yes **Expenses** Tuition $22,975; Room & Board $8420 **Undergraduates** 52% women, 4% part-time, 6% 25 or older, 0% Native American, 4% Hispanic American, 2% African American, 8% Asian American/Pacific Islander **The most frequently chosen baccalaureate fields are** education, visual/performing arts **Academic program** English as a second language, advanced placement, accelerated degree program, honors program, internships **Contact** Mr. David Lane, Director of Admissions, Peabody Conservatory of Music of The Johns Hopkins University, 1 East Mount Vernon Place, Baltimore, MD 21202-2397. Telephone: 410-659-8110 or toll-free 800-368-2521 (out-of-state). Web site: http://www.peabody.jhu.edu/.

ST. JOHN'S COLLEGE
ANNAPOLIS, MARYLAND

General Independent, comprehensive, coed **Entrance** Moderately difficult **Setting** 36-acre small-town campus **Total enrollment** 537 **Student/faculty ratio** 8:1 **Application deadline** Rolling (freshmen), rolling (transfer) **Freshmen** 79% were admitted **Housing** Yes **Expenses** Tuition 24,770; Room & Board 6576 **Undergraduates** 47% women, 0.2% part-time, 4% 25 or older, 0.4% Native American, 2% Hispanic American, 0.4% African American, 2% Asian American/Pacific Islander **The most frequently chosen baccalaureate field is** liberal arts/general studies **Academic program** Internships **Contact** Mr. John Christensen, Director of Admissions, St. John's College, PO Box 2800, 60 College Avenue, Annapolis, MD 21404. Telephone: 410-626-2522 or toll-free 800-727-9238. Fax: 410-269-7916. E-mail: admissions@sjca.edu. Web site: http://www.sjca.edu/.

ST. MARY'S COLLEGE OF MARYLAND
ST. MARY'S CITY, MARYLAND

General State-supported, 4-year, coed **Entrance** Moderately difficult **Setting** 275-acre rural campus **Total enrollment** 1,547 **Student/faculty ratio** 12:1 **Application deadline** 1/15 (freshmen), 3/15 (transfer) **Freshmen** 74% were admitted **Housing** Yes **Expenses** Tuition $7549; Room & Board $6555 **Undergraduates** 59% women, 10% part-time, 6% 25 or older, 0.4% Native American, 2% Hispanic American, 8% African American, 4% Asian American/Pacific Islander **The most frequently chosen baccalaureate fields are** psychology, biological/life sciences, social sciences and history **Academic program** Advanced placement, self-designed majors, honors program, summer session, adult/continuing education programs, internships **Contact** Mr. Richard J. Edgar, Director of Admissions, St. Mary's College of Maryland, 18952 East Fisher Road, St. Mary's City, MD 20686-3001. Telephone: 301-862-0292 or toll-free 800-492-7181. Fax: 301-862-0906. E-mail: admissions@honors.smcm.edu. Web site: http://www.smcm.edu/.

SALISBURY STATE UNIVERSITY
SALISBURY, MARYLAND

General State-supported, comprehensive, coed **Entrance** Moderately difficult **Setting** 140-acre small-town campus **Total enrollment** 6,421 **Student/faculty ratio** 17:1 **Application deadline** 1/15 (freshmen), rolling (transfer) **Freshmen** 21% were admitted **Housing** Yes **Expenses** Tuition 4312; Room & Board 5990 **Undergraduates** 57% women, 14% part-time, 12% 25 or older, 0.3% Native American, 1% Hispanic American, 6% African American, 2% Asian American/Pacific Islander **The most frequently chosen baccalaureate fields are** business/marketing, biological/life sciences, education **Academic program** English as a second language, advanced placement, self-designed majors, honors program, summer session, adult/continuing education programs, intern-

Salisbury State University *(continued)*

ships **Contact** Mrs. Jane H. Dané, Dean of Admissions, Salisbury State University, Admissions House, 1101 Camden Avenue, Salisbury, MD 21801. Telephone: 410-543-6161 or toll-free 888-543-0148. Fax: 410-546-6016. E-mail: d3adadm@ssa.ssu.umd.edu. Web site: http://www.ssu.edu/.

SOJOURNER-DOUGLASS COLLEGE
BALTIMORE, MARYLAND

General Independent, comprehensive, coed, primarily women **Entrance** Noncompetitive **Setting** 15-acre urban campus **Total enrollment** 844 **Student/faculty ratio** 10:1 **Application deadline** Rolling (freshmen), rolling (transfer) **Housing** No **Expenses** Tuition $4984 **Undergraduates** 83% women, 25% part-time, 95% 25 or older, 0.1% Native American, 98% African American **Academic program** Accelerated degree program, self-designed majors, honors program, summer session, adult/continuing education programs, internships **Contact** Ms. Diana Samuels, Manager, Office of Admissions, Sojourner-Douglass College, 500 North Caroline Street, Baltimore, MD 21205-1814. Telephone: 410-276-0306 Ext. 249. Fax: 410-675-1810. Web site: http://sdc.edu/.

TOWSON UNIVERSITY
TOWSON, MARYLAND

General State-supported, comprehensive, coed **Entrance** Moderately difficult **Setting** 321-acre suburban campus **Total enrollment** 16,729 **Student/faculty ratio** 15:1 **Application deadline** 5/1 (freshmen), rolling (transfer) **Freshmen** 62% were admitted **Housing** Yes **Expenses** Tuition $4984; Room & Board $6104 **Undergraduates** 60% women, 17% part-time, 14% 25 or older, 0.2% Native American, 2% Hispanic American, 10% African American, 3% Asian American/Pacific Islander **The most frequently chosen baccalaureate fields are** business/marketing, communications/communication technologies, education **Academic program** English as a second language, advanced placement, self-designed majors, honors program, summer session, adult/continuing education programs, internships **Contact** Ms. Louise Shulack, Director of Admissions, Towson University, 8000 York Road, Towson, MD 21252. Telephone: 410-704-3687 or toll-free 888-4TOWSON. Fax: 410-830-3030. E-mail: jackson-a@towson.edu. Web site: http://www.towson.edu/.

▶ **For more information, see page 476.**

UNITED STATES NAVAL ACADEMY
ANNAPOLIS, MARYLAND

General Federally supported, 4-year, coed **Entrance** Very difficult **Setting** 329-acre small-town campus **Total enrollment** 4,172 **Student/faculty ratio** 7:1 **Application deadline** 2/28 (freshmen) **Freshmen** 15% were admitted **Housing** Yes **Undergraduates** 15% women, 1% 25 or older, 1% Native American, 8% Hispanic American, 6% African American, 4% Asian American/Pacific Islander **The most frequently chosen baccalaureate fields are** engineering/engineering technologies, physical sciences, social sciences and history **Academic program** English as a second language, advanced placement, honors program, summer session **Contact** Col. David A. Vetter, Dean of Admissions, United States Naval Academy, 117 Decatur Road, Annapolis, MD 21402-5000. Telephone: 410-293-4361. Fax: 410-293-4348. Web site: http://www.usna.edu/.

UNIVERSITY OF BALTIMORE
BALTIMORE, MARYLAND

General State-supported, upper-level, coed **Entrance** Noncompetitive **Setting** 49-acre urban campus **Total enrollment** 4,674 **Student/faculty ratio** 14:1 **Application deadline** Rolling (transfer) **First-Year Students** 87% were admitted **Housing** No **Expenses** Tuition $4504 **Undergraduates** 59% women, 55% part-time, 73% 25 or older, 1% Native American, 2% Hispanic American, 30% African American, 2% Asian American/Pacific Islander **The most frequently chosen baccalaureate fields are** business/marketing, interdisciplinary studies, protective services/public administration **Academic program** Advanced placement, accelerated degree program, self-designed majors, honors program, summer session, adult/continuing education programs, internships **Contact** Mr. Daryl Minus, Assistant Director of Admissions, University of Baltimore, 1420 North Charles St., Baltimore, MD 21201-5779. Telephone: 410-837-4777 or toll-free 877-APPLYUB (in-state). Fax: 410-837-4793. E-mail: admissions@ubmail.ubalt.edu. Web site: http://www.ubalt.edu/.

UNIVERSITY OF MARYLAND, BALTIMORE COUNTY
BALTIMORE, MARYLAND

General State-supported, university, coed **Entrance** Moderately difficult **Setting** 500-acre suburban campus **Total enrollment** 10,759 **Student/faculty ratio** 16:1 **Application deadline** 3/15 (freshmen), rolling (transfer) **Freshmen** 66% were admitted **Housing** Yes **Expenses** Tuition $5490; Room & Board $5850 **Undergraduates** 50% women, 20% part-time, 19% 25 or older, 1% Native American, 3% Hispanic American, 16% African American, 18% Asian American/Pacific Islander **The most frequently chosen baccalaureate fields are** computer/information sciences, psychology, social sciences and history **Academic program** English as a second language, advanced placement, self-designed majors, honors program, summer session, adult/continuing education programs, internships **Contact** Ms. Yvette Mozie-Ross, Director of Admissions, University of Maryland, Baltimore County, 1000 Hilltop Circle, Baltimore, MD 21250-5398. Telephone: 410-455-3799 or toll-free 800-UMBC-4U2 (in-state); 800-862-2402 (out-of-state). Fax: 410-455-1094. E-mail: admissions@umbc.edu. Web site: http://www.umbc.edu/.

UNIVERSITY OF MARYLAND, COLLEGE PARK
COLLEGE PARK, MARYLAND

General State-supported, university, coed **Entrance** Moderately difficult **Setting** 3,650-acre suburban campus **Total enrollment** 33,189 **Student/faculty ratio** 13:1 **Application deadline** 2/15 (freshmen), 7/1 (transfer) **Freshmen** 51% were admitted **Housing** Yes **Expenses** Tuition 5136; Room & Board 6328 **Undergraduates** 49% women, 11% part-time, 10% 25 or older, 0.3% Native American, 5% Hispanic American, 14% African American, 14% Asian American/Pacific Islander **The most frequently chosen baccalaureate fields are** business/marketing, biological/life sciences, social sciences and history **Academic program** English as a second language, advanced placement, accelerated degree program, self-designed majors, honors program, summer session, adult/continuing education programs, internships **Contact** Dr. Linda Clement, Assistant Vice President Academic Affairs and Director of Undergraduate Admissions, University of Maryland, College Park, Mitchell Building, College Park, MD 20742-5235. Telephone: 301-314-8385 or toll-free 800-422-5867. Fax: 301-314-9693. E-mail: um-admit@uga.umd.edu. Web site: http://www.maryland.edu/.

▶ **For more information, see page 478.**

UNIVERSITY OF MARYLAND EASTERN SHORE
PRINCESS ANNE, MARYLAND

General State-supported, university, coed **Entrance** Moderately difficult **Setting** 700-acre rural campus **Total enrollment** 3,297 **Student/faculty ratio** 20:1 **Application deadline** Rolling (freshmen), rolling (transfer) **Freshmen** 66% were admitted **Housing** Yes **Expenses** Tuition 3994; Room & Board 5130 **Undergraduates** 58% women, 14% part-time, 13% 25 or older, 0.2% Native American, 1% Hispanic American, 78% African American, 1% Asian American/Pacific Islander **Academic program** Advanced placement, accelerated degree program, self-designed majors, honors program, summer session, adult/continuing education programs, internships **Contact** Ms. Cheryll Collier-Mills, Acting Director of Admissions, Registration and Recruitment, University of Maryland Eastern Shore, Princess Anne, MD 21853-1299. Telephone: 410-651-8410. Fax: 410-651-7922. Web site: http://www.umes.umd.edu/.

UNIVERSITY OF MARYLAND UNIVERSITY COLLEGE
ADELPHI, MARYLAND

General State-supported, comprehensive, coed **Entrance** Noncompetitive **Setting** suburban campus **Total enrollment** 18,276 **Application deadline** Rolling (freshmen), rolling (transfer) **Freshmen** 100% were admitted **Housing** No **Expenses** Tuition $4584 **Undergraduates** 58% women, 87% part-time, 84% 25 or older, 1% Native American, 4% Hispanic American, 32% African American, 7% Asian American/Pacific Islander **The most frequently chosen baccalaureate field is** interdisciplinary studies **Academic program** Advanced placement, accelerated degree program, summer session, adult/continuing education programs **Contact** Ms. Anne Rahill, Technical Director, Admissions, University of Maryland University College, 3501 University Boulevard, East, Adelphi, MD 20783. Telephone: 301-985-7000 or toll-free 800-888-UMUC (in-state). Fax: 301-985-7364. E-mail: umucinfo@nova.umuc.ed. Web site: http://www.umuc.edu/.

UNIVERSITY OF PHOENIX–MARYLAND CAMPUS
COLUMBIA, MARYLAND

General Proprietary, comprehensive, coed **Entrance** Noncompetitive **Total enrollment** 66,534 **Student/faculty ratio** 13:1 **Application deadline** Rolling (freshmen), rolling (transfer) **Expenses** Tuition $7740 **Undergraduates** 56% women, 86% 25 or older, 2% Native American, 18% Hispanic American, 13% African American, 6% Asian American/Pacific Islander **Academic program** Advanced placement, accelerated degree program, adult/continuing education programs **Contact** Ms. Beth Barilla, Director of Admissions, University of Phoenix–Maryland Campus, 4615 East Elwood Street, Phoenix, AZ 85040-1948. Telephone: 480-927-0099 Ext. 1218 or toll-free 800-228-7240. Fax: 480-894-1758. E-mail: beth.barilla@apollogrp.edu. Web site: http://www.phoenix.edu/.

VILLA JULIE COLLEGE
STEVENSON, MARYLAND

General Independent, comprehensive, coed **Entrance** Moderately difficult **Setting** 60-acre suburban campus **Total enrollment** 2,259 **Student/faculty ratio** 12:1 **Application deadline** 7/15 (freshmen), 7/15 (transfer) **Housing** Yes **Expenses** Tuition 11,500; Room only 3750 **Undergraduates** 72% women, 25% part-time, 23% 25 or older, 0.1% Native American, 1% Hispanic American, 9% African American, 3% Asian American/Pacific Islander **Academic program** English as a second language, advanced placement, accelerated degree program, self-designed majors, honors program, summer session, adult/continuing education programs, internships **Contact** Mr. Mark Hergan, Dean of Admissions, Villa Julie College, 125 Greenspring Valley Road, Stevenson, MD 21153. Telephone: 410-486-7001 or toll-free 877-468-6852 (in-state); 877-468-3852 (out-of-state). Fax: 410-602-6600. E-mail: admissions@vjc.edu. Web site: http://www.vjc.edu/.

WASHINGTON BIBLE COLLEGE
LANHAM, MARYLAND

General Independent nondenominational, 4-year, coed **Entrance** Moderately difficult **Setting** 63-acre suburban campus **Total enrollment** 313 **Student/faculty ratio** 12:1 **Application deadline** Rolling (freshmen), rolling (transfer) **Freshmen** 56% were

Washington Bible College *(continued)*

admitted **Housing** Yes **Expenses** Tuition $6680; Room & Board $4690 **Undergraduates** 44% women, 51% part-time, 63% 25 or older **The most frequently chosen baccalaureate field is** philosophy, religion, and theology **Academic program** English as a second language, advanced placement, accelerated degree program, summer session, adult/continuing education programs, internships **Contact** Mrs. Shea Kaurin, Director of Admissions, Washington Bible College, 6511 Princess Garden Parkway, Lanham, MD 20706. Telephone: 800-787-0256 Ext. 213 or toll-free 800-787-0256 Ext. 212. Fax: 301-552-2775 Ext. 212. E-mail: admiss@bible.edu. Web site: http://www.bible.edu/.

WASHINGTON COLLEGE
CHESTERTOWN, MARYLAND

General Independent, comprehensive, coed **Entrance** Moderately difficult **Setting** 120-acre small-town campus **Total enrollment** 1,225 **Student/faculty ratio** 12:1 **Application deadline** 2/15 (freshmen), rolling (transfer) **Freshmen** 88% were admitted **Housing** Yes **Expenses** Tuition 21,300; Room & Board 5740 **Undergraduates** 60% women, 4% part-time, 2% 25 or older, 0.3% Native American, 1% Hispanic American, 3% African American, 1% Asian American/Pacific Islander **The most frequently chosen baccalaureate fields are** business/marketing, foreign language/literature, social sciences and history **Academic program** English as a second language, advanced placement, self-designed majors, internships **Contact** Mr. Kevin Coveney, Vice President for Admissions, Washington College, 300 Washington Avenue, Chestertown, MD 21620-1197. Telephone: 410-778-7700 or toll-free 800-422-1782. E-mail: admissions_office@washcoll.edu. Web site: http://www.washcoll.edu/.

► **For more information, see page 486.**

WESTERN MARYLAND COLLEGE
WESTMINSTER, MARYLAND

General Independent, comprehensive, coed **Entrance** Moderately difficult **Setting** 160-acre small-town campus **Total enrollment** 3,147 **Student/faculty ratio** 12:1 **Application deadline** 3/15 (freshmen), 7/1 (transfer) **Freshmen** 77% were admitted **Housing** Yes **Expenses** Tuition 20,550; Room & Board 5450 **Undergraduates** 56% women, 3% part-time, 4% 25 or older, 0.1% Native American, 1% Hispanic American, 6% African American, 2% Asian American/Pacific Islander **The most frequently chosen baccalaureate fields are** business/marketing, psychology, social sciences and history **Academic program** Advanced placement, self-designed majors, honors program, summer session, adult/continuing education programs, internships **Contact** Ms. M. Martha O'Connell, Dean of Admissions, Western Maryland College, 2 College Hill, Westminster, MD 21157-4390. Telephone: 410-857-2230 or toll-free 800-638-5005. Fax: 410-857-2757. E-mail: admissio@ns1.wmc.car.md.us. Web site: http://www.wmdc.edu/.

► **For more information, see page 491.**

MASSACHUSETTS

AMERICAN INTERNATIONAL COLLEGE
SPRINGFIELD, MASSACHUSETTS

General Independent, comprehensive, coed **Entrance** Moderately difficult **Setting** 58-acre urban campus **Total enrollment** 1,274 **Student/faculty ratio** 14:1 **Application deadline** Rolling (freshmen), rolling (transfer) **Freshmen** 79% were admitted **Housing** Yes **Expenses** Tuition $14,756; Room & Board $7468 **Undergraduates** 55% women, 8% part-time, 25% 25 or older, 0.3% Native American, 5% Hispanic American, 21% African American, 1% Asian American/Pacific Islander **The most frequently chosen baccalaureate fields are** business/marketing, health professions and related sciences, protective services/public administration **Academic program** English as a second language, advanced placement, accelerated degree program, honors program, summer session, adult/continuing education programs, internships **Contact** Dean of Admissions, American International College, 1000 State Street, Springfield, MA 01109. Telephone: 413-205-3201 or toll-free 800-242-3142. Fax: 413-205-3943. E-mail: inquiry@www.aic.edu. Web site: http://www.aic.edu/.

AMHERST COLLEGE
AMHERST, MASSACHUSETTS

General Independent, 4-year, coed **Entrance** Most difficult **Setting** 964-acre small-town campus **Total enrollment** 1,682 **Student/faculty ratio** 8:1 **Application deadline** 12/31 (freshmen), 2/1 (transfer) **Freshmen** 19% were admitted **Housing** Yes **Expenses** Tuition 26,080; Room & Board 6800 **Undergraduates** 48% women, 0.2% Native American, 7% Hispanic American, 8% African American, 11% Asian American/Pacific Islander **The most frequently chosen baccalaureate fields are** English, foreign language/literature, social sciences and history **Academic program** Self-designed majors, honors program **Contact** Mr. Thomas Parker, Dean of Admission and Financial Aid, Amherst College, PO Box 5000, Amherst, MA 01002. Telephone: 413-542-2328. Fax: 413-542-2040. E-mail: admissions@amherst.edu. Web site: http://www.amherst.edu/.

ANNA MARIA COLLEGE
PAXTON, MASSACHUSETTS

General Independent Roman Catholic, comprehensive, coed **Entrance** Moderately difficult **Setting** 180-acre rural campus **Total enrollment** 1,255 **Student/faculty ratio** 15:1 **Application deadline** Rolling (freshmen), rolling (transfer) **Freshmen** 83% were admitted **Housing** Yes **Expenses** Tuition $14,645; Room & Board $6200 **Undergraduates** 63% women, 33% part-time, 33% 25 or older, 0.3% Native American, 3% Hispanic American, 3% African American, 2% Asian American/Pacific Islander **The most frequently chosen baccalaureate fields are** business/marketing, education, protective services/public administration **Academic program** English as a second language, advanced placement, accelerated degree program, self-designed majors, summer session, adult/continuing education programs, internships **Contact** Ms. Laurie Peltier, Director of Admissions, Anna Maria College, Box O, Sunset Lane, Paxton, MA 01612. Telephone: 508-849-3360 or toll-free 800-344-4586 Ext. 360. Fax: 508-849-3362. E-mail: admissions@amc.anna-maria.edu. Web site: http://www.annamaria.edu/.

THE ART INSTITUTE OF BOSTON AT LESLEY UNIVERSITY
BOSTON, MASSACHUSETTS

General Independent, 4-year, coed **Entrance** Moderately difficult **Setting** urban campus **Total enrollment** 791 **Student/faculty ratio** 11:1 **Application deadline** Rolling (freshmen), rolling (transfer) **Freshmen** 49% were admitted **Housing** Yes **Expenses** Tuition $14,090; Room & Board $7520 **Undergraduates** 58% women, 41% part-time, 7% 25 or older, 0% Native American, 3% Hispanic American, 2% African American, 6% Asian American/Pacific Islander **The most frequently chosen baccalaureate field is** visual/performing arts **Academic program** English as a second language, advanced placement, self-designed majors, honors program, summer session, adult/continuing education programs, internships **Contact** Bradford White, Director of Admissions, The Art Institute of Boston at Lesley University, 700 Beacon Street, Boston, MA 02215-2598. Telephone: 617-262-1223 Ext. 304 or toll-free 800-773-0494 (in-state). Fax: 617-437-1226. E-mail: admissions@aiboston.edu. Web site: http://www.aiboston.edu/.

ASSUMPTION COLLEGE
WORCESTER, MASSACHUSETTS

General Independent Roman Catholic, comprehensive, coed **Entrance** Moderately difficult **Setting** 145-acre urban campus **Total enrollment** 2,766 **Student/faculty ratio** 14:1 **Application deadline** 3/1 (freshmen), 5/1 (transfer) **Freshmen** 71% were admitted **Housing** Yes **Expenses** Tuition $18,945; Room & Board $7375 **Undergraduates** 64% women, 17% part-time, 1% 25 or older **The most frequently chosen baccalaureate fields are** business/marketing, health professions and related sciences, social sciences and history **Academic program** Advanced placement, self-designed majors, honors program, summer session, adult/continuing education programs, internships **Contact** Ms. Mary Bresnahan, Dean of Admission, Assumption College, 500 Salisbury Street, Worcester, MA 01109-1296. Telephone: 508-767-7362 or toll-free 888-882-7786. Fax: 508-799-4412. E-mail: admiss@assumption.edu. Web site: http://www.assumption.edu/.

ATLANTIC UNION COLLEGE
SOUTH LANCASTER, MASSACHUSETTS

General Independent Seventh-day Adventist, comprehensive, coed **Entrance** Moderately difficult **Setting** 314-acre small-town campus **Total enrollment** 742 **Student/faculty ratio** 13:1 **Application deadline** 8/1 (freshmen), 8/1 (transfer) **Freshmen** 42% were admitted **Housing** Yes **Expenses** Tuition $13,170; Room & Board $4552 **Undergraduates** 61% women, 35% part-time, 0.5% Native American, 20% Hispanic American, 47% African American, 2% Asian American/Pacific Islander **Academic program** English as a second language, advanced placement, honors program, summer session, adult/continuing education programs, internships **Contact** Mrs. Rosita Lashley, Associate Director for Admissions, Atlantic Union College, PO Box 1000, South Lancaster, MA 01561. Telephone: 978-368-2239 or toll-free 800-282-2030. Fax: 978-368-2015. E-mail: enroll@math.atlanticuc.edu. Web site: http://www.atlanticuc.edu/.

BABSON COLLEGE
WELLESLEY, MASSACHUSETTS

General Independent, comprehensive, coed **Entrance** Very difficult **Setting** 450-acre suburban campus **Total enrollment** 3,397 **Student/faculty ratio** 9:1 **Application deadline** 2/1 (freshmen), 4/1 (transfer) **Freshmen** 39% were admitted **Housing** Yes **Expenses** Tuition $21,952; Room & Board $8746 **Undergraduates** 36% women, 0.2% Native American, 3% Hispanic American, 2% African American, 7% Asian American/Pacific Islander **The most frequently chosen baccalaureate field is** business/marketing **Academic program** Advanced placement, self-designed majors, honors program, summer session, internships **Contact** Mrs. Monica Inzer, Dean of Undergraduate Admission and Student Financial Services, Babson College, Office of Undergraduate Admissions, Mustard Hall, Babson Park, MA 02457-0310. Telephone: 800-488-3696 or toll-free 800-488-3696. Fax: 781-239-4006. E-mail: ugradadmission@babson.edu. Web site: http://www.babson.edu/.

BAY PATH COLLEGE
LONGMEADOW, MASSACHUSETTS

General Independent, comprehensive, women only **Entrance** Moderately difficult **Setting** 44-acre suburban campus **Total enrollment** 799 **Student/faculty ratio** 13:1 **Application deadline** Rolling (freshmen), rolling (transfer) **Freshmen** 67% were admitted **Housing** Yes **Expenses** Tuition $13,660; Room & Board $6945 **Undergraduates** 29% part-time, 37% 25 or older, 0.1% Native American, 7% Hispanic American, 8% African American, 2% Asian American/Pacific Islander **The most frequently chosen baccalaureate fields are** business/marketing, law/legal studies, psychology **Academic program** English as a second language, advanced placement, self-designed majors, honors program, summer session, adult/continuing education programs, internships **Contact** Brenda Wishart, Director of Admissions, Bay Path College, 588 Longmeadow Street, Longmeadow, MA 01106-2292. Telephone: 413-565-1000 Ext. 229 or toll-free 800-782-7284. Fax: 413-565-1105. E-mail: chobin@baypath.edu. Web site: http://www.baypath.edu/.

Bay Path College *(continued)*

BECKER COLLEGE
WORCESTER, MASSACHUSETTS

General Independent, 4-year, coed **Entrance** Minimally difficult **Setting** urban campus **Total enrollment** 1,163 **Student/faculty ratio** 15:1 **Application deadline** Rolling (freshmen), rolling (transfer) **Freshmen** 87% were admitted **Housing** Yes **Expenses** Tuition $12,520; Room & Board $6420 **Undergraduates** 77% women, 35% part-time, 9% 25 or older, 0.2% Native American, 4% Hispanic American, 4% African American, 3% Asian American/Pacific Islander **The most frequently chosen baccalaureate fields are** business/marketing, law/legal studies, psychology **Academic program** English as a second language, advanced placement, accelerated degree program, summer session, adult/continuing education programs, internships **Contact** Admissions Receptionist, Becker College, 61 Sever Street, Worcester, MA 01609. Telephone: 508-791-9241 Ext. 245 or toll-free 877-5BECKER Ext. 245. Fax: 508-890-1500. E-mail: admissions@go.becker.edu. Web site: http://www.beckercollege.edu/.

BENTLEY COLLEGE
WALTHAM, MASSACHUSETTS

General Independent, comprehensive, coed **Entrance** Moderately difficult **Setting** 143-acre suburban campus **Total enrollment** 5,728 **Student/faculty ratio** 15:1 **Application deadline** 2/1 (freshmen), 5/15 (transfer) **Freshmen** 49% were admitted **Housing** Yes **Expenses** Tuition $18,910; Room & Board $8600 **Undergraduates** 44% women, 16% part-time, 12% 25 or older, 0.1% Native American, 3% Hispanic American, 3% African American, 8% Asian American/Pacific Islander **The most frequently chosen baccalaureate fields are** business/marketing, computer/information sciences, interdisciplinary studies **Academic program** English as a second language, advanced placement, accelerated degree program, self-designed majors, honors program, summer session, adult/continuing education programs, internships **Contact** Ms. Judith A. Pearson, Director of Admission, Bentley College, 175 Forest Street, Waltham, MA 02452-4705. Telephone: 781-891-2244 or toll-free 800-523-2354 (out-of-state). Fax: 781-891-3414. E-mail: moreinfo@bentley.edu. Web site: http://www.bentley.edu/.

BERKLEE COLLEGE OF MUSIC
BOSTON, MASSACHUSETTS

General Independent, 4-year, coed **Entrance** Moderately difficult **Setting** urban campus **Total enrollment** 3,361 **Student/faculty ratio** 13:1 **Application deadline** Rolling (freshmen), rolling (transfer) **Freshmen** 78% were admitted **Housing** Yes **Expenses** Tuition $16,916; Room & Board $8890 **Undergraduates** 14% 25 or older, 0.3% Native American, 3% Hispanic American, 4% African American, 2% Asian American/Pacific Islander **The most frequently chosen baccalaureate field is** visual/performing arts **Academic program** English as a second language, advanced placement, accelerated degree program, self-designed majors, summer session, internships **Contact** Ms. Marsha Ginn, Director of Admissions, Berklee College of Music, 1140 Boylston Street, Boston, MA 02215-3693. Telephone: 617-747-2222 or toll-free 800-BERKLEE. Fax: 617-747-2047. E-mail: admissions@berklee.edu. Web site: http://www.berklee.edu/.

BOSTON ARCHITECTURAL CENTER
BOSTON, MASSACHUSETTS

General Independent, comprehensive, coed **Entrance** Noncompetitive **Setting** urban campus **Total enrollment** 631 **Student/faculty ratio** 10:1 **Application deadline** Rolling (freshmen), rolling (transfer) **Freshmen** 95% were admitted **Housing** No **Expenses** Tuition $6767 **Undergraduates** 27% women, 13% part-time, 67% 25 or older, 3% Native American, 5% Hispanic American, 2% African American, 2% Asian American/Pacific Islander **The most frequently chosen baccalaureate field is** architecture **Academic program** Advanced placement, summer session, adult/continuing education programs, internships **Contact** Ms. Valerie Nichols, Director of Admissions, Boston Architectural Center, 320 Newbury Street, Boston, MA 02115-2795. Telephone: 617-585-0202 or toll-free 877-585-0100. Fax: 617-585-0121. E-mail: admissions@the-bac.edu. Web site: http://www.the-bac.edu/.

BOSTON COLLEGE
CHESTNUT HILL, MASSACHUSETTS

General Independent Roman Catholic (Jesuit), university, coed **Entrance** Very difficult **Setting** 240-acre suburban campus **Total enrollment** 13,551 **Student/faculty ratio** 14:1 **Application deadline** 1/15 (freshmen), 4/15 (transfer) **Freshmen** 32% were admitted **Housing** Yes **Expenses** Tuition 23,270; Room & Board 8510 **Undergraduates** 52% women, 0.4% Native American, 5% Hispanic American, 5% African American, 8% Asian American/Pacific Islander **The most frequently chosen baccalaureate fields are** business/marketing, education, social sciences and history **Academic program** Advanced placement, accelerated degree program, self-designed majors, honors program, summer session, adult/continuing education programs, internships **Contact** Mr. John L. Mahoney Jr., Director of Undergraduate Admission, Boston College, 140 Commonwealth Avenue, Devlin Hall 208, 140 Commonwealth Avenue, Chestnut Hill, MA 02167-3809. Telephone: 617-552-3100 or toll-free 800-360-2522. Fax: 617-552-0798. E-mail: admissions@bcvms.bc.edu. Web site: http://www.bc.edu/.

BOSTON CONSERVATORY
BOSTON, MASSACHUSETTS

General Independent, comprehensive, coed **Entrance** Moderately difficult **Setting** urban campus **Total enrollment** 500 **Application deadline** Rolling (freshmen), rolling (transfer) **Freshmen** 47% were admitted **Housing** Yes **Expenses** Tuition $19,250; Room & Board $9280 **Academic program** English as a second language, advanced placement, summer session, adult/continuing education programs **Contact** Ms. Halley Shefler, Dean of Enrollment, Boston Conservatory, 8 The Fenway, Boston, MA 02215. Telephone: 617-912-9153. Fax: 617-536-3176. Web site: http://www.bostonconservatory.edu/.

BOSTON UNIVERSITY
BOSTON, MASSACHUSETTS

General Independent, university, coed **Entrance** Very difficult **Setting** 132-acre urban campus **Total enrollment** 28,318 **Student/faculty ratio** 14:1 **Application deadline** 1/1 (freshmen), 4/1 (transfer) **Freshmen** 49% were admitted **Housing** Yes **Expenses** Tuition 26,228; Room & Board 8750 **Undergraduates** 59% women, 11% part-time, 3% 25 or older, 0.3% Native American, 5% Hispanic American, 3% African American, 11% Asian American/Pacific Islander **The most frequently chosen baccalaureate fields are** communications/communication technologies, business/marketing, social sciences and history **Academic program** English as a second language, advanced placement, accelerated degree program, self-designed majors, honors program, summer session, adult/continuing education programs, internships **Contact** Ms. Kelly A. Walter, Director of Undergraduate Admissions, Boston University, 121 Bay State Road, Boston, MA 02215. Telephone: 617-353-2300. Fax: 617-353-9695. E-mail: admissions@bu.edu. Web site: http://www.bu.edu/.

BRANDEIS UNIVERSITY
WALTHAM, MASSACHUSETTS

General Independent, university, coed **Entrance** Most difficult **Setting** 235-acre suburban campus **Total enrollment** 4,753 **Student/faculty ratio** 9:1 **Application deadline** 1/31 (freshmen), 4/1 (transfer) **Freshmen** 48% were admitted **Housing** Yes **Expenses** Tuition 26,166; Room & Board 7189 **Undergraduates** 57% women, 1% part-time, 1% 25 or older, 0.2% Native American, 3% Hispanic American, 2% African American, 10% Asian American/Pacific Islander **The most frequently chosen baccalaureate fields are** biological/life sciences, psychology, social sciences and history **Academic program** English as a second language, advanced placement, self-designed majors, summer session, adult/continuing education programs, internships **Contact** Mr. Michael Kalafatas, Director of Admissions, Brandeis University, 415 South Street, Waltham, MA 02254-9110. Telephone: 781-736-3500 or toll-free 800-622-0622 (out-of-state). Fax: 781-736-3536. E-mail: admitme@brandeis.edu. Web site: http://www.brandeis.edu/.

BRIDGEWATER STATE COLLEGE
BRIDGEWATER, MASSACHUSETTS

General State-supported, comprehensive, coed **Entrance** Moderately difficult **Setting** 235-acre suburban campus **Total enrollment** 8,839 **Student/faculty ratio** 18:1 **Application deadline** 3/1 (freshmen), 4/1 (transfer) **Freshmen** 81% were admitted **Housing** Yes **Expenses** Tuition $2895; Room & Board $4887 **Undergraduates** 61% women, 24% part-time, 20% 25 or older, 0.3% Native American, 2% Hispanic American, 4% African American, 1% Asian American/Pacific Islander **The most frequently chosen baccalaureate fields are** business/marketing, education, social sciences and history **Academic program** English as a second language, advanced placement, self-designed majors, honors program, summer session, adult/continuing education programs, internships **Contact** Mr. Steve King, Director of Admissions, Bridgewater State College, Admission Office, Bridgewater, MA 02325-0001. Telephone: 508-531-1237. Fax: 508-531-1746. E-mail: admission@bridgew.edu. Web site: http://www.bridgew.edu/.

CAMBRIDGE COLLEGE
CAMBRIDGE, MASSACHUSETTS

General Independent, comprehensive, coed **Entrance** Minimally difficult **Setting** urban campus **Total enrollment** 2,700 **Student/faculty ratio** 18:1 **Application deadline** Rolling (freshmen), rolling (transfer) **Freshmen** 100% were admitted **Housing** No **Expenses** Tuition $8550 **Undergraduates** 95% 25 or older **The most frequently chosen baccalaureate field is** psychology **Academic program** English as a second language, accelerated degree program, summer session, adult/continuing education programs, internships **Contact** Ms. Joy King, Undergraduate Enrollment Mgr., Cambridge College, 1000 Massachusetts Avenue, Cambridge, MA 02138-5304. Telephone: 617-868-1000 or toll-free 800-877-4723. Fax: 617-349-3545. E-mail: enroll@idea.cambridge.edu. Web site: http://www.cambridge.edu/.

CLARK UNIVERSITY
WORCESTER, MASSACHUSETTS

General Independent, university, coed **Entrance** Moderately difficult **Setting** 50-acre urban campus **Total enrollment** 2,910 **Student/faculty ratio** 11:1 **Application deadline** 2/1 (freshmen), 4/15 (transfer) **Freshmen** 70% were admitted **Housing** Yes **Expenses** Tuition $24,620; Room & Board $4350 **Undergraduates** 59% women, 10% part-time, 1% 25 or older, 0.2% Native American, 3% Hispanic American, 3% African American, 4% Asian American/Pacific Islander **The most frequently chosen baccalaureate fields are** psychology, biological/life sciences, social sciences and history **Academic program** English as a second language, advanced placement, accelerated degree program, self-designed majors, honors program, summer session, adult/continuing education programs, internships **Contact** Mr. Harold M. Wingood, Dean of Admissions, Clark University, 950 Main Street, Worcester, MA 01610-1477. Telephone: 508-793-7431 or toll-free 800-GO-CLARK (out-of-state). E-mail: admissions@clarku.edu. Web site: http://www.clarku.edu/.

COLLEGE OF OUR LADY OF THE ELMS
CHICOPEE, MASSACHUSETTS

General Independent Roman Catholic, comprehensive, coed, primarily women **Entrance** Moderately difficult **Setting** 32-acre suburban campus **Total enrollment** 956 **Student/faculty ratio** 11:1 **Application deadline** Rolling (freshmen), rolling (transfer) **Freshmen** 85% were admitted **Housing** Yes **Expenses** Tuition $14,720; Room & Board $5566 **Undergraduates** 88% women, 37% part-time, 52% 25 or older, 0.3% Native American, 5% Hispanic American, 5% African American, 1% Asian American/ Pacific Islander **The most frequently chosen baccalaureate fields are** health professions and related sciences, business/marketing, social sciences and history **Academic program** English as a second language, advanced placement, accelerated degree program, self-designed majors, honors program, summer session, adult/continuing education programs, internships **Contact** Mr. Michael Crowley, Director of Admissions, College of Our Lady of the Elms, 291 Springfield Street, Chicopee, MA 01013-2839. Telephone: 413-592-3189 Ext. 350 or toll-free 800-255-ELMS. Fax: 413-594-2781. E-mail: admissions@elms.edu. Web site: http://www.elms.edu/.

COLLEGE OF THE HOLY CROSS
WORCESTER, MASSACHUSETTS

General Independent Roman Catholic (Jesuit), 4-year, coed **Entrance** Very difficult **Setting** 174-acre suburban campus **Total enrollment** 2,826 **Student/faculty ratio** 12:1 **Application deadline** 1/15 (freshmen), 5/1 (transfer) **Freshmen** 41% were admitted **Housing** Yes **Expenses** Tuition $23,815; Room & Board $7540 **Undergraduates** 53% women, 1% part-time, 0% 25 or older, 0.3% Native American, 5% Hispanic American, 3% African American, 3% Asian American/Pacific Islander **The most frequently chosen baccalaureate fields are** English, psychology, social sciences and history **Academic program** Advanced placement, accelerated degree program, self-designed majors, honors program, internships **Contact** Ms. Ann Bowe McDermott, Director of Admissions, College of the Holy Cross, 1 College Street, Worcester, MA 01610. Telephone: 508-793-2443 or toll-free 800-442-2421. E-mail: admissions@holycross.edu. Web site: http://www.holycross.edu/.

CURRY COLLEGE
MILTON, MASSACHUSETTS

General Independent, comprehensive, coed **Entrance** Moderately difficult **Setting** 131-acre suburban campus **Total enrollment** 2,330 **Student/faculty ratio** 12:1 **Application deadline** 4/1 (freshmen), 7/1 (transfer) **Freshmen** 76% were admitted **Housing** Yes **Expenses** Tuition $17,960; Room & Board $6870 **Undergraduates** 50% women, 39% part-time, 43% 25 or older, 0.1% Native American, 3% Hispanic American, 5% African American, 1% Asian American/ Pacific Islander **The most frequently chosen baccalaureate fields are** health professions and related sciences, business/marketing, protective services/ public administration **Academic program** Advanced placement, accelerated degree program, self-designed majors, honors program, summer session, adult/ continuing education programs, internships **Contact** Mr. Michael Poll, Dean of Admission and Financial Aid, Curry College, 1071 Blue Hill Avenue, Milton, MA 02186. Telephone: 617-333-2210 or toll-free 800-669-0686. Fax: 617-333-2114. E-mail: curryadm@curry.edu. Web site: http://www.curry.edu/.

EASTERN NAZARENE COLLEGE
QUINCY, MASSACHUSETTS

General Independent, comprehensive, coed, affiliated with Church of the Nazarene **Entrance** Moderately difficult **Setting** 15-acre suburban campus **Total enrollment** 1,387 **Student/faculty ratio** 12:1 **Application deadline** Rolling (freshmen), rolling (transfer) **Freshmen** 69% were admitted **Housing** Yes **Expenses** Tuition $14,458; Room & Board $4975 **Undergraduates** 59% women, 2% part-time, 50% 25 or older, 1% Native American, 3% Hispanic American, 9% African American, 1% Asian American/ Pacific Islander **The most frequently chosen baccalaureate fields are** business/marketing, biological/ life sciences, education **Academic program** English as a second language, advanced placement, accelerated degree program, honors program, summer session, adult/continuing education programs, internships **Contact** Mr. James F. Heyward II, Director of Admissions, Eastern Nazarene College, 23 East Elm Avenue, Quincy, MA 02170. Telephone: 617-745-3868 or toll-free 800-88-ENC88. Fax: 617-745-3929. E-mail: admissions@enc.edu. Web site: http://www.enc.edu/.

ELMS COLLEGE
See College of Our Lady of the Elms

EMERSON COLLEGE
BOSTON, MASSACHUSETTS

General Independent, comprehensive, coed **Entrance** Very difficult **Setting** urban campus **Total enrollment** 4,074 **Student/faculty ratio** 16:1 **Application deadline** 2/1 (freshmen), 3/1 (transfer) **Freshmen** 52% were admitted **Housing** Yes **Expenses** Tuition 20,014; Room & Board 9020 **Undergraduates** 58% women, 13% part-time, 6% 25 or older, 0.3% Native American, 2% Hispanic American, 1% African American, 2% Asian American/Pacific Islander **Academic program** Advanced placement, self-designed majors, honors program, summer session, adult/continuing education programs, internships **Contact** Ms. Sara Ramirez, Director of Admission, Emerson College, 120 Boylston Street, Boston, MA 02116-4624. Telephone: 617-824-8600. Fax: 617-824-8609. E-mail: admission@emerson.edu. Web site: http://www.emerson.edu/.

► **For more information, see page 414.**

EMMANUEL COLLEGE
BOSTON, MASSACHUSETTS

General Independent Roman Catholic, comprehensive, coed **Entrance** Moderately difficult **Setting**

16-acre urban campus **Total enrollment** 1,524 **Student/faculty ratio** 15:1 **Application deadline** Rolling (freshmen), rolling (transfer) **Freshmen** 83% were admitted **Housing** Yes **Expenses** Tuition $16,412; Room & Board $7390 **Undergraduates** 89% women, 44% part-time, 54% 25 or older, 0.2% Native American, 5% Hispanic American, 10% African American, 3% Asian American/Pacific Islander **The most frequently chosen baccalaureate fields are** business/marketing, health professions and related sciences, interdisciplinary studies **Academic program** English as a second language, advanced placement, accelerated degree program, self-designed majors, honors program, summer session, adult/continuing education programs, internships **Contact** Ms. Sandra Robbins, Dean of Admissions, Emmanuel College, 400 The Fenway, Boston, MA 02115. Telephone: 617-735-9715. Fax: 617-735-9801. E-mail: enroll@emmanuel.edu. Web site: http://www.emmanuel.edu/.

ENDICOTT COLLEGE
BEVERLY, MASSACHUSETTS

General Independent, comprehensive, coed **Entrance** Moderately difficult **Setting** 200-acre suburban campus **Total enrollment** 1,958 **Student/faculty ratio** 13:1 **Application deadline** Rolling (freshmen), rolling (transfer) **Freshmen** 70% were admitted **Housing** Yes **Expenses** Tuition $15,116; Room & Board $7698 **Undergraduates** 67% women, 9% part-time, 10% 25 or older, 1% Native American, 2% Hispanic American, 1% African American, 1% Asian American/Pacific Islander **The most frequently chosen baccalaureate fields are** business/marketing, personal/miscellaneous services, psychology **Academic program** English as a second language, advanced placement, accelerated degree program, honors program, summer session, adult/continuing education programs, internships **Contact** Mr. Thomas J. Redman, Vice President of Admissions and Financial Aid, Endicott College, 376 Hale Street, Beverly, MA 01915. Telephone: 978-921-1000 or toll-free 800-325-1114 (out-of-state). Fax: 978-232-2520. E-mail: admissio@endicott.edu. Web site: http://www.endicott.edu/.

FITCHBURG STATE COLLEGE
FITCHBURG, MASSACHUSETTS

General State-supported, comprehensive, coed **Entrance** Moderately difficult **Setting** 45-acre small-town campus **Total enrollment** 5,715 **Student/faculty ratio** 11:1 **Application deadline** 4/1 (freshmen), rolling (transfer) **Freshmen** 66% were admitted **Housing** Yes **Expenses** Tuition $3018; Room & Board $4680 **Undergraduates** 58% women, 31% part-time, 23% 25 or older, 0.1% Native American, 3% Hispanic American, 4% African American, 2% Asian American/Pacific Islander **The most frequently chosen baccalaureate fields are** business/marketing, education, health professions and related sciences **Academic program** Advanced placement, accelerated degree program, self-designed majors, honors program, summer session, adult/continuing education programs, internships **Contact** Mr. James Dupont, Director of Admissions, Fitchburg State College, 160 Pearl Street, Fitchburg, MA 01420-2697. Telephone: 978-665-3144 or toll-free 800-705-9692. Fax: 978-665-4540. E-mail: admissions@fsc.edu. Web site: http://www.fsc.edu/.

▶ **For more information, see page 420.**

FRAMINGHAM STATE COLLEGE
FRAMINGHAM, MASSACHUSETTS

General State-supported, comprehensive, coed **Entrance** Moderately difficult **Setting** 73-acre suburban campus **Total enrollment** 6,626 **Student/faculty ratio** 15:1 **Application deadline** 3/1 (freshmen), 3/1 (transfer) **Freshmen** 62% were admitted **Housing** Yes **Expenses** Tuition $2830; Room & Board $4148 **Undergraduates** 65% women, 27% part-time, 17% 25 or older, 0.4% Native American, 3% Hispanic American, 4% African American, 3% Asian American/Pacific Islander **The most frequently chosen baccalaureate fields are** business/marketing, psychology, social sciences and history **Academic program** English as a second language, advanced placement, honors program, summer session, adult/continuing education programs, internships **Contact** Dr. Philip Dooher, Dean of Admissions and Enrollment Services, Framingham State College, P.O. Box 9101, Framingham, MA 01701-9101. Telephone: 508-626-4500. E-mail: admiss@frc.mass.edu. Web site: http://www.framingham.edu/.

GORDON COLLEGE
WENHAM, MASSACHUSETTS

General Independent nondenominational, comprehensive, coed **Entrance** Moderately difficult **Setting** 500-acre small-town campus **Total enrollment** 1,617 **Student/faculty ratio** 15:1 **Application deadline** Rolling (freshmen), rolling (transfer) **Freshmen** 80% were admitted **Housing** Yes **Expenses** Tuition 17,270; Room & Board 5200 **Undergraduates** 64% women, 3% part-time, 3% 25 or older, 0.2% Native American, 1% Hispanic American, 1% African American, 2% Asian American/Pacific Islander **The most frequently chosen baccalaureate fields are** English, philosophy, religion, and theology, social sciences and history **Academic program** Advanced placement, self-designed majors, honors program, internships **Contact** Mr. Silvio E. Vazquez, Dean of Admissions, Gordon College, 255 Grapevine Road, Wenham, MA 01984-1899. Telephone: 978-927-2300 Ext. 4218 or toll-free 800-343-1379. Fax: 978-524-3722. E-mail: admissions@hope.gordonc.edu. Web site: http://www.gordon.edu/.

HAMPSHIRE COLLEGE
AMHERST, MASSACHUSETTS

General Independent, 4-year, coed **Entrance** Moderately difficult **Setting** 800-acre rural campus **Total enrollment** 1,172 **Student/faculty ratio** 11:1 **Application deadline** 2/1 (freshmen), 3/15 (transfer) **Freshmen** 62% were admitted **Housing** Yes **Expenses** Tuition 26,125; Room & Board 6814 **Undergradu-**

Hampshire College *(continued)*

ates 56% women, 0.2% Native American, 3% Hispanic American, 4% African American, 4% Asian American/Pacific Islander **Academic program** Advanced placement, accelerated degree program, self-designed majors, internships **Contact** Ms. Karen S. Parker, Director of Admissions, Hampshire College, 839 West Street, Amherst, MA 01002. Telephone: 413-559-5471 or toll-free 877-937-4267 (out-of-state). Fax: 413-559-5631. E-mail: admissions@hamp.hampshire.edu. Web site: http://www.hampshire.edu/.

HARVARD UNIVERSITY
CAMBRIDGE, MASSACHUSETTS

General Independent, university, coed **Entrance** Most difficult **Setting** 380-acre urban campus **Total enrollment** 17,850 **Student/faculty ratio** 8:1 **Application deadline** 1/1 (freshmen), 2/1 (transfer) **Freshmen** 11% were admitted **Housing** Yes **Expenses** Tuition 25,128; Room & Board 7982 **Undergraduates** 1% 25 or older, 1% Native American, 8% Hispanic American, 8% African American, 17% Asian American/Pacific Islander **Academic program** English as a second language, advanced placement, accelerated degree program, self-designed majors, honors program, summer session, adult/continuing education programs, internships **Contact** Office of Admissions and Financial Aid, Harvard University, Byerly Hall, 8 Garden Street, Cambridge, MA 02138. Telephone: 617-495-1551. E-mail: college@harvard.edu. Web site: http://www.harvard.edu/.

HEBREW COLLEGE
BROOKLINE, MASSACHUSETTS

General Independent Jewish, comprehensive, coed **Entrance** Minimally difficult **Setting** 3-acre suburban campus **Application deadline** 4/15 (freshmen), 4/15 (transfer) **Housing** No **Expenses** Tuition $14,940 **Academic program** Summer session, adult/continuing education programs, internships **Contact** Mrs. Norma Frankel, Registrar, Hebrew College, 43 Hawes Street, Brookline, MA 02446-5495. Telephone: 617-278-4944 or toll-free 800-866-4814. Fax: 617-734-9769. E-mail: nfrankel@lynx.neu.edu. Web site: http://www.hebrewcollege.edu/.

HELLENIC COLLEGE
BROOKLINE, MASSACHUSETTS

General Independent Greek Orthodox, 4-year, coed **Entrance** Minimally difficult **Setting** 52-acre suburban campus **Total enrollment** 47 **Student/faculty ratio** 6:1 **Application deadline** Rolling (freshmen), rolling (transfer) **Freshmen** 48% were admitted **Housing** Yes **Expenses** Tuition 9215; Room & Board 7000 **Undergraduates** 28% women, 10% 25 or older, 0% Native American, 0% Hispanic American, 0% African American, 0% Asian American/Pacific Islander **The most frequently chosen baccalaureate fields are** education, foreign language/literature, philosophy, religion, and theology **Academic program** Advanced placement, summer session, internships **Contact** Rev. Deacon Gerasimos Michaleas, Director of Admissions and Records, Hellenic College, 50 Goddard Avenue, Brookline, MA 02445-7496. Telephone: 617-731-3500 Ext. 1260. Fax: 617-850-1460. E-mail: admissions@hchc.edu. Web site: http://www.hchc.edu/.

LASELL COLLEGE
NEWTON, MASSACHUSETTS

General Independent, 4-year, coed **Entrance** Moderately difficult **Setting** 50-acre suburban campus **Total enrollment** 841 **Student/faculty ratio** 10:1 **Application deadline** Rolling (freshmen), rolling (transfer) **Freshmen** 79% were admitted **Housing** Yes **Expenses** Tuition $15,500; Room & Board $7700 **Undergraduates** 76% women, 8% part-time, 15% 25 or older, 0.1% Native American, 6% Hispanic American, 12% African American, 4% Asian American/Pacific Islander **The most frequently chosen baccalaureate fields are** business/marketing, education, protective services/public administration **Academic program** English as a second language, advanced placement, honors program, internships **Contact** Ms. Wendy Ferrucci, Director of Admission, Lasell College, 1844 Commonwealth Avenue, Newton, MA 02466. Telephone: 617-243-2225 or toll-free 888-LASELL-4. Fax: 617-796-4343. E-mail: info@lasell.edu. Web site: http://www.lasell.edu/.

LESLEY UNIVERSITY
CAMBRIDGE, MASSACHUSETTS

General Independent, comprehensive, coed, primarily women **Entrance** Moderately difficult **Setting** 5-acre urban campus **Total enrollment** 5,630 **Student/faculty ratio** 14:1 **Application deadline** 3/17 (freshmen), 5/1 (transfer) **Freshmen** 79% were admitted **Housing** Yes **Expenses** Tuition $16,475; Room & Board $7520 **Undergraduates** 100% women, 5% part-time, 0% 25 or older, 0.4% Native American, 7% Hispanic American, 8% African American, 5% Asian American/Pacific Islander **The most frequently chosen baccalaureate fields are** health professions and related sciences, education, liberal arts/general studies **Academic program** English as a second language, advanced placement, summer session, adult/continuing education programs, internships **Contact** Jane A. Raley, Director of Women's College Admissions, Lesley University, 29 Everett Street, Cambridge, MA 02138-2790. Telephone: 617-349-8800 or toll-free 800-999-1959 Ext. 8800. Fax: 617-349-8810. E-mail: vgadm@mail.lesley.edu. Web site: http://www.lesley.edu/.

MASSACHUSETTS COLLEGE OF ART
BOSTON, MASSACHUSETTS

General State-supported, comprehensive, coed **Entrance** Very difficult **Setting** 5-acre urban campus **Total enrollment** 2,315 **Student/faculty ratio** 13:1 **Application deadline** 3/1 (freshmen), 4/1 (transfer) **Freshmen** 46% were admitted **Housing** Yes **Expenses** Tuition $3883; Room & Board $7192 **Undergradu-**

ates 65% women, 44% part-time, 18% 25 or older, 0.2% Native American, 5% Hispanic American, 4% African American, 4% Asian American/Pacific Islander **The most frequently chosen baccalaureate fields are** education, architecture, visual/performing arts **Academic program** Self-designed majors, summer session, internships **Contact** Ms. Kay Ransdell, Dean of Admissions, Massachusetts College of Art, 621 Huntington Avenue, Boston, MA 02115-5882. Telephone: 617-232-1555 Ext. 235. Fax: 617-879-7250. E-mail: admissions@massart.edu. Web site: http://www.massart.edu/.

MASSACHUSETTS COLLEGE OF LIBERAL ARTS
NORTH ADAMS, MASSACHUSETTS

General State-supported, comprehensive, coed **Entrance** Moderately difficult **Setting** 80-acre small-town campus **Total enrollment** 1,520 **Student/faculty ratio** 13:1 **Application deadline** Rolling (freshmen), rolling (transfer) **Freshmen** 70% were admitted **Housing** Yes **Expenses** Tuition $3357; Room & Board $4290 **Undergraduates** 61% women, 22% part-time, 1% Native American, 2% Hispanic American, 5% African American, 1% Asian American/Pacific Islander **The most frequently chosen baccalaureate fields are** business/marketing, English, social sciences and history **Academic program** Advanced placement, self-designed majors, honors program, summer session, internships **Contact** Ms. Denise Richardello, Dean of Enrollment Management, Massachusetts College of Liberal Arts, 375 Church Street, North Adams, MA 01247-4100. Telephone: 413-662-5410 Ext. 5416 or toll-free 800-292-6632 (in-state). Fax: 413-662-5179. E-mail: admissions@nasc.mass.edu. Web site: http://www.mcla.edu/.

MASSACHUSETTS COLLEGE OF PHARMACY AND HEALTH SCIENCES
BOSTON, MASSACHUSETTS

General Independent, university, coed **Entrance** Moderately difficult **Setting** 2-acre urban campus **Total enrollment** 1,886 **Student/faculty ratio** 14:1 **Application deadline** 3/1 (freshmen), 3/1 (transfer) **Freshmen** 76% were admitted **Housing** Yes **Expenses** Tuition $17,343; Room & Board $8400 **Undergraduates** 65% women, 38% part-time **The most frequently chosen baccalaureate field is** health professions and related sciences **Academic program** English as a second language, advanced placement, summer session, adult/continuing education programs, internships **Contact** Ms. Kathleen Houghton, Director of Admission, Massachusetts College of Pharmacy and Health Sciences, 179 Longwood Avenue, Boston, MA 02115. Telephone: 617-732-2850 Ext. 2987 or toll-free 800-225-5506 (out-of-state). Fax: 617-732-2801. E-mail: admissions@mcp.edu. Web site: http://www.mcp.edu/.

MASSACHUSETTS INSTITUTE OF TECHNOLOGY
CAMBRIDGE, MASSACHUSETTS

General Independent, university, coed **Entrance** Most difficult **Setting** 154-acre urban campus **Total enrollment** 10,090 **Application deadline** 1/1 (freshmen), 3/15 (transfer) **Freshmen** 16% were admitted **Housing** Yes **Expenses** Tuition 26,050; Room & Board 7175 **Undergraduates** 41% women, 1% part-time, 1% 25 or older, 2% Native American, 11% Hispanic American, 6% African American, 27% Asian American/Pacific Islander **The most frequently chosen baccalaureate fields are** computer/information sciences, biological/life sciences, engineering/engineering technologies **Academic program** English as a second language, advanced placement, accelerated degree program, self-designed majors, summer session, internships **Contact** Ms. Marilee Jones, Dean of Admissions, Massachusetts Institute of Technology, 77 Massachusetts Avenue, Cambridge, MA 02139-4307. Telephone: 617-253-4791. E-mail: mitfrosh@mit.edu. Web site: http://web.mit.edu/.

MASSACHUSETTS MARITIME ACADEMY
BUZZARDS BAY, MASSACHUSETTS

General State-supported, 4-year, coed, primarily men **Entrance** Moderately difficult **Setting** 55-acre small-town campus **Total enrollment** 831 **Student/faculty ratio** 12:1 **Application deadline** Rolling (freshmen), rolling (transfer) **Freshmen** 72% were admitted **Housing** Yes **Expenses** Tuition $4016; Room & Board $5403 **Undergraduates** 13% women, 6% part-time, 6% 25 or older **The most frequently chosen baccalaureate fields are** engineering/engineering technologies, natural resources/environmental science **Academic program** Advanced placement, summer session, adult/continuing education programs, internships **Contact** Roy Fulgueras, Director of Admissions, Massachusetts Maritime Academy, 101 Academy Drive, Buzzards Bay, MA 02532-1803. Telephone: 508-830-5031 or toll-free 800-544-3411. Fax: 508-830-5077. E-mail: mmadmit@bridge.mma.mass.edu. Web site: http://www.mma.mass.edu/.

MERRIMACK COLLEGE
NORTH ANDOVER, MASSACHUSETTS

General Independent Roman Catholic, comprehensive, coed **Entrance** Moderately difficult **Setting** 220-acre suburban campus **Total enrollment** 2,587 **Student/faculty ratio** 14:1 **Application deadline** 2/15 (freshmen), 6/1 (transfer) **Freshmen** 70% were admitted **Housing** Yes **Expenses** Tuition $16,775; Room & Board $7750 **Undergraduates** 52% women, 19% part-time, 16% 25 or older, 0.1% Native American, 3% Hispanic American, 1% African American, 1% Asian American/Pacific Islander **The most frequently chosen baccalaureate fields are** business/marketing, psychology, social sciences and history **Academic program** English as a second language, advanced placement, self-designed majors, honors program, summer session, adult/continuing educa-

Merrimack College *(continued)*

tion programs, internships **Contact** Ms. MaryLou Retelle, Dean of Admissions and Financial Aid, Merrimack College, Austin Hall, A22, North Andover, MA 01845. Telephone: 978-837-5100 Ext. 5120. Fax: 978-837-5133. E-mail: admissions@merrimack.edu. Web site: http://www.merrimack.edu/.

MONTSERRAT COLLEGE OF ART
BEVERLY, MASSACHUSETTS

General Independent, 4-year, coed **Entrance** Moderately difficult **Setting** 10-acre suburban campus **Total enrollment** 402 **Student/faculty ratio** 11:1 **Application deadline** 8/1 (freshmen), rolling (transfer) **Freshmen** 84% were admitted **Housing** Yes **Expenses** Tuition 15,490; Room only 4258 **Undergraduates** 57% women, 9% part-time, 1% 25 or older, 1% Native American, 1% Hispanic American, 1% African American, 3% Asian American/Pacific Islander **The most frequently chosen baccalaureate field is** visual/performing arts **Academic program** English as a second language, advanced placement, self-designed majors, summer session, adult/continuing education programs, internships **Contact** Mr. Stephen M. Negron, Director of Admissions, Montserrat College of Art, 41 Essex Street, Beverly, MA 01945. Telephone: 978-921-4242 Ext. 1153 or toll-free 800-836-0487. Fax: 978-921-4241. E-mail: admiss@montserrat.edu. Web site: http://www.montserrat.edu/.

MOUNT HOLYOKE COLLEGE
SOUTH HADLEY, MASSACHUSETTS

General Independent, comprehensive, women only **Entrance** Very difficult **Setting** 800-acre small-town campus **Total enrollment** 2,089 **Student/faculty ratio** 10:1 **Application deadline** 1/15 (freshmen), 5/31 (transfer) **Freshmen** 55% were admitted **Housing** Yes **Expenses** Tuition 25,370; Room & Board 7410 **Undergraduates** 3% part-time, 7% 25 or older, 0.4% Native American, 4% Hispanic American, 4% African American, 9% Asian American/Pacific Islander **The most frequently chosen baccalaureate fields are** biological/life sciences, English, social sciences and history **Academic program** Advanced placement, self-designed majors, honors program, adult/continuing education programs, internships **Contact** Diane Anci, Director of Admission, Mount Holyoke College, 50 College Street, South Hadley, MA 01075. Telephone: 413-538-2023. Fax: 413-538-2409. E-mail: admissions@mtholyoke.edu. Web site: http://www.mtholyoke.edu/.

MOUNT IDA COLLEGE
NEWTON CENTRE, MASSACHUSETTS

General Independent, 4-year, coed **Entrance** Minimally difficult **Setting** 85-acre suburban campus **Total enrollment** 1,471 **Application deadline** Rolling (freshmen), rolling (transfer) **Freshmen** 80% were admitted **Housing** Yes **Expenses** Tuition $15,830; Room & Board $8950 **Undergraduates** 59% women, 12% part-time, 8% 25 or older, 1% Native American, 6% Hispanic American, 18% African American, 5% Asian American/Pacific Islander **Academic program** English as a second language, accelerated degree program, self-designed majors, honors program, adult/continuing education programs, internships **Contact** Ms. Nancy Lemelman, Director of Admissions, Mount Ida College, 777 Dedham Street, Newton Centre, MA 02459. Telephone: 617-928-4500. E-mail: admissions@mountida.edu. Web site: http://www.mountida.edu/.

NEW ENGLAND CONSERVATORY OF MUSIC
BOSTON, MASSACHUSETTS

General Independent, comprehensive, coed **Entrance** Very difficult **Setting** urban campus **Total enrollment** 783 **Student/faculty ratio** 9:1 **Application deadline** 12/1 (freshmen), 12/1 (transfer) **Freshmen** 48% were admitted **Housing** Yes **Expenses** Tuition 20,800; Room & Board 8950 **Undergraduates** 45% women, 11% part-time, 7% 25 or older, 0.5% Native American, 3% Hispanic American, 4% African American, 7% Asian American/Pacific Islander **The most frequently chosen baccalaureate field is** visual/performing arts **Academic program** English as a second language, advanced placement, summer session, adult/continuing education programs, internships **Contact** Dean of Enrollment Services, New England Conservatory of Music, 290 Huntington Avenue, Boston, MA 02115-5000. Telephone: 617-585-1101. Fax: 617-585-1115. E-mail: admissions@newenglandconservatory.edu. Web site: http://www.newenglandconservatory.edu/.

NEW ENGLAND INSTITUTE OF APPLIED ARTS AND SCIENCES
See Mount Ida College

THE NEW ENGLAND SCHOOL OF ART AND DESIGN AT SUFFOLK UNIVERSITY
See Suffolk University

NICHOLS COLLEGE
DUDLEY, MASSACHUSETTS

General Independent, comprehensive, coed **Entrance** Moderately difficult **Setting** 210-acre rural campus **Total enrollment** 1,363 **Student/faculty ratio** 18:1 **Application deadline** Rolling (freshmen), rolling (transfer) **Freshmen** 85% were admitted **Housing** Yes **Expenses** Tuition $15,650; Room & Board $7810 **Undergraduates** 47% women, 42% part-time, 5% 25 or older **The most frequently chosen baccalaureate fields are** business/marketing, English, psychology **Academic program** Advanced placement, summer session, adult/continuing education programs, internships **Contact** Susan Montville, Admissions Assistant, Nichols College, P.O. Box 5000, Office of Admissions, Dudley, MA 01571. Telephone: 508-943-2055 or toll-free 800-470-3379. Fax:

508-943-9885. E-mail: sibolesl@nichols.edu. Web site: http://www.nichols.edu/.

NORTH ADAMS STATE COLLEGE

See Massachusetts College of Liberal Arts

NORTHEASTERN UNIVERSITY

BOSTON, MASSACHUSETTS

General Independent, university, coed **Entrance** Moderately difficult **Setting** 60-acre urban campus **Total enrollment** 17,990 **Student/faculty ratio** 16:1 **Application deadline** Rolling (freshmen), rolling (transfer) **Freshmen** 70% were admitted **Housing** Yes **Expenses** Tuition 19,590; Room & Board 9135 **Undergraduates** 50% women, 4% 25 or older, 0.2% Native American, 4% Hispanic American, 5% African American, 7% Asian American/Pacific Islander **The most frequently chosen baccalaureate fields are** business/marketing, engineering/engineering technologies, health professions and related sciences **Academic program** English as a second language, advanced placement, accelerated degree program, self-designed majors, honors program, summer session, adult/continuing education programs, internships **Contact** J. Robert Spatig, Interim Director of Admissions, Northeastern University, 150 Richards Hall, Boston, MA 02115-5096. Telephone: 617-373-2200. Fax: 617-373-8780. E-mail: admissions@neu.edu. Web site: http://www.neu.edu/.

► **For more information, see page 456.**

PINE MANOR COLLEGE

CHESTNUT HILL, MASSACHUSETTS

General Independent, 4-year, women only **Entrance** Moderately difficult **Setting** 65-acre suburban campus **Total enrollment** 370 **Student/faculty ratio** 13:1 **Application deadline** Rolling (freshmen), rolling (transfer) **Freshmen** 78% were admitted **Housing** Yes **Expenses** Tuition 11,894; Room & Board 7450 **Undergraduates** 3% part-time, 10% 25 or older **The most frequently chosen baccalaureate fields are** business/marketing, psychology, visual/performing arts **Academic program** English as a second language, advanced placement, self-designed majors, honors program, summer session, adult/continuing education programs, internships **Contact** Mr. Bill Nichols, Dean of Admissions, Pine Manor College, 400 Heath Street, Chestnut Hill, MA 02167-2332. Telephone: 617-731-7104 or toll-free 800-762-1357. Fax: 617-731-7199. E-mail: admisso@pmc.edu. Web site: http://www.pmc.edu/.

REGIS COLLEGE

WESTON, MASSACHUSETTS

General Independent Roman Catholic, comprehensive, women only **Entrance** Moderately difficult **Setting** 168-acre small-town campus **Total enrollment** 1,138 **Student/faculty ratio** 10:1 **Application deadline** Rolling (freshmen), rolling (transfer) **Freshmen** 89% were admitted **Housing** Yes **Expenses** Tuition $17,500; Room & Board $8100 **Undergraduates** 25% part-time, 12% 25 or older, 0.1% Native American, 6% Hispanic American, 4% African American, 5% Asian American/Pacific Islander **The most frequently chosen baccalaureate fields are** health professions and related sciences, communications/communication technologies, social sciences and history **Academic program** English as a second language, advanced placement, self-designed majors, honors program, summer session, adult/continuing education programs, internships **Contact** Ms. Donna L. Gibbons, Director of Admission, Regis College, 235 Wellesley Street, Weston, MA 02493. Telephone: 781-768-7065 or toll-free 800-456-1820. Fax: 781-768-7071. E-mail: admission@regiscollege.edu/. Web site: http://www.regiscollege.edu/.

SAINT JOHN'S SEMINARY COLLEGE OF LIBERAL ARTS

BRIGHTON, MASSACHUSETTS

General Independent Roman Catholic, 4-year, men only **Entrance** Minimally difficult **Setting** 70-acre urban campus **Total enrollment** 32 **Student/faculty ratio** 12:1 **Application deadline** 8/1 (freshmen), 8/1 (transfer) **Freshmen** 73% were admitted **Housing** Yes **Expenses** Tuition $10,000 **Undergraduates** 50% 25 or older, 9% Hispanic American, 13% Asian American/Pacific Islander **The most frequently chosen baccalaureate field is** philosophy, religion, and theology **Academic program** English as a second language, self-designed majors **Contact** Rev. Robert W. Flagg, Dean of the College, Saint John's Seminary College of Liberal Arts, 127 Lake Street, Brighton, MA 02135. Telephone: 617-746-5460. Fax: 617-746-5499.

SALEM STATE COLLEGE

SALEM, MASSACHUSETTS

General State-supported, comprehensive, coed **Entrance** Minimally difficult **Setting** 62-acre small-town campus **Total enrollment** 13,417 **Student/faculty ratio** 16:1 **Application deadline** Rolling (freshmen), rolling (transfer) **Freshmen** 58% were admitted **Housing** Yes **Expenses** Tuition $3583; Room & Board $2860 **Undergraduates** 63% women, 22% part-time, 18% 25 or older, 1% Native American, 3% Hispanic American, 5% African American, 2% Asian American/Pacific Islander **The most frequently chosen baccalaureate fields are** business/marketing, education, health professions and related sciences **Academic program** English as a second language, advanced placement, self-designed majors, honors program, summer session, adult/continuing education programs, internships **Contact** Mr. Nate Bryant, Director of Admissions, Salem State College, 352 Lafayette Street, Salem, MA 01970-5353. Telephone: 978-542-6200. Web site: http://www.salemstate.edu/.

Salem State College *(continued)*

SCHOOL OF THE MUSEUM OF FINE ARTS
BOSTON, MASSACHUSETTS

General Independent, comprehensive, coed **Entrance** Moderately difficult **Setting** 14-acre urban campus **Total enrollment** 900 **Application deadline** Rolling (freshmen), rolling (transfer) **Housing** No **Expenses** Tuition $18,560 **Undergraduates** 26% 25 or older, 0.2% Native American, 2% Hispanic American, 1% African American, 4% Asian American/Pacific Islander **Academic program** Self-designed majors, summer session, adult/continuing education programs, internships **Contact** Mr. John A. Williamson, Director of Enrollment and Student Services, School of the Museum of Fine Arts, 230 The Fenway, Boston, MA 02115. Telephone: 617-369-3626 or toll-free 800-643-6078 (in-state). Fax: 617-369-3679. E-mail: info@smfa.edu. Web site: http://www.smfa.edu/.

SIMMONS COLLEGE
BOSTON, MASSACHUSETTS

General Independent, comprehensive, coed, primarily women **Entrance** Moderately difficult **Setting** 12-acre urban campus **Total enrollment** 3,340 **Student/faculty ratio** 10:1 **Application deadline** 2/1 (freshmen), 4/1 (transfer) **Freshmen** 65% were admitted **Housing** Yes **Expenses** Tuition $20,890; Room & Board $8410 **Undergraduates** 100% women, 11% part-time, 16% 25 or older, 0.2% Native American, 3% Hispanic American, 7% African American, 6% Asian American/Pacific Islander **The most frequently chosen baccalaureate fields are** health professions and related sciences, biological/life sciences, social sciences and history **Academic program** English as a second language, advanced placement, accelerated degree program, self-designed majors, honors program, summer session, adult/continuing education programs, internships **Contact** Ms. Patricia A. Tencza, Director of Undergraduate Admissions, Simmons College, 300 The Fenway, Boston, MA 02115. Telephone: 617-521-2051 or toll-free 800-345-8468 (out-of-state). Fax: 617-521-3190. E-mail: yadm@vmsvax.simmons.edu. Web site: http://www.simmons.edu/.

SIMON'S ROCK COLLEGE OF BARD
GREAT BARRINGTON, MASSACHUSETTS

General Independent, 4-year, coed **Entrance** Very difficult **Setting** 275-acre rural campus **Total enrollment** 387 **Student/faculty ratio** 8:1 **Application deadline** 6/15 (freshmen), 7/15 (transfer) **Freshmen** 70% were admitted **Housing** Yes **Expenses** Tuition 24,350; Room & Board 6700 **Undergraduates** 57% women, 1% part-time, 0% 25 or older, 1% Native American, 3% Hispanic American, 4% African American, 8% Asian American/Pacific Islander **The most frequently chosen baccalaureate fields are** social sciences and history, physical sciences, visual/performing arts **Academic program** Self-designed majors, adult/continuing education programs, internships **Contact** Ms. Mary King Austin, Director of Admissions, Simon's Rock College of Bard, 84 Alford Road, Great Barrington, MA 01230-9702. Telephone: 413-528-7317 or toll-free 800-235-7186. Fax: 413-528-7334. E-mail: admit@simons-rock.edu. Web site: http://www.simons-rock.edu/.

SMITH COLLEGE
NORTHAMPTON, MASSACHUSETTS

General Independent, comprehensive, women only **Entrance** Very difficult **Setting** 125-acre urban campus **Total enrollment** 3,113 **Student/faculty ratio** 10:1 **Application deadline** 1/15 (freshmen), 6/15 (transfer) **Freshmen** 53% were admitted **Housing** Yes **Expenses** Tuition 23,400; Room & Board 8160 **Undergraduates** 2% part-time, 8% 25 or older, 1% Native American, 5% Hispanic American, 5% African American, 10% Asian American/Pacific Islander **The most frequently chosen baccalaureate fields are** social sciences and history, biological/life sciences, visual/performing arts **Academic program** Advanced placement, accelerated degree program, self-designed majors, honors program, adult/continuing education programs, internships **Contact** Ms. Audrey Y. Smith, Director of Admissions, Smith College, 7 College Lane, Northampton, MA 01063. Telephone: 413-585-2500. Fax: 413-585-2527. E-mail: admission@smith.edu. Web site: http://www.smith.edu/.

SPRINGFIELD COLLEGE
SPRINGFIELD, MASSACHUSETTS

General Independent, comprehensive, coed **Entrance** Moderately difficult **Setting** 167-acre suburban campus **Total enrollment** 3,946 **Student/faculty ratio** 12:1 **Application deadline** 4/1 (freshmen), 5/1 (transfer) **Freshmen** 58% were admitted **Housing** Yes **Expenses** Tuition 17,300; Room & Board 6035 **Academic program** English as a second language, advanced placement, accelerated degree program, honors program, summer session, adult/continuing education programs, internships **Contact** Ms. Mary DeAngelo, Director of Admissions, Springfield College, 263 Alden Street, Box M, Springfield, MA 01109. Telephone: 413-748-3136 or toll-free 800-343-1257 (out-of-state). Fax: 413-748-3694. E-mail: admissions@spfldcol.edu. Web site: http://www.spfldcol.edu/.

▶ **For more information, see page 471.**

STONEHILL COLLEGE
EASTON, MASSACHUSETTS

General Independent Roman Catholic, comprehensive, coed **Entrance** Very difficult **Setting** 375-acre suburban campus **Total enrollment** 2,649 **Student/faculty ratio** 12:1 **Application deadline** 1/15 (freshmen), 4/1 (transfer) **Freshmen** 44% were admitted **Housing** Yes **Expenses** Tuition $17,320; Room & Board $8166 **Undergraduates** 59% women, 17% part-time, 1% 25 or older, 0.2% Native American, 2% Hispanic American, 2% African American, 2% Asian American/Pacific Islander **The most frequently cho-**

sen baccalaureate fields are business/marketing, education, social sciences and history **Academic program** Advanced placement, self-designed majors, honors program, summer session, adult/continuing education programs, internships **Contact** Mr. Brian P. Murphy, Dean of Admissions and Enrollment, Stonehill College, 320 Washington Street, Easton, MA 02357-5610. Telephone: 508-565-1373. Fax: 508-565-1545. E-mail: admissions@stonehill.edu. Web site: http://www.stonehill.edu/.

SUFFOLK UNIVERSITY
BOSTON, MASSACHUSETTS

General Independent, comprehensive, coed **Entrance** Moderately difficult **Setting** 2-acre urban campus **Total enrollment** 6,982 **Student/faculty ratio** 12:1 **Application deadline** Rolling (freshmen), rolling (transfer) **Freshmen** 79% were admitted **Housing** Yes **Expenses** Tuition $16,616; Room & Board $9990 **Undergraduates** 58% women, 23% part-time, 14% 25 or older, 0.1% Native American, 4% Hispanic American, 6% African American, 5% Asian American/Pacific Islander **The most frequently chosen baccalaureate fields are** business/marketing, communications/communication technologies, social sciences and history **Academic program** English as a second language, advanced placement, accelerated degree program, honors program, summer session, adult/continuing education programs, internships **Contact** Mr. Walter Caffey, Director of Undergraduate Admission, Suffolk University, 8 Ashburton Place, Boston, MA 02108. Telephone: 617-573-8460 or toll-free 800-6-SUFFOLK. Fax: 617-742-4291. E-mail: admission@admin.suffolk.edu. Web site: http://www.suffolk.edu/.

TUFTS UNIVERSITY
MEDFORD, MASSACHUSETTS

General Independent, university, coed **Entrance** Most difficult **Setting** 150-acre suburban campus **Total enrollment** 8,933 **Student/faculty ratio** 9:1 **Application deadline** 1/1 (freshmen), 3/1 (transfer) **Freshmen** 26% were admitted **Housing** Yes **Expenses** Tuition 25,714; Room & Board 7680 **Undergraduates** 53% women, 1% part-time, 0.1% Native American, 7% Hispanic American, 6% African American, 13% Asian American/Pacific Islander **The most frequently chosen baccalaureate fields are** engineering/engineering technologies, biological/life sciences, social sciences and history **Academic program** Advanced placement, self-designed majors, honors program, summer session, adult/continuing education programs, internships **Contact** Mr. David D. Cuttino, Dean of Undergraduate Admissions, Tufts University, Bendetson Hall, Tufts University, Medford, MA 02155. Telephone: 617-627-3170. Fax: 617-627-3860. E-mail: admissions.inquiry@ase.tufts.edu. Web site: http://www.tufts.edu/.

UNIVERSITY OF MASSACHUSETTS AMHERST
AMHERST, MASSACHUSETTS

General State-supported, university, coed **Entrance** Moderately difficult **Setting** 1,463-acre small-town campus **Total enrollment** 24,416 **Student/faculty ratio** 18:1 **Application deadline** 2/1 (freshmen), 5/1 (transfer) **Freshmen** 67% were admitted **Housing** Yes **Expenses** Tuition $5370; Room & Board $4895 **Undergraduates** 51% women, 8% part-time, 6% 25 or older, 0.4% Native American, 4% Hispanic American, 5% African American, 7% Asian American/Pacific Islander **The most frequently chosen baccalaureate fields are** business/marketing, communications/communication technologies, social sciences and history **Academic program** English as a second language, advanced placement, self-designed majors, honors program, summer session, adult/continuing education programs, internships **Contact** Mr. Joseph Marshall, Assistant Dean for Enrollment Services, University of Massachusetts Amherst, 37 Mather Drive, Amherst, MA 01003-9291. Telephone: 413-545-0222. Fax: 413-545-4312. E-mail: amh.admis@dpc.umassp.edu. Web site: http://www.umass.edu/.

UNIVERSITY OF MASSACHUSETTS BOSTON
BOSTON, MASSACHUSETTS

General State-supported, university, coed **Entrance** Moderately difficult **Setting** 177-acre urban campus **Total enrollment** 13,346 **Student/faculty ratio** 15:1 **Application deadline** 3/1 (freshmen), 3/1 (transfer) **Freshmen** 59% were admitted **Housing** No **Expenses** Tuition 4222 **Undergraduates** 57% women, 44% part-time, 47% 25 or older, 0.5% Native American, 6% Hispanic American, 14% African American, 11% Asian American/Pacific Islander **The most frequently chosen baccalaureate fields are** business/marketing, psychology, social sciences and history **Academic program** English as a second language, advanced placement, accelerated degree program, self-designed majors, honors program, summer session, adult/continuing education programs, internships **Contact** Office of Admissions Information Service, University of Massachusetts Boston, Office of Undergraduate Admissions, 100 Morrissey Boulevard, Boston, MA 02125-3393. Telephone: 617-287-6100. Fax: 617-287-6242. E-mail: bos.admiss@umassp.edu. Web site: http://www.umb.edu/.

UNIVERSITY OF MASSACHUSETTS DARTMOUTH
NORTH DARTMOUTH, MASSACHUSETTS

General State-supported, comprehensive, coed **Entrance** Moderately difficult **Setting** 710-acre suburban campus **Total enrollment** 7,122 **Student/faculty ratio** 13:1 **Application deadline** Rolling (freshmen), rolling (transfer) **Freshmen** 73% were admitted **Housing** Yes **Expenses** Tuition $4129; Room & Board $5143 **Undergraduates** 53% women, 20% part-time, 11% 25 or older, 1% Native Ameri-

University of Massachusetts Dartmouth *(continued)*

can, 2% Hispanic American, 5% African American, 2% Asian American/Pacific Islander **The most frequently chosen baccalaureate fields are** business/marketing, psychology, social sciences and history **Academic program** Advanced placement, self-designed majors, honors program, summer session, adult/continuing education programs, internships **Contact** Mr. Steven Briggs, Director of Admissions, University of Massachusetts Dartmouth, 285 Old Westport Road, North Dartmouth, MA 02747-2300. Telephone: 508-999-8606. Fax: 508-999-8755. E-mail: athompson@umassd.edu. Web site: http://www.umassd.edu/.

▶ **For more information, see page 479.**

UNIVERSITY OF MASSACHUSETTS LOWELL
LOWELL, MASSACHUSETTS

General State-supported, university, coed **Entrance** Moderately difficult **Setting** 100-acre urban campus **Total enrollment** 12,189 **Application deadline** Rolling (freshmen), rolling (transfer) **Freshmen** 67% were admitted **Housing** Yes **Expenses** Tuition $4255; Room & Board $4994 **Undergraduates** 17% 25 or older, 0.1% Native American, 3% Hispanic American, 2% African American, 8% Asian American/Pacific Islander **The most frequently chosen baccalaureate fields are** business/marketing, engineering/engineering technologies, health professions and related sciences **Academic program** Advanced placement, accelerated degree program, honors program, summer session, adult/continuing education programs, internships **Contact** Ms. Lisa Johnson, Assistant Vice Chancellor of Enrollment Management, University of Massachusetts Lowell, 883 Broadway Street, Room 110, Lowell, MA 01854-5104. Telephone: 978-934-3944 or toll-free 800-410-4607. Fax: 978-934-3086. E-mail: admissions@uml.edu. Web site: http://www.uml.edu/.

WELLESLEY COLLEGE
WELLESLEY, MASSACHUSETTS

General Independent, 4-year, women only **Entrance** Most difficult **Setting** 500-acre suburban campus **Total enrollment** 2,267 **Student/faculty ratio** 9:1 **Application deadline** 1/15 (freshmen), 2/10 (transfer) **Freshmen** 43% were admitted **Housing** Yes **Expenses** Tuition 24,174; Room & Board 7480 **Undergraduates** 3% part-time, 5% 25 or older **The most frequently chosen baccalaureate fields are** psychology, English, social sciences and history **Academic program** Advanced placement, self-designed majors, summer session, adult/continuing education programs, internships **Contact** Ms. Janet Lavin Rapelye, Dean of Admission, Wellesley College, 106 Central Street, Wellesley, MA 02481-8203. Telephone: 781-283-2270. Fax: 781-283-3678. E-mail: admission@wellesley.edu. Web site: http://www.wellesley.edu/.

WENTWORTH INSTITUTE OF TECHNOLOGY
BOSTON, MASSACHUSETTS

General Independent, 4-year, coed **Entrance** Moderately difficult **Setting** 35-acre urban campus **Total enrollment** 3,152 **Application deadline** Rolling (freshmen), rolling (transfer) **Freshmen** 67% were admitted **Housing** Yes **Expenses** Tuition $13,000; Room & Board $6800 **Undergraduates** 20% women, 18% part-time, 3% 25 or older, 0.5% Native American, 4% Hispanic American, 7% African American, 10% Asian American/Pacific Islander **The most frequently chosen baccalaureate fields are** architecture, computer/information sciences, engineering/engineering technologies **Academic program** English as a second language, advanced placement, accelerated degree program, summer session, internships **Contact** Ms. Keiko S. Broomhead, Director of Admissions, Wentworth Institute of Technology, 550 Huntington Avenue, Boston, MA 02115-5998. Telephone: 617-989-4009 or toll-free 800-556-0610. Fax: 617-989-4010. E-mail: admissions@wit.edu. Web site: http://www.wit.edu/.

▶ **For more information, see page 489.**

WESTERN NEW ENGLAND COLLEGE
SPRINGFIELD, MASSACHUSETTS

General Independent, comprehensive, coed **Entrance** Moderately difficult **Setting** 185-acre suburban campus **Total enrollment** 3,136 **Student/faculty ratio** 17:1 **Application deadline** Rolling (freshmen), rolling (transfer) **Freshmen** 69% were admitted **Housing** Yes **Undergraduates** 36% 25 or older, 0.2% Native American, 3% Hispanic American, 3% African American, 2% Asian American/Pacific Islander **The most frequently chosen baccalaureate fields are** business/marketing, engineering/engineering technologies, protective services/public administration **Academic program** Advanced placement, self-designed majors, honors program, summer session, adult/continuing education programs, internships **Contact** Dr. Charles R. Pollock, Dean of Enrollment Management, Western New England College, 1215 Wilbraham Road, Springfield, MA 01119. Telephone: 413-782-1321 or toll-free 800-325-1122 Ext. 1321. Fax: 413-782-1777. E-mail: ugradmis@wnec.edu. Web site: http://www.wnec.edu/.

WESTFIELD STATE COLLEGE
WESTFIELD, MASSACHUSETTS

General State-supported, comprehensive, coed **Entrance** Moderately difficult **Setting** 227-acre small-town campus **Total enrollment** 5,008 **Student/faculty ratio** 17:1 **Application deadline** 3/1 (freshmen), 4/1 (transfer) **Freshmen** 64% were admitted **Housing** Yes **Expenses** Tuition 2916; Room & Board 4556 **Undergraduates** 55% women, 20% part-time, 4% 25 or older, 0.3% Native American, 2% Hispanic American, 3% African American, 1% Asian American/Pacific Islander **The most frequently chosen baccalaureate fields are** education, business/marketing, protective services/public administration **Academic program** Advanced placement, accelerated degree program, self-designed majors, honors program, summer session, adult/continuing education programs, internships **Contact** Ms. Michelle Mattie, Director of Student Administrative Services, Westfield State College, 333 Western Avenue, Westfield, MA 01086. Telephone: 413-572-5218 or toll-free 800-322-8401 (in-state). Fax: 413-572-0520. E-mail: admission@wsc.mass.edu. Web site: http://www.wsc.ma.edu/.

WHEATON COLLEGE
NORTON, MASSACHUSETTS

General Independent, 4-year, coed **Entrance** Moderately difficult **Setting** 385-acre small-town campus **Total enrollment** 1,474 **Student/faculty ratio** 12:1 **Application deadline** 2/1 (freshmen), 4/1 (transfer) **Freshmen** 65% were admitted **Housing** Yes **Expenses** Tuition $24,450; Room & Board $6920 **Undergraduates** 64% women, 1% part-time, 1% 25 or older, 0.3% Native American, 3% Hispanic American, 4% African American, 2% Asian American/Pacific Islander **The most frequently chosen baccalaureate fields are** psychology, social sciences and history, visual/performing arts **Academic program** Advanced placement, accelerated degree program, self-designed majors, honors program, adult/continuing education programs, internships **Contact** Ms. Lynne M. Stack, Director of Admission, Wheaton College, East Main Street, Norton, MA 02766. Telephone: 508-286-8251 or toll-free 800-394-6003. Fax: 508-286-8271. E-mail: admission@wheatonma.edu. Web site: http://www.wheatoncollege.edu/.

WHEELOCK COLLEGE
BOSTON, MASSACHUSETTS

General Independent, comprehensive, coed, primarily women **Entrance** Moderately difficult **Setting** 5-acre urban campus **Total enrollment** 1,077 **Student/faculty ratio** 11:1 **Application deadline** 3/1 (freshmen), 4/15 (transfer) **Freshmen** 83% were admitted **Housing** Yes **Expenses** Tuition $17,410; Room & Board $6950 **Undergraduates** 94% women, 3% part-time, 6% 25 or older, 1% Native American, 4% Hispanic American, 7% African American, 3% Asian American/Pacific Islander **The most frequently chosen baccalaureate fields are** education, health professions and related sciences, protective services/public administration **Academic program** Advanced placement, honors program, internships **Contact** Ms. Lynne E. Dailey, Dean of Admissions, Wheelock College, 200 The Riverway, Boston, MA 02215. Telephone: 617-879-2204 or toll-free 800-734-5212 (out-of-state). Fax: 617-566-4453. E-mail: undergrad@wheelock.edu. Web site: http://www.wheelock.edu/.

WILLIAMS COLLEGE
WILLIAMSTOWN, MASSACHUSETTS

General Independent, comprehensive, coed **Entrance** Most difficult **Setting** 450-acre small town campus **Total enrollment** 2,066 **Student/faculty ratio** 9:1 **Application deadline** 1/1 (freshmen), 3/1 (transfer) **Freshmen** 24% were admitted **Housing** Yes **Expenses** Tuition 24,740; Room & Board 6730 **Undergraduates** 48% women, 2% part-time, 1% 25 or older, 0.4% Native American, 6% Hispanic American, 7% African American, 9% Asian American/Pacific Islander **The most frequently chosen baccalaureate fields are** biological/life sciences, English, social sciences and history **Academic program** Advanced placement, accelerated degree program, self-designed majors, honors program, internships **Contact** Mr. Thomas H. Parker, Director of Admission, Williams College, PO Box 487, Williamstown, MA 01267. Telephone: 413-597-2211. Fax: 413-597-4052. E-mail: admission@williams.edu. Web site: http://www.williams.edu/.

WORCESTER POLYTECHNIC INSTITUTE
WORCESTER, MASSACHUSETTS

General Independent, university, coed **Entrance** Very difficult **Setting** 80-acre suburban campus **Total enrollment** 3,874 **Student/faculty ratio** 13:1 **Application deadline** 2/1 (freshmen), 4/15 (transfer) **Freshmen** 77% were admitted **Housing** Yes **Expenses** Tuition 23,452; Room & Board 7592 **Undergraduates** 23% women, 4% part-time, 2% 25 or older, 0.3% Native American, 2% Hispanic American, 1% African American, 7% Asian American/Pacific Islander **The most frequently chosen baccalaureate fields are** biological/life sciences, computer/information sciences, engineering/engineering technologies **Academic program** English as a second language, advanced placement, accelerated degree program, self-designed majors, summer session, adult/continuing education programs **Contact** Ms. Kristin Tichenor, Director of Admissions, Worcester Polytechnic Institute, 100 Institute Road, Worcester, MA 01609. Telephone: 508-831-5286. Fax: 508-831-5875. E-mail: rgvoss@wpi.edu. Web site: http://www.wpi.edu/.

WORCESTER STATE COLLEGE
WORCESTER, MASSACHUSETTS

General State-supported, comprehensive, coed **Entrance** Moderately difficult **Setting** 53-acre urban campus **Total enrollment** 5,303 **Student/faculty ratio** 20:1 **Application deadline** 8/1 (freshmen), 8/1 (transfer) **Freshmen** 52% were admitted **Housing** Yes **Expenses** Tuition 2508; Room & Board 5000 **Undergraduates** 34% 25 or older, 1% Native American, 3% Hispanic American, 4% African American, 3% Asian American/Pacific Islander **The most frequently chosen baccalaureate fields are** business/marketing, health professions and related sciences, psychology **Academic program** Advanced placement, accelerated degree program, honors program, summer session, adult/continuing education programs, internships **Contact** Mr. Alan Kines, Director of Admissions, Worcester State College, 486 Chandler Street, Worcester, MA 01602-2597. Telephone: 508-929-8758. Fax: 508-929-8131. E-mail: admissions@worcester.edu. Web site: http://www.worcester.edu/.

MICHIGAN

ADRIAN COLLEGE
ADRIAN, MICHIGAN

General Independent, 4-year, coed, affiliated with United Methodist Church **Entrance** Moderately difficult **Setting** 100-acre small-town campus **Total enrollment** 1,082 **Student/faculty ratio** 12:1 **Application deadline** 8/1 (freshmen), 8/1 (transfer) **Freshmen** 86% were admitted **Housing** Yes **Expenses** Tuition $14,250; Room & Board $4990 **Undergraduates** 54% women, 6% part-time, 1% 25 or older, 0.3% Native American, 2% Hispanic American, 7% African American, 0.4% Asian American/Pacific Islander **The most frequently chosen baccalaureate fields are** business/marketing, parks and recreation, social sciences and history **Academic program** English as a second language, advanced placement, self-designed majors, honors program, summer session, adult/continuing education programs, internships **Contact** Ms. Janel Sutkus, Director of Admissions, Adrian College, 110 South Madison Street, Adrian, MI 49221. Telephone: 517-265-5161 Ext. 4326 or toll-free 800-877-2246. Fax: 517-264-3331. E-mail: admission@adrian.adrian.edu. Web site: http://www.adrian.edu/.

ALBION COLLEGE
ALBION, MICHIGAN

General Independent Methodist, 4-year, coed **Entrance** Moderately difficult **Setting** 225-acre small-town campus **Total enrollment** 1,522 **Student/faculty ratio** 12:1 **Application deadline** 5/1 (freshmen), rolling (transfer) **Freshmen** 85% were admitted **Housing** Yes **Expenses** Tuition 19,522; Room & Board 5594 **Undergraduates** 58% women, 1% part-time, 2% 25 or older, 0.5% Native American, 1% Hispanic American, 2% African American, 2% Asian American/Pacific Islander **The most frequently chosen baccalaureate fields are** biological/life sciences, business/marketing, social sciences and history **Academic program** Advanced placement, self-designed majors, honors program, summer session, internships **Contact** Doug Kellar, Associate Vice President for Enrollment, Albion College, 611 East Porter Street, Albion, MI 48224. Telephone: 517-629-0600 or toll-free 800-858-6770. E-mail: admissions@albion.edu. Web site: http://www.albion.edu/.

ALMA COLLEGE
ALMA, MICHIGAN

General Independent Presbyterian, 4-year, coed **Entrance** Moderately difficult **Setting** 100-acre small-town campus **Total enrollment** 1,409 **Student/faculty ratio** 14:1 **Application deadline** Rolling (freshmen), rolling (transfer) **Freshmen** 82% were admitted **Housing** Yes **Expenses** Tuition 15,884; Room & Board 5726 **Undergraduates** 59% women, 4% part-time, 2% 25 or older, 1% Native American, 2% Hispanic American, 2% African American, 1% Asian American/Pacific Islander **The most frequently chosen baccalaureate fields are** biological/life sciences, business/marketing, health professions and related sciences **Academic program** English as a second language, advanced placement, accelerated degree program, self-designed majors, summer session, adult/continuing education programs, internships **Contact** Mr. Paul Pollatz, Director of Admissions, Alma College, Admissions Office, Alma, MI 48801-1599. Telephone: 517-463-7139 or toll-free 800-321-ALMA. Fax: 517-463-7057. E-mail: admissions@alma.edu. Web site: http://www.alma.edu/.

▶ **For more information, see page 384.**

ANDREWS UNIVERSITY
BERRIEN SPRINGS, MICHIGAN

General Independent Seventh-day Adventist, university, coed **Entrance** Moderately difficult **Setting** 1,650-acre small-town campus **Total enrollment** 2,749 **Student/faculty ratio** 10:1 **Application deadline** Rolling (freshmen), rolling (transfer) **Freshmen** 54% were admitted **Housing** Yes **Expenses** Tuition $12,916; Room & Board $4060 **Undergraduates** 56% women, 17% part-time, 18% 25 or older, 0.3% Native American, 9% Hispanic American, 20% African American, 9% Asian American/Pacific Islander **The most frequently chosen baccalaureate fields are** biological/life sciences, education, health professions and related sciences **Academic program** English as a second language, advanced placement, accelerated degree program, self-designed majors, honors program, summer session, adult/continuing education programs, internships **Contact** Ms. Charlotte Coy, Admissions Supervisor, Andrews University, Berrien Springs, MI 49104. Telephone: 616-471-7771 or toll-free 800-253-2874. Fax: 616-471-3228. E-mail: enroll@andrews.edu. Web site: http://www.andrews.edu/.

AQUINAS COLLEGE
GRAND RAPIDS, MICHIGAN

General Independent Roman Catholic, comprehensive, coed **Entrance** Moderately difficult **Setting** 107-acre suburban campus **Total enrollment** 2,605 **Student/faculty ratio** 16:1 **Application deadline** Rolling (freshmen), rolling (transfer) **Freshmen** 83% were admitted **Housing** Yes **Expenses** Tuition $14,876; Room & Board $5176 **Undergraduates** 61% women, 25% part-time, 2% 25 or older, 0.2% Native American, 2% Hispanic American, 6% African American, 1% Asian American/Pacific Islander **The most frequently chosen baccalaureate fields are** business/marketing, education, social sciences and history **Academic program** Advanced placement, accelerated degree program, self-designed majors, honors program, summer session, adult/continuing education programs, internships **Contact** Ms. Lynn Atkins-Ryert, Staff Assistant/Applications Secretary, Aquinas College, 1607 Robinson Road, SE, Grand Rapids, MI 49506-1799. Telephone: 616-732-4460 Ext. 5150 or toll-free 800-678-9593. Fax: 616-732-4469. E-mail: admissions@aquinas.edu. Web site: http://www.aquinas.edu/.

▶ **For more information, see page 385.**

AVE MARIA COLLEGE
YPSILANTI, MICHIGAN

General Independent Roman Catholic, 4-year, coed **Entrance** Very difficult **Total enrollment** 135 **Student/faculty ratio** 10:1 **Expenses** Tuition 7050; Room & Board 3200 **Undergraduates** 53% women, 30% part-time **Contact** Joshua J. F. McCallen, Director of Admissions, Ave Maria College, 300 West Forest Avenue, Ypsilanti, MI 48197. Telephone: 877-285-9002. Web site: http://www.avemaria.edu/.

BAKER COLLEGE OF AUBURN HILLS
AUBURN HILLS, MICHIGAN

General Independent, 4-year, coed **Entrance** Noncompetitive **Setting** 7-acre urban campus **Total enrollment** 1,910 **Student/faculty ratio** 22:1 **Application deadline** Rolling (freshmen), rolling (transfer) **Freshmen** 100% were admitted **Housing** No **Expenses** Tuition 5400 **Undergraduates** 67% women, 47% part-time, 41% 25 or older, 1% Native American, 4% Hispanic American, 17% African American, 2% Asian American/Pacific Islander **Academic program** Advanced placement, accelerated degree program, summer session, internships **Contact** Ms. Jan Bohlen, Vice President for Admissions, Baker College of Auburn Hills, 1500 University Drive, Auburn Hills, MI 48326-1586. Telephone: 248-340-0600 or toll-free 888-429-0410 (in-state). Fax: 248-340-0608. E-mail: love_j@auburnhills.baker.edu. Web site: http://www.baker.edu/.

BAKER COLLEGE OF CADILLAC
CADILLAC, MICHIGAN

General Independent, 4-year, coed **Entrance** Noncompetitive **Setting** 40-acre small-town campus **Total enrollment** 864 **Student/faculty ratio** 16:1 **Application deadline** Rolling (freshmen), rolling (transfer) **Freshmen** 100% were admitted **Housing** No **Expenses** Tuition 5400 **Undergraduates** 72% women, 52% part-time, 56% 25 or older, 0% Native American, 0.2% Hispanic American, 0.5% African American, 0.2% Asian American/Pacific Islander **Academic program** Advanced placement, summer session, internships **Contact** Eric Runstrom, Vice President for Admissions, Baker College of Cadillac, 9600 East 13th Street, Cadillac, MI 49601. Telephone: 616-775-8458 or toll-free 888-313-3463 (in-state); 231-876-3100 (out-of-state). Fax: 231-775-8505. E-mail: musolf_c@cadillac.baker.edu. Web site: http://www.baker.edu/.

BAKER COLLEGE OF CLINTON TOWNSHIP
CLINTON TOWNSHIP, MICHIGAN

General Independent, 4-year, coed **Entrance** Noncompetitive **Setting** urban campus **Total enrollment** 2,560 **Student/faculty ratio** 19:1 **Application deadline** Rolling (freshmen), rolling (transfer) **Freshmen** 46% were admitted **Housing** No **Expenses** Tuition 5400 **Undergraduates** 77% women, 51% part-time, 42% 25 or older, 1% Native American, 1% Hispanic American, 13% African American, 1% Asian American/Pacific Islander **Academic program** Advanced placement, summer session, internships **Contact** Ms. Annette M. Looser, Vice President for Admissions, Baker College of Clinton Township, 34950 Little Mack Avenue, Clinton Township, MI 48035. Telephone: 810-791-6610 or toll-free 888-272-2842. Fax: 810-791-6611. E-mail: looser_a@mt.clemens.baker.edu. Web site: http://www.baker.edu/.

BAKER COLLEGE OF FLINT
FLINT, MICHIGAN

General Independent, 4-year, coed **Entrance** Noncompetitive **Setting** 30-acre urban campus **Total enrollment** 3,901 **Student/faculty ratio** 37:1 **Application deadline** 9/20 (freshmen), 9/20 (transfer) **Freshmen** 100% were admitted **Housing** Yes **Expenses** Tuition $5580; Room only $1950 **Undergraduates** 67% women, 49% part-time, 1% Native American, 2% Hispanic American, 17% African American, 2% Asian American/Pacific Islander **The most frequently chosen baccalaureate fields are** business/marketing, health professions and related sciences, visual/performing arts **Academic program** Advanced placement, accelerated degree program, summer session, internships **Contact** Mr. Mark Heaton, Vice President for Admissions, Baker College of Flint, 1050 West Bristol Road, Flint, MI 48507-5508. Telephone: 810-766-4015 or toll-free 800-964-4299. Fax: 810-766-4049. E-mail: heaton_m@flint.baker.edu. Web site: http://www.baker.edu/.

BAKER COLLEGE OF JACKSON
JACKSON, MICHIGAN

General Independent, 4-year, coed **Entrance** Noncompetitive **Setting** 42-acre urban campus **Total enrollment** 1,201 **Student/faculty ratio** 13:1 **Application deadline** 9/19 (freshmen), rolling (transfer) **Freshmen** 100% were admitted **Housing** No **Expenses** Tuition $5400 **Undergraduates** 75% women, 54% part-time, 56% 25 or older, 1% Native American, 2% Hispanic American, 7% African American, 1% Asian American/Pacific Islander **The most frequently chosen baccalaureate field is** business/marketing **Academic program** Advanced placement, accelerated degree program, summer session, internships **Contact** Ms. Kelli Hoban, Director of Admissions, Baker College of Jackson, 2800 Springport Road, Jackson, MI 49202. Telephone: 517-788-7800 or toll-free 888-343-3683. Fax: 517-789-7331. E-mail: heldt_v@jackson.baker.edu. Web site: http://www.baker.edu/.

BAKER COLLEGE OF MUSKEGON
MUSKEGON, MICHIGAN

General Independent, 4-year, coed **Entrance** Noncompetitive **Setting** 40-acre suburban campus **Total**

Baker College of Muskegon *(continued)*

enrollment 2,727 **Student/faculty ratio** 30:1 **Application deadline** 9/24 (freshmen), rolling (transfer) **Freshmen** 75% were admitted **Housing** Yes **Expenses** Tuition $7440; Room only $2025 **Undergraduates** 68% women, 45% part-time, 45% 25 or older, 1% Native American, 3% Hispanic American, 13% African American, 1% Asian American/Pacific Islander **The most frequently chosen baccalaureate fields are** business/marketing, engineering/engineering technologies, health professions and related sciences **Academic program** Advanced placement, accelerated degree program, summer session, adult/continuing education programs, internships **Contact** Ms. Kathy Jacobson, Director of Admissions, Baker College of Muskegon, 1903 Marquette Avenue, Muskegon, MI 49442-3497. Telephone: 231-777-5207 or toll-free 800-937-0337 (in-state). Fax: 231-777-5201. E-mail: jacobs_k@muskegon.baker.edu. Web site: http://www.baker.edu/.

BAKER COLLEGE OF OWOSSO
OWOSSO, MICHIGAN

General Independent, 4-year, coed **Entrance** Noncompetitive **Setting** 32-acre small-town campus **Total enrollment** 1,905 **Student/faculty ratio** 38:1 **Application deadline** Rolling (freshmen), rolling (transfer) **Freshmen** 100% were admitted **Housing** Yes **Expenses** Tuition 7200; Room only 1950 **Undergraduates** 69% women, 40% part-time, 41% 25 or older, 1% Native American, 2% Hispanic American, 1% African American, 0.3% Asian American/Pacific Islander **The most frequently chosen baccalaureate fields are** business/marketing, computer/information sciences, health professions and related sciences **Academic program** Advanced placement, accelerated degree program, summer session, adult/continuing education programs, internships **Contact** Mr. Michael Konopacke, Director, Baker College of Owosso, 1020 South Washington Street, Owosso, MI 48867-4400. Telephone: 517-729-3353 or toll-free 800-879-3797. Fax: 517-729-3359. E-mail: lundee_b@owosso.baker.edu. Web site: http://www.baker.edu/.

BAKER COLLEGE OF PORT HURON
PORT HURON, MICHIGAN

General Independent, 4-year, coed **Entrance** Noncompetitive **Setting** 10-acre urban campus **Total enrollment** 1,230 **Student/faculty ratio** 13:1 **Application deadline** 9/24 (freshmen), rolling (transfer) **Freshmen** 100% were admitted **Housing** No **Expenses** Tuition $7440 **Undergraduates** 78% women, 47% part-time, 51% 25 or older, 0.5% Native American, 2% Hispanic American, 3% African American, 1% Asian American/Pacific Islander **Academic program** Advanced placement, accelerated degree program, summer session, internships **Contact** Mr. Daniel Kenny, Director of Admissions, Baker College of Port Huron, 3403 Lapeer Road, Port Huron, MI 48060-2597. Telephone: 810-985-7000 or toll-free 888-262-2442. Fax: 810-985-7066. E-mail: kenny_d@porthuron.baker.edu. Web site: http://www.baker.edu/.

CALVIN COLLEGE
GRAND RAPIDS, MICHIGAN

General Independent, comprehensive, coed, affiliated with Christian Reformed Church **Entrance** Moderately difficult **Setting** 370-acre suburban campus **Total enrollment** 4,309 **Student/faculty ratio** 15:1 **Application deadline** 8/15 (freshmen), rolling (transfer) **Freshmen** 99% were admitted **Housing** Yes **Expenses** Tuition $14,870; Room & Board $5180 **Undergraduates** 55% women, 5% part-time, 0% 25 or older, 0.4% Native American, 1% Hispanic American, 1% African American, 2% Asian American/Pacific Islander **The most frequently chosen baccalaureate fields are** business/marketing, education, social sciences and history **Academic program** English as a second language, advanced placement, accelerated degree program, self-designed majors, honors program, summer session, adult/continuing education programs, internships **Contact** Mr. Dale D. Kuiper, Director of Admissions, Calvin College, 3201 Burton Street, SE, Grand Rapids, MI 49546-4388. Telephone: 616-957-6106 or toll-free 800-668-0122. Fax: 616-957-6777. E-mail: admissions@calvin.edu. Web site: http://www.calvin.edu/.

▶ **For more information, see page 394.**

CENTER FOR CREATIVE STUDIES-COLLEGE OF ART AND DESIGN
DETROIT, MICHIGAN

General Independent, 4-year, coed **Entrance** Moderately difficult **Setting** 11-acre urban campus **Total enrollment** 1,086 **Student/faculty ratio** 9:1 **Application deadline** Rolling (freshmen), rolling (transfer) **Freshmen** 82% were admitted **Housing** Yes **Expenses** Tuition $17,640; Room only $3300 **Undergraduates** 41% women, 14% part-time, 1% Native American, 3% Hispanic American, 7% African American, 6% Asian American/Pacific Islander **The most frequently chosen baccalaureate field is** visual/performing arts **Academic program** English as a second language, advanced placement, summer session, internships **Contact** Office of Admissions, Center for Creative Studies-College of Art and Design, 201 East Kirby, Detroit, MI 48202-4034. Telephone: 313-664-7425 or toll-free 800-952-ARTS. Fax: 313-872-2739. E-mail: admissions@ccscad.edu. Web site: http://www.ccscad.edu/.

CENTRAL MICHIGAN UNIVERSITY
MOUNT PLEASANT, MICHIGAN

General State-supported, university, coed **Entrance** Moderately difficult **Setting** 854-acre small-town campus **Total enrollment** 26,775 **Student/faculty ratio** 23:1 **Application deadline** Rolling (freshmen), rolling (transfer) **Freshmen** 83% were admitted **Housing** Yes **Expenses** Tuition $3775; Room & Board $4828 **Undergraduates** 59% women, 15% part-time, 6% 25 or older, 1% Native American, 2% Hispanic American, 5% African American, 1% Asian American/Pacific Islander **The most frequently chosen baccalaureate fields are** business/marketing, education, health professions and related sciences **Academic program** English as a second language, advanced placement, accelerated degree program, self-designed majors, honors program, summer session, adult/continuing education programs, internships **Contact** Mrs. Betty J. Wagner, Director of Admissions, Central Michigan University, Office of Admissions, 105 Warriner Hall, Mt. Pleasant, MI 48859. Telephone: 517-774-3076. Fax: 517-774-7267. E-mail: 34inz2k@cmuvm.csv.cmich.edu. Web site: http://www.cmich.edu/.

CLEARY COLLEGE
HOWELL, MICHIGAN

General Independent, comprehensive, coed **Entrance** Moderately difficult **Setting** 27-acre small-town campus **Total enrollment** 885 **Student/faculty ratio** 10:1 **Application deadline** Rolling (freshmen), rolling (transfer) **Housing** No **Expenses** Tuition 9230 **Undergraduates** 62% women, 9% part-time, 84% 25 or older, 1% Native American, 0.5% Hispanic American, 7% African American, 1% Asian American/Pacific Islander **Academic program** Advanced placement, accelerated degree program, summer session, adult/continuing education programs, internships **Contact** Ms. Mary Krowleski, Admissions Representative, Cleary College, 3750 Cleary College Drive, Howell, MI 48843. Telephone: 517-548-3670 Ext. 2215 or toll-free 800-552-7805 Ext. 2249 (out-of-state). Fax: 517-552-7805. E-mail: admissions@cleary.edu. Web site: http://www.cleary.edu/.

► **For more information, see page 402.**

CONCORDIA COLLEGE
ANN ARBOR, MICHIGAN

General Independent, comprehensive, coed, affiliated with Lutheran Church–Missouri Synod **Entrance** Moderately difficult **Setting** 234-acre suburban campus **Total enrollment** 604 **Student/faculty ratio** 9:1 **Application deadline** Rolling (freshmen), rolling (transfer) **Freshmen** 85% were admitted **Housing** Yes **Expenses** Tuition $14,700; Room & Board $5800 **Undergraduates** 60% women, 17% part-time, 25% 25 or older, 1% Native American, 2% Hispanic American, 6% African American, 1% Asian American/Pacific Islander **The most frequently chosen baccalaureate fields are** business/marketing, education, health professions and related sciences **Academic program** Advanced placement, accelerated degree program, self-designed majors, summer session, adult/continuing education programs, internships **Contact** Ms. Kathleen Rowe, Director of Admissions, Concordia College, 4090 Geddes Road, Ann Arbor, MI 48105. Telephone: 734-995-7322 Ext. 7311 or toll-free 800-253-0680. Fax: 734-995-7455. E-mail: admissions@ccaa.edu. Web site: http://www.ccaa.edu/.

CORNERSTONE UNIVERSITY
GRAND RAPIDS, MICHIGAN

General Independent Baptist, 4-year, coed **Entrance** Moderately difficult **Setting** 132-acre suburban campus **Total enrollment** 1,848 **Student/faculty ratio** 16:1 **Application deadline** Rolling (freshmen), rolling (transfer) **Freshmen** 93% were admitted **Housing** Yes **Expenses** Tuition $12,005; Room & Board $4830 **Undergraduates** 60% women, 10% part-time, 5% 25 or older, 0.3% Native American, 2% Hispanic American, 5% African American, 1% Asian American/Pacific Islander **The most frequently chosen baccalaureate fields are** business/marketing, education, English **Academic program** Advanced placement, accelerated degree program, summer session, adult/continuing education programs, internships **Contact** Mr. Brent Rudin, Director of Admissions, Cornerstone University, 1001 East Beltline Avenue, NE, Grand Rapids, MI 49525. Telephone: 616-222-1426 or toll-free 800-787-9778. Fax: 616-222-1400. E-mail: admissions@cornerstone.edu. Web site: http://www.cornerstone.edu/.

DAVENPORT UNIVERSITY
DEARBORN, MICHIGAN

General Independent, comprehensive, coed **Entrance** Noncompetitive **Setting** 17-acre suburban campus **Total enrollment** 3,158 **Student/faculty ratio** 22:1 **Application deadline** Rolling (freshmen), rolling (transfer) **Freshmen** 100% were admitted **Housing** No **Expenses** Tuition $6984 **Undergraduates** 74% women, 49% part-time, 69% 25 or older, 1% Native American, 3% Hispanic American, 59% African American, 1% Asian American/Pacific Islander **The most frequently chosen baccalaureate fields are** business/marketing, health professions and related sciences **Academic program** Advanced placement, summer session, internships **Contact** Ms. Jennifer Salloum, Director of Admissions, Davenport University, 4801 Oakman Boulevard, Dearborn, MI 48126-3799. Telephone: 313-581-4400. Fax: 313-581-1985. E-mail: dbajmiller@davenport.edu. Web site: http://www.davenport.edu/.

DAVENPORT UNIVERSITY
GRAND RAPIDS, MICHIGAN

General Independent, comprehensive, coed **Entrance** Noncompetitive **Setting** 5-acre urban campus **Total enrollment** 2,214 **Student/faculty ratio** 19:1 **Application deadline** Rolling (freshmen), rolling (transfer) **Freshmen** 100% were admitted **Housing** Yes **Expenses** Tuition $9408; Room only $3200 **Undergraduates** 65% women, 62% part-time, 45% 25 or older, 1% Native American, 5% Hispanic American, 7% African American, 3% Asian American/Pacific Islander **The most frequently chosen baccalaureate fields are** business/marketing, computer/information sciences, law/legal studies **Academic program** English as a second language, advanced placement, accelerated degree program, summer session, adult/continuing education programs, internships **Contact** Mr. Paul David, Director of Admissions, Davenport University, 415 East Fulton, Grand Rapids, MI 49503. Telephone: 616-732-1200 or toll-free 800-632-9569 (out-of-state). Web site: http://www.davenport.edu/.

DAVENPORT UNIVERSITY
KALAMAZOO, MICHIGAN

General Independent, 4-year, coed **Entrance** Noncompetitive **Setting** 5-acre suburban campus **Total enrollment** 1,081 **Student/faculty ratio** 13:1 **Application deadline** Rolling (freshmen), rolling (transfer) **Housing** No **Expenses** Tuition $8940 **Undergraduates** 71% 25 or older, 0.5% Native American, 2% Hispanic American, 17% African American, 1% Asian American/Pacific Islander **The most frequently chosen baccalaureate fields are** computer/information sciences, business/marketing, law/legal studies **Academic program** English as a second language, summer session, adult/continuing education programs, internships **Contact** Ms. Deb Burley, Admissions Director, Davenport University, 4123 West Main Street, Kalamazoo, MI 49006-2791. Telephone: 616-382-2835 Ext. 3309 or toll-free 800-632-8928 Ext. 3308 (in-state). Fax: 616-382-2661. Web site: http://www.davenport.edu/.

DAVENPORT UNIVERSITY
LANSING, MICHIGAN

General Independent, 4-year, coed **Entrance** Noncompetitive **Setting** 2-acre suburban campus **Total enrollment** 1,140 **Application deadline** 9/15 (freshmen), 9/15 (transfer) **Housing** No **Expenses** Tuition $8364 **Undergraduates** 71% women, 60% part-time, 45% 25 or older, 0.3% Native American, 5% Hispanic American, 17% African American, 2% Asian American/Pacific Islander **Academic program** Advanced placement, accelerated degree program, self-designed majors, summer session, adult/continuing education programs, internships **Contact** Mr. Tom Woods, Associate Dean of Enrollment, Davenport University, 220 East Kalamazoo, Lansing, MI 48933-2197. Telephone: 517-484-2600 Ext. 288 or toll-free 800-331-3306 (in-state). Fax: 517-484-9719. E-mail: laadmissions@davenport.edu. Web site: http://www.davenport.edu/.

DAVENPORT UNIVERSITY
WARREN, MICHIGAN

General Independent, comprehensive, coed **Entrance** Noncompetitive **Setting** 9-acre suburban campus **Total enrollment** 2,561 **Student/faculty ratio** 20:1 **Application deadline** Rolling (freshmen), rolling (transfer) **Freshmen** 100% were admitted **Housing** No **Expenses** Tuition $6984 **Undergraduates** 77% women, 49% part-time, 68% 25 or older, 0.4% Native American, 1% Hispanic American, 40% African American, 2% Asian American/Pacific Islander **The most frequently chosen baccalaureate fields are** business/marketing, health professions and related sciences **Academic program** Advanced placement, summer session, internships **Contact** Ms. Gerri Pauvall, Director of Admissions, Davenport University, 27650 Dequindre Road, Warren, MI 48092-5209. Telephone: 810-558-8700. Fax: 810-558-7868. E-mail: wagpavone@davenport.edu. Web site: http://www.davenport.edu/.

EASTERN MICHIGAN UNIVERSITY
YPSILANTI, MICHIGAN

General State-supported, comprehensive, coed **Entrance** Moderately difficult **Setting** 460-acre suburban campus **Total enrollment** 23,181 **Student/faculty ratio** 19:1 **Application deadline** 6/30 (freshmen), 6/30 (transfer) **Freshmen** 73% were admitted **Housing** Yes **Expenses** Tuition $3900; Room & Board $5016 **Undergraduates** 61% women, 31% part-time, 24% 25 or older, 1% Native American, 2% Hispanic American, 16% African American, 2% Asian American/Pacific Islander **The most frequently chosen baccalaureate fields are** business/marketing, education, social sciences and history **Academic program** English as a second language, advanced placement, accelerated degree program, self-designed majors, honors program, summer session, adult/continuing education programs, internships **Contact** Ms. Judy Benfield-Tatum, Director of Admissions, Eastern Michigan University, Ypsilanti, MI 48197. Telephone: 734-487-3060 or toll-free 800-GO TO EMU. Fax: 734-487-1484. Web site: http://www.emich.edu/.

FERRIS STATE UNIVERSITY
BIG RAPIDS, MICHIGAN

General State-supported, comprehensive, coed **Entrance** Minimally difficult **Setting** 600-acre small-town campus **Total enrollment** 9,847 **Student/faculty ratio** 16:1 **Application deadline** Rolling (freshmen), rolling (transfer) **Freshmen** 87% were admitted **Housing** Yes **Expenses** Tuition $4386; Room & Board $5258 **Undergraduates** 44% women, 20% part-time, 1% Native American, 1% Hispanic American, 11% African American, 2% Asian American/Pacific Islander **The most frequently chosen baccalaureate fields are** business/marketing, engineering/engineering technologies, health professions and related sciences **Academic program** English as a second language, advanced placement, accelerated degree program, honors program, summer session, adult/continuing education programs, internships **Contact** Mr. Ronnie Higgs, Assistant Vice President/Dean of Enrollment Services, Ferris State University, PRK 110, Big Rapids, MI 49307-2742. Telephone: 231-591-2100 or toll-free 800-433-7747. Fax: 616-592-2978. E-mail: admissions@act01.ferris.edu. Web site: http://www.ferris.edu/.

▶ **For more information, see page 417.**

FINLANDIA UNIVERSITY
HANCOCK, MICHIGAN

General Independent, 4-year, coed, affiliated with Evangelical Lutheran Church in America **Entrance** Minimally difficult **Setting** 25-acre small-town campus **Total enrollment** 380 **Student/faculty ratio** 11:1 **Application deadline** 8/15 (freshmen), 8/15 (transfer) **Freshmen** 73% were admitted **Housing** Yes **Expenses** Tuition $12,150; Room & Board $4500 **Undergraduates** 67% women, 14% part-time, 34% 25 or older, 1% Native American, 0.3% Hispanic

American, 2% African American, 0% Asian American/ Pacific Islander **The most frequently chosen baccalaureate field is** business/marketing **Academic program** English as a second language, advanced placement, accelerated degree program, summer session, adult/continuing education programs, internships **Contact** Mr. Ben Larson, Director of Admissions, Finlandia University, 601 Quincy Street, Hancock, MI 49930. Telephone: 906-487-7311 Ext. 311 or toll-free 800-682-7604. Fax: 906-487-7383. E-mail: admissions@suomi.edu. Web site: http://www.suomi.edu/.

GMI ENGINEERING & MANAGEMENT INSTITUTE

See Kettering University

GRACE BIBLE COLLEGE

GRAND RAPIDS, MICHIGAN

General Independent, 4-year, coed, affiliated with Grace Gospel Fellowship **Entrance** Minimally difficult **Setting** 16-acre suburban campus **Total enrollment** 140 **Student/faculty ratio** 9:1 **Application deadline** 7/15 (freshmen) **Freshmen** 81% were admitted **Housing** Yes **Expenses** Tuition $7730; Room & Board $4500 **Undergraduates** 52% women, 14% part-time, 9% 25 or older, 1% Native American, 0% Hispanic American, 0% African American, 2% Asian American/Pacific Islander **The most frequently chosen baccalaureate fields are** business/marketing, education, visual/performing arts **Academic program** English as a second language, advanced placement, internships **Contact** Mr. Kevin Gilliam, Director of Enrollment, Grace Bible College, 1101 Aldon Street, SW, PO Box 910, Grand Rapids, MI 49509. Telephone: 616-538-2330 or toll-free 800-968-1887. Fax: 616-538-0599. E-mail: gbc@gbcol.edu. Web site: http://www.gbcol.edu/.

GRAND VALLEY STATE UNIVERSITY

ALLENDALE, MICHIGAN

General State-supported, comprehensive, coed **Entrance** Moderately difficult **Setting** 900-acre small-town campus **Total enrollment** 18,579 **Student/faculty ratio** 21:1 **Application deadline** 7/26 (freshmen), 7/26 (transfer) **Freshmen** 77% were admitted **Housing** Yes **Expenses** Tuition $4272; Room & Board $5030 **Undergraduates** 60% women, 19% part-time, 15% 25 or older, 1% Native American, 2% Hispanic American, 5% African American, 2% Asian American/Pacific Islander **The most frequently chosen baccalaureate fields are** business/marketing, health professions and related sciences, protective services/public administration **Academic program** English as a second language, advanced placement, accelerated degree program, honors program, summer session, adult/continuing education programs, internships **Contact** Ms. Jodi Chycinski, Director of Admissions, Grand Valley State University, 1 Campus Drive, Allendale, MI 49401. Telephone: 616-895-2025 or toll-free 800-748-0246. Fax: 616-895-2000. E-mail: go2gvsu@gvsu.edu. Web site: http://www.gvsu.edu/.

GREAT LAKES CHRISTIAN COLLEGE

LANSING, MICHIGAN

Contact Mr. Ray Maurer, Director of Admissions, Great Lakes Christian College, 6211 West Willow Highway, Lansing, MI 48917-1299. Telephone: 517-321-0242 or toll-free 800-YES-GLCC. Fax: 517-321-5902. Web site: http://www.glcc.edu/.

HILLSDALE COLLEGE

HILLSDALE, MICHIGAN

General Independent, 4-year, coed **Entrance** Very difficult **Setting** 200-acre small-town campus **Total enrollment** 1,138 **Student/faculty ratio** 11:1 **Application deadline** Rolling (freshmen), rolling (transfer) **Freshmen** 84% were admitted **Housing** Yes **Expenses** Tuition 13,840; Room & Board 5700 **Undergraduates** 50% women, 4% part-time, 1% 25 or older **The most frequently chosen baccalaureate fields are** business/marketing, biological/life sciences, social sciences and history **Academic program** Advanced placement, accelerated degree program, honors program, summer session, internships **Contact** Mr. Jeffrey S. Lantis, Director of Admissions, Hillsdale College, 33 East College Street, Hillsdale, MI 49242-1298. Telephone: 517-437-7341 Ext. 2327. Fax: 517-437-0190. E-mail: admissions@ac.hillsdale.edu. Web site: http://www.hillsdale.edu/.

HOPE COLLEGE

HOLLAND, MICHIGAN

General Independent, 4-year, coed, affiliated with Reformed Church in America **Entrance** Moderately difficult **Setting** 45-acre small-town campus **Total enrollment** 3,015 **Student/faculty ratio** 13:1 **Application deadline** Rolling (freshmen), rolling (transfer) **Freshmen** 89% were admitted **Housing** Yes **Expenses** Tuition $16,644; Room & Board $5224 **Undergraduates** 60% women, 5% part-time, 2% 25 or older, 0.3% Native American, 2% Hispanic American, 1% African American, 2% Asian American/Pacific Islander **The most frequently chosen baccalaureate fields are** biological/life sciences, business/marketing, English **Academic program** English as a second language, advanced placement, self-designed majors, summer session, internships **Contact** Office of Admissions, Hope College, 69 East 10th Street, PO Box 9000, Holland, MI 49422-9000. Telephone: 616-395-7850 or toll-free 800-968-7850. Fax: 616-395-7130. E-mail: admissions@hope.edu. Web site: http://www.hope.edu/.

KALAMAZOO COLLEGE

KALAMAZOO, MICHIGAN

General Independent, 4-year, coed, affiliated with American Baptist Churches in the U.S.A. **Entrance** Very difficult **Setting** 60-acre suburban campus **Total**

Kalamazoo College *(continued)*

enrollment 1,322 **Student/faculty ratio** 14:1 **Application deadline** 2/15 (freshmen), 2/15 (transfer) **Freshmen** 70% were admitted **Housing** Yes **Expenses** Tuition 19,764; Room & Board 5961 **Undergraduates** 57% women, 1% 25 or older, 0.2% Native American, 2% Hispanic American, 3% African American, 5% Asian American/Pacific Islander **The most frequently chosen baccalaureate fields are** biological/life sciences, business/marketing, social sciences and history **Academic program** English as a second language, advanced placement, adult/continuing education programs, internships **Contact** Mrs. Linda Wirgau, Records Manager, Kalamazoo College, Mandelle Hall, 1200 Academy Street, Kalamazoo, MI 49006-3295. Telephone: 616-337-7166 or toll-free 800-253-3602. E-mail: admissions@kzoo.edu. Web site: http://www.kzoo.edu/.

KENDALL COLLEGE OF ART AND DESIGN AT FERRIS STATE UNIVERSITY

GRAND RAPIDS, MICHIGAN

General Independent, 4-year, coed **Entrance** Minimally difficult **Setting** urban campus **Total enrollment** 744 **Student/faculty ratio** 13:1 **Application deadline** Rolling (freshmen), rolling (transfer) **Housing** No **Expenses** Tuition $8820 **Undergraduates** 57% women, 27% part-time, 28% 25 or older, 0.1% Native American, 2% Hispanic American, 4% African American, 2% Asian American/Pacific Islander **The most frequently chosen baccalaureate fields are** trade and industry, visual/performing arts **Academic program** Advanced placement, summer session, adult/continuing education programs, internships **Contact** Ms. Amy Packard, Director of Admissions, Kendall College of Art and Design at Ferris State University, 111 Division Avenue North, Grand Rapids, MI 49503-3194. Telephone: 616-451-2787 Ext. 109 or toll-free 800-676-2787. Fax: 616-831-9689. Web site: http://www.kcad.edu/.

KETTERING UNIVERSITY

FLINT, MICHIGAN

General Independent, comprehensive, coed **Entrance** Very difficult **Setting** 45-acre suburban campus **Total enrollment** 3,341 **Student/faculty ratio** 10:1 **Application deadline** Rolling (freshmen), rolling (transfer) **Freshmen** 72% were admitted **Housing** Yes **Expenses** Tuition 16,110; Room & Board 4340 **Undergraduates** 19% women, 3% 25 or older, 0.3% Native American, 2% Hispanic American, 7% African American, 4% Asian American/Pacific Islander **The most frequently chosen baccalaureate fields are** business/marketing, engineering/engineering technologies, mathematics **Academic program** Advanced placement, accelerated degree program, internships **Contact** Mr. Rawlan Lillard II, Director of Admissions, Kettering University, 1700 West Third Avenue, Flint, MI 48504-4898. Telephone: 810-762-7865 or toll-free 800-955-4464 Ext. 7865 (in-state); 800-955-4464 (out-of-state). Fax: 810-762-9837. E-mail: admissions@gmi.edu. Web site: http://www.kettering.edu/.

▶ **For more information, see page 436.**

LAKE SUPERIOR STATE UNIVERSITY

SAULT SAINTE MARIE, MICHIGAN

General State-supported, 4-year, coed **Entrance** Moderately difficult **Setting** 121-acre small-town campus **Total enrollment** 3,118 **Student/faculty ratio** 17:1 **Application deadline** 8/15 (freshmen), rolling (transfer) **Freshmen** 89% were admitted **Housing** Yes **Expenses** Tuition $4014; Room & Board $5078 **Undergraduates** 53% women, 22% part-time, 24% 25 or older, 8% Native American, 1% Hispanic American, 1% African American, 1% Asian American/Pacific Islander **The most frequently chosen baccalaureate fields are** business/marketing, engineering/engineering technologies, protective services/public administration **Academic program** Advanced placement, self-designed majors, honors program, summer session, adult/continuing education programs, internships **Contact** Mr. Kevin Pollock, Director of Admissions, Lake Superior State University, 650 West Easterday Avenue, Sault Saint Marie, MI 49783-1699. Telephone: 906-635-2670 or toll-free 888-800-LSSU Ext. 2231. Fax: 906-635-6669. E-mail: admissions@lakers.lssu.edu. Web site: http://www.lssu.edu/.

LAWRENCE TECHNOLOGICAL UNIVERSITY

SOUTHFIELD, MICHIGAN

General Independent, comprehensive, coed **Entrance** Moderately difficult **Setting** 110-acre suburban campus **Total enrollment** 4,117 **Student/faculty ratio** 12:1 **Application deadline** 4/15 (freshmen), 8/15 (transfer) **Freshmen** 78% were admitted **Housing** Yes **Expenses** Tuition 11,300; Room only 2400 **Academic program** Advanced placement, self-designed majors, honors program, summer session, adult/continuing education programs, internships **Contact** Mrs. Lisa Kujawa, Director of Admissions, Lawrence Technological University, 2100 West 10 Mile Road, Southfield, MI 48075. Telephone: 248-204-3180 or toll-free 800-225-5588. Fax: 248-204-3188. E-mail: admissions@ltu.edu. Web site: http://www.ltu.edu/.

MADONNA UNIVERSITY

LIVONIA, MICHIGAN

General Independent Roman Catholic, comprehensive, coed **Entrance** Moderately difficult **Setting** 49-acre suburban campus **Total enrollment** 3,819 **Student/faculty ratio** 17:1 **Application deadline** Rolling (freshmen), rolling (transfer) **Freshmen** 66% were admitted **Housing** Yes **Expenses** Tuition 7660; Room & Board 5054 **Undergraduates** 78% women, 55% part-time, 60% 25 or older, 0.4% Native American, 3% Hispanic American, 11% African American, 1% Asian American/Pacific Islander **The most frequently chosen baccalaureate fields are** health professions and related sciences, business/marketing, protective services/public administration **Academic program** English as a second language, advanced placement, accelerated degree program, summer session, adult/continuing education programs, internships **Contact** Mr. Frank J. Hribar, Director of

Enrollment Management, Madonna University, 36600 Schoolcraft Road, Livonia, MI 48150-1173. Telephone: 734-432-5317 or toll-free 800-852-4951. Fax: 734-432-5393. E-mail: muinfo@smtp.munet.edu. Web site: http://www.munet.edu/.

MARYGROVE COLLEGE
DETROIT, MICHIGAN

General Independent Roman Catholic, comprehensive, coed, primarily women **Entrance** Moderately difficult **Setting** 50-acre urban campus **Total enrollment** 5,644 **Student/faculty ratio** 15:1 **Application deadline** 8/15 (freshmen), 8/15 (transfer) **Freshmen** 58% were admitted **Housing** Yes **Expenses** Tuition $10,650; Room & Board $5200 **Undergraduates** 80% 25 or older, 0.3% Native American, 1% Hispanic American, 75% African American, 0.3% Asian American/Pacific Islander **The most frequently chosen baccalaureate fields are** business/marketing, education, protective services/public administration **Academic program** Advanced placement, self-designed majors, summer session, internships **Contact** Denise Williams, Interim Director, Marygrove College, 8425 West McNichols Road, Detroit, MI 48221-2599. Telephone: 313-927-1241. Fax: 313-927-1345. E-mail: info@marygrove.edu. Web site: http://www.marygrove.edu/.

MICHIGAN CHRISTIAN COLLEGE
See Rochester College

MICHIGAN STATE UNIVERSITY
EAST LANSING, MICHIGAN

General State-supported, university, coed **Entrance** Moderately difficult **Setting** suburban campus **Total enrollment** 43,366 **Student/faculty ratio** 18:1 **Application deadline** 7/30 (freshmen), 7/30 (transfer) **Freshmen** 69% were admitted **Housing** Yes **Expenses** Tuition $5772; Room & Board $4472 **Undergraduates** 53% women, 13% part-time, 5% 25 or older, 1% Native American, 2% Hispanic American, 9% African American, 4% Asian American/Pacific Islander **The most frequently chosen baccalaureate fields are** business/marketing, engineering/engineering technologies, social sciences and history **Academic program** English as a second language, advanced placement, accelerated degree program, self-designed majors, honors program, summer session, adult/continuing education programs, internships **Contact** Dr. Gordon Stanley, Assistant to the Provost for Enrollment and Director of Admissions, Michigan State University, East Lansing, MI 48824. Telephone: 517-355-8332. Fax: 517-353-1647. E-mail: adm00@msu.edu. Web site: http://www.msu.edu/.

MICHIGAN TECHNOLOGICAL UNIVERSITY
HOUGHTON, MICHIGAN

General State-supported, university, coed **Entrance** Moderately difficult **Setting** 240-acre small-town campus **Total enrollment** 6,336 **Student/faculty ratio** 12:1 **Application deadline** Rolling (freshmen), rolling (transfer) **Freshmen** 94% were admitted **Housing** Yes **Expenses** Tuition 4666; Room & Board 4917 **Undergraduates** 26% women, 13% part-time, 8% 25 or older, 1% Native American, 1% Hispanic American, 2% African American, 1% Asian American/Pacific Islander **The most frequently chosen baccalaureate fields are** business/marketing, computer/information sciences, engineering/engineering technologies **Academic program** English as a second language, advanced placement, self-designed majors, summer session, internships **Contact** Ms. Nancy Rehling, Director of Undergraduate Admissions, Michigan Technological University, 1400 Townsend Drive, Houghton, MI 49931-1295. Telephone: 906-487-2335. Fax: 906-487-3343. E-mail: mtu4u@mtu.edu. Web site: http://www.mtu.edu/.

NORTHERN MICHIGAN UNIVERSITY
MARQUETTE, MICHIGAN

General State-supported, comprehensive, coed **Entrance** Minimally difficult **Setting** 300-acre small-town campus **Total enrollment** 8,082 **Student/faculty ratio** 20:1 **Application deadline** Rolling (freshmen), rolling (transfer) **Freshmen** 85% were admitted **Housing** Yes **Expenses** Tuition $3234; Room & Board $4976 **Undergraduates** 54% women, 15% part-time, 16% 25 or older, 2% Native American, 1% Hispanic American, 1% African American, 0.5% Asian American/Pacific Islander **Academic program** Advanced placement, accelerated degree program, self-designed majors, summer session, adult/continuing education programs, internships **Contact** Ms. Gerri Daniels, Northern Michigan University, 1401 Presque Isle Avenue, Marquette, MI 49855. Telephone: 906-227-2650 or toll-free 800-682-9797 Ext. 1 (in-state); 800-682-9797 (out-of-state). Fax: 906-227-1747. E-mail: admiss@nmu.edu. Web site: http://www.nmu.edu/.

NORTHWOOD UNIVERSITY
MIDLAND, MICHIGAN

General Independent, comprehensive, coed **Entrance** Moderately difficult **Setting** 434-acre small-town campus **Total enrollment** 3,823 **Student/faculty ratio** 26:1 **Application deadline** Rolling (freshmen), rolling (transfer) **Freshmen** 96% were admitted **Housing** Yes **Expenses** Tuition 12,063; Room & Board 5592 **Undergraduates** 50% women, 43% part-time, 3% 25 or older **The most frequently chosen baccalaureate fields are** business/marketing, computer/information sciences **Academic program** English as a second language, advanced placement, accelerated degree program, honors program, summer session, adult/continuing education programs, internships **Contact** Dr. David D. Long, Vice President of Enrollment Management, Northwood University, 4000 Whiting Drive, Midland, MI 48640. Telephone: 517-837-4273 or toll-free 800-457-7878. Fax: 517-837-4490. E-mail: admissions@northwood.edu. Web site: http://www.northwood.edu/.

▶ **For more information, see page 458.**

OAKLAND UNIVERSITY
ROCHESTER, MICHIGAN

General State-supported, university, coed **Entrance** Moderately difficult **Setting** 1,444-acre suburban campus **Total enrollment** 15,235 **Student/faculty ratio** 21:1 **Application deadline** 8/28 (transfer) **Freshmen** 78% were admitted **Housing** Yes **Expenses** Tuition 4279; Room & Board 4833 **Undergraduates** 64% women, 32% part-time, 22% 25 or older, 0.4% Native American, 1% Hispanic American, 7% African American, 3% Asian American/Pacific Islander **The most frequently chosen baccalaureate fields are** business/marketing, education, health professions and related sciences **Academic program** English as a second language, advanced placement, accelerated degree program, self-designed majors, honors program, summer session, internships **Contact** Mr. Robert E. Johnson, Associate Vice President for Enrollment Management, Oakland University, 101 North Foundation Hall, Rochester, MI 48309-4401. Telephone: 248-370-3360 or toll-free 800-OAK-UNIV. Fax: 248-370-4462. E-mail: ouinfo@oakland.edu. Web site: http://www.oakland.edu/.

OLIVET COLLEGE
OLIVET, MICHIGAN

General Independent, comprehensive, coed, affiliated with Congregational Christian Church **Entrance** Minimally difficult **Setting** 92-acre small-town campus **Total enrollment** 960 **Student/faculty ratio** 14:1 **Application deadline** Rolling (freshmen), rolling (transfer) **Freshmen** 80% were admitted **Housing** Yes **Expenses** Tuition 13,592; Room & Board 4452 **Undergraduates** 48% women, 11% part-time, 8% 25 or older, 2% Native American, 2% Hispanic American, 20% African American, 5% Asian American/Pacific Islander **Academic program** Advanced placement, accelerated degree program, self-designed majors, honors program, summer session, internships **Contact** Mr. Kevin Leonard, Director of Admissions, Olivet College, 320 South Main Street, Olivet, MI 49076. Telephone: 616-749-7635 or toll-free 800-456-7189. Fax: 616-749-3821. E-mail: admissions@olivetcollege.edu. Web site: http://www.olivetcollege.edu/.

REFORMED BIBLE COLLEGE
GRAND RAPIDS, MICHIGAN

General Independent religious, 4-year, coed **Entrance** Moderately difficult **Setting** 27-acre suburban campus **Total enrollment** 280 **Student/faculty ratio** 10:1 **Application deadline** Rolling (freshmen), rolling (transfer) **Freshmen** 55% were admitted **Housing** Yes **Expenses** Tuition $7895; Room & Board $4200 **Undergraduates** 48% women, 17% part-time, 36% 25 or older, 1% Native American, 1% Hispanic American, 4% African American, 3% Asian American/Pacific Islander **The most frequently chosen baccalaureate field is** philosophy, religion, and theology **Academic program** Advanced placement, summer session, adult/continuing education programs, internships **Contact** Ms. Sarah Couwenhoven Behm, Associate Director of Admissions, Reformed Bible College, 3333 East Beltline North East, Grand Rapids, MI 49525. Telephone: 616-222-3000 Ext. 631 or toll-free 800-511-3749. Fax: 616-222-3045. E-mail: admissions@reformed.edu. Web site: http://www.reformed.edu/.

ROCHESTER COLLEGE
ROCHESTER HILLS, MICHIGAN

General Independent, 4-year, coed, affiliated with Church of Christ **Entrance** Minimally difficult **Setting** 83-acre suburban campus **Total enrollment** 830 **Student/faculty ratio** 11:1 **Application deadline** Rolling (freshmen), rolling (transfer) **Housing** Yes **Expenses** Tuition $8984; Room & Board $4768 **Undergraduates** 54% women, 31% part-time, 9% 25 or older, 1% Native American, 1% Hispanic American, 11% African American, 1% Asian American/Pacific Islander **The most frequently chosen baccalaureate fields are** business/marketing, English, psychology **Academic program** Advanced placement, accelerated degree program, summer session, adult/continuing education programs, internships **Contact** Mr. Larry Norman, Vice President for Enrollment Management, Rochester College, 800 West Avon Road, Rochester Hills, MI 48307-2764. Telephone: 248-218-2032 or toll-free 800-521-6010. Fax: 248-218-2005. E-mail: admissions@michchristian.edu. Web site: http://www.rc.edu/.

SACRED HEART MAJOR SEMINARY
DETROIT, MICHIGAN

General Independent Roman Catholic, comprehensive, coed **Entrance** Moderately difficult **Setting** 24-acre urban campus **Total enrollment** 377 **Student/faculty ratio** 8:1 **Application deadline** 7/31 (freshmen), 7/31 (transfer) **Freshmen** 100% were admitted **Housing** Yes **Expenses** Tuition $6862 **Undergraduates** 40% 25 or older, 7% Native American, 10% Hispanic American, 10% Asian American/Pacific Islander **The most frequently chosen baccalaureate field is** philosophy, religion, and theology **Academic program** Advanced placement, honors program **Contact** Mrs. Jane Jeffrey, Assistant Dean of Studies, Sacred Heart Major Seminary, 2701 Chicago Boulevard, Detroit, MI 48206. Telephone: 313-883-8712.

SAGINAW VALLEY STATE UNIVERSITY
UNIVERSITY CENTER, MICHIGAN

General State-supported, comprehensive, coed **Entrance** Moderately difficult **Setting** 782-acre rural campus **Total enrollment** 8,622 **Student/faculty ratio** 23:1 **Application deadline** Rolling (freshmen), rolling (transfer) **Housing** Yes **Expenses** Tuition $3607; Room & Board $5015 **Undergraduates** 29% 25 or older, 0.5% Native American, 3% Hispanic American, 6% African American, 1% Asian American/Pacific Islander **The most frequently chosen baccalaureate fields are** business/marketing, education, protective services/public administration **Academic**

program English as a second language, advanced placement, accelerated degree program, self-designed majors, honors program, summer session, internships **Contact** Mr. James P. Dwyer, Director of Admissions, Saginaw Valley State University, 7400 Bay Road, University Center, MI 48710. Telephone: 517-790-4200 or toll-free 800-968-9500. Fax: 517-790-0180. E-mail: admissions@tardis.svsu.edu. Web site: http://www.svsu.edu/.

SAINT MARY'S COLLEGE OF AVE MARIA UNIVERSITY

ORCHARD LAKE, MICHIGAN

General Independent Roman Catholic, 4-year, coed **Entrance** Moderately difficult **Setting** 120-acre suburban campus **Total enrollment** 479 **Student/faculty ratio** 12:1 **Application deadline** Rolling (freshmen), rolling (transfer) **Freshmen** 81% were admitted **Housing** Yes **Expenses** Tuition $6634; Room & Board $5140 **Undergraduates** 44% women, 46% part-time, 30% 25 or older, 1% Native American, 1% Hispanic American, 7% African American, 2% Asian American/Pacific Islander **The most frequently chosen baccalaureate fields are** biological/life sciences, communications/communication technologies, psychology **Academic program** English as a second language, advanced placement, accelerated degree program, internships **Contact** Mr. James Bass, Director of Admissions, Saint Mary's College of Ave Maria University, 3535 Indian Trail, Orchard Lake, MI 48324-1623. Telephone: 248-683-0523 or toll-free 877-252-3131 (in-state). Fax: 248-683-1756. E-mail: jbass@stmarys.ols.edu.

SIENA HEIGHTS UNIVERSITY

ADRIAN, MICHIGAN

General Independent Roman Catholic, comprehensive, coed **Entrance** Moderately difficult **Setting** 140-acre small-town campus **Total enrollment** 1,917 **Student/faculty ratio** 14:1 **Application deadline** Rolling (freshmen), rolling (transfer) **Freshmen** 73% were admitted **Housing** Yes **Expenses** Tuition $13,000; Room & Board $4750 **Undergraduates** 51% 25 or older, 0.3% Native American, 2% Hispanic American, 8% African American, 1% Asian American/Pacific Islander **The most frequently chosen baccalaureate fields are** business/marketing, education, health professions and related sciences **Academic program** Advanced placement, accelerated degree program, self-designed majors, summer session, adult/continuing education programs, internships **Contact** Mr. Kevin Kucera, Dean of Admissions and Enrollment Services, Siena Heights University, 1247 East Siena Heights Drive, Adrian, MI 49221-1796. Telephone: 517-264-7180 or toll-free 800-521-0009. Fax: 517-264-7745. E-mail: admssns@sienahts.edu. Web site: http://www.sienahts.edu.

SPRING ARBOR UNIVERSITY

SPRING ARBOR, MICHIGAN

General Independent Free Methodist, comprehensive, coed **Entrance** Moderately difficult **Setting** 70-acre small-town campus **Total enrollment** 2,558 **Student/faculty ratio** 16:1 **Application deadline** Rolling (freshmen), rolling (transfer) **Freshmen** 90% were admitted **Housing** Yes **Expenses** Tuition $12,416; Room & Board $4580 **Undergraduates** 69% women, 14% part-time **The most frequently chosen baccalaureate fields are** business/marketing, education, social sciences and history **Academic program** English as a second language, advanced placement, accelerated degree program, self-designed majors, honors program, summer session, adult/continuing education programs, internships **Contact** Mr. Jim Weidman, Director of Admissions, Spring Arbor University, 106 East Main Street, Spring Arbor, MI 49283-9799. Telephone: 517-750-1200 Ext. 1475 or toll-free 800-968-0011. Fax: 517-750-6620. E-mail: blouckes@admin.arbor.edu. Web site: http://www.arbor.edu/.

UNIVERSITY OF DETROIT MERCY

DETROIT, MICHIGAN

General Independent Roman Catholic (Jesuit), university, coed **Contact** Ms. Colleen Ezzeddine, Admissions Counselor, University of Detroit Mercy, PO Box 19900, Detroit, MI 48219-0900. Telephone: 313-993-1245 or toll-free 800-635-5020 (out-of-state). Fax: 313-993-3326. E-mail: admissions@udmercy.edu. Web site: http://www.udmercy.edu/.

UNIVERSITY OF MICHIGAN

ANN ARBOR, MICHIGAN

General State-supported, university, coed **Entrance** Very difficult **Setting** 2,861-acre suburban campus **Total enrollment** 37,595 **Student/faculty ratio** 16:1 **Application deadline** 2/1 (freshmen), 3/1 (transfer) **Freshmen** 55% were admitted **Housing** Yes **Expenses** Tuition 6513; Room & Board 5780 **Undergraduates** 52% women, 6% part-time, 4% 25 or older, 1% Native American, 4% Hispanic American, 8% African American, 12% Asian American/Pacific Islander **The most frequently chosen baccalaureate fields are** engineering/engineering technologies, psychology, social sciences and history **Academic program** English as a second language, advanced placement, accelerated degree program, self-designed majors, honors program, summer session, adult/continuing education programs, internships **Contact** Mr. Ted Spencer, Director of Undergraduate Admissions, University of Michigan, Ann Arbor, MI 48109-1316. Telephone: 734-764-7433. Fax: 734-936-0740. E-mail: ugadmiss@umich.edu. Web site: http://www.umich.edu/.

UNIVERSITY OF MICHIGAN–DEARBORN

DEARBORN, MICHIGAN

General State-supported, comprehensive, coed **Entrance** Moderately difficult **Setting** 210-acre suburban campus **Total enrollment** 8,484 **Application deadline** Rolling (freshmen), rolling (transfer) **Freshmen** 74% were admitted **Housing** No **Expenses** Tuition 4440 **Undergraduates** 31% 25 or older **The most frequently chosen baccalaureate fields are**

University of Michigan–Dearborn *(continued)*

business/marketing, engineering/engineering technologies, psychology **Academic program** Accelerated degree program, self-designed majors, honors program, summer session, adult/continuing education programs, internships **Contact** Mr. David Placey, Director of Admissions, University of Michigan–Dearborn, 4901 Evergreen Road, Dearborn, MI 48128-1491. Telephone: 313-593-5100. E-mail: umdgoblu@umd.umich.edu. Web site: http://www.umd.umich.edu/.

UNIVERSITY OF MICHIGAN–FLINT

FLINT, MICHIGAN

General State-supported, comprehensive, coed **Entrance** Moderately difficult **Setting** 72-acre urban campus **Total enrollment** 6,316 **Student/faculty ratio** 15:1 **Application deadline** 9/2 (freshmen), 8/21 (transfer) **Freshmen** 82% were admitted **Housing** No **Expenses** Tuition $3916 **Undergraduates** 65% women, 43% part-time, 38% 25 or older, 1% Native American, 2% Hispanic American, 11% African American, 1% Asian American/Pacific Islander **Academic program** Advanced placement, self-designed majors, honors program, summer session, adult/continuing education programs, internships **Contact** Dr. Virginia R. Allen, Vice Chancellor for Student Services and Enrollment, University of Michigan–Flint, 303 East Kearsley Street, Flint, MI 48502-1950. Telephone: 810-762-3434 or toll-free 800-942-5636 (in-state). Fax: 810-762-3272. E-mail: davis_m@pavilion.flint.umich.edu. Web site: http://www.flint.umich.edu/.

UNIVERSITY OF PHOENIX–GRAND RAPIDS CAMPUS

GRAND RAPIDS, MICHIGAN

General Proprietary, comprehensive, coed **Entrance** Noncompetitive **Total enrollment** 66,534 **Student/faculty ratio** 13:1 **Application deadline** Rolling (freshmen), rolling (transfer) **Expenses** Tuition 7740 **Undergraduates** 56% women, 86% 25 or older, 2% Native American, 18% Hispanic American, 13% African American, 6% Asian American/Pacific Islander **Academic program** Advanced placement, accelerated degree program, adult/continuing education programs **Contact** Ms. Beth Barilla, Director of Admissions, University of Phoenix–Grand Rapids Campus, 4615 East Elwood Street, Phoenix, AZ 85040-1948. Telephone: 480-927-0099 Ext. 1218 or toll-free 800-228-7240. Fax: 480-594-1758. E-mail: beth.barilla@apollogrp.edu. Web site: http://www.phoenix.edu/.

UNIVERSITY OF PHOENIX–METRO DETROIT CAMPUS

TROY, MICHIGAN

General Proprietary, comprehensive, coed **Entrance** Noncompetitive **Total enrollment** 66,534 **Student/faculty ratio** 13:1 **Application deadline** Rolling (freshmen), rolling (transfer) **Expenses** Tuition 7740 **Undergraduates** 56% women, 86% 25 or older, 2% Native American, 18% Hispanic American, 13% African American, 6% Asian American/Pacific Islander **Academic program** Advanced placement, accelerated degree program **Contact** Ms. Beth Barilla, Director of Admissions, University of Phoenix–Metro Detroit Campus, 4615 East Elwood Street, Phoenix, AZ 85040-1948. Telephone: 480-927-0099 Ext. 1218. Fax: 480-594-1758. E-mail: beth.barilla@apollogrp.edu. Web site: http://www.phoenix.edu.

WALSH COLLEGE OF ACCOUNTANCY AND BUSINESS ADMINISTRATION

TROY, MICHIGAN

General Independent, upper-level, coed **Entrance** Noncompetitive **Setting** 29-acre suburban campus **Total enrollment** 2,981 **Student/faculty ratio** 23:1 **Application deadline** Rolling (transfer) **First-Year Students** 74% were admitted **Housing** No **Expenses** Tuition $5264 **Undergraduates** 62% women, 81% part-time, 67% 25 or older, 0.3% Native American, 1% Hispanic American, 5% African American, 3% Asian American/Pacific Islander **Academic program** Advanced placement, summer session, adult/continuing education programs, internships **Contact** Ms. Diane Zalapi, Director of Admissions, Walsh College of Accountancy and Business Administration, 3838 Livernois, PO Box 7006, Troy, MI 48007-7006. Telephone: 248-689-8282 Ext. 294 or toll-free 800-925-7401 (in-state). Fax: 248-524-2520. E-mail: admissions@walshcollege.edu. Web site: http://www.walshcollege.edu/.

WAYNE STATE UNIVERSITY

DETROIT, MICHIGAN

General State-supported, university, coed **Entrance** Moderately difficult **Setting** 203-acre urban campus **Total enrollment** 30,408 **Student/faculty ratio** 11:1 **Application deadline** 8/1 (freshmen), 8/1 (transfer) **Freshmen** 78% were admitted **Housing** Yes **Expenses** Tuition $3970 **Undergraduates** 60% women, 50% part-time, 40% 25 or older, 0.4% Native American, 2% Hispanic American, 30% African American, 5% Asian American/Pacific Islander **The most frequently chosen baccalaureate fields are** education, engineering/engineering technologies, health professions and related sciences **Academic program** English as a second language, advanced placement, accelerated degree program, self-designed majors, honors program, summer session, adult/continuing education programs, internships **Contact** Mr. Michael Wood, Interim Director of University Admissions, Wayne State University, 3E HNJ, Detroit, MI 48202. Telephone: 313-577-3581. Fax: 313-577-7536. E-mail: credwine@cms.cc.wayne.edu. Web site: http://www.wayne.edu/.

WESTERN MICHIGAN UNIVERSITY

KALAMAZOO, MICHIGAN

General State-supported, university, coed **Entrance** Moderately difficult **Setting** 504-acre urban campus

Total enrollment 28,657 **Student/faculty ratio** 16:1 **Application deadline** Rolling (freshmen), rolling (transfer) **Freshmen** 85% were admitted **Housing** Yes **Expenses** Tuition $4094; Room & Board $5073 **Undergraduates** 53% women, 17% part-time, 0.4% Native American, 2% Hispanic American, 6% African American, 1% Asian American/Pacific Islander **The most frequently chosen baccalaureate fields are** business/marketing, education, social sciences and history **Academic program** English as a second language, advanced placement, accelerated degree program, self-designed majors, honors program, summer session, adult/continuing education programs, internships **Contact** Mr. John Fraire, Dean, Office of Admissions and Orientation, Western Michigan University, Office of Admissions and Orientation, Kalamazoo, MI 49008. Telephone: 616-387-2000 or toll-free 800-400-4968 (in-state). Fax: 616-387-2096. E-mail: ask-wmu@wmich.edu. Web site: http://www.wmich.edu/.

▶ **For more information, see page 492.**

WILLIAM TYNDALE COLLEGE
FARMINGTON HILLS, MICHIGAN

General Independent religious, 4-year, coed **Entrance** Minimally difficult **Setting** 28-acre suburban campus **Total enrollment** 625 **Student/faculty ratio** 12:1 **Application deadline** Rolling (freshmen), rolling (transfer) **Freshmen** 99% were admitted **Housing** Yes **Expenses** Tuition $7150; Room & Board $2800 **Undergraduates** 52% women, 33% part-time, 57% 25 or older, 0.3% Native American, 0.5% Hispanic American, 31% African American, 1% Asian American/Pacific Islander **The most frequently chosen baccalaureate fields are** business/marketing, philosophy, religion, and theology, psychology **Academic program** Advanced placement, accelerated degree program, summer session, adult/continuing education programs, internships **Contact** Mr. Fred Schebor, Dean of Admissions, William Tyndale College, 37500 West Twelve Mile Road, Farmington Hills, MI 48331. Telephone: 248-553-7200 Ext. 301 or toll-free 800-483-0707. Fax: 248-553-5963. E-mail: admissions@williamtyndale.edu. Web site: http://www.williamtyndale.edu.

YESHIVA GEDDOLAH OF GREATER DETROIT RABBINICAL COLLEGE
OAK PARK, MICHIGAN

Contact Mr. Eric Krohner, Executive Director, Yeshiva Geddolah of Greater Detroit Rabbinical College, 24600 Greenfield, Oak Park, MI 48237-1544. Telephone: 810-968-3360.

MINNESOTA

AUGSBURG COLLEGE
MINNEAPOLIS, MINNESOTA

General Independent Lutheran, comprehensive, coed **Entrance** Moderately difficult **Setting** 23-acre urban campus **Total enrollment** 3,040 **Student/faculty ratio** 15:1 **Application deadline** 8/15 (freshmen), 8/10 (transfer) **Freshmen** 75% were admitted **Housing** Yes **Expenses** Tuition $16,340; Room & Board $5320 **Undergraduates** 60% women, 19% part-time, 9% 25 or older, 1% Native American, 1% Hispanic American, 6% African American, 3% Asian American/Pacific Islander **The most frequently chosen baccalaureate fields are** business/marketing, education, psychology **Academic program** English as a second language, advanced placement, self-designed majors, honors program, summer session, adult/continuing education programs, internships **Contact** Ms. Sally Daniels, Director of Undergraduate Day Admissions, Augsburg College, 2211 Riverside Avenue, Minneapolis, MN 55454-1351. Telephone: 612-330-1001 or toll-free 800-788-5678. Fax: 612-330-1590. E-mail: admissions@augsburg.edu. Web site: http://www.augsburg.edu/.

BEMIDJI STATE UNIVERSITY
BEMIDJI, MINNESOTA

General State-supported, comprehensive, coed **Entrance** Moderately difficult **Setting** 89-acre small-town campus **Total enrollment** 4,608 **Student/faculty ratio** 20:1 **Application deadline** Rolling (freshmen), rolling (transfer) **Freshmen** 77% were admitted **Housing** Yes **Expenses** Tuition $4221; Room & Board $3982 **Undergraduates** 57% women, 25% part-time, 27% 25 or older, 4% Native American, 1% Hispanic American, 0.5% African American, 1% Asian American/Pacific Islander **The most frequently chosen baccalaureate fields are** business/marketing, education, protective services/public administration **Academic program** English as a second language, advanced placement, honors program, summer session, adult/continuing education programs, internships **Contact** Mr. Paul Muller, Director of Admissions, Bemidji State University, Deputy-102, Bemidji, MN 56601. Telephone: 218-755-2040 or toll-free 800-475-2001 (in-state); 800-652-9747 (out-of-state). Fax: 218-755-2074. E-mail: admissions@vax1.bemidji.msus.edu. Web site: http://www.bemidjistate.edu/.

BETHEL COLLEGE
ST. PAUL, MINNESOTA

General Independent, comprehensive, coed, affiliated with Baptist General Conference **Entrance** Moderately difficult **Setting** 231-acre suburban campus **Total enrollment** 2,953 **Student/faculty ratio** 14:1 **Application deadline** 6/1 (freshmen), 8/1 (transfer) **Freshmen** 77% were admitted **Housing** Yes **Expenses** Tuition 15,935; Room & Board 5700 **Undergraduates** 63% women, 8% part-time, 7% 25 or older, 0.4% Native American, 1% Hispanic American, 1% African American, 2% Asian American/Pacific Islander **The most frequently chosen baccalaureate fields are** business/marketing, health professions and related sciences, interdisciplinary studies **Academic program** English as a second language, advanced placement, accelerated degree program, self-designed

Bethel College *(continued)*

majors, honors program, summer session, adult/continuing education programs, internships **Contact** Mr. Jay Fedje, Director of Admissions, Bethel College, 3900 Bethel Drive, St. Paul, MN 55112. Telephone: 651-638-6438 or toll-free 800-255-8706 Ext. 6242. Fax: 651-635-1490. E-mail: bcoll-admit@bethel.edu. Web site: http://www.bethel.edu/.

▶ **For more information, see page 389.**

CAPELLA UNIVERSITY
MINNEAPOLIS, MINNESOTA

General Proprietary, upper-level, coed **Student/faculty ratio** 12:1 **Expenses** Tuition $2580 **Undergraduates** 1% Native American, 3% Hispanic American, 6% African American, 6% Asian American/Pacific Islander **Academic program** Self-designed majors, summer session, adult/continuing education programs, internships **Contact** Ms. Liz Krumman, Associate Director, Enrollment Services, Capella University, 222 South 9th Street, Minneapolis, MN 55402. Telephone: 612-252-4286 or toll-free 888-CAPELLA. E-mail: info@capella.edu. Web site: http://www.capellauniversity.edu/.

CARLETON COLLEGE
NORTHFIELD, MINNESOTA

General Independent, 4-year, coed **Entrance** Very difficult **Setting** 955-acre small-town campus **Total enrollment** 1,936 **Student/faculty ratio** 10:1 **Application deadline** 1/15 (freshmen), 3/31 (transfer) **Freshmen** 44% were admitted **Housing** Yes **Expenses** Tuition 24,570; Room & Board 4950 **Undergraduates** 52% women, 1% part-time, 0% 25 or older, 0.3% Native American, 4% Hispanic American, 3% African American, 8% Asian American/Pacific Islander **The most frequently chosen baccalaureate fields are** physical sciences, biological/life sciences, social sciences and history **Academic program** Advanced placement, accelerated degree program, self-designed majors, internships **Contact** Mr. Paul Thiboutot, Dean of Admissions, Carleton College, 100 South College Street, Northfield, MN 55057. Telephone: 507-646-4190 or toll-free 800-995-2275. Fax: 507-646-4526. E-mail: admissions@acs.carleton.edu. Web site: http://www.carleton.edu/.

COLLEGE OF SAINT BENEDICT
SAINT JOSEPH, MINNESOTA

General Independent Roman Catholic, 4-year, women only, coordinate institution with Saint John's University (MN) **Entrance** Moderately difficult **Setting** 315-acre small-town campus **Total enrollment** 2,024 **Student/faculty ratio** 13:1 **Application deadline** Rolling (freshmen), rolling (transfer) **Freshmen** 80% were admitted **Housing** Yes **Expenses** Tuition 17,241; Room & Board 5272 **Undergraduates** 3% part-time, 4% 25 or older, 0.3% Native American, 1% Hispanic American, 0.5% African American, 2% Asian American/Pacific Islander **The most frequently chosen baccalaureate fields are** business/marketing, health professions and related sciences, social sciences and history **Academic program** English as a second language, advanced placement, accelerated degree program, self-designed majors, honors program, internships **Contact** Ms. Mary Milbert, Dean of Admissions, College of Saint Benedict, 37 South College Avenue, St. Joseph, MN 56374. Telephone: 320-363-5308 or toll-free 800-544-1489. Fax: 320-363-5010. E-mail: admissions@csbsju.edu. Web site: http://www.csbsju.edu/.

COLLEGE OF ST. CATHERINE
ST. PAUL, MINNESOTA

General Independent Roman Catholic, comprehensive, women only **Entrance** Moderately difficult **Setting** 110-acre urban campus **Total enrollment** 4,487 **Student/faculty ratio** 10:1 **Application deadline** 8/15 (freshmen), rolling (transfer) **Freshmen** 85% were admitted **Housing** Yes **Expenses** Tuition 16,442; Room & Board 4690 **Undergraduates** 36% part-time, 49% 25 or older, 1% Native American, 2% Hispanic American, 5% African American, 4% Asian American/Pacific Islander **The most frequently chosen baccalaureate fields are** education, business/marketing, health professions and related sciences **Academic program** English as a second language, advanced placement, self-designed majors, honors program, summer session, adult/continuing education programs, internships **Contact** Ms. Cory Piper-Hauswirth, Associate Director of Admission and Financial Aid, College of St. Catherine, 2004 Randolph Avenue, St. Paul, MN 55105-1789. Telephone: 651-690-6047 or toll-free 800-945-4599 (in-state). Fax: 651-690-8824. E-mail: stkate@stkate.edu. Web site: http://www.stkate.edu/.

THE COLLEGE OF ST. SCHOLASTICA
DULUTH, MINNESOTA

General Independent, comprehensive, coed, affiliated with Roman Catholic Church **Entrance** Moderately difficult **Setting** 160-acre suburban campus **Total enrollment** 1,984 **Student/faculty ratio** 13:1 **Application deadline** Rolling (freshmen), rolling (transfer) **Freshmen** 36% were admitted **Housing** Yes **Expenses** Tuition 16,290; Room & Board 4952 **Undergraduates** 18% 25 or older, 1% Native American, 0.5% Hispanic American, 1% African American, 1% Asian American/Pacific Islander **The most frequently chosen baccalaureate fields are** biological/life sciences, health professions and related sciences, parks and recreation **Academic program** Advanced placement, accelerated degree program, self-designed majors, honors program, summer session, adult/continuing education programs, internships **Contact** Mr. Brian Dalton, Vice President for Enrollment Management, The College of St. Scholastica, 1200 Kenwood Avenue, Duluth, MN 55811-4199. Telephone: 218-723-6053 or toll-free 800-447-5444. Fax: 218-723-6290. E-mail: admissions@css1.css.edu. Web site: http://www.css.edu/.

COLLEGE OF VISUAL ARTS
ST. PAUL, MINNESOTA

General Independent, 4-year, coed **Entrance** Minimally difficult **Setting** 2-acre urban campus **Total enrollment** 278 **Student/faculty ratio** 10:1 **Application deadline** Rolling (freshmen), rolling (transfer) **Freshmen** 65% were admitted **Housing** No **Expenses** Tuition 12,230 **Undergraduates** 56% women, 8% part-time, 17% 25 or older, 1% Native American, 4% Hispanic American, 2% African American, 4% Asian American/Pacific Islander **The most frequently chosen baccalaureate field is** visual/performing arts **Academic program** Advanced placement, summer session, internships **Contact** Ms. Lynn E. Tanaka, Director of Admissions, College of Visual Arts, 344 Summit Avenue, St. Paul, MN 55102-2124. Telephone: 651-224-3416 or toll-free 800-224-1536. Fax: 651-224-8854. E-mail: info @cva.edu. Web site: http://www.cva.edu/.

CONCORDIA COLLEGE
MOORHEAD, MINNESOTA

General Independent, 4-year, coed, affiliated with Evangelical Lutheran Church in America **Entrance** Moderately difficult **Setting** 120-acre suburban campus **Total enrollment** 2,826 **Student/faculty ratio** 14:1 **Application deadline** Rolling (freshmen), rolling (transfer) **Freshmen** 84% were admitted **Housing** Yes **Expenses** Tuition $14,136; Room & Board $3900 **Undergraduates** 62% women, 3% part-time, 2% 25 or older, 0.5% Native American, 1% Hispanic American, 1% African American, 1% Asian American/Pacific Islander **The most frequently chosen baccalaureate fields are** business/marketing, biological/life sciences, education **Academic program** English as a second language, advanced placement, honors program, summer session, adult/continuing education programs, internships **Contact** Mr. Scott E. Ellingson, Associate Director of Admissions, Concordia College, 901 8th Street South, Moorhead, MN 56562. Telephone: 218-299-3004 or toll-free 800-699-9897. Fax: 218-299-3947. E-mail: admissions@gloria.cord.edu. Web site: http://www.cord.edu/.

CONCORDIA UNIVERSITY
ST. PAUL, MINNESOTA

General Independent, comprehensive, coed, affiliated with Lutheran Church–Missouri Synod **Contact** Mr. Tim Utter, Director of Admissions, Concordia University, 275 Syndicate North, St. Paul, MN 55104-5494. Telephone: 651-641-8230 or toll-free 800-333-4705. Fax: 651-659-0207. E-mail: admiss@luther.csp.edu. Web site: http://www.csp.edu/.

CROWN COLLEGE
ST. BONIFACIUS, MINNESOTA

General Independent, comprehensive, coed, affiliated with The Christian and Missionary Alliance **Entrance** Minimally difficult **Setting** 193-acre suburban campus **Total enrollment** 897 **Student/faculty ratio** 14:1 **Application deadline** Rolling (freshmen), rolling (transfer) **Freshmen** 65% were admitted **Housing** Yes **Expenses** Tuition 11,346; Room & Board 4698 **Undergraduates** 58% women, 23% part-time, 0.1% Native American, 1% Hispanic American, 2% African American, 2% Asian American/Pacific Islander **The most frequently chosen baccalaureate fields are** education, business/marketing, philosophy, religion, and theology **Academic program** English as a second language, advanced placement, honors program, summer session, adult/continuing education programs, internships **Contact** Ms. Kimberely LaQuay, Application Coordinator/Office Systems Manager, Crown College, 6425 County Road 30, St. Bonifacius, MN 55375-9001. Telephone: 952-446-4143 or toll-free 800-68-CROWN. Fax: 952-446-4149. E-mail: pearsont@gw.crown.edu. Web site: http://www.crown.edu/.

GUSTAVUS ADOLPHUS COLLEGE
ST. PETER, MINNESOTA

General Independent, 4-year, coed, affiliated with Evangelical Lutheran Church in America **Entrance** Very difficult **Setting** 330-acre small-town campus **Total enrollment** 2,560 **Student/faculty ratio** 13:1 **Application deadline** 4/1 (freshmen), 4/1 (transfer) **Freshmen** 76% were admitted **Housing** Yes **Expenses** Tuition 18,330; Room & Board 4605 **Undergraduates** 57% women, 1% part-time, 0% 25 or older, 0.2% Native American, 1% Hispanic American, 1% African American, 3% Asian American/Pacific Islander **The most frequently chosen baccalaureate fields are** business/marketing, biological/life sciences, social sciences and history **Academic program** Advanced placement, accelerated degree program, self-designed majors, honors program, summer session, internships **Contact** Mr. Mark H. Anderson, Dean of Admission, Gustavus Adolphus College, 800 West College Avenue, St. Peter, MN 56082-1498. Telephone: 507-933-7676 or toll-free 800-GUSTAVU(S). E-mail: admission@gac.edu. Web site: http://www.gustavus.edu/.

HAMLINE UNIVERSITY
ST. PAUL, MINNESOTA

General Independent, comprehensive, coed, affiliated with United Methodist Church **Entrance** Moderately difficult **Setting** 50-acre urban campus **Total enrollment** 3,380 **Student/faculty ratio** 14:1 **Application deadline** Rolling (freshmen), rolling (transfer) **Freshmen** 81% were admitted **Housing** Yes **Expenses** Tuition 16,275; Room & Board 5445 **Undergraduates** 65% women, 8% part-time, 7% 25 or older, 1% Native American, 1% Hispanic American, 3% African American, 4% Asian American/Pacific Islander **The most frequently chosen baccalaureate fields are** business/marketing, psychology, social sciences and history **Academic program** English as a second language, advanced placement, self-designed majors, honors program, summer session, adult/continuing education programs, internships **Contact** Mr. Steven Bjork, Director of Undergraduate Admission, Hamline University, 1536 Hewitt Avenue C1930, St. Paul, MN 55104-1284. Tele-

Hamline University *(continued)*

phone: 651-523-2207 or toll-free 800-753-9753. Fax: 651-523-2458. E-mail: admis@seq.hamline.edu. Web site: http://www.hamline.edu/.

MACALESTER COLLEGE
ST. PAUL, MINNESOTA

General Independent Presbyterian, 4-year, coed **Entrance** Very difficult **Setting** 53-acre urban campus **Total enrollment** 1,794 **Student/faculty ratio** 10:1 **Application deadline** 1/15 (freshmen), 3/15 (transfer) **Freshmen** 53% were admitted **Housing** Yes **Expenses** Tuition 21,614; Room & Board 5932 **Undergraduates** 60% women, 3% part-time, 0.3% 25 or older, 1% Native American, 3% Hispanic American, 4% African American, 5% Asian American/Pacific Islander **The most frequently chosen baccalaureate fields are** biological/life sciences, psychology, social sciences and history **Academic program** Self-designed majors, honors program, internships **Contact** Mr. Lorne T. Robinson, Dean of Admissions and Financial Aid, Macalester College, 1600 Grand Avenue, St. Paul, MN 55105-1899. Telephone: 651-696-6357 or toll-free 800-231-7974. Fax: 651-696-6724. E-mail: admissions@macalstr.edu. Web site: http://www.macalester.edu/.

MANKATO STATE UNIVERSITY
See Minnesota State University, Mankato

MARTIN LUTHER COLLEGE
NEW ULM, MINNESOTA

General Independent, 4-year, coed, affiliated with Wisconsin Evangelical Lutheran Synod **Entrance** Moderately difficult **Setting** 50-acre small-town campus **Total enrollment** 1,026 **Student/faculty ratio** 10:1 **Application deadline** 4/15 (freshmen), 5/1 (transfer) **Housing** Yes **Expenses** Tuition $5195; Room & Board $2340 **Undergraduates** 50% women, 0.2% part-time, 0.3% Native American, 1% Hispanic American, 1% African American, 1% Asian American/Pacific Islander **The most frequently chosen baccalaureate fields are** education, interdisciplinary studies, philosophy, religion, and theology **Academic program** Advanced placement, summer session, internships **Contact** Prof. Ronald B. Brutlag, Associate Director of Admissions, Martin Luther College, 1995 Luther Court, New Ulm, MN 56073. Telephone: 507-354-8221 Ext. 280. Fax: 507-354-8225. E-mail: sebaldja-fac@mlc-wels.edu. Web site: http://www.mlc-wels.edu/.

MAYO SCHOOL OF HEALTH-RELATED SCIENCES
ROCHESTER, MINNESOTA

Contact Ms. Kate Ray, Mayo School of Health-Related Sciences, 200 First Street, SW, Rochester, MN 55905. Telephone: 507-266-4077 or toll-free 800-626-9041. Fax: 507-284-0656. E-mail: kray@mayo.edu. Web site: http://www.mayo.edu/hrs/hrs.htm.

METROPOLITAN STATE UNIVERSITY
ST. PAUL, MINNESOTA

General State-supported, comprehensive, coed **Entrance** Minimally difficult **Setting** urban campus **Total enrollment** 5,623 **Student/faculty ratio** 11:1 **Application deadline** Rolling (freshmen), rolling (transfer) **Housing** No **Expenses** Tuition $2942 **Undergraduates** 60% women, 74% part-time, 86% 25 or older, 1% Native American, 1% Hispanic American, 7% African American, 5% Asian American/Pacific Islander **Academic program** English as a second language, self-designed majors, summer session, adult/continuing education programs, internships **Contact** Ms. Cindy Olson, Registrar, Metropolitan State University, 700 East 7th Street, St. Paul, MN 55106-5000. Telephone: 651-772-7776. Web site: http://www.metrostate.edu.

MINNEAPOLIS COLLEGE OF ART AND DESIGN
MINNEAPOLIS, MINNESOTA

General Independent, comprehensive, coed **Entrance** Moderately difficult **Setting** 7-acre urban campus **Total enrollment** 623 **Student/faculty ratio** 15:1 **Application deadline** Rolling (freshmen), rolling (transfer) **Freshmen** 71% were admitted **Housing** Yes **Expenses** Tuition $20,500; Room only $3150 **Undergraduates** 42% women, 9% part-time, 18% 25 or older, 1% Native American, 2% Hispanic American, 2% African American, 6% Asian American/Pacific Islander **The most frequently chosen baccalaureate field is** visual/performing arts **Academic program** Advanced placement, summer session, adult/continuing education programs, internships **Contact** Ms. Susan Neppl, Director of Enrollment and Student Financial Services, Minneapolis College of Art and Design, 2501 Stevens Avenue South, Minneapolis, MN 55404-4347. Telephone: 612-874-3762 or toll-free 800-874-6223. E-mail: admissions@mn.mcad.edu. Web site: http://www.mcad.edu/.

▶ **For more information, see page 450.**

MINNESOTA BIBLE COLLEGE
ROCHESTER, MINNESOTA

General Independent, 4-year, coed, affiliated with Christian Churches and Churches of Christ **Entrance** Noncompetitive **Setting** 40-acre urban campus **Total enrollment** 116 **Student/faculty ratio** 8:1 **Application deadline** 8/15 (freshmen), 8/15 (transfer) **Freshmen** 68% were admitted **Housing** Yes **Expenses** Tuition 5660; Room only 1900 **Undergraduates** 47% women, 13% part-time, 16% 25 or older, 0% Native American, 2% Hispanic American, 2% African American, 1% Asian American/Pacific Islander **The most frequently chosen baccalaureate field is** philosophy, religion, and theology **Academic program** Advanced placement, self-designed majors, internships **Contact** Mr. Alan Wager, Director of Admissions, Minnesota Bible College, 920 Mayowood Road, SW, Rochester, MN 55902-2382. Telephone: 507-288-4563 Ext. 246 or toll-free 800-456-7651. Fax: 507-288-9046. E-mail: admissions@mnbc.edu. Web site: http://www.mnbc.edu/.

MINNESOTA STATE UNIVERSITY, MANKATO
MANKATO, MINNESOTA

General State-supported, comprehensive, coed **Entrance** Moderately difficult **Setting** 303-acre small-town campus **Total enrollment** 12,085 **Student/faculty ratio** 20:1 **Application deadline** Rolling (freshmen), rolling (transfer) **Housing** Yes **Expenses** Tuition $3208; Room & Board $3344 **Undergraduates** 53% women, 14% part-time, 14% 25 or older **The most frequently chosen baccalaureate fields are** business/marketing, education, protective services/public administration **Academic program** English as a second language, advanced placement, accelerated degree program, self-designed majors, honors program, summer session, adult/continuing education programs, internships **Contact** Mr. Walt Wolff, Director of Admissions, Minnesota State University, Mankato, 122 Taylor Center, Mankato, MN 56001. Telephone: 507-389-6670 or toll-free 800-722-0544. Fax: 507-389-1511. E-mail: linda_meidl@msl.mankato.msus.edu. Web site: http://www.mnsu.edu.

MINNESOTA STATE UNIVERSITY MOORHEAD
MOORHEAD, MINNESOTA

General State-supported, comprehensive, coed **Entrance** Moderately difficult **Setting** 118-acre urban campus **Total enrollment** 7,060 **Application deadline** 8/7 (freshmen), 8/7 (transfer) **Freshmen** 91% were admitted **Housing** Yes **Expenses** Tuition 3520; Room & Board 3500 **Undergraduates** 19% 25 or older, 1% Native American, 1% Hispanic American, 1% African American, 1% Asian American/Pacific Islander **The most frequently chosen baccalaureate fields are** business/marketing, education, protective services/public administration **Academic program** Advanced placement, self-designed majors, honors program, summer session, adult/continuing education programs, internships **Contact** Ms. Gina Monson, Director of Admissions, Minnesota State University Moorhead, Owens Hall, Moorhead, MN 56563-0002. Telephone: 218-236-2161 or toll-free 800-593-7246. Fax: 218-236-2168. Web site: http://www.mnstate.edu/.

NATIONAL AMERICAN UNIVERSITY–ST. PAUL CAMPUS
ST. PAUL, MINNESOTA

General Proprietary, 4-year, coed **Contact** Mrs. Cindy Olson, Director of Admissions, National American University–St. Paul Campus, 1380 Energy Lane, Suite 13, St. Paul, MN 55108-9952. Telephone: 651-644-1265. E-mail: natcoll@iaxs.net. Web site: http://www.nationalcollege.edu/.

NORTH CENTRAL UNIVERSITY
MINNEAPOLIS, MINNESOTA

General Independent, 4-year, coed, affiliated with Assemblies of God **Entrance** Noncompetitive **Setting** 9-acre urban campus **Total enrollment** 1,163 **Student/faculty ratio** 18:1 **Application deadline** 6/1 (freshmen), 6/1 (transfer) **Freshmen** 77% were admitted **Housing** Yes **Expenses** Tuition $8554; Room & Board $2270 **Undergraduates** 16% 25 or older, 1% Native American, 3% Hispanic American, 5% African American, 1% Asian American/Pacific Islander **The most frequently chosen baccalaureate fields are** education, communications/communication technologies, philosophy, religion, and theology **Academic program** Advanced placement, self-designed majors, summer session, adult/continuing education programs, internships **Contact** Ms. Mary Jo Meier, Admissions Secretary, North Central University, 910 Elliot Avenue, Minneapolis, MN 55404. Telephone: 612-343-4401 or toll-free 800-289-6222. Fax: 612-343-4146. E-mail: akgoetz@topaz.ncbc.edu. Web site: http://www.northcentral.edu/.

NORTHWESTERN COLLEGE
ST. PAUL, MINNESOTA

General Independent nondenominational, 4-year, coed **Entrance** Moderately difficult **Setting** 100-acre suburban campus **Total enrollment** 2,084 **Student/faculty ratio** 16:1 **Application deadline** 8/15 (freshmen), 8/15 (transfer) **Freshmen** 75% were admitted **Housing** Yes **Expenses** Tuition $15,600; Room & Board $5050 **Undergraduates** 62% women, 15% part-time, 15% 25 or older, 0.2% Native American, 1% Hispanic American, 3% African American, 1% Asian American/Pacific Islander **The most frequently chosen baccalaureate fields are** business/marketing, education, psychology **Academic program** English as a second language, advanced placement, summer session, adult/continuing education programs, internships **Contact** Mr. Kenneth K. Faffler, Director of Recruitment, Northwestern College, 3003 Snelling Avenue North, Nazareth Hall, Room 229, St. Paul, MN 55113-1598. Telephone: 651-631-5209 or toll-free 800-827-6827. Fax: 651-631-5680. E-mail: admissions@nwc.edu. Web site: http://www.nwc.edu/.

OAK HILLS CHRISTIAN COLLEGE
BEMIDJI, MINNESOTA

General Independent interdenominational, 4-year, coed **Entrance** Minimally difficult **Setting** 180-acre rural campus **Total enrollment** 155 **Student/faculty ratio** 8:1 **Application deadline** Rolling (freshmen), rolling (transfer) **Freshmen** 80% were admitted **Housing** Yes **Expenses** Tuition $9450; Room & Board $3410 **Undergraduates** 50% women, 15% part-time, 18% 25 or older, 1% Native American, 0% Hispanic American, 0% African American, 0% Asian

Oak Hills Christian College *(continued)*

American/Pacific Islander **The most frequently chosen baccalaureate field is** philosophy, religion, and theology **Academic program** Advanced placement, honors program, internships **Contact** Mr. Dan Hovestol, Admissions Director, Oak Hills Christian College, 1600 Oak Hills Road, SW, Bemidji, MN 56601. Telephone: 218-751-8670 Ext. 220 or toll-free 888-751-8670 Ext. 285. Fax: 218-751-8825. E-mail: ohadmit@northernnet.com. Web site: http://www.oakhills.edu/.

PILLSBURY BAPTIST BIBLE COLLEGE
OWATONNA, MINNESOTA

Contact Mr. Paul Rumsey, Director of Admissions, Pillsbury Baptist Bible College, 315 South Grove, Owatonna, MN 55060-3097. Telephone: 507-451-2710 Ext. 279 or toll-free 800-747-4557. Fax: 507-451-6459. Web site: http://www.pillsbury.edu/.

ST. CLOUD STATE UNIVERSITY
ST. CLOUD, MINNESOTA

General State-supported, comprehensive, coed **Entrance** Moderately difficult **Setting** 108-acre suburban campus **Total enrollment** 15,140 **Student/faculty ratio** 20:1 **Application deadline** 8/1 (freshmen), 8/1 (transfer) **Freshmen** 83% were admitted **Housing** Yes **Expenses** Tuition $3067; Room & Board $3468 **Undergraduates** 55% women, 21% part-time, 14% 25 or older, 1% Native American, 1% Hispanic American, 1% African American, 1% Asian American/Pacific Islander **The most frequently chosen baccalaureate fields are** business/marketing, education, social sciences and history **Academic program** English as a second language, advanced placement, accelerated degree program, self-designed majors, honors program, summer session, adult/continuing education programs, internships **Contact** Ms. Annette Day, Director of Admissions, St. Cloud State University, 720 4th Avenue South, St. Cloud, MN 56301-4498. Telephone: 320-255-2244 or toll-free 877-654-7278. Fax: 320-255-2243. E-mail: scsu4u@tigger.stcloud.msus.edu. Web site: http://www.stcloudstate.edu/.

SAINT JOHN'S UNIVERSITY
COLLEGEVILLE, MINNESOTA

General Independent Roman Catholic, comprehensive, men only, coordinate institution with College of Saint Benedict **Entrance** Moderately difficult **Setting** 2,400-acre rural campus **Total enrollment** 2,020 **Student/faculty ratio** 13:1 **Application deadline** Rolling (freshmen), rolling (transfer) **Freshmen** 85% were admitted **Housing** Yes **Expenses** Tuition 17,241; Room & Board 5129 **Undergraduates** 3% part-time, 2% 25 or older, 0.2% Native American, 1% Hispanic American, 0.3% African American, 2% Asian American/Pacific Islander **The most frequently chosen baccalaureate fields are** business/marketing, biological/life sciences, social sciences and history **Academic program** English as a second language, advanced placement, accelerated degree program, self-designed majors, honors program, internships **Contact** Ms. Mary Milbert, Dean of Admissions, Saint John's University, PO Box 7155, Collegeville, MN 56321-7155. Telephone: 320-363-2196 or toll-free 800-24JOHNS. Fax: 320-363-3206. E-mail: admissions@csbsju.edu. Web site: http://www.csbsju.edu/.

SAINT MARY'S UNIVERSITY OF MINNESOTA
WINONA, MINNESOTA

General Independent Roman Catholic, comprehensive, coed **Entrance** Moderately difficult **Setting** 350-acre small-town campus **Total enrollment** 4,991 **Student/faculty ratio** 14:1 **Application deadline** Rolling (freshmen), rolling (transfer) **Freshmen** 91% were admitted **Housing** Yes **Expenses** Tuition $14,355; Room & Board $4620 **Undergraduates** 52% women, 22% part-time, 5% 25 or older, 0.2% Native American, 1% Hispanic American, 0.4% African American, 1% Asian American/Pacific Islander **The most frequently chosen baccalaureate fields are** business/marketing, education, protective services/public administration **Academic program** English as a second language, advanced placement, accelerated degree program, self-designed majors, honors program, summer session, adult/continuing education programs, internships **Contact** Mr. Anthony M. Piscitiello, Vice President for Admission, Saint Mary's University of Minnesota, 700 Terrace Heights, Winona, MN 55987-1399. Telephone: 507-457-1700 or toll-free 800-635-5987. Fax: 507-457-1722. E-mail: admissions@smumn.edu. Web site: http://www.smumn.edu/.

ST. OLAF COLLEGE
NORTHFIELD, MINNESOTA

General Independent Lutheran, 4-year, coed **Entrance** Very difficult **Setting** 350-acre small-town campus **Total enrollment** 3,014 **Student/faculty ratio** 13:1 **Application deadline** Rolling (freshmen), rolling (transfer) **Freshmen** 74% were admitted **Housing** Yes **Expenses** Tuition $19,400; Room & Board $4500 **Undergraduates** 57% women, 2% part-time, 1% 25 or older, 0.2% Native American, 1% Hispanic American, 1% African American, 3% Asian American/Pacific Islander **The most frequently chosen baccalaureate fields are** social sciences and history, English, visual/performing arts **Academic program** English as a second language, advanced placement, accelerated degree program, self-designed majors, summer session, adult/continuing education programs, internships **Contact** Ms. Sara Kyle, Director of Admissions, St. Olaf College, 1520 St. Olaf Avenue, Northfield, MN 55057. Telephone: 507-646-3025 or toll-free 800-800-3025 (in-state). Fax: 507-646-3832. E-mail: admiss@stolaf.edu. Web site: http://www.stolaf.edu/.

SOUTHWEST STATE UNIVERSITY
MARSHALL, MINNESOTA

General State-supported, comprehensive, coed **Entrance** Minimally difficult **Setting** 216-acre small-town campus **Total enrollment** 4,707 **Student/faculty ratio** 18:1 **Application deadline** Rolling (freshmen), rolling (transfer) **Freshmen** 48% were admitted **Housing** Yes **Expenses** Tuition 3428; Room & Board 3588 **Undergraduates** 59% women, 47% part-time, 7% 25 or older, 0.3% Native American, 0.5% Hispanic American, 1% African American, 1% Asian American/Pacific Islander **The most frequently chosen baccalaureate fields are** business/marketing, education, social sciences and history **Academic program** Advanced placement, accelerated degree program, self-designed majors, honors program, summer session, adult/continuing education programs, internships **Contact** Richard Shearer, Director of Enrollment Services, Southwest State University, 1501 State Street, Marshall, MN 56258-1598. Telephone: 507-537-6286 or toll-free 800-642-0684. Fax: 507-537-7154. E-mail: 509ras@rickyvs.southwest.msus.edu. Web site: http://www.southwest.msus.edu/.

UNIVERSITY OF MINNESOTA, CROOKSTON
CROOKSTON, MINNESOTA

General State-supported, 4-year, coed **Entrance** Moderately difficult **Setting** 95-acre rural campus **Total enrollment** 2,464 **Student/faculty ratio** 17:1 **Application deadline** 8/1 (freshmen), 8/1 (transfer) **Freshmen** 95% were admitted **Housing** Yes **Expenses** Tuition $5070; Room & Board $4100 **Undergraduates** 55% women, 58% part-time, 3% 25 or older, 1% Native American, 1% Hispanic American, 3% African American, 1% Asian American/Pacific Islander **Academic program** Advanced placement, summer session, adult/continuing education programs, internships **Contact** Mr. Russ Kreager, Director of Admissions and Enrollment Manager, University of Minnesota, Crookston, 2900 University Avenue, 170 Owen Hall, Crookston, MN 56716-5001. Telephone: 218-281-8568 or toll-free 800-232-6466. Fax: 218-281-8575. E-mail: info@crk.umn.edu. Web site: http://www.crk.umn.edu/.

► **For more information, see page 480.**

UNIVERSITY OF MINNESOTA, DULUTH
DULUTH, MINNESOTA

General State-supported, comprehensive, coed **Entrance** Moderately difficult **Setting** 250-acre suburban campus **Total enrollment** 9,089 **Student/faculty ratio** 20:1 **Application deadline** 2/1 (freshmen), 8/1 (transfer) **Freshmen** 78% were admitted **Housing** Yes **Expenses** Tuition 5017; Room & Board 4338 **Undergraduates** 51% women, 18% part-time, 10% 25 or older, 1% Native American, 1% Hispanic American, 1% African American, 2% Asian American/Pacific Islander **The most frequently chosen baccalaureate fields are** business/marketing, education, social sciences and history **Academic program** English as a second language, advanced placement, self-designed majors, honors program, summer session, adult/continuing education programs, internships **Contact** Ms. Beth Esselstrom, Director of Admissions, University of Minnesota, Duluth, 184 Darland Administration Building, 10 University Drive, Duluth, MN 55812. Telephone: 218-726-7171 or toll-free 800-232-1339. Fax: 218-726-6394. E-mail: umdadmis@d.umn.edu. Web site: http://www.d.umn.edu/.

UNIVERSITY OF MINNESOTA, MORRIS
MORRIS, MINNESOTA

General State-supported, 4-year, coed **Entrance** Moderately difficult **Setting** 130-acre small-town campus **Total enrollment** 1,944 **Student/faculty ratio** 16:1 **Application deadline** 3/15 (freshmen), 5/1 (transfer) **Freshmen** 87% were admitted **Housing** Yes **Expenses** Tuition $5567; Room & Board $4102 **Undergraduates** 58% women, 5% part-time, 5% 25 or older, 6% Native American, 1% Hispanic American, 6% African American, 3% Asian American/Pacific Islander **The most frequently chosen baccalaureate fields are** biological/life sciences, business/marketing, social sciences and history **Academic program** English as a second language, advanced placement, accelerated degree program, self-designed majors, honors program, summer session, adult/continuing education programs, internships **Contact** Mr. Scott K. Hagg, Acting Director of Admissions, University of Minnesota, Morris, 600 East 4th Street, Morris, MN 56267-2199. Telephone: 320-539-6035 or toll-free 800-992-8863. Fax: 320-589-1673. E-mail: admissions@mrs.umn.edu. Web site: http://www.mrs.umn.edu/.

UNIVERSITY OF MINNESOTA, TWIN CITIES CAMPUS
MINNEAPOLIS, MINNESOTA

General State-supported, university, coed **Entrance** Moderately difficult **Setting** 2,000-acre urban campus **Total enrollment** 45,481 **Application deadline** Rolling (freshmen), 3/1 (transfer) **Freshmen** 75% were admitted **Housing** Yes **Expenses** Tuition $4877; Room & Board $4914 **Undergraduates** 53% women, 28% part-time, 13% 25 or older, 1% Native American, 2% Hispanic American, 4% African American, 8% Asian American/Pacific Islander **The most frequently chosen baccalaureate fields are** engineering/engineering technologies, business/marketing, social sciences and history **Academic program** English as a second language, advanced placement, accelerated degree program, self-designed majors, honors program, summer session, adult/continuing education programs, internships **Contact** Ms. Patricia Jones Whyte, Associate Director of Admissions, University of Minnesota, Twin Cities Campus, 240 Williamson Hall, Minneapolis, MN 55455-0115. Telephone: 612-625-2008 or toll-free 800-752-1000. Fax: 612-626-1693. E-mail: admissions@tc.umn.edu. Web site: http://www.umn.edu/tc/.

UNIVERSITY OF ST. THOMAS
ST. PAUL, MINNESOTA

General Independent Roman Catholic, university, coed **Entrance** Moderately difficult **Setting** 78-acre

University of St. Thomas *(continued)*

urban campus **Total enrollment** 11,288 **Student/faculty ratio** 15:1 **Application deadline** Rolling (freshmen), 8/1 (transfer) **Freshmen** 82% were admitted **Housing** Yes **Expenses** Tuition $18,421; Room & Board $5623 **Undergraduates** 53% women, 14% part-time, 11% 25 or older, 0.5% Native American, 2% Hispanic American, 2% African American, 5% Asian American/Pacific Islander **The most frequently chosen baccalaureate fields are** business/marketing, communications/communication technologies, social sciences and history **Academic program** English as a second language, advanced placement, self-designed majors, honors program, summer session, adult/continuing education programs, internships **Contact** Ms. Marla Friederichs, Associate Vice President of Enrollment Management, University of St. Thomas, Mail #32F-1, 2115 Summit Avenue, St. Paul, MN 55105-1096. Telephone: 651-962-6150 or toll-free 800-328-6819 Ext. 26150. Fax: 651-962-6160. E-mail: admissions@stthomas.edu. Web site: http://www.stthomas.edu/.

WINONA STATE UNIVERSITY
WINONA, MINNESOTA

General State-supported, comprehensive, coed **Entrance** Moderately difficult **Setting** 40-acre small-town campus **Total enrollment** 7,318 **Student/faculty ratio** 19:1 **Application deadline** Rolling (freshmen), rolling (transfer) **Freshmen** 68% were admitted **Housing** Yes **Expenses** Tuition $3300; Room & Board $3600 **Undergraduates** 8% 25 or older, 0.2% Native American, 1% Hispanic American, 1% African American, 1% Asian American/Pacific Islander **The most frequently chosen baccalaureate fields are** business/marketing, education, health professions and related sciences **Academic program** English as a second language, advanced placement, accelerated degree program, self-designed majors, honors program, summer session, adult/continuing education programs, internships **Contact** Mr. Douglas Schacke, Director of Admissions, Winona State University, PO Box 5838, Winona, MN 55987. Telephone: 507-457-5100 or toll-free 800-DIAL WSU. Fax: 507-457-5620. E-mail: admissions@vax2.winona.msus.edu. Web site: http://www.winona.msus.edu/.

MISSISSIPPI

ALCORN STATE UNIVERSITY
ALCORN STATE, MISSISSIPPI

General State-supported, comprehensive, coed **Entrance** Minimally difficult **Setting** 1,756-acre rural campus **Total enrollment** 2,936 **Student/faculty ratio** 13:1 **Application deadline** Rolling (freshmen), rolling (transfer) **Housing** Yes **Expenses** Tuition $2785; Room & Board $2809 **Undergraduates** 60% women, 9% part-time, 15% 25 or older, 0.1% Native American, 0.04% Hispanic American, 94% African American, 0.04% Asian American/Pacific Islander **Academic program** Advanced placement, honors program, internships **Contact** Mr. Emanuel Barnes, Director of Admissions, Alcorn State University, 1000 ASU Drive, Alcorn State, MS 39096-7500. Telephone: 601-877-6147 or toll-free 800-222-6790 (in-state). Fax: 601-877-6347. E-mail: ebarnes@loman.alcorn.edu. Web site: http://www.alcorn.edu/.

BELHAVEN COLLEGE
JACKSON, MISSISSIPPI

General Independent Presbyterian, comprehensive, coed **Entrance** Moderately difficult **Setting** 42-acre urban campus **Total enrollment** 1,630 **Student/faculty ratio** 15:1 **Application deadline** Rolling (freshmen), rolling (transfer) **Freshmen** 70% were admitted **Housing** Yes **Expenses** Tuition $10,860; Room & Board $4010 **Undergraduates** 64% women, 10% part-time, 52% 25 or older, 0.5% Native American, 1% Hispanic American, 31% African American, 1% Asian American/Pacific Islander **The most frequently chosen baccalaureate fields are** business/marketing, education, psychology **Academic program** English as a second language, advanced placement, accelerated degree program, honors program, summer session, adult/continuing education programs, internships **Contact** Suzanne Teel, Director of Admissions, Belhaven College, 150 Peachtree Street, Jackson, MS 39202. Telephone: 601-968-5940 or toll-free 800-960-5940. Fax: 601-968-8946. E-mail: admissions@belhaven.edu. Web site: http://www.belhaven.edu/.

BLUE MOUNTAIN COLLEGE
BLUE MOUNTAIN, MISSISSIPPI

General Independent Southern Baptist, 4-year, women only **Entrance** Noncompetitive **Setting** 44-acre rural campus **Total enrollment** 371 **Student/faculty ratio** 13:1 **Application deadline** Rolling (freshmen), rolling (transfer) **Freshmen** 79% were admitted **Housing** Yes **Expenses** Tuition 6100; Room & Board 3004 **Undergraduates** 21% part-time, 27% 25 or older, 1% Native American, 0.3% Hispanic American, 11% African American, 1% Asian American/Pacific Islander **The most frequently chosen baccalaureate fields are** education, philosophy, religion, and theology, social sciences and history **Academic program** Advanced placement, accelerated degree program, honors program, summer session, internships **Contact** Ms. Tina Barkley, Director of Admissions, Blue Mountain College, PO Box 160, Blue Mountain, MS 38610-0160. Telephone: 662-685-4161 Ext. 176 or toll-free 800-235-0136. E-mail: tbarkley@bmc.edu. Web site: http://www.bmc.edu/.

DELTA STATE UNIVERSITY
CLEVELAND, MISSISSIPPI

General State-supported, comprehensive, coed **Entrance** Minimally difficult **Setting** 332-acre small-town campus **Total enrollment** 3,875 **Student/**

faculty ratio 14:1 **Application deadline** 8/1 (freshmen), rolling (transfer) **Housing** Yes **Expenses** Tuition $2696; Room & Board $2990 **Undergraduates** 60% women, 19% part-time, 22% 25 or older, 0.2% Native American, 0.3% Hispanic American, 28% African American, 1% Asian American/Pacific Islander **The most frequently chosen baccalaureate fields are** business/marketing, education, social sciences and history **Academic program** Advanced placement, honors program, summer session, internships **Contact** Ms. Debbie Heslep, Coordinator of Admissions, Delta State University, Highway 8 West, Cleveland, MS 38733. Telephone: 662-846-4018 or toll-free 800-468-6378. Fax: 662-846-4683. E-mail: jdcooper@dsu.deltast.edu. Web site: http://www.deltast.edu/.

JACKSON STATE UNIVERSITY
JACKSON, MISSISSIPPI

General State-supported, university, coed **Entrance** Minimally difficult **Setting** 128-acre urban campus **Total enrollment** 6,820 **Application deadline** 8/1 (freshmen), 8/1 (transfer) **Freshmen** 26% were admitted **Housing** Yes **Expenses** Tuition $2788; Room & Board $3492 **Undergraduates** 55% women, 12% part-time, 18% 25 or older, 0.1% Native American, 0.1% Hispanic American, 98% African American, 0.2% Asian American/Pacific Islander **Academic program** English as a second language, advanced placement, accelerated degree program, honors program, summer session, adult/continuing education programs, internships **Contact** Mrs. Linda Rush, Admissions Counselor, Jackson State University, PO Box 17330, 1400 John R. Lynch Street, Jackson, MS 39217. Telephone: 601-968-2911 or toll-free 800-682-5390 (in-state); 800-848-6817 (out-of-state). E-mail: schatman@ccaix.jsums.edu. Web site: http://www.jsums.edu/.

MAGNOLIA BIBLE COLLEGE
KOSCIUSKO, MISSISSIPPI

General Independent, 4-year, coed, primarily men, affiliated with Church of Christ **Entrance** Noncompetitive **Setting** 5-acre small-town campus **Total enrollment** 37 **Student/faculty ratio** 4:1 **Application deadline** 8/31 (freshmen), 8/31 (transfer) **Freshmen** 100% were admitted **Housing** Yes **Expenses** Tuition $4540; Room only $1000 **Undergraduates** 41% women, 43% part-time, 32% 25 or older, 3% Hispanic American, 33% African American **The most frequently chosen baccalaureate field is** philosophy, religion, and theology **Academic program** Summer session, internships **Contact** Mr. Allen Coker, Admissions Officer, Magnolia Bible College, PO Box 1109, Kosciusko, MS 39090-1109. Telephone: 601-289-2896 Ext. 106 or toll-free 800-748-8655 (in-state). Fax: 601-289-1850. E-mail: mbcgary@kopower.com. Web site: http://www.mbc.org/.

MILLSAPS COLLEGE
JACKSON, MISSISSIPPI

General Independent United Methodist, comprehensive, coed **Entrance** Moderately difficult **Setting** 100-acre urban campus **Total enrollment** 1,277 **Student/faculty ratio** 13:1 **Application deadline** 2/1 (freshmen), rolling (transfer) **Freshmen** 88% were admitted **Housing** Yes **Expenses** Tuition 15,814; Room & Board 6339 **Undergraduates** 54% women, 5% part-time, 11% 25 or older, 0.3% Native American, 1% Hispanic American, 11% African American, 3% Asian American/Pacific Islander **The most frequently chosen baccalaureate fields are** business/marketing, English, social sciences and history **Academic program** English as a second language, advanced placement, honors program, summer session, adult/continuing education programs, internships **Contact** Mr. John Gaines, Director of Admissions, Millsaps College, 1701 North State Street, Jackson, MS 39210-0001. Telephone: 601-974-1050 or toll-free 800-352-1050. Fax: 601-974-1059. E-mail: hinesfw@okra.millsaps.edu. Web site: http://www.millsaps.edu/.

MISSISSIPPI COLLEGE
CLINTON, MISSISSIPPI

General Independent Southern Baptist, comprehensive, coed **Entrance** Moderately difficult **Setting** 320-acre suburban campus **Total enrollment** 3,423 **Student/faculty ratio** 15:1 **Application deadline** Rolling (freshmen), rolling (transfer) **Freshmen** 98% were admitted **Housing** Yes **Expenses** Tuition $10,150; Room & Board $4424 **Undergraduates** 58% women, 14% part-time, 15% 25 or older, 0.2% Native American, 0.3% Hispanic American, 11% African American, 1% Asian American/Pacific Islander **The most frequently chosen baccalaureate fields are** business/marketing, education, health professions and related sciences **Academic program** Advanced placement, honors program, summer session, adult/continuing education programs, internships **Contact** Dr. Jim Turcotte, Dean of Enrollment Services, Mississippi College, PO Box 4026, Clinton, MS 39058. Telephone: 601-925-3240 or toll-free 800-738-1236. Fax: 601-925-3804. E-mail: admissions@mc.edu.

MISSISSIPPI STATE UNIVERSITY
MISSISSIPPI STATE, MISSISSIPPI

General State-supported, university, coed **Entrance** Moderately difficult **Setting** 4,200-acre small-town campus **Total enrollment** 16,561 **Student/faculty ratio** 15:1 **Application deadline** 4/1 (freshmen), 7/1 (transfer) **Freshmen** 71% were admitted **Housing** Yes **Expenses** Tuition 3430; Room & Board 3990 **Undergraduates** 46% women, 12% part-time, 14% 25 or older, 0.5% Native American, 1% Hispanic American, 19% African American, 1% Asian American/Pacific Islander **The most frequently chosen baccalaureate fields are** business/marketing, education, engineering/engineering technologies **Academic program** English as a second language, advanced placement, accelerated degree program, self-designed majors, honors program, summer session, adult/continuing education programs, internships **Contact** Mr. Jerry Inmon, Director of Admissions, Mississippi State University, PO Box 6305, Mississippi State,

Mississippi State University *(continued)*

MS 39762. Telephone: 662-325-2224. Fax: 662-325-7360. E-mail: admit@admissions.msstate.edu. Web site: http://www.msstate.edu/.

MISSISSIPPI UNIVERSITY FOR WOMEN
COLUMBUS, MISSISSIPPI

General State-supported, comprehensive, coed **Entrance** Moderately difficult **Setting** 110-acre small-town campus **Total enrollment** 2,814 **Application deadline** 9/6 (freshmen), 9/6 (transfer) **Freshmen** 79% were admitted **Housing** Yes **Expenses** Tuition 2656; Room & Board 2790 **Undergraduates** 42% 25 or older, 0.2% Native American, 1% Hispanic American, 28% African American, 0.3% Asian American/Pacific Islander **Academic program** English as a second language, advanced placement, accelerated degree program, honors program, summer session, adult/continuing education programs, internships **Contact** Ms. Terri Heath, Director of Admissions, Mississippi University for Women, PO Box 1613, Columbus, MS 39701-9998. Telephone: 601-329-7106 or toll-free 877-GO 2 THE W. Fax: 601-241-7481. E-mail: admissions@muw.edu. Web site: http://www.muw.edu/.

MISSISSIPPI VALLEY STATE UNIVERSITY
ITTA BENA, MISSISSIPPI

General State-supported, comprehensive, coed **Entrance** Minimally difficult **Setting** 450-acre small-town campus **Total enrollment** 2,687 **Student/faculty ratio** 20:1 **Application deadline** Rolling (freshmen), rolling (transfer) **Freshmen** 45% were admitted **Housing** Yes **Expenses** Tuition 2746; Room & Board 2825 **Undergraduates** 64% women, 14% part-time, 34% 25 or older, 0% Native American, 0.1% Hispanic American, 97% African American, 0.2% Asian American/Pacific Islander **The most frequently chosen baccalaureate fields are** business/marketing, education, protective services/public administration **Academic program** Honors program, summer session, adult/continuing education programs, internships **Contact** Ms. Laronistine Dyson, Director of Admissions and Recruitment, Mississippi Valley State University, 14000 Highway 82 West, Itta Bena, MS 38941-1400. Telephone: 662-254-3344 or toll-free 800-844-6885 (in-state). Fax: 662-254-7900. Web site: http://www.mvsu.edu/.

RUST COLLEGE
HOLLY SPRINGS, MISSISSIPPI

General Independent United Methodist, 4-year, coed **Entrance** Moderately difficult **Setting** 126-acre rural campus **Total enrollment** 852 **Student/faculty ratio** 16:1 **Application deadline** 7/15 (freshmen), 7/15 (transfer) **Freshmen** 40% were admitted **Housing** Yes **Expenses** Tuition $5400; Room & Board $2400 **Undergraduates** 65% women, 20% part-time, 20% 25 or older, 94% African American **The most frequently chosen baccalaureate fields are** business/marketing, computer/information sciences, social sciences and history **Academic program** Accelerated degree program, honors program, summer session, adult/continuing education programs, internships **Contact** Mr. Johnny McDonald, Director of Enrollment Services, Rust College, 150 Rust Avenue, Holly Springs, MS 38635-2328. Telephone: 601-252-8000 Ext. 4065 or toll-free 888-886-8492 Ext. 4065. Fax: 662-252-8895. E-mail: admissions@rustcollege.edu. Web site: http://www.rustcollege.edu/.

SOUTHEASTERN BAPTIST COLLEGE
LAUREL, MISSISSIPPI

Contact Mrs. Emma Bond, Director of Admissions, Southeastern Baptist College, 4229 Highway 15 North, Laurel, MS 39440-1096. Telephone: 601-426-6346.

TOUGALOO COLLEGE
TOUGALOO, MISSISSIPPI

General Independent, 4-year, coed, affiliated with United Church of Christ **Entrance** Minimally difficult **Setting** 500-acre suburban campus **Total enrollment** 1,000 **Student/faculty ratio** 18:1 **Application deadline** Rolling (freshmen), rolling (transfer) **Freshmen** 99% were admitted **Housing** Yes **Expenses** Tuition $7555; Room & Board $3200 **Undergraduates** 72% women, 10% part-time, 10% 25 or older, 0% Native American, 0% Hispanic American, 99% African American, 0% Asian American/Pacific Islander **The most frequently chosen baccalaureate fields are** psychology, business/marketing, social sciences and history **Academic program** Accelerated degree program, self-designed majors, honors program, adult/continuing education programs, internships **Contact** Ms. Adriene W. Walls, Data Entry Specialist, Tougaloo College, Student Enrollment Management Center, 500 West County Line Road, Tougaloo, MS 39174. Telephone: 601-977-7768 or toll-free 888-42GALOO. E-mail: carolyn.evans@tougaloo.edu. Web site: http://www.tougaloo.edu/.

UNIVERSITY OF MISSISSIPPI
OXFORD, MISSISSIPPI

General State-supported, university, coed **Entrance** Moderately difficult **Setting** 2,500-acre small-town campus **Total enrollment** 12,105 **Student/faculty ratio** 17:1 **Application deadline** 7/20 (freshmen), 7/24 (transfer) **Freshmen** 82% were admitted **Housing** Yes **Expenses** Tuition 3153; Room & Board 3790 **Undergraduates** 52% women, 9% part-time, 10% 25 or older, 0.4% Native American, 1% Hispanic American, 12% African American, 1% Asian American/Pacific Islander **The most frequently chosen baccalaureate fields are** business/marketing, education, health professions and related sciences **Academic program** English as a second language, advanced placement, accelerated degree program, honors program, summer session, adult/continuing education programs, internships **Contact** Mr. Beckett Howorth, Director of Admissions, University of Mississippi, Office of Admissions, 145 Martindale Student Services Center, University, MS 38677. Telephone: 662-915-7226 or toll-free 800-653-6477 (in-state). Fax: 662-915-5869. E-mail: info@olemiss.edu. Web site: http://www.olemiss.edu/.

UNIVERSITY OF MISSISSIPPI MEDICAL CENTER

JACKSON, MISSISSIPPI

General State-supported, upper-level, coed **Entrance** Moderately difficult **Setting** 164-acre urban campus **Total enrollment** 1,694 **Application deadline** 2/15 (transfer) **Housing** Yes **Expenses** Tuition $2478; Room only $1836 **Undergraduates** 91% women, 24% 25 or older, 0% Native American, 1% Hispanic American, 21% African American, 2% Asian American/ Pacific Islander **The most frequently chosen baccalaureate field is** health professions and related sciences **Academic program** Summer session, internships **Contact** Dr. Billy M. Bishop, Director of Student Services and Records, University of Mississippi Medical Center, 2500 North State Street, Jackson, MS 39216-4505. Telephone: 601-984-1080. Fax: 601-984-1079. Web site: http://umc.edu/.

UNIVERSITY OF SOUTHERN MISSISSIPPI

HATTIESBURG, MISSISSIPPI

General State-supported, university, coed **Entrance** Moderately difficult **Setting** 1,090-acre suburban campus **Total enrollment** 14,510 **Student/faculty ratio** 19:1 **Application deadline** Rolling (freshmen), rolling (transfer) **Freshmen** 65% were admitted **Housing** Yes **Expenses** Tuition 2970; Room & Board 4212 **Undergraduates** 61% women, 15% part-time, 20% 25 or older, 0.3% Native American, 1% Hispanic American, 23% African American, 0.5% Asian American/Pacific Islander **The most frequently chosen baccalaureate fields are** business/marketing, education, health professions and related sciences **Academic program** English as a second language, advanced placement, accelerated degree program, honors program, summer session, adult/continuing education programs **Contact** Dr. Homer Wesley, Dean of Admissions, University of Southern Mississippi, Box 5166, Hattiesburg, MS 39406-5166. Telephone: 601-266-5000. Fax: 601-266-5148. E-mail: admissions@usm.edu. Web site: http://www.usm.edu/.

WESLEY COLLEGE

FLORENCE, MISSISSIPPI

General Independent Congregational Methodist, 4-year, coed **Contact** Rev. Chris Lohrstorfer, Director of Admissions, Wesley College, PO Box 1070, Florence, MS 39073-1070. Telephone: 601-845-2265 Ext. 21 or toll-free 800-748-9972. Fax: 601-845-2266. E-mail: wcadmit@aol.com. Web site: http://www.wesleycollege.com/.

WILLIAM CAREY COLLEGE

HATTIESBURG, MISSISSIPPI

Contact Mr. Thomas M. Huebner Jr., Director of Admissions, William Carey College, 498 Tuscan Avenue, Hattiesburg, MS 39401-5499. Telephone: 601-582-5051 Ext. 103 or toll-free 800-962-5991 (in-state). E-mail: admiss@mail.wmcarey.edu. Web site: http://www.wmcarey.edu/.

MISSOURI

AVILA COLLEGE

KANSAS CITY, MISSOURI

General Independent Roman Catholic, comprehensive, coed **Entrance** Minimally difficult **Setting** 50-acre suburban campus **Total enrollment** 1,412 **Student/faculty ratio** 11:1 **Application deadline** Rolling (freshmen), rolling (transfer) **Freshmen** 97% were admitted **Housing** Yes **Expenses** Tuition $12,650; Room & Board $5000 **Undergraduates** 70% women, 33% part-time, 35% 25 or older, 1% Native American, 3% Hispanic American, 14% African American, 1% Asian American/Pacific Islander **The most frequently chosen baccalaureate fields are** business/ marketing, education, health professions and related sciences **Academic program** English as a second language, advanced placement, accelerated degree program, summer session, adult/continuing education programs, internships **Contact** Ms. Rebecca Colwell, Director of Admissions, Avila College, 11901 Wornall Rd, Kansas City, MO 64145. Telephone: 816-501-3773 or toll-free 800-GO-AVILA. Fax: 816-501-2453. E-mail: admissions@mail.avila.edu. Web site: http://www.avila.edu/.

BAPTIST BIBLE COLLEGE

SPRINGFIELD, MISSOURI

General Independent Baptist, comprehensive, coed **Entrance** Noncompetitive **Setting** 38-acre campus **Total enrollment** 929 **Application deadline** Rolling (freshmen), rolling (transfer) **Freshmen** 100% were admitted **Housing** Yes **Expenses** Tuition 3164; Room & Board 3864 **Academic program** Summer session, internships **Contact** Dr. Joseph Gleason, Director of Admissions, Baptist Bible College, 628 East Kearney, Springfield, MO 65803-3498. Telephone: 417-268-6000 Ext. 6013. Fax: 417-268-6694. Web site: http://www.bbcnet.edu/bbgst.html.

CALVARY BIBLE COLLEGE AND THEOLOGICAL SEMINARY

KANSAS CITY, MISSOURI

General Independent interdenominational, comprehensive, coed **Entrance** Minimally difficult **Setting** 55-acre suburban campus **Total enrollment** 265 **Student/faculty ratio** 7:1 **Application deadline** Rolling (freshmen), rolling (transfer) **Housing** Yes **Expenses** Tuition $5010; Room & Board $3040 **Undergraduates** 47% women, 35% part-time, 50% 25 or older, 0% Native American, 1% Hispanic American, 7% African American, 4% Asian American/ Pacific Islander **Academic program** Advanced place-

Calvary Bible College and Theological Seminary *(continued)*

ment, accelerated degree program, summer session, adult/continuing education programs **Contact** Mr. Timothy Smith, Director of Admissions, Calvary Bible College and Theological Seminary, 15800 Calvary Road, Kansas City, MO 64147-1341. Telephone: 816-322-0110 Ext. 1326 or toll-free 800-326-3960. Fax: 816-331-4474. E-mail: admissions@calvary.edu. Web site: http://www.calvary.edu/.

CENTRAL BIBLE COLLEGE
SPRINGFIELD, MISSOURI

General Independent, 4-year, coed, affiliated with Assemblies of God **Entrance** Moderately difficult **Setting** 108-acre suburban campus **Total enrollment** 849 **Student/faculty ratio** 18:1 **Application deadline** Rolling (freshmen), rolling (transfer) **Freshmen** 93% were admitted **Housing** Yes **Expenses** Tuition $6430; Room & Board $3500 **Undergraduates** 42% women, 10% part-time, 22% 25 or older, 0.5% Native American, 3% Hispanic American, 2% African American, 2% Asian American/Pacific Islander **The most frequently chosen baccalaureate field is** philosophy, religion, and theology **Academic program** Advanced placement, summer session, internships **Contact** Mrs. Eunice A. Bruegman, Director of Admissions and Records, Central Bible College, 3000 North Grant Avenue, Springfield, MO 65803-1096. Telephone: 417-833-2551 Ext. 1184 or toll-free 800-831-4222 Ext. 1184. Fax: 417-833-5141. E-mail: info@cbcag.edu. Web site: http://www.cbcag.edu/.

CENTRAL CHRISTIAN COLLEGE OF THE BIBLE
MOBERLY, MISSOURI

General Independent, 4-year, coed, affiliated with Christian Churches and Churches of Christ **Entrance** Noncompetitive **Setting** 40-acre small-town campus **Total enrollment** 133 **Application deadline** Rolling (freshmen), rolling (transfer) **Housing** Yes **Expenses** Tuition $4416; Room & Board $1450 **Undergraduates** 20% 25 or older **Academic program** Self-designed majors, internships **Contact** Mr. Jon Ralls, Director of Admissions, Central Christian College of the Bible, 911 Urbandale Drive East, Moberly, MO 65270-1997. Telephone: 660-263-3900 or toll-free 888-263-3900 (in-state). Fax: 660-263-3936. E-mail: iwant2be@cccb.edu. Web site: http://www.cccb.edu/.

CENTRAL METHODIST COLLEGE
FAYETTE, MISSOURI

General Independent Methodist, comprehensive, coed **Entrance** Moderately difficult **Setting** 52-acre small-town campus **Total enrollment** 1,232 **Student/faculty ratio** 14:1 **Application deadline** 8/15 (freshmen), rolling (transfer) **Freshmen** 85% were admitted **Housing** Yes **Expenses** Tuition $11,760; Room & Board $4330 **Undergraduates** 61% women, 11% part-time, 24% 25 or older, 1% Native American, 1% Hispanic American, 8% African American, 0.4% Asian American/Pacific Islander **The most frequently chosen baccalaureate fields are** business/marketing, education, health professions and related sciences **Academic program** Advanced placement, self-designed majors, honors program, summer session, internships **Contact** Mr. David Heringer, Vice President for Enrollment Management and Student Development, Central Methodist College, 411 Central Methodist Square, Fayette, MO 65248-1198. Telephone: 660-248-6247 or toll-free 888-262-1854 (in-state). Fax: 660-248-1872. E-mail: sdaris@cmc2.cmc.edu. Web site: http://www.cmc.edu/.

CENTRAL MISSOURI STATE UNIVERSITY
WARRENSBURG, MISSOURI

General State-supported, comprehensive, coed **Entrance** Moderately difficult **Setting** 1,240-acre small-town campus **Total enrollment** 10,936 **Student/faculty ratio** 17:1 **Application deadline** Rolling (freshmen), rolling (transfer) **Freshmen** 82% were admitted **Housing** Yes **Expenses** Tuition 3510; Room & Board 4410 **Undergraduates** 53% women, 19% part-time, 29% 25 or older, 1% Native American, 1% Hispanic American, 5% African American, 1% Asian American/Pacific Islander **The most frequently chosen baccalaureate fields are** business/marketing, education, protective services/public administration **Academic program** English as a second language, advanced placement, self-designed majors, honors program, summer session, adult/continuing education programs, internships **Contact** Ms. Margaret Herron, Director of Admissions, Central Missouri State University, Administration Building Room 104, Warrensburg, MO 64093. Telephone: 660-543-4290 or toll-free 800-729-2678 (in-state). Fax: 660-543-8517. E-mail: admit@cmsuvmb.cmsu.edu. Web site: http://www.cmsu.edu/.

CLEVELAND CHIROPRACTIC COLLEGE OF KANSAS CITY
KANSAS CITY, MISSOURI

General Independent, upper-level, coed **Total enrollment** 570 **Student/faculty ratio** 15:1 **Expenses** Tuition 15,150 **Academic program** Accelerated degree program, summer session, internships **Contact** Ms. Melissa Denton, Director of Admissions, Cleveland Chiropractic College of Kansas City, 6401 Rockhill Road, Kansas City, MO 64131. Telephone: 816-501-0100 or toll-free 800-467-2252. Fax: 816-501-0205. E-mail: mdenton@cleveland.edu. Web site: http://www.cleveland.edu/.

COLLEGE OF THE OZARKS
POINT LOOKOUT, MISSOURI

General Independent Presbyterian, 4-year, coed **Entrance** Moderately difficult **Setting** 1,000-acre small-town campus **Total enrollment** 1,404 **Student/faculty ratio** 14:1 **Application deadline** 8/20 (freshmen), 8/20 (transfer) **Freshmen** 17% were admitted **Housing** Yes **Expenses** Tuition $0 **Undergraduates** 56% women, 8% part-time, 11% 25 or older, 1%

Native American, 1% Hispanic American, 0.5% African American, 1% Asian American/Pacific Islander **The most frequently chosen baccalaureate fields are** business/marketing, agriculture, education **Academic program** Advanced placement, accelerated degree program, self-designed majors, honors program, summer session, internships **Contact** Ms. Betty McKenzie, Admissions Secretary, College of the Ozarks, PO Box 17, Point Lookout, MO 65726. Telephone: 417-334-6411 Ext. 4217 or toll-free 800-222-0525. Fax: 417-335-2618. E-mail: admiss4@cofo.edu. Web site: http://www.cofo.edu/.

COLUMBIA COLLEGE
COLUMBIA, MISSOURI

General Independent, comprehensive, coed, affiliated with Christian Church (Disciples of Christ) **Entrance** Minimally difficult **Setting** 29-acre small-town campus **Total enrollment** 906 **Student/faculty ratio** 11:1 **Application deadline** Rolling (freshmen), rolling (transfer) **Freshmen** 97% were admitted **Housing** Yes **Expenses** Tuition $10,102; Room & Board $4399 **Undergraduates** 59% women, 18% part-time, 22% 25 or older, 0.4% Native American, 1% Hispanic American, 6% African American, 3% Asian American/Pacific Islander **The most frequently chosen baccalaureate fields are** business/marketing, liberal arts/general studies, protective services/public administration **Academic program** English as a second language, advanced placement, accelerated degree program, self-designed majors, honors program, summer session, adult/continuing education programs, internships **Contact** Ms. Regina Morin, Director of Admissions, Columbia College, 1001 Rogers Street, Columbia, MO 65216. Telephone: 573-875-7352 or toll-free 800-231-2391 Ext. 7366. Fax: 573-875-7506. E-mail: admissions@ccishp.ccis.edu. Web site: http://www.ccis.edu/.

CONCEPTION SEMINARY COLLEGE
CONCEPTION, MISSOURI

General Independent Roman Catholic, 4-year, men only **Entrance** Noncompetitive **Setting** 30-acre rural campus **Total enrollment** 91 **Student/faculty ratio** 4:1 **Application deadline** 7/31 (freshmen), 7/31 (transfer) **Freshmen** 100% were admitted **Housing** Yes **Expenses** Tuition $8792; Room & Board $5068 **Undergraduates** 3% part-time, 36% 25 or older, 0% Native American, 11% Hispanic American, 1% African American, 15% Asian American/Pacific Islander **The most frequently chosen baccalaureate fields are** liberal arts/general studies, philosophy, religion, and theology **Academic program** English as a second language, advanced placement **Contact** Mr. Keith Jiron, Director of Recruitment and Admissions, Conception Seminary College, PO Box 502, Highway 136 & VV, 37174 State Highway VV, Conception, MO 64433. Telephone: 660-944-2886. E-mail: 0553004@acad.nwmissouri.edu. Web site: http://www.conceptionabbey.edu.

CULVER-STOCKTON COLLEGE
CANTON, MISSOURI

General Independent, 4-year, coed, affiliated with Christian Church (Disciples of Christ) **Entrance** Moderately difficult **Setting** 143-acre rural campus **Total enrollment** 821 **Student/faculty ratio** 15:1 **Application deadline** 2/1 (freshmen), 6/1 (transfer) **Freshmen** 77% were admitted **Housing** Yes **Expenses** Tuition $11,200; Room & Board $4975 **Undergraduates** 55% women, 8% part-time, 9% 25 or older, 0.2% Native American, 2% Hispanic American, 4% African American, 0.5% Asian American/Pacific Islander **The most frequently chosen baccalaureate fields are** business/marketing, education, health professions and related sciences **Academic program** Advanced placement, accelerated degree program, self-designed majors, honors program, summer session, internships **Contact** Culver-Stockton College, One College Hill, Canton, MO 63435-1299. Telephone: or toll-free 800-537-1883 (out-of-state). Fax: 217-231-6618. E-mail: enrollment@culver.edu. Web site: http://www.culver.edu/.

DEACONESS COLLEGE OF NURSING
ST. LOUIS, MISSOURI

General Proprietary, 4-year, coed **Entrance** Moderately difficult **Setting** 15-acre urban campus **Total enrollment** 220 **Student/faculty ratio** 12:1 **Application deadline** Rolling (freshmen), rolling (transfer) **Freshmen** 37% were admitted **Housing** Yes **Expenses** Tuition $8975; Room & Board $3990 **Undergraduates** 96% women, 22% part-time, 23% 25 or older, 0.5% Native American, 1% Hispanic American, 27% African American, 2% Asian American/Pacific Islander **The most frequently chosen baccalaureate field is** health professions and related sciences **Academic program** English as a second language, advanced placement, summer session **Contact** Ms. Peggy Hudson, Admissions Coordinator, Deaconess College of Nursing, 6150 Oakland Avenue, St. Louis, MO 63139-3215. Telephone: 314-768-3044 or toll-free 800-942-4310. Fax: 314-768-5673. Web site: http://www.deaconess.edu.

DEVRY INSTITUTE OF TECHNOLOGY
KANSAS CITY, MISSOURI

General Proprietary, 4-year, coed **Entrance** Minimally difficult **Setting** 12-acre urban campus **Total enrollment** 2,708 **Student/faculty ratio** 19:1 **Application deadline** Rolling (freshmen), rolling (transfer) **Freshmen** 70% were admitted **Housing** No **Expenses** Tuition $8740 **Undergraduates** 23% women, 32% part-time, 50% 25 or older, 1% Native American, 3% Hispanic American, 13% African American, 3% Asian American/Pacific Islander **The most frequently chosen baccalaureate fields are** business/marketing, computer/information sciences, engineering/engineering technologies **Academic program** Advanced placement, accelerated degree program, summer session, adult/continuing education programs **Contact** Mike Wimer, Director of Admis-

DeVry Institute of Technology *(continued)*

sions, DeVry Institute of Technology, 11224 Holmes Road, Kansas City, MO 64131. Telephone: 816-941-2810 or toll-free 800-821-3766 (out-of-state). Web site: http://www.kc.devry.edu/.

DRURY UNIVERSITY
SPRINGFIELD, MISSOURI

General Independent, comprehensive, coed **Entrance** Moderately difficult **Setting** 60-acre urban campus **Total enrollment** 1,762 **Student/faculty ratio** 12:1 **Application deadline** 3/15 (freshmen), rolling (transfer) **Freshmen** 88% were admitted **Housing** Yes **Expenses** Tuition $11,204; Room & Board $4304 **Undergraduates** 56% women, 2% part-time, 0.3% Native American, 1% Hispanic American, 25% African American, 1% Asian American/Pacific Islander **Academic program** English as a second language, advanced placement, accelerated degree program, self-designed majors, honors program, summer session, adult/continuing education programs, internships **Contact** Mr. Michael Thomas, Director of Admission, Drury University, 900 North Benton, Bay Hall, Springfield, MO 65802. Telephone: 417-873-7205 or toll-free 800-922-2274 (in-state). Fax: 417-866-3873. E-mail: druryad@lib.drury.edu. Web site: http://www.drury.edu/.

EVANGEL UNIVERSITY
SPRINGFIELD, MISSOURI

General Independent, comprehensive, coed, affiliated with Assemblies of God **Entrance** Moderately difficult **Setting** 80-acre urban campus **Total enrollment** 1,538 **Student/faculty ratio** 18:1 **Application deadline** 8/15 (freshmen), 8/15 (transfer) **Freshmen** 92% were admitted **Housing** Yes **Expenses** Tuition 10,186; Room & Board 3900 **Undergraduates** 56% women, 5% part-time, 3% 25 or older, 1% Native American, 4% Hispanic American, 3% African American, 1% Asian American/Pacific Islander **The most frequently chosen baccalaureate fields are** business/marketing, education, psychology **Academic program** Advanced placement, summer session **Contact** Andrew Denton, Director of Admissions, Evangel University, 1111 North Glenstone, Springfield, MO 65802-2191. Telephone: 417-865-2811 Ext. 7342 or toll-free 800-382-6435 (in-state). Fax: 417-865-9599. E-mail: admissions@mail4.evangel.edu. Web site: http://www.evangel.edu/.

FONTBONNE COLLEGE
ST. LOUIS, MISSOURI

General Independent Roman Catholic, comprehensive, coed **Entrance** Moderately difficult **Setting** 13-acre suburban campus **Total enrollment** 2,059 **Student/faculty ratio** 11:1 **Application deadline** 8/1 (freshmen), rolling (transfer) **Freshmen** 81% were admitted **Housing** Yes **Expenses** Tuition $11,843; Room & Board $5200 **Undergraduates** 70% women, 18% part-time, 37% 25 or older, 1% Native American, 1% Hispanic American, 18% African American, 1% Asian American/Pacific Islander **The most frequently chosen baccalaureate fields are** business/marketing, education, visual/performing arts **Academic program** English as a second language, advanced placement, accelerated degree program, self-designed majors, honors program, summer session, adult/continuing education programs, internships **Contact** Ms. Peggy Musen, Associate Dean for Enrollment Management, Fontbonne College, 6800 Wydown Boulevard, St. Louis, MO 63105-3098. Telephone: 314-889-1400. Fax: 314-719-8021. E-mail: pmusen@fontbonne.edu. Web site: http://www.fontbonne.edu/.

GLOBAL UNIVERSITY OF THE ASSEMBLIES OF GOD
SPRINGFIELD, MISSOURI

General Independent, comprehensive, coed, affiliated with Assemblies of God **Entrance** Noncompetitive **Total enrollment** 2,756 **Application deadline** Rolling (freshmen), rolling (transfer) **Housing** No **Expenses** Tuition $1800 **Undergraduates** 32% women, 89% part-time, 92% 25 or older **The most frequently chosen baccalaureate field is** philosophy, religion, and theology **Academic program** Advanced placement, accelerated degree program, honors program, adult/continuing education programs, internships **Contact** Lattice Campbell, Dean of Student Affairs, Global University of the Assemblies of God, 1211 South Glenstone Avenue, Springfield, MO 65804. Telephone: 800-443-1083 or toll-free 800-443-1083. E-mail: berean@ag.org. Web site: http://www.globaluniversity.edu/.

HANNIBAL-LAGRANGE COLLEGE
HANNIBAL, MISSOURI

General Independent Southern Baptist, 4-year, coed **Entrance** Moderately difficult **Setting** 110-acre small-town campus **Total enrollment** 1,104 **Student/faculty ratio** 16:1 **Application deadline** 8/26 (freshmen), rolling (transfer) **Freshmen** 41% were admitted **Housing** Yes **Expenses** Tuition $8830; Room & Board $3226 **Undergraduates** 20% 25 or older, 1% Native American, 1% Hispanic American, 3% African American, 1% Asian American/Pacific Islander **Academic program** Advanced placement, accelerated degree program, self-designed majors, honors program, summer session, adult/continuing education programs, internships **Contact** Mr. Raymond Carty, Dean of Enrollment Management, Hannibal-LaGrange College, 2800 Palmyra Road, Hannibal, MO 63401-1999. Telephone: 573-221-3113 or toll-free 800-HLG-1119. E-mail: admissio@hlg.edu. Web site: http://www.hlg.edu/.

HARRIS-STOWE STATE COLLEGE
ST. LOUIS, MISSOURI

General State-supported, 4-year, coed **Entrance** Moderately difficult **Setting** 22-acre urban campus **Total enrollment** 1,100 **Student/faculty ratio** 18:1 **Application deadline** Rolling (freshmen), rolling (transfer) **Freshmen** 66% were admitted **Housing** No **Expenses** Tuition $2160 **Undergraduates** 0.1% Native American, 1% Hispanic American, 76% African American, 0.2% Asian American/Pacific Islander **Academic program** Advanced placement, summer session, internships **Contact** Ms. Miranda Saddler, Interim Director of Admissions, Harris-Stowe State College, 3026 Laclede Avenue, St. Louis, MO 63103. Telephone: 314-340-3300. Fax: 314-340-3555. E-mail: currierd@mail1.hssc.edu. Web site: http://www.hssc.edu/.

JEWISH HOSPITAL COLLEGE OF NURSING AND ALLIED HEALTH

ST. LOUIS, MISSOURI

General Independent, comprehensive, coed, primarily women **Entrance** Moderately difficult **Setting** urban campus **Total enrollment** 432 **Application deadline** Rolling (freshmen), rolling (transfer) **Freshmen** 100% were admitted **Housing** Yes **Expenses** Tuition $11,090; Room only $2385 **Undergraduates** 86% women, 71% part-time, 60% 25 or older, 0% Native American, 1% Hispanic American, 19% African American, 2% Asian American/Pacific Islander **Academic program** Advanced placement, summer session **Contact** Ms. Constance J. Stohlman, Director of Enrollment and Management, Jewish Hospital College of Nursing and Allied Health, 306 South Kingshighway, St. Louis, MO 63110-1091. Telephone: 314-454-7057 or toll-free 800-832-9009 (in-state). Fax: 314-454-5239. E-mail: cal7374@bjcmail.carenet.org. Web site: http://jhconah.org/.

KANSAS CITY ART INSTITUTE

KANSAS CITY, MISSOURI

General Independent, 4-year, coed **Entrance** Moderately difficult **Setting** 12-acre urban campus **Total enrollment** 527 **Student/faculty ratio** 9:1 **Application deadline** Rolling (freshmen), rolling (transfer) **Freshmen** 77% were admitted **Housing** Yes **Expenses** Tuition $18,218; Room & Board $5500 **Undergraduates** 51% women, 2% part-time, 12% 25 or older, 1% Native American, 5% Hispanic American, 1% African American, 2% Asian American/Pacific Islander **The most frequently chosen baccalaureate field is** visual/performing arts **Academic program** English as a second language, advanced placement, summer session, adult/continuing education programs, internships **Contact** Mr. Gerald Valet, Director of Admission Technology, Kansas City Art Institute, 4415 Warwick Boulevard, Kansas City, MO 64111-1874. Telephone: 816-474-5224 or toll-free 800-522-5224. Fax: 816-802-3309. E-mail: admiss@kcai.edu. Web site: http://www.kcai.edu/.

KANSAS CITY COLLEGE OF LEGAL STUDIES

KANSAS CITY, MISSOURI

General Proprietary, 4-year, coed **Total enrollment** 102 **Expenses** Tuition 23,958 **Contact** Mrs. Rosemary Velez, Admissions Director, Kansas City College of Legal Studies, 402 East Bannister Road, Suite A, Kansas City, MO 64131. Telephone: 816-444-2232. Web site: http://www.metropolitancollege.edu/.

LESTER L. COX COLLEGE OF NURSING AND HEALTH SCIENCES

SPRINGFIELD, MISSOURI

General Independent, 4-year, coed, primarily women **Total enrollment** 294 **Application deadline** 2/1 (freshmen) **Freshmen** 69% were admitted **Housing** Yes **Expenses** Tuition $6928; Room only $1750 **Undergraduates** 93% women, 40% part-time, 44% 25 or older, 1% Native American, 1% Hispanic American, 1% African American, 1% Asian American/Pacific Islander **The most frequently chosen baccalaureate field is** health professions and related sciences **Academic program** Adult/continuing education programs **Contact** Ms. Virginia Mace, Admissions Counselor, Lester L. Cox College of Nursing and Health Sciences, 1423 North Jefferson, Springfield, MO 65802. Telephone: 417-269-3069. Fax: 417-269-3581. E-mail: vsmace@coxnet.org. Web site: http://www.coxnet.org/coxcollege/default.cfm.

LINCOLN UNIVERSITY

JEFFERSON CITY, MISSOURI

General State-supported, comprehensive, coed **Entrance** Noncompetitive **Setting** 152-acre small-town campus **Total enrollment** 3,347 **Student/faculty ratio** 17:1 **Application deadline** 7/15 (freshmen), 6/15 (transfer) **Freshmen** 80% were admitted **Housing** Yes **Expenses** Tuition $3598; Room & Board $3790 **Undergraduates** 58% women, 35% part-time, 5% 25 or older, 0.4% Native American, 1% Hispanic American, 33% African American, 1% Asian American/Pacific Islander **Academic program** Advanced placement, accelerated degree program, self-designed majors, honors program, summer session, adult/continuing education programs, internships **Contact** Executive Director of Enrollment Management, Lincoln University, 820 Chestnut, Jefferson City, MO 65102. Telephone: 573-681-5599 or toll-free 800-521-5052. Web site: http://www.lincolnu.edu/.

LINDENWOOD UNIVERSITY

ST. CHARLES, MISSOURI

General Independent Presbyterian, comprehensive, coed **Entrance** Moderately difficult **Setting** 358-acre suburban campus **Total enrollment** 6,056 **Student/faculty ratio** 17:1 **Application deadline** Rolling (freshmen), rolling (transfer) **Housing** Yes **Expenses** Tuition $11,250; Room & Board $5600 **Undergraduates** 54% women, 6% part-time, 35% 25 or older, 0.5% Native American, 1% Hispanic American, 7% African American, 1% Asian American/Pacific Islander **The most frequently chosen baccalaureate fields are** business/marketing, communications/communication technologies, education **Academic program** Advanced placement, accelerated degree program, self-designed majors, honors program, summer session, adult/continuing education programs, internships **Contact** John Guffey, Dean of Admis-

Lindenwood University *(continued)*

sions, Lindenwood University, 209 South Kingshighway, St. Charles, MO 63301-1695. Telephone: 636-949-4933. Fax: 636-949-4910. Web site: http://www.lindenwood.edu/.

LOGAN UNIVERSITY OF CHIROPRACTIC
CHESTERFIELD, MISSOURI

General Independent, upper-level, coed **Entrance** Moderately difficult **Setting** 100-acre suburban campus **Total enrollment** 852 **Application deadline** Rolling (freshmen), rolling (transfer) **Housing** No **Expenses** Tuition 9874 **Undergraduates** 44% women, 19% part-time, 44% 25 or older, 0% Native American, 3% Hispanic American, 6% African American, 3% Asian American/Pacific Islander **The most frequently chosen baccalaureate field is** biological/life sciences **Academic program** Advanced placement, adult/continuing education programs, internships **Contact** Dr. Patrick Browne, Dean of Admissions, Logan University of Chiropractic, 1851 Schoettler Road, Box 1065, Chesterfield, MO 63006-1065. Telephone: 636-227-2100 Ext. 149 or toll-free 800-533-9210. E-mail: loganadm@logan.edu. Web site: http://www.logan.edu/.

MARYVILLE UNIVERSITY OF SAINT LOUIS
ST. LOUIS, MISSOURI

General Independent, comprehensive, coed **Entrance** Moderately difficult **Setting** 130-acre suburban campus **Total enrollment** 3,055 **Student/faculty ratio** 13:1 **Application deadline** 8/15 (freshmen), rolling (transfer) **Freshmen** 78% were admitted **Housing** Yes **Expenses** Tuition 13,000; Room & Board 5600 **Undergraduates** 73% women, 46% part-time, 48% 25 or older, 0.4% Native American, 1% Hispanic American, 5% African American, 1% Asian American/Pacific Islander **The most frequently chosen baccalaureate fields are** business/marketing, health professions and related sciences, psychology **Academic program** English as a second language, advanced placement, accelerated degree program, honors program, summer session, adult/continuing education programs, internships **Contact** Dr. Martha Wade, Vice President of Admissions and Enrollment Management, Maryville University of Saint Louis, 13550 Conway Road, St. Louis, MO 63141-7299. Telephone: 314-529-9350 or toll-free 800-627-9855. Fax: 314-529-9927. E-mail: admissions@maryville.edu. Web site: http://www.maryville.edu/.

▶ **For more information, see page 448.**

MESSENGER COLLEGE
JOPLIN, MISSOURI

General Independent Pentecostal, 4-year, coed **Entrance** Moderately difficult **Setting** 16-acre small-town campus **Total enrollment** 90 **Application deadline** 9/1 (freshmen), 9/1 (transfer) **Freshmen** 100% were admitted **Housing** Yes **Expenses** Tuition $4170; Room & Board $3100 **Undergraduates** 46% women, 16% part-time, 20% 25 or older, 2% Native American, 1% Hispanic American, 3% African American, 1% Asian American/Pacific Islander **The most frequently chosen baccalaureate fields are** philosophy, religion, and theology, visual/performing arts **Academic program** Honors program, internships **Contact** Gwen Minor, Vice President of Academic Affairs, Messenger College, 300 East 50th, PO Box 4050, Joplin, MO 64803. Telephone: 417-624-7070 Ext. 102 or toll-free 800-385-8940 (in-state). Fax: 417-624-5070. E-mail: mc@pcg.org.

MISSOURI BAPTIST COLLEGE
ST. LOUIS, MISSOURI

General Independent Southern Baptist, comprehensive, coed **Entrance** Moderately difficult **Setting** 65-acre suburban campus **Total enrollment** 2,806 **Student/faculty ratio** 15:1 **Application deadline** Rolling (freshmen), rolling (transfer) **Freshmen** 75% were admitted **Housing** Yes **Expenses** Tuition 10,682; Room & Board 5080 **Undergraduates** 63% women, 65% part-time, 34% 25 or older, 0.1% Native American, 2% Hispanic American, 6% African American, 0.4% Asian American/Pacific Islander **The most frequently chosen baccalaureate fields are** business/marketing, education, psychology **Academic program** Advanced placement, accelerated degree program, self-designed majors, summer session, adult/continuing education programs, internships **Contact** Mr. Robert Cornwell, Associate Director of Admissions, Missouri Baptist College, One College Park Drive, St. Louis, MO 63141-8660. Telephone: 314-392-2293 or toll-free 877-434-1115 Ext. 2290. Fax: 314-434-7596. E-mail: admissions@mobap.edu. Web site: http://www.mobap.edu/.

MISSOURI SOUTHERN STATE COLLEGE
JOPLIN, MISSOURI

General State-supported, 4-year, coed **Entrance** Moderately difficult **Setting** 350-acre small-town campus **Total enrollment** 5,785 **Student/faculty ratio** 18:1 **Application deadline** 8/1 (freshmen), 8/1 (transfer) **Freshmen** 91% were admitted **Housing** Yes **Expenses** Tuition $2496; Room & Board $3610 **Undergraduates** 57% women, 35% part-time, 31% 25 or older, 3% Native American, 1% Hispanic American, 3% African American, 1% Asian American/Pacific Islander **The most frequently chosen baccalaureate fields are** business/marketing, education, protective services/public administration **Academic program** English as a second language, advanced placement, accelerated degree program, honors program, summer session, adult/continuing education programs, internships **Contact** Mr. Derek Skaggs, Director of Enrollment Services, Missouri Southern State College, 3950 East Newman Road, Joplin, MO 64801-1595. Telephone: 417-625-9537 or toll-free 800-606-MSSC. Fax: 417-659-4429. E-mail: admis@vm.mssc.edu. Web site: http://www.mssc.edu/.

▶ **For more information, see page 451.**

MISSOURI TECH
ST. LOUIS, MISSOURI

Contact Mr. Phil Eberle, Director of Admissions, Missouri Tech, 1167 Corporate Lake Drive, St. Louis, MO 63132-1716. Telephone: 314-569-3600 or toll-free 800-230-3600 (out-of-state). Fax: 314-569-1167. E-mail: rhonaber@motech.edu. Web site: http://www.motech.edu/.

MISSOURI VALLEY COLLEGE
MARSHALL, MISSOURI

General Independent, 4-year, coed, affiliated with Presbyterian Church **Entrance** Moderately difficult **Setting** 140-acre small-town campus **Total enrollment** 1,641 **Student/faculty ratio** 22:1 **Application deadline** Rolling (freshmen), rolling (transfer) **Freshmen** 84% were admitted **Housing** Yes **Expenses** Tuition $12,450; Room & Board $5000 **Undergraduates** 41% women, 14% part-time, 10% 25 or older, 1% Native American, 5% Hispanic American, 17% African American, 3% Asian American/Pacific Islander **Academic program** English as a second language, advanced placement, summer session, adult/continuing education programs, internships **Contact** Ms. Debbie Bultman, Admissions, Missouri Valley College, 500 East College, Marshall, MO 65340-3197. Telephone: 660-831-4114. Fax: 660-831-4039. E-mail: mo-valley@juno.com. Web site: http://www.murlin.com/~webfx/mvc/.

MISSOURI WESTERN STATE COLLEGE
ST. JOSEPH, MISSOURI

General State-supported, 4-year, coed **Entrance** Noncompetitive **Setting** 744-acre suburban campus **Total enrollment** 5,089 **Student/faculty ratio** 18:1 **Application deadline** 7/30 (freshmen), 7/30 (transfer) **Freshmen** 100% were admitted **Housing** Yes **Expenses** Tuition $3026; Room & Board $3476 **Undergraduates** 61% women, 25% part-time, 23% 25 or older, 1% Native American, 2% Hispanic American, 9% African American, 1% Asian American/Pacific Islander **The most frequently chosen baccalaureate fields are** business/marketing, education, protective services/public administration **Academic program** Advanced placement, accelerated degree program, honors program, summer session, adult/continuing education programs, internships **Contact** Mr. Howard McCauley, Director of Admissions, Missouri Western State College, 4525 Downs Drive, St. Joseph, MO 64507-2294. Telephone: 816-271-4267 or toll-free 800-662-7041 Ext. 60. Fax: 816-271-5833. E-mail: admissn@griffon.mwsc.edu. Web site: http://www.mwsc.edu/.

NATIONAL AMERICAN UNIVERSITY
KANSAS CITY, MISSOURI

General Proprietary, 4-year, coed **Entrance** Noncompetitive **Setting** 1-acre urban campus **Total enrollment** 380 **Student/faculty ratio** 12:1 **Application deadline** Rolling (freshmen) **Housing** No **Expenses** Tuition $9360 **Undergraduates** 97% 25 or older **Academic program** Summer session **Contact** Janet Miller, Director of Admissions, National American University, 4200 Blue Ridge Boulevard, Kansas City, MO 64133-1612. Telephone: 816-353-4554. Fax: 816-353-1176. Web site: http://www.national.edu/.

NORTHWEST MISSOURI STATE UNIVERSITY
MARYVILLE, MISSOURI

General State-supported, comprehensive, coed **Entrance** Moderately difficult **Setting** 240-acre small-town campus **Total enrollment** 6,442 **Student/faculty ratio** 21:1 **Application deadline** Rolling (freshmen), rolling (transfer) **Freshmen** 90% were admitted **Housing** Yes **Expenses** Tuition $3330; Room & Board $4150 **Undergraduates** 56% women, 11% part-time, 4% 25 or older, 0.3% Native American, 1% Hispanic American, 3% African American, 1% Asian American/Pacific Islander **Academic program** English as a second language, advanced placement, accelerated degree program, summer session, internships **Contact** Ms. Beverly Schenkel, Associate Director of Admission, Northwest Missouri State University, 800 University Drive, Maryville, MO 64468-6001. Telephone: 660-562-1149 or toll-free 800-633-1175. Fax: 660-562-1121. E-mail: admissions@acad.nwmissouri.edu. Web site: http://www.nwmissouri.edu/.

OZARK CHRISTIAN COLLEGE
JOPLIN, MISSOURI

General Independent Christian, 4-year, coed **Entrance** Noncompetitive **Setting** 110-acre suburban campus **Total enrollment** 750 **Student/faculty ratio** 21:1 **Application deadline** 8/15 (freshmen), rolling (transfer) **Freshmen** 100% were admitted **Housing** Yes **Expenses** Tuition $5230; Room & Board $3830 **Undergraduates** 50% women, 15% part-time, 25% 25 or older, 2% Native American, 2% Hispanic American, 1% African American, 1% Asian American/Pacific Islander **The most frequently chosen baccalaureate field is** philosophy, religion, and theology **Academic program** English as a second language, summer session, adult/continuing education programs, internships **Contact** Jim Marcum, Director of Admissions, Ozark Christian College, 1111 North Main Street, Joplin, MO 64801-4804. Telephone: 417-624-2518 Ext. 2021 or toll-free 800-299-4622. Fax: 417-624-0090. E-mail: occadmin@occ.edu. Web site: http://www.occ.edu/.

PARK UNIVERSITY
PARKVILLE, MISSOURI

General Independent, comprehensive, coed, affiliated with Reorganized Church of Jesus Christ of Latter Day Saints **Entrance** Moderately difficult **Setting** 800-acre suburban campus **Total enrollment** 1,367 **Student/faculty ratio** 14:1 **Application deadline** 8/1 (freshmen), 8/1 (transfer) **Freshmen** 77% were admitted **Housing** Yes **Expenses** Tuition $4950;

Park University *(continued)*

Room & Board $4850 **Undergraduates** 61% women, 26% part-time, 33% 25 or older, 1% Native American, 4% Hispanic American, 13% African American, 2% Asian American/Pacific Islander **The most frequently chosen baccalaureate fields are** business/ marketing, education, social sciences and history **Academic program** English as a second language, advanced placement, self-designed majors, honors program, summer session, adult/continuing education programs, internships **Contact** Dr. Ron Carruth, Director of Student Recruiting and Marketing, Park University, 8700 NW River Park Drive, Campus Box 1, Parkville, MO 64152. Telephone: 816-741-2000 Ext. 6215 or toll-free 800-745-7275. Fax: 816-741-4462. E-mail: admissions@mail.park.edu. Web site: http://www.park.edu/.

RESEARCH COLLEGE OF NURSING
KANSAS CITY, MISSOURI

General Independent, comprehensive, coed, primarily women **Entrance** Moderately difficult **Setting** 66-acre urban campus **Total enrollment** 216 **Student/faculty ratio** 7:1 **Application deadline** 6/30 (freshmen), 1/31 (transfer) **Freshmen** 78% were admitted **Housing** Yes **Expenses** Tuition $13,895; Room & Board $4850 **Undergraduates** 96% women, 7% part-time, 30% 25 or older **Academic program** Advanced placement, accelerated degree program, honors program, summer session **Contact** Ms. Marisa Ferrara, Rockhurst College Admission Office, Research College of Nursing, 2316 East Meyer Boulevard, Kansas City, MO 64132. Telephone: 816-501-4100 Ext. 4654 or toll-free 800-842-6776. Fax: 816-501-4588. E-mail: mendenhall@vax2.rockhurst.edu.

ROCKHURST UNIVERSITY
KANSAS CITY, MISSOURI

General Independent Roman Catholic (Jesuit), comprehensive, coed **Entrance** Moderately difficult **Setting** 35-acre urban campus **Total enrollment** 2,727 **Student/faculty ratio** 12:1 **Application deadline** 6/30 (freshmen), rolling (transfer) **Freshmen** 88% were admitted **Housing** Yes **Expenses** Tuition 13,800; Room & Board 4850 **Undergraduates** 58% women, 39% part-time, 15% 25 or older, 1% Native American, 5% Hispanic American, 8% African American, 2% Asian American/Pacific Islander **The most frequently chosen baccalaureate fields are** business/ marketing, health professions and related sciences, psychology **Academic program** Advanced placement, accelerated degree program, honors program, summer session, adult/continuing education programs, internships **Contact** Mr. Phillip Gebauer, Director of Undergraduate Admissions, Rockhurst University, 1100 Rockhurst Road, Kansas City, MO 64110-2561. Telephone: 816-501-4100 or toll-free 800-842-6776. Fax: 816-501-4241. E-mail: admission@ vax2.rockhurst.edu. Web site: http://www.rockhurst.edu/.

ST. LOUIS CHRISTIAN COLLEGE
FLORISSANT, MISSOURI

General Independent Christian, 4-year, coed **Entrance** Minimally difficult **Setting** 20-acre suburban campus **Total enrollment** 192 **Student/faculty ratio** 12:1 **Application deadline** 8/15 (freshmen), 8/15 (transfer) **Freshmen** 91% were admitted **Housing** Yes **Expenses** Tuition 5190; Room & Board 3180 **Undergraduates** 43% women, 46% part-time, 46% 25 or older, 1% Native American, 1% Hispanic American, 22% African American, 1% Asian American/ Pacific Islander **The most frequently chosen baccalaureate fields are** education, philosophy, religion, and theology, social sciences and history **Academic program** Advanced placement, accelerated degree program, adult/continuing education programs, internships **Contact** Mr. Richard Fordyce, Registrar, St. Louis Christian College, 1360 Grandview Drive, Florissant, MO 63033-6499. Telephone: 314-837-6777 Ext. 1500. Fax: 314-837-8291. E-mail: questions@ slcc4ministry.edu. Web site: http://www.slcc4ministry.edu/.

ST. LOUIS COLLEGE OF PHARMACY
ST. LOUIS, MISSOURI

General Independent, comprehensive, coed **Entrance** Moderately difficult **Setting** 5-acre urban campus **Total enrollment** 907 **Student/faculty ratio** 9:1 **Application deadline** Rolling (freshmen), 2/1 (transfer) **Freshmen** 79% were admitted **Housing** Yes **Expenses** Tuition 13,120; Room & Board 5220 **Undergraduates** 65% women, 0.1% part-time, 15% 25 or older, 0% Native American, 1% Hispanic American, 5% African American, 15% Asian American/ Pacific Islander **Academic program** Advanced placement, summer session, adult/continuing education programs, internships **Contact** Ms. Penny Bryant, Director of Admissions/Registrar, St. Louis College of Pharmacy, 4588 Parkview Place, St. Louis, MO 63110-1088. Telephone: 314-367-8700 Ext. 1067 or toll-free 800-278-5267 (in-state). Fax: 314-367-2784. E-mail: lboeschen@slcop.stlcop.edu. Web site: http://www.stlcop.edu/.

SAINT LOUIS UNIVERSITY
ST. LOUIS, MISSOURI

General Independent Roman Catholic (Jesuit), university, coed **Entrance** Moderately difficult **Setting** 279-acre urban campus **Total enrollment** 13,873 **Student/faculty ratio** 13:1 **Application deadline** Rolling (freshmen), rolling (transfer) **Freshmen** 67% were admitted **Housing** Yes **Expenses** Tuition 18,438; Room & Board 6140 **Undergraduates** 56% women, 41% part-time, 15% 25 or older, 0.3% Native American, 2% Hispanic American, 9% African American, 5% Asian American/Pacific Islander **The most frequently chosen baccalaureate fields are** business/ marketing, health professions and related sciences, psychology **Academic program** English as a second language, advanced placement, accelerated degree program, self-designed majors, honors program, summer session, adult/continuing education programs, internships **Contact** Mr. Scott Belobrajdic, Credential Evaluator for Undergraduate Admissions, Saint Louis University, 221 North Grand Boulevard, St. Louis, MO 63103-2097. Telephone: 314-977-2500 or toll-free 314-977-2500 (in-state); 800-758-3678 (out-of-state). Fax: 314-977-7136. E-mail: admitme@sluvca.slu.edu.. Web site: http://imagine.slu.edu/.

SAINT LUKE'S COLLEGE
KANSAS CITY, MISSOURI

General Independent Episcopal, upper-level, coed, primarily women **Entrance** Very difficult **Setting** 3-acre urban campus **Total enrollment** 107 **Student/faculty ratio** 7:1 **Application deadline** 12/31 (transfer) **Housing** Yes **Expenses** Tuition $8250 **Undergraduates** 96% women, 13% part-time, 80% 25 or older, 0% Native American, 3% Hispanic American, 6% African American, 4% Asian American/Pacific Islander **The most frequently chosen baccalaureate field is** health professions and related sciences **Academic program** Summer session **Contact** Ms. Marsha Thomas, Director, Admissions and Records, Saint Luke's College, 4426 Wornall Road, Kansas City, MO 64111. Telephone: 816-932-2073. E-mail: mjthomas@saint-lukes.org. Web site: http://www.saint-lukes.org/.

SOUTHEAST MISSOURI STATE UNIVERSITY
CAPE GIRARDEAU, MISSOURI

General State-supported, comprehensive, coed **Entrance** Moderately difficult **Setting** 693-acre small-town campus **Total enrollment** 8,948 **Student/faculty ratio** 18:1 **Application deadline** 7/15 (freshmen), 8/15 (transfer) **Freshmen** 48% were admitted **Housing** Yes **Expenses** Tuition $3390; Room & Board $4718 **Undergraduates** 58% women, 24% part-time, 18% 25 or older, 1% Native American, 1% Hispanic American, 6% African American, 1% Asian American/Pacific Islander **The most frequently chosen baccalaureate fields are** business/marketing, education, protective services/public administration **Academic program** English as a second language, advanced placement, self-designed majors, honors program, summer session, adult/continuing education programs, internships **Contact** Mr. Jay Goff, Director of Admissions, Southeast Missouri State University, MS 3550, Cape Girardeau, MO 63701. Telephone: 573-651-2590. Fax: 573-651-5936. E-mail: f333rec.@semoum.semo.edu. Web site: http://www.semo.edu/.

SOUTHWEST BAPTIST UNIVERSITY
BOLIVAR, MISSOURI

General Independent Southern Baptist, comprehensive, coed **Entrance** Moderately difficult **Setting** 152-acre small-town campus **Total enrollment** 2,701 **Student/faculty ratio** 19:1 **Application deadline** Rolling (freshmen), rolling (transfer) **Freshmen** 86% were admitted **Housing** Yes **Expenses** Tuition $9746, Room & Board $3010 **The most frequently chosen baccalaureate fields are** business/marketing, education, health professions and related sciences **Academic program** English as a second language, advanced placement, accelerated degree program, honors program, summer session, internships **Contact** Mr. Rob Harris, Director of Admissions, Southwest Baptist University, 1600 University Avenue, Bolivar, MO 65613-2597. Telephone: 417-328-1809 or toll-free 800-526-5859. Fax: 417-328-1514. E-mail: admitme@shuniv.edu. Web site: http://www.sbuniv.edu/.

SOUTHWEST MISSOURI STATE UNIVERSITY
SPRINGFIELD, MISSOURI

General State-supported, comprehensive, coed **Entrance** Moderately difficult **Setting** 225-acre suburban campus **Total enrollment** 17,703 **Student/faculty ratio** 18:1 **Application deadline** 8/1 (freshmen), 8/1 (transfer) **Freshmen** 87% were admitted **Housing** Yes **Expenses** Tuition $3748; Room & Board $4032 **Undergraduates** 55% women, 19% part-time, 15% 25 or older, 1% Native American, 1% Hispanic American, 3% African American, 1% Asian American/Pacific Islander **The most frequently chosen baccalaureate fields are** business/marketing, communications/communication technologies, education **Academic program** English as a second language, advanced placement, accelerated degree program, self-designed majors, honors program, summer session, adult/continuing education programs, internships **Contact** Ms. Jill Duncan, Associate Director of Admissions, Southwest Missouri State University, 901 South National, Springfield, MO 65804-0094. Telephone: 417-836-5517 or toll-free 800-492-7900. Fax: 417-836-6334. E-mail: smsuinfo@vma.smsu.edu. Web site: http://www.smsu.edu/.

STEPHENS COLLEGE
COLUMBIA, MISSOURI

General Independent, comprehensive, women only **Entrance** Moderately difficult **Setting** 202-acre urban campus **Total enrollment** 683 **Student/faculty ratio** 10:1 **Application deadline** 7/31 (freshmen), 7/31 (transfer) **Freshmen** 82% were admitted **Housing** Yes **Expenses** Tuition $15,770; Room & Board $5870 **Undergraduates** 33% part-time, 9% 25 or older, 1% Native American, 2% Hispanic American, 8% African American, 1% Asian American/Pacific Islander **The most frequently chosen baccalaureate fields are** education, communications/communication technologies, visual/performing arts **Academic program** English as a second language, advanced placement, accelerated degree program, self-designed majors, honors program, adult/continuing education programs, internships **Contact** Patricia M. Gibbs, Dean of Enrollment Services, Stephens College, Box 2121, Columbia, MO 65215-0002. Telephone: 573-876-7207 or toll-free 800-876-7207. Fax: 573-876-7237. E-mail: apply@stephens.edu. Web site: http://www.stephens.edu/.

TRUMAN STATE UNIVERSITY
KIRKSVILLE, MISSOURI

General State-supported, comprehensive, coed **Entrance** Moderately difficult **Setting** 140-acre small-town campus **Total enrollment** 6,009 **Student/faculty ratio** 15:1 **Application deadline** 3/1 (freshmen), 4/1 (transfer) **Freshmen** 79% were admitted **Housing** Yes **Expenses** Tuition 3712; Room & Board 4552 **Undergraduates** 58% women, 3% part-time, 2% 25 or older, 0.3% Native American, 2% Hispanic American, 3% African American, 2% Asian American/Pacific Islander **The most frequently chosen baccalaureate fields are** biological/life sciences, business/marketing, English **Academic program** English as a second language, advanced placement, accelerated degree program, honors program, summer session, internships **Contact** Mr. Brad Chambers, Co-Director of Admissions, Truman State University, 205 McClain Hall, Kirksville, MO 63501-4221. Telephone: 660-785-4114 or toll-free 800-892-7792 (in-state). Fax: 660-785-7456. E-mail: admissions@truman.edu. Web site: http://www.truman.edu/.

UNIVERSITY OF MISSOURI–COLUMBIA
COLUMBIA, MISSOURI

General State-supported, university, coed **Entrance** Moderately difficult **Setting** 1,348-acre small-town campus **Total enrollment** 23,309 **Student/faculty ratio** 16:1 **Application deadline** Rolling (freshmen), rolling (transfer) **Freshmen** 90% were admitted **Housing** Yes **Expenses** Tuition $4887; Room & Board $5043 **Undergraduates** 53% women, 6% part-time, 5% 25 or older, 0.5% Native American, 1% Hispanic American, 6% African American, 2% Asian American/Pacific Islander **The most frequently chosen baccalaureate fields are** business/marketing, communications/communication technologies, education **Academic program** English as a second language, advanced placement, accelerated degree program, self-designed majors, honors program, summer session, adult/continuing education programs, internships **Contact** Ms. Georgeanne Porter, Director of Undergraduate Admissions, University of Missouri–Columbia, 225 Jesse Hall, Columbia, MO 65211. Telephone: 573-882-7786 or toll-free 800-225-6075 (in-state). Fax: 573-882-7887. E-mail: mu4u@missouri.edu. Web site: http://www.missouri.edu/.

UNIVERSITY OF MISSOURI–KANSAS CITY
KANSAS CITY, MISSOURI

General State-supported, university, coed **Entrance** Moderately difficult **Setting** 191-acre urban campus **Total enrollment** 12,698 **Student/faculty ratio** 8:1 **Application deadline** Rolling (freshmen), rolling (transfer) **Freshmen** 71% were admitted **Housing** Yes **Expenses** Tuition $5050; Room & Board $4950 **Undergraduates** 58% women, 50% part-time, 24% 25 or older **The most frequently chosen baccalaureate fields are** biological/life sciences, business/marketing, liberal arts/general studies **Academic program** English as a second language, advanced placement, accelerated degree program, self-designed majors, honors program, summer session, adult/continuing education programs, internships **Contact** Mr. Melvin C. Tyler, Director of Admissions, University of Missouri–Kansas City, 5100 Rockhill Road, Kansas City, MO 64110-2499. Telephone: 816-235-1111. Fax: 816-235-5544. E-mail: admit@umkc.edu. Web site: http://www.umkc.edu/.

UNIVERSITY OF MISSOURI–ROLLA
ROLLA, MISSOURI

General State-supported, university, coed **Entrance** Very difficult **Setting** 284-acre small-town campus **Total enrollment** 4,626 **Student/faculty ratio** 12:1 **Application deadline** 6/1 (freshmen), rolling (transfer) **Freshmen** 92% were admitted **Housing** Yes **Expenses** Tuition 4805; Room & Board 4838 **Undergraduates** 23% women, 11% part-time, 10% 25 or older, 1% Native American, 1% Hispanic American, 4% African American, 3% Asian American/Pacific Islander **The most frequently chosen baccalaureate fields are** computer/information sciences, engineering/engineering technologies, physical sciences **Academic program** English as a second language, advanced placement, accelerated degree program, honors program, summer session, adult/continuing education programs, internships **Contact** Ms. Martina Hahn, Director of Admission and Student Financial Assistance, University of Missouri–Rolla, 102 Parker Hall, Rolla, MO 65409. Telephone: 573-341-4164 or toll-free 800-522-0938. Fax: 573-341-4082. E-mail: umrolla@umr.edu. Web site: http://www.umr.edu/.

UNIVERSITY OF MISSOURI–ST. LOUIS
ST. LOUIS, MISSOURI

General State-supported, university, coed **Entrance** Moderately difficult **Setting** 250-acre suburban campus **Total enrollment** 15,397 **Student/faculty ratio** 12:1 **Application deadline** Rolling (freshmen), rolling (transfer) **Freshmen** 57% were admitted **Housing** Yes **Expenses** Tuition 4944; Room & Board 4620 **Undergraduates** 60% women, 58% part-time, 36% 25 or older, 0.3% Native American, 1% Hispanic American, 14% African American, 3% Asian American/Pacific Islander **The most frequently chosen baccalaureate fields are** business/marketing, education, social sciences and history **Academic program** English as a second language, advanced placement, accelerated degree program, self-designed majors, honors program, summer session, adult/continuing education programs, internships **Contact** Mr. Curtis C. Coonrod, Director of Admissions, University of Missouri–St. Louis, 351 Millennuim Student Center, St. Louis, MO 63121-4499. Telephone: 314-516-5460. Fax: 314-516-5310. E-mail: don_morris@ccmail.umsl.edu. Web site: http://www.umsl.edu/.

UNIVERSITY OF PHOENIX–SAINT LOUIS CAMPUS
MARYLAND HEIGHTS, MISSOURI

General Proprietary, comprehensive, coed **Entrance** Noncompetitive **Total enrollment** 66,534 **Student/**

faculty ratio 13:1 **Expenses** Tuition $7740 **Undergraduates** 56% women, 86% 25 or older, 2% Native American, 18% Hispanic American, 13% African American, 6% Asian American/Pacific Islander **Academic program** Advanced placement, accelerated degree program, adult/continuing education programs **Contact** Ms. Beth Barilla, Director of Admissions, University of Phoenix–Saint Louis Campus, 4615 East Elwood Street, Phoenix, AZ 85040-1948. Telephone: 480-927-0099 Ext. 1218 or toll-free 888-326-7737 (in-state); 800-228-7240 (out-of-state). Fax: 480-594-1758. E-mail: beth.barilla@apollogrp.edu. Web site: http://www.phoenix.edu/.

WASHINGTON UNIVERSITY IN ST. LOUIS
ST. LOUIS, MISSOURI

General Independent, university, coed **Entrance** Most difficult **Setting** 169-acre suburban campus **Total enrollment** 12,118 **Student/faculty ratio** 7:1 **Application deadline** 1/15 (freshmen), 4/15 (transfer) **Freshmen** 30% were admitted **Housing** Yes **Expenses** Tuition $26,377; Room & Board $8216 **Undergraduates** 51% women, 12% part-time, 1% 25 or older, 0.2% Native American, 2% Hispanic American, 7% African American, 11% Asian American/Pacific Islander **The most frequently chosen baccalaureate fields are** engineering/engineering technologies, business/marketing, social sciences and history **Academic program** English as a second language, advanced placement, accelerated degree program, self-designed majors, summer session, adult/continuing education programs, internships **Contact** Ms. Nanette Tarbouni, Director of Admissions, Washington University in St. Louis, Campus Box 1089, 1 Brookings Drive, St. Louis, MO 63130-4899. Telephone: 314-935-6000 or toll-free 800-638-0700. Fax: 314-935-4290. E-mail: admission@wustl.edu. Web site: http://www.admissions.wustl.edu/.

WEBSTER UNIVERSITY
ST. LOUIS, MISSOURI

General Independent, comprehensive, coed **Entrance** Moderately difficult **Setting** 47-acre suburban campus **Total enrollment** 16,730 **Student/faculty ratio** 14:1 **Application deadline** 7/1 (freshmen), 8/1 (transfer) **Freshmen** 63% were admitted **Housing** Yes **Expenses** Tuition 13,080; Room & Board 5658 **Undergraduates** 61% women, 37% part-time, 40% 25 or older, 0.4% Native American, 2% Hispanic American, 9% African American, 1% Asian American/Pacific Islander **The most frequently chosen baccalaureate fields are** business/marketing, communications/communication technologies, health professions and related sciences **Academic program** English as a second language, advanced placement, accelerated degree program, self-designed majors, summer session, adult/continuing education programs, internships **Contact** Mr. Andrew Laue, Associate Director of Undergraduate Admission, Webster University, 470 East Lockwood Avenue, St. Louis, MO 63119-3194. Telephone: 314-961-2660 Ext. 7712 or toll-free 800-75-ENROL. Fax: 314-968-7115. E-mail: admit@websteruniv.edu. Web site: http://www.webster.edu/.

WESTMINSTER COLLEGE
FULTON, MISSOURI

General Independent, 4-year, coed, affiliated with Presbyterian Church **Entrance** Moderately difficult **Setting** 65-acre small-town campus **Total enrollment** 686 **Student/faculty ratio** 11:1 **Application deadline** Rolling (freshmen), rolling (transfer) **Freshmen** 86% were admitted **Housing** Yes **Expenses** Tuition 14,300; Room & Board 5020 **Undergraduates** 43% women, 3% part-time, 3% 25 or older, 0.3% Native American, 2% Hispanic American, 2% African American, 1% Asian American/Pacific Islander **The most frequently chosen baccalaureate fields are** business/marketing, psychology, social sciences and history **Academic program** English as a second language, advanced placement, self-designed majors, summer session, internships **Contact** Dr. Patrick Kirby, Dean of Enrollment Services, Westminster College, 501 Westminster Avenue, Fulton, MO 65251-1299. Telephone: 573-592-5251 or toll-free 800-475-3361. Fax: 573-592-5255. E-mail: admissions@micro.wcmo.edu. Web site: http://www.westminster-mo.edu/.

WILLIAM JEWELL COLLEGE
LIBERTY, MISSOURI

General Independent Baptist, 4-year, coed **Entrance** Moderately difficult **Setting** 149-acre small-town campus **Total enrollment** 1,153 **Student/faculty ratio** 10:1 **Application deadline** Rolling (freshmen), rolling (transfer) **Freshmen** 87% were admitted **Housing** Yes **Expenses** Tuition 13,800; Room & Board 4250 **Undergraduates** 59% women, 3% part-time, 4% 25 or older, 0.4% Native American, 2% Hispanic American, 3% African American, 1% Asian American/Pacific Islander **The most frequently chosen baccalaureate fields are** business/marketing, education, psychology **Academic program** Advanced placement, self-designed majors, honors program, summer session, adult/continuing education programs, internships **Contact** Mr. Chad Jolly, Dean of Enrollment Development, William Jewell College, 500 College Hill, Liberty, MO 64068. Telephone: 816-781-7700 or toll-free 800-753-7009. Fax: 816-415-5027. E-mail: admission@william.jewell.edu. Web site: http://www.jewell.edu/.

WILLIAM WOODS UNIVERSITY
FULTON, MISSOURI

General Independent, comprehensive, coed, affiliated with Christian Church (Disciples of Christ) **Entrance** Moderately difficult **Setting** 170-acre small-town campus **Total enrollment** 1,479 **Student/faculty ratio** 8:1 **Application deadline** Rolling (freshmen), rolling (transfer) **Freshmen** 84% were admitted **Housing** Yes **Expenses** Tuition $13,690; Room & Board $5600 **Academic program** English as a second language, advanced placement, accelerated degree program, self-designed majors, honors program, summer session, adult/continuing education programs, internships **Contact** Ms. Laura Archuleta, Executive

William Woods University *(continued)*

Director of Enrollment Services, William Woods University, One University Avenue, Fulton, MO 65251. Telephone: 573-592-4221 or toll-free 800-995-3159 Ext. 4221. Fax: 573-592-1146. E-mail: larchuleta@williamwoods.edu. Web site: http://www.williamwoods.edu/.

MONTANA

CARROLL COLLEGE
HELENA, MONTANA

General Independent Roman Catholic, 4-year, coed **Entrance** Moderately difficult **Setting** 64-acre small-town campus **Total enrollment** 1,251 **Student/faculty ratio** 13:1 **Application deadline** 6/1 (freshmen), 6/1 (transfer) **Freshmen** 89% were admitted **Housing** Yes **Expenses** Tuition 12,816; Room & Board 5168 **Undergraduates** 60% women, 17% part-time, 12% 25 or older, 1% Native American, 2% Hispanic American, 0% African American, 0.4% Asian American/Pacific Islander **Academic program** English as a second language, advanced placement, accelerated degree program, self-designed majors, honors program, summer session, adult/continuing education programs, internships **Contact** Ms. Candace A. Cain, Director of Admission, Carroll College, 1601 North Benton Avenue, Helena, MT 59625-0002. Telephone: 406-447-4384 or toll-free 800-992-3648. Fax: 406-447-4533. E-mail: enroll@carroll.edu. Web site: http://www.carroll.edu/.

MONTANA STATE UNIVERSITY–BILLINGS
BILLINGS, MONTANA

General State-supported, comprehensive, coed **Entrance** Moderately difficult **Setting** 92-acre urban campus **Total enrollment** 4,296 **Student/faculty ratio** 21:1 **Application deadline** 7/1 (freshmen), rolling (transfer) **Freshmen** 88% were admitted **Housing** Yes **Expenses** Tuition $3052; Room & Board $4500 **Undergraduates** 64% women, 23% part-time, 40% 25 or older, 6% Native American, 3% Hispanic American, 0.5% African American, 1% Asian American/Pacific Islander **The most frequently chosen baccalaureate fields are** business/marketing, education, liberal arts/general studies **Academic program** English as a second language, advanced placement, accelerated degree program, honors program, summer session, adult/continuing education programs, internships **Contact** Ms. Karen Everett, Director, Admissions and Records, Montana State University–Billings, 1500 North 30th Street, Billings, MT 59101. Telephone: 406-657-2158 or toll-free 800-565-6782. Fax: 406-657-2302. E-mail: adm_tempo@vicuna.emcmt.edu. Web site: http://www.msubillings.edu/.

MONTANA STATE UNIVERSITY–BOZEMAN
BOZEMAN, MONTANA

General State-supported, university, coed **Entrance** Moderately difficult **Setting** 1,170-acre small-town campus **Total enrollment** 11,658 **Student/faculty ratio** 20:1 **Application deadline** Rolling (freshmen), rolling (transfer) **Freshmen** 84% were admitted **Housing** Yes **Expenses** Tuition $3079; Room & Board $4650 **Undergraduates** 45% women, 12% part-time, 17% 25 or older, 2% Native American, 1% Hispanic American, 0.4% African American, 1% Asian American/Pacific Islander **The most frequently chosen baccalaureate fields are** business/marketing, education, engineering/engineering technologies **Academic program** English as a second language, advanced placement, self-designed majors, honors program, summer session, adult/continuing education programs, internships **Contact** Ms. Ronda Russell, Director of New Student Services, Montana State University–Bozeman, PO Box 172190, Bozeman, MT 59717-2190. Telephone: 406-994-2452 or toll-free 888-MSU-CATS. Fax: 406-994-1923. E-mail: zam1202@msu.oscs.montana.edu. Web site: http://www.montana.edu/.

MONTANA STATE UNIVERSITY–NORTHERN
HAVRE, MONTANA

General State-supported, comprehensive, coed **Entrance** Moderately difficult **Setting** 105-acre small-town campus **Total enrollment** 1,525 **Application deadline** Rolling (freshmen), rolling (transfer) **Freshmen** 100% were admitted **Housing** Yes **Expenses** Tuition $2692; Room & Board $3800 **Undergraduates** 52% women, 24% part-time, 65% 25 or older, 10% Native American, 1% Hispanic American, 1% African American, 1% Asian American/Pacific Islander **Academic program** English as a second language, advanced placement, honors program, summer session, adult/continuing education programs, internships **Contact** Ms. Rosalie Spinler, Director of Admissions, Montana State University–Northern, PO Box 7751, Havre, MT 59501-7751. Telephone: 406-265-3704 or toll-free 800-662-6132 (in-state). Fax: 406-265-3777. E-mail: msunadmit@nmc1.nmclites.edu. Web site: http://www.msun.edu/.

MONTANA TECH OF THE UNIVERSITY OF MONTANA
BUTTE, MONTANA

General State-supported, comprehensive, coed **Entrance** Moderately difficult **Setting** 56-acre small-town campus **Total enrollment** 2,067 **Student/faculty ratio** 16:1 **Application deadline** Rolling (freshmen), rolling (transfer) **Freshmen** 97% were admitted **Housing** Yes **Expenses** Tuition $3006; Room & Board $4278 **Undergraduates** 45% women, 15% part-time, 24% 25 or older, 2% Native American, 1% Hispanic American, 0.3% African American, 1% Asian American/Pacific Islander **The most fre-**

quently chosen baccalaureate fields are business/marketing, engineering/engineering technologies, health professions and related sciences **Academic program** Advanced placement, self-designed majors, summer session, adult/continuing education programs, internships **Contact** Tony Campeau, Associate Director of Admissions, Montana Tech of The University of Montana, 1300 West Park Street, Butte, MT 59701-8997. Telephone: 406-496-4178 Ext. 4632 or toll-free 800-445-TECH Ext. 1. Fax: 406-496-4170. E-mail: admissions@p01.mtech.edu. Web site: http://www.mtech.edu/.

ROCKY MOUNTAIN COLLEGE
BILLINGS, MONTANA

General Independent interdenominational, 4-year, coed **Entrance** Moderately difficult **Setting** 60-acre urban campus **Total enrollment** 792 **Student/faculty ratio** 14:1 **Application deadline** Rolling (freshmen), rolling (transfer) **Freshmen** 99% were admitted **Housing** Yes **Expenses** Tuition $12,243; Room & Board $4564 **Undergraduates** 29% 25 or older, 7% Native American, 1% Hispanic American, 0.4% African American, 1% Asian American/Pacific Islander **The most frequently chosen baccalaureate fields are** business/marketing, education, parks and recreation **Academic program** English as a second language, advanced placement, accelerated degree program, self-designed majors, honors program, summer session, adult/continuing education programs, internships **Contact** Mr. Craig Gould, Director of Admissions, Rocky Mountain College, 1511 Poly Drive, Billings, MT 59102-1796. Telephone: 406-657-1026 or toll-free 800-877-6259. Fax: 406-259-9751. E-mail: admissions@rocky.edu. Web site: http://www.rocky.edu/.

UNIVERSITY OF GREAT FALLS
GREAT FALLS, MONTANA

General Independent Roman Catholic, comprehensive, coed **Entrance** Noncompetitive **Setting** 40-acre urban campus **Total enrollment** 1,072 **Student/faculty ratio** 15:1 **Application deadline** Rolling (freshmen), rolling (transfer) **Freshmen** 100% were admitted **Housing** Yes **Expenses** Tuition 10,260; Room only 1500 **Undergraduates** 69% 25 or older, 8% Native American, 2% Hispanic American, 2% African American, 2% Asian American/Pacific Islander **The most frequently chosen baccalaureate fields are** computer/information sciences, health professions and related sciences, protective services/public administration **Academic program** Advanced placement, accelerated degree program, summer session, adult/continuing education programs, internships **Contact** Mr. Michael Myers, Assistant Director of Admissions, University of Great Falls, 1301 Twentieth Street South, Great Falls, MT 59405. Telephone: 406-791-5200 or toll-free 800-856-9544. Fax: 406-791-5209. E-mail: adminrec@ugf.edu. Web site: http://www.ugf.edu/.

THE UNIVERSITY OF MONTANA–MISSOULA
MISSOULA, MONTANA

General State-supported, university, coed **Entrance** Moderately difficult **Setting** 220-acre urban campus **Total enrollment** 12,406 **Student/faculty ratio** 22:1 **Application deadline** 7/1 (freshmen), rolling (transfer) **Freshmen** 86% were admitted **Housing** Yes **Expenses** Tuition $3360; Room & Board $4525 **Undergraduates** 53% women, 14% part-time, 21% 25 or older, 3% Native American, 1% Hispanic American, 0.5% African American, 1% Asian American/Pacific Islander **Academic program** English as a second language, advanced placement, honors program, summer session, adult/continuing education programs, internships **Contact** Office of New Student Services, The University of Montana–Missoula, Missoula, MT 59812-0002. Telephone: 406-243-6266 or toll-free 800-462-8636. Fax: 406-243-5711. E-mail: admiss@selway.umt.edu. Web site: http://www.umt.edu/.

WESTERN MONTANA COLLEGE OF THE UNIVERSITY OF MONTANA
DILLON, MONTANA

General State-supported, 4-year, coed **Entrance** Moderately difficult **Setting** 36-acre small-town campus **Total enrollment** 1,160 **Student/faculty ratio** 17:1 **Application deadline** 7/1 (freshmen), 7/1 (transfer) **Freshmen** 79% were admitted **Housing** Yes **Expenses** Tuition $2795; Room & Board $3810 **Undergraduates** 59% women, 22% part-time, 30% 25 or older, 4% Native American, 2% Hispanic American, 1% African American, 1% Asian American/Pacific Islander **The most frequently chosen baccalaureate fields are** business/marketing, biological/life sciences, education **Academic program** Advanced placement, accelerated degree program, self-designed majors, honors program, summer session, adult/continuing education programs, internships **Contact** Ms. Arlene Williams, Director of Admissions and New Student Services, Western Montana College of The University of Montana, 710 South Atlantic, Dillon, MT 59725. Telephone: 406-683-7331 or toll-free 800-WMC-MONT. Fax: 406-683-7493. E-mail: K_leum@wmc.edu. Web site: http://www.wmc.edu/.

NEBRASKA

BELLEVUE UNIVERSITY
BELLEVUE, NEBRASKA

General Independent, comprehensive, coed **Entrance** Noncompetitive **Setting** 19-acre suburban campus **Total enrollment** 3,445 **Student/faculty ratio** 23:1 **Application deadline** Rolling (freshmen), rolling (transfer) **Freshmen** 94% were admitted **Housing** No **Expenses** Tuition $3238 **Undergraduates** 50% women, 35% part-time, 80% 25 or older, 1% Native

Bellevue University *(continued)*

American, 1% Hispanic American, 7% African American, 1% Asian American/Pacific Islander **The most frequently chosen baccalaureate fields are** business/marketing, computer/information sciences, psychology **Academic program** English as a second language, advanced placement, accelerated degree program, summer session, adult/continuing education programs, internships **Contact** Ms. Sharon Thonen, Director of Admissions, Bellevue University, 1000 Galvin Road South, Bellevue, NE 68005-3098. Telephone: 402-293-3711 or toll-free 800-756-7920. Fax: 402-293-2020. E-mail: set@scholars.bellevue.edu. Web site: http://www.bellevue.edu/.

CHADRON STATE COLLEGE
CHADRON, NEBRASKA

General State-supported, comprehensive, coed **Entrance** Noncompetitive **Setting** 281-acre small-town campus **Total enrollment** 2,686 **Student/faculty ratio** 17:1 **Application deadline** Rolling (freshmen), rolling (transfer) **Freshmen** 100% were admitted **Housing** Yes **Expenses** Tuition 2361; Room & Board 3492 **Undergraduates** 58% women, 24% part-time, 13% 25 or older, 2% Native American, 3% Hispanic American, 1% African American, 0.5% Asian American/Pacific Islander **The most frequently chosen baccalaureate fields are** business/marketing, education, protective services/public administration **Academic program** Advanced placement, self-designed majors, honors program, summer session, adult/continuing education programs, internships **Contact** Ms. Terie Dawson, Director of Enrollment Management, Chadron State College, 1000 Main Street, Chadron, NE 69337-2690. Telephone: 308-432-6263 or toll-free 800-CHADRON (in-state). Fax: 308-432-6229. E-mail: admissions@csc1.csc.edu. Web site: http://www.csc.edu/.

CLARKSON COLLEGE
OMAHA, NEBRASKA

General Independent, comprehensive, coed, primarily women **Entrance** Moderately difficult **Setting** 3-acre urban campus **Total enrollment** 401 **Student/faculty ratio** 12:1 **Application deadline** Rolling (freshmen), rolling (transfer) **Freshmen** 72% were admitted **Housing** Yes **Expenses** Tuition $9078; Room only $2800 **Undergraduates** 89% women, 47% part-time, 41% 25 or older, 0.4% Native American, 3% Hispanic American, 5% African American, 0.4% Asian American/Pacific Islander **The most frequently chosen baccalaureate fields are** business/marketing, health professions and related sciences **Academic program** Advanced placement, accelerated degree program, summer session, adult/continuing education programs, internships **Contact** Mr. Tony Damewood, Director of Enrollment Services, Clarkson College, 101 South 42nd Street, Omaha, NE 68131-2739. Telephone: 402-552-6109 or toll-free 800-647-5500. Fax: 402-552-6057. E-mail: admiss@clrkcol.crhsnet.edu. Web site: http://www.clarksoncollege.edu/.

► **For more information, see page 401.**

COLLEGE OF SAINT MARY
OMAHA, NEBRASKA

General Independent Roman Catholic, 4-year, women only **Entrance** Minimally difficult **Setting** 25-acre suburban campus **Total enrollment** 947 **Student/faculty ratio** 10:1 **Application deadline** Rolling (freshmen), rolling (transfer) **Freshmen** 99% were admitted **Housing** Yes **Expenses** Tuition $13,350; Room & Board $4784 **Undergraduates** 44% part-time, 53% 25 or older, 0.5% Native American, 3% Hispanic American, 5% African American, 0.4% Asian American/Pacific Islander **The most frequently chosen baccalaureate fields are** business/marketing, education, health professions and related sciences **Academic program** Advanced placement, accelerated degree program, summer session, adult/continuing education programs, internships **Contact** Ms. Christy Whitfield JD, Vice President for Enrollment Services, College of Saint Mary, 1901 South 72nd Street, Omaha, NE 68124-2377. Telephone: 402-399-2407 or toll-free 800-926-5534. Fax: 402-399-2412. E-mail: enroll@csm.edu. Web site: http://www.csm.edu/.

CONCORDIA UNIVERSITY
SEWARD, NEBRASKA

General Independent, comprehensive, coed, affiliated with Lutheran Church–Missouri Synod **Entrance** Moderately difficult **Setting** 120-acre small-town campus **Total enrollment** 1,270 **Student/faculty ratio** 14:1 **Application deadline** 8/1 (freshmen), 8/1 (transfer) **Freshmen** 92% were admitted **Housing** Yes **Expenses** Tuition $12,470; Room & Board $4136 **Undergraduates** 55% women, 4% part-time, 4% 25 or older, 0.1% Native American, 1% Hispanic American, 1% African American, 1% Asian American/Pacific Islander **Academic program** English as a second language, advanced placement, accelerated degree program, honors program, summer session, adult/continuing education programs, internships **Contact** Mr. Don Vos, Director of Admissions, Concordia University, 800 North Columbia Avenue, Seward, NE 68434-1599. Telephone: 402-643-7233 or toll-free 800-535-5494. Fax: 402-643-4073. E-mail: admiss@seward.ccsn.edu. Web site: http://www.cune.edu/.

CREIGHTON UNIVERSITY
OMAHA, NEBRASKA

General Independent Roman Catholic (Jesuit), university, coed **Entrance** Moderately difficult **Setting** 90-acre urban campus **Total enrollment** 6,235 **Student/faculty ratio** 14:1 **Application deadline** 8/1 (freshmen), rolling (transfer) **Freshmen** 89% were admitted **Housing** Yes **Expenses** Tuition $14,910; Room & Board $5782 **Undergraduates** 59% women, 10% part-time, 1% Native American, 4% Hispanic American, 3% African American, 10% Asian American/Pacific Islander **The most frequently chosen baccalaureate fields are** business/marketing, biological/life sciences, health professions and related sciences **Academic program** English as a second language, advanced placement, accelerated degree program, honors program, summer session, adult/continuing education programs, internships **Contact** Mr. Dennis J. O'Driscoll, Director of Admissions, Creighton University, 2500 California Plaza, Omaha, NE 68178-0001. Telephone: 402-280-2703 or toll-free 800-282-5835. Fax: 402-280-2685. E-mail: admissions@creighton.edu. Web site: http://www.creighton.edu/.

DANA COLLEGE
BLAIR, NEBRASKA

General Independent, 4-year, coed, affiliated with Evangelical Lutheran Church in America **Entrance** Moderately difficult **Setting** 150-acre small-town campus **Total enrollment** 583 **Student/faculty ratio** 10:1 **Application deadline** Rolling (freshmen) **Freshmen** 97% were admitted **Housing** Yes **Expenses** Tuition $13,300; Room & Board $4202 **Undergraduates** 47% women, 3% part-time, 5% 25 or older, 1% Native American, 2% Hispanic American, 4% African American, 5% Asian American/Pacific Islander **The most frequently chosen baccalaureate fields are** business/marketing, education, protective services/public administration **Academic program** English as a second language, advanced placement, accelerated degree program, self-designed majors, honors program, summer session, adult/continuing education programs, internships **Contact** Ms. Judy Mathiesen, Office Manager, Dana College, 2848 College Drive, Blair, NE 68008-1099. Telephone: 402-426-7337 or toll-free 800-444-3262. Fax: 402-426-7386. E-mail: admissions@dana.edu. Web site: http://www.dana.edu/.

DOANE COLLEGE
CRETE, NEBRASKA

General Independent, comprehensive, coed, affiliated with United Church of Christ **Entrance** Moderately difficult **Setting** 300-acre small-town campus **Total enrollment** 2,135 **Student/faculty ratio** 12:1 **Application deadline** Rolling (freshmen), rolling (transfer) **Freshmen** 89% were admitted **Housing** Yes **Expenses** Tuition $12,826; Room & Board $3900 **Undergraduates** 53% women, 17% part-time, 0.1% Native American, 2% Hispanic American, 3% African American, 1% Asian American/Pacific Islander **The most frequently chosen baccalaureate fields are** business/marketing, education, social sciences and history **Academic program** English as a second language, advanced placement, accelerated degree program, self-designed majors, honors program, summer session, adult/continuing education programs, internships **Contact** Mr. Dan Kunzman, Dean of Admissions, Doane College, 1014 Boswell Avenue, Crete, NE 68333-2430. Telephone: 402-826-8222 or toll-free 800-333-6263. Fax: 402-826-8600. E-mail: admissions@doane.edu. Web site: http://www.doane.edu/.

GRACE UNIVERSITY
OMAHA, NEBRASKA

General Independent interdenominational, comprehensive, coed **Entrance** Moderately difficult **Setting** 15-acre urban campus **Total enrollment** 573 **Student/faculty ratio** 19:1 **Application deadline** Rolling (freshmen), rolling (transfer) **Freshmen** 47% were admitted **Housing** Yes **Expenses** Tuition 8324; Room & Board 3700 **Undergraduates** 55% women, 26% part-time, 20% 25 or older, 1% Native American, 2% Hispanic American, 3% African American, 0.4% Asian American/Pacific Islander **Academic program** Advanced placement, accelerated degree program, self-designed majors, summer session, adult/continuing education programs, internships **Contact** Mrs. Terri L. Dingfield, Director of Admissions, Grace University, 1311 South Ninth Street, Omaha, NE 68108. Telephone: 402-449-2831 or toll-free 800-383-1422. Fax: 402-341-9587. E-mail: admissions@graceuniversity.edu. Web site: http://www.graceuniversity.edu/.

HASTINGS COLLEGE
HASTINGS, NEBRASKA

General Independent Presbyterian, comprehensive, coed **Entrance** Moderately difficult **Setting** 88-acre small-town campus **Total enrollment** 1,130 **Student/faculty ratio** 13:1 **Application deadline** 8/1 (freshmen), rolling (transfer) **Freshmen** 87% were admitted **Housing** Yes **Expenses** Tuition $13,666; Room & Board $4188 **Undergraduates** 51% women, 3% part-time, 0.4% Native American, 2% Hispanic American, 1% African American, 0.5% Asian American/Pacific Islander **The most frequently chosen baccalaureate fields are** business/marketing, education, psychology **Academic program** Advanced placement, self-designed majors, summer session, adult/continuing education programs, internships **Contact** Mr. Michael Karloff, Director of Admissions, Hastings College, 800 North Turner Avenue, Hastings, NE 68901-7696. Telephone: 402-461-7316 or toll-free 800-532-7642. Fax: 402-461-7490. E-mail: admissions@hastings.edu. Web site: http://www.hastings.edu/.

MIDLAND LUTHERAN COLLEGE
FREMONT, NEBRASKA

General Independent Lutheran, 4-year, coed **Entrance** Moderately difficult **Setting** 27-acre small-town campus **Total enrollment** 1,025 **Student/faculty ratio** 15:1 **Application deadline** Rolling (freshmen), rolling (transfer) **Freshmen** 95% were admitted **Housing** Yes **Expenses** Tuition $14,600; Room & Board $4080 **Undergraduates** 59% women, 11% part-time, 5% 25 or older, 0% Native American, 1% Hispanic American, 5% African American, 0.3% Asian American/Pacific Islander **The most frequently chosen baccalaureate fields are** business/marketing, biological/life sciences, education **Academic program** English as a second language, advanced placement, accelerated degree program, self-designed majors, honors program, summer session, internships **Contact** Mr. John W. Klockentager, Vice President for Enrollment Management, Midland Lutheran College, Admissions Office, Fremont, NE 68025-4200. Telephone: 402-941-6508 or toll-free 800-642-8382 Ext. 6501. Fax: 402-721-0250. E-mail: rkahnk@admin.mlc.edu. Web site: http://www.mlc.edu/.

Midland Lutheran College *(continued)*

NEBRASKA CHRISTIAN COLLEGE
NORFOLK, NEBRASKA

General Independent, 4-year, coed, affiliated with Christian Churches and Churches of Christ **Entrance** Minimally difficult **Setting** 85-acre small-town campus **Total enrollment** 162 **Student/faculty ratio** 12:1 **Application deadline** Rolling (freshmen), rolling (transfer) **Freshmen** 65% were admitted **Housing** Yes **Expenses** Tuition $5250; Room & Board $3060 **Undergraduates** 49% women, 12% part-time, 12% 25 or older, 1% Native American, 2% Hispanic American, 1% African American, 1% Asian American/Pacific Islander **The most frequently chosen baccalaureate fields are** liberal arts/general studies, philosophy, religion, and theology **Academic program** Internships **Contact** Mr. Tim DeFor, Associate Director of Admissions, Nebraska Christian College, 1800 Syracuse Avenue, Norfolk, NE 68701-2458. Telephone: 402-378-5000 Ext. 413. Fax: 402-379-5100. Web site: http://www.nechristian.edu/.

NEBRASKA METHODIST COLLEGE
OMAHA, NEBRASKA

General Independent, comprehensive, coed, affiliated with United Methodist Church **Entrance** Moderately difficult **Setting** 5-acre urban campus **Total enrollment** 400 **Student/faculty ratio** 10:1 **Application deadline** 4/1 (freshmen), 4/1 (transfer) **Freshmen** 86% were admitted **Housing** Yes **Expenses** Tuition $9600; Room only $1300 **Undergraduates** 92% women, 29% part-time, 45% 25 or older, 0% Native American, 2% Hispanic American, 6% African American, 1% Asian American/Pacific Islander **The most frequently chosen baccalaureate field is** health professions and related sciences **Academic program** Advanced placement, accelerated degree program, summer session, internships **Contact** Ms. Deann Sterner, Director of Admissions, Nebraska Methodist College, 8501 West Dodge Road, Omaha, NE 68114. Telephone: 402-354-4922 or toll-free 800-335-5510. Fax: 402-354-8875. E-mail: dsterne@methodistcollege.edu. Web site: http://www.methodistcollege.edu/.

NEBRASKA WESLEYAN UNIVERSITY
LINCOLN, NEBRASKA

General Independent United Methodist, 4-year, coed **Entrance** Moderately difficult **Setting** 50-acre suburban campus **Total enrollment** 1,699 **Student/faculty ratio** 13:1 **Application deadline** 5/1 (freshmen), rolling (transfer) **Freshmen** 94% were admitted **Housing** Yes **Expenses** Tuition $13,704; Room & Board $4006 **Undergraduates** 57% women, 12% part-time, 9% 25 or older, 0.1% Native American, 1% Hispanic American, 1% African American, 1% Asian American/Pacific Islander **The most frequently chosen baccalaureate fields are** biological/life sciences, business/marketing, psychology **Academic program** Advanced placement, summer session, adult/continuing education programs, internships **Contact** Mr. Kendal E. Sieg, Director of Admissions, Nebraska Wesleyan University, 5000 Saint Paul Avenue, Lincoln, NE 68504. Telephone: 402-465-2218 or toll-free 800-541-3818. Fax: 402-465-2179. E-mail: adm@nebrwesleyan.edu. Web site: http://www.nebrwesleyan.edu/.

PERU STATE COLLEGE
PERU, NEBRASKA

General State-supported, comprehensive, coed **Entrance** Noncompetitive **Setting** 103-acre rural campus **Total enrollment** 1,664 **Student/faculty ratio** 16:1 **Application deadline** Rolling (freshmen), rolling (transfer) **Freshmen** 63% were admitted **Housing** Yes **Expenses** Tuition 2378; Room & Board 3526 **Undergraduates** 55% women, 40% part-time, 8% 25 or older, 1% Native American, 1% Hispanic American, 2% African American, 1% Asian American/Pacific Islander **The most frequently chosen baccalaureate fields are** biological/life sciences, education, interdisciplinary studies **Academic program** Advanced placement, honors program, adult/continuing education programs, internships **Contact** Mr. Robert J. Lopez, Director of Enrollment Management, Peru State College, Administration Building, Peru, NE 68421. Telephone: 402-872-3815 Ext. 2221 or toll-free 800-742-4412 (in-state). E-mail: rlopez@oakmail.peru.edu. Web site: http://www.peru.edu/.

UNION COLLEGE
LINCOLN, NEBRASKA

General Independent Seventh-day Adventist, 4-year, coed **Entrance** Moderately difficult **Setting** 26-acre suburban campus **Total enrollment** 801 **Student/faculty ratio** 12:1 **Application deadline** Rolling (freshmen), rolling (transfer) **Freshmen** 43% were admitted **Housing** Yes **Expenses** Tuition $11,504; Room & Board $3260 **Undergraduates** 54% women, 11% part-time, 16% 25 or older, 1% Native American, 4% Hispanic American, 3% African American, 2% Asian American/Pacific Islander **The most frequently chosen baccalaureate fields are** business/marketing, education, health professions and related sciences **Academic program** English as a second language, advanced placement, accelerated degree program, self-designed majors, honors program, summer session, adult/continuing education programs, internships **Contact** Huda McClelland, Director of Admissions, Union College, 3800 South 48th Street, Lincoln, NE 68516. Telephone: 402-486-2504 or toll-free 800-228-4600 (out-of-state). Fax: 402-486-2895. E-mail: ucenrol@ucollege.edu. Web site: http://www.ucollege.edu/.

UNIVERSITY OF NEBRASKA AT KEARNEY
KEARNEY, NEBRASKA

General State-supported, comprehensive, coed **Entrance** Moderately difficult **Setting** 235-acre small-town campus **Total enrollment** 6,506 **Student/faculty ratio** 16:1 **Application deadline** 8/1 (freshmen), 8/1 (transfer) **Freshmen** 93% were admitted

Housing Yes **Expenses** Room & Board 3832 **Undergraduates** 55% women, 12% part-time, 11% 25 or older, 0.2% Native American, 1% Hispanic American, 1% African American, 0.3% Asian American/ Pacific Islander **The most frequently chosen baccalaureate fields are** business/marketing, education, protective services/public administration **Academic program** English as a second language, advanced placement, honors program, summer session, internships **Contact** Mr. John Kundel, Director of Admissions, University of Nebraska at Kearney, 905 West 25th Street, Kearney, NE 68849-0001. Telephone: 308-865-8702 or toll-free 800-532-7639. Fax: 308-865-8987. E-mail: admissionsug@plattc.unk.edu. Web site: http://www.unk.edu/.

UNIVERSITY OF NEBRASKA AT OMAHA
OMAHA, NEBRASKA

General State-supported, university, coed **Entrance** Minimally difficult **Setting** 88-acre urban campus **Total enrollment** 13,479 **Student/faculty ratio** 18:1 **Application deadline** Rolling (freshmen), rolling (transfer) **Freshmen** 87% were admitted **Housing** Yes **Expenses** Tuition $2970; Room only $2619 **Undergraduates** 53% women, 31% part-time, 26% 25 or older, 1% Native American, 3% Hispanic American, 6% African American, 2% Asian American/ Pacific Islander **The most frequently chosen baccalaureate fields are** business/marketing, education, protective services/public administration **Academic program** English as a second language, advanced placement, self-designed majors, honors program, summer session, adult/continuing education programs, internships **Contact** Ms. Jolene Adams, Associate Director of Admissions, University of Nebraska at Omaha, 6001 Dodge Street, Omaha, NE 68182. Telephone: 402-554-2416 or toll-free 800-858-8648 (in-state). Fax: 402-554-3472. Web site: http://www.unomaha.edu/.

UNIVERSITY OF NEBRASKA–LINCOLN
LINCOLN, NEBRASKA

General State-supported, university, coed **Entrance** Moderately difficult **Setting** 623-acre urban campus **Total enrollment** 22,268 **Student/faculty ratio** 18:1 **Application deadline** 6/30 (freshmen), 6/30 (transfer) **Freshmen** 92% were admitted **Housing** Yes **Expenses** Tuition $3450; Room & Board $4310 **Undergraduates** 47% women, 11% part-time, 9% 25 or older, 1% Native American, 2% Hispanic American, 2% African American, 2% Asian American/ Pacific Islander **The most frequently chosen baccalaureate fields are** business/marketing, education, engineering/engineering technologies **Academic program** English as a second language, advanced placement, accelerated degree program, self-designed majors, honors program, summer session, adult/ continuing education programs, internships **Contact** Dr. Susanna Finnell, Director of Admissions, University of Nebraska–Lincoln, 1410 Q Street, Lincoln, NE 68588-0417. Telephone: 402-472-2030 or toll-free 800-742-8800. Fax: 402-472-0670. E-mail: lschmidt@unl.edu. Web site: http://www.unl.edu/.

UNIVERSITY OF NEBRASKA MEDICAL CENTER
OMAHA, NEBRASKA

General State-supported, upper-level, coed **Entrance** Moderately difficult **Setting** 51-acre urban campus **Total enrollment** 2,695 **Application deadline** Rolling (transfer) **First-Year Students** 33% were admitted **Housing** No **Expenses** Tuition $4,022 **Undergraduates** 93% women, 12% part-time, 0% Native American, 2% Hispanic American, 0.3% African American, 1% Asian American/Pacific Islander **The most frequently chosen baccalaureate field is** health professions and related sciences **Academic program** Honors program, summer session, internships **Contact** Ms. Jo Wagner, Assistant Director of Academic Records, University of Nebraska Medical Center, 984230 Nebraska Medical Center, Omaha, NE 68198-4230. Telephone: 402-559-6468 or toll-free 800-626-8431. Fax: 402-559-6796. Web site: http://www.unmc.edu/.

WAYNE STATE COLLEGE
WAYNE, NEBRASKA

General State-supported, comprehensive, coed **Entrance** Noncompetitive **Setting** 128-acre small-town campus **Total enrollment** 3,518 **Student/faculty ratio** 19:1 **Application deadline** Rolling (freshmen), rolling (transfer) **Freshmen** 100% were admitted **Housing** Yes **Expenses** Tuition $2513; Room & Board $3330 **Undergraduates** 58% women, 10% part-time, 12% 25 or older, 1% Native American, 2% Hispanic American, 3% African American, 0.5% Asian American/Pacific Islander **The most frequently chosen baccalaureate fields are** business/ marketing, education, parks and recreation **Academic program** Self-designed majors, honors program, summer session, adult/continuing education programs, internships **Contact** Mr. Brian Taylor, Director of Admissions, Wayne State College, 1111 Main Street, Wayne, NE 68787. Telephone: 402-375-7234 or toll-free 800-228-9972 (in-state). Fax: 402-375-7204. E-mail: wscadmit@wscgate.wsc.edu. Web site: http://www.wsc.edu/.

YORK COLLEGE
YORK, NEBRASKA

General Independent, 4-year, coed, affiliated with Church of Christ **Entrance** Moderately difficult **Setting** 44-acre small-town campus **Total enrollment** 497 **Student/faculty ratio** 12:1 **Application deadline** Rolling (freshmen), rolling (transfer) **Freshmen** 56% were admitted **Housing** Yes **Expenses** Tuition $9000; Room & Board $2900 **Undergraduates** 4% 25 or older, 1% Hispanic American, 4% African American **Academic program** Advanced placement, honors program, summer session, adult/continuing education programs, internships **Contact** Dr. James White, Vice President of Enrollment, York College, 1125 East 8th Street, York, NE 68467-2699. Telephone: 402-363-5668 or toll-free 800-950-9675. Fax: 402-363-5623. E-mail: enroll@yc.ne.edu. Web site: http://www.york.edu/.

NEVADA

MORRISON UNIVERSITY
RENO, NEVADA

Contact Ms. Teresa Sanders, Director of Admissions, Morrison University, 140 Washington Street, Reno, NV 89503-5600. Telephone: 775-323-4145 or toll-free 800-369-6144. Web site: http://www.morrison.edu/.

SIERRA NEVADA COLLEGE
INCLINE VILLAGE, NEVADA

General Independent, comprehensive, coed **Entrance** Moderately difficult **Setting** 20-acre small-town campus **Total enrollment** 354 **Student/faculty ratio** 14:1 **Application deadline** Rolling (freshmen), rolling (transfer) **Freshmen** 96% were admitted **Housing** Yes **Expenses** Tuition $12,200; Room & Board $5600 **Undergraduates** 52% women, 18% part-time, 29% 25 or older, 0.3% Native American, 1% Hispanic American, 1% African American, 0% Asian American/Pacific Islander **Academic program** Advanced placement, accelerated degree program, honors program, summer session, adult/continuing education programs, internships **Contact** Office of Admission, Sierra Nevada College, 999 Tahoe Boulevard, Incline Village, NV 89451. Telephone: 775-831-1314 Ext. 4046 or toll-free 800-332-8666 Ext. 4046 (out-of-state). Fax: 775-831-1347. E-mail: admissions@sierranevada.edu. Web site: http://www.sierranevada.edu/.

UNIVERSITY OF NEVADA, LAS VEGAS
LAS VEGAS, NEVADA

General State-supported, university, coed **Entrance** Moderately difficult **Setting** 335-acre urban campus **Total enrollment** 22,043 **Student/faculty ratio** 18:1 **Application deadline** 7/15 (freshmen), 8/15 (transfer) **Freshmen** 79% were admitted **Housing** Yes **Expenses** Tuition $2386; Room & Board $5800 **Undergraduates** 55% women, 41% part-time, 29% 25 or older, 1% Native American, 9% Hispanic American, 7% African American, 12% Asian American/Pacific Islander **The most frequently chosen baccalaureate fields are** business/marketing, education, social sciences and history **Academic program** English as a second language, advanced placement, self-designed majors, honors program, summer session, adult/continuing education programs, internships **Contact** Mrs. Susan Bozarth, Director of Admissions, University of Nevada, Las Vegas, 4505 Maryland Parkway, Box 451021, Las Vegas, NV 89154-1021. Telephone: 702-895-3443. Fax: 702-895-1118. E-mail: witter@ccmail.nevada.edu. Web site: http://www.unlv.edu/.

UNIVERSITY OF NEVADA, RENO
RENO, NEVADA

General State-supported, university, coed **Entrance** Moderately difficult **Setting** 200-acre urban campus **Total enrollment** 13,149 **Student/faculty ratio** 20:1 **Application deadline** 3/1 (freshmen), rolling (transfer) **Freshmen** 91% were admitted **Housing** Yes **Expenses** Tuition $2454; Room & Board $5650 **Undergraduates** 55% women, 27% part-time, 21% 25 or older, 1% Native American, 6% Hispanic American, 2% African American, 6% Asian American/Pacific Islander **The most frequently chosen baccalaureate fields are** business/marketing, education, social sciences and history **Academic program** English as a second language, advanced placement, honors program, summer session, adult/continuing education programs, internships **Contact** Dr. Melissa N. Choroszy, Associate Dean of Records and Enrollment Services, University of Nevada, Reno, Mail Stop 120, Reno, NV 89557. Telephone: 775-784-6865. Fax: 775-784-4283. E-mail: unrug@unr.edu. Web site: http://www.unr.edu/.

UNIVERSITY OF PHOENIX–NEVADA CAMPUS
LAS VEGAS, NEVADA

General Proprietary, comprehensive, coed **Entrance** Noncompetitive **Total enrollment** 66,534 **Student/faculty ratio** 13:1 **Application deadline** Rolling (freshmen), rolling (transfer) **Expenses** Tuition $7740 **Undergraduates** 56% women, 86% 25 or older, 2% Native American, 18% Hispanic American, 13% African American, 6% Asian American/Pacific Islander **Academic program** Advanced placement, accelerated degree program, adult/continuing education programs **Contact** Ms. Beth Barilla, Director of Admissions, University of Phoenix–Nevada Campus, 4615 East Elwood Street, Phoenix, AZ 85040-1948. Telephone: 480-927-0099 Ext. 1218 or toll-free 800-228-7240. Fax: 480-594-1758. E-mail: beth.barilla@apollogrp.edu. Web site: http://www.phoenix.edu/.

NEW HAMPSHIRE

COLBY-SAWYER COLLEGE
NEW LONDON, NEW HAMPSHIRE

General Independent, 4-year, coed **Entrance** Moderately difficult **Setting** 190-acre small-town campus **Total enrollment** 845 **Student/faculty ratio** 12:1 **Application deadline** Rolling (freshmen), rolling (transfer) **Freshmen** 84% were admitted **Housing** Yes **Expenses** Tuition $19,160; Room & Board $7240 **Undergraduates** 65% women, 4% part-time, 3% 25 or older, 0.4% Native American, 0.5% Hispanic American, 0.4% African American, 0.4% Asian American/Pacific Islander **The most frequently chosen baccalaureate fields are** parks and recreation, business/marketing, psychology **Academic program** English as a second language, advanced placement, accelerated degree program, self-designed majors, honors program, internships **Contact** Ms. Wendy Beckemeyer, Vice President for Enrollment Management and Dean of Admissions, Colby-Sawyer College, 100 Main Street, New London, NH 03257-

4648. Telephone: 603-526-3700 or toll-free 800-272-1015. Fax: 603-526-3452. E-mail: csadmiss@colby-sawyer.edu. Web site: http://www.colby-sawyer.edu/.

DANIEL WEBSTER COLLEGE
NASHUA, NEW HAMPSHIRE

General Independent, 4-year, coed **Entrance** Moderately difficult **Setting** 50-acre suburban campus **Total enrollment** 1,099 **Student/faculty ratio** 13:1 **Application deadline** Rolling (freshmen), rolling (transfer) **Freshmen** 84% were admitted **Housing** Yes **Expenses** Tuition $16,570; Room & Board $6340 **Undergraduates** 31% women, 28% part-time, 6% 25 or older, 0.2% Native American, 2% Hispanic American, 3% African American, 1% Asian American/Pacific Islander **The most frequently chosen baccalaureate fields are** business/marketing, computer/information sciences, trade and industry **Academic program** Advanced placement, summer session, adult/continuing education programs, internships **Contact** Mr. Paul D. LaBarre, Director of Enrollment Services, Daniel Webster College, 20 University Drive, Nashua, NH 03063. Telephone: 603-577-6603 or toll-free 800-325-6876. Fax: 603-577-6001. E-mail: admissions@dwc.edu. Web site: http://www.dwc.edu/.

DARTMOUTH COLLEGE
HANOVER, NEW HAMPSHIRE

General Independent, university, coed **Entrance** Most difficult **Setting** 265-acre rural campus **Total enrollment** 5,386 **Student/faculty ratio** 8:1 **Application deadline** 1/1 (freshmen), 3/1 (transfer) **Freshmen** 21% were admitted **Housing** Yes **Expenses** Tuition $26,562; Room & Board $7896 **Undergraduates** 48% women, 1% part-time, 2% Native American, 6% Hispanic American, 5% African American, 10% Asian American/Pacific Islander **The most frequently chosen baccalaureate fields are** biological/life sciences, English, social sciences and history **Academic program** Advanced placement, accelerated degree program, self-designed majors, honors program, summer session, internships **Contact** Mr. Karl M. Furstenberg, Dean of Admissions and Financial Aid, Dartmouth College, 6016 McNutt Hall, Hanover, NH 03755. Telephone: 603-646-2875. E-mail: admissions.office@dartmouth.edu. Web site: http://www.dartmouth.edu/.

FRANKLIN PIERCE COLLEGE
RINDGE, NEW HAMPSHIRE

General Independent, comprehensive, coed **Entrance** Moderately difficult **Setting** 1,000-acre rural campus **Total enrollment** 1,489 **Student/faculty ratio** 15:1 **Application deadline** Rolling (freshmen), rolling (transfer) **Freshmen** 75% were admitted **Housing** Yes **Expenses** Tuition $18,985; Room & Board $6250 **Undergraduates** 49% women, 2% part-time, 3% 25 or older, 0.3% Native American, 3% Hispanic American, 3% African American, 1% Asian American/Pacific Islander **The most frequently chosen baccalaureate fields are** business/marketing, communications/communication technologies, social sciences and history **Academic program** English as a second language, advanced placement, self-designed majors, honors program, summer session, adult/continuing education programs, internships **Contact** Ms. Lucy C. Shonk, Director of Admissions, Franklin Pierce College, Box 60, College Road, Franklin Pierce College, Rindge, NH 03461. Telephone: 603-899-4050 or toll-free 800-437-0048. Fax: 603-899-4394. E-mail: admissions@rindge.fpc.edu. Web site: http://www.fpc.edu/.

KEENE STATE COLLEGE
KEENE, NEW HAMPSHIRE

General State-supported, comprehensive, coed **Entrance** Moderately difficult **Setting** 160-acre small-town campus **Total enrollment** 4,573 **Student/faculty ratio** 18:1 **Application deadline** 4/1 (freshmen), 5/1 (transfer) **Freshmen** 77% were admitted **Housing** Yes **Expenses** Tuition $5304; Room & Board $5086 **Undergraduates** 58% women, 14% part-time, 9% 25 or older, 0.2% Native American, 1% Hispanic American, 0.3% African American, 1% Asian American/Pacific Islander **The most frequently chosen baccalaureate fields are** education, psychology, visual/performing arts **Academic program** English as a second language, advanced placement, self-designed majors, honors program, summer session, internships **Contact** Mrs. Kathryn G. Dodge, Director of Admissions, Keene State College, 229 Main Street, Keene, NH 03435-2604. Telephone: 603-358-2276 or toll-free 800-572-1909. Fax: 603-358-2767. E-mail: admissions@keene.edu. Web site: http://www.keene.edu/.

MAGDALEN COLLEGE
WARNER, NEW HAMPSHIRE

General Independent Roman Catholic, 4-year, coed **Entrance** Moderately difficult **Total enrollment** 75 **Student/faculty ratio** 9:1 **Application deadline** 5/1 (freshmen) **Freshmen** 67% were admitted **Housing** Yes **Expenses** Tuition $6950; Room & Board $5000 **Undergraduates** 47% women, 3% 25 or older, 5% Hispanic American **The most frequently chosen baccalaureate field is** liberal arts/general studies **Academic program** Summer session **Contact** Paul V. Sullivan, Director of Admissions, Magdalen College, 511 Kearsarge Mountain Road, Warner, NH 03278. Telephone: 603-456-2656 Ext. 11 or toll-free 877-498-1723 (out-of-state). Fax: 603-456-2660. E-mail: admissions@magdalen.edu. Web site: http://www.magdalen.edu/.

NEW ENGLAND COLLEGE
HENNIKER, NEW HAMPSHIRE

General Independent, comprehensive, coed **Entrance** Moderately difficult **Setting** 225-acre small-town campus **Total enrollment** 831 **Student/faculty ratio** 11:1 **Application deadline** Rolling (freshmen), rolling (transfer) **Freshmen** 92% were admitted **Housing** Yes **Expenses** Tuition $18,886; Room & Board

New England College *(continued)*

$6538 **Undergraduates** 51% women, 11% part-time, 11% 25 or older, 0% Native American, 0.1% Hispanic American, 4% African American, 1% Asian American/Pacific Islander **The most frequently chosen baccalaureate fields are** business/marketing, psychology, social sciences and history **Academic program** English as a second language, advanced placement, self-designed majors, honors program, summer session, adult/continuing education programs, internships **Contact** Mr. Donald N. Parker, Dean of Admission, New England College, 26 Bridge Street, Henniker, NH 03242. Telephone: 603-428-2223 or toll-free 800-521-7642 (out-of-state). Fax: 603-428-7230. E-mail: admis@nec1.nec.edu. Web site: http://www.nec.edu/.

NEW HAMPSHIRE COLLEGE

See Southern New Hampshire University

NOTRE DAME COLLEGE
MANCHESTER, NEW HAMPSHIRE

General Independent Roman Catholic, comprehensive, coed **Entrance** Moderately difficult **Setting** 8-acre suburban campus **Total enrollment** 1,120 **Student/faculty ratio** 13:1 **Application deadline** Rolling (freshmen), rolling (transfer) **Freshmen** 88% were admitted **Housing** Yes **Expenses** Tuition $15,647; Room & Board $6213 **Undergraduates** 34% 25 or older, 0.3% Native American, 1% Hispanic American, 2% African American, 1% Asian American/Pacific Islander **The most frequently chosen baccalaureate fields are** biological/life sciences, education, interdisciplinary studies **Academic program** Advanced placement, accelerated degree program, summer session, adult/continuing education programs, internships **Contact** Mr. Timothy Jones, Director of Admissions, Notre Dame College, 2321 Elm Street, Manchester, NH 03104. Telephone: 800-754-0405 or toll-free 800-754-0405. Fax: 603-644-8316. E-mail: admissions@notredame.edu. Web site: http://www.notredame.edu/.

PLYMOUTH STATE COLLEGE
PLYMOUTH, NEW HAMPSHIRE

General State-supported, comprehensive, coed **Entrance** Moderately difficult **Setting** 170-acre small-town campus **Total enrollment** 4,041 **Student/faculty ratio** 15:1 **Application deadline** 4/1 (freshmen), 4/1 (transfer) **Freshmen** 79% were admitted **Housing** Yes **Expenses** Tuition 5314; Room & Board 5206 **Undergraduates** 50% women, 8% part-time, 6% 25 or older, 1% Native American, 1% Hispanic American, 0.5% African American, 1% Asian American/Pacific Islander **The most frequently chosen baccalaureate fields are** business/marketing, education, social sciences and history **Academic program** Advanced placement, accelerated degree program, self-designed majors, honors program, summer session, internships **Contact** Mr. Eugene Fahey, Senior Associate Director of Admission, Plymouth State College, 17 High Street, MSC #52, Plymouth, NH 03264-1595. Telephone: 800-842-6900 or toll-free 800-842-6900. Fax: 603-535-2714. E-mail: pscadmit@psc.plymouth.edu. Web site: http://www.plymouth.edu/.

RIVIER COLLEGE
NASHUA, NEW HAMPSHIRE

General Independent Roman Catholic, comprehensive, coed **Entrance** Moderately difficult **Setting** 64-acre suburban campus **Total enrollment** 2,300 **Student/faculty ratio** 13:1 **Application deadline** Rolling (freshmen), rolling (transfer) **Freshmen** 70% were admitted **Housing** Yes **Expenses** Tuition $15,520; Room & Board $6100 **Undergraduates** 47% 25 or older, 0.3% Native American, 2% Hispanic American, 1% African American, 3% Asian American/Pacific Islander **The most frequently chosen baccalaureate fields are** education, health professions and related sciences, psychology **Academic program** English as a second language, advanced placement, honors program, summer session, adult/continuing education programs, internships **Contact** Mr. David Boisvert, (Interim Director of Undergraduate Admissions) Executive Assistant to President for Enrollment Management, Rivier College, Office of Undergraduate Admissions, 420 Main Street, Nashua, NH 03060. Telephone: 603-897-8502 or toll-free 800-44RIVIER. Fax: 603-891-1799. E-mail: rivadmit@mighty.riv.edu. Web site: http://www.rivier.edu/.

SAINT ANSELM COLLEGE
MANCHESTER, NEW HAMPSHIRE

General Independent Roman Catholic, 4-year, coed **Entrance** Moderately difficult **Setting** 450-acre suburban campus **Total enrollment** 1,985 **Student/faculty ratio** 15:1 **Application deadline** Rolling (freshmen), rolling (transfer) **Freshmen** 73% were admitted **Housing** Yes **Expenses** Tuition $18,950; Room & Board $7000 **Undergraduates** 56% women, 4% part-time, 0% 25 or older, 0.1% Native American, 1% Hispanic American, 0.4% African American, 1% Asian American/Pacific Islander **The most frequently chosen baccalaureate fields are** business/marketing, health professions and related sciences, social sciences and history **Academic program** Advanced placement, honors program, summer session, internships **Contact** Mr. Donald E. Healy, Director of Admissions, Saint Anselm College, 100 Saint Anselm Drive, Manchester, NH 03102-1310. Telephone: 603-641-7500 Ext. 7171 or toll-free 888-4ANSELM. Fax: 603-641-7550. E-mail: admissions@anselm.edu. Web site: http://www.anselm.edu/.

SOUTHERN NEW HAMPSHIRE UNIVERSITY
MANCHESTER, NEW HAMPSHIRE

General Independent, comprehensive, coed **Entrance** Moderately difficult **Setting** 280-acre suburban campus **Total enrollment** 5,363 **Student/faculty ratio** 18:1 **Application deadline** Rolling (freshmen), rolling (transfer) **Freshmen** 80% were admitted **Hous-**

ing Yes **Expenses** Tuition $15,850; Room & Board $6792 **Undergraduates** 56% women, 59% part-time, 1% 25 or older, 0.1% Native American, 2% Hispanic American, 2% African American, 1% Asian American/Pacific Islander **Academic program** English as a second language, advanced placement, accelerated degree program, honors program, summer session, adult/continuing education programs, internships **Contact** Mr. Brad Poznanski, Director of Admission and Enrollment Planning, Southern New Hampshire University, 2500 North River Road, Manchester, NH 03106-1045. Telephone: 603-645-9611 Ext. 9633 or toll-free 800-NHC-4YOU. Fax: 603-645-9693. E-mail: admission@nhc.edu. Web site: http://www.snhu.edu/.

THOMAS MORE COLLEGE OF LIBERAL ARTS
MERRIMACK, NEW HAMPSHIRE

General Independent, 4-year, coed, affiliated with Roman Catholic Church **Entrance** Moderately difficult **Setting** 14-acre small-town campus **Total enrollment** 72 **Student/faculty ratio** 7:1 **Application deadline** Rolling (freshmen), rolling (transfer) **Freshmen** 66% were admitted **Housing** Yes **Expenses** Tuition 10,000; Room & Board 7700 **Undergraduates** 56% women, 6% part-time, 2% 25 or older, 3% Native American, 4% Hispanic American, 0% African American, 1% Asian American/Pacific Islander **The most frequently chosen baccalaureate fields are** foreign language/literature, philosophy, religion, and theology, social sciences and history **Contact** Dr. Kristen S. Kelly, Director of Admissions, Thomas More College of Liberal Arts, 6 Manchester Street, Merrimack, NH 03054-4818. Telephone: 603-880-8308. Fax: 603-880-9280. E-mail: thomaemorae@earthlink.com. Web site: http://www.thomasmorecollege.edu/.

UNIVERSITY OF NEW HAMPSHIRE
DURHAM, NEW HAMPSHIRE

General State-supported, university, coed **Entrance** Moderately difficult **Setting** 200-acre small-town campus **Total enrollment** 13,426 **Student/faculty ratio** 14:1 **Application deadline** 2/1 (freshmen), 3/1 (transfer) **Freshmen** 76% were admitted **Housing** Yes **Expenses** Tuition $7395; Room & Board $5154 **Undergraduates** 58% women, 9% part-time, 5% 25 or older, 0.2% Native American, 1% Hispanic American, 1% African American, 2% Asian American/Pacific Islander **The most frequently chosen baccalaureate fields are** business/marketing, health professions and related sciences, social sciences and history **Academic program** English as a second language, advanced placement, accelerated degree program, self-designed majors, honors program, summer session, adult/continuing education programs, internships **Contact** Dr. Mark Rubinstein, Vice Provost for Enrollment Management, University of New Hampshire, Grant House, 4 Garrison Avenue, Durham, NH 03824. Telephone: 603-862-1360. Fax: 603-862-0077. E-mail: admissions@unh.edu. Web site: http://www.unh.edu/.

UNIVERSITY OF NEW HAMPSHIRE AT MANCHESTER
MANCHESTER, NEW HAMPSHIRE

General State-supported, comprehensive, coed **Entrance** Moderately difficult **Setting** 800-acre urban campus **Total enrollment** 1,086 **Student/faculty ratio** 13:1 **Application deadline** 6/15 (freshmen), 6/15 (transfer) **Freshmen** 73% were admitted **Housing** No **Expenses** Tuition 5064 **Undergraduates** 62% women, 60% part-time, 0.3% Native American, 1% Hispanic American, 2% African American, 1% Asian American/Pacific Islander **The most frequently chosen baccalaureate fields are** foreign language/literature, communications/communication technologies, psychology **Academic program** Advanced placement, self-designed majors, summer session, adult/continuing education programs, internships **Contact** Ms. Susan Miller, Administrative Assistant, University of New Hampshire at Manchester, 400 Commercial Street, Manchester, NH 03101. Telephone: 603-641-4150. Fax: 603-641-4125. E-mail: unhm@unh.edu. Web site: http://www.unh.edu/unhm/.

UNIVERSITY SYSTEM COLLEGE FOR LIFELONG LEARNING
CONCORD, NEW HAMPSHIRE

General State and locally supported, 4-year, coed **Entrance** Noncompetitive **Setting** rural campus **Student/faculty ratio** 10:1 **Application deadline** Rolling (freshmen), rolling (transfer) **Housing** No **Expenses** Tuition $4158 **The most frequently chosen baccalaureate fields are** business/marketing, liberal arts/general studies, social sciences and history **Academic program** Advanced placement, accelerated degree program, self-designed majors, summer session, adult/continuing education programs, internships **Contact** Ms. Teresa McDonnell, Associate Dean of Learner Services, University System College for Lifelong Learning, 125 North State Street, Concord, NH 03301. Telephone: 603-228-3000 Ext. 308 or toll-free 800-582-7248 Ext. 313 (in-state). Fax: 603-229-0964. E-mail: k_king@unhf.unh.edu. Web site: http://www.cll.edu/.

WHITE PINES COLLEGE
CHESTER, NEW HAMPSHIRE

General Independent, 4-year, coed **Entrance** Moderately difficult **Setting** 83-acre rural campus **Total enrollment** 129 **Student/faculty ratio** 8:1 **Application deadline** Rolling (freshmen), rolling (transfer) **Freshmen** 83% were admitted **Housing** Yes **Expenses** Tuition $12,100; Room & Board $5500 **Undergraduates** 55% women, 6% part-time, 9% 25 or older, 2% Native American, 2% Hispanic American, 0% African American, 2% Asian American/Pacific Islander **Academic program** English as a second language, advanced placement, self-designed majors, honors program, summer session, adult/continuing education programs, internships **Contact** Ms. Sue Dugas, Director of Admissions and Enrollment, White Pines

White Pines College *(continued)*

College, 40 Chester Street, Chester, NH 03036. Telephone: 603-887-7400 or toll-free 877-818-0492. Fax: 603-887-1777. E-mail: wpc@gsinet.net. Web site: http://www.whitepines.edu/.

NEW JERSEY

BETH MEDRASH GOVOHA
LAKEWOOD, NEW JERSEY

Contact Rabbi Yehuda Jacobs, Director of Admissions, Beth Medrash Govoha, 617 Sixth Street, Lakewood, NJ 08701-2797. Telephone: 908-367-1060.

BLOOMFIELD COLLEGE
BLOOMFIELD, NEW JERSEY

General Independent, 4-year, coed, affiliated with Presbyterian Church (U.S.A.) **Entrance** Minimally difficult **Setting** 12-acre suburban campus **Total enrollment** 1,771 **Student/faculty ratio** 13:1 **Application deadline** 8/1 (freshmen), rolling (transfer) **Freshmen** 55% were admitted **Housing** Yes **Expenses** Tuition $10,950; Room & Board $5350 **Undergraduates** 69% women, 30% part-time, 44% 25 or older, 0.2% Native American, 16% Hispanic American, 49% African American, 4% Asian American/Pacific Islander **The most frequently chosen baccalaureate fields are** business/marketing, biological/life sciences, social sciences and history **Academic program** English as a second language, advanced placement, accelerated degree program, self-designed majors, honors program, summer session, internships **Contact** Office of Admission, Bloomfield College, 467 Franklin Street, Bloomfield, NJ 07003-9981. Telephone: 973-748-9000 Ext. 230 or toll-free 800-848-4555. Fax: 973-748-0916. E-mail: admission@bloomfield.edu. Web site: http://www.bloomfield.edu/.

CALDWELL COLLEGE
CALDWELL, NEW JERSEY

General Independent Roman Catholic, comprehensive, coed **Entrance** Moderately difficult **Setting** 100-acre suburban campus **Total enrollment** 2,094 **Student/faculty ratio** 13:1 **Application deadline** Rolling (transfer) **Freshmen** 74% were admitted **Housing** Yes **Expenses** Tuition $13,200; Room & Board $6250 **Undergraduates** 69% women, 50% part-time, 53% 25 or older, 0.1% Native American, 8% Hispanic American, 15% African American, 3% Asian American/Pacific Islander **The most frequently chosen baccalaureate fields are** business/marketing, education, psychology **Academic program** English as a second language, advanced placement, accelerated degree program, self-designed majors, honors program, summer session, adult/continuing education programs, internships **Contact** Mr. Bob Costello, Vice President for Enrollment Management, Caldwell College, 9 Ryerson Avenue, Caldwell, NJ 07006. Telephone: 973-618-3224 or toll-free 888-864-9516 (out-of-state). Fax: 973-618-3600. E-mail: admissions@caldwell.edu. Web site: http://www.caldwell.edu/.

CENTENARY COLLEGE
HACKETTSTOWN, NEW JERSEY

General Independent, comprehensive, coed, affiliated with United Methodist Church **Entrance** Moderately difficult **Setting** 42-acre suburban campus **Total enrollment** 1,338 **Student/faculty ratio** 13:1 **Application deadline** Rolling (freshmen), rolling (transfer) **Freshmen** 77% were admitted **Housing** Yes **Expenses** Tuition $15,370; Room & Board $6250 **Undergraduates** 81% women, 28% part-time, 26% 25 or older, 0.3% Native American, 2% Hispanic American, 3% African American, 3% Asian American/Pacific Islander **The most frequently chosen baccalaureate fields are** business/marketing, liberal arts/general studies, psychology **Academic program** English as a second language, advanced placement, accelerated degree program, self-designed majors, honors program, summer session, internships **Contact** Mr. Michael Szarek, Assistant Dean of Admissions, Centenary College, 400 Jefferson Street, Hackettstown, NJ 07840-2100. Telephone: 908-852-1400 Ext. 2338 or toll-free 800-236-8679. Fax: 908-852-3454. E-mail: admissions@centenarycollege.edu. Web site: http://www.centenarycollege.edu/.

THE COLLEGE OF NEW JERSEY
EWING, NEW JERSEY

General State-supported, comprehensive, coed **Entrance** Very difficult **Setting** 255-acre suburban campus **Total enrollment** 6,859 **Student/faculty ratio** 12:1 **Application deadline** 2/15 (freshmen), 2/15 (transfer) **Freshmen** 50% were admitted **Housing** Yes **Expenses** Tuition 5991; Room & Board 6504 **Undergraduates** 59% women, 6% part-time, 6% 25 or older, 0.1% Native American, 5% Hispanic American, 6% African American, 5% Asian American/Pacific Islander **The most frequently chosen baccalaureate fields are** business/marketing, education, English **Academic program** Advanced placement, honors program, summer session, internships **Contact** Ms. Lisa Angeloni, Director of Admissions, The College of New Jersey, The College of New Jersey, Admission Office, PO Box 7718, Ewing, NJ 08628. Telephone: 609-771-2131 or toll-free 800-624-0967. Fax: 609-637-5174. E-mail: admiss@vm.tcnj.edu. Web site: http://www.tcnj.edu/.

COLLEGE OF SAINT ELIZABETH
MORRISTOWN, NEW JERSEY

General Independent Roman Catholic, comprehensive, women only **Entrance** Moderately difficult **Setting** 188-acre suburban campus **Total enrollment** 1,772 **Student/faculty ratio** 9:1 **Application deadline** 8/15 (freshmen), rolling (transfer) **Freshmen** 79% were admitted **Housing** Yes **Expenses** Tuition $14,610; Room & Board $6850 **Undergraduates**

56% part-time, 56% 25 or older, 0.2% Native American, 13% Hispanic American, 12% African American, 3% Asian American/Pacific Islander **The most frequently chosen baccalaureate fields are** business/marketing, education, psychology **Academic program** English as a second language, advanced placement, accelerated degree program, self-designed majors, honors program, summer session, internships **Contact** Ms. Donna Yamanis, Dean of Admissions and Financial Aid, College of Saint Elizabeth, 2 Convent Road, Morristown, NJ 07960. Telephone: 973-290-4700 or toll-free 800-210-7900. Fax: 973-290-4710. E-mail: apply@liza.st-elizabeth.edu. Web site: http://www.st-elizabeth.edu/.

DEVRY COLLEGE OF TECHNOLOGY
NORTH BRUNSWICK, NEW JERSEY

General Proprietary, 4-year, coed **Entrance** Minimally difficult **Setting** 10-acre urban campus **Total enrollment** 3,779 **Student/faculty ratio** 22:1 **Application deadline** Rolling (freshmen), rolling (transfer) **Freshmen** 57% were admitted **Housing** No **Expenses** Tuition $8805 **Undergraduates** 23% women, 38% part-time, 45% 25 or older, 0.2% Native American, 17% Hispanic American, 23% African American, 7% Asian American/Pacific Islander **Academic program** Advanced placement, summer session, adult/continuing education programs **Contact** Ms. Danielle DiNapoli, Director of Admission, DeVry College of Technology, 630 US Highway One, North Brunswick, NJ 08902-3362. Telephone: 732-435-4850 or toll-free 800-333-3879. Web site: http://www.nj.devry.edu/.

DREW UNIVERSITY
MADISON, NEW JERSEY

General Independent, university, coed, affiliated with United Methodist Church **Entrance** Very difficult **Setting** 186-acre suburban campus **Total enrollment** 2,412 **Student/faculty ratio** 11:1 **Application deadline** 2/15 (freshmen), 8/1 (transfer) **Freshmen** 71% were admitted **Housing** Yes **Expenses** Tuition 24,018; Room & Board 6782 **Undergraduates** 60% women, 3% part-time, 3% 25 or older, 0.3% Native American, 5% Hispanic American, 3% African American, 6% Asian American/Pacific Islander **The most frequently chosen baccalaureate fields are** psychology, English, social sciences and history **Academic program** Advanced placement, accelerated degree program, self-designed majors, summer session, adult/continuing education programs, internships **Contact** Mr. Roberto Noya, Dean of Admissions for the College of Liberal Arts, Drew University, 36 Madison Avenue, Madison, NJ 07940. Telephone: 973-408-3739. Fax: 973-408-3036. E-mail: cadm@drew.edu. Web site: http://www.drew.edu/.

FAIRLEIGH DICKINSON UNIVERSITY, FLORHAM-MADISON CAMPUS
MADISON, NEW JERSEY

General Independent, comprehensive, coed **Entrance** Moderately difficult **Setting** 178-acre suburban campus **Total enrollment** 3,451 **Student/faculty ratio** 16:1 **Application deadline** 3/1 (freshmen), 8/1 (transfer) **Freshmen** 76% were admitted **Housing** Yes **Expenses** Tuition $16,346; Room & Board $6842 **Undergraduates** 55% women, 21% part-time, 17% 25 or older, 0.2% Native American, 6% Hispanic American, 6% African American, 3% Asian American/Pacific Islander **The most frequently chosen baccalaureate fields are** business/marketing, liberal arts/general studies, psychology **Academic program** English as a second language, advanced placement, accelerated degree program, honors program, summer session, adult/continuing education programs, internships **Contact** Admissions Office, Fairleigh Dickinson University, Florham-Madison Campus, 285 Madison Avenue, Madison, NJ 07940. Telephone: 973-443-8900 or toll-free 800-338-8803. Fax: 973-443-8088. E-mail: globaleducation@fdu.edu. Web site: http://www.fdu.edu/.

FAIRLEIGH DICKINSON UNIVERSITY, TEANECK–HACKENSACK CAMPUS
TEANECK, NEW JERSEY

General Independent, comprehensive, coed **Entrance** Moderately difficult **Setting** 125-acre suburban campus **Total enrollment** 5,931 **Student/faculty ratio** 14:1 **Application deadline** 3/1 (freshmen), 8/1 (transfer) **Freshmen** 69% were admitted **Housing** Yes **Expenses** Tuition $16,346; Room & Board $6842 **Undergraduates** 59% women, 53% part-time, 30% 25 or older, 0.5% Native American, 13% Hispanic American, 23% African American, 6% Asian American/Pacific Islander **The most frequently chosen baccalaureate fields are** business/marketing, communications/communication technologies, health professions and related sciences **Academic program** English as a second language, advanced placement, accelerated degree program, honors program, summer session, adult/continuing education programs, internships **Contact** Dean of Admissions, Fairleigh Dickinson University, Teaneck–Hackensack Campus, 1000 River Road, Teaneck, NJ 07666. Telephone: 201-692-2000 or toll-free 800-338-8803. Fax: 201-692-2560. E-mail: globaleducation@fdu.edu. Web site: http://www.fdu.edu/.

FELICIAN COLLEGE
LODI, NEW JERSEY

General Independent Roman Catholic, comprehensive, coed **Entrance** Moderately difficult **Setting** 37-acre suburban campus **Total enrollment** 1,531 **Student/faculty ratio** 15:1 **Application deadline** Rolling (freshmen), rolling (transfer) **Freshmen** 66% were admitted **Housing** Yes **Expenses** Tuition $11,690; Room & Board $2980 **Undergraduates** 73% women, 33% part-time, 40% 25 or older, 0.2% Native American, 16% Hispanic American, 13% African American, 6% Asian American/Pacific Islander **The most frequently chosen baccalaureate fields are** education, English, health professions and related sciences **Academic program** English as a second language, advanced placement, accelerated degree program, self-designed majors, honors program, summer ses-

Felician College *(continued)*

sion, adult/continuing education programs, internships **Contact** Ms. Cynthia Sievewright, Director of Admission, Felician College, 262 South Main Street, Lodi, NJ 07644. Telephone: 201-559-6131. Fax: 201-559-6188. E-mail: admissions@inet.felician.edu. Web site: http://www.felician.edu/.

GEORGIAN COURT COLLEGE
LAKEWOOD, NEW JERSEY

General Independent Roman Catholic, comprehensive, women only **Entrance** Moderately difficult **Setting** 150-acre suburban campus **Total enrollment** 2,486 **Student/faculty ratio** 14:1 **Application deadline** 8/1 (freshmen), 8/1 (transfer) **Freshmen** 94% were admitted **Housing** Yes **Expenses** Tuition $13,092; Room & Board $4700 **Undergraduates** 33% part-time, 35% 25 or older, 0.2% Native American, 5% Hispanic American, 6% African American, 1% Asian American/Pacific Islander **The most frequently chosen baccalaureate fields are** business/marketing, education, psychology **Academic program** Advanced placement, honors program, summer session, adult/continuing education programs, internships **Contact** Ms. Marjorie Cooke, Dean of Admissions and Enrollment Services, Georgian Court College, Office of Admissions, 900 Lakewood Avenue, Lakewood, NJ 08701-2697. Telephone: 732-364-2200 Ext. 760 or toll-free 800-458-8422. Fax: 732-364-4442. E-mail: admissions-ugrad@georgian.edu. Web site: http://www.georgian.edu/.

JERSEY CITY STATE COLLEGE
See New Jersey City University

KEAN UNIVERSITY
UNION, NEW JERSEY

General State-supported, comprehensive, coed **Entrance** Moderately difficult **Setting** 151-acre urban campus **Total enrollment** 11,468 **Student/faculty ratio** 20:1 **Application deadline** 5/31 (freshmen), 7/15 (transfer) **Freshmen** 62% were admitted **Housing** Yes **Expenses** Tuition $4612; Room only $4500 **Undergraduates** 65% women, 31% part-time, 37% 25 or older, 0.2% Native American, 19% Hispanic American, 20% African American, 6% Asian American/Pacific Islander **The most frequently chosen baccalaureate fields are** business/marketing, education, protective services/public administration **Academic program** English as a second language, accelerated degree program, honors program, summer session, adult/continuing education programs, internships **Contact** Mr. Audley Bridges, Director of Admissions, Kean University, 1000 Morris Avenue, Union, NJ 07083. Telephone: 908-527-2195. E-mail: admitme@turbo.kean.edu. Web site: http://www.kean.edu/.

MONMOUTH UNIVERSITY
WEST LONG BRANCH, NEW JERSEY

General Independent, comprehensive, coed **Entrance** Moderately difficult **Setting** 147-acre suburban campus **Total enrollment** 5,636 **Student/faculty ratio** 16:1 **Application deadline** 3/1 (freshmen), rolling (transfer) **Freshmen** 84% were admitted **Housing** Yes **Expenses** Tuition $16,326; Room & Board $6900 **Undergraduates** 57% women, 14% part-time, 15% 25 or older, 0.3% Native American, 4% Hispanic American, 5% African American, 2% Asian American/Pacific Islander **The most frequently chosen baccalaureate fields are** business/marketing, communications/communication technologies, education **Academic program** Advanced placement, accelerated degree program, self-designed majors, honors program, summer session, adult/continuing education programs, internships **Contact** Ms. Christine Benol, Associate Director of Undergraduate Admission, Monmouth University, 400 Cedar Avenue, West Long Branch, NJ 07764-1898. Telephone: 732-571-3456 or toll-free 800-543-9671 (out-of-state). Fax: 732-263-5166. E-mail: barson@mondec.monmouth.edu. Web site: http://www.monmouth.edu/.

MONTCLAIR STATE UNIVERSITY
UPPER MONTCLAIR, NEW JERSEY

General State-supported, comprehensive, coed **Entrance** Moderately difficult **Setting** 200-acre suburban campus **Total enrollment** 13,502 **Student/faculty ratio** 15:1 **Application deadline** 3/1 (freshmen), 5/1 (transfer) **Freshmen** 23% were admitted **Housing** Yes **Expenses** Tuition $4864; Room & Board $6454 **Undergraduates** 62% women, 25% part-time, 26% 25 or older, 0.2% Native American, 16% Hispanic American, 11% African American, 5% Asian American/Pacific Islander **Academic program** English as a second language, advanced placement, accelerated degree program, honors program, summer session, adult/continuing education programs, internships **Contact** Dr. Alan L. Buechler, Director of Admissions, Montclair State University, One Normal Avenue, Upper Montclair, NJ 07043-1624. Telephone: 973-655-4444 or toll-free 800-331-9205. Fax: 973-893-5455. E-mail: msuadm@saturn.montclair.edu. Web site: http://www.montclair.edu/.

NEW JERSEY CITY UNIVERSITY
JERSEY CITY, NEW JERSEY

General State-supported, comprehensive, coed **Entrance** Moderately difficult **Setting** 46-acre urban campus **Total enrollment** 8,267 **Student/faculty ratio** 15:1 **Application deadline** 4/1 (freshmen), 4/1 (transfer) **Freshmen** 51% were admitted **Housing** Yes **Expenses** Tuition $4642; Room & Board $5600 **Undergraduates** 62% women, 41% part-time, 36% 25 or older, 0.2% Native American, 30% Hispanic American, 20% African American, 9% Asian American/Pacific Islander **The most frequently chosen baccalaureate fields are** business/marketing, health professions and related sciences, social sciences and history **Academic program** English as a second language, advanced placement, accelerated degree program, honors program, summer session, adult/continuing education programs, internships **Contact** Ms. Drusilla Blackman, Director of Admissions, New

Jersey City University, 2039 Kennedy Boulevard, Jersey City, NJ 07305-1597. Telephone: 201-200-3234 or toll-free 800-441-NJCU. E-mail: admissions@jcs1.jcstate.edu. Web site: http://www.njcu.edu/core.htm.

NEW JERSEY INSTITUTE OF TECHNOLOGY

NEWARK, NEW JERSEY

General State-supported, university, coed **Entrance** Moderately difficult **Setting** 45-acre urban campus **Total enrollment** 8,261 **Student/faculty ratio** 14:1 **Application deadline** 4/1 (freshmen), 6/1 (transfer) **Freshmen** 57% were admitted **Housing** Yes **Expenses** Tuition $6730; Room & Board $7300 **Undergraduates** 22% women, 30% part-time, 26% 25 or older, 0.2% Native American, 13% Hispanic American, 12% African American, 21% Asian American/Pacific Islander **The most frequently chosen baccalaureate fields are** computer/information sciences, architecture, engineering/engineering technologies **Academic program** English as a second language, advanced placement, accelerated degree program, honors program, summer session, adult/continuing education programs, internships **Contact** Ms. Kathy Kelly, Director of Admissions, New Jersey Institute of Technology, University Heights, Newark, NJ 07102-1982. Telephone: 973-596-3300 or toll-free 800-925-NJIT. Fax: 973-596-3461. E-mail: admissions@njit.edu. Web site: http://www.njit.edu/.

PRINCETON UNIVERSITY

PRINCETON, NEW JERSEY

General Independent, university, coed **Entrance** Most difficult **Setting** 600-acre suburban campus **Total enrollment** 6,547 **Application deadline** 1/1 (freshmen) **Freshmen** 12% were admitted **Housing** Yes **Expenses** Tuition 25,430; Room & Board 7206 **Undergraduates** 47% women, 2% part-time, 0% 25 or older, 1% Native American, 6% Hispanic American, 7% African American, 12% Asian American/Pacific Islander **The most frequently chosen baccalaureate fields are** engineering/engineering technologies, biological/life sciences, social sciences and history **Academic program** Advanced placement, accelerated degree program, self-designed majors, honors program, adult/continuing education programs, internships **Contact** Mr. Fred A. Hargadon, Dean of Admission, Princeton University, PO Box 430, Princeton, NJ 08544. Telephone: 609-258-3062. Fax: 609-258-6743. E-mail: g3516@princeton.edu. Web site: http://www.princeton.edu/.

RABBINICAL COLLEGE OF AMERICA

MORRISTOWN, NEW JERSEY

General Independent Jewish, 4-year, men only **Entrance** Minimally difficult **Setting** 81-acre small-town campus **Total enrollment** 250 **Application deadline** Rolling (freshmen) **Freshmen** 100% were admitted **Housing** Yes **Expenses** Tuition $7000 **Academic program** Accelerated degree program, summer session, internships **Contact** Rabbi Israel Teitelbaum, Registrar, Rabbinical College of America, Box 1996, Morristown, NJ 07962. Telephone: 973-267-9404.

RAMAPO COLLEGE OF NEW JERSEY

MAHWAH, NEW JERSEY

General State-supported, comprehensive, coed **Entrance** Moderately difficult **Setting** 315-acre suburban campus **Total enrollment** 5,195 **Student/faculty ratio** 17:1 **Application deadline** 3/15 (freshmen), 5/1 (transfer) **Freshmen** 48% were admitted **Housing** Yes **Expenses** Tuition $5638; Room & Board $7044 **Undergraduates** 59% women, 32% part-time, 26% 25 or older, 0.3% Native American, 8% Hispanic American, 7% African American, 4% Asian American/Pacific Islander **The most frequently chosen baccalaureate fields are** business/marketing, communications/communication technologies, psychology **Academic program** English as a second language, advanced placement, accelerated degree program, self-designed majors, honors program, summer session, adult/continuing education programs, internships **Contact** Ms. Nancy Jaeger, Director of Admissions, Ramapo College of New Jersey, 505 Ramapo Valley Road, Mahwah, NJ 07430-1680. Telephone: 201-684-7300 Ext. 7601 or toll-free 800-9RAMAPO (in-state). Fax: 201-684-7508. E-mail: adm@ramapo.edu. Web site: http://www.ramapo.edu/.

THE RICHARD STOCKTON COLLEGE OF NEW JERSEY

POMONA, NEW JERSEY

General State-supported, comprehensive, coed **Entrance** Very difficult **Setting** 1,600-acre suburban campus **Total enrollment** 6,312 **Student/faculty ratio** 20:1 **Application deadline** 5/1 (freshmen), 6/1 (transfer) **Freshmen** 48% were admitted **Housing** Yes **Expenses** Tuition 4784; Room & Board 5516 **Undergraduates** 21% 25 or older, 0.4% Native American, 5% Hispanic American, 8% African American, 4% Asian American/Pacific Islander **The most frequently chosen baccalaureate fields are** biological/life sciences, business/marketing, social sciences and history **Academic program** Advanced placement, accelerated degree program, self-designed majors, honors program, summer session, adult/continuing education programs, internships **Contact** Mr. Salvatore Catalfamo, Dean of Enrollment Management, The Richard Stockton College of New Jersey, PO Box 195, Jimmie Leeds Road, Pomona, NJ 08240-0195. Telephone: 609-652-4261. Fax: 609-748-5541. E-mail: admissions@pollux.stockton.edu. Web site: http://www.stockton.edu/.

► **For more information, see page 462.**

RIDER UNIVERSITY

LAWRENCEVILLE, NEW JERSEY

General Independent, comprehensive, coed **Entrance** Moderately difficult **Setting** 340-acre suburban cam-

Rider University *(continued)*

pus **Total enrollment** 5,274 **Student/faculty ratio** 13:1 **Application deadline** Rolling (freshmen), rolling (transfer) **Freshmen** 81% were admitted **Housing** Yes **Expenses** Tuition $18,320; Room & Board $7380 **Undergraduates** 58% women, 21% part-time, 19% 25 or older, 1% Native American, 4% Hispanic American, 8% African American, 3% Asian American/Pacific Islander **The most frequently chosen baccalaureate fields are** business/marketing, education, English **Academic program** English as a second language, advanced placement, honors program, summer session, adult/continuing education programs, internships **Contact** Mrs. Susan C. Christian, Director, Office of Admissions, Rider University, 2083 Lawrenceville Road, Lawrenceville, NJ 08648-3099. Telephone: 609-895-5768 or toll-free 800-257-9026. Fax: 609-895-6645. E-mail: admissions@rider.edu. Web site: http://www.rider.edu/.

▶ **For more information, see page 463.**

ROWAN UNIVERSITY
GLASSBORO, NEW JERSEY

General State-supported, comprehensive, coed **Entrance** Moderately difficult **Setting** 200-acre small-town campus **Total enrollment** 9,364 **Student/faculty ratio** 14:1 **Application deadline** 3/15 (freshmen), 3/15 (transfer) **Freshmen** 30% were admitted **Housing** Yes **Expenses** Tuition $5347; Room & Board $5776 **Undergraduates** 58% women, 22% part-time, 19% 25 or older, 0.4% Native American, 5% Hispanic American, 9% African American, 4% Asian American/Pacific Islander **The most frequently chosen baccalaureate fields are** business/marketing, communications/communication technologies, education **Academic program** English as a second language, advanced placement, accelerated degree program, honors program, summer session, adult/continuing education programs, internships **Contact** Mr. Marvin G. Sills, Director of Admissions, Rowan University, 201 Mullica Hill Road, Glassboro, NJ 08028. Telephone: 856-256-4200 or toll-free 800-447-1165 (in-state). Fax: 856-256-4430. E-mail: admissions@rowan.edu. Web site: http://www.rowan.edu/.

RUTGERS, THE STATE UNIVERSITY OF NEW JERSEY, CAMDEN
CAMDEN, NEW JERSEY

General State-supported, university, coed **Total enrollment** 5,125 **Student/faculty ratio** 12:1 **Application deadline** Rolling (freshmen) **Freshmen** 59% were admitted **Expenses** Tuition $6204; Room & Board $6519 **Undergraduates** 59% women, 27% part-time, 34% 25 or older, 0.5% Native American, 6% Hispanic American, 16% African American, 7% Asian American/Pacific Islander **Academic program** English as a second language, advanced placement, self-designed majors, honors program, summer session, internships **Contact** Ms. Diane Williams Harris, Associate Director of University Undergraduate Admissions, Rutgers, The State University of New Jersey, Camden, 65 Davidson Road, Piscataway, NJ 08854-8097. Telephone: 732-932-4636. Fax: 732-353-1440. E-mail: admissions@asb-ugadm.rutgers.edu. Web site: http://camden-www.rutgers.edu/.

RUTGERS, THE STATE UNIVERSITY OF NEW JERSEY, NEWARK
NEWARK, NEW JERSEY

General State-supported, university, coed **Entrance** Moderately difficult **Total enrollment** 9,352 **Student/faculty ratio** 12:1 **Application deadline** Rolling (freshmen) **Freshmen** 52% were admitted **Expenses** Tuition $6204; Room & Board $6519 **Undergraduates** 58% women, 31% part-time, 28% 25 or older, 0.3% Native American, 18% Hispanic American, 20% African American, 19% Asian American/Pacific Islander **Academic program** English as a second language, advanced placement, accelerated degree program, self-designed majors, honors program, summer session, adult/continuing education programs, internships **Contact** Ms. Diane William Harris, Associate Director of University Undergraduate Admissions, Rutgers, The State University of New Jersey, Newark, 65 Davidson Road, Piscataway, NJ 08854-8097. Telephone: 732-932-4636. Fax: 732-353-1440. E-mail: admissions@asb-ugadm.rutgers.edu. Web site: http://info.rutgers.edu/newark/.

RUTGERS, THE STATE UNIVERSITY OF NEW JERSEY, NEW BRUNSWICK
NEW BRUNSWICK, NEW JERSEY

General State-supported, university, coed **Entrance** Moderately difficult **Total enrollment** 35,237 **Student/faculty ratio** 17:1 **Application deadline** Rolling (freshmen) **Freshmen** 58% were admitted **Expenses** Tuition $6204; Room & Board $6519 **Undergraduates** 53% women, 10% part-time, 0.2% Native American, 8% Hispanic American, 8% African American, 19% Asian American/Pacific Islander **Academic program** English as a second language, advanced placement, accelerated degree program, self-designed majors, honors program **Contact** Ms. Diane Williams Harris, Associate Director of University Undergraduate Admissions, Rutgers, The State University of New Jersey, New Brunswick, 65 Davidson Road, Piscataway, NJ 08854-8097. Telephone: 732-932-4636. E-mail: admissions@sb-ugadm.rutgers.edu. Web site: http://www.rutgers.edu/.

SAINT PETER'S COLLEGE
JERSEY CITY, NEW JERSEY

General Independent Roman Catholic (Jesuit), comprehensive, coed **Entrance** Moderately difficult **Setting** 15-acre urban campus **Total enrollment** 3,282 **Student/faculty ratio** 20:1 **Application deadline** Rolling (freshmen), 6/1 (transfer) **Freshmen** 84% were admitted **Housing** Yes **Expenses** Tuition 16,468; Room only 4340 **Undergraduates** 19% 25 or older, 0.3% Native American, 27% Hispanic American, 16% African American, 8% Asian American/Pacific

Islander **The most frequently chosen baccalaureate fields are** business/marketing, education, health professions and related sciences **Academic program** Advanced placement, accelerated degree program, self-designed majors, honors program, summer session, adult/continuing education programs, internships **Contact** Stephanie Decker, Director of Recruitment, Saint Peter's College, 2627 Kennedy Blvd., Jersey City, NJ 07306. Telephone: 201-915-9213 or toll-free 888-SPC-9933. Fax: 201-432-5860. E-mail: admissions@spcvxa.spc.edu. Web site: http://www.spc.edu/.

SETON HALL UNIVERSITY
SOUTH ORANGE, NEW JERSEY

General Independent Roman Catholic, university, coed **Entrance** Moderately difficult **Setting** 58-acre suburban campus **Total enrollment** 9,920 **Student/faculty ratio** 14:1 **Application deadline** 3/1 (freshmen), 6/1 (transfer) **Freshmen** 76% were admitted **Housing** Yes **Expenses** Tuition $19,400; Room & Board $8060 **Undergraduates** 9% 25 or older, 0.1% Native American, 9% Hispanic American, 12% African American, 6% Asian American/Pacific Islander **The most frequently chosen baccalaureate fields are** business/marketing, communications/communication technologies, protective services/public administration **Academic program** English as a second language, advanced placement, accelerated degree program, honors program, summer session, internships **Contact** Ms. Alyssa McCloud, Acting Director of Admissions, Seton Hall University, Enrollment Services, Bayley Hall, South Orange, NJ 07079-2697. Telephone: 973-275-2576 or toll-free 800-THE HALL (out-of-state). Fax: 973-275-2040. E-mail: thehall@lanmail.shu.edu. Web site: http://www.shu.edu/.

STEVENS INSTITUTE OF TECHNOLOGY
HOBOKEN, NEW JERSEY

General Independent, university, coed **Entrance** Very difficult **Setting** 55-acre urban campus **Total enrollment** 3,714 **Student/faculty ratio** 9:1 **Application deadline** 2/15 (freshmen), 7/1 (transfer) **Freshmen** 54% were admitted **Housing** Yes **Expenses** Tuition 22,150; Room & Board 7492 **Undergraduates** 23% women, 1% part-time, 3% 25 or older, 0.2% Native American, 12% Hispanic American, 5% African American, 22% Asian American/Pacific Islander **The most frequently chosen baccalaureate fields are** computer/information sciences, biological/life sciences, engineering/engineering technologies **Academic program** Advanced placement, accelerated degree program, honors program, summer session, internships **Contact** Mr. Daniel Gallagher, Dean of Undergraduate Admissions, Stevens Institute of Technology, Castle Point on Hudson, Hoboken, NJ 07030. Telephone: 201-216-5197 or toll-free 800-458-5323. Fax: 201-216 8348. E-mail: admissions@stevens-tech.edu. Web site: http://www.stevens-tech.edu/.

TALMUDICAL ACADEMY OF NEW JERSEY
ADELPHIA, NEW JERSEY

Contact Rabbi G. Finkel, Director of Admissions, Talmudical Academy of New Jersey, Route 524, Adelphia, NJ 07710. Telephone: 201-431-1600.

THOMAS EDISON STATE COLLEGE
TRENTON, NEW JERSEY

General State-supported, comprehensive, coed **Entrance** Noncompetitive **Total enrollment** 8,137 **Application deadline** Rolling (transfer) **Housing** No **Undergraduates** 46% women, 100% part-time, 88% 25 or older, 1% Native American, 4% Hispanic American, 9% African American, 2% Asian American/Pacific Islander **The most frequently chosen baccalaureate fields are** business/marketing, physical sciences, social sciences and history **Academic program** Advanced placement, accelerated degree program, self-designed majors, summer session, adult/continuing education programs **Contact** Mr. Gordon Holly, Director of Admissions Services, Thomas Edison State College, 101 West State Street, Trenton, NJ 08608-1176. Telephone: 609-984-1150 or toll-free 888-442-8372. Fax: 609-984-8447. E-mail: admissions@call.tesc.edu. Web site: http://www.tesc.edu/.

WESTMINSTER CHOIR COLLEGE OF RIDER UNIVERSITY
PRINCETON, NEW JERSEY

General Independent, comprehensive, coed **Entrance** Moderately difficult **Setting** 23-acre small-town campus **Total enrollment** 481 **Student/faculty ratio** 7:1 **Application deadline** Rolling (freshmen), rolling (transfer) **Freshmen** 68% were admitted **Housing** Yes **Expenses** Tuition 18,240; Room & Board 7670 **Undergraduates** 59% women, 2% part-time **The most frequently chosen baccalaureate field is** visual/performing arts **Academic program** English as a second language, advanced placement, honors program, summer session, adult/continuing education programs, internships **Contact** Ms. Monica Thomas Tritto, Director of Admissions, Westminster Choir College of Rider University, 101 Walnut Lane, Princeton, NJ 08540-3899. Telephone: 609-921-7144 Ext. 103 or toll-free 800-96-CHOIR. Fax: 609-921-2538. E-mail: wccadmission@rider.edu. Web site: http://westminster.rider.edu/.

WILLIAM PATERSON UNIVERSITY OF NEW JERSEY
WAYNE, NEW JERSEY

General State-supported, comprehensive, coed **Entrance** Moderately difficult **Setting** 300-acre suburban campus **Total enrollment** 9,126 **Student/faculty ratio** 12:1 **Application deadline** 5/1 (freshmen), 5/1 (transfer) **Freshmen** 51% were admitted **Housing** Yes **Expenses** Tuition 5150; Room & Board 6350 **Undergraduates** 59% women, 22% part-time,

William Paterson University of New Jersey *(continued)*

23% 25 or older, 0.2% Native American, 14% Hispanic American, 12% African American, 3% Asian American/Pacific Islander **Academic program** English as a second language, advanced placement, accelerated degree program, honors program, summer session, adult/continuing education programs, internships **Contact** Mr. Leo DeBartolo, Director of Admissions, William Paterson University of New Jersey, 300 Pompton Road, Wayne, NJ 07470. Telephone: 973-720-2906 or toll-free 877-WPU-EXCEL (in-state). Fax: 973-720-2910. E-mail: christensen_@wpc.wilpaterson.edu. Web site: http://www.wpunj.edu/.

▶ **For more information, see page 493.**

NEW MEXICO

COLLEGE OF SANTA FE
SANTA FE, NEW MEXICO

General Independent, comprehensive, coed **Entrance** Moderately difficult **Setting** 100-acre suburban campus **Total enrollment** 1,618 **Student/faculty ratio** 11:1 **Application deadline** Rolling (freshmen), rolling (transfer) **Freshmen** 83% were admitted **Housing** Yes **Expenses** Tuition 17,154; Room & Board 5464 **Undergraduates** 61% women, 50% part-time, 19% 25 or older, 2% Native American, 18% Hispanic American, 1% African American, 1% Asian American/Pacific Islander **The most frequently chosen baccalaureate fields are** business/marketing, education, visual/performing arts **Academic program** Advanced placement, accelerated degree program, self-designed majors, summer session, adult/continuing education programs, internships **Contact** Mr. Dale H. Reinhart, Director of Admissions and Enrollment Management, College of Santa Fe, Admissions Office, 1600 St. Michael's Drive, Santa Fe, NM 87505-7634. Telephone: 505-473-6133 or toll-free 800-456-2673. Fax: 505-473-6129. E-mail: admissio@fogelson.csf.edu. Web site: http://www.csf.edu.

COLLEGE OF THE SOUTHWEST
HOBBS, NEW MEXICO

General Independent, comprehensive, coed **Entrance** Moderately difficult **Setting** 162-acre small-town campus **Total enrollment** 698 **Student/faculty ratio** 15:1 **Application deadline** Rolling (freshmen), rolling (transfer) **Freshmen** 55% were admitted **Housing** Yes **Expenses** Tuition $4990; Room & Board $3766 **Undergraduates** 69% women, 42% part-time, 62% 25 or older, 0.4% Native American, 23% Hispanic American, 2% African American, 0% Asian American/Pacific Islander **The most frequently chosen baccalaureate fields are** education, English, psychology **Academic program** Advanced placement, accelerated degree program, summer session, adult/continuing education programs, internships **Contact** Charlotte Smith, Admissions Counselor, College of the Southwest, 6610 Lovington Highway, Hobbs, NM 88240. Telephone: 505-392-6561 Ext. 1012 or toll-free 800-530-4400 Ext. 347. Fax: 505-392-6006. E-mail: csmith@csw.edu. Web site: http://www.csw.edu/.

EASTERN NEW MEXICO UNIVERSITY
PORTALES, NEW MEXICO

General State-supported, comprehensive, coed **Entrance** Minimally difficult **Setting** 240-acre rural campus **Total enrollment** 3,564 **Student/faculty ratio** 16:1 **Application deadline** Rolling (freshmen), rolling (transfer) **Freshmen** 47% were admitted **Housing** Yes **Expenses** Tuition 1944; Room & Board 3690 **Undergraduates** 60% women, 16% part-time, 27% 25 or older, 3% Native American, 29% Hispanic American, 4% African American, 1% Asian American/Pacific Islander **The most frequently chosen baccalaureate fields are** education, business/marketing, social sciences and history **Academic program** English as a second language, advanced placement, accelerated degree program, self-designed majors, honors program, summer session, adult/continuing education programs, internships **Contact** Dr. Karyl C. Lyne, Assistant Vice President for Student Affairs, Eastern New Mexico University, Station #7 ENMU, Portales, NM 88130. Telephone: 505-562-2178 or toll-free 800-367-3668. Fax: 505-562-2118. E-mail: austinr@email.enmu.edu. Web site: http://www.enmu.edu/.

METROPOLITAN COLLEGE OF COURT REPORTING
ALBUQUERQUE, NEW MEXICO

Contact Metropolitan College of Court Reporting, 1717 Louisiana Boulevard NE, Suite 207, Albuquerque, NM 87110-7027. Web site: http://www.metropolitancollege.edu/.

NATIONAL AMERICAN UNIVERSITY
ALBUQUERQUE, NEW MEXICO

General Proprietary, 4-year, coed **Entrance** Noncompetitive **Setting** suburban campus **Application deadline** Rolling (freshmen), rolling (transfer) **Housing** No **Expenses** Tuition 9195 **Academic program** Accelerated degree program, summer session, adult/continuing education programs, internships **Contact** Ms. Karina Elliott-Long, Executive Admissions Representative, National American University, 4775 Indian School, NE, Albuquerque, NM 87110. Telephone: 505-265-7517 or toll-free 800-843-8892. Fax: 505-265-7542.

NAZARENE INDIAN BIBLE COLLEGE
ALBUQUERQUE, NEW MEXICO

General Independent, 4-year, coed, affiliated with Church of the Nazarene **Contact** Ms. Yolanda Vielle, Registrar, Nazarene Indian Bible College, 2315

Markham Road, SW, Albuquerque, NM 87105. Telephone: 505-877-0240 Ext. 107 or toll-free 888-877-NIBC.

NEW MEXICO HIGHLANDS UNIVERSITY
LAS VEGAS, NEW MEXICO

General State-supported, comprehensive, coed **Entrance** Minimally difficult **Setting** 120-acre small-town campus **Total enrollment** 3,396 **Application deadline** Rolling (freshmen), rolling (transfer) **Freshmen** 79% were admitted **Housing** Yes **Expenses** Tuition $1992; Room & Board $3970 **Undergraduates** 26% 25 or older, 7% Native American, 65% Hispanic American, 3% African American, 2% Asian American/Pacific Islander **The most frequently chosen baccalaureate fields are** business/marketing, education, protective services/public administration **Academic program** Advanced placement, accelerated degree program, honors program, summer session, internships **Contact** Dr. Dianne Brimmer, Vice President/Dean of Students, New Mexico Highlands University, Box 9000, Las Vegas, NM 87701. Telephone: 505-454-3020 or toll-free 800-338-6648 (in-state). Fax: 505-454-3311. E-mail: johncoca@merlin.nmhu.edu. Web site: http://www.nmhu.edu/.

NEW MEXICO INSTITUTE OF MINING AND TECHNOLOGY
SOCORRO, NEW MEXICO

General State-supported, university, coed **Entrance** Moderately difficult **Setting** 320-acre small-town campus **Total enrollment** 1,548 **Student/faculty ratio** 12:1 **Application deadline** 8/1 (freshmen), 8/1 (transfer) **Freshmen** 68% were admitted **Housing** Yes **Expenses** Tuition 2499; Room & Board 3704 **Undergraduates** 36% women, 19% part-time, 18% 25 or older, 4% Native American, 19% Hispanic American, 1% African American, 3% Asian American/Pacific Islander **The most frequently chosen baccalaureate fields are** engineering/engineering technologies, biological/life sciences, physical sciences **Academic program** Advanced placement, accelerated degree program, self-designed majors, summer session, adult/continuing education programs, internships **Contact** Ms. Melissa Jaramillo-Fleming, Director of Admissions, New Mexico Institute of Mining and Technology, 801 Leroy Place, Socorro, NM 87801. Telephone: 505-835-5424 or toll-free 800-428-TECH. Fax: 505-835-5989. E-mail: admission@admin.nmt.edu. Web site: http://www.nmt.edu/.

NEW MEXICO STATE UNIVERSITY
LAS CRUCES, NEW MEXICO

General State-supported, university, coed **Entrance** Moderately difficult **Setting** 900-acre suburban campus **Total enrollment** 14,958 **Application deadline** 8/14 (freshmen), 8/14 (transfer) **Freshmen** 61% were admitted **Housing** Yes **Expenses** Tuition $2790; Room & Board $3892 **Undergraduates** 54% women, 22% part-time, 20% 25 or older, 3% Native American, 42% Hispanic American, 3% African American, 2% Asian American/Pacific Islander **The most frequently chosen baccalaureate fields are** business/marketing, education, engineering/engineering technologies **Academic program** Advanced placement, accelerated degree program, self-designed majors, honors program, summer session, adult/continuing education programs, internships **Contact** Ms. Angela Mora-Riley, Director of Admissions, New Mexico State University, Box 30001, MSC, Las Cruces, NM 88003-8001. Telephone: 505-646-3121 or toll-free 800-662-6678. Fax: 505-646-6330. E-mail: admssions@nmsu.edu. Web site: http://www.nmsu.edu/.

ST. JOHN'S COLLEGE
SANTA FE, NEW MEXICO

General Independent, comprehensive, coed **Entrance** Very difficult **Setting** 250-acre small-town campus **Total enrollment** 504 **Student/faculty ratio** 8:1 **Application deadline** Rolling (freshmen), rolling (transfer) **Freshmen** 81% were admitted **Housing** Yes **Expenses** Tuition 23,630; Room & Board 6576 **Undergraduates** 43% women, 1% part-time, 6% 25 or older, 2% Native American, 7% Hispanic American, 0.2% African American, 2% Asian American/Pacific Islander **The most frequently chosen baccalaureate field is** liberal arts/general studies **Academic program** Summer session **Contact** Mr. Larry Clendenin, Director of Admissions, St. John's College, 1160 Camino Cruz Blanca, Santa Fe, NM 87501. Telephone: 505-984-6060 or toll-free 800-331-5232. Fax: 505-984-6162. E-mail: admissions@shadow.sjcsf.edu. Web site: http://www.sjcsf.edu/.

UNIVERSITY OF NEW MEXICO
ALBUQUERQUE, NEW MEXICO

General State-supported, university, coed **Entrance** Moderately difficult **Setting** 625-acre urban campus **Total enrollment** 23,545 **Application deadline** 6/15 (freshmen), 6/15 (transfer) **Freshmen** 85% were admitted **Housing** Yes **Expenses** Tuition $2794; Room & Board $4860 **Undergraduates** 26% 25 or older, 6% Native American, 33% Hispanic American, 3% African American, 3% Asian American/Pacific Islander **The most frequently chosen baccalaureate fields are** education, business/marketing, health professions and related sciences **Academic program** English as a second language, advanced placement, accelerated degree program, self-designed majors, honors program, summer session, adult/continuing education programs, internships **Contact** Ms. Robin Ryan, Associate Director of Admissions, University of New Mexico, Albuquerque, NM 87131-2046. Telephone: 505-277-2446 or toll-free 800-CALLUNM (in-state). Fax: 505-277-6686. E-mail: apply@unm.edu. Web site: http://www.unm.edu/.

UNIVERSITY OF PHOENIX–NEW MEXICO CAMPUS
ALBUQUERQUE, NEW MEXICO

General Proprietary, comprehensive, coed **Entrance** Noncompetitive **Total enrollment** 66,534 **Student/**

University of Phoenix–New Mexico Campus *(continued)*

faculty ratio 13:1 **Application deadline** Rolling (freshmen), rolling (transfer) **Expenses** Tuition $7740 **Undergraduates** 56% women, 86% 25 or older, 2% Native American, 18% Hispanic American, 13% African American, 6% Asian American/Pacific Islander **Academic program** Advanced placement, accelerated degree program, adult/continuing education programs **Contact** Ms. Beth Barilla, Director of Admissions, University of Phoenix–New Mexico Campus, 4615 East Elwood Street, Phoenix, AZ 85040-1948. Telephone: 480-927-0099 Ext. 1218 or toll-free 800-228-7240. Fax: 480-594-1758. E-mail: beth.barilla@apollogrp.edu. Web site: http://www.phoenix.edu/.

WESTERN NEW MEXICO UNIVERSITY
SILVER CITY, NEW MEXICO

Contact Mr. Michael Alecksen, Director of Admissions, Western New Mexico University, College Avenue, Silver City, NM 88062-0680. Telephone: 505-538-6106 or toll-free 800-872-WNMU (in-state). Fax: 505-538-6155. Web site: http://www.wnmu.edu/.

NEW YORK

ADELPHI UNIVERSITY
GARDEN CITY, NEW YORK

General Independent, university, coed **Entrance** Moderately difficult **Setting** 75-acre suburban campus **Total enrollment** 5,908 **Student/faculty ratio** 14:1 **Application deadline** Rolling (freshmen), rolling (transfer) **Freshmen** 70% were admitted **Housing** Yes **Expenses** Tuition 15,690; Room & Board 7450 **Undergraduates** 69% women, 23% part-time, 31% 25 or older, 0.1% Native American, 7% Hispanic American, 12% African American, 3% Asian American/Pacific Islander **The most frequently chosen baccalaureate fields are** business/marketing, health professions and related sciences, trade and industry **Academic program** Advanced placement, honors program, summer session, internships **Contact** Mr. Joseph Posillico, Acting Director of Admissions/Director of Student Financial Services, Adelphi University, South Avenue, Garden City, NY 11530. Telephone: 516-877-3052 or toll-free 800-ADELPHI. Fax: 516-877-3039. E-mail: admissions@adelphi.edu. Web site: http://www.adelphi.edu/.

ALBANY COLLEGE OF PHARMACY OF UNION UNIVERSITY
ALBANY, NEW YORK

General Independent, comprehensive, coed **Entrance** Moderately difficult **Setting** 1-acre urban campus **Total enrollment** 691 **Student/faculty ratio** 14:1 **Application deadline** 2/1 (freshmen), 2/1 (transfer) **Freshmen** 80% were admitted **Housing** Yes **Expenses** Tuition $12,873; Room & Board $5100 **Undergraduates** 63% women, 1% part-time, 14% 25 or older, 0.3% Native American, 2% Hispanic American, 3% African American, 10% Asian American/Pacific Islander **Academic program** Advanced placement, accelerated degree program, summer session, internships **Contact** Mr. Robert Gould, Director of Admissions, Albany College of Pharmacy of Union University, 106 New Scotland Avenue, Albany, NY 12208-3425. Telephone: 518-445-7221 or toll-free 888-203-8010. Fax: 518-445-7202. E-mail: admissions@acp.edu. Web site: http://www.acp.edu/.

ALBERT A. LIST COLLEGE OF JEWISH STUDIES
See Jewish Theological Seminary of America

ALFRED UNIVERSITY
ALFRED, NEW YORK

General Independent, university, coed **Entrance** Moderately difficult **Setting** 232-acre rural campus **Total enrollment** 2,433 **Student/faculty ratio** 11:1 **Application deadline** 2/1 (freshmen), 8/1 (transfer) **Freshmen** 76% were admitted **Housing** Yes **Expenses** Tuition 19,150; Room & Board 7450 **Undergraduates** 52% women, 5% part-time, 8% 25 or older, 0.4% Native American, 3% Hispanic American, 4% African American, 2% Asian American/Pacific Islander **The most frequently chosen baccalaureate fields are** business/marketing, engineering/engineering technologies, psychology **Academic program** Advanced placement, accelerated degree program, self-designed majors, honors program, summer session, adult/continuing education programs, internships **Contact** Katherine M. McCarthy, Director of Admissions, Alfred University, Alumni Hall, Alfred, NY 14802-1205. Telephone: 607-871-2115 or toll-free 800-541-9229. Fax: 607-871-2198. E-mail: admssn@bigvax.alfred.edu. Web site: http://www.alfred.edu/.

▶ **For more information, see page 382.**

ARNOLD & MARIE SCHWARTZ COLLEGE OF PHARMACY AND HEALTH SCIENCES
See Long Island University, Brooklyn Campus

AUDREY COHEN COLLEGE
NEW YORK, NEW YORK

General Independent, comprehensive, coed **Entrance** Moderately difficult **Setting** urban campus **Total enrollment** 1,278 **Student/faculty ratio** 25:1 **Application deadline** 8/15 (freshmen), 8/15 (transfer) **Freshmen** 68% were admitted **Housing** No **Expenses** Tuition $14,750 **Undergraduates** 83% women, 65% 25 or older, 4% Native American, 20% Hispanic American, 63% African American, 2% Asian American/Pacific Islander **Academic program** English as a second language, accelerated degree program, summer session, adult/continuing education programs, internships **Contact** Ms. Jennifer Gass, Admissions Counselor, Audrey Cohen College, 75 Varick Street, 12th Floor, New York, NY 10013. Telephone: 212-343-1234 Ext. 2704 or toll-free 800-33-THINK Ext. 5001 (in-state). Fax: 212-343-8470. Web site: http://www.audreycohen.edu/.

BARD COLLEGE
ANNANDALE-ON-HUDSON, NEW YORK

General Independent, comprehensive, coed **Entrance** Very difficult **Setting** 600-acre rural campus **Total enrollment** 1,430 **Student/faculty ratio** 9:1 **Application deadline** 1/15 (freshmen), 1/15 (transfer) **Freshmen** 48% were admitted **Housing** Yes **Expenses** Tuition 24,950; Room & Board 7440 **Undergraduates** 56% women, 4% part-time, 1% 25 or older, 0.2% Native American, 4% Hispanic American, 2% African American, 2% Asian American/Pacific Islander **The most frequently chosen baccalaureate fields are** social sciences and history, foreign language/literature, visual/performing arts **Academic program** English as a second language, advanced placement, accelerated degree program, self-designed majors, adult/continuing education programs, internships **Contact** Ms. Mary Inga Backlund, Director of Admissions, Bard College, Ravine Road, PO Box 5000, Annandale-on-Hudson, NY 12504. Telephone: 845-758-7472. Fax: 845-758-5208. E-mail: admission@bard.edu. Web site: http://www.bard.edu/.

BARNARD COLLEGE
NEW YORK, NEW YORK

General Independent, 4-year, women only **Entrance** Most difficult **Setting** 4-acre urban campus **Total enrollment** 21,000 **Student/faculty ratio** 11:1 **Application deadline** 1/15 (freshmen), 5/1 (transfer) **Freshmen** 37% were admitted **Housing** Yes **Expenses** Tuition 23,056; Room & Board 9358 **Undergraduates** 2% part-time, 0.4% 25 or older, 0.4% Native American, 5% Hispanic American, 5% African American, 22% Asian American/Pacific Islander **The most frequently chosen baccalaureate fields are** English, psychology, social sciences and history **Academic program** Advanced placement, accelerated degree program, self-designed majors, honors program, internships **Contact** Ms. Jennifer Gill Fondiller, Dean of Admissions, Barnard College, 3009 Broadway, New York, NY 10027. Telephone: 212-854-2014. Fax: 212-854-6220. E-mail: admissions@barnard.columbia.edu. Web site: http://www.barnard.edu/.

BERNARD M. BARUCH COLLEGE OF THE CITY UNIVERSITY OF NEW YORK
NEW YORK, NEW YORK

General State and locally supported, comprehensive, coed **Entrance** Very difficult **Setting** urban campus **Total enrollment** 15,698 **Application deadline** 4/1 (freshmen), 5/1 (transfer) **Freshmen** 23% were admitted **Housing** No **Expenses** Tuition $3350 **Undergraduates** 57% women, 34% part-time, 37% 25 or older, 0.1% Native American, 19% Hispanic American, 21% African American, 24% Asian American/Pacific Islander **The most frequently chosen baccalaureate fields are** business/marketing, psychology, social sciences and history **Academic program** English as a second language, advanced placement, self-designed majors, honors program, summer session, adult/continuing education programs, internships **Contact** Mr. James F. Murphy, Director of Undergraduate Admissions and Financial Aid, Bernard M. Baruch College of the City University of New York, Box H-0720, New York, NY 10010-5585. Telephone: 212-802-2300. E-mail: udgbb@cunyvm.edu. Web site: http://www.baruch.cuny.edu/.

BETH HAMEDRASH SHAAREI YOSHER INSTITUTE
BROOKLYN, NEW YORK

Contact Mr. Menachem Steinberg, Director of Admissions, Beth HaMedrash Shaarei Yosher Institute, 4102-10 Sixteenth Avenue, Brooklyn, NY 11204. Telephone: 718-854-2290.

BETH HATALMUD RABBINICAL COLLEGE
BROOKLYN, NEW YORK

Contact Rabbi Osina, Director of Admissions, Beth Hatalmud Rabbinical College, 2127 Eighty-second Street, Brooklyn, NY 11214. Telephone: 718-259-2525.

BORICUA COLLEGE
NEW YORK, NEW YORK

General Independent, comprehensive, coed **Entrance** Moderately difficult **Setting** urban campus **Total enrollment** 1,520 **Student/faculty ratio** 20:1 **Application deadline** Rolling (freshmen), rolling (transfer) **Freshmen** 47% were admitted **Housing** No **Expenses** Tuition $7350 **Undergraduates** 89% 25 or older **Academic program** Accelerated degree program, honors program, summer session, adult/continuing education programs, internships **Contact** Dr. Alicea Mercedes, Director of Registration and Assessment, Boricua College, 3755 Broadway, New York, NY 10032-1560. Telephone: 212-694-1000 Ext. 525.

BRIARCLIFFE COLLEGE
BETHPAGE, NEW YORK

General Proprietary, 4-year, coed **Entrance** Moderately difficult **Setting** 18-acre suburban campus **Total enrollment** 1,790 **Student/faculty ratio** 14:1 **Application deadline** Rolling (freshmen), rolling (transfer) **Freshmen** 65% were admitted **Housing** No **Expenses** Tuition $10,400 **Undergraduates** 52% women, 30% part-time, 42% 25 or older, 3% Native American, 8% Hispanic American, 5% African American, 2% Asian American/Pacific Islander **Academic program** Advanced placement, accelerated degree program, summer session, adult/continuing education programs, internships **Contact** Ms. Theresa Donohue, Dean of Marketing and Admissions, Bri-

Briarcliffe College *(continued)*

arcliffe College, 1055 Stewart Avenue, Bethpage, NY 11714. Telephone: 516-918-3705. Fax: 516-470-6020. E-mail: donohuet@bcl.org. Web site: http://www.bcl.edu/.

BROOKLYN COLLEGE OF THE CITY UNIVERSITY OF NEW YORK
BROOKLYN, NEW YORK

General State and locally supported, comprehensive, coed **Entrance** Moderately difficult **Setting** 26-acre urban campus **Total enrollment** 15,039 **Student/faculty ratio** 15:1 **Application deadline** Rolling (freshmen), rolling (transfer) **Housing** No **Expenses** Tuition 3393; Room & Board 55 **Undergraduates** 61% women, 34% part-time, 29% 25 or older, 0.1% Native American, 9% Hispanic American, 22% African American, 7% Asian American/Pacific Islander **The most frequently chosen baccalaureate fields are** business/marketing, education, psychology **Academic program** English as a second language, advanced placement, honors program, summer session, adult/continuing education programs, internships **Contact** Ms. Celia Adams, Admissions Counselor/Recruiter, Brooklyn College of the City University of New York, 2900 Bedford Avenue, 1203 Plaza, Brooklyn, NY 11210-2889. Telephone: 718-951-5001. Fax: 718-951-4506. E-mail: admissions@brooklyn.cuny.edu. Web site: http://www.brooklyn.cuny.edu/.

CANISIUS COLLEGE
BUFFALO, NEW YORK

General Independent Roman Catholic (Jesuit), comprehensive, coed **Entrance** Moderately difficult **Setting** 26-acre urban campus **Total enrollment** 4,814 **Student/faculty ratio** 16:1 **Application deadline** Rolling (freshmen), rolling (transfer) **Freshmen** 83% were admitted **Housing** Yes **Expenses** Tuition 16,447; Room & Board 6730 **Undergraduates** 53% women, 14% part-time, 13% 25 or older, 0.3% Native American, 3% Hispanic American, 7% African American, 2% Asian American/Pacific Islander **The most frequently chosen baccalaureate fields are** business/marketing, education, liberal arts/general studies **Academic program** English as a second language, advanced placement, self-designed majors, honors program, summer session, internships **Contact** Miss Penelope H. Lips, Director of Admissions, Canisius College, 2001 Main Street, Buffalo, NY 14208-1098. Telephone: 716-888-2200 or toll-free 800-843-1517. Fax: 716-888-3230. E-mail: inquiry@gort.canisius.edu. Web site: http://www.canisius.edu/.

CAZENOVIA COLLEGE
CAZENOVIA, NEW YORK

General Independent, 4-year, coed **Entrance** Minimally difficult **Setting** 40-acre small-town campus **Total enrollment** 962 **Student/faculty ratio** 13:1 **Application deadline** Rolling (freshmen), rolling (transfer) **Freshmen** 100% were admitted **Housing** Yes **Expenses** Tuition $13,150; Room & Board $6054 **Undergraduates** 73% women, 23% part-time, 5% 25 or older, 1% Native American, 4% Hispanic American, 7% African American, 1% Asian American/Pacific Islander **The most frequently chosen baccalaureate fields are** business/marketing, home economics/vocational home economics, visual/performing arts **Academic program** Advanced placement, self-designed majors, honors program, summer session, adult/continuing education programs, internships **Contact** Mr. Robert A. Croot, Dean for Enrollment Management, Cazenovia College, Cazenovia, NY 13035. Telephone: 315-655-7208 or toll-free 800-654-3210. Fax: 315-655-4860. E-mail: admission@cazcollege.edu. Web site: http://www.cazcollege.edu/.

CENTRAL YESHIVA TOMCHEI TMIMIM-LUBAVITCH
BROOKLYN, NEW YORK

Contact Moses Gluckowsky, Director of Admissions, Central Yeshiva Tomchei Tmimim-Lubavitch, 841-853 Ocean Parkway, Brooklyn, NY 11230. Telephone: 718-859-7600.

CITY COLLEGE OF THE CITY UNIVERSITY OF NEW YORK
NEW YORK, NEW YORK

General State and locally supported, university, coed **Entrance** Moderately difficult **Setting** 35-acre urban campus **Total enrollment** 10,362 **Student/faculty ratio** 15:1 **Application deadline** Rolling (freshmen), rolling (transfer) **Freshmen** 74% were admitted **Housing** No **Expenses** Tuition $3309 **Undergraduates** 52% women, 37% part-time, 39% 25 or older, 0.2% Native American, 30% Hispanic American, 30% African American, 11% Asian American/Pacific Islander **Academic program** English as a second language, advanced placement, accelerated degree program, self-designed majors, honors program, summer session, adult/continuing education programs, internships **Contact** Mr. William Di Brienza, Acting Director of Admissions, City College of the City University of New York, Convent Avenue at 138th Street, New York, NY 10031-9198. Telephone: 212-650-6977. Fax: 212-650-6417. E-mail: adocc@cunyvm.cuny.edu. Web site: http://www.ccny.cuny.edu/.

CLARKSON UNIVERSITY
POTSDAM, NEW YORK

General Independent, university, coed **Entrance** Very difficult **Setting** 640-acre small-town campus **Total enrollment** 2,877 **Student/faculty ratio** 16:1 **Application deadline** 3/15 (freshmen), rolling (transfer) **Freshmen** 83% were admitted **Housing** Yes **Expenses** Tuition 21,000; Room & Board 7781 **Undergraduates** 26% women, 2% part-time, 3% 25 or older, 1% Native American, 1% Hispanic American, 2% African American, 3% Asian American/Pacific Islander **The most frequently chosen baccalaureate fields are** business/marketing, engineering/engineering technologies, interdisciplinary studies **Academic program** English as a second language, advanced placement, accelerated degree program, self-designed majors, honors program, summer session, internships **Contact** Mr. Brian T. Grant, Director of Enrollment Operations, Clarkson University, Holcroft House, Potsdam, NY 13699. Telephone: 315-268-6479 or toll-free 800-527-6577. Fax: 315-268-7647. E-mail: fradmis@agent.clarkson.edu. Web site: http://www.clarkson.edu/.

COLGATE UNIVERSITY
HAMILTON, NEW YORK

General Independent, comprehensive, coed **Entrance** Very difficult **Setting** 515-acre rural campus **Total enrollment** 2,781 **Student/faculty ratio** 11:1 **Application deadline** 1/15 (freshmen), 3/15 (transfer) **Freshmen** 38% were admitted **Housing** Yes **Expenses** Tuition 25,740; Room & Board 6330 **Undergraduates** 51% women, 0.2% part-time, 0% 25 or older, 1% Native American, 4% Hispanic American, 4% African American, 5% Asian American/Pacific Islander **The most frequently chosen baccalaureate fields are** biological/life sciences, English, social sciences and history **Academic program** Advanced placement, self-designed majors, honors program **Contact** Mr. Gary L. Ross, Dean of Admission, Colgate University, 13 Oak Drive, Hamilton, NY 13346-1386. Telephone: 315-228-7401. Fax: 315-228-7544. E-mail: admission@center.colgate.edu. Web site: http://www.colgate.edu/.

COLLEGE OF AERONAUTICS
FLUSHING, NEW YORK

General Independent, 4-year, coed, primarily men **Entrance** Minimally difficult **Setting** 6-acre urban campus **Total enrollment** 1,301 **Student/faculty ratio** 11:1 **Application deadline** Rolling (freshmen), rolling (transfer) **Freshmen** 88% were admitted **Expenses** Tuition 10,550 **Undergraduates** 8% women, 32% part-time, 35% 25 or older, 0.1% Native American, 35% Hispanic American, 20% African American, 14% Asian American/Pacific Islander **Academic program** Advanced placement, summer session, adult/continuing education programs, internships **Contact** Thomas Bracken, Associate Director, Admissions, College of Aeronautics, La Guardia Airport, 86-01 23rd Avenue, Flushing, NY 11369. Telephone: 718-429-6600 Ext. 167 or toll-free 800-776-2376 (in-state). Fax: 718-429-0256. E-mail: pro@aero.edu. Web site: http://www.aero.edu/.

THE COLLEGE OF INSURANCE
NEW YORK, NEW YORK

General Independent, comprehensive, coed **Entrance** Very difficult **Setting** 2-acre urban campus **Total enrollment** 329 **Student/faculty ratio** 11:1 **Application deadline** Rolling (freshmen), rolling (transfer) **Freshmen** 52% were admitted **Housing** Yes **Expenses** Tuition $14,612; Room & Board $9414 **Undergraduates** 49% women, 56% part-time, 24% 25 or older, 0% Native American, 9% Hispanic American, 18% African American, 15% Asian American/Pacific Islander **The most frequently chosen baccalaureate field is** business/marketing **Academic program** English as a second language, advanced placement, summer session, adult/continuing education programs **Contact** Andrew Ippolito, Director of Undergraduate Admissions, The College of Insurance, 101 Murray Street, New York, NY 10007. Telephone: 212-815-9235 or toll-free 800-356-5146. Fax: 212-964-3381. E-mail: admissions@tci.edu. Web site: http://www.tci.edu/.

COLLEGE OF MOUNT SAINT VINCENT
RIVERDALE, NEW YORK

General Independent, comprehensive, coed **Entrance** Moderately difficult **Setting** 70-acre suburban campus **Total enrollment** 1,512 **Student/faculty ratio** 12:1 **Application deadline** Rolling (freshmen), rolling (transfer) **Freshmen** 70% were admitted **Housing** Yes **Expenses** Tuition 16,330; Room & Board 7300 **Undergraduates** 79% women, 22% part-time, 23% 25 or older, 31% Hispanic American, 17% African American, 8% Asian American/Pacific Islander **The most frequently chosen baccalaureate fields are** education, health professions and related sciences, social sciences and history **Academic program** English as a second language, advanced placement, accelerated degree program, self-designed majors, honors program, summer session, adult/continuing education programs, internships **Contact** Mrs. Lenore M. Mott, Dean of Admissions and Financial Aid, College of Mount Saint Vincent, 6301 Riverdale Avenue, Riverdale, NY 10471-1093. Telephone: 718-405-3268 or toll-free 800-665-CMSV. Fax: 718-549-7945. E-mail: admissns@cmsv.edu. Web site: http://www.cmsv.edu/.

THE COLLEGE OF NEW ROCHELLE
NEW ROCHELLE, NEW YORK

General Independent, comprehensive, coed, primarily women **Entrance** Moderately difficult **Setting** 20-acre suburban campus **Total enrollment** 6,787 **Student/faculty ratio** 9:1 **Application deadline** Rolling (freshmen), rolling (transfer) **Freshmen** 55% were admitted **Housing** Yes **Expenses** Tuition $12,080; Room & Board $6250 **Undergraduates** 87% women, 15% part-time, 7% 25 or older, 0.3% Native American, 9% Hispanic American, 44% African American, 1% Asian American/Pacific Islander **The most frequently chosen baccalaureate fields are** health professions and related sciences, education, liberal arts/general studies **Academic program** English as a second language, advanced placement, accelerated degree program, self-designed majors, honors program, summer session, adult/continuing education programs, internships **Contact** Mrs. Kelly Getman-Crowley, Director of Admission, The College of New Rochelle, 29 Castle Place, New Rochelle, NY 10805-2339. Telephone: 914-654-5452 or toll-free 800-933-5923. Fax: 914-654-5486. Web site: http://cnr.edu/.

THE COLLEGE OF SAINT ROSE
ALBANY, NEW YORK

General Independent, comprehensive, coed **Entrance** Moderately difficult **Setting** 22-acre urban campus **Total enrollment** 4,231 **Student/faculty ratio** 15:1 **Application deadline** 2/1 (freshmen), 2/1 (transfer) **Freshmen** 75% were admitted **Housing** Yes **Expenses** Tuition $13,160; Room & Board $6550 **Undergraduates** 73% women, 21% part-time, 34% 25 or older, 0.3% Native American, 2% Hispanic American, 3% African American, 1% Asian American/Pacific Islander **The most frequently chosen baccalaureate fields are** business/marketing, education, health professions and related sciences **Academic program** Advanced placement, accelerated degree program, self-designed majors, summer session, adult/continuing education programs, internships **Contact** Ms. Mary Elizabeth Amico, Associate Dean of Admissions and Enrollment Services, The College of Saint Rose, 432 Western Avenue, Albany, NY 12203-1419. Telephone: 518-454-5150 or toll-free 800-637-8556. Fax: 518-454-2013. E-mail: admit@rosnet.strose.edu. Web site: http://www.strose.edu/.

COLLEGE OF STATEN ISLAND OF THE CITY UNIVERSITY OF NEW YORK
STATEN ISLAND, NEW YORK

General State and locally supported, comprehensive, coed **Entrance** Noncompetitive **Setting** 204-acre urban campus **Total enrollment** 11,115 **Student/faculty ratio** 17:1 **Application deadline** Rolling (freshmen), rolling (transfer) **Freshmen** 100% were admitted **Housing** No **Expenses** Tuition $3316 **Undergraduates** 59% women, 37% part-time, 36% 25 or older, 0.2% Native American, 10% Hispanic American, 10% African American, 8% Asian American/Pacific Islander **Academic program** English as a second language, advanced placement, accelerated degree program, honors program, summer session, adult/continuing education programs, internships **Contact** Ms. Mary-Beth Riley, Director of Admissions and Recruitment, College of Staten Island of the City University of New York, 2800 Victory Boulevard, Staten Island, NY 10314-6600. Telephone: 718-982-2011. Fax: 718-982-2500. Web site: http://www.csi.cuny.edu/.

COLUMBIA COLLEGE
NEW YORK, NEW YORK

General Independent, 4-year, coed **Entrance** Most difficult **Setting** 35-acre urban campus **Total enrollment** 3,913 **Student/faculty ratio** 7:1 **Application deadline** 1/1 (freshmen), 3/15 (transfer) **Freshmen** 13% were admitted **Housing** Yes **Expenses** Tuition 25,922; Room & Board 7939 **Undergraduates** 51% women, 0% 25 or older **Academic program** English as a second language, advanced placement, self-designed majors, honors program, summer session, internships **Contact** Mr. Eric Furda, Director of Undergraduate Admissions, Columbia College, 1130 Amsterdam Avenue MC 2807, New York, NY 10027. Telephone: 212-854-2522. Fax: 212-854-1209. E-mail: ugrad-admiss@columbia.edu. Web site: http://www.columbia.edu/.

COLUMBIA UNIVERSITY, BARNARD COLLEGE
See Barnard College

COLUMBIA UNIVERSITY, COLUMBIA COLLEGE
See Columbia College

COLUMBIA UNIVERSITY, SCHOOL OF GENERAL STUDIES
NEW YORK, NEW YORK

General Independent, 4-year, coed **Entrance** Most difficult **Setting** 36-acre urban campus **Total enrollment** 19,000 **Student/faculty ratio** 7:1 **Application deadline** 7/1 (freshmen), 7/1 (transfer) **Freshmen** 45% were admitted **Housing** Yes **Expenses** Tuition $24,944; Room & Board $9000 **Undergraduates** 55% women, 47% part-time, 75% 25 or older, 0.1% Native American, 9% Hispanic American, 8% African American, 9% Asian American/Pacific Islander **The most frequently chosen baccalaureate field is** liberal arts/general studies **Academic program** English as a second language, advanced placement, accelerated degree program, self-designed majors, honors program, summer session, adult/continuing education programs, internships **Contact** Mr. Carlos A. Porro, Director of Admissions, Columbia University, School of General Studies, Mail Code 4101, Lewisohn Hall, 2970 Broadway, New York, NY 10027-9829. Telephone: 212-854-2772 or toll-free 800-895-1169 (out-of-state). Fax: 212-854-6316. E-mail: gs-admit@columbia.edu.

▶ **For more information, see page 404.**

COLUMBIA UNIVERSITY, THE FU FOUNDATION SCHOOL OF ENGINEERING AND APPLIED SCIENCE
NEW YORK, NEW YORK

General Independent, university, coed **Entrance** Most difficult **Setting** urban campus **Total enrollment** 21,000 **Student/faculty ratio** 5:1 **Application deadline** 1/1 (freshmen), 3/15 (transfer) **Freshmen** 27% were admitted **Housing** Yes **Expenses** Tuition 25,922; Room & Board 7939 **Undergraduates** 27% women, 0% 25 or older **Academic program** English as a second language, advanced placement, accelerated degree program, honors program, summer session, adult/continuing education programs, internships **Contact** Mr. Eric J. Furda, Director of Undergraduate Admissions, Columbia University, The Fu Foundation School of Engineering and Applied Science, 1130 Amsterdam Avenue MC 2807, New York, NY 10027. Telephone: 212-854-2522. Fax: 212-854-1209. E-mail: ugrad-admiss@columbia.edu. Web site: http://www.columbia.edu/.

CONCORDIA COLLEGE
BRONXVILLE, NEW YORK

General Independent Lutheran, 4-year, coed **Entrance** Moderately difficult **Setting** 33-acre suburban campus **Total enrollment** 578 **Student/faculty ratio** 12:1 **Application deadline** 3/15 (freshmen), 7/15 (transfer) **Freshmen** 83% were admitted **Housing** Yes **Expenses** Tuition $14,350; Room & Board $6500 **Undergraduates** 57% women, 9% part-time, 18% 25 or older, 0.3% Native American, 7% Hispanic American, 12% African American, 2% Asian American/Pacific Islander **The most frequently chosen baccalaureate fields are** business/marketing, biological/life sciences, education **Academic program** English as a second language, advanced placement, accelerated degree program, self-designed majors, honors program, adult/continuing education programs, internships **Contact** Rebecca Hendricks, Director of Admission, Concordia College, 171 White Plains Road, Bronxville, NY 10708. Telephone: 914-337-9300 Ext. 2149 or toll-free 800-YES-COLLEGE. Fax: 914-395-4636. E-mail: admission@concordia-ny.edu. Web site: http://www.concordia-ny.edu/.

COOPER UNION FOR THE ADVANCEMENT OF SCIENCE AND ART
NEW YORK, NEW YORK

General Independent, comprehensive, coed **Entrance** Most difficult **Setting** urban campus **Total enrollment** 906 **Student/faculty ratio** 7:1 **Application deadline** 1/1 (freshmen), 1/1 (transfer) **Freshmen** 13% were admitted **Housing** Yes **Expenses** Room only 7400 **Undergraduates** 36% women, 2% part-time, 2% 25 or older, 0.5% Native American, 7% Hispanic American, 5% African American, 28% Asian American/Pacific Islander **The most frequently chosen baccalaureate fields are** engineering/engineering technologies, architecture, visual/performing arts **Academic program** Advanced placement, self-designed majors, honors program, summer session, internships **Contact** Mr. Richard Bory, Dean of Admissions and Records and Registrar, Cooper Union for the Advancement of Science and Art, 30 Cooper Square, New York, NY 10003. Telephone: 212-353-4120. Fax: 212-353-4342. E-mail: admissions@cooper.edu. Web site: http://www.cooper.edu/.

CORNELL UNIVERSITY
ITHACA, NEW YORK

General Independent, university, coed **Entrance** Most difficult **Setting** 745-acre small-town campus **Total enrollment** 18,995 **Student/faculty ratio** 11:1 **Application deadline** 1/1 (freshmen), 3/15 (transfer) **Freshmen** 31% were admitted **Housing** Yes **Expenses** Tuition 24,852; Room & Board 8086 **Undergraduates** 48% women, 2% 25 or older, 1% Native American, 6% Hispanic American, 4% African American, 16% Asian American/Pacific Islander **The most frequently chosen baccalaureate fields are** agriculture, business/marketing, engineering/engineering technologies **Academic program** English as a second language, advanced placement, accelerated degree program, self-designed majors, honors program, summer session, internships **Contact** Ms. Wendy Schaerer, Director of Undergraduate Admissions, Cornell University, 410 Thurston Avenue, Ithaca, NY 14850. Telephone: 607-255-5241. Fax: 607-255-0659. E-mail: admissions_mailbox@cornell.edu. Web site: http://www.cornell.edu/.

THE CULINARY INSTITUTE OF AMERICA
HYDE PARK, NEW YORK

General Independent, 4-year, coed **Entrance** Moderately difficult **Setting** 150-acre small-town campus **Total enrollment** 2,028 **Student/faculty ratio** 18:1 **Application deadline** Rolling (freshmen), rolling (transfer) **Freshmen** 41% were admitted **Housing** Yes **Expenses** Tuition $18,055; Room only $3650 **Undergraduates** 32% women, 25% 25 or older, 0.2% Native American, 4% Hispanic American, 3% African American, 3% Asian American/Pacific Islander **Academic program** Adult/continuing education programs, internships **Contact** Mr. Dennis Craig, Director of Admissions, The Culinary Institute of America, 1946 Campus Drive, Hyde Park, NY 12538-1499. Telephone: 845-451-1534 or toll-free 800-CULINARY. Fax: 845-451-1068. E-mail: admissions@culinary.edu. Web site: http://www.ciachef.edu/.

C.W. POST CAMPUS OF LONG ISLAND UNIVERSITY
See Long Island University, C.W. Post Campus

DAEMEN COLLEGE
AMHERST, NEW YORK

General Independent, comprehensive, coed **Entrance** Moderately difficult **Setting** 35-acre suburban campus **Total enrollment** 1,825 **Student/faculty ratio** 14:1 **Application deadline** Rolling (freshmen), rolling (transfer) **Freshmen** 74% were admitted **Housing** Yes **Expenses** Tuition 12,920; Room & Board 6100 **Undergraduates** 77% women, 22% part-time, 30% 25 or older, 1% Native American, 1% Hispanic American, 12% African American, 3% Asian American/Pacific Islander **The most frequently chosen baccalaureate fields are** education, business/marketing, health professions and related sciences **Academic program** Advanced placement, self-designed majors, summer session, adult/continuing education programs, internships **Contact** Ms. Maria P. Dillard, Dean of Admissions and Enrollment Management, Daemen College, 4380 Main Street, Amherst, NY 14226-3592. Telephone: 716-839-8225 or toll-free 800-462-7652. Fax: 716-839-8370. E-mail: admissions@daemen.edu. Web site: http://www.daemen.edu/.

DARKEI NOAM RABBINICAL COLLEGE
BROOKLYN, NEW YORK

Contact Rabbi Pinchas Horowitz, Director of Admissions, Darkei Noam Rabbinical College, 2822 Avenue J, Brooklyn, NY 11210. Telephone: 718-338-6464

DEVRY INSTITUTE OF TECHNOLOGY
LONG ISLAND CITY, NEW YORK

General Proprietary, 4-year, coed **Entrance** Minimally difficult **Setting** urban campus **Total enrollment** 1,652 **Student/faculty ratio** 20:1 **Application deadline** Rolling (freshmen), rolling (transfer) **Freshmen** 47% were admitted **Housing** No **Expenses** Tuition 9865 **Undergraduates** 20% women, 28% part-time, 37% 25 or older, 0.5% Native American, 18% Hispanic American, 25% African American, 5% Asian American/Pacific Islander **Academic program** Advanced placement, accelerated degree program, summer session, adult/continuing education programs **Contact** Mr. Christopher Wargo, Director of Admissions, DeVry Institute of Technology, 30-20 Thomson Avenue, Long Island, NY 11101. Telephone: 718-361-0004 or toll-free 888-713-3879 (out-of-state). Fax: 718-269-4288. Web site: http://www.ny.devry.edu/.

DOMINICAN COLLEGE
ORANGEBURG, NEW YORK

General Independent, comprehensive, coed **Entrance** Moderately difficult **Setting** 14-acre suburban campus **Total enrollment** 1,636 **Student/faculty ratio** 12:1 **Application deadline** Rolling (freshmen), rolling (transfer) **Freshmen** 86% were admitted **Housing** Yes **Expenses** Tuition $13,910; Room & Board $7400 **Undergraduates** 72% women, 51% part-time, 66% 25 or older, 11% Hispanic American, 15% African American, 5% Asian American/Pacific Islander **The most frequently chosen baccalaureate fields are** business/marketing, health professions and related sciences, social sciences and history **Academic program** English as a second language, advanced placement, accelerated degree program, honors program, summer session, adult/continuing education programs, internships **Contact** Joyce Elbe, Director of Admissions, Dominican College, 470 Western Highway, Orangeburg, NY 10962-1210. Telephone: 914-359-7800 Ext. 271. Fax: 914-365-3150. E-mail: admissions@dc.edu. Web site: http://www.dc.edu/.

DOWLING COLLEGE
OAKDALE, NEW YORK

General Independent, comprehensive, coed **Entrance** Moderately difficult **Setting** 156-acre suburban campus **Total enrollment** 6,885 **Application deadline** Rolling (freshmen), rolling (transfer) **Freshmen** 89% were admitted **Housing** Yes **Expenses** Tuition $14,090; Room only $4800 **Undergraduates** 63% women, 38% part-time, 54% 25 or older, 0.2% Native American, 6% Hispanic American, 6% African American, 2% Asian American/Pacific Islander **Academic program** English as a second language, advanced placement, accelerated degree program, self-designed majors, honors program, summer session, internships **Contact** Mr. Stephen Dougherty, Special Assistant for Student Recruitment, Dowling College, 150 Idle Hour Boulevard, Oakdale, NY 11769. Telephone: 631-244-3497 or toll-free 800-DOWLING. Fax: 631-563-3827. E-mail: rowek@dowling.edu. Web site: http://www.dowling.edu/.

D'YOUVILLE COLLEGE
BUFFALO, NEW YORK

General Independent, comprehensive, coed **Entrance** Moderately difficult **Setting** 7-acre urban campus **Total enrollment** 2,397 **Student/faculty ratio** 12:1 **Application deadline** Rolling (freshmen), rolling (transfer) **Freshmen** 75% were admitted **Housing** Yes **Expenses** Tuition $11,930; Room & Board $5720 **Undergraduates** 75% women, 20% part-time, 39% 25 or older, 1% Native American, 3% Hispanic American, 10% African American, 2% Asian American/Pacific Islander **The most frequently chosen baccalaureate fields are** health professions and related sciences, business/marketing, home economics/vocational home economics **Academic program** Accelerated degree program, summer session, adult/continuing education programs, internships **Contact** Mr. Ron Dannecker, Director of Admissions and Financial Aid, D'Youville College, 320 Porter Avenue, Buffalo, NY 14201-1084. Telephone: 716-881-7600 or toll-free 800-777-3921. Fax: 716-881-7790. E-mail: admiss@dyc.edu. Web site: http://www.dyc.edu/.

EASTMAN SCHOOL OF MUSIC
See University of Rochester

ELMIRA COLLEGE
ELMIRA, NEW YORK

General Independent, 4-year, coed **Entrance** Moderately difficult **Setting** 42-acre small-town campus **Total enrollment** 1,581 **Student/faculty ratio** 12:1 **Application deadline** 5/15 (freshmen), 8/1 (transfer) **Freshmen** 78% were admitted **Housing** Yes **Expenses** Tuition 23,540; Room & Board 7530 **Undergraduates** 70% women, 13% part-time, 4% 25 or older, 0.2% Native American, 1% Hispanic American, 3% African American, 1% Asian American/Pacific Islander **The most frequently chosen baccalaureate fields are** business/marketing, education, health professions and related sciences **Academic program** English as a second language, advanced placement, accelerated degree program, self-designed majors, summer session, adult/continuing education programs, internships **Contact** Mr. William S. Neal, Dean of Admissions, Elmira College, Office of Admissions, Elmira, NY 14901. Telephone: 607-735-1724 or toll-free 800-935-6472. Fax: 607-735-1718. E-mail: admissions@elmira.edu. Web site: http://www.elmira.edu/.

▶ **For more information, see page 412.**

EUGENE LANG COLLEGE, NEW SCHOOL UNIVERSITY
NEW YORK, NEW YORK

General Independent, 4-year, coed **Entrance** Moderately difficult **Setting** 5-acre urban campus **Total enrollment** 7,867 **Student/faculty ratio** 10:1 **Appli-**

cation deadline 2/1 (freshmen), 5/15 (transfer) **Freshmen** 56% were admitted **Housing** Yes **Expenses** Tuition $21,216; Room & Board $9083 **Undergraduates** 68% women, 7% part-time, 4% 25 or older, 1% Native American, 10% Hispanic American, 7% African American, 6% Asian American/Pacific Islander **The most frequently chosen baccalaureate field is** liberal arts/general studies **Academic program** Accelerated degree program, summer session, adult/continuing education programs, internships **Contact** Mr. Terence Peavy, Director of Admissions, Eugene Lang College, New School University, 65 West 11th Street, New York, NY 10011-8601. Telephone: 212-229-5665. E-mail: lang@newschool.edu. Web site: http://www.newschool.edu/.

EXCELSIOR COLLEGE
ALBANY, NEW YORK

General Independent, comprehensive, coed **Entrance** Noncompetitive **Setting** urban campus **Total enrollment** 18,041 **Application deadline** Rolling (freshmen), rolling (transfer) **Freshmen** 100% were admitted **Housing** No **Undergraduates** 60% women, 99% part-time, 98% 25 or older, 1% Native American, 5% Hispanic American, 12% African American, 5% Asian American/Pacific Islander **Academic program** Advanced placement, accelerated degree program, self-designed majors, adult/continuing education programs **Contact** Ms. Chari Leader, Vice President for Enrollment Management, Excelsior College, 7 Columbia Circle, Albany, NY 12203-5159. Telephone: 518-464-8500 or toll-free 888-647-2388. Fax: 518-464-8777. E-mail: rcinfo@cnsvax.albany.edu. Web site: http://www.excelsior.edu.

FASHION INSTITUTE OF TECHNOLOGY
NEW YORK, NEW YORK

General State and locally supported, comprehensive, coed **Entrance** Moderately difficult **Setting** 5-acre urban campus **Total enrollment** 10,813 **Student/faculty ratio** 18:1 **Application deadline** 1/15 (freshmen), 1/15 (transfer) **Freshmen** 41% were admitted **Housing** Yes **Expenses** Tuition 3314; Room & Board 7535 **Undergraduates** 81% women, 42% part-time, 35% 25 or older, 0.3% Native American, 10% Hispanic American, 7% African American, 11% Asian American/Pacific Islander **The most frequently chosen baccalaureate fields are** business/marketing, engineering/engineering technologies, visual/performing arts **Academic program** English as a second language, advanced placement, honors program, summer session, adult/continuing education programs, internships **Contact** Mr. Jim Pidgeon, Director of Admissions, Fashion Institute of Technology, Seventh Avenue at 27th Street, New York, NY 10001-5992. Telephone: 212-217-7675 or toll-free 800-GOTOFIT (out-of-state). Fax: 212-217-7481. E-mail: fitinfo@sfitva.cc.fitsuny.edu. Web site: http://www.fitnyc.suny.edu/.

FIVE TOWNS COLLEGE
DIX HILLS, NEW YORK

General Independent, comprehensive, coed **Setting** 40-acre suburban campus **Total enrollment** 946 **Student/faculty ratio** 13:1 **Application deadline** Rolling (freshmen), rolling (transfer) **Freshmen** 88% were admitted **Expenses** Tuition $10,300; Room & Board $6800 **Undergraduates** 37% women, 4% part-time, 0.1% Native American, 13% Hispanic American, 24% African American, 2% Asian American/Pacific Islander **The most frequently chosen baccalaureate fields are** education, visual/performing arts **Academic program** Advanced placement, summer session, internships **Contact** Mr. Jerry Cohen, Enrollment Services, Five Towns College, 305 North Service Road, Dix Hills, NY 11746-6055. Telephone: 631-424-7000 Ext. 110. Fax: 631-424-7008. Web site: http://www.fivetowns.edu/.

▶ **For more information, see page 421.**

FORDHAM UNIVERSITY
NEW YORK, NEW YORK

General Independent Roman Catholic (Jesuit), university, coed **Entrance** Very difficult **Setting** 85-acre urban campus **Total enrollment** 13,650 **Student/faculty ratio** 10:1 **Application deadline** 2/1 (freshmen), 7/1 (transfer) **Freshmen** 63% were admitted **Housing** Yes **Expenses** Tuition 20,660; Room & Board 8310 **Undergraduates** 59% women, 12% part-time, 10% 25 or older, 0.2% Native American, 12% Hispanic American, 5% African American, 5% Asian American/Pacific Islander **The most frequently chosen baccalaureate fields are** business/marketing, communications/communication technologies, social sciences and history **Academic program** English as a second language, advanced placement, accelerated degree program, self-designed majors, honors program, summer session, adult/continuing education programs, internships **Contact** Mr. John W. Buckley, Dean of Admission, Fordham University, 441 East Fordham Road, Theband Hall, New York, NY 10458. Telephone: 718-817-4000 or toll-free 800-FORDHAM. Fax: 718-367-9404. E-mail: ad_buckley@lars.fordham.edu. Web site: http://www.fordham.edu/.

▶ **For more information, see page 422.**

FRIENDS WORLD COLLEGE
See Long Island University, Southampton College, Friends World Program

GLOBE INSTITUTE OF TECHNOLOGY
NEW YORK, NEW YORK

General Proprietary, 4-year, coed **Total enrollment** 662 **Student/faculty ratio** 20:1 **Freshmen** 90% were admitted **Expenses** Tuition $8620 **Undergraduates** 41% women, 16% part-time, 0.3% Native American, 9% Hispanic American, 19% African American, 12% Asian American/Pacific Islander **Academic program** English as a second language, internships

Globe Institute of Technology *(continued)*

Contact Ms. Tatiana Garelik, Director of Admissions, Globe Institute of Technology, 291 Boradway, New York, NY 10007. Telephone: 212-349-4330. Fax: 212-227-5920. Web site: http://www.globe.edu.

HAMILTON COLLEGE
CLINTON, NEW YORK

General Independent, 4-year, coed **Entrance** Very difficult **Setting** 1,200-acre rural campus **Total enrollment** 1,767 **Student/faculty ratio** 10:1 **Application deadline** 1/15 (freshmen), 3/15 (transfer) **Freshmen** 39% were admitted **Housing** Yes **Expenses** Tuition $26,100; Room & Board $6440 **Undergraduates** 52% women, 1% part-time, 1% 25 or older, 0.2% Native American, 4% Hispanic American, 4% African American, 4% Asian American/Pacific Islander **The most frequently chosen baccalaureate fields are** English, social sciences and history, visual/performing arts **Academic program** English as a second language, advanced placement, accelerated degree program, self-designed majors, adult/continuing education programs, internships **Contact** Mr. Richard M. Fuller, Dean of Admission and Financial Aid, Hamilton College, 198 College Hill Road, Clinton, NY 13323-1296. Telephone: 315-859-4421 or toll-free 800-843-2655. Fax: 315-859-4457. E-mail: admissio@hamilton.edu. Web site: http://www.hamilton.edu/.

HARTWICK COLLEGE
ONEONTA, NEW YORK

General Independent, 4-year, coed **Entrance** Moderately difficult **Setting** 425-acre small-town campus **Total enrollment** 1,419 **Student/faculty ratio** 11:1 **Application deadline** 2/15 (freshmen), 8/1 (transfer) **Freshmen** 89% were admitted **Housing** Yes **Expenses** Tuition $25,085; Room & Board $6530 **Undergraduates** 12% 25 or older, 0.3% Native American, 3% Hispanic American, 4% African American, 1% Asian American/Pacific Islander **The most frequently chosen baccalaureate fields are** psychology, business/marketing, social sciences and history **Academic program** Advanced placement, accelerated degree program, self-designed majors, honors program, internships **Contact** Ms. Susan Dileno, Dean of Admissions, Hartwick College, One Hartwick Drive, P.O. Box 4022, Oneonta, NY 13820-4022. Telephone: 607-431-4150 or toll-free 888-HARTWICK (out-of-state). Fax: 607-431-4138. E-mail: admissions@hartwick.edu. Web site: http://www.hartwick.edu/.

HILBERT COLLEGE
HAMBURG, NEW YORK

General Independent, 4-year, coed **Entrance** Minimally difficult **Setting** 40-acre small-town campus **Total enrollment** 893 **Student/faculty ratio** 16:1 **Application deadline** 9/1 (freshmen), 8/1 (transfer) **Freshmen** 89% were admitted **Housing** Yes **Expenses** Tuition $11,850; Room & Board $4630 **Undergraduates** 65% women, 34% part-time, 39% 25 or older, 1% Native American, 1% Hispanic American, 4% African American, 0.2% Asian American/Pacific Islander **The most frequently chosen baccalaureate fields are** business/marketing, health professions and related sciences, protective services/public administration **Academic program** Advanced placement, honors program, summer session, internships **Contact** Ms. Michele Sojda, Admissions Counselor, Hilbert College, 5200 South Park Avenue, Hamburg, NY 14075-1597. Telephone: 716-649-7900 Ext. 211. Fax: 716-649-0702. Web site: http://www.hilbert.edu/.

HOBART AND WILLIAM SMITH COLLEGES
GENEVA, NEW YORK

General Independent, 4-year, coed **Entrance** Very difficult **Setting** 200-acre small-town campus **Total enrollment** 1,854 **Student/faculty ratio** 13:1 **Application deadline** 2/1 (freshmen), rolling (transfer) **Freshmen** 72% were admitted **Housing** Yes **Expenses** Tuition 25,192; Room & Board 6808 **Undergraduates** 53% women, 0.3% part-time, 0% 25 or older, 0.3% Native American, 4% Hispanic American, 5% African American, 2% Asian American/Pacific Islander **The most frequently chosen baccalaureate fields are** English, psychology, social sciences and history **Academic program** English as a second language, advanced placement, accelerated degree program, self-designed majors, honors program, adult/continuing education programs, internships **Contact** Ms. Mara O'Laughlin, Director of Admissions, Hobart and William Smith Colleges, 629 South Main Street, Geneva, NY 14456-3397. Telephone: 315-781-3472 or toll-free 800-245-0100. Fax: 315-781-5471. E-mail: hoadm@hws.edu. Web site: http://www.hws.edu/.

HOFSTRA UNIVERSITY
HEMPSTEAD, NEW YORK

General Independent, university, coed **Entrance** Moderately difficult **Setting** 240-acre suburban campus **Total enrollment** 13,144 **Student/faculty ratio** 13:1 **Application deadline** Rolling (freshmen), rolling (transfer) **Freshmen** 80% were admitted **Housing** Yes **Expenses** Tuition 15,042; Room & Board 7240 **Undergraduates** 54% women, 14% part-time, 13% 25 or older, 0.2% Native American, 6% Hispanic American, 9% African American, 5% Asian American/Pacific Islander **The most frequently chosen baccalaureate fields are** business/marketing, communications/communication technologies, psychology **Academic program** English as a second language, advanced placement, accelerated degree program, self-designed majors, honors program, summer session, adult/continuing education programs, internships **Contact** Ms. Suzanne Tang, Director of Admissions and Financial Aid, Hofstra University, 100 Hofstra University, Hempstead, NY 11549. Telephone: 516-463-6700 or toll-free 800-HOFSTRA. Fax: 516-560-7660. E-mail: hofstra@hofstra.edu. Web site: http://www.hofstra.edu/.

► **For more information, see page 432.**

HOLY TRINITY ORTHODOX SEMINARY
JORDANVILLE, NEW YORK

General Independent Russian Orthodox, 5-year, men only **Entrance** Noncompetitive **Setting** 900-acre rural campus **Total enrollment** 50 **Application deadline** 5/1 (freshmen), 5/1 (transfer) **Freshmen** 60% were admitted **Housing** Yes **Expenses** Tuition $2000 **Undergraduates** 30% 25 or older **Academic program** English as a second language, accelerated degree program **Contact** Fr. Vladimir Tsurikov, Secretary, Holy Trinity Orthodox Seminary, PO Box 36, Jordanville, NY 13361. Telephone: 315-858-0945. Fax: 315-858-0945. E-mail: seminary@telenet.net.

HOUGHTON COLLEGE
HOUGHTON, NEW YORK

General Independent Wesleyan, 4-year, coed **Entrance** Moderately difficult **Setting** 1,300-acre rural campus **Total enrollment** 1,409 **Student/faculty ratio** 14:1 **Application deadline** Rolling (freshmen), rolling (transfer) **Freshmen** 88% were admitted **Housing** Yes **Expenses** Tuition $15,180; Room & Board $5400 **Undergraduates** 63% women, 4% part-time, 13% 25 or older, 0.2% Native American, 1% Hispanic American, 1% African American, 1% Asian American/Pacific Islander **The most frequently chosen baccalaureate fields are** business/marketing, education, social sciences and history **Academic program** Advanced placement, honors program, summer session, adult/continuing education programs, internships **Contact** Mr. Timothy Fuller, Vice President for Enrollment, Houghton College, PO Box 128, Houghton, NY 14744. Telephone: 716-567-9353 or toll-free 800-777-2556. Fax: 716-567-9522. E-mail: admissions@houghton.edu. Web site: http://www.houghton.edu/.

HUNTER COLLEGE OF THE CITY UNIVERSITY OF NEW YORK
NEW YORK, NEW YORK

General State and locally supported, comprehensive, coed **Entrance** Moderately difficult **Setting** urban campus **Total enrollment** 20,012 **Application deadline** 1/15 (freshmen), 3/1 (transfer) **Freshmen** 53% were admitted **Housing** Yes **Expenses** Tuition 3,343; Room only 1890 **Undergraduates** 70% women, 37% part-time, 40% 25 or older, 0.2% Native American, 23% Hispanic American, 20% African American, 14% Asian American/Pacific Islander **Academic program** English as a second language, advanced placement, self-designed majors, honors program, summer session, internships **Contact** Office of Admissions, Hunter College of the City University of New York, 695 Park Avenue, New York, NY 10021-5085. Telephone: 212-772-4490. Web site: http://www.hunter.cuny.edu/.

IONA COLLEGE
NEW ROCHELLE, NEW YORK

General Independent, comprehensive, coed, affiliated with Roman Catholic Church **Entrance** Moderately difficult **Setting** 35-acre suburban campus **Total enrollment** 4,469 **Student/faculty ratio** 16:1 **Application deadline** 3/15 (freshmen), 8/15 (transfer) **Freshmen** 78% were admitted **Housing** Yes **Expenses** Tuition $15,870; Room & Board $8835 **Undergraduates** 52% women, 16% part-time, 17% 25 or older, 0.1% Native American, 12% Hispanic American, 10% African American, 2% Asian American/Pacific Islander **The most frequently chosen baccalaureate fields are** business/marketing, communications/communication technologies, protective services/public administration **Academic program** Advanced placement, accelerated degree program, honors program, summer session, adult/continuing education programs, internships **Contact** Mr. Thomas Weede, Director of Undergraduate Admissions, Iona College, Admissions, 715 North Avenue, New Rochelle, NY 10801. Telephone: 914-633-2502 or toll-free 800-231-IONA (in-state); 914-633-2502 (out-of-state). Fax: 914-637-2778. Web site: http://www.iona.edu/.

ITHACA COLLEGE
ITHACA, NEW YORK

General Independent, comprehensive, coed **Entrance** Moderately difficult **Setting** 757-acre small-town campus **Total enrollment** 6,170 **Student/faculty ratio** 12:1 **Application deadline** 3/1 (freshmen), 7/15 (transfer) **Freshmen** 70% were admitted **Housing** Yes **Expenses** Tuition 19,192; Room & Board 8284 **Undergraduates** 56% women, 3% part-time, 2% 25 or older, 0.3% Native American, 3% Hispanic American, 2% African American, 2% Asian American/Pacific Islander **The most frequently chosen baccalaureate fields are** communications/communication technologies, health professions and related sciences, visual/performing arts **Academic program** Advanced placement, accelerated degree program, self-designed majors, honors program, summer session, adult/continuing education programs, internships **Contact** Ms. Paula J. Mitchell, Director of Admission, Ithaca College, 100 Job Hall, Ithaca, NY 14850-7020. Telephone: 607-274-3124 or toll-free 800-429-4274. Fax: 607-274-1900. E-mail: admission@ithaca.edu. Web site: http://www.ithaca.edu/.

► **For more information, see page 434.**

JEWISH THEOLOGICAL SEMINARY OF AMERICA
NEW YORK, NEW YORK

General Independent Jewish, university, coed **Entrance** Very difficult **Setting** 1-acre urban campus **Total enrollment** 574 **Student/faculty ratio** 5:1 **Application deadline** 2/15 (freshmen), 5/1 (transfer) **Freshmen** 60% were admitted **Housing** Yes **Expenses** Tuition $9220; Room only $6100 **Undergraduates** 63% women, 1% 25 or older **The most frequently chosen baccalaureate field is** philosophy, religion, and theology **Academic program** Advanced placement, self-designed majors, honors program, summer session, adult/continuing education programs, internships **Contact** Ms. Reena Kamins, Assistant

Jewish Theological Seminary of America *(continued)*

Director of Admissions, Jewish Theological Seminary of America, Room 614 Schiff, 3080 Broadway, New York, NY 10027-4649. Telephone: 212-678-8832. Fax: 212-678-8947. E-mail: mablumenthal@jtsa.edu. Web site: http://www.jtsa.edu/.

JOHN JAY COLLEGE OF CRIMINAL JUSTICE OF THE CITY UNIVERSITY OF NEW YORK

NEW YORK, NEW YORK

General State and locally supported, comprehensive, coed **Entrance** Moderately difficult **Setting** urban campus **Total enrollment** 10,472 **Student/faculty ratio** 20:1 **Application deadline** Rolling (freshmen), rolling (transfer) **Freshmen** 73% were admitted **Housing** No **Expenses** Tuition $3312 **Undergraduates** 35% 25 or older, 0.2% Native American, 37% Hispanic American, 31% African American, 5% Asian American/Pacific Islander **The most frequently chosen baccalaureate fields are** protective services/public administration, psychology, social sciences and history **Academic program** English as a second language, advanced placement, honors program, summer session, internships **Contact** Mr. Richard Saulnier, Acting Dean for Admissions and Registration, John Jay College of Criminal Justice of the City University of New York, 899 Tenth Avenue, New York, NY 10019-1093. Telephone: 212-237-8878. Web site: http://www.jjay.cuny.edu/.

THE JUILLIARD SCHOOL

NEW YORK, NEW YORK

General Independent, comprehensive, coed **Entrance** Most difficult **Setting** urban campus **Total enrollment** 784 **Student/faculty ratio** 4:1 **Application deadline** 12/1 (freshmen), 12/1 (transfer) **Freshmen** 8% were admitted **Housing** Yes **Expenses** Tuition 18,000; Room & Board 7000 **Undergraduates** 51% women, 1% part-time, 5% 25 or older, 0.2% Native American, 4% Hispanic American, 11% African American, 14% Asian American/Pacific Islander **The most frequently chosen baccalaureate field is** visual/performing arts **Academic program** English as a second language, accelerated degree program, self-designed majors, adult/continuing education programs **Contact** Ms. Mary K. Gray, Associate Dean for Admissions, The Juilliard School, 60 Lincoln Center Plaza, New York, NY 10023-6588. Telephone: 212-799-5000 Ext. 223. Fax: 212-724-0263. E-mail: webmaster@juilliard.edu. Web site: http://www.juilliard.edu/.

KEHILATH YAKOV RABBINICAL SEMINARY

BROOKLYN, NEW YORK

Contact Rabbi Zalman Gombo, Admissions Officer, Kehilath Yakov Rabbinical Seminary, 206 Wilson Street, Brooklyn, NY 11211-7207. Telephone: 718-963-1212.

KEUKA COLLEGE

KEUKA PARK, NEW YORK

General Independent, 4-year, coed, affiliated with American Baptist Churches in the U.S.A. **Entrance** Moderately difficult **Setting** 173-acre rural campus **Total enrollment** 952 **Student/faculty ratio** 17:1 **Application deadline** Rolling (freshmen), rolling (transfer) **Freshmen** 86% were admitted **Housing** Yes **Expenses** Tuition $13,970; Room & Board $6750 **Undergraduates** 72% women, 2% part-time, 10% 25 or older, 0.1% Native American, 2% Hispanic American, 4% African American, 1% Asian American/Pacific Islander **The most frequently chosen baccalaureate fields are** education, business/marketing, health professions and related sciences **Academic program** Advanced placement, accelerated degree program, self-designed majors, summer session, adult/continuing education programs, internships **Contact** Mr. Joel Wincowski, Dean of Admissions and Financial Aid, Keuka College, Office of Admissions, Keuka Park, NY 14478-0098. Telephone: 315-279-4411 Ext. 5254 or toll-free 800-33-KEUKA. Fax: 315-279-5386. E-mail: admissions@mail.keuka.edu. Web site: http://www.keuka.edu/.

KOL YAAKOV TORAH CENTER

MONSEY, NEW YORK

General Independent Jewish, comprehensive, men only **Contact** Assistant Director of Admissions, Kol Yaakov Torah Center, 29 West Maple Avenue, Monsey, NY 10952-2954. Telephone: 914-425-3871. E-mail: horizonss@aol.com. Web site: http://horizons.edu/.

LABORATORY INSTITUTE OF MERCHANDISING

NEW YORK, NEW YORK

General Proprietary, 4-year, coed, primarily women **Entrance** Moderately difficult **Setting** urban campus **Total enrollment** 285 **Student/faculty ratio** 8:1 **Application deadline** Rolling (freshmen), rolling (transfer) **Freshmen** 74% were admitted **Housing** No **Expenses** Tuition $13,550 **Undergraduates** 98% women, 4% part-time, 1% 25 or older, 1% Native American, 14% Hispanic American, 12% African American, 6% Asian American/Pacific Islander **The most frequently chosen baccalaureate field is** business/marketing **Academic program** Advanced placement, summer session, internships **Contact** Mr. Adam Rosen, Director of Admissions, Laboratory Institute of Merchandising, 12 East 53rd Street, New York, NY 10022-5268. Telephone: 212-752-1530 or toll-free 800-677-1323. Fax: 212-421-4341. E-mail: limcollege@usa.pipeline.com. Web site: http://www.limcollege.edu/.

LEHMAN COLLEGE OF THE CITY UNIVERSITY OF NEW YORK

BRONX, NEW YORK

General State and locally supported, comprehensive, coed **Contact** Ms. Gloria Ortiz, Assistant Director of

Undergraduate Admissions, Lehman College of the City University of New York, 250 Bedford Park Boulevard West, Bronx, NY 10468. Telephone: 718-960-8096 or toll-free 877-Lehman1 (out-of-state). Fax: 718-960-8712. E-mail: cawic@cunyum.cunx.edu. Web site: http://www.lehman.cuny.edu/.

LE MOYNE COLLEGE
SYRACUSE, NEW YORK

General Independent Roman Catholic (Jesuit), comprehensive, coed **Entrance** Moderately difficult **Setting** 151-acre suburban campus **Total enrollment** 3,130 **Student/faculty ratio** 15:1 **Application deadline** 3/1 (freshmen), 6/1 (transfer) **Freshmen** 84% were admitted **Housing** Yes **Expenses** Tuition 15,870; Room & Board 6760 **Undergraduates** 59% women, 13% part-time, 10% 25 or older, 1% Native American, 4% Hispanic American, 4% African American, 2% Asian American/Pacific Islander **The most frequently chosen baccalaureate fields are** business/ marketing, psychology, social sciences and history **Academic program** Advanced placement, accelerated degree program, honors program, summer session, adult/continuing education programs, internships **Contact** Mr. Dennis J. Nicholson, Director of Admission, Le Moyne College, 1419 Salt Spring Road, Syracuse, NY 13214-1399. Telephone: 315-445-4300 or toll-free 800-333-4733. Fax: 315-445-4711. E-mail: admission@mail.lemoyne.edu. Web site: http://www.lemoyne.edu/.

▶ **For more information, see page 438.**

LIST COLLEGE OF JEWISH STUDIES
See Jewish Theological Seminary of America

LONG ISLAND UNIVERSITY, BRENTWOOD CAMPUS
BRENTWOOD, NEW YORK

General Independent, upper-level, coed **Total enrollment** 856 **Application deadline** 9/14 (transfer) **First-Year Students** 100% were admitted **Expenses** Tuition $17,510 **Undergraduates** 95% 25 or older, 1% Native American, 12% Hispanic American, 7% African American, 1% Asian American/Pacific Islander **The most frequently chosen baccalaureate fields are** business/marketing, protective services/public administration **Contact** Mr. John P. Metcalfe, Director of Admissions, Long Island University, Brentwood Campus, 100 Second Avenue, Brentwood, NY 11717. Telephone: 631-273-5112 Ext. 26. E-mail: brentwd@raptor.liu.edu. Web site: http://www.liunet.edu/cwis/brent/brent.htm.

LONG ISLAND UNIVERSITY, BROOKLYN CAMPUS
BROOKLYN, NEW YORK

General Independent, university, coed **Entrance** Minimally difficult **Setting** 10-acre urban campus **Total enrollment** 7,782 **Student/faculty ratio** 10:1 **Application deadline** Rolling (freshmen), rolling (transfer) **Freshmen** 79% were admitted **Housing** Yes **Expenses** Tuition $16,920; Room & Board $573 **Undergraduates** 71% women, 18% part-time, 0.3% Native American, 15% Hispanic American, 48% African American, 11% Asian American/Pacific Islander **Academic program** English as a second language, advanced placement, self-designed majors, honors program, summer session, adult/continuing education programs, internships **Contact** Mr. Alan B. Chaves, Dean of Admissions, Long Island University, Brooklyn Campus, One University Plaza, Brooklyn, NY 11201-8423. Telephone: 718-488-1011 or toll-free 800-LIU-PLAN (in-state). Fax: 718-797-2399. E-mail: adm_sunday@eagle.liunet.edu. Web site: http://www.liu.edu/.

LONG ISLAND UNIVERSITY, C.W. POST CAMPUS
BROOKVILLE, NEW YORK

General Independent, comprehensive, coed **Entrance** Moderately difficult **Setting** 308-acre suburban campus **Total enrollment** 13,147 **Student/faculty ratio** 18:1 **Application deadline** Rolling (freshmen), rolling (transfer) **Freshmen** 85% were admitted **Housing** Yes **Expenses** Tuition $16,840; Room & Board $6790 **Undergraduates** 23% 25 or older, 1% Native American, 8% Hispanic American, 9% African American, 3% Asian American/Pacific Islander **The most frequently chosen baccalaureate fields are** computer/ information sciences, education, health professions and related sciences **Academic program** English as a second language, advanced placement, accelerated degree program, self-designed majors, honors program, summer session, adult/continuing education programs, internships **Contact** Mr. Jeffrey Lang, Associate Director of Admissions, Long Island University, C.W. Post Campus, 720 Northern Boulevard, Brookville, NY 11548-1300. Telephone: 516-299-2900 or toll-free 800-LIU-PLAN. Fax: 516-299-2137. E-mail: admissions@collegehall.liunet.edu. Web site: http://www.cwpost.liunet.edu/cwis/cwp/post.html.

LONG ISLAND UNIVERSITY, SOUTHAMPTON COLLEGE
SOUTHAMPTON, NEW YORK

General Independent, comprehensive, coed **Entrance** Moderately difficult **Setting** 110-acre rural campus **Total enrollment** 2,254 **Student/faculty ratio** 11:1 **Application deadline** Rolling (freshmen), rolling (transfer) **Freshmen** 67% were admitted **Housing** Yes **Expenses** Tuition 16,950; Room & Board 7760 **Undergraduates** 1% Native American, 5% Hispanic American, 4% African American, 2% Asian American/ Pacific Islander **The most frequently chosen baccalaureate fields are** biological/life sciences, business/ marketing, liberal arts/general studies **Academic program** English as a second language, advanced placement, self-designed majors, honors program, summer session, adult/continuing education programs, internships **Contact** Mr. Michael Brophy,

Long Island University, Southampton College *(continued)*

Associate Provost, Long Island University, Southampton College, 239 Montauk Highway, Southampton, NY 11968-9822. Telephone: 631-287-8200 or toll-free 800-LIU PLAN Ext. 2. Fax: 631-287-8125. E-mail: sc_info@sand.liunet.edu. Web site: http://www.southampton.liu.edu/.

LONG ISLAND UNIVERSITY, SOUTHAMPTON COLLEGE, FRIENDS WORLD PROGRAM

SOUTHAMPTON, NEW YORK

General Independent, 4-year, coed **Entrance** Non-competitive **Setting** 110-acre rural campus **Total enrollment** 216 **Student/faculty ratio** 8:1 **Application deadline** Rolling (freshmen), rolling (transfer) **Freshmen** 80% were admitted **Housing** Yes **Expenses** Tuition 16,750; Room & Board 7400 **Undergraduates** 70% women, 2% part-time, 7% 25 or older, 1% Native American, 4% Hispanic American, 4% African American, 3% Asian American/Pacific Islander **The most frequently chosen baccalaureate field is** interdisciplinary studies **Academic program** Advanced placement, self-designed majors, internships **Contact** Ms. Joyce Tuttle, Director of Enrollment, Friends World Program, Long Island University, Southampton College, Friends World Program, 239 Montauk Highway, Southampton, NY 11968. Telephone: 631-287-8465 or toll-free 800-LIU PLAN (out-of-state). Fax: 631-287-8463. E-mail: fw@southampton.liunet.edu. Web site: http://www.southampton.liu.edu/fw/.

MACHZIKEI HADATH RABBINICAL COLLEGE

BROOKLYN, NEW YORK

General Independent Jewish, comprehensive, men only **Contact** Rabbi Abraham M. Lezerowitz, Director of Admissions, Machzikei Hadath Rabbinical College, 5407 Sixteenth Avenue, Brooklyn, NY 11204-1805. Telephone: 718-854-8777. Web site: 8991.

MANHATTAN COLLEGE

RIVERDALE, NEW YORK

General Independent, comprehensive, coed, affiliated with Roman Catholic Church **Entrance** Moderately difficult **Setting** 31-acre urban campus **Total enrollment** 2,943 **Student/faculty ratio** 14:1 **Application deadline** 3/1 (freshmen), 7/1 (transfer) **Freshmen** 63% were admitted **Housing** Yes **Expenses** Tuition $19,500; Room & Board $7550 **Undergraduates** 47% women, 7% part-time, 7% 25 or older, 0.1% Native American, 17% Hispanic American, 6% African American, 6% Asian American/Pacific Islander **The most frequently chosen baccalaureate fields are** business/marketing, education, engineering/engineering technologies **Academic program** English as a second language, advanced placement, accelerated degree program, honors program, summer session, adult/continuing education programs, internships **Contact** Mr. William J. Bisset Jr., Dean of Admissions and Financial Aid, Manhattan College, 4513 Manhattan College Parkway, Riverdale, NY 10471. Telephone: 718-862-7200 or toll-free 800-622-9235 (in-state). Fax: 718-862-8019. E-mail: admit@manhattan.edu. Web site: http://www.manhattan.edu/.

MANHATTAN SCHOOL OF MUSIC

NEW YORK, NEW YORK

General Independent, comprehensive, coed **Entrance** Very difficult **Setting** 1-acre urban campus **Total enrollment** 723 **Student/faculty ratio** 8:1 **Application deadline** 12/15 (freshmen), 12/15 (transfer) **Freshmen** 32% were admitted **Housing** Yes **Expenses** Tuition 20,500; Room only 5900 **Undergraduates** 50% women, 5% part-time, 28% 25 or older, 1% Native American, 6% Hispanic American, 4% African American, 11% Asian American/Pacific Islander **The most frequently chosen baccalaureate field is** visual/performing arts **Academic program** English as a second language, advanced placement **Contact** Ms. Lee Cioppa, Director of Admission, Manhattan School of Music, 120 Claremont Avenue, New York, NY 10027. Telephone: 212-749-2802 Ext. 2. Fax: 212-749-3025. E-mail: admission@msnnyc.edu. Web site: http://www.msmnyc.edu/.

MANHATTANVILLE COLLEGE

PURCHASE, NEW YORK

General Independent, comprehensive, coed **Entrance** Moderately difficult **Setting** 100-acre suburban campus **Total enrollment** 2,200 **Student/faculty ratio** 10:1 **Application deadline** 3/1 (freshmen), rolling (transfer) **Freshmen** 66% were admitted **Housing** Yes **Expenses** Tuition $20,410; Room & Board $8320 **Undergraduates** 5% 25 or older, 0.2% Native American, 13% Hispanic American, 6% African American, 3% Asian American/Pacific Islander **Academic program** English as a second language, advanced placement, accelerated degree program, self-designed majors, honors program, summer session, adult/continuing education programs, internships **Contact** Mr. Jose Flores, Director of Admissions, Manhattanville College, 2900 Purchase Street, Purchase, NY 10577-2132. Telephone: 914-323-5124 or toll-free 800-328-4553. Fax: 914-694-1732. E-mail: admission@mville.edu. Web site: http://www.manhattanville.edu/.

MANNES COLLEGE OF MUSIC, NEW SCHOOL UNIVERSITY

NEW YORK, NEW YORK

General Independent, comprehensive, coed **Entrance** Very difficult **Setting** urban campus **Total enrollment** 7,867 **Student/faculty ratio** 2:1 **Application deadline** 12/15 (freshmen), rolling (transfer) **Freshmen** 16% were admitted **Housing** Yes **Expenses** Tuition $19,316; Room & Board $9083 **Undergraduates** 63% women, 13% 25 or older, 1% Native American, 2% Hispanic American, 2% African American, 10% Asian American/Pacific Islander **The most**

frequently chosen baccalaureate field is visual/performing arts **Academic program** English as a second language, advanced placement, accelerated degree program, summer session, adult/continuing education programs **Contact** Ms. Allison Scola, Director of Enrollment, Mannes College of Music, New School University, 150 West 85th Street, New York, NY 10024-4402. Telephone: 212-580-0210 Ext. 246 or toll-free 800-292-3040 (out-of-state). Fax: 212-580-1738. E-mail: mannasadmissions@newschool.edu. Web site: http://www.mannes.edu/.

MARIST COLLEGE
POUGHKEEPSIE, NEW YORK

General Independent, comprehensive, coed **Entrance** Moderately difficult **Setting** 135-acre small-town campus **Total enrollment** 5,498 **Student/faculty ratio** 14:1 **Application deadline** 2/15 (freshmen), rolling (transfer) **Freshmen** 53% were admitted **Housing** Yes **Expenses** Tuition $15,746; Room & Board $7828 **Undergraduates** 58% women, 16% part-time, 16% 25 or older, 0.1% Native American, 5% Hispanic American, 5% African American, 1% Asian American/Pacific Islander **The most frequently chosen baccalaureate fields are** business/marketing, communications/communication technologies, protective services/public administration **Academic program** English as a second language, advanced placement, accelerated degree program, honors program, summer session, adult/continuing education programs, internships **Contact** Mr. Jay Murray, Associate Director of Admissions, Marist College, 3399 North Road, Poughkeepsie, NY 12601-1387. Telephone: 914-575-3226 Ext. 2441 or toll-free 800-436-5483. E-mail: admissions@marist.edu. Web site: http://www.marist.edu/.

MARYMOUNT COLLEGE
TARRYTOWN, NEW YORK

General Independent, 4-year, women only **Entrance** Moderately difficult **Setting** 25-acre suburban campus **Total enrollment** 938 **Student/faculty ratio** 11:1 **Application deadline** Rolling (transfer) **Freshmen** 81% were admitted **Housing** Yes **Expenses** Tuition $15,750; Room & Board $8100 **Undergraduates** 19% part-time, 35% 25 or older, 0.1% Native American, 16% Hispanic American, 15% African American, 5% Asian American/Pacific Islander **The most frequently chosen baccalaureate fields are** business/marketing, computer/information sciences, psychology **Academic program** English as a second language, advanced placement, self-designed majors, honors program, summer session, adult/continuing education programs, internships **Contact** Daniela Esposito, Director of Admissions, Marymount College, 100 Marymount Avenue, Tarrytown, NY 10591-3796. Telephone: 914-332-8295 or toll-free 800-724-4312. Fax: 914-332-7442. E-mail: admiss@mmc.marymt.edu. Web site: http://www.marymt.edu/.

▶ **For more information, see page 446.**

MARYMOUNT MANHATTAN COLLEGE
NEW YORK, NEW YORK

General Independent, 4-year, coed **Entrance** Moderately difficult **Setting** 1-acre urban campus **Total enrollment** 2,497 **Student/faculty ratio** 18:1 **Application deadline** Rolling (freshmen), rolling (transfer) **Freshmen** 65% were admitted **Housing** Yes **Expenses** Tuition $14,180; Room only $7000 **Undergraduates** 79% women, 34% part-time, 40% 25 or older, 0.3% Native American, 23% Hispanic American, 20% African American, 4% Asian American/Pacific Islander **The most frequently chosen baccalaureate fields are** business/marketing, communications/communication technologies, visual/performing arts **Academic program** English as a second language, advanced placement, accelerated degree program, honors program, summer session, adult/continuing education programs, internships **Contact** Mr. Thomas Friebel, Associate Vice President for Enrollment Services, Marymount Manhattan College, 221 East 71st Street, New York, NY 10021. Telephone: 212-517-0430 or toll-free 800-MARYMOUNT (out-of-state). Fax: 212-517-0448. E-mail: admissions@marymou.edu. Web site: http://www.marymount.mmm.edu/.

MEDAILLE COLLEGE
BUFFALO, NEW YORK

General Independent, comprehensive, coed **Entrance** Moderately difficult **Setting** 13-acre urban campus **Total enrollment** 1,618 **Student/faculty ratio** 17:1 **Application deadline** 8/1 (freshmen), rolling (transfer) **Freshmen** 70% were admitted **Housing** Yes **Expenses** Tuition $11,960; Room & Board $5500 **Undergraduates** 70% women, 16% part-time, 53% 25 or older, 0.4% Native American, 2% Hispanic American, 15% African American, 1% Asian American/Pacific Islander **The most frequently chosen baccalaureate fields are** business/marketing, education, liberal arts/general studies **Academic program** Advanced placement, accelerated degree program, self-designed majors, summer session, adult/continuing education programs, internships **Contact** Mrs. Jacqueline S. Matheny, Director of Enrollment Management, Medaille College, Medaille College, Office of Admissions, Buffalo, NY 14214. Telephone: 716-884-3281 Ext. 203 or toll-free 800-292-1582 (in-state). Fax: 716-884-0291. E-mail: jmatheny@medaille.edu. Web site: http://www.medaille.edu/.

MEDGAR EVERS COLLEGE OF THE CITY UNIVERSITY OF NEW YORK
BROOKLYN, NEW YORK

General State and locally supported, 4-year, coed **Entrance** Noncompetitive **Setting** 1-acre urban campus **Total enrollment** 4,700 **Student/faculty ratio** 18:1 **Application deadline** Rolling (freshmen), rolling (transfer) **Housing** No **Expenses** Tuition $3282 **Undergraduates** 78% women, 49% part-time, 70% 25 or older, 0.1% Native American, 4% Hispanic American, 68% African American, 1% Asian American/

Medgar Evers College of the City University of New York *(continued)*

Pacific Islander **The most frequently chosen baccalaureate fields are** business/marketing, education, health professions and related sciences **Academic program** English as a second language, advanced placement, honors program, summer session, adult/continuing education programs, internships **Contact** Mr. Eric Hilton, Acting Director of Admissions, Medgar Evers College of the City University of New York, 1650 Bedford Avenue, Brooklyn, NY 11225. Telephone: 718-270-6025. Fax: 718-270-6198. Web site: http://www.mec.cuny.edu/.

MERCY COLLEGE
DOBBS FERRY, NEW YORK

General Independent, comprehensive, coed **Entrance** Noncompetitive **Setting** 60-acre suburban campus **Total enrollment** 10,000 **Application deadline** Rolling (freshmen), rolling (transfer) **Housing** Yes **Expenses** Tuition $8500; Room & Board $7700 **Undergraduates** 58% 25 or older **Academic program** English as a second language, advanced placement, accelerated degree program, self-designed majors, honors program, summer session, adult/continuing education programs, internships **Contact** Ms. Kathy O'Brien, Assistant Dean for Admissions, Mercy College, 555 Broadway, Dobbs Ferry, NY 10522-1189. Telephone: 914-674-7535 or toll-free 800-MERCY-NY. Fax: 914-674-7382. E-mail: admissions@merlin.mercynet.edu. Web site: http://www.mercynet.edu/.

MESIVTA OF EASTERN PARKWAY RABBINICAL SEMINARY
BROOKLYN, NEW YORK

Contact Rabbi Joseph Halberstadt, Dean, Mesivta of Eastern Parkway Rabbinical Seminary, 510 Dahill Road, Brooklyn, NY 11218-5559. Telephone: 718-438-1002.

MESIVTA TIFERETH JERUSALEM OF AMERICA
NEW YORK, NEW YORK

Contact Rabbi Fishellis, Director of Admissions, Mesivta Tifereth Jerusalem of America, 141 East Broadway, New York, NY 10002-6301. Telephone: 212-964-2830.

MESIVTA TORAH VODAATH RABBINICAL SEMINARY
BROOKLYN, NEW YORK

General Independent Jewish, comprehensive, men only **Contact** Rabbi Issac Braun, Administrator, Mesivta Torah Vodaath Rabbinical Seminary, 425 East Ninth Street, Brooklyn, NY 11218-5209. Telephone: 718-941-8000. Fax: 718-941-8032.

MIRRER YESHIVA
BROOKLYN, NEW YORK

Contact Director of Admissions, Mirrer Yeshiva, 1795 Ocean Parkway, Brooklyn, NY 11223-2010. Telephone: 718-645-0536.

MOLLOY COLLEGE
ROCKVILLE CENTRE, NEW YORK

General Independent, comprehensive, coed **Entrance** Moderately difficult **Setting** 25-acre suburban campus **Total enrollment** 2,490 **Student/faculty ratio** 9:1 **Application deadline** Rolling (freshmen), rolling (transfer) **Freshmen** 90% were admitted **Housing** No **Expenses** Tuition $13,250 **Undergraduates** 77% women, 30% part-time, 38% 25 or older, 0.2% Native American, 7% Hispanic American, 16% African American, 3% Asian American/Pacific Islander **The most frequently chosen baccalaureate fields are** health professions and related sciences, business/marketing, psychology **Academic program** English as a second language, advanced placement, self-designed majors, honors program, summer session, adult/continuing education programs, internships **Contact** Mrs. Linda Finley Albanese, Director of Admissions, Molloy College, 1000 Hempstead Avenue, PO Box 5002, Rockville Centre, NY 11571-5002. Telephone: 516-678-5000 Ext. 6240 or toll-free 888-4MOLLOY. Fax: 516-256-2247. E-mail: jforgione@molloy.edu.

MOUNT SAINT MARY COLLEGE
NEWBURGH, NEW YORK

General Independent, comprehensive, coed **Entrance** Moderately difficult **Setting** 72-acre suburban campus **Total enrollment** 2,019 **Student/faculty ratio** 16:1 **Application deadline** Rolling (freshmen), rolling (transfer) **Freshmen** 82% were admitted **Housing** Yes **Expenses** Tuition $11,960; Room & Board $5980 **Undergraduates** 30% 25 or older, 0.3% Native American, 8% Hispanic American, 8% African American, 2% Asian American/Pacific Islander **Academic program** Advanced placement, accelerated degree program, honors program, summer session, adult/continuing education programs, internships **Contact** Mr. J. Randall Ognibene, Director of Admissions, Mount Saint Mary College, 330 Powell Avenue, Newburgh, NY 12550. Telephone: 845-569-3248 or toll-free 888-937-6762. Fax: 845-562-6762. E-mail: ogrady@msmc.edu. Web site: http://www.msmc.edu/.

NAZARETH COLLEGE OF ROCHESTER
ROCHESTER, NEW YORK

General Independent, comprehensive, coed **Entrance** Moderately difficult **Setting** 75-acre suburban campus **Total enrollment** 2,975 **Student/faculty ratio** 12:1 **Application deadline** 2/15 (freshmen), 3/15 (transfer) **Freshmen** 78% were admitted **Housing** Yes **Expenses** Tuition 14,666; Room & Board 6470 **Undergraduates** 74% women, 14% part-time, 14% 25 or older, 0.4% Native American, 2% Hispanic

American, 4% African American, 1% Asian American/Pacific Islander **Academic program** Advanced placement, honors program, summer session, adult/continuing education programs, internships **Contact** Mr. Thomas K. DaRin, Vice President for Enrollment Management, Nazareth College of Rochester, 4245 East Avenue, Rochester, NY 14618-3790. Telephone: 716-389-2860 or toll-free 800-462-3944 (in-state). Fax: 716-389-2826. E-mail: tkdarin@naz.edu. Web site: http://www.naz.edu/.

NEW SCHOOL BACHELOR OF ARTS, NEW SCHOOL UNIVERSITY

NEW YORK, NEW YORK

General Independent, upper-level, coed **Entrance** Moderately difficult **Setting** urban campus **Total enrollment** 1,395 **Application deadline** 8/1 (transfer) **Housing** Yes **Expenses** Tuition $13,808; Room only $6508 **Undergraduates** 65% women, 71% part-time, 72% 25 or older, 1% Native American, 7% Hispanic American, 11% African American, 3% Asian American/Pacific Islander **The most frequently chosen baccalaureate fields are** liberal arts/general studies, visual/performing arts **Academic program** English as a second language, advanced placement, accelerated degree program, self-designed majors, summer session, adult/continuing education programs, internships **Contact** Ms. Gerianne Brusati, Director of Educational Advising and Admissions, New School Bachelor of Arts, New School University, 66 West 12th Street, New York, NY 10011-8603. Telephone: 212-229-5630. E-mail: admissions@dialnsa.edu. Web site: http://www.newschool.edu/.

NEW SCHOOL UNIVERSITY, EUGENE LANG COLLEGE

See Eugene Lang College, New School University

NEW SCHOOL UNIVERSITY, MANNES COLLEGE OF MUSIC

See Mannes College of Music, New School University

NEW SCHOOL UNIVERSITY, PARSONS SCHOOL OF DESIGN

See Parsons School of Design, New School University

NEW YORK INSTITUTE OF TECHNOLOGY

OLD WESTBURY, NEW YORK

General Independent, comprehensive, coed **Entrance** Moderately difficult **Setting** 1,050-acre suburban campus **Total enrollment** 8,965 **Student/faculty ratio** 16:1 **Application deadline** Rolling (freshmen), rolling (transfer) **Freshmen** 75% were admitted **Housing** Yes **Expenses** Tuition $13,700; Room & Board $7310 **Undergraduates** 39% women, 30% part-time, 33% 25 or older, 0.3% Native American, 10% Hispanic American, 14% African American, 12% Asian American/Pacific Islander **The most frequently chosen baccalaureate fields are** architecture, business/marketing, engineering/engineering technologies **Academic program** English as a second language, advanced placement, accelerated degree program, self-designed majors, honors program, summer session, adult/continuing education programs, internships **Contact** Mr. James Newell, Director of Financial Aid, New York Institute of Technology, PO Box 8000, Old Westbury, NY 11568. Telephone: 516-686-7680 or toll-free 800-345-NYIT. Fax: 516-686-7613. E-mail: admissions@aol.nuit.edu. Web site: http://www.nyit.edu/.

NEW YORK SCHOOL OF INTERIOR DESIGN

NEW YORK, NEW YORK

General Independent, comprehensive, coed **Entrance** Moderately difficult **Setting** urban campus **Total enrollment** 698 **Student/faculty ratio** 9:1 **Application deadline** Rolling (freshmen), rolling (transfer) **Housing** No **Expenses** Tuition $16,140 **Undergraduates** 86% women, 82% part-time, 65% 25 or older **The most frequently chosen baccalaureate field is** visual/performing arts **Academic program** English as a second language, advanced placement, summer session, internships **Contact** Ms. Valerie Gomez, Admissions Associate, New York School of Interior Design, 170 East 70th Street, New York, NY 10021-5110. Telephone: 212-472-1500 Ext. 204 or toll-free 800-336-9743. Fax: 212-472-1867. E-mail: admissions@nysid.edu. Web site: http://www.nysid.edu/.

NEW YORK STATE COLLEGE OF CERAMICS

See Alfred University

NEW YORK UNIVERSITY

NEW YORK, NEW YORK

General Independent, university, coed **Entrance** Most difficult **Setting** 28-acre urban campus **Total enrollment** 37,150 **Student/faculty ratio** 12:1 **Application deadline** 1/15 (freshmen), 4/1 (transfer) **Freshmen** 29% were admitted **Housing** Yes **Expenses** Tuition 24,336; Room & Board 9226 **Undergraduates** 60% women, 11% part-time, 11% 25 or older, 0.1% Native American, 7% Hispanic American, 6% African American, 14% Asian American/Pacific Islander **The most frequently chosen baccalaureate fields are** business/marketing, social sciences and history, visual/performing arts **Academic program** English as a second language, advanced placement, accelerated degree program, self-designed majors, honors program, summer session, adult/continuing education programs, internships **Contact** Assistant Vice President for Enrollment Services, New York University, 22 Washington Square North, New York, NY 10011. Telephone: 212-998-4500. Fax: 212-995-4902. E-mail: nyuadmit@uccvm.nyu.edu. Web site: http://www.nyu.edu/.

▶ **For more information, see page 454.**

NIAGARA UNIVERSITY
NIAGARA FALLS, NEW YORK

General Independent, comprehensive, coed, affiliated with Roman Catholic Church **Entrance** Moderately difficult **Setting** 160-acre suburban campus **Total enrollment** 3,146 **Student/faculty ratio** 16:1 **Application deadline** 8/1 (freshmen), 8/15 (transfer) **Freshmen** 84% were admitted **Housing** Yes **Expenses** Tuition 14,560; Room & Board 6660 **Undergraduates** 62% women, 9% part-time, 11% 25 or older, 1% Native American, 2% Hispanic American, 4% African American, 1% Asian American/Pacific Islander **The most frequently chosen baccalaureate fields are** business/marketing, education, social sciences and history **Academic program** English as a second language, advanced placement, accelerated degree program, honors program, summer session, adult/continuing education programs, internships **Contact** Ms. Christine M. McDermott, Associate Director of Admissions, Niagara University, Niagara University, NY 14109. Telephone: 716-286-8700 Ext. 8715 or toll-free 800-462-2111. Fax: 716-286-8733. E-mail: admissions@niagara.edu. Web site: http://www.niagara.edu/.

NYACK COLLEGE
NYACK, NEW YORK

General Independent, 4-year, coed, affiliated with The Christian and Missionary Alliance **Entrance** Moderately difficult **Setting** 102-acre suburban campus **Total enrollment** 2,160 **Student/faculty ratio** 16:1 **Application deadline** Rolling (freshmen), rolling (transfer) **Freshmen** 65% were admitted **Housing** Yes **Expenses** Tuition 13,280; Room & Board 6200 **Undergraduates** 59% women, 6% part-time, 40% 25 or older, 0.2% Native American, 19% Hispanic American, 28% African American, 6% Asian American/Pacific Islander **The most frequently chosen baccalaureate fields are** business/marketing, education, philosophy, religion, and theology **Academic program** English as a second language, advanced placement, accelerated degree program, honors program, summer session, adult/continuing education programs, internships **Contact** Mr. Miguel Sanchez, Director of Admissions, ADCP, Nyack College, 1 South Boulevard, Nyack, NY 10960-3698. Telephone: 845-358-1710 Ext. 350 or toll-free 800-33-NYACK. Fax: 845-358-3047. E-mail: enroll@nyack.edu. Web site: http://www.nyackcollege.edu/.

OHR HAMEIR THEOLOGICAL SEMINARY
PEEKSKILL, NEW YORK

Contact Rabbi M. Z. Weisverg, Director of Admissions, Ohr Hameir Theological Seminary, Furnace Woods Road, Peekskill, NY 10566. Telephone: 914-736-1500.

OHR SOMAYACH/JOSEPH TANENBAUM EDUCATIONAL CENTER
MONSEY, NEW YORK

Contact Rabbi Avrohom Braun, Dean of Students, Ohr Somayach/Joseph Tanenbaum Educational Center, PO Box 334, Monsey, NY 10952-0334. Telephone: 914-425-1370 Ext. 22.

PACE UNIVERSITY, NEW YORK CITY CAMPUS
NEW YORK, NEW YORK

General Independent, university, coed **Entrance** Moderately difficult **Total enrollment** 7,911 **Student/faculty ratio** 15:1 **Application deadline** Rolling (freshmen), rolling (transfer) **Freshmen** 75% were admitted **Housing** Yes **Expenses** Tuition 16,230; Room & Board 6900 **Undergraduates** 62% women, 24% part-time, 22% 25 or older, 0.1% Native American, 12% Hispanic American, 13% African American, 16% Asian American/Pacific Islander **The most frequently chosen baccalaureate fields are** business/marketing, computer/information sciences, health professions and related sciences **Academic program** English as a second language, advanced placement, accelerated degree program, honors program, summer session, adult/continuing education programs, internships **Contact** Mr. Richard Alvarez, Director of Admission, Pace University, New York City Campus, One Pace Plaza, New York, NY 10038. Telephone: 212-346-1323 or toll-free 800-874-7223. Fax: 212-346-1040. E-mail: infoctr@ny027.wan.pace.edu. Web site: http://www.pace.edu/.

PACE UNIVERSITY, PLEASANTVILLE/BRIARCLIFF CAMPUS
PLEASANTVILLE, NEW YORK

General Independent, comprehensive, coed **Entrance** Moderately difficult **Total enrollment** 3,533 **Student/faculty ratio** 13:1 **Application deadline** Rolling (freshmen), rolling (transfer) **Freshmen** 82% were admitted **Housing** Yes **Expenses** Tuition $16,230; Room & Board $6900 **Undergraduates** 57% women, 29% part-time, 22% 25 or older, 0.4% Native American, 9% Hispanic American, 9% African American, 5% Asian American/Pacific Islander **The most frequently chosen baccalaureate fields are** business/marketing, computer/information sciences, health professions and related sciences **Academic program** English as a second language, advanced placement, accelerated degree program, honors program, summer session, adult/continuing education programs, internships **Contact** Joanna Broda, Director of Admission, Pace University, Pleasantville/Briarcliff Campus, 861 Bedford Road, Pleasantville, NY 10570. Telephone: 914-773-3746 or toll-free 800-874-7223. Fax: 914-773-3851. E-mail: infoctr@pace.edu. Web site: http://www.pace.edu/.

PARSONS SCHOOL OF DESIGN, NEW SCHOOL UNIVERSITY
NEW YORK, NEW YORK

General Independent, comprehensive, coed **Entrance** Very difficult **Setting** 2-acre urban campus **Total enrollment** 7,867 **Student/faculty ratio** 15:1 **Application deadline** 7/1 (freshmen), 7/1 (transfer) **Fresh-**

men 41% were admitted **Housing** Yes **Expenses** Tuition $21,930; Room & Board $9083 **Undergraduates** 73% women, 10% part-time, 21% 25 or older, 0.2% Native American, 7% Hispanic American, 4% African American, 19% Asian American/Pacific Islander **The most frequently chosen baccalaureate fields are** communications/communication technologies, business/marketing, visual/performing arts **Academic program** English as a second language, advanced placement, accelerated degree program, honors program, summer session, adult/continuing education programs, internships **Contact** Ms. Nadine M. Bourgeois, Director of Admissions and Associate Dean of Enrollment Management, Parsons School of Design, New School University, 66 Fifth Avenue, New York, NY 10011-8878. Telephone: 212-229-8910 or toll-free 800-252-0852. E-mail: parsadm@newschool.edu. Web site: http://www.parsons.edu/.

PLATTSBURGH STATE UNIVERSITY OF NEW YORK

PLATTSBURGH, NEW YORK

General State-supported, comprehensive, coed **Entrance** Moderately difficult **Setting** 265-acre small-town campus **Total enrollment** 6,153 **Student/faculty ratio** 17:1 **Application deadline** Rolling (freshmen), rolling (transfer) **Freshmen** 63% were admitted **Housing** Yes **Expenses** Tuition $4065; Room & Board $5116 **Undergraduates** 57% women, 7% part-time, 6% 25 or older, 1% Native American, 3% Hispanic American, 3% African American, 2% Asian American/Pacific Islander **The most frequently chosen baccalaureate fields are** business/marketing, communications/communication technologies, education **Academic program** English as a second language, advanced placement, accelerated degree program, self-designed majors, honors program, summer session, adult/continuing education programs, internships **Contact** Mr. Richard Higgins, Director of Admissions, Plattsburgh State University of New York, 101 Broad Street, Plattsburgh, NY 12901-2681. Telephone: 518-564-2040 or toll-free 888-673-0012 (in-state). Fax: 518-564-2045. E-mail: admissions@splava.cc.plattsburgh.edu. Web site: http://www.plattsburgh.edu/.

POLYTECHNIC UNIVERSITY, BROOKLYN CAMPUS

BROOKLYN, NEW YORK

General Independent, university, coed **Entrance** Very difficult **Setting** 3-acre urban campus **Total enrollment** 3,059 **Student/faculty ratio** 12:1 **Application deadline** Rolling (freshmen), rolling (transfer) **Freshmen** 66% were admitted **Housing** No **Expenses** Tuition $21,780; Room & Board $5250 **Undergraduates** 19% women, 8% part-time, 6% 25 or older, 0.2% Native American, 6% Hispanic American, 10% African American, 39% Asian American/Pacific Islander **The most frequently chosen baccalaureate fields are** computer/information sciences, engineering/engineering technologies, physical sciences **Academic program** English as a second language, advanced placement, accelerated degree program, honors program, summer session, internships **Contact** Mr. John S. Kerge, Dean of Admissions, Polytechnic University, Brooklyn Campus, Six Metrotech Center, Brooklyn, NY 11201-2990. Telephone: 718-260-3100 or toll-free 800-POLYTECH. Fax: 718-260-3446. E-mail: admitme@poly.edu. Web site: http://www.poly.edu/.

PRACTICAL BIBLE COLLEGE

BIBLE SCHOOL PARK, NEW YORK

General Independent nondenominational, 4-year, coed **Entrance** Minimally difficult **Setting** 22-acre suburban campus **Total enrollment** 252 **Student/faculty ratio** 17:1 **Application deadline** Rolling (freshmen), rolling (transfer) **Freshmen** 53% were admitted **Housing** Yes **Expenses** Tuition $6965; Room & Board $4300 **Undergraduates** 40% women, 20% part-time, 22% 25 or older, 0% Native American, 2% Hispanic American, 1% African American, 1% Asian American/Pacific Islander **The most frequently chosen baccalaureate field is** philosophy, religion, and theology **Academic program** English as a second language, advanced placement, summer session, adult/continuing education programs, internships **Contact** Mrs. Suzanne VanWormer, Associate Director of Admissions, Practical Bible College, PO Box 601, Bible School Park, NY 13737-0601. Telephone: 607-729-1581 Ext. 406 or toll-free 800-331-4137 Ext. 406. Fax: 607-729-2962. E-mail: pettyjohn1@juno.com. Web site: http://www.practical.edu/.

PRATT INSTITUTE

BROOKLYN, NEW YORK

General Independent, comprehensive, coed **Entrance** Very difficult **Setting** 25-acre urban campus **Total enrollment** 4,199 **Student/faculty ratio** 9:1 **Application deadline** 2/1 (freshmen), 2/11 (transfer) **Freshmen** 43% were admitted **Housing** Yes **Expenses** Tuition $21,354; Room & Board $7940 **Undergraduates** 51% women, 12% part-time, 27% 25 or older, 0.1% Native American, 8% Hispanic American, 7% African American, 10% Asian American/Pacific Islander **Academic program** English as a second language, advanced placement, summer session, internships **Contact** Ms. Heidi Metcalf, Director of Admissions, Pratt Institute, DeKalb Hall, 200 Willoughby Avenue, Brooklyn, NY 11205-3899. Telephone: 718-636-3780 or toll-free 800-331-0834. Fax: 718-636-3670. E-mail: admissions@pratt.edu. Web site: http://www.pratt.edu/.

▶ **For more information, see page 460.**

PURCHASE COLLEGE, STATE UNIVERSITY OF NEW YORK

PURCHASE, NEW YORK

General State-supported, comprehensive, coed **Entrance** Moderately difficult **Setting** 500-acre small-town campus **Total enrollment** 4,078 **Student/faculty ratio** 16:1 **Application deadline** 7/1 (freshmen), rolling (transfer) **Freshmen** 33% were admitted **Housing** Yes **Expenses** Tuition $3997; Room &

Purchase College, State University of New York *(continued)*

Board $5654 **Undergraduates** 56% women, 24% part-time, 14% 25 or older, 0.2% Native American, 10% Hispanic American, 9% African American, 3% Asian American/Pacific Islander **The most frequently chosen baccalaureate fields are** liberal arts/general studies, English, visual/performing arts **Academic program** English as a second language, advanced placement, self-designed majors, summer session, adult/continuing education programs, internships **Contact** Ms. Betsy Immergut, Director of Admissions, Purchase College, State University of New York, 735 Anderson Hill Road, Purchase, NY 10577-1400. Telephone: 914-251-6300. Fax: 914-251-6314. E-mail: admissn@brick.purchase.edu. Web site: http://www.purchase.edu/.

QUEENS COLLEGE OF THE CITY UNIVERSITY OF NEW YORK
FLUSHING, NEW YORK

General State and locally supported, comprehensive, coed **Entrance** Very difficult **Setting** 76-acre urban campus **Total enrollment** 15,686 **Student/faculty ratio** 19:1 **Application deadline** Rolling (freshmen), 3/1 (transfer) **Freshmen** 49% were admitted **Housing** No **Expenses** Tuition $3403 **Undergraduates** 63% women, 38% part-time, 39% 25 or older, 0.1% Native American, 16% Hispanic American, 10% African American, 16% Asian American/Pacific Islander **The most frequently chosen baccalaureate fields are** business/marketing, education, social sciences and history **Academic program** English as a second language, advanced placement, accelerated degree program, self-designed majors, honors program, summer session, adult/continuing education programs, internships **Contact** Undergraduate Admissions Office, Queens College of the City University of New York, Undergraduate Admissions, Kiely Hall 217, 65-30 Kissena Boulevard, Flushing, NY 11367. Telephone: 718-997-5600. Fax: 718-997-5617. E-mail: admissions@qc.edu. Web site: http://www.qc.edu/.

RABBINICAL ACADEMY MESIVTA RABBI CHAIM BERLIN
BROOKLYN, NEW YORK

Contact Mr. Mayer Weinberger, Executive Administrator, Office of Admissions, Rabbinical Academy Mesivta Rabbi Chaim Berlin, 1605 Coney Island Avenue, Brooklyn, NY 11230-4715. Telephone: 718-377-0777. Fax: 718-338-5578.

RABBINICAL COLLEGE BETH SHRAGA
MONSEY, NEW YORK

Contact Rabbi Schiff, Director of Admissions, Rabbinical College Beth Shraga, 28 Saddle River Road, Monsey, NY 10952-3035. Telephone: 914-356-1980.

RABBINICAL COLLEGE BOBOVER YESHIVA B'NEI ZION
BROOKLYN, NEW YORK

Contact Mr. Israel Licht, Director of Admissions, Rabbinical College Bobover Yeshiva B'nei Zion, 1577 Forty-eighth Street, Brooklyn, NY 11219. Telephone: 718-438-2018.

RABBINICAL COLLEGE CH'SAN SOFER
BROOKLYN, NEW YORK

Contact Director of Admissions, Rabbinical College Ch'san Sofer, 1876 Fiftieth Street, Brooklyn, NY 11204. Telephone: 718-236-1171.

RABBINICAL COLLEGE OF LONG ISLAND
LONG BEACH, NEW YORK

Contact Director of Admissions, Rabbinical College of Long Island, 201 Magnolia Boulevard, Long Beach, NY 11561-3305. Telephone: 516-431-7414.

RABBINICAL SEMINARY ADAS YEREIM
BROOKLYN, NEW YORK

Contact Mr. Hersch Greenschweig, Director of Admissions, Rabbinical Seminary Adas Yereim, 185 Wilson Street, Brooklyn, NY 11211-7206. Telephone: 718-388-1751.

RABBINICAL SEMINARY M'KOR CHAIM
BROOKLYN, NEW YORK

Contact Rabbi Benjamin Paler, Director of Admissions, Rabbinical Seminary M'kor Chaim, 1571 Fifty-fifth Street, Brooklyn, NY 11219. Telephone: 718-851-0183.

RABBINICAL SEMINARY OF AMERICA
FOREST HILLS, NEW YORK

General Independent Jewish, comprehensive, men only **Contact** Rabbi Abraham Semmel, Director of Admissions, Rabbinical Seminary of America, 92-15 Sixty-ninth Avenue, Forest Hills, NY 11375. Telephone: 718-268-4700.

REGENTS COLLEGE
See Excelsior College

RENSSELAER POLYTECHNIC INSTITUTE
TROY, NEW YORK

General Independent, university, coed **Entrance** Very difficult **Setting** 260-acre suburban campus **Total enrollment** 8,022 **Student/faculty ratio** 16:1 **Application deadline** 1/1 (freshmen), 7/1 (transfer) **Freshmen** 73% were admitted **Housing** Yes **Expenses** Tuition $25,538; Room & Board $8308 **Undergraduates** 24% women, 1% part-time, 3% 25 or older, 0.4% Native American, 5% Hispanic American, 4% African American, 11% Asian American/Pacific

Islander **The most frequently chosen baccalaureate fields are** business/marketing, architecture, engineering/engineering technologies **Academic program** English as a second language, advanced placement, accelerated degree program, self-designed majors, honors program, summer session, adult/continuing education programs, internships **Contact** Ms. Teresa Duffy, Dean of Enrollment Management, Rensselaer Polytechnic Institute, 110 8th Street, Troy, NY 12180-3590. Telephone: 518-276-6216 or toll-free 800-448-6562. Fax: 518-276-4072. E-mail: admissions@rpi.edu. Web site: http://www.rpi.edu/.

▶ **For more information, see page 461.**

ROBERTS WESLEYAN COLLEGE
ROCHESTER, NEW YORK

General Independent, comprehensive, coed, affiliated with Free Methodist Church of North America **Entrance** Moderately difficult **Setting** 75-acre suburban campus **Total enrollment** 1,596 **Student/faculty ratio** 14:1 **Application deadline** 2/1 (freshmen), rolling (transfer) **Freshmen** 92% were admitted **Housing** Yes **Expenses** Tuition $14,220; Room & Board $4758 **Undergraduates** 65% women, 8% part-time, 0.2% Native American, 2% Hispanic American, 5% African American, 1% Asian American/Pacific Islander **The most frequently chosen baccalaureate fields are** business/marketing, education, health professions and related sciences **Academic program** English as a second language, advanced placement, honors program, summer session, adult/continuing education programs, internships **Contact** Ms. Linda Kurtz, Dean of Admissions, Roberts Wesleyan College, 2301 Westside Drive, Rochester, NY 14624. Telephone: 716-594-6400 or toll-free 800-777-4RWC. Fax: 716-594-6371. E-mail: admissions@roberts.edu. Web site: http://www.roberts.edu/.

ROCHESTER INSTITUTE OF TECHNOLOGY
ROCHESTER, NEW YORK

General Independent, comprehensive, coed **Entrance** Moderately difficult **Setting** 1,300-acre suburban campus **Total enrollment** 13,274 **Student/faculty ratio** 13:1 **Application deadline** 7/1 (freshmen), rolling (transfer) **Freshmen** 74% were admitted **Housing** Yes **Expenses** Tuition 18,252; Room & Board 6996 **Undergraduates** 33% women, 20% part-time, 24% 25 or older, 0.4% Native American, 3% Hispanic American, 5% African American, 5% Asian American/Pacific Islander **The most frequently chosen baccalaureate fields are** engineering/engineering technologies, business/marketing, visual/performing arts **Academic program** English as a second language, advanced placement, accelerated degree program, self-designed majors, honors program, summer session, adult/continuing education programs, internships **Contact** Mr. Daniel Shelley, Director of Admissions, Rochester Institute of Technology, 60 Lomb Memorial Drive, Rochester, NY 14623-5604. Telephone: 716-475-6631. Fax: 716-475-7424. E-mail: admissions@rit.edu. Web site: http://www.rit.edu/.

RUSSELL SAGE COLLEGE
TROY, NEW YORK

General Independent, 4-year, women only **Entrance** Moderately difficult **Setting** 8-acre urban campus **Total enrollment** 819 **Student/faculty ratio** 10:1 **Application deadline** 8/1 (freshmen), rolling (transfer) **Freshmen** 76% were admitted **Housing** Yes **Expenses** Tuition $16,400; Room & Board $6038 **Undergraduates** 8% part-time, 20% 25 or older, 0.5% Native American, 2% Hispanic American, 7% African American, 3% Asian American/Pacific Islander **The most frequently chosen baccalaureate fields are** education, health professions and related sciences, visual/performing arts **Academic program** English as a second language, advanced placement, accelerated degree program, self-designed majors, honors program, summer session, adult/continuing education programs, internships **Contact** Ms. Beth Robertson, Senior Associate Director of Admissions, Russell Sage College, 45 Ferry Street, Troy, NY 12180. Telephone: 518-244-2217 or toll-free 888-VERY-SAGE (in-state); 888-VERY SAGE (out-of-state). Fax: 518-244-6880. E-mail: rscadmin@sage.edu. Web site: http://www.sage.edu/html/rsc/welcome.html.

ST. BONAVENTURE UNIVERSITY
ST. BONAVENTURE, NEW YORK

General Independent, comprehensive, coed, affiliated with Roman Catholic Church **Entrance** Moderately difficult **Setting** 600-acre small-town campus **Total enrollment** 2,801 **Student/faculty ratio** 16:1 **Application deadline** 4/1 (freshmen), 8/1 (transfer) **Freshmen** 89% were admitted **Housing** Yes **Expenses** Tuition $15,140; Room & Board $5800 **Undergraduates** 54% women, 5% part-time, 3% 25 or older, 0.1% Native American, 1% Hispanic American, 1% African American, 0.4% Asian American/Pacific Islander **The most frequently chosen baccalaureate fields are** business/marketing, education, social sciences and history **Academic program** Advanced placement, self-designed majors, honors program, summer session, internships **Contact** Mr. James Dirisio, Director of Admissions, St. Bonaventure University, PO Box D, St. Bonaventure, NY 14778-2284. Telephone: 716-375-2400 or toll-free 800-462-5050. Fax: 716-375-4005. E-mail: admissions@sbu.edu. Web site: http://www.sbu.edu/.

ST. FRANCIS COLLEGE
BROOKLYN HEIGHTS, NEW YORK

General Independent Roman Catholic, 4-year, coed **Entrance** Moderately difficult **Setting** 1-acre urban campus **Total enrollment** 2,336 **Student/faculty ratio** 20:1 **Application deadline** Rolling (freshmen), rolling (transfer) **Freshmen** 75% were admitted **Housing** No **Expenses** Tuition $8990 **Undergraduates** 60% women, 19% part-time, 20% 25 or older, 0.2% Native American, 14% Hispanic American, 19% African American, 3% Asian American/Pacific Islander **Academic program** English as a second language,

St. Francis College *(continued)*

advanced placement, accelerated degree program, honors program, summer session, adult/continuing education programs, internships **Contact** Br. George Larkin OSF, Dean of Admissions, St. Francis College, 180 Remsen Street, Brooklyn Heights, NY 11201-4398. Telephone: 718-489-5200. Fax: 718-522-1274. Web site: http://www.stfranciscollege.edu/.

► **For more information, see page 473.**

ST. JOHN FISHER COLLEGE
ROCHESTER, NEW YORK

General Independent, comprehensive, coed, affiliated with Roman Catholic Church **Entrance** Moderately difficult **Setting** 136-acre suburban campus **Total enrollment** 2,739 **Student/faculty ratio** 16:1 **Application deadline** Rolling (freshmen), rolling (transfer) **Freshmen** 73% were admitted **Housing** Yes **Expenses** Tuition 15,400; Room & Board 6600 **Undergraduates** 62% women, 23% part-time **Academic program** Advanced placement, accelerated degree program, self-designed majors, honors program, summer session, adult/continuing education programs, internships **Contact** Mr. Gerard J. Rooney, Vice President of Enrollment Management, St. John Fisher College, 3690 East Avenue, Rochester, NY 14610. Telephone: 716-385-8064 or toll-free 800-444-4640. Fax: 716-385-8386. E-mail: admissions@fisher.sjfc.edu. Web site: http://www.sjfc.edu/.

ST. JOHN'S UNIVERSITY
JAMAICA, NEW YORK

General Independent, university, coed, affiliated with Roman Catholic Church **Entrance** Moderately difficult **Setting** 95-acre urban campus **Total enrollment** 18,621 **Student/faculty ratio** 20:1 **Application deadline** Rolling (freshmen), rolling (transfer) **Freshmen** 80% were admitted **Housing** Yes **Expenses** Tuition $15,930; Room & Board $8950 **Undergraduates** 57% women, 20% part-time, 9% 25 or older, 0.2% Native American, 15% Hispanic American, 12% African American, 14% Asian American/Pacific Islander **The most frequently chosen baccalaureate fields are** business/marketing, education, health professions and related sciences **Academic program** English as a second language, advanced placement, accelerated degree program, honors program, summer session, adult/continuing education programs, internships **Contact** Mr. Glenn Sklarin, St. John's University, 8000 Utopia Parkway, Jamaica, NY 11439. Telephone: 718-990-2000 or toll-free 888-9STJOHNS (in-state). Fax: 718-990-1677. E-mail: admissions@stjohns.edu. Web site: http://www.stjohns.edu/.

ST. JOSEPH'S COLLEGE, NEW YORK
BROOKLYN, NEW YORK

General Independent, 4-year, coed **Entrance** Moderately difficult **Setting** urban campus **Total enrollment** 1,283 **Student/faculty ratio** 11:1 **Application deadline** 8/15 (freshmen), 8/15 (transfer) **Freshmen** 56% were admitted **Housing** No **Expenses** Tuition $9030 **Undergraduates** 78% women, 53% part-time, 66% 25 or older, 0% Native American, 8% Hispanic American, 40% African American, 5% Asian American/Pacific Islander **The most frequently chosen baccalaureate fields are** education, business/marketing, health professions and related sciences **Academic program** Advanced placement, honors program, summer session, adult/continuing education programs, internships **Contact** Ms. Mary Elizabeth Rohan, Director of Admissions, St. Joseph's College, New York, 245 Clinton Avenue, Brooklyn, NY 11205-3688. Telephone: 718-636-6868. E-mail: asinfob@sjcny.edu. Web site: http://www.sjcnj.edu/.

ST. JOSEPH'S COLLEGE, SUFFOLK CAMPUS
PATCHOGUE, NEW YORK

General Independent, comprehensive, coed **Entrance** Moderately difficult **Setting** 28-acre small-town campus **Total enrollment** 3,236 **Student/faculty ratio** 16:1 **Application deadline** Rolling (freshmen), rolling (transfer) **Freshmen** 75% were admitted **Housing** No **Expenses** Tuition $9622 **Undergraduates** 78% women, 30% part-time, 36% 25 or older, 0.3% Native American, 5% Hispanic American, 3% African American, 1% Asian American/Pacific Islander **The most frequently chosen baccalaureate fields are** business/marketing, education, health professions and related sciences **Academic program** Advanced placement, summer session, adult/continuing education programs **Contact** Mrs. Marion E. Salgado, Director of Admissions, St. Joseph's College, Suffolk Campus, 155 West Roe Boulevard, Patchogue, NY 11772. Telephone: 631-447-3219 or toll-free 866-AT ST JOE (in-state). Fax: 631-447-1734. E-mail: admissions_patchogue@sjcny.edu. Web site: http://www.sjcny.edu/.

ST. LAWRENCE UNIVERSITY
CANTON, NEW YORK

General Independent, comprehensive, coed **Entrance** Very difficult **Setting** 1,000-acre small-town campus **Total enrollment** 2,061 **Student/faculty ratio** 11:1 **Application deadline** 2/15 (freshmen), 4/1 (transfer) **Freshmen** 69% were admitted **Housing** Yes **Expenses** Tuition 23,955; Room & Board 7475 **Undergraduates** 53% women, 2% part-time, 0.2% 25 or older, 1% Native American, 2% Hispanic American, 2% African American, 1% Asian American/Pacific Islander **The most frequently chosen baccalaureate fields are** biological/life sciences, psychology, social sciences and history **Academic program** Advanced placement, self-designed majors, summer session, internships **Contact** Ms. Terry Cowdrey, Dean of Admissions and Financial Aid, St. Lawrence University, Canton, NY 13617-1455. Telephone: 315-229-5261 or toll-free 800-285-1856. Fax: 315-229-5818. E-mail: admiss@music.stlawu.edu. Web site: http://www.stlawu.edu/.

ST. THOMAS AQUINAS COLLEGE
SPARKILL, NEW YORK

General Independent, comprehensive, coed **Entrance** Moderately difficult **Setting** 46-acre suburban campus **Total enrollment** 2,185 **Student/faculty ratio** 17:1 **Application deadline** Rolling (freshmen), rolling (transfer) **Freshmen** 75% were admitted **Housing** Yes **Expenses** Tuition 12,820; Room & Board 7350 **Undergraduates** 21% 25 or older **Academic program** English as a second language, advanced placement, accelerated degree program, honors program, summer session, adult/continuing education programs, internships **Contact** Mr. Gregg Meyer, Dean of Enrollment Management, St. Thomas Aquinas College, 125 Route 340, Sparkill, NY 10976. Telephone: 914-398-4100 or toll-free 800-999-STAC. E-mail: joestacenroll@rockland.net. Web site: http://www.stac.edu/.

SARAH LAWRENCE COLLEGE
BRONXVILLE, NEW YORK

General Independent, comprehensive, coed **Entrance** Very difficult **Setting** 40-acre suburban campus **Total enrollment** 1,449 **Student/faculty ratio** 6:1 **Application deadline** 1/15 (freshmen), 3/1 (transfer) **Freshmen** 38% were admitted **Housing** Yes **Expenses** Tuition $27,982; Room & Board $8778 **Undergraduates** 75% women, 6% part-time, 4% 25 or older, 0.5% Native American, 5% Hispanic American, 6% African American, 5% Asian American/Pacific Islander **The most frequently chosen baccalaureate field is** liberal arts/general studies **Academic program** Advanced placement, self-designed majors, adult/continuing education programs, internships **Contact** Ms. Thyra L. Briggs, Dean of Admission, Sarah Lawrence College, 1 Mead Way, Bronxville, NY 10708-5999. Telephone: 914-395-2510 or toll-free 800-888-2858. Fax: 914-395-2515. E-mail: slcadmit@mail.slc.edu. Web site: http://www.slc.edu/.

SCHOOL OF VISUAL ARTS
NEW YORK, NEW YORK

General Proprietary, comprehensive, coed **Entrance** Moderately difficult **Setting** 1-acre urban campus **Total enrollment** 5,312 **Student/faculty ratio** 4:1 **Application deadline** Rolling (freshmen), rolling (transfer) **Freshmen** 60% were admitted **Housing** Yes **Expenses** Tuition 16,110; Room only 6600 **Undergraduates** 54% women, 44% part-time, 16% 25 or older, 0.4% Native American, 9% Hispanic American, 4% African American, 11% Asian American/Pacific Islander **The most frequently chosen baccalaureate field is** visual/performing arts **Academic program** English as a second language, summer session, adult/continuing education programs, internships **Contact** Mr. Richard M. Longo, Executive Director of Admissions, School of Visual Arts, 209 East 23rd Street, New York, NY 10010-3994. Telephone: 212-592-2100 or toll-free 800-436-4204. Fax: 212-592-2116. E-mail: admissions@adm.schoolofvisualarts.edu. Web site: http://www.schoolofvisualarts.edu/.

SH'OR YOSHUV RABBINICAL COLLEGE
FAR ROCKAWAY, NEW YORK

Contact Rabbi Avrohom Halpern, Executive Director, Sh'or Yoshuv Rabbinical College, 1284 Central Avenue, Far Rockaway, NY 11691-4002. Telephone: 718-327-7244.

SIENA COLLEGE
LOUDONVILLE, NEW YORK

General Independent Roman Catholic, 4-year, coed **Entrance** Moderately difficult **Setting** 155-acre suburban campus **Total enrollment** 3,314 **Student/faculty ratio** 14:1 **Application deadline** 3/1 (freshmen), 9/1 (transfer) **Freshmen** 67% were admitted **Housing** Yes **Expenses** Tuition 15,800; Room & Board 6680 **Undergraduates** 52% women, 15% part-time, 9% 25 or older, 0.2% Native American, 2% Hispanic American, 2% African American, 2% Asian American/Pacific Islander **The most frequently chosen baccalaureate fields are** business/marketing, English, social sciences and history **Academic program** Advanced placement, honors program, summer session, adult/continuing education programs, internships **Contact** Mr. Edward Jones, Director of Admissions, Siena College, 515 Loudon Road, Loudonville, NY 12211-1462. Telephone: 518-783-2423 or toll-free 888-ATSIENA. Fax: 518-783-2436. E-mail: admit@siena.edu. Web site: http://www.siena.edu/.

SKIDMORE COLLEGE
SARATOGA SPRINGS, NEW YORK

General Independent, comprehensive, coed **Entrance** Very difficult **Setting** 800-acre small-town campus **Total enrollment** 2,503 **Student/faculty ratio** 11:1 **Application deadline** 1/15 (freshmen), 4/1 (transfer) **Freshmen** 43% were admitted **Housing** Yes **Expenses** Tuition 25,475; Room & Board 7260 **Undergraduates** 61% women, 10% part-time, 0% 25 or older, 0.3% Native American, 5% Hispanic American, 2% African American, 4% Asian American/Pacific Islander **The most frequently chosen baccalaureate fields are** business/marketing, social sciences and history, visual/performing arts **Academic program** Advanced placement, accelerated degree program, self-designed majors, honors program, summer session, adult/continuing education programs, internships **Contact** Ms. Mary Lou W. Bates, Director of Admissions, Skidmore College, 815 North Broadway, Saratoga Springs, NY 12866-1632. Telephone: 518-580-5570 or toll-free 800-867-6007. Fax: 518-580-5584. E-mail: admissions@scott.skidmore.edu. Web site: http://www.skidmore.edu/.

SOUTHAMPTON CAMPUS OF LONG ISLAND UNIVERSITY

See Long Island University, Southampton College

STATE UNIVERSITY OF NEW YORK AT ALBANY
ALBANY, NEW YORK

General State-supported, university, coed **Entrance** Moderately difficult **Setting** 560-acre suburban campus **Total enrollment** 16,831 **Student/faculty ratio** 19:1 **Application deadline** 3/1 (freshmen), 4/1 (transfer) **Freshmen** 58% were admitted **Housing** Yes **Expenses** Tuition $4625; Room & Board $3290 **Undergraduates** 49% women, 9% part-time, 10% 25 or older, 0.2% Native American, 7% Hispanic American, 9% African American, 7% Asian American/Pacific Islander **The most frequently chosen baccalaureate fields are** mathematics, health professions and related sciences, protective services/public administration **Academic program** English as a second language, advanced placement, self-designed majors, honors program, summer session, internships **Contact** Mr. Harry Wood, Director of Undergraduate Admissions, State University of New York at Albany, 1400 Washington Avenue, University Administrtion Building 101, Albany, NY 12222-0001. Telephone: 518-442-5435. E-mail: ugadmit@safnet.albany.edu. Web site: http://www.albany.edu/.

STATE UNIVERSITY OF NEW YORK AT BINGHAMTON
BINGHAMTON, NEW YORK

General State-supported, university, coed **Entrance** Very difficult **Setting** 606-acre suburban campus **Total enrollment** 12,473 **Student/faculty ratio** 19:1 **Application deadline** Rolling (freshmen), rolling (transfer) **Freshmen** 42% were admitted **Housing** Yes **Expenses** Tuition 4463; Room & Board 5772 **Undergraduates** 54% women, 4% part-time, 4% 25 or older, 0.1% Native American, 5% Hispanic American, 5% African American, 17% Asian American/Pacific Islander **The most frequently chosen baccalaureate fields are** business/marketing, psychology, social sciences and history **Academic program** English as a second language, advanced placement, accelerated degree program, self-designed majors, honors program, summer session, adult/continuing education programs, internships **Contact** Cheryl S. Brown, Acting Director of Admissions, State University of New York at Binghamton, PO Box 6001, Binghamton, NY 13902-6001. Telephone: 607-777-2000. Fax: 607-777-4445. E-mail: admit@binghamton.edu. Web site: http://www.binghamton.edu/.

STATE UNIVERSITY OF NEW YORK AT BUFFALO
See University at Buffalo, The State University of New York

STATE UNIVERSITY OF NEW YORK AT FARMINGDALE
FARMINGDALE, NEW YORK

General State-supported, 4-year, coed **Entrance** Moderately difficult **Setting** 380-acre small-town campus **Total enrollment** 5,045 **Student/faculty ratio** 20:1 **Application deadline** Rolling (freshmen), rolling (transfer) **Freshmen** 69% were admitted **Housing** Yes **Expenses** Tuition $4085; Room & Board $6400 **Undergraduates** 44% women, 40% part-time, 33% 25 or older, 0.2% Native American, 10% Hispanic American, 16% African American, 4% Asian American/Pacific Islander **The most frequently chosen baccalaureate fields are** business/marketing, engineering/engineering technologies **Academic program** Advanced placement, summer session, internships **Contact** Ms. Kathleen Fitzwilliam, Assistant Dean for Enrollment Services, State University of New York at Farmingdale, Route 110, Farmingdale, NY 11735-1021. Telephone: 631-420-2457 or toll-free 877-4-FARMINGDALE. Fax: 631-420-2633. E-mail: admissions@farmingdale.edu. Web site: http://www.farmingdale.edu/.

STATE UNIVERSITY OF NEW YORK AT NEW PALTZ
NEW PALTZ, NEW YORK

General State-supported, comprehensive, coed **Entrance** Moderately difficult **Setting** 216-acre small-town campus **Total enrollment** 7,720 **Student/faculty ratio** 21:1 **Application deadline** 3/30 (freshmen), 6/1 (transfer) **Freshmen** 46% were admitted **Housing** Yes **Expenses** Tuition $4000; Room & Board $5800 **Undergraduates** 64% women, 15% part-time, 12% 25 or older, 0.3% Native American, 9% Hispanic American, 8% African American, 4% Asian American/Pacific Islander **The most frequently chosen baccalaureate fields are** communications/communication technologies, education, social sciences and history **Academic program** English as a second language, advanced placement, honors program, summer session, adult/continuing education programs, internships **Contact** Ms. Mary Claire Bauer, Dean of Undergraduate Admission, State University of New York at New Paltz, 75 South Manheim Boulevard, Suite 1, New Paltz, NY 12561-2499. Telephone: 845-257-3200 or toll-free 888-639-7589 (in-state). Fax: 845-257-3209. E-mail: admiss@newpaltz.edu. Web site: http://www.newpaltz.edu/.

STATE UNIVERSITY OF NEW YORK AT OSWEGO
OSWEGO, NEW YORK

General State-supported, comprehensive, coed **Entrance** Moderately difficult **Setting** 696-acre small-town campus **Total enrollment** 8,159 **Student/faculty ratio** 20:1 **Application deadline** Rolling (freshmen), rolling (transfer) **Freshmen** 57% were admitted **Housing** Yes **Expenses** Tuition $4011; Room & Board $6350 **Undergraduates** 54% women, 11% part-time, 16% 25 or older, 0.5% Native American, 3% Hispanic American, 4% African American, 1% Asian American/Pacific Islander **The most frequently chosen baccalaureate fields are** business/marketing, communications/communication technologies, education **Academic program** English as a second language, advanced placement, accelerated degree program, self-designed majors, honors program, summer session, adult/continuing education programs, internships **Contact** Mr. Daniel Griffin, Associate Director, State University of New York at Oswego, 7060 State Route 104, Oswego, NY 13126. Telephone: 315-312-2250. Fax: 315-312-3260. E-mail: admiss@oswego.edu. Web site: http://www.oswego.edu/.

STATE UNIVERSITY OF NEW YORK AT STONY BROOK

See Stony Brook University, State University of New York

STATE UNIVERSITY OF NEW YORK COLLEGE AT BROCKPORT

BROCKPORT, NEW YORK

General State-supported, comprehensive, coed **Entrance** Moderately difficult **Setting** 435-acre small-town campus **Total enrollment** 8,524 **Student/faculty ratio** 19:1 **Application deadline** Rolling (freshmen), rolling (transfer) **Freshmen** 54% were admitted **Housing** Yes **Expenses** Tuition $4103; Room & Board $5800 **Undergraduates** 58% women, 15% part-time, 22% 25 or older, 0.3% Native American, 2% Hispanic American, 7% African American, 1% Asian American/Pacific Islander **The most frequently chosen baccalaureate fields are** health professions and related sciences, business/marketing, protective services/public administration **Academic program** Advanced placement, accelerated degree program, self-designed majors, honors program, summer session, internships **Contact** Bernie Valento, Associate Director of Undergraduate Admissions, State University of New York College at Brockport, 350 New Campus Drive, Brockport, NY 14420-2997. Telephone: 716-395-5059 Ext. 5059 or toll-free 800-382-8447 (in-state). Fax: 716-395-5452. E-mail: ccasalin@brockuma.cc.brockport.edu. Web site: http://www.brockport.edu/.

STATE UNIVERSITY OF NEW YORK COLLEGE AT BUFFALO

BUFFALO, NEW YORK

General State-supported, comprehensive, coed **Entrance** Moderately difficult **Setting** 115-acre urban campus **Total enrollment** 11,402 **Student/faculty ratio** 22:1 **Application deadline** Rolling (freshmen), rolling (transfer) **Freshmen** 59% were admitted **Housing** Yes **Expenses** Tuition $3909; Room & Board $5170 **Undergraduates** 58% women, 19% part-time, 24% 25 or older, 1% Native American, 4% Hispanic American, 11% African American, 1% Asian American/Pacific Islander **The most frequently chosen baccalaureate fields are** business/marketing, education, social sciences and history **Academic program** English as a second language, advanced placement, honors program, summer session, adult/continuing education programs, internships **Contact** Ms. Lesa Loritts, Director of Admissions, State University of New York College at Buffalo, 1300 Elmwood Avenue, Buffalo, NY 14222-1095. Telephone: 716-878-5519. Fax: 716-878-6100. E-mail: admissio@snybufaa.cs.snybuf.edu. Web site: http://www.buffalostate.edu/.

STATE UNIVERSITY OF NEW YORK COLLEGE AT CORTLAND

CORTLAND, NEW YORK

General State-supported, comprehensive, coed **Entrance** Moderately difficult **Setting** 191-acre small-town campus **Total enrollment** 7,178 **Student/faculty ratio** 16:1 **Freshmen** 62% were admitted **Housing** Yes **Expenses** Tuition $4104; Room & Board $5750 **Undergraduates** 58% women, 5% part-time, 18% 25 or older, 0.3% Native American, 3% Hispanic American, 2% African American, 1% Asian American/Pacific Islander **The most frequently chosen baccalaureate fields are** education, health professions and related sciences, social sciences and history **Academic program** Advanced placement, self-designed majors, honors program, summer session, adult/continuing education programs, internships **Contact** Mr. Gradon Avery, Director of Admission, State University of New York College at Cortland, PO Box 2000, Cortland, NY 13045. Telephone: 607-753-4711. Fax: 607-753-5998. E-mail: admssn_info@snycorva.cortland.edu. Web site: http://www.cortland.edu/.

STATE UNIVERSITY OF NEW YORK COLLEGE AT FREDONIA

FREDONIA, NEW YORK

General State-supported, comprehensive, coed **Entrance** Moderately difficult **Setting** 266-acre small-town campus **Total enrollment** 5,086 **Student/faculty ratio** 20:1 **Application deadline** Rolling (freshmen), rolling (transfer) **Freshmen** 60% were admitted **Housing** Yes **Expenses** Tuition $4225; Room & Board $5330 **Undergraduates** 59% women, 6% part-time, 7% 25 or older, 1% Native American, 1% Hispanic American, 1% African American, 1% Asian American/Pacific Islander **The most frequently chosen baccalaureate fields are** business/marketing, education, visual/performing arts **Academic program** Advanced placement, accelerated degree program, self-designed majors, honors program, summer session, adult/continuing education programs, internships **Contact** Mr. J. Denis Bolton, Director of Admissions, State University of New York College at Fredonia, Fredonia, NY 14063. Telephone: 716-673-3251 or toll-free 800-252-1212. Fax: 716-673-3249. E-mail: admissionsinq@fredonia.edu. Web site: http://www.fredonia.edu/.

STATE UNIVERSITY OF NEW YORK COLLEGE AT GENESEO

GENESEO, NEW YORK

General State-supported, comprehensive, coed **Entrance** Very difficult **Setting** 220-acre small-town campus **Total enrollment** 5,477 **Student/faculty ratio** 19:1 **Application deadline** 2/15 (freshmen),

State University of New York College at Geneseo *(continued)*

1/15 (transfer) **Freshmen** 47% were admitted **Housing** Yes **Expenses** Tuition 4221; Room & Board 4890 **Undergraduates** 66% women, 3% part-time, 2% 25 or older, 0.3% Native American, 3% Hispanic American, 2% African American, 5% Asian American/Pacific Islander **The most frequently chosen baccalaureate fields are** education, business/marketing, social sciences and history **Academic program** English as a second language, advanced placement, honors program, summer session, internships **Contact** Mr. Scott Hooker, Director of Admissions, State University of New York College at Geneseo, 1 College Circle, Geneseo, NY 14454-1401. Telephone: 716-245-5571. Fax: 716-245-5550. E-mail: admissions@sgenva.cc.geneseo.edu. Web site: http://www.geneseo.edu/.

STATE UNIVERSITY OF NEW YORK COLLEGE AT OLD WESTBURY

OLD WESTBURY, NEW YORK

General State-supported, comprehensive, coed **Entrance** Minimally difficult **Setting** 605-acre suburban campus **Total enrollment** 2,992 **Student/faculty ratio** 22:1 **Application deadline** Rolling (freshmen), 12/15 (transfer) **Freshmen** 56% were admitted **Housing** Yes **Expenses** Tuition $3946; Room & Board $5345 **Undergraduates** 60% women, 22% part-time, 36% 25 or older, 0.3% Native American, 15% Hispanic American, 30% African American, 8% Asian American/Pacific Islander **The most frequently chosen baccalaureate fields are** business/marketing, education, psychology **Academic program** English as a second language, advanced placement, summer session, internships **Contact** Ms. Mary Marquez Bell, Director, State University of New York College at Old Westbury, PO Box 307, Old Westbury, NY 11568. Telephone: 516-876-3073. Fax: 516-876-3307. Web site: http://www.oldwestbury.edu/.

STATE UNIVERSITY OF NEW YORK COLLEGE AT ONEONTA

ONEONTA, NEW YORK

General State-supported, comprehensive, coed **Entrance** Moderately difficult **Setting** 250-acre small-town campus **Total enrollment** 5,584 **Student/faculty ratio** 20:1 **Application deadline** Rolling (freshmen), rolling (transfer) **Freshmen** 71% were admitted **Housing** Yes **Expenses** Tuition 4185; Room & Board 5626 **Undergraduates** 60% women, 4% part-time, 9% 25 or older, 0.2% Native American, 4% Hispanic American, 3% African American, 2% Asian American/Pacific Islander **The most frequently chosen baccalaureate fields are** business/marketing, education, home economics/vocational home economics **Academic program** English as a second language, advanced placement, honors program, summer session, adult/continuing education programs, internships **Contact** Ms. Karen A. Brown, Director of Admissions, State University of New York College at Oneonta, Alumni Hall 116, Oneonta, NY 13820-4015. Telephone: 607-436-2524 or toll-free 800-SUNY-123. Fax: 607-436-3074. E-mail: admissions@oneonta.edu. Web site: http://www.oneonta.edu/.

STATE UNIVERSITY OF NEW YORK COLLEGE AT PLATTSBURGH

See Plattsburgh State University of New York

STATE UNIVERSITY OF NEW YORK COLLEGE AT POTSDAM

POTSDAM, NEW YORK

General State-supported, comprehensive, coed **Entrance** Moderately difficult **Setting** 240-acre small-town campus **Total enrollment** 4,231 **Student/faculty ratio** 19:1 **Application deadline** Rolling (freshmen), rolling (transfer) **Freshmen** 69% were admitted **Housing** Yes **Expenses** Tuition $4099; Room & Board $6100 **Undergraduates** 60% women, 6% part-time, 14% 25 or older, 2% Native American, 2% Hispanic American, 3% African American, 1% Asian American/Pacific Islander **The most frequently chosen baccalaureate fields are** psychology, education, social sciences and history **Academic program** Advanced placement, self-designed majors, honors program, summer session, adult/continuing education programs, internships **Contact** Mr. Thomas Nesbitt, Director of Admissions, State University of New York College at Potsdam, 44 Pierrepont Avenue, Potsdam, NY 13676. Telephone: 315-267-2180. Fax: 315-267-2163. E-mail: admissions@potsdam.edu. Web site: http://www.potsdam.edu/.

STATE UNIVERSITY OF NEW YORK COLLEGE AT PURCHASE

See Purchase College, State University of New York

STATE UNIVERSITY OF NEW YORK COLLEGE OF AGRICULTURE AND TECHNOLOGY AT COBLESKILL

COBLESKILL, NEW YORK

General State-supported, 4-year, coed **Entrance** Moderately difficult **Setting** 750-acre rural campus **Total enrollment** 2,301 **Student/faculty ratio** 18:1 **Application deadline** Rolling (freshmen), rolling (transfer) **Freshmen** 34% were admitted **Housing** Yes **Expenses** Tuition $3971; Room & Board $6100 **Undergraduates** 46% women, 7% part-time, 12% 25 or older, 0.3% Native American, 3% Hispanic American, 5% African American, 1% Asian American/Pacific Islander **Academic program** Advanced placement, honors program, summer session, adult/continuing education programs, internships **Contact** Mr. Clayton Smith, Director of Admissions, State University of New York College of Agriculture and Technology at Cobleskill, Cobleskill, NY 12043. Telephone: 518-255-5525 or toll-free 800-295-8988. Fax: 518-255-6769. E-mail: admissions@snycob.cobleskill.edu. Web site: http://www.cobleskill.edu/.

STATE UNIVERSITY OF NEW YORK COLLEGE OF ENVIRONMENTAL SCIENCE AND FORESTRY
SYRACUSE, NEW YORK

General State-supported, university, coed **Entrance** Very difficult **Setting** 12-acre urban campus **Total enrollment** 1,749 **Student/faculty ratio** 12:1 **Application deadline** Rolling (freshmen), rolling (transfer) **Freshmen** 57% were admitted **Housing** Yes **Expenses** Tuition 3702; Room & Board 8310 **Undergraduates** 39% women, 4% part-time, 12% 25 or older, 0.4% Native American, 3% Hispanic American, 3% African American, 2% Asian American/Pacific Islander **Academic program** English as a second language, advanced placement, accelerated degree program, honors program, adult/continuing education programs, internships **Contact** Ms. Susan Sanford, Director of Admissions, State University of New York College of Environmental Science and Forestry, 1 Forestry Drive, Syracuse, NY 13210-2779. Telephone: 315-470-6600 or toll-free 800-777-7373. Fax: 315-470-6933. E-mail: esfinfo@lmailbox.syr.edu. Web site: http://www.esf.edu/.

STATE UNIVERSITY OF NEW YORK COLLEGE OF TECHNOLOGY AT CANTON
CANTON, NEW YORK

General State-supported, 4-year, coed **Entrance** Minimally difficult **Setting** 555-acre small-town campus **Total enrollment** 2,126 **Student/faculty ratio** 17:1 **Application deadline** Rolling (freshmen), rolling (transfer) **Freshmen** 90% were admitted **Housing** Yes **Expenses** Room & Board 4800 **Undergraduates** 50% women, 21% part-time, 22% 25 or older, 2% Native American, 2% Hispanic American, 9% African American, 0.4% Asian American/Pacific Islander **Academic program** Advanced placement, self-designed majors, summer session, adult/continuing education programs, internships **Contact** Mr. David M. Gerlach, Dean of Enrollment Management, State University of New York College of Technology at Canton, Cornell Drive, Canton, NY 13617. Telephone: 315-386-7123 or toll-free 800-388-7123. Fax: 315-386-7929. E-mail: williama@scanva.canton.edu. Web site: http://www.canton.edu/.

STATE UNIVERSITY OF NEW YORK EMPIRE STATE COLLEGE
SARATOGA SPRINGS, NEW YORK

General State-supported, comprehensive, coed **Entrance** Minimally difficult **Setting** small-town campus **Total enrollment** 8,009 **Student/faculty ratio** 30:1 **Application deadline** Rolling (freshmen), rolling (transfer) **Housing** No **Expenses** Tuition $3555 **Undergraduates** 54% women, 72% part-time, 85% 25 or older, 0.4% Native American, 7% Hispanic American, 12% African American, 1% Asian American/Pacific Islander **Academic program** Advanced placement, self-designed majors, adult/continuing education programs **Contact** Ms. Jennifer Riley, Assistant Director of Admissions, State University of New York Empire State College, 2 Union Avenue, Saratoga Springs, NY 12866-4397. Telephone: 518-587-2100 Ext. 214 or toll-free 800-847-3000 (out-of-state). Fax: 518-580-0105. Web site: http://www.esc.edu/.

STATE UNIVERSITY OF NEW YORK HEALTH SCIENCE CENTER AT BROOKLYN
BROOKLYN, NEW YORK

General State-supported, upper-level, coed **Entrance** Moderately difficult **Setting** urban campus **Total enrollment** 1,470 **Application deadline** 5/1 (transfer) **Housing** Yes **Expenses** Tuition $4004; Room & Board $9041 **Undergraduates** 87% women, 48% part-time, 5% Hispanic American, 46% African American, 7% Asian American/Pacific Islander **Academic program** Advanced placement, accelerated degree program, summer session, adult/continuing education programs, internships **Contact** Mr. Thomas Lo, Director of Admissions, State University of New York Health Science Center at Brooklyn, 450 Clarkson Avenue, Box 60, Brooklyn, NY 11203. Telephone: 718-270-4744 or toll-free 718-270-2446 (in-state). Fax: 718-270-7592. Web site: http://www.downstate.edu/.

STATE UNIVERSITY OF NEW YORK INSTITUTE OF TECHNOLOGY AT UTICA/ROME
UTICA, NEW YORK

General State-supported, upper-level, coed **Setting** 800-acre suburban campus **Total enrollment** 2,660 **Student/faculty ratio** 19:1 **Application deadline** Rolling (transfer) **Housing** Yes **Expenses** Tuition $4045; Room & Board $6030 **Undergraduates** 50% women, 42% part-time, 0.4% Native American, 3% Hispanic American, 6% African American, 3% Asian American/Pacific Islander **The most frequently chosen baccalaureate fields are** business/marketing, engineering/engineering technologies, health professions and related sciences **Academic program** English as a second language, advanced placement, accelerated degree program, summer session, adult/continuing education programs, internships **Contact** Ms. Marybeth Lyons, Director of Admissions, State University of New York Institute of Technology at Utica/Rome, PO Box 3050, Utica, NY 13504-3050. Telephone: 315-792-7500 or toll-free 800-SUNYTEC. Fax: 315-792-7837. E-mail: admissions@sunyit.edu. Web site: http://www.sunyit.edu/.

STATE UNIVERSITY OF NEW YORK MARITIME COLLEGE
THROGGS NECK, NEW YORK

General State-supported, comprehensive, coed **Entrance** Moderately difficult **Setting** 56-acre suburban campus **Total enrollment** 918 **Student/faculty ratio** 11:1 **Application deadline** Rolling (freshmen), rolling (transfer) **Freshmen** 76% were admitted **Hous-**

State University of New York Maritime College *(continued)*

ing Yes **Expenses** Tuition $4900; Room & Board $5700 **Undergraduates** 8% 25 or older, 0.3% Native American, 6% Hispanic American, 7% African American, 3% Asian American/Pacific Islander **Academic program** Advanced placement, self-designed majors, summer session, adult/continuing education programs, internships **Contact** Ms. Deidre Whitman, Vice President of Enrollment and Campus Life, State University of New York Maritime College, 6 Pennyfield Avenue, Throggs Neck, NY 10465-4198. Telephone: 718-409-7220 Ext. 7222 or toll-free 800-654-1874 (in-state); 800-642-1874 (out-of-state). Fax: 718-409-7465. E-mail: dwhitman@sunymaritime.edu. Web site: http://www.sunymaritime.edu/.

STATE UNIVERSITY OF NEW YORK UPSTATE MEDICAL UNIVERSITY
SYRACUSE, NEW YORK

General State-supported, upper-level, coed **Entrance** Moderately difficult **Setting** 25-acre urban campus **Total enrollment** 1,173 **Application deadline** Rolling (freshmen), rolling (transfer) **Housing** Yes **Expenses** Tuition 3810; Room & Board 6515 **Undergraduates** 1% Native American, 0% Hispanic American, 3% African American, 1% Asian American/Pacific Islander **The most frequently chosen baccalaureate field is** health professions and related sciences **Academic program** Advanced placement, summer session, internships **Contact** Ms. Donna L. Vavonese, Assistant Director of Admissions, State University of New York Upstate Medical University, 155 Elizabeth Blackwell Street, Syracuse, NY 13210. Telephone: 315-464-4570. Fax: 315-464-8867. E-mail: admiss@upstate.edu. Web site: http://www.upstate.edu/.

STERN COLLEGE FOR WOMEN
See Yeshiva University

STONY BROOK UNIVERSITY, STATE UNIVERSITY OF NEW YORK
STONY BROOK, NEW YORK

General State-supported, university, coed **Entrance** Very difficult **Setting** 1,100-acre small-town campus **Total enrollment** 19,924 **Student/faculty ratio** 18:1 **Application deadline** Rolling (freshmen), rolling (transfer) **Freshmen** 56% were admitted **Housing** Yes **Expenses** Tuition $4228; Room & Board $6524 **Undergraduates** 49% women, 10% part-time, 11% 25 or older, 0.1% Native American, 7% Hispanic American, 9% African American, 23% Asian American/Pacific Islander **The most frequently chosen baccalaureate fields are** psychology, biological/life sciences, social sciences and history **Academic program** English as a second language, advanced placement, self-designed majors, honors program, summer session, adult/continuing education programs, internships **Contact** Ms. Gigi Lamens, Director of Admissions and Enrollment Planning, Stony Brook University, State University of New York, Nicolls Road, Stony Brook, NY 11794. Telephone: 631-632-6868 or toll-free 800-USB-SUNY (out-of-state). E-mail: admiss@mail.upsa.sunysb.edu. Web site: http://www.sunysb.edu/.

SYRACUSE UNIVERSITY
SYRACUSE, NEW YORK

General Independent, university, coed **Entrance** Very difficult **Setting** 200-acre urban campus **Total enrollment** 14,478 **Student/faculty ratio** 12:1 **Application deadline** 1/15 (freshmen), 1/15 (transfer) **Freshmen** 58% were admitted **Housing** Yes **Expenses** Tuition 20,816; Room & Board 8750 **Undergraduates** 54% women, 1% part-time, 2% 25 or older, 0.2% Native American, 4% Hispanic American, 7% African American, 5% Asian American/Pacific Islander **The most frequently chosen baccalaureate fields are** business/marketing, communications/communication technologies, social sciences and history **Academic program** English as a second language, advanced placement, accelerated degree program, self-designed majors, honors program, summer session, adult/continuing education programs, internships **Contact** Office of Admissions, Syracuse University, 201 Tolley Administration Building, Syracuse, NY 13244-1100. Telephone: 315-443-3611. E-mail: orange@suadmin.syr.edu. Web site: http://www.syracuse.edu/.

SYRACUSE UNIVERSITY, UTICA COLLEGE
See Utica College of Syracuse University

TALMUDICAL INSTITUTE OF UPSTATE NEW YORK
ROCHESTER, NEW YORK

General Independent Jewish, 5-year, men only **Entrance** Noncompetitive **Setting** 1-acre urban campus **Total enrollment** 30 **Application deadline** Rolling (freshmen), rolling (transfer) **Freshmen** 100% were admitted **Housing** Yes **Undergraduates** 0% 25 or older **Academic program** Self-designed majors **Contact** Director of Admissions, Talmudical Institute of Upstate New York, 769 Park Avenue, Rochester, NY 14607-3046. Telephone: 716-473-2810.

TALMUDICAL SEMINARY OHOLEI TORAH
BROOKLYN, NEW YORK

Contact Rabbi E. Piekarski, Director of Academic Affairs, Talmudical Seminary Oholei Torah, 667 Eastern Parkway, Brooklyn, NY 11213-3310. Telephone: 718-363-2034.

TORAH TEMIMAH TALMUDICAL SEMINARY
BROOKLYN, NEW YORK

Contact Rabbi I. Hisiger, Principal, Torah Temimah Talmudical Seminary, 555 Ocean Parkway, Brooklyn, NY 11218-5913. Telephone: 718-853-8500.

TOURO COLLEGE
NEW YORK, NEW YORK

General Independent, comprehensive, coed **Entrance** Moderately difficult **Setting** urban campus **Total enrollment** 7,791 **Student/faculty ratio** 12:1 **Application deadline** Rolling (freshmen), rolling (transfer) **Freshmen** 74% were admitted **Housing** Yes **Expenses** Tuition $9950; Room only $4500 **Undergraduates** 69% women, 12% part-time, 51% 25 or older **Academic program** English as a second language, advanced placement, accelerated degree program, self-designed majors, honors program, summer session, internships **Contact** Mr. Andre Baron, Director of Admissions, Touro College, 27-33 West 23rd Street, New York, NY 10010. Telephone: 212-463-0400 Ext. 665. Web site: http://www.touro.edu/.

UNION COLLEGE
SCHENECTADY, NEW YORK

General Independent, comprehensive, coed **Entrance** Very difficult **Setting** 100-acre suburban campus **Total enrollment** 2,439 **Student/faculty ratio** 11:1 **Application deadline** 2/1 (freshmen), 6/1 (transfer) **Freshmen** 47% were admitted **Housing** Yes **Expenses** Tuition 24,963; Room & Board 6639 **Undergraduates** 48% women, 2% part-time, 1% 25 or older, 0.1% Native American, 4% Hispanic American, 4% African American, 4% Asian American/Pacific Islander **The most frequently chosen baccalaureate fields are** biological/life sciences, psychology, social sciences and history **Academic program** English as a second language, advanced placement, accelerated degree program, self-designed majors, honors program, summer session, internships **Contact** Mr. Daniel Lundquist, Vice President for Admissions and Financial Aid, Union College, Becker Hall, Schenectady, NY 12308. Telephone: 518-388-6112 or toll-free 888-843-6688 (in-state). Fax: 518-388-6986. E-mail: admissions@union.edu. Web site: http://www.union.edu/.

UNITED STATES MERCHANT MARINE ACADEMY
KINGS POINT, NEW YORK

General Federally supported, 4-year, coed **Entrance** Very difficult **Setting** 80-acre suburban campus **Total enrollment** 921 **Student/faculty ratio** 12:1 **Application deadline** 3/1 (freshmen), 3/1 (transfer) **Freshmen** 24% were admitted **Housing** Yes **Undergraduates** 10% women, 0% 25 or older **The most frequently chosen baccalaureate fields are** engineering/engineering technologies, military science/technologies **Academic program** Honors program, internships **Contact** Capt. James M. Skinner, Director of Admissions, United States Merchant Marine Academy, 300 Steamboat Road, Wiley Hall, Kings Point, NY 11024-1699. Telephone: 516-773-5391 or toll-free 800-732-6267 (out-of state). Fax: 516-773-5390. E-mail: admissions@usmma.edu. Web site: http://www.usmma.edu/.

UNITED STATES MILITARY ACADEMY
WEST POINT, NEW YORK

General Federally supported, 4-year, coed, primarily men **Entrance** Most difficult **Setting** 16,080-acre small-town campus **Total enrollment** 4,088 **Student/faculty ratio** 7:1 **Application deadline** 3/21 (freshmen), 3/21 (transfer) **Freshmen** 14% were admitted **Housing** Yes **Undergraduates** 16% women, 0% 25 or older, 1% Native American, 6% Hispanic American, 8% African American, 5% Asian American/Pacific Islander **The most frequently chosen baccalaureate fields are** engineering/engineering technologies, physical sciences, social sciences and history **Academic program** Advanced placement, summer session **Contact** Col. Michael C. Jones, Director of Admissions, United States Military Academy, United States Military Academy, West Point, NY 10996. Telephone: 845-938-4041. E-mail: 8dad@sunams.usma.army.mil. Web site: http://www.usma.edu/.

► **For more information, see page 482.**

UNITED TALMUDICAL SEMINARY
BROOKLYN, NEW YORK

Contact Director of Admissions, United Talmudical Seminary, 82 Lee Avenue, Brooklyn, NY 11211-7900. Telephone: 719-963-9770.

UNIVERSITY AT ALBANY, STATE UNIVERSITY OF NEW YORK
See State University of New York at Albany

UNIVERSITY AT BUFFALO, THE STATE UNIVERSITY OF NEW YORK
BUFFALO, NEW YORK

General State-supported, university, coed **Entrance** Moderately difficult **Setting** 1,350-acre suburban campus **Total enrollment** 24,830 **Student/faculty ratio** 14:1 **Application deadline** Rolling (freshmen), rolling (transfer) **Freshmen** 68% were admitted **Housing** Yes **Expenses** Tuition 4715; Room & Board 6054 **Undergraduates** 46% women, 12% part-time, 16% 25 or older, 1% Native American, 4% Hispanic American, 8% African American, 10% Asian American/Pacific Islander **The most frequently chosen baccalaureate fields are** business/marketing, health professions and related sciences, social sciences and history **Academic program** English as a second language, advanced placement, self-designed majors, honors program, summer session, adult/continuing education programs, internships **Contact** Ms. Regina Toomey, Director of Admissions, University at Buffalo, The State University of New York, Capen Hall, Room 17, North Campus, Buffalo, NY 14260-1660. Telephone: 716-645-6900. Fax: 716-645-6411. E-mail: ub-admissions@acsu.buffalo.edu. Web site: http://www.buffalo.edu/.

UNIVERSITY OF ROCHESTER
ROCHESTER, NEW YORK

General Independent, university, coed **Entrance** Very difficult **Setting** 534-acre suburban campus **Total**

University of Rochester *(continued)*

enrollment 8,336 **Student/faculty ratio** 12:1 **Application deadline** 1/15 (freshmen), rolling (transfer) **Freshmen** 50% were admitted **Housing** Yes **Expenses** Tuition 23,730; Room & Board 7740 **Undergraduates** 46% women, 6% part-time, 0.4% Native American, 4% Hispanic American, 5% African American, 13% Asian American/Pacific Islander **The most frequently chosen baccalaureate fields are** biological/life sciences, psychology, visual/performing arts **Academic program** English as a second language, advanced placement, self-designed majors, summer session, internships **Contact** Mr. Jamie Hobba, Director of Admissions, University of Rochester, PO Box 270251, Rochester, NY 14627-0001. Telephone: 716-275-3221 or toll-free 888-822-2256. Fax: 716-461-4595. E-mail: admit@macmail.cc.rochester.edu. Web site: http://www.rochester.edu/.

UTICA COLLEGE OF SYRACUSE UNIVERSITY
UTICA, NEW YORK

General Independent, comprehensive, coed **Entrance** Moderately difficult **Setting** 138-acre suburban campus **Total enrollment** 2,189 **Student/faculty ratio** 13:1 **Application deadline** Rolling (freshmen), rolling (transfer) **Freshmen** 82% were admitted **Housing** Yes **Expenses** Tuition $17,104; Room & Board $6660 **Undergraduates** 62% women, 17% part-time, 20% 25 or older, 1% Native American, 4% Hispanic American, 9% African American, 2% Asian American/Pacific Islander **The most frequently chosen baccalaureate fields are** business/marketing, health professions and related sciences, psychology **Academic program** English as a second language, advanced placement, accelerated degree program, honors program, summer session, adult/continuing education programs, internships **Contact** Ms. Leslie North, Vice President for Enrollment Management, Utica College of Syracuse University, 160 Burrstone Road, Utica, NY 13502. Telephone: 315-792-3006 or toll-free 800-782-8884. Fax: 315-792-3003. E-mail: admiss@utica.ucsu.edu. Web site: http://www.utica.edu/.

VASSAR COLLEGE
POUGHKEEPSIE, NEW YORK

General Independent, comprehensive, coed **Entrance** Very difficult **Setting** 1,000-acre suburban campus **Total enrollment** 2,400 **Student/faculty ratio** 9:1 **Application deadline** 1/1 (freshmen), 4/1 (transfer) **Freshmen** 35% were admitted **Housing** Yes **Expenses** Tuition 24,940; Room & Board 6940 **Undergraduates** 61% women, 2% part-time, 1% 25 or older, 0.3% Native American, 5% Hispanic American, 5% African American, 9% Asian American/Pacific Islander **The most frequently chosen baccalaureate fields are** English, social sciences and history, visual/performing arts **Academic program** Advanced placement, self-designed majors, internships **Contact** Dr. David M. Borus, Dean of Admission and Financial Aid, Vassar College, 124 Raymond Avenue, Poughkeepsie, NY 12604. Telephone: 914-437-7300 or toll-free 800-827-7270. Fax: 914-437-7063. E-mail: admissions@vassar.edu. Web site: http://www.vassar.edu/.

WADHAMS HALL SEMINARY-COLLEGE
OGDENSBURG, NEW YORK

General Independent Roman Catholic, 4-year, men only **Entrance** Moderately difficult **Setting** 208-acre rural campus **Total enrollment** 21 **Student/faculty ratio** 2:1 **Application deadline** 8/15 (freshmen), 8/15 (transfer) **Freshmen** 100% were admitted **Housing** Yes **Expenses** Tuition 5745; Room & Board 4970 **Undergraduates** 26% 25 or older, 5% Hispanic American **The most frequently chosen baccalaureate field is** philosophy, religion, and theology **Academic program** Advanced placement, adult/continuing education programs **Contact** Rev. Timothy G. Canaan, Director of Admissions, Wadhams Hall Seminary-College, 6866 State Highway 37, Ogdensburg, NY 13669. Telephone: 315-393-4231 Ext. 224. Fax: 315-393-4249. Web site: http://www.wadhams.edu/.

WAGNER COLLEGE
STATEN ISLAND, NEW YORK

General Independent, comprehensive, coed **Entrance** Moderately difficult **Setting** 105-acre urban campus **Total enrollment** 2,013 **Student/faculty ratio** 15:1 **Application deadline** 2/15 (freshmen), rolling (transfer) **Freshmen** 69% were admitted **Housing** Yes **Expenses** Tuition $19,200; Room & Board $6800 **Undergraduates** 9% 25 or older, 0.3% Native American, 5% Hispanic American, 5% African American, 3% Asian American/Pacific Islander **The most frequently chosen baccalaureate fields are** biological/life sciences, business/marketing, education **Academic program** English as a second language, advanced placement, accelerated degree program, self-designed majors, honors program, summer session, internships **Contact** Mr. Angelo Araimo, Dean of Admissions, Wagner College, One Campus Road, Staten Island, NY 10301. Telephone: 718-390-3411 or toll-free 800-221-1010 (out-of-state). Fax: 718-390-3105. E-mail: adm@wagner.edu. Web site: http://www.wagner.edu/.

WEBB INSTITUTE
GLEN COVE, NEW YORK

General Independent, 4-year, coed **Entrance** Most difficult **Setting** 26-acre suburban campus **Total enrollment** 74 **Student/faculty ratio** 7:1 **Application deadline** 2/15 (freshmen), 2/15 (transfer) **Freshmen** 41% were admitted **Housing** Yes **Expenses** Tuition 0; Room & Board 6250 **Undergraduates** 19% women, 0% 25 or older, 0% Native American, 0% Hispanic American, 0% African American, 1% Asian American/Pacific Islander **The most frequently chosen baccalaureate field is** engineering/engineering technologies **Academic program** Internships **Contact** Mr. William G. Murray, Executive Director of Student Administrative Services, Webb Institute, Crescent Beach Road, Glen Cove, NY 11542-1398. Telephone: 516-671-2213. Fax: 516-674-

9838. E-mail: admissions@webb-institute.edu. Web site: http://www.webb-institute.edu/.

WELLS COLLEGE
AURORA, NEW YORK

General Independent, 4-year, women only **Entrance** Moderately difficult **Setting** 365-acre rural campus **Total enrollment** 462 **Student/faculty ratio** 8:1 **Application deadline** 3/1 (freshmen), rolling (transfer) **Freshmen** 89% were admitted **Housing** Yes **Expenses** Tuition $12,660; Room & Board $6200 **Undergraduates** 5% part-time, 8% 25 or older, 0.2% Native American, 3% Hispanic American, 5% African American, 3% Asian American/Pacific Islander **The most frequently chosen baccalaureate fields are** biological/life sciences, social sciences and history, visual/performing arts **Academic program** Advanced placement, accelerated degree program, self-designed majors, adult/continuing education programs, internships **Contact** Ms. Susan Raith Sloan, Director of Admissions, Wells College, MacMillan Hall, Aurora, NY 13026. Telephone: 315-364-3264 or toll-free 800-952-9355. Fax: 315-364-3227. E-mail: admissions@wells.edu. Web site: http://www.wells.edu/.

► **For more information, see page 488.**

WILLIAM SMITH COLLEGE
See Hobart and William Smith Colleges

YESHIVA COLLEGE
See Yeshiva University

YESHIVA DERECH CHAIM
BROOKLYN, NEW YORK

Contact Mr. Y. Borchardt, Administrator, Yeshiva Derech Chaim, 4907 18th Avenue, Brooklyn, NY 11218. Telephone: 718-438-5476.

YESHIVA KARLIN STOLIN RABBINICAL INSTITUTE
BROOKLYN, NEW YORK

General Independent Jewish, comprehensive, men only **Entrance** Very difficult **Setting** urban campus **Total enrollment** 53 **Application deadline** Rolling (freshmen), rolling (transfer) **Housing** Yes **Expenses** Tuition $5200; Room & Board $3200 **Contact** Mr. Aryeh L. Wolpin, Director of Admissions, Yeshiva Karlin Stolin Rabbinical Institute, 1818 Fifty-fourth Street, Brooklyn, NY 11204. Telephone: 718-232-7800 Ext. 26. Fax: 718-331-4833.

YESHIVA OF NITRA RABBINICAL COLLEGE
MOUNT KISCO, NEW YORK

General Independent Jewish, comprehensive, men only **Contact** Mr. Ernest Schwartz, Administrator, Yeshiva of Nitra Rabbinical College, Pines Bridge Road, Mount Kisco, NY 10549. Telephone: 718-384-5460. Fax: 718-387-9400.

YESHIVA SHAAR HATORAH TALMUDIC RESEARCH INSTITUTE
KEW GARDENS, NEW YORK

Contact Rabbi Kalman Epstein, Assistant Dean, Yeshiva Shaar Hatorah Talmudic Research Institute, 83-96 117th Street, Kew Gardens, NY 11418-1469. Telephone: 718-846-1940.

YESHIVATH VIZNITZ
MONSEY, NEW YORK

Contact Rabbi Bernard Rosenfeld, Registrar, Yeshivath Viznitz, Phyllis Terrace, PO Box 446, Monsey, NY 10952. Telephone: 914-356-1010.

YESHIVATH ZICHRON MOSHE
SOUTH FALLSBURG, NEW YORK

Contact Rabbi Abba Gorelick, Dean, Yeshivath Zichron Moshe, Laurel Park Road, South Fallsburg, NY 12779. Telephone: 914-434-5240.

YESHIVAT MIKDASH MELECH
BROOKLYN, NEW YORK

Contact Rabbi S. Churba, Director of Admissions, Yeshivat Mikdash Melech, 1326 Ocean Parkway, Brooklyn, NY 11230-5601. Telephone: 718-339-1090.

YESHIVA UNIVERSITY
NEW YORK, NEW YORK

General Independent, university, coed **Entrance** Moderately difficult **Setting** urban campus **Total enrollment** 5,481 **Application deadline** 2/15 (freshmen), 2/15 (transfer) **Freshmen** 79% were admitted **Housing** Yes **Expenses** Tuition 17,295; Room & Board 5520 **Undergraduates** 44% women, 2% part-time, 1% 25 or older **Academic program** English as a second language, advanced placement, self-designed majors, honors program, summer session, internships **Contact** Mr. Michael Kranzler, Director of Undergraduate Admissions, Yeshiva University, 500 West 185th Street, New York, NY 10033-3201. Telephone: 212-960-5400 Ext. 277. Fax: 212-960-0086. E-mail: yuadmit@ymail.yu.edu. Web site: http://www.yu.edu/.

YORK COLLEGE OF THE CITY UNIVERSITY OF NEW YORK
JAMAICA, NEW YORK

General State and locally supported, 4-year, coed **Entrance** Noncompetitive **Setting** 50-acre urban campus **Total enrollment** 5,389 **Student/faculty ratio** 18:1 **Application deadline** Rolling (freshmen), rolling (transfer) **Freshmen** 71% were admitted **Housing** No **Expenses** Tuition $3292 **Undergraduates**

York College of the City University of New York *(continued)*

70% women, 47% part-time, 57% 25 or older, 0.3% Native American, 14% Hispanic American, 46% African American, 8% Asian American/Pacific Islander **The most frequently chosen baccalaureate fields are** business/marketing, education, psychology **Academic program** English as a second language, advanced placement, self-designed majors, honors program, summer session, adult/continuing education programs, internships **Contact** Ms. Sally Nelson, Director of Admissions, York College of the City University of New York, 94-20 Guy R. Brewer Boulevard, Jamaica, NY 11451. Telephone: 718-262-2165. Fax: 718-262-2601. Web site: http://www.york.cuny.edu/.

NORTH CAROLINA

APPALACHIAN STATE UNIVERSITY
BOONE, NORTH CAROLINA

General State-supported, comprehensive, coed **Entrance** Moderately difficult **Setting** 255-acre small-town campus **Total enrollment** 13,227 **Student/faculty ratio** 17:1 **Application deadline** Rolling (freshmen), rolling (transfer) **Freshmen** 70% were admitted **Housing** Yes **Expenses** Tuition $1988; Room & Board $3810 **Undergraduates** 51% women, 9% part-time, 7% 25 or older, 0.4% Native American, 1% Hispanic American, 3% African American, 1% Asian American/Pacific Islander **The most frequently chosen baccalaureate fields are** business/marketing, education, social sciences and history **Academic program** English as a second language, advanced placement, accelerated degree program, self-designed majors, honors program, summer session, adult/continuing education programs, internships **Contact** Mr. Joe Watts, Associate Vice Chancellor, Appalachian State University, John Thomas Hall, Boone, NC 28608. Telephone: 828-262-2120. Fax: 828-262-3296. E-mail: admissions@conrad.appstate.edu. Web site: http://www.appstate.edu/.

BARBER-SCOTIA COLLEGE
CONCORD, NORTH CAROLINA

General Independent, 4-year, coed, affiliated with Presbyterian Church (U.S.A.) **Entrance** Minimally difficult **Setting** 23-acre small-town campus **Total enrollment** 543 **Student/faculty ratio** 18:1 **Application deadline** Rolling (freshmen), rolling (transfer) **Freshmen** 31% were admitted **Housing** Yes **Expenses** Tuition $13,220; Room & Board $3800 **Undergraduates** 9% 25 or older, 94% African American **The most frequently chosen baccalaureate fields are** business/marketing, parks and recreation, social sciences and history **Academic program** Advanced placement, honors program, summer session, internships **Contact** Dr. Alexander Erwin, Academic Dean, Barber-Scotia College, 145 Cabarrus Avenue, West, Concord, NC 28025-5187. Telephone: 704-789-2948 or toll-free 800-610-0778. Fax: 704-784-3817. Web site: http://www.barber-scotia.edu/.

BARTON COLLEGE
WILSON, NORTH CAROLINA

General Independent, 4-year, coed, affiliated with Christian Church (Disciples of Christ) **Entrance** Minimally difficult **Setting** 62-acre small-town campus **Total enrollment** 1,202 **Student/faculty ratio** 13:1 **Application deadline** Rolling (freshmen), rolling (transfer) **Freshmen** 87% were admitted **Housing** Yes **Expenses** Tuition 11,462; Room & Board 4270 **Undergraduates** 69% women, 19% part-time, 25% 25 or older, 0.4% Native American, 2% Hispanic American, 16% African American, 1% Asian American/Pacific Islander **The most frequently chosen baccalaureate fields are** business/marketing, education, health professions and related sciences **Academic program** Advanced placement, summer session, adult/continuing education programs, internships **Contact** Ms. Amy Denton, Director of In-State Admissions, Barton College, Box 500, College Station, Hardy Center, Wilson, NC 27893. Telephone: 252-399-6314 or toll-free 800-345-4973. Fax: 252-399-6572. E-mail: adenton@barton.edu. Web site: http://www.barton.edu.

BELMONT ABBEY COLLEGE
BELMONT, NORTH CAROLINA

General Independent Roman Catholic, 4-year, coed **Entrance** Moderately difficult **Setting** 650-acre small-town campus **Total enrollment** 918 **Student/faculty ratio** 17:1 **Application deadline** 8/1 (freshmen), 8/15 (transfer) **Freshmen** 31% were admitted **Housing** Yes **Expenses** Tuition $13,976; Room & Board $6856 **Undergraduates** 56% women **The most frequently chosen baccalaureate fields are** business/marketing, computer/information sciences, education **Academic program** Advanced placement, accelerated degree program, honors program, summer session, adult/continuing education programs, internships **Contact** Mr. R. Lawton Blandford, Director of Administration, Belmont Abbey College, 100 Belmont-Mt. Holly Road, Belmont, NC 28012-1802. Telephone: 704-825-6665 or toll-free 888-BAC-0110. Fax: 704-825-6220. E-mail: admissions@bac.edu. Web site: http://www.belmontabbeycollege.edu/.

BENNETT COLLEGE
GREENSBORO, NORTH CAROLINA

General Independent United Methodist, 4-year, women only **Entrance** Moderately difficult **Setting** 55-acre urban campus **Total enrollment** 619 **Student/faculty ratio** 10:1 **Application deadline** Rolling (freshmen), rolling (transfer) **Freshmen** 16% were admitted **Housing** Yes **Expenses** Tuition $9222; Room & Board $4034 **Undergraduates** 3% part-time, 4% 25 or older, 98% African American **The most frequently chosen baccalaureate fields are** biological/life sciences, business/marketing, psychology **Academic program** Self-designed majors, honors program, summer session, adult/continuing education programs, internships **Contact** Ms. Linda K. Torrence, Director of Admissions, Bennett College, Campus Box H, Greensboro, NC 27401. Telephone: 336-517-2167. E-mail: admiss@bennett.edu. Web site: http://www.bennett.edu/.

BREVARD COLLEGE
BREVARD, NORTH CAROLINA

General Independent United Methodist, 4-year, coed **Entrance** Minimally difficult **Setting** 120-acre small-town campus **Total enrollment** 710 **Student/faculty ratio** 10:1 **Application deadline** Rolling (freshmen), rolling (transfer) **Freshmen** 89% were admitted **Housing** Yes **Expenses** Tuition 12,300; Room & Board 5060 **Undergraduates** 46% women, 6% part-time, 7% 25 or older, 0% Native American, 1% Hispanic American, 8% African American, 0% Asian American/Pacific Islander **The most frequently chosen baccalaureate fields are** parks and recreation, English, visual/performing arts **Academic program** English as a second language, advanced placement, self-designed majors, honors program, adult/continuing education programs, internships **Contact** Mr. Theodore J. Wiard, Dean for Admissions and Financial Aid, Brevard College, 400 North Broad Street, Brevard, NC 28712-3306. Telephone: 828-884-8300 or toll-free 800-527-9090. Fax: 828-884-3790. E-mail: admissions@lightnin.brevard.edu. Web site: http://www.brevard.edu/.

▶ **For more information, see page 391.**

CAMPBELL UNIVERSITY
BUIES CREEK, NORTH CAROLINA

General Independent Baptist, university, coed **Entrance** Moderately difficult **Setting** 850-acre rural campus **Total enrollment** 3,490 **Student/faculty ratio** 18:1 **Application deadline** Rolling (freshmen), rolling (transfer) **Freshmen** 75% were admitted **Housing** Yes **Expenses** Tuition $11,539; Room & Board $4122 **Undergraduates** 53% women, 3% part-time, 10% 25 or older, 0.4% Native American, 2% Hispanic American, 10% African American, 0% Asian American/Pacific Islander **The most frequently chosen baccalaureate fields are** business/marketing, psychology, social sciences and history **Academic program** Advanced placement, accelerated degree program, honors program, summer session, adult/continuing education programs, internships **Contact** Laura Boivert Boyd, Director of Admissions, Campbell University, PO Box 546, Buies Creek, NC 27506. Telephone: 910-893-1300 or toll-free 800-334-4111 (out-of-state). Fax: 910-893-1288. E-mail: satterfia@mailcenter.campbell.edu. Web site: http://www.campbell.edu/.

▶ **For more information, see page 395.**

CATAWBA COLLEGE
SALISBURY, NORTH CAROLINA

General Independent, comprehensive, coed, affiliated with United Church of Christ **Entrance** Moderately difficult **Setting** 210-acre small-town campus **Total enrollment** 1,342 **Student/faculty ratio** 16:1 **Application deadline** Rolling (freshmen), rolling (transfer) **Freshmen** 83% were admitted **Housing** Yes **Expenses** Tuition $13,330; Room & Board $4980 **Undergraduates** 51% women, 3% part-time, 21% 25 or older, 0.4% Native American, 2% Hispanic American, 16% African American, 1% Asian American/Pacific Islander **The most frequently chosen baccalaureate fields are** business/marketing, education, social sciences and history **Academic program** Advanced placement, self-designed majors, honors program, summer session, adult/continuing education programs, internships **Contact** Mr. Brian Best, Chief Enrollment Officer, Catawba College, 2300 West Innes Street, Salisbury, NC 28144-2488. Telephone: 800-CATAWBA or toll-free 800-CATAWBA. Fax: 704-637-4222. E-mail: bdbest@catawba.edu. Web site: http://www.catawba.edu/.

CHOWAN COLLEGE
MURFREESBORO, NORTH CAROLINA

General Independent Baptist, 4-year, coed **Entrance** Minimally difficult **Setting** 300-acre rural campus **Total enrollment** 773 **Student/faculty ratio** 12:1 **Application deadline** Rolling (freshmen), rolling (transfer) **Freshmen** 71% were admitted **Housing** Yes **Expenses** Tuition $11,920; Room & Board $4780 **Undergraduates** 45% women, 5% part-time, 12% 25 or older **The most frequently chosen baccalaureate fields are** business/marketing, computer/information sciences, education **Academic program** Advanced placement, self-designed majors, summer session, internships **Contact** Mrs. Stephanie Harrell, Director of Admissions, Chowan College, 200 Jones Drive, Murfreesboro, NC 27855. Telephone: 252-398-6314 or toll-free 800-488-4101. Fax: 252-398-1190. E-mail: admissions@micah.chowan.edu. Web site: http://www.chowan.edu/.

DAVIDSON COLLEGE
DAVIDSON, NORTH CAROLINA

General Independent Presbyterian, 4-year, coed **Entrance** Very difficult **Setting** 464-acre small-town campus **Total enrollment** 1,679 **Student/faculty ratio** 11:1 **Application deadline** 1/2 (freshmen), 3/15 (transfer) **Freshmen** 36% were admitted **Housing** Yes **Expenses** Tuition 25,095; Room & Board 6571 **Undergraduates** 50% women, 0.1% part-time, 0.4% 25 or older, 0.4% Native American, 2% Hispanic American, 5% African American, 2% Asian American/Pacific Islander **The most frequently chosen baccalaureate fields are** biological/life sciences, English, social sciences and history **Academic program** Advanced placement, accelerated degree program, self-designed majors, honors program **Contact** Dr. Nancy J. Cable, Dean of Admission and Financial Aid, Davidson College, PO Box 1719, Davidson, NC 28036-1719. Telephone: 704-894-2230 or toll-free 800-768-0380. Fax: 704-894-2016. E-mail: admission@davidson.edu. Web site: http://www.davidson.edu/.

▶ **For more information, see page 407.**

DUKE UNIVERSITY
DURHAM, NORTH CAROLINA

General Independent, university, coed, affiliated with United Methodist Church **Entrance** Most difficult **Setting** 8,500-acre suburban campus **Total enrollment** 12,192 **Student/faculty ratio** 11:1 **Application deadline** 1/2 (freshmen), 3/15 (transfer) **Freshmen** 26% were admitted **Housing** Yes **Expenses** Tuition 25,630; Room & Board 7387 **Undergraduates** 48% women, 1% part-time, 1% 25 or older, 0.3% Native American, 5% Hispanic American, 10% African American, 12% Asian American/Pacific Islander **The most frequently chosen baccalaureate fields are** biological/life sciences, engineering/engineering technologies, social sciences and history **Academic program** English as a second language, advanced placement, accelerated degree program, self-designed majors, honors program, summer session, adult/continuing education programs, internships **Contact** Mr. Christoph Guttentag, Director of Admissions, Duke University, Durham, NC 27708-0586. Telephone: 919-684-3214. Fax: 919-684-8941. E-mail: askduke@admiss.duke.edu. Web site: http://www.duke.edu/.

EAST CAROLINA UNIVERSITY
GREENVILLE, NORTH CAROLINA

General State-supported, university, coed **Entrance** Moderately difficult **Setting** 465-acre urban campus **Total enrollment** 18,750 **Student/faculty ratio** 18:1 **Application deadline** 3/15 (freshmen), 4/15 (transfer) **Freshmen** 74% were admitted **Housing** Yes **Expenses** Tuition 2257; Room & Board 4220 **Undergraduates** 58% women, 9% part-time, 12% 25 or older, 1% Native American, 2% Hispanic American, 14% African American, 2% Asian American/Pacific Islander **The most frequently chosen baccalaureate fields are** business/marketing, education, health professions and related sciences **Academic program** Advanced placement, accelerated degree program, honors program, summer session, adult/continuing education programs, internships **Contact** Dr. Thomas Powell Jr., Director of Admissions, East Carolina University, East Fifth Street, Whichard Building 106, Greenville, NC 27858-4353. Telephone: 252-328-6640. Fax: 252-328-6945. E-mail: admis@mail.ecu.edu. Web site: http://www.ecu.edu/.

ELIZABETH CITY STATE UNIVERSITY
ELIZABETH CITY, NORTH CAROLINA

General State-supported, 4-year, coed **Entrance** Moderately difficult **Setting** 125-acre small-town campus **Total enrollment** 1,920 **Application deadline** Rolling (freshmen), rolling (transfer) **Freshmen** 27% were admitted **Housing** Yes **Expenses** Tuition 1684; Room & Board 4008 **Undergraduates** 25% 25 or older, 75% African American **Academic program** Advanced placement, honors program, summer session, adult/continuing education programs, internships **Contact** Ms. Bridgett N. Golman, Director of Admissions, Elizabeth City State University, Campus Box 901, Elizabeth City, NC 27909-7806. Telephone: 252-335-3305 or toll-free 800-347-3278. Fax: 252-335-3537. E-mail: admissions@mail.ecsu.edu.

ELON UNIVERSITY
ELON COLLEGE, NORTH CAROLINA

General Independent, comprehensive, coed, affiliated with United Church of Christ **Entrance** Moderately difficult **Setting** 500-acre suburban campus **Total enrollment** 4,138 **Student/faculty ratio** 16:1 **Application deadline** Rolling (freshmen), rolling (transfer) **Freshmen** 61% were admitted **Housing** Yes **Expenses** Tuition $14,560; Room & Board $4870 **Undergraduates** 61% women, 3% part-time, 2% 25 or older, 0.1% Native American, 1% Hispanic American, 6% African American, 1% Asian American/Pacific Islander **The most frequently chosen baccalaureate fields are** business/marketing, communications/communication technologies, education **Academic program** English as a second language, advanced placement, accelerated degree program, self-designed majors, honors program, summer session, internships **Contact** Director of Admissions Records, Elon University, 2700 Campus Box, Elon College, NC 27244. Telephone: 336-278-3566 or toll-free 800-334-8448. Fax: 336-278-7699. E-mail: admissns@numen.elon.edu. Web site: http://www.elon.edu/.

FAYETTEVILLE STATE UNIVERSITY
FAYETTEVILLE, NORTH CAROLINA

Contact Director of Enrollment Management and Admissions, Fayetteville State University, 1200 Murchison Road, Fayetteville, NC 28301-4298. Telephone: 910-486-1371 or toll-free 800-672-6667 (in-state); 800-222-2594 (out-of-state). Fax: 910-437-2512.

GARDNER-WEBB UNIVERSITY
BOILING SPRINGS, NORTH CAROLINA

General Independent Baptist, comprehensive, coed **Entrance** Moderately difficult **Setting** 200-acre small-town campus **Total enrollment** 3,194 **Student/faculty ratio** 16:1 **Application deadline** Rolling (freshmen), rolling (transfer) **Freshmen** 81% were admitted **Housing** Yes **Expenses** Tuition 12,010; Room & Board 4760 **Undergraduates** 64% women, 17% part-time, 34% 25 or older, 0.4% Native American, 1% Hispanic American, 13% African American, 1% Asian American/Pacific Islander **The most frequently chosen baccalaureate fields are** business/marketing, education, social sciences and history **Academic program** English as a second language, advanced placement, accelerated degree program, honors program, summer session, adult/continuing education programs, internships **Contact** Mr. Ray McKay Hardee, Dean of Admissions and Enrollment Management, Gardner-Webb University, PO Box 817, Boiling Springs, NC 28017. Telephone: 704-434-4491 or toll-free 800-253-6472. Fax: 704-434-4488. E-mail: admissions@gardner-webb.edu. Web site: http://www.gardner-webb.edu/.

► **For more information, see page 423.**

GREENSBORO COLLEGE
GREENSBORO, NORTH CAROLINA

General Independent United Methodist, 4-year, coed **Entrance** Moderately difficult **Setting** 40-acre urban campus **Total enrollment** 973 **Student/faculty ratio** 12:1 **Application deadline** Rolling (freshmen), rolling (transfer) **Freshmen** 75% were admitted **Housing** Yes **Expenses** Tuition $12,700; Room & Board $5100 **Undergraduates** 52% women, 17% part-time, 22% 25 or older, 1% Native American, 2% Hispanic American, 15% African American, 1% Asian American/Pacific Islander **The most frequently chosen baccalaureate fields are** business/marketing, biological/life sciences, education **Academic program** Advanced placement, accelerated degree program, self-designed majors, honors program, summer session, adult/continuing education programs, internships **Contact** Mr. Timothy L. Jackson, Director of Admissions, Greensboro College, 815 West Market Street, Greensboro, NC 27401-1875. Telephone: 336-272-7102 Ext. 211 or toll-free 800-346-8226. Fax: 336-378-0154. E-mail: admissions@gborocollege.edu. Web site: http://www.gborocollege.edu/.

GUILFORD COLLEGE
GREENSBORO, NORTH CAROLINA

General Independent, 4-year, coed, affiliated with Society of Friends **Entrance** Moderately difficult **Setting** 340-acre suburban campus **Total enrollment** 1,246 **Student/faculty ratio** 13:1 **Application deadline** 2/15 (freshmen), 4/1 (transfer) **Freshmen** 78% were admitted **Housing** Yes **Expenses** Tuition 17,800; Room & Board 5800 **Undergraduates** 53% women, 11% part-time, 1% 25 or older, 1% Native American, 3% Hispanic American, 9% African American, 1% Asian American/Pacific Islander **The most frequently chosen baccalaureate fields are** business/marketing, psychology, social sciences and history **Academic program** English as a second language, advanced placement, accelerated degree program, self-designed majors, honors program, summer session, adult/continuing education programs, internships **Contact** Mr. Randy Doss, Vice President of Enrollment, Guilford College, 5800 West Friendly Avenue, Greensboro, NC 27410-4173. Telephone: 336-316-2100 or toll-free 800-992-7759. Fax: 336-316-2954. E-mail: admission@rascal.guilford.edu. Web site: http://www.guilford.edu/.

HERITAGE BIBLE COLLEGE
DUNN, NORTH CAROLINA

General Independent Pentecostal Free Will Baptist, 4-year, coed **Entrance** Minimally difficult **Setting** 82-acre small-town campus **Total enrollment** 76 **Student/faculty ratio** 20:1 **Application deadline** Rolling (freshmen), rolling (transfer) **Housing** Yes **Expenses** Tuition $4000; Room & Board $2236 **Undergraduates** 25% women, 36% part-time, 66% 25 or older, 0% Native American, 9% Hispanic American, 21% African American, 1% Asian American/Pacific Islander **Academic program** Summer session, adult/continuing education programs, internships **Contact** Elvin Butts, Dean of Students/Registrar, Heritage Bible College, PO Box 1628, Dunn, NC 28335. Telephone: 910-892-3198. Fax: 910-891-1660. Web site: http://www.pfwb.org/non-frames/hbc/index.htm.

HIGH POINT UNIVERSITY
HIGH POINT, NORTH CAROLINA

General Independent United Methodist, comprehensive, coed **Entrance** Moderately difficult **Setting** 77-acre suburban campus **Total enrollment** 2,788 **Student/faculty ratio** 12:1 **Application deadline** 8/15 (freshmen), 8/15 (transfer) **Freshmen** 86% were admitted **Housing** Yes **Expenses** Tuition 13,150; Room & Board 6030 **Undergraduates** 61% women, 9% part-time, 8% 25 or older, 0.2% Native American, 1% Hispanic American, 18% African American, 1% Asian American/Pacific Islander **The most frequently chosen baccalaureate fields are** business/marketing, computer/information sciences, education **Academic program** English as a second language, advanced placement, accelerated degree program, self-designed majors, honors program, summer session, adult/continuing education programs, internships **Contact** Mr. James L. Schlimmer, Dean of Enrollment Management, High Point University, University Station 3188, 833 Montlieu Avenue, High Point, NC 2726-3598. Telephone: 336-841-9216 or toll-free 800-345-6993. Fax: 336-841-5123. E-mail: admiss@acme.highpoint.edu. Web site: http://www.highpoint.edu/.

JOHNSON C. SMITH UNIVERSITY
CHARLOTTE, NORTH CAROLINA

General Independent, 4-year, coed **Entrance** Minimally difficult **Setting** 105-acre urban campus **Total enrollment** 1,585 **Student/faculty ratio** 16:1 **Application deadline** 8/1 (freshmen), 8/1 (transfer) **Freshmen** 33% were admitted **Housing** Yes **Expenses** Tuition $11,605; Room & Board $4035 **Undergraduates** 60% women, 5% part-time, 6% 25 or older, 0.2% Hispanic American, 99% African American **Academic program** Advanced placement, accelerated degree program, honors program, summer session, adult/continuing education programs, internships **Contact** Mr. Jeffrey Smith, Director of Admissions, Johnson C. Smith University, 100 Beatties Ford Road, Charlotte, NC 28216. Telephone: 704-378-1010 or toll-free 800-782-7303. Web site: http://www.jcsu.edu/.

JOHN WESLEY COLLEGE
HIGH POINT, NORTH CAROLINA

General Independent interdenominational, 4-year, coed **Entrance** Minimally difficult **Setting** 24-acre urban campus **Total enrollment** 172 **Student/faculty ratio** 12:1 **Application deadline** 8/1 (freshmen), 8/1 (transfer) **Freshmen** 64% were admitted **Housing** Yes **Expenses** Tuition $6074; Room only $1760 **Undergraduates** 42% women, 19% part-time, 75% 25 or older, 20% African American, 0% Asian

John Wesley College *(continued)*

American/Pacific Islander **The most frequently chosen baccalaureate fields are** business/marketing, education, philosophy, religion, and theology **Academic program** Advanced placement, summer session, adult/continuing education programs, internships **Contact** Mr. Greg Workman, Admissions Officer, John Wesley College, 2314 North Centennial Street, High Point, NC 27265-3197. Telephone: 336-889-2262 Ext. 127. Fax: 336-889-2261. E-mail: gworkman@johnwesley.edu. Web site: http://www.johnwesley.edu/.

LEES-MCRAE COLLEGE
BANNER ELK, NORTH CAROLINA

General Independent, 4-year, coed, affiliated with Presbyterian Church (U.S.A.) **Entrance** Minimally difficult **Setting** 400-acre rural campus **Total enrollment** 712 **Student/faculty ratio** 15:1 **Application deadline** 8/1 (freshmen), 8/1 (transfer) **Freshmen** 92% were admitted **Housing** Yes **Expenses** Tuition $11,340; Room & Board $4100 **Undergraduates** 54% women, 2% part-time, 17% 25 or older, 1% Native American, 1% Hispanic American, 7% African American, 1% Asian American/Pacific Islander **Academic program** Advanced placement, self-designed majors, honors program, summer session, adult/continuing education programs, internships **Contact** Mr. Bart Walker, Director of Admissions, Lees-McRae College, PO Box 128, Banner Elk, NC 28604-0128. Telephone: 828-898-8702 or toll-free 800-280-4562. Fax: 828-898-8707. E-mail: admissions@bobcat.lmc.edu. Web site: http://www.lmc.edu/.

LENOIR-RHYNE COLLEGE
HICKORY, NORTH CAROLINA

General Independent Lutheran, comprehensive, coed **Entrance** Moderately difficult **Setting** 100-acre small-town campus **Total enrollment** 1,483 **Student/faculty ratio** 12:1 **Application deadline** Rolling (freshmen), rolling (transfer) **Freshmen** 85% were admitted **Housing** Yes **Expenses** Tuition $13,356; Room & Board $4920 **Undergraduates** 22% 25 or older, 0.1% Native American, 1% Hispanic American, 7% African American, 1% Asian American/Pacific Islander **Academic program** English as a second language, advanced placement, accelerated degree program, self-designed majors, honors program, summer session, adult/continuing education programs, internships **Contact** Mrs. Rachel Nichols, Director of Admissions, Lenoir-Rhyne College, PO Box 7227, Hickory, NC 28603. Telephone: 828-328-7300 Ext. 300 or toll-free 800-277-5721. Fax: 828-328-7338. E-mail: admission@lrc.edu. Web site: http://www.lrc.edu/.

LIVINGSTONE COLLEGE
SALISBURY, NORTH CAROLINA

General Independent, 4-year, coed, affiliated with African Methodist Episcopal Zion Church **Entrance** Minimally difficult **Setting** 272-acre small-town campus **Total enrollment** 917 **Student/faculty ratio** 17:1 **Application deadline** Rolling (freshmen), rolling (transfer) **Freshmen** 71% were admitted **Housing** Yes **Expenses** Tuition $8820; Room & Board $3700 **Undergraduates** 48% women, 5% part-time, 18% 25 or older, 0.4% Hispanic American, 94% African American, 0.2% Asian American/Pacific Islander **Academic program** Advanced placement, honors program, summer session, adult/continuing education programs, internships **Contact** Ms. Marjorie Kinard, Director of Enrollment Management, Livingstone College, 701 West Monroe Street, Salisburg, NC 28144. Telephone: 704-216-6183 or toll-free 800-835-3435. Fax: 704-216-6215. E-mail: admissions@livingstone.edu. Web site: http://www.livingstone.edu/.

MARS HILL COLLEGE
MARS HILL, NORTH CAROLINA

General Independent Baptist, 4-year, coed **Entrance** Moderately difficult **Setting** 194-acre small-town campus **Total enrollment** 1,224 **Student/faculty ratio** 13:1 **Application deadline** Rolling (freshmen), rolling (transfer) **Freshmen** 90% were admitted **Housing** Yes **Expenses** Tuition $13,800; Room & Board $4800 **Undergraduates** 57% women, 12% part-time, 18% 25 or older, 1% Native American, 1% Hispanic American, 10% African American, 0.2% Asian American/Pacific Islander **The most frequently chosen baccalaureate fields are** business/marketing, education, social sciences and history **Academic program** English as a second language, advanced placement, accelerated degree program, self-designed majors, honors program, summer session, adult/continuing education programs, internships **Contact** Ms. Cathy Beard, Director of Admissions, Mars Hill College, PO Box 370, Mars Hill, NC 28754. Telephone: 828-689-1201 or toll-free 800-543-1514. Fax: 828-689-1473. E-mail: admissions@mhc.edu. Web site: http://www.mhc.edu/.

MEREDITH COLLEGE
RALEIGH, NORTH CAROLINA

General Independent, comprehensive, women only, affiliated with Baptist Church **Entrance** Moderately difficult **Setting** 225-acre urban campus **Total enrollment** 2,595 **Student/faculty ratio** 12:1 **Application deadline** 2/15 (freshmen), 2/15 (transfer) **Freshmen** 80% were admitted **Housing** Yes **Expenses** Tuition $12,300; Room & Board $4400 **Undergraduates** 22% part-time, 22% 25 or older, 0.2% Native American, 2% Hispanic American, 6% African American, 2% Asian American/Pacific Islander **The most frequently chosen baccalaureate fields are** business/marketing, home economics/vocational home economics, visual/performing arts **Academic program** Advanced placement, accelerated degree program, self-designed majors, honors program, summer session, adult/continuing education programs, internships **Contact** Ms. Carol R. Kercheval, Director of Admissions, Meredith College, 3800 Hillsborough Street, Raleigh, NC 27607-5298. Telephone: 919-760-8581 or toll-free 800-MEREDITH. Fax: 919-760-2348. E-mail: admissions@meredith.edu. Web site: http://www.meredith.edu/.

METHODIST COLLEGE
FAYETTEVILLE, NORTH CAROLINA

General Independent United Methodist, comprehensive, coed **Entrance** Moderately difficult **Setting** 600-acre suburban campus **Total enrollment** 2,134 **Student/faculty ratio** 17:1 **Application deadline** Rolling (freshmen), rolling (transfer) **Freshmen** 65% were admitted **Housing** Yes **Expenses** Tuition 13,410; Room & Board 5080 **Undergraduates** 46% women, 22% part-time, 2% 25 or older, 1% Native American, 6% Hispanic American, 19% African American, 1% Asian American/Pacific Islander **The most frequently chosen baccalaureate fields are** business/marketing, health professions and related sciences, social sciences and history **Academic program** English as a second language, advanced placement, accelerated degree program, honors program, summer session, adult/continuing education programs, internships **Contact** Mr. Rick Lowe, Vice President of Enrollment Services, Methodist College, Admissions Office, 5400 Ramsey Street, Fayetteville, NC 28311. Telephone: 910-630-7027 or toll-free 800-488-7110 Ext. 7027. Fax: 910-630-7285. E-mail: admissions@methodist.edu. Web site: http://www.methodist.edu/.

MONTREAT COLLEGE
MONTREAT, NORTH CAROLINA

General Independent Presbyterian, comprehensive, coed **Entrance** Moderately difficult **Setting** 100-acre small-town campus **Total enrollment** 1,203 **Application deadline** 8/15 (freshmen), 8/15 (transfer) **Freshmen** 86% were admitted **Housing** Yes **Expenses** Tuition 12,318; Room & Board 4846 **Undergraduates** 57% women, 2% part-time, 58% 25 or older **Academic program** Advanced placement, adult/continuing education programs, internships **Contact** Ms. Anita Darby, Director of Admissions, Montreat College, PO Box 1267, 310 Gaither Circle, Montreat, NC 28757-1267. Telephone: 828-669-8012 Ext. 3784 or toll-free 800-622-6968 (in-state). Fax: 828-669-0120. E-mail: kbuckwalter@montreat.edu. Web site: http://www.montreat.edu/.

▶ **For more information, see page 452.**

MOUNT OLIVE COLLEGE
MOUNT OLIVE, NORTH CAROLINA

General Independent Free Will Baptist, 4-year, coed **Entrance** Minimally difficult **Setting** 123-acre small-town campus **Total enrollment** 1,713 **Student/faculty ratio** 17:1 **Application deadline** Rolling (freshmen), rolling (transfer) **Freshmen** 87% were admitted **Housing** Yes **Expenses** Tuition $9210; Room & Board $4000 **Undergraduates** 54% women, 26% part-time, 49% 25 or older, 0% Native American, 1% Hispanic American, 25% African American, 0.4% Asian American/Pacific Islander **The most frequently chosen baccalaureate fields are** business/marketing, parks and recreation, protective services/public administration **Academic program** Advanced placement, accelerated degree program, honors program, summer session, adult/continuing education programs, internships **Contact** Mr. Tim Woodard, Director of Admissions, Mount Olive College, 634 Henderson Street, Mount Olive, NC 28365. Telephone: 919-658-2502 Ext. 3009 or toll-free 800-653-0854 (in-state). Fax: 919-658-8934. E-mail: bkornegay@exchange.moc.edu. Web site: http://www.mountolivecollege.edu/.

NORTH CAROLINA AGRICULTURAL AND TECHNICAL STATE UNIVERSITY
GREENSBORO, NORTH CAROLINA

General State-supported, university, coed **Entrance** Moderately difficult **Setting** 191-acre urban campus **Total enrollment** 7,748 **Application deadline** 6/1 (freshmen), 6/1 (transfer) **Freshmen** 93% were admitted **Housing** Yes **Expenses** Room & Board 5100 **Undergraduates** 53% women, 11% part-time, 21% 25 or older, 0.3% Native American, 0.4% Hispanic American, 93% African American, 1% Asian American/Pacific Islander **Academic program** Advanced placement, honors program, summer session, adult/continuing education programs, internships **Contact** Mr. John Smith, Director of Admissions, North Carolina Agricultural and Technical State University, 1601 East Market Street, Webb Hall, Greensboro, NC 27411. Telephone: 336-334-7946 or toll-free 800-443-8964 (in-state). Fax: 336-334-7478. Web site: http://www.ncat.edu/.

NORTH CAROLINA CENTRAL UNIVERSITY
DURHAM, NORTH CAROLINA

General State-supported, comprehensive, coed **Entrance** Minimally difficult **Setting** 103-acre urban campus **Total enrollment** 5,476 **Student/faculty ratio** 14:1 **Application deadline** 7/1 (freshmen), 7/1 (transfer) **Freshmen** 74% were admitted **Housing** Yes **Expenses** Tuition $1975; Room & Board $3837 **Undergraduates** 64% women, 20% part-time, 26% 25 or older, 0.2% Native American, 1% Hispanic American, 91% African American, 0.4% Asian American/Pacific Islander **The most frequently chosen baccalaureate fields are** education, health professions and related sciences, liberal arts/general studies **Academic program** Advanced placement, honors program, summer session, adult/continuing education programs, internships **Contact** Ms. Jocelyn L. Foy, Undergraduate Director of Admissions, North Carolina Central University, 1801 Fayetteville Street, Durham, NC 27707-3129. Telephone: 919-560-6298. Fax: 919-530-7625. E-mail: ebridges@wpo.nccu.edu. Web site: http://www.nccu.edu/.

NORTH CAROLINA SCHOOL OF THE ARTS
WINSTON-SALEM, NORTH CAROLINA

General State-supported, comprehensive, coed **Entrance** Very difficult **Setting** 57-acre urban campus **Total enrollment** 768 **Student/faculty ratio** 8:1 **Application deadline** Rolling (freshmen), rolling

North Carolina School of the Arts *(continued)*

(transfer) **Freshmen** 42% were admitted **Housing** Yes **Expenses** Tuition 2592; Room & Board 4686 **Undergraduates** 41% women, 4% part-time, 12% 25 or older, 1% Native American, 2% Hispanic American, 8% African American, 2% Asian American/Pacific Islander **The most frequently chosen baccalaureate field is** visual/performing arts **Contact** Ms. Sheeler Lawson, Director of Admissions, North Carolina School of the Arts, 1533 South Main Street, PO Box 12189, Winston-Salem, NC 27127-2188. Telephone: 336-770-3290. Fax: 336-770-3370. E-mail: palmc.@ncsavx.ncarts.edu. Web site: http://www.ncarts.edu/.

NORTH CAROLINA STATE UNIVERSITY
RALEIGH, NORTH CAROLINA

General State-supported, university, coed **Entrance** Very difficult **Setting** 1,623-acre suburban campus **Total enrollment** 28,619 **Student/faculty ratio** 13:1 **Application deadline** 2/1 (freshmen), 4/1 (transfer) **Freshmen** 65% were admitted **Housing** Yes **Expenses** Tuition 2746; Room & Board 5274 **Undergraduates** 42% women, 19% part-time, 9% 25 or older, 1% Native American, 2% Hispanic American, 10% African American, 5% Asian American/Pacific Islander **The most frequently chosen baccalaureate fields are** business/marketing, agriculture, engineering/engineering technologies **Academic program** Advanced placement, accelerated degree program, self-designed majors, honors program, summer session, adult/continuing education programs, internships **Contact** Dr. George R. Dixon, Vice Provost and Director of Admissions, North Carolina State University, Box 7103, 112 Peele Hall, Raleigh, NC 27695. Telephone: 919-515-2434. E-mail: undergrad_admissions@ncsu.edu. Web site: http://www.ncsu.edu/.

NORTH CAROLINA WESLEYAN COLLEGE
ROCKY MOUNT, NORTH CAROLINA

General Independent, 4-year, coed, affiliated with United Methodist Church **Entrance** Moderately difficult **Setting** 200-acre suburban campus **Total enrollment** 1,956 **Student/faculty ratio** 15:1 **Application deadline** 7/15 (freshmen), 7/15 (transfer) **Freshmen** 91% were admitted **Housing** Yes **Expenses** Tuition 9236; Room & Board 5802 **Undergraduates** 56% women, 42% part-time, 57% 25 or older, 0.2% Native American, 1% Hispanic American, 36% African American, 0.2% Asian American/Pacific Islander **Academic program** Advanced placement, honors program, summer session, adult/continuing education programs, internships **Contact** Cecelia Summers, Associate Director of Admissions, North Carolina Wesleyan College, 3400 N Wesleyan Blvd., Attn: Office of Admission, Rocky Mount, NC 27804. Telephone: 800-488-6292 Ext. 5202 or toll-free 800-488-6292. Fax: 252-985-5295. E-mail: adm@ncwc.edu. Web site: http://www.ncwc.edu/.

PEACE COLLEGE
RALEIGH, NORTH CAROLINA

General Independent, 4-year, women only, affiliated with Presbyterian Church (U.S.A.) **Entrance** Moderately difficult **Setting** 16-acre urban campus **Total enrollment** 604 **Student/faculty ratio** 14:1 **Application deadline** Rolling (freshmen), rolling (transfer) **Freshmen** 83% were admitted **Housing** Yes **Expenses** Tuition $9949; Room & Board $5200 **Undergraduates** 5% part-time, 83% 25 or older, 0.3% Native American, 1% Hispanic American, 6% African American, 2% Asian American/Pacific Islander **The most frequently chosen baccalaureate fields are** business/marketing, communications/communication technologies, liberal arts/general studies **Academic program** English as a second language, advanced placement, honors program, adult/continuing education programs, internships **Contact** Dr. E. Carole Tyler, Dean of Admissions and Financial Aid, Peace College, Admissions and Financial Aid, Raleigh, NC 27604. Telephone: 919-508-2000 Ext. 2202 or toll-free 800-PEACE-47. Fax: 919-508-2306. E-mail: chill@peace.edu. Web site: http://www.peace.edu/.

PFEIFFER UNIVERSITY
MISENHEIMER, NORTH CAROLINA

General Independent United Methodist, comprehensive, coed **Entrance** Moderately difficult **Setting** 300-acre rural campus **Total enrollment** 1,494 **Student/faculty ratio** 14:1 **Application deadline** Rolling (freshmen), rolling (transfer) **Freshmen** 84% were admitted **Housing** Yes **Expenses** Tuition $12,066; Room & Board $4734 **Undergraduates** 57% women, 11% part-time **The most frequently chosen baccalaureate fields are** business/marketing, health professions and related sciences, protective services/public administration **Academic program** English as a second language, advanced placement, accelerated degree program, honors program, summer session, internships **Contact** Mr. Steve Cumming, Director of Admissions, Pfeiffer University, PO Box 960, Highway 52 North, Misenheimer, NC 28109. Telephone: 704-463-1360 Ext. 2079 or toll-free 800-338-2060. Fax: 704-463-1363. E-mail: admiss@jfh.pfeiffer.edu. Web site: http://www.pfeiffer.edu/.

PIEDMONT BAPTIST COLLEGE
WINSTON-SALEM, NORTH CAROLINA

General Independent Baptist, comprehensive, coed **Entrance** Noncompetitive **Setting** 12-acre urban campus **Total enrollment** 320 **Student/faculty ratio** 11:1 **Application deadline** Rolling (freshmen), rolling (transfer) **Freshmen** 59% were admitted **Housing** Yes **Expenses** Tuition 5970; Room & Board 3700 **Undergraduates** 40% women, 26% part-time, 32% 25 or older, 0.3% Native American, 0% Hispanic American, 4% African American, 8% Asian American/Pacific Islander **Academic program** Advanced placement, summer session, adult/continuing education programs, internships **Contact** Mrs. Carole Beverly, Director of Admissions, Piedmont Baptist College,

716 Franklin Street, Winston-Salem, NC 27101-5197. Telephone: 336-725-8344 Ext. 2327 or toll-free 800-937-5097. Fax: 336-725-5522. E-mail: admissions@pbc.edu. Web site: http://www.pbc.edu/.

QUEENS COLLEGE
CHARLOTTE, NORTH CAROLINA

General Independent Presbyterian, comprehensive, coed **Entrance** Moderately difficult **Setting** 25-acre suburban campus **Total enrollment** 1,596 **Student/faculty ratio** 12:1 **Application deadline** Rolling (freshmen), rolling (transfer) **Freshmen** 77% were admitted **Housing** Yes **Expenses** Tuition $11,360; Room & Board $5890 **Undergraduates** 76% women, 40% part-time, 0.4% Native American, 2% Hispanic American, 16% African American, 1% Asian American/Pacific Islander **Academic program** Advanced placement, self-designed majors, honors program, summer session, adult/continuing education programs, internships **Contact** Ms. Eileen T. Dills, Dean of Admissions and Financial Aid, Queens College, 1900 Selwyn Avenue, Charlotte, NC 28274. Telephone: 704-337-2212 or toll-free 800-849-0202. Fax: 704-337-2403. E-mail: case@rex.queens.edu. Web site: http://www.queens.edu/.

ROANOKE BIBLE COLLEGE
ELIZABETH CITY, NORTH CAROLINA

General Independent Christian, 4-year, coed **Entrance** Minimally difficult **Setting** 19-acre small-town campus **Total enrollment** 159 **Student/faculty ratio** 11:1 **Application deadline** 8/1 (freshmen), 8/1 (transfer) **Freshmen** 62% were admitted **Housing** Yes **Expenses** Tuition $5990; Room & Board $3860 **Undergraduates** 43% women, 18% part-time, 1% Native American, 1% Hispanic American, 8% African American, 0% Asian American/Pacific Islander **Academic program** Advanced placement, internships **Contact** Mrs. Deborah T. Roach, Director of Admissions, Roanoke Bible College, 715 North Poindexter Street, Elizabeth City, NC 27909-4054. Telephone: 252-334-2019 or toll-free 800-RBC-8980. Fax: 252-334-2071. E-mail: roanoke@interpath.com. Web site: http://www.roanokebible.edu/.

ST. ANDREWS PRESBYTERIAN COLLEGE
LAURINBURG, NORTH CAROLINA

General Independent Presbyterian, 4-year, coed **Entrance** Moderately difficult **Setting** 600-acre small-town campus **Total enrollment** 638 **Student/faculty ratio** 10:1 **Application deadline** Rolling (freshmen), rolling (transfer) **Freshmen** 81% were admitted **Housing** Yes **Expenses** Tuition $14,310; Room & Board $5410 **Undergraduates** 60% women, 14% part-time, 19% 25 or older, 0.5% Native American, 1% Hispanic American, 13% African American, 2% Asian American/Pacific Islander **The most frequently chosen baccalaureate fields are** business/marketing, education, psychology **Academic program** Advanced placement, accelerated degree program, self-designed majors, honors program, summer session, adult/continuing education programs, internships **Contact** Ms. Peggy Crawford, Dean for Student Affairs and Enrollment, St. Andrews Presbyterian College, 1700 Dogwood Mile, Laurinburg, NC 28352. Telephone: 910-277-5555 or toll-free 800-763-0198. Fax: 910-277-5087. E-mail: admission@sapc.edu. Web site: http://www.sapc.edu/.

SAINT AUGUSTINE'S COLLEGE
RALEIGH, NORTH CAROLINA

General Independent Episcopal, 4-year, coed **Entrance** Minimally difficult **Setting** 110-acre urban campus **Total enrollment** 1,465 **Student/faculty ratio** 16:1 **Application deadline** 7/1 (freshmen), rolling (transfer) **Freshmen** 45% were admitted **Housing** Yes **Expenses** Tuition 7900; Room & Board 4960 **Undergraduates** 17% 25 or older, 0% Native American, 0.2% Hispanic American, 90% African American, 0% Asian American/Pacific Islander **The most frequently chosen baccalaureate fields are** business/marketing, psychology, social sciences and history **Academic program** Accelerated degree program, honors program, summer session, adult/continuing education programs, internships **Contact** Mr. Sha-Ron Jones, Dean for Enrollment Management, Saint Augustine's College, 1315 Oakwood Avenue, Raleigh, NC 27610-2298. Telephone: 919-516-4011 or toll-free 800-948-1126. Fax: 919-516-4415. E-mail: admissions@es.st-aug.edu. Web site: http://www.st-aug.edu/.

SALEM COLLEGE
WINSTON-SALEM, NORTH CAROLINA

General Independent Moravian, comprehensive, women only **Entrance** Moderately difficult **Setting** 57-acre urban campus **Total enrollment** 1,027 **Student/faculty ratio** 13:1 **Application deadline** Rolling (freshmen), rolling (transfer) **Freshmen** 81% were admitted **Housing** Yes **Expenses** Tuition 13,945; Room & Board 8240 **Undergraduates** 27% part-time, 38% 25 or older, 1% Native American, 2% Hispanic American, 15% African American, 2% Asian American/Pacific Islander **The most frequently chosen baccalaureate fields are** business/marketing, social sciences and history, visual/performing arts **Academic program** Advanced placement, self-designed majors, honors program, summer session, adult/continuing education programs, internships **Contact** Ms. Katherine Knapp-Watts, Dean of Admissions and Financial Aid, Salem College, PO Box 10548, Shober House, Winston-Salem, NC 27108. Telephone: 336-721-2621 or toll-free 800-327-2536. Fax: 336-724-7102. E-mail: admissions@salem.edu. Web site: http://www.salem.edu/.

SHAW UNIVERSITY
RALEIGH, NORTH CAROLINA

General Independent Baptist, comprehensive, coed **Entrance** Minimally difficult **Setting** 18-acre urban campus **Total enrollment** 2,527 **Student/faculty ratio** 15:1 **Application deadline** 7/30 (freshmen),

Shaw University *(continued)*

7/30 (transfer) **Freshmen** 67% were admitted **Housing** Yes **Expenses** Tuition 7430; Room & Board 4648 **Undergraduates** 66% women, 14% part-time, 46% 25 or older, 0.2% Native American, 0.3% Hispanic American, 85% African American, 0.1% Asian American/Pacific Islander **The most frequently chosen baccalaureate fields are** business/marketing, protective services/public administration, social sciences and history **Academic program** English as a second language, advanced placement, accelerated degree program, self-designed majors, honors program, summer session, adult/continuing education programs, internships **Contact** Mr. Paul Vandergrift, Director of Admissions and Recruitment, Shaw University, 118 East South Street, Raleigh, NC 27601-2399. Telephone: 919-546-8275 or toll-free 800-214-6683. Fax: 919-546-8271. E-mail: ksmith@shawu.edu. Web site: http://www.shawuniversity.edu/.

THE UNIVERSITY OF NORTH CAROLINA AT ASHEVILLE

ASHEVILLE, NORTH CAROLINA

General State-supported, comprehensive, coed **Entrance** Moderately difficult **Setting** 265-acre suburban campus **Total enrollment** 3,234 **Student/faculty ratio** 13:1 **Application deadline** 3/15 (freshmen), 6/1 (transfer) **Freshmen** 64% were admitted **Housing** Yes **Expenses** Tuition 2063; Room & Board 4300 **Undergraduates** 57% women, 25% part-time, 20% 25 or older, 1% Native American, 1% Hispanic American, 3% African American, 1% Asian American/Pacific Islander **The most frequently chosen baccalaureate fields are** business/marketing, psychology, social sciences and history **Academic program** Advanced placement, self-designed majors, honors program, summer session, adult/continuing education programs, internships **Contact** Mr. John W. White, Director of Admissions, The University of North Carolina at Asheville, 117 Lipinsky Hall, CPO 2210, One University Heights, Asheville, NC 28804-8510. Telephone: 828-251-6481 or toll-free 800-531-9842. Fax: 828-251-6482. E-mail: admissions@unca.edu. Web site: http://www.unca.edu/.

THE UNIVERSITY OF NORTH CAROLINA AT CHAPEL HILL

CHAPEL HILL, NORTH CAROLINA

General State-supported, university, coed **Entrance** Very difficult **Setting** 789-acre suburban campus **Total enrollment** 24,892 **Student/faculty ratio** 14:1 **Application deadline** 1/15 (freshmen), 3/1 (transfer) **Freshmen** 37% were admitted **Housing** Yes **Expenses** Tuition 2768; Room & Board 5630 **Undergraduates** 61% women, 6% part-time, 3% 25 or older, 1% Native American, 1% Hispanic American, 11% African American, 5% Asian American/Pacific Islander **The most frequently chosen baccalaureate fields are** communications/communication technologies, biological/life sciences, social sciences and history **Academic program** Advanced placement, self-designed majors, honors program, summer session, internships **Contact** Mr. Jerome A. Lucido, Associate Vice Chancellor/Director of Undergraduate Admissions, The University of North Carolina at Chapel Hill, Office of Undergraduate Admissions, Jackson Hall 153A, Campus Box 2200, Chapel Hill, NC 27599-2200. Telephone: 919-966-3621. Fax: 919-962-3045. E-mail: uadm@email.unc.edu. Web site: http://www.unc.edu/.

THE UNIVERSITY OF NORTH CAROLINA AT CHARLOTTE

CHARLOTTE, NORTH CAROLINA

General State-supported, university, coed **Entrance** Moderately difficult **Setting** 1,000-acre suburban campus **Total enrollment** 17,241 **Student/faculty ratio** 16:1 **Application deadline** 7/1 (freshmen), 7/1 (transfer) **Freshmen** 71% were admitted **Housing** Yes **Expenses** Tuition 2138; Room & Board 4354 **Undergraduates** 54% women, 26% part-time, 22% 25 or older, 0.4% Native American, 2% Hispanic American, 17% African American, 5% Asian American/Pacific Islander **The most frequently chosen baccalaureate fields are** business/marketing, engineering/engineering technologies, social sciences and history **Academic program** English as a second language, advanced placement, honors program, summer session, adult/continuing education programs, internships **Contact** Mr. Craig Fulton, Director of Admissions, The University of North Carolina at Charlotte, 9201 University City Boulevard, Charlotte, NC 28223-0001. Telephone: 704-687-2213. Fax: 704-687-6483. E-mail: unccadm@email.uncc.edu. Web site: http://www.uncc.edu/.

THE UNIVERSITY OF NORTH CAROLINA AT GREENSBORO

GREENSBORO, NORTH CAROLINA

General State-supported, university, coed **Entrance** Moderately difficult **Setting** 200-acre urban campus **Total enrollment** 12,831 **Student/faculty ratio** 15:1 **Application deadline** 8/1 (freshmen), 8/1 (transfer) **Freshmen** 75% were admitted **Housing** Yes **Expenses** Tuition 2201; Room & Board 5422 **Undergraduates** 67% women, 17% part-time, 20% 25 or older, 0.5% Native American, 2% Hispanic American, 19% African American, 2% Asian American/Pacific Islander **The most frequently chosen baccalaureate fields are** business/marketing, health professions and related sciences, home economics/vocational home economics **Academic program** English as a second language, advanced placement, accelerated degree program, self-designed majors, honors program, summer session, adult/continuing education programs, internships **Contact** Mr. Peter Lindsey, Director of Admissions, The University of North Carolina at Greensboro, 1000 Spring Garden Street, Greensboro, NC 27412-5001. Telephone: 336-334-5243. Fax: 336-334-4180. E-mail: undergrad_admissions@uncg.edu. Web site: http://www.uncg.edu/.

THE UNIVERSITY OF NORTH CAROLINA AT PEMBROKE

PEMBROKE, NORTH CAROLINA

General State-supported, comprehensive, coed **Entrance** Moderately difficult **Setting** 126-acre rural campus **Total enrollment** 3,445 **Student/faculty ratio** 18:1 **Application deadline** Rolling (freshmen), rolling (transfer) **Freshmen** 86% were admitted **Housing** Yes **Expenses** Tuition $1860; Room & Board $3680 **Undergraduates** 63% women, 23% part-time, 30% 25 or older, 23% Native American, 2% Hispanic American, 20% African American, 2% Asian American/Pacific Islander **The most frequently chosen baccalaureate fields are** education, business/marketing, protective services/public administration **Academic program** English as a second language, advanced placement, accelerated degree program, honors program, summer session, adult/continuing education programs, internships **Contact** Ms. Jacqueline Clark, Director of Admissions, The University of North Carolina at Pembroke, PO Box 1510, Pembroke, NC 28372-1510. Telephone: 910-521-6262 or toll-free 800-949-UNCP (in-state); 800-949-uncp (out-of-state). Fax: 910-521-6497. Web site: http://www.uncp.edu/.

THE UNIVERSITY OF NORTH CAROLINA AT WILMINGTON

WILMINGTON, NORTH CAROLINA

General State-supported, comprehensive, coed **Entrance** Moderately difficult **Setting** 650-acre urban campus **Total enrollment** 9,885 **Student/faculty ratio** 18:1 **Application deadline** 2/15 (freshmen), rolling (transfer) **Freshmen** 61% were admitted **Housing** Yes **Expenses** Tuition $2360; Room & Board $4862 **Undergraduates** 60% women, 13% part-time, 16% 25 or older, 1% Native American, 2% Hispanic American, 5% African American, 1% Asian American/Pacific Islander **The most frequently chosen baccalaureate fields are** business/marketing, biological/life sciences, English **Academic program** English as a second language, advanced placement, accelerated degree program, honors program, summer session, adult/continuing education programs, internships **Contact** Mr. Ronald E. Whittaker, Registrar, The University of North Carolina at Wilmington, 601 South College Road, Wilmington, NC 28403-3201. Telephone: 910-962-3243 or toll-free 800-228-5571 (out-of-state). Fax: 910-962-3038. E-mail: admissions@uncwil.edu. Web site: http://www.uncwil.edu/.

WAKE FOREST UNIVERSITY

WINSTON-SALEM, NORTH CAROLINA

General Independent, university, coed, affiliated with North Carolina Baptist State Convention **Entrance** Very difficult **Setting** 340-acre suburban campus **Total enrollment** 6,124 **Student/faculty ratio** 11:1 **Application deadline** 1/15 (freshmen), 2/15 (transfer) **Freshmen** 49% were admitted **Housing** Yes **Expenses** Tuition 22,410; Room & Board 6340 **Undergraduates** 51% women, 1% part-time, 3% 25 or older **The most frequently chosen baccalaureate fields are** business/marketing, psychology, social sciences and history **Academic program** Advanced placement, accelerated degree program, self-designed majors, honors program, summer session, internships **Contact** Mr. William G. Starling, Director of Admissions, Wake Forest University, PO Box 7305, Winston-Salem, NC 27109. Telephone: 336-758-5201. Fax: 336-758-6074. E-mail: admissions@wfu.edu. Web site: http://www.wfu.edu/.

WARREN WILSON COLLEGE

ASHEVILLE, NORTH CAROLINA

General Independent, comprehensive, coed, affiliated with Presbyterian Church (U.S.A.) **Entrance** Moderately difficult **Setting** 1,100-acre small-town campus **Total enrollment** 799 **Student/faculty ratio** 10:1 **Application deadline** 3/15 (freshmen), 3/15 (transfer) **Freshmen** 81% were admitted **Housing** Yes **Expenses** Tuition $15,094; Room & Board $4874 **Undergraduates** 63% women, 2% part-time, 4% 25 or older, 1% Native American, 2% Hispanic American, 2% African American, 1% Asian American/Pacific Islander **The most frequently chosen baccalaureate fields are** natural resources/environmental science, English, social sciences and history **Academic program** English as a second language, advanced placement, self-designed majors, honors program, internships **Contact** Mr. Richard Blomgren, Dean of Admission, Warren Wilson College, PO Box 9000, Asheville, NC 28815-9000. Telephone: 828-771-2073 or toll-free 800-934-3536. Fax: 828-298-1440. E-mail: admit@warren-wilson.edu. Web site: http://www.warren-wilson.edu/.

► **For more information, see page 485.**

WESTERN CAROLINA UNIVERSITY

CULLOWHEE, NORTH CAROLINA

General State-supported, comprehensive, coed **Entrance** Moderately difficult **Setting** 260-acre rural campus **Total enrollment** 6,699 **Student/faculty ratio** 15:1 **Application deadline** 8/1 (freshmen), 7/1 (transfer) **Freshmen** 87% were admitted **Housing** Yes **Expenses** Tuition $2345; Room & Board $3424 **Undergraduates** 52% women, 12% part-time, 27% 25 or older, 2% Native American, 1% Hispanic American, 5% African American, 1% Asian American/Pacific Islander **The most frequently chosen baccalaureate fields are** business/marketing, education, health professions and related sciences **Academic program** English as a second language, advanced placement, accelerated degree program, self-designed majors, honors program, summer session, adult/continuing education programs, internships **Contact** Mr. Philip Cauley, Director of Admissions, Western Carolina University, Cullowhee, NC 28723. Telephone: 828-227-7317. Fax: 828-277-7319. E-mail: cauley@wcu.edu. Web site: http://www.wcu.edu/.

WINGATE UNIVERSITY

WINGATE, NORTH CAROLINA

General Independent Baptist, comprehensive, coed **Entrance** Moderately difficult **Setting** 330-acre

Wingate University *(continued)*

small-town campus **Total enrollment** 1,283 **Student/faculty ratio** 13:1 **Application deadline** Rolling (freshmen), rolling (transfer) **Freshmen** 83% were admitted **Housing** Yes **Expenses** Tuition 13,680; Room & Board 5460 **Undergraduates** 49% women, 5% part-time, 3% 25 or older, 0.2% Native American, 2% Hispanic American, 12% African American, 1% Asian American/Pacific Islander **The most frequently chosen baccalaureate fields are** business/marketing, parks and recreation, psychology **Academic program** Advanced placement, accelerated degree program, honors program, summer session, adult/continuing education programs, internships **Contact** Mr. Walter P. Crutchfield III, Dean of Admissions, Wingate University, PO Box 159, Wingate, NC 28174. Telephone: 704-233-8000 or toll-free 800-755-5550. Fax: 704-233-8110. E-mail: admit@wingate.edu. Web site: http://www.wingate.edu/.

WINSTON-SALEM STATE UNIVERSITY
WINSTON-SALEM, NORTH CAROLINA

General State-supported, 4-year, coed **Entrance** Minimally difficult **Setting** 94-acre urban campus **Total enrollment** 2,717 **Student/faculty ratio** 15:1 **Application deadline** Rolling (freshmen), rolling (transfer) **Freshmen** 67% were admitted **Housing** Yes **Expenses** Tuition $1805; Room & Board $3628 **Undergraduates** 67% women, 19% part-time, 32% 25 or older, 0.1% Native American, 1% Hispanic American, 86% African American, 1% Asian American/Pacific Islander **The most frequently chosen baccalaureate fields are** education, business/marketing, health professions and related sciences **Academic program** Advanced placement, accelerated degree program, honors program, summer session, adult/continuing education programs, internships **Contact** Mr. Van C. Wilson, Director of Admissions, Winston-Salem State University, 601 Martin Luther King Jr Drive, Winston-Salem, NC 27110-0003. Telephone: 336-750-2070 or toll-free 800-257-4052. Fax: 336-750-2079. E-mail: wilsonv@wssu1.adp.edu. Web site: http://www.wssu.edu.

NORTH DAKOTA

DICKINSON STATE UNIVERSITY
DICKINSON, NORTH DAKOTA

General State-supported, 4-year, coed **Entrance** Noncompetitive **Setting** 100-acre small-town campus **Total enrollment** 2,012 **Student/faculty ratio** 19:1 **Application deadline** Rolling (freshmen), rolling (transfer) **Freshmen** 100% were admitted **Housing** Yes **Expenses** Tuition $2378; Room & Board $2716 **Undergraduates** 58% women, 25% part-time, 20% 25 or older, 2% Native American, 0.4% Hispanic American, 1% African American, 0.2% Asian American/Pacific Islander **The most frequently chosen baccalaureate fields are** business/marketing, education, liberal arts/general studies **Academic program** Advanced placement, accelerated degree program, self-designed majors, summer session, adult/continuing education programs, internships **Contact** Deb Dazell, Director of Student Recruitment, Dickinson State University, 8th Avenue West and 3rd Street West, Dickinson, ND 58601. Telephone: 701-483-2175 or toll-free 800-279-4295. Fax: 701-483-2409. E-mail: dsuhawk@eagle.dsu.nodak.edu. Web site: http://www.dsu.nodak.edu/.

JAMESTOWN COLLEGE
JAMESTOWN, NORTH DAKOTA

General Independent Presbyterian, 4-year, coed **Entrance** Minimally difficult **Setting** 107-acre small-town campus **Total enrollment** 1,195 **Student/faculty ratio** 17:1 **Application deadline** Rolling (freshmen), rolling (transfer) **Freshmen** 99% were admitted **Housing** Yes **Expenses** Tuition 7925; Room & Board 3385 **Undergraduates** 58% women, 9% part-time, 5% 25 or older, 1% Native American, 1% Hispanic American, 1% African American, 1% Asian American/Pacific Islander **The most frequently chosen baccalaureate fields are** business/marketing, education, health professions and related sciences **Academic program** Advanced placement, self-designed majors, honors program, summer session, internships **Contact** Judy Erickson, Director of Admissions, Jamestown College, 6081 College Lane, Jamestown, ND 58405. Telephone: 701-252-3467 Ext. 2548 or toll-free 800-336-2554. Fax: 701-253-4318. E-mail: admissions@jc.edu. Web site: http://www.jc.edu/.

MAYVILLE STATE UNIVERSITY
MAYVILLE, NORTH DAKOTA

General State-supported, 4-year, coed **Entrance** Noncompetitive **Setting** 60-acre rural campus **Total enrollment** 776 **Student/faculty ratio** 14:1 **Application deadline** Rolling (freshmen), rolling (transfer) **Freshmen** 96% were admitted **Housing** Yes **Expenses** Tuition 3182; Room & Board 3026 **Undergraduates** 55% women, 24% part-time, 29% 25 or older **The most frequently chosen baccalaureate fields are** business/marketing, biological/life sciences, education **Academic program** Advanced placement, accelerated degree program, self-designed majors, summer session, adult/continuing education programs, internships **Contact** Brian Larson, Director of Enrollment Services, Mayville State University, 330 3rd Street, NE, Mayville, ND 58257-1299. Telephone: 701-786-4768 Ext. 34768 or toll-free 800-437-4104. Fax: 701-786-4748. E-mail: mvadmiss@plains.nodak.edu. Web site: http://www.masu.nodak.edu/.

MEDCENTER ONE COLLEGE OF NURSING
BISMARCK, NORTH DAKOTA

General Independent, upper-level, coed, primarily women **Entrance** Moderately difficult **Setting** 15-acre small-town campus **Total enrollment** 83 **Student/faculty ratio** 9:1 **Application deadline** 11/7 (transfer) **First-Year Students** 53% were admitted **Housing**

Yes **Expenses** Tuition 3772; Room only 900 **Undergraduates** 92% women, 18% part-time, 37% 25 or older, 5% Native American, 1% Hispanic American, 1% Asian American/Pacific Islander **The most frequently chosen baccalaureate field is** health professions and related sciences **Academic program** Honors program, summer session, internships **Contact** Dr. Karen Latham, Dean/Provost, Medcenter One College of Nursing, 512 North 7th Street, Bismarck, ND 58501-4494. Telephone: 701-323-6832. Fax: 701-323-6967. Web site: http://www.medcenterone.com/nursing/nursing.htm/.

MINOT STATE UNIVERSITY
MINOT, NORTH DAKOTA

General State-supported, comprehensive, coed **Entrance** Minimally difficult **Setting** 103-acre small-town campus **Total enrollment** 3,081 **Student/faculty ratio** 14:1 **Application deadline** Rolling (freshmen), rolling (transfer) **Freshmen** 97% were admitted **Housing** Yes **Expenses** Tuition $2454; Room & Board $3080 **Undergraduates** 63% women, 21% part-time, 27% 25 or older, 5% Native American, 1% Hispanic American, 2% African American, 1% Asian American/Pacific Islander **Academic program** Advanced placement, accelerated degree program, self-designed majors, honors program, summer session, adult/continuing education programs, internships **Contact** Ms. Ann Hendrick, Admissions Specialist, Minot State University, 500 University Avenue West, Minot, ND 58707-0002. Telephone: 701-858-3346 or toll-free 800-777-0750 Ext. 3350. Fax: 701-839-6933. E-mail: beltz@warp6.cs.misu.nodak.edu. Web site: http://www.minotstateu.edu/.

NORTH DAKOTA STATE UNIVERSITY
FARGO, NORTH DAKOTA

General State-supported, university, coed **Entrance** Moderately difficult **Setting** 2,100-acre urban campus **Total enrollment** 9,894 **Student/faculty ratio** 19:1 **Application deadline** 8/15 (freshmen), 8/15 (transfer) **Freshmen** 78% were admitted **Housing** Yes **Expenses** Tuition $3010; Room & Board $3542 **Undergraduates** 43% women, 12% part-time, 12% 25 or older, 1% Native American, 0.4% Hispanic American, 1% African American, 1% Asian American/Pacific Islander **The most frequently chosen baccalaureate fields are** business/marketing, engineering/engineering technologies, health professions and related sciences **Academic program** English as a second language, advanced placement, accelerated degree program, self-designed majors, honors program, summer session, internships **Contact** Dr. Kate Haugen, Director of Admission, North Dakota State University, PO Box 5454, Fargo, ND 58105-5454. Telephone: 701-231-8643 or toll-free 800-488-NDSU. Fax: 701-231-8802. E-mail: nuadmiss@plains.nodak.edu. Web site: http://www.ndsu.edu/.

TRINITY BIBLE COLLEGE
ELLENDALE, NORTH DAKOTA

General Independent, 4-year, coed, affiliated with Assemblies of God **Entrance** Noncompetitive **Setting** 28-acre rural campus **Total enrollment** 360 **Student/faculty ratio** 11:1 **Application deadline** Rolling (freshmen), rolling (transfer) **Freshmen** 55% were admitted **Housing** Yes **Expenses** Tuition $6520; Room & Board $3420 **Undergraduates** 49% women, 22% part-time, 18% 25 or older, 2% Native American, 2% Hispanic American, 0.3% African American, 0.3% Asian American/Pacific Islander **The most frequently chosen baccalaureate fields are** health professions and related sciences, business/marketing, liberal arts/general studies **Academic program** Advanced placement, accelerated degree program, summer session, internships **Contact** Rev. Jerry Grimshaw, Enrollment Manager, Trinity Bible College, 50 South Sixth Avenue, Ellendale, ND 58436. Telephone: 701-349-3621 Ext. 2045 or toll-free 800-TBC-2DAY. Fax: 701-349-5443. E-mail: TBC@DAY.edu.

UNIVERSITY OF MARY
BISMARCK, NORTH DAKOTA

General Independent Roman Catholic, comprehensive, coed **Entrance** Moderately difficult **Setting** 107-acre suburban campus **Total enrollment** 2,119 **Application deadline** Rolling (freshmen), rolling (transfer) **Housing** Yes **Expenses** Room & Board $3600 **Undergraduates** 20% 25 or older **Academic program** Advanced placement, accelerated degree program, summer session, adult/continuing education programs, internships **Contact** Mrs. Steph Storey, Director of Admissions, University of Mary, 7500 University Drive, Bismarck, ND 58504-9652. Telephone: 701-255-7500 Ext. 429 or toll-free 800-288-6279. Fax: 701-255-7687. E-mail: marauder@umary.edu. Web site: http://www.umary.edu/.

UNIVERSITY OF NORTH DAKOTA
GRAND FORKS, NORTH DAKOTA

General State-supported, university, coed **Entrance** Minimally difficult **Setting** 570-acre small-town campus **Total enrollment** 11,031 **Student/faculty ratio** 18:1 **Application deadline** 7/1 (freshmen), 7/1 (transfer) **Freshmen** 59% were admitted **Housing** Yes **Expenses** Tuition $3572; Room & Board $3614 **Undergraduates** 48% women, 9% part-time, 13% 25 or older, 3% Native American, 1% Hispanic American, 1% African American, 1% Asian American/Pacific Islander **The most frequently chosen baccalaureate fields are** business/marketing, health professions and related sciences, trade and industry **Academic program** Advanced placement, accelerated degree program, self-designed majors, honors program, summer session, adult/continuing education programs, internships **Contact** Ms. Heidi Kippenhan, Assistant Director of Admissions, University of North Dakota, Box 8382, Grand Forks, ND 58202. Telephone: 701-777-3821 or toll-free 800-CALL UND. Fax: 701-777-2696. E-mail: rob_carolin@mail.und.nodak.edu. Web site: http://www.und.edu/.

VALLEY CITY STATE UNIVERSITY
VALLEY CITY, NORTH DAKOTA

General State-supported, 4-year, coed **Entrance** Noncompetitive **Setting** 55-acre small-town campus **Total**

Valley City State University *(continued)*

enrollment 1,090 **Student/faculty ratio** 17:1 **Application deadline** Rolling (freshmen), rolling (transfer) **Freshmen** 94% were admitted **Housing** Yes **Expenses** Tuition 3173; Room & Board 2892 **Undergraduates** 55% women, 26% part-time, 21% 25 or older, 2% Native American, 1% Hispanic American, 1% African American, 0.5% Asian American/Pacific Islander **The most frequently chosen baccalaureate fields are** business/marketing, education, liberal arts/general studies **Academic program** English as a second language, self-designed majors, summer session, internships **Contact** Mr. Monte Johnson, Director of Admissions, Valley City State University, 101 College Street Southwest, Valley City, ND 58072. Telephone: 701-845-7101 or toll-free 800-532-8641 Ext. 37101. Fax: 701-845-7299. E-mail: vcadmiss@plains.nodak.edu. Web site: http://www.vcsu.nodak.edu/.

OHIO

ANTIOCH COLLEGE
YELLOW SPRINGS, OHIO

General Independent, 4-year, coed **Entrance** Moderately difficult **Setting** 100-acre small-town campus **Total enrollment** 628 **Student/faculty ratio** 9:1 **Application deadline** 2/1 (freshmen), rolling (transfer) **Freshmen** 80% were admitted **Housing** Yes **Expenses** Tuition $25,072 **Undergraduates** 66% women, 4% part-time, 4% 25 or older, 1% Native American, 3% Hispanic American, 6% African American, 1% Asian American/Pacific Islander **Academic program** Advanced placement, self-designed majors, summer session, internships **Contact** Ms. Cathy Paige, Information Manager, Antioch College, 795 Livermore Street, Yellow Springs, OH 45387-1697. Telephone: 937-767-6400 Ext. 6559 or toll-free 800-543-9436 (out-of-state). Fax: 937-767-6473. E-mail: admissions@college.antioch.edu. Web site: http://www.antioch-college.edu/.

ANTIOCH UNIVERSITY MCGREGOR
YELLOW SPRINGS, OHIO

Contact Ms. Terri J. Haney, Director of Admissions and Community Relations, Antioch University McGregor, 800 Livermore Street, Yellow Springs, OH 45387-1609. Telephone: 937-767-6325. E-mail: admiss@unibase.antioch.edu. Web site: http://www.mcgregor.edu/.

ART ACADEMY OF CINCINNATI
CINCINNATI, OHIO

General Independent, comprehensive, coed **Entrance** Moderately difficult **Setting** 184-acre urban campus **Total enrollment** 255 **Student/faculty ratio** 12:1 **Application deadline** 6/30 (freshmen), 6/30 (transfer) **Freshmen** 83% were admitted **Housing** No **Expenses** Tuition $13,000 **Undergraduates** 58% women, 6% part-time, 27% 25 or older, 0% Native American, 0.4% Hispanic American, 1% African American, 2% Asian American/Pacific Islander **Academic program** Advanced placement, self-designed majors, summer session, adult/continuing education programs, internships **Contact** Mary Jane Zumwalde, Director of Admissions, Art Academy of Cincinnati, 1125 Saint Gregory Street, Cincinnati, OH 45202. Telephone: 513-562-8744 or toll-free 800-323-5692 (in-state). Fax: 513-562-8778. E-mail: dotto@tso.cin.ix.net. Web site: http://www.artacademy.edu/.

ASHLAND UNIVERSITY
ASHLAND, OHIO

General Independent, comprehensive, coed, affiliated with Brethren Church **Entrance** Moderately difficult **Setting** 98-acre small-town campus **Total enrollment** 6,055 **Student/faculty ratio** 13:1 **Application deadline** 8/30 (freshmen), rolling (transfer) **Freshmen** 90% were admitted **Housing** Yes **Expenses** Tuition $16,270; Room & Board $5862 **Undergraduates** 57% women, 24% part-time, 30% 25 or older, 0.3% Native American, 1% Hispanic American, 3% African American, 0.4% Asian American/Pacific Islander **The most frequently chosen baccalaureate fields are** business/marketing, education, protective services/public administration **Academic program** English as a second language, advanced placement, accelerated degree program, honors program, summer session, adult/continuing education programs, internships **Contact** Mr. Tom Mansperger, Director of Admissions, Ashland University, 401 College Avenue, Ashland, OH 44805. Telephone: 419-289-5080 or toll-free 800-882-1548. Fax: 419-289-5999. E-mail: auadmsn@ashland.edu. Web site: http://www.ashland.edu/.

BALDWIN-WALLACE COLLEGE
BEREA, OHIO

General Independent Methodist, comprehensive, coed **Entrance** Moderately difficult **Setting** 92-acre suburban campus **Total enrollment** 4,831 **Student/faculty ratio** 15:1 **Application deadline** Rolling (freshmen), rolling (transfer) **Freshmen** 82% were admitted **Housing** Yes **Expenses** Tuition $15,340; Room & Board $5460 **Undergraduates** 62% women, 26% part-time, 19% 25 or older, 0.2% Native American, 1% Hispanic American, 4% African American, 1% Asian American/Pacific Islander **The most frequently chosen baccalaureate fields are** business/marketing, education, social sciences and history **Academic program** English as a second language, advanced placement, accelerated degree program, self-designed majors, honors program, summer session, adult/continuing education programs, internships **Contact** Mrs. Julie Baker, Director of Undergraduate Admission, Baldwin-Wallace College, 275 Eastland Road, Berea, OH 44017-2088. Telephone: 440-826-2222 or toll-free 877-BWAPPLY (in-state). Fax: 440-826-3830. E-mail: admission@baldwinw.edu. Web site: http://www.bw.edu/.

BLUFFTON COLLEGE
BLUFFTON, OHIO

General Independent Mennonite, comprehensive, coed **Entrance** Moderately difficult **Setting** 65-acre small-town campus **Total enrollment** 1,063 **Student/faculty ratio** 13:1 **Application deadline** 5/31 (freshmen), rolling (transfer) **Freshmen** 86% were admitted **Housing** Yes **Expenses** Tuition $15,346; Room & Board $5268 **Undergraduates** 54% women, 11% part-time, 9% 25 or older, 0.4% Native American, 2% Hispanic American, 6% African American, 1% Asian American/Pacific Islander **The most frequently chosen baccalaureate fields are** business/marketing, education, social sciences and history **Academic program** English as a second language, advanced placement, accelerated degree program, self-designed majors, honors program, summer session, adult/continuing education programs, internships **Contact** Mr. Eric Fulcomer, Dean of Admissions, Bluffton College, 280 West College Avenue, Bluffton, OH 45817. Telephone: 419-358-3254 or toll-free 800-488-3257. Fax: 419-358-3232. E-mail: admissions@bluffton.edu. Web site: http://www.bluffton.edu/.

BOWLING GREEN STATE UNIVERSITY
BOWLING GREEN, OHIO

General State-supported, university, coed **Entrance** Moderately difficult **Setting** 1,230-acre small-town campus **Total enrollment** 18,096 **Student/faculty ratio** 20:1 **Application deadline** 7/15 (freshmen), 7/15 (transfer) **Freshmen** 88% were admitted **Housing** Yes **Expenses** Tuition $5184; Room & Board $5768 **Undergraduates** 57% women, 8% part-time, 7% 25 or older, 0.2% Native American, 2% Hispanic American, 4% African American, 1% Asian American/Pacific Islander **The most frequently chosen baccalaureate fields are** business/marketing, education, health professions and related sciences **Academic program** English as a second language, advanced placement, accelerated degree program, self-designed majors, honors program, summer session, adult/continuing education programs, internships **Contact** Mr. Gary Swegan, Director of Admissions, Bowling Green State University, 110 McFall, Bowling Green, OH 43403. Telephone: 419-372-2086. Fax: 419-372-6955. E-mail: admissions@bgnet.bgsu.edu. Web site: http://www.bgsu.edu/.

BRYANT AND STRATTON COLLEGE
CLEVELAND, OHIO

General Proprietary, 4-year, coed **Entrance** Minimally difficult **Setting** urban campus **Total enrollment** 205 **Student/faculty ratio** 10:1 **Application deadline** Rolling (freshmen), rolling (transfer) **Freshmen** 93% were admitted **Housing** Yes **Expenses** Tuition 9472; Room only 4200 **Undergraduates** 40% women, 46% part-time, 59% 25 or older, 0% Native American, 4% Hispanic American, 50% African American, 0% Asian American/Pacific Islander **The most frequently chosen baccalaureate field is** engineering/engineering technologies **Academic program** Summer session, adult/continuing education programs, internships **Contact** Kerry Burton, Director of Admissions, Bryant and Stratton College, 1700 East 13th Street, Cleveland, OH 44114-3203. Telephone: 216-771-1700. Fax: 216-771-7787. Web site: http://www.bryantstratton.edu/.

CAPITAL UNIVERSITY
COLUMBUS, OHIO

General Independent, comprehensive, coed, affiliated with Evangelical Lutheran Church in America **Entrance** Moderately difficult **Setting** 48-acre suburban campus **Total enrollment** 3,897 **Student/faculty ratio** 11:1 **Application deadline** 4/15 (freshmen), rolling (transfer) **Freshmen** 81% were admitted **Housing** Yes **Expenses** Tuition $16,880; Room & Board $5170 **Undergraduates** 63% women, 29% part-time, 3% 25 or older, 0.3% Native American, 1% Hispanic American, 16% African American, 1% Asian American/Pacific Islander **The most frequently chosen baccalaureate fields are** business/marketing, education, health professions and related sciences **Academic program** English as a second language, advanced placement, self-designed majors, summer session, adult/continuing education programs, internships **Contact** Mrs. Kimberly V. Ebbrecht, Director of Admission, Capital University, 2199 East Main Street, Columbus, OH 43209. Telephone: 614-236-6101 or toll-free 800-289-6289. Fax: 614-236-6926. E-mail: admissions@capital.edu. Web site: http://www.capital.edu/.

CASE WESTERN RESERVE UNIVERSITY
CLEVELAND, OHIO

General Independent, university, coed **Entrance** Very difficult **Setting** 128-acre urban campus **Total enrollment** 9,304 **Student/faculty ratio** 8:1 **Application deadline** 2/1 (freshmen), 6/30 (transfer) **Freshmen** 71% were admitted **Housing** Yes **Expenses** Tuition $20,260; Room & Board $5815 **Undergraduates** 39% women, 8% part-time, 3% 25 or older, 0.2% Native American, 2% Hispanic American, 4% African American, 13% Asian American/Pacific Islander **The most frequently chosen baccalaureate fields are** engineering/engineering technologies, biological/life sciences, social sciences and history **Academic program** English as a second language, advanced placement, accelerated degree program, self-designed majors, honors program, summer session, adult/continuing education programs, internships **Contact** Mr. William T. Conley, Dean of Undergraduate Admission, Case Western Reserve University, 10900 Euclid Avenue, Cleveland, OH 44106. Telephone: 216-368-4450. E-mail: xx329@po.cwru.edu. Web site: http://www.cwru.edu/.

CEDARVILLE UNIVERSITY
CEDARVILLE, OHIO

General Independent Baptist, comprehensive, coed **Entrance** Moderately difficult **Setting** 300-acre rural campus **Total enrollment** 2,857 **Student/faculty**

Cedarville University *(continued)*

ratio 18:1 **Application deadline** Rolling (freshmen), rolling (transfer) **Freshmen** 74% were admitted **Housing** Yes **Expenses** Tuition 11,562; Room & Board 4929 **Undergraduates** 54% women, 4% part-time, 1% 25 or older, 0.2% Native American, 1% Hispanic American, 1% African American, 1% Asian American/Pacific Islander **The most frequently chosen baccalaureate fields are** education, business/marketing, philosophy, religion, and theology **Academic program** Advanced placement, accelerated degree program, honors program, summer session, internships **Contact** Mr. Roscoe Smith, Director of Admissions, Cedarville University, 251 North Main Street, Cedarville, OH 45314-0601. Telephone: 937-766-7700 or toll-free 800-CEDARVILLE. Fax: 937-766-7575. E-mail: admiss@cedarville.edu. Web site: http://www.cedarville.edu/.

CENTRAL STATE UNIVERSITY
WILBERFORCE, OHIO

General State-supported, comprehensive, coed **Entrance** Minimally difficult **Setting** 60-acre rural campus **Total enrollment** 1,129 **Student/faculty ratio** 12:1 **Application deadline** 6/15 (freshmen), 6/15 (transfer) **Freshmen** 34% were admitted **Housing** Yes **Expenses** Tuition 3573; Room & Board 5031 **Undergraduates** 54% women, 11% part-time, 19% 25 or older, 0% Native American, 0% Hispanic American, 95% African American, 0.4% Asian American/Pacific Islander **Academic program** Honors program, summer session, adult/continuing education programs, internships **Contact** Mr. Thandabantu Maceo, Director, Admissions, Central State University, PO Box 1004, 1400 Blush Row Road, Wilber Force, OH 45384. Telephone: 937-376-6348 or toll-free 800-388-CSU1 (in-state). Fax: 937-376-6648. E-mail: admissions@csu.ces.edu. Web site: http://www.centralstate.edu/.

CINCINNATI BIBLE COLLEGE AND SEMINARY
CINCINNATI, OHIO

General Independent, comprehensive, coed, affiliated with Church of Christ **Entrance** Minimally difficult **Setting** 40-acre urban campus **Total enrollment** 927 **Student/faculty ratio** 17:1 **Application deadline** 8/10 (freshmen), 8/10 (transfer) **Freshmen** 97% were admitted **Housing** Yes **Expenses** Tuition $7500; Room & Board $4340 **Undergraduates** 44% women, 14% part-time, 20% 25 or older **Academic program** Advanced placement, summer session, adult/continuing education programs, internships **Contact** Mr. Alex Eady, Director of Undergraduate Admissions, Cincinnati Bible College and Seminary, 2700 Glenway Avenue, Cincinnati, OH 45204-1799. Telephone: 800-949-4222 Ext. 8610 or toll-free 800-949-4CBC. Fax: 513-244-8140. E-mail: admissions@cincybible.edu. Web site: http://www.cincybible.edu/.

CIRCLEVILLE BIBLE COLLEGE
CIRCLEVILLE, OHIO

General Independent, 4-year, coed, affiliated with Churches of Christ in Christian Union **Entrance** Minimally difficult **Setting** 40-acre small-town campus **Total enrollment** 216 **Student/faculty ratio** 12:1 **Application deadline** Rolling (freshmen), rolling (transfer) **Freshmen** 65% were admitted **Housing** Yes **Expenses** Tuition 8164; Room & Board 4856 **Undergraduates** 45% women, 14% part-time, 42% 25 or older, 1% Native American, 1% Hispanic American, 3% African American, 0% Asian American/Pacific Islander **The most frequently chosen baccalaureate fields are** interdisciplinary studies, philosophy, religion, and theology, psychology **Academic program** Advanced placement, self-designed majors, honors program, summer session, adult/continuing education programs, internships **Contact** Rev. Matt Taylor, Director of Enrollment, Circleville Bible College, PO Box 458, Circleville, OH 43113-9487. Telephone: 740-477-7701 or toll-free 800-701-0222. Fax: 740-477-7755. E-mail: enroll@biblecollege.edu. Web site: http://www.biblecollege.edu/.

CLEVELAND COLLEGE OF JEWISH STUDIES
BEACHWOOD, OHIO

General Independent, comprehensive, coed **Entrance** Noncompetitive **Setting** 2-acre suburban campus **Total enrollment** 105 **Student/faculty ratio** 8:1 **Application deadline** Rolling (freshmen), rolling (transfer) **Freshmen** 75% were admitted **Housing** No **Expenses** Tuition $6320 **Undergraduates** 88% women, 100% part-time, 100% 25 or older, 0% Native American, 0% Hispanic American, 0% African American, 0% Asian American/Pacific Islander **The most frequently chosen baccalaureate fields are** education, philosophy, religion, and theology **Academic program** Summer session, adult/continuing education programs, internships **Contact** Ms. Linda L. Rosen, Director of Student Services, Cleveland College of Jewish Studies, 26500 Shaker Boulevard, 26500 Shaker Boulevard, Beachwood, OH 44122-7116. Telephone: 216-464-4050 Ext. 101 or toll-free 888-336-2257. Fax: 216-464-5827. E-mail: admissions@ccjs.edu. Web site: http://www.ccjs.edu/.

THE CLEVELAND INSTITUTE OF ART
CLEVELAND, OHIO

General Independent, 5-year, coed **Entrance** Moderately difficult **Setting** 488-acre urban campus **Total enrollment** 553 **Student/faculty ratio** 10:1 **Application deadline** Rolling (freshmen), rolling (transfer) **Freshmen** 72% were admitted **Housing** Yes **Expenses** Tuition $16,167; Room & Board $5334 **Undergraduates** 51% women, 6% part-time, 13% 25 or older, 0.4% Native American, 1% Hispanic American, 4% African American, 2% Asian American/Pacific Islander **The most frequently chosen baccalaureate fields are** health professions and related sciences, visual/performing arts **Academic program**

Advanced placement, internships **Contact** Office of Admissions, The Cleveland Institute of Art, 11141 East Boulevard, Cleveland, OH 44106. Telephone: 216-421-7418 or toll-free 800-223-4700. Fax: 216-421-7438. E-mail: 74527.17@compuserve.com. Web site: http://www.cia.edu/.

CLEVELAND INSTITUTE OF MUSIC
CLEVELAND, OHIO

General Independent, comprehensive, coed **Entrance** Very difficult **Setting** 488-acre urban campus **Total enrollment** 386 **Student/faculty ratio** 7:1 **Application deadline** 12/1 (freshmen), 12/1 (transfer) **Freshmen** 29% were admitted **Housing** Yes **Expenses** Tuition 19,425; Room & Board 5210 **Undergraduates** 3% 25 or older, 0% Native American, 4% Hispanic American, 1% African American, 7% Asian American/Pacific Islander **The most frequently chosen baccalaureate field is** visual/performing arts **Academic program** English as a second language, advanced placement, accelerated degree program, summer session, internships **Contact** Mr. William Fay, Director of Admission, Cleveland Institute of Music, 11021 East Boulevard, Cleveland, OH 44106-1776. Telephone: 216-795-3107. Fax: 216-791-1530. E-mail: cimadmission@po.cwru.edu. Web site: http://www.cim.edu/.

CLEVELAND STATE UNIVERSITY
CLEVELAND, OHIO

General State-supported, university, coed **Entrance** Noncompetitive **Setting** 70-acre urban campus **Total enrollment** 15,293 **Student/faculty ratio** 16:1 **Application deadline** 7/15 (freshmen), 7/15 (transfer) **Freshmen** 86% were admitted **Housing** Yes **Expenses** Tuition 4110; Room & Board 5200 **Undergraduates** 55% women, 35% part-time, 40% 25 or older, 0.4% Native American, 3% Hispanic American, 20% African American, 3% Asian American/Pacific Islander **The most frequently chosen baccalaureate fields are** business/marketing, education, social sciences and history **Academic program** English as a second language, advanced placement, accelerated degree program, self-designed majors, summer session, adult/continuing education programs, internships **Contact** Office of Admissions, Cleveland State University, 1983 East 24th Street, Rhodes Tower West, Room 204, Cleveland, OH 44115. Telephone: 216-687-3754 or toll-free 800-CSU-OHIO (in-state). Fax: 216-687-9210. E-mail: d.norris@csuohio.edu. Web site: http://www.csuohio.edu/.

COLLEGE OF MOUNT ST. JOSEPH
CINCINNATI, OHIO

General Independent Roman Catholic, comprehensive, coed **Entrance** Moderately difficult **Setting** 75-acre suburban campus **Total enrollment** 2,216 **Student/faculty ratio** 14:1 **Application deadline** 8/15 (freshmen), 8/15 (transfer) **Freshmen** 85% were admitted **Housing** Yes **Expenses** Tuition $14,000; Room & Board $5100 **Undergraduates** 71% women, 35% part-time, 36% 25 or older, 0.1% Native American, 1% Hispanic American, 8% African American, 2% Asian American/Pacific Islander **The most frequently chosen baccalaureate fields are** business/marketing, education, health professions and related sciences **Academic program** English as a second language, advanced placement, accelerated degree program, honors program, summer session, adult/continuing education programs, internships **Contact** Mr. Edward C. Eckel, Director of Admission, College of Mount St. Joseph, 5701 Delhi Road, Cincinnati, OH 45233-1672. Telephone: 513-244-4302 or toll-free 800-654-9314. Fax: 513-244-4629. E-mail: edward_eckel@mail.msj.edu. Web site: http://www.msj.edu/.

THE COLLEGE OF WOOSTER
WOOSTER, OHIO

General Independent, 4-year, coed, affiliated with Presbyterian Church (U.S.A.) **Entrance** Moderately difficult **Setting** 320-acre small-town campus **Total enrollment** 1,837 **Student/faculty ratio** 12:1 **Application deadline** 2/15 (freshmen), 6/1 (transfer) **Freshmen** 74% were admitted **Housing** Yes **Expenses** Tuition 21,520; Room & Board 5680 **Undergraduates** 53% women, 2% part-time, 45% 25 or older, 0.2% Native American, 1% Hispanic American, 4% African American, 2% Asian American/Pacific Islander **The most frequently chosen baccalaureate fields are** English, biological/life sciences, social sciences and history **Academic program** Advanced placement, self-designed majors, summer session, internships **Contact** Ms. Carol D. Wheatley, Director of Admissions, The College of Wooster, 1189 Beall Avenue, Wooster, OH 44691. Telephone: 330-263-2270 Ext. 2118 or toll-free 800-877-9905. Fax: 330-263-2621. E-mail: admissions@acs.wooster.edu. Web site: http://www.wooster.edu/.

► **For more information, see page 403.**

COLUMBUS COLLEGE OF ART AND DESIGN
COLUMBUS, OHIO

General Independent, 4-year, coed **Entrance** Moderately difficult **Setting** 7-acre urban campus **Total enrollment** 1,546 **Student/faculty ratio** 10:1 **Application deadline** Rolling (freshmen), rolling (transfer) **Freshmen** 70% were admitted **Housing** Yes **Expenses** Tuition $15,010; Room & Board $6100 **Undergraduates** 51% women, 24% part-time, 10% 25 or older, 1% Native American, 2% Hispanic American, 5% African American, 5% Asian American/Pacific Islander **Academic program** English as a second language, advanced placement, summer session, internships **Contact** Mr. Thomas E. Green, Director of Admissions, Columbus College of Art and Design, 107 North Ninth Street, Columbus, OH 43215-1758. Telephone: 614-224-9101. Fax: 614-232-8344. E-mail: brooke@ccad.edu. Web site: http://www.ccad.edu/.

DAVID N. MYERS COLLEGE
CLEVELAND, OHIO

General Independent, 4-year, coed **Contact** Ms. Tiffiney Payton, Interim Director of Admissions, David N. Myers College, 112 Prospect Avenue, Cleveland, OH 44115. Telephone: 216-523-3806 Ext. 805 or toll-free 800-424-3953. Fax: 216-696-6430. E-mail: lhice@dnmyers.edu. Web site: http://www.dnmyers.edu/.

DEFIANCE COLLEGE
DEFIANCE, OHIO

General Independent, comprehensive, coed, affiliated with United Church of Christ **Entrance** Moderately difficult **Setting** 150-acre small-town campus **Total enrollment** 991 **Student/faculty ratio** 14:1 **Application deadline** 8/15 (freshmen), 8/15 (transfer) **Freshmen** 78% were admitted **Housing** Yes **Expenses** Tuition $15,780; Room & Board $4700 **Undergraduates** 55% women, 24% part-time, 35% 25 or older, 0.2% Native American, 3% Hispanic American, 5% African American, 1% Asian American/Pacific Islander **Academic program** Advanced placement, self-designed majors, honors program, summer session, adult/continuing education programs, internships **Contact** Ms. Sarah Evans Bates, Director of Admissions, Defiance College, 701 North Clinton Street, Defiance, OH 43512-1610. Telephone: 419-783-2354 or toll-free 800-520-4632 Ext. 2359. Fax: 419-783-2468. E-mail: admissions@defiance.edu. Web site: http://www.defiance.edu/.

DENISON UNIVERSITY
GRANVILLE, OHIO

General Independent, 4-year, coed **Entrance** Moderately difficult **Setting** 1,200-acre small-town campus **Total enrollment** 2,108 **Student/faculty ratio** 11:1 **Application deadline** 2/1 (freshmen), 5/1 (transfer) **Freshmen** 68% were admitted **Housing** Yes **Expenses** Tuition $22,210; Room & Board $6300 **Undergraduates** 57% women, 1% part-time, 1% 25 or older, 0.2% Native American, 2% Hispanic American, 5% African American, 2% Asian American/Pacific Islander **The most frequently chosen baccalaureate fields are** biological/life sciences, social sciences and history, visual/performing arts **Academic program** Advanced placement, self-designed majors, honors program, internships **Contact** Mollie Rodenbeck, Campus Visit Coordinator, Denison University, Box H, Granville, OH 43023. Telephone: 740-587-6276 or toll-free 800-DENISON. E-mail: admissions@denison.edu. Web site: http://www.denison.edu/.

DEVRY INSTITUTE OF TECHNOLOGY
COLUMBUS, OHIO

General Proprietary, 4-year, coed **Entrance** Minimally difficult **Setting** 21-acre urban campus **Total enrollment** 3,570 **Student/faculty ratio** 28:1 **Application deadline** Rolling (freshmen), rolling (transfer) **Freshmen** 62% were admitted **Housing** No **Expenses** Tuition 8805 **Undergraduates** 25% women, 26% part-time, 41% 25 or older, 0.5% Native American, 1% Hispanic American, 18% African American, 3% Asian American/Pacific Islander **The most frequently chosen baccalaureate fields are** business/marketing, computer/information sciences, engineering/engineering technologies **Academic program** Advanced placement, accelerated degree program, summer session, adult/continuing education programs **Contact** Mr. Curt Hemmeler, Acting Director of Admissions, DeVry Institute of Technology, 1350 Alum Creek Drive, Columbus, OH 43209-2705. Telephone: 614-253-7291 Ext. 700 or toll-free 800-426-3916 (in-state); 800-426-3090 (out-of-state). E-mail: admissions@devrycol5.edu.

FRANCISCAN UNIVERSITY OF STEUBENVILLE
STEUBENVILLE, OHIO

General Independent Roman Catholic, comprehensive, coed **Entrance** Moderately difficult **Setting** 116-acre suburban campus **Total enrollment** 2,154 **Student/faculty ratio** 15:1 **Application deadline** 5/1 (freshmen), 5/1 (transfer) **Freshmen** 90% were admitted **Housing** Yes **Expenses** Tuition $12,970; Room & Board $5070 **Undergraduates** 60% women, 9% part-time, 13% 25 or older, 0.1% Native American, 4% Hispanic American, 1% African American, 2% Asian American/Pacific Islander **The most frequently chosen baccalaureate fields are** education, health professions and related sciences, philosophy, religion, and theology **Academic program** Advanced placement, accelerated degree program, honors program, summer session, adult/continuing education programs, internships **Contact** Mrs. Margaret Weber, Director of Admissions, Franciscan University of Steubenville, 1235 University Boulevard, Steubenville, OH 43952-1763. Telephone: 740-283-6226 or toll-free 800-783-6220. Fax: 740-284-5456. E-mail: admissions@franuniv.edu. Web site: http://www.franuniv.edu/.

FRANKLIN UNIVERSITY
COLUMBUS, OHIO

General Independent, comprehensive, coed **Entrance** Noncompetitive **Setting** 14-acre urban campus **Total enrollment** 5,087 **Student/faculty ratio** 18:1 **Application deadline** Rolling (freshmen), rolling (transfer) **Freshmen** 100% were admitted **Housing** No **Expenses** Tuition 5983 **Undergraduates** 74% 25 or older, 0.4% Native American, 1% Hispanic American, 14% African American, 3% Asian American/Pacific Islander **The most frequently chosen baccalaureate fields are** business/marketing, computer/information sciences, health professions and related sciences **Academic program** English as a second language, advanced placement, accelerated degree program, self-designed majors, summer session, adult/continuing education programs, internships **Contact** Ms. Ellen Levino, Vice President for Students, Franklin University, 201 S. Grant Avenue, Columbus, OH 43215. Telephone: 614-341-6256 or toll-free 877-341-6300. Fax: 614-224-8027. E-mail: info@franklin.edu. Web site: http://www.franklin.edu/.

GOD'S BIBLE SCHOOL AND COLLEGE
CINCINNATI, OHIO

General Independent interdenominational, 4-year, coed **Entrance** Minimally difficult **Setting** 14-acre urban campus **Total enrollment** 238 **Application deadline** Rolling (freshmen), rolling (transfer) **Housing** Yes **Expenses** Tuition $3780; Room & Board $2800 **Undergraduates** 18% 25 or older **Academic program** Advanced placement, summer session, internships **Contact** Ms. Laura Ellison, Director of Admissions, God's Bible School and College, 1810 Young Street, Cincinnati, OH 45210-1599. Telephone: 513-721-7944 Ext. 204 or toll-free 800-486-4637. Fax: 513-721-3971. E-mail: gbs4u@juno.com.

HEIDELBERG COLLEGE
TIFFIN, OHIO

General Independent, comprehensive, coed, affiliated with United Church of Christ **Entrance** Moderately difficult **Setting** 110-acre small-town campus **Total enrollment** 1,562 **Student/faculty ratio** 13:1 **Application deadline** 8/1 (freshmen), 8/1 (transfer) **Freshmen** 87% were admitted **Housing** Yes **Expenses** Tuition 17,278; Room & Board 5974 **Undergraduates** 53% women, 26% part-time, 4% 25 or older, 0.4% Native American, 1% Hispanic American, 3% African American, 0.4% Asian American/Pacific Islander **The most frequently chosen baccalaureate fields are** business/marketing, education, parks and recreation **Academic program** English as a second language, advanced placement, accelerated degree program, honors program, summer session, adult/continuing education programs, internships **Contact** Ms. Sharon Pugh, Director of Admission, Heidelberg College, 310 East Market Street, Tiffin, OH 44883-2462. Telephone: 419-448-2330 or toll-free 800-434-3352. Fax: 419-448-2334. E-mail: adminfo@nike.heidelberg.edu. Web site: http://www.heidelberg.edu/.

HIRAM COLLEGE
HIRAM, OHIO

General Independent, 4-year, coed, affiliated with Christian Church (Disciples of Christ) **Entrance** Very difficult **Setting** 110-acre rural campus **Total enrollment** 1,199 **Student/faculty ratio** 12:1 **Application deadline** 3/15 (freshmen), 7/15 (transfer) **Freshmen** 87% were admitted **Housing** Yes **Expenses** Tuition 18,440; Room & Board 6254 **Undergraduates** 57% women, 22% part-time, 26% 25 or older, 0.2% Native American, 1% Hispanic American, 9% African American, 1% Asian American/Pacific Islander **The most frequently chosen baccalaureate fields are** business/marketing, biological/life sciences, social sciences and history **Academic program** English as a second language, advanced placement, accelerated degree program, self-designed majors, summer session, adult/continuing education programs, internships **Contact** Mr. Ed Frato Sweeney, Director of Admission, Hiram College, Box 96, Hiram, OH 44234-0067. Telephone: 330-569-5169 or toll-free 800-362-5280. Fax: 330-569-5944. E-mail: admission@hiram.edu. Web site: http://www.hiram.edu/.

► **For more information, see page 431.**

JOHN CARROLL UNIVERSITY
UNIVERSITY HEIGHTS, OHIO

General Independent Roman Catholic (Jesuit), comprehensive, coed **Entrance** Moderately difficult **Setting** 60-acre suburban campus **Total enrollment** 4,384 **Student/faculty ratio** 14:1 **Application deadline** 2/1 (freshmen), rolling (transfer) **Freshmen** 87% were admitted **Housing** Yes **Expenses** Tuition $17,837; Room & Board $6312 **Undergraduates** 54% women, 6% part-time, 2% 25 or older, 0.2% Native American, 2% Hispanic American, 5% African American, 3% Asian American/Pacific Islander **The most frequently chosen baccalaureate fields are** business/marketing, communications/communication technologies, social sciences and history **Academic program** Advanced placement, accelerated degree program, self-designed majors, honors program, summer session, adult/continuing education programs, internships **Contact** Mr. Thomas P. Fanning, Director of Admission, John Carroll University, 20700 North Park Boulevard, University Heights, OH 44118-4581. Telephone: 216-397-4294. Fax: 216-397-4981. E-mail: admission@jcvaxa.jcu.edu. Web site: http://www.jcu.edu/.

KENT STATE UNIVERSITY
KENT, OHIO

General State-supported, university, coed **Entrance** Moderately difficult **Setting** 1,200-acre small-town campus **Total enrollment** 21,924 **Student/faculty ratio** 19:1 **Application deadline** 3/15 (freshmen), 7/1 (transfer) **Freshmen** 92% were admitted **Housing** Yes **Expenses** Tuition 5285; Room & Board 4764 **Undergraduates** 60% women, 17% part-time, 16% 25 or older **The most frequently chosen baccalaureate fields are** business/marketing, education, health professions and related sciences **Academic program** English as a second language, advanced placement, self-designed majors, honors program, summer session, adult/continuing education programs, internships **Contact** Mr. Christopher Buttenschon, Assistant Director of Admissions, Kent State University, 161 Michael Schwartz Center, Kent, OH 44242-0001. Telephone: 330-672-2444 or toll-free 800-988-KENT. Fax: 330-672-2499. E-mail: kentadm@admissions.kent.edu. Web site: http://www.kent.edu/.

KENYON COLLEGE
GAMBIER, OHIO

General Independent, 4-year, coed **Entrance** Very difficult **Setting** 800-acre rural campus **Total enrollment** 1,599 **Student/faculty ratio** 11:1 **Application deadline** 1/15 (freshmen), 4/1 (transfer) **Freshmen** 65% were admitted **Housing** Yes **Expenses** Tuition

Kenyon College *(continued)*

26,080; Room & Board 4370 **Undergraduates** 55% women, 1% part-time, 0% 25 or older, 0% Native American, 3% Hispanic American, 4% African American, 3% Asian American/Pacific Islander **The most frequently chosen baccalaureate fields are** English, psychology, social sciences and history **Academic program** Advanced placement, accelerated degree program, self-designed majors, honors program, internships **Contact** Mr. John W. Anderson, Dean of Admissions, Kenyon College, Office of Admissions, Gambier, OH 43022-9623. Telephone: 740-427-5776 or toll-free 800-848-2468. Fax: 740-427-5770. E-mail: admissions@kenyon.edu. Web site: http://www.kenyon.edu/.

LAKE ERIE COLLEGE
PAINESVILLE, OHIO

General Independent, comprehensive, coed **Entrance** Minimally difficult **Setting** 57-acre small-town campus **Total enrollment** 815 **Student/faculty ratio** 12:1 **Freshmen** 83% were admitted **Housing** Yes **Expenses** Tuition $16,392; Room & Board $5420 **Undergraduates** 77% women, 23% part-time, 23% 25 or older, 0.2% Native American, 2% Hispanic American, 4% African American, 1% Asian American/Pacific Islander **Academic program** Advanced placement, accelerated degree program, self-designed majors, summer session, adult/continuing education programs, internships **Contact** Kevin Coughlin, Dean of Admissions and Financial Aid, Lake Erie College, 391 West Washington Street, Painesville, OH 44077-3389. Telephone: 440-639-7879 or toll-free 800-916-0904. Fax: 440-352-3533. E-mail: lecadmit@lakeerie.edu. Web site: http://www.lec.edu/.

LOURDES COLLEGE
SYLVANIA, OHIO

General Independent Roman Catholic, 4-year, coed **Entrance** Moderately difficult **Setting** 90-acre suburban campus **Total enrollment** 1,270 **Student/faculty ratio** 14:1 **Application deadline** Rolling (freshmen), rolling (transfer) **Freshmen** 66% were admitted **Housing** No **Expenses** Tuition $9624 **Undergraduates** 81% women, 66% part-time, 70% 25 or older, 1% Native American, 2% Hispanic American, 10% African American, 0.2% Asian American/Pacific Islander **The most frequently chosen baccalaureate fields are** business/marketing, health professions and related sciences, home economics/vocational home economics **Academic program** Advanced placement, accelerated degree program, self-designed majors, summer session, adult/continuing education programs, internships **Contact** Ms. Beth Csortos, Director of Admissions, Lourdes College, 6832 Convent Boulevard, Sylvania, OH 43560. Telephone: 419-885-5291 Ext. 299 or toll-free 800-878-3210 Ext. 1299. Fax: 419-882-3987. E-mail: btanesky@lourdes.edu. Web site: http://www.lourdes.edu/.

MALONE COLLEGE
CANTON, OHIO

General Independent, comprehensive, coed, affiliated with Evangelical Friends Church–Eastern Region **Entrance** Moderately difficult **Setting** 78-acre suburban campus **Total enrollment** 2,162 **Student/faculty ratio** 14:1 **Application deadline** 7/1 (freshmen), 7/1 (transfer) **Freshmen** 84% were admitted **Housing** Yes **Expenses** Tuition $13,030; Room & Board $5450 **Undergraduates** 62% women, 11% part-time, 22% 25 or older, 0.2% Native American, 1% Hispanic American, 4% African American, 0.3% Asian American/Pacific Islander **The most frequently chosen baccalaureate fields are** business/marketing, education, health professions and related sciences **Academic program** Advanced placement, accelerated degree program, self-designed majors, honors program, summer session, adult/continuing education programs, internships **Contact** Mr. John Chopka, Dean of Admissions, Malone College, 515 25th Street, NW, Canton, OH 44709-3897. Telephone: 330-471-8145 or toll-free 800-521-1146. Fax: 330-471-8149. E-mail: lgonot@malone.malone.edu. Web site: http://www.malone.edu/.

MARIETTA COLLEGE
MARIETTA, OHIO

General Independent, comprehensive, coed **Entrance** Moderately difficult **Setting** 120-acre small-town campus **Total enrollment** 1,262 **Student/faculty ratio** 12:1 **Application deadline** 4/15 (freshmen), rolling (transfer) **Freshmen** 94% were admitted **Housing** Yes **Expenses** Tuition $18,240; Room & Board $5196 **Undergraduates** 52% women, 10% part-time, 4% 25 or older, 0.4% Native American, 1% Hispanic American, 2% African American, 1% Asian American/Pacific Islander **The most frequently chosen baccalaureate fields are** business/marketing, education, social sciences and history **Academic program** English as a second language, advanced placement, accelerated degree program, self-designed majors, honors program, summer session, adult/continuing education programs, internships **Contact** Ms. Marke Vickers, Director of Admission, Marietta College, 215 Fifth Street, Marietta, OH 45750-4000. Telephone: 740-376-4600 or toll-free 800-331-7896. Fax: 740-376-8888. E-mail: admit@mcnet.marietta.edu. Web site: http://www.marietta.edu/.

THE MCGREGOR SCHOOL OF ANTIOCH UNIVERSITY
See Antioch University McGregor

MIAMI UNIVERSITY
OXFORD, OHIO

General State-related, university, coed **Entrance** Moderately difficult **Setting** 2,000-acre small-town campus **Total enrollment** 16,290 **Student/faculty ratio** 18:1 **Application deadline** 1/31 (freshmen), 5/1 (transfer) **Freshmen** 69% were admitted **Hous-**

ing Yes **Expenses** Tuition 6403; Room & Board 5590 **Undergraduates** 55% women, 3% part-time, 3% 25 or older, 0.5% Native American, 2% Hispanic American, 4% African American, 2% Asian American/Pacific Islander **The most frequently chosen baccalaureate fields are** business/marketing, education, social sciences and history **Academic program** Advanced placement, self-designed majors, honors program, summer session, adult/continuing education programs, internships **Contact** Michael E. Mills, Director, Undergraduate Admissions, Miami University, Oxford, OH 45056. Telephone: 513-529-5040. Fax: 513-529-1550. E-mail: admission@muohio.edu. Web site: http://www.muohio.edu/.

MOUNT CARMEL COLLEGE OF NURSING
COLUMBUS, OHIO

General Independent, 4-year **Total enrollment** 350 **Expenses** Tuition $8700; Room only $2592 **Contact** Ms. Merschel Menefield, Director of Admissions, Mount Carmel College of Nursing, 127 South Davis Avenue, Columbus, OH 43222. Telephone: 614-234-5800.

MOUNT UNION COLLEGE
ALLIANCE, OHIO

General Independent United Methodist, 4-year, coed **Entrance** Moderately difficult **Setting** 105-acre suburban campus **Total enrollment** 2,334 **Student/faculty ratio** 15:1 **Application deadline** Rolling (freshmen), rolling (transfer) **Freshmen** 84% were admitted **Housing** Yes **Expenses** Tuition 15,550; Room & Board 4560 **Undergraduates** 57% women, 10% part-time, 2% 25 or older, 0.4% Native American, 1% Hispanic American, 4% African American, 0.4% Asian American/Pacific Islander **The most frequently chosen baccalaureate fields are** business/marketing, education, parks and recreation **Academic program** English as a second language, advanced placement, accelerated degree program, self-designed majors, honors program, summer session, adult/continuing education programs, internships **Contact** Mr. Greg King, Director of Admissions and Enrollment Management, Mount Union College, 1972 Clark Avenue, Alliance, OH 44601. Telephone: 330-823-2590 or toll-free 800-334-6682 (in-state); 800-992-6682 (out-of-state). Fax: 330-823-3457. E-mail: admissn@muc.edu. Web site: http://www.muc.edu/.

MOUNT VERNON NAZARENE COLLEGE
MOUNT VERNON, OHIO

General Independent Nazarene, comprehensive, coed **Entrance** Moderately difficult **Setting** 210-acre small-town campus **Total enrollment** 1,961 **Student/faculty ratio** 18:1 **Application deadline** 5/30 (freshmen), 5/30 (transfer) **Freshmen** 88% were admitted **Housing** Yes **Expenses** Tuition $11,926; Room & Board $4203 **Undergraduates** 58% women, 5% part-time, 1% 25 or older, 0.3% Native American, 1% Hispanic American, 1% African American, 1% Asian American/Pacific Islander **The most frequently chosen baccalaureate fields are** business/marketing, biological/life sciences, education **Academic program** Advanced placement, honors program, summer session, adult/continuing education programs, internships **Contact** Rev. Ron Fox, Director of Admissions and Student Recruitment, Mount Vernon Nazarene College, 800 Martinsburg Road, Mount Vernon, OH 43050-9500. Telephone: 740-397-6862 Ext. 4510 or toll-free 800-782-2435. Fax: 740-393-0511. E-mail: admissions@mvnc.edu. Web site: http://www.mvnc.edu/.

MUSKINGUM COLLEGE
NEW CONCORD, OHIO

General Independent, comprehensive, coed, affiliated with Presbyterian Church (U.S.A.) **Contact** Mr. Doug Kellar, Director of Admission, Muskingum College, 163 Stormont Street, New Concord, OH 43762. Telephone: 740-826-8137 or toll-free 800-752-6082. Fax: 740-826-8100. E-mail: adminfo@muskingum.edu. Web site: http://www.muskingum.edu/.

NOTRE DAME COLLEGE OF OHIO
SOUTH EUCLID, OHIO

General Independent Roman Catholic, comprehensive, coed **Entrance** Moderately difficult **Setting** 53-acre suburban campus **Total enrollment** 878 **Student/faculty ratio** 9:1 **Application deadline** Rolling (freshmen), rolling (transfer) **Freshmen** 55% were admitted **Housing** Yes **Expenses** Tuition 13,886; Room & Board 5416 **Undergraduates** 75% 25 or older, 0% Native American, 1% Hispanic American, 31% African American, 1% Asian American/Pacific Islander **The most frequently chosen baccalaureate fields are** biological/life sciences, business/marketing, communications/communication technologies **Academic program** Advanced placement, accelerated degree program, self-designed majors, summer session, adult/continuing education programs, internships **Contact** Ms. Meredith Young, Director of Admissions, Notre Dame College of Ohio, 4545 College Road, South Euclid, OH 44121-4293. Telephone: 216-381-1680 Ext. 355 or toll-free 800-NDC-1680 Ext. 355. Fax: 216-381-3802. E-mail: admissions@ndc.edu. Web site: http://www.ndc.edu/.

OBERLIN COLLEGE
OBERLIN, OHIO

General Independent, comprehensive, coed **Entrance** Very difficult **Setting** 440-acre small-town campus **Total enrollment** 2,955 **Student/faculty ratio** 10:1 **Application deadline** 1/15 (freshmen), 3/15 (transfer) **Freshmen** 43% were admitted **Housing** Yes **Expenses** Tuition 25,530; Room & Board 6364 **Undergraduates** 59% women, 3% part-time, 1% 25 or older, 0% Native American, 3% Hispanic American, 7% African American, 6% Asian American/Pacific Islander **The most frequently chosen baccalaureate fields are** English, social sciences and history, visual/performing arts **Academic program** English as a second language, advanced placement,

Oberlin College *(continued)*

accelerated degree program, self-designed majors, honors program, internships **Contact** Ms. Debra Chermonte, Dean of Admissions and Financial Aid, Oberlin College, Admissions Office, Carnegie Building, Oberlin, OH 44074-1090. Telephone: 440-775-8411 or toll-free 800-622-OBIE. Fax: 440-775-6905. E-mail: college.admissions@oberlin.edu. Web site: http://www.oberlin.edu/.

OHIO DOMINICAN COLLEGE
COLUMBUS, OHIO

General Independent Roman Catholic, 4-year, coed **Entrance** Moderately difficult **Setting** 62-acre urban campus **Total enrollment** 2,085 **Student/faculty ratio** 18:1 **Application deadline** Rolling (freshmen), rolling (transfer) **Freshmen** 67% were admitted **Housing** Yes **Expenses** Tuition $10,910; Room & Board $5220 **Undergraduates** 69% women, 30% part-time, 41% 25 or older, 0.3% Native American, 1% Hispanic American, 26% African American, 1% Asian American/Pacific Islander **The most frequently chosen baccalaureate fields are** business/marketing, education, social sciences and history **Academic program** English as a second language, advanced placement, self-designed majors, honors program, summer session, adult/continuing education programs, internships **Contact** Ms. Vicki Thompson-Campbell, Director of Admissions, Ohio Dominican College, 1216 Sunbury Road, Columbus, OH 43219-2099. Telephone: 614-251-4500 or toll-free 800-854-2670. Fax: 614-251-0156. E-mail: admissions@odc.edu. Web site: http://www.odc.edu/.

OHIO NORTHERN UNIVERSITY
ADA, OHIO

General Independent United Methodist, comprehensive, coed **Entrance** Moderately difficult **Setting** 260-acre small-town campus **Total enrollment** 3,227 **Student/faculty ratio** 13:1 **Application deadline** 8/15 (freshmen), 8/15 (transfer) **Freshmen** 95% were admitted **Housing** Yes **Expenses** Tuition $21,435; Room & Board $5265 **Undergraduates** 50% women, 3% part-time, 3% 25 or older, 0.2% Native American, 0.5% Hispanic American, 2% African American, 2% Asian American/Pacific Islander **The most frequently chosen baccalaureate fields are** business/marketing, engineering/engineering technologies, health professions and related sciences **Academic program** Advanced placement, honors program, summer session, internships **Contact** Ms. Karen Condeni, Vice President of Admissions and Financial Aid, Ohio Northern University, 525 South Main, Ada, OH 45810-1599. Telephone: 419-772-2260 or toll-free 888-408-4ONU. Fax: 419-772-2313. E-mail: admissions-ug@onu.edu. Web site: http://www.onu.edu/.

THE OHIO STATE UNIVERSITY
COLUMBUS, OHIO

General State-supported, university, coed **Entrance** Moderately difficult **Setting** urban campus **Total enrollment** 47,952 **Student/faculty ratio** 13:1 **Application deadline** 2/15 (freshmen), 6/25 (transfer) **Freshmen** 72% were admitted **Housing** Yes **Expenses** Tuition 4761; Room & Board 5807 **Undergraduates** 49% women, 14% part-time, 11% 25 or older, 0.4% Native American, 2% Hispanic American, 8% African American, 5% Asian American/Pacific Islander **The most frequently chosen baccalaureate fields are** business/marketing, home economics/vocational home economics, social sciences and history **Academic program** English as a second language, advanced placement, accelerated degree program, self-designed majors, honors program, summer session, adult/continuing education programs, internships **Contact** Dr. Mabel G. Freeman, Director of Undergraduate Admissions and Vice President for First-Year Experience, The Ohio State University, 3rd Floor, Lincoln Tower, Columbus, OH 43210-1200. Telephone: 614-292-3974. Fax: 614-292-4818. E-mail: telecounseling@fa.adm.ohio-state.edu. Web site: http://www.osu.edu/.

THE OHIO STATE UNIVERSITY AT LIMA
LIMA, OHIO

General State-supported, 4-year, coed **Entrance** Noncompetitive **Setting** 565-acre small-town campus **Total enrollment** 1,600 **Student/faculty ratio** 13:1 **Application deadline** 7/1 (freshmen), 7/1 (transfer) **Freshmen** 72% were admitted **Housing** No **Expenses** Tuition 3351 **Undergraduates** 63% women, 16% part-time, 25% 25 or older **Academic program** English as a second language, advanced placement, accelerated degree program, honors program, summer session, adult/continuing education programs **Contact** Marissa Christoff Snyder, Admissions Counselor, The Ohio State University at Lima, 4240 Campus Drive, Lima, OH 45804. Telephone: 419-995-8220. E-mail: admissions@lima.ohio-state.edu. Web site: http://www.ohio-state.edu/.

THE OHIO STATE UNIVERSITY AT MARION
MARION, OHIO

Contact Mr. Mathrey Moreau, Admissions Coordinator, The Ohio State University at Marion, 1465 Mount Vernon Avenue, Marion, OH 43302-5695. Telephone: 740-389-6786 Ext. 6337. Web site: http://www.ohio-state.edu/.

THE OHIO STATE UNIVERSITY–MANSFIELD CAMPUS
MANSFIELD, OHIO

General State-supported, 4-year, coed **Entrance** Noncompetitive **Setting** 593-acre small-town campus **Total enrollment** 1,583 **Application deadline** 7/1 (freshmen), 7/1 (transfer) **Freshmen** 94% were admitted **Housing** No **Expenses** Tuition $3351 **Undergraduates** 24% 25 or older **Academic program** English as a second language, advanced placement, accelerated degree program, honors program, summer session, adult/continuing education programs

Contact Mr. Henry D. Thomas, Coordinator of Admissions and Financial Aid, The Ohio State University–Mansfield Campus, 1680 University Drive, Mansfield, OH 44906-1599. Telephone: 419-755-4226. Web site: http://www.ohio-state.edu/.

THE OHIO STATE UNIVERSITY–NEWARK CAMPUS
NEWARK, OHIO

General State-supported, 4-year, coed **Entrance** Noncompetitive **Setting** 101-acre small-town campus **Total enrollment** 2,025 **Student/faculty ratio** 23:1 **Application deadline** 7/1 (freshmen), 7/1 (transfer) **Freshmen** 97% were admitted **Housing** No **Expenses** Tuition $3351; Room only $3600 **Undergraduates** 24% 25 or older, 1% Native American, 1% Hispanic American, 3% African American, 1% Asian American/Pacific Islander **Academic program** English as a second language, advanced placement, accelerated degree program, honors program, summer session, adult/continuing education programs **Contact** Ms. Ann Donahue, Director of Enrollment, The Ohio State University–Newark Campus, 1179 University Drive, Newark, OH 43055-1797. Telephone: 614-366-9333. Web site: http://www.ohio-state.edu/.

OHIO UNIVERSITY
ATHENS, OHIO

General State-supported, university, coed **Entrance** Moderately difficult **Setting** 1,700-acre small-town campus **Total enrollment** 19,667 **Student/faculty ratio** 21:1 **Application deadline** 2/1 (freshmen), 5/15 (transfer) **Freshmen** 77% were admitted **Housing** Yes **Expenses** Tuition $5085; Room & Board $5922 **Undergraduates** 55% women, 6% part-time, 6% 25 or older, 0.3% Native American, 1% Hispanic American, 3% African American, 1% Asian American/Pacific Islander **The most frequently chosen baccalaureate fields are** business/marketing, education, English **Academic program** English as a second language, advanced placement, accelerated degree program, self-designed majors, honors program, summer session, adult/continuing education programs, internships **Contact** Mr. N. Kip Howard Jr., Director of Admissions, Ohio University, Athens, OH 45701-2979. Telephone: 740-593-4100. E-mail: uadmiss1@ohiou.edu. Web site: http://www.ohio.edu/.

OHIO UNIVERSITY–CHILLICOTHE
CHILLICOTHE, OHIO

General State-supported, 4-year, coed **Entrance** Noncompetitive **Setting** 124-acre small-town campus **Total enrollment** 1,726 **Application deadline** 9/1 (freshmen), 9/1 (transfer) **Freshmen** 94% were admitted **Housing** No **Expenses** Tuition 3033 **Undergraduates** 35% 25 or older **Academic program** Advanced placement, accelerated degree program, self-designed majors, summer session, adult/continuing education programs, internships **Contact** Mr. Richard R. Whitney, Director of Student Services, Ohio University–Chillicothe, 571 West Fifth Street, Chillicothe, OH 45601. Telephone: 740-774-7242 or toll-free 877-462-6824 (in-state). Fax: 740-774-7295. Web site: http://www.ohio.edu/chillicothe/.

OHIO UNIVERSITY–EASTERN
ST. CLAIRSVILLE, OHIO

General State-supported, 4-year, coed **Entrance** Noncompetitive **Setting** 300-acre rural campus **Total enrollment** 1,118 **Application deadline** Rolling (freshmen), rolling (transfer) **Housing** No **Expenses** Tuition $3033 **Undergraduates** 68% women, 27% part-time, 32% 25 or older, 0% Native American, 0.1% Hispanic American, 2% African American, 0.1% Asian American/Pacific Islander **Academic program** Advanced placement, accelerated degree program, self-designed majors, summer session, adult/continuing education programs **Contact** Mr. Kevin Chenoweth, Student Services Manager, Ohio University–Eastern, 45425 National Road, St. Clairsville, OH 43950-9724. Telephone: 614-695-1720 Ext. 209 or toll-free 800-648-3331 (in-state). E-mail: chenowet@ohio.edu.

OHIO UNIVERSITY–LANCASTER
LANCASTER, OHIO

General State-supported, comprehensive, coed **Entrance** Noncompetitive **Setting** 360-acre small-town campus **Total enrollment** 1,585 **Application deadline** Rolling (freshmen), rolling (transfer) **Housing** No **Expenses** Tuition $3033 **Undergraduates** 46% 25 or older **Academic program** Advanced placement, accelerated degree program, self-designed majors, summer session, adult/continuing education programs **Contact** Dr. Scott Shepherd, Director of Student Services, Ohio University–Lancaster, 1570 Granville Pike, Lancaster, OH 43130-1097. Telephone: 740-654-6711 Ext. 209 or toll-free 888-446-4468. E-mail: shepherd@ohiou.edu.

OHIO UNIVERSITY–ZANESVILLE
ZANESVILLE, OHIO

General State-supported, comprehensive, coed **Entrance** Noncompetitive **Setting** 179-acre rural campus **Total enrollment** 1,357 **Application deadline** Rolling (freshmen), rolling (transfer) **Freshmen** 100% were admitted **Housing** No **Expenses** Tuition $3048 **Undergraduates** 68% women, 33% part-time, 33% 25 or older, 0.4% Native American, 1% Hispanic American, 3% African American, 1% Asian American/Pacific Islander **Academic program** Advanced placement, self-designed majors, summer session, adult/continuing education programs **Contact** Mrs. Karen Ragsdale, Student Services Secretary, Ohio University–Zanesville, 1425 Newark Road, Zanesville, OH 43701-2695. Telephone: 740-588-1440. Fax: 740-453-6161. Web site: http://www.zanesvile.ohiou.edu/.

OHIO WESLEYAN UNIVERSITY
DELAWARE, OHIO

General Independent United Methodist, 4-year, coed **Entrance** Very difficult **Setting** 200-acre small-town

Ohio Wesleyan University *(continued)*

campus **Total enrollment** 1,880 **Student/faculty ratio** 13:1 **Application deadline** 3/15 (freshmen), 5/15 (transfer) **Freshmen** 81% were admitted **Housing** Yes **Expenses** Tuition $21,880; Room & Board $6610 **Undergraduates** 52% women, 2% part-time, 1% 25 or older, 0.2% Native American, 2% Hispanic American, 5% African American, 2% Asian American/Pacific Islander **The most frequently chosen baccalaureate fields are** business/marketing, psychology, social sciences and history **Academic program** Advanced placement, self-designed majors, honors program, summer session, internships **Contact** Ms. Karen L. Raftus, Director of Admission, Ohio Wesleyan University, 61 South Sandusky Street, Delaware, OH 43015. Telephone: 740-368-3039 or toll-free 800-922-8953. Fax: 740-368-3315. E-mail: owuadmit@cc.owu.edu. Web site: http://www.owu.edu/.

OTTERBEIN COLLEGE
WESTERVILLE, OHIO

General Independent United Methodist, comprehensive, coed **Entrance** Moderately difficult **Setting** 140-acre suburban campus **Total enrollment** 2,917 **Student/faculty ratio** 14:1 **Application deadline** Rolling (freshmen), rolling (transfer) **Freshmen** 85% were admitted **Housing** Yes **Expenses** Tuition $16,911; Room & Board $5289 **Undergraduates** 64% women, 27% part-time, 37% 25 or older **The most frequently chosen baccalaureate fields are** business/marketing, communications/communication technologies, education **Academic program** English as a second language, advanced placement, self-designed majors, honors program, summer session, adult/continuing education programs, internships **Contact** Dr. Cass Johnson, Director of Admissions, Otterbein College, One Otterbein College, Westerville, OH 43081-9924. Telephone: 614-823-1500 or toll-free 800-488-8144. Fax: 614-823-1200. E-mail: uotterb@otterbein.edu. Web site: http://www.otterbein.edu/.

PONTIFICAL COLLEGE JOSEPHINUM
COLUMBUS, OHIO

General Independent Roman Catholic, comprehensive, coed, primarily men **Entrance** Minimally difficult **Setting** 100-acre suburban campus **Total enrollment** 106 **Application deadline** Rolling (freshmen), rolling (transfer) **Freshmen** 86% were admitted **Housing** Yes **Expenses** Tuition $8276; Room & Board $5136 **Undergraduates** 16% 25 or older **Academic program** English as a second language, advanced placement, internships **Contact** Arminda Crawford, Secretary for Admissions, Pontifical College Josephinum, 7625 North High Street, Columbus, OH 43235-1498. Telephone: 614-885-5585 Ext. 436. Web site: http://www.pcj.edu/.

SHAWNEE STATE UNIVERSITY
PORTSMOUTH, OHIO

General State-supported, 4-year, coed **Entrance** Noncompetitive **Setting** small-town campus **Total enrollment** 3,280 **Student/faculty ratio** 17:1 **Application deadline** Rolling (freshmen), rolling (transfer) **Freshmen** 100% were admitted **Housing** Yes **Expenses** Tuition $3162; Room & Board $4588 **Undergraduates** 63% women, 22% part-time, 32% 25 or older, 1% Native American, 1% Hispanic American, 2% African American, 0.2% Asian American/Pacific Islander **The most frequently chosen baccalaureate fields are** business/marketing, education, social sciences and history **Academic program** Advanced placement, honors program, summer session, adult/continuing education programs, internships **Contact** Mr. Bob Trusz, Director of Admission, Shawnee State University, 940 Second Street, Commons Building, Portsmouth, OH 45662. Telephone: 740-355-2610 Ext. 610 or toll-free 800-959-2SSU. Fax: 740-355-2111. E-mail: admsn@shawnee.edu. Web site: http://www.shawnee.edu/.

TIFFIN UNIVERSITY
TIFFIN, OHIO

General Independent, comprehensive, coed **Entrance** Minimally difficult **Setting** 108-acre small-town campus **Total enrollment** 1,558 **Student/faculty ratio** 21:1 **Application deadline** Rolling (freshmen), rolling (transfer) **Freshmen** 80% were admitted **Housing** Yes **Expenses** Tuition $11,130; Room & Board $5100 **Undergraduates** 52% women, 25% part-time, 22% 25 or older, 2% Hispanic American, 12% African American, 5% Asian American/Pacific Islander **The most frequently chosen baccalaureate fields are** business/marketing, computer/information sciences, protective services/public administration **Academic program** Advanced placement, accelerated degree program, summer session, adult/continuing education programs, internships **Contact** Mr. Ron Schumacher, Director of Admissions, Tiffin University, 155 Miami Street, Tiffin, OH 44883-2161. Telephone: 419-448-3425 or toll-free 800-968-6446. Fax: 419-443-5006. E-mail: admiss@tiffin.edu. Web site: http://www.tiffin.edu/.

THE UNION INSTITUTE
CINCINNATI, OHIO

General Independent, university, coed **Entrance** Moderately difficult **Setting** 5-acre urban campus **Total enrollment** 1,812 **Student/faculty ratio** 16:1 **Application deadline** 10/1 (freshmen), 10/1 (transfer) **Freshmen** 83% were admitted **Housing** No **Expenses** Tuition 6528 **Undergraduates** 66% women, 43% part-time, 98% 25 or older, 1% Native American, 9% Hispanic American, 37% African American, 1% Asian American/Pacific Islander **The most frequently chosen baccalaureate fields are** business/marketing, protective services/public administration, psychology **Academic program** Advanced placement, accelerated degree program, self-designed majors, summer session, adult/continuing education programs **Contact** Ms. Lisa Schrenger, Director, Admissions, The Union Institute, 440 East McMillan Street, Cincinnati, OH 45206-1925. Telephone: 513-861-6400 or toll-free 800-486-3116. E-mail: admissions@tui.edu. Web site: http://www.tui.edu/.

THE UNIVERSITY OF AKRON
AKRON, OHIO

General State-supported, university, coed **Entrance** Noncompetitive **Setting** 170-acre urban campus **Total enrollment** 21,556 **Student/faculty ratio** 17:1 **Application deadline** 8/15 (freshmen), 8/15 (transfer) **Freshmen** 90% were admitted **Housing** Yes **Expenses** Tuition $4496; Room & Board $5350 **Undergraduates** 54% women, 35% part-time, 30% 25 or older, 1% Native American, 1% Hispanic American, 14% African American, 2% Asian American/Pacific Islander **The most frequently chosen baccalaureate fields are** business/marketing, education, engineering/engineering technologies **Academic program** English as a second language, advanced placement, accelerated degree program, self-designed majors, honors program, summer session, adult/continuing education programs, internships **Contact** Ms. Kim Gentile, Interim Director of Admissions, The University of Akron, 381 Buchtel Common, Akron, OH 44325-2001. Telephone: 330-972-6428 or toll-free 800-655-4884. Fax: 330-972-7676. E-mail: admissions@uakron.edu. Web site: http://www.uakron.edu/.

UNIVERSITY OF CINCINNATI
CINCINNATI, OHIO

General State-supported, university, coed **Entrance** Moderately difficult **Setting** 137-acre urban campus **Total enrollment** 27,327 **Application deadline** Rolling (freshmen), rolling (transfer) **Freshmen** 82% were admitted **Housing** Yes **Expenses** Tuition $5716; Room & Board $6720 **Undergraduates** 49% women, 27% part-time, 16% 25 or older, 0.4% Native American, 1% Hispanic American, 14% African American, 3% Asian American/Pacific Islander **The most frequently chosen baccalaureate fields are** business/marketing, engineering/engineering technologies, health professions and related sciences **Academic program** English as a second language, advanced placement, accelerated degree program, self-designed majors, honors program, summer session, adult/continuing education programs, internships **Contact** Terry Davis, Director of Admissions, University of Cincinnati, PO Box 210091, Cincinnati, OH 45221-0091. Telephone: 513-556-1100 or toll-free 800-827-8728 (in-state). Fax: 513-556-1105. E-mail: admissions@uc.edu. Web site: http://www.uc.edu/.

UNIVERSITY OF DAYTON
DAYTON, OHIO

General Independent Roman Catholic, university, coed **Entrance** Moderately difficult **Setting** 110-acre suburban campus **Total enrollment** 10,310 **Student/faculty ratio** 15:1 **Application deadline** Rolling (freshmen), 6/15 (transfer) **Freshmen** 79% were admitted **Housing** Yes **Expenses** Tuition 16,070; Room & Board 5080 **Undergraduates** 51% women, 7% part-time, 4% 25 or older, 0.1% Native American, 2% Hispanic American, 3% African American, 1% Asian American/Pacific Islander **Academic program** English as a second language, advanced placement, accelerated degree program, honors program, summer session, adult/continuing education programs, internships **Contact** Mr. Myron H. Achbach, Director of Admission, University of Dayton, 300 College Park, Dayton, OH 45469-1300. Telephone: 937-229-4411 or toll-free 800-837-7433. Fax: 937-229-4729. E-mail: admission@udayton.edu. Web site: http://www.udayton.edu/.

THE UNIVERSITY OF FINDLAY
FINDLAY, OHIO

General Independent, comprehensive, coed, affiliated with Church of God **Entrance** Moderately difficult **Setting** 160-acre small-town campus **Total enrollment** 4,510 **Student/faculty ratio** 19:1 **Application deadline** 7/1 (freshmen), 8/1 (transfer) **Freshmen** 81% were admitted **Housing** Yes **Expenses** Tuition 16,020; Room & Board 5960 **Undergraduates** 57% women, 22% part-time, 31% 25 or older, 0.5% Native American, 3% Hispanic American, 4% African American, 4% Asian American/Pacific Islander **The most frequently chosen baccalaureate fields are** business/marketing, engineering/engineering technologies, health professions and related sciences **Academic program** English as a second language, advanced placement, accelerated degree program, self-designed majors, honors program, summer session, adult/continuing education programs, internships **Contact** Curtis Davidson, Director, Undergraduate Admissions, The University of Findlay, 1000 North Main Street, Findlay, OH 45840-3653. Telephone: 419-424-4638 or toll-free 800-548-0932. Fax: 419-424-4898. E-mail: admissions@findlay.edu. Web site: http://www.findlay.edu/.

UNIVERSITY OF PHOENIX–OHIO CAMPUS
INDEPENDENCE, OHIO

General Proprietary, comprehensive, coed **Entrance** Noncompetitive **Total enrollment** 66,534 **Student/faculty ratio** 13:1 **Application deadline** Rolling (freshmen), rolling (transfer) **Expenses** Tuition $7740 **Undergraduates** 56% women, 86% 25 or older, 2% Native American, 18% Hispanic American, 13% African American, 6% Asian American/Pacific Islander **Academic program** Advanced placement, accelerated degree program, adult/continuing education programs **Contact** Ms. Beth Barilla, Director of Admissions, University of Phoenix–Ohio Campus, 4615 East Elwood Street, Phoenix, AZ 85040-1948. Telephone: 480-927-0099 Ext. 1218. Fax: 480-594-1758. E-mail: beth.barilla@apollogrp.edu. Web site: http://www.phoenix.edu/.

UNIVERSITY OF RIO GRANDE
RIO GRANDE, OHIO

General Independent, comprehensive, coed **Entrance** Noncompetitive **Setting** 170-acre rural campus **Total enrollment** 2,107 **Student/faculty ratio** 17:1 **Application deadline** Rolling (freshmen), rolling (transfer) **Freshmen** 100% were admitted **Housing** Yes

University of Rio Grande *(continued)*

Expenses Tuition $8805; Room & Board $5169 **Undergraduates** 25% 25 or older **The most frequently chosen baccalaureate fields are** business/ marketing, communications/communication technologies, education **Academic program** English as a second language, advanced placement, accelerated degree program, self-designed majors, honors program, summer session, adult/continuing education programs, internships **Contact** Mr. Mark F. Abell, Executive Director of Admissions, University of Rio Grande, PO Box 500, Rio Grande, OH 45674. Telephone: 740-245-5353 Ext. 7206 or toll-free 800-282-7201 (in-state). Fax: 740-245-7260. E-mail: mabell@urgrgcc.edu. Web site: http://www.rio.edu/.

UNIVERSITY OF TOLEDO
TOLEDO, OHIO

General State-supported, university, coed **Entrance** Noncompetitive **Setting** 407-acre suburban campus **Total enrollment** 20,411 **Application deadline** Rolling (freshmen), rolling (transfer) **Freshmen** 95% were admitted **Housing** Yes **Expenses** Tuition $4681; Room & Board $4798 **Undergraduates** 54% women, 29% part-time, 25% 25 or older, 1% Native American, 2% Hispanic American, 14% African American, 2% Asian American/Pacific Islander **Academic program** English as a second language, advanced placement, accelerated degree program, self-designed majors, honors program, summer session, adult/continuing education programs, internships **Contact** Mr. Scott Lingrell, Associate Director for High School Relations, University of Toledo, 2801 West Bancroft, Toledo, OH 43606-3398. Telephone: 419-530-2077 or toll-free 800-5TOLEDO (in-state). Fax: 419-530-4504. E-mail: adm0017@uofT01.utoledo.edu. Web site: http://www.utoledo.edu/.

URBANA UNIVERSITY
URBANA, OHIO

General Independent, comprehensive, coed, affiliated with Church of the New Jerusalem **Entrance** Moderately difficult **Setting** 128-acre small-town campus **Total enrollment** 1,372 **Student/faculty ratio** 18:1 **Application deadline** Rolling (freshmen), rolling (transfer) **Freshmen** 73% were admitted **Housing** Yes **Expenses** Tuition 11,548; Room & Board 5000 **Undergraduates** 51% women, 34% part-time, 0.3% Native American, 1% Hispanic American, 16% African American, 0.2% Asian American/Pacific Islander **Academic program** English as a second language, advanced placement, accelerated degree program, self-designed majors, summer session, adult/continuing education programs, internships **Contact** Ms. Mona Newcomer, Admissions Office Manager, Urbana University, 579 College Way, Urbana, OH 43078-2091. Telephone: 937-484-1356 or toll-free 800-787-2262 (in-state). Fax: 937-484-1389. E-mail: admiss@urbana.edu. Web site: http://www.urbana.edu/.

URSULINE COLLEGE
PEPPER PIKE, OHIO

General Independent Roman Catholic, comprehensive, coed, primarily women **Entrance** Minimally difficult **Setting** 112-acre suburban campus **Total enrollment** 1,252 **Student/faculty ratio** 10:1 **Application deadline** Rolling (freshmen), rolling (transfer) **Freshmen** 94% were admitted **Housing** Yes **Expenses** Tuition $13,500; Room & Board $4560 **Undergraduates** 93% women, 51% part-time, 57% 25 or older, 0.2% Native American, 2% Hispanic American, 23% African American, 2% Asian American/ Pacific Islander **Academic program** Advanced placement, self-designed majors, summer session, adult/ continuing education programs, internships **Contact** Ms. Jill Bakley-Jeppe, Director of Admissions, Ursuline College, 2550 Lander Road, Pepper Pike, OH 44124. Telephone: 440-449-4203 or toll-free 888-URSULINE (in-state). Fax: 440-684-6138. E-mail: dgiaco@en.com. Web site: http://www.ursuline.edu/.

WALSH UNIVERSITY
NORTH CANTON, OHIO

General Independent Roman Catholic, comprehensive, coed **Entrance** Moderately difficult **Setting** 100-acre small-town campus **Total enrollment** 1,545 **Student/faculty ratio** 12:1 **Application deadline** Rolling (freshmen), rolling (transfer) **Freshmen** 82% were admitted **Housing** Yes **Expenses** Tuition $12,410; Room & Board $5600 **Undergraduates** 60% women, 28% part-time, 1% Native American, 1% Hispanic American, 6% African American, 1% Asian American/ Pacific Islander **The most frequently chosen baccalaureate fields are** business/marketing, biological/ life sciences, education **Academic program** English as a second language, advanced placement, accelerated degree program, self-designed majors, honors program, summer session, adult/continuing education programs, internships **Contact** Mr. Doug Swartz, Director of Admissions, Walsh University, 2020 Easton Street, NW, North Canton, OH 44720-3396. Telephone: 330-490-7172 or toll-free 800-362-9846 (in-state); 800-362-8846 (out-of-state). Fax: 330-490-7165. E-mail: admissions@alex.walsh.edu. Web site: http://www.walsh.edu/.

WILBERFORCE UNIVERSITY
WILBERFORCE, OHIO

General Independent, 4-year, coed, affiliated with African Methodist Episcopal Church **Entrance** Minimally difficult **Setting** 125-acre rural campus **Total enrollment** 908 **Student/faculty ratio** 13:1 **Application deadline** 7/1 (freshmen), 7/1 (transfer) **Freshmen** 22% were admitted **Housing** Yes **Expenses** Tuition 9800; Room & Board 5060 **Undergraduates** 59% women, 10% 25 or older, 0.4% Hispanic American, 91% African American, 0.2% Asian American/ Pacific Islander **Academic program** Advanced placement, honors program **Contact** Mr. Kenneth C. Christmon, Director of Admissions, Wilberforce University,)(Box 1001, Wilberforce, OH 45384-1001.

Telephone: 937-708-5789 or toll-free 800-367-8568. Fax: 937-376-4751. E-mail: admissions@shorter.wilberforce.edu. Web site: http://www.wilberforce.edu/.

WILMINGTON COLLEGE
WILMINGTON, OHIO

General Independent Friends, 4-year, coed **Entrance** Moderately difficult **Setting** 1,465-acre small-town campus **Total enrollment** 1,262 **Student/faculty ratio** 18:1 **Application deadline** Rolling (freshmen), rolling (transfer) **Freshmen** 81% were admitted **Housing** Yes **Expenses** Tuition $14,566; Room & Board $5220 **Undergraduates** 54% women, 5% part-time, 0.1% Native American, 0.1% Hispanic American, 7% African American, 0.1% Asian American/Pacific Islander **Academic program** Advanced placement, self-designed majors, honors program, summer session, adult/continuing education programs, internships **Contact** Tina Garland, Interim Director of Admission and Financial Aid, Wilmington College, Pyle Center Box 1325, 251 Ludovic Street, Wilmington, OH 45177. Telephone: 937-382-6661 Ext. 260 or toll-free 800-341-9318 Ext. 260. Fax: 937-382-7077. E-mail: admission@wilmington.edu. Web site: http://www.wilmington.edu/.

WITTENBERG UNIVERSITY
SPRINGFIELD, OHIO

General Independent, comprehensive, coed, affiliated with Evangelical Lutheran Church **Entrance** Moderately difficult **Setting** 71-acre suburban campus **Total enrollment** 2,274 **Student/faculty ratio** 14:1 **Application deadline** 3/15 (freshmen), rolling (transfer) **Freshmen** 88% were admitted **Housing** Yes **Expenses** Tuition $21,182; Room & Board $5336 **Undergraduates** 57% women, 6% part-time, 2% 25 or older, 0.3% Native American, 1% Hispanic American, 6% African American, 1% Asian American/Pacific Islander **Academic program** English as a second language, advanced placement, accelerated degree program, self-designed majors, honors program, summer session, adult/continuing education programs, internships **Contact** Mr. Kenneth G. Benne, Dean of Admissions, Wittenberg University, PO Box 720, Springfield, OH 45501-0720. Telephone: 937-327-6314 Ext. 6366 or toll-free 800-677-7558 Ext. 6314. Fax: 937-327-6379. E-mail: admission@wittenberg.edu. Web site: http://www.wittenberg.edu/.

WRIGHT STATE UNIVERSITY
DAYTON, OHIO

General State-supported, university, coed **Entrance** Minimally difficult **Setting** 557-acre suburban campus **Total enrollment** 14,773 **Student/faculty ratio** 18:1 **Application deadline** Rolling (freshmen), rolling (transfer) **Freshmen** 91% were admitted **Housing** Yes **Expenses** Tuition $4335; Room & Board $4700 **Undergraduates** 57% women, 19% part-time, 31% 25 or older, 0.3% Native American, 1% Hispanic American, 11% African American, 2% Asian American/Pacific Islander **The most frequently chosen baccalaureate fields are** business/marketing, education, liberal arts/general studies **Academic program** English as a second language, advanced placement, self-designed majors, honors program, summer session, adult/continuing education programs, internships **Contact** Ms. Cathy Davis, Director of Undergraduate Admissions, Wright State University, 3640 Colonel Glenn Highway, Dayton, OH 45435. Telephone: 937-775-5700 or toll-free 800-247-1770. Fax: 937-775-5795. E-mail: admissions@wright.edu. Web site: http://www.wright.edu/.

XAVIER UNIVERSITY
CINCINNATI, OHIO

General Independent Roman Catholic, comprehensive, coed **Entrance** Moderately difficult **Setting** 100-acre suburban campus **Total enrollment** 6,523 **Student/faculty ratio** 15:1 **Application deadline** 3/15 (freshmen), rolling (transfer) **Freshmen** 88% were admitted **Housing** Yes **Expenses** Tuition $15,880; Room & Board $6940 **Undergraduates** 59% women, 17% part-time, 16% 25 or older, 0.1% Native American, 1% Hispanic American, 9% African American, 2% Asian American/Pacific Islander **The most frequently chosen baccalaureate fields are** business/marketing, education, liberal arts/general studies **Academic program** English as a second language, advanced placement, honors program, summer session, adult/continuing education programs, internships **Contact** Mr. Marc Camille, Dean of Admission, Xavier University, 3800 Victory Parkway, Cincinnati, OH 45207-5311. Telephone: 513-745-3301 or toll-free 800-344-4698. Fax: 513-745-4319. E-mail: xuadmit@admin.xu.edu. Web site: http://www.xu.edu/.

YOUNGSTOWN STATE UNIVERSITY
YOUNGSTOWN, OHIO

General State-supported, comprehensive, coed **Entrance** Noncompetitive **Setting** 150-acre urban campus **Total enrollment** 11,787 **Application deadline** 7/15 (freshmen), 7/15 (transfer) **Freshmen** 62% were admitted **Housing** Yes **Expenses** Tuition 3994; Room & Board 4800 **Undergraduates** 53% women, 23% part-time, 25% 25 or older, 0.3% Native American, 2% Hispanic American, 9% African American, 1% Asian American/Pacific Islander **The most frequently chosen baccalaureate fields are** business/marketing, education, protective services/public administration **Academic program** English as a second language, advanced placement, accelerated degree program, self-designed majors, honors program, summer session, adult/continuing education programs, internships **Contact** Dr. Jane S. Reid, Director of Undergraduate Recruitment and Admissions, Youngstown State University, One University Plaza, Youngstown, OH 44555-0001. Telephone: 330-742-2000 or toll-free 877-468-6978. Fax: 330-742-3674. E-mail: nsrysu@ysub.edu. Web site: http://www.ysu.edu/.

OKLAHOMA

AMERICAN BIBLE COLLEGE AND SEMINARY
OKLAHOMA CITY, OKLAHOMA

General Independent interdenominational, comprehensive, coed **Entrance** Noncompetitive **Setting** 1-acre small-town campus **Total enrollment** 484 **Student/faculty ratio** 8:1 **Housing** No **Expenses** Tuition 2916 **Undergraduates** 45% women, 62% part-time, 90% 25 or older, 0% Native American, 22% Hispanic American, 36% African American, 10% Asian American/Pacific Islander **Academic program** Advanced placement, summer session, adult/continuing education programs, internships **Contact** Dr. Mitchel Beville, Director of Admissions, American Bible College and Seminary, 4300 Highline Boulevard #202, Oklahoma City, OK 73108. Telephone: 405-945-0100 or toll-free 800-488-2528. Fax: 405-945-0311. E-mail: info@abcs.edu. Web site: http://www.abcs.edu/.

BARTLESVILLE WESLEYAN COLLEGE
See Oklahoma Wesleyan College

CAMERON UNIVERSITY
LAWTON, OKLAHOMA

General State-supported, comprehensive, coed **Entrance** Minimally difficult **Setting** 160-acre suburban campus **Total enrollment** 5,002 **Student/faculty ratio** 20:1 **Application deadline** Rolling (freshmen), rolling (transfer) **Freshmen** 91% were admitted **Housing** Yes **Expenses** Tuition $2090; Room & Board $2746 **Undergraduates** 56% women, 44% part-time, 46% 25 or older, 5% Native American, 7% Hispanic American, 20% African American, 4% Asian American/Pacific Islander **The most frequently chosen baccalaureate fields are** business/marketing, education, social sciences and history **Academic program** Advanced placement, accelerated degree program, honors program, summer session, adult/continuing education programs **Contact** Ms. Brenda Dally, Coordinator of Student Recruitment, Cameron University, Cameron University, Attention: Admissions, 2800 West Gore Boulevard, Lawton, OK 73505. Telephone: 580-581-2837 or toll-free 888-454-7600. Fax: 580-581-5514. E-mail: admiss@cua.cameron.edu. Web site: http://www.cameron.edu/.

EAST CENTRAL UNIVERSITY
ADA, OKLAHOMA

General State-supported, comprehensive, coed **Entrance** Moderately difficult **Setting** 140-acre small-town campus **Total enrollment** 4,110 **Student/faculty ratio** 19:1 **Application deadline** 9/1 (freshmen), 9/1 (transfer) **Housing** Yes **Expenses** Tuition $1962; Room & Board $1167 **Undergraduates** 60% women, 15% part-time, 37% 25 or older, 18% Native American, 1% Hispanic American, 3% African American, 1% Asian American/Pacific Islander **The most frequently chosen baccalaureate fields are** business/marketing, education, parks and recreation **Academic program** Advanced placement, accelerated degree program, honors program, summer session, adult/continuing education programs, internships **Contact** Ms. Pamela Armstrong, Registrar, East Central University, Registry Office PMBJ8, 1100 East 14th Street, Ada, OK 74820-6999. Telephone: 580-332-8000 Ext. 239. Fax: 580-310-5432. E-mail: parmstro@mailclerk.ecok.edu. Web site: http://www.ecok.edu/.

HILLSDALE FREE WILL BAPTIST COLLEGE
MOORE, OKLAHOMA

General Independent Free Will Baptist, 4-year, coed **Entrance** Noncompetitive **Setting** 40-acre suburban campus **Total enrollment** 256 **Student/faculty ratio** 15:1 **Application deadline** Rolling (freshmen), rolling (transfer) **Housing** Yes **Expenses** Tuition 6290; Room & Board 4040 **Undergraduates** 37% women, 16% part-time, 12% 25 or older, 8% Native American, 2% Hispanic American, 7% African American, 0% Asian American/Pacific Islander **The most frequently chosen baccalaureate field is** philosophy, religion, and theology **Academic program** English as a second language, advanced placement, accelerated degree program, summer session, adult/continuing education programs, internships **Contact** Ms. Sue Chaffin, Registrar/Assistant Director of Admissions, Hillsdale Free Will Baptist College, PO Box 7208, Moore, OK 73153-1208. Telephone: 405-912-9005. Fax: 405-912-9050. E-mail: gosaints@flash.net. Web site: http://www.hc.edu.

LANGSTON UNIVERSITY
LANGSTON, OKLAHOMA

General State-supported, comprehensive, coed **Entrance** Minimally difficult **Setting** 40-acre rural campus **Total enrollment** 3,398 **Application deadline** Rolling (freshmen), rolling (transfer) **Freshmen** 18% were admitted **Housing** Yes **Expenses** Tuition $1713; Room & Board $2964 **Undergraduates** 58% women, 39% part-time, 20% 25 or older **The most frequently chosen baccalaureate fields are** education, health professions and related sciences, psychology **Academic program** Advanced placement, accelerated degree program, honors program, summer session, adult/continuing education programs, internships **Contact** Ms. Vickie Alexander, Langston University, Langston, OK 73050. Telephone: 405-466-3231. Fax: 405-466-3381. Web site: http://www.lunet.edu/.

METROPOLITAN COLLEGE
OKLAHOMA CITY, OKLAHOMA

General Proprietary, 4-year, coed, primarily women **Entrance** Minimally difficult **Total enrollment** 140 **Expenses** Tuition $6593 **Undergraduates** 94%

women, 45% part-time, 7% Native American, 1% Hispanic American, 34% African American **Contact** Mr. Keith Wells, Admissions Director, Metropolitan College, 2901 North Classen Boulevard, Suite 200, Oklahoma City, OK 73106. Telephone: 405-528-5000. Web site: http://www.metropolitancollege.edu/.

METROPOLITAN COLLEGE
TULSA, OKLAHOMA

General Proprietary, 4-year, coed, primarily women **Entrance** Minimally difficult **Total enrollment** 96 **Freshmen** 67% were admitted **Expenses** Tuition 6535 **Undergraduates** 96% women, 85% 25 or older, 13% Native American, 2% Hispanic American, 22% African American **Academic program** Accelerated degree program, adult/continuing education programs, internships **Contact** Ms. Sandra Pella, Admission Representative, Metropolitan College, 4528 South Sheridan Road, Suite 105, Tulsa, OK 74145-1011. Telephone: 918-627-9300. Web site: http://www.metropolitancollege.edu/.

MID-AMERICA BIBLE COLLEGE
OKLAHOMA CITY, OKLAHOMA

General Independent, 4-year, coed, affiliated with Church of God **Entrance** Noncompetitive **Setting** 145-acre suburban campus **Total enrollment** 613 **Student/faculty ratio** 19:1 **Application deadline** Rolling (freshmen), rolling (transfer) **Freshmen** 100% were admitted **Housing** Yes **Expenses** Tuition $6244; Room & Board $5266 **Undergraduates** 48% women, 11% part-time, 53% 25 or older, 3% Native American, 4% Hispanic American, 9% African American, 1% Asian American/Pacific Islander **The most frequently chosen baccalaureate fields are** business/marketing, philosophy, religion, and theology, psychology **Academic program** Advanced placement, accelerated degree program, summer session, adult/continuing education programs, internships **Contact** Ms. Dianna Rea, Director of College Relations, Mid-America Bible College, 3500 Southwest 119th Street, Oklahoma City, OK 73170. Telephone: 405-692-3180. Fax: 405-692-3165. E-mail: mbcok@cris.com. Web site: http://www.mabc.edu/.

NORTHEASTERN STATE UNIVERSITY
TAHLEQUAH, OKLAHOMA

General State-supported, comprehensive, coed **Entrance** Moderately difficult **Setting** 160-acre small-town campus **Total enrollment** 8,351 **Student/faculty ratio** 21:1 **Application deadline** 8/5 (freshmen), 8/5 (transfer) **Freshmen** 74% were admitted **Housing** Yes **Expenses** Tuition $2375; Room & Board $2724 **Undergraduates** 60% women, 26% part-time, 35% 25 or older **Academic program** Advanced placement, honors program, summer session, adult/continuing education programs, internships **Contact** Mr. Bill Nowlin, Dean, Enrollment Management and Registrar, Northeastern State University, 601 North Grand, Tahlequah, OK 74464. Telephone: 918-456-5511 Ext. 2200 or toll-free 800-722-9614 (in-state). Fax: 918-458-2342. E-mail: nowlin@cherokee.nsuok.edu. Web site: http://www.nsuok.edu/.

NORTHWESTERN OKLAHOMA STATE UNIVERSITY
ALVA, OKLAHOMA

General State-supported, comprehensive, coed **Entrance** Moderately difficult **Setting** 70-acre small-town campus **Total enrollment** 2,019 **Student/faculty ratio** 17:1 **Application deadline** Rolling (freshmen), rolling (transfer) **Freshmen** 100% were admitted **Housing** Yes **Expenses** Tuition 1993; Room & Board 2500 **Undergraduates** 54% women, 32% part-time, 26% 25 or older, 4% Native American, 2% Hispanic American, 4% African American, 0.3% Asian American/Pacific Islander **The most frequently chosen baccalaureate fields are** business/marketing, education, health professions and related sciences **Academic program** Advanced placement, summer session, adult/continuing education programs **Contact** Dr. Timothy A. Zwink, Vice President for Academic Affairs, Northwestern Oklahoma State University, 709 Oklahoma Boulevard, Alva, OK 73717-2799. Telephone: 580-327-8407. Fax: 580-327-1881. E-mail: krschroc@ranger1.nwalva.edu. Web site: http://www.nwalva.edu/.

OKLAHOMA BAPTIST UNIVERSITY
SHAWNEE, OKLAHOMA

General Independent Southern Baptist, comprehensive, coed **Entrance** Moderately difficult **Setting** 125-acre small-town campus **Total enrollment** 2,017 **Student/faculty ratio** 14:1 **Application deadline** 8/1 (freshmen), 8/1 (transfer) **Freshmen** 86% were admitted **Housing** Yes **Expenses** Tuition $9440; Room & Board $3510 **Undergraduates** 56% women, 19% part-time, 18% 25 or older, 5% Native American, 2% Hispanic American, 3% African American, 2% Asian American/Pacific Islander **Academic program** Advanced placement, self-designed majors, honors program, summer session, internships **Contact** Mr. Michael Cappo, Dean of Admissions, Oklahoma Baptist University, Box 61174, Shawnee, OK 74804. Telephone: 405-878-2033 or toll-free 800-654-3285. Fax: 405-878-2046. E-mail: admissions@mail.okbu.edu. Web site: http://www.okbu.edu/.

OKLAHOMA CHRISTIAN UNIVERSITY
OKLAHOMA CITY, OKLAHOMA

General Independent, comprehensive, coed, affiliated with Church of Christ **Entrance** Noncompetitive **Setting** 200-acre suburban campus **Total enrollment** 1,808 **Student/faculty ratio** 19:1 **Application deadline** Rolling (freshmen), rolling (transfer) **Freshmen** 90% were admitted **Housing** Yes **Expenses** Tuition $12,100; Room & Board $4400 **Undergraduates** 3% Native American, 2% Hispanic American, 5% African American, 2% Asian American/Pacific Islander **The most frequently chosen baccalaureate fields are** communications/communication tech-

Oklahoma Christian University *(continued)*

nologies, education, engineering/engineering technologies **Academic program** English as a second language, advanced placement, accelerated degree program, honors program, summer session, adult/continuing education programs, internships **Contact** Mr. Kyle Ray, Director of Admissions, Oklahoma Christian University, Box 11000, Oklahoma City, OK 73136-1100. Telephone: 405-425-5050 or toll-free 800-877-5010 (in-state). Fax: 405-425-5208. E-mail: kyleray@oc.edu. Web site: http://www.oc.edu/.

OKLAHOMA CITY UNIVERSITY

OKLAHOMA CITY, OKLAHOMA

General Independent United Methodist, comprehensive, coed **Entrance** Moderately difficult **Setting** 68-acre urban campus **Total enrollment** 4,041 **Student/faculty ratio** 14:1 **Application deadline** 8/29 (freshmen), rolling (transfer) **Freshmen** 82% were admitted **Housing** Yes **Expenses** Tuition 10,170; Room & Board 9300 **Undergraduates** 58% women, 25% part-time, 27% 25 or older, 4% Native American, 3% Hispanic American, 5% African American, 2% Asian American/Pacific Islander **The most frequently chosen baccalaureate fields are** liberal arts/general studies, business/marketing, visual/performing arts **Academic program** English as a second language, advanced placement, accelerated degree program, self-designed majors, honors program, summer session, adult/continuing education programs, internships **Contact** Ms. Stacy Messinger, Dean of Admissions and Enrollment Management, Oklahoma City University, 2501 North Blackwelder, Oklahoma City, OK 73106. Telephone: 405-521-5050 or toll-free 800-633-7242 (in-state). Fax: 405-521-5916. E-mail: uadmissions@frodo.okcu.edu. Web site: http://www.okcu.edu/.

OKLAHOMA PANHANDLE STATE UNIVERSITY

GOODWELL, OKLAHOMA

General State-supported, 4-year, coed **Entrance** Noncompetitive **Setting** 40-acre rural campus **Total enrollment** 1,178 **Student/faculty ratio** 24:1 **Application deadline** Rolling (freshmen), rolling (transfer) **Freshmen** 100% were admitted **Housing** Yes **Expenses** Tuition $1911; Room & Board $2580 **Undergraduates** 53% women, 17% part-time, 23% 25 or older, 2% Native American, 11% Hispanic American, 4% African American, 1% Asian American/Pacific Islander **The most frequently chosen baccalaureate fields are** agriculture, business/marketing, education **Academic program** English as a second language, advanced placement, accelerated degree program, summer session, adult/continuing education programs, internships **Contact** Registrar and Director of Admissions, Oklahoma Panhandle State University, PO Box 430, 323 Eagle Boulevard, Goodwell, OK 73939-0430. Telephone: 580-349-2611 Ext. 212 or toll-free 800-664-6778. Fax: 580-349-2302. E-mail: opsu@opsu.edu. Web site: http://www.opsu.edu/.

OKLAHOMA STATE UNIVERSITY

STILLWATER, OKLAHOMA

General State-supported, university, coed **Entrance** Moderately difficult **Setting** 840-acre small-town campus **Total enrollment** 21,252 **Student/faculty ratio** 18:1 **Application deadline** Rolling (freshmen), rolling (transfer) **Freshmen** 92% were admitted **Housing** Yes **Expenses** Tuition $2587; Room & Board $4716 **Undergraduates** 48% women, 10% part-time, 12% 25 or older, 8% Native American, 2% Hispanic American, 3% African American, 2% Asian American/Pacific Islander **The most frequently chosen baccalaureate fields are** business/marketing, education, engineering/engineering technologies **Academic program** English as a second language, advanced placement, accelerated degree program, self-designed majors, honors program, summer session, adult/continuing education programs, internships **Contact** Ms. Paulette Cundiff, Coordinator of Admissions Processing, Oklahoma State University, 324 Student Union, Stillwater, OK 74078. Telephone: 405-744-6858 or toll-free 800-233-5019 (in-state); 800-852-1255 (out-of-state). Fax: 405-744-5285. E-mail: grl6458@okway.okstate.edu. Web site: http://www.okstate.edu/.

OKLAHOMA WESLEYAN COLLEGE

BARTLESVILLE, OKLAHOMA

General Independent, 4-year, coed, affiliated with Wesleyan Church **Entrance** Minimally difficult **Setting** 127-acre small-town campus **Total enrollment** 768 **Application deadline** Rolling (freshmen), rolling (transfer) **Housing** Yes **Expenses** Tuition $9800; Room & Board $4100 **Undergraduates** 40% 25 or older **Academic program** English as a second language, advanced placement, self-designed majors, summer session, adult/continuing education programs, internships **Contact** Mr. Marty Carver, Director of Enrollment Services, Oklahoma Wesleyan College, 2201 Silver Lake Road, Bartlesville, OK 74006-6299. Telephone: 918-335-6219 or toll-free 800-468-6292 (in-state). Fax: 918-335-6229. E-mail: gotobwc@aol.com.

ORAL ROBERTS UNIVERSITY

TULSA, OKLAHOMA

General Independent interdenominational, comprehensive, coed **Entrance** Moderately difficult **Setting** 263-acre urban campus **Total enrollment** 3,552 **Student/faculty ratio** 18:1 **Application deadline** Rolling (freshmen), rolling (transfer) **Freshmen** 81% were admitted **Housing** Yes **Expenses** Tuition $12,260; Room & Board $5228 **Undergraduates** 58% women, 7% part-time, 9% 25 or older, 1% Native American, 5% Hispanic American, 16% African American, 2% Asian American/Pacific Islander **The most frequently chosen baccalaureate fields are** business/marketing, education, philosophy, religion, and theology **Academic program** English as a second language, advanced placement, self-designed majors, honors program, summer session, adult/continuing education programs, internships **Contact** Chris Miller, Director of Undergraduate Admissions, Oral Roberts University, 7777 South Lewis Avenue, Tulsa, OK 74171. Telephone: 918-495-6518 or toll-free 800-678-8876. Fax: 918-495-6222. E-mail: admissions@oru.edu. Web site: http://www.oru.edu/.

ROGERS STATE UNIVERSITY
CLAREMORE, OKLAHOMA

General State-supported, 4-year, coed **Entrance** Non-competitive **Setting** small-town campus **Total enrollment** 2,622 **Student/faculty ratio** 20:1 **Application deadline** Rolling (freshmen), rolling (transfer) **Freshmen** 100% were admitted **Housing** Yes **Expenses** Tuition 1650; Room & Board 2063 **Undergraduates** 64% women, 55% part-time, 50% 25 or older, 23% Native American, 2% Hispanic American, 2% African American, 1% Asian American/Pacific Islander **Academic program** Advanced placement, summer session, adult/continuing education programs, internships **Contact** Ms. Becky Noah, Director of Enrollment Management, Rogers State University, Roger's State University, Office of Admissions, 1701 West Will Rogers Boulevard, Claremore, OK 74017. Telephone: 918-343-7545 or toll-free 800-256-7511. Fax: 918-343-7595. E-mail: bnoah@rsu.edu. Web site: http://www.rsu.edu/.

ST. GREGORY'S UNIVERSITY
SHAWNEE, OKLAHOMA

General Independent Roman Catholic, 4-year, coed **Entrance** Minimally difficult **Setting** 640-acre small-town campus **Total enrollment** 754 **Student/faculty ratio** 18:1 **Application deadline** Rolling (freshmen), rolling (transfer) **Freshmen** 77% were admitted **Housing** Yes **Expenses** Tuition $9084; Room & Board $4338 **Undergraduates** 53% women, 20% part-time, 19% 25 or older, 9% Native American, 5% Hispanic American, 5% African American, 1% Asian American/Pacific Islander **The most frequently chosen baccalaureate fields are** health professions and related sciences, psychology, visual/performing arts **Academic program** English as a second language, advanced placement, self-designed majors, honors program, summer session, adult/continuing education programs, internships **Contact** Mr. Joe Carter, Director of Admissions, St. Gregory's University, 1900 West MacArthur Drive, Shawnee, OK 74804. Telephone: 405-878-5444 Ext. 447 or toll-free 888-STGREGS. Fax: 405-878-5198. E-mail: admissions@sgc.edu. Web site: http://www.sgc.edu/.

SOUTHEASTERN OKLAHOMA STATE UNIVERSITY
DURANT, OKLAHOMA

General State-supported, comprehensive, coed **Entrance** Moderately difficult **Setting** 176-acre small-town campus **Total enrollment** 3,776 **Student/faculty ratio** 18:1 **Application deadline** 8/15 (transfer) **Freshmen** 77% were admitted **Housing** Yes **Expenses** Tuition $1670; Room & Board $1246 **Undergraduates** 54% women, 21% part-time, 26% 25 or older, 30% Native American, 1% Hispanic American, 5% African American, 1% Asian American/Pacific Islander **The most frequently chosen baccalaureate fields are** business/marketing, education, engineering/engineering technologies **Academic program** Advanced placement, accelerated degree program, honors program, summer session, adult/continuing education programs, internships **Contact** Mr. Rudy Manley, Director of Enrollment Management, Southeastern Oklahoma State University, Box 4225, Durant, OK 74701-0609. Telephone: 580-924-0121 Ext. 2050 or toll-free 800-435-1327 Ext. 2307. Fax: 580-920-7472. Web site: http://www.sosu.edu/.

SOUTHERN NAZARENE UNIVERSITY
BETHANY, OKLAHOMA

Contact Mr. Brad Townley, Director of Admissions, Southern Nazarene University, 6729 Northwest 39th Expressway, Bethany, OK 73008. Telephone: 405-491-6324 or toll-free 800-648-9899. Fax: 405-491-6320. E-mail: tspindle@snu.edu. Web site: http://www.snu.edu/.

SOUTHWESTERN COLLEGE OF CHRISTIAN MINISTRIES
BETHANY, OKLAHOMA

General Independent, comprehensive, coed, affiliated with Pentecostal Holiness Church **Entrance** Minimally difficult **Setting** 7-acre suburban campus **Total enrollment** 199 **Student/faculty ratio** 15:1 **Application deadline** Rolling (freshmen), rolling (transfer) **Housing** Yes **Expenses** Tuition $4744; Room & Board $3200 **Undergraduates** 45% women, 5% part-time, 20% 25 or older, 5% Native American, 3% Hispanic American, 9% African American, 1% Asian American/Pacific Islander **The most frequently chosen baccalaureate field is** philosophy, religion, and theology **Academic program** Advanced placement, summer session, internships **Contact** Mr. Johnny Lipton, Director of Admissions, Southwestern College of Christian Ministries, PO Box 340, Bethany, OK 73008-0340. Telephone: 405-789-7661 Ext. 3449. E-mail: admissions@sccm.edu. Web site: http://www.sccm.edu/.

SOUTHWESTERN OKLAHOMA STATE UNIVERSITY
WEATHERFORD, OKLAHOMA

General State-supported, comprehensive, coed **Entrance** Moderately difficult **Setting** 73-acre small-town campus **Total enrollment** 4,862 **Student/faculty ratio** 19:1 **Freshmen** 93% were admitted **Housing** Yes **Expenses** Tuition $2089; Room & Board $2506 **Undergraduates** 17% 25 or older, 5% Native American, 3% Hispanic American, 4% African American, 3% Asian American/Pacific Islander **The most frequently chosen baccalaureate fields are** education, business/marketing, health professions and related sciences **Academic program** Advanced placement, accelerated degree program,

Southwestern Oklahoma State University *(continued)*

summer session, adult/continuing education programs, internships **Contact** Ms. Connie Phillips, Admission Counselor, Southwestern Oklahoma State University, Registrar's Office, 100 Campus Drive, Weatherford, OK 73096. Telephone: 580-774-3009. Fax: 580-774-3795. E-mail: ropers@swosu.edu. Web site: http://www.swosu.edu/.

UNIVERSITY OF BIBLICAL STUDIES AND SEMINARY

See American Bible College and Seminary

UNIVERSITY OF CENTRAL OKLAHOMA

EDMOND, OKLAHOMA

General State-supported, comprehensive, coed **Entrance** Minimally difficult **Setting** 200-acre suburban campus **Total enrollment** 14,173 **Student/faculty ratio** 21:1 **Application deadline** Rolling (freshmen), rolling (transfer) **Freshmen** 95% were admitted **Housing** Yes **Expenses** Tuition $1965; Room & Board $2905 **Undergraduates** 56% women, 34% part-time, 24% 25 or older, 4% Native American, 3% Hispanic American, 7% African American, 3% Asian American/Pacific Islander **The most frequently chosen baccalaureate fields are** business/marketing, education, liberal arts/general studies **Academic program** English as a second language, advanced placement, accelerated degree program, honors program, summer session, adult/continuing education programs, internships **Contact** Ms. Evelyn Wilson, Dean of Enrollment Services, University of Central Oklahoma, 100 North University Drive, Edmond, OK 73034. Telephone: 405-974-2338 Ext. 2338 or toll-free 800-254-4215 (in-state). Fax: 405-341-4964. Web site: http://www.cwc.cc.wy.us/.

UNIVERSITY OF OKLAHOMA

NORMAN, OKLAHOMA

General State-supported, university, coed **Entrance** Moderately difficult **Setting** 3,500-acre suburban campus **Total enrollment** 21,607 **Student/faculty ratio** 20:1 **Application deadline** 6/1 (freshmen), rolling (transfer) **Freshmen** 86% were admitted **Housing** Yes **Expenses** Tuition $2581; Room & Board $4610 **Undergraduates** 48% women, 15% part-time, 13% 25 or older, 8% Native American, 4% Hispanic American, 7% African American, 6% Asian American/Pacific Islander **The most frequently chosen baccalaureate fields are** business/marketing, engineering/engineering technologies, social sciences and history **Academic program** English as a second language, advanced placement, accelerated degree program, self-designed majors, honors program, summer session, adult/continuing education programs, internships **Contact** Karen Renfroe, Director of Prospective Student Services, University of Oklahoma, 1000 Asp Avenue, Norman, OK 73019. Telephone: 405-325-2151 or toll-free 800-234-6868. Fax: 405-325-7124. E-mail: admrec@ouwww.ucs.ou.edu. Web site: http://www.ou.edu/.

UNIVERSITY OF OKLAHOMA HEALTH SCIENCES CENTER

OKLAHOMA CITY, OKLAHOMA

General State-supported, upper-level, coed **Entrance** Moderately difficult **Setting** 200-acre urban campus **Total enrollment** 2,831 **Application deadline** 10/1 (transfer) **Housing** No **Expenses** Tuition $2978 **Undergraduates** 89% women, 17% part-time, 36% 25 or older, 10% Native American, 4% Hispanic American, 4% African American, 3% Asian American/Pacific Islander **The most frequently chosen baccalaureate field is** health professions and related sciences **Academic program** Advanced placement, honors program, summer session, internships **Contact** Dr. Willie V. Bryan, Vice Provost for Educational Services and Registrar, University of Oklahoma Health Sciences Center, PO Box 26901, Oklahoma City, OK 73190. Telephone: 405-271-2655. Fax: 405-271-2480. E-mail: sophie-mack@uokhsc.edu.

UNIVERSITY OF PHOENIX–OKLAHOMA CITY CAMPUS

OKLAHOMA CITY, OKLAHOMA

General Proprietary, comprehensive, coed **Entrance** Noncompetitive **Total enrollment** 66,534 **Student/faculty ratio** 13:1 **Application deadline** Rolling (freshmen), rolling (transfer) **Expenses** Tuition $7740 **Undergraduates** 56% women, 86% 25 or older, 2% Native American, 18% Hispanic American, 13% African American, 6% Asian American/Pacific Islander **Academic program** Advanced placement, accelerated degree program, adult/continuing education programs **Contact** Ms. Beth Barilla, Director of Admissions, University of Phoenix–Oklahoma City Campus, 4615 East Elwood Street, Phoenix, AZ 85040-1948. Telephone: 480-927-0099 Ext. 1218 or toll-free 800-228-7240. Fax: 480-594-1758. E-mail: beth.barilla@apollogrp.edu. Web site: http://www.phoenix.edu/.

UNIVERSITY OF PHOENIX–TULSA CAMPUS

TULSA, OKLAHOMA

General Proprietary, comprehensive, coed **Entrance** Noncompetitive **Total enrollment** 66,534 **Student/faculty ratio** 13:1 **Application deadline** Rolling (freshmen), rolling (transfer) **Expenses** Tuition $7740 **Undergraduates** 56% women, 86% 25 or older, 2% Native American, 18% Hispanic American, 13% African American, 6% Asian American/Pacific Islander **Academic program** Advanced placement, accelerated degree program, adult/continuing education programs **Contact** Ms. Beth Barilla, Director of Admissions, University of Phoenix–Tulsa Campus, 4615 East Elwood Street, Phoenix, AZ 85040-1948. Telephone: 480-927-0099 Ext. 1218 or toll-free 800-228-

7240. Fax: 480-594-1758. E-mail: beth.barilla@apollogrp.edu. Web site: http://www.phoenix.edu.

UNIVERSITY OF SCIENCE AND ARTS OF OKLAHOMA
CHICKASHA, OKLAHOMA

General State-supported, 4-year, coed **Entrance** Moderately difficult **Setting** 75-acre small-town campus **Total enrollment** 1,409 **Student/faculty ratio** 16:1 **Application deadline** Rolling (freshmen), rolling (transfer) **Freshmen** 83% were admitted **Housing** Yes **Expenses** Tuition $2021; Room & Board $2390 **Undergraduates** 64% women, 31% part-time, 25% 25 or older, 13% Native American, 3% Hispanic American, 5% African American, 1% Asian American/Pacific Islander **The most frequently chosen baccalaureate fields are** business/marketing, education, social sciences and history **Academic program** English as a second language, advanced placement, accelerated degree program, self-designed majors, honors program, summer session, adult/continuing education programs, internships **Contact** Mr. Joseph Evans, Registrar and Director of Admissions and Records, University of Science and Arts of Oklahoma, PO Box 82345, Chickasha, OK 73018-0001. Telephone: 405-574-1204 or toll-free 800-933-8726 Ext. 1204. Fax: 405-574-1220. E-mail: registrar@mercur.usao.edu. Web site: http://www.usao.edu/.

UNIVERSITY OF TULSA
TULSA, OKLAHOMA

General Independent, university, coed, affiliated with Presbyterian Church **Entrance** Moderately difficult **Setting** 160-acre urban campus **Total enrollment** 4,158 **Student/faculty ratio** 11:1 **Application deadline** Rolling (transfer) **Freshmen** 75% were admitted **Housing** Yes **Expenses** Tuition 13,810; Room & Board 4810 **Undergraduates** 52% women, 8% part-time, 9% 25 or older, 6% Native American, 3% Hispanic American, 7% African American, 2% Asian American/Pacific Islander **The most frequently chosen baccalaureate fields are** business/marketing, engineering/engineering technologies, health professions and related sciences **Academic program** English as a second language, advanced placement, accelerated degree program, self-designed majors, honors program, summer session, adult/continuing education programs, internships **Contact** Mr. John C. Corso, Associate VP for Administration/Dean of Admission, University of Tulsa, Office of Admission, The University of Tulsa, 600 South College Avenue, Tulsa, OK 74104. Telephone: 918-631-2307 or toll-free 800-331-3050. Fax: 918-631-5003. E-mail: admission@utulsa.edu. Web site: http://www.utulsa.edu/.

OREGON

THE ART INSTITUTE OF PORTLAND
PORTLAND, OREGON

General Proprietary, 4-year, coed **Entrance** Minimally difficult **Setting** 1-acre urban campus **Total enrollment** 668 **Student/faculty ratio** 17:1 **Application deadline** Rolling (freshmen), rolling (transfer) **Housing** No **Expenses** Tuition $13,365 **Undergraduates** 55% women, 20% part-time, 39% 25 or older **The most frequently chosen baccalaureate field is** visual/performing arts **Academic program** Advanced placement, summer session, internships **Contact** Ms. Kelly Alston, Director of Admissions, The Art Institute of Portland, 2000 Southwest Fifth Avenue, Portland, OR 97201-4907. Telephone: 503-228-6528 Ext. 103 or toll-free 888-228-6528. Fax: 503-525-8331. E-mail: admissions@bassist.edu. Web site: http://www.aipd.artinstitutes.edu/.

BASSIST COLLEGE
See The Art Institute of Portland

CASCADE COLLEGE
PORTLAND, OREGON

General Independent, 4-year, coed, affiliated with Church of Christ **Entrance** Noncompetitive **Setting** 13-acre urban campus **Total enrollment** 321 **Student/faculty ratio** 18:1 **Application deadline** Rolling (freshmen), rolling (transfer) **Freshmen** 100% were admitted **Housing** Yes **Expenses** Tuition $9200; Room & Board $4800 **Undergraduates** 53% women, 4% part-time, 4% 25 or older, 1% Native American, 3% Hispanic American, 7% African American, 2% Asian American/Pacific Islander **The most frequently chosen baccalaureate fields are** liberal arts/general studies, business/marketing, philosophy, religion, and theology **Academic program** Advanced placement, accelerated degree program, summer session, internships **Contact** Mr. Clint La Rue, Director of Admissions, Cascade College, 9101 East Burnside, Portland, OR 97216-1515. Telephone: 503-257-1202 or toll-free 800-550-7678. E-mail: admissions@cascade.edu. Web site: http://www.cascade.edu/.

CONCORDIA UNIVERSITY
PORTLAND, OREGON

General Independent, comprehensive, coed, affiliated with Lutheran Church–Missouri Synod **Entrance** Moderately difficult **Setting** 13-acre urban campus **Total enrollment** 1,040 **Student/faculty ratio** 13:1 **Application deadline** Rolling (freshmen), rolling (transfer) **Freshmen** 67% were admitted **Housing** Yes **Expenses** Tuition $16,200; Room & Board $4300 **Undergraduates** 64% women, 15% part-time, 41% 25 or older, 1% Native American, 3% Hispanic American, 6% African American, 3% Asian American/Pacific Islander **The most frequently chosen baccalaureate fields are** business/marketing, education, health professions and related sciences **Academic program** English as a second language, advanced placement, accelerated degree program, self-designed majors, summer session, adult/continuing education programs, internships **Contact** Mr. Peter D. Johnson, Director of Admission, Concordia University, 2811 Northeast Holman, Portland, OR 97211-6099. Telephone: 503-493-6521 or toll-free 800-321-9371. Fax:

Concordia University *(continued)*

503-280-8531. E-mail: cu-admissions@cu-portland.edu. Web site: http://www.cu-portland.edu/.

▶ **For more information, see page 406.**

EASTERN OREGON UNIVERSITY
LA GRANDE, OREGON

General State-supported, comprehensive, coed **Entrance** Moderately difficult **Setting** 121-acre rural campus **Total enrollment** 2,782 **Student/faculty ratio** 14:1 **Application deadline** 9/15 (freshmen), 9/15 (transfer) **Freshmen** 92% were admitted **Housing** Yes **Expenses** Tuition $3366; Room & Board $4830 **Undergraduates** 58% women, 27% part-time, 42% 25 or older, 3% Native American, 3% Hispanic American, 1% African American, 3% Asian American/Pacific Islander **The most frequently chosen baccalaureate fields are** interdisciplinary studies, business/marketing, liberal arts/general studies **Academic program** English as a second language, advanced placement, self-designed majors, summer session, adult/continuing education programs, internships **Contact** Ms. Christian Steinmetz, Director, Admissions, Eastern Oregon University, One University Boulevard, La Grande, OR 97850. Telephone: 541-962-3393 or toll-free 800-452-8639. Fax: 541-962-3418. E-mail: admissions@eosc.osshe.edu. Web site: http://www.eou.edu/.

EUGENE BIBLE COLLEGE
EUGENE, OREGON

General Independent, 4-year, coed, affiliated with Open Bible Standard Churches **Entrance** Minimally difficult **Setting** 40-acre suburban campus **Total enrollment** 210 **Student/faculty ratio** 15:1 **Application deadline** 9/1 (freshmen), 9/1 (transfer) **Freshmen** 60% were admitted **Housing** Yes **Expenses** Tuition $6276; Room & Board $3723 **Undergraduates** 47% women, 18% part-time, 19% 25 or older, 1% Native American, 1% Hispanic American, 1% African American, 1% Asian American/Pacific Islander **Academic program** Advanced placement, summer session, internships **Contact** Mr. Trent Combs, Director of Admissions, Eugene Bible College, 2155 Bailey Hill Road, Eugene, OR 97405. Telephone: 541-485-1780 Ext. 135 or toll-free 800-322-2638. Fax: 541-343-5801. E-mail: admissions@ebc.edu. Web site: http://www.ebc.edu/.

GEORGE FOX UNIVERSITY
NEWBERG, OREGON

General Independent Friends, university, coed **Entrance** Moderately difficult **Setting** 73-acre small-town campus **Total enrollment** 2,635 **Student/faculty ratio** 15:1 **Application deadline** 6/1 (freshmen), 6/1 (transfer) **Freshmen** 90% were admitted **Housing** Yes **Expenses** Tuition $17,610; Room & Board $5550 **Undergraduates** 59% women, 21% part-time, 22% 25 or older, 1% Native American, 3% Hispanic American, 1% African American, 3% Asian American/Pacific Islander **The most frequently chosen baccalaureate fields are** business/marketing, education, social sciences and history **Academic program** English as a second language, advanced placement, accelerated degree program, self-designed majors, honors program, adult/continuing education programs, internships **Contact** Mr. Dale Seipp, Director of Admissions, George Fox University, 414 North Meridian, Newberg, CT 97132. Telephone: 503-554-2240 or toll-free 800-765-4369. Fax: 503-554-3110. E-mail: admissions@georgefox.edu. Web site: http://www.georgefox.edu/.

▶ **For more information, see page 424.**

LEWIS & CLARK COLLEGE
PORTLAND, OREGON

General Independent, comprehensive, coed **Entrance** Very difficult **Setting** 115-acre suburban campus **Total enrollment** 3,014 **Student/faculty ratio** 13:1 **Application deadline** 2/1 (freshmen) **Freshmen** 68% were admitted **Housing** Yes **Expenses** Tuition $22,610; Room & Board $6400 **Undergraduates** 60% women, 2% part-time, 1% 25 or older, 1% Native American, 3% Hispanic American, 1% African American, 7% Asian American/Pacific Islander **The most frequently chosen baccalaureate fields are** biological/life sciences, social sciences and history, visual/performing arts **Academic program** English as a second language, advanced placement, accelerated degree program, self-designed majors, honors program, summer session, internships **Contact** Mr. Michael Sexton, Dean of Admissions, Lewis & Clark College, 0615 SW Palatine Hill Road, Portland, OR 97219-7899. Telephone: 503-768-7040 or toll-free 800-444-4111. Fax: 503-768-7055. E-mail: admissions@lclark.edu. Web site: http://www.lclark.edu/.

LINFIELD COLLEGE
MCMINNVILLE, OREGON

General Independent American Baptist, 4-year, coed **Entrance** Moderately difficult **Setting** 95-acre small-town campus **Total enrollment** 1,534 **Student/faculty ratio** 12:1 **Application deadline** 2/15 (freshmen), 4/15 (transfer) **Freshmen** 92% were admitted **Housing** Yes **Expenses** Tuition 18,600; Room & Board 5350 **Undergraduates** 56% women, 2% part-time, 2% 25 or older, 1% Native American, 3% Hispanic American, 2% African American, 5% Asian American/Pacific Islander **The most frequently chosen baccalaureate fields are** business/marketing, health professions and related sciences, social sciences and history **Academic program** English as a second language, advanced placement, accelerated degree program, self-designed majors, honors program, summer session, adult/continuing education programs, internships **Contact** Ms. Lisa Knodle-Bragiel, Interim Director of Admissions, Linfield College, 900 SE Baker Street, McMinnville, OR 97128-6894. Telephone: 503-434-2489 or toll-free 800-640-2287. Fax: 503-434-2472. E-mail: admissions@linfield.edu. Web site: http://www.linfield.edu/.

MARYLHURST UNIVERSITY
MARYLHURST, OREGON

General Independent Roman Catholic, comprehensive, coed **Contact** Ms. Jennifer Damian, Admission Specialist, Marylhurst University, 17600 Pacific Highway (Hwy 43), PO Box 261, Marylhurst, OR 97036. Telephone: 503-699-6268 Ext. 3320 or toll-free 800-634-9982 Ext. 3317 (out-of-state). Fax: 503-636-9526. E-mail: admissions@marylhurst.edu. Web site: http://www.marylhurst.edu/.

MOUNT ANGEL SEMINARY
SAINT BENEDICT, OREGON

Contact Registrar/Admissions Officer, Mount Angel Seminary, Saint Benedict, OR 97373. Telephone: 503-845-3951 Ext. 14.

MULTNOMAH BIBLE COLLEGE AND BIBLICAL SEMINARY
PORTLAND, OREGON

General Independent interdenominational, comprehensive, coed **Entrance** Moderately difficult **Setting** 22-acre urban campus **Total enrollment** 838 **Student/faculty ratio** 17:1 **Application deadline** 7/15 (freshmen), 7/15 (transfer) **Freshmen** 80% were admitted **Housing** Yes **Expenses** Tuition $9050; Room & Board $3880 **Undergraduates** 46% women, 8% part-time, 14% 25 or older, 0% Native American, 2% Hispanic American, 1% African American, 2% Asian American/Pacific Islander **The most frequently chosen baccalaureate field is** philosophy, religion, and theology **Academic program** Advanced placement, summer session, adult/continuing education programs, internships **Contact** Ms. Nancy Gerecz, Admissions Assistant, Multnomah Bible College and Biblical Seminary, 8435 Northeast Glisan Street, Portland, OR 97220-5898. Telephone: 503-255-0332 Ext. 373 or toll-free 800-275-4672. Fax: 503-254-1268. E-mail: admiss@multnomah.edu. Web site: http://www.multnomah.edu/.

NORTHWEST CHRISTIAN COLLEGE
EUGENE, OREGON

General Independent interdenominational, comprehensive, coed **Entrance** Moderately difficult **Setting** 8-acre urban campus **Total enrollment** 513 **Student/faculty ratio** 13:1 **Application deadline** Rolling (freshmen), rolling (transfer) **Freshmen** 100% were admitted **Housing** Yes **Expenses** Tuition $13,905; Room & Board $5207 **Undergraduates** 39% 25 or older, 3% Native American, 2% Hispanic American, 2% African American, 3% Asian American/Pacific Islander **The most frequently chosen baccalaureate fields are** business/marketing, education, psychology **Academic program** Advanced placement, accelerated degree program, self-designed majors, adult/continuing education programs, internships **Contact** Mr. Bill Stenberg, Director of Admissions, Northwest Christian College, 828 East 11th Avenue, Eugene, OR 97401-3727. Telephone: 541-684-7209 or toll-free 877-463-6622. Fax: 541-684-7317. E-mail: admissions@nwcc.edu. Web site: http://www.nwcc.edu/.

OREGON COLLEGE OF ART AND CRAFT
PORTLAND, OREGON

General Independent, 4-year, coed **Entrance** Minimally difficult **Setting** 7-acre urban campus **Total enrollment** 95 **Student/faculty ratio** 6:1 **Application deadline** Rolling (freshmen), rolling (transfer) **Freshmen** 67% were admitted **Housing** No **Expenses** Tuition 12,642 **Undergraduates** 73% women, 57% part-time, 71% 25 or older, 2% Native American, 0% Hispanic American, 0% African American, 4% Asian American/Pacific Islander **The most frequently chosen baccalaureate field is** visual/performing arts **Academic program** Advanced placement, adult/continuing education programs, internships **Contact** Sarah Turner, Admissions Officer, Oregon College of Art and Craft, 8245 Southwest Barnes Road, Portland, OR 97225. Telephone: 503-297-5544 Ext. 141 or toll-free 800-390-0632. Fax: 503-297-9651. E-mail: admissions@ocac.edu. Web site: http://www.ocac.edu/.

OREGON HEALTH & SCIENCE UNIVERSITY
PORTLAND, OREGON

General State-related, upper-level, coed **Contact** Ms. Victoria Souza, Registrar and Director of Financial Aid, Oregon Health & Science University, 3181 Southwest Sam Jackson Park Road, Portland, OR 97201-3098. Telephone: 503-494-7800. E-mail: porterts@ohsu.edu. Web site: http://www.ohsu.edu/.

OREGON INSTITUTE OF TECHNOLOGY
KLAMATH FALLS, OREGON

General State-supported, comprehensive, coed **Entrance** Moderately difficult **Setting** 173-acre small-town campus **Total enrollment** 2,842 **Student/faculty ratio** 14:1 **Application deadline** 6/1 (freshmen), 6/1 (transfer) **Freshmen** 77% were admitted **Housing** Yes **Expenses** Tuition $3459; Room & Board $4898 **Undergraduates** 43% women, 38% part-time, 38% 25 or older, 2% Native American, 3% Hispanic American, 1% African American, 7% Asian American/Pacific Islander **Academic program** English as a second language, advanced placement, summer session, adult/continuing education programs, internships **Contact** Palmer Muntz, Director of Admissions, Oregon Institute of Technology, 3201 Campus Drive, Klamath Falls, OR 97601-8801. Telephone: 541-885-1150 or toll-free 800-422-2017 (in-state); 800-343-6653 (out-of-state). Fax: 541-885-1115. E-mail: oit@oit.edu. Web site: http://www.oit.edu/.

OREGON STATE UNIVERSITY
CORVALLIS, OREGON

General State-supported, university, coed **Entrance** Moderately difficult **Setting** 422-acre small-town campus **Total enrollment** 16,788 **Student/faculty ratio** 13:1 **Application deadline** 3/1 (freshmen), 3/1

Oregon State University *(continued)*

(transfer) **Freshmen** 87% were admitted **Housing** Yes **Expenses** Tuition $3014; Room & Board $5508 **Undergraduates** 46% women, 10% part-time, 8% 25 or older, 1% Native American, 3% Hispanic American, 1% African American, 8% Asian American/ Pacific Islander **The most frequently chosen baccalaureate fields are** business/marketing, education, natural resources/environmental science **Academic program** English as a second language, advanced placement, self-designed majors, honors program, summer session, internships **Contact** Ms. Michele Sandlin, Associate Director of Processing, Oregon State University, Corvallis, OR 97331. Telephone: 541-737-4411 or toll-free 800-291-4192 (in-state). E-mail: osuadmit@ccmail.orst.edu. Web site: http://osu.orst.edu/.

PACIFIC NORTHWEST COLLEGE OF ART
PORTLAND, OREGON

General Independent, 4-year, coed **Entrance** Moderately difficult **Setting** urban campus **Total enrollment** 317 **Student/faculty ratio** 10:1 **Application deadline** 7/1 (freshmen) **Freshmen** 86% were admitted **Housing** Yes **Expenses** Tuition $13,420; Room only $3840 **Undergraduates** 61% women, 18% part-time, 34% 25 or older, 2% Native American, 4% Hispanic American, 2% African American, 2% Asian American/Pacific Islander **The most frequently chosen baccalaureate field is** visual/performing arts **Academic program** Advanced placement, self-designed majors, summer session, adult/continuing education programs, internships **Contact** Mr. Clarence Goodman, Enrollment Counselor, Pacific Northwest College of Art, 1241 NW Johnson Street, Portland, OR 97209. Telephone: 503-821-8975 or toll-free 800-818-PNCA. Fax: 503-821-8978. E-mail: colin@pnca.edu. Web site: http://www.pnca.edu/.

PACIFIC UNIVERSITY
FOREST GROVE, OREGON

General Independent, comprehensive, coed **Entrance** Moderately difficult **Setting** 55-acre small-town campus **Total enrollment** 2,148 **Student/faculty ratio** 10:1 **Application deadline** Rolling (freshmen), rolling (transfer) **Freshmen** 86% were admitted **Housing** Yes **Expenses** Tuition 17,840; Room & Board 5465 **Undergraduates** 61% women, 5% part-time, 4% 25 or older, 1% Native American, 2% Hispanic American, 1% African American, 18% Asian American/ Pacific Islander **The most frequently chosen baccalaureate fields are** biological/life sciences, business/ marketing, social sciences and history **Academic program** English as a second language, advanced placement, accelerated degree program, honors program, summer session, internships **Contact** Ms. Beth Woodward, Director of Undergraduate Admissions, Pacific University, 2043 College Way, Forest Grove, OR 97116-1797. Telephone: 503-359-2218 or toll-free 800-677-6712. Fax: 503-359-2975. E-mail: admissions@pacificu.edu. Web site: http://www.pacificu.edu/.

PORTLAND STATE UNIVERSITY
PORTLAND, OREGON

General State-supported, university, coed **Entrance** Minimally difficult **Setting** 36-acre urban campus **Total enrollment** 18,889 **Student/faculty ratio** 20:1 **Application deadline** Rolling (freshmen), rolling (transfer) **Freshmen** 86% were admitted **Housing** Yes **Expenses** Tuition $3525; Room & Board $6150 **Undergraduates** 56% women, 43% part-time, 38% 25 or older, 1% Native American, 4% Hispanic American, 3% African American, 10% Asian American/ Pacific Islander **The most frequently chosen baccalaureate fields are** business/marketing, psychology, social sciences and history **Academic program** English as a second language, advanced placement, accelerated degree program, self-designed majors, honors program, summer session, adult/continuing education programs, internships **Contact** Ms. Agnes A. Hoffman, Director of Admissions and Records, Portland State University, PO Box 751, Portland, OR 97207-0751. Telephone: 503-725-3511 or toll-free 800-547-8887. Fax: 503-725-5525. E-mail: askadm@ofa.pdx.edu. Web site: http://www.pdx.edu/.

REED COLLEGE
PORTLAND, OREGON

General Independent, comprehensive, coed **Entrance** Very difficult **Setting** 98-acre suburban campus **Total enrollment** 1,385 **Student/faculty ratio** 10:1 **Application deadline** 1/15 (freshmen), 3/1 (transfer) **Freshmen** 74% were admitted **Housing** Yes **Expenses** Tuition 25,020; Room & Board 6820 **Undergraduates** 53% women, 4% part-time, 3% 25 or older, 1% Native American, 4% Hispanic American, 1% African American, 6% Asian American/Pacific Islander **The most frequently chosen baccalaureate fields are** biological/life sciences, English, psychology **Academic program** Advanced placement, accelerated degree program, self-designed majors **Contact** Mr. Tom Marlitt, Acting Dean of Admission, Reed College, 3203 Southeast Woodstock Boulevard, Portland, OR 97202-8199. Telephone: 503-777-7511 or toll-free 800-547-4750 (out-of-state). Fax: 503-777-7553. E-mail: admission@reed.edu. Web site: http://web.reed.edu/.

SOUTHERN OREGON UNIVERSITY
ASHLAND, OREGON

General State-supported, comprehensive, coed **Entrance** Moderately difficult **Setting** 175-acre small-town campus **Total enrollment** 5,493 **Student/faculty ratio** 18:1 **Application deadline** Rolling (freshmen), rolling (transfer) **Freshmen** 96% were admitted **Housing** Yes **Expenses** Tuition $3369; Room & Board $5649 **Undergraduates** 57% women, 28% part-time, 26% 25 or older, 2% Native American, 3% Hispanic American, 1% African American, 3% Asian American/Pacific Islander **The most frequently chosen baccalaureate fields are** business/ marketing, communications/communication technologies, social sciences and history **Academic program**

Advanced placement, accelerated degree program, self-designed majors, honors program, summer session, adult/continuing education programs **Contact** Ms. Mara A. Affre, Director of Admissions, Southern Oregon University, 1250 Siskiyou Boulevard, Ashland, OR 97520. Telephone: 541-552-6411 or toll-free 800-482-7672 (in-state). Fax: 541-552-6614. E-mail: admissions@wpo.sosc.osshe.edu. Web site: http://www.sou.edu/.

UNIVERSITY OF OREGON
EUGENE, OREGON

General State-supported, university, coed **Entrance** Moderately difficult **Setting** 280-acre urban campus **Total enrollment** 17,801 **Student/faculty ratio** 18:1 **Application deadline** 2/1 (freshmen), 5/15 (transfer) **Freshmen** 90% were admitted **Housing** Yes **Expenses** Tuition $3825; Room & Board $5564 **Undergraduates** 53% women, 11% part-time, 2% 25 or older, 1% Native American, 3% Hispanic American, 2% African American, 6% Asian American/Pacific Islander **The most frequently chosen baccalaureate fields are** business/marketing, communications/communication technologies, social sciences and history **Academic program** English as a second language, advanced placement, accelerated degree program, self-designed majors, honors program, summer session, adult/continuing education programs, internships **Contact** Ms. Martha Pitts, Director of Admissions, University of Oregon, Eugene, OR 97403. Telephone: 541-346-3201 or toll-free 800-232-3825 (in-state). Fax: 541-346-5815. E-mail: uoadmit@oregon.uoregon.edu. Web site: http://www.uoregon.edu/.

UNIVERSITY OF PHOENIX–OREGON CAMPUS
PORTLAND, OREGON

General Proprietary, comprehensive, coed **Entrance** Noncompetitive **Total enrollment** 66,534 **Student/faculty ratio** 13:1 **Application deadline** Rolling (freshmen), rolling (transfer) **Expenses** Tuition $7740 **Undergraduates** 56% women, 86% 25 or older, 2% Native American, 18% Hispanic American, 13% African American, 6% Asian American/Pacific Islander **Academic program** Advanced placement, accelerated degree program, adult/continuing education programs **Contact** Ms. Beth Barilla, Director of Admissions, University of Phoenix–Oregon Campus, 4615 East Elwood Street, Phoenix, AZ 85040-1948. Telephone: 480-927-0099 Ext. 1218 or toll-free 800-228-7240. Fax: 480-594-1758. E-mail: beth.barilla@apollogrp.edu. Web site: http://www.phoenix.edu/.

UNIVERSITY OF PORTLAND
PORTLAND, OREGON

General Independent Roman Catholic, comprehensive, coed **Entrance** Moderately difficult **Setting** 125-acre suburban campus **Total enrollment** 2,926 **Student/faculty ratio** 13:1 **Application deadline** 3/1 (freshmen), 6/1 (transfer) **Freshmen** 88% were admitted **Housing** Yes **Expenses** Tuition $18,450; Room & Board $5398 **Undergraduates** 57% women, 4% part-time, 5% 25 or older, 0.5% Native American, 4% Hispanic American, 1% African American, 9% Asian American/Pacific Islander **The most frequently chosen baccalaureate fields are** biological/life sciences, education, foreign language/literature **Academic program** English as a second language, advanced placement, accelerated degree program, self-designed majors, honors program, summer session, adult/continuing education programs, internships **Contact** Mr. James C. Lyons, Dean of Admissions, University of Portland, 5000 North Willamette Boulevard, Portland, OR 97203-5798. Telephone: 503-943-7147 or toll-free 888-627-5601 (out-of-state). Fax: 503-943-7315. E-mail: admissions@uofport.edu. Web site: http://www.up.edu/.

WARNER PACIFIC COLLEGE
PORTLAND, OREGON

General Independent, comprehensive, coed, affiliated with Church of God **Entrance** Moderately difficult **Setting** 15-acre urban campus **Total enrollment** 638 **Student/faculty ratio** 14:1 **Application deadline** Rolling (freshmen), rolling (transfer) **Freshmen** 79% were admitted **Housing** Yes **Expenses** Tuition $14,635; Room & Board $4400 **Undergraduates** 64% women, 15% part-time, 39% 25 or older, 1% Native American, 2% Hispanic American, 4% African American, 3% Asian American/Pacific Islander **The most frequently chosen baccalaureate fields are** business/marketing, philosophy, religion, and theology, psychology **Academic program** Advanced placement, self-designed majors, honors program, summer session, adult/continuing education programs, internships **Contact** Office of Admissions and Financial Aid, Warner Pacific College, 2219 Southeast 68th Avenue, Portland, OR 97215. Telephone: 503-517-1020 or toll-free 800-582-7885 (in-state); 800-804-1510 (out-of-state). Fax: 503-517-1352. E-mail: admiss@warnerpacific.edu. Web site: http://www.warnerpacific.edu/.

WESTERN BAPTIST COLLEGE
SALEM, OREGON

General Independent religious, 4-year, coed **Entrance** Moderately difficult **Setting** 107-acre suburban campus **Total enrollment** 696 **Student/faculty ratio** 18:1 **Application deadline** 8/1 (freshmen), 8/1 (transfer) **Freshmen** 72% were admitted **Housing** Yes **Expenses** Tuition 14,360; Room & Board 5340 **Undergraduates** 58% women, 7% part-time, 21% 25 or older, 1% Native American, 2% Hispanic American, 1% African American, 1% Asian American/Pacific Islander **The most frequently chosen baccalaureate fields are** business/marketing, education, psychology **Academic program** Advanced placement, accelerated degree program, honors program, summer session, adult/continuing education programs, internships **Contact** Mr. Marty Ziesemer, Director of Admissions, Western Baptist College, 5000 Deer Park Drive, SE, Salem, OR 97301-9392. Telephone: 503-375-7005 or toll-free 800-845-3005 (out-of-state). E-mail: dmilionis@wbc.edu. Web site: http://www.wbc.edu/.

WESTERN OREGON UNIVERSITY
MONMOUTH, OREGON

General State-supported, comprehensive, coed **Entrance** Moderately difficult **Setting** 157-acre rural campus **Total enrollment** 4,729 **Student/faculty ratio** 20:1 **Application deadline** Rolling (freshmen), rolling (transfer) **Freshmen** 93% were admitted **Housing** Yes **Expenses** Tuition $3342; Room & Board $5043 **Undergraduates** 60% women, 11% part-time, 20% 25 or older, 1% Native American, 4% Hispanic American, 1% African American, 3% Asian American/Pacific Islander **Academic program** English as a second language, advanced placement, self-designed majors, honors program, summer session, adult/continuing education programs, internships **Contact** Ms. Alison Marshall-Sanchez, Director of Admissions, Western Oregon University, 345 North Monmouth Avenue, Monmouth, OR 97361. Telephone: 503-838-8211 or toll-free 877-877-1593. Fax: 503-838-8067. E-mail: wolfgram@fsa.wosc.osshe.edu. Web site: http://www.wou.edu/.

WESTERN STATES CHIROPRACTIC COLLEGE
PORTLAND, OREGON

General Independent, upper-level, coed **Contact** Dr. Randell Hand, Dean of Enrollment Management, Western States Chiropractic College, 2900 Northeast 132nd Avenue, Portland, OR 97230-3099. Telephone: 503-251-5734 Ext. 707 or toll-free 800-641-5641. Fax: 503-251-5723. Web site: http://www.wschiro.edu/.

WILLAMETTE UNIVERSITY
SALEM, OREGON

General Independent United Methodist, comprehensive, coed **Entrance** Very difficult **Setting** 72-acre urban campus **Total enrollment** 2,405 **Student/faculty ratio** 11:1 **Application deadline** 2/1 (freshmen), 2/1 (transfer) **Freshmen** 90% were admitted **Housing** Yes **Expenses** Tuition 22,822; Room & Board 5930 **Undergraduates** 55% women, 6% part-time, 3% 25 or older, 1% Native American, 5% Hispanic American, 2% African American, 7% Asian American/Pacific Islander **The most frequently chosen baccalaureate fields are** biological/life sciences, business/marketing, social sciences and history **Academic program** Advanced placement, accelerated degree program, self-designed majors, honors program, internships **Contact** Ms. Robin Brown, Vice President for Enrollment, Willamette University, 900 State Street, Salem, OR 97301-3931. Telephone: 503-370-6303 or toll-free 877-542-2787. Fax: 503-375-5363. E-mail: undergrad-admission@willamette.edu. Web site: http://www.willamette.edu/.

PENNSYLVANIA

ALBRIGHT COLLEGE
READING, PENNSYLVANIA

General Independent, 4-year, coed, affiliated with United Methodist Church **Entrance** Moderately difficult **Setting** 110-acre suburban campus **Total enrollment** 1,728 **Student/faculty ratio** 14:1 **Application deadline** Rolling (freshmen), 8/15 (transfer) **Freshmen** 76% were admitted **Housing** Yes **Expenses** Tuition 20,310; Room & Board 6040 **Undergraduates** 57% women, 6% part-time, 2% 25 or older, 1% Native American, 3% Hispanic American, 7% African American, 2% Asian American/Pacific Islander **The most frequently chosen baccalaureate fields are** business/marketing, psychology, social sciences and history **Academic program** English as a second language, advanced placement, accelerated degree program, self-designed majors, honors program, summer session, internships **Contact** Mr. Gregory E. Eichhorn, Vice President for Enrollment Management, Albright College, P.O. Box 15234, 13th and Bern Streets, Reading, PA 19612-5234. Telephone: 610-921-7260 or toll-free 800-252-1856. Fax: 610-921-7294. E-mail: albright@joe.alb.edu. Web site: http://www.albright.edu/.

ALLEGHENY COLLEGE
MEADVILLE, PENNSYLVANIA

General Independent, 4-year, coed, affiliated with United Methodist Church **Entrance** Very difficult **Setting** 254-acre small-town campus **Total enrollment** 1,904 **Student/faculty ratio** 14:1 **Application deadline** 2/15 (freshmen), 7/1 (transfer) **Freshmen** 76% were admitted **Housing** Yes **Expenses** Tuition 22,490; Room & Board 5290 **Undergraduates** 52% women, 2% part-time, 1% 25 or older, 1% Native American, 1% Hispanic American, 2% African American, 1% Asian American/Pacific Islander **The most frequently chosen baccalaureate fields are** psychology, biological/life sciences, social sciences and history **Academic program** Advanced placement, accelerated degree program, self-designed majors, internships **Contact** Ms. Megan K. Murphy, Dean of Admissions and Enrollment Management, Allegheny College, 520 North Main Street, Box 5, Meadville, PA 16335. Telephone: 814-332-4351 or toll-free 800-521-5293. Fax: 814-337-0431. E-mail: admiss@admin.alleg.edu. Web site: http://www.allegheny.edu/.

▶ **For more information, see page 383.**

ALLEGHENY UNIVERSITY OF THE HEALTH SCIENCES
See MCP Hahnemann University

ALLENTOWN COLLEGE OF ST. FRANCIS DE SALES
See DeSales University

ALVERNIA COLLEGE
READING, PENNSYLVANIA

General Independent Roman Catholic, comprehensive, coed **Entrance** Moderately difficult **Setting** 85-acre suburban campus **Total enrollment** 1,647 **Student/faculty ratio** 14:1 **Application deadline** Rolling (freshmen), rolling (transfer) **Freshmen** 76% were admitted **Housing** Yes **Expenses** Tuition $13,435; Room & Board $5840 **Undergraduates** 66% women, 30% part-time, 44% 25 or older, 0.4% Native American, 3% Hispanic American, 8% African American, 2% Asian American/Pacific Islander **The most frequently chosen baccalaureate fields are** business/marketing, health professions and related sciences, protective services/public administration **Academic program** Advanced placement, accelerated degree program, honors program, summer session, adult/continuing education programs, internships **Contact** Mr. Francis Schodowski, Director of Admissions, Alvernia College, 400 Saint Bernardine Street, Reading, PA 19607. Telephone: 610-796-8220 or toll-free 888-ALVERNIA (in-state). Fax: 610-796-8336. Web site: http://www.alvernia.edu/.

ARCADIA UNIVERSITY
GLENSIDE, PENNSYLVANIA

General Independent, comprehensive, coed, affiliated with Presbyterian Church (U.S.A.) **Entrance** Moderately difficult **Setting** 55-acre suburban campus **Total enrollment** 2,756 **Student/faculty ratio** 12:1 **Application deadline** Rolling (freshmen), rolling (transfer) **Freshmen** 76% were admitted **Housing** Yes **Expenses** Tuition $17,830; Room & Board $7740 **Undergraduates** 74% women, 22% part-time, 29% 25 or older, 0.1% Native American, 2% Hispanic American, 13% African American, 3% Asian American/Pacific Islander **Academic program** English as a second language, advanced placement, self-designed majors, honors program, summer session, adult/continuing education programs, internships **Contact** Mr. Dennis L. Nostrand, Director of Enrollment Management, Arcadia University, 450 South Easton Road, Glenside, PA 19038. Telephone: 215-572-2910 or toll-free 888-BEAVER3. Fax: 215-572-4049. E-mail: admiss@beaver.edu. Web site: http://www.arcadia.edu.

BAPTIST BIBLE COLLEGE OF PENNSYLVANIA
CLARKS SUMMIT, PENNSYLVANIA

General Independent Baptist, comprehensive, coed **Entrance** Minimally difficult **Setting** 124-acre suburban campus **Total enrollment** 750 **Application deadline** 8/15 (freshmen), rolling (transfer) **Freshmen** 79% were admitted **Housing** Yes **Expenses** Tuition $9870; Room & Board $4892 **Undergraduates** 59% women, 8% part-time, 7% 25 or older **Academic program** Advanced placement, summer session, internships **Contact** Mr. Andy Giessman, Applications Coordinator, Baptist Bible College of Pennsylvania, PO Box 800, Clarks Summit, PA 18411-1297. Telephone: 570-586-2400 Ext. 9376 or toll-free 800-451-7664. Fax: 570-585-9400. E-mail: gamos@bbc.edu. Web site: http://www.bbc.edu/.

BEAVER COLLEGE
See Arcadia University

BLOOMSBURG UNIVERSITY OF PENNSYLVANIA
BLOOMSBURG, PENNSYLVANIA

General State-supported, comprehensive, coed **Entrance** Moderately difficult **Setting** 282-acre small-town campus **Total enrollment** 7,548 **Student/faculty ratio** 19:1 **Application deadline** Rolling (freshmen), rolling (transfer) **Freshmen** 61% were admitted **Housing** Yes **Expenses** Tuition 4668; Room & Board 4032 **Undergraduates** 61% women, 9% part-time, 8% 25 or older, 0.2% Native American, 2% Hispanic American, 3% African American, 1% Asian American/Pacific Islander **The most frequently chosen baccalaureate fields are** business/marketing, education, social sciences and history **Academic program** Advanced placement, honors program, summer session, adult/continuing education programs, internships **Contact** Mr. Christopher Keller, Director of Admissions, Bloomsburg University of Pennsylvania, Ben Franklin Hall, Room 10, Bloomsburg, PA 17815-1905. Telephone: 570-389-4316. E-mail: buadmiss@bloomu.edu. Web site: http://www.bloomu.edu/.

BRYN ATHYN COLLEGE OF THE NEW CHURCH
BRYN ATHYN, PENNSYLVANIA

General Independent Swedenborgian, comprehensive, coed **Entrance** Minimally difficult **Setting** 130-acre small-town campus **Total enrollment** 166 **Student/faculty ratio** 6:1 **Application deadline** 6/1 (freshmen), rolling (transfer) **Freshmen** 100% were admitted **Housing** Yes **Expenses** Tuition $6009; Room & Board $4581 **Undergraduates** 58% women, 9% part-time, 15% 25 or older **The most frequently chosen baccalaureate fields are** education, English, interdisciplinary studies **Academic program** Advanced placement, accelerated degree program, self-designed majors, internships **Contact** Dr. Dan Synnestvedt, Director of Admissions, Bryn Athyn College of the New Church, PO Box 717, Bryn Athyn, PA 19009-0717. Telephone: 215-938-2503. Fax: 215-938-2658. Web site: http://www.newchurch.edu/college/.

BRYN MAWR COLLEGE
BRYN MAWR, PENNSYLVANIA

General Independent, university, women only **Entrance** Most difficult **Setting** 135-acre suburban campus **Total enrollment** 1,784 **Student/faculty ratio** 9:1 **Application deadline** 1/15 (freshmen), 3/15 (transfer) **Freshmen** 61% were admitted **Housing** Yes **Expenses** Tuition 24,160; Room & Board 8340 **Undergraduates** 5% part-time, 5% 25 or older, 0.1% Native American, 3% Hispanic American, 4%

Bryn Mawr College *(continued)*

African American, 17% Asian American/Pacific Islander **The most frequently chosen baccalaureate fields are** biological/life sciences, English, social sciences and history **Academic program** Advanced placement, accelerated degree program, self-designed majors, honors program, summer session, adult/continuing education programs **Contact** Ms. Nancy Monnich, Director of Admissions, Bryn Mawr College, 101 North Merion Avenue, Bryn Mawr, PA 19010. Telephone: 610-526-5152 or toll-free 800-BMC-1885 (out-of-state). E-mail: admissions@brynmawr.edu. Web site: http://www.brynmawr.edu/.

BUCKNELL UNIVERSITY
LEWISBURG, PENNSYLVANIA

General Independent, comprehensive, coed **Entrance** Very difficult **Setting** 393-acre small-town campus **Total enrollment** 3,582 **Student/faculty ratio** 12:1 **Application deadline** 1/1 (freshmen), 4/1 (transfer) **Freshmen** 42% were admitted **Housing** Yes **Expenses** Tuition 23,839; Room & Board 5596 **Undergraduates** 48% women, 1% part-time, 1% 25 or older, 0.3% Native American, 2% Hispanic American, 3% African American, 5% Asian American/Pacific Islander **The most frequently chosen baccalaureate fields are** business/marketing, engineering/engineering technologies, social sciences and history **Academic program** Advanced placement, self-designed majors, honors program, summer session, internships **Contact** Mr. Mark D. Davies, Dean of Admissions, Bucknell University, Lewisburg, PA 17837. Telephone: 570-577-1101. Fax: 570-577-3538. E-mail: admissions@bucknell.edu. Web site: http://www.bucknell.edu/.

CABRINI COLLEGE
RADNOR, PENNSYLVANIA

General Independent Roman Catholic, comprehensive, coed **Entrance** Minimally difficult **Setting** 112-acre suburban campus **Total enrollment** 2,062 **Student/faculty ratio** 14:1 **Application deadline** Rolling (freshmen), rolling (transfer) **Freshmen** 87% were admitted **Housing** Yes **Expenses** Tuition 16,900; Room & Board 7560 **Undergraduates** 66% women, 27% part-time, 24% 25 or older, 0.4% Native American, 2% Hispanic American, 6% African American, 1% Asian American/Pacific Islander **The most frequently chosen baccalaureate fields are** business/marketing, communications/communication technologies, education **Academic program** Advanced placement, accelerated degree program, self-designed majors, honors program, summer session, adult/continuing education programs, internships **Contact** Mr. Mark Osborn, Director of Admissions, Cabrini College, 610 King of Prussia Road, Radnor, PA 19087-3698. Telephone: 610-902-8552 or toll-free 800-848-1003. Fax: 610-902-8508. E-mail: admit@cabrini.edu. Web site: http://www.cabrini.edu/.

CALIFORNIA UNIVERSITY OF PENNSYLVANIA
CALIFORNIA, PENNSYLVANIA

General State-supported, comprehensive, coed **Entrance** Moderately difficult **Setting** 148-acre small-town campus **Total enrollment** 5,899 **Application deadline** 7/30 (freshmen), 7/30 (transfer) **Freshmen** 78% were admitted **Housing** Yes **Expenses** Tuition $4937; Room & Board $4662 **Undergraduates** 53% women, 12% part-time, 20% 25 or older, 0.4% Native American, 1% Hispanic American, 4% African American, 0.4% Asian American/Pacific Islander **The most frequently chosen baccalaureate fields are** business/marketing, education, social sciences and history **Academic program** Advanced placement, accelerated degree program, honors program, summer session, adult/continuing education programs, internships **Contact** Mr. William A. Edmonds, Dean of Enrollment Management and Academic Services, California University of Pennsylvania, 250 University Avenue, California, PA 15419. Telephone: 724-938-4404. Fax: 724-938-4564. E-mail: inquiry@cup.edu. Web site: http://www.cup.edu/.

CARLOW COLLEGE
PITTSBURGH, PENNSYLVANIA

General Independent Roman Catholic, comprehensive, coed, primarily women **Entrance** Moderately difficult **Setting** 13-acre urban campus **Total enrollment** 1,925 **Student/faculty ratio** 15:1 **Application deadline** Rolling (freshmen), rolling (transfer) **Freshmen** 70% were admitted **Housing** Yes **Expenses** Tuition $13,342; Room & Board $5280 **Undergraduates** 93% women, 47% part-time, 57% 25 or older, 1% Native American, 1% Hispanic American, 17% African American, 1% Asian American/Pacific Islander **The most frequently chosen baccalaureate fields are** health professions and related sciences, education, interdisciplinary studies **Academic program** English as a second language, advanced placement, accelerated degree program, self-designed majors, honors program, summer session, adult/continuing education programs, internships **Contact** Ms. Susan Winstel, Assistant Director of Admissions, Carlow College, 3333 Fifth Avenue, Pittsburgh, PA 15213. Telephone: 412-578-6330 or toll-free 800-333-CARLOW. Fax: 412-578-6668. E-mail: admissions@carlow.edu. Web site: http://www.carlow.edu/.

CARNEGIE MELLON UNIVERSITY
PITTSBURGH, PENNSYLVANIA

General Independent, university, coed **Entrance** Very difficult **Setting** 103-acre urban campus **Total enrollment** 8,514 **Student/faculty ratio** 10:1 **Application deadline** 1/1 (freshmen), 3/15 (transfer) **Freshmen** 36% were admitted **Housing** Yes **Expenses** Tuition 23,022; Room & Board 7028 **Undergraduates** 37% women, 4% part-time, 1% 25 or older, 1% Native American, 5% Hispanic American, 3% African American, 20% Asian American/Pacific Islander **The most frequently chosen baccalaureate fields are** engineering/

engineering technologies, business/marketing, visual/performing arts **Academic program** English as a second language, advanced placement, accelerated degree program, self-designed majors, honors program, summer session, adult/continuing education programs, internships **Contact** Mr. Michael Steidel, Director of Admissions, Carnegie Mellon University, 5000 Forbes Avenue, Warner Hall, Room 101, Pittsburgh, PA 15213. Telephone: 412-268-2082. Fax: 412-268-7838. E-mail: undergraduate-admissions+@andrew.cmu.edu. Web site: http://www.cmu.edu/.

CEDAR CREST COLLEGE
ALLENTOWN, PENNSYLVANIA

General Independent, 4-year, women only, affiliated with United Church of Christ **Entrance** Moderately difficult **Setting** 84-acre suburban campus **Total enrollment** 1,566 **Student/faculty ratio** 11:1 **Application deadline** Rolling (freshmen), rolling (transfer) **Freshmen** 73% were admitted **Housing** Yes **Expenses** Tuition $17,790; Room & Board $6465 **Undergraduates** 48% part-time, 48% 25 or older, 0.2% Native American, 3% Hispanic American, 3% African American, 2% Asian American/Pacific Islander **The most frequently chosen baccalaureate fields are** psychology, biological/life sciences, social sciences and history **Academic program** English as a second language, advanced placement, accelerated degree program, self-designed majors, honors program, summer session, adult/continuing education programs, internships **Contact** Ms. Judith A. Neyhart, Vice President for Enrollment and Advancement, Cedar Crest College, 100 College Drive, Allentown, PA 18104-6196. Telephone: 610-740-3780 or toll-free 800-360-1222. Fax: 610-606-4647. E-mail: cccadmis@cedarcrest.edu. Web site: http://www.cedarcrest.edu/.

► **For more information, see page 397.**

CHATHAM COLLEGE
PITTSBURGH, PENNSYLVANIA

General Independent, comprehensive, women only **Entrance** Moderately difficult **Setting** 34-acre urban campus **Total enrollment** 1,004 **Student/faculty ratio** 10:1 **Application deadline** Rolling (freshmen), rolling (transfer) **Freshmen** 87% were admitted **Housing** Yes **Expenses** Tuition $18,236; Room & Board $6246 **Undergraduates** 16% part-time, 18% 25 or older, 1% Native American, 2% Hispanic American, 11% African American, 3% Asian American/Pacific Islander **The most frequently chosen baccalaureate fields are** biological/life sciences, English, psychology **Academic program** English as a second language, advanced placement, accelerated degree program, self-designed majors, summer session, adult/continuing education programs, internships **Contact** Ms. Karina J. Dayich, Dean of Admissions and Financial Aid, Chatham College, Woodland Road, Pittsburgh, PA 15232. Telephone: 412-365-1290 or toll free 800-837-1290. Fax: 412-365-1609. E-mail: admissions@chat.edu. Web site: http://www.chatham.edu/.

CHESTNUT HILL COLLEGE
PHILADELPHIA, PENNSYLVANIA

General Independent Roman Catholic, comprehensive, women only **Entrance** Moderately difficult **Setting** 45-acre suburban campus **Total enrollment** 1,561 **Student/faculty ratio** 10:1 **Application deadline** Rolling (freshmen), rolling (transfer) **Freshmen** 75% were admitted **Housing** Yes **Expenses** Tuition 17,620; Room & Board 7170 **Undergraduates** 38% part-time, 25% 25 or older **The most frequently chosen baccalaureate fields are** business/marketing, education, protective services/public administration **Academic program** English as a second language, advanced placement, self-designed majors, honors program, summer session, adult/continuing education programs, internships **Contact** Ms. Elizabeth Becker, Director of Admissions, Chestnut Hill College, 9601 Germantown Avenue, Philadelphia, PA 19118-2693. Telephone: 215-248-7001 or toll-free 800-248-0052 (out-of-state). Fax: 215-248-7082. E-mail: chcapply@chc.edu. Web site: http://www.chc.edu/.

► **For more information, see page 399.**

CHEYNEY UNIVERSITY OF PENNSYLVANIA
CHEYNEY, PENNSYLVANIA

General State-supported, comprehensive, coed **Entrance** Minimally difficult **Setting** 275-acre suburban campus **Total enrollment** 1,496 **Student/faculty ratio** 13:1 **Application deadline** Rolling (freshmen), rolling (transfer) **Freshmen** 82% were admitted **Housing** Yes **Expenses** Tuition $4447; Room & Board $4983 **Undergraduates** 56% women, 12% part-time, 13% 25 or older, 0.1% Native American, 1% Hispanic American, 98% African American, 0.2% Asian American/Pacific Islander **The most frequently chosen baccalaureate fields are** business/marketing, education, social sciences and history **Academic program** Summer session, adult/continuing education programs, internships **Contact** Mr. James V. Brown, Interim Director of Admissions, Cheyney University of Pennsylvania, Cheyney and Creek Roads, Cheyney, PA 19319. Telephone: 610-399-2000 or toll-free 800-CHEYNEY. Fax: 610-399-2099. Web site: http://www.cheyney.edu/.

CLARION UNIVERSITY OF PENNSYLVANIA
CLARION, PENNSYLVANIA

General State-supported, comprehensive, coed **Entrance** Minimally difficult **Setting** 100-acre rural campus **Total enrollment** 6,192 **Student/faculty ratio** 18:1 **Application deadline** Rolling (freshmen), rolling (transfer) **Freshmen** 86% were admitted **Housing** Yes **Expenses** Tuition $4359; Room & Board $2420 **Undergraduates** 61% women, 8% part-time, 14% 25 or older, 0.2% Native American, 1% Hispanic American, 5% African American, 1% Asian American/Pacific Islander **The most frequently chosen baccalaureate fields are** business/marketing,

Clarion University of Pennsylvania *(continued)*

education, health professions and related sciences **Academic program** Advanced placement, accelerated degree program, honors program, summer session, adult/continuing education programs, internships **Contact** Ms. Sue McMillen, Interim Director of Admissions, Clarion University of Pennsylvania, Clarion, PA 16214. Telephone: 814-393-2306 or toll-free 800-672-7171 (in-state). Fax: 814-393-2030. E-mail: pstewart@mail.clarion.edu. Web site: http://www.clarion.edu/.

COLLEGE MISERICORDIA
DALLAS, PENNSYLVANIA

General Independent Roman Catholic, comprehensive, coed **Entrance** Moderately difficult **Setting** 100-acre small-town campus **Total enrollment** 1,765 **Student/faculty ratio** 14:1 **Application deadline** Rolling (freshmen), rolling (transfer) **Freshmen** 84% were admitted **Housing** Yes **Expenses** Tuition $16,010; Room & Board $6470 **Undergraduates** 73% women, 30% part-time, 0.1% Native American, 1% Hispanic American, 0.4% African American, 0.4% Asian American/Pacific Islander **The most frequently chosen baccalaureate fields are** health professions and related sciences, education, liberal arts/general studies **Academic program** Advanced placement, accelerated degree program, self-designed majors, honors program, summer session, adult/continuing education programs, internships **Contact** Ms. Jane Dessoye, Executive Director of Admissions and Financial Aid, College Misericordia, 301 Lake Street, Dallas, PA 18612. Telephone: 570-675-4449 Ext. 6168 or toll-free 800-852-7675. Fax: 570-675-2441. E-mail: admiss@miseri.edu. Web site: http://www.miseri.edu/.

THE CURTIS INSTITUTE OF MUSIC
PHILADELPHIA, PENNSYLVANIA

General Independent, comprehensive, coed **Entrance** Most difficult **Setting** urban campus **Total enrollment** 168 **Application deadline** 1/15 (freshmen), 1/15 (transfer) **Freshmen** 7% were admitted **Housing** No **Expenses** Tuition 695 **The most frequently chosen baccalaureate field is** visual/performing arts **Academic program** English as a second language, advanced placement, accelerated degree program **Contact** Mr. Christopher Hodges, Admissions Officer, The Curtis Institute of Music, 1726 Locust Street, Philadelphia, PA 19103-6107. Telephone: 215-893-5262. Fax: 215-893-7900.

DELAWARE VALLEY COLLEGE
DOYLESTOWN, PENNSYLVANIA

General Independent, comprehensive, coed **Entrance** Moderately difficult **Setting** 600-acre suburban campus **Total enrollment** 1,887 **Student/faculty ratio** 15:1 **Application deadline** Rolling (freshmen), rolling (transfer) **Freshmen** 82% were admitted **Housing** Yes **Expenses** Tuition $16,448; Room & Board $6340 **Undergraduates** 51% women, 27% part-time, 24% 25 or older, 0.2% Native American, 2% Hispanic American, 4% African American, 0.4% Asian American/Pacific Islander **The most frequently chosen baccalaureate fields are** agriculture, biological/life sciences, business/marketing **Academic program** Advanced placement, honors program, summer session, adult/continuing education programs, internships **Contact** Mr. Stephen Zenko, Director of Admissions, Delaware Valley College, 700 East Butler Avenue, Doylestown, PA 18901. Telephone: 215-489-2211 Ext. 2211 or toll-free 800-2DELVAL (in-state). Fax: 215-230-2968. E-mail: admitme@devalcol.edu. Web site: http://www.devalcol.edu/.

DESALES UNIVERSITY
CENTER VALLEY, PENNSYLVANIA

General Independent Roman Catholic, comprehensive, coed **Entrance** Moderately difficult **Setting** 300-acre suburban campus **Total enrollment** 2,549 **Student/faculty ratio** 14:1 **Application deadline** 8/1 (freshmen), 8/1 (transfer) **Freshmen** 72% were admitted **Housing** Yes **Expenses** Tuition $14,790; Room & Board $6090 **Undergraduates** 57% women, 25% part-time, 1% 25 or older, 0.1% Native American, 2% Hispanic American, 1% African American, 1% Asian American/Pacific Islander **The most frequently chosen baccalaureate fields are** business/marketing, protective services/public administration, visual/performing arts **Academic program** Advanced placement, accelerated degree program, summer session, adult/continuing education programs, internships **Contact** Ms. Angie Waters, Director of Admissions, DeSales University, 2755 Station Avenue, Center Valley, PA 18034-9568. Telephone: 610-282-1100 Ext. 1206 or toll-free 800-228-5114. Fax: 610-282-2254. E-mail: kelly@accnov.allencol.edu. Web site: http://www.desales.edu.

DICKINSON COLLEGE
CARLISLE, PENNSYLVANIA

General Independent, 4-year, coed **Entrance** Very difficult **Setting** 103-acre suburban campus **Total enrollment** 2,115 **Student/faculty ratio** 12:1 **Application deadline** 2/1 (freshmen), 6/1 (transfer) **Freshmen** 64% were admitted **Housing** Yes **Expenses** Tuition $25,485; Room & Board $6725 **Undergraduates** 61% women, 1% part-time, 1% 25 or older, 0.1% Native American, 2% Hispanic American, 1% African American, 3% Asian American/Pacific Islander **The most frequently chosen baccalaureate fields are** foreign language/literature, English, social sciences and history **Academic program** Advanced placement, accelerated degree program, self-designed majors, summer session, adult/continuing education programs, internships **Contact** Mr. Christopher Seth Allen, Director of Admissions, Dickinson College, PO Box 1773, Carlisle, PA 17013-2896. Telephone: 717-245-1231 or toll-free 800-644-1773. Fax: 717-245-1231. E-mail: admit@dickinson.edu. Web site: http://www.dickinson.edu/.

DREXEL UNIVERSITY
PHILADELPHIA, PENNSYLVANIA

General Independent, university, coed **Entrance** Moderately difficult **Setting** 42-acre urban campus **Total enrollment** 13,128 **Student/faculty ratio** 14:1 **Application deadline** 3/1 (freshmen), rolling (transfer) **Freshmen** 78% were admitted **Housing** Yes **Expenses** Tuition 18,962; Room & Board 8705 **Undergraduates** 38% women, 18% part-time, 13% 25 or older, 0.2% Native American, 2% Hispanic American, 9% African American, 13% Asian American/Pacific Islander **The most frequently chosen baccalaureate fields are** business/marketing, computer/information sciences, engineering/engineering technologies **Academic program** English as a second language, advanced placement, accelerated degree program, honors program, summer session, adult/continuing education programs, internships **Contact** Ms. Joan MacDonald, Dean of Enrollment Management and Career Services, Drexel University, 3141 Chestnut Street, Room 220, Philadelphia, PA 19104-2875. Telephone: 215-895-2400 or toll-free 800-2-DREXEL. Fax: 215-895-5939. E-mail: undergrad-admissions@post.drexel.edu. Web site: http://www.drexel.edu/.

▶ **For more information, see page 408.**

DUQUESNE UNIVERSITY
PITTSBURGH, PENNSYLVANIA

General Independent Roman Catholic, university, coed **Entrance** Moderately difficult **Setting** 43-acre urban campus **Total enrollment** 9,667 **Student/faculty ratio** 15:1 **Application deadline** 7/1 (freshmen), 7/1 (transfer) **Freshmen** 84% were admitted **Housing** Yes **Expenses** Tuition 16,520; Room & Board 6504 **Undergraduates** 58% women, 9% part-time, 13% 25 or older, 0.2% Native American, 2% Hispanic American, 4% African American, 2% Asian American/Pacific Islander **The most frequently chosen baccalaureate fields are** business/marketing, education, health professions and related sciences **Academic program** English as a second language, advanced placement, accelerated degree program, self-designed majors, honors program, summer session, adult/continuing education programs, internships **Contact** Office of Admissions, Duquesne University, 600 Forbes Avenue, Pittsburgh, PA 15282-0201. Telephone: 412-396-5000 or toll-free 800-456-0590. Fax: 412-396-5644. E-mail: admissions@duq2.cc.duq.edu. Web site: http://www.duq.edu/.

EASTERN COLLEGE
ST. DAVIDS, PENNSYLVANIA

General Independent American Baptist, comprehensive, coed **Entrance** Moderately difficult **Setting** 107-acre small-town campus **Total enrollment** 2,400 **Student/faculty ratio** 14:1 **Application deadline** Rolling (freshmen), rolling (transfer) **Freshmen** 84% were admitted **Housing** Yes **Expenses** Tuition $15,150; Room & Board $6490 **Undergraduates** 39% 25 or older, 0.2% Native American, 2% Hispanic American, 14% African American, 1% Asian American/Pacific Islander **The most frequently chosen baccalaureate fields are** business/marketing, education, philosophy, religion, and theology **Academic program** English as a second language, advanced placement, accelerated degree program, self-designed majors, honors program, summer session, adult/continuing education programs, internships **Contact** Mr. David Urban, Director of Undergraduate Admissions, Eastern College, 1300 Eagle Road, St. Davids, PA 19087-3696. Telephone: 610-225-5005 or toll-free 800-452-0996. Fax: 610-341-1723. E-mail: ugadm@eastern.edu. Web site: http://www.eastern.edu/.

▶ **For more information, see page 410.**

EAST STROUDSBURG UNIVERSITY OF PENNSYLVANIA
EAST STROUDSBURG, PENNSYLVANIA

General State-supported, comprehensive, coed **Contact** Mr. Alan T. Chesterton, Director of Admissions, East Stroudsburg University of Pennsylvania, 200 Prospect Street, East Stroudsburg, PA 18301. Telephone: 570-422-3542 or toll-free 877-230-5547. Fax: 570-422-3933. E-mail: atc@po-box.esu.edu. Web site: http://www.esu.edu/.

EDINBORO UNIVERSITY OF PENNSYLVANIA
EDINBORO, PENNSYLVANIA

General State-supported, comprehensive, coed **Entrance** Moderately difficult **Setting** 585-acre small-town campus **Total enrollment** 7,212 **Student/faculty ratio** 18:1 **Application deadline** Rolling (freshmen), rolling (transfer) **Freshmen** 80% were admitted **Housing** Yes **Expenses** Tuition $4569; Room & Board $4104 **Undergraduates** 57% women, 10% part-time, 16% 25 or older, 0.3% Native American, 1% Hispanic American, 5% African American, 1% Asian American/Pacific Islander **The most frequently chosen baccalaureate fields are** education, protective services/public administration, visual/performing arts **Academic program** Advanced placement, accelerated degree program, self-designed majors, honors program, summer session, adult/continuing education programs, internships **Contact** Mr. Terrence Carlin, Assistant Vice President for Admissions, Edinboro University of Pennsylvania, Biggers House, Edinboro, PA 16444. Telephone: 814-732-2761 or toll-free 888-846-2676 (in-state); 800-626-2203 (out-of-state). Fax: 814-732-2420. E-mail: carlin@edinboro.edu. Web site: http://www.edinboro.edu/.

ELIZABETHTOWN COLLEGE
ELIZABETHTOWN, PENNSYLVANIA

General Independent, comprehensive, coed, affiliated with Church of the Brethren **Entrance** Moderately difficult **Setting** 185-acre small-town campus **Total enrollment** 1,825 **Student/faculty ratio** 12:1 **Application deadline** Rolling (freshmen), rolling

Elizabethtown College *(continued)*

(transfer) **Freshmen** 77% were admitted **Housing** Yes **Expenses** Tuition 19,100; Room & Board 5600 **Undergraduates** 65% women, 10% part-time, 0.1% Native American, 2% Hispanic American, 1% African American, 2% Asian American/Pacific Islander **The most frequently chosen baccalaureate fields are** business/marketing, education, health professions and related sciences **Academic program** English as a second language, advanced placement, honors program, summer session, adult/continuing education programs, internships **Contact** W. Kent Barnds, Director of Admissions, Elizabethtown College, 1 Alpha Drive, Elizabethtown, PA 17022-2298. Telephone: 717-361-1400. Fax: 717-361-1365. E-mail: admissions@acad.etown.edu. Web site: http://www.etown.edu/.

FRANKLIN AND MARSHALL COLLEGE
LANCASTER, PENNSYLVANIA

General Independent, 4-year, coed **Entrance** Very difficult **Setting** 125-acre suburban campus **Total enrollment** 1,892 **Student/faculty ratio** 11:1 **Application deadline** 2/1 (freshmen), 5/1 (transfer) **Freshmen** 56% were admitted **Housing** Yes **Expenses** Tuition 24,866; Room & Board 5994 **Undergraduates** 50% women, 2% part-time, 0% 25 or older, 0.1% Native American, 3% Hispanic American, 3% African American, 4% Asian American/Pacific Islander **The most frequently chosen baccalaureate fields are** business/marketing, English, social sciences and history **Academic program** Advanced placement, accelerated degree program, self-designed majors, honors program, summer session, internships **Contact** Gregory Goldsmith, Director of Admissions, Franklin and Marshall College, PO Box 3003, Lancaster, PA 17604-3003. Telephone: 717-291-3953. Fax: 717-291-4389. E-mail: admission@fandm.edu. Web site: http://www.fandm.edu/.

GANNON UNIVERSITY
ERIE, PENNSYLVANIA

General Independent Roman Catholic, comprehensive, coed **Entrance** Moderately difficult **Setting** 13-acre urban campus **Total enrollment** 3,377 **Student/faculty ratio** 13:1 **Application deadline** Rolling (freshmen), rolling (transfer) **Freshmen** 90% were admitted **Housing** Yes **Expenses** Tuition $14,112; Room & Board $5670 **Undergraduates** 59% women, 14% part-time, 15% 25 or older, 0.3% Native American, 1% Hispanic American, 3% African American, 1% Asian American/Pacific Islander **The most frequently chosen baccalaureate fields are** business/marketing, education, health professions and related sciences **Academic program** English as a second language, advanced placement, accelerated degree program, honors program, summer session, adult/continuing education programs, internships **Contact** Ms. Beth Nemenz, Director of Admissions, Gannon University, University Square, Erie, PA 16541. Telephone: 814-871-7240 or toll-free 800-GANNONU. Fax: 814-871-5803. E-mail: admissions@cluster.gannon.edu. Web site: http://www.gannon.edu/.

GENEVA COLLEGE
BEAVER FALLS, PENNSYLVANIA

General Independent, comprehensive, coed, affiliated with Reformed Presbyterian Church of North America **Entrance** Moderately difficult **Setting** 55-acre small-town campus **Total enrollment** 2,286 **Student/faculty ratio** 19:1 **Application deadline** 8/1 (freshmen), rolling (transfer) **Freshmen** 78% were admitted **Housing** Yes **Expenses** Tuition $14,050; Room & Board $5940 **Undergraduates** 56% women, 19% part-time, 4% 25 or older, 0.3% Native American, 2% Hispanic American, 15% African American, 1% Asian American/Pacific Islander **The most frequently chosen baccalaureate fields are** business/marketing, education, liberal arts/general studies **Academic program** English as a second language, advanced placement, accelerated degree program, self-designed majors, honors program, summer session, adult/continuing education programs, internships **Contact** Mr. David Layton, Director of Admissions, Geneva College, 3200 College Avenue, Beaver Falls, PA 15010. Telephone: 724-847-6500 or toll-free 800-847-8255. Fax: 724-847-6776. E-mail: admissions@geneva.edu. Web site: http://www.geneva.edu/.

GETTYSBURG COLLEGE
GETTYSBURG, PENNSYLVANIA

General Independent, 4-year, coed, affiliated with Evangelical Lutheran Church in America **Entrance** Very difficult **Setting** 200-acre small-town campus **Total enrollment** 2,218 **Student/faculty ratio** 11:1 **Application deadline** 2/15 (freshmen) **Freshmen** 68% were admitted **Housing** Yes **Expenses** Tuition $24,875; Room & Board $5956 **Undergraduates** 52% women, 0.5% part-time, 0.2% Native American, 1% Hispanic American, 2% African American, 1% Asian American/Pacific Islander **The most frequently chosen baccalaureate fields are** business/marketing, biological/life sciences, social sciences and history **Academic program** Advanced placement, accelerated degree program, self-designed majors, adult/continuing education programs, internships **Contact** Ms. Gail Sweezey, Director of Admissions, Gettysburg College, 300 North Washington Street, Gettysburg, PA 17325. Telephone: 717-337-6100 or toll-free 800-431-0803. Fax: 717-337-6145. E-mail: admiss@gettysburg.edu. Web site: http://www.gettysburg.edu/.

GRATZ COLLEGE
MELROSE PARK, PENNSYLVANIA

General Independent Jewish, comprehensive, coed **Entrance** Moderately difficult **Setting** 28-acre suburban campus **Total enrollment** 503 **Student/faculty ratio** 12:1 **Application deadline** Rolling (freshmen), rolling (transfer) **Freshmen** 75% were admitted **Housing** No **Expenses** Tuition 7560 **Undergraduates** 64% women, 73% part-time, 89% 25 or older **The**

most frequently chosen baccalaureate field is philosophy, religion, and theology **Academic program** Summer session, adult/continuing education programs, internships **Contact** Ms. Adena E. Johnston, Director of Admissions, Gratz College, 7605 Old York Road, Melrose Park, PA 19027. Telephone: 215-635-7300 Ext. 140 or toll-free 800-475-4635 Ext. 140 (out-of-state). Fax: 215-635-7320 Ext. 140. E-mail: gratzgen@hslc.org. Web site: http://www.gratzcollege.edu/.

GROVE CITY COLLEGE

GROVE CITY, PENNSYLVANIA

General Independent Presbyterian, 4-year, coed **Entrance** Very difficult **Setting** 150-acre small-town campus **Total enrollment** 2,332 **Student/faculty ratio** 19:1 **Application deadline** 2/15 (freshmen), rolling (transfer) **Freshmen** 51% were admitted **Housing** Yes **Expenses** Tuition 7710; Room & Board 4206 **Undergraduates** 50% women, 2% part-time, 1% 25 or older, 0% Native American, 0.2% Hispanic American, 0.3% African American, 1% Asian American/Pacific Islander **The most frequently chosen baccalaureate fields are** biological/life sciences, business/marketing, education **Academic program** Advanced placement, self-designed majors, summer session, internships **Contact** Mr. Jeffrey C. Mincey, Director of Admissions, Grove City College, 100 Campus Drive, Grove City, PA 16127-2104. Telephone: 724-458-2100. Fax: 724-458-3395. E-mail: admissionsinformation@gcc.edu. Web site: http://www.gcc.edu/.

► **For more information, see page 428.**

GWYNEDD-MERCY COLLEGE

GWYNEDD VALLEY, PENNSYLVANIA

General Independent Roman Catholic, comprehensive, coed **Entrance** Moderately difficult **Setting** 170-acre suburban campus **Total enrollment** 1,941 **Student/faculty ratio** 17:1 **Application deadline** Rolling (freshmen), 8/1 (transfer) **Freshmen** 79% were admitted **Housing** Yes **Expenses** Tuition $15,226; Room & Board $7540 **Undergraduates** 75% women, 48% part-time, 46% 25 or older, 0.1% Native American, 2% Hispanic American, 10% African American, 3% Asian American/Pacific Islander **The most frequently chosen baccalaureate fields are** education, business/marketing, health professions and related sciences **Academic program** English as a second language, advanced placement, accelerated degree program, honors program, summer session, adult/continuing education programs, internships **Contact** Mr. Dennis Murphy, Vice President of Enrollment Management, Gwynedd-Mercy College, 1325 Sumneytown Pike, Gwynedd Valley, PA 19437-0901. Telephone: 215-646-7300 or toll-free 800-DIAL-GMC (in-state). E-mail: admissions@gmc.edu. Web site: http://www.gmc.edu/.

HAVERFORD COLLEGE

HAVERFORD, PENNSYLVANIA

General Independent, 4-year, coed **Entrance** Most difficult **Setting** 200-acre suburban campus **Total enrollment** 1,135 **Student/faculty ratio** 9:1 **Application deadline** 1/15 (freshmen), 3/31 (transfer) **Freshmen** 32% were admitted **Housing** Yes **Expenses** Tuition 24,940; Room & Board 7910 **Undergraduates** 52% women, 0% 25 or older, 0.4% Native American, 6% Hispanic American, 6% African American, 10% Asian American/Pacific Islander **The most frequently chosen baccalaureate fields are** biological/life sciences, English, social sciences and history **Academic program** Advanced placement, accelerated degree program, self-designed majors, internships **Contact** Ms. Delsie Z. Phillips, Director of Admission, Haverford College, 370 Lancaster Avenue, Haverford, PA 19041-1392. Telephone: 610-896-1350. Fax: 610-896-1338. E-mail: admitme@haverford.edu. Web site: http://www.haverford.edu/.

► **For more information, see page 429.**

HOLY FAMILY COLLEGE

PHILADELPHIA, PENNSYLVANIA

General Independent Roman Catholic, comprehensive, coed **Entrance** Moderately difficult **Setting** 47-acre suburban campus **Total enrollment** 2,546 **Student/faculty ratio** 11:1 **Application deadline** Rolling (freshmen), rolling (transfer) **Freshmen** 89% were admitted **Housing** No **Expenses** Tuition 12,760 **Undergraduates** 77% women, 42% part-time, 12% 25 or older, 0.2% Native American, 2% Hispanic American, 3% African American, 3% Asian American/Pacific Islander **The most frequently chosen baccalaureate fields are** education, business/marketing, health professions and related sciences **Academic program** Advanced placement, accelerated degree program, honors program, summer session, adult/continuing education programs, internships **Contact** Mrs. Roberta Nolan, Director of Admissions, Holy Family College, Grant and Frankford Avenues, Philadelphia, PA 19114-2094. Telephone: 215-637-3050 or toll-free 800-637-1191. Fax: 215-281-1022. E-mail: rnolan@hfc.edu. Web site: http://www.hfc.edu/.

IMMACULATA COLLEGE

IMMACULATA, PENNSYLVANIA

General Independent Roman Catholic, comprehensive, women only **Entrance** Moderately difficult **Setting** 400-acre suburban campus **Total enrollment** 3,278 **Student/faculty ratio** 13:1 **Application deadline** 8/15 (freshmen), rolling (transfer) **Freshmen** 86% were admitted **Housing** Yes **Expenses** Tuition $13,950; Room & Board $6800 **Undergraduates** 47% part-time, 77% 25 or older, 0.2% Native American, 1% Hispanic American, 8% African American, 1% Asian American/Pacific Islander **The most frequently chosen baccalaureate fields are** business/marketing, home economics/vocational home economics, psychology **Academic program** English as a second language, advanced placement, accelerated degree program, self-designed majors, honors program, summer session, adult/continuing education programs, internships **Contact** Mr. Ken Rasp, Dean of Enrollment Management, Immaculata College, 1145 King Road, Immaculata, PA 19345-0500. Tele-

Immaculata College *(continued)*

phone: 610-647-4400 Ext. 3015 or toll-free 877-428-6328. Fax: 610-640-0836. E-mail: admiss@immaculata.edu. Web site: http://www.immaculata.edu/.

INDIANA UNIVERSITY OF PENNSYLVANIA

INDIANA, PENNSYLVANIA

General State-supported, university, coed **Entrance** Moderately difficult **Setting** 350-acre small-town campus **Total enrollment** 13,410 **Student/faculty ratio** 18:1 **Application deadline** Rolling (freshmen), rolling (transfer) **Freshmen** 58% were admitted **Housing** Yes **Expenses** Tuition $4617; Room & Board $3966 **Undergraduates** 56% women, 6% part-time, 7% 25 or older, 0.1% Native American, 1% Hispanic American, 5% African American, 1% Asian American/Pacific Islander **The most frequently chosen baccalaureate fields are** business/marketing, education, social sciences and history **Academic program** English as a second language, advanced placement, accelerated degree program, honors program, summer session, adult/continuing education programs, internships **Contact** Mr. William Nunn, Dean of Admissions, Indiana University of Pennsylvania, 216 Pratt Hall, Indiana, PA 15705. Telephone: 724-357-2230 or toll-free 800-442-6830. E-mail: admissions_inquiry@grove.iup.edu. Web site: http://www.iup.edu/.

JUNIATA COLLEGE

HUNTINGDON, PENNSYLVANIA

General Independent, 4-year, coed, affiliated with Church of the Brethren **Entrance** Moderately difficult **Setting** 110-acre small-town campus **Total enrollment** 1,291 **Student/faculty ratio** 14:1 **Application deadline** 3/15 (freshmen), 6/15 (transfer) **Freshmen** 81% were admitted **Housing** Yes **Expenses** Tuition $19,360; Room & Board $5290 **Undergraduates** 57% women, 3% part-time, 5% 25 or older, 0.2% Native American, 1% Hispanic American, 0.4% African American, 1% Asian American/Pacific Islander **The most frequently chosen baccalaureate fields are** biological/life sciences, education, social sciences and history **Academic program** English as a second language, advanced placement, self-designed majors, honors program, summer session, adult/continuing education programs, internships **Contact** Ms. Michelle Bartol, Dean of Admissions, Juniata College, 1700 Moore Street, Huntingdon, PA 16652-2119. Telephone: 814-641-3432 or toll-free 877-JUNIATA. Fax: 814-641-3100. E-mail: info@juncol.juniata.edu. Web site: http://www.juniata.edu/.

KING'S COLLEGE

WILKES-BARRE, PENNSYLVANIA

General Independent Roman Catholic, comprehensive, coed **Entrance** Moderately difficult **Setting** 48-acre suburban campus **Total enrollment** 2,233 **Student/faculty ratio** 15:1 **Application deadline** Rolling (freshmen), rolling (transfer) **Freshmen** 86% were admitted **Housing** Yes **Expenses** Tuition $16,700; Room & Board $6890 **Undergraduates** 52% women, 17% part-time, 4% 25 or older, 0.2% Native American, 1% Hispanic American, 2% African American, 1% Asian American/Pacific Islander **The most frequently chosen baccalaureate fields are** business/marketing, health professions and related sciences, protective services/public administration **Academic program** English as a second language, advanced placement, accelerated degree program, self-designed majors, honors program, summer session, adult/continuing education programs, internships **Contact** Ms. Susan McGarry-Hannon, Director of Admissions, King's College, 133 North River Street, Wilkes-Barre, PA 18711-0801. Telephone: 570-208-5858 or toll-free 888-KINGSPA. Fax: 570-208-5971. E-mail: admssns@rs01.kings.edu. Web site: http://www.kings.edu/.

KUTZTOWN UNIVERSITY OF PENNSYLVANIA

KUTZTOWN, PENNSYLVANIA

General State-supported, comprehensive, coed **Entrance** Moderately difficult **Setting** 326-acre rural campus **Total enrollment** 8,068 **Student/faculty ratio** 16:1 **Application deadline** Rolling (freshmen), rolling (transfer) **Freshmen** 73% were admitted **Housing** Yes **Expenses** Tuition $4667; Room & Board $4522 **Undergraduates** 60% women, 10% part-time, 10% 25 or older, 0.3% Native American, 2% Hispanic American, 3% African American, 1% Asian American/Pacific Islander **The most frequently chosen baccalaureate fields are** business/marketing, education, visual/performing arts **Academic program** Advanced placement, accelerated degree program, self-designed majors, honors program, summer session, adult/continuing education programs, internships **Contact** Dr. Robert McGowan, Director of Admissions, Kutztown University of Pennsylvania, 15200 Kutztown Road, Kutztown, PA 19530-0730. Telephone: 610-683-4060 Ext. 4053 or toll-free 877-628-1915. Fax: 610-683-1375. E-mail: admission@kutztown.edu. Web site: http://www.kutztown.edu/.

LAFAYETTE COLLEGE

EASTON, PENNSYLVANIA

General Independent, 4-year, coed, affiliated with Presbyterian Church (U.S.A.) **Entrance** Very difficult **Setting** 110-acre suburban campus **Total enrollment** 2,279 **Student/faculty ratio** 11:1 **Application deadline** 1/1 (freshmen), 6/1 (transfer) **Freshmen** 40% were admitted **Housing** Yes **Expenses** Tuition $24,921; Room & Board $7734 **Undergraduates** 49% women, 4% part-time, 0% 25 or older, 0.3% Native American, 2% Hispanic American, 4% African American, 2% Asian American/Pacific Islander **The most frequently chosen baccalaureate fields are** engineering/engineering technologies, biological/life sciences, social sciences and history **Academic program** Advanced placement, accelerated degree program, self-designed majors, honors program, summer session, adult/continuing education programs, internships **Contact** Ms. Carol Rowlands, Director of

Admissions, Lafayette College, Easton, PA 18042-1798. Telephone: 610-330-5100. Fax: 610-330-5355. E-mail: rippleg@lafayette.edu. Web site: http://www.lafayette.edu/.

LANCASTER BIBLE COLLEGE
LANCASTER, PENNSYLVANIA

General Independent nondenominational, comprehensive, coed **Entrance** Minimally difficult **Setting** 100-acre suburban campus **Total enrollment** 760 **Student/faculty ratio** 16:1 **Application deadline** Rolling (freshmen), rolling (transfer) **Freshmen** 82% were admitted **Housing** Yes **Expenses** Tuition $9980; Room & Board $4550 **Undergraduates** 54% women, 26% part-time, 19% 25 or older, 0.2% Native American, 1% Hispanic American, 2% African American, 0.3% Asian American/Pacific Islander **The most frequently chosen baccalaureate fields are** education, philosophy, religion, and theology **Academic program** Advanced placement, summer session, adult/continuing education programs, internships **Contact** Mrs. Joanne M. Roper, Director of Admissions, Lancaster Bible College, 901 Eden Road, Lancaster, PA 17601-5036. Telephone: 717-560-8271 or toll-free 888-866-LBC-4-YOU. Fax: 717-560-8213. E-mail: admissions@lbc.edu. Web site: http://www.lbc.edu/.

LA ROCHE COLLEGE
PITTSBURGH, PENNSYLVANIA

General Independent, comprehensive, coed, affiliated with Roman Catholic Church **Entrance** Minimally difficult **Setting** 80-acre suburban campus **Total enrollment** 1,875 **Student/faculty ratio** 15:1 **Application deadline** Rolling (freshmen), rolling (transfer) **Freshmen** 86% were admitted **Housing** Yes **Expenses** Tuition $12,000; Room & Board $6474 **Undergraduates** 63% women, 24% part-time, 27% 25 or older, 0.2% Native American, 1% Hispanic American, 3% African American, 0.4% Asian American/Pacific Islander **The most frequently chosen baccalaureate fields are** business/marketing, psychology, visual/performing arts **Academic program** English as a second language, advanced placement, honors program, summer session, adult/continuing education programs, internships **Contact** Ms. Dayna R. McNally, Director of Enrollment Services, La Roche College, 9000 Babcock Boulevard, Pittsburgh, PA 15237. Telephone: 412-536-1274 or toll-free 800-838-4LRC. Fax: 412-536-1048. E-mail: admsns@laroche.edu. Web site: http://www.laroche.edu/.

LA SALLE UNIVERSITY
PHILADELPHIA, PENNSYLVANIA

General Independent Roman Catholic, comprehensive, coed **Entrance** Moderately difficult **Setting** 100-acre urban campus **Total enrollment** 5,567 **Student/faculty ratio** 17:1 **Application deadline** 4/1 (freshmen), 8/1 (transfer) **Freshmen** 72% were admitted **Housing** Yes **Expenses** Tuition 18,400; Room & Board 7676 **Undergraduates** 57% women, 21% part-time, 2% 25 or older, 0.1% Native American, 5% Hispanic American, 11% African American, 2% Asian American/Pacific Islander **Academic program** Advanced placement, accelerated degree program, self-designed majors, honors program, summer session, adult/continuing education programs, internships **Contact** Mr. Robert G. Voss, Acting Dean of Admission and Financial Aid, La Salle University, 1900 West Olney Avenue, Philadelphia, PA 19141-1199. Telephone: 215-951-1500 or toll-free 800-328-1910. Fax: 215-951-1656. E-mail: admiss@lasalle.edu. Web site: http://www.lasalle.edu/.

LEBANON VALLEY COLLEGE
ANNVILLE, PENNSYLVANIA

General Independent United Methodist, comprehensive, coed **Entrance** Moderately difficult **Setting** 275-acre small-town campus **Total enrollment** 2,100 **Student/faculty ratio** 14:1 **Application deadline** Rolling (freshmen), rolling (transfer) **Freshmen** 73% were admitted **Housing** Yes **Expenses** Tuition 18,420; Room & Board 5680 **Undergraduates** 60% women, 24% part-time, 17% 25 or older, 0.2% Native American, 1% Hispanic American, 2% African American, 2% Asian American/Pacific Islander **The most frequently chosen baccalaureate fields are** biological/life sciences, computer/information sciences, psychology **Academic program** Advanced placement, self-designed majors, summer session, adult/continuing education programs, internships **Contact** William J. Brown Jr., Dean of Admission and Financial Aid, Lebanon Valley College, 101 N. College Avenue, Annville, PA 17003-1400. Telephone: 717-867-6181 or toll-free 866-582-4236 (out-of-state). Fax: 717-867-6026. E-mail: admiss@lvc.edu. Web site: http://www.lvc.edu/.

LEHIGH UNIVERSITY
BETHLEHEM, PENNSYLVANIA

General Independent, university, coed **Entrance** Most difficult **Setting** 1,600-acre suburban campus **Total enrollment** 6,509 **Student/faculty ratio** 11:1 **Application deadline** 1/1 (freshmen) **Freshmen** 46% were admitted **Housing** Yes **Expenses** Tuition 24,000; Room & Board 6440 **Undergraduates** 41% women, 5% part-time, 1% 25 or older, 0.1% Native American, 3% Hispanic American, 3% African American, 5% Asian American/Pacific Islander **The most frequently chosen baccalaureate fields are** business/marketing, engineering/engineering technologies, social sciences and history **Academic program** English as a second language, advanced placement, accelerated degree program, honors program, summer session, adult/continuing education programs, internships **Contact** Mrs. Lorna Hunter, Dean of Admissions and Financial Aid, Lehigh University, 27 Memorial Drive West, Bethlehem, PA 18015. Telephone: 610-758-3100. Fax: 610-758-4361. E-mail: inado@lehigh.edu. Web site: http://www.lehigh.edu/.

Lehigh University *(continued)*

LINCOLN UNIVERSITY
LINCOLN UNIVERSITY, PENNSYLVANIA

General State-related, comprehensive, coed **Entrance** Moderately difficult **Setting** 442-acre rural campus **Total enrollment** 2,008 **Student/faculty ratio** 16:1 **Application deadline** Rolling (freshmen), rolling (transfer) **Freshmen** 53% were admitted **Housing** Yes **Expenses** Tuition 5621; Room & Board 5256 **Undergraduates** 59% women, 4% part-time, 4% 25 or older, 0% Native American, 0.2% Hispanic American, 94% African American, 0.2% Asian American/Pacific Islander **The most frequently chosen baccalaureate fields are** business/marketing, education, social sciences and history **Academic program** Advanced placement, accelerated degree program, self-designed majors, honors program, summer session, adult/continuing education programs, internships **Contact** Dr. Robert Laney Jr., Director of Admissions, Lincoln University, MSC 147, Lincoln University, PO Box 179, Lincoln University, PA 19352-0999. Telephone: 610-932-8300 Ext. 306 or toll-free 800-215-4858. Fax: 610-932-1209. E-mail: admiss@lu.lincoln.edu. Web site: http://www.lincoln.edu/.

LOCK HAVEN UNIVERSITY OF PENNSYLVANIA
LOCK HAVEN, PENNSYLVANIA

General State-supported, comprehensive, coed **Entrance** Moderately difficult **Setting** 165-acre small-town campus **Total enrollment** 4,105 **Student/faculty ratio** 14:1 **Application deadline** Rolling (freshmen), rolling (transfer) **Freshmen** 77% were admitted **Housing** Yes **Expenses** Tuition $4548; Room & Board $4264 **Undergraduates** 57% women, 10% part-time, 10% 25 or older, 0.2% Native American, 1% Hispanic American, 3% African American, 1% Asian American/Pacific Islander **The most frequently chosen baccalaureate fields are** education, health professions and related sciences, parks and recreation **Academic program** Advanced placement, accelerated degree program, self-designed majors, honors program, summer session, adult/continuing education programs, internships **Contact** Mr. James Reeser, Director of Admissions, Lock Haven University of Pennsylvania, Office of Admission, Akeley Hall, Lock Haven, PA 17745. Telephone: 570-893-2027 or toll-free 800-332-8900 (in-state); 800-233-8978 (out-of-state). Fax: 570-893-2201. E-mail: admissions@eagle.lhup.edu. Web site: http://www.lhup.edu/.

LYCOMING COLLEGE
WILLIAMSPORT, PENNSYLVANIA

General Independent United Methodist, 4-year, coed **Entrance** Moderately difficult **Setting** 35-acre small-town campus **Total enrollment** 1,402 **Student/faculty ratio** 13:1 **Application deadline** 4/1 (freshmen), 6/1 (transfer) **Freshmen** 79% were admitted **Housing** Yes **Expenses** Tuition 18,540; Room & Board 5145 **Undergraduates** 56% women, 4% part-time, 6% 25 or older, 0.1% Native American, 1% Hispanic American, 2% African American, 1% Asian American/Pacific Islander **The most frequently chosen baccalaureate fields are** biological/life sciences, business/marketing, psychology **Academic program** Advanced placement, accelerated degree program, self-designed majors, honors program, summer session, internships **Contact** Mr. James Spencer, Dean of Admissions and Financial Aid, Lycoming College, Admissions House, 700, College Place, Williamsport, PA 17701. Telephone: 570-321-4026 or toll-free 800-345-3920. E-mail: admissions@lycoming.edu. Web site: http://www.lycoming.edu/.

MANSFIELD UNIVERSITY OF PENNSYLVANIA
MANSFIELD, PENNSYLVANIA

General State-supported, comprehensive, coed **Entrance** Moderately difficult **Setting** 205-acre small-town campus **Total enrollment** 3,113 **Student/faculty ratio** 16:1 **Application deadline** Rolling (freshmen), rolling (transfer) **Freshmen** 78% were admitted **Housing** Yes **Expenses** Tuition $4766; Room & Board $4198 **Undergraduates** 59% women, 25% part-time, 16% 25 or older, 1% Native American, 1% Hispanic American, 4% African American, 1% Asian American/Pacific Islander **The most frequently chosen baccalaureate fields are** education, business/marketing, protective services/public administration **Academic program** Advanced placement, accelerated degree program, self-designed majors, honors program, summer session, adult/continuing education programs, internships **Contact** Mr. Brian D. Barden, Director of Admissions, Mansfield University of Pennsylvania, Alumni Hall, Mansfield, PA 16933. Telephone: 570-662-4813 or toll-free 800-577-6826. Fax: 570-662-4121. E-mail: admissions@mnsfld.edu. Web site: http://www.mansfield.edu/.

MARYWOOD UNIVERSITY
SCRANTON, PENNSYLVANIA

General Independent Roman Catholic, comprehensive, coed **Entrance** Moderately difficult **Setting** 115-acre suburban campus **Total enrollment** 2,859 **Student/faculty ratio** 12:1 **Application deadline** Rolling (freshmen), rolling (transfer) **Freshmen** 81% were admitted **Housing** Yes **Expenses** Tuition $16,487; Room & Board $6900 **Undergraduates** 73% women, 14% part-time, 19% 25 or older, 0.3% Native American, 1% Hispanic American, 1% African American, 1% Asian American/Pacific Islander **The most frequently chosen baccalaureate fields are** business/marketing, education, health professions and related sciences **Academic program** English as a second language, advanced placement, accelerated degree program, self-designed majors, honors program, summer session, adult/continuing education programs, internships **Contact** Mr. Robert W. Reese, Director of Admissions, Marywood University, 2300 Adams Avenue, Scranton, PA 18509-1598. Telephone: 570-348-6234 or toll-free 800-346-5014. Fax: 570-961-

4763. E-mail: ugadm@ac.marywood.edu. Web site: http://www.marywood.edu/.

MCP HAHNEMANN UNIVERSITY
PHILADELPHIA, PENNSYLVANIA

General Independent, university, coed **Entrance** Moderately difficult **Setting** urban campus **Total enrollment** 2,451 **Student/faculty ratio** 9:1 **Application deadline** 6/1 (freshmen), 6/1 (transfer) **Freshmen** 69% were admitted **Housing** Yes **Expenses** Tuition 11,155; Room & Board 8526 **Undergraduates** 65% women, 42% part-time, 75% 25 or older, 1% Native American, 3% Hispanic American, 20% African American, 7% Asian American/Pacific Islander **The most frequently chosen baccalaureate fields are** health professions and related sciences, liberal arts/general studies **Academic program** Summer session, adult/continuing education programs, internships **Contact** Ms. Jarmila H. Force, Associate Director of Enrollment Management, MCP Hahnemann University, 245 North 15th Street, Mail Stop 472, Philadelphia, PA 19102-1192. Telephone: 215-762-4671 or toll-free 800-2-DREXEL Ext. 6333. Fax: 215-762-6194. E-mail: enroll@mcphu.edu. Web site: http://www.mcphu.edu/.

► **For more information, see page 444.**

MERCYHURST COLLEGE
ERIE, PENNSYLVANIA

General Independent Roman Catholic, comprehensive, coed **Entrance** Moderately difficult **Setting** 88-acre suburban campus **Total enrollment** 3,222 **Student/faculty ratio** 17:1 **Application deadline** Rolling (freshmen), rolling (transfer) **Freshmen** 80% were admitted **Housing** Yes **Expenses** Tuition $14,340; Room & Board $5364 **Undergraduates** 60% women, 18% part-time, 19% 25 or older, 0.3% Native American, 1% Hispanic American, 4% African American, 1% Asian American/Pacific Islander **The most frequently chosen baccalaureate fields are** business/marketing, education, social sciences and history **Academic program** Advanced placement, accelerated degree program, self-designed majors, honors program, summer session, adult/continuing education programs, internships **Contact** Ms. Robin Engel, Director of Undergraduate Admissions, Mercyhurst College, 501 East 38th Street, Erie, PA 16546-0001. Telephone: 814-824-2573 or toll-free 800-825-1926. Fax: 814-824-2071. E-mail: admug@paradise.mercy.edu. Web site: http://www.mercyhurst.edu/.

MESSIAH COLLEGE
GRANTHAM, PENNSYLVANIA

General Independent interdenominational, 4-year, coed **Entrance** Moderately difficult **Setting** 400-acre small-town campus **Total enrollment** 2,797 **Student/faculty ratio** 14:1 **Application deadline** Rolling (freshmen), rolling (transfer) **Freshmen** 78% were admitted **Housing** Yes **Expenses** Tuition 16,130; Room & Board 5770 **Undergraduates** 61% women, 2% part-time, 1% 25 or older, 0.2% Native American, 1% Hispanic American, 1% African American, 2% Asian American/Pacific Islander **The most frequently chosen baccalaureate fields are** business/marketing, education, health professions and related sciences **Academic program** Advanced placement, accelerated degree program, self-designed majors, honors program, summer session, adult/continuing education programs, internships **Contact** Mr. William G. Strausbaugh, Dean for Enrollment Management, Messiah College, One College Avenue, Grantham, PA 17027. Telephone: 717-691-6000 or toll-free 800-382-1349 (in-state); 800-233-4220 (out-of-state). Fax: 717-796-5374. E-mail: admiss@messiah.edu. Web site: http://www.messiah.edu/.

MILLERSVILLE UNIVERSITY OF PENNSYLVANIA
MILLERSVILLE, PENNSYLVANIA

General State-supported, comprehensive, coed **Entrance** Moderately difficult **Setting** 190-acre suburban campus **Total enrollment** 7,378 **Student/faculty ratio** 17:1 **Application deadline** Rolling (freshmen), rolling (transfer) **Freshmen** 71% were admitted **Housing** Yes **Expenses** Tuition $4804; Room & Board $4900 **Undergraduates** 58% women, 14% part-time, 14% 25 or older, 0.2% Native American, 2% Hispanic American, 6% African American, 1% Asian American/Pacific Islander **The most frequently chosen baccalaureate fields are** business/marketing, education, social sciences and history **Academic program** English as a second language, advanced placement, honors program, summer session, adult/continuing education programs, internships **Contact** Mr. Darrell Davis, Director of Admissions, Millersville University of Pennsylvania, Millersville University, Admissions Office, PO Box 1002, Millersville, PA 17551-0302. Telephone: 717-872-3371 or toll-free 800-MU-ADMIT (out-of-state). Fax: 717-871-2147. E-mail: adm_info@mu3.millersv.edu. Web site: http://www.millersville.edu/.

MOORE COLLEGE OF ART AND DESIGN
PHILADELPHIA, PENNSYLVANIA

General Independent, 4-year, women only **Entrance** Moderately difficult **Setting** 3-acre urban campus **Total enrollment** 530 **Student/faculty ratio** 8:1 **Application deadline** 8/15 (freshmen), rolling (transfer) **Freshmen** 57% were admitted **Housing** Yes **Expenses** Tuition $15,995; Room & Board $6100 **Undergraduates** 24% part-time, 13% 25 or older, 0.5% Native American, 3% Hispanic American, 7% African American, 6% Asian American/Pacific Islander **The most frequently chosen baccalaureate field is** visual/performing arts **Academic program** Advanced placement, accelerated degree program, summer session, adult/continuing education programs, internships **Contact** Ms. Heesung Lee, Director of Admissions, Moore College of Art and Design, 20th and the Parkway, Philadelphia, PA 19103. Telephone: 215-568-4515 Ext. 1108 or toll-free 800-523-2025. Fax: 215-965-8544. E-mail: admiss@moore.edu. Web site: http://www.moore.edu/.

MORAVIAN COLLEGE
BETHLEHEM, PENNSYLVANIA

General Independent, comprehensive, coed, affiliated with Moravian Church **Entrance** Moderately difficult **Setting** 70-acre suburban campus **Student/faculty ratio** 14:1 **Application deadline** 3/1 (freshmen), 3/1 (transfer) **Freshmen** 69% were admitted **Housing** Yes **Expenses** Tuition $20,465; Room & Board $6570 **Undergraduates** 4% 25 or older **The most frequently chosen baccalaureate fields are** business/marketing, psychology, social sciences and history **Academic program** Advanced placement, accelerated degree program, self-designed majors, honors program, summer session, adult/continuing education programs, internships **Contact** Mr. James P. Mackin, Director of Admission, Moravian College, 1200 Main Street, Bethlehem, PA 18018. Telephone: 610-861-1320 or toll-free 800-441-3191. Fax: 610-861-3956. E-mail: admissions@moravian.edu. Web site: http://www.moravian.edu/.

MOUNT ALOYSIUS COLLEGE
CRESSON, PENNSYLVANIA

General Independent Roman Catholic, 4-year, coed **Entrance** Minimally difficult **Setting** 125-acre rural campus **Total enrollment** 1,297 **Student/faculty ratio** 13:1 **Application deadline** Rolling (freshmen), rolling (transfer) **Freshmen** 53% were admitted **Housing** Yes **Expenses** Tuition 13,826; Room & Board 5190 **Undergraduates** 71% women, 38% part-time, 43% 25 or older, 0.2% Native American, 1% Hispanic American, 2% African American, 0.5% Asian American/Pacific Islander **The most frequently chosen baccalaureate fields are** health professions and related sciences, interdisciplinary studies, protective services/public administration **Academic program** Advanced placement, summer session, adult/continuing education programs, internships **Contact** Mr. Mike Macekura, Dean of Enrollment Management, Mount Aloysius College, 7373 Admiral Peary Highway, Cresson, PA 16630. Telephone: 814-886-6383 or toll-free 888-823-2220. Fax: 814-886-6441. E-mail: admissions@mtaloy.edu. Web site: http://www.mtaloy.edu/.

MUHLENBERG COLLEGE
ALLENTOWN, PENNSYLVANIA

General Independent, 4-year, coed, affiliated with Lutheran Church **Entrance** Very difficult **Setting** 75-acre suburban campus **Total enrollment** 2,470 **Student/faculty ratio** 13:1 **Application deadline** 2/15 (freshmen), 6/1 (transfer) **Freshmen** 44% were admitted **Housing** Yes **Expenses** Tuition 21,050; Room & Board 5650 **Undergraduates** 58% women, 12% part-time, 5% 25 or older, 0.1% Native American, 2% Hispanic American, 2% African American, 3% Asian American/Pacific Islander **The most frequently chosen baccalaureate fields are** biological/life sciences, psychology, social sciences and history **Academic program** Advanced placement, accelerated degree program, self-designed majors, honors program, summer session, adult/continuing education programs, internships **Contact** Mr. Christopher Hooker-Haring, Dean of Admissions, Muhlenberg College, 2400 Chew Street, Allentown, PA 18104-5586. Telephone: 484-664-3245. Fax: 484-664-3234. E-mail: adm@max.muhlberg.edu. Web site: http://www.muhlenberg.edu/.

▶ **For more information, see page 453.**

NEUMANN COLLEGE
ASTON, PENNSYLVANIA

General Independent Roman Catholic, comprehensive, coed **Entrance** Moderately difficult **Setting** 28-acre suburban campus **Total enrollment** 1,625 **Student/faculty ratio** 14:1 **Application deadline** Rolling (freshmen), rolling (transfer) **Freshmen** 87% were admitted **Housing** Yes **Expenses** Tuition $14,320; Room & Board $6760 **Undergraduates** 67% women, 26% part-time, 33% 25 or older, 0.2% Native American, 2% Hispanic American, 13% African American, 1% Asian American/Pacific Islander **The most frequently chosen baccalaureate fields are** health professions and related sciences, education, liberal arts/general studies **Academic program** Advanced placement, accelerated degree program, self-designed majors, honors program, summer session, adult/continuing education programs, internships **Contact** Mr. Scott Bogard, Director of Admissions, Neumann College, One Neumann Drive, Aston, PA 19014-1298. Telephone: 610-558-5612 or toll-free 800-963-8626. Fax: 610-558-5652. E-mail: neucoladm@hslc.org. Web site: http://www.neumann.edu/.

PEIRCE COLLEGE
PHILADELPHIA, PENNSYLVANIA

General Independent, 4-year, coed, primarily women **Entrance** Minimally difficult **Setting** 1-acre urban campus **Total enrollment** 2,334 **Student/faculty ratio** 12:1 **Application deadline** Rolling (freshmen), rolling (transfer) **Freshmen** 64% were admitted **Housing** No **Expenses** Tuition 9100 **Undergraduates** 81% women, 61% part-time, 70% 25 or older, 0.2% Native American, 5% Hispanic American, 63% African American, 3% Asian American/Pacific Islander **The most frequently chosen baccalaureate field is** law/legal studies **Academic program** Advanced placement, accelerated degree program, summer session, internships **Contact** Mr. Steve W. Bird, College Representative, Peirce College, 1420 Pine Street, Philadelphia, PA 19102. Telephone: 215-545-6400 Ext. 9375 or toll-free 877-670-9190 Ext. 9214. Fax: 215-545-3682. E-mail: info@peirce.edu. Web site: http://www.peirce.edu/.

PENNSYLVANIA COLLEGE OF TECHNOLOGY
WILLIAMSPORT, PENNSYLVANIA

General State-related, 4-year, coed **Entrance** Noncompetitive **Setting** 927-acre small-town campus **Total enrollment** 5,320 **Student/faculty ratio** 18:1 **Application deadline** Rolling (freshmen), rolling (transfer) **Freshmen** 57% were admitted **Housing** Yes **Undergraduates** 33% women, 21% part-time, 24% 25 or older, 1% Native American, 0.5% Hispanic American, 2% African American, 1% Asian American/Pacific Islander **The most frequently chosen baccalaureate fields are** engineering/engineering technologies, business/marketing, health professions and related sciences **Academic program** English as a second language, advanced placement, self-designed majors, summer session, internships **Contact** Mr. Chester D. Schuman, Director of Admissions, Pennsylvania College of Technology, One College Avenue, Williamsport, PA 17701. Telephone: 570-327-4761 or toll-free 800-367-9222 (in-state). Fax: 570-321-5551. E-mail: cschuman@pct.edu. Web site: http://www.pct.edu/.

PENNSYLVANIA SCHOOL OF ART & DESIGN

LANCASTER, PENNSYLVANIA

General Independent, 4-year, coed **Entrance** Moderately difficult **Total enrollment** 180 **Application deadline** 5/1 (freshmen), 5/1 (transfer) **Freshmen** 50% were admitted **Housing** No **Expenses** Tuition $10,875 **Academic program** Advanced placement, internships **Contact** Ms. Wendy Sweigart, Director of Admissions, Pennsylvania School of Art & Design, Admissions Office, PO Box 59, Lancaster, PA 17608-0059. Telephone: 717-396-7833 Ext. 19. Fax: 717-396-1339. E-mail: term1@psad.edu. Web site: http://www.psad.edu/.

THE PENNSYLVANIA STATE UNIVERSITY ABINGTON COLLEGE

ABINGTON, PENNSYLVANIA

General State-related, 4-year, coed **Entrance** Moderately difficult **Setting** 45-acre small-town campus **Total enrollment** 3,049 **Student/faculty ratio** 20:1 **Application deadline** Rolling (freshmen), rolling (transfer) **Freshmen** 81% were admitted **Housing** No **Expenses** Tuition $6722 **Undergraduates** 50% women, 25% part-time, 16% 25 or older, 0.1% Native American, 4% Hispanic American, 10% African American, 10% Asian American/Pacific Islander **The most frequently chosen baccalaureate fields are** liberal arts/general studies, business/marketing, protective services/public administration **Academic program** English as a second language, advanced placement, self-designed majors, honors program, summer session, adult/continuing education programs, internships **Contact** Ms. Erica George, Admissions Counselor, The Pennsylvania State University Abington College, 1600 Woodland Road, Abington, PA 19001. Telephone: 215-881-7600. Fax: 215-881-7317. E-mail: admissions@psu.edu. Web site: http://www.psu.edu/.

THE PENNSYLVANIA STATE UNIVERSITY ALTOONA COLLEGE

ALTOONA, PENNSYLVANIA

General State-related, 4-year, coed **Entrance** Moderately difficult **Setting** 115-acre suburban campus **Total enrollment** 3,765 **Student/faculty ratio** 21:1 **Application deadline** Rolling (freshmen), rolling (transfer) **Freshmen** 84% were admitted **Housing** Yes **Expenses** Tuition 6742; Room & Board 4910 **Undergraduates** 50% women, 11% part-time, 7% 25 or older, 0.1% Native American, 2% Hispanic American, 4% African American, 2% Asian American/Pacific Islander **The most frequently chosen baccalaureate fields are** business/marketing, liberal arts/general studies **Academic program** English as a second language, advanced placement, self-designed majors, honors program, summer session, adult/continuing education programs, internships **Contact** Mr. Richard Shaffer, Director of Admissions and Enrollment Services, The Pennsylvania State University Altoona College, E108 Smith Building, 3000 Ivyside Park, Altoona, PA 16601-3760. Telephone: 814-949-5466. Fax: 814-949-5564. E-mail: admissions@psu.edu. Web site: http://www.psu.edu/.

THE PENNSYLVANIA STATE UNIVERSITY AT ERIE, THE BEHREND COLLEGE

ERIE, PENNSYLVANIA

General State-related, comprehensive, coed **Entrance** Very difficult **Setting** 727-acre suburban campus **Total enrollment** 3,791 **Student/faculty ratio** 18:1 **Application deadline** Rolling (freshmen), rolling (transfer) **Freshmen** 73% were admitted **Housing** Yes **Expenses** Tuition 6852; Room & Board 4910 **Undergraduates** 38% women, 9% part-time, 9% 25 or older, 0.03% Native American, 1% Hispanic American, 3% African American, 2% Asian American/Pacific Islander **The most frequently chosen baccalaureate fields are** business/marketing, biological/life sciences, engineering/engineering technologies **Academic program** Advanced placement, honors program, summer session, adult/continuing education programs, internships **Contact** Ms. Mary-Ellen Madigan, Admissions Director, The Pennsylvania State University at Erie, The Behrend College, 5091 Station Road, Erie, PA 16563. Telephone: 814-898-6100. Fax: 814-898-6044. E-mail: admissions@psu.edu. Web site: http://www.psu.edu/.

THE PENNSYLVANIA STATE UNIVERSITY BERKS CAMPUS OF THE BERKS–LEHIGH VALLEY COLLEGE

READING, PENNSYLVANIA

General State-related, 4-year, coed **Entrance** Moderately difficult **Setting** 240-acre suburban campus **Total enrollment** 2,197 **Student/faculty ratio** 20:1 **Application deadline** Rolling (freshmen), rolling (transfer) **Freshmen** 85% were admitted **Housing** Yes **Expenses** Tuition 6742; Room & Board 4910 **Undergraduates** 39% women, 14% part-time, 10% 25 or older, 0.1% Native American, 2% Hispanic American, 5% African American, 4% Asian American/Pacific Islander **Academic program** Advanced placement, honors program, summer session, adult/continuing education programs, internships **Contact** Jennifer Peters, Admissions Counselor, The Pennsylvania State University Berks Campus of the Berks–

The Pennsylvania State University Berks Campus of the Berks–Lehigh Valley College *(continued)*

Lehigh Valley College, 14 Perkins Student Center, PO Box 7009, Reading, PA 19610-6009. Telephone: 610-396-6066. Fax: 610-396-6077. E-mail: admissions@psu.edu. Web site: http://www.psu.edu/.

THE PENNSYLVANIA STATE UNIVERSITY HARRISBURG CAMPUS OF THE CAPITAL COLLEGE

MIDDLETOWN, PENNSYLVANIA

General State-related, comprehensive, coed **Entrance** Moderately difficult **Setting** 218-acre small-town campus **Total enrollment** 3,258 **Student/faculty ratio** 11:1 **Application deadline** Rolling (freshmen), rolling (transfer) **Freshmen** 100% were admitted **Housing** Yes **Expenses** Tuition 6832; Room & Board 4910 **Undergraduates** 52% women, 35% part-time, 41% 25 or older, 0.2% Native American, 2% Hispanic American, 5% African American, 5% Asian American/Pacific Islander **The most frequently chosen baccalaureate fields are** business/marketing, engineering/engineering technologies, protective services/public administration **Academic program** Advanced placement, honors program, summer session, adult/continuing education programs, internships **Contact** Dr. Thomas Streveler, Director of Enrollment Services, The Pennsylvania State University Harrisburg Campus of the Capital College, 777 West Harrisburg Pike, Middletown, PA 17057-4898. Telephone: 717-948-6250. Fax: 717-948-6325. E-mail: admissions@psu.edu. Web site: http://www.psu.edu/.

THE PENNSYLVANIA STATE UNIVERSITY LEHIGH VALLEY CAMPUS OF THE BERKS-LEHIGH VALLEY COLLEGE

FOGELSVILLE, PENNSYLVANIA

General State-related, 4-year, coed **Entrance** Moderately difficult **Setting** 42-acre small-town campus **Total enrollment** 693 **Student/faculty ratio** 16:1 **Application deadline** Rolling (freshmen), rolling (transfer) **Freshmen** 83% were admitted **Housing** No **Expenses** Tuition $6646 **Undergraduates** 38% women, 23% part-time, 16% 25 or older, 0.2% Native American, 5% Hispanic American, 2% African American, 7% Asian American/Pacific Islander **Academic program** Advanced placement, honors program, summer session, adult/continuing education programs, internships **Contact** Mr. Emory Guffrovich Jr., Admissions Coordinator, The Pennsylvania State University Lehigh Valley Campus of the Berks-Lehigh Valley College, 8380 Mohr Lane, Fogelsville, PA 18051. Telephone: 610-821-6577. Fax: 610-285-5220. E-mail: admissions@psu.edu. Web site: http://www.psu.edu/.

THE PENNSYLVANIA STATE UNIVERSITY SCHUYLKILL CAMPUS OF THE CAPITAL COLLEGE

SCHUYLKILL HAVEN, PENNSYLVANIA

General State-related, 4-year, coed **Entrance** Moderately difficult **Setting** 42-acre small-town campus **Total enrollment** 1,124 **Student/faculty ratio** 16:1 **Application deadline** Rolling (freshmen), rolling (transfer) **Freshmen** 89% were admitted **Housing** Yes **Expenses** Tuition 6626; Room & Board 4910 **Undergraduates** 54% women, 19% part-time, 17% 25 or older, 0.1% Native American, 3% Hispanic American, 13% African American, 4% Asian American/Pacific Islander **Academic program** Advanced placement, summer session, adult/continuing education programs, internships **Contact** Mr. Jerry Bowman, Director of Student Programs and Services, The Pennsylvania State University Schuylkill Campus of the Capital College, 200 University Dirve, Schuylkill Haven, PA 17972-2208. Telephone: 570-385-6252. Fax: 570-385-3672. E-mail: admissions@psu.edu. Web site: http://www.psu.edu/.

THE PENNSYLVANIA STATE UNIVERSITY UNIVERSITY PARK CAMPUS

STATE COLLEGE, PENNSYLVANIA

General State-related, university, coed **Entrance** Very difficult **Setting** 5,617-acre small-town campus **Total enrollment** 40,571 **Student/faculty ratio** 18:1 **Application deadline** Rolling (freshmen), rolling (transfer) **Freshmen** 48% were admitted **Housing** Yes **Expenses** Tuition 6852; Room & Board 4910 **Undergraduates** 47% women, 5% part-time, 4% 25 or older, 0.1% Native American, 3% Hispanic American, 4% African American, 5% Asian American/Pacific Islander **The most frequently chosen baccalaureate fields are** business/marketing, engineering/engineering technologies, health professions and related sciences **Academic program** English as a second language, advanced placement, self-designed majors, honors program, summer session, adult/continuing education programs, internships **Contact** Mr. Geoffrey Harford, Director-Admissions Services and Evaluation, The Pennsylvania State University University Park Campus, 201 Old Main, University Park, PA 16802. Telephone: 814-863-0233. Fax: 814-863-7590. E-mail: admissions@psu.edu. Web site: http://www.psu.edu/.

PHILADELPHIA BIBLICAL UNIVERSITY

LANGHORNE, PENNSYLVANIA

General Independent nondenominational, comprehensive, coed **Entrance** Moderately difficult **Setting** 105-acre suburban campus **Total enrollment** 1,434 **Student/faculty ratio** 14:1 **Application deadline** Rolling (freshmen), rolling (transfer) **Freshmen** 67% were admitted **Housing** Yes **Expenses** Tuition $11,100; Room & Board $5195 **Undergraduates** 53% women, 16% part-time, 22% 25 or older, 0% Native American, 1% Hispanic American, 11% African American, 2% Asian American/Pacific Islander **The most fre-**

quently chosen baccalaureate fields are education, philosophy, religion, and theology, protective services/public administration **Academic program** Advanced placement, accelerated degree program, honors program, summer session, adult/continuing education programs, internships **Contact** Mrs. Fran Emmons, Vice President Admissions and Financial Aid, Philadelphia Biblical University, 200 Manor Avenue, Langhorne, PA 19047. Telephone: 215-702-4239 or toll-free 800-366-0049 (out-of-state). Fax: 215-752-4248. E-mail: admissions@pcb.edu. Web site: http://www.pbu.edu/.

PHILADELPHIA COLLEGE OF PHARMACY AND SCIENCE

See University of the Sciences in Philadelphia

PHILADELPHIA COLLEGE OF TEXTILES AND SCIENCE

See Philadelphia University

PHILADELPHIA UNIVERSITY

PHILADELPHIA, PENNSYLVANIA

General Independent, comprehensive, coed **Entrance** Moderately difficult **Setting** 100-acre suburban campus **Total enrollment** 3,316 **Student/faculty ratio** 12:1 **Application deadline** Rolling (freshmen), rolling (transfer) **Freshmen** 79% were admitted **Housing** Yes **Expenses** Tuition 15,458; Room & Board 6882 **Undergraduates** 65% women, 22% part-time, 22% 25 or older, 0% Native American, 2% Hispanic American, 11% African American, 3% Asian American/Pacific Islander **The most frequently chosen baccalaureate fields are** business/marketing, architecture, visual/performing arts **Academic program** English as a second language, advanced placement, accelerated degree program, honors program, summer session, adult/continuing education programs, internships **Contact** Ms. Laurie C. Grover, Dean of Admissions, Philadelphia University, School House Lane and Henry Avenue, Philadelphia, PA 19144-5497. Telephone: 215-951-2800. Fax: 215-951-2907. E-mail: admissions@laurel.texsci.edu. Web site: http://www.philau.edu/.

POINT PARK COLLEGE

PITTSBURGH, PENNSYLVANIA

General Independent, comprehensive, coed **Entrance** Moderately difficult **Setting** urban campus **Total enrollment** 2,619 **Student/faculty ratio** 14:1 **Application deadline** Rolling (freshmen), rolling (transfer) **Freshmen** 81% were admitted **Housing** Yes **Expenses** Tuition 12,996; Room & Board 5718 **Undergraduates** 54% women, 39% part-time, 51% 25 or older, 0.2% Native American, 1% Hispanic American, 13% African American, 0.5% Asian American/Pacific Islander **The most frequently chosen baccalaureate fields are** business/marketing, engineering/engineering technologies, visual/performing arts **Academic program** English as a second language, advanced placement, accelerated degree program, self-designed majors, summer session, adult/continuing education programs, internships **Contact** Ms. Michele Lawrence, Director of Admissions, Point Park College, Point Park College, 201 Wood Street, Pittsburgh, PA 15222. Telephone: 412-392-3430 or toll-free 800-321-0129. Fax: 412-391-1980. E-mail: enroll@ppc.edu. Web site: http://www.ppc.edu/.

ROBERT MORRIS COLLEGE

MOON TOWNSHIP, PENNSYLVANIA

General Independent, comprehensive, coed **Entrance** Moderately difficult **Setting** 230-acre suburban campus **Total enrollment** 4,660 **Student/faculty ratio** 16:1 **Application deadline** Rolling (freshmen), rolling (transfer) **Freshmen** 72% were admitted **Housing** Yes **Expenses** Tuition $10,034; Room & Board $6320 **Undergraduates** 49% women, 30% part-time, 32% 25 or older, 0.2% Native American, 1% Hispanic American, 8% African American, 1% Asian American/Pacific Islander **The most frequently chosen baccalaureate fields are** business/marketing, computer/information sciences, health professions and related sciences **Academic program** Advanced placement, accelerated degree program, honors program, summer session, adult/continuing education programs, internships **Contact** Keith A. Paylo, Assistant Dean of Enrollment Services, Robert Morris College, Enrollment Services Department, 881 Narrows Run Road, Moon Township, PA 15108-1189. Telephone: 412-262-8402 or toll-free 800-762-0097. Fax: 412-299-2425. E-mail: budzisze@robert-morris.edu. Web site: http://www.robert-morris.edu/.

ROSEMONT COLLEGE

ROSEMONT, PENNSYLVANIA

General Independent Roman Catholic, comprehensive, women only **Entrance** Moderately difficult **Setting** 56-acre suburban campus **Total enrollment** 1,178 **Student/faculty ratio** 8:1 **Application deadline** Rolling (freshmen), rolling (transfer) **Freshmen** 97% were admitted **Housing** Yes **Expenses** Tuition $15,270; Room & Board $7030 **Undergraduates** 49% part-time, 55% 25 or older, 0.3% Native American, 2% Hispanic American, 20% African American, 3% Asian American/Pacific Islander **The most frequently chosen baccalaureate fields are** business/marketing, English, psychology **Academic program** English as a second language, advanced placement, accelerated degree program, self-designed majors, honors program, summer session, adult/continuing education programs, internships **Contact** Admissions Office, Rosemont College, 1400 Montgomery Avenue, Rosemont, PA 19010. Telephone: 610-526-2966 or toll-free 800-331-0708. Fax: 610-520-4399. E-mail: rosecoladmit@rosemont.edu. Web site: http://www.rosemont.edu/.

ST. CHARLES BORROMEO SEMINARY, OVERBROOK
WYNNEWOOD, PENNSYLVANIA

General Independent Roman Catholic, comprehensive, coed, primarily men **Entrance** Moderately difficult **Setting** 77-acre suburban campus **Total enrollment** 484 **Student/faculty ratio** 8:1 **Application deadline** 7/15 (freshmen), 7/15 (transfer) **Freshmen** 100% were admitted **Housing** Yes **Expenses** Tuition $8450; Room & Board $5800 **Undergraduates** 55% women, 71% part-time, 19% 25 or older, 0% Native American, 9% Hispanic American, 2% African American, 14% Asian American/Pacific Islander **The most frequently chosen baccalaureate field is** philosophy, religion, and theology **Academic program** English as a second language, advanced placement, accelerated degree program, summer session, adult/continuing education programs **Contact** Rev. Christopher J. Schreck, Vice Rector for Educational Administration, St. Charles Borromeo Seminary, Overbrook, 100 East Wynnewood Road, Wynnewood, PA 19096. Telephone: 610-785-6271 Ext. 271.

SAINT FRANCIS UNIVERSITY
LORETTO, PENNSYLVANIA

General Independent Roman Catholic, comprehensive, coed **Entrance** Moderately difficult **Setting** 600-acre rural campus **Total enrollment** 2,129 **Application deadline** Rolling (freshmen), rolling (transfer) **Freshmen** 87% were admitted **Housing** Yes **Expenses** Tuition $16,519; Room & Board $7075 **Undergraduates** 13% 25 or older, 0.2% Native American, 1% Hispanic American, 2% African American, 1% Asian American/Pacific Islander **The most frequently chosen baccalaureate fields are** business/marketing, education, health professions and related sciences **Academic program** Advanced placement, accelerated degree program, self-designed majors, honors program, summer session, adult/continuing education programs, internships **Contact** Evan E. Lipp, Dean for Enrollment Management, Saint Francis University, PO Box 600, Loretto, PA 15940-0600. Telephone: 814-472-3000 or toll-free 800-342-5732. Fax: 814-472-3335. E-mail: admission@sfcpa.edu. Web site: http://www.sfcpa.edu/.

SAINT JOSEPH'S UNIVERSITY
PHILADELPHIA, PENNSYLVANIA

General Independent Roman Catholic (Jesuit), comprehensive, coed **Entrance** Very difficult **Setting** 60-acre suburban campus **Total enrollment** 6,961 **Student/faculty ratio** 13:1 **Application deadline** 7/1 (transfer) **Freshmen** 60% were admitted **Housing** Yes **Expenses** Tuition $19,965; Room & Board $7856 **Undergraduates** 56% women, 21% part-time, 0.1% Native American, 2% Hispanic American, 7% African American, 2% Asian American/Pacific Islander **Academic program** English as a second language, advanced placement, accelerated degree program, self-designed majors, honors program, summer session, adult/continuing education programs, internships **Contact** Mr. David Conway, Assistant Vice President of Enrollment Management, Saint Joseph's University, 5600 City Avenue, Philadelphia, PA 19131-1395. Telephone: 610-660-1300 or toll-free 888-BEAHAWK (in-state). Fax: 610-660-1314. E-mail: admi@sju.edu. Web site: http://www.sju.edu/.

SAINT VINCENT COLLEGE
LATROBE, PENNSYLVANIA

General Independent Roman Catholic, 4-year, coed **Entrance** Moderately difficult **Setting** 200-acre suburban campus **Total enrollment** 1,206 **Student/faculty ratio** 13:1 **Application deadline** 5/1 (freshmen), 7/1 (transfer) **Freshmen** 84% were admitted **Housing** Yes **Expenses** Tuition $15,781; Room & Board $5168 **Undergraduates** 49% women, 9% part-time, 8% 25 or older, 0.1% Native American, 1% Hispanic American, 3% African American, 1% Asian American/Pacific Islander **The most frequently chosen baccalaureate fields are** business/marketing, psychology, social sciences and history **Academic program** Advanced placement, accelerated degree program, honors program, summer session, adult/continuing education programs, internships **Contact** Rev. Paul Taylor OSB, Director of Admission and Financial Aid, Saint Vincent College, 300 Fraser Purchase Road, Latrobe, PA 15650. Telephone: 724-537-4540 or toll-free 800-SVC-5549. Fax: 724-532-5069. E-mail: tpratt@admin.stvicent.edu. Web site: http://www.stvincent.edu/.

SETON HILL COLLEGE
GREENSBURG, PENNSYLVANIA

General Independent Roman Catholic, comprehensive, coed, primarily women **Entrance** Moderately difficult **Setting** 200-acre small-town campus **Total enrollment** 1,366 **Student/faculty ratio** 13:1 **Application deadline** Rolling (freshmen), rolling (transfer) **Freshmen** 79% were admitted **Housing** Yes **Expenses** Tuition $15,225; Room & Board $5200 **Undergraduates** 83% women, 30% part-time, 13% 25 or older, 0.4% Native American, 2% Hispanic American, 5% African American, 1% Asian American/Pacific Islander **The most frequently chosen baccalaureate fields are** business/marketing, social sciences and history, visual/performing arts **Academic program** English as a second language, advanced placement, accelerated degree program, self-designed majors, honors program, summer session, adult/continuing education programs, internships **Contact** Ms. Kathleen Berard, Director of Admissions, Seton Hill College, Seton Hill Drive, Greensburg, PA 15601. Telephone: 724-838-4255 or toll-free 800-826-6234. Fax: 724-830-1294. E-mail: admit@setonhill.edu. Web site: http://www.setonhill.edu/.

▶ **For more information, see page 466.**

SHIPPENSBURG UNIVERSITY OF PENNSYLVANIA
SHIPPENSBURG, PENNSYLVANIA

General State-supported, comprehensive, coed **Entrance** Moderately difficult **Setting** 200-acre rural campus **Total enrollment** 7,011 **Student/faculty ratio** 21:1 **Application deadline** Rolling (freshmen), rolling (transfer) **Freshmen** 65% were admitted **Housing** Yes **Expenses** Tuition 4746; Room & Board 4274 **Undergraduates** 54% women, 4% part-time, 6% 25 or older, 0.2% Native American, 1% Hispanic American, 3% African American, 1% Asian American/Pacific Islander **The most frequently chosen baccalaureate fields are** business/marketing, education, protective services/public administration **Academic program** Advanced placement, accelerated degree program, honors program, summer session, internships **Contact** Mr. Joseph Cretella, Dean of Undergraduate and Graduate Admissions, Shippensburg University of Pennsylvania, 1871 Old Main Drive, Shippensburg, PA 17257-2299. Telephone: 717-477-1231 or toll-free 800-822-8028 (in-state). Fax: 717-477-4016. E-mail: admiss@ark.ship.edu. Web site: http://www.ship.edu/.

SLIPPERY ROCK UNIVERSITY OF PENNSYLVANIA
SLIPPERY ROCK, PENNSYLVANIA

General State-supported, comprehensive, coed **Entrance** Moderately difficult **Setting** 611-acre rural campus **Total enrollment** 6,952 **Student/faculty ratio** 21:1 **Application deadline** 5/1 (freshmen), 5/1 (transfer) **Freshmen** 83% were admitted **Housing** Yes **Expenses** Tuition $4684; Room & Board $3988 **Undergraduates** 57% women, 9% part-time, 13% 25 or older, 0.2% Native American, 1% Hispanic American, 3% African American, 1% Asian American/Pacific Islander **The most frequently chosen baccalaureate fields are** business/marketing, education, health professions and related sciences **Academic program** Advanced placement, accelerated degree program, honors program, summer session, adult/continuing education programs, internships **Contact** Ms. Marian Hargrave, Director of Admissions, Slippery Rock University of Pennsylvania, Maltby Center, Slippery Rock, PA 16057. Telephone: 724-738-2111 or toll-free 800-SRU-9111. Fax: 724-738-2913. E-mail: apply@sru.edu. Web site: http://www.sru.edu/.

SUSQUEHANNA UNIVERSITY
SELINSGROVE, PENNSYLVANIA

General Independent, 4-year, coed, affiliated with Lutheran Church **Entrance** Moderately difficult **Setting** 210-acre small-town campus **Total enrollment** 1,829 **Student/faculty ratio** 14:1 **Application deadline** 3/1 (freshmen), 7/1 (transfer) **Freshmen** 75% were admitted **Housing** Yes **Expenses** Tuition $20,440; Room & Board $5770 **Undergraduates** 58% women, 7% part-time, 2% 25 or older, 0.4% Native American, 2% Hispanic American, 2% African American, 2% Asian American/Pacific Islander **The most frequently chosen baccalaureate fields are** business/marketing, communications/communication technologies, social sciences and history **Academic program** Advanced placement, accelerated degree program, self-designed majors, honors program, summer session, adult/continuing education programs, internships **Contact** Mr. Chris Markle, Director of Admissions, Susquehanna University, 514 University Avenue, Selinsgrove, PA 17870-1040. Telephone: 570-372-4260 or toll-free 800-326-9672. Fax: 570-372-2722. E-mail: suadmiss@susqu.edu. Web site: http://www.susqu.edu/.

SWARTHMORE COLLEGE
SWARTHMORE, PENNSYLVANIA

General Independent, 4-year, coed **Entrance** Most difficult **Setting** 330-acre suburban campus **Total enrollment** 1,428 **Student/faculty ratio** 8:1 **Application deadline** 1/1 (freshmen), 4/1 (transfer) **Freshmen** 24% were admitted **Housing** Yes **Expenses** Tuition 25,200; Room & Board 7804 **Undergraduates** 53% women, 0.4% part-time, 0% 25 or older, 1% Native American, 10% Hispanic American, 8% African American, 14% Asian American/Pacific Islander **The most frequently chosen baccalaureate fields are** biological/life sciences, English, social sciences and history **Academic program** Advanced placement, self-designed majors, honors program, internships **Contact** Office of Admissions, Swarthmore College, 500 College Avenue, Swarthmore, PA 19081. Telephone: 610-328-8300 or toll-free 800-667-3110. Fax: 610-328-8580. E-mail: admissions@swarthmore.edu. Web site: http://www.swarthmore.edu/.

TALMUDICAL YESHIVA OF PHILADELPHIA
PHILADELPHIA, PENNSYLVANIA

General Independent Jewish, 4-year, men only **Contact** Rabbi Shmuel Kamenetsky, Co-Dean, Talmudical Yeshiva of Philadelphia, 6063 Drexel Road, Philadelphia, PA 19131-1296. Telephone: 215-473-1212.

TEMPLE UNIVERSITY
PHILADELPHIA, PENNSYLVANIA

General State-related, university, coed **Entrance** Moderately difficult **Setting** 76-acre urban campus **Total enrollment** 28,355 **Student/faculty ratio** 15:1 **Application deadline** 4/1 (freshmen), 6/15 (transfer) **Freshmen** 71% were admitted **Housing** Yes **Expenses** Tuition 6948; Room & Board 6482 **Undergraduates** 58% women, 19% part-time, 22% 25 or older, 0.2% Native American, 4% Hispanic American, 27% African American, 9% Asian American/Pacific Islander **The most frequently chosen baccalaureate fields are** business/marketing, education, health professions and related sciences **Academic program** English as a second language, advanced placement, self-designed majors, honors program, summer session, adult/continuing education programs, internships **Contact** Dr. Timm Rinehart, Acting Director of Admissions, Temple University, 1801 North Broad Street, Philadelphia, PA 19122-6096. Telephone: 215-204-8556 or toll-free 888-340-2222. Fax: 215-204-5694. E-mail: tuadm@vm.temple.edu. Web site: http://www.temple.edu/.

THIEL COLLEGE

GREENVILLE, PENNSYLVANIA

General Independent, 4-year, coed, affiliated with Evangelical Lutheran Church in America **Entrance** Moderately difficult **Setting** 135-acre rural campus **Total enrollment** 1,039 **Student/faculty ratio** 14:1 **Application deadline** 8/15 (freshmen), rolling (transfer) **Freshmen** 78% were admitted **Housing** Yes **Expenses** Tuition $11,464; Room & Board $5674 **Undergraduates** 53% women, 11% part-time, 10% 25 or older, 0% Native American, 1% Hispanic American, 7% African American, 0.1% Asian American/Pacific Islander **The most frequently chosen baccalaureate fields are** business/marketing, psychology, social sciences and history **Academic program** English as a second language, advanced placement, honors program, summer session, adult/continuing education programs, internships **Contact** Mr. Mark Thompson, Director of Admissions, Thiel College, 75 College Avenue, Greenville, PA 16125-2181. Telephone: 724-589-2176 or toll-free 800-24THIEL. Fax: 724-589-2013. E-mail: thieladmis@shrsys.hslc.org. Web site: http://www.thiel.edu/.

THOMAS JEFFERSON UNIVERSITY

PHILADELPHIA, PENNSYLVANIA

General Independent, upper-level, coed **Entrance** Moderately difficult **Setting** 13-acre urban campus **Total enrollment** 2,260 **Student/faculty ratio** 9:1 **Application deadline** Rolling (transfer) **Housing** Yes **Expenses** Tuition $17,500; Room only $2340 **Undergraduates** 81% women, 48% part-time, 58% 25 or older, 1% Native American, 2% Hispanic American, 19% African American, 7% Asian American/Pacific Islander **The most frequently chosen baccalaureate field is** health professions and related sciences **Academic program** Advanced placement, adult/continuing education programs **Contact** Assistant Director of Admissions, Thomas Jefferson University, Edison Building, Suite 1610, 130 South Ninth Street, Philadelphia, PA 19107. Telephone: 215-503-8890 or toll-free 877-533-3247. Fax: 215-503-7241. E-mail: chp.admissions@mail.tju.edu. Web site: http://www.tju.edu/.

UNIVERSITY OF PENNSYLVANIA

PHILADELPHIA, PENNSYLVANIA

General Independent, university, coed **Entrance** Most difficult **Setting** 260-acre urban campus **Total enrollment** 18,145 **Student/faculty ratio** 7:1 **Application deadline** 1/1 (freshmen), 4/1 (transfer) **Freshmen** 23% were admitted **Housing** Yes **Expenses** Tuition 25,170; Room & Board 7826 **Undergraduates** 48% women, 4% part-time, 1% 25 or older, 0.2% Native American, 5% Hispanic American, 6% African American, 19% Asian American/Pacific Islander **The most frequently chosen baccalaureate fields are** business/marketing, engineering/engineering technologies, social sciences and history **Academic program** English as a second language, advanced placement, accelerated degree program, self-designed majors, honors program, summer session, adult/continuing education programs, internships **Contact** Mr. Willis J. Stetson Jr., Dean of Admissions, University of Pennsylvania, 1 College Hall, Levy Park, Philadelphia, PA 19104. Telephone: 215-898-7507. Web site: http://www.upenn.edu/.

UNIVERSITY OF PHOENIX–PHILADELPHIA CAMPUS

WAYNE, PENNSYLVANIA

General Proprietary, comprehensive, coed **Entrance** Noncompetitive **Total enrollment** 66,534 **Student/faculty ratio** 13:1 **Application deadline** Rolling (freshmen), rolling (transfer) **Expenses** Tuition $7740 **Undergraduates** 56% women, 86% 25 or older, 2% Native American, 18% Hispanic American, 13% African American, 6% Asian American/Pacific Islander **Academic program** Advanced placement, accelerated degree program, adult/continuing education programs **Contact** Ms. Beth Barilla, Director of Admissions, University of Phoenix–Philadelphia Campus, 4615 East Elwood Street, Phoenix, AZ 85040-1948. Telephone: 480-927-0099 Ext. 1218 or toll-free 800-228-7240. Fax: 480-594-1758. E-mail: beth.barilla@apollogrp.edu. Web site: http://www.phoenix.edu/.

UNIVERSITY OF PHOENIX–PITTSBURGH CAMPUS

PITTSBURGH, PENNSYLVANIA

General Proprietary, comprehensive, coed **Entrance** Noncompetitive **Total enrollment** 66,534 **Student/faculty ratio** 13:1 **Application deadline** Rolling (freshmen), rolling (transfer) **Expenses** Tuition $7740 **Undergraduates** 56% women, 86% 25 or older, 2% Native American, 18% Hispanic American, 13% African American, 6% Asian American/Pacific Islander **Academic program** Accelerated degree program, adult/continuing education programs **Contact** Ms. Beth Barilla, Director of Admissions, University of Phoenix–Pittsburgh Campus, 4615 East Elwood Street, Phoenix, AZ 85040-1948. Telephone: 480-927-0099 Ext. 1218 or toll-free 800-228-7240. Fax: 480-594-1758. E-mail: beth.barilla@apollogrp.edu. Web site: http://www.phoenix.edu/.

UNIVERSITY OF PITTSBURGH

PITTSBURGH, PENNSYLVANIA

General State-related, university, coed **Entrance** Moderately difficult **Setting** 132-acre urban campus **Total enrollment** 26,329 **Student/faculty ratio** 17:1 **Application deadline** Rolling (freshmen), rolling (transfer) **Freshmen** 62% were admitted **Housing** Yes **Expenses** Tuition 7002; Room & Board 5936 **Undergraduates** 53% women, 14% part-time, 15% 25 or older, 0.2% Native American, 1% Hispanic American, 9% African American, 4% Asian American/Pacific Islander **The most frequently chosen baccalaureate fields are** English, health professions and related sciences, social sciences and history **Academic program** English as a second language, advanced placement, self-designed majors, honors program, summer session, adult/continuing education programs, internships **Contact** Dr. Betsy A. Porter, Director, Office of Admissions and Financial Aid, University of Pittsburgh, 4227 Fifth Avenue, First Floor, Masonic Temple, Pittsburgh, PA 115213. Telephone: 412-624-7488. Fax: 412-648-8815. E-mail: oafa@pitt.edu. Web site: http://www.pitt.edu/.

UNIVERSITY OF PITTSBURGH AT BRADFORD

BRADFORD, PENNSYLVANIA

General State-related, 4-year, coed **Entrance** Moderately difficult **Setting** 145-acre small-town campus **Total enrollment** 1,204 **Student/faculty ratio** 12:1 **Application deadline** Rolling (freshmen), rolling (transfer) **Freshmen** 82% were admitted **Housing** Yes **Expenses** Tuition $6876; Room & Board $5150 **Undergraduates** 59% women, 26% part-time, 25% 25 or older, 0.5% Native American, 1% Hispanic American, 1% African American, 1% Asian American/ Pacific Islander **Academic program** Advanced placement, accelerated degree program, summer session, adult/continuing education programs, internships **Contact** Janet Shade, Administrative Secretary, University of Pittsburgh at Bradford, 300 Campus Drive, Bradford, PA 16701-2812. Telephone: 814-362-7555 or toll-free 800-872-1787. E-mail: shade@imap.pitt.edu. Web site: http://www.upb.pitt.edu/.

UNIVERSITY OF PITTSBURGH AT GREENSBURG

GREENSBURG, PENNSYLVANIA

General State-related, 4-year, coed **Entrance** Moderately difficult **Setting** 217-acre small-town campus **Total enrollment** 1,587 **Student/faculty ratio** 18:1 **Application deadline** 8/1 (freshmen), 8/1 (transfer) **Freshmen** 80% were admitted **Housing** Yes **Expenses** Tuition $6936; Room & Board $5540 **Undergraduates** 55% women, 16% part-time, 12% 25 or older, 0.4% Native American, 1% Hispanic American, 2% African American, 2% Asian American/Pacific Islander **The most frequently chosen baccalaureate fields are** business/marketing, English, psychology **Academic program** Advanced placement, accelerated degree program, self-designed majors, summer session, adult/continuing education programs, internships **Contact** Mr. John R. Sparks, Director of Admissions and Financial Aid, University of Pittsburgh at Greensburg, 1150 Mount Pleasant Road, Greensburg, PA 15601-5860. Telephone: 724-836-9880. Fax: 724-836-7160. E-mail: upgadmit@pitt.edu. Web site: http://www.pitt.edu/~upg/.

UNIVERSITY OF PITTSBURGH AT JOHNSTOWN

JOHNSTOWN, PENNSYLVANIA

General State-related, 4-year, coed **Entrance** Moderately difficult **Setting** 650-acre suburban campus **Total enrollment** 3,031 **Student/faculty ratio** 19:1 **Application deadline** Rolling (freshmen), rolling (transfer) **Freshmen** 83% were admitted **Housing** Yes **Expenses** Tuition $6984; Room & Board $5400 **Undergraduates** 55% women, 10% part-time, 0.1% Native American, 0.4% Hispanic American, 1% African American, 1% Asian American/Pacific Islander **Academic program** Advanced placement, accelerated degree program, self-designed majors, summer session, adult/continuing education programs, internships **Contact** Mr. James F. Gyure, Director of Admissions, University of Pittsburgh at Johnstown, 157 Blackington Hall, Johnstown, PA 15904-2990. Telephone: 814-269-7050 or toll-free 800-765-4875. Fax: 814-269-7044. Web site: http://info.pitt.edu/~upjweb/.

THE UNIVERSITY OF SCRANTON

SCRANTON, PENNSYLVANIA

General Independent Roman Catholic (Jesuit), comprehensive, coed **Entrance** Moderately difficult **Setting** 50-acre urban campus **Total enrollment** 4,615 **Student/faculty ratio** 13:1 **Application deadline** 3/1 (freshmen), 7/1 (transfer) **Freshmen** 84% were admitted **Housing** Yes **Expenses** Tuition $18,660; Room & Board $8112 **Undergraduates** 58% women, 11% part-time, 9% 25 or older, 0.2% Native American, 2% Hispanic American, 1% African American, 2% Asian American/Pacific Islander **The most frequently chosen baccalaureate fields are** business/marketing, education, health professions and related sciences **Academic program** Advanced placement, self-designed majors, honors program, summer session, adult/continuing education programs, internships **Contact** Mr. Joseph Roback, Director of Admissions, The University of Scranton, Scranton, PA 18510-4622. Telephone: 570-941-7540 or toll-free 888-SCRANTON. Fax: 570-941-4370. E-mail: admissions@uofs.edu. Web site: http://www.scranton.edu/.

THE UNIVERSITY OF THE ARTS

PHILADELPHIA, PENNSYLVANIA

General Independent, comprehensive, coed **Entrance** Moderately difficult **Setting** 18-acre urban campus **Total enrollment** 2,063 **Student/faculty ratio** 10:1 **Application deadline** Rolling (freshmen), rolling (transfer) **Freshmen** 54% were admitted **Housing** Yes **Expenses** Tuition 17,850; Room only 4800 **Undergraduates** 53% women, 3% part-time, 6% 25 or older, 0.3% Native American, 3% Hispanic American, 8% African American, 3% Asian American/ Pacific Islander **The most frequently chosen baccalaureate field is** visual/performing arts **Academic program** English as a second language, advanced placement, adult/continuing education programs, internships **Contact** Barbara Elliott, Director of Admissions, The University of the Arts, 320 South Broad Street, Philadelphia, PA 19102-4944. Telephone: 215-717-6030 or toll-free 800-616-ARTS. Fax: 215-717-6045. E-mail: admissions@uarts.edu. Web site: http://www.uarts.edu/.

▶ **For more information, see page 481.**

UNIVERSITY OF THE SCIENCES IN PHILADELPHIA
PHILADELPHIA, PENNSYLVANIA

General Independent, university, coed **Entrance** Moderately difficult **Setting** 35-acre urban campus **Total enrollment** 2,262 **Student/faculty ratio** 13:1 **Application deadline** Rolling (freshmen), rolling (transfer) **Freshmen** 82% were admitted **Housing** Yes **Expenses** Tuition 16,100; Room & Board 7600 **Undergraduates** 67% women, 2% part-time, 6% 25 or older, 0% Native American, 2% Hispanic American, 6% African American, 32% Asian American/Pacific Islander **Academic program** English as a second language, advanced placement, honors program, summer session, adult/continuing education programs, internships **Contact** Louis L. Hegyes, Director of Admission, University of the Sciences in Philadelphia, 600 South 43rd Street, Philadelphia, PA 19104-4495. Telephone: 215-596-8810 or toll-free 888-996-8747 (in-state). Fax: 215-596-8821. E-mail: admit@pcps.edu. Web site: http://www.usip.edu/.

URSINUS COLLEGE
COLLEGEVILLE, PENNSYLVANIA

General Independent, 4-year, coed, affiliated with United Church of Christ **Entrance** Very difficult **Setting** 140-acre suburban campus **Total enrollment** 1,290 **Student/faculty ratio** 12:1 **Application deadline** 2/15 (freshmen), 8/1 (transfer) **Freshmen** 72% were admitted **Housing** Yes **Expenses** Tuition $23,770; Room & Board $6140 **Undergraduates** 54% women, 1% part-time, 1% 25 or older, 0.1% Native American, 2% Hispanic American, 8% African American, 3% Asian American/Pacific Islander **The most frequently chosen baccalaureate fields are** biological/life sciences, business/marketing, social sciences and history **Academic program** English as a second language, advanced placement, self-designed majors, honors program, adult/continuing education programs, internships **Contact** Mr. Paul M. Cramer, Director of Admissions, Ursinus College, Box 1000, Collegeville, PA 19426. Telephone: 610-409-3200. Fax: 610-409-3662. E-mail: admissions@ursinus.edu. Web site: http://www.ursinus.edu/.

VALLEY FORGE CHRISTIAN COLLEGE
PHOENIXVILLE, PENNSYLVANIA

Contact Mr. Craig Tavani, Director of Admissions, Valley Forge Christian College, 1401 Charlestown Road, Phoenixville, PA 19460. Telephone: 610-935-0450 Ext. 1430 or toll-free 800-432-8322. Fax: 610-935-9353. E-mail: vfcccomp@boicenet.com. Web site: http://www.vfcc.edu/.

VILLANOVA UNIVERSITY
VILLANOVA, PENNSYLVANIA

General Independent Roman Catholic, comprehensive, coed **Entrance** Moderately difficult **Setting** 222-acre suburban campus **Total enrollment** 10,003 **Student/faculty ratio** 12:1 **Application deadline** 1/7 (freshmen), 7/15 (transfer) **Freshmen** 52% were admitted **Housing** Yes **Expenses** Tuition $22,825; Room & Board $8050 **Undergraduates** 50% women, 10% part-time, 1% 25 or older, 0.2% Native American, 4% Hispanic American, 3% African American, 4% Asian American/Pacific Islander **The most frequently chosen baccalaureate fields are** business/marketing, engineering/engineering technologies, social sciences and history **Academic program** English as a second language, advanced placement, accelerated degree program, honors program, summer session, adult/continuing education programs, internships **Contact** Mr. Michael M. Gaynor, Director of University Admission, Villanova University, 800 Lancaster Avenue, Villanova, PA 19085-1672. Telephone: 610-519-4000 or toll-free 800-338-7927. Fax: 610-519-6450. E-mail: gotovu@ucis.vill.edu. Web site: http://www.villanova.edu/.

WASHINGTON & JEFFERSON COLLEGE
WASHINGTON, PENNSYLVANIA

General Independent, 4-year, coed **Entrance** Moderately difficult **Setting** 40-acre small-town campus **Total enrollment** 1,241 **Student/faculty ratio** 12:1 **Application deadline** 3/1 (freshmen), rolling (transfer) **Freshmen** 79% were admitted **Housing** Yes **Expenses** Tuition $19,650; Room & Board $5160 **Undergraduates** 49% women, 5% part-time, 1% 25 or older, 0.3% Native American, 1% Hispanic American, 2% African American, 2% Asian American/Pacific Islander **The most frequently chosen baccalaureate fields are** business/marketing, biological/life sciences, psychology **Academic program** Advanced placement, accelerated degree program, self-designed majors, honors program, summer session, internships **Contact** Mr. Alton E. Newell, Dean of Enrollment, Washington & Jefferson College, 60 South Lincoln Street, Washington, PA 15301-4601. Telephone: 724-223-6025 or toll-free 888-WANDJAY. Fax: 724-223-5271. E-mail: admission@washjeff.edu. Web site: http://www.washjeff.edu/.

WAYNESBURG COLLEGE
WAYNESBURG, PENNSYLVANIA

General Independent, comprehensive, coed, affiliated with Presbyterian Church (U.S.A.) **Entrance** Moderately difficult **Setting** 30-acre small-town campus **Total enrollment** 1,692 **Student/faculty ratio** 16:1 **Application deadline** Rolling (freshmen), rolling (transfer) **Freshmen** 91% were admitted **Housing** Yes **Expenses** Tuition 11,950; Room & Board 2460 **Undergraduates** 54% women, 12% part-time, 22% 25 or older, 0.1% Native American, 0.3% Hispanic American, 4% African American, 1% Asian American/Pacific Islander **The most frequently chosen baccalaureate fields are** business/marketing, health professions and related sciences, protective services/public administration **Academic program** English as a second language, advanced placement, accelerated degree program, honors program, adult/continuing education programs, internships **Contact** Ms. Robin L. Moore, Dean of Admissions, Waynesburg College, 51 West College Street, Waynesburg, PA 15070. Telephone: 724-852-3333 or toll-free 800-225-7393. Fax: 724-627-8124. E-mail: admissions@waynesburg.edu. Web site: http://www.waynesburg.edu/.

WEST CHESTER UNIVERSITY OF PENNSYLVANIA
WEST CHESTER, PENNSYLVANIA

General State-supported, comprehensive, coed **Entrance** Moderately difficult **Setting** 547-acre suburban campus **Total enrollment** 12,274 **Student/faculty ratio** 17:1 **Application deadline** Rolling (freshmen), rolling (transfer) **Freshmen** 57% were admitted **Housing** Yes **Expenses** Tuition 4630; Room & Board 4650 **Undergraduates** 60% women, 15% part-time, 13% 25 or older, 0.2% Native American, 2% Hispanic American, 8% African American, 2% Asian American/Pacific Islander **The most frequently chosen baccalaureate fields are** business/marketing, education, English **Academic program** English as a second language, advanced placement, self-designed majors, honors program, summer session, adult/continuing education programs, internships **Contact** Ms. Marsha Haug, Director of Admissions, West Chester University of Pennsylvania, Messikomer Hall, Rosedale Avenue, West Chester, PA 19383. Telephone: 610-436-3411 or toll-free 877-315-2165 (in-state). Fax: 610-436-2907. E-mail: ugadmiss@wcupa.edu. Web site: http://www.wcupa.edu/.

WESTMINSTER COLLEGE
NEW WILMINGTON, PENNSYLVANIA

General Independent, comprehensive, coed, affiliated with Presbyterian Church (U.S.A.) **Entrance** Moderately difficult **Setting** 300-acre small-town campus **Total enrollment** 1,599 **Student/faculty ratio** 13:1 **Application deadline** Rolling (freshmen), rolling (transfer) **Freshmen** 89% were admitted **Housing** Yes **Expenses** Tuition $17,750; Room & Board $5210 **Undergraduates** 62% women, 5% part-time, 1% 25 or older, 0% Native American, 0.3% Hispanic American, 1% African American, 1% Asian American/Pacific Islander **The most frequently chosen baccalaureate fields are** business/marketing, biological/life sciences, social sciences and history **Academic program** Advanced placement, accelerated degree program, self-designed majors, honors program, summer session, adult/continuing education programs, internships **Contact** Mr. Doug Swartz, Director of Admissions, Westminster College, 319 South Market Street, New Wilmington, PA 16172-0001. Telephone: 724-946-7100 or toll-free 800-942-8033 (in-state). Fax: 724-946-7171. E-mail: paulrd@westminster.edu. Web site: http://www.westminster.edu/.

WIDENER UNIVERSITY
CHESTER, PENNSYLVANIA

General Independent, comprehensive, coed **Entrance** Moderately difficult **Setting** 110-acre suburban campus **Total enrollment** 5,680 **Student/faculty ratio** 12:1 **Application deadline** Rolling (freshmen), rolling (transfer) **Freshmen** 76% were admitted **Housing** Yes **Expenses** Tuition $17,950; Room & Board $7325 **Undergraduates** 45% women, 9% part-time, 5% 25 or older, 0.3% Native American, 1% Hispanic American, 10% African American, 3% Asian American/Pacific Islander **The most frequently chosen baccalaureate fields are** business/marketing, engineering/engineering technologies, health professions and related sciences **Academic program** English as a second language, advanced placement, accelerated degree program, self-designed majors, honors program, summer session, adult/continuing education programs, internships **Contact** Michael Hendricks, Dean of Admissions, Widener University, One University Place, Chester, PA 19013. Telephone: 610-499-4126 or toll-free 888-WIDENER (in-state). Fax: 610-499-4676. E-mail: admissions.office@widener.edu. Web site: http://www.widener.edu/.

WILKES UNIVERSITY
WILKES-BARRE, PENNSYLVANIA

General Independent, comprehensive, coed **Entrance** Moderately difficult **Setting** 25-acre urban campus **Total enrollment** 3,570 **Student/faculty ratio** 13:1 **Application deadline** Rolling (freshmen), rolling (transfer) **Freshmen** 84% were admitted **Housing** Yes **Expenses** Tuition $17,220; Room & Board $7438 **Undergraduates** 48% women, 18% part-time, 17% 25 or older, 0.2% Native American, 1% Hispanic American, 2% African American, 1% Asian American/Pacific Islander **The most frequently chosen baccalaureate fields are** business/marketing, biological/life sciences, psychology **Academic program** Advanced placement, accelerated degree program, self-designed majors, honors program, summer session, adult/continuing education programs, internships **Contact** Mike Frantz, Dean, Enrollment, Wilkes University, PO Box 111, Wilkes-Barre, PA 18766. Telephone: 570-408-4400 or toll-free 800-945-5378 Ext. 4400. Fax: 570-408-4904. E-mail: admissions@wilkes.edu. Web site: http://www.wilkes.edu/.

WILSON COLLEGE
CHAMBERSBURG, PENNSYLVANIA

General Independent, 4-year, women only, affiliated with Presbyterian Church (U.S.A.) **Entrance** Moderately difficult **Setting** 262-acre small-town campus **Total enrollment** 818 **Student/faculty ratio** 10:1 **Application deadline** Rolling (freshmen), rolling (transfer) **Freshmen** 90% were admitted **Housing** Yes **Expenses** Tuition $14,600; Room & Board $6562 **Undergraduates** 47% part-time, 40% 25 or older, 0.4% Native American, 1% Hispanic American, 2% African American, 1% Asian American/Pacific Islander **The most frequently chosen baccalaureate fields are** biological/life sciences, agriculture, business/marketing **Academic program** English as a second language, advanced placement, accelerated degree program, self-designed majors, summer session, adult/continuing education programs, internships **Contact** Edgerton Deuel II, Director of Admissions, Wilson College, 1015 Philadelphia Avenue, Chambersburg,

Wilson College *(continued)*

PA 17201. Telephone: 717-262-2002 or toll-free 800-421-8402. Fax: 717-264-1578. E-mail: wilson@pa.net. Web site: http://www.wilson.edu/.

YESHIVA BETH MOSHE
SCRANTON, PENNSYLVANIA

Contact Rabbi I. Bressler, Dean, Yeshiva Beth Moshe, 930 Hickory Street, PO Box 1141, Scranton, PA 18505-2124. Telephone: 717-346-1747.

YORK COLLEGE OF PENNSYLVANIA
YORK, PENNSYLVANIA

General Independent, comprehensive, coed **Entrance** Moderately difficult **Setting** 80-acre suburban campus **Total enrollment** 5,254 **Student/faculty ratio** 15:1 **Application deadline** Rolling (freshmen), rolling (transfer) **Freshmen** 67% were admitted **Housing** Yes **Expenses** Tuition $6978; Room & Board $4860 **Undergraduates** 59% women, 24% part-time, 21% 25 or older, 0.1% Native American, 1% Hispanic American, 1% African American, 1% Asian American/Pacific Islander **The most frequently chosen baccalaureate fields are** business/marketing, education, health professions and related sciences **Academic program** Advanced placement, accelerated degree program, self-designed majors, summer session, adult/continuing education programs, internships **Contact** Mrs. Nancy L. Spataro, Director of Admissions, York College of Pennsylvania, York, PA 17405-7199. Telephone: 717-849-1600 or toll-free 800-455-8018. Fax: 717-849-1607. E-mail: admissions@ycp.edu. Web site: http://www.ycp.edu/.

RHODE ISLAND

BROWN UNIVERSITY
PROVIDENCE, RHODE ISLAND

General Independent, university, coed **Entrance** Most difficult **Setting** 140-acre urban campus **Total enrollment** 7,723 **Student/faculty ratio** 8:1 **Application deadline** 1/1 (freshmen), 4/1 (transfer) **Freshmen** 16% were admitted **Housing** Yes **Expenses** Tuition $26,184; Room & Board $7346 **Undergraduates** 53% women, 6% part-time, 1% 25 or older, 1% Native American, 6% Hispanic American, 6% African American, 15% Asian American/Pacific Islander **The most frequently chosen baccalaureate fields are** liberal arts/general studies, biological/life sciences, social sciences and history **Academic program** Advanced placement, accelerated degree program, self-designed majors, honors program, summer session, adult/continuing education programs, internships **Contact** Mr. Michael Goldberger, Director of Admission, Brown University, Box 1876, Providence, RI 02912. Telephone: 401-863-2378. Fax: 401-863-9300. E-mail: admission_undergraduate@brown.edu. Web site: http://www.brown.edu/.

BRYANT COLLEGE
SMITHFIELD, RHODE ISLAND

General Independent, comprehensive, coed **Entrance** Moderately difficult **Setting** 387-acre suburban campus **Total enrollment** 3,373 **Student/faculty ratio** 19:1 **Application deadline** Rolling (freshmen), 8/15 (transfer) **Freshmen** 73% were admitted **Housing** Yes **Expenses** Tuition $18,480; Room & Board $7500 **Undergraduates** 41% women, 11% part-time, 9% 25 or older, 0.2% Native American, 3% Hispanic American, 3% African American, 3% Asian American/Pacific Islander **The most frequently chosen baccalaureate fields are** business/marketing, computer/information sciences, social sciences and history **Academic program** English as a second language, advanced placement, honors program, summer session, adult/continuing education programs, internships **Contact** Ms. Cynthia Bonn, Director of Freshman Admission, Bryant College, 1150 Douglas Pike, Smithfield, RI 02917. Telephone: 401-232-6100 or toll-free 800-622-7001. Fax: 401-232-6741. E-mail: admissions@bryant.edu. Web site: http://www.bryant.edu/.

JOHNSON & WALES UNIVERSITY
PROVIDENCE, RHODE ISLAND

General Independent, comprehensive, coed **Entrance** Minimally difficult **Setting** 47-acre urban campus **Total enrollment** 9,172 **Student/faculty ratio** 30:1 **Application deadline** Rolling (freshmen), rolling (transfer) **Freshmen** 82% were admitted **Housing** Yes **Expenses** Tuition 14,340; Room & Board 6150 **Undergraduates** 48% women, 17% part-time, 11% 25 or older, 0.2% Native American, 6% Hispanic American, 12% African American, 3% Asian American/Pacific Islander **Academic program** English as a second language, advanced placement, accelerated degree program, honors program, summer session, adult/continuing education programs, internships **Contact** Ms. Maureen Dumas, Dean of Admissions, Johnson & Wales University, 8 Abbott Park Place, Providence, RI 02903-3703. Telephone: 401-598-2310 or toll-free 800-342-5598 (out-of-state). Fax: 401-598-2948. E-mail: admissions@jwu.edu. Web site: http://www.jwu.edu/.

PROVIDENCE COLLEGE
PROVIDENCE, RHODE ISLAND

General Independent Roman Catholic, comprehensive, coed **Entrance** Very difficult **Setting** 105-acre suburban campus **Total enrollment** 5,336 **Student/faculty ratio** 13:1 **Application deadline** 1/15 (freshmen), 4/15 (transfer) **Freshmen** 57% were admitted **Housing** Yes **Expenses** Tuition 18,750; Room & Board 7625 **Undergraduates** 58% women, 13% part-time, 9% 25 or older, 0.1% Native American, 4% Hispanic American, 1% African American, 2% Asian American/Pacific Islander **The most frequently chosen baccalaureate fields are** business/marketing, education, social sciences and history **Academic program** Advanced placement, self-designed majors, honors program, summer session, adult/continuing education programs, internships **Contact** Mr. Christopher Lydon, Dean of Enrollment Management, Providence College, River Avenue and Eaton Street, Providence, RI 02918. Telephone: 401-865-2535 or toll-free 800-721-6444. Fax: 401-865-2826. E-mail: pcadmiss@providence.edu. Web site: http://www.providence.edu/.

RHODE ISLAND COLLEGE
PROVIDENCE, RHODE ISLAND

General State-supported, comprehensive, coed **Entrance** Moderately difficult **Setting** 170-acre suburban campus **Total enrollment** 8,513 **Student/faculty ratio** 14:1 **Application deadline** 5/1 (freshmen), 6/1 (transfer) **Freshmen** 72% were admitted **Housing** Yes **Expenses** Tuition $3521; Room & Board $5946 **Undergraduates** 68% women, 36% part-time, 30% 25 or older, 0.3% Native American, 5% Hispanic American, 5% African American, 3% Asian American/Pacific Islander **Academic program** Advanced placement, self-designed majors, honors program, summer session, adult/continuing education programs, internships **Contact** Dr. Holly Shadoian, Director of Admissions, Rhode Island College, 600 Mount Pleasant Avenue, Providence, RI 02908-1924. Telephone: 401-456-8234 or toll-free 800-669-5760 (in-state). Fax: 401-456-8817. E-mail: admissions@ric.edu. Web site: http://www.ric.edu/.

RHODE ISLAND SCHOOL OF DESIGN
PROVIDENCE, RHODE ISLAND

General Independent, comprehensive, coed **Entrance** Very difficult **Setting** 13-acre urban campus **Total enrollment** 2,086 **Student/faculty ratio** 10:1 **Application deadline** 2/15 (freshmen), 3/31 (transfer) **Freshmen** 35% were admitted **Housing** Yes **Expenses** Tuition 22,305; Room & Board 6600 **Undergraduates** 61% women, 14% 25 or older, 0.3% Native American, 4% Hispanic American, 3% African American, 11% Asian American/Pacific Islander **The most frequently chosen baccalaureate fields are** architecture, visual/performing arts **Academic program** English as a second language, advanced placement, adult/continuing education programs, internships **Contact** Mr. Edward Newhall, Director of Admissions, Rhode Island School of Design, 2 College Street, Providence, RI 02905-2791. Telephone: 401-454-6300 or toll-free 800-364-RISD. Fax: 401-454-6309. E-mail: admissions@risd.edu. Web site: http://www.risd.edu/.

ROGER WILLIAMS UNIVERSITY
BRISTOL, RHODE ISLAND

General Independent, comprehensive, coed **Entrance** Moderately difficult **Setting** 140-acre small-town campus **Total enrollment** 4,115 **Student/faculty ratio** 16:1 **Application deadline** Rolling (freshmen), rolling (transfer) **Freshmen** 86% were admitted **Housing** Yes **Expenses** Tuition $19,035; Room & Board $8530 **Undergraduates** 51% women, 32% part time, 0.3% Native American, 2% Hispanic American, 2% African American, 1% Asian American/Pacific Islander **The most frequently chosen baccalaureate fields are** business/marketing, protective services/public administration, social sciences and history **Academic program** English as a second language, advanced placement, self-designed majors, honors program, summer session, adult/continuing education programs, internships **Contact** Ms. Julie H. Cairns, Office of Admissions, Roger Williams University, 1 Old Ferry Road, Bristol, RI 02809. Telephone: 401-254-3500 or toll-free 800-458-7144 (out-of-state). Fax: 401-254-3557. E-mail: admit@alpha.rwu.edu. Web site: http://www.rwu.edu/.

SALVE REGINA UNIVERSITY
NEWPORT, RHODE ISLAND

General Independent Roman Catholic, comprehensive, coed **Entrance** Moderately difficult **Setting** 65-acre suburban campus **Total enrollment** 2,246 **Student/faculty ratio** 13:1 **Application deadline** Rolling (freshmen), rolling (transfer) **Freshmen** 67% were admitted **Housing** Yes **Expenses** Tuition $18,360; Room & Board $8100 **Undergraduates** 69% women, 7% part-time, 6% 25 or older, 0.4% Native American, 2% Hispanic American, 2% African American, 1% Asian American/Pacific Islander **The most frequently chosen baccalaureate fields are** business/marketing, education, protective services/public administration **Academic program** English as a second language, advanced placement, accelerated degree program, honors program, summer session, adult/continuing education programs, internships **Contact** Colleen Emerson, Director of Admissions, Salve Regina University, 100 Ochre Point Avenue, Newport, RI 02840-4192. Telephone: 401-341-2109 or toll-free 888-GO SALVE. Fax: 401-848-2823. E-mail: sruadmis@salve3.salve.edu. Web site: http://www.salve.edu/.

UNIVERSITY OF RHODE ISLAND
KINGSTON, RHODE ISLAND

General State-supported, university, coed **Entrance** Moderately difficult **Setting** 1,200-acre small-town campus **Total enrollment** 14,362 **Student/faculty ratio** 18:1 **Application deadline** 3/1 (freshmen), 5/1 (transfer) **Freshmen** 75% were admitted **Housing** Yes **Expenses** Tuition 5154; Room & Board 6688 **Undergraduates** 56% women, 18% part-time, 16% 25 or older, 1% Native American, 4% Hispanic American, 4% African American, 4% Asian American/Pacific Islander **The most frequently chosen baccalaureate fields are** business/marketing, education, health professions and related sciences **Academic program** Advanced placement, accelerated degree program, self-designed majors, honors program, summer session, adult/continuing education programs, internships **Contact** Ms. Catherine Zeiser, Assistant Dean of Admissions, University of Rhode Island, 8 Ranger Road, Suite 1, Kingston, RI 02881-2020. Telephone: 401-874-7100. Fax: 401-874-5523. E-mail: uriadmit@riacc.uri.edu. Web site: http://www.uri.edu

University of Rhode Island *(continued)*

SOUTH CAROLINA

ALLEN UNIVERSITY
COLUMBIA, SOUTH CAROLINA

General Independent African Methodist Episcopal, 4-year, coed **Entrance** Minimally difficult **Setting** suburban campus **Total enrollment** 466 **Student/faculty ratio** 10:1 **Application deadline** Rolling (freshmen) **Freshmen** 81% were admitted **Housing** Yes **Expenses** Tuition $4750; Room & Board $4210 **Undergraduates** 60% women, 2% 25 or older, 92% Native American, 0.2% Hispanic American, 1% Asian American/Pacific Islander **The most frequently chosen baccalaureate fields are** business/marketing, liberal arts/general studies, social sciences and history **Academic program** Honors program, summer session, adult/continuing education programs, internships **Contact** Admissions Office, Allen University, 1530 Harden Street, Columbia, SC 29204-1085. Telephone: 803-254-4165. Fax: 803-376-5731. E-mail: auniv@mindspring.com.

ANDERSON COLLEGE
ANDERSON, SOUTH CAROLINA

General Independent Baptist, 4-year, coed **Entrance** Moderately difficult **Setting** 44-acre suburban campus **Total enrollment** 1,398 **Student/faculty ratio** 15:1 **Application deadline** 6/30 (freshmen), 8/1 (transfer) **Freshmen** 78% were admitted **Housing** Yes **Expenses** Tuition $10,515; Room & Board $4605 **Undergraduates** 62% women, 23% part-time, 25% 25 or older, 0.4% Native American, 1% Hispanic American, 12% African American, 1% Asian American/Pacific Islander **The most frequently chosen baccalaureate fields are** business/marketing, education, visual/performing arts **Academic program** Advanced placement, honors program, summer session, adult/continuing education programs, internships **Contact** Ms. Pam Bryant, Director of Admissions, Anderson College, 316 Boulevard, Anderson, SC 29621. Telephone: 864-231-5607 or toll-free 800-542-3594. Fax: 864-231-3033. E-mail: admissions@anderson-college.edu. Web site: http://www.anderson-college.edu/.

BENEDICT COLLEGE
COLUMBIA, SOUTH CAROLINA

Contact Dr. Marcia Conston, Associate Vice President, Institutional Effectiveness, Benedict College, PO Box 98, Columbia, SC 29204. Telephone: 803-253-5526 or toll-free 800-868-6598 (in-state). Fax: 803-253-5167. Web site: http://bchome.benedict.edu/.

CHARLESTON SOUTHERN UNIVERSITY
CHARLESTON, SOUTH CAROLINA

General Independent Baptist, comprehensive, coed **Entrance** Moderately difficult **Setting** 500-acre suburban campus **Total enrollment** 2,603 **Student/faculty ratio** 16:1 **Application deadline** Rolling (freshmen), rolling (transfer) **Freshmen** 93% were admitted **Housing** Yes **Expenses** Tuition $11,346; Room & Board $4362 **Undergraduates** 59% women, 17% part-time, 28% 25 or older, 0.2% Native American, 1% Hispanic American, 19% African American, 1% Asian American/Pacific Islander **The most frequently chosen baccalaureate fields are** business/marketing, education, protective services/public administration **Academic program** Advanced placement, accelerated degree program, summer session, internships **Contact** Mrs. Debbie Williamson, Director of Enrollment Management, Charleston Southern University, PO Box 118087, Charleston, SC 29423-8087. Telephone: 843-863-7050 or toll-free 800-947-7474. E-mail: enroll@csuniv.edu. Web site: http://www.charlestonsouthern.edu/.

THE CITADEL, THE MILITARY COLLEGE OF SOUTH CAROLINA
CHARLESTON, SOUTH CAROLINA

General State-supported, comprehensive, coed, primarily men **Entrance** Moderately difficult **Setting** 130-acre urban campus **Total enrollment** 3,872 **Student/faculty ratio** 15:1 **Application deadline** Rolling (freshmen), rolling (transfer) **Freshmen** 81% were admitted **Housing** Yes **Expenses** Tuition $4288; Room & Board $4350 **Undergraduates** 7% women, 6% part-time, 6% 25 or older, 0.2% Native American, 4% Hispanic American, 8% African American, 2% Asian American/Pacific Islander **The most frequently chosen baccalaureate fields are** business/marketing, engineering/engineering technologies, social sciences and history **Academic program** English as a second language, advanced placement, honors program, summer session, adult/continuing education programs, internships **Contact** Lt. Col. Steven D. Klein, Dean of Enrollment Management, The Citadel, The Military College of South Carolina, 171 Moultrie Street, Charleston, SC 29409. Telephone: 843-953-5230 or toll-free 800-868-1842. Fax: 843-953-7036. E-mail: admissions@citadel.edu. Web site: http://www.citadel.edu.

CLAFLIN UNIVERSITY
ORANGEBURG, SOUTH CAROLINA

General Independent United Methodist, 4-year, coed **Entrance** Minimally difficult **Setting** 32-acre small-town campus **Total enrollment** 1,315 **Student/faculty ratio** 14:1 **Application deadline** Rolling (freshmen), rolling (transfer) **Freshmen** 56% were admitted **Housing** Yes **Expenses** Tuition $7538; Room & Board $4116 **The most frequently chosen baccalaureate fields are** education, biological/life sciences, social sciences and history **Academic program** Advanced placement, honors program, summer session, adult/continuing education programs, internships **Contact** Mr. Michael Zeigler, Director of Admissions, Claflin University, 400 Magnolia Street, Orangeburg, SC 29115. Telephone: 803-535-5340 or toll-free 800-922-1276 (in-state). Fax: 803-535-5387. E-mail: glee@claf1.claflin.edu.

CLEMSON UNIVERSITY
CLEMSON, SOUTH CAROLINA

General State-supported, university, coed **Entrance** Moderately difficult **Setting** 1,400-acre small-town campus **Total enrollment** 17,465 **Student/faculty ratio** 16:1 **Application deadline** 5/1 (freshmen), 8/1 (transfer) **Freshmen** 64% were admitted **Housing** Yes **Expenses** Tuition 3780; Room & Board 4325 **Undergraduates** 45% women, 6% part-time, 4% 25 or older, 0.2% Native American, 1% Hispanic American, 7% African American, 1% Asian American/Pacific Islander **The most frequently chosen baccalaureate fields are** business/marketing, education, engineering/engineering technologies **Academic program** Advanced placement, accelerated degree program, honors program, summer session, internships **Contact** Mr. Robert S. Barkley, Director of Admissions, Clemson University, 105 Sikes Hall, PO Box 345124, Clemson, SC 29634. Telephone: 864-656-2287. Fax: 864-656-2464. E-mail: cuadmissions@clemson.edu. Web site: http://www.clemson.edu/.

COASTAL CAROLINA UNIVERSITY
CONWAY, SOUTH CAROLINA

General State-supported, comprehensive, coed **Entrance** Moderately difficult **Setting** 244-acre suburban campus **Total enrollment** 4,653 **Student/faculty ratio** 17:1 **Application deadline** 8/15 (freshmen), 8/15 (transfer) **Freshmen** 72% were admitted **Housing** Yes **Expenses** Tuition 3500; Room & Board 5240 **Undergraduates** 56% women, 17% part-time, 18% 25 or older, 1% Native American, 1% Hispanic American, 9% African American, 1% Asian American/Pacific Islander **The most frequently chosen baccalaureate fields are** business/marketing, biological/life sciences, education **Academic program** Advanced placement, accelerated degree program, self-designed majors, honors program, summer session, adult/continuing education programs, internships **Contact** Dr. Judy Vogt, Director of Financial Aid and Admissions, Coastal Carolina University, PO Box 261954, Conway, SC 29528. Telephone: 843-349-2037 or toll-free 800-277-7000. Fax: 843-349-2127. E-mail: admis@coastal.edu. Web site: http://www.coastal.edu/.

COKER COLLEGE
HARTSVILLE, SOUTH CAROLINA

General Independent, 4-year, coed **Entrance** Moderately difficult **Setting** 30-acre small-town campus **Total enrollment** 445 **Student/faculty ratio** 9:1 **Application deadline** Rolling (freshmen), rolling (transfer) **Freshmen** 88% were admitted **Housing** Yes **Expenses** Tuition $15,361; Room & Board $4820 **Undergraduates** 64% women, 2% part-time, 22% 25 or older, 0.5% Native American, 2% Hispanic American, 19% African American, 0.5% Asian American/Pacific Islander **Academic program** English as a second language, advanced placement, accelerated degree program, self-designed majors, honors program, summer session, adult/continuing education programs, internships **Contact** Mr. David Anthony, Director of Admissions and Student Financial Planning, Coker College, 300 East College Avenue, Hartsville, SC 29550. Telephone: 843-383-8050 or toll-free 800-950-1908. Fax: 843-383-8056. E-mail: admissions@coker.edu. Web site: http://www.coker.edu/.

COLLEGE OF CHARLESTON
CHARLESTON, SOUTH CAROLINA

General State-supported, 4-year, coed **Entrance** Moderately difficult **Setting** 52-acre urban campus **Total enrollment** 11,129 **Student/faculty ratio** 18:1 **Application deadline** 6/1 (freshmen), 6/1 (transfer) **Freshmen** 67% were admitted **Housing** Yes **Expenses** Tuition $3630; Room & Board $4260 **Undergraduates** 63% women, 11% part-time, 11% 25 or older, 0.2% Native American, 1% Hispanic American, 8% African American, 1% Asian American/Pacific Islander **The most frequently chosen baccalaureate fields are** business/marketing, education, social sciences and history **Academic program** English as a second language, advanced placement, accelerated degree program, honors program, summer session, adult/continuing education programs, internships **Contact** Mr. Donald Burkard, Dean of Admissions, College of Charleston, 66 George Street, Charleston, SC 29424-0001. Telephone: 843-953-5670. Fax: 843-953-6322. E-mail: admissions@cofc.edu. Web site: http://www.cofc.edu/.

COLUMBIA COLLEGE
COLUMBIA, SOUTH CAROLINA

General Independent United Methodist, comprehensive, women only **Entrance** Moderately difficult **Setting** 33-acre suburban campus **Total enrollment** 1,398 **Student/faculty ratio** 14:1 **Application deadline** Rolling (freshmen), rolling (transfer) **Freshmen** 79% were admitted **Housing** Yes **Expenses** Tuition 15,870; Room & Board 5240 **Undergraduates** 23% 25 or older, 0% Native American, 1% Hispanic American, 39% African American, 0.2% Asian American/Pacific Islander **The most frequently chosen baccalaureate fields are** business/marketing, education, personal/miscellaneous services **Academic program** Advanced placement, accelerated degree program, self-designed majors, honors program, summer session, adult/continuing education programs, internships **Contact** Ms. Julie King, Director of Admissions, Columbia College, 1301 Columbia College Drive, Columbia, SC 29203. Telephone: 803-786-3871 or toll-free 800-277-1301. Fax: 803-786-3674. E-mail: admissions@colacoll.edu. Web site: http://www.columbiacollegesc.edu/.

COLUMBIA INTERNATIONAL UNIVERSITY
COLUMBIA, SOUTH CAROLINA

General Independent nondenominational, comprehensive, coed **Entrance** Minimally difficult **Setting** 450-acre suburban campus **Total enrollment** 808

Columbia International University *(continued)*

Student/faculty ratio 19:1 **Application deadline** Rolling (freshmen), rolling (transfer) **Freshmen** 61% were admitted **Housing** Yes **Expenses** Tuition $9140; Room & Board $4520 **Undergraduates** 55% women, 8% part-time, 15% 25 or older, 0% Native American, 0.2% Hispanic American, 4% African American, 1% Asian American/Pacific Islander **The most frequently chosen baccalaureate field is** philosophy, religion, and theology **Academic program** Advanced placement, accelerated degree program, summer session, internships **Contact** Miss Kandi A. Mulligan, Director of College Admissions, Columbia International University, P.O. Box 3122, 7435 Monticello Road, Columbia, SC 29230-3122. Telephone: 803-754-4100 Ext. 3024 or toll-free 800-777-2227 Ext. 3024. Fax: 803-786-4209. E-mail: yesciu@ciu.edu. Web site: http://www.ciu.edu/.

CONVERSE COLLEGE
SPARTANBURG, SOUTH CAROLINA

General Independent, comprehensive, women only **Entrance** Moderately difficult **Setting** 70-acre urban campus **Total enrollment** 1,513 **Student/faculty ratio** 9:1 **Application deadline** 8/1 (freshmen), 8/1 (transfer) **Freshmen** 81% were admitted **Housing** Yes **Expenses** Tuition 15,840; Room & Board 4830 **Undergraduates** 9% part-time, 13% 25 or older, 1% Native American, 2% Hispanic American, 13% African American, 1% Asian American/Pacific Islander **The most frequently chosen baccalaureate fields are** education, business/marketing, visual/performing arts **Academic program** English as a second language, advanced placement, accelerated degree program, honors program, summer session, adult/continuing education programs, internships **Contact** Ms. Susan Ikerd, Vice President for Enrollment, Converse College, 580 East Main Street, Spartanburg, SC 29302-0006. Telephone: 864-596-9040 Ext. 9041. Fax: 864-596-9158. Web site: http://www.converse.edu/.

ERSKINE COLLEGE
DUE WEST, SOUTH CAROLINA

General Independent, 4-year, coed, affiliated with Associate Reformed Presbyterian Church **Entrance** Moderately difficult **Setting** 85-acre rural campus **Total enrollment** 868 **Student/faculty ratio** 12:1 **Application deadline** Rolling (freshmen), rolling (transfer) **Freshmen** 78% were admitted **Housing** Yes **Expenses** Tuition 15,712; Room & Board 4987 **Undergraduates** 61% women, 2% part-time, 1% 25 or older, 0% Native American, 1% Hispanic American, 6% African American, 1% Asian American/Pacific Islander **The most frequently chosen baccalaureate fields are** biological/life sciences, business/marketing, social sciences and history **Academic program** Advanced placement, accelerated degree program, summer session, internships **Contact** Mr. Jeff Craft, Director of Admissions, Erskine College, PO Box 176, Due West, SC 29639. Telephone: 864-379-8830 or toll-free 800-241-8721. Fax: 864-379-8759. E-mail: admissions@erskine.edu. Web site: http://www.erskine.edu/.

FRANCIS MARION UNIVERSITY
FLORENCE, SOUTH CAROLINA

General State-supported, comprehensive, coed **Entrance** Moderately difficult **Setting** 309-acre rural campus **Total enrollment** 3,569 **Student/faculty ratio** 16:1 **Application deadline** Rolling (freshmen), rolling (transfer) **Freshmen** 77% were admitted **Housing** Yes **Expenses** Tuition $3600; Room & Board $3720 **Undergraduates** 61% women, 11% part-time, 15% 25 or older, 1% Native American, 1% Hispanic American, 31% African American, 1% Asian American/Pacific Islander **The most frequently chosen baccalaureate fields are** business/marketing, education, social sciences and history **Academic program** Advanced placement, accelerated degree program, honors program, summer session, adult/continuing education programs, internships **Contact** Ms. Drucilla P. Shelton, Director of Admissions, Francis Marion University, PO Box 100547, Florence, SC 29501-0547. Telephone: 843-661-1231 or toll-free 800-368-7551. Fax: 843-661-4635. E-mail: admission@fmarion.edu. Web site: http://www.fmarion.edu/.

FURMAN UNIVERSITY
GREENVILLE, SOUTH CAROLINA

General Independent, comprehensive, coed **Entrance** Very difficult **Setting** 750-acre suburban campus **Total enrollment** 3,272 **Student/faculty ratio** 12:1 **Application deadline** 1/15 (freshmen), 6/1 (transfer) **Freshmen** 60% were admitted **Housing** Yes **Expenses** Tuition $20,076; Room & Board $5416 **Undergraduates** 56% women, 6% part-time, 4% 25 or older, 0.1% Native American, 1% Hispanic American, 6% African American, 2% Asian American/Pacific Islander **The most frequently chosen baccalaureate fields are** business/marketing, education, social sciences and history **Academic program** Advanced placement, accelerated degree program, self-designed majors, summer session, adult/continuing education programs, internships **Contact** Mr. David R. O'Cain, Director of Admissions, Furman University, 3300 Poinsett Highway, Greenville, SC 29613. Telephone: 864-294-2034. Fax: 864-294-3127. E-mail: admissions@furman.edu. Web site: http://www.furman.edu/.

JOHNSON & WALES UNIVERSITY
CHARLESTON, SOUTH CAROLINA

Contact Ms. Deborah Langenstein, Director of Admissions, Johnson & Wales University, 701 East Bay Street, Charleston, SC 29403. Telephone: 843-727-3000 or toll-free 800-868-1522 (out-of-state). Fax: 843-763-0318. E-mail: admissions@jwu.edu. Web site: http://www.jwu.edu/.

LANDER UNIVERSITY
GREENWOOD, SOUTH CAROLINA

General State-supported, comprehensive, coed **Entrance** Moderately difficult **Setting** 100-acre small-town campus **Total enrollment** 2,935 **Student/**

faculty ratio 16:1 **Application deadline** Rolling (freshmen), rolling (transfer) **Freshmen** 81% were admitted **Housing** Yes **Expenses** Tuition 3955; Room & Board 3950 **Undergraduates** 63% women, 13% part-time, 26% 25 or older, 0.2% Native American, 1% Hispanic American, 20% African American, 1% Asian American/Pacific Islander **Academic program** Advanced placement, accelerated degree program, self-designed majors, honors program, summer session, adult/continuing education programs, internships **Contact** Mr. Jeffrey A. Constant, Assistant Director of Admissions, Lander University, 320 Stanley Avenue, Greenwood, SC 29649. Telephone: 864-388-8307 or toll-free 888-452-6337. Fax: 864-388-8125. E-mail: wmarceng@lander.edu. Web site: http://www.lander.edu/.

LIMESTONE COLLEGE
GAFFNEY, SOUTH CAROLINA

General Independent, 4-year, coed **Entrance** Minimally difficult **Setting** 115-acre small-town campus **Total enrollment** 1,967 **Student/faculty ratio** 9:1 **Application deadline** Rolling (freshmen), rolling (transfer) **Freshmen** 70% were admitted **Housing** Yes **Expenses** Tuition $10,800; Room & Board $5100 **Undergraduates** 56% women, 47% part-time, 14% 25 or older, 0.4% Native American, 1% Hispanic American, 30% African American, 1% Asian American/Pacific Islander **The most frequently chosen baccalaureate fields are** business/marketing, computer/information sciences, social sciences and history **Academic program** English as a second language, advanced placement, accelerated degree program, self-designed majors, honors program, summer session, adult/continuing education programs, internships **Contact** Ms. Debbie Borders, Office Manager of Admissions, Limestone College, Limestone College, 1115 College Drive, Gaffney, SC 29340-3799. Telephone: 864-489-7151 Ext. 554 or toll-free 800-795-7151 Ext. 554 (in-state); 800-795-7151 Ext. 553 (out-of-state). Fax: 864-487-8706. E-mail: cphenicie@limestone.edu. Web site: http://www.limestone.edu.

MEDICAL UNIVERSITY OF SOUTH CAROLINA
CHARLESTON, SOUTH CAROLINA

General State-supported, upper-level, coed **Entrance** Very difficult **Setting** 61-acre urban campus **Total enrollment** 2,346 **Student/faculty ratio** 12:1 **Application deadline** Rolling (transfer) **First-Year Students** 37% were admitted **Housing** No **Expenses** Tuition $5180 **Undergraduates** 83% women, 27% part-time, 63% 25 or older, 1% Native American, 1% Hispanic American, 16% African American, 2% Asian American/Pacific Islander **The most frequently chosen baccalaureate field is** health professions and related sciences **Academic program** Advanced placement, internships **Contact** Mr. James F. Menzel, Executive Director, Office of Enrollment Services, Medical University of South Carolina, 171 Ashley Avenue, Charleston, SC 29425-0002. Telephone: 843-792-5396. Fax: 843-792-3764. E-mail: smithman@musc.edu. Web site: http://www.musc.edu/.

MORRIS COLLEGE
SUMTER, SOUTH CAROLINA

General Independent, 4-year, coed, affiliated with Baptist Educational and Missionary Convention of South Carolina **Entrance** Minimally difficult **Setting** 34-acre small-town campus **Total enrollment** 940 **Student/faculty ratio** 17:1 **Application deadline** Rolling (freshmen), rolling (transfer) **Freshmen** 48% were admitted **Housing** Yes **Expenses** Tuition $6090; Room & Board $3051 **Undergraduates** 66% women, 2% part-time, 12% 25 or older, 100% African American **The most frequently chosen baccalaureate fields are** business/marketing, communications/communication technologies, protective services/public administration **Academic program** Accelerated degree program, honors program, summer session, adult/continuing education programs, internships **Contact** Ms. Deborah Calhoun, Director of Admissions and Records, Morris College, 100 West College Street, Sumter, SC 29150-3599. Telephone: 803-934-3225 or toll-free 888-775-1345. Fax: 803-773-3687. Web site: http://www.morris.edu/.

NEWBERRY COLLEGE
NEWBERRY, SOUTH CAROLINA

General Independent Lutheran, 4-year, coed **Entrance** Moderately difficult **Setting** 60-acre small-town campus **Total enrollment** 727 **Student/faculty ratio** 12:1 **Application deadline** Rolling (freshmen), rolling (transfer) **Freshmen** 86% were admitted **Housing** Yes **Expenses** Tuition $14,632; Room & Board $4230 **Undergraduates** 46% women, 11% part-time, 5% 25 or older, 0.3% Native American, 1% Hispanic American, 19% African American, 0.4% Asian American/Pacific Islander **The most frequently chosen baccalaureate fields are** business/marketing, education, social sciences and history **Academic program** Advanced placement, self-designed majors, honors program, summer session, adult/continuing education programs, internships **Contact** Mr. Jonathan Reece, Director of Admissions, Newberry College, 2100 College Street, Smeltzer Hall, Newberry, SC 29108. Telephone: 803-321-5127 or toll-free 800-845-4955 Ext. 5127. Fax: 803-321-5138. E-mail: admissions@newberry.edu. Web site: http://www.newberry.edu/.

NORTH GREENVILLE COLLEGE
TIGERVILLE, SOUTH CAROLINA

General Independent Southern Baptist, 4-year, coed **Entrance** Minimally difficult **Setting** 500-acre rural campus **Total enrollment** 1,282 **Application deadline** 8/22 (freshmen), 8/22 (transfer) **Freshmen** 66% were admitted **Housing** Yes **Expenses** Tuition $8000; Room & Board $4570 **Undergraduates** 46% women, 9% part-time, 13% 25 or older, 0% Native American, 1% Hispanic American, 11% African American, 0.3% Asian American/Pacific Islander **The most fre-**

North Greenville College *(continued)*

quently chosen baccalaureate fields are education, business/marketing, philosophy, religion, and theology **Academic program** English as a second language, advanced placement, accelerated degree program, self-designed majors, honors program, summer session, internships **Contact** Mr. Buddy Freeman, Executive Director of Admissions, North Greenville College, PO Box 1892, Tigerville, SC 29688-1892. Telephone: 864-977-7052 or toll-free 800-468-6642. Fax: 864-977-7177. E-mail: ngccwf@infoave.net. Web site: http://www.ngc.edu/.

PRESBYTERIAN COLLEGE
CLINTON, SOUTH CAROLINA

General Independent Presbyterian, 4-year, coed **Entrance** Very difficult **Setting** 215-acre small-town campus **Total enrollment** 1,147 **Student/faculty ratio** 15:1 **Application deadline** 4/1 (freshmen), 7/1 (transfer) **Freshmen** 82% were admitted **Housing** Yes **Expenses** Tuition $18,200; Room & Board $5156 **Undergraduates** 55% women, 3% part-time, 1% 25 or older, 0% Native American, 0.4% Hispanic American, 5% African American, 1% Asian American/Pacific Islander **The most frequently chosen baccalaureate fields are** business/marketing, biological/life sciences, social sciences and history **Academic program** Advanced placement, honors program, summer session, internships **Contact** Mr. Richard Dana Paul, Vice President of Enrollment and Dean of Admissions, Presbyterian College, South Broad Street, Clinton, SC 29325. Telephone: 864-833-8229 or toll-free 800-476-7272. Fax: 864-833-8481. E-mail: mwill@admin.presby.edu. Web site: http://www.presby.edu/.

SOUTH CAROLINA STATE UNIVERSITY
ORANGEBURG, SOUTH CAROLINA

General State-supported, comprehensive, coed **Entrance** Minimally difficult **Setting** 160-acre small-town campus **Total enrollment** 4,525 **Application deadline** 7/31 (freshmen), 7/31 (transfer) **Freshmen** 59% were admitted **Housing** Yes **Expenses** Tuition $3724 **Undergraduates** 12% 25 or older **Academic program** Advanced placement, honors program, summer session, adult/continuing education programs, internships **Contact** Lillian Adderson, Interim Director of Admissions, South Carolina State University, 300 College Street Northeast, Orangeburg, SC 29117-0001. Telephone: 803-536-8408 or toll-free 800-260-5956. Fax: 803-536-8990. E-mail: carolyn-free@scsu.scsu.edu. Web site: http://www.scsu.edu/.

SOUTHERN METHODIST COLLEGE
ORANGEBURG, SOUTH CAROLINA

General Independent religious, 4-year, coed **Entrance** Moderately difficult **Total enrollment** 82 **Expenses** Tuition $3860; Room & Board $3630 **Contact** Mr. John Hucks, Director of Admissions, Southern Methodist College, 541 Broughton Stret, PO Box 1027, Orangeburg, SC 29116-1027. Telephone: 803-534-7826.

SOUTHERN WESLEYAN UNIVERSITY
CENTRAL, SOUTH CAROLINA

General Independent, comprehensive, coed, affiliated with Wesleyan Church **Entrance** Minimally difficult **Setting** 230-acre small-town campus **Total enrollment** 1,803 **Student/faculty ratio** 13:1 **Application deadline** 8/10 (freshmen), 8/10 (transfer) **Freshmen** 66% were admitted **Housing** Yes **Expenses** Tuition $12,104; Room & Board $4290 **Undergraduates** 62% women, 5% part-time, 1% Native American, 1% Hispanic American, 24% African American, 0.2% Asian American/Pacific Islander **The most frequently chosen baccalaureate fields are** business/marketing, education, psychology **Academic program** Advanced placement, accelerated degree program, honors program, summer session, adult/continuing education programs, internships **Contact** Mrs. Joy Bryant, Director of Admissions, Southern Wesleyan University, 907 Wesleyan Drive, PO Box 1020, Central, SC 29630-1020. Telephone: 864-644-5550 or toll-free 800-CUATSWU. Fax: 864-644-5972. E-mail: 103134.1317@compuserve.com. Web site: http://www.swu.edu/.

UNIVERSITY OF SOUTH CAROLINA
COLUMBIA, SOUTH CAROLINA

General State-supported, university, coed **Entrance** Moderately difficult **Setting** 315-acre urban campus **Total enrollment** 23,728 **Student/faculty ratio** 14:1 **Application deadline** Rolling (freshmen), rolling (transfer) **Freshmen** 69% were admitted **Housing** Yes **Expenses** Tuition 3918; Room & Board 4588 **Undergraduates** 55% women, 18% part-time, 12% 25 or older, 0.3% Native American, 1% Hispanic American, 19% African American, 3% Asian American/Pacific Islander **The most frequently chosen baccalaureate fields are** business/marketing, communications/communication technologies, social sciences and history **Academic program** English as a second language, advanced placement, accelerated degree program, self-designed majors, honors program, summer session, adult/continuing education programs, internships **Contact** Ms. Terry L. Davis, Director of Undergraduate Admissions, University of South Carolina, Columbia, SC 29208. Telephone: 803-777-7700 or toll-free 800-868-5872 (in-state). Fax: 803-777-0101. E-mail: admissions-ugrad@scarolina.edu. Web site: http://www.sc.edu/.

UNIVERSITY OF SOUTH CAROLINA AIKEN
AIKEN, SOUTH CAROLINA

General State-supported, comprehensive, coed **Entrance** Minimally difficult **Setting** 453-acre suburban campus **Total enrollment** 3,278 **Student/faculty ratio** 15:1 **Application deadline** 8/1 (freshmen), rolling (transfer) **Freshmen** 64% were admitted

Housing Yes **Expenses** Tuition 3598; Room & Board 4090 **Undergraduates** 66% women, 30% part-time, 25% 25 or older, 0.4% Native American, 1% Hispanic American, 22% African American, 1% Asian American/Pacific Islander **Academic program** English as a second language, advanced placement, accelerated degree program, self-designed majors, honors program, summer session, adult/continuing education programs, internships **Contact** Mr. Randy R. Duckett, Dean of Enrollment Services, University of South Carolina Aiken, 471 University Parkway, Aiken, SC 29801-6309. Telephone: 803-648-6851 Ext. 3366 or toll-free 888-WOW-USCA. Fax: 803-641-3727. E-mail: admit@aiken.sc.edu. Web site: http://www.usca.sc.edu/.

UNIVERSITY OF SOUTH CAROLINA SPARTANBURG
SPARTANBURG, SOUTH CAROLINA

General State-supported, comprehensive, coed **Entrance** Moderately difficult **Setting** 298-acre urban campus **Total enrollment** 3,709 **Student/faculty ratio** 16:1 **Freshmen** 62% were admitted **Housing** Yes **Expenses** Tuition $3714; Room & Board $40,404 **Undergraduates** 65% women, 28% part-time, 29% 25 or older, 0.2% Native American, 1% Hispanic American, 23% African American, 1% Asian American/Pacific Islander **The most frequently chosen baccalaureate fields are** business/marketing, education, interdisciplinary studies **Academic program** Advanced placement, accelerated degree program, self-designed majors, summer session, adult/continuing education programs, internships **Contact** Ms. Donette Stewart, Director of Admissions, University of South Carolina Spartanburg, 800 University Way, Spartanburg, SC 29303. Telephone: 864-503-5280 or toll-free 800-277-8727. Fax: 864-503-5727. E-mail: dstawart@uscs.edu. Web site: http://www.uscs.edu/.

VOORHEES COLLEGE
DENMARK, SOUTH CAROLINA

General Independent Episcopal, 4-year, coed **Entrance** Minimally difficult **Setting** 350-acre rural campus **Total enrollment** 677 **Application deadline** Rolling (freshmen), rolling (transfer) **Freshmen** 80% were admitted **Housing** Yes **Expenses** Tuition $6460; Room & Board $3516 **Undergraduates** 10% 25 or older **Academic program** Advanced placement, honors program, summer session, adult/continuing education programs, internships **Contact** Ms. E. E. Phillips, Director of Admissions, Voorhees College, Massachusetts Hall, PO Box 678, Denmark, SC 29042. Telephone: 803-703-7111 Ext. 7115 or toll-free 800-446-6250. Fax: 803-793-1117. E-mail: elfphi@voorhees.edu.

WINTHROP UNIVERSITY
ROCK HILL, SOUTH CAROLINA

General State-supported, comprehensive, coed **Entrance** Moderately difficult **Setting** 418-acre suburban campus **Total enrollment** 6,062 **Student/faculty ratio** 15:1 **Application deadline** 6/1 (freshmen), 7/1 (transfer) **Freshmen** 72% were admitted **Housing** Yes **Expenses** Tuition 4282; Room & Board 4150 **Undergraduates** 69% women, 13% part-time, 12% 25 or older, 0.4% Native American, 1% Hispanic American, 25% African American, 1% Asian American/Pacific Islander **The most frequently chosen baccalaureate fields are** business/marketing, education, social sciences and history **Academic program** Advanced placement, honors program, summer session, adult/continuing education programs, internships **Contact** Ms. Deborah Barber, Director of Admissions, Winthrop University, Stewart House, Rock Hill, SC 29733. Telephone: 803-323-2191 or toll-free 800-763-0230. Fax: 803-323-2137. E-mail: admissions@winthrop.edu. Web site: http://www.winthrop.edu/.

WOFFORD COLLEGE
SPARTANBURG, SOUTH CAROLINA

General Independent, 4-year, coed, affiliated with United Methodist Church **Entrance** Very difficult **Setting** 140-acre urban campus **Total enrollment** 1,087 **Student/faculty ratio** 13:1 **Application deadline** 2/1 (freshmen), rolling (transfer) **Freshmen** 83% were admitted **Housing** Yes **Expenses** Tuition $17,730; Room & Board $5235 **Undergraduates** 47% women, 1% part-time, 0% 25 or older, 0.2% Native American, 1% Hispanic American, 8% African American, 1% Asian American/Pacific Islander **The most frequently chosen baccalaureate fields are** business/marketing, biological/life sciences, social sciences and history **Academic program** Advanced placement, accelerated degree program, self-designed majors, summer session, internships **Contact** Mr. Brand Stille, Director of Admissions, Wofford College, 429 North Church Street, Spartanburg, SC 29303-3663. Telephone: 864-597-4130. Fax: 864-597-4147. E-mail: admissions@wofford.edu. Web site: http://www.wofford.edu/.

SOUTH DAKOTA

AUGUSTANA COLLEGE
SIOUX FALLS, SOUTH DAKOTA

General Independent, comprehensive, coed, affiliated with Evangelical Lutheran Church in America **Entrance** Moderately difficult **Setting** 100-acre urban campus **Total enrollment** 1,783 **Student/faculty ratio** 12:1 **Application deadline** 8/1 (freshmen), rolling (transfer) **Freshmen** 83% were admitted **Housing** Yes **Expenses** Tuition 15,460; Room & Board 4478 **Undergraduates** 64% women, 6% part-time, 5% 25 or older, 0.5% Native American, 0.2% Hispanic American, 1% African American, 0.4% Asian American/Pacific Islander **The most frequently chosen baccalaureate fields are** education, business/marketing, health professions and related sciences **Academic program** Advanced placement, acceler-

Augustana College *(continued)*

ated degree program, self-designed majors, honors program, summer session, adult/continuing education programs, internships **Contact** Robert Preloger, Vice President for Enrollment, Augustana College, 2001 South Summit Avenue, Sioux Falls, SD 57197. Telephone: 605-274-5516 Ext. 5504 or toll-free 800-727-2844. Fax: 605-274-5518. E-mail: info@inst.augie.edu. Web site: http://www.augie.edu/.

BLACK HILLS STATE UNIVERSITY
SPEARFISH, SOUTH DAKOTA

General State-supported, comprehensive, coed **Entrance** Minimally difficult **Setting** 123-acre small-town campus **Total enrollment** 4,171 **Student/faculty ratio** 28:1 **Application deadline** Rolling (freshmen), rolling (transfer) **Freshmen** 66% were admitted **Housing** Yes **Expenses** Tuition $3629; Room & Board $2883 **Undergraduates** 62% women, 28% part-time, 29% 25 or older, 3% Native American, 1% Hispanic American, 1% African American, 1% Asian American/Pacific Islander **The most frequently chosen baccalaureate fields are** business/marketing, education, social sciences and history **Academic program** Advanced placement, accelerated degree program, summer session, internships **Contact** Ms. Judy Berry, Assistant Director of Admissions, Black Hills State University, University Station Box 9502, Spearfish, SD 57799-9502. Telephone: 605-642-6343 or toll-free 800-255-2478. E-mail: jberry@mystic.bhsu.edu. Web site: http://www.bhsu.edu/.

COLORADO TECHNICAL UNIVERSITY SIOUX FALLS CAMPUS
SIOUX FALLS, SOUTH DAKOTA

General Proprietary, comprehensive, coed **Entrance** Minimally difficult **Total enrollment** 850 **Student/faculty ratio** 18:1 **Application deadline** 9/15 (freshmen) **Freshmen** 97% were admitted **Housing** No **Expenses** Tuition 8040 **Undergraduates** 56% women, 65% part-time, 52% 25 or older, 2% Native American, 1% Hispanic American, 2% African American, 0.5% Asian American/Pacific Islander **Academic program** Accelerated degree program, summer session, adult/continuing education programs, internships **Contact** Ms. Trista L. Brown, Admissions Advisor/Mentor, Colorado Technical University Sioux Falls Campus, 3901 West 59th Street, Sioux Falls, SD 57108. Telephone: 605-361-0200 Ext. 113. Fax: 605-361-5954. E-mail: callen@sf.coloradotech.edu. Web site: http://www.colotechu.edu/.

DAKOTA STATE UNIVERSITY
MADISON, SOUTH DAKOTA

General State-supported, comprehensive, coed **Entrance** Minimally difficult **Setting** 40-acre rural campus **Total enrollment** 1,807 **Student/faculty ratio** 18:1 **Application deadline** Rolling (freshmen), rolling (transfer) **Freshmen** 91% were admitted **Housing** Yes **Expenses** Tuition 3805; Room & Board 2840 **Undergraduates** 49% women, 23% part-time, 1% Native American, 1% Hispanic American, 0.4% African American, 1% Asian American/Pacific Islander **Academic program** English as a second language, advanced placement, honors program, summer session, adult/continuing education programs, internships **Contact** Ms. Katy O'Hara, Admissions Secretary, Dakota State University, 820 North Washington, Madison, SD 57042-1799. Telephone: 605-256-5139 or toll-free 888-DSU-9988. Fax: 605-256-5316. E-mail: yourfuture@dsu.edu. Web site: http://www.dsu.edu/.

DAKOTA WESLEYAN UNIVERSITY
MITCHELL, SOUTH DAKOTA

General Independent United Methodist, 4-year, coed **Entrance** Moderately difficult **Setting** 40-acre small-town campus **Total enrollment** 692 **Student/faculty ratio** 14:1 **Application deadline** 9/10 (freshmen), 9/10 (transfer) **Freshmen** 87% were admitted **Housing** Yes **Expenses** Tuition 11,654; Room & Board 3858 **Undergraduates** 61% women, 11% part-time, 19% 25 or older, 4% Native American, 2% Hispanic American, 4% African American, 1% Asian American/Pacific Islander **The most frequently chosen baccalaureate fields are** education, protective services/public administration, social sciences and history **Academic program** English as a second language, self-designed majors, honors program, summer session, adult/continuing education programs, internships **Contact** Ms. Laura Miller, Director of Enrollment Services, Dakota Wesleyan University, Enrollment Services, Mitchell, SD 57301-4398. Telephone: 605-995-2650 or toll-free 800-333-8506. Fax: 605-995-2699. E-mail: admissions@cc.dwu.edu. Web site: http://www.dwu.edu/.

HURON UNIVERSITY
HURON, SOUTH DAKOTA

General Proprietary, 4-year, coed **Entrance** Minimally difficult **Setting** 15-acre small-town campus **Total enrollment** 598 **Student/faculty ratio** 11:1 **Application deadline** Rolling (freshmen), rolling (transfer) **Freshmen** 39% were admitted **Housing** Yes **Expenses** Tuition 9750; Room & Board 2850 **Undergraduates** 52% women, 15% part-time, 23% 25 or older, 3% Native American, 5% Hispanic American, 11% African American, 1% Asian American/Pacific Islander **The most frequently chosen baccalaureate fields are** business/marketing, education, protective services/public administration **Academic program** Advanced placement, accelerated degree program, honors program, summer session, adult/continuing education programs **Contact** Mr. Mike Riggin, Director of Admissions, Huron University, 333 9th Street Southwest, Huron, SD 57350. Telephone: 605-352-8721 or toll-free 800-710-7159. Fax: 605-352-7421. Web site: http://www.huron.edu/.

MOUNT MARTY COLLEGE
YANKTON, SOUTH DAKOTA

General Independent Roman Catholic, comprehensive, coed **Entrance** Moderately difficult **Setting**

80-acre small-town campus **Total enrollment** 1,125 **Student/faculty ratio** 12:1 **Application deadline** Rolling (freshmen), rolling (transfer) **Freshmen** 93% were admitted **Housing** Yes **Expenses** Tuition $10,634; Room & Board $4272 **Undergraduates** 67% women, 38% part-time, 35% 25 or older, 1% Native American, 1% Hispanic American, 1% African American, 1% Asian American/Pacific Islander **The most frequently chosen baccalaureate fields are** education, business/marketing, health professions and related sciences **Academic program** Advanced placement, accelerated degree program, self-designed majors, honors program, summer session, adult/continuing education programs, internships **Contact** Office of Admissions, Mount Marty College, 1105 West 8th Street, Yankton, SD 57078. Telephone: 605-668-1011 or toll-free 800-658-4552. Fax: 605-668-1607. E-mail: mmcadmit@rs1.mtmc.edu. Web site: http://www.mtmc.edu/.

NATIONAL AMERICAN UNIVERSITY
RAPID CITY, SOUTH DAKOTA

General Proprietary, comprehensive, coed **Entrance** Noncompetitive **Setting** 8-acre urban campus **Total enrollment** 1,049 **Application deadline** Rolling (freshmen), rolling (transfer) **Housing** Yes **Expenses** Tuition 9600; Room & Board 3675 **Undergraduates** 47% women, 36% part-time, 43% 25 or older **Academic program** English as a second language, advanced placement, accelerated degree program, summer session, adult/continuing education programs, internships **Contact** Mr. Tom Shea, Vice President of Enrollment Management, National American University, PO Box 1780, Rapid City, SD 57709-1780. Telephone: 605-394-4902 or toll-free 800-843-8892. Fax: 605-394-4871. E-mail: apply@national.edu. Web site: http://www.national.edu/.

NATIONAL AMERICAN UNIVERSITY–SIOUX FALLS BRANCH
SIOUX FALLS, SOUTH DAKOTA

General Proprietary, 4-year, coed **Entrance** Noncompetitive **Setting** urban campus **Total enrollment** 325 **Application deadline** Rolling (freshmen), rolling (transfer) **Housing** No **Expenses** Tuition 7320 **Undergraduates** 76% 25 or older **Academic program** English as a second language, advanced placement, accelerated degree program, summer session, adult/continuing education programs, internships **Contact** Ms. Lisa Houtsma, Director of Admissions, National American University–Sioux Falls Branch, 2801 South Kiwanis Avenue, Suite 100, Sioux Falls, SD 57105. Telephone: 605-334-5430. E-mail: lhoutsma@national.edu.

NORTHERN STATE UNIVERSITY
ABERDEEN, SOUTH DAKOTA

General State-supported, comprehensive, coed **Entrance** Minimally difficult **Setting** 52-acre small-town campus **Total enrollment** 3,283 **Student/faculty ratio** 22:1 **Application deadline** 9/1 (freshmen), 9/1 (transfer) **Freshmen** 91% were admitted **Housing** Yes **Expenses** Tuition $3312; Room & Board $2663 **Undergraduates** 60% women, 39% part-time, 19% 25 or older, 7% Native American, 1% Hispanic American, 1% African American, 1% Asian American/Pacific Islander **The most frequently chosen baccalaureate fields are** business/marketing, education, psychology **Academic program** English as a second language, advanced placement, accelerated degree program, self-designed majors, honors program, summer session, adult/continuing education programs, internships **Contact** Mr. Mike Mutzinger, Director of Admissions, Northern State University, 1200 South Jay Street, Aberdeen, SD 57401-7198. Telephone: 605-626-2544 or toll-free 800-678-5330. Fax: 605-626-2587. E-mail: admission1@wolf.northern.edu. Web site: http://www.northern.edu/.

OGLALA LAKOTA COLLEGE
KYLE, SOUTH DAKOTA

Contact Miss Billi K. Hornbeck, Registrar, Oglala Lakota College, 490 Piya Wiconi Road, Kyle, SD 57752-0490. Telephone: 605-455-2321 Ext. 236.

PRESENTATION COLLEGE
ABERDEEN, SOUTH DAKOTA

General Independent Roman Catholic, 4-year, coed **Entrance** Noncompetitive **Setting** 100-acre small-town campus **Total enrollment** 462 **Application deadline** Rolling (freshmen), rolling (transfer) **Freshmen** 100% were admitted **Housing** Yes **Expenses** Tuition $8698; Room & Board $4150 **Undergraduates** 32% 25 or older, 11% Native American, 0.2% Hispanic American, 3% African American, 0% Asian American/Pacific Islander **The most frequently chosen baccalaureate fields are** business/marketing, health professions and related sciences, liberal arts/general studies **Academic program** Advanced placement, accelerated degree program, summer session, adult/continuing education programs, internships **Contact** Mr. Joddy Meidinger, Director of Admissions, Presentation College, 1500 North Main Street, Aberdeen, SC 57401. Telephone: 605-229-8493 Ext. 492 or toll-free 800-437-6060. E-mail: admit@presentation.edu. Web site: http://www.presentation.edu/.

SINTE GLESKA UNIVERSITY
ROSEBUD, SOUTH DAKOTA

General Independent, comprehensive, coed **Entrance** Noncompetitive **Setting** 52-acre rural campus **Total enrollment** 907 **Application deadline** 8/20 (freshmen), 8/20 (transfer) **Housing** No **Expenses** Tuition $1770 **Undergraduates** 73% 25 or older **Academic program** Honors program, summer session, adult/continuing education programs, internships **Contact** Mr. Jack Herman, Registrar and Director of Admissions, Sinte Gleska University, PO Box 490, Rosebud, SD 57570-0490. Telephone: 605-747-2263 Ext. 224. Fax: 605-747-2098.

SOUTH DAKOTA SCHOOL OF MINES AND TECHNOLOGY
RAPID CITY, SOUTH DAKOTA

General State-supported, university, coed **Entrance** Moderately difficult **Setting** 120-acre suburban campus **Total enrollment** 2,307 **Student/faculty ratio** 13:1 **Application deadline** Rolling (freshmen), rolling (transfer) **Freshmen** 95% were admitted **Housing** Yes **Expenses** Tuition $4161; Room & Board $3224 **Undergraduates** 30% women, 20% part-time, 12% 25 or older, 2% Native American, 1% Hispanic American, 1% African American, 1% Asian American/Pacific Islander **The most frequently chosen baccalaureate fields are** computer/information sciences, engineering/engineering technologies, mathematics **Academic program** English as a second language, advanced placement, summer session, adult/continuing education programs, internships **Contact** Donald Hapward, Director of Admissions, South Dakota School of Mines and Technology, 501 East Saint Joseph, Rapid City, SD 57701-3995. Telephone: 605-394-2414 Ext. 1266 or toll-free 800-544-8162 Ext. 2414. Fax: 605-394-1268. E-mail: undergraduate_admissions@silver.sdsmt.ed. Web site: http://www.sdsmt.edu/.

SOUTH DAKOTA STATE UNIVERSITY
BROOKINGS, SOUTH DAKOTA

General State-supported, university, coed **Entrance** Moderately difficult **Setting** 260-acre small-town campus **Total enrollment** 8,662 **Student/faculty ratio** 15:1 **Application deadline** Rolling (freshmen), rolling (transfer) **Freshmen** 94% were admitted **Housing** Yes **Expenses** Tuition $3588; Room & Board $2922 **Undergraduates** 51% women, 15% part-time, 0.3% Native American, 0.1% Hispanic American, 0.1% African American, 0.1% Asian American/Pacific Islander **The most frequently chosen baccalaureate fields are** agriculture, health professions and related sciences, social sciences and history **Academic program** English as a second language, advanced placement, accelerated degree program, honors program, summer session, adult/continuing education programs, internships **Contact** Ms. Michelle Kuebler, Assistant Director of Admissions, South Dakota State University, PO Box 2201, Brookings, SD 57007. Telephone: 605-688-4121 or toll-free 800-952-3541. Fax: 605-688-6384. E-mail: sdsuadms@adm.sdstate.edu. Web site: http://www.sdstate.edu/.

UNIVERSITY OF SIOUX FALLS
SIOUX FALLS, SOUTH DAKOTA

General Independent American Baptist, comprehensive, coed **Entrance** Moderately difficult **Setting** 22-acre suburban campus **Total enrollment** 1,272 **Student/faculty ratio** 17:1 **Application deadline** Rolling (freshmen), rolling (transfer) **Freshmen** 94% were admitted **Housing** Yes **Expenses** Tuition 12,600; Room & Board 3850 **Undergraduates** 56% women, 21% part-time, 21% 25 or older, 1% Native American, 0.5% Hispanic American, 1% African American, 1% Asian American/Pacific Islander **Academic program** Advanced placement, accelerated degree program, self-designed majors, honors program, summer session, adult/continuing education programs, internships **Contact** Mr. Greg A. Fritz, Associate Vice President of Admissions and Marketing, University of Sioux Falls, 1101 West 22nd Street, Sioux Falls, SD 57105. Telephone: 605-331-6600 or toll-free 800-888-1047 Ext. 6 (out-of-state). Fax: 605-331-6615. E-mail: terry.okken@thecoo.edu. Web site: http://www.usiouxfalls.edu/.

UNIVERSITY OF SOUTH DAKOTA
VERMILLION, SOUTH DAKOTA

General State-supported, university, coed **Entrance** Moderately difficult **Setting** 216-acre small-town campus **Total enrollment** 7,488 **Student/faculty ratio** 15:1 **Application deadline** Rolling (freshmen), rolling (transfer) **Housing** Yes **Expenses** Tuition 3678; Room & Board 3037 **Undergraduates** 57% women, 21% part-time, 22% 25 or older, 2% Native American, 1% Hispanic American, 1% African American, 1% Asian American/Pacific Islander **The most frequently chosen baccalaureate fields are** business/marketing, education, health professions and related sciences **Academic program** English as a second language, advanced placement, honors program, summer session, internships **Contact** Ms. Paula Tacke, Director of Admissions, University of South Dakota, 414 East Clark Street, Vermillion, SD 57069. Telephone: 605-677-5434 or toll-free 877-269-6837. Fax: 605-677-6753. E-mail: admiss@usd.edu. Web site: http://www.usd.edu/.

TENNESSEE

AMERICAN BAPTIST COLLEGE OF AMERICAN BAPTIST THEOLOGICAL SEMINARY
NASHVILLE, TENNESSEE

General Independent Baptist, 4-year, coed **Entrance** Noncompetitive **Setting** 52-acre urban campus **Total enrollment** 106 **Application deadline** 7/1 (freshmen), 7/1 (transfer) **Freshmen** 100% were admitted **Housing** Yes **Expenses** Tuition $3045; Room only $1600 **Undergraduates** 85% 25 or older **Academic program** English as a second language, accelerated degree program, self-designed majors, summer session, adult/continuing education programs **Contact** Ms. Marcella Lockhart, Director of Enrollment Management, American Baptist College of American Baptist Theological Seminary, 1800 Baptist World Center Drive, Nashville, TN 37207. Telephone: 615-228-7877 Ext. 35. Fax: 615-226-7855. E-mail: mlockhart@abcnash.edu.

AQUINAS COLLEGE
NASHVILLE, TENNESSEE

General Independent Roman Catholic, 4-year, coed **Entrance** Moderately difficult **Setting** 92-acre urban campus **Total enrollment** 435 **Student/faculty ratio** 15:1 **Application deadline** Rolling (freshmen), rolling (transfer) **Freshmen** 9% were admitted **Housing** No **Expenses** Tuition 8130 **Undergraduates** 61% 25 or older **Academic program** Advanced placement, summer session, internships **Contact** Neil J. Devine, Director of Career Planning and Admission, Aquinas College, 4210 Harding Road, Nashville, TN 37205-2005. Telephone: 615-297-7545 Ext. 426. Fax: 615-297-7970 Ext. 460. Web site: http://www.aquinas-tn.edu/.

AUSTIN PEAY STATE UNIVERSITY
CLARKSVILLE, TENNESSEE

General State-supported, comprehensive, coed **Entrance** Moderately difficult **Setting** 200-acre suburban campus **Total enrollment** 7,121 **Application deadline** 8/15 (freshmen), rolling (transfer) **Freshmen** 48% were admitted **Housing** Yes **Expenses** Tuition $2831; Room & Board $3350 **Undergraduates** 59% women, 30% part-time, 40% 25 or older, 1% Native American, 5% Hispanic American, 19% African American, 3% Asian American/Pacific Islander **The most frequently chosen baccalaureate fields are** business/marketing, health professions and related sciences, interdisciplinary studies **Academic program** English as a second language, advanced placement, honors program, summer session, adult/continuing education programs, internships **Contact** Mr. Charles McCorkle, Director of Admissions, Austin Peay State University, PO Box 4548, Clarksville, TN 37044-4548. Telephone: 931-221-7661 or toll-free 800-844-2778 (out-of-state). Fax: 931-221-6168. E-mail: mccorklec@apsu02.apsu.edu. Web site: http://www.apsu.edu/.

BAPTIST MEMORIAL COLLEGE OF HEALTH SCIENCES
MEMPHIS, TENNESSEE

Contact Baptist Memorial College of Health Sciences, 1003 Monroe Avenue, Memphis, TN 38104. Telephone: or toll-free 800-796-7171. Web site: http://www.bmhcc.org/services/bchs/index.asp.

BELMONT UNIVERSITY
NASHVILLE, TENNESSEE

General Independent Baptist, comprehensive, coed **Entrance** Moderately difficult **Setting** 34-acre urban campus **Total enrollment** 2,976 **Student/faculty ratio** 10:1 **Application deadline** 5/1 (freshmen), 5/1 (transfer) **Freshmen** 74% were admitted **Housing** Yes **Expenses** Tuition 12,330; Room & Board 5437 **Undergraduates** 62% women, 14% part-time, 16% 25 or older, 0.3% Native American, 1% Hispanic American, 3% African American, 1% Asian American/Pacific Islander **The most frequently chosen baccalaureate fields are** business/marketing, health professions and related sciences, visual/performing arts **Academic program** Advanced placement, accelerated degree program, self-designed majors, honors program, summer session, adult/continuing education programs, internships **Contact** Dr. Kathryn Baugher, Dean of Enrollment Services, Belmont University, 1900 Belmont Boulevard, Nashville, TN 37212. Telephone: 615-460-6785 or toll-free 800-56E-NROL. Fax: 615-460-5434. E-mail: buadmission@belmont.edu. Web site: http://www.belmont.edu/.

► **For more information, see page 387.**

BETHEL COLLEGE
MCKENZIE, TENNESSEE

General Independent Cumberland Presbyterian, comprehensive, coed **Entrance** Minimally difficult **Setting** 100-acre small-town campus **Total enrollment** 843 **Student/faculty ratio** 14:1 **Application deadline** Rolling (freshmen), rolling (transfer) **Freshmen** 62% were admitted **Housing** Yes **Expenses** Tuition $8425; Room & Board $4732 **Undergraduates** 50% women, 14% part-time, 50% 25 or older, 1% Native American, 1% Hispanic American, 16% African American, 0.3% Asian American/Pacific Islander **The most frequently chosen baccalaureate fields are** business/marketing, biological/life sciences, education **Academic program** Advanced placement, accelerated degree program, self-designed majors, summer session, adult/continuing education programs, internships **Contact** Mr. Steve Trapp, Director of Admissions and Marketing, Bethel College, 325 Cherry Avenue, McKenzie, TN 38201. Telephone: 731-352-4030. Fax: 731-352-4069. E-mail: zakowiczd@bethel-college.edu. Web site: http://www.bethel-college.edu/.

BRYAN COLLEGE
DAYTON, TENNESSEE

General Independent interdenominational, 4-year, coed **Entrance** Moderately difficult **Setting** 100-acre small-town campus **Total enrollment** 616 **Application deadline** Rolling (freshmen), rolling (transfer) **Freshmen** 37% were admitted **Housing** Yes **Expenses** Tuition 12,200; Room & Board 4200 **Undergraduates** 1% 25 or older **Academic program** Advanced placement, honors program, summer session, adult/continuing education programs, internships **Contact** Mr. Ronald D. Petitte, Registrar, Bryan College, PO Box 7000, Dayton, TN 37321-7000. Telephone: 423-775-7237 or toll-free 800-277-9522. Fax: 423-775-7330. E-mail: admiss@bryannet.bryan.edu. Web site: http://www.bryan.edu/.

CARSON-NEWMAN COLLEGE
JEFFERSON CITY, TENNESSEE

General Independent Southern Baptist, comprehensive, coed **Entrance** Moderately difficult **Setting** 90-acre small-town campus **Total enrollment** 2,230 **Student/faculty ratio** 13:1 **Application deadline** 8/1 (freshmen), 8/1 (transfer) **Freshmen** 90% were admitted **Housing** Yes **Expenses** Tuition 11,920;

Carson-Newman College *(continued)*

Room & Board 3980 **Undergraduates** 58% women, 8% part-time, 13% 25 or older, 0.2% Native American, 0.4% Hispanic American, 6% African American, 1% Asian American/Pacific Islander **The most frequently chosen baccalaureate fields are** business/marketing, biological/life sciences, education **Academic program** English as a second language, advanced placement, accelerated degree program, self-designed majors, honors program, summer session, adult/continuing education programs, internships **Contact** Mrs. Sheryl M. Gray, Director of Undergraduate Admissions, Carson-Newman College, PO Box 72025, Jefferson City, TN 37760. Telephone: 423-471-3223 or toll-free 800-678-9061. Fax: 423-471-3502. E-mail: cnadmiss@cncacc.cn.edu. Web site: http://www.cn.edu/.

CHRISTIAN BROTHERS UNIVERSITY
MEMPHIS, TENNESSEE

General Independent Roman Catholic, comprehensive, coed **Entrance** Moderately difficult **Setting** 70-acre urban campus **Total enrollment** 2,156 **Student/faculty ratio** 14:1 **Application deadline** 8/23 (freshmen), 8/23 (transfer) **Freshmen** 82% were admitted **Housing** Yes **Expenses** Tuition 14,330; Room & Board 4470 **Undergraduates** 55% women, 23% part-time, 24% 25 or older, 0.3% Native American, 2% Hispanic American, 25% African American, 3% Asian American/Pacific Islander **The most frequently chosen baccalaureate fields are** business/marketing, engineering/engineering technologies, psychology **Academic program** Advanced placement, accelerated degree program, honors program, summer session, internships **Contact** Ms. Courtney Fee, Dean of Admission, Christian Brothers University, 650 East Parkway South, Memphis, TN 38104. Telephone: 901-321-3205 or toll-free 800-288-7576. Fax: 901-321-3202. E-mail: admissions@bucs.cbu.edu. Web site: http://www.cbu.edu/.

CRICHTON COLLEGE
MEMPHIS, TENNESSEE

General Independent, 4-year, coed **Entrance** Moderately difficult **Setting** 55-acre urban campus **Total enrollment** 973 **Student/faculty ratio** 16:1 **Application deadline** 8/31 (freshmen), 8/31 (transfer) **Freshmen** 63% were admitted **Housing** Yes **Expenses** Tuition $9480; Room only $3200 **Undergraduates** 62% women, 21% part-time, 72% 25 or older, 1% Native American, 0.4% Hispanic American, 48% African American, 0.4% Asian American/Pacific Islander **The most frequently chosen baccalaureate fields are** business/marketing, education, psychology **Academic program** Advanced placement, accelerated degree program, self-designed majors, summer session, adult/continuing education programs, internships **Contact** Mr. David Wilson, Associate Director of Admissions, Crichton College, 6655 Winchester Road, PO Box 757830, Memphis, TN 38175-7830. Telephone: 901-367-3888 or toll-free 800-960-9777. Fax: 901-367-2650. E-mail: info@crichton.edu. Web site: http://www.crichton.edu/.

CUMBERLAND UNIVERSITY
LEBANON, TENNESSEE

Contact Ms. Stephanie Walker, Director of Admissions, Cumberland University, One Cumberland Square, Lebanon, TN 37087-3554. Telephone: 615-444-2562 Ext. 1232 or toll-free 800-467-0562 (out-of-state). Fax: 615-444-2569. E-mail: admissions@cumberland.edu. Web site: http://www.cumberland.edu/.

DAVID LIPSCOMB UNIVERSITY
See Lipscomb University

EAST TENNESSEE STATE UNIVERSITY
JOHNSON CITY, TENNESSEE

General State-supported, university, coed **Entrance** Moderately difficult **Setting** 366-acre small-town campus **Total enrollment** 11,063 **Student/faculty ratio** 16:1 **Application deadline** Rolling (freshmen), rolling (transfer) **Freshmen** 79% were admitted **Housing** Yes **Expenses** Tuition 2759; Room & Board 3818 **Undergraduates** 57% women, 18% part-time, 28% 25 or older, 0.4% Native American, 1% Hispanic American, 4% African American, 1% Asian American/Pacific Islander **The most frequently chosen baccalaureate fields are** business/marketing, health professions and related sciences, protective services/public administration **Academic program** Advanced placement, accelerated degree program, honors program, summer session, adult/continuing education programs, internships **Contact** Mr. Mike Pitts, Director of Admissions, East Tennessee State University, PO Box 70731, Johnson City, TN 37614-0734. Telephone: 423-439-6861 or toll-free 800-462-3878. Fax: 423-439-4630. E-mail: pitts@etsuvax.etsu-tn.edu. Web site: http://www.etsu.edu/.

FISK UNIVERSITY
NASHVILLE, TENNESSEE

General Independent, comprehensive, coed, affiliated with United Church of Christ **Entrance** Moderately difficult **Setting** 40-acre urban campus **Total enrollment** 959 **Student/faculty ratio** 12:1 **Application deadline** 6/15 (freshmen), 6/15 (transfer) **Freshmen** 41% were admitted **Housing** Yes **Expenses** Tuition 9589; Room & Board 5156 **Undergraduates** 70% women, 4% part-time, 4% 25 or older, 0% Native American, 0% Hispanic American, 95% African American, 0.1% Asian American/Pacific Islander **The most frequently chosen baccalaureate fields are** business/marketing, biological/life sciences, psychology **Academic program** Advanced placement, self-designed majors, honors program, internships **Contact** Mr. Rodney Smith, Director of Admissions, Fisk University, 1000 17th Avenue North, Nashville, TN 37208-3051. Telephone: 615-329-8665 or toll-free 800-443-FISK. E-mail: lcampbel@dubois.fisk.edu. Web site: http://www.fisk.edu/.

▶ **For more information, see page 419.**

FREED-HARDEMAN UNIVERSITY
HENDERSON, TENNESSEE

General Independent, comprehensive, coed, affiliated with Church of Christ **Entrance** Moderately difficult **Setting** 96-acre small-town campus **Total enrollment** 1,886 **Student/faculty ratio** 19:1 **Application deadline** Rolling (freshmen), rolling (transfer) **Freshmen** 71% were admitted **Housing** Yes **Expenses** Tuition $8990; Room & Board $4620 **Undergraduates** 54% women, 6% part-time, 9% 25 or older, 0.4% Native American, 1% Hispanic American, 6% African American, 1% Asian American/Pacific Islander **The most frequently chosen baccalaureate fields are** business/marketing, education, philosophy, religion, and theology **Academic program** Advanced placement, accelerated degree program, self-designed majors, honors program, summer session, internships **Contact** Mr. Jim Brown, Director of Admissions, Freed-Hardeman University, 158 East Main Street, Henderson, TN 38340-2399. Telephone: 901-989-6651 or toll-free 800-630-3480. Fax: 901-989-6047. E-mail: admissions@fhu.edu. Web site: http://www.fhu.edu/.

FREE WILL BAPTIST BIBLE COLLEGE
NASHVILLE, TENNESSEE

General Independent Free Will Baptist, 4-year, coed **Entrance** Noncompetitive **Setting** 10-acre suburban campus **Total enrollment** 318 **Application deadline** Rolling (freshmen) **Housing** Yes **Expenses** Tuition $7112; Room & Board $3788 **Undergraduates** 7% 25 or older, 0.3% Native American, 2% African American, 0.3% Asian American/Pacific Islander **Academic program** English as a second language, advanced placement, self-designed majors, summer session, internships **Contact** Dr. Milton Fields, Academic Dean, Free Will Baptist Bible College, 3606 West End Avenue, Nashville, TN 37205-2498. Telephone: 615-383-1340 or toll-free 800-763-9222. Fax: 615-269-6028. Web site: http://www.fwbbc.edu.

JOHNSON BIBLE COLLEGE
KNOXVILLE, TENNESSEE

General Independent, comprehensive, coed, affiliated with Christian Churches and Churches of Christ **Entrance** Minimally difficult **Setting** 75-acre rural campus **Total enrollment** 636 **Student/faculty ratio** 16:1 **Application deadline** 8/1 (freshmen), 8/1 (transfer) **Freshmen** 85% were admitted **Housing** Yes **Expenses** Tuition 5500; Room & Board 3500 **Undergraduates** 48% women, 4% part-time, 17% 25 or older, 0.2% Native American, 1% Hispanic American, 1% African American, 0.4% Asian American/Pacific Islander **The most frequently chosen baccalaureate fields are** education, philosophy, religion, and theology **Academic program** English as a second language, advanced placement, accelerated degree program, summer session, adult/continuing education programs, internships **Contact** Mr. Tim Wingfield, Director of Admissions, Johnson Bible College, 7900 Johnson Drive, Knoxville, TN 37998. Telephone: 865-251-2346 or toll-free 800-827-2122. Fax: 423-251-2336. E-mail: lgreen@jbc.edu. Web site: http://www.jbc.edu/.

KING COLLEGE
BRISTOL, TENNESSEE

General Independent, 4-year, coed, affiliated with Presbyterian Church (U.S.A.) **Entrance** Moderately difficult **Setting** 135-acre suburban campus **Total enrollment** 602 **Student/faculty ratio** 11:1 **Application deadline** Rolling (freshmen), rolling (transfer) **Freshmen** 64% were admitted **Housing** Yes **Expenses** Tuition $12,700; Room & Board $4250 **Undergraduates** 55% women, 12% part-time, 9% 25 or older, 0% Native American, 1% Hispanic American, 2% African American, 1% Asian American/Pacific Islander **The most frequently chosen baccalaureate fields are** English, biological/life sciences, social sciences and history **Academic program** English as a second language, advanced placement, accelerated degree program, honors program, summer session, internships **Contact** Ms. Mindy Clark, Director of Admissions, King College, 1350 King College Road, Bristol, TN 37620-2699. Telephone: 423-652-4861 or toll-free 800-362-0014. Fax: 423-652-4727. E-mail: admissions@king2.king.bristol.tn.us. Web site: http://www.king.edu/.

LAMBUTH UNIVERSITY
JACKSON, TENNESSEE

General Independent United Methodist, 4-year, coed **Entrance** Moderately difficult **Setting** 50-acre urban campus **Total enrollment** 979 **Student/faculty ratio** 14:1 **Application deadline** Rolling (freshmen), rolling (transfer) **Freshmen** 72% were admitted **Housing** Yes **Expenses** Tuition $8648; Room & Board $4482 **Undergraduates** 57% women, 9% part-time, 17% 25 or older, 0% Native American, 1% Hispanic American, 15% African American, 0.4% Asian American/Pacific Islander **The most frequently chosen baccalaureate fields are** business/marketing, education, social sciences and history **Academic program** English as a second language, advanced placement, self-designed majors, summer session, adult/continuing education programs, internships **Contact** Dr. Joseph R. Thornton III, Vice President for Enrollment Management, Lambuth University, 705 Lambuth Boulevard, Jackson, TN 38301. Telephone: 901-425-3240 or toll-free 800-526-2884. Fax: 901-425-3496. E-mail: admit@lambuth.edu. Web site: http://www.lambuth.edu/.

LANE COLLEGE
JACKSON, TENNESSEE

General Independent, 4-year, coed, affiliated with Christian Methodist Episcopal Church **Entrance** Minimally difficult **Setting** 25-acre suburban cam-

Lane College *(continued)*

pus **Total enrollment** 702 **Student/faculty ratio** 15:1 **Application deadline** Rolling (freshmen), rolling (transfer) **Freshmen** 55% were admitted **Housing** Yes **Expenses** Tuition 6350; Room & Board 3800 **Undergraduates** 49% women, 2% part-time, 5% 25 or older, 0% Hispanic American, 99% African American **The most frequently chosen baccalaureate fields are** business/marketing, education, protective services/public administration **Academic program** Advanced placement, honors program, summer session, internships **Contact** Ms. E. Brown, Director of Admissions, Lane College, 545 Lane Avenue, Bray Administration Building 2nd Floor, Jackson, TN 38301-4598. Telephone: 901-426-7532 or toll-free 800-960-7533. Fax: 901-426-7559. E-mail: admissions@lanecollege.edu. Web site: http://lanecollege.edu/.

LEE UNIVERSITY
CLEVELAND, TENNESSEE

General Independent, comprehensive, coed, affiliated with Church of God **Entrance** Minimally difficult **Setting** 45-acre small-town campus **Total enrollment** 3,361 **Student/faculty ratio** 19:1 **Application deadline** 9/1 (freshmen), rolling (transfer) **Freshmen** 91% were admitted **Housing** Yes **Expenses** Tuition $7496; Room & Board $4550 **Undergraduates** 57% women, 8% part-time, 9% 25 or older **The most frequently chosen baccalaureate fields are** education, business/marketing, philosophy, religion, and theology **Academic program** English as a second language, advanced placement, honors program, summer session, adult/continuing education programs, internships **Contact** Admissions Coordinator, Lee University, PO Box 3450, Cleveland, TN 37311. Telephone: 423-614-8500 or toll-free 800-LEE-9930. Fax: 423-614-8533. E-mail: admissions@leeuniversity.edu. Web site: http://www.leeuniversity.edu/.

LEMOYNE-OWEN COLLEGE
MEMPHIS, TENNESSEE

General Independent, 4-year, coed, affiliated with United Church of Christ **Entrance** Minimally difficult **Setting** 15-acre urban campus **Total enrollment** 1,013 **Application deadline** 4/1 (freshmen), rolling (transfer) **Freshmen** 100% were admitted **Housing** Yes **Expenses** Tuition $7500; Room & Board $4200 **Undergraduates** 66% women, 20% part-time, 42% 25 or older, 0% Native American, 0.1% Hispanic American, 98% African American, 0% Asian American/Pacific Islander **The most frequently chosen baccalaureate fields are** business/marketing, education, social sciences and history **Academic program** Advanced placement, accelerated degree program, honors program, summer session, adult/continuing education programs, internships **Contact** Ms. Frankie Jeffries, Director of Admissions/Recruitment, LeMoyne-Owen College, 807 Walker Avenue, Memphis, TN 38126. Telephone: 901-942-7302 or toll-free 800-737-7778 (in-state). E-mail: admissions@locness.lemoyne-owen.edu. Web site: http://www.lemoyne-owen.edu/.

LINCOLN MEMORIAL UNIVERSITY
HARROGATE, TENNESSEE

General Independent, comprehensive, coed **Entrance** Moderately difficult **Setting** 1,000-acre small-town campus **Total enrollment** 1,753 **Student/faculty ratio** 9:1 **Application deadline** Rolling (freshmen), rolling (transfer) **Freshmen** 77% were admitted **Housing** Yes **Expenses** Tuition 10,800; Room & Board 4150 **Undergraduates** 69% women, 23% part-time, 28% 25 or older, 0% Native American, 0.3% Hispanic American, 4% African American, 0.2% Asian American/Pacific Islander **The most frequently chosen baccalaureate fields are** business/marketing, education, parks and recreation **Academic program** English as a second language, advanced placement, accelerated degree program, self-designed majors, honors program, summer session, adult/continuing education programs **Contact** Mr. Conrad Daniels, Dean of Admissions and Recruitment, Lincoln Memorial University, Cumberland Gap Parkway, Harrogate, TN 37752-1901. Telephone: 423-869-6280 or toll-free 800-325-0900. Fax: 423-869-6250. E-mail: admissions@inetlmu.lmunet.edu. Web site: http://www.lmunet.edu/.

LIPSCOMB UNIVERSITY
NASHVILLE, TENNESSEE

General Independent, comprehensive, coed, affiliated with Church of Christ **Entrance** Moderately difficult **Setting** 65-acre urban campus **Total enrollment** 2,545 **Student/faculty ratio** 16:1 **Application deadline** Rolling (freshmen), rolling (transfer) **Freshmen** 83% were admitted **Housing** Yes **Expenses** Tuition 10,268; Room & Board 5080 **Undergraduates** 56% women, 13% part-time, 10% 25 or older, 0.2% Native American, 1% Hispanic American, 4% African American, 1% Asian American/Pacific Islander **The most frequently chosen baccalaureate fields are** business/marketing, communications/communication technologies, education **Academic program** Advanced placement, accelerated degree program, honors program, summer session, adult/continuing education programs, internships **Contact** Mr. Scott Gilmer, Director of Admissions, Lipscomb University, 3901 Granny White Pike, Nashville, TN 37204-3951. Telephone: 615-269-1776 or toll-free 800-333-4358. Fax: 615-269-1804. E-mail: admissions@dlu.edu. Web site: http://www.lipscomb.edu/.

MARTIN METHODIST COLLEGE
PULASKI, TENNESSEE

General Independent United Methodist, 4-year, coed **Entrance** Minimally difficult **Setting** 6-acre small-town campus **Total enrollment** 582 **Student/faculty ratio** 18:1 **Application deadline** 8/30 (freshmen), 8/30 (transfer) **Freshmen** 97% were admitted **Housing** Yes **Expenses** Tuition $9920; Room & Board $3600 **Undergraduates** 62% women, 32% part-time, 31% 25 or older, 1% Native American, 2% Hispanic American, 11% African American, 0.2% Asian American/Pacific Islander **The most fre-**

quently chosen baccalaureate fields are** business/marketing, education, social sciences and history **Academic program** English as a second language, advanced placement, self-designed majors, summer session, adult/continuing education programs **Contact** Mr. Robby Shelton, Vice President for Enrollment Management, Martin Methodist College, 433 West Madison Street, Pulaski, TN 38478-2716. Telephone: 931-363-9807 or toll-free 800-467-1273. Fax: 931-363-9818. E-mail: admissions@martinmethodist.edu. Web site: http://www.martinmethodist.edu/.

MARYVILLE COLLEGE
MARYVILLE, TENNESSEE

General Independent Presbyterian, 4-year, coed **Entrance** Moderately difficult **Setting** 350-acre suburban campus **Total enrollment** 982 **Student/faculty ratio** 14:1 **Application deadline** 3/1 (freshmen), rolling (transfer) **Freshmen** 81% were admitted **Housing** Yes **Expenses** Tuition $16,649; Room & Board $5310 **Undergraduates** 56% women, 4% part-time, 7% 25 or older, 0.4% Native American, 1% Hispanic American, 5% African American, 1% Asian American/Pacific Islander **The most frequently chosen baccalaureate fields are** business/marketing, education, social sciences and history **Academic program** English as a second language, advanced placement, self-designed majors, honors program, summer session, adult/continuing education programs, internships **Contact** Ms. Linda L. Moore, Administrative Assistant of Admissions, Maryville College, 502 East Lamar Alexander Parkway, Maryville, TN 37804-5907. Telephone: 865-981-8092 or toll-free 800-597-2687. Fax: 865-981-8005. E-mail: admissions@maryvillecollege.edu. Web site: http://www.maryvillecollege.edu/.

MEMPHIS COLLEGE OF ART
MEMPHIS, TENNESSEE

General Independent, comprehensive, coed **Entrance** Moderately difficult **Setting** 200-acre urban campus **Total enrollment** 289 **Student/faculty ratio** 11:1 **Application deadline** Rolling (freshmen), rolling (transfer) **Freshmen** 83% were admitted **Housing** Yes **Expenses** Tuition $12,790; Room & Board $5200 **Undergraduates** 52% women, 11% part-time, 30% 25 or older, 0% Native American, 0.4% Hispanic American, 16% African American, 2% Asian American/Pacific Islander **The most frequently chosen baccalaureate field is** visual/performing arts **Academic program** Advanced placement, summer session, adult/continuing education programs, internships **Contact** Ms. Annette Moore, Director of Admission, Memphis College of Art, 1930 Poplar Avenue, Memphis, TN 38104. Telephone: 901-272-5153 or toll-free 800-727-1088. Fax: 901-272-5158. E-mail: info@mca.edu. Web site: http://www.mca.edu/.

MIDDLE TENNESSEE STATE UNIVERSITY
MURFREESBORO, TENNESSEE

General State-supported, university, coed **Entrance** Moderately difficult **Setting** 500-acre urban campus **Total enrollment** 19,121 **Student/faculty ratio** 23:1 **Application deadline** Rolling (freshmen), rolling (transfer) **Freshmen** 79% were admitted **Housing** Yes **Expenses** Tuition 2808; Room & Board 3436 **Undergraduates** 54% women, 16% part-time, 24% 25 or older, 1% Native American, 1% Hispanic American, 11% African American, 2% Asian American/Pacific Islander **The most frequently chosen baccalaureate fields are** business/marketing, communications/communication technologies, interdisciplinary studies **Academic program** English as a second language, advanced placement, accelerated degree program, self-designed majors, honors program, summer session, adult/continuing education programs, internships **Contact** Ms. Lynn Palmer, Director of Admissions, Middle Tennessee State University, 1301 East Main Street, Murfreesboro, TN 37132. Telephone: 615-898-2111. Fax: 615-898-5478. E-mail: admissions@mtsu.edu. Web site: http://www.mtsu.edu/.

MILLIGAN COLLEGE
MILLIGAN COLLEGE, TENNESSEE

General Independent Christian, comprehensive, coed **Entrance** Moderately difficult **Setting** 145-acre suburban campus **Total enrollment** 906 **Student/faculty ratio** 13:1 **Application deadline** Rolling (freshmen), rolling (transfer) **Freshmen** 69% were admitted **Housing** Yes **Expenses** Tuition 12,300; Room & Board 4200 **Undergraduates** 60% women, 3% part-time, 13% 25 or older, 0.3% Native American, 1% Hispanic American, 1% African American, 1% Asian American/Pacific Islander **The most frequently chosen baccalaureate fields are** business/marketing, education, health professions and related sciences **Academic program** Advanced placement, accelerated degree program, summer session, adult/continuing education programs, internships **Contact** Mr. Michael A. Johnson, Vice President for Enrollment Management, Milligan College, PO Box 210, Milligan College, TN 37682. Telephone: 423-461-8730 or toll-free 800-262-8337 (in-state). Fax: 423-461-8960. E-mail: admissions@kegley.milligan.milligan-coll. Web site: http://www.milligan.edu/.

O'MORE COLLEGE OF DESIGN
FRANKLIN, TENNESSEE

General Independent, 4-year, coed **Contact** Ms. Amy Shelton, Vice President for Admissions and Records, O'More College of Design, 423 South Margin Street, Franklin, TN 37064-2816. Telephone: 615-794-4254 Ext. 25. Fax: 615-790-1662. Web site: http://www.omorecollege.edu/.

RHODES COLLEGE
MEMPHIS, TENNESSEE

General Independent Presbyterian, comprehensive, coed **Entrance** Very difficult **Setting** 100-acre suburban campus **Total enrollment** 1,554 **Student/faculty ratio** 12:1 **Application deadline** 2/1 (freshmen), 2/1 (transfer) **Freshmen** 70% were admitted **Housing** Yes **Expenses** Tuition $19,503; Room &

Rhodes College *(continued)*

Board $5671 **Undergraduates** 57% women, 2% part-time, 0.1% 25 or older, 0.1% Native American, 2% Hispanic American, 4% African American, 3% Asian American/Pacific Islander **The most frequently chosen baccalaureate fields are** business/marketing, biological/life sciences, social sciences and history **Academic program** Advanced placement, accelerated degree program, self-designed majors, honors program, summer session, internships **Contact** Mr. David J. Wottle, Dean of Admissions and Financial Aid, Rhodes College, 2000 North Parkway, Memphis, TN 38112-1690. Telephone: 901-843-3700 or toll-free 800-844-5969 (out-of-state). Fax: 901-843-3719. E-mail: adminfo@rhodes.edu. Web site: http://www.rhodes.edu/.

SOUTHERN ADVENTIST UNIVERSITY
COLLEGEDALE, TENNESSEE

General Independent Seventh-day Adventist, comprehensive, coed **Entrance** Moderately difficult **Setting** 1,000-acre small-town campus **Total enrollment** 2,046 **Student/faculty ratio** 16:1 **Application deadline** Rolling (freshmen), rolling (transfer) **Freshmen** 72% were admitted **Housing** Yes **Expenses** Tuition $11,610; Room & Board $4040 **Undergraduates** 54% women, 10% part-time, 10% 25 or older, 1% Native American, 10% Hispanic American, 6% African American, 4% Asian American/Pacific Islander **The most frequently chosen baccalaureate fields are** business/marketing, education, health professions and related sciences **Academic program** English as a second language, advanced placement, honors program, summer session, internships **Contact** Mr. Victor Czerkasij, Director of Admissions and Recruitment, Southern Adventist University, PO Box 370, Collegedale, TN 37315-0370. Telephone: 423-238-2843 or toll-free 800-768-8437. Fax: 423-238-3005. E-mail: admissions@southern.edu. Web site: http://www.southern.edu/.

TENNESSEE STATE UNIVERSITY
NASHVILLE, TENNESSEE

General State-supported, comprehensive, coed **Entrance** Minimally difficult **Setting** 450-acre urban campus **Total enrollment** 8,640 **Student/faculty ratio** 28:1 **Application deadline** 8/1 (freshmen), 8/1 (transfer) **Freshmen** 54% were admitted **Housing** Yes **Expenses** Tuition $2697; Room & Board $3600 **Undergraduates** 62% women, 15% part-time, 36% 25 or older, 0.01% Native American, 0.4% Hispanic American, 83% African American, 1% Asian American/Pacific Islander **The most frequently chosen baccalaureate fields are** health professions and related sciences, business/marketing, interdisciplinary studies **Academic program** Accelerated degree program, honors program, summer session, adult/continuing education programs, internships **Contact** Ms. Vernella Smith, Admissions Coordinator, Tennessee State University, 3500 John A Merritt Boulevard, Nashville, TN 37209-1561. Telephone: 615-963-5104. Fax: 615-963-5108. E-mail: jcade@picard.tnstate.edu. Web site: http://www.tnstate.edu/.

TENNESSEE TECHNOLOGICAL UNIVERSITY
COOKEVILLE, TENNESSEE

General State-supported, university, coed **Entrance** Moderately difficult **Setting** 235-acre small-town campus **Total enrollment** 8,410 **Student/faculty ratio** 17:1 **Application deadline** Rolling (freshmen), rolling (transfer) **Freshmen** 94% were admitted **Housing** Yes **Expenses** Tuition 2704; Room & Board 3650 **Undergraduates** 47% women, 11% part-time, 28% 25 or older, 0.3% Native American, 1% Hispanic American, 4% African American, 1% Asian American/Pacific Islander **The most frequently chosen baccalaureate fields are** business/marketing, engineering/engineering technologies, interdisciplinary studies **Academic program** English as a second language, advanced placement, accelerated degree program, honors program, summer session, adult/continuing education programs, internships **Contact** Mrs. Rebecca Tolbert, Associate Vice President for Enrollment and Records, Tennessee Technological University, TTU Box 5006, Cookeville, TN 38505. Telephone: 931-372-3888 or toll-free 800-255-8881. Fax: 931-372-6250. E-mail: u_admissions@tntech.edu. Web site: http://www.tntech.edu/.

TENNESSEE TEMPLE UNIVERSITY
CHATTANOOGA, TENNESSEE

General Independent Baptist, comprehensive, coed **Entrance** Minimally difficult **Setting** 55-acre urban campus **Total enrollment** 772 **Application deadline** 8/20 (freshmen), 8/15 (transfer) **Freshmen** 99% were admitted **Housing** Yes **Expenses** Tuition $6450; Room & Board $5120 **Undergraduates** 9% 25 or older, 0.3% Native American, 2% Hispanic American, 3% African American, 1% Asian American/Pacific Islander **Academic program** Advanced placement, honors program, summer session, adult/continuing education programs, internships **Contact** Mr. David Delmotte, Director of Admissions, Tennessee Temple University, 1815 Union Avenue, Chattanooga, TN 37404-3587. Telephone: 423-493-4100 or toll-free 800-553-4050. Fax: 423-493-4497. E-mail: ttuinfo@tntemple.edu. Web site: http://www.tntemple.edu/.

TENNESSEE WESLEYAN COLLEGE
ATHENS, TENNESSEE

General Independent United Methodist, 4-year, coed **Entrance** Moderately difficult **Setting** 40-acre small-town campus **Total enrollment** 795 **Student/faculty ratio** 14:1 **Application deadline** Rolling (freshmen), rolling (transfer) **Freshmen** 29% were admitted **Housing** Yes **Expenses** Tuition 8050; Room & Board 4150 **Undergraduates** 63% women, 25% part-time, 32% 25 or older, 0.1% Native American, 1% Hispanic American, 3% African American, 0% Asian American/Pacific Islander **The most frequently chosen baccalaureate fields are** business/marketing, protective services/public administration, psychology **Academic program** English as a second language, advanced placement, accelerated degree program, self-designed majors, honors program, summer session, adult/continuing education programs, internships **Contact** Mrs. Ruthie Cawood, Director of Admission, Tennessee Wesleyan College, PO Box 40, Athens, TN 37371-0040. Telephone: 423-746-5287 or toll-free 800-PICK-TWC. Fax: 423-745-9335. Web site: http://www.twcnet.edu/.

TREVECCA NAZARENE UNIVERSITY
NASHVILLE, TENNESSEE

General Independent Nazarene, comprehensive, coed **Entrance** Noncompetitive **Setting** 65-acre urban campus **Total enrollment** 1,709 **Student/faculty ratio** 14:1 **Application deadline** Rolling (freshmen), rolling (transfer) **Freshmen** 82% were admitted **Housing** Yes **Expenses** Tuition $10,848; Room & Board $4904 **Undergraduates** 59% women, 21% part-time, 26% 25 or older, 1% Native American, 2% Hispanic American, 7% African American, 1% Asian American/Pacific Islander **The most frequently chosen baccalaureate fields are** business/marketing, education, health professions and related sciences **Academic program** Advanced placement, accelerated degree program, summer session, adult/continuing education programs, internships **Contact** Ms. Patricia D. Cook, Director of Admissions, Trevecca Nazarene University, 333 Murfreesboro Road, Nashville, TN 37210-2834. Telephone: 615-248-1320 or toll-free 888-210-4TNU. Fax: 615-248-7728. E-mail: admissions_und@trevecca.edu. Web site: http://www.trevecca.edu/.

TUSCULUM COLLEGE
GREENEVILLE, TENNESSEE

General Independent Presbyterian, comprehensive, coed **Entrance** Moderately difficult **Setting** 140-acre small-town campus **Total enrollment** 1,681 **Student/faculty ratio** 12:1 **Application deadline** Rolling (freshmen), rolling (transfer) **Freshmen** 88% were admitted **Housing** Yes **Expenses** Tuition $13,500; Room & Board $4500 **Undergraduates** 55% women, 2% part-time, 53% 25 or older, 1% Native American, 0.1% Hispanic American, 10% African American, 0.1% Asian American/Pacific Islander **The most frequently chosen baccalaureate fields are** business/marketing, education, health professions and related sciences **Academic program** English as a second language, advanced placement, self-designed majors, summer session, adult/continuing education programs, internships **Contact** Mr. George Wolf, Director of Admissions, Tusculum College, PO Box 5047, Greeneville, TN 37743-9997. Telephone: 423-636-7300 Ext. 611 or toll-free 800-729-0256. Fax: 423-638-7166 Ext. 312. E-mail: admissions@tusculum.edu. Web site: http://www.tusculum.edu/.

UNION UNIVERSITY
JACKSON, TENNESSEE

General Independent Southern Baptist, comprehensive, coed **Entrance** Moderately difficult **Setting** 290-acre small-town campus **Total enrollment** 2,392 **Student/faculty ratio** 12:1 **Application deadline** Rolling (freshmen), rolling (transfer) **Freshmen** 83% were admitted **Housing** Yes **Expenses** Tuition 12,670; Room & Board 4110 **Undergraduates** 61% women, 17% part-time, 22% 25 or older, 0.3% Native American, 0.4% Hispanic American, 6% African American, 1% Asian American/Pacific Islander **The most frequently chosen baccalaureate fields are** education, business/marketing, health professions and related sciences **Academic program** English as a second language, advanced placement, accelerated degree program, honors program, summer session, adult/continuing education programs, internships **Contact** Mr. Robbie Graves, Director of Enrollment Services, Union University, 1050 Union University Drive, Jackson, TN 38305-3697. Telephone: 901-661-5008 or toll-free 800-33-UNION. Fax: 901-661-5017. E-mail: cgriffin@buster.uu.edu. Web site: http://www.uu.edu/.

THE UNIVERSITY OF MEMPHIS
MEMPHIS, TENNESSEE

General State-supported, university, coed **Entrance** Moderately difficult **Setting** 1,100-acre urban campus **Total enrollment** 19,986 **Student/faculty ratio** 13:1 **Application deadline** 8/1 (freshmen), 8/1 (transfer) **Freshmen** 71% were admitted **Housing** Yes **Expenses** Tuition $3087; Room & Board $3908 **Undergraduates** 58% women, 28% part-time, 69% 25 or older, 0.3% Native American, 1% Hispanic American, 34% African American, 2% Asian American/Pacific Islander **The most frequently chosen baccalaureate fields are** business/marketing, education, social sciences and history **Academic program** English as a second language, advanced placement, accelerated degree program, self-designed majors, honors program, summer session, adult/continuing education programs, internships **Contact** Mr. David Wallace, Director of Admissions, The University of Memphis, Memphis, TN 38152. Telephone: 901-678-2101. Fax: 901-678-3053. E-mail: dwallace@memphis.edu. Web site: http://www.memphis.edu/.

THE UNIVERSITY OF TENNESSEE
KNOXVILLE, TENNESSEE

General State-supported, university, coed **Entrance** Moderately difficult **Setting** 533-acre urban campus **Total enrollment** 25,890 **Student/faculty ratio** 14:1 **Application deadline** 1/15 (freshmen), 6/1 (transfer) **Freshmen** 62% were admitted **Housing** Yes **Expenses** Tuition $3612; Room & Board $4490 **Undergraduates** 51% women, 11% part-time, 13% 25 or older, 0.3% Native American, 1% Hispanic American, 6% African American, 2% Asian American/Pacific Islander **The most frequently chosen baccalaureate fields are** business/marketing, engineering/engineering technologies, social sciences and history **Academic program** English as a second language, advanced placement, accelerated degree program, self-designed majors, honors program, summer session, adult/continuing education programs, internships **Contact** Mr. Marshall Rose, Acting Director of Admissions, The University of Tennessee, 320 Student Services

The University of Tennessee *(continued)*

Building, Knoxville, TN 37996-0230. Telephone: 865-974-2184 or toll-free 800-221-8657 (in-state). Fax: 865-974-6341. E-mail: admissions@tennessee.edu. Web site: http://www.tennessee.edu/.

THE UNIVERSITY OF TENNESSEE AT CHATTANOOGA

CHATTANOOGA, TENNESSEE

General State-supported, comprehensive, coed **Entrance** Moderately difficult **Setting** 102-acre urban campus **Total enrollment** 8,319 **Student/faculty ratio** 16:1 **Application deadline** Rolling (freshmen), rolling (transfer) **Freshmen** 56% were admitted **Housing** Yes **Expenses** Tuition 2834; Room only 2200 **Undergraduates** 57% women, 20% part-time, 22% 25 or older, 1% Native American, 1% Hispanic American, 17% African American, 3% Asian American/Pacific Islander **The most frequently chosen baccalaureate fields are** business/marketing, education, health professions and related sciences **Academic program** English as a second language, advanced placement, honors program, summer session, adult/continuing education programs, internships **Contact** Mr. Yancy Freeman, Director of Student Recruitment, The University of Tennessee at Chattanooga, 131 Hooper Hall, Chattanooga, TN 37403. Telephone: 423-755-4597 or toll-free 800-UTC-6627 (in-state). Fax: 423-755-4157. E-mail: steve-king@utc.edu. Web site: http://www.utc.edu/.

THE UNIVERSITY OF TENNESSEE AT MARTIN

MARTIN, TENNESSEE

General State-supported, comprehensive, coed **Entrance** Moderately difficult **Setting** 250-acre small-town campus **Total enrollment** 5,877 **Student/faculty ratio** 19:1 **Application deadline** Rolling (freshmen), rolling (transfer) **Freshmen** 61% were admitted **Housing** Yes **Expenses** Tuition $3330; Room & Board $3800 **Undergraduates** 57% women, 16% part-time, 25% 25 or older, 0.3% Native American, 1% Hispanic American, 16% African American, 0.4% Asian American/Pacific Islander **The most frequently chosen baccalaureate fields are** business/marketing, education, interdisciplinary studies **Academic program** English as a second language, advanced placement, accelerated degree program, self-designed majors, honors program, summer session, adult/continuing education programs, internships **Contact** Ms. Judy Rayburn, Director of Admission, The University of Tennessee at Martin, 200 Hall-Moody Administration Building, Martin, TN 38238. Telephone: 901-587-7032 or toll-free 800-829-8861. Fax: 731-587-7029. E-mail: admitme@utm.edu. Web site: http://www.utm.edu/.

THE UNIVERSITY OF TENNESSEE HEALTH SCIENCE CENTER

MEMPHIS, TENNESSEE

Contact Ms. June Peoples, Director of Admissions, The University of Tennessee Health Science Center, 800 Madison Avenue, Memphis, TN 38163-0002. Telephone: 901-448-5560. Fax: 901-448-7585. E-mail: jpeoples@utmen1.utmem.edu. Web site: http://www.utmem.edu/.

UNIVERSITY OF THE SOUTH

SEWANEE, TENNESSEE

General Independent Episcopal, comprehensive, coed **Entrance** Very difficult **Setting** 10,000-acre small-town campus **Total enrollment** 1,494 **Student/faculty ratio** 11:1 **Application deadline** 2/1 (freshmen), 4/1 (transfer) **Freshmen** 68% were admitted **Housing** Yes **Expenses** Tuition 20,130; Room & Board 5610 **Undergraduates** 53% women, 2% part-time, 1% 25 or older, 0.1% Native American, 1% Hispanic American, 4% African American, 1% Asian American/Pacific Islander **The most frequently chosen baccalaureate fields are** English, foreign language/literature, social sciences and history **Academic program** Advanced placement, self-designed majors, summer session, internships **Contact** Mr. Robert M. Hedrick, Director of Admission, University of the South, 735 University Avenue, Sewanee, TN 37383-1000. Telephone: 931-598-1238 or toll-free 800-522-2234. Fax: 931-598-3248. E-mail: admiss@sewanee.edu. Web site: http://www.sewanee.edu/.

VANDERBILT UNIVERSITY

NASHVILLE, TENNESSEE

General Independent, university, coed **Entrance** Very difficult **Setting** 330-acre urban campus **Total enrollment** 10,092 **Student/faculty ratio** 9:1 **Application deadline** 1/4 (freshmen) **Freshmen** 55% were admitted **Housing** Yes **Expenses** Tuition 24,712; Room & Board 5364 **Undergraduates** 53% women, 1% part-time, 1% 25 or older, 0.2% Native American, 3% Hispanic American, 5% African American, 6% Asian American/Pacific Islander **The most frequently chosen baccalaureate fields are** engineering/engineering technologies, psychology, social sciences and history **Academic program** English as a second language, advanced placement, accelerated degree program, self-designed majors, honors program, summer session **Contact** Mr. Bill Shain, Dean of Undergraduate Admissions, Vanderbilt University, Nashville, TN 37203-1727. Telephone: 615-322-2561 or toll-free 800-288-0432. Fax: 615-343-7765. E-mail: admissions@vanderbilt.edu. Web site: http://www.vanderbilt.edu/.

TEXAS

ABILENE CHRISTIAN UNIVERSITY

ABILENE, TEXAS

General Independent, comprehensive, coed, affiliated with Church of Christ **Entrance** Moderately difficult **Setting** 208-acre urban campus **Total enrollment** 4,739 **Student/faculty ratio** 17:1 **Application deadline** 8/1 (freshmen), rolling (transfer) **Fresh-**

men 72% were admitted **Housing** Yes **Expenses** Tuition $10,910; Room & Board $4420 **Undergraduates** 55% women, 8% part-time, 8% 25 or older, 0.5% Native American, 6% Hispanic American, 6% African American, 1% Asian American/Pacific Islander **The most frequently chosen baccalaureate fields are** business/marketing, education, interdisciplinary studies **Academic program** English as a second language, advanced placement, self-designed majors, honors program, summer session, adult/continuing education programs, internships **Contact** Mr. Tim Johnston, Director of Admissions, Abilene Christian University, ACU Box 29100, Abilene, TX 79699-9100. Telephone: 915-674-2650 or toll-free 800-460-6228 Ext. 2650. E-mail: info@admissions.acu.edu. Web site: http://www.acu.edu/.

AMBERTON UNIVERSITY
GARLAND, TEXAS

General Independent nondenominational, upper-level, coed **Entrance** Minimally difficult **Setting** 5-acre suburban campus **Total enrollment** 1,648 **Student/faculty ratio** 25:1 **Application deadline** Rolling (transfer) **Housing** No **Expenses** Tuition $4050 **Undergraduates** 67% women, 80% part-time, 98% 25 or older, 1% Native American, 6% Hispanic American, 31% African American, 1% Asian American/Pacific Islander **The most frequently chosen baccalaureate field is** interdisciplinary studies **Academic program** Self-designed majors, summer session, adult/continuing education programs, internships **Contact** Dr. Algia Allen, Vice President for Academic Services, Amberton University, 1700 Eastgate Drive, Garland, TX 75041-5595. Telephone: 972-279-6511 Ext. 135. E-mail: webteam@amberu.edu. Web site: http://www.amberton.edu/.

ANGELO STATE UNIVERSITY
SAN ANGELO, TEXAS

General State-supported, comprehensive, coed **Entrance** Moderately difficult **Setting** 268-acre urban campus **Total enrollment** 6,309 **Student/faculty ratio** 22:1 **Application deadline** 8/1 (freshmen), 8/1 (transfer) **Freshmen** 76% were admitted **Housing** Yes **Expenses** Tuition $2572; Room & Board $4140 **Undergraduates** 55% women, 19% part-time, 22% 25 or older, 0.3% Native American, 20% Hispanic American, 5% African American, 1% Asian American/Pacific Islander **The most frequently chosen baccalaureate fields are** business/marketing, education, social sciences and history **Academic program** Advanced placement, accelerated degree program, summer session, adult/continuing education programs, internships **Contact** Mrs. Monique Cossich, Director of Admissions and Retention, Angelo State University, Box 11014, ASU Station, Hardeman Administration and Journalism Building, San Angelo, TX 76909. Telephone: 915-942-2185 Ext. 231 or toll-free 800-946-8627 (in-state). Fax: 915-942-2078. E-mail: admissions@angelo.edu. Web site: http://www.angelo.edu/.

ARLINGTON BAPTIST COLLEGE
ARLINGTON, TEXAS

General Independent Baptist, 4-year, coed **Entrance** Minimally difficult **Setting** 32-acre urban campus **Total enrollment** 220 **Student/faculty ratio** 19:1 **Application deadline** Rolling (freshmen), rolling (transfer) **Freshmen** 100% were admitted **Housing** Yes **Expenses** Tuition $3900; Room only $1700 **Undergraduates** 37% women, 16% part-time, 26% 25 or older, 0% Native American, 5% Hispanic American, 1% African American, 0.5% Asian American/Pacific Islander **The most frequently chosen baccalaureate fields are** education, philosophy, religion, and theology **Academic program** Advanced placement, accelerated degree program, summer session, internships **Contact** Ms. Janie Hall, Registrar/Admissions, Arlington Baptist College, 3001 West Division, Arlington, TX 76012-3425. Telephone: 817-461-8741 Ext. 105. Fax: 817-274-1138. E-mail: jhall@abconline.edu. Web site: http://www.abconline.edu/.

AUSTIN COLLEGE
SHERMAN, TEXAS

General Independent Presbyterian, comprehensive, coed **Entrance** Very difficult **Setting** 60-acre suburban campus **Total enrollment** 1,234 **Student/faculty ratio** 13:1 **Application deadline** 8/15 (freshmen), 8/15 (transfer) **Freshmen** 84% were admitted **Housing** Yes **Expenses** Tuition 15,907; Room & Board 6187 **Undergraduates** 55% women, 1% part-time, 2% 25 or older, 1% Native American, 6% Hispanic American, 5% African American, 8% Asian American/Pacific Islander **The most frequently chosen baccalaureate fields are** area/ethnic studies, biological/life sciences, social sciences and history **Academic program** Advanced placement, accelerated degree program, self-designed majors, honors program, summer session, adult/continuing education programs, internships **Contact** Ms. Nan Massingill, Vice President for Institutional Enrollment, Austin College, 900 North Grand Avenue, Sherman, TX 75090-4400. Telephone: 903-813-3000 or toll-free 800-442-5363. Fax: 903-813-3198. E-mail: admissions@austinc.edu. Web site: http://www.austinc.edu/.

BAPTIST MISSIONARY ASSOCIATION THEOLOGICAL SEMINARY
JACKSONVILLE, TEXAS

General Independent Baptist, comprehensive, coed, primarily men **Entrance** Noncompetitive **Setting** 17-acre small-town campus **Total enrollment** 50 **Student/faculty ratio** 14:1 **Application deadline** 7/17 (freshmen), 8/1 (transfer) **Freshmen** 100% were admitted **Housing** Yes **Expenses** Tuition $12,200 **Undergraduates** 7% women, 74% part-time, 80% 25 or older, 7% Native American, 7% Hispanic American, 11% African American, 0% Asian American/Pacific Islander **The most frequently chosen baccalaureate field is** philosophy, religion, and theology **Academic program** Summer session, adult/continuing education programs, internships **Contact**

Baptist Missionary Association Theological Seminary *(continued)*

Dr. Philip Attebery, Dean and Registrar, Baptist Missionary Association Theological Seminary, 1530 East Pine Street, Jacksonville, TX 75766-5407. Telephone: 903-586-2501. Fax: 903-586-0378. E-mail: bmatsem@flash.net. Web site: http://www.geocities.com/athens/acropolis/3386/.

BAYLOR COLLEGE OF DENTISTRY

See Texas A&M University System Health Science Center

BAYLOR UNIVERSITY

WACO, TEXAS

General Independent Baptist, university, coed **Entrance** Moderately difficult **Setting** 432-acre urban campus **Total enrollment** 13,719 **Student/faculty ratio** 18:1 **Application deadline** Rolling (freshmen), rolling (transfer) **Freshmen** 84% were admitted **Housing** Yes **Expenses** Tuition 12,754; Room & Board 5481 **Undergraduates** 58% women, 4% part-time, 3% 25 or older, 1% Native American, 7% Hispanic American, 6% African American, 5% Asian American/Pacific Islander **Academic program** English as a second language, advanced placement, accelerated degree program, self-designed majors, honors program, summer session, internships **Contact** Mr. James Steen, Director of Recruitment, Baylor University, PO Box 97056, Waco, TX 76798-7056. Telephone: 254-710-3435 or toll-free 800-BAYLOR U. Fax: 254-710-3436. E-mail: admissions_office@baylor.edu. Web site: http://www.baylor.edu/.

CONCORDIA UNIVERSITY AT AUSTIN

AUSTIN, TEXAS

General Independent, comprehensive, coed, affiliated with Lutheran Church–Missouri Synod **Entrance** Moderately difficult **Setting** 20-acre urban campus **Total enrollment** 806 **Student/faculty ratio** 12:1 **Application deadline** 8/15 (freshmen), 8/1 (transfer) **Freshmen** 64% were admitted **Housing** Yes **Expenses** Tuition 12,570; Room & Board 5460 **Undergraduates** 55% women, 36% part-time, 30% 25 or older, 0.5% Native American, 13% Hispanic American, 4% African American, 0.5% Asian American/Pacific Islander **The most frequently chosen baccalaureate fields are** business/marketing, education, psychology **Academic program** English as a second language, advanced placement, accelerated degree program, honors program, summer session, adult/continuing education programs, internships **Contact** Mr. Jay Krause, Vice President for Enrollment Services, Concordia University at Austin, 3400 Interstate 35 North, Austin, TX 78705-2799. Telephone: 512-486-2000 Ext. 1107 or toll-free 800-285-4252. Fax: 512-459-8517. E-mail: ctxadmis@crf.cuis.edu. Web site: http://www.concordia.edu/.

THE CRISWELL COLLEGE

DALLAS, TEXAS

General Independent, comprehensive, coed, affiliated with Southern Baptist Convention **Entrance** Minimally difficult **Setting** 1-acre urban campus **Total enrollment** 451 **Application deadline** 8/15 (freshmen), 8/15 (transfer) **Housing** No **Expenses** Tuition 3900 **Academic program** Advanced placement, summer session, internships **Contact** Mr. Tommy Weir, Vice President for Institutional Advancement, The Criswell College, 4010 Gaston Avenue, Dallas, TX 75246-1537. Telephone: 214-818-1302 or toll-free 800-899-0012. Fax: 214-818-1310. E-mail: tweir@criswell.edu. Web site: http://www.criswell.edu/.

DALLAS BAPTIST UNIVERSITY

DALLAS, TEXAS

General Independent, comprehensive, coed, affiliated with Baptist Church **Entrance** Moderately difficult **Setting** 288-acre urban campus **Total enrollment** 4,032 **Student/faculty ratio** 19:1 **Application deadline** Rolling (freshmen), rolling (transfer) **Freshmen** 43% were admitted **Housing** Yes **Expenses** Tuition 9150; Room & Board 3774 **Undergraduates** 62% women, 58% part-time, 55% 25 or older, 3% Native American, 7% Hispanic American, 21% African American, 2% Asian American/Pacific Islander **The most frequently chosen baccalaureate fields are** business/marketing, education, liberal arts/general studies **Academic program** English as a second language, advanced placement, summer session, adult/continuing education programs, internships **Contact** Mr. Robert Sullivan, Director of Admissions, Dallas Baptist University, 3000 Mountain Creek Parkway, Dallas, TX 75211-9299. Telephone: 214-333-5360 or toll-free 800-460-1328. Fax: 214-333-5447. E-mail: admiss@dbu.edu. Web site: http://www.dbu.edu/.

DALLAS CHRISTIAN COLLEGE

DALLAS, TEXAS

General Independent, 4-year, coed, affiliated with Christian Churches and Churches of Christ **Entrance** Minimally difficult **Setting** 22-acre urban campus **Total enrollment** 254 **Student/faculty ratio** 13:1 **Application deadline** Rolling (freshmen), rolling (transfer) **Freshmen** 64% were admitted **Housing** Yes **Expenses** Tuition $6580; Room & Board $3900 **Undergraduates** 47% women, 39% part-time, 51% 25 or older, 1% Native American, 5% Hispanic American, 19% African American, 0.4% Asian American/Pacific Islander **The most frequently chosen baccalaureate fields are** business/marketing, philosophy, religion, and theology **Academic program** Advanced placement, accelerated degree program, summer session, adult/continuing education programs, internships **Contact** Mr. Marty McKee, Director of Admissions, Dallas Christian College, 2700 Christian Parkway, Dallas, TX 75234-7299. Telephone: 972-241-3371 Ext. 153. Fax: 972-241-8021. E-mail: dcc@dallas.edu. Web site: http://www.dallas.edu/.

DEVRY INSTITUTE OF TECHNOLOGY
IRVING, TEXAS

General Proprietary, 4-year, coed **Entrance** Minimally difficult **Setting** 13-acre suburban campus **Total enrollment** 3,462 **Student/faculty ratio** 18:1 **Application deadline** Rolling (freshmen), rolling (transfer) **Freshmen** 64% were admitted **Housing** No **Expenses** Tuition 8740 **Undergraduates** 29% women, 39% part-time, 55% 25 or older, 0.4% Native American, 27% Hispanic American, 28% African American, 16% Asian American/Pacific Islander **The most frequently chosen baccalaureate fields are** business/marketing, computer/information sciences, engineering/engineering technologies **Academic program** Advanced placement, accelerated degree program, summer session, adult/continuing education programs **Contact** Mr. Daniel Millan, Director of Admissions, DeVry Institute of Technology, 4000 Millenia Drive, Orlando, FL 32839. Telephone: 972-929-5777 or toll-free 800-443-3879 (in-state); 800-633-3879 (out-of-state). Web site: http://www.dal.devry.edu/.

EAST TEXAS BAPTIST UNIVERSITY
MARSHALL, TEXAS

General Independent Baptist, 4-year, coed **Entrance** Moderately difficult **Setting** 200-acre small-town campus **Total enrollment** 1,402 **Student/faculty ratio** 17:1 **Application deadline** Rolling (freshmen), rolling (transfer) **Freshmen** 92% were admitted **Housing** Yes **Expenses** Tuition $8450; Room & Board $3126 **Undergraduates** 55% women, 10% part-time, 7% 25 or older, 1% Native American, 3% Hispanic American, 10% African American, 0.2% Asian American/Pacific Islander **The most frequently chosen baccalaureate fields are** business/marketing, education, philosophy, religion, and theology **Academic program** English as a second language, advanced placement, accelerated degree program, honors program, summer session, adult/continuing education programs, internships **Contact** Mr. Vince Blankenship, Director of Admissions, East Texas Baptist University, 1209 North Grove, Marshall, TX 75670-1498. Telephone: 903-935-7963 Ext. 226 or toll-free 800-804-ETBU. Fax: 903-938-1705. E-mail: admissions@etbu.edu. Web site: http://www.etbu.edu/.

HARDIN-SIMMONS UNIVERSITY
ABILENE, TEXAS

General Independent Baptist, comprehensive, coed **Entrance** Moderately difficult **Setting** 40-acre urban campus **Total enrollment** 2,304 **Student/faculty ratio** 14:1 **Application deadline** Rolling (freshmen), rolling (transfer) **Freshmen** 45% were admitted **Housing** Yes **Expenses** Tuition 9950; Room & Board 3405 **Undergraduates** 54% women, 12% part-time, 11% 25 or older, 1% Native American, 7% Hispanic American, 4% African American, 1% Asian American/Pacific Islander **The most frequently chosen baccalaureate fields are** business/marketing, education, health professions and related sciences **Academic program** Advanced placement, accelerated degree program, summer session, adult/continuing education programs, internships **Contact** Mrs. Stacey Martin, Enrollment Services Counselor, Hardin-Simmons University, Box 16050, Abilene, TX 79698-6050. Telephone: 915-670-5813 or toll-free 800-568-2692. Fax: 915-670-1527. E-mail: enroll.services@hsutx.edu. Web site: http://www.hsutx.edu/.

HOUSTON BAPTIST UNIVERSITY
HOUSTON, TEXAS

General Independent Baptist, comprehensive, coed **Entrance** Moderately difficult **Setting** 158-acre urban campus **Total enrollment** 2,416 **Student/faculty ratio** 18:1 **Application deadline** Rolling (freshmen), rolling (transfer) **Freshmen** 70% were admitted **Housing** Yes **Expenses** Tuition $11,142; Room & Board $4080 **Undergraduates** 70% women, 15% part-time, 24% 25 or older, 0% Native American, 14% Hispanic American, 18% African American, 14% Asian American/Pacific Islander **Academic program** English as a second language, advanced placement, honors program, summer session, adult/continuing education programs, internships **Contact** Mr. David Melton, Director of Admissions, Houston Baptist University, 7502 Fondren Road, Houston, TX 77074-3298. Telephone: 281-649-3211 Ext. 3208 or toll-free 800-969-3210. Fax: 281-649-3217. E-mail: unadm@hbu.edu. Web site: http://www.hbu.edu/.

HOWARD PAYNE UNIVERSITY
BROWNWOOD, TEXAS

General Independent Southern Baptist, 4-year, coed **Entrance** Minimally difficult **Setting** 30-acre small-town campus **Total enrollment** 1,480 **Student/faculty ratio** 13:1 **Application deadline** Rolling (freshmen), rolling (transfer) **Freshmen** 80% were admitted **Housing** Yes **Expenses** Tuition $9000; Room & Board $3820 **Undergraduates** 47% women, 19% part-time, 25% 25 or older, 1% Native American, 9% Hispanic American, 7% African American, 2% Asian American/Pacific Islander **The most frequently chosen baccalaureate fields are** business/marketing, education, philosophy, religion, and theology **Academic program** English as a second language, advanced placement, honors program, summer session, adult/continuing education programs, internships **Contact** Ms. Cheryl Mangrum, Coordinator of Admission Services, Howard Payne University, HPU Station Box 828, 1000 Fisk Avenue, Brownwood, TX 76801. Telephone: 915-649-8027 or toll-free 800-880-4478. Fax: 915-649-8901. E-mail: admissions@hputx.edu. Web site: http://www.hputx.edu/.

HUSTON-TILLOTSON COLLEGE
AUSTIN, TEXAS

General Independent interdenominational, 4-year, coed **Contact** Tmitria A. Glenn, Admissions Counselor, Huston-Tillotson College, 900 Chicon Street, Austin, TX 78702. Telephone: 512-505-3029. Fax: 512-505-3192. E-mail: taglenn@htc.edu. Web site: http://www.htc.edu.

INSTITUTE FOR CHRISTIAN STUDIES
AUSTIN, TEXAS

General Independent, upper-level, coed, affiliated with Church of Christ **Entrance** Minimally difficult **Setting** urban campus **Total enrollment** 48 **Student/faculty ratio** 10:1 **Application deadline** Rolling (transfer) **Housing** Yes **Expenses** Tuition $1800; Room only $1500 **Undergraduates** 31% women, 77% part-time, 57% 25 or older, 10% Hispanic American, 29% African American **The most frequently chosen baccalaureate field is** philosophy, religion, and theology **Academic program** Advanced placement, summer session, adult/continuing education programs **Contact** Mr. Mark Martin, Director of Admissions and Registrar, Institute for Christian Studies, 1909 University Avenue, Austin, TX 78705-5610. Telephone: 512-476-2772 Ext. 203 or toll-free 888-ICS-AUSTIN (in-state). Fax: 512-476-3919. E-mail: instchrst@aol.com. Web site: http://www.ics.edu/.

JARVIS CHRISTIAN COLLEGE
HAWKINS, TEXAS

General Independent, 4-year, coed, affiliated with Christian Church (Disciples of Christ) **Contact** Ms. Serena Sentell, Admissions Counselor, Jarvis Christian College, PO Drawer G, Hawkins, TX 75765-9989. Telephone: 903-769-0417 or toll-free 800-292-9517. Fax: 903-769-4842. Web site: http://www.jarvis.edu/.

LAMAR UNIVERSITY
BEAUMONT, TEXAS

General State-supported, university, coed **Entrance** Minimally difficult **Setting** 200-acre suburban campus **Total enrollment** 8,568 **Student/faculty ratio** 15:1 **Application deadline** 8/1 (freshmen), 8/1 (transfer) **Freshmen** 74% were admitted **Housing** Yes **Expenses** Tuition $2776; Room & Board $3591 **Undergraduates** 59% women, 30% part-time, 39% 25 or older, 0.5% Native American, 5% Hispanic American, 19% African American, 3% Asian American/Pacific Islander **Academic program** English as a second language, advanced placement, accelerated degree program, self-designed majors, honors program, summer session, adult/continuing education programs, internships **Contact** Ms. Melissa Chesser, Director of Recruitment, Lamar University, PO Box 10009, Beaumont, TX 77710. Telephone: 409-880-8888. Fax: 409-880-8463. E-mail: hunterre@hal.lamar.edu. Web site: http://www.lamar.edu/.

LETOURNEAU UNIVERSITY
LONGVIEW, TEXAS

General Independent nondenominational, comprehensive, coed **Entrance** Moderately difficult **Setting** 162-acre suburban campus **Total enrollment** 2,981 **Student/faculty ratio** 15:1 **Application deadline** 8/1 (freshmen), 8/1 (transfer) **Freshmen** 86% were admitted **Housing** Yes **Expenses** Tuition $12,840; Room & Board $5420 **Undergraduates** 47% women, 44% part-time, 8% 25 or older, 1% Native American, 6% Hispanic American, 15% African American, 1% Asian American/Pacific Islander **The most frequently chosen baccalaureate fields are** business/marketing, biological/life sciences, engineering/engineering technologies **Academic program** Advanced placement, honors program, summer session, adult/continuing education programs, internships **Contact** Mr. Rodney Stanford, Director of Admissions, LeTourneau University, PO Box 7001, Longview, TX 75607. Telephone: 903-233-3400 or toll-free 800-759-8811. Fax: 903-233-3411. E-mail: admissions@james.letu.edu. Web site: http://www.letu.edu/.

LUBBOCK CHRISTIAN UNIVERSITY
LUBBOCK, TEXAS

General Independent, comprehensive, coed, affiliated with Church of Christ **Entrance** Moderately difficult **Setting** 120-acre suburban campus **Total enrollment** 1,617 **Student/faculty ratio** 16:1 **Application deadline** Rolling (freshmen), rolling (transfer) **Freshmen** 77% were admitted **Housing** Yes **Expenses** Tuition 9824; Room & Board 3588 **Undergraduates** 58% women, 17% part-time, 30% 25 or older, 1% Native American, 12% Hispanic American, 4% African American, 0.4% Asian American/Pacific Islander **The most frequently chosen baccalaureate fields are** business/marketing, education, liberal arts/general studies **Academic program** Advanced placement, accelerated degree program, self-designed majors, honors program, summer session, adult/continuing education programs, internships **Contact** Mrs. Rhonda Crawford, Director of Admissions, Lubbock Christian University, 5601 19th Street, Lubbock, TX 79407. Telephone: 806-796-8800 Ext. 260 or toll-free 800-933-7601 Ext. 260. Fax: 806-796-8917 Ext. 260. E-mail: admissions@lcu.edu.

MCMURRY UNIVERSITY
ABILENE, TEXAS

General Independent United Methodist, 4-year, coed **Entrance** Moderately difficult **Setting** 41-acre urban campus **Total enrollment** 1,344 **Student/faculty ratio** 14:1 **Application deadline** 8/15 (freshmen), 8/15 (transfer) **Freshmen** 70% were admitted **Housing** Yes **Expenses** Tuition $10,875; Room & Board $4512 **Undergraduates** 50% women, 17% part-time, 21% 25 or older, 1% Native American, 12% Hispanic American, 8% African American, 2% Asian American/Pacific Islander **The most frequently chosen baccalaureate fields are** business/marketing, education, social sciences and history **Academic program** Advanced placement, accelerated degree program, honors program, summer session, internships **Contact** Dr. L. Russell Watjen, Vice President, Enrollment Management and Student Relations, McMurry University, Box 947, Abilene, TX 79697. Telephone: 915-793-4720 or toll-free 800-477-0077. Fax: 915-793-4718. E-mail: rwatjen@mcm.edu. Web site: http://www.mcm.edu/.

MIDWESTERN STATE UNIVERSITY
WICHITA FALLS, TEXAS

General State-supported, comprehensive, coed **Entrance** Minimally difficult **Setting** 172-acre urban campus **Total enrollment** 5,809 **Student/faculty ratio** 18:1 **Application deadline** 8/7 (freshmen), 8/7 (transfer) **Housing** Yes **Expenses** Tuition $3112; Room & Board $4024 **Undergraduates** 57% women, 28% part-time, 28% 25 or older, 1% Native American, 8% Hispanic American, 8% African American, 3% Asian American/Pacific Islander **The most frequently chosen baccalaureate fields are** business/marketing, health professions and related sciences, interdisciplinary studies **Academic program** English as a second language, advanced placement, accelerated degree program, honors program, summer session, adult/continuing education programs, internships **Contact** Ms. Billye Tims, Registrar and Director of Admissions, Midwestern State University, 3410 Taft Boulevard, Wichita Falls, TX 76308. Telephone: 940-397-4321 or toll-free 800-842-1922 (in-state). E-mail: school.relations@nexus.mwsu.edu. Web site: http://www.mwsu.edu/.

NORTHWOOD UNIVERSITY, TEXAS CAMPUS
CEDAR HILL, TEXAS

General Independent, 4-year, coed **Entrance** Moderately difficult **Setting** 360-acre small-town campus **Total enrollment** 1,014 **Student/faculty ratio** 35:1 **Application deadline** 9/1 (freshmen), 9/1 (transfer) **Freshmen** 68% were admitted **Housing** Yes **Expenses** Tuition 12,063; Room & Board 5160 **Undergraduates** 56% women, 26% part-time, 5% 25 or older **The most frequently chosen baccalaureate fields are** business/marketing, computer/information sciences **Academic program** Advanced placement, honors program, summer session, adult/continuing education programs, internships **Contact** Mr. James R. Hickerson, Director of Admissions, Northwood University, Texas Campus, 1114 W FM 1382, PO Box 58, Cedar Hill, TX 75104-1204. Telephone: 972-293-5400 or toll-free 800-927-9663. Fax: 972-291-3824. E-mail: admissions@northwood.edu. Web site: http://www.northwood.edu/.

OUR LADY OF THE LAKE UNIVERSITY OF SAN ANTONIO
SAN ANTONIO, TEXAS

General Independent Roman Catholic, comprehensive, coed **Entrance** Moderately difficult **Setting** 75-acre urban campus **Total enrollment** 3,474 **Student/faculty ratio** 13:1 **Application deadline** Rolling (freshmen), rolling (transfer) **Freshmen** 65% were admitted **Housing** Yes **Expenses** Tuition $11,966; Room & Board $4466 **Undergraduates** 77% women, 44% part-time, 48% 25 or older, 0.3% Native American, 63% Hispanic American, 6% African American, 1% Asian American/Pacific Islander **The most frequently chosen baccalaureate fields are** business/marketing, liberal arts/general studies, psychology **Academic program** English as a second language, advanced placement, summer session, adult/continuing education programs, internships **Contact** Mr. Michael Boatner, Acting Director of Admissions, Our Lady of the Lake University of San Antonio, 411 Southwest 24th Street, San Antonio, TX 78207-4689. Telephone: 210-434-6711 Ext. 314 or toll-free 800-436-6558. Fax: 210-431-4036. E-mail: hamid@lake.occusa.edu. Web site: http://www.ollusa.edu/.

PAUL QUINN COLLEGE
DALLAS, TEXAS

Contact Don Robinson, Director of Admissions, Paul Quinn College, 3837 Simpson-Stuart Road, Dallas, TX 75241-4331. Telephone: 214-302-3520 or toll-free 800-237-2648. Fax: 214-302-3559.

PRAIRIE VIEW A&M UNIVERSITY
PRAIRIE VIEW, TEXAS

General State-supported, comprehensive, coed **Entrance** Moderately difficult **Setting** 1,440-acre small-town campus **Total enrollment** 6,609 **Student/faculty ratio** 19:1 **Application deadline** 7/1 (transfer) **Freshmen** 97% were admitted **Housing** Yes **Expenses** Tuition $2693 **Undergraduates** 56% women, 7% part-time, 16% 25 or older, 0.02% Native American, 2% Hispanic American, 93% African American, 1% Asian American/Pacific Islander **The most frequently chosen baccalaureate fields are** engineering/engineering technologies, business/marketing, health professions and related sciences **Academic program** English as a second language, advanced placement, accelerated degree program, honors program, summer session, internships **Contact** Ms. Mary Gooch, Director of Admissions, Prairie View A&M University, PO Box 3089, Prairie View, TX 77446-0188. Telephone: 936-857-2626. Fax: 936-857-2699. E-mail: mary_gooch@pvamu.edu. Web site: http://www.pvamu.edu/.

RICE UNIVERSITY
HOUSTON, TEXAS

General Independent, university, coed **Entrance** Most difficult **Setting** 300-acre urban campus **Total enrollment** 4,171 **Student/faculty ratio** 5:1 **Application deadline** 1/2 (freshmen), 4/1 (transfer) **Freshmen** 23% were admitted **Housing** Yes **Expenses** Tuition $16,400; Room & Board $6850 **Undergraduates** 47% women, 1% part-time, 0.5% Native American, 10% Hispanic American, 6% African American, 15% Asian American/Pacific Islander **Academic program** Advanced placement, accelerated degree program, self-designed majors, honors program, summer session, internships **Contact** Ms. Julie M. Browning, Dean for Undergraduate Admission, Rice University, PO Box 1892, MS 17, Houston, TX 77251-1892. Telephone: 713-348-RICE or toll-free 800-527-OWLS. E-mail: admi@rice.edu. Web site: http://www.rice.edu/.

ST. EDWARD'S UNIVERSITY

AUSTIN, TEXAS

General Independent Roman Catholic, comprehensive, coed **Entrance** Moderately difficult **Setting** 180-acre urban campus **Total enrollment** 3,824 **Student/faculty ratio** 14:1 **Application deadline** 8/1 (freshmen), 8/1 (transfer) **Freshmen** 78% were admitted **Housing** Yes **Expenses** Tuition $11,896; Room & Board $5000 **Undergraduates** 55% women, 31% part-time, 11% 25 or older, 0.4% Native American, 28% Hispanic American, 5% African American, 2% Asian American/Pacific Islander **The most frequently chosen baccalaureate fields are** business/marketing, liberal arts/general studies, social sciences and history **Academic program** Advanced placement, accelerated degree program, honors program, summer session, adult/continuing education programs, internships **Contact** Ms. Elizabeth Stanley, Director of Admission, St. Edward's University, 3001 South Congress Avenue, Austin, TX 78704-6489. Telephone: 512-448-8500 or toll-free 800-555-0164. Fax: 512-464-8877. E-mail: seu.admit@admin.stedwards.edu. Web site: http://www.stedwards.edu/.

ST. MARY'S UNIVERSITY OF SAN ANTONIO

SAN ANTONIO, TEXAS

General Independent Roman Catholic, comprehensive, coed **Entrance** Moderately difficult **Setting** 135-acre urban campus **Total enrollment** 4,137 **Student/faculty ratio** 14:1 **Application deadline** Rolling (freshmen), rolling (transfer) **Freshmen** 87% were admitted **Housing** Yes **Expenses** Tuition 13,480; Room & Board 5535 **Undergraduates** 59% women, 11% part-time, 13% 25 or older, 0.5% Native American, 68% Hispanic American, 3% African American, 3% Asian American/Pacific Islander **The most frequently chosen baccalaureate fields are** biological/life sciences, business/marketing, social sciences and history **Academic program** English as a second language, advanced placement, honors program, summer session, adult/continuing education programs, internships **Contact** Mr. Richard Castillo, Director of Admissions, St. Mary's University of San Antonio, 1 Camino Santa Maria, San Antonio, TX 78228-8503. Telephone: 210-436-3126 or toll-free 800-FOR-STMU (out-of-state). Fax: 210-431-6742. E-mail: vadm@stmarytx.edu. Web site: http://www.stmarytx.edu/.

▶ **For more information, see page 474.**

SAM HOUSTON STATE UNIVERSITY

HUNTSVILLE, TEXAS

General State-supported, comprehensive, coed **Entrance** Moderately difficult **Setting** 2,143-acre small-town campus **Total enrollment** 12,385 **Student/faculty ratio** 21:1 **Application deadline** Rolling (freshmen), rolling (transfer) **Freshmen** 81% were admitted **Housing** Yes **Expenses** Tuition 2228; Room & Board 3672 **Undergraduates** 57% women, 19% part-time, 18% 25 or older, 1% Native American, 9% Hispanic American, 15% African American, 1% Asian American/Pacific Islander **The most frequently chosen baccalaureate fields are** business/marketing, education, protective services/public administration **Academic program** English as a second language, advanced placement, accelerated degree program, honors program, summer session, adult/continuing education programs, internships **Contact** Ms. Joey Chandler, Director of Admissions and Recruitment, Sam Houston State University, PO Box 2418, Huntsville, TX 77341. Telephone: 936-294-1828. Fax: 936-294-3758. Web site: http://www.shsu.edu/.

SCHREINER UNIVERSITY

KERRVILLE, TEXAS

General Independent Presbyterian, comprehensive, coed **Entrance** Moderately difficult **Setting** 175-acre small-town campus **Total enrollment** 803 **Student/faculty ratio** 13:1 **Application deadline** 8/1 (freshmen), 8/15 (transfer) **Freshmen** 72% were admitted **Housing** Yes **Expenses** Tuition $11,740; Room & Board $6520 **Undergraduates** 60% women, 15% part-time, 23% 25 or older, 1% Native American, 14% Hispanic American, 3% African American, 1% Asian American/Pacific Islander **The most frequently chosen baccalaureate fields are** business/marketing, English, parks and recreation **Academic program** English as a second language, advanced placement, self-designed majors, honors program, summer session, internships **Contact** Mr. Todd Brown, Dean of Admission and Financial Aid, Schreiner University, 2100 Memorial Boulevard, Kerrville, TX 78028. Telephone: 830-792-7217 or toll-free 800-343-4919. Fax: 830-792-7226. E-mail: admissions@schreiner.edu. Web site: http://www.schreiner.edu/.

SOUTHERN METHODIST UNIVERSITY

DALLAS, TEXAS

General Independent, university, coed, affiliated with United Methodist Church **Entrance** Moderately difficult **Setting** 163-acre suburban campus **Total enrollment** 10,064 **Student/faculty ratio** 11:1 **Application deadline** 1/15 (freshmen), 7/1 (transfer) **Freshmen** 82% were admitted **Housing** Yes **Expenses** Tuition 19,620; Room & Board 7177 **Undergraduates** 55% women, 6% part-time, 7% 25 or older, 1% Native American, 8% Hispanic American, 6% African American, 6% Asian American/Pacific Islander **The most frequently chosen baccalaureate fields are** business/marketing, communications/communication technologies, social sciences and history **Academic program** English as a second language, advanced placement, accelerated degree program, self-designed majors, honors program, summer session, adult/continuing education programs, internships **Contact** Mr. Ron W. Moss, Director of Admission and Enrollment Management, Southern Methodist University, PO Box 750181, Dallas, TX 75275-0181. Telephone: 214-768-2058 or toll-free 800-323-0672. Fax: 214-768-0103. E-mail: ugadmission@smu.edu.

SOUTHWESTERN ADVENTIST UNIVERSITY
KEENE, TEXAS

General Independent Seventh-day Adventist, comprehensive, coed **Entrance** Minimally difficult **Setting** 150-acre rural campus **Total enrollment** 1,187 **Student/faculty ratio** 15:1 **Application deadline** 8/31 (freshmen), 8/31 (transfer) **Freshmen** 62% were admitted **Housing** Yes **Expenses** Tuition 10,020; Room & Board 4778 **Undergraduates** 57% women, 27% part-time, 1% Native American, 14% Hispanic American, 15% African American, 4% Asian American/Pacific Islander **The most frequently chosen baccalaureate fields are** business/marketing, education, philosophy, religion, and theology **Academic program** English as a second language, accelerated degree program, self-designed majors, honors program, summer session, internships **Contact** Mrs. Danna Burt, Admissions Counselor, Southwestern Adventist University, PO Box 567, Keene, TX 76059. Telephone: 817-645-3921 or toll-free 800-433-2240. Fax: 817-556-4744. E-mail: illingworth@vaxine.swac.edu. Web site: http://www.swau.edu/.

SOUTHWESTERN ASSEMBLIES OF GOD UNIVERSITY
WAXAHACHIE, TEXAS

General Independent, comprehensive, coed, affiliated with Assemblies of God **Entrance** Noncompetitive **Setting** 70-acre small-town campus **Total enrollment** 1,782 **Application deadline** Rolling (freshmen), rolling (transfer) **Housing** Yes **Expenses** Tuition $6480; Room & Board $3990 **Undergraduates** 24% 25 or older **Academic program** Advanced placement, summer session, adult/continuing education programs, internships **Contact** Eddie Davis, Enrollment Services, Southwestern Assemblies of God University, 1200 Sycamore Street, Waxahachie, TX 75165-2397. Telephone: 972-937-4010 Ext. 1121 or toll-free 800-262-SAGU. Fax: 972-923-0006. E-mail: edavis@fagu.edu. Web site: http://www.sagu.edu/.

SOUTHWESTERN CHRISTIAN COLLEGE
TERRELL, TEXAS

Contact Admissions Department, Southwestern Christian College, Box 10, Terrell, TX 75160-0010. Telephone: 214-524-3341. Web site: http://www.swcc.edu/.

SOUTHWESTERN UNIVERSITY
GEORGETOWN, TEXAS

General Independent Methodist, 4-year, coed **Entrance** Very difficult **Setting** 500-acre suburban campus **Total enrollment** 1,312 **Student/faculty ratio** 11:1 **Application deadline** 2/15 (freshmen), 4/1 (transfer) **Freshmen** 59% were admitted **Housing** Yes **Expenses** Tuition $15,750; Room & Board $6318 **Undergraduates** 58% women, 2% part-time, 2% 25 or older, 0.4% Native American, 12% Hispanic American, 2% African American, 3% Asian American/Pacific Islander **The most frequently chosen baccalaureate fields are** biological/life sciences, business/marketing, social sciences and history **Academic program** Advanced placement, accelerated degree program, self-designed majors, honors program, summer session, internships **Contact** Mr. John W. Lind, Vice President for Enrollment Management, Southwestern University, 1001 East University Avenue, Georgetown, TX 78626. Telephone: 512-863-1200 or toll-free 800-252-3166. Fax: 512-863-9601. E-mail: admission@southwestern.edu. Web site: http://www.southwestern.edu/.

SOUTHWEST TEXAS STATE UNIVERSITY
SAN MARCOS, TEXAS

General State-supported, comprehensive, coed **Entrance** Moderately difficult **Setting** 423-acre small-town campus **Total enrollment** 22,423 **Student/faculty ratio** 22:1 **Application deadline** 7/1 (freshmen), 7/1 (transfer) **Freshmen** 64% were admitted **Housing** Yes **Expenses** Tuition $3296; Room & Board $4564 **Undergraduates** 55% women, 20% part-time, 19% 25 or older, 1% Native American, 19% Hispanic American, 5% African American, 2% Asian American/Pacific Islander **The most frequently chosen baccalaureate fields are** business/marketing, interdisciplinary studies, social sciences and history **Academic program** English as a second language, advanced placement, accelerated degree program, honors program, summer session, adult/continuing education programs, internships **Contact** Mrs. Christie Kangas, Director of Admissions, Southwest Texas State University, Admissions and Visitors Center, San Marcos, TX 78666. Telephone: 512-245-2364 Ext. 2803. Fax: 512-245-8044. E-mail: admissions@swt.edu. Web site: http://www.swt.edu/.

▶ **For more information, see page 470.**

STEPHEN F. AUSTIN STATE UNIVERSITY
NACOGDOCHES, TEXAS

General State-supported, comprehensive, coed **Entrance** Moderately difficult **Setting** 400-acre small-town campus **Total enrollment** 11,284 **Student/faculty ratio** 20:1 **Application deadline** Rolling (freshmen), rolling (transfer) **Freshmen** 71% were admitted **Housing** Yes **Expenses** Tuition $2168; Room & Board $4370 **Undergraduates** 57% women, 13% part-time, 19% 25 or older, 1% Native American, 6% Hispanic American, 14% African American, 1% Asian American/Pacific Islander **The most frequently chosen baccalaureate fields are** business/marketing, health professions and related sciences, interdisciplinary studies **Academic program** English as a second language, advanced placement, accelerated degree program, self-designed majors, honors program, summer session, adult/continuing education programs, internships **Contact** Ms. Beth Smith, Assistant Director of Admissions, Stephen F. Austin State University, SFA Box 13051, Nacogdoches, TX 75962. Telephone: 936-468-2504 or toll-free 800-259-9SFA. Fax: 936-468-3849. E-mail: mbsmith@sfasu.edu. Web site: http://www.sfasu.edu/.

SUL ROSS STATE UNIVERSITY
ALPINE, TEXAS

General State-supported, comprehensive, coed **Entrance** Noncompetitive **Setting** 640-acre small-town campus **Total enrollment** 2,010 **Student/faculty ratio** 17:1 **Application deadline** Rolling (freshmen), rolling (transfer) **Freshmen** 99% were admitted **Housing** Yes **Expenses** Tuition $2792; Room & Board $3690 **Undergraduates** 24% 25 or older, 1% Native American, 46% Hispanic American, 4% African American, 0.5% Asian American/Pacific Islander **The most frequently chosen baccalaureate fields are** agriculture, business/marketing, education **Academic program** Advanced placement, honors program, summer session, internships **Contact** Mr. Robert Cullins, Dean of Admissions and Records, Sul Ross State University, Box C-2, Alpine, TX 79832. Telephone: 915-837-8050. Fax: 915-837-8431. E-mail: rcullins@sulross-.edu. Web site: http://www.sulross.edu/.

TARLETON STATE UNIVERSITY
STEPHENVILLE, TEXAS

General State-supported, comprehensive, coed **Entrance** Moderately difficult **Setting** 165-acre small-town campus **Total enrollment** 7,667 **Student/faculty ratio** 18:1 **Application deadline** 8/1 (freshmen), 8/1 (transfer) **Freshmen** 71% were admitted **Housing** Yes **Expenses** Tuition $3440; Room & Board $3802 **Undergraduates** 54% women, 23% part-time, 27% 25 or older, 1% Native American, 7% Hispanic American, 6% African American, 1% Asian American/Pacific Islander **The most frequently chosen baccalaureate fields are** agriculture, business/marketing, education **Academic program** Advanced placement, accelerated degree program, honors program, summer session, adult/continuing education programs, internships **Contact** Ms. Denise Siler, Director of Admissions, Tarleton State University, Box T-0030, Tarleton Station, Stephenville, TX 76402. Telephone: 254-968-9125 or toll-free 800-687-4878. Fax: 254-968-9951. Web site: http://www.tarleton.edu/.

TEXAS A&M INTERNATIONAL UNIVERSITY
LAREDO, TEXAS

General State-supported, comprehensive, coed **Entrance** Moderately difficult **Setting** 300-acre urban campus **Total enrollment** 3,016 **Student/faculty ratio** 19:1 **Application deadline** 7/1 (freshmen), 7/1 (transfer) **Freshmen** 92% were admitted **Expenses** Tuition $2533; Room only $3120 **Undergraduates** 64% women, 38% part-time, 37% 25 or older, 0.04% Native American, 93% Hispanic American, 0.2% African American, 0.4% Asian American/Pacific Islander **The most frequently chosen baccalaureate fields are** business/marketing, English, liberal arts/general studies **Academic program** English as a second language, advanced placement, honors program, summer session, internships **Contact** Ms. Veronica Gonzalez, Director of Enrollment Management and School Relations, Texas A&M International University, 5201 University Boulevard, Laredo, TX 78041-1900. Telephone: 956-326-2270. Fax: 956-326-2199. E-mail: mchayez@tamiu.edu. Web site: http://www.tamiu.edu/.

TEXAS A&M UNIVERSITY
COLLEGE STATION, TEXAS

General State-supported, university, coed **Entrance** Moderately difficult **Setting** 5,200-acre suburban campus **Total enrollment** 44,026 **Student/faculty ratio** 21:1 **Application deadline** 2/15 (freshmen), 4/1 (transfer) **Freshmen** 66% were admitted **Housing** Yes **Expenses** Tuition 3374; Room & Board 5164 **Undergraduates** 49% women, 8% part-time, 4% 25 or older, 0.5% Native American, 9% Hispanic American, 2% African American, 3% Asian American/Pacific Islander **The most frequently chosen baccalaureate fields are** business/marketing, education, home economics/vocational home economics **Academic program** English as a second language, advanced placement, honors program, summer session, internships **Contact** Ms. Stephanie D. Hays, Associate Director of Admissions, Texas A&M University, 217 John J. Koldus Building, College Station, TX 77843-1265. Telephone: 409-979-3741. Fax: 409-979-8737. E-mail: adminfo@tamu.edu. Web site: http://www.tamu.edu/.

TEXAS A&M UNIVERSITY AT GALVESTON
GALVESTON, TEXAS

General State-supported, 4-year, coed **Entrance** Moderately difficult **Setting** 100-acre suburban campus **Total enrollment** 1,363 **Student/faculty ratio** 16:1 **Application deadline** Rolling (freshmen), rolling (transfer) **Freshmen** 90% were admitted **Housing** Yes **Expenses** Tuition $2915; Room & Board $3977 **Undergraduates** 51% women, 8% part-time, 11% 25 or older, 0.4% Native American, 9% Hispanic American, 1% African American, 2% Asian American/Pacific Islander **The most frequently chosen baccalaureate fields are** biological/life sciences, business/marketing, interdisciplinary studies **Academic program** English as a second language, advanced placement, accelerated degree program, summer session, internships **Contact** Sarah Wilson, Academic Advisor II, Texas A&M University at Galveston, PO Box 1675, Galveston, TX 77553-1675. Telephone: 409-740-4448 or toll-free 87—SEAAGIE. Fax: 409-740-4731. E-mail: langd@tamug3.tamu.edu. Web site: http://www.tamug.tamu.edu/.

TEXAS A&M UNIVERSITY–COMMERCE
COMMERCE, TEXAS

General State-supported, university, coed **Entrance** Moderately difficult **Setting** 140-acre small-town campus **Total enrollment** 7,483 **Student/faculty ratio** 19:1 **Application deadline** 8/6 (freshmen), rolling (transfer) **Freshmen** 60% were admitted **Housing** Yes **Expenses** Tuition $2711; Room & Board

$4550 **Undergraduates** 57% women, 22% part-time, 13% 25 or older, 1% Native American, 5% Hispanic American, 15% African American, 1% Asian American/Pacific Islander **The most frequently chosen baccalaureate fields are** business/marketing, interdisciplinary studies, protective services/public administration **Academic program** Advanced placement, honors program, summer session, adult/continuing education programs, internships **Contact** Mr. Randy McDonald, Director of School Relations, Texas A&M University–Commerce, PO Box 3011, Commerce, TX 75429. Telephone: 903-886-5072 or toll-free 800-331-3878. Fax: 903-886-5888. E-mail: cathy_griffin@tamu-commerce.edu. Web site: http://www.tamu-commerce.edu/.

TEXAS A&M UNIVERSITY–CORPUS CHRISTI
CORPUS CHRISTI, TEXAS

General State-supported, comprehensive, coed **Entrance** Moderately difficult **Setting** 240-acre suburban campus **Total enrollment** 6,823 **Student/faculty ratio** 18:1 **Application deadline** 7/1 (freshmen), rolling (transfer) **Freshmen** 87% were admitted **Housing** Yes **Expenses** Tuition 2306; Room & Board 5661 **Undergraduates** 60% women, 25% part-time, 29% 25 or older, 1% Native American, 39% Hispanic American, 3% African American, 2% Asian American/Pacific Islander **The most frequently chosen baccalaureate fields are** business/marketing, health professions and related sciences, interdisciplinary studies **Academic program** Advanced placement, summer session, internships **Contact** Ms. Margaret Dechant, Director of Admissions, Texas A&M University–Corpus Christi, 6300 Ocean Drive, Corpus Christi, TX 78412-5503. Telephone: 361-825-2414 or toll-free 800-482-6822. Fax: 361-825-5887. E-mail: jmorgan@falcon.tamucc.edu. Web site: http://www.tamucc.edu/.

TEXAS A&M UNIVERSITY–KINGSVILLE
KINGSVILLE, TEXAS

General State-supported, university, coed **Entrance** Moderately difficult **Setting** 255-acre small-town campus **Total enrollment** 5,946 **Student/faculty ratio** 15:1 **Application deadline** Rolling (freshmen), rolling (transfer) **Freshmen** 84% were admitted **Housing** Yes **Expenses** Tuition $2607; Room & Board $3584 **Undergraduates** 48% women, 21% part-time, 24% 25 or older, 0.3% Native American, 66% Hispanic American, 6% African American, 1% Asian American/Pacific Islander **The most frequently chosen baccalaureate fields are** engineering/engineering technologies, business/marketing, interdisciplinary studies **Academic program** English as a second language, advanced placement, summer session, adult/continuing education programs, internships **Contact** Ms. Laura Knippers, Director of Admissions, Texas A&M University–Kingsville, Campus Box 105, Kingsville, TX 78363. Telephone: 361-593-2811 or toll-free 800-687-6000. Fax: 361-593-2195. Web site: http://www.tamuk.edu/.

TEXAS A&M UNIVERSITY SYSTEM HEALTH SCIENCE CENTER
COLLEGE STATION, TEXAS

General State-supported, upper-level, coed **Total enrollment** 541 **Application deadline** Rolling (transfer) **Housing** No **Undergraduates** 97% women, 36% 25 or older **The most frequently chosen baccalaureate field is** health professions and related sciences **Contact** Dr. Jack L. Long, Director of Admissions and Records, Texas A&M University System Health Science Center, PO Box 660677, Dallas, TX 75266-0677. Telephone: 214-828-8230. Fax: 214-874-4567. Web site: http://tamushsc.tamu.edu/.

TEXAS A&M UNIVERSITY–TEXARKANA
TEXARKANA, TEXAS

General State-supported, upper-level, coed **Entrance** Noncompetitive **Setting** 1-acre small-town campus **Total enrollment** 1,233 **Student/faculty ratio** 15:1 **Application deadline** Rolling (transfer) **Housing** No **Expenses** Tuition $1848 **Undergraduates** 71% women, 62% part-time, 1% Native American, 2% Hispanic American, 11% African American, 1% Asian American/Pacific Islander **The most frequently chosen baccalaureate fields are** business/marketing, health professions and related sciences, liberal arts/general studies **Academic program** Advanced placement, self-designed majors, summer session, internships **Contact** Mrs. Patricia E. Black, Director of Admissions and Registrar, Texas A&M University–Texarkana, PO Box 5518, Texarkana, TX 75505-5518. Telephone: 903-223-3068. Fax: 903-223-3140. E-mail: patblack@etsu.edu. Web site: http://www.tamut.edu/.

TEXAS CHIROPRACTIC COLLEGE
PASADENA, TEXAS

Contact Mr. Robert Cooper, Director of Admissions, Texas Chiropractic College, 5912 Spencer Highway, Pasadena, TX 77505-1699. Telephone: 281-998-6017 or toll-free 800-468-6839. Web site: http://www.txchiro.edu/.

TEXAS CHRISTIAN UNIVERSITY
FORT WORTH, TEXAS

General Independent, university, coed, affiliated with Christian Church (Disciples of Christ) **Entrance** Moderately difficult **Setting** 237-acre suburban campus **Total enrollment** 7,775 **Student/faculty ratio** 15:1 **Application deadline** 2/15 (freshmen), 6/15 (transfer) **Freshmen** 76% were admitted **Housing** Yes **Expenses** Tuition 13,125; Room & Board 4290 **Undergraduates** 59% women, 9% part-time, 7% 25 or older, 1% Native American, 6% Hispanic American, 4% African American, 2% Asian American/Pacific Islander **The most frequently chosen baccalaureate fields are** business/marketing, communications/communication technologies, education **Academic program** English as a second language, advanced placement, accelerated degree program, self-designed

Texas Christian University *(continued)*

majors, honors program, summer session, adult/continuing education programs, internships **Contact** Mr. Ray Brown, Dean of Admissions, Texas Christian University, TCU Box 297013, Fort Worth, TX 76129-0002. Telephone: 817-257-7490 or toll-free 800-828-3764. Fax: 817-257-7268. E-mail: frogmail@tcu.edu. Web site: http://www.tcu.edu/.

TEXAS COLLEGE
TYLER, TEXAS

Contact Ms. J'Nieta Hancock-Dickey, Director for Admissions and Recruitment, Texas College, 2404 North Grand Avenue, PO Box 4500, Tyler, TX 75712-4500. Telephone: 903-593-8311 Ext. 224. Web site: http://168.44.174.253/.

TEXAS LUTHERAN UNIVERSITY
SEGUIN, TEXAS

General Independent, 4-year, coed, affiliated with Evangelical Lutheran Church **Entrance** Moderately difficult **Setting** 196-acre suburban campus **Total enrollment** 1,506 **Student/faculty ratio** 15:1 **Application deadline** Rolling (freshmen), rolling (transfer) **Freshmen** 81% were admitted **Housing** Yes **Expenses** Tuition $12,570; Room & Board $4880 **Undergraduates** 53% women, 18% part-time, 3% 25 or older, 1% Native American, 17% Hispanic American, 6% African American, 2% Asian American/Pacific Islander **The most frequently chosen baccalaureate fields are** business/marketing, biological/life sciences, education **Academic program** English as a second language, advanced placement, accelerated degree program, honors program, summer session, adult/continuing education programs, internships **Contact** Mr. E. Norman Jones, Vice President for Enrollment Services, Texas Lutheran University, 1000 West Court Street, Seguin, TX 78155-5999. Telephone: 830-372-8050 or toll-free 800-771-8521. Fax: 830-372-8096. E-mail: admissions@txlutheran.edu. Web site: http://www.tlu.edu/.

TEXAS SOUTHERN UNIVERSITY
HOUSTON, TEXAS

General State-supported, university, coed **Entrance** Noncompetitive **Setting** 147-acre urban campus **Total enrollment** 6,886 **Student/faculty ratio** 23:1 **Application deadline** 8/10 (freshmen), 8/10 (transfer) **Freshmen** 49% were admitted **Housing** Yes **Expenses** Tuition $2078; Room & Board $4116 **Undergraduates** 56% women, 20% part-time, 72% 25 or older, 0.1% Native American, 3% Hispanic American, 91% African American, 3% Asian American/Pacific Islander **The most frequently chosen baccalaureate fields are** business/marketing, biological/life sciences, health professions and related sciences **Academic program** English as a second language, accelerated degree program, honors program, summer session, adult/continuing education programs, internships **Contact** Mrs. Joyce Waddell, Director of Admissions, Texas Southern University, 3100 Cleburne, Houston, TX 77004-4598. Telephone: 713-313-7472. Web site: http://www.tsu.edu/.

TEXAS TECH UNIVERSITY
LUBBOCK, TEXAS

General State-supported, university, coed **Entrance** Moderately difficult **Setting** 1,839-acre urban campus **Total enrollment** 24,558 **Student/faculty ratio** 20:1 **Application deadline** Rolling (freshmen), rolling (transfer) **Freshmen** 70% were admitted **Housing** Yes **Expenses** Tuition 3400; Room & Board 5079 **Undergraduates** 46% women, 10% part-time, 10% 25 or older, 0.5% Native American, 10% Hispanic American, 3% African American, 2% Asian American/Pacific Islander **The most frequently chosen baccalaureate fields are** business/marketing, engineering/engineering technologies, interdisciplinary studies **Academic program** English as a second language, advanced placement, accelerated degree program, self-designed majors, honors program, summer session, adult/continuing education programs, internships **Contact** Mrs. Marty Grassel, Director Admissions and School Relations, Texas Tech University, Box 45005, Lubbock, TX 79409-5005. Telephone: 806-742-1482. Fax: 806-742-0980. E-mail: a5adms@ttuvm1.ttu.edu. Web site: http://www.ttu.edu/.

▶ **For more information, see page 475.**

TEXAS WESLEYAN UNIVERSITY
FORT WORTH, TEXAS

General Independent United Methodist, comprehensive, coed **Entrance** Moderately difficult **Setting** 74-acre urban campus **Total enrollment** 3,133 **Student/faculty ratio** 15:1 **Application deadline** Rolling (freshmen), rolling (transfer) **Freshmen** 79% were admitted **Housing** Yes **Expenses** Tuition $10,010; Room & Board $3964 **Undergraduates** 65% women, 34% part-time, 31% 25 or older, 1% Native American, 16% Hispanic American, 16% African American, 3% Asian American/Pacific Islander **The most frequently chosen baccalaureate fields are** education, communications/communication technologies, psychology **Academic program** English as a second language, advanced placement, summer session, adult/continuing education programs, internships **Contact** Ms. Stephanie Lewis-Boatner, Director of Freshman Admissions, Texas Wesleyan University, 1201 Wesleyan Street, Fort Worth, TX 76105-1536. Telephone: 817-531-4422 or toll-free 800-580-8980 (in-state). Fax: 817-531-7515. E-mail: freshman@txwesleyan.edu. Web site: http://www.txwesleyan.edu/.

TEXAS WOMAN'S UNIVERSITY
DENTON, TEXAS

General State-supported, university, coed, primarily women **Entrance** Minimally difficult **Setting** 270-acre suburban campus **Total enrollment** 8,404 **Student/faculty ratio** 13:1 **Application deadline** 7/15 (freshmen), 7/15 (transfer) **Freshmen** 69% were admitted **Housing** Yes **Expenses** Tuition $2670;

Room & Board $4113 **Undergraduates** 43% 25 or older **The most frequently chosen baccalaureate fields are** health professions and related sciences, home economics/vocational home economics, interdisciplinary studies **Academic program** Advanced placement, accelerated degree program, honors program, summer session, adult/continuing education programs, internships **Contact** Director of Undergraduate Admissions, Texas Woman's University, PO Box 425589, Denton, TX 76204-5589. Telephone: 940-898-3040 or toll-free 888-948-9984. Fax: 940-898-3081. E-mail: admissions@twu.edu. Web site: http://www.twu.edu/.

TRINITY UNIVERSITY
SAN ANTONIO, TEXAS

General Independent, comprehensive, coed, affiliated with Presbyterian Church **Entrance** Very difficult **Setting** 113-acre urban campus **Total enrollment** 2,571 **Student/faculty ratio** 11:1 **Application deadline** 2/1 (freshmen), 2/1 (transfer) **Freshmen** 65% were admitted **Housing** Yes **Expenses** Tuition 15,804; Room & Board 6330 **Undergraduates** 52% women, 2% part-time, 1% 25 or older, 0.5% Native American, 9% Hispanic American, 2% African American, 7% Asian American/Pacific Islander **The most frequently chosen baccalaureate fields are** business/marketing, biological/life sciences, social sciences and history **Academic program** Advanced placement, accelerated degree program, honors program, summer session, internships **Contact** Christopher Ellertson, Dean of Admissions and Financial Aid, Trinity University, 715 Stadium Drive, San Antonio, TX 78212-7200. Telephone: 210-999-7207 or toll-free 800-TRINITY. Fax: 210-999-8164. E-mail: gboyd@trinity.edu. Web site: http://www.trinity.edu/.

UNIVERSITY OF DALLAS
IRVING, TEXAS

General Independent Roman Catholic, university, coed **Entrance** Very difficult **Setting** 750-acre suburban campus **Total enrollment** 3,300 **Student/faculty ratio** 13:1 **Application deadline** 2/15 (freshmen), 7/1 (transfer) **Freshmen** 76% were admitted **Housing** Yes **Expenses** Tuition 14,994; Room & Board 5600 **Undergraduates** 7% 25 or older, 1% Native American, 14% Hispanic American, 2% African American, 6% Asian American/Pacific Islander **The most frequently chosen baccalaureate fields are** social sciences and history, philosophy, religion, and theology, visual/performing arts **Academic program** English as a second language, advanced placement, accelerated degree program, self-designed majors, summer session, adult/continuing education programs, internships **Contact** Mr. Larry Webb, Director of Enrollment, University of Dallas, 1845 East Northgate Drive, Irving, TX 75062-4799. Telephone: 972-721-5266 or toll-free 800-628-6999. Fax: 972-721-5017. E-mail: undadmis@acad.udallas.edu. Web site: http://www.udallas.edu/.

UNIVERSITY OF HOUSTON
HOUSTON, TEXAS

General State-supported, university, coed **Entrance** Moderately difficult **Setting** 550-acre urban campus **Total enrollment** 32,123 **Student/faculty ratio** 19:1 **Application deadline** 5/1 (freshmen), 5/1 (transfer) **Freshmen** 81% were admitted **Housing** Yes **Expenses** Tuition 2616; Room & Board 5242 **Undergraduates** 53% women, 31% part-time, 24% 25 or older, 0.5% Native American, 19% Hispanic American, 15% African American, 20% Asian American/Pacific Islander **The most frequently chosen baccalaureate fields are** business/marketing, engineering/engineering technologies, psychology **Academic program** English as a second language, advanced placement, accelerated degree program, honors program, summer session, adult/continuing education programs, internships **Contact** Mr. Jose Cantu, Co-Assistant Director of Student Outreach Services, University of Houston, 4800 Calhoun, Houston, TX 77204-2161. Telephone: 713-743-9617. Fax: 713-743-9633. E-mail: admissions@uh.edu. Web site: http://www.uh.edu/.

UNIVERSITY OF HOUSTON–CLEAR LAKE
HOUSTON, TEXAS

General State-supported, upper-level, coed **Entrance** Minimally difficult **Setting** 487-acre suburban campus **Total enrollment** 7,580 **Application deadline** Rolling (transfer) **First-Year Students** 66% were admitted **Housing** No **Expenses** Tuition $4402 **Undergraduates** 63% women, 51% part-time, 62% 25 or older, 0.3% Native American, 15% Hispanic American, 8% African American, 6% Asian American/Pacific Islander **The most frequently chosen baccalaureate fields are** business/marketing, computer/information sciences, education **Academic program** English as a second language, accelerated degree program, self-designed majors, summer session, internships **Contact** Mr. John Smith, Executive Director of Enrollment Services, University of Houston–Clear Lake, 2700 Bay Area Boulevard, Box 13, Houston, TX 77058-1098. Telephone: 281-283-2517. Fax: 281-283-2530. E-mail: admissions@cl.uh.edu. Web site: http://www.cl.uh.edu/.

UNIVERSITY OF HOUSTON–DOWNTOWN
HOUSTON, TEXAS

General State-supported, 4-year, coed **Entrance** Noncompetitive **Setting** 20-acre urban campus **Total enrollment** 8,951 **Student/faculty ratio** 25:1 **Application deadline** 8/1 (freshmen), 8/1 (transfer) **Freshmen** 100% were admitted **Housing** No **Expenses** Tuition $2414 **Undergraduates** 59% women, 51% part-time, 49% 25 or older, 0.3% Native American, 32% Hispanic American, 29% African American, 11% Asian American/Pacific Islander **The most frequently chosen baccalaureate fields are** business/marketing, liberal arts/general studies, protective services/public administration **Academic program** English as a second language, advanced placement, accelerated degree program, summer session, adult/

University of Houston–Downtown *(continued)*

continuing education programs, internships **Contact** Mr. Mike Kerrendal, Director, Admissions and Records, University of Houston–Downtown, One Main Street, Houston, TX 77002. Telephone: 713-221-8931. Fax: 713-221-8157. E-mail: uhdadmit@dt.uh.edu. Web site: http://www.uhd.edu/.

UNIVERSITY OF HOUSTON–VICTORIA
VICTORIA, TEXAS

General State-supported, upper-level, coed **Entrance** Minimally difficult **Setting** small-town campus **Total enrollment** 1,698 **Student/faculty ratio** 16:1 **Application deadline** Rolling (transfer) **First-Year Students** 85% were admitted **Housing** No **Expenses** Tuition $2124 **Undergraduates** 72% women, 67% part-time, 59% 25 or older, 0% Native American, 17% Hispanic American, 8% African American, 4% Asian American/Pacific Islander **The most frequently chosen baccalaureate fields are** business/marketing, computer/information sciences, education **Academic program** Summer session, adult/continuing education programs, internships **Contact** Mr. Richard Phillips, Director of Enrollment Management, University of Houston–Victoria, 3007 North Ben Wilson, Victoria, TX 77901-4450. Telephone: 361-570-4110 or toll-free 800-687-8648 (in-state). Fax: 361-570-4114. E-mail: voarabjh@vicvx2.vic.uh.edu. Web site: http://www.vic.uh.edu/.

UNIVERSITY OF MARY HARDIN-BAYLOR
BELTON, TEXAS

General Independent Southern Baptist, comprehensive, coed **Entrance** Moderately difficult **Setting** 100-acre small-town campus **Total enrollment** 2,590 **Student/faculty ratio** 17:1 **Application deadline** Rolling (freshmen), rolling (transfer) **Freshmen** 60% were admitted **Housing** Yes **Expenses** Tuition $9300; Room & Board $3931 **Undergraduates** 62% women, 16% part-time, 21% 25 or older, 1% Native American, 10% Hispanic American, 10% African American, 1% Asian American/Pacific Islander **The most frequently chosen baccalaureate fields are** education, health professions and related sciences, liberal arts/general studies **Academic program** English as a second language, advanced placement, accelerated degree program, honors program, summer session, adult/continuing education programs, internships **Contact** Ms. Valerie Hampton, Admissions Clerk, University of Mary Hardin-Baylor, UMHB Station Box 8004, 900 College Street, Belton, TX 76513-2599. Telephone: 254-295-4520 or toll-free 800-727-8642. Fax: 254-295-5049. E-mail: admissions@umhb.edu. Web site: http://www.umhb.edu/.

UNIVERSITY OF NORTH TEXAS
DENTON, TEXAS

General State-supported, university, coed **Entrance** Moderately difficult **Setting** 500-acre urban campus **Total enrollment** 27,054 **Student/faculty ratio** 16:1 **Application deadline** 6/15 (freshmen), 6/15 (transfer) **Freshmen** 75% were admitted **Housing** Yes **Expenses** Tuition 3055; Room & Board 4202 **Undergraduates** 55% women, 23% part-time, 20% 25 or older, 1% Native American, 9% Hispanic American, 10% African American, 4% Asian American/Pacific Islander **The most frequently chosen baccalaureate fields are** business/marketing, communications/communication technologies, home economics/vocational home economics **Academic program** English as a second language, advanced placement, accelerated degree program, self-designed majors, honors program, summer session, internships **Contact** Mr. Joel Daboub, Senior Assistant Director of Admissions and Director of Freshman Orientation, University of North Texas, Box 311277, Denton, TX 76203-9988. Telephone: 940-565-2681 or toll-free 800-868-8211 (in-state). Fax: 940-565-2408. E-mail: undergrad@abn.unt.edu. Web site: http://www.unt.edu/.

UNIVERSITY OF ST. THOMAS
HOUSTON, TEXAS

General Independent Roman Catholic, comprehensive, coed **Setting** 20-acre urban campus **Total enrollment** 4,073 **Student/faculty ratio** 13:1 **Application deadline** Rolling (freshmen), rolling (transfer) **Freshmen** 78% were admitted **Housing** Yes **Expenses** Tuition $12,412; Room & Board $5550 **Undergraduates** 65% women, 30% part-time, 36% 25 or older, 0.4% Native American, 30% Hispanic American, 6% African American, 12% Asian American/Pacific Islander **The most frequently chosen baccalaureate fields are** business/marketing, liberal arts/general studies, social sciences and history **Academic program** English as a second language, advanced placement, accelerated degree program, self-designed majors, honors program, summer session, adult/continuing education programs, internships **Contact** Mrs. Elsie Biron, Dean of Admissions, University of St. Thomas, 3800 Montrose Boulevard, Houston, TX 77006-4696. Telephone: 713-525-3500 or toll-free 800-856-8565. Fax: 713-525-3558. E-mail: admissions@basil.stthom.edu. Web site: http://www.stthom.edu/.

THE UNIVERSITY OF TEXAS AT ARLINGTON
ARLINGTON, TEXAS

General State-supported, university, coed **Entrance** Moderately difficult **Setting** 395-acre urban campus **Total enrollment** 20,424 **Student/faculty ratio** 21:1 **Application deadline** Rolling (freshmen), rolling (transfer) **Freshmen** 86% were admitted **Housing** Yes **Expenses** Room & Board $3795 **Undergraduates** 53% women, 33% part-time, 34% 25 or older, 1% Native American, 12% Hispanic American, 13% African American, 11% Asian American/Pacific Islander **The most frequently chosen baccalaureate fields are** business/marketing, health professions and related sciences, social sciences and history **Academic program** English as a second language, advanced placement, self-designed majors, honors program, summer session, adult/continuing education programs, internships **Contact** Mr. George E.

Norton, Interim Director of Admissions, The University of Texas at Arlington, PO Box 19111, 701 South Nedderman Drive, Room 110, Davis Hall, Arlington, TX 76019-0088. Telephone: 817-272-3254. Fax: 817-272-3435. E-mail: adm@uta.edu. Web site: http://www.uta.edu/.

THE UNIVERSITY OF TEXAS AT AUSTIN
AUSTIN, TEXAS

General State-supported, university, coed **Entrance** Very difficult **Setting** 350-acre urban campus **Total enrollment** 49,996 **Student/faculty ratio** 19:1 **Application deadline** 2/1 (freshmen), 3/1 (transfer) **Freshmen** 62% were admitted **Housing** Yes **Expenses** Tuition 3575; Room & Board 5113 **Undergraduates** 50% women, 12% part-time, 8% 25 or older, 0.5% Native American, 13% Hispanic American, 3% African American, 15% Asian American/Pacific Islander **The most frequently chosen baccalaureate fields are** business/marketing, communications/communication technologies, social sciences and history **Academic program** English as a second language, advanced placement, accelerated degree program, self-designed majors, honors program, summer session, adult/continuing education programs, internships **Contact** Freshman Admissions Center, The University of Texas at Austin, John Hargis Hall, Campus Mail Code D0700, Austin, TX 78712-1111. Telephone: 512-475-7440. Fax: 512-475-7475. E-mail: adfre@utxdp.dp.utexas.edu. Web site: http://www.utexas.edu/.

THE UNIVERSITY OF TEXAS AT BROWNSVILLE
BROWNSVILLE, TEXAS

Contact Mr. Ernesto Garcia, Director of Enrollment, The University of Texas at Brownsville, 80 Fort Brown, Brownsville, TX 78520-4991. Telephone: 956-544-8254. Fax: 956-544-8832. Web site: http://www.utb.edu/.

THE UNIVERSITY OF TEXAS AT DALLAS
RICHARDSON, TEXAS

General State-supported, university, coed **Entrance** Very difficult **Setting** 455-acre suburban campus **Total enrollment** 10,945 **Student/faculty ratio** 19:1 **Application deadline** 8/1 (freshmen) **Freshmen** 49% were admitted **Housing** Yes **Expenses** Tuition 3287; Room & Board 5799 **Undergraduates** 47% women, 37% part-time, 33% 25 or older, 1% Native American, 8% Hispanic American, 7% African American, 21% Asian American/Pacific Islander **The most frequently chosen baccalaureate fields are** business/marketing, computer/information sciences, social sciences and history **Academic program** Advanced placement, accelerated degree program, self-designed majors, honors program, summer session, adult/continuing education programs, internships **Contact** Admissions Office, The University of Texas at Dallas, PO Box 830688 Mail Station MC11, Richardson, TX 75083-0688. Telephone: 972-883 2342 or toll-free 800-889-2443. Fax: 972-883-2599. E-mail: ugrad-admissions@utdallas.edu. Web site: http://www.utdallas.edu/.

THE UNIVERSITY OF TEXAS AT EL PASO
EL PASO, TEXAS

General State-supported, university, coed **Entrance** Minimally difficult **Setting** 360-acre urban campus **Total enrollment** 15,224 **Student/faculty ratio** 18:1 **Application deadline** 7/1 (freshmen), 7/31 (transfer) **Freshmen** 93% were admitted **Housing** Yes **Expenses** Tuition $2541; Room & Board $5165 **Undergraduates** 54% women, 29% part-time, 44% 25 or older, 0.3% Native American, 72% Hispanic American, 2% African American, 1% Asian American/Pacific Islander **Academic program** English as a second language, advanced placement, accelerated degree program, honors program, summer session, adult/continuing education programs, internships **Contact** Ms. Diana Guerrero, Director of Admissions, The University of Texas at El Paso, 500 West University Avenue, El Paso, TX 79968-0001. Telephone: 915-747-5588. Fax: 915-747-5122. E-mail: admission@utep.edu. Web site: http://www.utep.edu/.

THE UNIVERSITY OF TEXAS AT SAN ANTONIO
SAN ANTONIO, TEXAS

General State-supported, university, coed **Entrance** Moderately difficult **Setting** 600-acre suburban campus **Total enrollment** 18,830 **Student/faculty ratio** 22:1 **Application deadline** 7/1 (freshmen), 7/1 (transfer) **Freshmen** 99% were admitted **Housing** Yes **Expenses** Tuition $3455; Room & Board $5994 **Undergraduates** 55% women, 31% part-time, 34% 25 or older, 0.5% Native American, 47% Hispanic American, 5% African American, 3% Asian American/Pacific Islander **The most frequently chosen baccalaureate fields are** business/marketing, biological/life sciences, interdisciplinary studies **Academic program** English as a second language, advanced placement, accelerated degree program, honors program, summer session, adult/continuing education programs, internships **Contact** Ms. Sandy Speed, Interim Director, The University of Texas at San Antonio, 6900 North Loop 1604 West, San Antonio, TX 78249-0617. Telephone: 210-458-4530 or toll-free 800-669-0919 (out-of-state). Web site: http://www.utsa.edu/.

THE UNIVERSITY OF TEXAS AT TYLER
TYLER, TEXAS

General State-supported, comprehensive, coed **Setting** 200-acre urban campus **Total enrollment** 3,594 **Student/faculty ratio** 10:1 **Freshmen** 45% were admitted **Housing** Yes **Expenses** Tuition $2336; Room only $2464 **Undergraduates** 66% women, 41% part-time, 47% 25 or older, 1% Native American, 3% Hispanic American, 9% African American, 1% Asian American/Pacific Islander **The most frequently chosen baccalaureate fields are** health pro-

The University of Texas at Tyler *(continued)*

fessions and related sciences, business/marketing, interdisciplinary studies **Academic program** English as a second language, advanced placement, self-designed majors, honors program, summer session, adult/continuing education programs, internships **Contact** Ms. Shawnda Kennedy, Director of Admissions, The University of Texas at Tyler, 3900 University Boulevard, Tyler, TX 75799-0001. Telephone: 903-566-7207 or toll-free 800-UTTYLER (in-state). Fax: 903-566-7068. Web site: http://www.uttyler.edu/.

THE UNIVERSITY OF TEXAS HEALTH SCIENCE CENTER AT HOUSTON

HOUSTON, TEXAS

General State-supported, upper-level, coed **Entrance** Moderately difficult **Setting** urban campus **Total enrollment** 3,143 **Application deadline** 12/31 (transfer) **Housing** Yes **Expenses** Tuition $3463 **Undergraduates** 51% 25 or older, 0.4% Native American, 16% Hispanic American, 11% African American, 10% Asian American/Pacific Islander **The most frequently chosen baccalaureate field is** health professions and related sciences **Academic program** Accelerated degree program **Contact** Mr. Robert L. Jenkins, Associate Registrar, The University of Texas Health Science Center at Houston, 7000 Fannin, PO Box 20036, Houston, TX 77225-0036. Telephone: 713-500-3333. Fax: 713-500-3356. E-mail: uthschro@admin4.hsc.uth.tmc.edu. Web site: http://www.uth.tmc.edu/.

THE UNIVERSITY OF TEXAS HEALTH SCIENCE CENTER AT SAN ANTONIO

SAN ANTONIO, TEXAS

Contact Mr. James Peak, Registrar, The University of Texas Health Science Center at San Antonio, 7703 Floyd Curl Drive, San Antonio, TX 78229-3900. Telephone: 210-567-2629.

THE UNIVERSITY OF TEXAS MEDICAL BRANCH AT GALVESTON

GALVESTON, TEXAS

General State-supported, upper-level, coed **Entrance** Most difficult **Setting** 100-acre small-town campus **Total enrollment** 1,927 **First-Year Students** 51% were admitted **Housing** Yes **Expenses** Tuition 1832; Room only 6480 **Undergraduates** 85% women, 34% part-time, 59% 25 or older, 0% Native American, 15% Hispanic American, 13% African American, 9% Asian American/Pacific Islander **The most frequently chosen baccalaureate field is** health professions and related sciences **Academic program** Advanced placement, summer session, internships **Contact** Mr. Richard Lewis, University Registrar, The University of Texas Medical Branch at Galveston, 1212 Ashbel Smith, Galveston, TX 77555-1305. Telephone: 409-772-1215. Fax: 409-772-5056. E-mail: inet:ccoonrod@msp06.med.utmb.edu. Web site: http://www.utmb.edu/.

THE UNIVERSITY OF TEXAS OF THE PERMIAN BASIN

ODESSA, TEXAS

General State-supported, comprehensive, coed **Entrance** Moderately difficult **Setting** 600-acre urban campus **Total enrollment** 2,272 **Student/faculty ratio** 17:1 **Application deadline** 8/1 (freshmen), rolling (transfer) **Freshmen** 89% were admitted **Housing** Yes **Expenses** Tuition $2530; Room & Board $3950 **Undergraduates** 64% women, 34% part-time, 75% 25 or older, 1% Native American, 34% Hispanic American, 4% African American, 1% Asian American/Pacific Islander **The most frequently chosen baccalaureate fields are** business/marketing, English, social sciences and history **Academic program** Advanced placement, summer session, internships **Contact** Ms. Vicki Gomez, Assistant Vice President for Admissions, The University of Texas of the Permian Basin, 4901 East University, Odessa, TX 79762-0001. Telephone: 915-552-2605. Fax: 915-552-2374. E-mail: gomez-v@gusher.pb.utexas.edu. Web site: http://www.utpb.edu/.

THE UNIVERSITY OF TEXAS–PAN AMERICAN

EDINBURG, TEXAS

General State-supported, comprehensive, coed **Entrance** Noncompetitive **Setting** 200-acre rural campus **Total enrollment** 12,759 **Student/faculty ratio** 27:1 **Application deadline** 7/10 (freshmen), 7/10 (transfer) **Freshmen** 76% were admitted **Housing** Yes **Expenses** Tuition $2363; Room & Board $5531 **Undergraduates** 58% women, 35% part-time, 28% 25 or older, 0.1% Native American, 85% Hispanic American, 1% African American, 1% Asian American/Pacific Islander **The most frequently chosen baccalaureate fields are** business/marketing, interdisciplinary studies, protective services/public administration **Academic program** Honors program, summer session, adult/continuing education programs, internships **Contact** Mr. David Zuniga, Director of Admissions, The University of Texas–Pan American, Office of Admissions and Records, 1201 West University Drive, Edinburg, TX 78539. Telephone: 956-381-2201. Web site: http://www.panam.edu/.

THE UNIVERSITY OF TEXAS SOUTHWESTERN MEDICAL CENTER AT DALLAS

DALLAS, TEXAS

General State-supported, upper-level, coed **Entrance** Moderately difficult **Setting** 98-acre urban campus **Total enrollment** 1,505 **Application deadline** Rolling (transfer) **Housing** No **Expenses** Tuition $1941 **Undergraduates** 76% women, 34% part-time, 64% 25 or older, 0.4% Native American, 8% Hispanic American, 13% African American, 7% Asian American/Pacific Islander **The most frequently chosen baccalaureate fields are** health professions and related sciences, home economics/vocational home economics **Academic program** Advanced placement, internships **Contact** Dr. Scott Wright, Director of Admissions, The University of Texas Southwestern Medical Center at Dallas, 5323 Harry Hines Boulevard, Dallas, TX 75390-9096. Telephone: 214-648-5617. Fax: 214-648-3289. E-mail: admissions@mednet.swmed.edu. Web site: http://www.swmed.edu/.

UNIVERSITY OF THE INCARNATE WORD
SAN ANTONIO, TEXAS

General Independent Roman Catholic, comprehensive, coed **Entrance** Moderately difficult **Setting** 200-acre urban campus **Total enrollment** 3,702 **Student/faculty ratio** 15:1 **Application deadline** Rolling (freshmen), rolling (transfer) **Freshmen** 94% were admitted **Housing** Yes **Expenses** Tuition $12,670; Room & Board $5010 **Undergraduates** 68% women, 34% part-time, 13% 25 or older, 0.4% Native American, 54% Hispanic American, 6% African American, 2% Asian American/Pacific Islander **The most frequently chosen baccalaureate fields are** business/marketing, education, health professions and related sciences **Academic program** English as a second language, advanced placement, accelerated degree program, summer session, adult/continuing education programs, internships **Contact** Ms. Andrea Cyterski, Director of Admissions, University of the Incarnate Word, Box 285, San Antonio, TX 78209-6397. Telephone: 210-829-6005 or toll-free 800-749-WORD. Fax: 210-829-3921. E-mail: admis@universe.viwtx.edu. Web site: http://www.uiw.edu/.

WAYLAND BAPTIST UNIVERSITY
PLAINVIEW, TEXAS

General Independent Baptist, comprehensive, coed **Entrance** Minimally difficult **Setting** 80-acre small-town campus **Total enrollment** 5,093 **Student/faculty ratio** 15:1 **Application deadline** Rolling (freshmen), rolling (transfer) **Freshmen** 99% were admitted **Housing** Yes **Expenses** Tuition $7850; Room & Board $3121 **Undergraduates** 42% women, 80% part-time, 70% 25 or older, 1% Native American, 14% Hispanic American, 16% African American, 2% Asian American/Pacific Islander **The most frequently chosen baccalaureate fields are** business/marketing, education, social sciences and history **Academic program** Advanced placement, accelerated degree program, honors program, summer session, adult/continuing education programs, internships **Contact** Mr. Shawn Thomas, Director of Student Admissions, Wayland Baptist University, 1900 West 7th Street #712, Plainview, TX 79072. Telephone: 806-296-4709 or toll-free 800-588-1-WBU. E-mail: admityou@mail.wbu.edu. Web site: http://www.wbu.edu/.

WEST TEXAS A&M UNIVERSITY
CANYON, TEXAS

General State-supported, comprehensive, coed **Entrance** Moderately difficult **Setting** 128-acre small-town campus **Total enrollment** 6,775 **Student/faculty ratio** 21:1 **Application deadline** Rolling (freshmen), rolling (transfer) **Freshmen** 72% were admitted **Housing** Yes **Expenses** Tuition $2075; Room & Board $3474 **Undergraduates** 55% women, 22% part-time, 20% 25 or older, 1% Native American, 12% Hispanic American, 4% African American, 1% Asian American/Pacific Islander **The most frequently chosen baccalaureate fields are** business/marketing, health professions and related sciences, interdisciplinary studies **Academic program** English as a second language, advanced placement, self-designed majors, honors program, summer session, adult/continuing education programs, internships **Contact** Ms. Lila Vars, Director of Admissions, West Texas A&M University, WT Box 60907, Canyon, TX 79016-0001. Telephone: 806-651-2020 or toll-free 800-99-WTAMU (in-state); 800-99-WTMAU (out-of-state). Fax: 806-651-2017. E-mail: lilav@wtamu.edu. Web site: http://www.wtamu.edu/.

WILEY COLLEGE
MARSHALL, TEXAS

General Independent, 4-year, coed, affiliated with United Methodist Church **Entrance** Noncompetitive **Setting** 58-acre small-town campus **Total enrollment** 552 **Student/faculty ratio** 14:1 **Application deadline** 8/1 (freshmen), 8/1 (transfer) **Freshmen** 71% were admitted **Housing** Yes **Expenses** Tuition 5840; Room & Board 3732 **Undergraduates** 56% women, 2% part-time, 34% 25 or older, 1% Hispanic American, 88% African American **Academic program** Self-designed majors, summer session, adult/continuing education programs **Contact** Dr. Rory Bedford, Director of Admissions and Recruitment, Wiley College, 711 Wiley Avenue, Marshall, TX 75670. Telephone: 903-927-3311 Ext. 356 or toll-free 800-658-6889. E-mail: vvalentine@wileyc.edu. Web site: http://www.wileyc.edu/.

UTAH

BRIGHAM YOUNG UNIVERSITY
PROVO, UTAH

General Independent, university, coed, affiliated with Church of Jesus Christ of Latter-day Saints **Entrance** Moderately difficult **Setting** 638-acre suburban campus **Total enrollment** 32,554 **Student/faculty ratio** 20:1 **Application deadline** 2/15 (freshmen), 3/15 (transfer) **Freshmen** 64% were admitted **Housing** Yes **Expenses** Tuition $3060; Room & Board $4780 **Undergraduates** 51% women, 11% part-time, 8% 25 or older, 1% Native American, 3% Hispanic American, 0.3% African American, 3% Asian American/Pacific Islander **The most frequently chosen baccalaureate fields are** education, business/marketing, social sciences and history **Academic program** English as a second language, advanced placement, accelerated degree program, honors program, summer session, adult/continuing education programs,

Brigham Young University *(continued)*

internships **Contact** Mr. Erlend D. Peterson, Dean of Admissions and Records, Brigham Young University, Provo, UT 84602-1110. Telephone: 801-378-2539. Fax: 801-378-4264. E-mail: admissions@byu.edu. Web site: http://www.byu.edu/.

SOUTHERN UTAH UNIVERSITY
CEDAR CITY, UTAH

General State-supported, comprehensive, coed **Entrance** Moderately difficult **Setting** 113-acre small-town campus **Total enrollment** 5,963 **Student/faculty ratio** 22:1 **Application deadline** 7/1 (freshmen), rolling (transfer) **Freshmen** 84% were admitted **Housing** Yes **Expenses** Tuition $2066; Room & Board $2866 **Undergraduates** 56% women, 22% part-time, 19% 25 or older, 1% Native American, 2% Hispanic American, 1% African American, 1% Asian American/Pacific Islander **The most frequently chosen baccalaureate fields are** business/marketing, education, social sciences and history **Academic program** English as a second language, advanced placement, honors program, summer session, adult/continuing education programs, internships **Contact** Mr. Dale S. Orton, Director of Admissions, Southern Utah University, 351 West Center Street, Cedar City, UT 84720. Telephone: 801-586-7740. Fax: 435-865-8223. E-mail: adminfo@suu.edu. Web site: http://www.suu.edu/.

UNIVERSITY OF PHOENIX–UTAH CAMPUS
SALT LAKE CITY, UTAH

General Proprietary, comprehensive, coed **Entrance** Noncompetitive **Total enrollment** 66,534 **Student/faculty ratio** 13:1 **Application deadline** Rolling (freshmen), rolling (transfer) **Expenses** Tuition $7740 **Undergraduates** 56% women, 86% 25 or older, 2% Native American, 18% Hispanic American, 13% African American, 6% Asian American/Pacific Islander **Academic program** Advanced placement, accelerated degree program, adult/continuing education programs **Contact** Ms. Beth Barilla, Director of Admissions, University of Phoenix–Utah Campus, 4615 East Elwood Street, Phoenix, AZ 85040-1948. Telephone: 480-927-0099 Ext. 1218 or toll-free 800-224-2844. Fax: 480-594-1758. E-mail: beth.barilla@apollogrp.edu. Web site: http://www.phoenix.edu/.

UNIVERSITY OF UTAH
SALT LAKE CITY, UTAH

General State-supported, university, coed **Entrance** Moderately difficult **Setting** 1,500-acre urban campus **Total enrollment** 26,031 **Student/faculty ratio** 14:1 **Application deadline** 5/1 (freshmen), 5/1 (transfer) **Freshmen** 94% were admitted **Housing** Yes **Expenses** Tuition $2897; Room & Board $4669 **Undergraduates** 46% women, 37% part-time, 20% 25 or older, 1% Native American, 3% Hispanic American, 1% African American, 4% Asian American/Pacific Islander **The most frequently chosen baccalaureate fields are** business/marketing, communications/communication technologies, social sciences and history **Academic program** English as a second language, advanced placement, accelerated degree program, self-designed majors, honors program, summer session, adult/continuing education programs, internships **Contact** Ms. Suzanne Espinoza, Director of High School Services, University of Utah, 250 South Student Services Building, 201 South, 460 E Rm 205, Salt Lake City, UT 84112. Telephone: 801-581-8761 or toll-free 800-444-8638. Fax: 801-585-7864. Web site: http://www.utah.edu/.

UTAH STATE UNIVERSITY
LOGAN, UTAH

General State-supported, university, coed **Entrance** Moderately difficult **Setting** 456-acre urban campus **Total enrollment** 21,490 **Student/faculty ratio** 25:1 **Application deadline** Rolling (transfer) **Freshmen** 98% were admitted **Housing** Yes **Expenses** Tuition $2403; Room & Board $4040 **Undergraduates** 52% women, 33% part-time, 19% 25 or older, 1% Native American, 2% Hispanic American, 0.4% African American, 1% Asian American/Pacific Islander **The most frequently chosen baccalaureate fields are** business/marketing, education, engineering/engineering technologies **Academic program** English as a second language, advanced placement, accelerated degree program, self-designed majors, honors program, summer session, adult/continuing education programs, internships **Contact** Mr. Lynn Poulsen, Associate Vice President, Student Services, Utah State University, 1600 Old Main Hill, Logan, UT 84322-1600. Telephone: 435-797-1107. Fax: 435-797-4077. E-mail: admit@admission.usu.edu. Web site: http://www.usu.edu/.

WEBER STATE UNIVERSITY
OGDEN, UTAH

General State-supported, comprehensive, coed **Entrance** Noncompetitive **Setting** 526-acre urban campus **Total enrollment** 16,051 **Student/faculty ratio** 22:1 **Application deadline** 8/24 (freshmen), rolling (transfer) **Freshmen** 100% were admitted **Housing** Yes **Expenses** Tuition 2252; Room & Board 4625 **Undergraduates** 52% women, 41% part-time, 33% 25 or older, 1% Native American, 3% Hispanic American, 1% African American, 2% Asian American/Pacific Islander **The most frequently chosen baccalaureate fields are** business/marketing, education, protective services/public administration **Academic program** English as a second language, advanced placement, accelerated degree program, self-designed majors, honors program, summer session, adult/continuing education programs, internships **Contact** John Allred, Admissions Advisor, Weber State University, 1137 University Circle, 3750 Harrison Boulevard, oGDEN, UT 84408-1137. Telephone: 801-626-6050 or toll-free 800-634-6568 (in-state). Fax: 801-626-6744. E-mail: kolsen4@weber.edu. Web site: http://weber.edu/.

WESTERN GOVERNORS UNIVERSITY
SALT LAKE CITY, UTAH

General Independent, comprehensive, coed **Total enrollment** 500 **Student/faculty ratio** 36:1 **Expenses** Tuition 3650 **Undergraduates** 97% 25 or older, 0.4% Native American, 2% Hispanic American, 1% African American, 1% Asian American/Pacific Islander **Academic program** Accelerated degree program, adult/continuing education programs **Contact** Ms. Wendy Gregory, Enrollment Manager, Western Governors University, 2040 East Murray Holladay Road, Suite 106, Salt Lake City, UT 84117. Telephone: 801-274-3280 Ext. 15 or toll-free 877-435-7948. Fax: 801-274-3305. E-mail: info@wgu.edu. Web site: http://www.wgu.edu/.

WESTMINSTER COLLEGE
SALT LAKE CITY, UTAH

General Independent, comprehensive, coed **Entrance** Moderately difficult **Setting** 27-acre suburban campus **Total enrollment** 2,403 **Student/faculty ratio** 14:1 **Application deadline** Rolling (freshmen), rolling (transfer) **Freshmen** 86% were admitted **Housing** Yes **Expenses** Tuition 13,730; Room & Board 4570 **Undergraduates** 63% women, 17% part-time, 25% 25 or older, 1% Native American, 5% Hispanic American, 0.3% African American, 2% Asian American/Pacific Islander **The most frequently chosen baccalaureate fields are** business/marketing, communications/communication technologies, education **Academic program** English as a second language, advanced placement, accelerated degree program, self-designed majors, honors program, summer session, internships **Contact** Mr. Philip J. Alletto, Vice President of Student Development and Enrollment Management, Westminster College, 1840 South 1300 East, Salt Lake City, UT 84105-3697. Telephone: 801-832-2200 or toll-free 800-748-4753. Fax: 801-484-3252. E-mail: admispub@wcslc.edu. Web site: http://www.wcslc.edu/.

VERMONT

BENNINGTON COLLEGE
BENNINGTON, VERMONT

General Independent, comprehensive, coed **Entrance** Very difficult **Setting** 550-acre small-town campus **Total enrollment** 671 **Student/faculty ratio** 9:1 **Application deadline** 1/1 (freshmen), 3/1 (transfer) **Freshmen** 70% were admitted **Housing** Yes **Expenses** Tuition 23,600; Room & Board 6150 **Undergraduates** 69% women, 4% 25 or older, 0.4% Native American, 2% Hispanic American, 2% African American, 2% Asian American/Pacific Islander **The most frequently chosen baccalaureate fields are** interdisciplinary studies, English, visual/performing arts **Academic program** English as a second language, self-designed majors, internships **Contact** Mr. Deane Bogardus, Director of Admissions, Bennington College, Route 67A, Bennington, VT 05201. Telephone: 802-440-4312 or toll-free 800-833-6845. Fax: 802-440-4320. E-mail: admissions@bennington.edu. Web site: http://www.bennington.edu/.

BURLINGTON COLLEGE
BURLINGTON, VERMONT

General Independent, 4-year, coed **Entrance** Noncompetitive **Setting** 1-acre urban campus **Total enrollment** 209 **Student/faculty ratio** 8:1 **Application deadline** 8/16 (freshmen), rolling (transfer) **Freshmen** 94% were admitted **Housing** Yes **Expenses** Tuition $10,640 **Undergraduates** 59% women, 44% part-time, 66% 25 or older, 1% Native American, 1% Hispanic American, 3% African American, 1% Asian American/Pacific Islander **The most frequently chosen baccalaureate fields are** English, psychology, social sciences and history **Academic program** Accelerated degree program, self-designed majors, summer session, adult/continuing education programs, internships **Contact** Ms. Cathleen Sullivan, Assistant Director of Admissions, Burlington College, 95 North Avenue, Burlington, VT 05401-2998. Telephone: 802-862-9616 Ext. 24 or toll-free 800-862-9616. Fax: 802-660-4331. E-mail: admissions@burlcol.edu. Web site: http://www.burlcol.edu/.

CASTLETON STATE COLLEGE
CASTLETON, VERMONT

General State-supported, comprehensive, coed **Entrance** Moderately difficult **Setting** 130-acre rural campus **Total enrollment** 1,632 **Student/faculty ratio** 13:1 **Application deadline** Rolling (freshmen), rolling (transfer) **Freshmen** 85% were admitted **Housing** Yes **Expenses** Tuition 5392; Room & Board 5530 **Undergraduates** 58% women, 13% part-time, 15% 25 or older, 0.1% Native American, 1% Hispanic American, 0.1% African American, 1% Asian American/Pacific Islander **The most frequently chosen baccalaureate fields are** business/marketing, communications/communication technologies, social sciences and history **Academic program** Advanced placement, self-designed majors, honors program, summer session, internships **Contact** Mr. Bill Allen, Dean of Enrollment, Castleton State College, Seminary Street, Castleton, VT 05735. Telephone: 802-468-1214 or toll-free 800-639-8521. Fax: 802-468-1476. E-mail: tenczap@sparrow.csc.vsc.edu. Web site: http://www.castleton.edu/.

CHAMPLAIN COLLEGE
BURLINGTON, VERMONT

General Independent, 4-year, coed **Entrance** Minimally difficult **Setting** 19-acre suburban campus **Total enrollment** 2,876 **Student/faculty ratio** 14:1 **Application deadline** Rolling (freshmen), rolling (transfer) **Freshmen** 77% were admitted **Housing** Yes **Expenses** Tuition $11,005; Room & Board $7965 **Undergraduates** 61% women, 37% part-time, 16% 25 or older, 1% Native American, 1% Hispanic

Champlain College *(continued)*

American, 1% African American, 1% Asian American/Pacific Islander **Academic program** Advanced placement, honors program, summer session, adult/continuing education programs, internships **Contact** Ms. Josephine H. Churchill, Director of Admissions, Champlain College, 163 South Willard Street, Burlington, VT 05401. Telephone: 802-860-2727 or toll-free 800-570-5858. Fax: 802-860-2767. E-mail: admission@champlain.edu. Web site: http://www.champlain.edu/.

COLLEGE OF ST. JOSEPH
RUTLAND, VERMONT

General Independent Roman Catholic, comprehensive, coed **Entrance** Minimally difficult **Setting** 90-acre small-town campus **Total enrollment** 529 **Student/faculty ratio** 11:1 **Application deadline** Rolling (freshmen), rolling (transfer) **Freshmen** 95% were admitted **Housing** Yes **Expenses** Tuition 11,700; Room & Board 6200 **Undergraduates** 66% women, 40% part-time, 53% 25 or older, 0.3% Native American, 1% Hispanic American, 3% African American, 1% Asian American/Pacific Islander **The most frequently chosen baccalaureate fields are** business/marketing, psychology, social sciences and history **Academic program** English as a second language, advanced placement, accelerated degree program, summer session, adult/continuing education programs, internships **Contact** Mr. Maurice Ouimet, Assistant Dean of Admissions, College of St. Joseph, 71 Clement Road, Rutland, VT 05701-3899. Telephone: 802-773-5900 Ext. 217. Fax: 802-773-5900 Ext. 258. E-mail: admissions@csj.edu. Web site: http://www.csj.edu/.

GODDARD COLLEGE
PLAINFIELD, VERMONT

General Independent, comprehensive, coed **Entrance** Moderately difficult **Setting** 250-acre rural campus **Total enrollment** 584 **Student/faculty ratio** 11:1 **Application deadline** Rolling (freshmen), rolling (transfer) **Freshmen** 75% were admitted **Housing** Yes **Expenses** Tuition $18,080; Room & Board $1482 **Undergraduates** 63% women, 36% 25 or older, 1% Native American, 4% Hispanic American, 4% African American, 1% Asian American/Pacific Islander **Academic program** Advanced placement, self-designed majors, adult/continuing education programs, internships **Contact** Mr. Josh Castle, Admissions Counselor, Goddard College, 123 Pitkin Road, Plainfield, VT 05667-9432. Telephone: 802-454-8311 Ext. 322 or toll-free 800-468-4888 Ext. 307. Fax: 802-454-1029. E-mail: admissions@earth.goddard.edu. Web site: http://www.goddard.edu/.

GREEN MOUNTAIN COLLEGE
POULTNEY, VERMONT

General Independent, 4-year, coed, affiliated with United Methodist Church **Entrance** Moderately difficult **Setting** 155-acre small-town campus **Total enrollment** 672 **Application deadline** Rolling (freshmen), rolling (transfer) **Freshmen** 65% were admitted **Housing** Yes **Expenses** Tuition $17,400; Room & Board $5300 **Undergraduates** 49% women, 8% part-time, 5% 25 or older, 0.5% Native American, 2% Hispanic American, 2% African American, 0.5% Asian American/Pacific Islander **The most frequently chosen baccalaureate fields are** education, health professions and related sciences, parks and recreation **Academic program** English as a second language, advanced placement, accelerated degree program, self-designed majors, honors program, summer session, adult/continuing education programs, internships **Contact** Ms. Merrilyn Tatarczuch-Koff, Dean of Enrollment Services, Green Mountain College, One College Circle, Poultney, VT 05764. Telephone: 802-287-8000 Ext. 8305 or toll-free 800-776-6675 (out-of-state). Fax: 802-287-8099. E-mail: admiss@greenmtn.edu. Web site: http://www.greenmtn.edu/.

JOHNSON STATE COLLEGE
JOHNSON, VERMONT

General State-supported, comprehensive, coed **Entrance** Moderately difficult **Setting** 350-acre rural campus **Total enrollment** 1,450 **Student/faculty ratio** 16:1 **Application deadline** Rolling (freshmen), rolling (transfer) **Freshmen** 83% were admitted **Housing** Yes **Expenses** Tuition $5047; Room & Board $5346 **Undergraduates** 61% women, 26% part-time, 10% 25 or older, 2% Native American, 1% Hispanic American, 0.5% African American, 0.2% Asian American/Pacific Islander **The most frequently chosen baccalaureate fields are** business/marketing, education, liberal arts/general studies **Academic program** English as a second language, advanced placement, accelerated degree program, honors program, summer session, internships **Contact** Ms. Kellie Rose, Assistant Director of Admissions, Johnson State College, 337 College Hill, Johnson, VT 05656-9405. Telephone: 802-635-1219 or toll-free 800-635-2356. Fax: 802-635-1230. E-mail: jscapply@badger.jsc.vsc.edu. Web site: http://www.jsc.vsc.edu/.

LYNDON STATE COLLEGE
LYNDONVILLE, VERMONT

General State-supported, comprehensive, coed **Entrance** Moderately difficult **Setting** 175-acre rural campus **Total enrollment** 1,179 **Student/faculty ratio** 17:1 **Application deadline** Rolling (freshmen), rolling (transfer) **Freshmen** 93% were admitted **Housing** Yes **Expenses** Tuition $5028; Room & Board $5346 **Undergraduates** 45% women, 15% part-time, 14% 25 or older, 0.2% Native American, 0.3% Hispanic American, 0% African American, 0.3% Asian American/Pacific Islander **The most frequently chosen baccalaureate fields are** business/marketing, communications/communication technologies, parks and recreation **Academic program** Advanced placement, self-designed majors, summer session, adult/continuing education programs, internships **Contact** Ms. Michelle Keenan, Director of Admissions, Lyndon State College, 1001 College Road, PO Box 919, Lyndonville, VT 05851. Telephone: 802-626-6413 or toll-free 800-225-1998 (in-state). Fax: 802-626-6335. E-mail: butlers@king.lsc.vsc.edu. Web site: http://www.lsc.vsc.edu/.

MARLBORO COLLEGE
MARLBORO, VERMONT

General Independent, comprehensive, coed **Entrance** Moderately difficult **Setting** 350-acre rural campus **Total enrollment** 417 **Student/faculty ratio** 7:1 **Application deadline** 3/1 (freshmen), 4/1 (transfer) **Freshmen** 70% were admitted **Housing** Yes **Expenses** Tuition 19,660; Room & Board 6750 **Undergraduates** 59% women, 6% part-time, 10% 25 or older, 1% Native American, 2% Hispanic American, 1% African American, 2% Asian American/Pacific Islander **The most frequently chosen baccalaureate fields are** social sciences and history, biological/life sciences, visual/performing arts **Academic program** Advanced placement, accelerated degree program, self-designed majors, internships **Contact** Ms. Julie E. Richardson, Vice President, Enrollment and Financial Aid, Marlboro College, PO Box A, South Road, Marlboro, VT 05344. Telephone: 802-258-9261 or toll-free 800-343-0049 (out-of-state). Fax: 802-257-4154. E-mail: admissions@marlboro.edu. Web site: http://www.marlboro.edu/.

MIDDLEBURY COLLEGE
MIDDLEBURY, VERMONT

General Independent, comprehensive, coed **Entrance** Very difficult **Setting** 350-acre small-town campus **Total enrollment** 2,284 **Student/faculty ratio** 10:1 **Application deadline** 12/15 (freshmen), 3/1 (transfer) **Freshmen** 25% were admitted **Housing** Yes **Expenses** Tuition 32,765 **Undergraduates** 51% women, 1% part-time, 20% 25 or older, 1% Native American, 4% Hispanic American, 3% African American, 7% Asian American/Pacific Islander **The most frequently chosen baccalaureate fields are** English, foreign language/literature, social sciences and history **Academic program** Advanced placement, accelerated degree program, self-designed majors, honors program, summer session, internships **Contact** Mr. John Hanson, Director of Admissions, Middlebury College, Emma Willard House, Middlebury, VT 05753-6002. Telephone: 802-443-3000. Fax: 802-443-2056. E-mail: admit@midd-unix.middlebury.edu. Web site: http://www.middlebury.edu/.

NORWICH UNIVERSITY
NORTHFIELD, VERMONT

General Independent, comprehensive, coed **Entrance** Moderately difficult **Setting** 1,125-acre small-town campus **Total enrollment** 2,703 **Student/faculty ratio** 12:1 **Application deadline** Rolling (freshmen), rolling (transfer) **Freshmen** 89% were admitted **Housing** Yes **Expenses** Tuition $15,626; Room & Board $5890 **Undergraduates** 39% women, 7% part-time, 23% 25 or older, 1% Native American, 4% Hispanic American, 3% African American, 2% Asian American/Pacific Islander **Academic program** English as a second language, advanced placement, summer session, adult/continuing education programs, internships **Contact** Ms. Karen McGrath, Dean of Enrollment Management, Norwich University, 158 Harmon Drive, Northfield, VT 05663. Telephone: 802-485-2013 or toll-free 800-468-6679 (in-state). Fax: 802-485-2580. E-mail: nuadm@norwich.edu. Web site: http://www.norwich.edu/.

▶ **For more information, see page 459.**

SAINT MICHAEL'S COLLEGE
COLCHESTER, VERMONT

General Independent Roman Catholic, comprehensive, coed **Entrance** Moderately difficult **Setting** 440-acre small-town campus **Total enrollment** 2,687 **Student/faculty ratio** 13:1 **Application deadline** 2/1 (freshmen), 2/1 (transfer) **Freshmen** 71% were admitted **Housing** Yes **Expenses** Tuition $19,680; Room & Board $7255 **Undergraduates** 55% women, 6% part-time, 3% 25 or older, 0% Native American, 1% Hispanic American, 1% African American, 1% Asian American/Pacific Islander **The most frequently chosen baccalaureate fields are** business/marketing, psychology, social sciences and history **Academic program** English as a second language, advanced placement, self-designed majors, honors program, summer session, internships **Contact** Ms. Jacqueline Murphy, Director of Admission, Saint Michael's College, One Winooski Park, Colchester, VT 05439. Telephone: 802-654-3000 or toll-free 800-762-8000. Fax: 802-654-2591. E-mail: admission@smcvt.edu. Web site: http://www.smcvt.edu/.

SOUTHERN VERMONT COLLEGE
BENNINGTON, VERMONT

General Independent, 4-year, coed **Entrance** Minimally difficult **Setting** 371-acre small-town campus **Total enrollment** 479 **Student/faculty ratio** 10:1 **Application deadline** Rolling (freshmen), rolling (transfer) **Freshmen** 75% were admitted **Housing** Yes **Expenses** Tuition $11,290; Room & Board $5648 **Undergraduates** 64% women, 41% part-time, 35% 25 or older, 1% Native American, 2% Hispanic American, 1% African American, 0.4% Asian American/Pacific Islander **The most frequently chosen baccalaureate fields are** business/marketing, protective services/public administration, psychology **Academic program** Advanced placement, accelerated degree program, self-designed majors, honors program, summer session, adult/continuing education programs, internships **Contact** Elizabeth Gatti, Director of Admissions, Southern Vermont College, 982 Mansion Drive, Bennington, VT 05201. Telephone: 802-447-6304 or toll-free 800-378-2782 (in-state). Fax: 802-447-4695. E-mail: admis@svc.edu. Web site: http://www.svc.edu/.

STERLING COLLEGE

CRAFTSBURY COMMON, VERMONT

General Independent, 4-year, coed **Entrance** Moderately difficult **Setting** 150-acre rural campus **Total enrollment** 74 **Student/faculty ratio** 6:1 **Application deadline** Rolling (freshmen), rolling (transfer) **Freshmen** 77% were admitted **Housing** Yes **Expenses** Tuition $13,300; Room & Board $5600 **Undergraduates** 49% women, 5% part-time, 4% 25 or older **Academic program** Self-designed majors, honors program, summer session, internships **Contact** John Zaber, Director of Admissions, Sterling College, PO Box 72, Craftsbury Common, VT 05827. Telephone: 802-586-7711 Ext. 40 or toll-free 800-648-3591. Fax: 802-586-2596. E-mail: admissns@sterlingcollege.crftsbury.vt.us. Web site: http://www.sterlingcollege.edu/.

UNIVERSITY OF VERMONT

BURLINGTON, VERMONT

General State-supported, university, coed **Entrance** Moderately difficult **Setting** 425-acre suburban campus **Total enrollment** 10,118 **Student/faculty ratio** 14:1 **Application deadline** 1/15 (freshmen), 4/1 (transfer) **Freshmen** 80% were admitted **Housing** Yes **Expenses** Tuition $8288; Room & Board $5806 **Undergraduates** 56% women, 17% part-time, 5% 25 or older, 0.2% Native American, 1% Hispanic American, 0.3% African American, 1% Asian American/Pacific Islander **The most frequently chosen baccalaureate fields are** natural resources/environmental science, business/marketing, social sciences and history **Academic program** English as a second language, advanced placement, self-designed majors, honors program, summer session, internships **Contact** Mr. Donald M. Honeman, Director of Admissions, University of Vermont, Office of Admissions, Burlington, VT 05401-3596. Telephone: 802-656-3370. Fax: 802-656-8611. E-mail: admissions@uvm.edu. Web site: http://www.uvm.edu/.

VERMONT TECHNICAL COLLEGE

RANDOLPH CENTER, VERMONT

General State-supported, 4-year, coed **Entrance** Minimally difficult **Setting** 544-acre rural campus **Total enrollment** 1,145 **Student/faculty ratio** 11:1 **Application deadline** Rolling (freshmen), rolling (transfer) **Freshmen** 71% were admitted **Housing** Yes **Expenses** Tuition 5830; Room & Board 5346 **Undergraduates** 31% women, 27% part-time, 22% 25 or older, 0.4% Native American, 1% Hispanic American, 0.4% African American, 1% Asian American/Pacific Islander **The most frequently chosen baccalaureate fields are** architecture, engineering/engineering technologies **Academic program** English as a second language, advanced placement, accelerated degree program, honors program, summer session, internships **Contact** Ms. Rosemary W. Distel, Director of Admissions, Vermont Technical College, PO Box 500, Randolph Center, VT 05061. Telephone: 802-728-1245 or toll-free 800-442-VTC1. Fax: 802-728-1390. E-mail: admissions@vtc.vsc.edu. Web site: http://www.vtc.vsc.edu/.

VIRGINIA

AMERICAN MILITARY UNIVERSITY

MANASSAS PARK, VIRGINIA

General Proprietary, comprehensive, coed, primarily men **Entrance** Noncompetitive **Total enrollment** 2,080 **Student/faculty ratio** 13:1 **Application deadline** Rolling (freshmen), rolling (transfer) **Freshmen** 95% were admitted **Housing** No **Expenses** Tuition $9000 **Undergraduates** 14% women, 85% part-time, 92% 25 or older, 8% African American **The most frequently chosen baccalaureate field is** military science/technologies **Academic program** Adult/continuing education programs **Contact** Ms. Nancy Tilton, Director of Admissions, American Military University, 9104-P Manassas Drive, Manassas Park, VA 20111. Telephone: 703-330-5398 Ext. 114 or toll-free 877-468-6268 Ext. 114 (in-state); 877-468-6268 (out-of-state). Fax: 703-330-5109. E-mail: amugen@amunet.edu. Web site: http://www.amunet.edu/.

THE ART INSTITUTE OF WASHINGTON

ARLINGTON, VIRGINIA

General Proprietary, 4-year, coed **Student/faculty ratio** 20:1 **Housing** No **Expenses** Tuition 28,722 **Contact** Ms. Ann Marie Drucker, Director of Admissions, The Art Institute of Washington, 1820 North Fort Myer Drive, Arlington, VA 22209. Telephone: 703-358-9550 or toll-free 877-303-3771. Web site: http://www.aiw.artinstitutes.edu/.

AVERETT UNIVERSITY

DANVILLE, VIRGINIA

General Independent Baptist, comprehensive, coed **Entrance** Moderately difficult **Setting** 25-acre suburban campus **Total enrollment** 2,030 **Student/faculty ratio** 15:1 **Application deadline** Rolling (transfer) **Freshmen** 82% were admitted **Housing** Yes **Expenses** Tuition $14,190; Room & Board $4797 **Undergraduates** 60% women, 33% part-time, 17% 25 or older, 0.4% Native American, 2% Hispanic American, 24% African American, 1% Asian American/Pacific Islander **The most frequently chosen baccalaureate fields are** business/marketing, education, psychology **Academic program** Advanced placement, accelerated degree program, self-designed majors, honors program, summer session, adult/continuing education programs, internships **Contact** Mr. Gary Sherman, Vice President of Enrollment Management, Averett University, English Hall, Danville, VA 24541. Telephone: 804-791-5660 or toll-free 800-AVERETT. Fax: 804-797-2784. E-mail: admit@averett.edu. Web site: http://www.averett.edu/.

BLUEFIELD COLLEGE
BLUEFIELD, VIRGINIA

General Independent Southern Baptist, 4-year, coed **Entrance** Moderately difficult **Setting** 85-acre small-town campus **Total enrollment** 827 **Student/faculty ratio** 13:1 **Application deadline** Rolling (freshmen), rolling (transfer) **Freshmen** 82% were admitted **Housing** Yes **Expenses** Tuition $9140; Room & Board $5060 **Undergraduates** 56% women, 10% part-time, 34% 25 or older, 2% Native American, 0.2% Hispanic American, 9% African American, 1% Asian American/Pacific Islander **Academic program** Advanced placement, accelerated degree program, self-designed majors, honors program, summer session, adult/continuing education programs, internships **Contact** Office of Admissions, Bluefield College, 3000 College Drive, Bluefield, VA 24605-1799. Telephone: 540-326-4214 or toll-free 800-872-0175. Fax: 540-326-4288. E-mail: admissions@mail.bluefield.edu. Web site: http://www.bluefield.edu/.

BRIDGEWATER COLLEGE
BRIDGEWATER, VIRGINIA

General Independent, 4-year, coed, affiliated with Church of the Brethren **Entrance** Moderately difficult **Setting** 190-acre small-town campus **Total enrollment** 1,223 **Student/faculty ratio** 15:1 **Application deadline** Rolling (freshmen), rolling (transfer) **Freshmen** 92% were admitted **Housing** Yes **Expenses** Tuition $15,490; Room & Board $7460 **Undergraduates** 57% women, 2% part-time, 1% 25 or older, 0.4% Native American, 1% Hispanic American, 6% African American, 1% Asian American/Pacific Islander **The most frequently chosen baccalaureate fields are** business/marketing, psychology, social sciences and history **Academic program** Advanced placement, honors program, summer session, adult/continuing education programs, internships **Contact** Mr. Brian C. Hildebrand, Dean for Enrollment Management, Bridgewater College, 402 East College Street, Bridgewater, VA 22812-1599. Telephone: 540-828-5375 or toll-free 800-759-8328. Fax: 540-828-5481. E-mail: admissions@bridgewater.edu. Web site: http://www.bridgewater.edu/.

CHRISTENDOM COLLEGE
FRONT ROYAL, VIRGINIA

General Independent Roman Catholic, comprehensive, coed **Entrance** Moderately difficult **Setting** 100-acre rural campus **Total enrollment** 356 **Student/faculty ratio** 12:1 **Application deadline** Rolling (freshmen), rolling (transfer) **Freshmen** 82% were admitted **Housing** Yes **Expenses** Tuition $11,530; Room & Board $4570 **Undergraduates** 57% women, 1% part-time, 3% 25 or older, 0% Native American, 3% Hispanic American, 1% African American, 1% Asian American/Pacific Islander **The most frequently chosen baccalaureate fields are** philosophy, religion, and theology, English, social sciences and history **Academic program** Advanced placement, accelerated degree program, summer session, internships **Contact** Mr. Paul Heisler, Director of Admissions, Christendom College, 134 Christendom Drive, Front Royal, VA 22630-5103. Telephone: 540-636-2900 Ext. 290 or toll-free 800-877-5456 Ext. 290. Fax: 540-636-1655. E-mail: cc_adm@shentel.net. Web site: http://www.christendom.edu/.

CHRISTOPHER NEWPORT UNIVERSITY
NEWPORT NEWS, VIRGINIA

General State-supported, comprehensive, coed **Entrance** Moderately difficult **Setting** 113-acre suburban campus **Total enrollment** 5,249 **Student/faculty ratio** 17:1 **Application deadline** 3/15 (freshmen), 7/1 (transfer) **Freshmen** 59% were admitted **Housing** Yes **Expenses** Tuition $3056; Room & Board $5350 **Undergraduates** 61% women, 25% part-time, 26% 25 or older, 1% Native American, 2% Hispanic American, 15% African American, 3% Asian American/Pacific Islander **The most frequently chosen baccalaureate fields are** business/marketing, psychology, social sciences and history **Academic program** Advanced placement, accelerated degree program, self-designed majors, honors program, summer session, adult/continuing education programs, internships **Contact** Ms. Angela Boyd, Associate Director of Admissions, Christopher Newport University, 1 University Place, Newport News, VA 23606-2998. Telephone: 757-594-7045 or toll-free 800-333-4CNU. Fax: 757-594-7333. E-mail: admit@cnu.edu. Web site: http://www.cnu.edu/.

CLINCH VALLEY COLLEGE OF THE UNIVERSITY OF VIRGINIA
See The University of Virginia's College at Wise

THE COLLEGE OF WILLIAM AND MARY
WILLIAMSBURG, VIRGINIA

General State-supported, university, coed **Entrance** Very difficult **Setting** 1,200-acre small-town campus **Total enrollment** 7,530 **Student/faculty ratio** 12:1 **Application deadline** 1/5 (freshmen), 2/15 (transfer) **Freshmen** 41% were admitted **Housing** Yes **Expenses** Tuition 4687; Room & Board 5096 **Undergraduates** 57% women, 2% part-time, 1% 25 or older, 0.3% Native American, 3% Hispanic American, 5% African American, 7% Asian American/Pacific Islander **The most frequently chosen baccalaureate fields are** business/marketing, biological/life sciences, social sciences and history **Academic program** Advanced placement, accelerated degree program, self-designed majors, honors program, summer session **Contact** Ms. Virginia Carey, Dean of Admission, The College of William and Mary, Office of Admission, PO Box 8795, Williamsburg, VA 23187-8795. Telephone: 757-221-4223. Fax: 757-221-1242. E-mail: admiss@facstaff.wm.edu. Web site: http://www.wm.edu/.

COMMUNITY HOSPITAL OF ROANOKE VALLEY–COLLEGE OF HEALTH SCIENCES
ROANOKE, VIRGINIA

General Independent, 4-year, coed **Entrance** Moderately difficult **Setting** 1-acre urban campus **Total enrollment** 508 **Student/faculty ratio** 20:1 **Application deadline** 7/31 (freshmen) **Freshmen** 61% were admitted **Housing** Yes **Expenses** Tuition $5430; Room only $2000 **Undergraduates** 77% women, 25% part-time, 51% 25 or older, 0.2% Native American, 0.4% Hispanic American, 8% African American, 4% Asian American/Pacific Islander **Academic program** Advanced placement, accelerated degree program, summer session, adult/continuing education programs, internships **Contact** Ms. Connie Cook, Admissions Representative, Community Hospital of Roanoke Valley–College of Health Sciences, PO Box 13186, Roanoke, VA 24031-3186. Telephone: 540-985-8563 or toll-free 888-985-8483. Fax: 540-985-9773. E-mail: rrobertson@health.chs.edu. Web site: http://www.chs.edu/.

EASTERN MENNONITE UNIVERSITY
HARRISONBURG, VIRGINIA

General Independent Mennonite, comprehensive, coed **Entrance** Moderately difficult **Setting** 92-acre small-town campus **Total enrollment** 1,398 **Student/faculty ratio** 13:1 **Application deadline** 8/1 (freshmen), 8/1 (transfer) **Freshmen** 83% were admitted **Housing** Yes **Expenses** Tuition $14,150; Room & Board $5120 **Undergraduates** 58% women, 6% part-time, 6% 25 or older, 0.4% Native American, 2% Hispanic American, 5% African American, 1% Asian American/Pacific Islander **The most frequently chosen baccalaureate fields are** business/marketing, education, health professions and related sciences **Academic program** English as a second language, advanced placement, honors program, summer session, adult/continuing education programs, internships **Contact** Ms. Ellen B. Miller, Director of Admissions, Eastern Mennonite University, 1200 Park Road, Harrisonburg, VA 22802-2462. Telephone: 540-432-4118 or toll-free 800-368-2665. Fax: 540-432-4444. E-mail: admiss@emu.edu. Web site: http://www.emu.edu/.

▶ **For more information, see page 411.**

EMORY & HENRY COLLEGE
EMORY, VIRGINIA

General Independent United Methodist, comprehensive, coed **Entrance** Moderately difficult **Setting** 163-acre rural campus **Total enrollment** 977 **Student/faculty ratio** 14:1 **Application deadline** Rolling (freshmen), rolling (transfer) **Freshmen** 74% were admitted **Housing** Yes **Expenses** Tuition $14,100; Room & Board $5362 **Undergraduates** 53% women, 4% part-time, 6% 25 or older, 0% Native American, 0.1% Hispanic American, 5% African American, 1% Asian American/Pacific Islander **The most frequently chosen baccalaureate fields are** business/marketing, communications/communication technologies, social sciences and history **Academic program** English as a second language, advanced placement, self-designed majors, honors program, summer session, internships **Contact** Ms. Debbie Jones Thompson, Dean of Admissions and Financial Aid, Emory & Henry College, 30479 Armbrister Drive, PO Box 10, Emory, VA 24327. Telephone: 540-944-6133 or toll-free 800-848-5493. Fax: 540-944-6935. E-mail: ehadmiss@ehc.edu. Web site: http://www.ehc.edu/.

▶ **For more information, see page 415.**

FERRUM COLLEGE
FERRUM, VIRGINIA

General Independent United Methodist, 4-year, coed **Entrance** Minimally difficult **Setting** 720-acre rural campus **Total enrollment** 920 **Student/faculty ratio** 13:1 **Application deadline** Rolling (freshmen), rolling (transfer) **Freshmen** 81% were admitted **Housing** Yes **Expenses** Tuition $11,900; Room & Board $5250 **Undergraduates** 41% women, 5% part-time, 8% 25 or older, 0.2% Native American, 2% Hispanic American, 19% African American, 1% Asian American/Pacific Islander **The most frequently chosen baccalaureate fields are** business/marketing, natural resources/environmental science, protective services/public administration **Academic program** Advanced placement, self-designed majors, summer session, adult/continuing education programs, internships **Contact** Ms. Gilda Q. Woods, Director of Admissions, Ferrum College, Spilman-Daniel House, PO Box 1000, Ferrum, VA 24088-9001. Telephone: 540-365-4290 or toll-free 800-868-9797. Fax: 540-365-4266. E-mail: admissions@ferrum.edu. Web site: http://www.ferrum.edu/.

▶ **For more information, see page 418.**

GEORGE MASON UNIVERSITY
FAIRFAX, VIRGINIA

General State-supported, university, coed **Entrance** Moderately difficult **Setting** 677-acre suburban campus **Total enrollment** 23,408 **Student/faculty ratio** 16:1 **Application deadline** 2/1 (freshmen), 3/15 (transfer) **Freshmen** 61% were admitted **Housing** Yes **Expenses** Tuition $3768; Room & Board $5240 **Undergraduates** 56% women, 29% part-time, 32% 25 or older, 0.4% Native American, 7% Hispanic American, 9% African American, 16% Asian American/Pacific Islander **The most frequently chosen baccalaureate fields are** business/marketing, education, social sciences and history **Academic program** English as a second language, advanced placement, accelerated degree program, self-designed majors, honors program, summer session, adult/continuing education programs, internships **Contact** Mr. Eddie Tallent, Director of Admissions, George Mason University, 4400 University Drive, MSN 3A4, Fairfax, VA 22030-4444. Telephone: 703-993-2398. Fax: 703-993-2392. E-mail: admissions@gmu.edu. Web site: http://www.gmu.edu/.

HAMPDEN-SYDNEY COLLEGE
HAMPDEN-SYDNEY, VIRGINIA

General Independent Presbyterian, 4-year, men only **Entrance** Moderately difficult **Setting** 660-acre rural campus **Total enrollment** 976 **Student/faculty ratio** 11:1 **Application deadline** 3/1 (freshmen), 7/1 (transfer) **Freshmen** 72% were admitted **Housing** Yes **Expenses** Tuition 17,688; Room & Board 6110 **Undergraduates** 0% 25 or older, 0.3% Native American, 1% Hispanic American, 3% African American, 0.4% Asian American/Pacific Islander **The most frequently chosen baccalaureate fields are** business/marketing, psychology, social sciences and history **Academic program** Advanced placement, accelerated degree program, honors program, summer session, internships **Contact** Ms. Anita H. Garland, Dean of Admissions, Hampden-Sydney College, PO Box 667, Hampden-Sydney, VA 23943-0667. Telephone: 804-223-6120 or toll-free 800-755-0733. Fax: 804-223-6346. E-mail: hsapp@hsc.edu. Web site: http://www.hsc.edu/.

HAMPTON UNIVERSITY
HAMPTON, VIRGINIA

General Independent, comprehensive, coed **Entrance** Moderately difficult **Setting** 210-acre urban campus **Total enrollment** 5,743 **Student/faculty ratio** 16:1 **Application deadline** 3/15 (freshmen), 3/15 (transfer) **Freshmen** 48% were admitted **Housing** Yes **Expenses** Tuition 16,200 **Undergraduates** 61% women, 6% part-time, 9% 25 or older, 0.3% Native American, 1% Hispanic American, 95% African American, 0.4% Asian American/Pacific Islander **The most frequently chosen baccalaureate fields are** business/marketing, psychology, social sciences and history **Academic program** Advanced placement, accelerated degree program, honors program, summer session, adult/continuing education programs, internships **Contact** Mr. Leonard M. Jones Jr., Director of Admissions, Hampton University, Office of Admissions, Hampton, VA 23668. Telephone: 757-727-5328 or toll-free 800-624-3328. Fax: 757-727-5084. E-mail: admit@hamptonu.edu. Web site: http://www.hamptonu.edu/.

HOLLINS UNIVERSITY
ROANOKE, VIRGINIA

General Independent, comprehensive, women only **Entrance** Moderately difficult **Setting** 475-acre suburban campus **Total enrollment** 1,033 **Student/faculty ratio** 9:1 **Application deadline** 2/15 (freshmen), 7/1 (transfer) **Freshmen** 81% were admitted **Housing** Yes **Expenses** Tuition 17,210; Room & Board 6415 **Undergraduates** 5% part-time, 9% 25 or older, 0% Native American, 2% Hispanic American, 5% African American, 2% Asian American/Pacific Islander **The most frequently chosen baccalaureate fields are** social sciences and history, psychology, visual/performing arts **Academic program** Advanced placement, accelerated degree program, self-designed majors, honors program, adult/continuing education programs, internships **Contact** Ms. Terri Reddings, Dean of Admissions, Hollins University, PO Box 9707, Roanoke, VA 24020-1707. Telephone: 540-362-6401 or toll-free 800-456-9595. Fax: 540-362-6218. E-mail: hcadm@matty.hollins.edu. Web site: http://www.hollins.edu/.

JAMES MADISON UNIVERSITY
HARRISONBURG, VIRGINIA

General State-supported, comprehensive, coed **Entrance** Very difficult **Setting** 472-acre small-town campus **Total enrollment** 15,326 **Student/faculty ratio** 17:1 **Application deadline** 1/15 (freshmen), 3/1 (transfer) **Freshmen** 64% were admitted **Housing** Yes **Expenses** Tuition $4000; Room & Board $5290 **Undergraduates** 58% women, 6% part-time, 2% 25 or older, 0.2% Native American, 2% Hispanic American, 4% African American, 4% Asian American/Pacific Islander **The most frequently chosen baccalaureate fields are** business/marketing, psychology, social sciences and history **Academic program** English as a second language, advanced placement, accelerated degree program, honors program, summer session, adult/continuing education programs, internships **Contact** Ms. Laika Tamny, Associate Director of Admission, James Madison University, Office of Admission, Sonner Hall MSC 0101, Harrisonburg, VA 22807. Telephone: 540-568-6147. Fax: 540-568-3332. E-mail: gotojmu@jmu.edu. Web site: http://www.jmu.edu/.

LIBERTY UNIVERSITY
LYNCHBURG, VIRGINIA

General Independent nondenominational, comprehensive, coed **Entrance** Minimally difficult **Setting** 160-acre suburban campus **Total enrollment** 6,192 **Student/faculty ratio** 23:1 **Application deadline** 6/30 (freshmen), 6/30 (transfer) **Freshmen** 60% were admitted **Housing** Yes **Expenses** Tuition $9500; Room & Board $5000 **Undergraduates** 51% women, 15% part-time, 17% 25 or older, 1% Native American, 3% Hispanic American, 8% African American, 2% Asian American/Pacific Islander **The most frequently chosen baccalaureate fields are** business/marketing, philosophy, religion, and theology, psychology **Academic program** English as a second language, advanced placement, accelerated degree program, self-designed majors, honors program, summer session, internships **Contact** Mr. David Hart, Associate Director of Admissions, Liberty University, 1971 University Boulevard, Lynchburg, VA 24502. Telephone: 804-582-7307 or toll-free 800-543-5317. Fax: 804-582-2421. E-mail: admissions@liberty.edu. Web site: http://www.liberty.edu/.

LONGWOOD COLLEGE
FARMVILLE, VIRGINIA

General State-supported, comprehensive, coed **Entrance** Moderately difficult **Setting** 160-acre small-town campus **Total enrollment** 3,961 **Student/faculty ratio** 19:1 **Application deadline** 3/1 (fresh-

Longwood College *(continued)*

men), 6/1 (transfer) **Freshmen** 77% were admitted **Housing** Yes **Expenses** Tuition 4003; Room & Board 4820 **Undergraduates** 65% women, 4% part-time, 3% 25 or older, 0.2% Native American, 2% Hispanic American, 9% African American, 2% Asian American/ Pacific Islander **The most frequently chosen baccalaureate fields are** business/marketing, education, social sciences and history **Academic program** English as a second language, advanced placement, accelerated degree program, honors program, summer session, adult/continuing education programs, internships **Contact** Mr. Robert J. Chonko, Director of Admissions, Longwood College, 201 High Street, Farmville, VA 23909. Telephone: 804-395-2060 or toll-free 800-281-4677. Fax: 804-395-2332. E-mail: lcadmit@longwood.lwc.edu. Web site: http://www.lwc.edu/.

LYNCHBURG COLLEGE
LYNCHBURG, VIRGINIA

General Independent, comprehensive, coed, affiliated with Christian Church (Disciples of Christ) **Entrance** Moderately difficult **Setting** 214-acre suburban campus **Total enrollment** 1,932 **Student/ faculty ratio** 15:1 **Application deadline** Rolling (freshmen), rolling (transfer) **Freshmen** 82% were admitted **Housing** Yes **Expenses** Tuition $19,005; Room & Board $4400 **Undergraduates** 15% 25 or older, 1% Native American, 2% Hispanic American, 10% African American, 1% Asian American/Pacific Islander **The most frequently chosen baccalaureate fields are** business/marketing, education, social sciences and history **Academic program** Advanced placement, accelerated degree program, honors program, summer session, adult/continuing education programs, internships **Contact** Ms. Sharon Walters-Bower, Director of Recruitment, Lynchburg College, 1501 Lakeside Drive, Lynchburg, VA 24501-3199. Telephone: 804-544-8300 or toll-free 800-426-8101. Fax: 804-544-8653. E-mail: admissions@lynchburg.edu. Web site: http://www.lynchburg.edu/.

MARY BALDWIN COLLEGE
STAUNTON, VIRGINIA

General Independent, comprehensive, coed, primarily women, affiliated with Presbyterian Church (U.S.A.) **Entrance** Moderately difficult **Setting** 54-acre small-town campus **Total enrollment** 1,451 **Student/faculty ratio** 11:1 **Application deadline** Rolling (freshmen), rolling (transfer) **Freshmen** 93% were admitted **Housing** Yes **Expenses** Tuition $15,310; Room & Board $7450 **Undergraduates** 95% women, 28% part-time, 41% 25 or older, 0.2% Native American, 3% Hispanic American, 15% African American, 2% Asian American/Pacific Islander **The most frequently chosen baccalaureate fields are** business/ marketing, psychology, social sciences and history **Academic program** English as a second language, advanced placement, accelerated degree program, self-designed majors, honors program, adult/ continuing education programs, internships **Contact** Ms. Lisa Branson, Assistant Director for Freshmen Services, Mary Baldwin College, Frederick and New Streets, Staunton, VA 24401. Telephone: 540-887-7221 Ext. 7287 or toll-free 800-468-2262. Fax: 540-886-6634. E-mail: dcampbel@cit.mbc.edu. Web site: http://www.mbc.edu/.

MARYMOUNT UNIVERSITY
ARLINGTON, VIRGINIA

General Independent, comprehensive, coed, affiliated with Roman Catholic Church **Entrance** Moderately difficult **Setting** 21-acre suburban campus **Total enrollment** 3,422 **Student/faculty ratio** 11:1 **Application deadline** Rolling (freshmen), rolling (transfer) **Freshmen** 78% were admitted **Housing** Yes **Expenses** Tuition $14,420; Room & Board $6350 **Undergraduates** 72% women, 27% part-time, 33% 25 or older, 0.2% Native American, 7% Hispanic American, 16% African American, 7% Asian American/ Pacific Islander **Academic program** English as a second language, advanced placement, self-designed majors, summer session, internships **Contact** Mr. Mike Canfield, Associate Director of Undergraduate Admissions, Marymount University, 2807 North Glebe Road, Arlington, VA 22207-4299. Telephone: 703-284-1500 or toll-free 800-548-7638. Fax: 703-522-0349. E-mail: admissions@marymount.edu. Web site: http://www.marymount.edu/.

▶ **For more information, see page 447.**

MARY WASHINGTON COLLEGE
FREDERICKSBURG, VIRGINIA

General State-supported, comprehensive, coed **Entrance** Very difficult **Setting** 176-acre small-town campus **Total enrollment** 4,282 **Student/faculty ratio** 17:1 **Application deadline** 2/1 (freshmen), 3/1 (transfer) **Freshmen** 56% were admitted **Housing** Yes **Expenses** Tuition 3246; Room & Board 5448 **Undergraduates** 69% women, 18% part-time, 24% 25 or older, 0.3% Native American, 2% Hispanic American, 4% African American, 4% Asian American/ Pacific Islander **The most frequently chosen baccalaureate fields are** liberal arts/general studies, business/marketing, social sciences and history **Academic program** Advanced placement, accelerated degree program, self-designed majors, summer session, adult/continuing education programs, internships **Contact** Dr. Jenifer Blair, Dean of Undergraduate Admissions, Mary Washington College, 1301 College Avenue, Fredericksburg, VA 22401-5358. Telephone: 540-654-2000 or toll-free 800-468-5614. E-mail: admit@mwc.edu. Web site: http://www.mwc.edu/.

NORFOLK STATE UNIVERSITY
NORFOLK, VIRGINIA

General State-supported, comprehensive, coed **Entrance** Moderately difficult **Setting** 130-acre urban campus **Total enrollment** 6,668 **Student/faculty ratio** 19:1 **Application deadline** Rolling (freshmen), rolling (transfer) **Freshmen** 82% were admitted **Housing** Yes **Expenses** Tuition $2856; Room & Board

$5267 **Undergraduates** 64% women, 15% part-time, 30% 25 or older, 0.4% Native American, 1% Hispanic American, 92% African American, 1% Asian American/Pacific Islander **The most frequently chosen baccalaureate fields are** interdisciplinary studies, business/marketing, social sciences and history **Academic program** Advanced placement, accelerated degree program, self-designed majors, honors program, summer session, adult/continuing education programs, internships **Contact** Ms. Michelle Marable, Director of Admissions, Norfolk State University, 700 Park Avenue, Norfolk, VA 23504. Telephone: 757-823-8396. Fax: 757-683-2078. Web site: http://www.nsu.edu/.

OLD DOMINION UNIVERSITY
NORFOLK, VIRGINIA

General State-supported, university, coed **Entrance** Moderately difficult **Setting** 186-acre urban campus **Total enrollment** 18,969 **Student/faculty ratio** 17:1 **Application deadline** 2/15 (freshmen), 6/1 (transfer) **Freshmen** 70% were admitted **Housing** Yes **Expenses** Tuition $3916; Room & Board $5232 **Undergraduates** 57% women, 35% part-time, 33% 25 or older, 1% Native American, 3% Hispanic American, 23% African American, 6% Asian American/Pacific Islander **The most frequently chosen baccalaureate fields are** engineering/engineering technologies, business/marketing, health professions and related sciences **Academic program** English as a second language, advanced placement, accelerated degree program, self-designed majors, honors program, summer session, adult/continuing education programs, internships **Contact** Ms. Alice McAdory, (Acting) Director of Admissions, Old Dominion University, 108 Rollins Hall, Norfolk, VA 23529-0050. Telephone: 757-683-3637 or toll-free 800-348-7926. Fax: 757-683-3255. E-mail: aos@shawnee.oa.odu.edu. Web site: http://odu.edu/.

RADFORD UNIVERSITY
RADFORD, VIRGINIA

General State-supported, comprehensive, coed **Entrance** Moderately difficult **Setting** 177-acre small-town campus **Total enrollment** 8,837 **Student/faculty ratio** 19:1 **Application deadline** 5/1 (freshmen), rolling (transfer) **Freshmen** 76% were admitted **Housing** Yes **Expenses** Tuition $2950; Room & Board $4938 **Undergraduates** 60% women, 7% part-time, 0.3% Native American, 1% Hispanic American, 7% African American, 2% Asian American/Pacific Islander **The most frequently chosen baccalaureate fields are** business/marketing, interdisciplinary studies, protective services/public administration **Academic program** English as a second language, advanced placement, accelerated degree program, self-designed majors, honors program, summer session, adult/continuing education programs, internships **Contact** Dr. David Kraus, Director of Admissions and Records, Radford University, PO Box 6903, RU Station, Radford, VA 24142. Telephone: 540-831-5371 or toll-free 800-890-4265. Fax: 540-831-5038. E-mail: pwhite@runet.edu. Web site: http://www.radford.edu/.

RANDOLPH-MACON COLLEGE
ASHLAND, VIRGINIA

General Independent United Methodist, 4-year, coed **Entrance** Moderately difficult **Setting** 110-acre suburban campus **Total enrollment** 1,171 **Student/faculty ratio** 11:1 **Application deadline** 3/1 (freshmen), 3/1 (transfer) **Freshmen** 72% were admitted **Housing** Yes **Expenses** Tuition $18,350; Room & Board $4205 **Undergraduates** 51% women, 3% part-time, 1% 25 or older, 0.2% Native American, 1% Hispanic American, 5% African American, 1% Asian American/Pacific Islander **The most frequently chosen baccalaureate fields are** business/marketing, English, social sciences and history **Academic program** Advanced placement, accelerated degree program, honors program, summer session, internships **Contact** Mr. John C. Conkright, Dean of Admissions and Financial Aid, Randolph-Macon College, PO Box 5005, Ashland, VA 23005-5505. Telephone: 804-752-7305 or toll-free 800-888-1762. Fax: 804-752-4707. E-mail: admissions_office@rmc.edu. Web site: http://www.rmc.edu/.

RANDOLPH-MACON WOMAN'S COLLEGE
LYNCHBURG, VIRGINIA

General Independent Methodist, 4-year, women only **Entrance** Moderately difficult **Setting** 100-acre suburban campus **Total enrollment** 748 **Student/faculty ratio** 9:1 **Application deadline** 2/15 (freshmen), 6/1 (transfer) **Freshmen** 82% were admitted **Housing** Yes **Expenses** Tuition 17,680; Room & Board 7160 **Undergraduates** 6% part-time, 9% 25 or older, 0.4% Native American, 4% Hispanic American, 7% African American, 3% Asian American/Pacific Islander **The most frequently chosen baccalaureate fields are** psychology, biological/life sciences, social sciences and history **Academic program** Advanced placement, accelerated degree program, self-designed majors, honors program, adult/continuing education programs, internships **Contact** Pat LeDonne, Director of Admissions, Randolph-Macon Woman's College, 2500 Rivermont Avenue, Lynchburg, VA 24503-1526. Telephone: 804-947-8100 or toll-free 800-745-7692. Fax: 804-947-8996. E-mail: admissions@rmwc.edu. Web site: http://www.rmwc.edu/.

ROANOKE COLLEGE
SALEM, VIRGINIA

General Independent, 4-year, coed, affiliated with Evangelical Lutheran Church in America **Entrance** Moderately difficult **Setting** 68-acre suburban campus **Total enrollment** 1,677 **Student/faculty ratio** 14:1 **Application deadline** 3/1 (freshmen), 8/1 (transfer) **Freshmen** 81% were admitted **Housing** Yes **Expenses** Tuition $17,765; Room & Board $5722 **Undergraduates** 61% women, 6% part-time, 6% 25 or older, 0.2% Native American, 1% Hispanic American, 3% African American, 2% Asian American/Pacific Islander **The most frequently chosen baccalaureate fields are** business/marketing, English, social sciences and history **Academic program**

Roanoke College *(continued)*

English as a second language, advanced placement, accelerated degree program, honors program, summer session, adult/continuing education programs, internships **Contact** Mr. Michael C. Maxey, Vice President of Admissions, Roanoke College, 221 College Lane, Salem, VA 24153. Telephone: 540-375-2270 or toll-free 800-388-2276. Fax: 540-375-2267. E-mail: admissions@roanoke.edu. Web site: http://www.roanoke.edu/.

SAINT PAUL'S COLLEGE
LAWRENCEVILLE, VIRGINIA

General Independent Episcopal, 4-year, coed **Entrance** Minimally difficult **Setting** 75-acre small-town campus **Total enrollment** 531 **Student/faculty ratio** 17:1 **Freshmen** 88% were admitted **Housing** Yes **Expenses** Tuition 8380; Room & Board 4568 **Undergraduates** 1% 25 or older, 0% Native American, 0% Hispanic American, 97% African American, 0% Asian American/Pacific Islander **Academic program** Honors program, summer session, adult/continuing education programs, internships **Contact** Mr. Michael C Taylor, Director of Admissions, Saint Paul's College, 115 College Drive, Lawrenceville, VA 23868. Telephone: 804-848-4268 or toll-free 800-678-7071. Fax: 804-848-0229. E-mail: mtaylor@saintpauls.edu. Web site: http://www.saintpauls.edu.

SHENANDOAH UNIVERSITY
WINCHESTER, VIRGINIA

General Independent United Methodist, comprehensive, coed **Entrance** Moderately difficult **Setting** 100-acre small-town campus **Total enrollment** 2,428 **Student/faculty ratio** 10:1 **Application deadline** Rolling (freshmen), rolling (transfer) **Freshmen** 97% were admitted **Housing** Yes **Expenses** Tuition 16,300; Room & Board 6000 **Undergraduates** 57% women, 9% part-time, 15% 25 or older, 0.2% Native American, 2% Hispanic American, 10% African American, 1% Asian American/Pacific Islander **The most frequently chosen baccalaureate fields are** business/marketing, education, health professions and related sciences **Academic program** English as a second language, advanced placement, accelerated degree program, summer session, adult/continuing education programs, internships **Contact** Mr. Michael Carpenter, Director of Admissions, Shenandoah University, 1460 University Drive, Winchester, VA 22601-5195. Telephone: 540-665-4581 or toll-free 800-432-2266. Fax: 540-665-4627. E-mail: admit@su.edu. Web site: http://www.su.edu/.

▶ **For more information, see page 467.**

SOUTHERN VIRGINIA COLLEGE
BUENA VISTA, VIRGINIA

General Independent, 4-year, coed **Total enrollment** 420 **Freshmen** 99% were admitted **Expenses** Tuition 11,060; Room & Board 4400 **Undergraduates** 60% women, 5% 25 or older, 0.2% Native American, 2% Hispanic American, 1% African American, 2% Asian American/Pacific Islander **Academic program** Summer session **Contact** Ms. Lorie Davis, Director of Admissions, Southern Virginia College, One College Hill Drive, Buena Vista, VA 24416. Telephone: 703-261-8420 or toll-free 800-229-8420. Web site: http://www.southernvirginia.edu/.

SWEET BRIAR COLLEGE
SWEET BRIAR, VIRGINIA

General Independent, 4-year, women only **Entrance** Moderately difficult **Setting** 3,300-acre rural campus **Total enrollment** 749 **Student/faculty ratio** 7:1 **Application deadline** 2/15 (freshmen), 7/1 (transfer) **Freshmen** 89% were admitted **Housing** Yes **Expenses** Tuition $18,010; Room & Board $7300 **Undergraduates** 7% part-time, 2% 25 or older, 1% Native American, 3% Hispanic American, 4% African American, 2% Asian American/Pacific Islander **The most frequently chosen baccalaureate fields are** psychology, English, social sciences and history **Academic program** Advanced placement, accelerated degree program, self-designed majors, honors program, summer session, adult/continuing education programs, internships **Contact** Ms. Margaret Williams Blount, Director of Admissions, Sweet Briar College, PO Box B, Sweet Briar, VA 24595. Telephone: 804-381-6142 or toll-free 800-381-6142. Fax: 804-381-6152. E-mail: admissions@sbc.edu. Web site: http://www.sbc.edu/.

UNIVERSITY OF RICHMOND
RICHMOND, VIRGINIA

General Independent, comprehensive, coed **Entrance** Very difficult **Setting** 350-acre suburban campus **Total enrollment** 3,583 **Student/faculty ratio** 10:1 **Application deadline** 1/15 (freshmen), 2/15 (transfer) **Freshmen** 42% were admitted **Housing** Yes **Expenses** Tuition $22,570; Room & Board $4730 **Undergraduates** 51% women, 0% 25 or older, 0.1% Native American, 2% Hispanic American, 5% African American, 3% Asian American/Pacific Islander **The most frequently chosen baccalaureate fields are** business/marketing, area/ethnic studies, social sciences and history **Academic program** English as a second language, advanced placement, accelerated degree program, self-designed majors, honors program, summer session, adult/continuing education programs, internships **Contact** Ms. Pamela Spence, Dean of Admission, University of Richmond, 28 Westhampton Way, University of Richmond, VA 23173. Telephone: 804-289-8640 or toll-free 800-700-1662. Fax: 804-287-6003. E-mail: admissions@urich.edu. Web site: http://www.richmond.edu/.

UNIVERSITY OF VIRGINIA
CHARLOTTESVILLE, VIRGINIA

General State-supported, university, coed **Entrance** Most difficult **Setting** 1,133-acre suburban campus **Total enrollment** 22,411 **Student/faculty ratio** 15:1 **Application deadline** 1/2 (freshmen), 3/1 (transfer) **Freshmen** 39% were admitted **Housing** Yes **Expenses**

Tuition $4335; Room & Board $4767 **Undergraduates** 54% women, 8% part-time, 2% 25 or older, 0.3% Native American, 2% Hispanic American, 10% African American, 10% Asian American/Pacific Islander **The most frequently chosen baccalaureate fields are** business/marketing, engineering/engineering technologies, social sciences and history **Academic program** Advanced placement, accelerated degree program, self-designed majors, honors program, summer session, adult/continuing education programs, internships **Contact** Mr. John A. Blackburn, Dean of Admission, University of Virginia, PO Box 400160, Charlottesville, VA 22904-4160. Telephone: 804-982-3200. Fax: 804-924-3587. E-mail: undergrad-admission@virginia.edu. Web site: http://www.virginia.edu/.

THE UNIVERSITY OF VIRGINIA'S COLLEGE AT WISE
WISE, VIRGINIA

General State-supported, 4-year, coed **Entrance** Moderately difficult **Setting** 350-acre small-town campus **Total enrollment** 1,447 **Student/faculty ratio** 18:1 **Application deadline** 8/1 (freshmen), 8/15 (transfer) **Freshmen** 73% were admitted **Housing** Yes **Expenses** Tuition 3330; Room & Board 5080 **Undergraduates** 56% women, 20% part-time, 21% 25 or older, 0.2% Native American, 1% Hispanic American, 4% African American, 1% Asian American/Pacific Islander **The most frequently chosen baccalaureate fields are** business/marketing, psychology, social sciences and history **Academic program** Advanced placement, accelerated degree program, self-designed majors, honors program, summer session, adult/continuing education programs, internships **Contact** Mr. Russell Necessary, Director of Admissions and Financial Aid, The University of Virginia's College at Wise, 1 College Avenue, Wise, VA 24293. Telephone: 540-328-0322 or toll-free 888-282-9324. Fax: 540-328-0251. E-mail: admissions@uvawise.edu. Web site: http://www.uvawise.edu.

VIRGINIA COMMONWEALTH UNIVERSITY
RICHMOND, VIRGINIA

General State-supported, university, coed **Entrance** Moderately difficult **Setting** 126-acre urban campus **Total enrollment** 24,066 **Student/faculty ratio** 13:1 **Application deadline** 2/1 (freshmen), 8/1 (transfer) **Freshmen** 76% were admitted **Housing** Yes **Expenses** Tuition 3650; Room & Board 4955 **Undergraduates** 60% women, 30% part-time, 20% 25 or older, 1% Native American, 3% Hispanic American, 23% African American, 8% Asian American/Pacific Islander **The most frequently chosen baccalaureate fields are** business/marketing, health professions and related sciences, visual/performing arts **Academic program** English as a second language, advanced placement, accelerated degree program, self-designed majors, honors program, summer session, adult/continuing education programs, internships **Contact** Counseling Staff, Virginia Commonwealth University, 821 West Franklin Street, Box 842526, Richmond, VA 23284-9005. Telephone: 804-828-1222 or toll-free 800-841-3638. Fax: 804-828-1899. E-mail: vcuinfo@vcu.edu. Web site: http://www.vcu.edu/.

VIRGINIA INTERMONT COLLEGE
BRISTOL, VIRGINIA

General Independent, 4-year, coed, affiliated with Baptist Church **Entrance** Minimally difficult **Setting** 27-acre small-town campus **Total enrollment** 835 **Student/faculty ratio** 14:1 **Application deadline** Rolling (freshmen), rolling (transfer) **Freshmen** 69% were admitted **Housing** Yes **Expenses** Tuition 12,210; Room & Board 5300 **Undergraduates** 75% women, 12% part-time, 42% 25 or older, 1% Native American, 0.5% Hispanic American, 4% African American, 0.5% Asian American/Pacific Islander **The most frequently chosen baccalaureate fields are** business/marketing, agriculture, education **Academic program** Advanced placement, summer session, adult/continuing education programs, internships **Contact** Ms. Robin B. Cozart, Director of Admissions, Virginia Intermont College, 1013 Moore Street, Bristol, VA 24201-4298. Telephone: 540-466-7854 or toll-free 800-451-1842. Fax: 540-466-7855. E-mail: viadmit@vic.edu. Web site: http://www.vic.edu/.

VIRGINIA MILITARY INSTITUTE
LEXINGTON, VIRGINIA

General State-supported, 4-year, coed, primarily men **Entrance** Moderately difficult **Setting** 140-acre small-town campus **Total enrollment** 1,300 **Student/faculty ratio** 12:1 **Application deadline** 3/1 (freshmen), 3/1 (transfer) **Freshmen** 66% were admitted **Housing** Yes **Expenses** Tuition 5072; Room & Board 4564 **Undergraduates** 5% women, 0% 25 or older, 0.2% Native American, 3% Hispanic American, 6% African American, 4% Asian American/Pacific Islander **The most frequently chosen baccalaureate fields are** engineering/engineering technologies, English, social sciences and history **Academic program** Advanced placement, accelerated degree program, honors program, summer session, internships **Contact** Lt. Col. Tom Mortenson, Associate Director of Admissions, Virginia Military Institute, Admissions Office, 309 Letcher Avenue, Lexington, VA 24450. Telephone: 540-464-7211 or toll-free 800-767-4207. Fax: 540-464-7746. E-mail: admissions@vmi.edu. Web site: http://www.vmi.edu/.

VIRGINIA POLYTECHNIC INSTITUTE AND STATE UNIVERSITY
BLACKSBURG, VIRGINIA

General State-supported, university, coed **Entrance** Moderately difficult **Setting** 2,600-acre small-town campus **Total enrollment** 25,643 **Student/faculty ratio** 19:1 **Application deadline** 1/15 (freshmen), 3/1 (transfer) **Freshmen** 63% were admitted **Housing** Yes **Expenses** Tuition 3640; Room & Board 3954 **Undergraduates** 41% women, 3% part-time, 0.2% Native American, 2% Hispanic American, 4% African American, 6% Asian American/Pacific Islander

Virginia Polytechnic Institute and State University *(continued)*

The most frequently chosen baccalaureate fields are business/marketing, engineering/engineering technologies, home economics/vocational home economics **Academic program** English as a second language, advanced placement, accelerated degree program, honors program, summer session, adult/continuing education programs, internships **Contact** Ms. Mildred Johnson, Associate Director for Freshmen Admissions, Virginia Polytechnic Institute and State University, 201 Burruss Hall, Blacksburg, VA 24061. Telephone: 540-231-6267. Fax: 540-231-3242. E-mail: vtadmiss@vt.edu. Web site: http://www.vt.edu/.

VIRGINIA STATE UNIVERSITY
PETERSBURG, VIRGINIA

General State-supported, comprehensive, coed **Entrance** Minimally difficult **Setting** 236-acre suburban campus **Total enrollment** 4,353 **Student/faculty ratio** 17:1 **Application deadline** 5/1 (freshmen), 5/1 (transfer) **Freshmen** 89% were admitted **Housing** Yes **Expenses** Tuition $3312; Room & Board $5594 **Undergraduates** 56% women, 9% part-time, 7% 25 or older, 0.03% Native American, 1% Hispanic American, 96% African American, 0.2% Asian American/Pacific Islander **Academic program** Advanced placement, self-designed majors, honors program, summer session, adult/continuing education programs, internships **Contact** Ms. Lisa Winn, Director of Admissions, Virginia State University, PO Box 9018, Petersburg, VA 23806-2096. Telephone: 804-524-5902 or toll-free 800-871-7611. E-mail: lwinn@vsu.edu. Web site: http://www.vsu.edu/.

VIRGINIA UNION UNIVERSITY
RICHMOND, VIRGINIA

General Independent Baptist, comprehensive, coed **Entrance** Moderately difficult **Setting** 72-acre urban campus **Total enrollment** 1,700 **Student/faculty ratio** 16:1 **Application deadline** Rolling (freshmen), rolling (transfer) **Housing** Yes **Expenses** Tuition 9580; Room & Board 4250 **Academic program** English as a second language, advanced placement, honors program, summer session, adult/continuing education programs, internships **Contact** Mr. Gil Powell, Director of Admissions, Virginia Union University, 1500 North Lombardy Street, Richmond, VA 23220-1170. Telephone: 804-257-5881 or toll-free 800-368-3227 (out-of-state).

VIRGINIA WESLEYAN COLLEGE
NORFOLK, VIRGINIA

General Independent United Methodist, 4-year, coed **Entrance** Moderately difficult **Setting** 300-acre urban campus **Total enrollment** 1,421 **Student/faculty ratio** 13:1 **Application deadline** Rolling (freshmen), rolling (transfer) **Freshmen** 95% were admitted **Housing** Yes **Expenses** Tuition $16,500; Room & Board $5850 **Undergraduates** 68% women, 25% part-time, 35% 25 or older, 1% Native American, 2% Hispanic American, 12% African American, 2% Asian American/Pacific Islander **The most frequently chosen baccalaureate fields are** business/marketing, interdisciplinary studies, social sciences and history **Academic program** Advanced placement, self-designed majors, honors program, summer session, adult/continuing education programs, internships **Contact** Mr. Richard T. Hinshaw, Vice President for Enrollment Management, Dean of Admissions, Virginia Wesleyan College, Office of Admissions, Virginia Wesleyan College, 1584 Wesleyan Drive, Norfolk, VA 23502-5599. Telephone: 757-455-3208 or toll-free 800-737-8684. Fax: 757-461-5238. E-mail: admissions@vwc.edu. Web site: http://www.vwc.edu/.

▶ **For more information, see page 484.**

WASHINGTON AND LEE UNIVERSITY
LEXINGTON, VIRGINIA

General Independent, comprehensive, coed **Entrance** Most difficult **Setting** 322-acre small-town campus **Total enrollment** 2,100 **Student/faculty ratio** 9:1 **Application deadline** 1/15 (freshmen), 4/1 (transfer) **Freshmen** 35% were admitted **Housing** Yes **Expenses** Tuition 17,965; Room & Board 5690 **Undergraduates** 46% women, 0.2% part-time, 0.2% 25 or older, 0.1% Native American, 1% Hispanic American, 3% African American, 1% Asian American/Pacific Islander **The most frequently chosen baccalaureate fields are** business/marketing, biological/life sciences, social sciences and history **Academic program** Advanced placement, accelerated degree program, self-designed majors, honors program, internships **Contact** Mr. William M. Hartog, Dean of Admissions and Financial Aid, Washington and Lee University, Lexington, VA 24450-0303. Telephone: 540-463-8710. Fax: 540-463-8062. E-mail: admissions@wlu.edu. Web site: http://www.wlu.edu/.

WORLD COLLEGE
VIRGINIA BEACH, VIRGINIA

General Proprietary, 4-year, coed **Entrance** Noncompetitive **Setting** suburban campus **Total enrollment** 348 **Application deadline** Rolling (freshmen) **Housing** No **Expenses** Tuition $2243 **Undergraduates** 92% 25 or older **Academic program** Accelerated degree program, adult/continuing education programs **Contact** Michael Smith, Director of Operations and Registrar, World College, 5193 Shore Drive, Suite 105, Virginia Beach, VA 23455. Telephone: 757-464-4600 or toll-free 800-696-7532. Fax: 757-464-3687. E-mail: instruct@cie-wc.edu.

WASHINGTON

ANTIOCH UNIVERSITY SEATTLE
SEATTLE, WASHINGTON

General Independent, upper-level, coed **Entrance** Noncompetitive **Setting** urban campus **Total enroll-**

ment 834 **Student/faculty ratio** 8:1 **Application deadline** 9/15 (transfer) **Housing** No **Expenses** Tuition 11,070 **Undergraduates** 78% women, 75% part-time, 95% 25 or older, 3% Native American, 3% Hispanic American, 8% African American, 1% Asian American/Pacific Islander **Academic program** Advanced placement, accelerated degree program, self-designed majors, summer session, adult/continuing education programs **Contact** Ms. Dianne Larsen, Admissions Director, Antioch University Seattle, 2326 Sixth Avenue, Seattle, WA 98121. Telephone: 206-441-5352 Ext. 5200. E-mail: dawn_rhodes@cloud.seattleantioch.edu. Web site: http://www.antiochsea.edu/.

BASTYR UNIVERSITY
KENMORE, WASHINGTON

General Independent, upper-level, coed **Setting** 50-acre suburban campus **Total enrollment** 911 **Student/faculty ratio** 15:1 **Application deadline** 3/15 (transfer) **First-Year Students** 77% were admitted **Housing** Yes **Expenses** Tuition $10,000; Room only $3500 **Undergraduates** 79% women, 21% part-time, 56% 25 or older, 0% Native American, 3% Hispanic American, 1% African American, 3% Asian American/Pacific Islander **The most frequently chosen baccalaureate field is** biological/life sciences **Academic program** Summer session, internships **Contact** Mr. Richard Dent, Director of Student Enrollment, Bastyr University, 14500 Juanita Drive, NE, Kenmore, WA 98028-4966. Telephone: 425-602-3080. Fax: 425-823-6222. Web site: http://www.bastyr.edu/.

CENTRAL WASHINGTON UNIVERSITY
ELLENSBURG, WASHINGTON

General State-supported, comprehensive, coed **Entrance** Moderately difficult **Setting** 380-acre small-town campus **Total enrollment** 8,050 **Student/faculty ratio** 16:1 **Application deadline** Rolling (freshmen), rolling (transfer) **Freshmen** 85% were admitted **Housing** Yes **Expenses** Tuition $3162; Room & Board $4821 **Undergraduates** 54% women, 11% part-time, 20% 25 or older, 2% Native American, 5% Hispanic American, 2% African American, 4% Asian American/Pacific Islander **The most frequently chosen baccalaureate fields are** business/marketing, education, social sciences and history **Academic program** English as a second language, advanced placement, self-designed majors, honors program, summer session, adult/continuing education programs, internships **Contact** Mr. Mike Reilly, Director of Admissions, Central Washington University, 400 East 8th Avenue, Ellensburg, WA 98926-7463. Telephone: 509-963-1211 or toll-free 866-298-4968. Fax: 509-963-3022. E-mail: cwuadmis@cwu.edu. Web site: http://www.cwu.edu/.

CITY UNIVERSITY
BELLEVUE, WASHINGTON

General Independent, upper level, coed **Entrance** Noncompetitive **Setting** suburban campus **Total enrollment** 5,410 **Application deadline** Rolling (freshmen), rolling (transfer) **First-Year Students** 100% were admitted **Housing** No **Expenses** Tuition $6920 **Undergraduates** 46% women, 49% part-time, 90% 25 or older, 1% Native American, 1% Hispanic American, 2% African American, 5% Asian American/Pacific Islander **The most frequently chosen baccalaureate fields are** business/marketing, computer/information sciences, liberal arts/general studies **Academic program** English as a second language, advanced placement, accelerated degree program, honors program, summer session, adult/continuing education programs, internships **Contact** Dr. Marie Low, Vice President, Admissions and Student Relations, City University, 919 SW Grady Way, Renton, WA 98055. Telephone: 800-426-5596 Ext. 3803 or toll-free 800-426-5596. Fax: 425-277-2437. E-mail: info@cityu.edu. Web site: http://www.cityu.edu/.

CORNISH COLLEGE OF THE ARTS
SEATTLE, WASHINGTON

General Independent, 4-year, coed **Entrance** Moderately difficult **Setting** 4-acre urban campus **Total enrollment** 659 **Student/faculty ratio** 9:1 **Application deadline** 8/15 (freshmen), 8/15 (transfer) **Freshmen** 79% were admitted **Housing** No **Expenses** Tuition 15,100 **Undergraduates** 61% women, 6% part-time, 24% 25 or older **The most frequently chosen baccalaureate field is** visual/performing arts **Academic program** Advanced placement, summer session, internships **Contact** Ms. Sharron Starling, Associate Director of Admissions, Cornish College of the Arts, 710 East Roy Street, Seattle, WA 98102-4696. Telephone: 206-726-5017 or toll-free 800-726-ARTS. Fax: 206-720-1011. Web site: http://www.cornish.edu/.

EASTERN WASHINGTON UNIVERSITY
CHENEY, WASHINGTON

General State-supported, comprehensive, coed **Entrance** Moderately difficult **Setting** 335-acre small-town campus **Total enrollment** 8,597 **Student/faculty ratio** 17:1 **Application deadline** Rolling (freshmen), rolling (transfer) **Freshmen** 89% were admitted **Housing** Yes **Expenses** Tuition $3012; Room & Board $4558 **Undergraduates** 58% women, 9% part-time, 28% 25 or older, 2% Native American, 3% Hispanic American, 3% African American, 3% Asian American/Pacific Islander **The most frequently chosen baccalaureate fields are** business/marketing, education, social sciences and history **Academic program** English as a second language, advanced placement, self-designed majors, honors program, summer session, internships **Contact** Ms. Michelle Whittingham, Director of Admissions, Eastern Washington University, 526 Fifth Street, SUT 101, Sutton Hall 101, Cheney, WA 99004-2447. Telephone: 509-359-6582 or toll-free 888-740-1914. Fax: 509-359-6692. E-mail: admissions@ewu.edu. Web site: http://www.ewu.edu/.

THE EVERGREEN STATE COLLEGE
OLYMPIA, WASHINGTON

General State-supported, comprehensive, coed **Entrance** Moderately difficult **Setting** 1,000-acre small-town campus **Total enrollment** 4,125 **Student/faculty ratio** 22:1 **Application deadline** 3/1 (freshmen), 3/1 (transfer) **Freshmen** 87% were admitted **Housing** Yes **Expenses** Tuition $2997; Room & Board $5244 **Undergraduates** 58% women, 13% part-time, 36% 25 or older, 4% Native American, 4% Hispanic American, 4% African American, 4% Asian American/Pacific Islander **Academic program** Advanced placement, self-designed majors, summer session, internships **Contact** Ms. Christine Licht, Interim Director of Admissions, The Evergreen State College, 2700 Evergreen Parkway NW, Olympia, WA 98505. Telephone: 360-867-6170. Fax: 360-867-6576. E-mail: admissions@elwha.evergreen.edu. Web site: http://www.evergreen.edu/.

GONZAGA UNIVERSITY
SPOKANE, WASHINGTON

General Independent Roman Catholic, comprehensive, coed **Entrance** Moderately difficult **Setting** 94-acre urban campus **Total enrollment** 4,347 **Student/faculty ratio** 11:1 **Application deadline** 3/1 (freshmen), 6/1 (transfer) **Freshmen** 82% were admitted **Housing** Yes **Expenses** Tuition $18,400; Room & Board $5680 **Undergraduates** 55% women, 7% part-time, 9% 25 or older, 2% Native American, 3% Hispanic American, 1% African American, 5% Asian American/Pacific Islander **The most frequently chosen baccalaureate fields are** business/marketing, engineering/engineering technologies, social sciences and history **Academic program** English as a second language, advanced placement, self-designed majors, honors program, summer session, adult/continuing education programs, internships **Contact** Ms. Julie McCulloh, Associate Dean of Admission, Gonzaga University, Ad Box 102, Spokane, WA 99258-0102. Telephone: 509-323-6591 or toll-free 800-322-2584 Ext. 6572. Fax: 509-323-5780. E-mail: ballinger@gu.gonzaga.edu. Web site: http://www.gonzaga.edu/.

► **For more information, see page 425.**

HENRY COGSWELL COLLEGE
EVERETT, WASHINGTON

General Independent, 4-year, coed, primarily men **Entrance** Noncompetitive **Setting** 1-acre urban campus **Total enrollment** 249 **Student/faculty ratio** 6:1 **Application deadline** 4/1 (freshmen), rolling (transfer) **Freshmen** 100% were admitted **Housing** No **Expenses** Tuition 11,880 **Undergraduates** 16% women, 64% part-time, 82% 25 or older, 0.4% Native American, 4% Hispanic American, 3% African American, 10% Asian American/Pacific Islander **The most frequently chosen baccalaureate fields are** computer/information sciences, engineering/engineering technologies **Academic program** Advanced placement, accelerated degree program, summer session, adult/continuing education programs, internships **Contact** Ms. Cristy Null, Director of Admissions, Henry Cogswell College, 3002 Colby Avenue, Everett, WA 98201. Telephone: 425-258-3351 Ext. 116. Fax: 425-257-0405. E-mail: ccn_all@ccn.edu. Web site: http://www.henrycogswell.edu/.

HERITAGE COLLEGE
TOPPENISH, WASHINGTON

General Independent, comprehensive, coed **Entrance** Noncompetitive **Setting** 10-acre rural campus **Total enrollment** 1,127 **Student/faculty ratio** 9:1 **Application deadline** Rolling (freshmen), rolling (transfer) **Freshmen** 9% were admitted **Housing** No **Expenses** Tuition 5430 **Undergraduates** 80% women, 62% part-time, 71% 25 or older, 17% Native American, 48% Hispanic American, 1% African American, 2% Asian American/Pacific Islander **The most frequently chosen baccalaureate fields are** education, law/legal studies, protective services/public administration **Academic program** English as a second language, advanced placement, self-designed majors, honors program, summer session, adult/continuing education programs, internships **Contact** Mr. Norberto T. Espindola, Director of Admissions and Recruitment, Heritage College, 3240 Fort Road, Toppenish, WA 98948-9599. Telephone: 509-865-8500 Ext. 2002 or toll-free 509-865-8508. Fax: 509-865-4469. E-mail: espindola_b@heritage.edu. Web site: http://www.heritage.edu/.

THE LEADERSHIP INSTITUTE OF SEATTLE
KENMORE, WASHINGTON

Contact Mr. Don Werner, Coordinator of Undergraduate Admissions, The Leadership Institute of Seattle, 1450 114th Avenue SE, Suite 230, Bellevue, WA 98004-6934. Telephone: 425-635-1187 Ext. 254 or toll-free 800-789-5467. E-mail: lios@lios.org. Web site: http://www.lios.org/.

NORTHWEST COLLEGE
KIRKLAND, WASHINGTON

General Independent, comprehensive, coed, affiliated with Assemblies of God **Entrance** Moderately difficult **Setting** 65-acre suburban campus **Total enrollment** 1,096 **Student/faculty ratio** 18:1 **Application deadline** 8/1 (freshmen), 8/1 (transfer) **Freshmen** 53% were admitted **Housing** Yes **Expenses** Tuition $10,748; Room & Board $5490 **Undergraduates** 56% women, 5% part-time, 27% 25 or older, 1% Native American, 3% Hispanic American, 3% African American, 6% Asian American/Pacific Islander **The most frequently chosen baccalaureate fields are** business/marketing, education, philosophy, religion, and theology **Academic program** English as a second language, advanced placement, accelerated degree program, self-designed majors, summer session, adult/continuing education programs, internships **Contact** Mr. Myles Corrigan, Associate Vice President of Enrollment, Northwest College, PO Box

579, Kirkland, WA 98083-0579. Telephone: 425-889-5209 or toll-free 800-669-3781. Fax: 425-889-5224. E-mail: admissions@ncag.edu. Web site: http://www.nwcollege.edu/.

NORTHWEST COLLEGE OF ART
POULSBO, WASHINGTON

General Proprietary, 4-year, coed **Entrance** Moderately difficult **Setting** 26-acre small-town campus **Total enrollment** 83 **Application deadline** 6/1 (freshmen), 6/1 (transfer) **Housing** No **Expenses** Tuition $10,700 **Academic program** Summer session, internships **Contact** Mr. Craig Freeman, President, Northwest College of Art, 16464 State Highway 305, Poulsbo, WA 98370. Telephone: 360-779-9993 or toll-free 800-769-ARTS. Fax: 360-779-9933. E-mail: kimatnca@silverlink.net. Web site: http://www.nca.edu/.

PACIFIC LUTHERAN UNIVERSITY
TACOMA, WASHINGTON

General Independent, comprehensive, coed, affiliated with Evangelical Lutheran Church in America **Entrance** Moderately difficult **Setting** 126-acre suburban campus **Total enrollment** 3,515 **Student/faculty ratio** 14:1 **Application deadline** Rolling (freshmen), rolling (transfer) **Freshmen** 82% were admitted **Housing** Yes **Expenses** Tuition 16,800; Room & Board 5300 **Undergraduates** 61% women, 9% part-time, 16% 25 or older, 1% Native American, 2% Hispanic American, 2% African American, 5% Asian American/Pacific Islander **The most frequently chosen baccalaureate fields are** business/marketing, education, health professions and related sciences **Academic program** English as a second language, advanced placement, accelerated degree program, self-designed majors, honors program, summer session, adult/continuing education programs, internships **Contact** Office of Admissions, Pacific Lutheran University, Tacoma, WA 98447. Telephone: 253-535-7151 or toll-free 800-274-6758. Fax: 253-536-5136. E-mail: admissions@plu.edu. Web site: http://www.plu.edu/.

PUGET SOUND CHRISTIAN COLLEGE
EDMONDS, WASHINGTON

Contact Mr. Greg Kaler, Recruitment Director, Puget Sound Christian College, 410 4th Avenue North, Edmonds, WA 98020-3171. Telephone: 425-775-8686 Ext. 247. Fax: 425-775-8688. E-mail: psccdeve@ricochet.net.

SAINT MARTIN'S COLLEGE
LACEY, WASHINGTON

General Independent Roman Catholic, comprehensive, coed **Entrance** Moderately difficult **Setting** 380-acre suburban campus **Total enrollment** 1,498 **Student/faculty ratio** 12:1 **Application deadline** 8/1 (freshmen), 8/1 (transfer) **Freshmen** 92% were admitted **Housing** Yes **Expenses** Tuition 14,930; Room & Board 4768 **Undergraduates** 52% women, 26% part-time, 46% 25 or older, 1% Native American, 5% Hispanic American, 9% African American, 7% Asian American/Pacific Islander **The most frequently chosen baccalaureate fields are** business/marketing, education, psychology **Academic program** English as a second language, advanced placement, accelerated degree program, summer session, adult/continuing education programs, internships **Contact** Mr. Todd Abbott, Director of Admission, Saint Martin's College, 5300 Pacific Avenue, SE, Lacey, WA 98503. Telephone: 360-438-4590 or toll-free 800-368-8803. Fax: 37—412-6189. E-mail: admissions@stmartin.edu. Web site: http://www.stmartin.edu/.

SEATTLE PACIFIC UNIVERSITY
SEATTLE, WASHINGTON

General Independent Free Methodist, comprehensive, coed **Entrance** Moderately difficult **Setting** 35-acre urban campus **Total enrollment** 3,491 **Student/faculty ratio** 16:1 **Application deadline** 6/1 (freshmen), 8/1 (transfer) **Freshmen** 91% were admitted **Housing** Yes **Expenses** Tuition $16,425; Room & Board $6249 **Undergraduates** 66% women, 8% part-time, 8% 25 or older, 1% Native American, 2% Hispanic American, 1% African American, 6% Asian American/Pacific Islander **The most frequently chosen baccalaureate fields are** business/marketing, health professions and related sciences, psychology **Academic program** English as a second language, advanced placement, self-designed majors, honors program, summer session, adult/continuing education programs, internships **Contact** Mrs. Jennifer Feddern Kenney, Director of Admissions, Seattle Pacific University, 3307 Third Avenue West, Seattle, WA 98119-1997. Telephone: 206-281-2517 or toll-free 800-366-3344. Fax: 206-281-2669. E-mail: admissions@spu.edu. Web site: http://www.spu.edu/.

SEATTLE UNIVERSITY
SEATTLE, WASHINGTON

General Independent Roman Catholic, comprehensive, coed **Entrance** Moderately difficult **Setting** 46-acre urban campus **Total enrollment** 5,790 **Student/faculty ratio** 12:1 **Application deadline** 7/1 (freshmen), 8/1 (transfer) **Freshmen** 80% were admitted **Housing** Yes **Expenses** Tuition 17,010; Room & Board 6075 **Undergraduates** 60% women, 13% part-time, 14% 25 or older, 1% Native American, 5% Hispanic American, 5% African American, 21% Asian American/Pacific Islander **The most frequently chosen baccalaureate fields are** business/marketing, health professions and related sciences, psychology **Academic program** English as a second language, advanced placement, accelerated degree program, self-designed majors, honors program, summer session, adult/continuing education programs, internships **Contact** Mr. Michael K. McKeon, Dean of Admissions, Seattle University, 900 Broadway, Seattle, WA 98122-4340. Telephone: 206-296-2000 or toll-free 800-542-0833 (in-state); 800-426-7123 (out-of-state). Fax: 206-296-5656. E-mail: admissions@seattleu.edu. Web site: http://www.seattleu.edu/.

TRINITY LUTHERAN COLLEGE
ISSAQUAH, WASHINGTON

General Independent Lutheran, 4-year, coed **Entrance** Minimally difficult **Setting** 46-acre suburban campus **Total enrollment** 129 **Student/faculty ratio** 9:1 **Application deadline** 8/15 (freshmen), 8/15 (transfer) **Freshmen** 77% were admitted **Housing** Yes **Expenses** Tuition 8240; Room & Board 4600 **Undergraduates** 63% women, 16% part-time, 22% 25 or older, 2% Native American, 1% Hispanic American, 4% African American, 6% Asian American/Pacific Islander **The most frequently chosen baccalaureate field is** philosophy, religion, and theology **Academic program** English as a second language, advanced placement, adult/continuing education programs, internships **Contact** Ms. Sigrid Olsen Cutler, Trinity Lutheran College, 4221 228th Avenue, SE, Issaquah, WA 98029-9299. Telephone: 425-392-0400 or toll-free 800-843-5659. Fax: 425-392-0404. E-mail: admissn@lbi.edu. Web site: http://www.tlc.edu/.

UNIVERSITY OF PHOENIX–WASHINGTON CAMPUS
SEATTLE, WASHINGTON

General Proprietary, comprehensive, coed **Entrance** Noncompetitive **Total enrollment** 66,534 **Student/faculty ratio** 13:1 **Application deadline** Rolling (freshmen), rolling (transfer) **Expenses** Tuition $7740 **Undergraduates** 56% women, 86% 25 or older, 2% Native American, 18% Hispanic American, 13% African American, 6% Asian American/Pacific Islander **Academic program** Advanced placement, accelerated degree program, adult/continuing education programs **Contact** Ms. Beth Barilla, Director of Admissions, University of Phoenix–Washington Campus, 4615 East Elwood Street, Phoenix, AZ 85040-1948. Telephone: 480-927-0099 Ext. 1218 or toll-free 800-228-7240. Fax: 480-894-1758. E-mail: beth.barilla@apollogrp.edu. Web site: http://www.phoenix.edu/.

UNIVERSITY OF PUGET SOUND
TACOMA, WASHINGTON

General Independent, comprehensive, coed **Entrance** Very difficult **Setting** 97-acre suburban campus **Total enrollment** 2,867 **Student/faculty ratio** 11:1 **Application deadline** 2/1 (freshmen), 6/1 (transfer) **Freshmen** 72% were admitted **Housing** Yes **Expenses** Tuition 21,425; Room & Board 5510 **Undergraduates** 61% women, 4% part-time, 4% 25 or older, 1% Native American, 3% Hispanic American, 2% African American, 12% Asian American/Pacific Islander **The most frequently chosen baccalaureate fields are** business/marketing, English, social sciences and history **Academic program** Advanced placement, self-designed majors, honors program, summer session, internships **Contact** Daniel F. Evans, Director of Admission, University of Puget Sound, 1500 North Warner Street, Tacoma, WA 98416-0005. Telephone: 253-879-3211 or toll-free 800-396-7191. Fax: 253-879-3993. E-mail: admission@ups.edu. Web site: http://www.ups.edu/.

UNIVERSITY OF WASHINGTON
SEATTLE, WASHINGTON

General State-supported, university, coed **Entrance** Moderately difficult **Setting** 703-acre urban campus **Total enrollment** 36,134 **Student/faculty ratio** 11:1 **Application deadline** 1/15 (freshmen), 4/15 (transfer) **Freshmen** 78% were admitted **Housing** Yes **Expenses** Tuition 3761; Room & Board 6060 **Undergraduates** 52% women, 15% part-time, 14% 25 or older, 1% Native American, 4% Hispanic American, 3% African American, 23% Asian American/Pacific Islander **The most frequently chosen baccalaureate fields are** business/marketing, engineering/engineering technologies, social sciences and history **Academic program** English as a second language, advanced placement, accelerated degree program, self-designed majors, honors program, summer session, adult/continuing education programs, internships **Contact** Ms. Stephanie Preston, Assistant Director of Admissions, University of Washington, Box 355840, Seattle, WA 98195-5840. Telephone: 206-543-9686. E-mail: askuwadm@u.washington.edu. Web site: http://www.washington.edu/.

WALLA WALLA COLLEGE
COLLEGE PLACE, WASHINGTON

General Independent Seventh-day Adventist, comprehensive, coed **Entrance** Moderately difficult **Setting** 77-acre small-town campus **Total enrollment** 1,795 **Student/faculty ratio** 12:1 **Application deadline** Rolling (freshmen), rolling (transfer) **Freshmen** 83% were admitted **Housing** Yes **Expenses** Tuition 14,568; Room & Board 4176 **Undergraduates** 49% women, 14% part-time, 11% 25 or older, 0.2% Native American, 5% Hispanic American, 2% African American, 4% Asian American/Pacific Islander **The most frequently chosen baccalaureate fields are** engineering/engineering technologies, education, health professions and related sciences **Academic program** English as a second language, advanced placement, honors program, summer session, internships **Contact** Mr. Dallas Weis, Director of Admissions, Walla Walla College, 204 South College Avenue, College Place, WA 99324. Telephone: 509-527-2327 or toll-free 800-541-8900. Fax: 509-527-2397. E-mail: weisda@wwc.edu. Web site: http://www.wwc.edu/.

WASHINGTON STATE UNIVERSITY
PULLMAN, WASHINGTON

General State-supported, university, coed **Entrance** Moderately difficult **Setting** 620-acre rural campus **Total enrollment** 21,122 **Student/faculty ratio** 16:1 **Application deadline** 5/1 (freshmen) **Freshmen** 84% were admitted **Housing** Yes **Expenses** Tuition $3894; Room & Board $4826 **Undergraduates** 50% women, 16% part-time, 19% 25 or older, 1% Native American, 3% Hispanic American, 3% African American, 5% Asian American/Pacific Islander **The most frequently chosen baccalaureate fields are** business/marketing, communications/communication technologies, social sciences and history **Academic program**

English as a second language, advanced placement, honors program, summer session, adult/continuing education programs, internships **Contact** Kenneth Vreeland, Interim Director of Admissions, Washington State University, PO Box 641009, Pullman, WA 99164-1009. Telephone: 509-335-5586 or toll-free 888-468-6978. Fax: 509-335-7468. E-mail: admiss@wsu.edu. Web site: http://www.wsu.edu/.

WESTERN WASHINGTON UNIVERSITY
BELLINGHAM, WASHINGTON

General State-supported, comprehensive, coed **Entrance** Moderately difficult **Setting** 223-acre small-town campus **Total enrollment** 11,708 **Student/faculty ratio** 21:1 **Application deadline** 3/1 (freshmen), 4/1 (transfer) **Freshmen** 86% were admitted **Housing** Yes **Expenses** Tuition 3102; Room & Board 5100 **Undergraduates** 56% women, 5% part-time, 3% 25 or older, 2% Native American, 3% Hispanic American, 2% African American, 7% Asian American/Pacific Islander **The most frequently chosen baccalaureate fields are** business/marketing, education, social sciences and history **Academic program** English as a second language, advanced placement, accelerated degree program, self-designed majors, honors program, summer session, adult/continuing education programs, internships **Contact** Ms. Karen Copetas, Director of Admissions, Western Washington University, 516 High Street, Bellingham, WA 98225-9009. Telephone: 360-650-3440 Ext. 3440. Fax: 360-650-7369. E-mail: admit@cc.wwu.edu. Web site: http://www.wwu.edu/.

WHITMAN COLLEGE
WALLA WALLA, WASHINGTON

General Independent, 4-year, coed **Entrance** Very difficult **Setting** 55-acre small-town campus **Total enrollment** 1,424 **Student/faculty ratio** 11:1 **Application deadline** 2/1 (freshmen), 2/1 (transfer) **Freshmen** 50% were admitted **Housing** Yes **Expenses** Tuition $21,742; Room & Board $6090 **Undergraduates** 58% women, 3% part-time, 0.4% 25 or older, 1% Native American, 3% Hispanic American, 1% African American, 6% Asian American/Pacific Islander **The most frequently chosen baccalaureate fields are** biological/life sciences, English, social sciences and history **Academic program** Advanced placement, self-designed majors, honors program, internships **Contact** Mr. John Bogley, Dean of Admission and Financial Aid, Whitman College, 345 Boyer Avenue, Walla Walla, WA 99362-2083. Telephone: 509-527-5176. Fax: 509-527-4967. E-mail: admission@whitman.edu. Web site: http://www.whitman.edu/.

WHITWORTH COLLEGE
SPOKANE, WASHINGTON

General Independent Presbyterian, comprehensive, coed **Entrance** Very difficult **Setting** 200-acre suburban campus **Total enrollment** 2,012 **Student/faculty ratio** 15:1 **Application deadline** 3/1 (freshmen), 7/1 (transfer) **Freshmen** 90% were admitted **Housing** Yes **Expenses** Tuition $16,928; Room & Board $5500 **Undergraduates** 60% women, 8% part-time, 15% 25 or older, 1% Native American, 3% Hispanic American, 1% African American, 5% Asian American/Pacific Islander **The most frequently chosen baccalaureate fields are** business/marketing, education, visual/performing arts **Academic program** English as a second language, advanced placement, self-designed majors, summer session, adult/continuing education programs, internships **Contact** Admissions Office, Whitworth College, 300 West Hawthorne Road, Spokane, WA 99251-0001. Telephone: 800-533-4668 or toll-free 800-533-4668 (out-of-state). Fax: 509-777-3758. E-mail: admissions@whiteworth.edu. Web site: http://www.whitworth.edu/.

WEST VIRGINIA

ALDERSON-BROADDUS COLLEGE
PHILIPPI, WEST VIRGINIA

General Independent, comprehensive, coed, affiliated with American Baptist Churches in the U.S.A. **Entrance** Moderately difficult **Setting** 170-acre rural campus **Total enrollment** 749 **Student/faculty ratio** 13:1 **Application deadline** Rolling (freshmen), rolling (transfer) **Freshmen** 74% were admitted **Housing** Yes **Expenses** Tuition $14,440; Room & Board $5200 **Undergraduates** 62% women, 4% part-time, 33% 25 or older, 1% Native American, 1% Hispanic American, 4% African American, 3% Asian American/Pacific Islander **The most frequently chosen baccalaureate fields are** education, health professions and related sciences, social sciences and history **Academic program** Advanced placement, self-designed majors, honors program, summer session, internships **Contact** Kimberly Klaus, Assistant Director of Admissions, Alderson-Broaddus College, PO Box 2003, Philippi, WV 26416. Telephone: 304-457-1700 Ext. 6255 or toll-free 800-263-1549. Fax: 304-457-6239. E-mail: admissions@ab.wvnet.edu. Web site: http://www.ab.edu/.

► **For more information, see page 381.**

APPALACHIAN BIBLE COLLEGE
BRADLEY, WEST VIRGINIA

General Independent nondenominational, 4-year, coed **Entrance** Minimally difficult **Setting** 110-acre small-town campus **Total enrollment** 264 **Student/faculty ratio** 17:1 **Application deadline** Rolling (freshmen), rolling (transfer) **Housing** Yes **Expenses** Tuition $6132; Room & Board $3310 **The most frequently chosen baccalaureate field is** philosophy, religion, and theology **Academic program** Advanced placement, summer session, adult/continuing education programs, internships **Contact** Ms. Angela Harding, Admissions Counselor, Appalachian Bible College, PO Box ABC, Bradley, WV 25818. Telephone: 800-678-9ABC Ext. 3213 or toll-

Appalachian Bible College *(continued)*

free 800-678-9ABC. Fax: 304-877-5082. E-mail: admissions@abc.edu. Web site: http://www.abc.edu.

BETHANY COLLEGE
BETHANY, WEST VIRGINIA

General Independent, 4-year, coed, affiliated with Christian Church (Disciples of Christ) **Entrance** Moderately difficult **Setting** 1,600-acre rural campus **Total enrollment** 750 **Student/faculty ratio** 12:1 **Application deadline** 8/15 (freshmen), rolling (transfer) **Freshmen** 71% were admitted **Housing** Yes **Expenses** Tuition $19,495; Room & Board $6909 **Undergraduates** 46% women, 1% part-time, 2% 25 or older, 0% Native American, 1% Hispanic American, 3% African American, 0.3% Asian American/Pacific Islander **The most frequently chosen baccalaureate fields are** education, psychology, social sciences and history **Academic program** English as a second language, advanced placement, self-designed majors, internships **Contact** Brian Ralph, Vice President for Enrollment Management, Bethany College, Office of Admission, Bethany, WV 26032. Telephone: 304-829-7611 or toll-free 800-922-7611 (out-of-state). Fax: 304-829-7142. E-mail: g.forney@mail.bethany.wvnet.edu. Web site: http://www.bethanywv.edu/.

BLUEFIELD STATE COLLEGE
BLUEFIELD, WEST VIRGINIA

General State-supported, 4-year, coed **Entrance** Noncompetitive **Setting** 45-acre small-town campus **Total enrollment** 2,648 **Student/faculty ratio** 17:1 **Application deadline** Rolling (freshmen), rolling (transfer) **Freshmen** 99% were admitted **Housing** No **Expenses** Tuition $2288 **Undergraduates** 60% women, 35% part-time, 41% 25 or older, 0.4% Native American, 1% Hispanic American, 10% African American, 0.2% Asian American/Pacific Islander **The most frequently chosen baccalaureate fields are** business/marketing, engineering/engineering technologies, protective services/public administration **Academic program** Advanced placement, self-designed majors, summer session, adult/continuing education programs, internships **Contact** Mr. John C. Cardwell, Director of Enrollment Management, Bluefield State College, 219 Rock Street, Bluefield, WV 24701-2198. Telephone: 304-327-4567 or toll-free 800-344-8892 Ext. 4065 (in-state); 800-654-7798 Ext. 4065 (out-of-state). Fax: 304-325-7747. E-mail: jcardwell@bscvax.wvnet.edu. Web site: http://www.bluefield.wvnet.edu/.

THE COLLEGE OF WEST VIRGINIA
See Mountain State University

CONCORD COLLEGE
ATHENS, WEST VIRGINIA

General State-supported, 4-year, coed **Entrance** Minimally difficult **Setting** 100-acre rural campus **Total enrollment** 2,955 **Student/faculty ratio** 19:1 **Application deadline** Rolling (freshmen), rolling (transfer) **Freshmen** 98% were admitted **Housing** Yes **Expenses** Tuition $2620; Room & Board $4150 **Undergraduates** 57% women, 23% part-time, 16% 25 or older, 0.3% Native American, 0.5% Hispanic American, 5% African American, 1% Asian American/Pacific Islander **The most frequently chosen baccalaureate fields are** business/marketing, education, social sciences and history **Academic program** English as a second language, advanced placement, self-designed majors, honors program, summer session **Contact** Mr. Michael Curry, Vice President of Admissions and Financial Aid, Concord College, 1000 Vermillion Street, Athens, WV 24712. Telephone: 304-384-5248 or toll-free 888-384-5249 (out-of-state). Fax: 304-384-9044. E-mail: addsm@ccvms.wvnet.edu. Web site: http://www.concord.edu/.

► **For more information, see page 405.**

DAVIS & ELKINS COLLEGE
ELKINS, WEST VIRGINIA

General Independent Presbyterian, 4-year, coed **Entrance** Minimally difficult **Setting** 170-acre small-town campus **Total enrollment** 658 **Application deadline** Rolling (freshmen), rolling (transfer) **Freshmen** 94% were admitted **Housing** Yes **Expenses** Tuition $12,824; Room & Board $5570 **Undergraduates** 56% women, 9% part-time, 0.2% Native American, 1% Hispanic American, 2% African American, 3% Asian American/Pacific Islander **Academic program** English as a second language, advanced placement, accelerated degree program, self-designed majors, honors program, summer session, adult/continuing education programs, internships **Contact** Mr. Matt Shiflett, Director of Admissions, Davis & Elkins College, 100 Campus Drive, Elkins, WV 26241. Telephone: 304-637-1332 or toll-free 800-624-3157. Fax: 304-637-1800. E-mail: admiss@dne.wvnet.edu. Web site: http://www.dne.edu/.

FAIRMONT STATE COLLEGE
FAIRMONT, WEST VIRGINIA

General State-supported, 4-year, coed **Entrance** Minimally difficult **Setting** 80-acre small-town campus **Total enrollment** 6,496 **Student/faculty ratio** 17:1 **Application deadline** 6/15 (freshmen), 6/15 (transfer) **Freshmen** 100% were admitted **Housing** Yes **Expenses** Tuition $2316; Room & Board $4084 **Undergraduates** 56% women, 30% part-time, 26% 25 or older, 0.3% Native American, 1% Hispanic American, 3% African American, 0.5% Asian American/Pacific Islander **The most frequently chosen baccalaureate fields are** business/marketing, education, protective services/public administration **Academic program** English as a second language, advanced placement, accelerated degree program, honors program, summer session, adult/continuing education programs, internships **Contact** Dr. John G. Conaway, Director of Admissions, Fairmont State College, 1201 Locust Avenue, Fairmont, WV 26554. Telephone: 304-367-4141 or toll-free 800-641-5678. Fax: 304-

367-4789. E-mail: admit@fscvax.fairmont.wvnet.edu. Web site: http://www.fscwv.edu/.

▶ **For more information, see page 416.**

GLENVILLE STATE COLLEGE
GLENVILLE, WEST VIRGINIA

General State-supported, 4-year, coed **Entrance** Noncompetitive **Setting** 331-acre rural campus **Total enrollment** 2,198 **Application deadline** 8/1 (freshmen), 6/1 (transfer) **Freshmen** 100% were admitted **Housing** Yes **Expenses** Tuition 2376; Room & Board 3900 **Undergraduates** 59% women, 23% part-time, 0.5% Native American, 0.3% Hispanic American, 3% African American, 2% Asian American/Pacific Islander **The most frequently chosen baccalaureate fields are** business/marketing, education, psychology **Academic program** English as a second language, advanced placement, accelerated degree program, self-designed majors, honors program, summer session, adult/continuing education programs, internships **Contact** Ms. Brenda McCartney, Associate Registrar, Glenville State College, 200 High Street, Glenville, WV 26351-1200. Telephone: 304-462-4117 Ext. 347 or toll-free 800-924-2010 (in-state). Fax: 304-462-8619. E-mail: cottrill@glenville.wvnet.edu. Web site: http://www.glenville.edu/.

MARSHALL UNIVERSITY
HUNTINGTON, WEST VIRGINIA

General State-supported, university, coed **Entrance** Minimally difficult **Setting** 70-acre urban campus **Total enrollment** 13,643 **Student/faculty ratio** 20:1 **Application deadline** Rolling (freshmen), rolling (transfer) **Freshmen** 74% were admitted **Housing** Yes **Expenses** Tuition $2620; Room & Board $4772 **Undergraduates** 55% women, 16% part-time, 17% 25 or older, 1% Native American, 0.5% Hispanic American, 4% African American, 1% Asian American/Pacific Islander **The most frequently chosen baccalaureate fields are** business/marketing, education, liberal arts/general studies **Academic program** English as a second language, advanced placement, accelerated degree program, honors program, summer session, adult/continuing education programs, internships **Contact** Dr. James W. Harless, Admissions Director, Marshall University, 400 Hal Greer Boulevard, Huntington, WV 25755. Telephone: 304-696-3160 or toll-free 800-642-3499 (in-state). Fax: 304-696-3135. E-mail: admissions@marshall.edu. Web site: http://www.marshall.edu/.

MOUNTAIN STATE UNIVERSITY
BECKLEY, WEST VIRGINIA

General Independent, comprehensive, coed **Entrance** Noncompetitive **Setting** 7-acre small-town campus **Total enrollment** 2,110 **Student/faculty ratio** 29:1 **Application deadline** Rolling (freshmen), rolling (transfer) **Freshmen** 50% were admitted **Housing** Yes **Expenses** Tuition 4080; Room & Board 1824 **Undergraduates** 43% 25 or older, 1% Native American, 1% Hispanic American, 8% African American, 3% Asian American/Pacific Islander **The most frequently chosen baccalaureate fields are** business/marketing, health professions and related sciences, interdisciplinary studies **Academic program** English as a second language, advanced placement, accelerated degree program, self-designed majors, summer session, adult/continuing education programs, internships **Contact** Marketing Department, Mountain State University, P.O. Box 9003, Beckley, WV 25802-9003. Telephone: 304-253-7351 Ext. 1433 or toll-free 800-766-6067. Fax: 304-253-5072. E-mail: gocwv@cwv.edu. Web site: http://www.mountainstate.edu/.

OHIO VALLEY COLLEGE
VIENNA, WEST VIRGINIA

General Independent, 4-year, coed, affiliated with Church of Christ **Entrance** Minimally difficult **Setting** 299-acre small-town campus **Total enrollment** 417 **Student/faculty ratio** 10:1 **Application deadline** Rolling (freshmen), rolling (transfer) **Freshmen** 45% were admitted **Housing** Yes **Expenses** Tuition $9390; Room & Board $4210 **Undergraduates** 53% women, 3% part-time, 20% 25 or older, 0.5% Native American, 1% Hispanic American, 5% African American, 0.5% Asian American/Pacific Islander **The most frequently chosen baccalaureate fields are** business/marketing, education, psychology **Academic program** English as a second language, advanced placement, honors program, summer session, adult/continuing education programs, internships **Contact** Mr. Denver Lucky, Director of Admissions, Vice President for Enrollment, Ohio Valley College, #1 Campus View Drive, Vienna, WV 26105. Telephone: 304-485-7384 Ext. 215 or toll-free 800-446-8668 Ext. 142 (out-of-state). Fax: 304-485-3106. E-mail: admissions@juno.com. Web site: http://www.ovc.edu/.

SALEM INTERNATIONAL UNIVERSITY
SALEM, WEST VIRGINIA

General Independent, comprehensive, coed **Entrance** Minimally difficult **Setting** 300-acre rural campus **Total enrollment** 607 **Student/faculty ratio** 13:1 **Application deadline** Rolling (freshmen), rolling (transfer) **Freshmen** 83% were admitted **Housing** Yes **Expenses** Tuition 13,120; Room & Board 4430 **Undergraduates** 44% women, 1% part-time, 9% 25 or older, 1% Native American, 4% Hispanic American, 9% African American, 1% Asian American/Pacific Islander **Academic program** English as a second language, advanced placement, accelerated degree program, internships **Contact** Mrs. Carolyn S. Ritter, Director of Admissions, Salem International University, PO Box 500, Salem, WV 26426-0500. Telephone: 304-782-5336 Ext. 336 or toll-free 800-283-4562. E-mail: admis_new@salem.wvnet.edu. Web site: http://www.salemiu.edu/.

SHEPHERD COLLEGE
SHEPHERDSTOWN, WEST VIRGINIA

General State-supported, 4-year, coed **Entrance** Moderately difficult **Setting** 320-acre small-town

Shepherd College *(continued)*

campus **Total enrollment** 4,603 **Student/faculty ratio** 19:1 **Application deadline** 2/1 (freshmen), 3/15 (transfer) **Freshmen** 94% were admitted **Housing** Yes **Expenses** Tuition 2508; Room & Board 4112 **Undergraduates** 58% women, 39% part-time, 24% 25 or older, 1% Native American, 2% Hispanic American, 6% African American, 1% Asian American/Pacific Islander **The most frequently chosen baccalaureate fields are** business/marketing, education, liberal arts/general studies **Academic program** English as a second language, advanced placement, accelerated degree program, honors program, summer session, adult/continuing education programs, internships **Contact** Mr. Karl L. Wolf, Director of Admissions, Shepherd College, PO Box 3210, Shepherdstown, WV 25443-3210. Telephone: 304-876-5212 or toll-free 800-344-5231. Fax: 304-876-5165. E-mail: admoff@shepherd.wunet.edu. Web site: http://www.shepherd.edu/.

UNIVERSITY OF CHARLESTON
CHARLESTON, WEST VIRGINIA

General Independent, comprehensive, coed **Entrance** Moderately difficult **Setting** 40-acre urban campus **Total enrollment** 1,280 **Student/faculty ratio** 12:1 **Application deadline** Rolling (freshmen), rolling (transfer) **Freshmen** 72% were admitted **Housing** Yes **Expenses** Tuition $13,200; Room & Board $4637 **Undergraduates** 64% women, 28% part-time, 31% 25 or older, 1% Native American, 1% Hispanic American, 4% African American, 2% Asian American/Pacific Islander **The most frequently chosen baccalaureate fields are** business/marketing, biological/life sciences, health professions and related sciences **Academic program** English as a second language, advanced placement, accelerated degree program, self-designed majors, summer session, adult/continuing education programs, internships **Contact** Ms. Kim Scranage, Associate Director of Admissions, University of Charleston, 2300 MacCorkle Avenue, SE, Charleston, WV 25304-1099. Telephone: 304-357-4750 or toll-free 800-995-GOUC. Fax: 304-357-4781. E-mail: admissions@uchaswv.edu. Web site: http://www.uchaswv.edu/.

WEST LIBERTY STATE COLLEGE
WEST LIBERTY, WEST VIRGINIA

General State-supported, 4-year, coed **Entrance** Minimally difficult **Setting** 290-acre rural campus **Total enrollment** 2,606 **Student/faculty ratio** 19:1 **Freshmen** 96% were admitted **Housing** Yes **Expenses** Tuition $2420; Room & Board $3340 **Undergraduates** 55% women, 10% part-time, 17% 25 or older, 0.2% Native American, 1% Hispanic American, 2% African American, 0.3% Asian American/Pacific Islander **The most frequently chosen baccalaureate fields are** business/marketing, education, health professions and related sciences **Academic program** Advanced placement, accelerated degree program, self-designed majors, honors program, summer session, adult/continuing education programs, internships **Contact** Ms. Stephanie North, Admissions Counselor, West Liberty State College, PO Box 295, West Liberty, WV 26074. Telephone: 304-336-8078 or toll-free 800-732-6204 Ext. 8076. Fax: 304-336-8403. E-mail: wladmsn1@wlsvax.wvnet.edu. Web site: http://www.wlsc.wvnet.edu/.

WEST VIRGINIA STATE COLLEGE
INSTITUTE, WEST VIRGINIA

General State-supported, 4-year, coed **Entrance** Minimally difficult **Setting** 90-acre suburban campus **Total enrollment** 4,823 **Student/faculty ratio** 21:1 **Application deadline** 8/11 (freshmen), 8/11 (transfer) **Freshmen** 100% were admitted **Housing** Yes **Expenses** Tuition $2464; Room & Board $3800 **Undergraduates** 59% women, 40% part-time, 29% 25 or older, 0.4% Native American, 0.4% Hispanic American, 14% African American, 1% Asian American/Pacific Islander **The most frequently chosen baccalaureate fields are** education, business/marketing, liberal arts/general studies **Academic program** Advanced placement, accelerated degree program, summer session, adult/continuing education programs, internships **Contact** Ms. Alice Ruhnke, Director of Admissions, West Virginia State College, Campus Box 197, PO Box 1000, Ferrell Hall, Room 106, Institute, WV 25112-1000. Telephone: 304-766-3221 or toll-free 800-987-2112. Fax: 304-766-4158. E-mail: greenrl@ernie.wvsc.wvnet.edu. Web site: http://www.wvsc.edu/.

WEST VIRGINIA UNIVERSITY
MORGANTOWN, WEST VIRGINIA

General State-supported, university, coed **Entrance** Moderately difficult **Setting** 541-acre small-town campus **Total enrollment** 21,987 **Student/faculty ratio** 20:1 **Application deadline** 8/1 (freshmen), 8/1 (transfer) **Freshmen** 94% were admitted **Housing** Yes **Expenses** Tuition 2836; Room & Board 5152 **Undergraduates** 46% women, 5% part-time, 8% 25 or older, 0.4% Native American, 1% Hispanic American, 4% African American, 2% Asian American/Pacific Islander **The most frequently chosen baccalaureate fields are** business/marketing, engineering/engineering technologies, health professions and related sciences **Academic program** English as a second language, advanced placement, accelerated degree program, self-designed majors, honors program, summer session, adult/continuing education programs, internships **Contact** Mr. Cheng H. Khoo, Director of Admissions and Records, West Virginia University, Box 6009, Morgantown, WV 26506-6009. Telephone: 304-293-2121 Ext. 1511 or toll-free 800-344-9881. Fax: 304-293-3080. E-mail: wvuinfo@wvnvm.wvnet.edu. Web site: http://www.wvu.edu/.

WEST VIRGINIA UNIVERSITY INSTITUTE OF TECHNOLOGY
MONTGOMERY, WEST VIRGINIA

General State-supported, comprehensive, coed **Entrance** Noncompetitive **Setting** 200-acre small-town campus **Total enrollment** 2,326 **Student/faculty ratio** 16:1 **Application deadline** Rolling (freshmen), rolling (transfer) **Freshmen** 99% were admitted **Housing** Yes **Expenses** Tuition 3064; Room & Board 4210 **Undergraduates** 28% 25 or older **The most frequently chosen baccalaureate fields are** business/marketing, engineering/engineering technologies, interdisciplinary studies **Academic program** English as a second language, advanced placement, accelerated degree program, self-designed majors, summer session, adult/continuing education programs, internships **Contact** Ms. Donna Varney, Director of Admissions I, West Virginia University Institute of Technology, Box 10, Old Main, Montgomery, WV 25136. Telephone: 304-442-3071 or toll-free 888-554-8324. Fax: 304-442-3097. E-mail: wvutech@wvit.wvnet.edu. Web site: http://www.wvutech.edu.

WEST VIRGINIA WESLEYAN COLLEGE

BUCKHANNON, WEST VIRGINIA

General Independent, comprehensive, coed, affiliated with United Methodist Church **Entrance** Moderately difficult **Setting** 80-acre small-town campus **Total enrollment** 1,622 **Student/faculty ratio** 14:1 **Application deadline** 8/1 (freshmen), rolling (transfer) **Freshmen** 82% were admitted **Housing** Yes **Expenses** Tuition $18,700; Room & Board $4450 **Undergraduates** 57% women, 6% part-time, 2% 25 or older, 0.1% Native American, 1% Hispanic American, 5% African American, 1% Asian American/Pacific Islander **The most frequently chosen baccalaureate fields are** business/marketing, education, social sciences and history **Academic program** English as a second language, advanced placement, accelerated degree program, self-designed majors, honors program, summer session, adult/continuing education programs, internships **Contact** Mr. Robert N. Skinner II, Director of Admission, West Virginia Wesleyan College, 59 College Avenue, Buckhannon, WV 26201. Telephone: 304-473-8510 or toll-free 800-722-9933 (out-of-state). Fax: 304-472-2571. E-mail: admissions@academ.wvwc.edu. Web site: http://www.wvwc.edu/.

WHEELING JESUIT UNIVERSITY

WHEELING, WEST VIRGINIA

General Independent Roman Catholic (Jesuit), comprehensive, coed **Entrance** Moderately difficult **Setting** 70-acre suburban campus **Total enrollment** 1,515 **Student/faculty ratio** 13:1 **Application deadline** Rolling (freshmen), rolling (transfer) **Freshmen** 86% were admitted **Housing** Yes **Expenses** Tuition $16,230; Room & Board $5250 **Undergraduates** 59% women, 18% part-time, 25% 25 or older, 0.2% Native American, 1% Hispanic American, 2% African American, 1% Asian American/Pacific Islander **The most frequently chosen baccalaureate fields are** business/marketing, health professions and related sciences, psychology **Academic program** English as a second language, advanced placement, self-designed majors, honors program, summer session, adult/continuing education programs, internships **Contact** Mr. Thomas M. Pie, Director of Admissions, Wheeling Jesuit University, 316 Washington Avenue, Wheeling, WV 26003-6295. Telephone: 304-243-2359 or toll-free 800-624-6992. Fax: 304-243-2397. E-mail: admis@wju.edu. Web site: http://www.wju.edu/.

WISCONSIN

ALVERNO COLLEGE

MILWAUKEE, WISCONSIN

General Independent Roman Catholic, comprehensive, women only **Entrance** Moderately difficult **Setting** 46-acre suburban campus **Total enrollment** 1,872 **Student/faculty ratio** 14:1 **Application deadline** 8/1 (freshmen), 8/1 (transfer) **Freshmen** 70% were admitted **Housing** Yes **Expenses** Tuition $11,530; Room & Board $4610 **Undergraduates** 49% part-time, 18% 25 or older, 1% Native American, 9% Hispanic American, 25% African American, 2% Asian American/Pacific Islander **The most frequently chosen baccalaureate fields are** business/marketing, communications/communication technologies, health professions and related sciences **Academic program** Advanced placement, summer session, adult/continuing education programs, internships **Contact** Mr. Owen Smith, Director of Admissions, Alverno College, 3400 South 43 Street, PO Box 343922, Milwaukee, WI 53234-3922. Telephone: 414-382-6113 or toll-free 800-933-3401. Fax: 414-382-6354. E-mail: alvadm5h@exepc.com. Web site: http://www.alverno.edu/.

BELLIN COLLEGE OF NURSING

GREEN BAY, WISCONSIN

General Independent, 4-year, coed, primarily women **Entrance** Moderately difficult **Setting** urban campus **Total enrollment** 151 **Student/faculty ratio** 9:1 **Application deadline** Rolling (freshmen), rolling (transfer) **Freshmen** 50% were admitted **Housing** No **Expenses** Tuition $9919 **Undergraduates** 93% women, 7% part-time, 20% 25 or older, 3% Native American, 0% Hispanic American, 1% African American, 2% Asian American/Pacific Islander **The most frequently chosen baccalaureate field is** health professions and related sciences **Academic program** Advanced placement, accelerated degree program, summer session **Contact** Dr. Penny Croghan, Admissions Director, Bellin College of Nursing, 725 South Webster Ave, PO Box 23400, Green Bay, WI 54305-3400. Telephone: 920-433-5803 or toll-free 800-236-8707 (in-state). Fax: 920-433-7416. E-mail: admissio@bcon.edu. Web site: http://www.bcon.edu.

BELOIT COLLEGE

BELOIT, WISCONSIN

General Independent, 4-year, coed **Entrance** Very difficult **Setting** 65-acre small-town campus **Total**

Beloit College *(continued)*

enrollment 1,254 **Student/faculty ratio** 11:1 **Application deadline** Rolling (freshmen), rolling (transfer) **Freshmen** 67% were admitted **Housing** Yes **Expenses** Tuition 21,550; Room & Board 4882 **Undergraduates** 58% women, 4% part-time, 5% 25 or older, 0.2% Native American, 4% Hispanic American, 4% African American, 4% Asian American/Pacific Islander **The most frequently chosen baccalaureate fields are** social sciences and history, English, visual/performing arts **Academic program** English as a second language, advanced placement, self-designed majors, summer session, adult/continuing education programs, internships **Contact** Mr. James S. Zielinski, Director of Admissions, Beloit College, 700 College Street, Beloit, WI 53511-5596. Telephone: 608-363-2500 or toll-free 800-356-0751. Fax: 608-363-2075. E-mail: admiss@beloit.edu. Web site: http://www.beloit.edu/.

CARDINAL STRITCH UNIVERSITY
MILWAUKEE, WISCONSIN

General Independent Roman Catholic, comprehensive, coed **Entrance** Moderately difficult **Setting** 40-acre suburban campus **Total enrollment** 5,994 **Student/faculty ratio** 17:1 **Application deadline** Rolling (freshmen), rolling (transfer) **Freshmen** 77% were admitted **Housing** Yes **Expenses** Tuition 11,800; Room & Board 4820 **Undergraduates** 68% women, 7% part-time, 70% 25 or older **The most frequently chosen baccalaureate fields are** business/marketing, education, health professions and related sciences **Academic program** English as a second language, advanced placement, accelerated degree program, self-designed majors, honors program, summer session, adult/continuing education programs, internships **Contact** Mr. David Wegener, Director of Admissions, Cardinal Stritch University, 6801 North Yates Road, Milwaukee, WI 53217-3985. Telephone: 414-410-4040 or toll-free 800-347-8822 Ext. 4040. Fax: 414-410-4058. E-mail: admityou@stritch.edu. Web site: http://www.stritch.edu/.

CARROLL COLLEGE
WAUKESHA, WISCONSIN

General Independent Presbyterian, comprehensive, coed **Entrance** Moderately difficult **Setting** 52-acre suburban campus **Total enrollment** 2,902 **Student/faculty ratio** 17:1 **Application deadline** Rolling (freshmen), rolling (transfer) **Freshmen** 85% were admitted **Housing** Yes **Expenses** Tuition $16,200; Room & Board $4970 **Undergraduates** 66% women, 29% part-time, 23% 25 or older, 0.2% Native American, 2% Hispanic American, 2% African American, 1% Asian American/Pacific Islander **The most frequently chosen baccalaureate fields are** business/marketing, health professions and related sciences, psychology **Academic program** Advanced placement, self-designed majors, honors program, summer session, adult/continuing education programs, internships **Contact** Mr. James V. Wiseman III, Vice President of Enrollment, Carroll College, 100 North East Avenue, Waukesha, WI 53186-5593. Telephone: 262-524-7221 or toll-free 800-CARROLL. Fax: 262-524-7139. E-mail: cc.info@ccadmin.cc.edu. Web site: http://www.cc.edu/.

CARTHAGE COLLEGE
KENOSHA, WISCONSIN

General Independent, comprehensive, coed, affiliated with Evangelical Lutheran Church in America **Entrance** Moderately difficult **Setting** 72-acre suburban campus **Total enrollment** 2,222 **Student/faculty ratio** 16:1 **Application deadline** Rolling (freshmen), rolling (transfer) **Freshmen** 89% were admitted **Housing** Yes **Expenses** Tuition $17,350; Room & Board $5210 **Undergraduates** 57% women, 27% part-time, 11% 25 or older, 0.3% Native American, 3% Hispanic American, 5% African American, 1% Asian American/Pacific Islander **The most frequently chosen baccalaureate fields are** business/marketing, education, social sciences and history **Academic program** Advanced placement, accelerated degree program, self-designed majors, honors program, summer session, adult/continuing education programs, internships **Contact** Mr. Tom Augustine, Director of Admission, Carthage College, 2001 Alford Park Drive, Kenosha, WI 53140-1994. Telephone: 262-551-6000 or toll-free 800-351-4058. Fax: 262-551-5762. E-mail: admissions@carthage.edu. Web site: http://www.carthage.edu/.

COLUMBIA COLLEGE OF NURSING
MILWAUKEE, WISCONSIN

General Independent, 4-year, coed, primarily women **Entrance** Moderately difficult **Setting** urban campus **Total enrollment** 194 **Student/faculty ratio** 16:1 **Application deadline** Rolling (freshmen), rolling (transfer) **Freshmen** 77% were admitted **Housing** Yes **Expenses** Tuition $16,480; Room & Board $3700 **Undergraduates** 94% women, 23% part-time, 26% 25 or older, 0% Native American, 3% Hispanic American, 4% African American, 1% Asian American/Pacific Islander **The most frequently chosen baccalaureate field is** health professions and related sciences **Academic program** Advanced placement, honors program, summer session **Contact** Mr. James Wiseman, Dean of Admissions, Columbia College of Nursing, Carroll College, 100 North East Avenue, Milwaukee, WI 53186. Telephone: 262-524-7220. Fax: 262-524-7646. E-mail: jwiseman@ccadmin.cc.edu. Web site: http://www.ccon.edu/.

CONCORDIA UNIVERSITY WISCONSIN
MEQUON, WISCONSIN

General Independent, comprehensive, coed, affiliated with Lutheran Church–Missouri Synod **Entrance** Moderately difficult **Setting** 155-acre suburban campus **Total enrollment** 4,603 **Student/faculty ratio** 11:1 **Application deadline** 8/15 (freshmen), 8/15 (transfer) **Freshmen** 82% were admitted **Housing** Yes **Expenses** Tuition $13,610; Room & Board $5070 **Undergraduates** 64% women, 32% part-time, 1%

Native American, 1% Hispanic American, 8% African American, 0.4% Asian American/Pacific Islander **Academic program** English as a second language, advanced placement, accelerated degree program, self-designed majors, honors program, summer session, adult/continuing education programs, internships **Contact** Mr. Ken Gaschk, Director of Admissions, Concordia University Wisconsin, 12800 North Lake Shore Drive, Mequon, WI 53097-2402. Telephone: 262-243-4304 Ext. 305. E-mail: kgaschk@bach.cuw.edu. Web site: http://www.cuw.edu/.

EDGEWOOD COLLEGE
MADISON, WISCONSIN

General Independent Roman Catholic, comprehensive, coed **Entrance** Moderately difficult **Setting** 55-acre urban campus **Total enrollment** 2,077 **Student/faculty ratio** 13:1 **Application deadline** Rolling (freshmen), rolling (transfer) **Freshmen** 48% were admitted **Housing** Yes **Expenses** Tuition 12,450; Room & Board 4516 **Undergraduates** 72% women, 28% part-time, 22% 25 or older, 0.5% Native American, 1% Hispanic American, 1% African American, 1% Asian American/Pacific Islander **The most frequently chosen baccalaureate fields are** business/marketing, education, home economics/vocational home economics **Academic program** Advanced placement, summer session, adult/continuing education programs **Contact** Mr. Scott Flanagan, Dean of Admissions and Financial Aid, Edgewood College, 1000 Edgewood College Drive, Madison, WI 53711-1997. Telephone: 608-663-2254 or toll-free 800-444-4861. Fax: 608-663-3291. E-mail: admissions@edgewood.edu. Web site: http://www.edgewood.edu/.

LAKELAND COLLEGE
SHEBOYGAN, WISCONSIN

General Independent, comprehensive, coed, affiliated with United Church of Christ **Entrance** Moderately difficult **Setting** 240-acre rural campus **Total enrollment** 3,482 **Student/faculty ratio** 19:1 **Application deadline** Rolling (freshmen), rolling (transfer) **Freshmen** 76% were admitted **Housing** Yes **Undergraduates** 61% women, 65% part-time, 22% 25 or older, 1% Native American, 1% Hispanic American, 5% African American, 2% Asian American/Pacific Islander **The most frequently chosen baccalaureate fields are** business/marketing, computer/information sciences, education **Academic program** English as a second language, advanced placement, honors program, summer session, adult/continuing education programs, internships **Contact** Mr. Leo Gavrilos, Director of Admissions, Lakeland College, PO Box 359, Nash Visitors Center, Sheboygan, WI 53082. Telephone: 920-565-1217 or toll-free 800-242-3347 (in-state). E-mail: admissions@lakeland.edu. Web site: http://www.lakeland.edu/.

LAWRENCE UNIVERSITY
APPLETON, WISCONSIN

General Independent, 4-year, coed **Entrance** Very difficult **Setting** 84-acre small-town campus **Total enrollment** 1,289 **Student/faculty ratio** 11:1 **Application deadline** 1/15 (freshmen), rolling (transfer) **Freshmen** 73% were admitted **Housing** Yes **Expenses** Tuition 21,855; Room & Board 4791 **Undergraduates** 54% women, 9% part-time, 1% 25 or older, 0.5% Native American, 2% Hispanic American, 1% African American, 3% Asian American/Pacific Islander **The most frequently chosen baccalaureate fields are** biological/life sciences, psychology, social sciences and history **Academic program** Advanced placement, self-designed majors, internships **Contact** Mr. Steven T. Syverson, Dean of Admissions and Financial Aid, Lawrence University, PO Box 599, Appleton, WI 54912-0599. Telephone: 920-832-6500 or toll-free 800-227-0982. Fax: 920-832-6782. E-mail: excel@lawrence.edu. Web site: http://www.lawrence.edu.

MARANATHA BAPTIST BIBLE COLLEGE
WATERTOWN, WISCONSIN

General Independent Baptist, comprehensive, coed **Entrance** Noncompetitive **Setting** 60-acre small-town campus **Total enrollment** 673 **Student/faculty ratio** 15:1 **Application deadline** Rolling (freshmen), rolling (transfer) **Freshmen** 58% were admitted **Housing** Yes **Expenses** Tuition 6760; Room & Board 4050 **Undergraduates** 54% women, 8% 25 or older, 0.3% Native American, 1% Hispanic American, 1% African American, 1% Asian American/Pacific Islander **Academic program** Accelerated degree program, summer session, internships **Contact** James H. Harrison, Director of Admissions, Maranatha Baptist Bible College, 745 West Main Street, Watertown, WI 53094. Telephone: 920-206-2327 or toll-free 800-622-2947. Fax: 920-261-9109. E-mail: admissions@mbbc.edu. Web site: http://www.mbbc.edu/.

MARIAN COLLEGE OF FOND DU LAC
FOND DU LAC, WISCONSIN

General Independent Roman Catholic, comprehensive, coed **Entrance** Moderately difficult **Setting** 50-acre small-town campus **Total enrollment** 2,016 **Student/faculty ratio** 13:1 **Application deadline** Rolling (freshmen), rolling (transfer) **Freshmen** 79% were admitted **Housing** Yes **Expenses** Tuition $12,979; Room & Board $4482 **Undergraduates** 69% women, 10% part-time, 42% 25 or older, 0.5% Native American, 2% Hispanic American, 3% African American, 1% Asian American/Pacific Islander **The most frequently chosen baccalaureate fields are** business/marketing, education, health professions and related sciences **Academic program** Advanced placement, accelerated degree program, self-designed majors, honors program, summer session, adult/continuing education programs, internships **Contact** Stacey L. Akey, Dean of Admissions, Marian College of Fond du Lac, 45 South National Avenue, Fond du Lac, WI 54935. Telephone: 920-923-7652 or toll-free 800-2-MARIAN Ext. 7652 (in-state). Fax: 920-923-8755. E-mail: admit@mariancoll.edu. Web site: http://www.mariancollege.edu/

► **For more information, see page 445.**

MARQUETTE UNIVERSITY
MILWAUKEE, WISCONSIN

General Independent Roman Catholic (Jesuit), university, coed **Entrance** Moderately difficult **Setting** 80-acre urban campus **Total enrollment** 10,887 **Student/faculty ratio** 15:1 **Application deadline** Rolling (freshmen), rolling (transfer) **Freshmen** 84% were admitted **Housing** Yes **Expenses** Tuition 18,482; Room & Board 6362 **Undergraduates** 55% women, 8% part-time, 0.2% Native American, 4% Hispanic American, 5% African American, 4% Asian American/Pacific Islander **The most frequently chosen baccalaureate fields are** business/marketing, engineering/engineering technologies, health professions and related sciences **Academic program** English as a second language, advanced placement, accelerated degree program, honors program, summer session, adult/continuing education programs, internships **Contact** Mr. Robert Blust, Acting Dean of Undergraduate Admissions, Marquette University, PO Box 1881, Milwaukee, WI 53201-1881. Telephone: 414-288-7004 or toll-free 800-222-6544. Fax: 414-288-3764. E-mail: go2marquette@ums.csd.mu.edu. Web site: http://www.marquette.edu/.

MILWAUKEE INSTITUTE OF ART AND DESIGN
MILWAUKEE, WISCONSIN

General Independent, 4-year, coed **Entrance** Moderately difficult **Setting** urban campus **Total enrollment** 656 **Student/faculty ratio** 11:1 **Application deadline** Rolling (freshmen), rolling (transfer) **Freshmen** 86% were admitted **Housing** Yes **Expenses** Tuition $16,930; Room & Board $6459 **Undergraduates** 51% women, 12% part-time, 14% 25 or older, 1% Native American, 8% Hispanic American, 3% African American, 2% Asian American/Pacific Islander **The most frequently chosen baccalaureate field is** visual/performing arts **Academic program** Advanced placement, summer session, adult/continuing education programs, internships **Contact** Ms. Mary Schopp, Vice President of Enrollment Management, Milwaukee Institute of Art and Design, 273 East Erie Street, Milwaukee, WI 53202. Telephone: 414-291-8070 or toll-free 888-749-MIAD. Fax: 414-291-8077. E-mail: miadadm@miad.edu. Web site: http://www.miad.edu/.

MILWAUKEE SCHOOL OF ENGINEERING
MILWAUKEE, WISCONSIN

General Independent, comprehensive, coed, primarily men **Entrance** Moderately difficult **Setting** 12-acre urban campus **Total enrollment** 2,620 **Student/faculty ratio** 12:1 **Application deadline** Rolling (freshmen), rolling (transfer) **Freshmen** 82% were admitted **Housing** Yes **Expenses** Tuition $20,835; Room & Board $4845 **Undergraduates** 18% women, 26% part-time, 12% 25 or older, 0.3% Native American, 2% Hispanic American, 3% African American, 3% Asian American/Pacific Islander **The most frequently chosen baccalaureate fields are** business/marketing, engineering/engineering technologies, health professions and related sciences **Academic program** Advanced placement, accelerated degree program, summer session, adult/continuing education programs, internships **Contact** Mr. Tim A. Valley, Dean of Enrollment Management, Milwaukee School of Engineering, 1025 North Broadway, Milwaukee, WI 53202-3109. Telephone: 414-277-6763 or toll-free 800-332-6763. Fax: 414-277-7475. E-mail: explore@msoe.edu. Web site: http://www.msoe.edu/.

MOUNT MARY COLLEGE
MILWAUKEE, WISCONSIN

General Independent Roman Catholic, comprehensive, women only **Entrance** Moderately difficult **Setting** 80-acre suburban campus **Total enrollment** 1,246 **Student/faculty ratio** 8:1 **Application deadline** 8/15 (freshmen), 8/15 (transfer) **Freshmen** 63% were admitted **Housing** Yes **Expenses** Tuition 12,646; Room & Board 4380 **Undergraduates** 52% part-time, 45% 25 or older, 1% Native American, 3% Hispanic American, 10% African American, 3% Asian American/Pacific Islander **The most frequently chosen baccalaureate fields are** business/marketing, education, protective services/public administration **Academic program** English as a second language, advanced placement, accelerated degree program, self-designed majors, honors program, summer session, adult/continuing education programs, internships **Contact** Ms. Yvonne Hennigan, Dean of Enrollment Management, Mount Mary College, 2900 North Menomonee River Parkway, Milwaukee, WI 53222-4597. Telephone: 414-258-4810 Ext. 360. Fax: 414-256-1205. E-mail: admiss@mtmary.edu. Web site: http://www.mtmary.edu/.

MOUNT SENARIO COLLEGE
LADYSMITH, WISCONSIN

General Independent, 4-year, coed **Entrance** Minimally difficult **Setting** 110-acre small-town campus **Total enrollment** 830 **Student/faculty ratio** 13:1 **Application deadline** 8/20 (freshmen), rolling (transfer) **Freshmen** 64% were admitted **Housing** Yes **Expenses** Tuition $12,800; Room & Board $4950 **Undergraduates** 36% women, 48% part-time, 46% 25 or older, 1% Native American, 3% Hispanic American, 14% African American, 3% Asian American/Pacific Islander **The most frequently chosen baccalaureate fields are** business/marketing, education, protective services/public administration **Academic program** English as a second language, summer session, adult/continuing education programs, internships **Contact** Mr. Max M. Waits, Admissions Consultant/Foreign Student Advisor, Mount Senario College, 1500 College Avenue West, Ladysmith, WI 54848-2128. Telephone: 715-532-5511 Ext. 110 or toll-free 800-281-6514 (out-of-state). Fax: 715-532-7690. E-mail: admissions@mscfs.edu. Web site: http://www.mountsenario.edu/.

NORTHLAND COLLEGE
ASHLAND, WISCONSIN

General Independent, 4-year, coed, affiliated with United Church of Christ **Entrance** Moderately difficult **Setting** 130-acre small-town campus **Total enrollment** 531 **Student/faculty ratio** 14:1 **Application deadline** 8/1 (freshmen), 8/1 (transfer) **Freshmen** 87% were admitted **Housing** Yes **Expenses** Tuition 15,820; Room & Board 4610 **Undergraduates** 36% women, 16% part-time, 17% 25 or older, 3% Native American, 3% Hispanic American, 1% African American, 2% Asian American/Pacific Islander **Academic program** Advanced placement, accelerated degree program, self-designed majors, summer session, adult/continuing education programs, internships **Contact** Mr. Eric Peterson, Director of Admission, Northland College, 1411 Ellis Avenue, Ashland, WI 54806. Telephone: 715-682-1224 or toll-free 800-753-1840 (in-state); 800-753-1040 (out-of-state). Fax: 715-682-1258. E-mail: admit@wakefield.northland.edu. Web site: http://www.northland.edu/.

RIPON COLLEGE
RIPON, WISCONSIN

General Independent, 4-year, coed **Entrance** Moderately difficult **Setting** 250-acre small-town campus **Total enrollment** 862 **Student/faculty ratio** 10:1 **Application deadline** Rolling (freshmen), rolling (transfer) **Freshmen** 83% were admitted **Housing** Yes **Expenses** Tuition 18,240; Room & Board 4400 **Undergraduates** 53% women, 3% part-time, 1% 25 or older, 0.4% Native American, 2% Hispanic American, 1% African American, 1% Asian American/Pacific Islander **The most frequently chosen baccalaureate fields are** biological/life sciences, English, social sciences and history **Academic program** Advanced placement, accelerated degree program, self-designed majors, internships **Contact** Mr. Scott J. Goplin, Vice President and Dean of Admission and Financial Aid, Ripon College, 300 Seward Street, PO Box 248, Ripon, WI 54971. Telephone: 920-748-8185 or toll-free 800-947-4766. Fax: 920-748-8335. E-mail: adminfo@mac.ripon.edu. Web site: http://www.ripon.edu/.

▶ **For more information, see page 464.**

ST. NORBERT COLLEGE
DE PERE, WISCONSIN

General Independent Roman Catholic, comprehensive, coed **Entrance** Moderately difficult **Setting** 84-acre suburban campus **Total enrollment** 2,140 **Student/faculty ratio** 14:1 **Application deadline** Rolling (freshmen), rolling (transfer) **Freshmen** 88% were admitted **Housing** Yes **Expenses** Tuition $17,957; Room & Board $5162 **Undergraduates** 59% women, 3% part-time, 3% 25 or older, 1% Native American, 1% Hispanic American, 1% African American, 1% Asian American/Pacific Islander **The most frequently chosen baccalaureate fields are** business/marketing, education, social sciences and history **Academic program** English as a second language, advanced placement, accelerated degree program, self-designed majors, honors program, summer session, internships **Contact** Mr. Daniel L. Meyer, Dean of Admission and Enrollment Management, St. Norbert College, 100 Grant Street, Office of Admission, De Pere, WI 54115-2099. Telephone: 920-403-3005 or toll-free 800-236-4878. Fax: 920-403-4072. E-mail: admit@sncac.snc.edu. Web site: http://www.snc.edu/.

SILVER LAKE COLLEGE
MANITOWOC, WISCONSIN

General Independent Roman Catholic, comprehensive, coed **Entrance** Minimally difficult **Setting** 30-acre rural campus **Total enrollment** 956 **Student/faculty ratio** 8:1 **Application deadline** 8/31 (freshmen), 8/31 (transfer) **Freshmen** 86% were admitted **Housing** Yes **Expenses** Tuition $12,050; Room & Board $4444 **Undergraduates** 71% women, 65% part-time, 70% 25 or older, 2% Native American, 2% Hispanic American, 0.2% African American, 1% Asian American/Pacific Islander **The most frequently chosen baccalaureate fields are** business/marketing, education, engineering/engineering technologies **Academic program** English as a second language, advanced placement, accelerated degree program, self-designed majors, summer session, adult/continuing education programs, internships **Contact** Ms. Janis Algozine, Vice President, Dean of Students, Silver Lake College, 2406 South Alverno Road, Manitowoc, WI 54220-9319. Telephone: 920-684-5955 Ext. 175 or toll-free 800-236-4752 Ext. 175 (in-state). Fax: 920-684-7082. E-mail: admslc@sl.edu. Web site: http://www.sl.edu/.

UNIVERSITY OF WISCONSIN–EAU CLAIRE
EAU CLAIRE, WISCONSIN

General State-supported, comprehensive, coed **Entrance** Moderately difficult **Setting** 333-acre urban campus **Total enrollment** 10,549 **Student/faculty ratio** 20:1 **Application deadline** Rolling (freshmen), 7/1 (transfer) **Freshmen** 74% were admitted **Housing** Yes **Expenses** Tuition $3252; Room & Board $3435 **Undergraduates** 60% women, 8% part-time, 7% 25 or older, 1% Native American, 1% Hispanic American, 1% African American, 2% Asian American/Pacific Islander **The most frequently chosen baccalaureate fields are** business/marketing, education, health professions and related sciences **Academic program** English as a second language, advanced placement, honors program, summer session, adult/continuing education programs, internships **Contact** Ms. Kristine Anding, Interim Director of Admissions, University of Wisconsin–Eau Claire, PO Box 4004, Eau Claire, WI 54702-4004. Telephone: 715-836-5415. E-mail: ask-uwec@uwec.edu. Web site: http://www.uwec.edu/.

UNIVERSITY OF WISCONSIN–GREEN BAY
GREEN BAY, WISCONSIN

General State-supported, comprehensive, coed **Entrance** Moderately difficult **Setting** 700-acre suburban campus **Total enrollment** 5,507 **Student/faculty ratio** 21:1 **Application deadline** 2/1 (freshmen), 4/15 (transfer) **Freshmen** 81% were admitted

University of Wisconsin–Green Bay *(continued)*

Housing Yes **Expenses** Tuition $3306; Room only $2106 **Undergraduates** 65% women, 20% part-time, 20% 25 or older, 2% Native American, 1% Hispanic American, 1% African American, 2% Asian American/Pacific Islander **The most frequently chosen baccalaureate fields are** business/marketing, biological/life sciences, interdisciplinary studies **Academic program** English as a second language, advanced placement, accelerated degree program, self-designed majors, summer session, adult/continuing education programs, internships **Contact** Ms. Pam Harvey-Jacobs, Interim Director of Admissions, University of Wisconsin–Green Bay, 2420 Nicolet Drive, Green Bay, WI 54311-7001. Telephone: 920-465-2111 or toll-free 888-367-8942 (out-of-state). Fax: 920-465-5754. E-mail: admissns@uwgb.edu. Web site: http://www.uwgb.edu/.

UNIVERSITY OF WISCONSIN–LA CROSSE
LA CROSSE, WISCONSIN

General State-supported, comprehensive, coed **Entrance** Moderately difficult **Setting** 121-acre suburban campus **Total enrollment** 9,013 **Student/faculty ratio** 21:1 **Application deadline** Rolling (freshmen), rolling (transfer) **Freshmen** 67% were admitted **Housing** Yes **Expenses** Tuition $2697; Room & Board $3450 **Undergraduates** 58% women, 8% part-time, 6% 25 or older, 1% Native American, 1% Hispanic American, 1% African American, 2% Asian American/Pacific Islander **The most frequently chosen baccalaureate fields are** biological/life sciences, business/marketing, education **Academic program** English as a second language, advanced placement, honors program, summer session, adult/continuing education programs, internships **Contact** Mr. Tim Lewis, Director of Admissions, University of Wisconsin–La Crosse, 1725 State Street, LaCrosse, WI 54601. Telephone: 608-785-8939. Fax: 608-785-8940. E-mail: admissions@post.uwlax.edu. Web site: http://www.uwlax.edu/.

UNIVERSITY OF WISCONSIN–MADISON
MADISON, WISCONSIN

General State-supported, university, coed **Entrance** Very difficult **Setting** 1,050-acre urban campus **Total enrollment** 41,219 **Student/faculty ratio** 14:1 **Application deadline** 2/1 (freshmen), 2/1 (transfer) **Freshmen** 64% were admitted **Housing** Yes **Expenses** Tuition 3780; Room & Board 4500 **Undergraduates** 2% 25 or older, 0.5% Native American, 2% Hispanic American, 2% African American, 4% Asian American/Pacific Islander **Academic program** English as a second language, advanced placement, accelerated degree program, self-designed majors, honors program, summer session, adult/continuing education programs, internships **Contact** Mr. Keith White, Office of Admissions, University of Wisconsin–Madison, 716 Langdon Street, Madison, WI 53706-1400. Telephone: 608-262-3961. Fax: 608-262-7706. E-mail: on.wisconsion@mail.admin.wisc.edu. Web site: http://www.wisc.edu/.

UNIVERSITY OF WISCONSIN–MILWAUKEE
MILWAUKEE, WISCONSIN

General State-supported, university, coed **Entrance** Moderately difficult **Setting** 90-acre urban campus **Total enrollment** 23,578 **Student/faculty ratio** 19:1 **Application deadline** Rolling (freshmen), rolling (transfer) **Freshmen** 69% were admitted **Housing** Yes **Expenses** Tuition $3785; Room only $2611 **Undergraduates** 55% women, 25% part-time, 24% 25 or older, 1% Native American, 4% Hispanic American, 9% African American, 4% Asian American/Pacific Islander **The most frequently chosen baccalaureate fields are** business/marketing, education, health professions and related sciences **Academic program** English as a second language, advanced placement, self-designed majors, honors program, summer session, adult/continuing education programs, internships **Contact** Ms. Jan Ford, Director, Recruitment and Outreach, University of Wisconsin–Milwaukee, PO Box 749, Milwaukee, WI 53201. Telephone: 414-229-4397. Fax: 414-229-6940. E-mail: deswcb@des.uwm.edu. Web site: http://www.uwm.edu/.

UNIVERSITY OF WISCONSIN–OSHKOSH
OSHKOSH, WISCONSIN

General State-supported, comprehensive, coed **Entrance** Moderately difficult **Setting** 192-acre suburban campus **Total enrollment** 10,756 **Student/faculty ratio** 18:1 **Application deadline** 8/1 (freshmen), 8/1 (transfer) **Freshmen** 78% were admitted **Housing** Yes **Expenses** Tuition $3024; Room & Board $3234 **Undergraduates** 59% women, 15% part-time, 14% 25 or older, 1% Native American, 1% Hispanic American, 1% African American, 1% Asian American/Pacific Islander **Academic program** English as a second language, advanced placement, accelerated degree program, self-designed majors, honors program, summer session, adult/continuing education programs, internships **Contact** Mr. Richard Hillman, Associate Director of Admissions, University of Wisconsin–Oshkosh, 800 Algoma Boulevard, Oshkosh, WI 54901-8602. Telephone: 920-424-0202. Fax: 920-424-1098. E-mail: oshadmuw@uwosh.edu. Web site: http://www.uwosh.edu/.

UNIVERSITY OF WISCONSIN–PARKSIDE
KENOSHA, WISCONSIN

General State-supported, comprehensive, coed **Entrance** Moderately difficult **Setting** 700-acre suburban campus **Total enrollment** 4,856 **Student/faculty ratio** 27:1 **Application deadline** 8/15 (freshmen), rolling (transfer) **Freshmen** 94% were admitted **Housing** Yes **Expenses** Tuition $3094; Room & Board $4230 **Undergraduates** 59% women, 36% part-time, 78% 25 or older, 0.5% Native American, 5% Hispanic American, 8% African American, 1% Asian American/Pacific Islander **The most frequently chosen baccalaureate fields are** business/marketing, psychology, social sciences and history **Academic program** English as a second language, advanced placement, accelerated degree program, honors program, summer session, adult/continuing education programs, internships **Contact** Mr. Charles Murphy, Director of Admissions, University of Wisconsin–Parkside, 900 Wood Road, PO Box 2000, Kenosha, WI 53141-2000. Telephone: 262-595-2355 or toll-free 877-633-3897 (in-state). E-mail: jucha@it.uwp.edu. Web site: http://www.uwp.edu/.

UNIVERSITY OF WISCONSIN–PLATTEVILLE
PLATTEVILLE, WISCONSIN

General State-supported, comprehensive, coed **Contact** Dr. Richard Schumacher, Dean of Admissions and Enrollment Management, University of Wisconsin–Platteville, 1 University Plaza, Platteville, WI 53818-3099. Telephone: 608-342-1125 or toll-free 800-362-5515 (in-state). E-mail: admit@uwplatt.edu. Web site: http://www.uwplatt.edu/.

UNIVERSITY OF WISCONSIN–RIVER FALLS
RIVER FALLS, WISCONSIN

General State-supported, comprehensive, coed **Entrance** Moderately difficult **Setting** 225-acre suburban campus **Total enrollment** 6,743 **Student/faculty ratio** 19:1 **Application deadline** Rolling (freshmen), rolling (transfer) **Freshmen** 43% were admitted **Housing** Yes **Expenses** Tuition $3138; Room & Board $3452 **Undergraduates** 61% women, 10% part-time, 9% 25 or older, 0.5% Native American, 1% Hispanic American, 1% African American, 4% Asian American/Pacific Islander **Academic program** Advanced placement, accelerated degree program, self-designed majors, honors program, summer session, adult/continuing education programs, internships **Contact** Mr. Alan Tuchtenhagen, Director of Admissions, University of Wisconsin–River Falls, 410 South Third Street, 112 South Hall, River Falls, WI 54022-5001. Telephone: 715-425-3500. Fax: 715-425-0676. E-mail: admit@uwrf.edu. Web site: http://www.uwrf.edu/.

UNIVERSITY OF WISCONSIN–STEVENS POINT
STEVENS POINT, WISCONSIN

General State-supported, comprehensive, coed **Entrance** Moderately difficult **Setting** 335-acre small-town campus **Total enrollment** 8,858 **Student/faculty ratio** 20:1 **Application deadline** Rolling (freshmen), rolling (transfer) **Freshmen** 58% were admitted **Housing** Yes **Expenses** Tuition $3165; Room & Board $3616 **Undergraduates** 57% women, 9% part-time, 13% 25 or older, 1% Native American, 1% Hispanic American, 0.5% African American, 1% Asian American/Pacific Islander **The most frequently chosen baccalaureate fields are** education, business/marketing, natural resources/environmental science **Academic program** English as a second language, advanced placement, accelerated degree program, self-designed majors, summer session, adult/continuing education programs, internships **Contact** Dr. David Eckholm, Director of Admissions, University of Wisconsin–Stevens Point, 2100 Main Street, Stevens Point, WI 54481-3897. Telephone: 715-346-2441. Fax: 715-346-3296. E-mail: admiss@uwsp.edu. Web site: http://www.uwsp.edu/.

UNIVERSITY OF WISCONSIN–STOUT
MENOMONIE, WISCONSIN

General State-supported, comprehensive, coed **Entrance** Moderately difficult **Setting** 120-acre small-town campus **Total enrollment** 7,702 **Student/faculty ratio** 20:1 **Application deadline** Rolling (freshmen), rolling (transfer) **Freshmen** 81% were admitted **Housing** Yes **Expenses** Tuition $3286; Room & Board $3530 **Undergraduates** 49% women, 12% part-time, 11% 25 or older, 0.4% Native American, 1% Hispanic American, 1% African American, 2% Asian American/Pacific Islander **The most frequently chosen baccalaureate fields are** business/marketing, education, engineering/engineering technologies **Academic program** English as a second language, advanced placement, accelerated degree program, honors program, summer session, adult/continuing education programs, internships **Contact** Ms. Cynthia Jenkins, Director of Admissions, University of Wisconsin–Stout, Menomonie, WI 54751. Telephone: 715-232-2639 or toll-free 800-HI-STOUT (in-state). Fax: 715-232-1667. E-mail: jenkinsc@uwstout.edu. Web site: http://www.uwstout.edu/.

UNIVERSITY OF WISCONSIN–SUPERIOR
SUPERIOR, WISCONSIN

General State-supported, comprehensive, coed **Contact** Ms. Lorraine Washa, Student Application Contact, University of Wisconsin–Superior, Belknap and Catlin, PO Box 2000, Superior, WI 54880-4500. Telephone: 715-394-8230. Fax: 715-394-8407. E-mail: admissions@uwsuper.edu. Web site: http://www.uwsuper.edu/.

UNIVERSITY OF WISCONSIN–WHITEWATER
WHITEWATER, WISCONSIN

General State-supported, comprehensive, coed **Entrance** Moderately difficult **Setting** 385-acre small-town campus **Total enrollment** 10,540 **Student/faculty ratio** 21:1 **Application deadline** Rolling (freshmen), rolling (transfer) **Freshmen** 79% were admitted **Housing** Yes **Expenses** Tuition $3144; Room & Board $3324 **Undergraduates** 53% women, 16% part-time, 10% 25 or older, 0.4% Native American, 2% Hispanic American, 4% African American, 1% Asian American/Pacific Islander **The most frequently chosen baccalaureate fields are** business/marketing, education, social sciences and history **Academic program** Advanced placement, accelerated degree program, self-designed majors, honors program, summer session, adult/continuing education programs, internships **Contact** Dr. Tori A.

University of Wisconsin–Whitewater *(continued)*

McGuire, Executive Director of Admissions, University of Wisconsin–Whitewater, 800 West Main Street, Whitewater, WI 53190-1790. Telephone: 262-472-1440 Ext. 1512. Fax: 262-472-1515. E-mail: uwwadmit@uwwvax.uww.edu. Web site: http://www.uww.edu/.

VITERBO UNIVERSITY
LA CROSSE, WISCONSIN

General Independent Roman Catholic, comprehensive, coed **Entrance** Moderately difficult **Setting** 5-acre urban campus **Total enrollment** 2,106 **Student/faculty ratio** 14:1 **Application deadline** Rolling (freshmen), rolling (transfer) **Freshmen** 88% were admitted **Housing** Yes **Expenses** Tuition 13,630; Room & Board 4710 **Undergraduates** 75% women, 21% part-time, 34% 25 or older, 0.4% Native American, 1% Hispanic American, 1% African American, 1% Asian American/Pacific Islander **Academic program** Advanced placement, accelerated degree program, self-designed majors, summer session, adult/continuing education programs, internships **Contact** Mr. Joe Fischer, Admission Counselor, Viterbo University, 815 South Ninth Street, LaCrosse, WI 54601. Telephone: 608-796-3016 Ext. 3016 or toll-free 800-VIT-ERBO Ext. 3010. Fax: 608-796-3020. E-mail: admission@viterbo.edu. Web site: http://www.viterbo.edu/.

WISCONSIN LUTHERAN COLLEGE
MILWAUKEE, WISCONSIN

General Independent, 4-year, coed, affiliated with Wisconsin Evangelical Lutheran Synod **Entrance** Moderately difficult **Setting** 16-acre suburban campus **Total enrollment** 634 **Student/faculty ratio** 12:1 **Freshmen** 89% were admitted **Housing** Yes **Expenses** Tuition $14,116; Room & Board $5050 **Undergraduates** 61% women, 6% part-time, 4% 25 or older, 0% Native American, 1% Hispanic American, 1% African American, 1% Asian American/Pacific Islander **The most frequently chosen baccalaureate fields are** business/marketing, communications/communication technologies, education **Academic program** Advanced placement, self-designed majors, summer session, internships **Contact** Mr. Jeff Weber, Director of Admissions, Wisconsin Lutheran College, 8800 West Bluemound Road, Milwaukee, WI 53226-9942. Telephone: 414-443-8819 or toll-free 888-WIS LUTH. Fax: 414-443-8514. E-mail: jaweber@post.its.mcw.edu. Web site: http://www.wlc.edu/.

WYOMING

UNIVERSITY OF WYOMING
LARAMIE, WYOMING

General State-supported, university, coed **Entrance** Moderately difficult **Setting** small-town campus **Total enrollment** 11,057 **Student/faculty ratio** 14:1 **Application deadline** 8/10 (freshmen), 8/10 (transfer) **Freshmen** 97% were admitted **Housing** Yes **Expenses** Tuition $2,807; Room & Board $4744 **Undergraduates** 53% women, 15% part-time, 19% 25 or older, 1% Native American, 3% Hispanic American, 1% African American, 1% Asian American/Pacific Islander **The most frequently chosen baccalaureate fields are** business/marketing, education, engineering/engineering technologies **Academic program** Advanced placement, accelerated degree program, self-designed majors, honors program, summer session, adult/continuing education programs, internships **Contact** Ms. Sara Axelson, Associate Vice President Enrollment and Director of Admissions, University of Wyoming, Box 3435, Laramie, WY 82071. Telephone: 307-766-5160 or toll-free 800-342-5996. Fax: 307-766-4042. E-mail: undergraduate.admissions@uwyo.edu. Web site: http://www.uwyo.edu/.

DESCRIPTIONS

The full-page descriptions in this section provide a broad overview of some of the colleges and universities profiled in the previous section. These descriptions are offered to help give students a better sense of the individuality of each institution, in terms that include mission statements, campus environments, and academic programs. The absence from this section of any college or university does not constitute an editorial decision on the part of Peterson's. In essence, this section is an open forum for colleges and universities, on a voluntary basis, to communicate their particular messages to prospective college students. The descriptions are arranged alphabetically by the official name of the institution.

ALDERSON–BROADDUS COLLEGE

■ PHILIPPI, WEST VIRGINIA

THE COLLEGE

Located on a mountaintop overlooking the Tygart River valley in Philippi, West Virginia, Alderson-Broaddus College is a four-year, coeducational, independent liberal arts college with a history of educational excellence and innovation. Affiliated with the American Baptist Churches, U.S.A., the College has been preparing men and women for leadership for more than 130 years. Today, more than 750 men and women from thirty-eight states and eight countries study at Alderson-Broaddus, preparing for the future with quality programs in a variety of fields. Alderson-Broaddus emphasizes an innovative approach to quality liberal arts education. For example, the College pioneered the first undergraduate physician assistant program in the nation. With a state-of-the-art computer network in advance of most universities, the College also makes extensive computer resources available to all students and programs of study. Close student-faculty relationships and an average class size of 15 encourage involvement. Hands-on experience begins in the freshman year in all fields—from nursing to broadcasting, education to political science, biology to music. Alderson-Broaddus is accredited by the North Central Association of Colleges and Schools. The baccalaureate program in nursing is accredited by the National League for Nursing. The Physician Assistant Program is accredited by the Commission on Accreditation of Allied Health Programs (CAAHEP). The teacher education programs are accredited by the National Council for Accreditation of Teacher Education (NCATE). More than fifty student organizations and hundreds of activities provide opportunities for recreation, personal development, and service. The A-B Battlers have a championship tradition in intercollegiate athletics that includes baseball, basketball, cross-country, and soccer for men and basketball, cross-country, softball, and volleyball for women. A wide range of intramural sports involves most of the student body. The attractions of West Virginia's unspoiled state and national parks are nearby. The wooded 170-acre campus offers outstanding facilities, including modern academic facilities, a 7,200-watt FM radio station, an on-campus cafe, an art gallery, a bookstore, a post office, student lounges, and a sports coliseum with a pool, two gyms, a racquetball court, and a fitness center. The College provides varied, comfortable residential options and a flexible, high-quality meal plan. There are excellent medical facilities on campus and in the surrounding area.

For more information, students should contact:

Admissions Office
Alderson-Broaddus College
P.O. Box 2003
Philippi, West Virginia 26416
Telephone: 800-263-1549 (toll-free)
E-mail: admissions@ab.edu

ACADEMIC PROGRAM

The academic year consists of two 15-week semesters. Students generally take 15 to 18 semester hours each semester. In addition, the College offers a 10-week summer term. Completion of 128 hours of study is required for graduation. Most of the degree requirements are fulfilled through on-campus study, but some majors require off-campus field work and internships for which credit is awarded. With the help of their academic advisers, students select courses to fulfill requirements for liberal studies and a major. Students may choose elective minors in such areas as business, computer science, education, recreation, and technical writing. An honors program offers academically talented students opportunities for independent scholarship and research.

FINANCIAL AID

Alderson-Broaddus College has an excellent program of financial aid that includes merit, performance, and need-based grants and scholarships, loans, and college work-study. Applicants requesting financial aid are required to submit the Free Application for Federal Student Aid (FAFSA). Nearly 99 percent of all students receive some form of financial assistance.

ALFRED UNIVERSITY

■ ALFRED, NEW YORK

THE UNIVERSITY

Alfred University is a residential institution of 2,500 graduate and undergraduate students, located 70 miles south of Rochester, between the Finger Lakes region and the Allegheny Mountains in western New York State. Alfred is composed of the privately endowed Colleges of Business, Liberal Arts and Sciences, and Engineering and Professional Studies, as well as the publicly supported New York State College of Ceramics, which is composed of the School of Art and Design and the School of Ceramic Engineering and Materials Science. Alfred is noted for its superior academic quality, outstanding faculty, and commitment to student development. The New York State College of Ceramics is regarded as the world leader in the field of ceramic engineering. The state of New York has identified Alfred University as one of its ten centers for advanced technology research.

For more information, students should contact:

Katherine McCarthy
Director of Admissions
Alumni Hall
Alfred University
Saxon Drive
Alfred, New York 14802
Telephone: 607-871-2115
800-541-9229 (toll-free)
Fax: 607-871-2198
E-mail: admwww@alfred.edu
World Wide Web:
http://www.alfred.edu

ACADEMIC PROGRAM

All academic programs require courses in the liberal arts and sciences; however, specific graduation requirements differ for each college and school within the University. All candidates are required to satisfy a physical education requirement through courses or proficiency examinations. To encourage students with strong ability and initiative, the University recognizes the Advanced Placement and International Baccalaureate programs. In addition, the University offers its own challenge examination program for currently enrolled students. The University Honors Program is open to all majors and requires an additional essay application for admission to the program. Army ROTC is also available.

FINANCIAL AID

During the 2000–01 academic year, University-funded aid sources provided more than $14 million to undergraduate students. For private-sector programs, 95 percent of freshmen received some form of financial assistance. In the New York State College of Ceramics, 88 percent of freshmen received some form of aid. Aid administered by the University usually consists of a combination of scholarships or grants, loans, and part-time work. Students may be eligible for financial assistance under the Federal Pell Grant, Federal Supplemental Educational Opportunity Grant, Federal Perkins Loan, and Federal Work-Study programs. New York State residents may be eligible for aid under the Tuition Assistance Program. The University sponsors National Merit Scholarships; departmental talent awards; Presidential, Southern Tier, and transfer scholarships; and the Johnathan Allen Award for Leadership.

APPLICATION AND INFORMATION

Candidates must submit a completed Alfred University application form or the Common Application form, SAT I or ACT results, a letter of recommendation, and a $40 application fee. Students who visit campus receive an application fee waiver certificate that may be used on that day or at a later time. They must also have their high school guidance office submit an official transcript. Applicants to the School of Art and Design must submit a portfolio of their work, typically fifteen to twenty slides. The application and portfolio deadline under the early decision plan is December 1, with notification by December 15. The application and portfolio deadline for regular admission is February 1, with notification by mid-March. Transfer applicants should file an application by August 1 for September admission or December 1 for January admission. The School of Art and Design has different application and portfolio deadlines for transfer students, dependent upon the student's previous course work in art. Students should contact the Office of Admissions for further information regarding these deadlines.

ALLEGHENY COLLEGE

■ MEADVILLE, PENNSYLVANIA

THE COLLEGE

Founded on America's western frontier in 1815, Allegheny is a classical, selective college of the liberal arts and sciences. Although highly regarded as a preprofessional school, its impact on students goes well beyond preparation for careers. Allegheny not only develops in its students such essential skills as writing, critical thinking, and problem solving, it also fosters a capacity for lifelong learning, the ability to manage everyday affairs, responsible citizenship, social skills, and values. While nonsectarian in outlook and practice, Allegheny has been affiliated with the United Methodist Church since 1833. The 1,900 students come from thirty-eight states and seventeen other countries. Six percent are members of minority groups and three fourths reside on campus. On-campus residence is required of freshmen and sophomores and optional for other students, but it is guaranteed for all four years for all who seek it. Faculty members describe Allegheny students as active and hardworking. Approximately 70 percent come from the highest fifth of their high school class, 1 in 3 was a leader of a student organization, and 70 percent were active in volunteer service groups. At Allegheny, students sustain more than 100 clubs, committees, and organizations in drama, dance, vocal and instrumental music, publications, radio, religious life, politics, social service, professional and multicultural interest areas, and the governance of student life. Intramural athletics involve three fourths of the students, and the varsity program is one of the best in NCAA Division III. Of the twenty teams for men and women, about half are nationally ranked each year.

For more information, students should contact:

Office of Admissions
Allegheny College
Meadville, Pennsylvania 16335-3902
Telephone: 814-332-4351
800-521-5293 (toll-free)
E-mail: admiss@allegheny.edu
World Wide Web:
http://www.allegheny.edu

ACADEMIC PROGRAM

Allegheny ensures that students develop wholeness across the divisions of knowledge (arts and humanities, social sciences, and natural sciences) as well as expertise in one or more fields. Each student must complete 131 semester credit hours; the major may require 32 to 48 semester credit hours, including a junior seminar and the distinctive Senior Project, while the remainder are electives and Liberal Studies Program courses. The innovative Liberal Studies Program includes two freshman seminars, with strong advising, writing, and speaking components; a sophomore writing and speaking course; and some in-depth study in a subject outside the division of the major. Writing proficiency is emphasized throughout the Allegheny years—it is a central objective of the seminars. It is developed further in the sophomore writing course, after students have mastered some college-level material, and it must be demonstrated in all other courses.

FINANCIAL AID

A large number of merit-based scholarships are awarded annually, making the College more affordable even to families who do not qualify for need-based financial aid. Trustee Scholarships, which award up to $40,000, are guaranteed for four years of study at Allegheny. Also, scholarships, grants, loans, and campus employment are awarded to students who need assistance to meet College expenses. The Free Application for Federal Student Aid (FAFSA), which establishes an applicant's eligibility for virtually all institutional, state, and federal assistance, must be submitted by February 15. Notices about the receipt of financial aid are sent to students shortly after their acceptance by the College. Nine out of ten students receive some form of financial aid.

APPLICATION AND INFORMATION

The application for admission should be submitted by February 15 (January 15 for early decision), and the SAT I or ACT results should be forwarded to the College by each candidate. Applicants for early decision are notified on a rolling basis through January 31. Regular applicants are informed of the admission decision by April 1.

ALMA COLLEGE

■ ALMA, MICHIGAN

THE COLLEGE

Regarded as one of the nation's best liberal arts colleges, Alma College is in its second century of superior education and professional distinction. Founded by Presbyterians in 1886, Alma remains a private liberal arts institution committed to a values-oriented style of education. In a time when many professionals find that their technical training is already out of date, Alma's graduates are entering the job market with an education that will always serve them. Alma's academic philosophy, rooted in the liberal arts tradition and providing a broad educational base with flexible, innovative course work, has earned Alma a Phi Beta Kappa chapter. Classes are small—the average size is 19—enabling students to do more than just listen. Students enjoy the rigorous academic atmosphere; 82 percent of the faculty members hold the highest degree in their field.

For more information, students should contact:

Admissions Office
Alma College
614 West Superior Street
Alma, Michigan 48801-1599
Telephone: 800-321-ALMA (toll-free)
E-mail: admissions@alma.edu
World Wide Web:
http://www.alma.edu
http://www.alma.edu/admissions/application.htm (to apply)

ACADEMIC PROGRAM

The College operates on a 4-4-1 calendar—two 4-month terms in the fall and winter and one 1-month term in the spring. During the spring term, there are opportunities for international study as well as for on-campus instruction and research. In keeping with Alma's philosophy of educating the whole person, the College requires that all students complete liberal arts courses spanning the humanities, the natural sciences, and the social sciences. The B.A. and B.S. degree programs require the completion of 136 credits; the B.F.A. and B.M. degree programs, 148 credits. Highly qualified students are challenged by Alma's honors program, featuring a specially designed freshman course that explores the methods of communication used in the liberal arts disciplines. The honors concept extends throughout the four years at Alma. Alma accepts credits earned through the Advanced Placement (AP) Program, the College-Level Examination Program (CLEP), the International Baccalaureate Diploma (I.B.) program, and examinations designed by Alma's academic departments.

FINANCIAL AID

At Alma, students can achieve scholarship recognition regardless of need on the basis of outstanding scholastic achievement. Several academically competitive scholarship programs provide awards for eligible students, including a full tuition scholarship for National Merit Finalists. The College also offers performance scholarships in recognition of individual talent, as well as grants, loans, and deferred-payment plans. Up to 400 campus and community jobs are filled by Alma students yearly. To apply for aid, students are required only to file the Free Application for Federal Student Aid (FAFSA) in January of the year of prospective enrollment at Alma.

APPLICATION AND INFORMATION

Students may apply at any time after completing their junior year of high school. Freshman applicants should send the completed application for admission along with a $20 nonrefundable application fee, high school transcripts, and ACT or SAT I scores. Students are required to submit a recommendation from their high school guidance counselor. Early action applications are due by November 1. Transfer students should submit transcripts from all colleges and high schools attended, the completed application for admission, a $20 nonrefundable application fee, a financial aid transcript, and a Transfer Recommendation Form from the last college attended. Applications are handled on a rolling basis; students should hear about admission decisions within three weeks after sending an application and records. Alma College's nondiscrimination policy includes age, color, creed, gender, national origin, physical ability, race, religion, and sexual orientation.

AQUINAS COLLEGE

■ GRAND RAPIDS, MICHIGAN

THE COLLEGE

Located on the eastern edge of the city of Grand Rapids, Aquinas enjoys all of the advantages of Michigan's second-largest city and is just a 3-hour drive from Detroit or Chicago. The Aquinas College campus is an interesting blend of early-nineteenth-century architecture coupled with modern-day structures. The campus abounds with natural beauty; it has been called the most beautiful small campus in Michigan. Its ninety species of trees, winding woodland paths, and inviting creeks and ponds create a peaceful 107-acre environment that students of all ages find welcoming. Founded by the Dominican Sisters of Grand Rapids in 1886, Aquinas has a Catholic heritage and a Christian tradition. The Dominican tradition of working and serving remains alive at Aquinas. The Aquinas general education plan exposes students to the necessary skills that enable them to become critical thinkers, articulate speakers, strong writers, and effective problem solvers. Aquinas faculty members insist that students carry values as well as skills into the workplace. The College's curriculum, with its more than forty majors and cognates, is designed to provide students with both breadth and depth and to foster a thirst for knowledge and truth and a spirit of intellectual dialogue and inquiry. Coupled with nationally recognized co-op and internship programs, it prepares students to both live and work in the rapidly changing world of today and tomorrow.

For more information, students should contact:

Paula Meehan
Dean of Admissions
Aquinas College
1607 Robinson Road, SE
Grand Rapids, Michigan 49506
Telephone: 616-732-4460
800-678-9593 (toll-free)
E-mail: admissions@aquinas.edu
World Wide Web:
http://www.aquinas.edu

ACADEMIC PROGRAM

In addition to their major and minor fields of study, students take an integrated skills course called Inquiry and Expression. This course spans the entire freshman year and has an emphasis on writing integrated with reading critically, oral communication skills, critical thinking, library/electronic research methods, computer utilization, and basic quantitative reasoning. The thematic content is American Pluralism: The Individual in a Diverse America. Sophomores take a yearlong course in the humanities. As juniors they are required to take 3 hours in Religious Dimensions of Human Existence, with a choice among three categories: Scripture, Catholic/Christian Thought, or Contemporary Religious Experience. The senior year includes a capstone course called Global Perspective. Students are also required to be proficient in a second language through the 201 level. There also is a distribution plan in the general education plan covering The Individual in a Global Community; Myth, Mind, Body, and Spirit; Natural World; Artistic and Creative Studies; and Quantitative Reasoning and Technology. Aquinas also accepts credit through CLEP and Advanced Placement.

FINANCIAL AID

Aquinas College awards both merit-based financial assistance and traditional need-based assistance to qualified students. The Spectrum Scholarship Program was developed to recognize students' achievements in academics, leadership, and service. More than 50 percent of entering freshmen receive some form of financial assistance. The College administers the traditional grant and loan programs, including Federal Stafford Student Loans and Federal PLUS loans. Athletic grants are also available. The College participates in the Facts Tuition Management Plan. This plan assists students in paying costs over a period of time. To apply for financial assistance, students must complete the Free Application for Federal Student Aid (FAFSA).

ATLANTA COLLEGE OF ART

■ ATLANTA, GEORGIA

THE COLLEGE

The Atlanta College of Art provides an educational environment for the career-minded student with a talent and passion for art or design. Founded in 1928, the College is an accredited institutional member of the National Association of Schools of Art and Design and the Commission on Colleges of the Southern Association of Colleges and Schools. Approximately 430 students from across the U.S. and from abroad compose a highly charged, creative community that nurtures the development of educated, effective, and successful professionals in the visual arts.

For an application and more information, students should contact:

Director of Enrollment Management
Atlanta College of Art
Woodruff Arts Center
1280 Peachtree Street, NE
Atlanta, Georgia 30309

Telephone: 404-733-5100
800-832-2104 (toll-free)
E-mail: acainfo@woodruffcenter.org
World Wide Web:
http://www.aca.edu

ACADEMIC PROGRAM

The College's first-year Foundation Program combines visual studies courses, which emphasize visual thinking and problem solving, with courses in drawing and liberal arts as well as work in a studio area of choice. In the sophomore year, students develop their own course of study with a faculty adviser, either electing an established major or designing their own individualized major program. During the course of study, studio work is combined with courses in art history and criticism, English, literature, philosophy, psychology, anthropology, sociology, science, and math in a ratio of 2:1. These liberal arts courses reflect the notion that the making of art and the making of the artist are imaginative and reflective tasks and not simply technical ones, and they embody the conviction that the best artists and designers are those who can appreciate how tradition influences their work and is affected by it. Operating on a two-semester academic year with an optional concentrated summer session, the College requires that students complete 120 credit hours for the B.F.A. degree: 78 in studio (12 credits in visual studies, 12 credits in drawing, 30–36 credits in the major, and 18–24 credits in studio electives) and 42 in liberal arts (12 credits in art history, 18 credits in the humanities, 3 credits in natural science, 6 credits in social science, and 3 credits in math).

FINANCIAL AID

The Atlanta College of Art offers extensive financial assistance to students, combining institutional funds with funds from federal and state grant and loan programs. Each year, need-based grants, loans, and work-study jobs are awarded to students who apply for financial assistance using the Free Application of Federal Student Aid and the College's own financial aid form. While the priority deadline for applying for financial aid is March 15, awards are made on a first-come, first-served basis. The College also offers Merit Scholarships to both entering students and returning students. The Presidential Scholarship is awarded on the basis of the excellence of the portfolio and scholastic achievement. The School of Excellence award is given in recognition of the high quality of the student's high school or two-year college art program and the students' achievement in that program. The Dean's Scholarship is awarded on the basis of ACT or SAT I scores. Georgia residents are eligible for the Georgia Tuition Equalization Grant and the Hope Scholarship program.

APPLICATION AND INFORMATION

Students are admitted to the College on a rolling basis, and an admission decision is made as soon as the applicant file is complete. While there is no official deadline for submission of an application, students are encouraged to apply by March 1 for priority consideration for admission, financial aid, and scholarships.

BELMONT UNIVERSITY

■ NASHVILLE, TENNESSEE

THE UNIVERSITY

For more information, students should contact:

Office of Admissions
Belmont University
1900 Belmont Boulevard
Nashville, Tennessee 37212
Telephone: 615-460-6785
800-56ENROLL (toll-free)
Fax: 615-460-5434
E-mail:
buadmission@mail.belmont.edu
World Wide Web:
http://www.belmont.edu

Nationally recognized programs thrive on the Belmont University campus, which is located in the heart of the state capital, known both as Music City, U.S.A., and the Athens of the South (for its many educational institutions). Nashville offers big-city advantages with small-town charm. Belmont's vision is to be a premier teaching university, bringing together the best of liberal arts and professional education in a consistently caring Christian environment. Central to the fulfillment of that vision are faculty members who have a passion for teaching and the belief that premier teaching is interactive, technology-supported, motivational, creative, and exciting. With an enrollment of more than 3,000 students, Belmont is the second-largest private college or university in Tennessee. Affiliated with the Tennessee Baptist Convention, it is the state's largest private college or university with a religious affiliation. In addition to the many international countries represented in the student body, Belmont University attracts students from almost every state in the United States. The culturally diverse institution is committed to listening and learning from everyone. Students of today are helping shape the way students of tomorrow will be educated.

ACADEMIC PROGRAM

Uniquely positioned to provide the best of liberal arts and professional education, Belmont University offers celebrated professional programs structured to provide an academically well-rounded education. Belmont University operates on a two-semester schedule with classes beginning in late August and ending in early May. Two summer sessions are also offered. The academic program is arranged by school: the College of Arts and Sciences, the College of Business Administration, the College of Health Sciences, the College of Visual and Performing Arts, and the School of Religion. In addition to the degrees offered through the schools, Belmont University offers an honors program, which was created to provide an enrichment opportunity for students who have potential for superior academic performance and who seek added challenge and breadth to their studies. Students enrolled in the honors program are led in designing and working through a flexible, individual curriculum and interdisciplinary general education curriculum by a private tutor who is an honors faculty member. The University's advancements in undergraduate research are credited to a faculty committed to helping students practice their disciplines. The annual Belmont Undergraduate Research Symposium puts Belmont at the forefront of this national movement by providing a public forum for in-depth research at the undergraduate level.

FINANCIAL AID

The financial aid program at Belmont combines merit-based assistance with need-based assistance to make the University program affordable. Institutional merit awards range from full tuition Presidential Scholarships to performance scholarships. Also included are many levels of academic merit awards. Belmont University also administers traditional state and federal programs, including the Federal Pell Grant, Federal Stafford Student Loan, Federal Perkins Loan, Federal PLUS loan, and Tennessee Student Assistance Grants and Scholarships. Campus employment is available. Parents may arrange monthly tuition payments through an outside vendor. To apply for assistance, the student must complete the Free Application for Federal Student Aid (FAFSA).

BENEDICTINE UNIVERSITY

■ LISLE, ILLINOIS

THE UNIVERSITY

Benedictine University was founded in 1887 as St. Procopius College. One hundred fourteen years later, the University remains committed to providing a high-quality, Catholic, liberal education for men and women. The undergraduate enrollment is 2,000 students. The student body comprises students of diverse ages, religions, races, and national origins. Twenty-eight percent of the full-time students reside on campus. Benedictine University is situated on a rolling, tree-covered 108-acre campus of ten major buildings with air-conditioned classrooms and modern, well-equipped laboratories. A student athletic center features three full-size basketball courts, a competition-size swimming pool, three tennis courts, and training facilities. All of the residence halls are comfortable and spacious and have access to the Internet. Other features include a scenic campus pond, spacious and well-kept athletic fields, a student center with dining halls, a game room, lounges, a bookstore, and meeting rooms. At Benedictine University, the environment is strengthened by success, not size. Renowned faculty members know students by name and care as much about each student's progress as they do about their own research. Those personal relationships have produced superb results. The rate of acceptance of Benedictine University graduates to medical, dental, and professional schools is significantly above regional and national averages. The liberal arts curriculum has helped place the University among some of the finest small private schools in the nation. *U.S. News & World Report's* 2001 rankings listed Benedictine University as one of the top universities in the Midwest. The magazine also ranked the school one of the top five in the region for campus diversity.

For further information, students should contact:

Undergraduate Admissions
Benedictine University
5700 College Road
Lisle, Illinois 60532-0900

Telephone: 630-829-6300
888-829-6363 (toll-free oustide Illinois)
Fax: 630-829-6301
E-mail: admissions@ben.edu
World Wide Web:
http://www.ben.edu

ACADEMIC PROGRAM

For graduation, a student must earn at least 120 semester hours, at least 55 of which must be completed at a four-year regionally accredited college. At least the final 45 semester hours must be completed at Benedictine University. The University makes selective exceptions to the normal academic residency requirement of 45 semester hours for adults who are eligible for the Degree Completion Program. Eligibility is limited to those who have nearly completed their undergraduate studies but who, for reasons of employment, career change, or family situation, found it necessary to interrupt their studies. The Second Major Program is designed for people who already have a degree in one area and would like to gain expertise in another. This program allows the student to concentrate on courses that fulfill the requirements of a second major. The student receives a certificate upon completion.

FINANCIAL AID

In 1999-2000, Benedictine University freshmen received assistance totaling $3.3 million from sources that included loans, scholarships and grants, tuition remission, and employment opportunities. Nearly 93 percent of the freshman class participated, receiving an average package of $11,565. Benedictine University has dedicated more than $5 million of the annual budget to providing grants and scholarships to students, including scholarships for study in the humanities and a separate scholarship program designed to attract and serve members of minority groups. Students who wish to apply for aid must complete the Free Application for Federal Student Aid (FAFSA), the Benedictine University application for financial aid, and the Benedictine University application for admission.

APPLICATION AND INFORMATION

Applications are reviewed on a rolling basis. Students are encouraged to apply for admission at any time after completing their junior year of high school. Transfer students may apply for admission during their last semester or quarter before anticipated transfer to Benedictine University. Earlier applications are encouraged.

BETHEL COLLEGE

■ ST. PAUL, MINNESOTA

THE COLLEGE

Bethel College began its four-year Christian liberal arts program in 1945 but traces its roots to Bethel Theological Seminary, founded in 1871. Bethel is a ministry of the churches of the Baptist General Conference. The College encourages growth and learning in a distinctly Christian environment, continually striving to help students discover and develop the skills God has given them. Bethel's more than 3,000 students represent a wide range of national and international cultures and more than thirty denominations. Most of Bethel's students are between 18 and 22 years of age, but older and younger students bring a welcome diversity to campus life. Bethel students are involved in a wealth of cocurricular activities, from music to ministry, Bible study to broadcasting, theater to tennis, and art to athletics. Bethel sports teams compete in NCAA Division III and the Minnesota Intercollegiate Athletic Conference. The campus, built in the 1970s, is the newest among Minnesota colleges. Versatile buildings are centers for the sciences, humanities, physical education, learning resources, and fine arts. In addition to the undergraduate degree programs, Bethel offers Master of Arts degrees in communication, counseling psychology, nursing, and organizational leadership and a Master of Education degree with programs in educational leadership and special education.

For more information, students should contact:

Office of Admissions
Bethel College
3900 Bethel Drive
St. Paul, Minnesota 55112
Telephone: 651-638-6242
800-255-8706 Ext. 6242
(toll-free)
Fax: 651-635-1490
E-mail: bcoll-admit@bethel.edu
World Wide Web:
http://www.bethel.edu
AOL Keyword: Bethel

ACADEMIC PROGRAM

Bethel was named among the top ten liberal arts colleges in the Midwest by *U.S. News & World Report* in 2000. Bethel's general education curriculum has become a model for many other liberal arts colleges nationwide. Students are required to take classes that will give them a broad view of the world and their role as Christians. General education classes are grouped around the following themes: Bible and theology, Western heritage, world citizenship, self-understanding, science and technology, and health and wholeness. In addition, in order to graduate, all Bethel students must demonstrate competence in mathematics, writing, speaking, and computing. Bethel College follows a 4-1-4 academic calendar, consisting of two 15-week semesters and a 3-week Interim in January. A full-time academic load for each semester is 12 to 18 credits. To graduate, a student must complete a minimum of 122 credits with a cumulative grade point average of at least 2.0 and a minimum 2.25 grade point average in his or her major. Also required are 50 credits of general education.

FINANCIAL AID

Bethel College strives to make it financially possible for every qualified student to attend. Each year, nearly 90 percent of the students receive some kind of financial aid, including scholarships, grants, loans, and assistance in the form of on-campus employment. Students who wish to be considered for financial aid must first be admitted to the College and then submit a Family Financial Statement (FFS). Bethel's priority deadline is April 15 of each year. Students who have completed and mailed all necessary forms by this date receive first consideration.

APPLICATION AND INFORMATION

Students wishing to apply for admission to Bethel must send the following: a completed Bethel application form with a $25 nonrefundable application fee; test scores from the PSAT, SAT I, or ACT; transcripts of all course work completed at the high school and college levels; and references from a pastor and an adult friend or employer. Admission decisions are made on a rolling basis. Although there is no deadline, applicants for fall admission are encouraged to complete their files before May 1.

BOWIE STATE UNIVERSITY

■ BOWIE, MARYLAND

THE UNIVERSITY

Bowie State University began as a normal school in the city of Baltimore in 1865, and it has evolved over the years into a four-year, coeducational, liberal arts institution. It is currently situated on a beautiful 312-acre campus in Prince Georges County, Maryland, and offers both graduate and undergraduate programs of study. Teacher education programs were established in 1925; in 1935, with state authorization, a four-year program for the training of elementary school teachers was begun and the school became the Maryland State Teachers College at Bowie. In 1951, with the approval of the State Board of Education, its governing body at the time, the college established a teacher-preparation curriculum for the training of teachers for the core program in the junior high schools. Ten years later, permission was granted to institute a teacher-training program for secondary education. A liberal arts program was established in 1963, and the institution's name was changed to Bowie State College. In 1988, Bowie State achieved university status and joined the University System of Maryland (USM).

For more information, students should contact:

Office of Enrollment, Recruitment and Registration
Bowie State University
Bowie, Maryland 20715-9465
Telephone: 301-464-6566
410-880-4100 Ext. 6566
(from the Baltimore-Columbia area)
E-mail: admissions@bowiestate.edu
World Wide Web:
http://www.bowiestate.edu

ACADEMIC PROGRAM

The University operates on a semester calendar. Academic offerings can be divided into four main areas: humanities, science and mathematics, social sciences, and education. To receive a bachelor's degree, a student must earn a minimum of 120 semester hours with a cumulative grade point average of 2.0 or better. Students who enter through the University College of Excellence (UCE) are provided the opportunity to complete the General Education Program, acquire lifelong learning skills for a competitive world, and make a successful transition into their junior year. General studies requirements include communication skills, 9 hours; humanities, 9 hours; social sciences, 18 hours; science and mathematics, 9 hours; and physical education, 2 hours. The remaining credit hours can be electives or from major and minor areas of interest. Students must also pass the test of Proficiency in the English Language and must take the national standardized test in their major area. The Honors Program is designed for students with outstanding academic records and potential and provides a special educational opportunity for young adults with exceptional talent. The program is comprehensive and multidisciplinary in structure and interdisciplinary in application. It has been designed to provide a creative approach to the teaching/learning process and to present activities that will encourage the shaping of students' own experiences. The Special Services Project is a federally funded program designed to retain and graduate first-generation, low-income, and disabled students who have been admitted to Bowie State University. The purpose of the project is to help students overcome academic and nonacademic barriers to academic success, through participation in specially designed activities, including counseling, tutoring, and workshops on test taking and study skills. Bowie State University offers an Army ROTC program. Two-year and three-year scholarships are available.

FINANCIAL AID

Federal Pell Grants, Supplemental Grants, Work-Study, Perkins Loans, and Direct Loans are available. University scholarships, tuition waivers, and diversity grants are awarded. Most awards are based on need. Merit scholarships could be offered to students with cumulative grade point averages of at least 3.2 and minimum SAT I scores of 1150. Full-tuition awards are possible for out-of-state students who have a minimum cumulative grade point average of 3.4 and a minimum SAT I score of 1250. More than 65 percent of all undergraduate students receive some form of financial aid. Scholarships and assistantships are offered through the Model Institutions for Excellence Program for Science, Engineering, and Mathematics. Deadlines are April 1 for the fall semester and November 15 for the spring semester.

APPLICATION AND INFORMATION

The application deadline is April 1 for the fall semester and November 1 for spring.

BREVARD COLLEGE

■ BREVARD, NORTH CAROLINA

THE COLLEGE

Founded in 1853, Brevard is a church-related, coeducational liberal arts college that offers innovative four-year and two-year curriculums, with specialties in music, art, environmental studies, wilderness leadership, and other interdisciplinary majors, on a beautiful mountain campus near Asheville, North Carolina. The College's low student-faculty ratio of 10:1, a covenant that binds faculty members and students in a nurturing community of learning, rich cultural offerings, numerous opportunities for student leadership, nationally competitive athletic programs, and incomparable access to national parks, forest, wilderness areas, and white-water recreational rivers make Brevard distinctive. Inspired by its setting among the world's oldest mountains and founded upon the principles of the Christian faith, Brevard College has the purpose of educating students in the tradition of the liberal arts and in the spirit of love and service. The College's faculty and staff, academic and cocurricular programs, financial resources, and support services are devoted to providing an educational climate that fosters respect for learning and beauty, creativity and hard work, tolerance and personal integrity, intellect and love of knowledge, and vigorous activity and spiritual reflection.

For more information, students should contact:

Vice President and Dean for Admissions and Financial Aid
Brevard College
400 North Broad Street
Brevard, North Carolina 28712
Telephone: 828-884-8300
800-527-9090 (toll-free)
Fax: 828-884-3790
E-mail: admissions@brevard.edu
World Wide Web:
http://www.brevard.edu

ACADEMIC PROGRAM

The core liberal arts curriculum of the College requires each student to build a strong base in languages and literature, religion, humanities, mathematics and analytical reasoning, history, natural and social sciences, fine arts, and environmental studies. Students are exposed to other cultures and have significant opportunities for volunteer work in the community. The curriculum utilizes classroom studies in the Pisgah National Forest, Davidson and French Broad River ecosystems, Great Smoky Mountain National Park, and the Cradle of Forestry in America, which is designated as a National Historic Site. Through the "Voice of the Rivers," Brevard College offers select students the opportunity to make the world their classroom in an experiential program that combines wilderness leadership and environmental studies.

FINANCIAL AID

Opportunities for student financial aid are available to every student who can show financial need, superior academic achievement, or talent in athletics, art, drama, or music. All students desiring financial aid must submit the Free Application for Federal Student Aid (FAFSA). The College annually awards more than $200,000 in merit scholarships to select students who display academic excellence, unselfish character, and leadership potential as Brevard Scholars. These students participate in a variety of enriched intellectual, cultural, and leadership programs and work closely with distinguished professors who serve both as advisers and program directors.

APPLICATION AND INFORMATION

Students must submit an application for admission, a recommendation from the guidance counselor on the form provided by the Office of Admissions, official SAT I or ACT scores, and an official high school transcript. Students are advised of the admission decision as soon as all required application materials are received. In addition, Brevard College requires a medical history and a physical examination of each applicant prior to enrollment to the College.

CALIFORNIA COLLEGE OF ARTS AND CRAFTS

■ OAKLAND AND SAN FRANCISCO, CALIFORNIA

THE COLLEGE

The California College of Arts and Crafts (CCAC) was founded in 1907 with a new approach to art education—to offer training in a wide range of disciplines, creating a spirit of collaboration between artists, craftspeople, and designers. In the ensuing years, the College has expanded its commitment by offering an interdisciplinary curriculum that educates students in the full range of fine arts, architecture, and design studies in the context of a small, private four-year college. Today, CCAC's undergraduate enrollment is about 1,200 men and women. The College maintains close ties with the professional art community as well as with the community at large. Founded in 1998, the CCAC Institute offers a wide range of leading-edge programs, including exhibitions, lectures, artist residencies, performances, symposia, and publications in the fields of art, architecture, and design. Other programs for the public include extended education classes for adults and students in grades 6–12.

For more information, students should contact:

Office of Enrollment Services
California College of Arts and Crafts
1111 Eighth Street
San Francisco, California 94107-2247
Telephone: 800-447-1ART (toll-free)
World Wide Web: http://www.ccac-art.edu

ACADEMIC PROGRAM

The Bachelor of Fine Arts requires the completion of a minimum of 126 semester units, of which 75 must be in studio work and 51 must be in humanities and sciences. Most undergraduates at CCAC begin in a foundation—or core—program designed to orient them to a variety of two- and three-dimensional art and design media as well as to strengthen their communication skills and develop and refine their knowledge of history. Students select a major after completing this program. A diversified program of arts and humanities reflects CCAC's philosophy that a professional art education occurs in the context of the education of the whole person. The relative flexibility of CCAC's curriculum enables students to explore a variety of media, to change majors without changing schools, to receive supplementary training in the arts, and to develop programs related to individual interests, abilities, and long-range career goals. The Bachelor of Architecture, a five-year program, requires the completion of a minimum of 162 units, including the one-semester core program with an orientation to two-dimensional and three-dimensional media and a nine-semester major program.

FINANCIAL AID

Scholarships, grants, loans, and work-study awards are available for students on the basis of merit and financial need. Students applying for aid in 2000–01 should submit the Free Application for Federal Student Aid (FAFSA) to the Federal Student Aid Processing Agency by March 1 for priority consideration. CCAC continues to fund students after the priority deadline as long as funds remain available. Applications for Federal Pell Grants and Federal Direct Student Loans may be submitted throughout the school year. CCAC is approved for veterans attending under the Veterans Administration Educational Benefits Program. Approximately 65 percent of students attending CCAC during the 2000–01 year received some type of financial aid. CCAC also offers an extended interest-free payment plan.

APPLICATION AND INFORMATION

Individuals interested in applying for CCAC's merit scholarships should complete their applications by February 15. CCAC's priority deadline for all fall semester applications is March 1. The priority deadline for spring applicants is October 1. Students meeting these deadlines will have priority consideration regarding admission, housing, and financial aid. CCAC reviews undergraduate applications on a rolling admission basis; that is, applications are reviewed in the order in which they are received, and students are accepted and awarded financial aid after the priority dates. The application fee is $40. Persons who wish to take one or more individual courses may register as nondegree students on a space-available basis and receive College credit for courses completed.

CALIFORNIA STATE POLYTECHNIC UNIVERSITY, POMONA

■ POMONA, CALIFORNIA

THE UNIVERSITY

California State Polytechnic University, Pomona (Cal Poly Pomona) is located on the eastern edge of Southern California's San Gabriel Valley. Its 1400-acre campus, featuring lush rolling hills, was once the winter ranch of cereal magnate W.K. Kellogg. While the land and its contents were donated to the state in 1949, Kellogg's hilltop home and award-winning Arabian horses remain as lasting reminders of the university's heritage. As one of a few polytechnical universities in the nation, Cal Poly Pomona's mission is to advance learning and knowledge by linking theory and practice and integrating technology, while preparing students for lifelong learning, leadership, and careers. Its learn-by-doing, polytechnic philosophy has created a reputation of producing well-balance individuals who make an immediate impact. This is the reason Cal Poly Pomona graduates are among the most sought-after in today's marketplace. Cal Poly Pomona is well-known for the quality of its degree programs. The University has more than sixty undergraduate majors in eight colleges and schools: agriculture; business administration; education and integrative studies; engineering; environmental design; hospitality management; letters, arts, and social sciences; and science.

For more information, students should contact:

Office of Admissions & Outreach
Cal Poly Pomona
3801 West Temple Avenue
Pomona, California 91768
Telephone: 909-869-3210

ACADEMIC PROGRAM

Classes are offered in four 11-week quarters. Candidates for Bachelor of Arts degrees must earn at least 186 quarter units. The Bachelor of Science degree requires at least 198 quarter units. A graduation writing requirement exists for all baccalaureate degrees. Currently, Architecture, Computer Information Systems, and Computer Science are open to California residents only. Cal Poly Pomona offers Air Force and Army Reserve Officers' Training Corps, a California Pre-Doctoral Program, an Educational Opportunity Program, a Teacher Aide Path to Teaching, University Equity Programs, and other special programs. The University features special centers and institutes, such as the innovative Lyle Center for Regenerative Studies, the Apparel Technology and Research Center, the Center for Turf, Irrigation and Landscape Technology, the Equine Research Center, the Ocean Studies Institute, and the Institute for Cellular and Molecular Biology.

FINANCIAL AID

The University administers extensive financial aid programs, and each year more than 49 percent of Cal Poly Pomona students receive more than $50 million in financial aid. Applications for academic and merit scholarships must be completed by March 2. Applications for financial aid should be completed as early as possible after January 1 and no later than March 2 for the following academic year. Applicants should contact the financial aid office for information and application material.

APPLICATION AND INFORMATION

Applications are accepted for the following fall on November 1 of the preceding year. Deadlines: for fall and summer quarters are, April 1 for freshmen and lower-division transfers and May 1 for upper-division transfers; for winter quarter, September 1 for freshmen and lower-division transfers and October 1 for upper-division transfers; and for spring quarter, November 15 for all applicants. The application fee is $55, but waivers may be granted. Applications may be requested from a California high school, community college, or CSU campus; by contacting the Office of Admissions & Outreach; or by filling out an online request card at http://www.csupomona.edu/~enroll/admissions/contact. The University encourages students to apply online at http://www.csumentor.edu. Students can access Cal Poly Pomona's home page at http://www.csupomona.edu.

CALVIN COLLEGE

■ GRAND RAPIDS, MICHIGAN

THE COLLEGE

Calvin College is dedicated to relating the Christian faith to the whole learning process; this view affects every area of campus life from the content of each course to volunteer service and life in the residence halls. Calvin is one of the nation's largest and most respected evangelical Christian colleges. The 2000 fall enrollment was 4,314. Calvin maintains a strong affiliation with the Christian Reformed Church, and students from more than sixty other church denominations across North America and the world choose Calvin for its extensive curriculum and Christ-centered mission. Calvin is deeply committed to being a diverse community and is taking deliberate steps to increase opportunities for women, members of minority groups, and the disabled. Students are challenged not only to obtain a fine education and to prepare for a career but also to live lives of commitment and service.

For more information, students should contact:

Admissions Office
Calvin College
3201 Burton Street, SE
Grand Rapids, Michigan 49546
Telephone: 800-688-0122 (toll-free in North America)
Fax: 616-957-6777
E-mail: admissions@calvin.edu
World Wide Web: http://www.calvin.edu

ACADEMIC PROGRAM

Calvin College maintains a strong commitment to a liberal arts curriculum as an integral avenue to help students understand God's world and their place in it. The College follows a 4-1-4 academic calendar, consisting of two 4-month semesters with a three-week Interim term during January. Typically, students take four or five courses each semester and one course during the Interim. Graduation requires the successful completion of 124 semester hours. Calvin's new core curriculum begins with a first-year gateway course, Developing a Christian Mind, and ends with a capstone course in the senior year. Core curriculum requirements include foreign language, history, literature and arts, mathematics, natural sciences, philosophy, physical education, religion, social sciences, and written and spoken rhetoric. Some requirements can be satisfied by advanced high school work in foreign language, literature, and natural sciences. Qualified students can earn course exemption and/or credit by completing college-level work in high school or by examination. Satisfactory scores on Advanced Placement (AP), International Baccalaureate (I.B.), and/or CLEP exams are also accepted.

FINANCIAL AID

Sixty percent of Calvin students receive need-based financial aid; demonstrated need is the most important criterion in determining eligibility. Students wishing to be considered for financial aid must be admitted to the College and must submit the Free Application for Federal Student Aid (FAFSA) and Calvin's Supplemental Application for Financial Aid. February 15 is the suggested filing deadline for maximum consideration. Financial awards to eligible applicants consist of state and federal grants, loans, Federal Work-Study funds, and institutional grants and scholarships. Part-time employment is available on campus, and placement preference is given to needy students. Calvin also helps students find off-campus employment and runs a job transportation service that drives them to and from their jobs for a fee.

APPLICATION AND INFORMATION

Applicants must submit a completed application form, a high school or college transcript, results of either the ACT or SAT I, and an educational recommendation completed by a teacher or counselor. Admission decisions are made on a rolling basis beginning in mid-October. Applicants for fall admission are urged to complete their file before February 1, although there is no deadline as long as space remains in the entering class. Campus visits are strongly recommended, although not required. Students and parents are welcome to visit at any time that is convenient for them. The "Fridays at Calvin" campus visit program also provides an excellent opportunity to experience life at Calvin firsthand.

CAMPBELL UNIVERSITY

■ BUIES CREEK, NORTH CAROLINA

THE UNIVERSITY

Founded in 1887, Campbell University has had the distinction of being North Carolina's second-largest private undergraduate institution. Graduate programs were established, and in 1979 the name of the institution was changed from Campbell College to Campbell University. Its current enrollment is more than 7,800 students. In an average year, the student body comes from about ninety North Carolina counties, fifty states, and forty-six countries. Sixty-six percent of the students come from North Carolina. Campbell University has established a law school and schools of business, pharmacy, education, and divinity and now awards the J.D., Pharm.D., M.Ed., M.A., M.B.A., M.S., and M.Div. degrees. These additions have increased interest in the general program of the undergraduate college. Completed projects include a $1.2-million classroom building, the Keith Hills housing development and golf course, an indoor swimming pool, a welcome center, and a $3.5-million fine arts complex. A $3.5-million addition to the Norman Adrian Wiggins School of Law, an addition to the Campbell University School of Pharmacy, and the 76,000-square-foot, $11-million Lundy Fetterman School of Business are the newest expansion projects that have been completed. Campbell University is nonsectarian. Approximately 60 percent of its students are Baptist, but young people of twenty-two other faiths complete its student body. It is concerned with maintaining, for living and learning, an environment consistent with Christian ideals. Among the extracurricular activities available at Campbell are band, choir, and drama groups; religious, political, professional, social, and academic groups; and intercollegiate and intramural sports organizations.

For more information, students should contact:

Office of Admissions
Campbell University
P.O. Box 546
Buies Creek, North Carolina 27506
Telephone: 910-893-1320
910-893-1415 (international)
800-334-4111 (toll-free)
E-mail: adm@mailcenter.campbell.edu
World Wide Web:
http://www.campbell.edu/

ACADEMIC PROGRAM

The curriculum of Campbell University is designed to meet individual needs and interests. During the first two years, students follow a general course of study, the General College Curriculum, to broaden their backgrounds in the basic fields of knowledge. By the end of the sophomore year, they should have selected a major subject for specialized study during the final two years. Basic curriculum requirements for the first two years in semester hours are English, 12; social studies, 6; natural science, 8; religion, 6; music, art appreciation, or drama, 3; foreign language, up to 9, depending on high school credits and the program of study; and health and physical education, 3. Candidates for a bachelor's degree must earn a minimum of 128 credits, including the 3 in health and physical education, while maintaining at least a C average in academic course work; must complete a minimum of 32 semester hours in the departmental major at Campbell; and must average C or better in all courses required for the major. Candidates for the Associate in Arts degree must complete 64 semester hours of work and have at least a 2.0 GPA on all work required for graduation and at least a 2.0 GPA on 80 percent of all work attempted. The University calendar enables students to complete first-semester course work and examinations before Christmas vacation and end the spring session by the middle of May.

FINANCIAL AID

Campbell University has private and institutional scholarships, federal grants, loans, and Federal Work-Study Program awards. Loans are available through the Federal Stafford Student Loan Program and the Federal Perkins Loan Program. Needs analysis forms (Free Application for Federal Student Aid) are available January 1 and are due in the Financial Aid Office by March 15 if the applicant wishes to be considered for a maximum award. Ninety-one percent of the student body received financial assistance in 2000–01. All assistance is offered without regard to race, creed, or national origin.

THE CATHOLIC UNIVERSITY OF AMERICA

■ WASHINGTON, D.C.

THE UNIVERSITY

The Catholic University of America (CUA) offers an outstanding collegiate experience, with challenging undergraduate programs based in the liberal arts. CUA is the national university of the Catholic Church and the only higher education institution established by the U.S. Catholic bishops. Founded as a graduate institution more than a century ago, CUA introduced undergraduate education in 1904. The University today serves 5,600 students, including 2,400 undergraduates, from all fifty states and more than 100 other countries. Students from all religious traditions are welcome. While the University maintains a small-college atmosphere with a student-faculty ratio of 10:1, CUA is a major research institution. Undergraduates learn from the same professors that conduct research and teach graduate students.

For more information, students should contact:

Director of Admissions
The Catholic University of America
Washington, D.C. 20064
Telephone: 202-319-5305
800-673-2772 (toll-free)
Fax: 202-319-6533
E-mail: cua-admissions@cua.edu
World Wide Web:
http://www.cua.edu

ACADEMIC PROGRAM

Engineering, nursing, music, and architecture students follow study courses that provide professional training integrated with a broad range of academic disciplines. Students in the School of Arts and Sciences undertake a major course of study within a liberal arts curriculum that encompasses the humanities, languages and literature, philosophy, the social sciences, mathematics and natural sciences, and religion. Most majors require the satisfactory completion of forty courses that are 3 credits each for graduation. Certain majors under the Bachelor of Science degree may require additional credits. In addition to the major, students may complete a minor course sequence by utilizing the elective courses included in the undergraduate program.

FINANCIAL AID

CUA administers two separate and distinct financial assistance programs: merit scholarships and need-based financial aid. A number of scholarships, awarded on the basis of academic achievement in secondary school, are available. The University offers financial aid to students based on need as demonstrated by the Free Application for Federal Student Aid (FAFSA) and the Institutional Aid Form, which can be found in the CUA admissions application. Loans, work-study, and University grants are available. Candidates who complete the admission application process before February 15 of their senior year of secondary school are considered for academic scholarships and receive priority for financial aid. Candidates apply for financial aid at the same time they apply for admission. CUA has a need-blind admissions policy and makes admission decisions without regard to financial aid status.

APPLICATION AND INFORMATION

Admissions decisions are made on a rolling basis. Applicants for the Early Cardinal Program must apply by November 15 and will be notified by December 15. Regular action scholarship awards and financial aid decisions will be made shortly after the February 15 deadline. Candidates for freshman admission must submit CUA's secondary school report, high school transcripts, scores on the SAT I or ACT, and a $55 application fee. CUA accepts transfer applicants each semester. Transfer candidates should request applications for transfer admission from the Office of Admissions and Financial Aid. In addition to the high school records and SAT I or ACT scores, transfer students must furnish transcripts from the school the students are attending (a minimum 2.8 GPA is recommended). Transfer applicants are notified of their status on a rolling basis and at least one month prior to the opening of the semester for which they are applying for admission. Financial aid is awarded on the same basis as for freshman students.

CEDAR CREST COLLEGE

■ ALLENTOWN, PENNSYLVANIA

THE COLLEGE

Since its founding in 1867 as an independent liberal arts college for women, Cedar Crest has educated women for leadership in a changing world. Of the approximately 1,700 students who come to the College annually from twenty-six states and twenty other countries, 814 are full-time undergraduates. The 11:1 student-faculty ratio provides for small classes, individual advising, and independent work in an environment that emphasizes interdisciplinary, values-oriented education. The Honor Philosophy is the most compelling statement of each student's rights and responsibilities for her own academic and cocurricular performance.

For more information, students should contact:

Vice President for Enrollment
Cedar Crest College
100 College Drive
Allentown, Pennsylvania 18104-6196
Telephone: 800-360-1222 (toll-free)
Fax: 610-606-4647
E-mail: cccadmis@cedarcrest.edu
World Wide Web:
http://www.cedarcrest.edu

ACADEMIC PROGRAM

Self-designed majors, double majors, minors, independent study programs, and individual and group research projects support serious concentration at the undergraduate level. Working with her adviser, each student designs a program of study that meets the 120-credit College (nursing: 126 credits) and major requirements as well as her personal interests and professional goals. The College's curriculum is structured to provide course work in the areas that define a liberal arts education: a knowledge-based curriculum with Basic Composition and Construction of Knowledge taught in a computer classroom environment, Scientific Knowledge (The Human Agenda, The Environment), a departmentally determined mathematics requirement, and electives constitute the freshman-year program. The Sophomore Ethical Life Course integrates applied ethics and service-learning opportunities. Acquisition of Knowledge courses are selected in four categories: The Study of Humankind, The Study of Written Texts, The Study of Creativity and Creativity in Practice, and Global Issues and Distinct Cultures. Many of these courses also meet the requirements of majors and minors. Science majors begin conducting advanced research at the freshman level, opening opportunities that often lead to internships at major research institutions.

FINANCIAL AID

Cedar Crest offers a generous program of financial aid based on academic achievement and financial need, including scholarships, grants, loans, and employment. Federal funds available are Federal Pell Grants, Federal Supplemental Educational Opportunity Grants, Federal Perkins Loans, Federal Work-Study Program awards, and Nursing Student Loans. The size of an award varies with need. More than 80 percent of the students at Cedar Crest receive aid. Students applying for financial aid should file the Free Application for Federal Student Aid (FAFSA). Outstanding international students may also qualify for financial aid. Students can receive an early estimate of aid eligibility by completing a Cedar Crest financial aid application/planner.

APPLICATION AND INFORMATION

Students need to submit the application form, an official transcript of the secondary school record, examination results from the SAT I or ACT, and a personal essay. Cedar Crest has a rolling admission policy; applications are reviewed on a continuing basis. Students are encouraged to apply early in their senior year of high school. Admission is awarded for the fall or spring semester. Transfer students applying to Cedar Crest must fulfill all of the requirements stated above. They must also submit official transcripts and a catalog from each college previously attended. International students must complete the international student application form; students educated in non-English-speaking countries must also submit TOEFL examination scores.

CHAMINADE UNIVERSITY OF HONOLULU

■ HONOLULU, HAWAII

THE UNIVERSITY

Chaminade University of Honolulu, a private, coeducational institution, was established in 1955 by the Society of Mary (Marianists). Named after Father William Joseph Chaminade, a French Catholic priest who ministered to his people during the late eighteenth and early nineteenth centuries and who founded the Society in 1817, the University today continues the Marianist mission of educating leaders through faith and reason. To achieve this mission, Chaminade forms a community encompassing people from diverse cultural origins, both traditional and nontraditional, who hold a variety of religious beliefs. The University encourages learning through cooperation, self-discipline, caring, and mutual respect while offering individualized attention that promotes personal and intellectual growth. A major goal of the University is to educate and train students for leadership both within Chaminade and in communities beyond the campus.

For more information, students should contact:

Admission Office
Chaminade University
3140 Waialae Avenue
Honolulu, Hawaii 96816
Telephone: 808-735-4735
800-735-3733 (toll-free)
Fax: 808-739-4647
E-mail: admissions@chaminade.edu
World Wide Web:
http://www.chaminade.edu

ACADEMIC PROGRAM

The core curriculum at Chaminade is in liberal arts. The University is committed to a broad liberal education for its students and believes that such an education provides a basis for long-term personal growth, a foundation for a career that may encounter job changes, and a background that allows students to rise to leadership positions in their chosen fields and communities. Through undergraduate programs based on the liberal arts tradition, Chaminade seeks to heighten cultural awareness. Coupled with understanding diverse methods of inquiry and participation in Chaminade's multicultural interdependent community, cultural awareness prepares all students for lifelong learning—about themselves, each other, and the world in which they live.

FINANCIAL AID

Those with a high school GPA between 3.5 and 4.0 are eligible for a $5000 yearly scholarship; between 3.0 and 3.49, a $4500 yearly scholarship; between 2.5 and 2.99, a $3500 yearly grant; and between 2.25 to 2.49, a $3000 yearly grant. The Hawaii Grant for new full-time day session students from Hawaii is $1500 per semester. Scholarships and grants, available to regular full-time undergraduate students, are renewable for four years and are awarded without regard to financial need. Students may obtain only one of the Chaminade scholarships or grants. A tuition discount of 20 percent is offered to additional family members when one member of the family is paying full-time tuition.

APPLICATION AND INFORMATION

Chaminade University has a rolling admission process. As soon as all required information is received by the Admission Office, the application is reviewed by an application committee. Students are notified of the committee's decision usually within three to four weeks. Applications are accepted throughout the year. A $50 fee is payable upon application. Web site applications are also available for a $25 fee. All students desiring housing must file an application along with a $300 deposit applicable to the total cost per semester. Space and placement are not guaranteed without this deposit. A housing damage deposit of $100 is also required. Evidence of health insurance coverage from a U.S. insurer is required of all dormitory residents and international students. To ensure full consideration for scholarships or grants, students are urged to complete the appropriate application by April 1. Award notices are mailed by April 30.

CHESTNUT HILL COLLEGE

■ PHILADELPHIA, PENNSYLVANIA

THE COLLEGE

Chestnut Hill College (CHC) is a four-year Catholic liberal arts college for women. Founded in 1924 by the Sisters of St. Joseph, it is situated on a 45-acre campus overlooking Wissahickon Creek. Conscious of women's roles in society, Chestnut Hill College has chosen to remain a women's college at the traditional-age undergraduate level. It answers a need for well-educated, values-oriented women who can exert a positive influence on the society of the future. Since opportunities for leadership and self-expression are frequent, the Chestnut Hill graduate can enter a competitive world well prepared for success. Students come from fifteen states, thirteen countries, and every imaginable background. There are 372 full-time and 116 part-time undergraduate women in the day programs and 426 women and men enrolled in the accelerated evening and weekend undergraduate program. In addition to its undergraduate degrees, Chestnut Hill awards the M.Ed., M.A., and M.S. in six fields, including elementary education, counseling psychology and human services, holistic spirituality, and technology in education as well as a doctoral degree in clinical psychology (Psy.D.).

For more information, students should contact:

Elizabeth Becker
Director of Admissions
Chestnut Hill College
9601 Germantown Avenue
Philadelphia, Pennsylvania 19118-2695
Telephone: 215-248-7001
800-248-0052 (toll-free)
E-mail: chcapply@chc.edu
World Wide Web:
http://www.chc.edu

ACADEMIC PROGRAM

The academic year consists of two 15-week semesters. There are also two 6-week summer sessions. As a liberal arts college, CHC offers courses of study that provide the student with a broad background in the fine arts and humanities, a knowledge of science, and a keen awareness of the social problems of the day, as well as intensive, in-depth study in a major field. CHC confers a B.S. or B.A. degree to students who earn 120 semester hours of credit and satisfy specific requirements set by the faculty. Distribution requirements are as follows: 11 semester hours in natural sciences (8 hours of which must be a laboratory science), 9 semester hours in social sciences, and 21 semester hours in the humanities. In addition to these 41 hours of credit, every student must take 6 semester hours of religious studies, 6 hours beyond the elementary level in a classical or modern foreign language, and 3 hours in a writing course (unless exempted by the English department). As many as 45 of the 120 semester hours may be within the major area. A student with the ability and proper motivation may be permitted to major in two departments. The student must consult with the chair of each department to determine the feasibility of the proposal and then submit it to the dean of the college for approval. It is understood that she will satisfy the requirements of both departments.

FINANCIAL AID

Financial aid is available in the form of academic scholarships, guaranteed loans, work-study programs, federal grants, and Chestnut Hill College grants. Most of these are based on financial need and are awarded in financial aid packages that combine various forms of aid and are tailored to each student's need. More than 75 percent of CHC students receive financial aid to meet college costs. All applicants for aid should file a copy of the Free Application for Federal Student Aid (FAFSA). Full tuition scholarships are awarded each year strictly on the basis of achievement. Students should submit a completed application, the application essay, SAT I or ACT scores, a high school transcript, and a letter of recommendation. An interview is recommended and may be required.

APPLICATION AND INFORMATION

Applications are processed on a rolling admission system.

CLAREMONT MCKENNA COLLEGE

■ CLAREMONT, CALIFORNIA

THE COLLEGE

Founded in 1946 as the third undergraduate college in the cluster of the Claremont Colleges, Claremont McKenna College (CMC) occupies a unique place among American colleges. Through a grounding in the traditional liberal arts, CMC's purpose is to educate future leaders in business, the professions, and public affairs. Economics, government, and international relations are the most popular among twenty-one majors offered at CMC. The College is especially appropriate for students seeking to pursue careers in law, politics, government, international relations, business, management, and finance. Because approximately 95 percent of CMC students live on campus in coed residence halls and apartments, campus life is vibrant and active. Dorms provide the foundation for social life at CMC; the student-run dorm government often plans field trips, movie nights, barbecues, dinners, and socials for each dorm or apartment group. Intramural athletic teams are typically formed by each residence hall.

For more information, students should contact:

Richard C. Vos, Vice President and Dean of Admission and Financial Aid
Claremont McKenna College
890 Columbia Avenue
Claremont, California 91711-6425
Telephone: 909-621-8088
E-mail: admission@claremontmckenna.edu
World Wide Web: http://www.claremontmckenna.edu

ACADEMIC PROGRAM

Students must satisfactorily complete thirty-two semester courses, including general education and major requirements, in order to graduate. General education requirements include one course in mathematics, one course in English composition and analysis, two courses in the natural sciences, two courses in the humanities, three courses in the social sciences, and a senior thesis. In addition, students must complete a third semester of a foreign language and a Questions of Civilization course. Depending on the department, credit or advanced placement, or both, may be granted for college courses taken while in high school. Also, CMC may grant credit for scores of 4 or 5 on Advanced Placement (AP) examinations and for scores of 6 or 7 on higher level International Baccalaureate (I.B.) examinations. CMC sponsors a joint science program with two other Claremont Colleges, Pitzer and Scripps. The Keck Science Center houses modern laboratories for teaching and research, and a large biological field station is located adjacent to the campus. Virtually all students in the joint science program do independent research, and reports on many student-faculty projects have been published in professional journals. By intercollegiate agreement, CMC students may take courses not offered at Claremont McKenna at any of the Claremont Colleges. Up to one third of a student's courses may be taken at the other Claremont Colleges. CMC operates on an early semester calendar, beginning the first week in September and ending in mid-May.

FINANCIAL AID

Financial aid is awarded in the form of grants (nonrepayable gift aid), student loans, and part-time employment. Grants range from $1000 to $20,000 per year and average $13,000; loans for entering freshmen average $3000 per year. The total amount of aid a student is awarded is based on need. The College offers thirty McKenna Achievement Awards to members of each entering freshman class. These awards are valued at $5000 each and are renewable for each of the four years, provided the student earns at least a B average. To be considered for one of these awards, a student usually must rank among the top 5 percent in his or her high school class and earn a score of more than 680 on both the mathematical and verbal portions of the SAT I. Candidates must also have excellent school recommendations and strong extracurricular involvement, including leadership, and must have filed a completed application by December 15.

CLARKSON COLLEGE

■ OMAHA, NEBRASKA

THE COLLEGE

Clarkson College is a regionally accredited private institution, with exceptional programs in nursing, radiologic technology, medical imaging, occupational therapy assistant and physical therapist assistant studies, patient information management, and health-related business. The College offers the personal qualities of a small institution and the technological advantages found within a larger educational environment. Founded in 1888, it was the first school of nursing in Nebraska and the thirty-fifth in the nation and was approved to grant academic degrees in 1984. The baccalaureate and master's programs in nursing and the associate programs have professional accreditation. The current Clarkson enrollment of more than 400 students consists of individuals of diverse ages and ethnic and cultural backgrounds. The College's Distance Education programs enroll more than 125 students. Student support resources at the College are exceptional. Professional staff members in the offices of admissions, financial aid, student services, and housing are readily available to assist students. Both faculty and staff members are committed to providing the support services needed to ensure that students grow and learn to the maximum of their abilities.

For additional information, students should contact:

Enrollment Services
Clarkson College
101 South 42nd Street
Omaha, Nebraska 68131-2739
Telephone: 402-552-3100
800-647-5500 (toll-free)
E-mail: admiss@clarksoncollege.edu
World Wide Web:
http://www.clarksoncollege.edu

ACADEMIC PROGRAM

The goal of Clarkson College is to prepare individuals to be competent in the technical aspects of their profession and broadly educated in the liberal arts and sciences. The curriculum is supported by courses in the liberal arts and sciences and combines knowledge of course content with the development of intellectual and clinical competencies. Each student's curriculum plan reflects the individual's needs and interest. Although degree requirements remain constant, the scheduling of courses within the curriculum may be individualized. The flexibility of the programs permits full-time or part-time enrollment. The academic year begins with the fall semester in August, is followed by the spring semester in January, and ends with the summer semester. Candidates for the baccalaureate degree must complete 128 semester hours of course work, including 60 hours of general education and support courses. Advanced placement into the curriculum beyond the beginning of the freshman year is accomplished through transfer of credits or credit by examination and other means. The associate degree program requirements also include a general education component.

FINANCIAL AID

In 2000–01, the College awarded financial aid to approximately 90 percent of its undergraduate students. Scholarships, grants, loans, and work-study are available to meet the individual financial needs of students who qualify. Scholarships are awarded to outstanding applicants. Students are required to submit the completed Free Application for Federal Student Aid (FAFSA) or the Renewal Application as well as the Clarkson College Financial Aid Information Form for consideration for all forms of aid.

APPLICATION AND INFORMATION

The enrollment policy of Clarkson College allows potential students to apply anytime during the year. A completed application form, accompanied by the application fee, an official high school transcript or certification of successful completion of the GED, and ACT or SAT scores should be submitted when seeking admission. Students with previous postsecondary course work should also submit an official transcript from each institution of higher education attended.

CLEARY COLLEGE

■ ANN ARBOR AND HOWELL, MICHIGAN

THE COLLEGE

Cleary College, founded in 1883, is a private business college whose mission is to prepare students for a career in business with skills that exceed the expectations of their employers. Cleary College operates from two campuses in Michigan. The Washtenaw Campus, located in Ann Arbor, and the Livingston Campus, located in Howell, feature flexible classroom arrangements and meeting rooms as well as the computer, satellite, and telecommunications technology. Cleary College enrolls approximately 1,100 commuter students. Cleary students are focused on business careers and most students work while completing their degrees—either on their own or as part of an internship or degree program requirements. Cleary College emphasizes practical application of business theory and enjoys an excellent reputation among area employers for graduating students who succeed in the workplace. In addition to the on-campus offerings, Cleary College also offers a one-year bachelor's degree completion program at extension sites throughout southeastern Michigan.

For more information, students should contact:

Cleary College Admissions Office
3750 Cleary College Drive
Howell, Michigan 48845
Telephone: 888-5-CLEARY (toll-free)
World Wide Web:
http://www.cleary.edu

ACADEMIC PROGRAM

Cleary programs are intended for the serious student who has a clear goal—a career in business—and is motivated to apply energy to reach that goal. Emphasis is placed on providing a learning environment that fosters a mastery of current business theory and technology and the application of these skills to real-life business situations. Candidates for the B.B.A. degree must earn a minimum of 180 quarter credit hours and complete all requisite courses with an average of two honor points for each quarter of credit. Cleary's B.B.A. programs consist of a set of core courses in the major and electives courses. Required core courses are grouped into four areas: communication core (24 quarter credits); critical thinking core (18 quarter credits); civic preparation core (24 quarter credits); and leadership core (18 quarter credits). Cleary offers nine B.B.A. majors that support individual career interests and goals.

FINANCIAL AID

More than 60 percent of students receive some form of financial assistance. Cleary College participates in state and federal financial aid programs and accepts the Free Application for Federal Student Aid (FAFSA). Some of the financial aid programs Cleary participates in include: the Federal Pell Grant, Federal SEOG, Federal College Work-Study, Federal Stafford Loan, and Michigan Tuition Grant. In addition, a number of Cleary College scholarships and grants are available to students.

APPLICATION AND INFORMATION

Applications to the undergraduate program are accepted all year and must be submitted with a $25 nonrefundable application fee payable to Cleary College. It is recommended that applications to the BusinessTrack program be submitted at least six weeks prior to the start of the term. BusinessTrack terms begin in September, January, April, and July. It is recommended that applications to the Direct Degree program be submitted at least eight weeks prior to the start of the term. Direct Degree terms begin in September, October, January, February, April, May, and July.

THE COLLEGE OF WOOSTER

■ WOOSTER, OHIO

THE COLLEGE

One of the first coeducational colleges in the country, the College of Wooster was founded in 1866 by Presbyterians who wanted to do "their proper part in the great work of educating those who are to mold society and give shape to all its institutions." Today it is a fully independent, privately endowed liberal arts college with a rich tradition of academic excellence. That tradition defines student life at Wooster, beginning with the First-Year Seminar in Critical Inquiry and culminating in the Independent Study program. The current enrollment is about 1,700 men and women. Almost all students live on campus, selecting from a variety of housing options. These include Babcock International House for students interested in international studies, Douglass Hall for students with an interest in the humanities and sciences, and Luce Hall, a modern, ninety-six-bed facility arranged in living suites. There are also thirty houses on the edge of campus, many of which serve as living-learning centers for those in community service and volunteer programs.

For more information, students should contact:

Director of Admissions
The College of Wooster
Wooster, Ohio 44691
Telephone: 330-263-2000 Ext. 2270
or 2322
800-877-9905 (toll-free)
Fax: 330-263-2621
E-mail: admissions@wooster.edu
World Wide Web:
http://www.wooster.edu

ACADEMIC PROGRAM

Wooster's academic program is designed to provide a liberal education that prepares undergraduates for a lifetime of intellectual adventure, allows them to develop harmoniously and independently, and helps them meet new situations as they arise. To be eligible for a Bachelor of Arts degree, a student must successfully complete thirty-two courses, including a First-Year Seminar in Critical Inquiry and three courses of Independent Study. An overall grade point average of at least 2.0 (on a 4.0 scale) is required for graduation. Students may receive credit for work done at other colleges and for scores of 4 or better on the Advanced Placement tests offered by the College Board. Courses are graded A–D or No Credit unless the student exercises an option to take certain courses on a Satisfactory/No Credit basis.

FINANCIAL AID

Almost all financial assistance is awarded on the basis of need, as determined by the Free Application for Federal Student Aid (FAFSA). Aid is allocated when students are admitted to the College. Financial assistance information and forms should be requested at the time of application. Applications for aid should be submitted by March 1. Merit aid is available on a competitive basis. The College Scholar program offers eight awards of $18,000 each per year, based on a competitive examination. Additional awards of $13,000 per year are available. Selected entering students receive academic and achievement awards independent of the College Scholars program. Synod of the Covenant Scholarships for Presbyterian communicants are available, as are Scottish Arts awards. The Clarence B. Allen Scholarship program awards up to five scholarships of $18,000 a year to entering African-American students with a demonstrated record of academic achievement and promise of continued success in college. The Arthur Holly Compton Scholarships are awarded to students who demonstrate unusual aptitude for Wooster's program of Independent Study. Compton Scholarships of $8000 to $16,000 are awarded annually. Music scholarships are awarded to entering first-year students based on auditions in voice or on an instrument. A 15-minute performance of works representing several styles of music is required. Theater scholarships are awarded on a competitive basis. An audition is required. Byron E. Morris Scholarships of up to $6000 are awarded to students who have a demonstrated record of achievement in their school or community in the areas of volunteer/community service or leadership.

COLUMBIA UNIVERSITY, School of General Studies

■ NEW YORK, NEW YORK

THE UNIVERSITY

One of the best kept secrets in American higher education, the School of General Studies at Columbia University is the nation's premier college for returning college students. One of the four undergraduate colleges that grace Columbia, the School of General Studies is the liberal arts division dedicated to those students who have interrupted or postponed their education by at least one academic year. Unlike the division of the University dedicated to continuing education, the School of General Studies is a degree-granting liberal arts college. Classes are integrated with students from each of the other three undergraduate colleges on campus, allowing students access to world-class professors and an Ivy League education. General Studies students come from all walks of life and from varied backgrounds, and for that reason may study full- or part- time. Many degree candidates hold jobs as well as study, and many have family responsibilities. Others attend full-time, experiencing Columbia's more traditional college life. It is this diversity in the student body that makes attendance at Columbia so attractive. It is the varied personal experience represented in each classroom that allows for discussion and debate and, in turn, for the academic rigor and intellectual development that characterize a Columbia education. The School has more than 1,100 undergraduate degree candidates and about 250 postbaccalaureate premedical students. In addition to its bachelor's degree program, the School of General Studies offers combined undergraduate/graduate degree programs with Columbia's Schools of Social Work, International and Public Affairs, Law, Business, and Dental and Oral Surgery, as well as with Teachers College, the College of Physicians and Surgeons, and the Juilliard School.

For more information, students should contact:

Office of Admissions and Financial Aid
School of General Studies
408 Lewisohn Hall
2970 Broadway
Columbia University, Mail Code 4101
New York, New York 10027
Telephone: 212-854-2772
E-mail: gsdegree@columbia.edu
World Wide Web:
http://www.gs.columbia.edu

ACADEMIC PROGRAM

The School of General Studies offers a traditional liberal arts education designed to provide students with the broad knowledge and intellectual skills that make possible continued education and growth in the years after college and that constitute the soundest possible foundation on which to build competence for positions of responsibility in the professional world. Requirements for the bachelor's degree comprise three elements: (1) core requirements, intended to develop in students the ability to write and communicate clearly; to understand the modes of thought that characterize the humanities, the social sciences, and the sciences; to gain some familiarity with central cultural ideas through literature, fine arts, and music; and to acquire a working proficiency in a foreign language; (2) major requirements, designed to give students sustained and coherent exposure to a particular discipline in an area of strong intellectual interest; and (3) elective courses, in which students pursue particular interests and skills for their own sake or for their relationship to future professional or personal objectives. Students are required to complete a minimum of 124 points for the bachelor's degree; 60 of these may be in transfer credit, but at least 64 points (including the last 30 points) must be completed at Columbia. In addition to the usual graduation honors (cum laude, magna cum laude, and summa cum laude), honors programs for superior students are available in sixteen of the School's twenty-nine departments.

FINANCIAL AID

The School of General Studies awards financial aid based upon need and academic ability. Approximately 70 percent of General Studies degree candidates receive some form of financial aid, including Federal Pell Grants, New York State TAP Grants, Federal Stafford and unsubsidized Stafford Loans, Federal Perkins Loans, General Studies Scholarships, and Federal Work-Study Program awards. Application deadlines are July 1 for the fall 2001 semester and November 15 for the spring 2002 semester.

CONCORD COLLEGE

■ ATHENS, WEST VIRGINIA

THE COLLEGE

For further information, students may contact:

Michael Curry
Vice President for Enrollment Services
Concord College
P.O. Box 1000
Athens, West Virginia 24712
Telephone: 304-384-5248 or 5249
888-384-5249 (toll-free)
E-mail: admissions@concord.edu
World Wide Web:
http://www.concord.edu
http://www.concord.edu/admissions/download.html (to apply on line)

Concord College, a growing state-supported college committed exclusively to undergraduate instruction, was founded 128 years ago. Concord features accredited career-oriented education with a strong liberal arts base and focuses on the needs of the individual student as its fundamental concern. The beautiful 95-acre campus stands on a ridge of the Appalachian Mountains. Four residence halls and adult studio apartments house up to 1,100 students from twenty-eight states, predominantly from the East, South, and Midwest. Concord also has a large international student population, with thirty nations represented. With a total student population of 2,877, Concord serves the needs of active commuter students who join the residential students in following courses of study in the arts and sciences, business administration, teacher education, and such fields as advertising/graphic design and social work. Preparation for advanced and professional study is a Concord hallmark. Each year, the Alexander Fine Arts Center presents the Artist-Lecture Series, which includes recitals, plays, art exhibitions, and guest speakers. Special events have included the North Carolina Dance Theatre; the West Virginia Symphony; lecturers Dr. Homer Hickam, NASA scientist and author of the book *Rocket Boys* (which was later made into the hit movie *October Sky*), and Dr. Cornel West, a preeminent African-American scholar from Harvard; and professional art exhibits. Theatrical productions range from Shakespeare and Chekhov to Woody Allen.

ACADEMIC PROGRAM

All students must complete a minimum of 128 semester hours with a grade point average of 2.0 (C) or better to receive a degree. A program of general studies, required of all students, includes courses in communication and literature, fine arts, social sciences, natural sciences, mathematics, foreign languages (optional in most majors), and physical education. Credit is awarded for satisfactory scores on the College-Level Examination Program (CLEP), Advanced Placement (AP), and International Baccalaureate tests. An outstanding honors program is also available to qualifying students. Honors courses and independent study projects are available in most departments. Semesters begin in late August and mid-January; there are summer terms as well.

FINANCIAL AID

Concord College has the most generous scholarship program in the West Virginia State College System. Merit awards, athletic and talent scholarships, transfer scholarships, and scholarships for nontraditional students are readily available for qualifying students. Federal Pell Grants, Federal Supplemental Educational Opportunity Grants, Federal Perkins Loans, West Virginia Higher Education Grants, Federal PLUS loans, and Federal Stafford Student Loans are available through the College. The State Student Assistance Program and the Federal Work-Study Program offer opportunities for student employment. To receive priority, the Free Application for Federal Student Aid (FAFSA) must be on file by April 15. Concord offers scholarships to international students. The average scholarship covers about 35 percent of the total institutional cost. Incoming freshmen who are willing to perform community service may apply for the Bonner Scholars Program, which pays up to $3050 per year for four years as long as its criteria are met. Funded by the Corella and Bertram F. Bonner Foundation of Princeton, New Jersey, the award is primarily based on need and prior service. Approximately 65 percent of the students receive some form of financial assistance.

APPLICATION AND INFORMATION

Applications should be submitted by January 15 for early admission consideration and by August 1 for admission for the fall semester, which begins in late August and ends in December.

CONCORDIA UNIVERSITY

■ PORTLAND, OREGON

THE UNIVERSITY

Concordia University, Portland, is a private, four-year Lutheran university dedicated to the intellectual and professional development of the whole student. Founded in 1905 as an academy, Concordia grew from a junior college to a four-year college in the late 1970s, awarding its first bachelor's degrees in 1980 and graduate degrees in 1996. Concordia attained university status in 1995. The institution's mission statement is, "Concordia University is a Christian University preparing leaders for the transformation of society." The University is composed of three academic colleges: the College of Education, the School of Management and the College of Theology, Arts, and Sciences. Programmatic development through the 1980s and 1990s increased the University's commitment to local and regional needs through several academic additions. These include a nationally recognized health-care administration program, a concentration in e-business within the bachelor's in business administration, and a progressive program emphasis in environmental management. Concordia University (CU) further demonstrates its commitment to remain on the cutting edge of program development with its participation in the nationwide Concordia University System. An innovative intercampus partnership of the ten Concordia institutions of The Lutheran Church–Missouri Synod, the system has a combined enrollment of 15,000 students. Opportunities for enrollment in any one of the ten campuses and the benefits of high-tech distance learning and alternative timelines for degree completion are examples of the advantages of a small college within the framework of a nationwide educational system. Through the resource of compressed video, all system campuses are linked to provide academic offerings via a comprehensive telecommunications system. CU's electronic classroom increases educational accessibility and allows students to benefit from the academic expertise at other member institutions.

For more information, students should contact:

Office of Admissions
Concordia University
2811 Northeast Holman Street
Portland, Oregon 97211
Telephone: 503-288-9371
800-321-9371 (toll-free)
Fax: 503-280-8531
E-mail: admissions@cu-portland.edu
World Wide Web: http://www.cu-portland.edu

ACADEMIC PROGRAM

Concordia operates on a semester calendar with two 15-week semesters. A summer session is offered in selected programs. Academic work is measured in semester hours, and courses are assigned from .5 to 5 semester hours each. For a baccalaureate degree, 124 semester hours are required; for the associate degree, 63 hours are required. All degree-seeking students, regardless of their major, must complete the general education requirements, which include courses in communications, fine arts, humanities, physical education, religion, science, math, and social science. In several academic areas, students may earn credit through successful completion of Advanced Placement and College-Level Examination Program (CLEP) tests.

FINANCIAL AID

The Free Application for Federal Student Aid (FAFSA) is used to determine a student's financial need for the awarding of scholarships, grants, work-study programs, and loans. Most awards are made in the spring for the following academic year. Approximately 95 percent of CU's first-year students receive some form of scholarships and grants. Merit-based scholarships are awarded based on academic history.

APPLICATION AND INFORMATION

Candidates for admission must complete a formal Concordia application for admission, submit test scores and/or high school/college transcripts, and furnish one reference. Applicants are encouraged to apply as early in the academic year as possible. Concordia follows a rolling admission procedure, and candidates are notified of a decision shortly after all the necessary credentials have been received.

DAVIDSON COLLEGE

■ DAVIDSON, NORTH CAROLINA

THE COLLEGE

Founded in 1837, Davidson College consistently ranks as one of the most competitive liberal arts and sciences colleges in the United States. Davidson's student body is made up of 1,600 students from forty-three states and twenty-four other countries, chosen not only for their academic promise but also for their character and leadership. The liberal arts curriculum at Davidson is designed to give students knowledge and skills that they will put to use throughout their lives. Davidson offers more than 850 courses in twenty major fields and in special interdisciplinary programs. Students benefit from the careful attention of 137 full-time faculty members who are dedicated to teaching and guiding undergraduates. Close relationships between faculty members and students are a hallmark of the Davidson experience.

For more information, students should contact:

Nancy J. Cable, Ph.D.
Dean of Admission and Financial Aid
Davidson College
P.O. Box 1737
Davidson, North Carolina 28036
Telephone: 704-892-2230
800-768-0380 (toll-free)
World Wide Web:
http://www.davidson.edu

ACADEMIC PROGRAM

The liberal arts curriculum at Davidson gives students a broad-based and rich education, exposing them to many different academic areas. Through reading and writing assignments across every discipline, students learn to analyze information, think critically, and communicate effectively. Davidson requires a total of thirty-two courses to graduate. Through the required core curriculum, every Davidson student takes courses in six areas: the fine arts, natural sciences and mathematics, philosophy and religion, literature, history, and the social sciences. Additional courses are taken in composition, foreign language, cultural diversity, and physical education. In addition to the core curriculum, students choose a major by the end of their sophomore year. A major normally requires up to twelve courses, including at least five upper-level courses. The academic year at Davidson consists of two 15-week semesters. Notably, 92 percent of those who enroll at Davidson graduate within four academic years.

FINANCIAL AID

Admission decisions are made without regard to a student's financial need. Through a combination of state, federal, and private sources, Davidson grants in excess of $6.5 million to students who qualify. The instructions for applying for need-based aid are included with Davidson's application for admission. Students with financial need are assisted through a combination of Davidson scholarships, federal and state grants, loans, and work-study. Davidson awards merit scholarships to approximately 15 percent of each entering first-year class. These awards recognize students' academic promise, special talents, and personal qualities. Recipients are selected based on the strength of their admission application. For some scholarships, selection may also be based on the outcome of an audition, interview, portfolio review, or writing sample. Merit scholarships range from $2500 to the comprehensive fee and include the following top awards: the Thomas S. and Sarah B. Baker Scholarship (two awarded, comprehensive fee), the John Montgomery Belk Scholarship (one awarded to a student from the southeastern U.S., comprehensive fee), the William Holt Terry Scholarship (two awarded to students with exceptional leadership qualities, full tuition), the Bryan Scholarship (two awarded to students who contribute in a superlative manner to their sport as well as to the academic and cocurricular life at Davidson), and the Missy and John Kuykendall Scholarship (three awarded to students who provide service leadership).

DREXEL UNIVERSITY

■ PHILADELPHIA, PENNSYLVANIA

THE UNIVERSITY

Drexel is a private, nonsectarian, coeducational university that has maintained a reputation for academic excellence since its founding in 1891. Its academic programs offer students practical preparation for graduate school and a variety of careers. Full-time, paid professional experience through Drexel's cooperative education program is a vital part of a Drexel education. Students gain professional experience in jobs related to their career interests by alternating classroom study with periods of employment in business, industry, and government. More than 2,300 employers from twenty-eight states and fourteen other countries participate in this program. Another distinctive element is the University's microcomputer requirement, through which all undergraduates participate in a computer-enhanced education.

For more information, students should contact:

Office of Undergraduate Admissions
Drexel University
3141 Chestnut Streets
Philadelphia, Pennsylvania 19104
Telephone: 800-2-DREXEL (toll-free)
World Wide Web:
http://www.drexel.edu

ACADEMIC PROGRAM

Drexel's distinguishing feature is Drexel Co-op: "The Ultimate Internship™." Combined with rigorous academic programs, this feature provides an education that enables students to bridge the gap between academic studies and the working world. The co-op/internship program generates a two-way educational force: academic knowledge finds concrete form in the workplace, while personal growth and experiential learning on the job enrich the academic experience. All undergraduates are prepared for full-time professional internships through Drexel's cooperative education program. With the new flexible degree programs, studies in engineering, information systems, and commerce and engineering, as well as science programs in the College of Arts and Sciences, are designed to be completed in four or five years, including eighteen months of co-op experience. Most of the design arts programs require four years to complete and include six months of co-op. Business, humanities, and social science programs offer both four-year and five-year co-op/internship options. Each college has its own sequence of graduation requirements, including a common core of subjects and the opportunity for specialization after the core is complete.

FINANCIAL AID

Approximately 87 percent of all freshmen receive financial aid. The aid package may contain academic, athletic, or performing arts scholarships; grants; or loans; or part-time employment. Federal programs are also included. All students applying for aid must submit the Free Application for Federal Student Aid by May 1. Notification of incoming freshmen and transfer students begins about March 1. Drexel offers a unique achievement-based award, the A. J. Drexel Scholarship, to all qualified incoming freshmen and transfer students. With an annual award value of up to $10,000, the A. J. Drexel Scholarship is renewable on a yearly basis, provided the student maintains a 3.0 grade point average and full-time status. Criteria include a strong academic record and involvement in extracurricular and community service activities.

APPLICATION AND INFORMATION

Application forms with complete instructions for admission and financial aid and the appropriate college prospectus may be obtained by writing to the address given below. Each application must be accompanied by a nonrefundable application fee of $35; however, the fee may be waived in cases of extreme hardship if requested by the secondary school or if the student visits the campus. Students may access Drexel's online application at the Web site listed below. Applications for regular full-time undergraduate status are accepted throughout the senior year. Drexel subscribes to the College Board's Candidates Reply Date of May 1. Transfer students should apply at least three months before the beginning of the term in which they wish to enroll.

EARLHAM COLLEGE

■ RICHMOND, INDIANA

THE COLLEGE

Earlham College offers a challenging intellectual environment that attracts a diverse group of students with a variety of motivations—academic, political, social, athletic, ethical, and career-minded—who want to make an impact on the world. The College's 1,105 students—579 women and 526 men—represent forty-eight states and twenty-five countries. Students of many races, religious backgrounds, economic levels, and ethnic traditions join together on this Midwestern campus to create and experience the Earlham Effect. They share an experience rooted in the Quaker values of tolerance, equality, justice, respect, and collaboration. They explore an unending desire to see the world differently and to bring about change when necessary. Earlham's commitment to engaging students in a changing world is at the heart of its own mission. The College was founded in 1847 by the Religious Society of Friends (Quakers) and to this day believes that a strong liberal arts education is the best intellectual preparation for life. Students at Earlham get involved and nearly every interest and taste is satisfied by the variety of associations and organizations offered.

For more information, students should contact:

Office of Admissions
Earlham College
801 National Road West
Richmond, Indiana 47374-4095
Telephone: 765-983-1600
800-EARLHAM (toll-free)
Fax: 765-983-1560
E-mail: admission@earlham.edu
World Wide Web:
http://www.earlham.edu

ACADEMIC PROGRAM

Earlham aims to educate for depth and breadth, believing that one's success in the twenty-first century will depend heavily on an ability to understand and make well-educated connections across different intellectual and experiential boundaries. Earlham's General Education Program encourages students to develop competencies in language, social science, natural science, philosophy or religion, and fine arts. Students also complete some course work having multicultural and intercultural dimensions. First-year core courses, Humanities A and B, emphasize critical reading and writing skills. Students gain an in-depth understanding of one or more disciplines in their major area of academic concentration. An academic major usually consists of eight to ten courses in one department, a senior research project or seminar, and a departmental comprehensive examination. Earlham grants credit for Advanced Placement examinations and higher-level International Baccalaureate subjects. Students may also receive credit for independent studies and academic internships. The academic year consists of two semesters plus an optional May term. During the summer the College sponsors a two-week academic experience for high school students called Explore-A-College.

FINANCIAL AID

Most financial aid is awarded on the basis of demonstrated need; more than 80 percent of Earlham's students receive financial assistance. Earlham usually meets the full need of all accepted students with a combination of Earlham Grants, endowed scholarships, loans, federal and state grants, and campus work. Students must file both the Free Application for Federal Student Aid (FAFSA) and a special Earlham form. Scholarships are awarded without regard to financial need and recognize academic achievement. Earlham also offers scholarships through the National Merit Scholarship Corporation. Special scholarships are available to members of the Religious Society of Friends (Quakers) and students who will enhance the diversity of the student body. Scholarships and limited financial aid are available for international students.

APPLICATION AND INFORMATION

Earlham offers several admission options. The early decision deadline is December 1 (notification by December 15); the early action deadline is January 1 (notification on February 1); the regular decision deadline is February 15 (notification by March 15); and the transfer deadline is April 1. International students (non U.S. citizens) should apply by February 1. Applications are accepted after these deadlines as long as places remain in the entering class.

EASTERN COLLEGE

■ ST. DAVIDS, PENNSYLVANIA

THE COLLEGE

For more information, students should contact:

Mark Seymour
Vice President of Enrollment Management
Eastern College
1300 Eagle Road
St. Davids, Pennsylvania 19087-3696
Telephone: 800-452-0996 (toll-free)
E-mail: ugadm@eastern.edu
World Wide Web:
http://www.eastern.edu

Eastern College brings a special purpose to its mission as a Christian institution of higher education. The College wants to produce world Christians, capable of confronting injustice and indifference with the character, competence, and commitment Eastern has helped them develop. First and foremost, Eastern remains true to its biblical heritage. The power of the prophetic Word and the Lordship of Jesus Christ provide the context for the College's theological position. The College is sure of its Christian stand, and this encourages it to strengthen its faith by confronting serious contemporary issues. Neither narrow-minded nor staid, the College affirms and embraces Christians whose doctrinal positions may be broader or more restrictive. As a result, those at the College can actively pursue the full dynamic of an abundant Christian life and take an obedient walk with Him. In addition, the academic process revolves around a curriculum that emphasizes foundational skills as well as the understanding and application of knowledge in an increasingly complex society. Classroom experience is intellectually rigorous. A creative core curriculum builds on basic truths and continually challenges the potential of an expanding mind. Practical experience is generated through an extensive internship program as well as through relationships with established ministries such as World Vision, Young Life, Youth for Christ, foreign missions, and Christian outreach programs. The academic climate is enhanced through the presence of graduate programs. Knowledge, ultimately, is written as indelibly on the heart as it is on the mind. Justice and a will obedient to the Lord result from such an academic experience.

ACADEMIC PROGRAM

In the core curriculum, students take courses designed to fulfill the basic mission of Eastern: to provide biblical foundations to which all learning and action can be related, to ensure acquisition of certain basic skills, and to broaden the student's view of the world. Courses in the breadth area of the core are planned and taught in such a way that central themes of the Christian faith are integrated into the course content. The Fixed Core includes courses such as justice and diversity in a pluralistic society and science, technology, and values.

FINANCIAL AID

Eastern is committed to providing education to qualified students regardless of their means. The financial aid program offers scholarships, grants, loans, and employment. The College utilizes the Pennsylvania Higher Education Assistance Agency (PHEAA) for needs analysis forms processing. The student is required to complete the Free Application for Federal Student Aid (FAFSA) to determine financial aid eligibility. Overall, the College views financial assistance to students as a cooperative investment. If parents contribute to the maximum of their ability and if the student contributes his or her fair share through earnings and personal savings, the College attempts to complete the partnership. In addition, estimates of financial aid eligibility may be obtained from the Financial Aid Office whether or not the student is an applicant. Non-need academic scholarships ranging from $500 to $6000 are available. These scholarships are awarded on the basis of SAT I or ACT scores and high school class rank information. Music, leadership, honors college, and church-matching grants are other college-based grant programs that are available.

APPLICATION AND INFORMATION

Applications are generally accepted until the beginning of each term. Admission decisions are made on a rolling basis. Students should see Eastern's Web site for more information.

EASTERN MENNONITE UNIVERSITY

■ HARRISONBURG, VIRGINIA

THE UNIVERSITY

For more information, students should contact:

Ellen B. Miller
Director of Admissions
Eastern Mennonite University
Harrisonburg, Virginia 22802
Telephone: 800-368-2665 (toll-free)
Fax: 540-432-4444
E-mail: admiss@emu.edu
World Wide Web:
http://www.emu.edu

Eastern Mennonite, a private Christian university founded in 1917, provides a high-quality liberal arts education that emphasizes spiritual growth and cross-cultural awareness. The nurturing environment of EMU's student-oriented campus not only prepares students for a wide variety of careers but also challenges students to answer Christ's call to a life of nonviolence, witness, service, and peacebuilding. The undergraduate experience is enriched by graduate programs in business administration, conflict transformation, counseling, and education. The University also has a seminary. EMU is accredited by the Southern Association of Colleges and Schools. In addition, the nursing, teacher education, and social work programs are accredited by their specialty organizations at the national level. Undergraduate students make up about 1,000 of the 1,400 students. Of the undergraduates, 60 percent are women and 8 percent are American multiethnic students. Eight percent come from international settings. Students represent thirty-seven states and twenty-two other countries. Most students are traditional college age. Religious backgrounds vary widely, with 60 percent representing Mennonites. EMU is a residential community in which students live on campus until age 21 (unless they are married or live at home). Housing options include traditional residence halls, coed buildings, suite arrangements, apartments for upperclass students, and group houses. An energetic residence staff provides a dynamic residential life program focused on education and support. After the freshman year, a housing lottery is used to determine certain housing options.

ACADEMIC PROGRAM

The academic calendar consists of two 15-week semesters from late August to late April. The baccalaureate degree requires 128 semester hours. All students complete a major, the Global Village general education curriculum, and electives. The Global Village curriculum is a sequence of courses consisting of 49 semester hours distributed as follows: faith (11), humanities (9), cross-cultural studies (9), math/natural science (9), social science (3), writing (3), speech (2), physical education (2), and the first-year experience (1). Associate degrees require 64 semester hours of general education requirements, a concentration in a major, and electives. Thirty semester hours are needed to complete a certificate. Cross-cultural studies take students to another culture for a semester or a three- to nine-week summer session. An honors program provides academic challenges and leadership opportunities for a select group of students through faculty mentoring, seminars, research opportunities, and special projects. Twelve honors students are selected from each first-year class. Two of the 12 receive full-tuition scholarships, and 10 are awarded half-tuition scholarships. Other special academic opportunities include credit by examination and extension credit for special programs with outside organizations.

FINANCIAL AID

More than 90 percent of EMU students receive financial aid. Scholarships include those given for academic achievement and an award of $1000 given to new first-year students who are children of alumni. Other grant aid, given to meet financial need, includes federal aid and EMU grants. Admission is need-blind. In addition, students with financial need may obtain federal loans or participate in the work-study program. Virginia residents receive the Virginia Tuition Assistance Grant, regardless of need, which amounts to $2850 or more annually. If students receive grants from their churches, EMU matches up to $1000 per year. No application is needed for academic scholarships except for honors awards. Students applying for need-based aid must complete the Free Application for Federal Student Aid (FAFSA). Applications should be completed by February 15.

ELMIRA COLLEGE

■ ELMIRA, NEW YORK

THE COLLEGE

For more information, students should contact:

Dean of Admissions
Elmira College
Elmira, New York 14901
Telephone: 800-935-6472 (toll-free)
E-mail: admissions@elmira.edu
World Wide Web:
http://www.elmira.edu

Elmira College is a small, independent college that is recognized for its emphasis on education of high quality in the liberal arts and preprofessional preparation. One of the oldest colleges in the United States, Elmira was founded in 1855. The College has always produced graduates interested in both community service and successful careers. Friendliness, personal attention, strong college spirit, and support for learning beyond the classroom help to make Elmira a special place. Elmira College is one of only 258 colleges in the nation to be granted a chapter of the prestigious Phi Beta Kappa honor society. The full-time undergraduate enrollment is about 1,150 men and women. The students at Elmira represent more than twenty-seven states, primarily those in the Northeast, with the highest representation coming from New York, New Jersey, Massachusetts, Connecticut, Maine, and Pennsylvania. International students from twenty-three countries were enrolled in September 1999. Ninety-five percent of the full-time undergraduates live in College residence halls. The intercollegiate sports program includes men's and women's basketball, golf, ice hockey, lacrosse, soccer, and tennis and women's cheerleading, field hockey, softball, and volleyball. An intramural program is also available. Emerson Hall houses the student fitness center, a pool, and a gym capable of seating 1000, as well as the Gibson Theatre, which has a state-of-the-art sound and lighting system. Professional societies; clubs; music, dance, and drama groups; a student-operated FM radio station; and the student newspaper, yearbook, and literary magazine also provide numerous opportunities for extracurricular activity.

ACADEMIC PROGRAM

The College's calendar is composed of two 12-week terms followed by a 6-week spring term. Students enroll for four subjects during the 12-week terms, completing the first term by mid-December and the second during the first week of April. The 6-week term, from mid-April through May, may be devoted to a particular project involving travel, internship, research, or independent study. Students are required to participate in internships in order to gain practical and meaningful experience related to their program of study. Credit is awarded for these projects. Special opportunities for outstanding students include participation in thirteen national honorary societies on campus and a chance to assist faculty members in teaching and research. The College also offers an accelerated three-year graduation option for outstanding students. Army and Air Force ROTC are available.

FINANCIAL AID

Financial aid is available for both freshmen and transfer students. Awards are based upon the Free Application for Federal Student Aid (FAFSA) and Financial Aid PROFILE as well as the student's academic potential. Types of aid include grants, scholarships, federal loans, Elmira College loans, and work opportunities. In addition, superior students may qualify for no-need Elmira College Honors Scholarships, which are available to both freshmen and transfer students and range fom $4000 to full tuition per year. For 2000–01, the average freshman aid package (including all types of aid) amounted to more than $19,000. Transfer students applying for financial aid must submit a financial aid transcript from all colleges previously attended, whether or not they received financial aid. About 80 percent of the full-time undergraduates receive financial aid.

EMBRY-RIDDLE AERONAUTICAL UNIVERSITY

■ DAYTONA BEACH, FLORIDA

THE UNIVERSITY

The purpose of Embry-Riddle Aeronautical University is to provide a comprehensive education of such excellence that graduates are responsible citizens and well prepared for productive careers in aviation and aerospace. In addition to its traditional residential campuses in Daytona Beach, Florida, and Prescott, Arizona, Embry-Riddle serves the continuing education needs of the aviation industry through an extensive network of off-campus centers in the United States and Europe and through its division of continuing education's training seminars and management development programs. The total University enrollment (full-time and part-time) is more than 12,000. Approximately 4,500 undergraduate students are currently enrolled at the Daytona Beach residential campus, and more than 6,000 students are enrolled in graduate programs University-wide. Students come from all fifty states and more than 100 countries, which makes Embry-Riddle truly an international university. Graduate programs leading to the degrees of Master of Science in Aerospace Engineering, Master of Business Administration in Aviation, Master of Aeronautical Science, Master of Science in Technical Management, Master of Human Factors and Systems, Master of Industrial Relations, and Master of Software Engineering are available at the Daytona Beach campus as well as at many college of continuing education locations. Embry-Riddle provides cocurricular activities that appeal to almost every taste. Students take advantage of the many opportunities for personal growth and development through social and preprofessional fraternities and sororities and cultural and recreational activities. Embry-Riddle's award-winning Precision Flight Demonstration teams offer students the opportunity to compete nationally in air and ground events. Embry-Riddle athletes participate in intercollegiate and intramural competitions in many sports, including baseball, basketball, cross-country, golf, lacrosse, rugby, soccer, tennis, and volleyball.

For more information, students should contact:

Director of Admissions
Embry-Riddle Aeronautical University
P.O. Box 11767
Daytona Beach, Florida 32120-1767
Telephone: 904-226-6100
800-862-2416 (toll-free nationwide)
E-mail: admit@db.erau.edu
World Wide Web:
http://www.embryriddle.edu

ACADEMIC PROGRAM

Even a field as specialized as aviation requires a broad background. General education courses required of all students who are pursuing a baccalaureate program include communication skills, such as English composition, literature, and technical report writing; humanities; social sciences; mathematics; physical science; economics; and computer science. To ensure academic success, Embry-Riddle provides free tutorial services. The calendar year is divided into two semesters of fifteen weeks each, with the summer session divided into two terms. The average course load for each fall or spring semester is 15 credit hours.

FINANCIAL AID

Applicants for financial aid are required to complete the Department of Education's Free Application for Federal Student Aid (FAFSA) and any other documents requested by the University. Students are encouraged to apply early if they wish to be considered for all types of programs. Florida residents may also apply for several additional programs available through the state.

APPLICATION AND INFORMATION

Embry-Riddle requires each applicant to submit an application form and fee, SAT I or ACT scores, and an official high school/college transcript. Flight students must provide an FAA Class I or Class II medical certificate. When a student is accepted for admission, tuition and housing deposits are required by May 1.

EMERSON COLLEGE

■ BOSTON, MASSACHUSETTS

THE COLLEGE

For more information, students should contact:

Office of Undergraduate Admission
Emerson College
120 Bolyston Street
Boston, Massachusetts 02116-4624
Telephone: 617-824-8600
Fax: 617-824-8609
E-mail: admission@emerson.edu
World Wide Web:
http://www.emerson.edu

Founded in 1880, Emerson is one of the premier colleges in the United States for the study of communication and the performing arts. Students may choose from over twenty undergraduate majors and twelve graduate programs supported by state-of-the-art facilities and a nationally renowned faculty. The campus is home to WERS 88.9 FM, the oldest noncommercial radio station in New England; the 850-seat Emerson Majestic Theatre; and *Ploughshares*, the award-winning journal for new writing. A pioneer in the fields of communication and performing arts, Emerson was one of the first colleges in the nation to establish a program in children's theater (1919) as well as an undergraduate program in broadcasting (1937). Professional-level training in speech pathology and audiology was inaugurated in 1935, educational FM radio in 1949, closed-circuit television in 1955, and a B.F.A. degree in film as early as 1972. In 1980, the College created the country's first graduate program in professional writing and publishing. Today, Emerson's 2,700 undergraduate and 800 graduate students come from more than sixty countries and forty-five states and territories. Approximately 1,300 students live on campus, some on special theme floors, such as the Writer's Block and Wellness and Digital Culture Floors. The campus also boasts a 10,000-square-foot fitness center, health services center, student union, cabaret, and cultural center. In addition, students are supported by several College offices, such as the Learning Assistance Center, Office of AHANA Student Affairs, Center for Spiritual Life, Office of Off-Campus Services, International Student Affairs Office, Counseling Center, Office of Student Life, and Career Services Office. Emerson College is fully accredited by the New England Association of Schools and Colleges.

ACADEMIC PROGRAM

Emerson's academic calendar consists of two 15-week semesters, plus two 6-week summer sessions. The requirements for graduation combine a general liberal arts curriculum with advanced, specialized courses that are specific to individual departments. Internships for academic credit are available in almost every major, and the Institute for Liberal Arts and Interdisciplinary Studies offers first-year seminars, exclusive honors program classes, independent study options, and innovative courses that cut across academic disciplines.

FINANCIAL AID

Each year, more than 70 percent of Emerson's student body receives some form of financial assistance. The College provides more than $38 million in need-based financial support that typically combines grant and scholarship, loan, and college work-study. Academic scholarships ranged from $5000 to half-tuition are awarded on a limited basis to students who meet high academic standards. Special performance-based scholarships, averaging $4000, are available to exceptional students in the performing arts. In order to apply for financial assistance, students must complete the FAFSA form, CSS PROFILE, and an Emerson College financial aid application by March 1 (for September entrance) or December 1 (for January entrance). More information about financial assistance at Emerson can be found online at http://www.emerson.edu/fin_aid, or by contacting the Office of Financial Assistance (telephone: 617-824-9655; fax: 617-824-8619; e-mail: finaid@emerson.edu).

EMORY & HENRY COLLEGE

■ EMORY, VIRGINIA

THE COLLEGE

Since its founding in 1836, Emory & Henry College has instilled a strong sense of values in students and has prepared them for lifelong learning and success. Among the College's alumni have been congressmen, businesspeople, scientists, teachers, artists, ministers, authors, and many public servants. The College's 900 students (almost equally divided between men and women) constitute a diverse group, coming from rural areas of southwestern Virginia as well as from urban centers nationwide. They represent more than twenty states and several countries. The campus stretches over 150 acres of rolling hills and has many trees and broad open spaces. The buildings are a mixture of historic structures renovated for contemporary use and modern facilities designed to blend with the environment. The College was named in honor of Bishop John Emory, an outstanding United Methodist churchman, and Patrick Henry, a Revolutionary War patriot from Virginia.

For more information, students should contact:

Office of Admissions and Financial Aid
Emory & Henry College
P.O. Box 947
Emory, Virginia 24327-0947
Telephone: 540-944-6133
800-848-5493 (toll-free)
Fax: 540-944-6935
E-mail: ehadmiss@ehc.edu
World Wide Web:
http://www.ehc.edu

ACADEMIC PROGRAM

Emory & Henry offers a liberal arts program with emphasis on writing, reasoning, value inquiry, and knowledge of global concerns, as well as a broad introduction to liberal arts subjects. All students complete a core curriculum, which includes a yearlong, interdisciplinary Western Tradition course and a writing course for all first-year students. Sophomores complete an ambitious Great Books program, and upperclass students take courses related to value inquiry and global studies. Along with the core curriculum, each student completes a major and a minor or a combined program referred to as an area of concentration. Students also have the opportunity to choose elective courses and to participate in international exchange programs.

FINANCIAL AID

Forms of aid include need-based and non-need-based scholarships, loans, and part-time jobs. A Bonner Scholars program provides substantial scholarships for selected students who do volunteer work in the surrounding region. Virginia residents are eligible for a special grant based on residence. Merit scholarships are awarded based on academic performance, and many can be renewed based on continued academic success. Ninety-six percent of fall 2000 undergraduates received financial aid. The average aided first-year student received an aid package worth $12,803, meeting 91 percent of need. The priority application deadline for financial aid is April 1 and the deadline is August 1.

APPLICATION AND INFORMATION

To apply for admission, students should submit the basic application form, an essay, a copy of the high school transcript, scores from either the SAT I or the ACT, and a nonrefundable $30 application fee. Transfer applicants must submit a transcript from any college previously attended and a statement of good standing. A rolling admission policy allows notification of the admission decision within two weeks after a file has been completed. Students who have thoroughly researched their college options and have determined that Emory & Henry College is their first choice are encouraged to consider applying under the Early Decision Plan. Although these students may file regular applications with other colleges, it is understood that they are applying for Early Decision only at Emory & Henry College and intend to enroll if admitted. To be considered for Early Decision, a student should submit the completed Application for Admission, including the Early Decision Agreement; the secondary school transcript; and a report of either SAT I or ACT test scores by December 1.

FAIRMONT STATE COLLEGE

■ FAIRMONT, WEST VIRGINIA

THE COLLEGE

Fairmont State College (FSC) is the largest state-supported four-year college in West Virginia, with an enrollment of approximately 6,600 students. Founded in 1867, the College is located in the north-central portion of the state in the city of Fairmont, West Virginia. In addition to the main campus, which includes thirteen major buildings, classes are also offered at the FSC Robert C. Byrd National Aerospace Education Center in Bridgeport as well as at the FSC Gaston Caperton Center, a 36,000-square-foot state-of-the-art facility in Clarksburg. The College also has satellite facilities reaching across the north-central region of West Virginia and at the Center for Workforce Education at the I-79 Technology Park. Fairmont State College has a rich and proud athletic tradition. The College is a member of NCAA Division II and offers men's teams in baseball, basketball, cross-country, football, golf, tennis, and swimming. The College sponsors women's teams in basketball, cross-country, golf, softball, swimming, tennis, and volleyball. Fairmont State's cheerleaders are consistently among the top teams in the state and the nation. FSC also has an extensive and well-organized intramural program and provides other recreational facilities across campus. Students who live on campus are housed in one of three residence halls and take their meals at a centrally located dining hall or at the food court in the student center. For those students who prefer to live off campus, private accommodations close to the College are available. Parents who are taking classes at the College may find it convenient to enroll their young children in the day-care center located on the main campus. The Newman Center and the Wesley Foundation are available to minister to the spiritual needs of students; both organizations are adjacent to the FSC campus. There are also various student organizations, honor societies, and social fraternities and sororities to enhance extracurricular life at the College.

For more information or to schedule a tour, students should contact:

Office of Enrollment Services
Fairmont State College
1201 Locust Avenue
Fairmont, West Virginia 26554
Telephone: 304-367-4892
800-641-5678 (toll-free)
304-367-4141 (admissions and records)
304-367-4213 (financial aid)
304-367-4216 (housing)
304-367-4000 (campus operator)
304-623-5721 (Caperton Center)
304-842-8300 (Aerospace Education Center)

ACADEMIC PROGRAM

Fairmont State College offers more than 130 program areas in the Schools of Business and Economics, Education, Fine Arts, Health Careers, Language and Literature, Science and Mathematics, Social Science, and Technology. Special degrees such as the Regents Bachelor of Arts degree offer nontraditional approaches for individual career or personal requirements. Certificate programs are designed to provide basic skills or increased proficiency in specific occupational areas. Preprofessional studies are designed to prepare students for a wide variety of professional programs beyond a four-year degree.

FINANCIAL AID

Sixty-five percent of Fairmont State College students receive some form of financial aid. Guidelines and forms for West Virginia and out-of-state residents are available from high school guidance counselors or FSC's Financial Aid Office.

APPLICATION AND INFORMATION

Campus tours are available Monday through Friday by appointment. Fairmont State College also sponsors a Saturday Campus Visitation Day once each fall and spring semester.

FERRIS STATE UNIVERSITY

■ BIG RAPIDS, MICHIGAN

THE UNIVERSITY

Ferris State University is Michigan's foremost professional and technical university, providing career-oriented education to nearly 10,000 students. Accredited by the North Central Association of Colleges and Schools, the University offers more than 120 programs through the Colleges of Allied Health Sciences, Arts and Sciences, Business, Education, Pharmacy, Technology, University College, and the Michigan College of Optometry. These offerings lead to bachelor's and associate degrees and certificates, master's degrees in accountancy, criminal justice administration, information systems management, and career and technical education, and doctorates in optometry and pharmacy. One of Michigan's fifteen public universities, Ferris State University is recognized for its career-oriented educational programs that are designed to meet the technology and workforce demands of business and industry, the health-care professions, and society in general through applied research and practical education. Ferris was founded in 1884 by Woodbridge N. Ferris (1853–1928), a distinguished Michigan educator and politician who served two terms as the state's governor and was elected to the United States Senate. Ferris was a private institution until 1950 when it joined the state higher education system. The college obtained university status in 1987. Ferris graduates consistently have experienced high job placement rates because Ferris programs are tailored to the needs of employers. The most recent annual survey of graduates showed that 98 percent of Ferris's 1999–2000 graduates were employed or continued as full-time students. Of those in the job market, 91 percent found employment in a position related to their major field of study.

For more information, students should contact:

Admissions Office
Ferris State University
420 Oak Street, PRK 101
Big Rapids, Michigan 49307-2020
Telephone: 231-591-2100
800-4FERRIS (toll-free)
E-mail: admissions@ferris.edu

ACADEMIC PROGRAM

Ferris is dedicated to the ideal of blending career-oriented professional training with a solid base of general education. While major programs of study provide graduates with the skills and knowledge required to enter a chosen career, general education provides graduates with the academic skills, analytic flexibility, and broad base of knowledge required for continued learning, performance, and advancement in their personal and professional lives. Ferris currently is on the semester system, and the minimum requirement for a baccalaureate degree is 120 semester hours. The average program requires between 120 and 130 semester hours. The minimum number of hours required for an associate degree is 60. The University's academic year begins in August and ends in early May.

FINANCIAL AID

Approximately 71 percent of Ferris students receive some type of financial aid through federal, state, and University programs. In 1999–2000, student financial aid included more than $43 million in scholarships, grants, loans, work-study, or a combination of these. The Free Application for Federal Student Aid (FAFSA) must be submitted by April 1 to receive priority consideration for need-based financial aid. The University also provides merit-based scholarships in recognition of superior academic performance and residence-based scholarships for students living on campus who maintain high academic grades. The Woodbridge N. Ferris Scholarship Program offers competitive awards ranging from $500 to $6000 per year to those who qualify. The Residential Life Scholarship offers $2000 per year for entering students who live in a residence hall on campus, have a 3.0 or better high school GPA, and have a minimum score of 20 on the ACT. Information and counseling are available from the Office of Scholarships and Financial Aid (telephone: 231-591-2110 or 800-940-4-AID, toll-free).

FERRUM COLLEGE

■ FERRUM, VIRGINIA

THE COLLEGE

Ferrum College is a four-year, independent, coeducational college situated on a 700-acre wooded campus in the foothills of southcentral Virginia's Blue Ridge Mountains. Ferrum is a self-contained community; 81 percent of the student body lives on campus, and many faculty members live on or near campus and are closely involved in campus life. Ferrum also provides in-room Dell computers at no extra charge. Founded in 1913 by the United Methodist Church, Ferrum is a comprehensive liberal arts college accredited by the Southern Association of Colleges and Schools. Ferrum's student body of about 950 (56 percent men, 44 percent women) is a diverse group; while the largest contingent comes from Virginia, twenty-five other states and a number of other countries are also represented. Ferrum's curriculum provides solid career preparation that includes rigorous academics, a strong experiential learning component, and a practical, broad-based, "real-life" emphasis. Ferrum students take what they learn in the classroom and apply it in the community through internships, volunteer opportunities, and fieldwork. The result: a successful start to a meaningful career. Ferrum recently surveyed the graduating class of 1999 and 95 percent of the respondents reported being either employed, attending graduate school, or both.

Further information may be obtained by contacting:

Director of Admissions
Spilman-Daniel House
Ferrum College
Ferrum, Virginia 24088-9000
Telephone: 540-365-4290
800-868-9797 (toll-free)
540-365-4290
E-mail: admissions@ferrum.edu
World Wide Web:
http://www.ferrum.edu

ACADEMIC PROGRAM

Ferrum College's comprehensive approach to higher education provides the benefits of liberal arts education with solid, practical career preparation. To graduate, students must complete 127 semester hours of academic work, meet the appropriate distribution and major/minor requirements, and achieve a cumulative grade point average of at least 2.0. Faculty members encourage students to take advantage of the wide variety of experiential learning opportunities available. Internships are required for programs such as environmental science, agriculture, teacher education, social work, recreation and leisure, and sports medicine and strongly recommended for all others, reflecting the College's belief in the value of hands-on learning. Ferrum students can also do volunteer work, join student government and/or the residence life staff, or work on campus in jobs ranging from student trainers to ropes course facilitators to public relations interns.

FINANCIAL AID

In 2000–01, 95 percent of Ferrum students were offered some form of financial assistance. For the 75 percent of students receiving need-based aid, the average financial aid package totaled $10,675. Ferrum makes every effort to provide financial assistance consistent with the ability of students and their families to meet college expenses. A comprehensive assistance program includes campus jobs, scholarships, grants, and loans. A typical package consists of 58 percent scholarships and grants, 34 percent low-interest loans, and 8 percent campus-based jobs. Ferrum College is one of a small group of colleges nationwide that offers a unique financial aid opportunity known as the Bonner Scholars Program, which gives qualified students a chance to receive scholarship funds and to become involved in various service projects. The Free Application for Federal Student Aid (FAFSA) and forms concerning grants and scholarships are sent to all applicants and should be completed and submitted no later than April 1 for priority consideration. Virginia residents are eligible for grants under the Tuition Assistance Grant (TAG) Program, and out-of-state students receive a comparable TAG offered by the College.

APPLICATION AND INFORMATION

Applicants should submit a completed application (available on request from the Admissions Office or online at the Web address below), a high school transcript (and a college transcript, if applicable), and scores from the SAT I or ACT.

FISK UNIVERSITY

■ NASHVILLE, TENNESSEE

THE UNIVERSITY

Money magazine recently listed Fisk University as the nineteenth-best bargain for the dollar among 1,011 public and private colleges and universities in America. Founded in 1866, the University is coeducational, private, and one of America's older historically black universities. It serves a national student body, with an enrollment of 820 students. There are two residence halls for men and three for women. The focal point of the 40-acre campus and architectural symbol of the University is Jubilee Hall, the first permanent building for education of blacks in the South. The Victorian-Gothic structure is named for the internationally renowned Fisk Jubilee Singers, who continue their tradition of singing the Negro spiritual. The original Jubilee Singers toured this country and abroad in 1871. Their selflessness is the saga of Fisk. From its earliest days, Fisk has played a leadership role in the education of African Americans. Faculty and alumni have been among America's intellectual, artistic, and civic leaders. Among them are W. E. B. DuBois, the great social critic and cofounder of the NAACP, and the distinguished artist of the Harlem Renaissance, Aaron Douglas, who taught at Fisk. In proportion to its size, Fisk continues to contribute more alumni to the ranks of scholars pursuing doctoral degrees than any other institution in the United States. In addition to the undergraduate degrees listed below, Fisk offers the Master of Arts in biology, chemistry, physics, psychology (general or clinical), social gerontology, and sociology. Fisk also offers a master's degree in business administration in cooperation with Owen School of Management at Vanderbilt University, as well as an early admission program with Meharry Medical College. The mission of the University is to prepare students to be skilled, resourceful, and imaginative leaders who will address effectively the challenges of life in a technological society, a pluralistic nation, and a multicultural world.

For further information, students should contact:

Director of Admissions
Fisk University
Nashville, Tennessee 37208-3051
Telephone: 615-329-8665
800-443-3475 (toll-free)

ACADEMIC PROGRAM

The academic year comprises two semesters. All undergraduates are required to complete the core curriculum, which provides a common intellectual background for all students. Its purposes include developing a level of skill in written and oral communication and in quantitative thinking that is appropriate to support a lifelong program of study in the liberal arts. Requirements for graduation vary by program but are approximately 120 credit hours. Fisk is accredited by the Southern Association of Colleges and Schools.

FINANCIAL AID

Student financial aid is based on the principle that all qualified and motivated students who earnestly seek an education should be able to attend college, regardless of the economic status of the student's family. Aid is awarded on an individual basis, and the amount to be offered is determined by an examination of the family's financial position. Assistance is offered to the student from grants, loans, or work, or from a combination of funds. Eligibility requirements vary depending on the financial aid source. Applicants are urged to complete financial aid forms by April 20 to receive consideration while funds are available.

Applications are processed on a rolling basis; that is, the application is acted upon when the file is complete. For an early decision, applications should be filed prior to November 15; students are notified by January 17. Early decision applicants must then notify the University of their decision by January 30.

FITCHBURG STATE COLLEGE

■ FITCHBURG, MASSACHUSETTS

THE COLLEGE

For further information, students should contact:

Director of Admissions
Fitchburg State College
Fitchburg, Massachusetts 01420

Telephone: 978-665-3144
Fax: 978-665-4540
E-mail: admissions@fsc.edu
World Wide Web: http://www.fsc.edu

Fitchburg State College, the Leadership College, is a liberal arts institution where career-oriented and professional education programs thrive. Under the leadership of its president, Dr. Michael Riccards, Fitchburg State has undertaken a number of major initiatives. The College now offers a three-year baccalaureate program, more internship opportunities, a substantially increased Merit Scholarship program, and a guarantee that its graduates will be qualified for jobs in their fields. The College is investing in new technologies in every curriculum to assure that Fitchburg State continues to place more than 85 percent of its graduates in their chosen professions. Fitchburg State's excellent academic reputation and graduate placement can be attributed to a nationally recognized faculty and a commitment to teaching that is unparalleled in Massachusetts. The College serves 3,000 students in its day division and another 4,000 students in its evening and graduate programs. The average class size is 25, and the overall student-teacher ratio remains low at 15:1. Each student is assigned to an academic adviser to assist with the planning of a program of study. In addition, each department has access to state-of-the-art equipment and an internship network that spreads throughout New England. Student life at Fitchburg State is friendly and informal. There are numerous and varied opportunities for student leadership through the Student Government Association, the Athletic Council, the All-College Committee, the Campus Center Advisory Committee, the Residence Hall Councils, publications, and student-faculty-administration committees. Three student publications offer creative opportunities—the *Point,* a weekly newspaper; the *Scrimshaw,* a literary magazine; and the *Saxifrage,* the College yearbook. A number of special interest clubs are open to all students. Several sororities and fraternities contribute to the social and recreational life of the campus. Hundreds of popular and well-attended activities take place during the year, including films, lectures, concerts, seminars, coffeehouses, pub entertainment, recreational tournaments, performing arts series, and visual arts exhibits.

ACADEMIC PROGRAM

The College operates on a two-semester basis. The first semester begins in early September and ends in mid-December, and the second semester begins in mid-January and ends in mid-May. The curriculum has a strong liberal arts and sciences requirement, providing a strong foundation for either further academic study or a career. Students may obtain practical experience through volunteer placement in social agencies, government offices, and businesses related to their interests. Some major programs require an extensive supervised practicum to complete degree requirements. For education majors, a broad spectrum of student-teaching experiences is available. The four-year honors program, for students with excellent high school records, culminates in a senior thesis or project.

FINANCIAL AID

Many sources of financial aid are available to Fitchburg State students. The College participates in federal and state programs, including the Federal Direct Student Loan Program. Packages consisting of grants, loans, work-study awards, and scholarships are given to students demonstrating financial need. Financial aid applications for the fall semester must be completed by the preceding March 15 to be given priority consideration.

APPLICATION AND INFORMATION

Acceptance of qualified applicants begins in January and proceeds on a rolling basis until all available spaces are taken. Students should apply by April 1 for the fall semester and by December 1 for the spring semester.

FIVE TOWNS COLLEGE

■ DIX HILLS, NEW YORK

THE COLLEGE

Nestled in the rolling hills of Long Island's North Shore, Five Towns College offers students the opportunity to study in a suburban environment that is close to New York City. Founded in 1972 by a group of educators and community leaders, Five Towns College is an independent, nonsectarian, coeducational institution that places its emphasis on the student as an individual. Many students are drawn to the College because of its strong reputation in music, media, and the performing arts. The College offers associate, bachelor's, and master's degrees. The College also offers programs leading to the Master of Music (M.M.) degree in jazz/commercial music and in music education. From as far away as England and Japan and from as close as Long Island and New York City, the 860 full-time students reflect a rich cultural diversity. The College's enrollment is 65 percent men and 35 percent women, with a minority population of approximately 34 percent. The College's music programs are contemporary in nature, although classical musicians are also part of this creative community. The most popular programs are audio recording technology, music performance, music business, teacher education, theater, and film/video production.

For further information, students should contact:

Director of Admissions
Five Towns College
305 North Service Road
Dix Hills, New York 11746-5871
Telephone: 631-424-7000 Ext. 110
Fax: 631-424-7008
E-mail: admissions@ftc.edu
World Wide Web: http://www.ftc.edu

ACADEMIC PROGRAM

Concentrations are offered in audio recording technology, music business, composition/songwriting, performance, video music, theater arts, and film/video. To earn a bachelor's degree, students must accumulate between 120 and 128 credits, depending upon the program of study, with a proper distribution of courses and a GPA of at least 2.0. To earn an associate degree, students must accumulate between 60 and 64 credits.

FINANCIAL AID

The annual tuition at Five Towns College is among the lowest of all the private colleges in the region. Nevertheless, approximately 68 percent of all students receive some form of financial assistance. Need-based and/or merit-based grants, scholarships, loans, and work-study programs are available to qualified recipients, including transfer students. Prospective students are urged to contact the Financial Aid Office as early as possible.

APPLICATION AND INFORMATION

Admission into any music program is contingent upon passing an audition demonstrating skill in performance on a major instrument or vocally. Music students must also take written and aural examinations in harmony, sight singing, and ear training in order to demonstrate talent, well-developed musicianship, and artistic sensibilities. Admission into any theater program is also contingent upon passing an audition. In some cases, the Admissions Committee may request an on-campus interview with an applicant. Music, theater, video arts, and film/video students are encouraged to submit a portfolio tape or reel, if available. Except for applicants applying on an early decision basis, new students are accepted on a rolling basis, with decisions for the fall and spring semesters mailed starting January 15 and September 15, respectively. There is an application fee of $25.

FORDHAM UNIVERSITY

■ NEW YORK, NEW YORK

THE UNIVERSITY

Fordham, New York City's Jesuit University, offers a distinctive educational experience that is rooted in the 450-year-old Jesuit tradition of intellectual rigor and personal respect for the individual. The University enrolls 13,551 students, of whom 6,578 are undergraduates. Fordham has four undergraduate colleges and six graduate schools. In addition to its full-time undergraduate programs, the University offers part-time undergraduate study at Fordham College of Liberal Studies and during two summer sessions. Fordham College at Rose Hill and the College of Business Administration, located on the Rose Hill campus, are adjacent to the New York Botanical Garden and the Bronx Zoo. The Rose Hill campus is a self-contained 85-acre campus with residential facilities for 2,520 students and ample parking for commuters. It is easily accessible by public and private transportation. Fordham also provides an intercampus van service to transport students to and from Manhattan. Fordham College at Lincoln Center is located in Manhattan, overlooking the famous Lincoln Center for the Performing Arts complex. The Lincoln Center campus houses McMahon Hall, a new 850-bed apartment-style residence, and is accessible via the West Side Highway and major subway lines.

For additional details and application forms, students should contact:

Office of Undergraduate Admission
Thebaud Hall
Fordham University
441 East Fordham Road
New York, New York 10458-9993
Telephone: 800-FORDHAM (367-3426) (toll-free)
E-mail: enroll@fordham.edu

ACADEMIC PROGRAM

Students in all the undergraduate colleges pursue a common core curriculum designed to provide them with the breadth of knowledge necessary for life in twenty-first century. Drawn from nine disciplines, the common core curriculum includes the study of philosophy, English composition and literature, history, theology, mathematical reasoning, natural science, social sciences, the fine arts, and foreign language. Business students benefit from the common core as well as additional business core courses.

FINANCIAL AID

More than 80 percent of the entering students enroll with aid from Fordham and from outside sources. Among the major aid programs are the Federal Pell Grants, Federal Supplemental Educational Opportunity Grants, Federal Perkins Loans, work grants sponsored by both the government and the University, and University grants-in-aid. Outside sources of aid include state scholarships (more than 20,000 are awarded to students entering colleges in New York State each year), the New York State Tuition Assistance Program (TAP), privately sponsored scholarships, state government loan programs, and deferred-payment programs. The University also offers academic scholarships ranging from $7500 to the full cost of tuition and room. Applicants for aid must submit the Free Application for Federal Student Aid (FAFSA) and the College Scholarship Service PROFILE. Inquiries should be directed to the Fordham Office of Undergraduate Admission.

APPLICATION AND INFORMATION

Application may be made for either September or January enrollment. The application deadline is February 1 for fall admission. The completed application, the secondary school report, the results of the SAT I or ACT, all financial aid forms, and an application fee of $50 (check or money order made payable to Fordham University) should be submitted by this date. Students are notified by April 1. Candidates for early decision should apply by November 1 and receive notification by December 15. Transfer students must apply by December 1 for spring admission or by July 1 for fall admission.

GARDNER-WEBB UNIVERSITY

■ BOILING SPRINGS, NORTH CAROLINA

THE UNIVERSITY

Gardner-Webb University was founded in 1905 as a private high school by a group of Baptist associations. It became a junior college in 1928, was renamed Gardner-Webb College in 1942 in honor of former governor O. Max Gardner, and became a fully accredited senior college in 1971. Gardner-Webb moved to University status in 1993. Gardner-Webb's mission is to provide a high-quality liberal arts education in a Christian environment with the personal touch. The most outstanding characteristics of the University are its Christian environment, sense of community, and proven record of academic distinction. Its origins are obviously deep in Christian tradition, which is exemplified in the lives of staff and faculty members. Because the University is small, students can be well known by a large percentage of the faculty and administration. The Program for the Blind at Gardner-Webb University has been developed to allow students with visual handicaps to receive a liberal arts education. Special support services and job opportunities are provided for every entering student who is visually impaired. The Degree Program for the Deaf provides interpreters, note takers, and tutors skilled in sign language so that hearing-impaired students have full access to all University programs.

For further information, students should contact:

Dean of Undergraduate Admissions
and Enrollment Management
Gardner-Webb University
Boiling Springs, North Carolina
28017
Telephone: 704-434-4GWU
800-253-6472 (toll-free)
World Wide Web:
http://www.gardner-webb.edu

ACADEMIC PROGRAM

The total program is marked by flexibility for the student but encourages, through active faculty advisement, choosing a substantial course of study. Elements of the humanities, the social and physical sciences, and mathematics or related disciplines must be taken. A typical bachelor's degree program requires 128 semester hours for graduation: 59 to 63 in the core (humanities and social and physical sciences), 30 in the major, and 39 to 42 in supporting subjects and free electives. Requirements for science curricula vary somewhat. The associate degree requires the completion of 64 semester hours. A cumulative average of C (2.0 on a 4.0 scale) or better is required for graduation.

FINANCIAL AID

Gardner-Webb University makes available to its students a variety of scholarships, loans, grants-in-aid, and work-study awards. Prospective applicants with financial need should contact the financial aid director early in their senior year of high school for a financial need estimate. Applications received after April 1 can be considered only in terms of available funds. An applicant must be accepted for admission before being awarded aid. Students must file the Free Application for Federal Student Aid (FAFSA). Scholarships and other types of aid include academic awards, Christian service awards, endowed scholarships, and annual scholarships. There are several Gardner-Webb loan funds. The University also administers aid from the full range of federal programs: Federal Pell Grants, Federal Work-Study Program awards, Federal Perkins Loans, and federally guaranteed Federal Stafford Student and Federal PLUS loans. North Carolina students have access to state grant funds administered by the University. Scholarships based on academic promise are also granted each year. Of all students, 90 percent receive aid in some form. The two criteria for receiving financial aid are financial need and academic promise.

APPLICATION AND INFORMATION

Applications, together with a nonrefundable $25 application fee, may be submitted for either semester. Early application is advised. Notification of the admission decision is given on a rolling basis upon receipt of all application data. A $150 room deposit for boarding students is due thirty days after acceptance and is refundable until May 1. A $50 deposit is required of commuting students.

GEORGE FOX UNIVERSITY

■ NEWBERG, OREGON

THE UNIVERSITY

George Fox University was founded 110 years ago by the Society of Friends (Quakers) with the purpose of providing students a challenging academic atmosphere and a commitment to Christian faith. From a modest beginning of 15 students in 1891, George Fox has grown to an enrollment of 2,300 students from thirteen countries. Students find George Fox to be a place where the integration of spiritual and intellectual challenge takes place in a friendly, caring environment. This tradition of integration has been recognized by the Templeton Foundation by naming George Fox University to the honor roll of character-building colleges. Seventy-five percent of George Fox students live in campus residence halls, suites, and apartments. Opportunities for extracurricular involvement are available in music, drama, journalism, student government, radio, clubs, and athletics. George Fox is a member of the NCAA Division III and competes in six men's sports (baseball, basketball, cross-country, soccer, tennis, and track) and seven women's sports (basketball, cross-country, soccer, softball, tennis, track, and volleyball). A number of intramural sports are also available. Regular chapel services bring the campus community together in worship. Students have the opportunity to put their faith into action on volunteer mission trips and during community outreach activities. In addition to its undergraduate degrees, George Fox confers the Master of Business Administration, Master of Education, Doctor of Education, Master of Arts in Teaching, and Doctor of Psychology degrees, and seven master's degrees through George Fox Evangelical Seminary.

For more information, students should contact:

Office of Undergraduate Admission
George Fox University
Newberg, Oregon 97132-2697
Telephone: 800-765-4369 Ext. 2240 (toll-free)
E-mail: admissions@georgefox.edu
World Wide Web: http://www.georgefox.edu

ACADEMIC PROGRAM

The academic year at George Fox University is divided into two semesters of fifteen weeks. In addition to the two semesters, the University sponsors a three-week May Term. For graduation, students are required to earn 126 credit hours, including 54 general education and 42 upper-division credits. Students may reduce the number of required courses and add flexibility to their undergraduate years with credit earned through Advanced Placement, International Baccalaureate (IB), the College-Level Examination Program, and credit by examination. An innovative program called "Computers Across the Curriculum" expands the computer literacy of students. The University issues every incoming freshman a computer for school and personal use. The computer becomes the property of the student upon graduation. To meet the needs of this program, the University has a full-service computer store, a campus network, and a CD-ROM computer center on campus. George Fox demonstrates its commitment to freshmen by providing a Freshman Seminar Program to assist students as they integrate themselves into the academic and social life of the University community.

FINANCIAL AID

George Fox maintains that every qualified student should be able to attend the university of his or her choice without letting limited finances stand in the way. To this end, federal, state, and institutional need-based funds are available, as are merit awards. About 87 percent of all students receive financial aid.

GONZAGA UNIVERSITY

■ SPOKANE, WASHINGTON

THE UNIVERSITY

Gonzaga, founded in 1887, is an independent, comprehensive university with a distinguished background in the Catholic, Jesuit, and humanistic tradition. Gonzaga emphasizes the moral and ethical implications of learning, living, and working in today's global society. Through the University Core Curriculum, each student develops a strong liberal arts foundation, which many alumni cite as a most valuable asset. In addition, students specialize in any of more than seventy-five academic areas of study. Gonzaga's 108-acre campus is characterized by sprawling green lawns and majestic evergreen trees. Towering above the campus are the stately spires of St. Aloysius Church, the well-recognized landmark featured in the University logo. Because personal growth is as important as intellectual development, Gonzaga places great emphasis on student life outside of class. Ten of the fourteen residence halls house only 25 to 35 students each, providing an intimate atmosphere. Each hall has a chaplain or a resident Jesuit. Since 98 percent of the freshmen and 43 percent of the total undergraduate student body live on campus, campus-based activities ranging from current affairs symposiums to intramural sports keep students informed and entertained. Students in all academic majors integrate with the Spokane community through a variety of activities, such as volunteer opportunities and internships at numerous businesses and agencies. Gonzaga provides both career and counseling centers.

For more information, students should contact:

Dean of Admission
Gonzaga University
Spokane, Washington 99258-0102
Telephone: 800-322-2584 (toll-free)
E-mail: ballinger@gu.gonzaga.edu
World Wide Web:
http://www.gonzaga.edu

ACADEMIC PROGRAM

Gonzaga University believes that it is necessary for all students, regardless of their chosen major or profession, to attain an education that goes beyond specialization. Therefore, all students attending Gonzaga receive a strong liberal arts background as well as depth in their major. The Core Curriculum is a very important component of the 128 semester units a student must earn for graduation. The Honors Program challenges special achievers with an integrated curriculum compatible with any major and most double majors. The program requires a separate application. The Hogan Entrepreneurial Leadership Program is for motivated and imaginative student leaders who are interested in creating new ventures and who want to make a difference in the world. A separate application is required. Gonzaga University Summer Term (GUST) offers motivated high school students intensive course work in a variety of academic disciplines. Academic and cocurricular activities are included in the six-week session. Credits earned through the Washington State Running Start Program or International Baccalaureate (I.B.) program are accepted on a class-by-class basis. College credit is given for certain test scores in most Advanced Placement (AP) subjects. The academic year follows a two-semester system, beginning in early September. Two summer sessions also are available.

FINANCIAL AID

Gonzaga University offers many different types of financial aid to qualified students, including scholarships, Federal Pell Grants, Federal Supplemental Educational Opportunity Grants, work-study jobs, Federal Perkins Loans, Federal Stafford Student Loans, and on- and off-campus employment. In order to apply for financial aid awards, a student must first be accepted by the University and must see that the Free Application for Federal Student Aid (FAFSA) is submitted by February 1. After this date, awards are made on a funds-available basis. Approximately 90 percent of the students at Gonzaga receive financial assistance.

GOUCHER COLLEGE

■ BALTIMORE, MARYLAND

THE COLLEGE

Since its inception in 1885, Goucher College has maintained a reputation for academic excellence and a tradition of high quality combined with flexibility. The past few decades have seen many changes in academic programs and the student population, during which time Goucher has held fast to its commitment to a superior liberal arts education designed to help students achieve their fullest potential. The 1,100 men and women enrolled as undergraduates come from all parts of the United States and many other countries; they represent diverse backgrounds, interests, and points of view. Goucher's strength in the liberal arts comes from its attention to learning both inside and outside the classroom. Academic departments are organized into five divisions: arts, humanities, interdisciplinary studies, natural sciences and mathematics, and social sciences. The Goucher College curriculum encompasses courses from all five divisions; a freshman colloquium; an off-campus learning experience that is satisfied through an internship, study abroad, or an independent research project; and demonstrated proficiency in writing, computers, and a foreign language. Goucher's fieldstone buildings on a 287-acre wooded, residential campus provide an ideal setting for learning. The residence halls are an important part of the students' educational and social experience. Residence on campus is generally required of all students who do not live at home. The four halls are divided into fifteen residential houses of about 50 students each; housing space is guaranteed for all four years. There are areas for socializing, meeting rooms, and kitchenettes in each hall, and there is one main dining room. A kosher dining hall is also available. Students from all four classes are represented in each house, and there is a staff of 15 resident assistants to serve as peer counselors.

For more information, students should contact:

Director of Admissions
Goucher College
1021 Dulaney Valley Road
Baltimore, Maryland 21204-2794
Telephone: 410-337-6100
800-GOUCHER (toll-free)
E-mail: admissions@goucher.edu
World Wide Web:
http://www.goucher.edu

ACADEMIC PROGRAM

The core curriculum is the foundation for a Goucher education. Recently revised, the core retains Goucher's tradition of academic rigor while becoming more relevant to a changing world. There is a strong emphasis on both interdisciplinary study and the development of a global perspective. Requirements include a demonstrated proficiency in a foreign language, English composition, and computer technology, along with courses in the arts, natural sciences, humanities, social sciences, and mathematics as well as a 3-credit off-campus requirement that reflects the College's belief in balancing classroom theory with real-world experience and that may take the form of an internship, a period of study abroad, or an independent project. All freshmen take the semester-long Freshman Colloquium. Taught in small sections, the course integrates humanities and social sciences perspectives. There is an interdisciplinary honors program in addition to honors courses in each department. The Goucher degree requires 120 semester hours of credit. The departmental major consists of at least 30 credits (about ten courses); the double major requires 60 credits. Goucher's calendar is based on the semester system.

FINANCIAL AID

In an average year, more than half of Goucher's students receive some form of aid; 45 percent are awarded grants, ranging from $400 to the total cost of the education. The average financial aid award is more than $15,000. Goucher participates in the Federal Work-Study Program and helps students benefit from Federal Supplemental Educational Opportunity Grants, Federal Pell Grants, Federal Perkins Loans, Federal Stafford Student Loans, and College loans. Goucher also offers a competitive merit award program.

GRACE COLLEGE

■ WINONA LAKE, INDIANA

THE COLLEGE

Grace College is a Christian undergraduate college of arts and sciences founded in 1948 and affiliated with the Fellowship of Grace Brethren Churches, a conservative evangelical denomination. Grace College attracts students from a variety of conservative evangelical backgrounds and from around the United States and several other countries. The College offers an environment and academic program that are conservative in theology and progressive in spirit and that emphasize three qualities for students as they reach adulthood—mature Christian character, academic and career competence, and a heart for service to mankind. Enrollment at Grace College is 1,090, providing an ideal atmosphere in which students can learn, grow, and develop lasting friendships. Grace College has a campus of 165 acres. Approximately 69 percent of the College's students live on campus. The majority of students range in age from 18 to 23 years. More than 44 percent of the students come from Indiana; students also come from thirty-six other states and seven countries. Approximately one third of the students are affiliated with the Fellowship of Grace Brethren Churches; the other two thirds are from other conservative Christian denominations, particularly Baptist and independent church backgrounds.

For more information, students should contact:

Grace College
200 Seminary Drive
Winona Lake, Indiana 46590
Telephone: 800-54-GRACE (toll-free)
World Wide Web:
http://www.grace.edu

ACADEMIC PROGRAM

The Christian liberal arts philosophy of Grace College pervades each program of study and reflects the College's recognition that a broad common core of course work is central to each student's education. When combined with detailed study in a major field, this core establishes the foundation for successful graduate study and for a career. The requirements for the bachelor's degree include the successful completion of one major (36–56 semester hours) and one minor (20–28 semester hours) area of concentration in addition to the specified program of general education courses. Students are required to complete a total of 124 semester hours of course work. Through the January session (Winterim) offered each year, students have an opportunity to take courses off campus as well as on the campus. Grace College operates on a two-semester calendar and offers a summer session in addition to Winterim. Advanced Placement (AP) and College-Level Examination Program (CLEP) test scores are considered for college credit and advanced placement. One outstanding strength of Grace College is the Student Academic Counseling Center. The center offers academic advising and tutorial services.

FINANCIAL AID

The College offers extensive financial assistance to qualified students. Most students receive some sort of financial assistance—in the form of a scholarship, grant, loan, or campus employment—to help pay college costs. The average amount of financial aid awarded to a Grace College student totals $7500 per year. To be considered for financial assistance at Grace College, students must submit the Free Application for Federal Student Aid (FAFSA). Students may receive Federal Pell Grants, Federal Perkins Loans, and Federal Supplemental Educational Opportunity Grants. In addition, students may be eligible for Federal Work-Study Program awards. The FAFSA should be on file by March 1 for priority consideration. To renew financial aid, students must refile the FAFSA each year.

APPLICATION AND INFORMATION

Students may apply for admission to any semester. Applications are accepted on a rolling basis until January 1 for the spring term and August 1 for the fall term. There is a $20 nonrefundable application fee. Students may also apply on the Grace Web site at no cost. Interested students and their parents are encouraged to visit the campus and to arrange for an interview at that time in order to get a clear picture of Grace College. Arrangements can be made for housing and meals for applicants by contacting the Grace College Visitor's Center.

GROVE CITY COLLEGE

■ GROVE CITY, PENNSYLVANIA

THE COLLEGE

The beautifully landscaped campus of Grove City College stretches more than 150 acres and includes twenty-seven neo-Gothic buildings valued at more than $100 million. The campus is considered one of the loveliest in the nation. While the College has changed to meet the needs of the society it serves, its basic philosophy has remained unchanged since its founding in 1876. It is a Christian liberal arts and sciences institution of ideal size and dedicated to the principle of providing the highest-quality education at the lowest possible cost. Wishing to remain truly independent and to retain its distinctive qualities as a private school governed by private citizens (trustees), it is one of the very few colleges in the country that does not accept any state or federal monies. Affiliated with the Presbyterian Church (U.S.A.) but not narrowly denominational, the College believes that to be well educated a student should be exposed to the central ideas of the Judeo-Christian tradition. A 20-minute chapel program offered Tuesday and Thursday mornings, along with a Sunday evening worship service, challenge students in their faith. Sixteen chapel services per semester are required out of forty opportunities. Religious organizations and activities exist to provide fellowship and spiritual growth.

For more information, students should contact:

Jeffrey C. Mincey
Director of Admissions
Grove City College
100 Campus Drive
Grove City, Pennsylvania 16127-2104
Telephone: 724-458-2100
Fax: 724-458-3395
E-mail: admissions@gcc.edu
World Wide Web:
http://www.gcc.edu

ACADEMIC PROGRAM

Grove City College's goal is to assist young men and women in developing as complete individuals—academically, spiritually, and physically. The general education requirements provide all students with a high level of cultural literacy and communication skills. They include 38–50 semester hours of courses with emphases in the humanities, social sciences, and natural sciences and in quantitative and logical reasoning, as well as a language requirement for nonengineering and science majors. Degree candidates must also complete the requirements in their field of concentration, physical education, electives, and convocation. To graduate, a student must have completed 128 semester hours (136 in engineering) plus 4 convocation credits. About 70 percent of those entering as freshmen stay and receive a diploma in four years.

FINANCIAL AID

Because the College's tuition charges are low, every student, in effect, receives significant financial assistance. Fifty-seven percent of the freshmen receive additional aid from GCC. Students applying for financial assistance must complete Grove City College's financial aid form. Job opportunities are available both on and off campus.

APPLICATION AND INFORMATION

A regular admission applicant should take the SAT I or ACT by October or November of the senior year in high school. The application should include scores on the SAT I (preferred) or the ACT, a high school transcript, references, a recommendation from the student's principal or counselor, and a nonrefundable application fee of $30. An application may be submitted after the eleventh grade. An early decision applicant should take the entrance test in the eleventh grade, visit the College for an interview, and submit the application by November 15; notification of the admission decision is mailed on December 15. Approved early decision applicants must accept by January 15 and submit a nonrefundable deposit of $200. Applicants seeking regular decision must submit the completed application and supporting documents by February 15 of their senior year. Notification of the admission decision is mailed on March 15. Students who are offered admission should reply as soon as possible, but no later than May 1, and include a nonrefundable deposit of $150. Applications received after February 15 will be considered as space permits. The College receives four applications for every freshman vacancy.

HAVERFORD COLLEGE

■ HAVERFORD, PENNSYLVANIA

THE COLLEGE

Haverford is the first college established by members of the Society of Friends (Quakers). Founded in 1833, Haverford has chosen to remain small, undergraduate, and residential to carry out its educational philosophy and to maintain a strong sense of community. Haverford's 1,100 students represent forty-five states, Puerto Rico, the District of Columbia, and twenty countries. Twenty-three percent of the students are students of color, while an additional 4 percent are international students. Haverford is a residential campus with 98 percent of the students and 70 percent of the faculty living on campus. Students may also choose to live at nearby Bryn Mawr College.

For more information or to arrange an interview or tour appointment, students should contact:

Office of Admission
Haverford College
370 Lancaster Avenue
Haverford, Pennsylvania 19041-1392
Telephone: 610-896-1350
610-896-1436 (TTY/TDD)
Fax: 610-896-1338
E-mail: admitme@haverford.edu
finaid@haverford.edu
World Wide Web:
http://www.haverford.edu

ACADEMIC PROGRAM

Students plan their programs using established guidelines and with the help of faculty advisers. They must have at least three courses in each of the divisions of the College: humanities, social science, and natural science. In addition, they must fulfill requirements in foreign language, social justice, writing, and quantitative course work. Flexibility in the curriculum allows opportunities for independent study, foreign study, and noncollegiate academic study. Majors are selected at the end of the sophomore year. Normally, students take four courses per semester and thirty-two courses over four years. Scheduling is flexible, however, and students may arrange programs to meet individual needs, including six-semester, seven-semester, and five-year programs. Credit is given on the basis of Advanced Placement (AP) examinations, A-Level examinations, and International Baccalaureate Higher Level examinations. One of Haverford's distinctive features is its extensive academic and social cooperation with Bryn Mawr College. Students may take courses or major at either school, live on either campus, and eat on either campus. A free bus service between the two campuses, which are a mile apart, facilitates cooperative arrangements. Haverford and Bryn Mawr also share library resources with nearby Swarthmore College. All three college libraries are linked electronically, and students have instant access to library resources through the campus computer network.

FINANCIAL AID

The College has an extensive financial aid program. Approximately 40 percent of Haverford's students receive College grant aid. Candidates for Haverford College funded aid must file the Financial Aid PROFILE with the College Scholarship Service, along with the FAFSA. Applicants may register for the PROFILE by completing a short form, available from their local high school guidance office, and sending it to the College Scholarship Service or by calling the College Scholarship Service at (800) 778-6888. Regular decision students should complete the PROFILE registration process by January 2, so the College Scholarship Service can send the form and have students complete it by the January 31 deadline. The FAFSA is also available from high school guidance offices and must also be filed by January 31. Early decision candidates should complete the PROFILE registration process by October 15 and file the PROFILE form with the College Scholarship Service by November 15.

APPLICATION AND INFORMATION

The application deadlines for admission are November 15 for early decision candidates, January 15 for regular decision candidates, and March 31 for transfer candidates. Haverford also accepts the Common Application, which is available in school guidance offices. The admission office is open from 9 a.m. to 5 p.m. on weekdays (8:30 a.m. to 4:30 p.m. from June to August) and, during the fall, from 9 a.m. to noon on Saturday.

HAWAII PACIFIC UNIVERSITY

■ HONOLULU, HAWAII

THE UNIVERSITY

Hawaii Pacific University (HPU) is an independent, coeducational, career-oriented comprehensive university with a foundation in the liberal arts. Undergraduate and graduate degrees are offered in close to fifty different areas. Hawaii Pacific prides itself on maintaining small class size (averaging 25 students) and individual attention to students. Students at HPU come from every state in the union and more than 100 countries around the world. The diversity of the student body stimulates learning about other cultures firsthand, both in and out of the classroom. There is no majority population at HPU. Students are encouraged to examine the values, customs, traditions, and principles of others to gain a clearer understanding of their own perspectives. HPU students develop friendships with students from throughout the United States and the world, important connections for success in the global economy of the twenty-first century. In addition to the undergraduate programs described below, HPU offers several graduate programs: the M.B.A. (with twelve concentrations), the M.S. in Information Systems (M.S.I.S.), the master's in nursing, and the M.A. in communications, diplomacy and military studies, human resource management, management, organizational change, and teaching English as a second language (TESL). HPU has NCAA intercollegiate sports. Men's athletic programs include baseball, basketball, cheerleading, cross-country, and tennis. Women's athletics include cheerleading, cross-country, softball, tennis, and volleyball. The Housing Office at HPU offers many services and options for students. Residence halls with cafeteria service are available on the Windward campus, while University-sponsored apartments are available in the Waikiki area for those seeking more independent living arrangements.

For further information and for application materials, students should contact:

Office of Admissions
Hawaii Pacific University
1164 Bishop Street, Suite 200
Honolulu, Hawaii 96813
Telephone: 808-544-0238
866-225-5478
Fax: 808-544-1136
E-mail: admissions@hpu.edu
World Wide Web:
http://www.hpu.edu/

ACADEMIC PROGRAM

The baccalaureate student must complete at least 124 semester hours of credit. Forty-five of these credits provide the student with a strong foundation in the liberal arts, with the remaining credits composed of appropriate upper-division classes in the student's major and related areas. The academic year operates on a modified 4-1-4 semester system, featuring a five-week winter intersession. The University also offers extensive summer sessions. A student can earn up to 15 semester hours of credit during the summer. By attending these supplemental sessions, a student may complete the baccalaureate degree program in three years. A five-year B.S.B.A./M.B.A. program is also available.

FINANCIAL AID

The University provides financial aid for qualified students through institutional, state, and federal aid programs. Approximately 50 percent of the University's students receive financial aid. Among the forms of aid available are Federal Perkins Loans, Federal Stafford Student Loans, Guaranteed Parental Loans, Federal Pell Grants, and Federal Supplemental Educational Opportunity Grants. To apply for aid, students must submit the Free Application for Federal Student Aid (FAFSA). The FAFSA may be submitted at any time, but the priority deadline is March 1.

APPLICATION AND INFORMATION

Candidates are notified of admission decisions on a rolling basis, usually within two weeks of receipt of application materials. Early entrance and deferred entrance are available. HPU accepts the Common Application form.

HIRAM COLLEGE

■ HIRAM, OHIO

THE COLLEGE

Founded in 1850, Hiram College cherishes its heritage as an institution of academic excellence and rare distinction. Hiram's 900 students come from twenty-five states and nineteen countries and represent more than twenty-five different religions. SAT I and ACT scores of Hiram's entering freshmen exceed national norms: in 2000, SAT I medians were 580 (verbal) and 570 (math); the ACT composite median was 25. Between 50 and 60 percent of the College's graduates go on to graduate school or professional school within five years. The College was awarded a Phi Beta Kappa chapter in 1971.

For more information, students should contact:

Dean of Admission
Hiram College
Hiram, Ohio 44234
Telephone: 330-569-5169
800-362-5280 (toll-free)
E-mail: admission@hiram.edu
World Wide Web:
http://www.hiram.edu

ACADEMIC PROGRAM

Hiram's academic calendar, the Hiram Plan, is unique among colleges and universities. Each fifteen-week semester is divided into a twelve-week and a three-week session. During the three-week session, students take only one intensive course. The plan provides two formats for learning, which increases opportunity for small group study with faculty, study in special topics, hands-on learning through field trips and internships, and study abroad. Hiram College's commitment to the liberal arts is manifested in a core curriculum required of all students. Required courses include the Freshman Colloquium, a small, seminar course on a special topic taught by a student's adviser; First Year Seminar, providing an introduction to Western thought and emphasizing critical thinking, effective writing, and speaking; and a sequence of interdisciplinary courses. The course of study in most areas of major concentration is specified by the departments and divisions. Students generally take ten courses from within a department, as well as two or three courses from related or supporting departments. Alternatively, a student, with the assistance of the adviser, may develop an area of concentration that consists of related courses from different academic areas, crossing departmental lines to focus on particular needs or interests. A student may also submit a proposal for an individually designed program to the Area of Concentration Board.

FINANCIAL AID

More than 75 percent of Hiram's students receive financial aid based on need. All financial aid awards are made on a one-year basis, and each year a new Free Application for Federal Student Aid (FAFSA) must be submitted to determine eligibility. Most financial aid at Hiram is a combination of a loan, a job, and a scholarship or grant-in-aid. Scholarships awarded on the basis of merit are also available and range from $3000 to $12,000 per year. Aid includes Federal Pell Grants, Federal Supplemental Educational Opportunity Grants, Federal Perkins Loans, Federal Stafford Student Loans, state grants, Federal Work-Study awards, and veterans' benefits. Campus employment is available regardless of aid eligibility.

APPLICATION AND INFORMATION

Application materials include the completed application form; a secondary school report, which must be completed and returned to Hiram directly by the high school guidance counselor; the results of the SAT I or ACT; and an essay. Teacher recommendations are also required. The application deadline is February 1. An early decision option is also available. Applicants are encouraged to visit the campus. The Office of Admission, located in Teachout-Price Hall, is open year-round for interviews from 9 a.m. to 4 p.m. on weekdays and from 9 a.m. to noon on Saturday (except during the summer months).

HOFSTRA UNIVERSITY

■ HEMPSTEAD, NEW YORK

THE UNIVERSITY

Hofstra University is traditional, contemporary, and innovative. As universities go, Hofstra is young, but the extraordinary vigor and growth shown in the brief span of its life have marked it as an educational phenomenon. The University offers the student with ability a good education and unusual opportunities for choice. In many fields, special facilities—clinics, Hofstra's Television Institute, the radio station, a reading center, and a playhouse—enrich the curriculum. Hofstra's philosophy is to provide a strong foundation in the liberal arts and sciences. The University's ultimate goal for its students is "the pursuit of knowledge, understanding, and wisdom upon which a good life can be built." The extracurricular program is full and varied. As a result of the Program for the Higher Education of the Disabled, Hofstra is 100 percent accessible to persons with disabilities. Necessary services are provided for wheelchair-bound and other disabled students who meet all academic requirements for admission.

For additional information, students should contact:

Dean of Admissions
Hofstra University
Hempstead, New York 11549
Telephone: 516-463-6700
800-HOFSTRA (toll-free)
Fax: 516-463-5100
World Wide Web:
http://www.hofstra.edu

ACADEMIC PROGRAM

The requirement for the B.A. degree is 124 semester hours, of which 94 must be in liberal arts and 30 in free electives. Successful completion of at least 124 semester hours with a quality point average of 2.0 or better is required for graduation. For the major, each academic department defines the special pattern of required and suggested study that suits its discipline. Beyond this major requirement, five general requirements in humanities, natural sciences, social sciences, English, and foreign languages must be fulfilled. A candidate for graduation with the degree of B.B.A. must successfully complete at least 128 semester hours with a quality point average of 2.0 or better, completing at least 64 hours in liberal arts subjects (humanities, mathematics, natural sciences, and social sciences), 40 hours in general business courses (accounting, business law, finance, general business, international business, management, marketing, and quantitative methods), and all major and additional requirements as listed under the department of specialization. Each of the scientific-technical programs leading to the B.S. degree requires a total of 124 to 134 semester hours, of which approximately half must be in liberal arts courses exclusive of those offered by the academic department of major specialization.

FINANCIAL AID

Financial aid options range from scholarships through assistance grants to loans and part-time jobs. About 84 percent of all students receive financial help, and almost 65 percent work to earn part of their expenses. Scholarships average $3825 per year; loans average $2625 per year. Hofstra subscribes to the principles of the College Scholarship Service in determining the amount of awards. Federal funds include Federal Perkins Loans, Federal Pell and Federal Supplemental Educational Opportunity grants, and Federal Work-Study Program awards. To be considered for financial aid, completed financial aid applications and credentials (including the Free Application for Federal Student Aid) should be received on or before March 1.

APPLICATION AND INFORMATION

Freshman applicants must submit the application, a $40 application fee, the high school transcript, test scores, and a guidance counselor's recommendation. Transfer students must submit an application, the application fee, high school and college transcripts, and test scores (if fewer than 24 semester hours were attempted at the previous college).

IDAHO STATE UNIVERSITY

■ POCATELLO, IDAHO

THE UNIVERSITY

Idaho State University (ISU) has existed as an institution since 1901, when it was first established as the Academy of Idaho. It gained university status in 1963. Offering instruction in nearly every area of the arts and sciences, the University also conducts well-rounded programs of training in vocational and technical fields. Bachelor's and master's degrees in a variety of areas are awarded by the College of Arts and Sciences, the College of Business, the College of Education, the College of Engineering, the College of Health Professions, the College of Pharmacy, and the Graduate School. Doctoral degrees offered at ISU include the Doctor of Philosophy, Doctor of Arts, and Doctor of Education. Certificate programs of varying lengths and B.S. and M.S. degrees are included in the curricula of the School of Applied Technology. Because of its location and character, ISU serves a diverse population that includes traditional-age students, nontraditional students, working professionals, and senior citizens. ISU has a total enrollment of 13,040 (10,703 undergraduate); they represent nearly every state in the Union and fifty-seven other countries. U.S. and international students attend the University because of its reputation as an academic and vocational institution of high quality; its relaxed, safe, and rural atmosphere; and its location at the foot of the Rocky Mountains. Through its programs in pharmacy and other health-related professions, ISU is a center for education in the health field. Its programs in education, business, and engineering respond to a variety of current and emerging demands. It serves as a national center for Doctor of Arts degree programs. ISU also has responsibility for Idaho's dental education program. Several of the programs in the School of Applied Technology, the largest such school in the state, are nationally recognized.

For more information, students should contact:

Office of Enrollment Planning and Academic Services
Campus Box 8054
Idaho State University
Pocatello, Idaho 83209-0009
Telephone: 208-282-3277
Fax: 208-282-4314
E-mail: info@isu.edu
World Wide Web: http://www.isu.edu

ACADEMIC PROGRAM

ISU requires a broad liberal arts education of all candidates for the bachelor's degree. Students are required to complete credits in math, English, speech, the physical and natural sciences, the humanities, and the social sciences before concentrating on their major field. All bachelor's degree candidates must complete a minimum of 128 credit hours. The University operates on the semester system; opportunities are available for receiving credit by examination or tailoring a degree through the Bachelor of University Studies program. Internships are also arranged for students through the Career Development Center and individual departments.

FINANCIAL AID

The goal of the University's financial assistance program is twofold: to reward those students who demonstrate outstanding academic, leadership, or other talents and to aid those students unable to bear the costs of attending the University. ISU provides financial assistance for some 80 percent of its students through grant, loan, work, and scholarship programs. ISU accepts the Free Application for Federal Student Aid (FAFSA). The priority deadline for mailing the FAFSA is March 1. The scholarship application deadline for new and transfer students is February 20. A number of competitive out-of-state-student tuition and reduced fee waivers are also available to domestic and international students, as are campus and off-campus job placement programs.

APPLICATION AND INFORMATION

Deadlines for submission of all application materials are August 1 for the fall semester and December 1 for the spring semester. Notification is made within two weeks of application.

ITHACA COLLEGE

■ ITHACA, NEW YORK

THE COLLEGE

Coeducational and nonsectarian since its founding in 1892, Ithaca College enrolls approximately 6,200 students. The College community is a diverse one; virtually every state is represented in the student population, as are more than seventy-five other countries. Students come to Ithaca College to get active, hands-on learning that brings together the best of liberal arts and professional studies. The program is offered in five schools: the School of Humanities and Sciences (2,250 students), School of Business (600 students), Roy H. Park School of Communications (1,250 students), School of Health Sciences and Human Performance (1,300 students), and School of Music (500 students). There are approximately 300 graduate students.

For additional information and application forms, students should contact:

Paula J. Mitchell
Director of Admission
Office of Admission
Ithaca College
100 Job Hall
Ithaca, New York 14850-7020
Telephone: 800-429-4274 (toll-free)
607-274-3124
Fax: 607-274-1900
E-mail: admission@ithaca.edu
World Wide Web:
http://www.ithaca.edu

ACADEMIC PROGRAM

Undergraduate programs of study address two primary issues: the need for rigorous academic preparation in highly specialized professional fields and the need for students to prepare for the complex demands of society by acquiring an intellectual breadth that extends beyond their chosen profession. Each degree offered requires a minimum of 120 credit hours and a specified number of liberal arts credits. Minors, academic concentrations, and numerous teacher certification programs are available. The academic year comprises two 15-week semesters, from late August to mid-December and from mid-January to mid-May.

FINANCIAL AID

Financial aid, which totals more than $80 million from all sources, is extended to approximately 80 percent of Ithaca students. To apply for financial aid, students should check the proper space on the College's admission application, and if seeking federal aid, submit the Free Application for Federal Student Aid (FAFSA) by February 1 with the U.S. Department of Education at the address indicated on the form. Early decision and physical therapy candidates should follow the time line outlined under the Application and Information section below. All accepted applicants are considered for merit aid in recognition of their academic and personal achievement. Programs providing grants and loans include the Federal Work-Study, Federal Pell Grant, Federal Perkins Loan, Federal Stafford Student Loan, and Federal Supplemental Educational Opportunity Grant.

APPLICATION AND INFORMATION

For freshman regular decision, prospective students should apply by March 1; applicants are notified of a decision on a rolling basis no later than April 15 and must confirm their enrollment by May 1. Freshman applicants seeking institutional and federal aid should file the FAFSA by February 1 with the federal processor. For freshman early decision, which is binding, students should apply by November 1; applicants are notified by December 15 and must confirm their enrollment by February 1. Early decision applicants seeking institutional and federal financial aid should submit the Financial Aid PROFILE, available from the College Scholarship Service, by November 1 and the FAFSA by February 1. For physical therapy (both freshman and transfer), students should apply by January 15; applicants are notified by March 10 and must confirm their enrollment by May 1. Applicants seeking institutional and federal financial aid should submit the CSS PROFILE and the FAFSA by January 15. Students who want to transfer into Ithaca College should apply by July 15 for fall admission and by December 1 for spring admission. Applicants seeking institutional and federal financial aid should file the FAFSA by February 1. All applicants must submit a $45 application fee. Ithaca's application for admission is available on line (http://www.ithaca.edu/admission).

KENTUCKY WESLEYAN COLLEGE

■ OWENSBORO, KENTUCKY

THE COLLEGE

The tradition of high-quality teaching and a talent for translating a liberal arts education into usable and useful service have long been hallmarks of Kentucky Wesleyan College (KWC). Founded by the United Methodist Church in 1858, the College's mission is to prepare leaders for the twenty-first century through a coordinated and integrated liberal arts education. To fulfill its mission, Kentucky Wesleyan offers Leadership KWC, a nationally recognized leadership program established with an $800,000 grant from the W.K. Kellogg Foundation. Liberal arts course work forms the basis of Leadership KWC and represents the College's belief that a solid liberal arts education provides the communication, problem-solving, and creative-thinking skills necessary for tomorrow's leaders. Kentucky Wesleyan is home to approximately 700 students from twenty-three states and several other countries. There are one women's, one men's, and two coed residence halls. Each residence hall room is air conditioned and has a cable television hookup and access to the campus computer network.

For more information, students should contact:

Office of Admission
Kentucky Wesleyan College
3000 Frederica Street
Box 1039
Owensboro, Kentucky 42302-1039
Telephone: 270-926-3111
800-999-0592 (toll free)
E-mail: admitme@kwc.edu
World Wide Web:
http://www.kwc.edu

ACADEMIC PROGRAM

There are three academic divisions in the Kentucky Wesleyan College curriculum: the Natural Sciences, the Humanities and Fine Arts, and the Social Sciences. The requirements for the degrees of Bachelor of Science and Bachelor of Arts are based on the principle of a broad distribution of studies among the representative fields of human culture and a concentration of studies in a specific field. In most cases, 128 semester hours are required to obtain a bachelor's degree. Students have the opportunity to develop and carry out individual programs of studies related to their particular vocational or professional goals through the Interdisciplinary Studies (IDS) Program.

FINANCIAL AID

Kentucky Wesleyan participates in all federal student aid programs and is committed to helping each student meet his or her demonstrated financial need. No student should hesitate to apply for admission due to financial reasons. Kentucky Wesleyan awards more than $6.2 million each year in financial aid to eligible students. Kentucky residents may qualify for Kentucky Higher Education Assistance Authority Grants. In addition to federal and state financial aid programs, Kentucky Wesleyan invests more than $2.6 million annually in scholarships and grants for its students. Academic scholarships are awarded to students who attend one of several on-campus scholarship days. These scholarships range from $2000 to full tuition and are renewable annually. Students who demonstrate a strong record of leadership in their school, church, place of employment, or community are encouraged to apply for Stanley Reed Leadership Awards. These awards range from $2000 to $4000 and are renewable annually (applications are available from the Office of Admission). For maximum financial aid consideration, students are requested to submit the Free Application for Federal Student Aid (FAFSA) by March 1. Kentucky Wesleyan is need-blind in its admission process.

APPLICATION AND INFORMATION

The Office of Admission is open from 8 a.m. to 5 p.m., Monday through Friday, and on Saturday by appointment. Interested students are encouraged to visit the campus during one of the College's weekend open houses in the fall and winter or by individual appointment during the week. Students who wish to stay on campus overnight are welcome to do so at no charge. Students may apply for admission after completing their junior year. Applications are evaluated on a rolling basis, and students can expect to be notified of a decision within two weeks of completing their application for admission.

KETTERING UNIVERSITY

■ FLINT, MICHIGAN

THE UNIVERSITY

Kettering University (formerly GMI Engineering & Management Institute) offers education for the real world. Nearly 100 percent of Kettering's students receive a job offer or are accepted by graduate schools before receiving their diplomas. Kettering University has a unique partnership that offers students, business, and industry an opportunity found at no other undergraduate college in America. Kettering, a five-year cooperative engineering, management, science, and math university, is the only institution that assists incoming freshmen to be selected by companies for cooperative employment, a process initiated for all accepted students. Kettering University successfully integrates the practical aspects of the workplace into the world of higher education through its more than 750 corporate partners, corporations, and agencies located throughout the United States, Canada, and selected countries. Kettering's corporate partners represent most major industrial groups; many are recognized as worldwide leaders in business innovation and manufacturing technology. Kettering's corporate partners invest in students' futures by providing a five-year program of progressive work experience that exposes them to processes, products, corporate culture, and the technology necessary to compete in tomorrow's business environment.

For more information, students should contact:

Admissions Office
Kettering University
1700 West Third Avenue
Flint, Michigan 48504-4898
Telephone: 810-762-7865
800-955-4464 (toll-free in the United States and Canada)
E-mail: admissions@kettering.edu
World Wide Web:
http://www.kettering.edu

ACADEMIC PROGRAM

Although each program at Kettering University has its own sequence requirements, 180 credit hours are generally required, including thesis credit hours. The program involves nine academic terms and up to eleven co-op terms, two of which are focused on the capstone fifth-year thesis project, which is done on behalf of the student's co-op employer. Students alternate between twelve-week periods of academic study on the campus in Flint and twelve-week periods of related work experience with their corporate employer. The academic year consists of two 3–month academic terms on campus and two 3–month terms of paid work experience. A typical Kettering University cooperative student may earn up to $65,000 in co-op wages through the complete program.

FINANCIAL AID

In addition to all traditional sources of aid, all Kettering students benefit from a special resource that is significant and not need based. One of the many advantages of attending Kettering University is the opportunity for students to earn a salary during their co-op work terms. Co-op income is substantial and can help cover part of the cost of a Kettering education by supplementing the family contribution and the standard forms of need-based and merit-based financial aid. Students who live at home during work experience periods are able to contribute a greater proportion of earnings directly to educational expenses. About 70 percent of students are able to live at home during work terms. The typical range of co-op earnings over the five-year program is $40,000 to $65,000. The primary purpose of financial aid at Kettering University is to supplement a student's unmet financial need after cooperative earnings and parents' contributions. Students who wish to apply for financial aid should complete the Free Application for Federal Student Aid (FAFSA) and request that a copy of the analysis be sent to Kettering University. Aid is given as grants, scholarships, loans, and work-study awards.

APPLICATION AND INFORMATION

Prospective freshmen are encouraged to file their application early in their senior year. Admission decisions for transfer applicants are based on college record for those who have completed at least 30 credits. Applications are accepted all year long; however, early application greatly increases visibility for early employment possibilities in the co-op search process. The application fee is $25.

LAGRANGE COLLEGE

■ LAGRANGE, GEORGIA

THE COLLEGE

Founded in 1831, LaGrange College is the oldest private college in Georgia. A four-year liberal arts and sciences college affiliated with the United Methodist Church, the College is ranked in the top tier and as one of the top ten best values among Southern liberal arts schools by *U.S. News & World Report.* The College has an enrollment of approximately 1,000 men and women and a student-faculty ratio of 13:1. With only 17 students in the average classroom, LaGrange College provides a challenging and supportive academic environment. Students live in College residence halls that provide quick online access via the College's fiber-optic network. In addition to network access, each room is outfitted with cable TV, central air-conditioning, and local telephone service. The College is located in a residential section of LaGrange, Georgia, which has a population of 30,000 and was named Intelligent City of the Year by the World Teleport Association for its telecommunications infrastructure and Internet initiatives. LaGrange is home to Fortune 500 companies, unique shops and restaurants, and historic landmarks. Nearby are the world-famous Callaway Gardens, the Warm Springs Foundation, and Franklin D. Roosevelt's Little White House. The West Point Dam on the Chattahoochee River provides one of the largest lakes in the region; waterfronts and a marina are within the city limits of LaGrange. The city is located 65 miles southwest of Atlanta and 55 miles southwest of Hartsfield Atlanta International Airport.

For more information, students should contact:

Office of Admission
LaGrange College
601 Broad Street
LaGrange, Georgia 30240
Telephone: 706-880-8005
800-593-2885 (toll-free)
Fax: 706-880-8010
E-mail: lgcadmis@lgc.edu
World Wide Web: http://www.lgc.edu

ACADEMIC PROGRAM

Each program of study contains a substantial interdisciplinary core component. Providing a background in the natural and social sciences, arts, and humanities, the core helps students see how subjects interrelate while developing the research and problem-solving skills employers and graduate schools seek most. A minimum of 108 semester hours is required to earn a bachelor's degree; 48 semester hours of liberal studies core courses are required for all bachelor's degrees. Most majors require an additional 36 to 56 semester hours of credit beyond the liberal studies curriculum. Students may be eligible for credit and/or exemption in certain areas through Advanced Placement (AP) tests or the College-Level Examination Program (CLEP).

FINANCIAL AID

As a private college, LaGrange is committed to helping meet the difference between the funds any student has available and the cost of attending LaGrange College. More than 80 percent of LaGrange students receive some combination of financial awards, with more than $8 million awarded annually. These awards may include grants, loans, scholarships, and employment opportunities. Federal financial aid and institutional funds are available to all students who qualify. The state of Georgia provides additional funding for Georgia residents. All Georgia residents who enroll as full-time students receive the Georgia Tuition Equalization Grant in the amount of $1050 per year. The HOPE Scholarship, which totals $3000 per year, is awarded to all Georgia residents who have graduated from high school since 1996 with a B average and who enter as freshmen. Georgia residents who do not qualify for the HOPE Scholarship as freshmen may be able to obtain the HOPE Scholarship by maintaining a 3.0 grade point average through the freshman and sophomore years. Academic scholarships that range from $1000 to full scholarships are also awarded. All accepted students are considered for scholarships; a separate application is not required. In 2000–01, all financial aid applicants were awarded financial aid.

APPLICATION AND INFORMATION

Applications for admission are evaluated on a rolling basis and should be submitted at least one month prior to the beginning of the semester in which entrance is desired.

LE MOYNE COLLEGE

■ SYRACUSE, NEW YORK

THE COLLEGE

Le Moyne College is a four-year Jesuit college of approximately 2,000 undergraduate students that uniquely balances a comprehensive liberal arts education with preparation for specific career paths or graduate study. Founded by the Society of Jesus in 1946, Le Moyne is the second-youngest of the twenty-eight Jesuit colleges and universities in the United States. The campus environment is one of a closely knit community. Le Moyne's personal approach to education is reflected in the quality of contact between students and faculty members. A wide range of student-directed activities, athletics, clubs, and service organizations complement the academic experience. Intramural sports are very popular with Le Moyne students, and approximately 75 percent of the students participate in athletics. More than 75 percent of students live in residence halls and town houses on campus. The Residence Hall Councils and the Le Moyne Student Programming Board organize many campus activities, including concerts, dances, a weekly film series, student talent programs, and special lectures as well as off-campus trips and skiing excursions.

For more information, students should contact:

Dennis J. Nicholson
Director of Admission
Le Moyne College
Syracuse, New York 13214-1399
Telephone: 315-445-4300
800-333-4733 (toll-free)
E-mail: admission@mail.lemoyne.edu
World Wide Web:
http://www.lemoyne.edu

ACADEMIC PROGRAM

While each major department has its own sequence requirements for the minimum 120 credit hours needed for the Le Moyne degree, the College is convinced that there is a fundamental intellectual discipline that should characterize the graduate of a superior liberal arts college. Le Moyne's core curriculum provides this foundation by including studies of English language and literature, philosophy, history, religious studies, science, mathematics, and social sciences. For exceptional students, Le Moyne offers an integral honors program that includes an interdisciplinary humanities sequence as well as departmental honors courses. Le Moyne also offers a part-time course of study during evening hours through its Center for Continuous Learning. Le Moyne students may enroll in Army and Air Force ROTC programs at Syracuse University.

FINANCIAL AID

Financial aid is offered to 95 percent of Le Moyne's students through scholarships, grants, loans, and work-study assignments. Le Moyne offers a generous program of merit-based academic and athletic scholarships as well as financial aid based on a student's need and academic promise. Federal funds are available through the Federal Pell Grant, Federal Work-Study, Federal Supplemental Educational Opportunity Grant, and Federal Perkins Loan programs. A student's eligibility for need-based financial aid is determined from both the Free Application for Federal Student Aid (FAFSA) and the Le Moyne Financial Aid Application Form. It is recommended that these forms be mailed by February 1.

APPLICATION AND INFORMATION

The Admission Committee reviews applications and mails decisions on a rolling admission cycle beginning January 1. The priority deadline for applications is March 1; all students who wish to be considered for academic non-need scholarships should have a completed application on file in the Office of Admission before this date. Students who wish to be considered under the early decision program must have a completed application submitted by December 1. Early decision applicants will by notified by December 15. Transfer students are encouraged to apply before May 1 for the fall semester and December 1 for the spring semester. A fun-filled two-day orientation program takes place in mid-summer.

LOYOLA MARYMOUNT UNIVERSITY

■ LOS ANGELES, CALIFORNIA

THE UNIVERSITY

Loyola Marymount University, situated on a picturesque campus, offers competitive students an education of high quality in a friendly and relaxed atmosphere. As successor of the oldest institution of learning in southern California, St. Vincent's College, the University is steeped in a tradition and history of dedication to academic excellence and the total development of its students. Although the emphasis is within the undergraduate school (full-time enrollment is 4,540 and part-time enrollment is 311), 1,300 students attend the Graduate Division, primarily in the evening hours, working toward master's degrees in the fields of arts, arts in teaching, business administration, education, and science (including engineering). The School of Law, situated at a separate campus, has both day and evening divisions and offers the Juris Doctor degree. Law school enrollment is 1,412. Approximately 65 percent of the undergraduate students live on campus and are able to choose accommodations in one of ten residential halls or four apartment complexes. Students have access to a sports pavilion, two swimming pools, baseball and soccer fields, tennis and volleyball courts, and four indoor racquetball courts. A new recreation center includes three additional courts and a fitness center. LMU fields teams in eleven intercollegiate sports (baseball, basketball, crew, cross-country, golf, soccer, softball, swimming, tennis, volleyball, and water polo) and has club teams in lacrosse and rugby. More than 2,000 undergraduate students participate in the active intramural program, which includes coed sports. Student organizations include the AM/FM radio station (KXLU), Biology Society, Black Students Freedom Alliance, Chinese Club, MEChA, Pre-Legal Society, Student Activities Board, University Choruses, fraternities and sororities, and various honor and service groups. The Debate Squad and LMU's Air Force ROTC detachment have received national recognition in their respective areas.

For more information about Loyola Marymount University, prospective students should contact:

Matthew X. Fissinger
Director of Admissions
Loyola Marymount University
7900 Loyola Boulevard
Los Angeles, California 90045
Telephone: 310-338-2750
800-LMU-INFO (toll-free)
Fax: 310-338-2797

ACADEMIC PROGRAM

While premajor and major requirements differ with each area of study, a core curriculum is maintained as a degree requirement in the fields of American cultures, communication skills, fine arts, history, literature/psychology, mathematics/science, philosophy, social science, and theology, thus ensuring each student a balanced education. The maximum requirement in each of the core fields is 6 units of academic work. The interdepartmental honors program provides challenges for the exceptional student.

FINANCIAL AID

Approximately 75 percent of the University's undergraduate students receive some type of financial assistance. The total amount of financial aid awarded to students is approximately $60 million. Students applying for aid must file the Free Application for Student Aid (FAFSA) and the CSS PROFILE. All students are expected to apply for the Federal Pell Grant, and California residents must apply for the California grants. Most aid is awarded on the basis of need, but the University does offer merit scholarships (including full-tuition scholarships). The priority date for financial aid is February 15. Aid is awarded after that date on a funds-available basis.

APPLICATION AND INFORMATION

Applicants must submit official transcripts from the last high school attended and from each college attended, arrange for SAT I or ACT scores to be sent to the Office of Admissions, submit a recommendation form from an official of the last school attended, and file an application with the $45 nonrefundable fee. Applications are considered when all necessary documents have been received prior to the deadline of the semester for which application is made. The deadlines are February 1 for the fall semester and December 1 for the spring semester.

LOYOLA UNIVERSITY CHICAGO

■ CHICAGO, ILLINOIS

THE UNIVERSITY

Loyola University Chicago is the most comprehensive Jesuit university in the United States. Founded in 1870 by priests of the Society of Jesus, Loyola continues the Jesuit commitment to education, which is well-grounded in the liberal arts and based on excellence in teaching and research. Loyola attracts students from all fifty states and seventy-four countries to its nine schools and colleges: the Stritch School of Medicine, the School of Law, the College of Arts and Sciences, the School of Business Administration, the Niehoff School of Nursing, the School of Education, the School of Social Work, the Graduate School, and Mundelein College (for adult and lifelong learning). Each year, Loyola enrolls nearly 1,000 freshmen and 400 transfer students. These students choose Loyola because of its personal attention, its environment of academic excellence, and its reputation for career preparation.

For more information, students should contact:

Undergraduate Admission Office
Loyola University Chicago
820 North Michigan Avenue
Chicago, Illinois 60611
Telephone: 312-915-6500
800-262-2373 (toll-free)
E-mail: admission@luc.edu
World Wide Web:
http://www.luc.edu/

ACADEMIC PROGRAM

Jesuit educators believe that a solid foundation in the liberal arts and sciences is essential for students entering all professions. Loyola's Core Curriculum is designed to give students this foundation. The core requirements vary by college but usually include courses in literature, expressive arts, history, social sciences, mathematical and natural sciences, philosophy, and theology. The core allows students who are undecided about their majors to explore all possibilities before deciding upon a field of study. Most majors require 128 semester hours for graduation. Exceptionally well qualified students may apply to the Honors Program. Students may receive credit through the Advanced Placement Program (AP Program) tests, the International Baccalaureate (I.B.), and certain College-Level Examination Program (CLEP) tests are accepted. Loyola students may participate in the Army and Naval ROTC programs through neighboring universities.

FINANCIAL AID

Loyola attempts to meet the financial need of as many students as possible. Seventy-five percent of Loyola students receive some form of aid, including University-funded scholarships and grants, federal and state grants, work-study, and loans. Students are encouraged to file the Free Application for Federal Student Aid (FAFSA) by mid-February in order to receive consideration for all types of aid. Merit scholarships are awarded to entering freshmen who have outstanding academic records. Presidential, Damen, and Loyola scholarships are awarded to students who rank at the top of their high school graduating class and score well on the ACT or SAT I. Scholarship amounts for these programs are $5000–$10,000 per year. These awards are renewable for up to three years. Other scholarships available include competitive awards for students admitted to the Honors Program and students from Jesuit/BVM/Sisters of Christian Charity high schools, National Merit/National Achievement finalists, theater scholarships (awarded by audition), and debate, leadership, nursing, and public accounting awards. Transfer students who have completed 30 hours of college credit with an outstanding record of academic achievement may receive a Transfer Academic Scholarship. These awards are renewable for up to three years.

APPLICATION AND INFORMATION

Applicants are notified of the admission decision three to four weeks after the application, supporting credentials, secondary school counselor recommendation, and $25 application fee are received. Prospective students are encouraged to visit the campus. The Undergraduate Admission Office encourages students to schedule individual appointments and campus tours or to participate in one of the many campus programs offered throughout the year.

LOYOLA UNIVERSITY NEW ORLEANS

■ NEW ORLEANS, LOUISIANA

THE UNIVERSITY

Founded by the Jesuits in 1912, Loyola University's more than 35,000 graduates have excelled in innumerable professional fields for more than eighty years. Approximately 3,500 undergraduate students enjoy the individual attention of a caring faculty in a university dedicated to creating community and fostering individualism while educating the whole person, not only intellectually, but spiritually, socially, and athletically. Loyola students represent forty-nine states and forty-eight countries. This diversity is found in a setting where the average class size is 22 students. More than 53 percent of the students permanently reside outside Louisiana, and 30 percent belong to minority groups. Loyola's 20-acre main campus and 4-acre Broadway campus are located in the historic uptown area of New Orleans and are hubs of student activity. The University's residence halls, equipped with computer labs, kitchen, laundry, and study facilities, are home to almost 1,000 students. The Joseph A. Danna Center, the student center, houses four food venues, including the remodeled Orleans Room, Pizza Hut, N'Awlins Poboys, and a gourmet coffee shop. Also found in the Danna Center are an art gallery, travel agency, hair salon, concierge desk, and post office. Nationally affiliated fraternities and sororities are among Loyola's more than 120 student organizations. During the fall's Organizational Fair, students can join the award-winning newspaper, the Loyola University Community Action Program (a volunteer community service organization, the largest such club on campus), or one of the many special interest groups. Students can also take this opportunity to sign up for one of Loyola's club sports.

For more information, students should contact:

Office of Admissions
Loyola University
6363 St. Charles Avenue, Box 18
New Orleans, Louisiana 70118
Telephone: 504-865-3240
800-4-LOYOLA (toll-free)
Fax: 504-865-3383
E-mail: admit@loyno.edu
World Wide Web:
http://www.loyno.edu

ACADEMIC PROGRAM

Once enrolled at Loyola, students are introduced to the common curriculum, designed to give them a well-rounded preparation in their major field of concentration, as well as the ability to understand and reflect on disciplines allied to or outside their major. The curriculum is divided into four categories: major, minor, common curriculum, and elective courses. Students must meet the requirements of their degree program as specified by their particular college; the minimum four-year program requires 128 hours. Common curriculum courses include seven introductory courses in English composition, math, science, philosophy, religion, literature, and history and nine upper-division courses in humanities, social science, and natural science. Through the Early Scholars/Early Artists Program, academically gifted and artistically talented local high school sophomores, juniors, and seniors may participate in challenging college courses and earn academic credit. (Interested students should contact the Office of Admissions for more information.) The College of Arts and Sciences also requires a minimum of one year of study in a modern foreign language. The honors program and independent studies provide special opportunities for qualified students.

FINANCIAL AID

Loyola University's endowment provides money for financial aid in addition to that provided by federal funding. Assistance in the forms of merit- and talent-based scholarships, loans, work-study program awards, and grants is awarded on the basis of academic achievement and need. More than 450 scholarships are awarded annually to students with competitive grades and test scores. To apply for one of the scholarships, students must have a GPA of at least 3.2 and competitive standardized test scores. Offers of financial aid are not made until after admission. Notifications of awards are sent in early February. Awards of need-based financial aid packages are made on a first-come, first-served basis.

LUTHER COLLEGE

■ DECORAH, IOWA

THE COLLEGE

Luther College, founded in 1861, is a four-year residential liberal arts college of the Evangelical Lutheran Church in America. The College, which was founded by Norwegian immigrants, is an academic community of faith and learning where students of promise from all beliefs and backgrounds have the freedom to learn, to express themselves, to perform, to compete, and to grow. The College, located in Decorah, Iowa, is home to 2,600 students from thirty-seven states and thirty-six countries. Thirty-six percent of the students are from Iowa; 86 percent come from the four-state area of Iowa, Minnesota, Wisconsin, and Illinois. Each year, approximately 150 international students choose to study at Luther. The College provides a stimulating cultural and educational atmosphere by bringing distinguished public figures, theater groups, musicians, and educators to the campus. Cocurricular activities are an important part of College life. The College sponsors seven choirs, two orchestras, two bands, three jazz bands, and a full theater and dance program. Numerous student organizations and societies provide ample opportunities for student involvement in meaningful activities. Nineteen intercollegiate sports are offered.

For more information, students should contact:

Admissions Office
Luther College
Decorah, Iowa 52101-1042
Telephone: 319-387-1287
800-458-8437 (toll-free)
Fax: 319-387-2159
319-387-1060 (international)
E-mail: admissions@luther.edu (admissions)
lutherfa@luther.edu (financial planning)
lundsony@luther.edu (international)
World Wide Web:
http://www.luther.edu

ACADEMIC PROGRAM

Luther operates on a 4-1-4 academic calendar. The first semester runs from September to December, followed by a 3-week January Term and the second semester, which runs from February to May. Two four-week summer sessions are offered in June and July. Each candidate is required to complete a total of 128 semester hours of credit with a C average or better. At least 76 of the required 128 semester hours must be earned outside the major discipline. Each senior writes a research paper in his or her major. Students are required to complete the following number of semester hours of credit in designated areas: 12 of Paideia, an interdisciplinary course; 9–12 of religion/philosophy; 7–8 of natural science (4 of which may be in mathematics); 6–8 of social science; 3–9 of foreign language (proficiency based); 3–4 of fine arts; and 2 of physical education. Demonstration of competency in mathematics is required. Advanced placement and credit by examination are available. A qualified student may develop an interdisciplinary major with a faculty adviser.

FINANCIAL AID

More than 97 percent of all Luther students receive financial aid in the form of grants, such as the Federal Pell Grant; scholarships from Luther and other sources; loans; and jobs on campus. Luther awards Regent and Presidential Scholarships to those demonstrating superior academic achievement. The amount of aid given is determined by the College's analysis of the Free Application for Federal Student Aid. The priority deadline for a financial aid application is March 1. Students receive notification of financial aid awards after their acceptance for admission.

APPLICATION AND INFORMATION

An application, SAT I or ACT scores, an educator's reference, a transcript of previous academic work, and a $25 application fee are required for admission. On-campus interviews are recommended but not required.

LYNN UNIVERSITY

■ BOCA RATON, FLORIDA

THE UNIVERSITY

Founded in 1962, Lynn University is a private, coeducational institution located in Boca Raton, Florida. The University, small by design, provides an environment within and outside the classroom in which a community of learners can pursue academic excellence. Faculty, staff, and students contribute to an atmosphere that nurtures creativity, fosters achievement, and values diversity. Accredited in 1967 by the Southern Association of Colleges and Schools, Lynn University has steadily grown to become a comprehensive university offering undergraduate and graduate programs in more than thirty disciplines. Lynn leads the country in offering majors in many of the world's fastest-growing professions, thus preparing its students to meet the career demands of the twenty-first century. The 2,000 students who are currently enrolled come from all parts of the United States and nearly seventy nations. Lynn is a residential institution with four air-conditioned residence halls that house 55 percent of the undergraduates. University life is designed to provide a learning situation through which students are guided toward responsible decision-making and leadership.

For more information, students should contact:

Office of Admission
Lynn University
3601 North Military Trail
Boca Raton, Florida 33431-5598
Telephone: 561-237-7900
800-544-8035 (toll-free)
Fax: 561-237-7100
E-mail: admission@lynn.edu
World Wide Web:
http://www.lynn.edu

ACADEMIC PROGRAM

The University is committed to student-centered learning, where faculty and staff members provide personalized attention to students who have varying levels of academic proficiency with a motivation to excel. A full range of academic and support programs is coordinated to serve the increasingly diverse needs of all students. These are enhanced by the favorable 19:1 student-faculty ratio. The Freshman Seminar is the cornerstone to freshman advising at Lynn and provides an introduction to college life for all new students. The course includes academic success strategies, time management, communication skills, study and test-taking techniques, academic advisement, and career development. The course is taught by select members of the faculty and staff who serve as mentors to new students throughout their freshman year. Lynn University's approach to the development of academic programs has been one that focuses on the balance of a carefully selected core of liberal arts subjects within the framework of a curriculum that is career-oriented and provides both theoretical and practical preparation. Upon this solid liberal arts foundation, students build special competence in their chosen fields of concentration. The practical application of knowledge is a vital component of Lynn's academic program; therefore, residencies, student teaching, community service projects, and internships are required for many degrees. The University follows a semester calendar and offers a summer session. Most graduate programs are scheduled on ten-week term cycles.

FINANCIAL AID

A student's education is not only a commitment of intellect and time, but a substantial financial investment as well. The University has a broad program of student financial aid, including scholarships, grants, work-study, and loans. Academic, athletic, and need-based scholarships are awarded. Inquiries may be made to the Office of Financial Aid.

APPLICATION AND INFORMATION

There is no formal deadline for admission, and applicants are notified on a rolling basis upon receipt of all credentials. The application fee is $25.

MCP HAHNEMANN UNIVERSITY
College of Nursing and Health Professions

■ PHILADELPHIA, PENNSYLVANIA

THE UNIVERSITY AND THE SCHOOL

MCP Hahnemann University (MCPHU) is an academic health center that includes more than 2,700 students in its School of Medicine, College of Nursing and Health Professions, and School of Public Health. The University grants degrees from the associate through the doctorate in more than eighty programs. It has a rich heritage spanning two centuries of health-care education. Hahnemann University was founded in 1848, while Medical College of Pennsylvania was founded in 1850. In 1993 the two schools consolidated into one institution. In the College of Nursing and Health Professions, there are 588 undergraduate students. The student population is not only culturally diverse but also age-diverse, ranging from high school graduates to older adults. The University is also sensitive to the many time constraints placed on today's students, so many programs offer flexible scheduling. The University offers undergraduate and graduate programs in the College of Nursing and Health Professions as well as graduate programs in the School of Public Health. Biomedical graduate programs, such as the M.D. degree, and dual-degree programs, such as M.D./M.B.A., M.D./M.P.H., and M.D./Ph.D., are offered through the University's School of Medicine. Stiles Alumni Hall, a sixteen-story building, is the University's housing facility, located one block north of the Center City campus. It contains 195 carpeted apartments, furnished and unfurnished, with various floor plans to accommodate single or shared occupancy. Information about off-campus housing may be obtained from the Office of Residential Life.

For more information, students should contact:

Office of Enrollment
MCP Hahnemann University
245 North 15th Street
Mail Stop 472
Philadelphia, Pennsylvania 19102-1192
Telephone: 215-762-8288
800-2-DREXEL Ext. 6333
E-mail: enroll@mcphu.edu
World Wide Web: http://www.mcphu.edu

ACADEMIC PROGRAM

Candidates for graduation must have fulfilled all course requirements in the major curriculum prescribed by the program director. Associate degree candidates must have completed course work equivalent to a minimum of 60 semester hours with a minimum cumulative grade point average of 2.0 on a 4.0 scale. In addition, the following distributional requirements must be met: 3 semester hours each of social sciences, humanities, and natural sciences and 6 semester hours of English (6 semester hours in college-level composition, 6 semester hours in combined college-level composition and literature, or 3 semester hours in college-level composition and 3 semester hours in literature). Bachelor's degree candidates must have completed course work equivalent to a minimum of 120 semester hours with a minimum cumulative grade point average of 2.0. In addition, the following distributional requirements must be met: 3 semester hours each of mathematics/statistics and computer science; 6 semester hours each of humanities and natural sciences; 6 semester hours of English (see above); and 12 semester hours of social sciences (3 semester hours of health administration and management may be selected in lieu of 3 semester hours of a social science at the program director's discretion).

FINANCIAL AID

MCPHU awards funds to students from loan programs and numerous scholarship and grant programs. Awards are based on financial need, with the neediest students funded first. Some scholarship funds are awarded to students based on both financial need and academic merit. Students must complete the Free Application for Federal Student Aid (FAFSA) form to be considered for any aid from the University.

MARIAN COLLEGE OF FOND DU LAC

■ FOND DU LAC, WISCONSIN

THE COLLEGE

Marian College is a community of students and faculty and staff members working together toward the pursuit of excellence in education. Founded in 1936 by the Sisters of the Congregation of Saint Agnes as a private school for teacher education, Marian now offers more than forty majors and minors in professional and preprofessional programs. A strong liberal arts curriculum, combined with outstanding experiential education opportunities, gives students the reasoning, problem-solving, and communication skills essential for any career choice. An active campus life provides many opportunities for the 1,100 traditional undergraduate students, 600 adult completion students, and 700 students pursuing master's degrees. The Marian community has many social organizations and clubs as well as twelve NCAA Division III athletic programs, including men's baseball, basketball, golf, ice hockey, soccer, and tennis and women's basketball, golf, soccer, tennis, and volleyball. Student life is further enhanced by the Dale R. Michels Performance Series for Students that brings national entertainers to the Marian campus. Through its programming, Marian shows a continuous commitment to the service of diverse populations. Students enjoy a variety of modern housing options while residing on campus. One traditional residence hall (completely renovated in 2000) and town house and courtyard complexes, with spacious living rooms, kitchens, bedrooms, and private bathrooms, are where Marian students make their home away from home. The Todd Wehr Alumni Center and coffee house and the atrium of the Stayer Center for Technology and Executive Learning are two locations that not only enhance the beautiful 97-acre campus but provide an atmosphere where students and faculty and staff members can relax and socialize. In addition to the undergraduate degrees offered, Marian also provides executive education and degree completion programs for adults and master's degrees in education and organizational leadership and quality.

For more information, students should contact:

Stacey Akey
Dean of Enrollment Management
Marian College of Fond du Lac
45 South National Avenue
Fond du Lac, Wisconsin 54935
Telephone: 920-923-7650
800-2-MARIAN (toll-free)
E-mail: admissions@mariancollege.edu
World Wide Web:
http://www.mariancollege.edu

ACADEMIC PROGRAM

Six instructional divisions comprise Marian academic programming: the Division of Arts and Humanities, the Division of Business, the Division of Educational Studies, the Division of Mathematics and Natural Sciences, the Division of Nursing, and the Division of Social and Behavioral Science. In addition to classroom learning, more than 90 percent of Marian students receive hands-on work experience through internships, co-ops, and clinical experiences prior to graduation. All students, regardless of their specific degree program, must successfully complete 48 credits in the liberal arts general curriculum. Marian students must complete the requirements for at least one major and take at least 128 total hours of credit with a minimum average of 2 grade points for each credit hour.

FINANCIAL AID

The Marian College Financial Aid Office coordinates an active program of financial assistance for students. More than 90 percent of students are recipients of aid, which is based on need and/or academic merit. The principal sources of aid include the Federal Pell Grant Programs, the Federal Work-Study Program, and Marian assistance. Academic scholarships, including the Academic Achievement Award ($7500), the Presidential Scholarship ($5000), the Naber Leadership Award ($3000), the Sister Shelia Burns Award, and numerous other renewable scholarships and awards are available to entering students.

MARYMOUNT COLLEGE

■ TARRYTOWN, NEW YORK

THE COLLEGE

Founded in 1907, Marymount is an independent, four-year liberal arts college whose mission is to prepare women for leadership in the twenty-first century. A pioneer in women's education for more than ninety years, the College encourages women to explore their goals and ideas. Marymount also offers a special weekend session to serve the needs of working women and men wishing to pursue a bachelor's degree. The College enrolls 700 students in the Women's College and 300 in the Weekend College. Marymount accommodates both commuting and residential students. The College's physical facilities consist of twelve buildings, seven of which have been constructed since 1950. The facilities include new computer labs, a newly renovated athletic center with an Olympic-size pool, and a science building with state-of-the-art laboratory equipment. The four dormitories accommodate approximately 650 students. Students come from many parts of the country to take advantage of the academic facilities of the College and the cultural offerings of New York City. Student organizations include numerous special interest clubs, community service programs, and honor societies. Cocurricular programs include numerous special interest clubs, community service programs, and honor societies. The College provides frequent social and cultural activities in which students may participate, as well as dramatic performances, art exhibits, film festival series, fashion shows, and dance concerts. Nearby New York City serves as a cultural classroom and social destination for students. Marymount has intercollegiate teams and an extensive intramural program.

For further information, prospective students should contact:

Daniela Esposito
Director of Admissions
Marymount College
100 Marymount Avenue
Tarrytown, New York 10591-3796
Telephone: 914-332-8295
800-724-4312 (toll-free)
Fax: 914-332-7442
E-mail: admiss@mmc.marymt.edu
World Wide Web:
http://www.marymt.edu

ACADEMIC PROGRAM

Marymount students have great flexibility in their course selection, although there is a general education requirement. In consultation with their academic adviser, they may choose from the wide variety of courses offered in some thirty majors. From this broad background, they are guided in their choice of a major field, which comprises ten to twenty-one of their courses. Candidates for a bachelor's degree must complete 120 semester credits and fulfill the requirements of their major program. Candidates for the Associate of Arts degree must complete 60 credits; candidates for the Associate of Science degree must complete 66 credits. Students are also encouraged to participate in the internship program for college credit. The College awards credit for successful scores on the College-Level Examination Program (CLEP) general and subject examinations. Students may also earn credit through Advanced Placement (AP) examinations. Credit for life/work experience is also available to adult students on presentation of a portfolio.

FINANCIAL AID

In 1999–2000, Marymount students received more than $8.8 million in student financial aid. Of this, $5.1 million came from federal programs, $810,000 from state programs, and more than $2.8 million from Marymount. Trustee grants and scholarships are also available. Financial aid applicants are required to file the FAFSA. It is recommended that the form be submitted by February 1. Early applicants can expect to receive their award notifications beginning April 15.

APPLICATION AND INFORMATION

The application, a $30 fee, official high school records, essay, recommendation, and test scores should be submitted by April 15 for admission to the fall term or by December 1 for the spring term. Notification of the admission decision, which is given on a rolling basis, begins in the late fall. Deferred admission and early admission are available.

MARYMOUNT UNIVERSITY

■ ARLINGTON, VIRGINIA

THE UNIVERSITY

Marymount University is a comprehensive, coeducational Catholic institution, founded in 1950 by the Religious of the Sacred Heart of Mary. Marymount emphasizes excellence in teaching, attention to the individual, and values and ethics across the curriculum. Approximately 2,100 undergraduate and 1,600 graduate students are enrolled, representing forty states and seventy-nine countries. The University offers thirty-seven undergraduate majors and twenty-five graduate degrees through its four schools: Arts and Sciences, Business Administration, Education and Human Services, and Health Professions. The University is accredited by the Commission on Colleges of the Southern Association of Colleges and Schools. Located in Arlington, VA, minutes from the heart of Washington, D.C., Marymount takes full advantage of resources in the nation's capital. Nationally and internationally known speakers frequently visit Marymount's campus, enriching the university experience.

For more information, students should contact:

Chris Domes, Vice President of
Enrollment Management
Marymount University
2807 North Glebe Road
Arlington, Virginia 22207-4299
Telephone: 703-284-1500
800-548-7638 (toll-free)
E-mail: admissions@marymount.edu
World Wide Web:
http://www.marymount.edu

ACADEMIC PROGRAM

Marymount University's goal is to help each student achieve his or her full potential. While students study a liberal arts core curriculum and the required elements of their discipline, they are able to work with their faculty adviser to tailor an academic program that fits their personal and career objectives. Requirements for earning a degree include a cumulative GPA of 2.0 or better and a minimum of 36 credits as a student at Marymount. The total number of credits required to earn a degree varies by program. Marymount operates on a semester system. Small classes and personal attention help ensure student success and a strong sense of community. An honor system guides academic and social conduct. The cultural and educational resources of the nation's capital add to the curriculum through off-campus activities. Excellent academics, ethics across the curriculum, and a focus on service complete the solid foundation Marymount provides students.

FINANCIAL AID

Marymount provides an extensive scholarship and grant program and participates in all federal and state aid programs. To be considered for aid, students must file the Free Application for Federal Student Aid (FAFSA) with the College Scholarship Service. Approximately 69 percent of full-time, first-year students receive need-based aid and 20 percent receive non-need-based aid. The financial compensation is in the form of scholarships, grants, loans, work-study awards, or on-campus employment. The average financial aid package for freshman is $16,057, which includes all forms of financial aid.

APPLICATION AND INFORMATION

High school students seeking admission are advised to apply early during their senior year. They should submit an application, a nonrefundable fee of $35, a high school transcript, SAT I or ACT scores, evidence of expected graduation from an accredited high school, and a recommendation from a high school counselor or an appropriate school official. Those who have attended another college or university must submit the application, $35 fee, test scores, evidence of high school graduation, transcripts of college-level study, and a recommendation from the Dean of Students at the previous institution. The University has a rolling admission policy and notifies applicants soon after the application process is completed and the Admissions Committee has acted on the application.

MARYVILLE UNIVERSITY OF SAINT LOUIS

■ ST. LOUIS, MISSOURI

THE UNIVERSITY

Maryville University of Saint Louis is an independent coeducational university with an enrollment of more than 3,000 undergraduate and graduate students. The quality and variety of its curriculum—solid liberal arts studies and professional programs covering more than fifty fields (undergraduate and graduate)—have attracted an increasing number of students in recent years. A special feature is the large measure of personal concern for each student demonstrated by everyone on campus, from the faculty members through the administrative staff to the president. The University was founded in 1872 by the Religious of the Sacred Heart, moved to its present site in suburban St. Louis in 1961, became an independent college in 1972, and became a university in 1991. The two residence halls house 350 students.

For further information, students should contact:

Dr. Martha Wade
Vice President for Admissions and Enrollment Management
Maryville University of Saint Louis
13550 Conway Road
St. Louis, Missouri 63141-7299
Telephone: 314-529-9350
800-627-9855 (toll-free)
Fax: 314-529-9927
E-mail: admissions@maryville.edu
World Wide Web:
http://www.maryville.edu

ACADEMIC PROGRAM

The academic curriculum and programs are based on a semester calendar with a summer session. Professional programs combine education toward a career with a strong liberal arts base to ensure that students in all fields develop a high degree of competence in professional areas closely related to their academic interests. A cooperative education program combines supervised, paid work experience with classroom studies. An intensive English program is offered for international students. Weekend College enables students to attend classes on alternate weekends to earn a bachelor's degree in accountancy, accounting information systems, business administration, communications, criminology, health-care management, information systems, liberal studies, management, marketing, nursing (one of the nation's few weekend programs in nursing; it includes a B.S.N. degree-completion program for RNs), organizational leadership, psychology, psychology/sociology, and sociology.

FINANCIAL AID

Financial aid is available in the form of employment, loans, and grants; awards are based on need as determined by the FAFSA and University-administered forms. Scholarships, which are awarded on merit rather than on a need basis, are also available. Students are free to accept employment or a grant without being obligated to accept a loan, which may be offered as part of a financial aid package. Last year, more than 80 percent of the University's full-time students received financial aid; the average award was $9654. Deferred payment plans are available through arrangements with the University for those who wish to pay their educational expenses in installments.

APPLICATION AND INFORMATION

Freshman applicants must submit an application for admission with a $20 application fee, an official high school transcript, and ACT or SAT I scores. Under Maryville's rolling admission policy, applications are reviewed immediately upon receipt of all necessary material. Transfer students must submit an application for admission with a $20 application fee and high school and college transcripts. Certain programs require additional credentials. The physical therapy and occupational therapy programs require submission of a letter of recommendation; physical therapy also requires a personal interview. Admission of students to the B.F.A. or B.A. in art program requires a portfolio evaluation by the art and design faculty. Acceptance into the nursing program requires a personal interview. Applications may be submitted by mail or electronically.

MILLS COLLEGE

■ OAKLAND, CALIFORNIA

THE COLLEGE

Mills is the only women's college among the many fine educational institutions in the San Francisco Bay Area. Founded in 1852 as the first women's college west of the Rockies, it is committed to remaining a women's college because it believes that such an environment offers women special advantages in preparing for new roles and responsibilities. A small, liberal arts college, Mills enrolls more than 700 undergraduate women and 300 graduate women and men. The faculty is equally divided between women and men, and the ratio of students to faculty is approximately 11:1. The College has remained small because ideas and enthusiasm are more readily transmitted in a community of this size. Classes are normally small; 87 percent have 20 or fewer students. Faculty members observe each person's work closely, encouraging high performance and offering individual instruction when appropriate.

For more information, students should contact:

Avis E. Hinkson
Dean of Admission
Mills College
5000 MacArthur Boulevard
Oakland, California 94613
Telephone: 510-430-2135
800-87-MILLS (toll-free)
Fax: 510-430-3314
E-mail: admission@mills.edu
World Wide Web:
http://www.mills.edu

ACADEMIC PROGRAM

To earn a Mills B.A., students must take thirty-four semester courses (usually four courses each semester). Grading is traditional, and a pass-fail option is available outside the major. First-year students take interdisciplinary seminars on such topics as Science and Pseudoscience, Tribal Cultures in Fact and Fiction, and Music and the Written Word. Students are also expected to choose two courses from each of four areas (natural sciences and mathematics, social sciences, humanities, and fine arts), a one-semester multicultural or cross-cultural course, and one course that heavily stresses writing skills. They also must choose at least half their courses from outside their major field. Students complete their chosen major with a senior project or thesis. A comprehensive program in mathematics and computer science offers basic grounding in mathematics for women who have had insufficient high school preparation but need math skills for their prospective careers.

FINANCIAL AID

More than 80 percent of Mills students are awarded a financial aid package that includes a loan, campus work-study, and a scholarship grant from Mills, outside sources, or both. Awards are based on both need and academic merit. Scholarship grants range from $200 to full tuition per year. Mills makes a special effort to provide financial aid to members of minority groups who demonstrate need. Almost 90 percent of Mills undergraduates who apply for financial aid are offered assistance. Financial aid applicants are expected to apply for assistance from appropriate outside sources, such as the National Merit Scholarship, Federal Pell Grant, and California State Grant programs. More than 40 percent of Mills students have some of their determined need offset by such outside awards. Loans may be obtained by most students, and 45 percent of undergraduates are offered campus work opportunities; some students take off-campus jobs. All freshman and transfer candidates who are California residents must file the Free Application for Federal Student Aid (FAFSA) to be considered for all types of government aid and must also file the Cal Grant GPA Verification Form. Students who seek Mills scholarship funds must also file the Mills Financial Aid Form. Priority is given to applicants who meet the published deadlines.

MINNEAPOLIS COLLEGE OF ART AND DESIGN

■ MINNEAPOLIS, MINNESOTA

THE COLLEGE

The 114-year-old Minneapolis College of Art and Design, along with The Minneapolis Institute of Arts and the Children's Theatre Company, occupies three square blocks in a residential neighborhood just south of the downtown district. The three institutions constitute one of the largest art centers in the nation. There are currently 348 men and 250 women enrolled in the B.F.A. program. The College maintains furnished apartments in modern residences, which can accommodate approximately 185 students (35 percent of the entire student population). In addition to its regular academic program, the College offers evening, Saturday, and summer school classes and art-related films, lectures, performances, and conferences through the Continuing Studies Office. The MCAD Gallery hosts exhibitions during the academic year, providing students with an excellent opportunity to view the work of important contemporary artists and designers. As part of a visiting artists program, nationally prominent artists, designers, and critics visit the campus for varying periods of time to teach, lecture, and work with students and faculty members. Although there are a variety of campus social events each year, students who apply to the College should be aware that its standards of professionalism and performance demand a significant commitment.

For more information, students should contact:

Admissions Office
Minneapolis College of Art and Design
2501 Stevens Avenue South
Minneapolis, Minnesota 55404
Telephone: 612-874-3760
800-874-6223 (toll-free)
Fax: 612-874-3701
E-mail: admissions@mcad.edu
World Wide Web:
http://www.mcad.edu/

ACADEMIC PROGRAM

In order to be awarded the B.S. degree, students are required to complete 120 semester credits, 36 of which concentrate in courses relating to visualization (e.g., communication theory and marketing: history, strategies, forms and perceptions, media analysis, hypermedia), and 18 credits, which are taken within MCAD's studio offerings. Students are also required to participate in team-based projects, an externship or study abroad program, and a senior project/exhibit. This degree program offers course work in visual persuasion and information techniques applicable to the fields of advertising/marketing, science/technology, entertainment, education, and corporate communications. The B.F.A. program requires students to complete 120 semester credits. Eighteen of these are in the first-year Foundation Studies program, 39 are in the liberal arts area, and 63 are in the studio. To facilitate the growth of the perception and judgment necessary for meaningful creative endeavor, the College has developed a curriculum that stresses critical thinking, artistic inquiry, professional responsibility, and interdisciplinary dialogue. The goals of the first-year Foundation Studies Program are to develop a student's ability to integrate verbal and visual communication skills and enhance personal expression while preparing for the major areas of study. Course work within the various majors provides students with a solid foundation in craftsmanship and offers both technical and conceptual information. All students are encouraged to expand their interests and technical abilities in other disciplines through elective courses. Complementing work in the studio courses, the Liberal Arts Division offers study in history, criticism, literature, philosophy, religion, and the social and behavioral sciences.

FINANCIAL AID

More than 87 percent of the College student body receive financial aid to meet education costs. Financial aid administered by the College comes from federal, state, and private sources and includes Federal Pell Grants, Federal Stafford Student Loans, Federal Supplemental Educational Opportunity Grants, Federal Perkins Loans, and Minnesota State Scholarships and Grants-in-Aid. College-controlled aid includes a variety of College grants, scholarships, and work-study contracts. Aid from private sources is also available. To qualify, applicants must submit the Free Application for Federal Student Aid (FAFSA).

MISSOURI SOUTHERN STATE COLLEGE

■ JOPLIN, MISSOURI

THE COLLEGE

Missouri Southern State College is a four-year institution that specializes in undergraduate university education with an international perspective. The College focuses on classroom teaching, resulting in a tradition of small classes and close, personal interaction between faculty members and approximately 5,600 students. This approach is maintained through an 18:1 student-teacher ratio. Southern's faculty members come from all over the world, with degrees from prestigious universities and professional experience in the disciplines they teach. Southern stresses the development of independent learners and their ability to conceptualize, solve problems, manipulate thoughts and patterns, and work cooperatively. Those elements, coupled with an international emphasis, enable Southern's graduates to compete successfully in the rapidly changing world. This international emphasis, a distinctive theme of the College's mission, is the focus of the Institute of International Studies, which coordinates all international programs and activities, including a pervasive global dimension in all curricula, study-abroad opportunities for faculty members and students, internships abroad for students, and expanded foreign language offerings.

For more information, students should contact:

Admission Office
Missouri Southern State College
3950 East Newman Road
Joplin, Missouri 64801-1595
Telephone: 417-782-6772
800-606-MSSC (6772) (toll-free)
Fax: 417-659-4429
E-mail: admissions@mail.mssc.edu
World Wide Web:
http://www.mssc.edu

ACADEMIC PROGRAM

Because graduates may change occupations and careers several times during their working lives, all students pursuing a degree complete the core curriculum, a series of courses carefully designed to instill certain lifelong thinking and learning skills. Core courses emphasize critical thinking, problem-solving, and communications skills; a general understanding of scientific and artistic aspects of this culture; and the ability to function in a global society through knowledge and understanding of other cultures. In both the core and major studies, writing skills and computer literacy are developed, and an international perspective is stressed in every possible course. The baccalaureate degree requires 51 credit hours of the core with a total of 124 hours; the Associate of Arts degree requires 64 hours, with 42 hours from the core; and the Associate of Science degree requires 64 hours, with 26 hours from the core curriculum. Several degree programs are designed to provide a seamless path for students wishing to transfer from a two-year institution to Missouri Southern, to transfer from Missouri Southern to another institution to continue undergraduate studies in areas such as engineering or medicine, or to proceed to graduate school in an area such as environmental health.

FINANCIAL AID

A wide variety of financial aid options assist students with college costs. Approximately $14 million is distributed each year to 70 percent of the students, with an average award of approximately $3500. Federal programs include the Federal Pell Grant, Federal Supplemental Educational Opportunity Grant, Federal Work-Study Program, Federal Perkins Loan, and Federal Stafford Loan, among others. Several state programs aid prospective teachers and students with high academic standing. In addition, the College provides a wide range of academic scholarships, performing awards, and student employment. Special scholarships are available for qualified junior college transfer students, and out-of-state tuition waivers are offered to students in a designated surrounding area.

APPLICATION AND INFORMATION

The College has a priority deadline of August 1. Students may apply any time during their senior year of high school. There is a $15 nonrefundable application fee.

MONTREAT COLLEGE

■ MONTREAT, NORTH CAROLINA

THE COLLEGE

For more information, students should call the Financial Aid Office at 800-545-4656 (toll-free).

Office of Admissions
Montreat College
P.O. Box 1267
Montreat, North Carolina 28757
Telephone: 828-669-8012 Ext. 3781
800-622-6968 (toll-free)
Fax: 828-669-0120
E-mail: admissions@montreat.edu
World Wide Web:
http://www.montreat.edu

Montreat is a four-year Christian liberal arts college affiliated with the Presbyterian Church (USA). At Montreat College, a student's experience is enhanced by an education of value, grounded in a strong liberal arts core, taught by an outstanding Christian faculty, and prized by today's employers and graduate schools. Students benefit from Montreat's small classes where their opinions matter, and they grow through one-on-one interaction with professors and classmates. Studies challenge them to integrate faith and learning while considering subjects in ways never thought possible. Hands-on experiences in the majors (internships, field studies, mission programs, community service, and independent research) enable students to gain practical career and life preparation. Montreat College enrollment is rapidly growing. Enrollment is more than 1,000 in the traditional Montreat campus program and in the off-campus School of Professional and Adult Studies. The student body typically represents approximately thirty states and ten other countries. The natural beauty of the Montreat campus both calms the spirit and awakens the senses. In a diverse and multicultural environment, students learn how to investigate the unfamiliar, think critically, and communicate and clarify their ideas. In the process, they develop the skills, personal values, and faith to take their places in the world with confidence.

ACADEMIC PROGRAM

Upon enrollment, students are assigned a faculty adviser to assist them in clarifying their educational objectives and meeting the requirements for graduation. Students and faculty advisers work together in arranging a program of study leading to graduation. Graduation requirements are a minimum of 126 semester hours, cumulative quality point average of at least 2.0, completion of the general education core requirements, 33 semester hours in 300-level or above courses, completion of all major requirements, a grade of C or better in courses needed for the major or minor, and completion of at least 31 semester hours at Montreat College. Students interested in careers in medicine, law, criminology, and other professional areas are reminded that the best preparation, according to graduate school advisers in these areas, is a solid liberal arts degree program such as that found at Montreat College.

FINANCIAL AID

Through generous financial aid and scholarship packages, deserving students receive the quality academics of a private college at a modest cost. Each year, more than 90 percent of Montreat students receive some form of financial aid. Working individually with each student, the College awards financial aid packages that include scholarships, grants, loans, and work-study jobs. Scholarships are also made available to transfer students. All students must submit the Free Application for Federal Student Aid (FAFSA) and the Montreat College Application for Scholarship and Financial Assistance. To drastically reduce processing time, the FAFSA can be electronically submitted by the College to the federal government for students who have applied, been accepted, and submitted a $100 deposit.

MUHLENBERG COLLEGE

■ ALLENTOWN, PENNSYLVANIA

THE COLLEGE

Founded in 1848 and affiliated with the Lutheran Church, Muhlenberg College has the primary purpose of helping students develop those capacities of imaginative and critical thinking that make possible humane and responsible living within a free society. A secondary, but related, purpose is to provide students with excellent undergraduate preparation for socially useful and fulfilling occupations. Muhlenberg students achieve the College's goals by assuming strong individual responsibility for intense involvement in vigorous academic work and for personal involvement within the College community. The more than 100 student organizations provide outlets for the diversified cultural, athletic, religious, social, leadership, and service interests of the students. The campus is primarily residential; more than 90 percent of the 2,050 students live on campus. A close sense of community develops naturally, one in which their diversified academic and personal interests enable students to contribute positively to the intellectual and personal growth of their peers. Students are aided by an active Career Planning and Placement Service in relating academic and personal knowledge and skills to appropriate career goals and in obtaining positions upon graduation. More than one third of a typical graduating class proceeds immediately to graduate or professional school.

For further information, interested students should contact:

Christopher Hooker-Haring
Dean of Admission and Financial Aid
Muhlenberg College
Allentown, Pennsylvania 18104-5586

Telephone: 484-664-3200
E-mail: admissions@muhlenberg.edu
World Wide Web:
http://www.muhlenberg.edu

ACADEMIC PROGRAM

The A.B. and B.S. programs emphasize breadth of study in the liberal arts as well as in-depth study of a particular academic major. All students must fulfill requirements in the humanities, social sciences, natural sciences, and physical education and must demonstrate proficiency in one foreign language. Strong achievement on Advanced Placement examinations may enable a student to receive advanced placement, possibly with credit. Scores of 4 or 5 earn automatic credit. Scores of 3 are evaluated by the appropriate department. Students work closely with academic advisers to formulate programs well suited to their individual interests, abilities, needs, and goals. Generally, students are expected to declare their major at the end of the freshman year; however, many students later change their academic major with no difficulty. A double major is possible, and several fields are available as minor programs. These minor fields are accounting, anthropology, business administration, chemistry, computer science, economics, English, French, German, history, Latin, mathematics, music, philosophy, physics, political science, religion, sociology, Spanish, and women's studies. In addition, independent study and research are available. The College also enriches the freshman-year experience through more than thirty special-focus Freshman Seminars.

FINANCIAL AID

Muhlenberg College endeavors to make its educational opportunities available to all qualified students regardless of their financial circumstances. While most financial aid at Muhlenberg is based on financial need as demonstrated by the College Scholarship Service Financial Aid PROFILE, there is also a limited amount of merit aid available. Typically, about 65 percent of Muhlenberg's students qualify for and receive financial aid.

APPLICATION AND INFORMATION

Students who wish to be considered for admission should submit a completed application form as early as possible during their senior year of secondary school and no later than February 15. Candidates receive notice of admission decisions in late March. Early decision and early admission plans and transfer admission are possible.

NEW YORK UNIVERSITY

■ NEW YORK, NEW YORK

THE UNIVERSITY

New York University (NYU) was founded in 1831 by Albert Gallatin, Secretary of the Treasury under Thomas Jefferson; he believed that the place for a university was not in "the seclusion of cloistered halls but in the throbbing heart of a great city." NYU draws top students from every state and more than 120 countries. The distinguished academic atmosphere attracts the teachers, and the teachers and the atmosphere together attract the students who are capable of benefiting from both. Within three years of graduation, 80 percent of NYU's students go on to postbaccalaureate work. Of those who apply for admission to medical school, 85 percent are accepted, placing NYU well above the national average. The faculty includes world-famous scholars, researchers, and artists, among them Nobel laureates, winners of the Pulitzer Prize, and members of the National Science Foundation. NYU is a member of the prestigious Association of American Universities. A study sponsored by the National Science Foundation placed NYU among the top four universities in the country in the number of "leading intellectuals" on the faculty. Full professors teach on both the graduate and undergraduate levels. Seven undergraduate divisions provide extensive offerings in a wide range of subjects: more than 2,500 courses in 160 major fields are available to NYU's full-time undergraduates. The average class size is under 30, and the faculty-student ratio is 1:13—benefits generally associated with a much smaller institution.

For more information, students should contact:

Office of Undergraduate Admissions
New York University
22 Washington Square North
New York, New York 10011
Telephone: 212-998-4500
World Wide Web:
http://www.nyu.edu/ugadmissions/

ACADEMIC PROGRAM

Requirements for graduation vary among departments and schools. A liberal arts core curriculum is an integral part of all areas of concentration. The baccalaureate degree requires completion of at least 128 credits. The University calendar is organized on the traditional semester system, including two 6-week summer sessions. Some divisions offer part-time programs during the day and evening and on weekends.

FINANCIAL AID

Financial aid at NYU comes from many sources. All students are encouraged to apply for financial assistance or one of NYU's innovative financing plans. Seventy-seven percent of NYU's undergraduates receive financial assistance. Each year more than 1,700 entering freshmen are awarded scholarships based on academic promise and/or financial need. The University may offer a package of aid that includes scholarships or grants, loans, or work-study programs. NYU requires the submission of the Free Application for Federal Student Aid (FAFSA). The deadline for filing this financial aid form is February 15 for the fall semester and November 1 for the spring semester.

APPLICATION AND INFORMATION

For entrance in the fall term, the application for admission—including all supporting credentials—must be received by November 15 (early decision freshman candidates), January 15 (freshmen), or March 1 (transfer students). For entrance in the spring term, the application materials must be received by November 1 for both freshman and transfer candidates. For entrance in the summer, the application materials should be received by April 15 for both freshman and transfer candidates. Applications for admission received after these dates are considered only if space remains. Official notification of fall admission is made on April 1 and on a rolling basis thereafter. A campus tour or an appointment for an information session can be arranged by calling 212-998-4524.

NORTH GEORGIA COLLEGE & STATE UNIVERSITY
The Military College of Georgia

■ DAHLONEGA, GEORGIA

THE COLLEGE

Following the Civil War, abandoned U.S. Mint property was given to the state of Georgia for educational purposes; thus, what is now North Georgia College & State University (NGCSU) was born. Originally named North Georgia Agricultural College, the institution was established in 1873 as a land-grant school of agriculture and mechanical arts, particularly mining engineering. As area gold resources were depleted and agricultural education was assumed by the University of Georgia, the mission of the institution evolved into one emphasizing arts and sciences. The school was renamed North Georgia College in summer 1929 and North Georgia College & State University in fall 1996. NGCSU is a member of the University System of Georgia. North Georgia College & State University's first class of students requested that military training be a part of the curriculum. During the fall semester of 2000, approximately 15 percent of the student body enrolled in NGCSU's nationally prominent ROTC program, which is administered by the U.S. Army. NGCSU is the senior military college of Georgia and is one of only six senior military colleges in the nation. In fact, NGCSU is the only public, coeducational, liberal arts, military school in the country. NGCSU is unique in that it serves as a military college for its Corps of Cadets and as a liberal arts academic institution for all of its students. Among the institution's many distinctions are its firsts for women: NGCSU was the first public college in Georgia to award a degree to a woman, the first to grant athletic scholarships to women, and the first military college in the nation to accept women in the Corps of Cadets. Women have been fully qualified members of the Corps of Cadets since 1973.

For more information, students should contact:

Office of Undergraduate Admission and Recruiting
North Georgia College & State University
Dahlonega, Georgia 30597
Telephone: 706-864-1800
800-498-9581 (toll-free)
Fax: 706-864-1478
E-mail: admissions@ngcsu.edu
World Wide Web:
http://www.ngcsu.edu

ACADEMIC PROGRAM

North Georgia requires all students to complete core curriculum requirements. The core curriculum consists of 9 semester hours of English and mathematics; 4 semester hours of institutional requirements (ethics, speech, philosophy); 6 semester hours of humanities/fine arts; 11 semester hours of science, mathematics, and technology; 12 semester hours of social science; and 18 semester hours related to the major. The minimum requirement for a baccalaureate degree is 120 semester hours, including 12 hours of military science for members of the Corps of Cadets. All students must complete an additional 3 semester hours of physical education. The state of Georgia requires all graduates to meet U.S. and Georgia history and U.S. and Georgia Constitution requirements. These are met upon completion of the core curriculum. All students must also pass the Regents' Test of Reading and Writing before graduating. Participation in the Honors Program is limited to 20 freshmen each year. In addition to completing approximately 20 semester hours of the required honors-only course work, honors students participate in numerous on- and off-campus enrichment programs, such as field trips and faculty mentoring opportunities. Completion of a senior research paper is required of all Honors Program participants.

FINANCIAL AID

Of those students who apply for financial assistance, more than 80 percent receive financial aid. Aid is available through a combination of scholarships, grants, loans, and campus employment. Among the federal funds available are grants, student loans, the Federal Work-Study Program, and ROTC scholarships. Georgia residents who participate in the Corps of Cadets receive $750 per semester, provided they maintain a cumulative average of at least 2.0. Nonresidents who participate in the Corps of Cadets may have their out-of-state tuition waived, provided that they meet specific academic criteria.

NORTHEASTERN UNIVERSITY

▪ BOSTON, MASSACHUSETTS

THE UNIVERSITY

Located at the center of Boston's thriving educational and cultural life, Northeastern University is dedicated to excellence in research and scholarship and is committed to responding to individual and community educational needs. Since its founding in 1898, Northeastern has pioneered a wide range of educational programs and services for students of all ages. The University is an internationally recognized leader in cooperative education—a unique approach to undergraduate education that joins the challenges of traditional classroom instruction on campus with the adventure of learning in a variety of paid professional employment situations in industry, government, or public service organizations. Each year students graduate from Northeastern with a solid sense of themselves and their relationship to the community as well as a valuable head start on their careers.

For more information, students should contact:

Office of Undergraduate Admissions
Northeastern University
360 Huntington Avenue
Boston, Massachusetts 02115

Telephone: 617-373-2200 (voice)
617-373-3100 (TTY)

E-mail:
undergrad-admissions@neu.edu
World Wide Web:
http://www.neu.edu

ACADEMIC PROGRAM

A University-wide honors program gives students opportunities to participate in enriched educational experiences, such as honors equivalents of required academic courses and interdisciplinary colloquia. These experiences are designed to help students expand special interests and develop an understanding of new fields. Honors students are selected on the basis of demonstrated ability and academic promise. The Cooperative Education Program enables students to gain practical experience in the workplace that is integrated with their academic studies. The program is both national and international in scope. Alternate quarters of work and study (after a traditional freshman year) constitute a five-year program leading to a bachelor's degree. A four-year co-op option is available to speech, language pathology and audiology, engineering, business, and computer science students, and a four-year non–co-op schedule is available in the College of Arts and Sciences.

FINANCIAL AID

The University operates a substantial aid program designed to make attendance at Northeastern feasible for all qualified students. By coordinating the resources of the University and various public and private scholarship programs, the Office of Student Financial Services was able to provide more than $100 million to more than 8,630 students last year. Approximately 76 percent of the freshman class received financial assistance from University-based sources, and another 5 percent received aid through the Federal Stafford Student Loan Program. Financial aid is based on need and academic promise and may consist of a grant, a loan, part-time employment, or any combination of these three. To apply, students must file a Free Application for Federal Student Aid (FAFSA) and a PROFILE form with the College Scholarship Service by February 15. Students who are accepted by March 2 have priority in receiving funds.

APPLICATION AND INFORMATION

Under Northeastern's rolling admission plan, candidates may apply and be accepted at the point in their secondary school careers where there is sufficient evidence that they can profit from University study. Applications completed by March 1 will secure a decision in time for the April 15 Candidates Reply Date (applies to fall quarter freshman applicants only). Junior-year and deferred admissions are available, and students who have successfully completed study at other accredited institutions are eligible for advanced standing. Freshmen may enroll in all programs in September and, depending on the availability of courses, in January, April, and June. Transfer students in most programs may apply for entrance at the beginning of each quarter. Personal interviews are recommended but not required. Campus tours and group information sessions are held daily, and open house programs are scheduled throughout the year.

NORTHERN KENTUCKY UNIVERSITY

■ HIGHLAND HEIGHTS, KENTUCKY

THE UNIVERSITY

Northern Kentucky University (NKU) was founded in 1968 and is the newest of Kentucky's eight state universities. The atmosphere of the campus is futuristic, emphasizing a high-quality education by supporting the liberal arts. Twelve major buildings are of modern, contemporary architectural design and are set on 300 acres of rolling countryside. NKU has an enrollment of approximately 12,000 students from thirty states and forty-nine countries and is accredited by the Southern Association of Colleges and Schools. The Salmon P. Chase College of Law is accredited by both the American Bar Association and the Association of American Law Schools. There are more than 100 student organizations. NKU competes in the NCAA Division II Great Lakes Valley Conference. Intercollegiate sports are offered for men and women in basketball, cross-country, soccer, and tennis; for men in baseball and golf; and for women in fast-pitch softball and volleyball. Intramural activities are archery, badminton, basketball, canoeing, flag football, innertube water polo, racquetball, soccer, softball, track and field, volleyball, water basketball, and water volleyball.

For more information, students should contact:

Office of Admissions
Northern Kentucky University
Highland Heights, Kentucky 41099
Telephone: 859-572-5220
800-637-9948 (toll-free)
E-mail: admitnku@nku.edu
World Wide Web:
http://www.nku.edu

ACADEMIC PROGRAM

NKU operates on a semester calendar. To receive a bachelor's degree, students must complete a minimum of 128 credit hours. At least 64 credit hours are required for the associate degree. The University offers a variety of career planning and placement, internship, independent study, work-study, and cooperative education programs. There is also an Advising, Counseling, and Testing Center available. Other programs include an honors program, a program that allows for the dual enrollment of high school students, a program where students can combine their career interests in the liberal arts and engineering fields, and University 101, an orientation program for freshmen. NKU recognizes credit earned through the Advanced Placement Program and the general, subject, and institutional tests of the College-Level Examination Program. A maximum of 45 credit hours may be applied toward the bachelor's degree from the AP and CLEP examinations. The International Baccalaureate Program allows students to earn credit in science, mathematics, psychology, and languages.

FINANCIAL AID

Last year, 51 percent of undergraduates received some form of financial assistance. To receive financial aid, applicants must complete the Free Application for Federal Student Aid (FAFSA). Academic, athletic, music-drama, and art scholarships and scholarships for members of minority groups are available at Northern Kentucky University. The application deadline for all academic scholarships is February 1. There is no deadline for the University's financial aid application; however, students who wish to receive institutional aid must apply by April 1 for priority consideration. Applicants are notified of acceptance on a rolling basis.

APPLICATION AND INFORMATION

There is a $25 fee that may be waived for applicants with demonstrated need. The fall semester early action and scholarship deadline is February 1; the priority application deadline is May 1. The priority application deadline for the nursing program is January 31. The deadline for the radiologic technology program is February 15. The priority application deadline for the respiratory care program is April 15.

NORTHWOOD UNIVERSITY

■ MIDLAND, MICHIGAN; CEDAR HILL, TEXAS; AND WEST PALM BEACH, FLORIDA

THE UNIVERSITY

Northwood University was founded in 1959 by Dr. Arthur E. Turner and Dr. R. Gary Stauffer, who had decided that the liberal arts approach to business did not really expose students to the wealth of opportunities the world of work had to offer. Established originally in Alma, Michigan, the school moved to Midland in 1961. The Texas campus was opened in 1966. Other expansions include the Florida campus in West Palm Beach and the Northwood University Margaret Chase Smith Library Center in Skowhegan, Maine. Northwood University also coordinates a nontraditional program, University College, headquartered at the Midland, Michigan, campus; extension centers are located on all three campuses and in Carlsbad, New Mexico; Chicago, Illinois; Fort Worth, Texas; Detroit, Flint, and Lansing, Michigan; Tampa, Florida; Indianapolis, Indiana; Louisville, Kentucky; New Orleans, Louisiana; and Selfridge ANG Base, Michigan. University College is dedicated to providing nontraditional options for earning management degrees for students who are balancing work schedules, family responsibilities, community involvement, and educational goals.

For more information, students should contact:

Director of Admissions
Northwood University
4000 Whiting Drive
Midland, Michigan 48640
Telephone: 517-837-4273
800-457-7878 (toll-free)
World Wide Web:
http://www.northwood.edu
Director of Admissions
Northwood University, Florida Campus
2600 North Military Trail
West Palm Beach, Florida 33409
Telephone: 561-478-5500
800-458-8325 (toll-free)
Director of Admissions
Northwood University, Texas Campus
1114 West FM 1382
P.O. Box 58
Cedar Hill, Texas 75104
Telephone: 214-291-1541
800-927-9663 (toll-free)
Director of Admissions
University College
3225 Cook Road
Midland, Michigan 48640
Telephone: 517-837-4411
800-445-5873 (toll-free)

ACADEMIC PROGRAM

Northwood University's programs have been designed to prepare men and women for specific career goals. The courses for the major (approximately 30 percent of the total requirements) are reinforced by classes in general business (30 percent) and the humanities (40 percent). Associate degree candidates are required to complete 90 term hours with a minimum GPA of 2.0. Bachelor's degree candidates must complete 180 term hours with a minimum GPA of 2.0. Northwood's terms last ten weeks. The fall term runs from September through November, the winter term from December through February, and the spring term from March through May. In addition, the college offers three 3-week summer sessions. Northwood believes strongly in the free enterprise system and, accordingly, has designed its curriculum to reflect this belief. All students must satisfactorily complete core courses in accounting, business law, economics, management, and marketing. No matter what the ultimate career goal of a student may be, he or she will have acquired a set of basic skills as preparation for the productive world of work. This academic program, however, does not prohibit students from appreciating the arts. Northwood strongly promotes the interrelationship between the business and art worlds by providing on- and off-campus voluntary programs.

FINANCIAL AID

Students should file the Free Application for Federal Student Aid (FAFSA). Available aid includes Federal Pell Grants, Federal Supplemental Educational Opportunity Grants, state and institutional grants and scholarships, Federal Stafford Student Loans, loans for parents, and Federal Work-Study awards. Approximately 70 percent of students receive some type of financial aid.

NORWICH UNIVERSITY

■ NORTHFIELD, VERMONT

THE UNIVERSITY

Norwich University is unique among institutions of higher education. No other university combines a military tradition of nearly two centuries, a broad range of traditional undergraduate degree programs, and five of the more innovative low-residency and nonresidency programs in higher education. Students on the Northfield campus may enroll in the Corps of Cadets and follow a disciplined military regime or join civilian students who lead a more traditional collegiate lifestyle. Both groups are coeducational and attend classes and participate in sports and other activities together. There are approximately 1,600 students enrolled on the Northfield campus. Norwich students have come from forty-eight states and twenty-nine countries. The University's minority enrollment is consistently the largest representation by percentage of any Vermont college or university.

For more information, students should contact:

Dean of Enrollment Management
Norwich University
158 Harmon Drive
Northfield, Vermont 05663
Telephone: 800-468-NORWICH (6679) (toll-free)
E-mail: nuadm@norwich.edu
World Wide Web: http://www.norwich.edu

ACADEMIC PROGRAM

To qualify for the baccalaureate degree, students must have a final cumulative quality point average of at least 2.0. Teacher licensure candidates reserve the eighth semester for sixteen weeks of student teaching. Individual departmental requirements are outlined in the Norwich catalog. Approximately 25 percent of entering freshmen have undeclared majors. For military cadets, eight semesters of Army, Air Force, or Naval ROTC are required. Prior to the start of the junior year, a cadet may elect to contract with his or her ROTC program of study for consideration for a commission upon graduation as a second lieutenant in the Army, Air Force, or Marine Corps or as an ensign in the Navy. A cadet not wishing to contract for a commission has no military obligation upon completion of the required four years of ROTC courses. Norwich students entering their junior year may enroll in the nation's first college-based Peace Corps Preparatory Program. Participants in the program take specialized courses designed to prepare them for assignments in Third World countries, perform voluntary community service during the school year, and spend six weeks in a foreign country, during the summer between their junior and senior years, with an established service agency. The curriculum is an acceptable alternative to the Military College requirement for junior and senior year ROTC participation for those students not seeking an officer's commission.

FINANCIAL AID

All applicants for financial aid must submit both the CSS PROFILE form and the Free Application for Federal Student Aid (FAFSA). Financial awards are made on the basis of need, but academic and extracurricular activities are taken into consideration. Most awards consist of an aid package of University scholarships, work-study programs, federal grants, and student loans. Winners of three- and four-year Army, Air Force, and Naval ROTC scholarships are strongly encouraged to consider the Norwich program. ROTC scholarship winners attending Norwich University receive full scholarships for room and board as long as they maintain scholarship status each year. ROTC students receive an annual uniform allowance, and students who are working toward a commission through advanced ROTC receive a monthly subsistence allowance during the school year. Eligible students may also apply for three- and two-year Air Force, Army, and Naval ROTC scholarships while attending Norwich. For further ROTC scholarship information, students should write to the Admissions Office.

APPLICATION AND INFORMATION

There is no deadline for applications. The University uses a rolling admission system; an admission decision is announced as soon as all of an applicant's materials have been received, processed, and reviewed.

PRATT INSTITUTE

■ BROOKLYN, NEW YORK

THE INSTITUTE

Founded in 1887 on its present site in Brooklyn by industrialist and philanthropist Charles Pratt, the Institute educated on nonbaccalaureate levels for its first half-century. As the educational preparation necessary for various professions expanded, Pratt Institute moved with the times. It granted its first baccalaureate degree in 1938 and started its first graduate program in 1950. Pratt continues to add programs at all educational levels, including undergraduate and graduate programs in art history and graduate programs in art education and design management. Although the characteristics and educational requirements of the professions for which Pratt prepares people have changed over the course of a century, the Institute has succeeded in pursuing its abiding purpose—to blend theoretical learning with professional and humanistic development. In educating more than four generations of students to be creative, technically skilled, and adaptable professionals as well as responsible citizens, Pratt has gained a national and international reputation that attracts undergraduate and graduate students from more than forty-six states, the District of Columbia, Puerto Rico, the Virgin Islands, and seventy countries.

For more information about Pratt Institute, students should contact:

Office of Admissions
Pratt Institute
200 Willoughby Avenue
Brooklyn, New York 11205
Telephone: 718-636-3669
800-331-0834 (toll-free)
E-mail: admissions@pratt.edu
World Wide Web:
http://www.pratt.edu

ACADEMIC PROGRAM

Educating professionals for productive careers in artistic and technical fields has been the mission of Pratt Institute since it assembled its first group of students in 1887. Within the structure of that professional education, Pratt students are encouraged to acquire the diverse knowledge that is necessary for them to succeed in their chosen fields. In addition to the professional studies, the curriculum in each of Pratt's schools includes a broad range of liberal arts courses. Students from all schools take these courses together and have the opportunity to examine the interrelationships of art, science, technology, and human need. At the time of graduation, students in the associate degree programs have completed 66 credit hours of course work. In the bachelor's programs, credit-hour requirements range from 132 to 135 credits, depending on the particular program. For the Bachelor of Architecture degree, 175 credits are required. With an additional 27 or 49 credits of study, students in the School of Architecture can choose a combined B.Arch./M.S. in urban design or a combined B.Arch./M.S. in city and regional planning degree program. Pratt's academic calendar consists of two semesters plus a winter term that allows students to choose alternative courses or various options usually not offered during the fall or spring semester. A number of summer sessions are offered.

FINANCIAL AID

Pratt Institute offers a large number of grants, scholarships, loans, and awards on the basis of academic achievement, financial need, or both. More than 75 percent of Pratt students receive aid in one or more of these forms. Through funds from the federal and state governments, contributions from Pratt alumni, and industry scholarships, Pratt is able to maintain an effective aid program in a time of escalating costs. Pratt attempts to ensure that no student is prevented by lack of funds from completing his or her education.

APPLICATION AND INFORMATION

Pratt has two admissions deadlines: January 1 and February 1. To receive full consideration, students must submit applications by February 1 for anticipated entrance in the fall semester and by October 15 for anticipated entrance in the spring semester. All applicants must submit transcripts from high schools and any college attended and letters of recommendation. Additional professional requirements are requested by each department.

RENSSELAER POLYTECHNIC INSTITUTE

■ TROY, NEW YORK

THE INSTITUTE

The oldest technological university in the English-speaking world, Rensselaer Polytechnic Institute was founded in 1824 "for the purpose of instructing persons in the application of science to the common purposes of life." Still pursuing that original mission, Rensselaer has become one of the world's premier research universities. More than 100 programs and 1,000 courses lead to bachelor's, master's, and doctoral degrees. Undergraduates pursue their studies in the Schools of Architecture, Engineering, Humanities and Social Sciences, Management and Technology, and Science and in the interdisciplinary program in information technology (IT). Rensselaer's long tradition of cross-disciplinary, real-world, industry-oriented research and education is clearly reflected in cross-school programs, such as product design and innovation, and unusual degree offerings, such as bioinformatics and molecular biology; electronic media, arts, and communication; and information technology. Rensselaer's unique B.S. degree program in information technology requires students to choose an area in which they wish to apply IT from more than thirty second disciplines that are taught by experts from across the University. Rensselaer's more than twenty interdisciplinary research and academic centers have achieved international recognition in such fields as microelectronics, simulation-based engineering, advanced computing, student leadership, multimedia arts, and composite materials. Strong and deep ties to a broad range of firms, from large multinational corporations to fast-growing entrepreneurial ventures, help ensure the relevance of educational and research initiatives and offer rich co-op, internship, and employment opportunities for students.

For more information, students should contact:

Admissions Office, Undergraduate Programs
Rensselaer Polytechnic Institute
Troy, New York 12180
Telephone: 518-276-6216
Fax: 518-276-4072
E-mail: admissions@rpi.edu
World Wide Web: http://admissions.rpi.edu

ACADEMIC PROGRAM

Rensselaer leads the nation in educational reform with its award-winning, studio-based interactive approach to teaching. Although there are still lectures, more and more classes involve lively discussion, team problem solving, and faculty mentoring as opposed to instructing. In the past two years, faculty members have also renewed the curriculum, replacing the traditional five or six 3-credit-course model with a "4x4" curriculum of four 4-credit-hour courses. All incoming students are required to have a laptop computer that meets Rensselaer's specifications. While each school has its own sequence requirements, the following minimums apply to all students: 124 credit hours and a 1.8 quality point average in total courses; 24 credit hours in physical, life, and engineering sciences; 24 in humanities and social sciences; 30 in a selected discipline; and 24 in electives. Students are strongly encouraged to learn outside of the classroom with independent projects, faculty research, study abroad, and cooperative education. The Undergraduate Research Program offers hands-on experience to students in hundreds of areas. Any full-time undergraduate can participate for credit or pay during the academic year or the summer. Co-op assignments give students the opportunity to add practical experience to their academic study. The study-work schedule is such that students graduate in the class with which they matriculated. Air Force, Army, and Naval/Marine ROTC programs are available on an elective basis.

FINANCIAL AID

Nearly all freshmen who have financial need are offered assistance under a comprehensive program of scholarships, loans, and part-time employment that provides annual assistance ranging from $100 up to full tuition, room, and board. Available federal funds include student loans, Federal Work-Study Program awards, and ROTC scholarships.

THE RICHARD STOCKTON COLLEGE OF NEW JERSEY

■ POMONA, NEW JERSEY

THE COLLEGE

The Richard Stockton College of New Jersey is an undergraduate college of arts, sciences, and professional studies within the New Jersey System of Higher Education. Named for Richard Stockton, one of the New Jersey signers of the Declaration of Independence, the College was authorized by the passage of the state's 1968 bond referendum for higher education and accepted its charter class in 1971. More than 6,000 students are enrolled at the College, which provides distinctive traditional and alternative approaches to education. Stockton seeks to develop the analytic and creative capabilities of its students by encouraging them to undertake individually planned courses of study that promote self-reliance and an acceptance of and responsiveness to change. On-campus housing for more than 2,000 students is available in the Housing I garden apartments, the Housing II and III residence halls, and the Housing IV complex, which opened in fall 1999. All types of units are fully furnished and air conditioned and are within easy walking distance of the College's main academic complex.

For more information, students should contact:

Dean of Enrollment Management
The Richard Stockton College of New Jersey
P.O. Box 195
Pomona, New Jersey 08240-0195
Telephone: 609-652-4261
Fax: 609-748-5541
E-mail: admissions@stockton.edu
World Wide Web: http://www.stockton.edu

ACADEMIC PROGRAM

To earn a baccalaureate degree at Stockton, a student must satisfactorily complete a minimum of 128 semester credits. Degree programs include a combination of general studies and program (major field) studies. The Bachelor of Arts student must earn a total of 64 credits in general studies; the Bachelor of Science student must earn 48. General studies courses are broad cross-disciplinary courses designed to introduce students to all major areas of the curriculum and to the broadly applicable intellectual skills necessary for success in college. Students must select some courses from each major curricular area. The only specifically required courses within general studies are the basic studies courses (up to three), from which students may be exempted on the basis of diagnostic testing. The Bachelor of Arts student must earn a total of 64 credits in program studies; the Bachelor of Science student must earn 80. Program studies (major field) requirements are carefully structured and emphasize sequences of specific courses. Students at Stockton have special opportunities to influence what and how they learn by participating in the major decisions that shape their academic lives. The main avenue of participation is the preceptorial system, which enables students to work, on a personalized basis, with an assigned faculty-staff preceptor in the planning and evaluation of individualized courses of study and in the exploration of various career alternatives. Stockton's academic programs emphasize curricular organization and methods of instruction that promote independent learning and research, cross-disciplinary study, problem solving, and decision making through analysis and synthesis.

FINANCIAL AID

Financial aid is available in the form of scholarships, grants, loans, and jobs. Aid is awarded both on a competitive (merit) basis and according to need. Students seeking financial aid should file the Free Application for Federal Student Aid (FAFSA) by March 1. This form is used by the College in evaluating all applications for financial aid.

RIDER UNIVERSITY

■ LAWRENCEVILLE, NEW JERSEY

THE UNIVERSITY

Founded in 1865, Rider University is an independent, coeducational, nonsectarian institution accredited by the Middle States Association of Colleges and Schools. Rider has two campuses, one in Lawrenceville, New Jersey, and one in Princeton, New Jersey. Rider's four academic units include the College of Business Administration; the College of Liberal Arts, Education, and Sciences; the College of Continuing Studies; and Westminster Choir College, located in Princeton, New Jersey. More than 95 percent of Rider's full-time faculty members hold a doctorate or other appropriate advanced degree. Primarily a teaching institution, Rider University selects instructors who are committed to imparting the knowledge and skills of a particular discipline. Full professors teach at all levels. There are no teaching assistants in the classrooms or laboratories. Rider University is located on a 353-acre campus that contains large open areas and thirty-eight modern buildings constructed within the past thirty years. Approximately 70 percent of the 3,000 undergraduates live in University residence halls or in fraternities or sororities on the campus. Entering students and returning students are guaranteed housing on the campus provided that they meet the stated deadlines for submission of housing applications and deposits.

For more information, students should contact:

Director of Admissions
Rider University
2083 Lawrenceville Road
Lawrenceville, New Jersey 08648-3099
Telephone: 609-896-5042
800-257-9026 (toll-free)
E-mail: admissions@rider.edu
World Wide Web:
http://www.rider.edu

ACADEMIC PROGRAM

Rider University operates on the semester system. Each College requires a minimum of 120 semester hours of credit for graduation; the last 30 semester hours of credit must be earned at Rider University. The College of Business Administration requires that a student earn at least 45 semester hours, including the last 30, at Rider University. The Baccalaureate Honors Program is available to students in all programs. To be considered for the program, incoming freshmen must be in the top 10 percent of their high school class and have a combined SAT I score of 1150 or higher. Students currently enrolled in the University and transfer students must have at least a 3.25 cumulative grade point average. All applicants are interviewed by the Baccalaureate Honors Program Committee.

FINANCIAL AID

Most financial aid is based upon demonstrated financial need. Students and their parents are required to file the Free Application for Federal Student Aid (FAFSA) prior to March 1 to be considered for financial assistance administered by Rider University. The University maintains a need-blind admission policy and attempts to meet the full financial need of all eligible applicants. Entering students are eligible for consideration for various forms of institutional aid. Rider University offers six merit-based scholarship programs for qualified applicants. These scholarships, the Presidential, Diversity, Provost, Dean's, Founders, and Transfer scholarships, are for up to $15,000 and are renewable for up to four years of study if the student maintains the minimum grade point average specified by the Scholarship Committee. Rider also offers two full-tuition actors scholarships.

APPLICATION AND INFORMATION

Rider University works on a rolling admissions basis, but it encourages applications for the fall semester to be submitted by February 15 if the student wishes to obtain housing on the campus. Applications for the spring semester should be submitted by December 15. An early action option is available. Students must submit all necessary documentation by November 15 and are notified of an admissions decision by December 15. The application fee of $40 should be included with the application. Students are notified of the admission decision in approximately 3 to 4 weeks, in accordance with the rolling admission policy. Transfer applicants receive the same priority for admission, housing, and financial aid as freshman applicants.

RIPON COLLEGE

■ RIPON, WISCONSIN

THE COLLEGE

One key reason why students choose Ripon College from among the more than 3,500 colleges and universities in the country is that Ripon offers an intensely personal undergraduate education. Since 1851, Ripon has provided a personal liberal arts education that makes a remarkable difference in the lives of students. *U.S. News & World Report* recently ranked Ripon in a fifth-place tie among those national liberal arts colleges that offer "high quality education at a reasonable cost." Companies look for college graduates who can adapt to change and who can write, use modern technology with confidence, communicate, and make a contribution to a team. These are the skills that a Ripon education offers students. Ripon's curricular emphasis focuses on Communicating Plus. This program aims to assist students in the development of superior written and oral communication, critical-thinking, and problem-solving skills. Ripon is a residential college; 90 percent of students live on campus, and because students remain on campus after classes have ended, learning occurs around the clock. All students are encouraged to participate in Ripon's numerous extracurricular activities, including the campus radio station and the Student Senate. Ripon College is fully accredited by the North Central Association of Colleges and Schools.

For further information, students should contact:

Dean of Admission
Ripon College
300 Seward Street
P.O. Box 248
Ripon, Wisconsin 54971-0248

Telephone: 800-94-RIPON (toll-free)
E-mail: adminfo@ripon.edu
World Wide Web:
http://www.ripon.edu

ACADEMIC PROGRAM

Since its founding, Ripon has been a liberal arts college. Students have the opportunity to study all fields of human knowledge, including the social sciences, the natural sciences, the humanities, and the fine arts. While other colleges have become increasingly specialized, Ripon has remained steadfast in its belief that the liberal arts are the key for a life of both personal and professional success. Ripon operates on a schedule of two 15-week semesters and an optional 3-week "Maymester."

FINANCIAL AID

Ninety percent of Ripon students receive financial assistance that meets 100 percent of their financial need. The average financial aid award equals 78 percent of a student's total costs. Ripon's extensive scholarship program is designed to recognize and reward applicants for their talents and abilities. Currently, seventeen types of scholarships that range from $1000 to full tuition annually are available.

APPLICATION AND INFORMATION

Prospective students who value a challenging liberal arts and sciences education in a small, caring community are invited to visit the campus, sit in on Ripon classes, and see firsthand how Ripon students and professors interact with one another. Students who wish to apply to Ripon College should submit a completed application form, a secondary school transcript, results of standardized tests, and the $30 application fee. Ripon College application forms are available from the admission office and at the College's Web site (address below). Ripon participates in the Common Application Plan and accepts photocopies of the Common Application in place of the Ripon College application form. Common Application forms are available in many secondary school guidance offices. Ripon also accepts applications that are made through the Wisconsin Mentor site (http://www.wisconsinmentor.org/admissionapp). Candidates for fall term consideration are encouraged to apply early. Notification of fall term admission occurs within two weeks of the completion of the student's application. Students applying for spring term consideration should submit applications by December 15. Notification occurs shortly thereafter.

SAVANNAH COLLEGE OF ART AND DESIGN

■ SAVANNAH, GEORGIA

THE COLLEGE

The Savannah College of Art and Design (SCAD) is a private coeducational college, preparing students for careers in the visual and performing arts, building arts, design, and the history of art and architecture. The College emphasizes individual attention in a positively oriented environment and is open to both resident and nonresident students. The College offers intellectual diversity that enriches, a learning experience that challenges, and an environment that is creatively centered. A balanced fine arts and liberal arts curriculum has attracted students from every state and from more than seventy-five countries, making SCAD one the largest art and design colleges in the United States; current enrollment is approximately 5,000 students.

For more information, students should contact:

Admission Department
Savannah College of Art and Design
P.O. Box 2072
Savannah, Georgia 31402-2072
Telephone: 912-525-5100
800-869-7223 (toll-free)
Fax: 912-525-5986
E-mail: admission@scad.edu
World Wide Web:
http://www.scad.edu

ACADEMIC PROGRAM

The College operates on the quarter system. Fall, winter, and spring sessions extend from mid-September through May. Summer sessions in Savannah run from mid-June through mid-September and include short sessions in New York and abroad through the off-campus programs. Students may earn credits during all sessions. The uniquely balanced curriculum prepares students for careers and offers a well-rounded liberal arts education, the traditional components of a fine arts education, the opportunity to acquire contemporary high-tech skills through the use of state-of-the-art facilities, and the option of pursuing double majors and multidisciplinary explorations. The total course of study for a B.F.A. degree consists of 180 quarter credit hours (thirty-six courses). Of these, a student takes 35–50 hours in the foundation studies program, 55–65 hours in the liberal arts program (with a concentration on art history classes), 60–70 hours in the major area of study, and 10–20 hours of electives. The five-year B.F.A./M.Arch. degree requires 225 hours, which include 35 foundation hours, 60 hours of liberal arts study, 95 hours in the major program, and 35 hours of electives. Independent study programs are also available to students wishing to pursue a highly specialized area of study. To enhance the academic programs, the College offers seminars, lectures, and workshops by distinguished artists, scholars, and other professionalsduring the academic year at no charge.

FINANCIAL AID

Approximately 54 percent of undergraduates and 45 percent of freshmen receive financial assistance. The Savannah College of Art and Design has a number of financial aid programs, which may consist of scholarships, grants, loans, or any combination of these, from federal (including the Federal Direct Loan Program), state, and College sources. Application may be made at any time during the academic year; however, early application is advised. Students may also help finance educational expenses by jobs secured through the Federal Work-Study Program and the College's Student Placement Service. Many employment opportunities exist in the Savannah area, and the College refers interested students to appropriate part-time or freelance jobs when they are available. A detailed listing of the financial aid programs may be obtained from the financial aid office. Scholarships for incoming students are awarded through the Admission Department.

APPLICATION AND INFORMATION

Applicants are encouraged to apply as early as possible. The nonrefundable application fee is $50. Admission decisions are made on a rolling basis.

SETON HILL COLLEGE

■ GREENSBURG, PENNSYLVANIA

THE COLLEGE

In 1918, the Sisters of Charity founded Seton Hill College to help women open new doors through the power of education. Since that time, Seton Hill has been recognized as a leader in liberal arts education. Today, Seton Hill College is ranked by *U.S. News & World Report* as a top institution for its academic reputation among northern liberal arts colleges. Seton Hill College, a liberal arts and sciences, coeducational institution, is situated in the Laurel Highlands, an area of southwestern Pennsylvania known for its beautiful scenery and wealth of outdoor activities such as skiing, cycling, hiking, and white-water rafting. Recreational opportunities include on-campus lectures, theater productions, a fitness center, and aerobics classes, as well as College-sponsored trips to Pittsburgh for cultural and sports events. Seton Hill has varsity teams in basketball, cross-country, equestrian competition, golf, soccer, softball, tennis, and volleyball, plus a variety of intramural teams. At the graduate level, Seton Hill grants the Master of Arts degree in art therapy, counseling psychology, elementary education, special education, and writing popular fiction, a Master of Science in management, and a Master of Education in technologies-enhanced learning.

For more information, students should contact:

Kathleen H. Berard
Director of Admissions
Seton Hill College
Seton Hill Drive
Greensburg, Pennsylvania 15601-1599
Telephone: 724-838-4255
800-826-6234 (toll-free)
Fax: 724-830-1294
E-mail: admit@setonhill.edu
World Wide Web:
http://www.setonhill.edu

ACADEMIC PROGRAM

Seton Hill offers five divisions, with the opportunity to self-design a major, all enhanced by the College's award-winning core curriculum. Special programs are available for students who are undecided about their major. The Seton Hill College Honors Program is available for students who have distinguished themselves academically in high school. Prior to graduation all students complete a portfolio, a four-year compilation of their academic, professional, and personal achievements at Seton Hill. Portfolios allow students to showcase their learning and assist them in documenting their accomplishments as they transition from students to practicing professionals. Students hoping to one day own a business may be interested in Seton Hill College's National Education Center for Women in Business. The center is the first organization of its kind in the United States to offer courses in business ownership and entrepreneurial activities to students in any major.

FINANCIAL AID

Seton Hill College's Financial Aid Office works with each student to develop an aid package from the wide variety of scholarships, grants, loans, and work-study programs available. Seton Hill offers Presidential Scholarships valued annually from $4106 to $8212, which are automatically awarded to students who rank in the top 10 percent, 20 percent, or 30 percent of their high school class and meet the admission criteria. In addition, valedictorian, leadership, community service, art, music, theater, biology, chemistry, math, and athletic scholarships are awarded based on merit.

APPLICATION AND INFORMATION

Seton Hill College has a rolling admissions policy. Decisions of the Admissions Committee are rendered shortly after all application materials have been submitted. The first-time freshman applicant should submit a completed application form, a $30 nonrefundable application fee, an official secondary school transcript that includes the applicant's rank and cumulative grade point average, and official score reports from either the SAT or ACT. Prospective students who do not have SAT or ACT scores may submit two graded written assignments from their junior or senior year for consideration.

SHENANDOAH UNIVERSITY

■ WINCHESTER, VIRGINIA

THE UNIVERSITY

Shenandoah University was founded at Dayton, Virginia, in 1875. Although the institution was established to provide "classical" and music studies, by 1888 an unusual blend of educational opportunities had been formulated that included arts, sciences, music, medical arts, and business management. These programs, on a much more sophisticated basis, are found at Shenandoah today. In 1960, Shenandoah moved to a 62-acre campus in Winchester, Virginia. The main campus is now more than 100 acres with nineteen buildings, including six residence halls. Of these six facilities for boarding students, one is for women and five are coeducational. There are five additional buildings at off-campus locations. Shenandoah's historical relationship with the United Methodist Church does not place sectarian obligations on any student. Shenandoah's students have the distinct advantage of being on a small campus near large metropolitan cultural centers. Such student organizations as academic fraternities, service and honor organizations, and various departmental clubs provide opportunities for leadership and recreation. Students come to Shenandoah because they want an educational experience of superior quality and believe that the facilities of a small campus, with a personal atmosphere, are the most conducive to achieving this experience.

For more information, students should contact:

Director of Admissions
Shenandoah University
1460 University Drive
Winchester, Virginia 22601
Telephone: 540-665-4581
800-432-2266 (toll-free)
Fax: 540-665-4627
E-mail: admit@su.edu

ACADEMIC PROGRAM

Shenandoah's academic calendar is divided into fall and spring semesters. Summer terms, ranging in length from two to eleven weeks, are also available. Each academic division (arts and sciences, business, conservatory, and health professions) offers diversified programs, with specific courses required by the various accreditation agencies. Credit is available through the tests of the College-Level Examination Program (CLEP), Proficiency Examination Program (PEP), and Advanced Placement (AP) Program and through various departmental challenge examinations.

FINANCIAL AID

Shenandoah makes every effort to assist students in finding resources to finance their education. Approximately 91 percent of the University's students receive some type of financial aid. Shenandoah annually awards more than $18 million in aid to students in the form of grants, loans, scholarships, and employment on the campus. Previous financial aid packages have averaged approximately $13,000 per undergraduate student per year. To qualify for scholarships and financial aid, students must submit the Free Application for Federal Student Aid (FAFSA). Aid is awarded on a first-come, first-served basis, as funds are available. A student must be accepted for admission to a degree program before a financial aid offer is made. Specific information regarding financial aid should be requested from the Director of Financial Aid.

APPLICATION AND INFORMATION

To apply, a student must submit an application with a $30 nonrefundable application fee, SAT I or ACT scores, and an official high school transcript. Transfer students must submit an official college transcript for all postsecondary course work in addition to meeting the freshman score and transcript requirements. Applicants are notified of the admission decision after receipt of all credentials.

SIMPSON COLLEGE

■ INDIANOLA, IOWA

THE COLLEGE

Simpson College was founded in 1860. The institution was named Simpson College to honor Bishop Matthew Simpson (1811–1884), one of the best-known and most influential religious leaders of his day. The College is coeducational; although it is affiliated with the United Methodist Church, it is nonsectarian in spirit and accepts students without regard to race, color, creed, national origin, religion, sex, age, or disability. For more than a century, Simpson has played a vital role in the educational, cultural, intellectual, political, and religious life of the nation. The College has thirty-two buildings on 73 acres of beautiful campus and enrolls 1,900 students. Extracurricular activities at Simpson are designed to supplement and reinforce the academic program and contribute toward a total learning experience. Students may participate in student government, publications, music, theater, and social groups. Simpson competes in eighteen intercollegiate sports and has an extensive intramural program for both men and women. Men's and women's athletics at Simpson are governed by the NCAA. Simpson also has chapters of three national fraternities, one local fraternity, and four national sororities.

For additional information or to obtain application materials, students should contact:

Office of Admissions
Simpson College
701 North "C" Street
Indianola, Iowa 50125
Telephone: 515-961-1624
800-362-2454 (toll-free)
E-mail: admiss@simpson.edu
World Wide Web:
http://www.simpson.edu

ACADEMIC PROGRAM

Simpson operates on a 4-4-1 academic calendar. The first semester starts in late August and ends in mid-December; the second semester starts in mid-January and ends in late April. A three-week session takes place during the month of May. During this period, students have the opportunity to take one class that focuses on a single subject, to study abroad, or to participate in a field experience or internship. New students are assigned faculty advisers who aid them in constructing academically sound majors. Students must participate in one May Term class or program for each year of full-time study or its equivalent at Simpson College. All students must complete the requirements of the Cornerstone Studies in liberal arts and competencies in foreign language, math, and writing. To earn the Bachelor of Arts degree, students may take no more than 42 hours in the major department, excluding May Term programs, and 84 hours in the division of the major, including May Term programs. Also, at least 128 semester hours of course work must be accumulated with a grade point average of C (2.0) or better. For a Bachelor of Music degree, the same requirements apply, except that 84 hours must be earned in the major, excluding May Terms, and the candidate is limited to 12 additional hours in the division of fine arts. Also, at least 132 hours of course work must be completed with a cumulative grade point average of C (2.0) or better.

FINANCIAL AID

Simpson College seeks to make it financially possible for qualified students to experience the advantages of a college education. Generous gifts from alumni, trustees, and friends of the College, in addition to state and federal programs of student aid, make this opportunity possible. Simpson offers financial aid on both a need and non-need basis. Need is determined by filing the Free Application for Federal Student Aid. Financial aid granted on a non-need basis includes academic scholarships, which are awarded on the basis of prior academic records, and talent scholarships, which are available in theater, music, and art. The talent scholarships are determined by audition/portfolio.

APPLICATION AND INFORMATION

Simpson's rolling admission policy allows flexibility; however, early application is recommended. Transfer and foreign students are welcome. Students are strongly encouraged to visit the campus.

SOUTHERN CONNECTICUT STATE UNIVERSITY

■ NEW HAVEN, CONNECTICUT

THE UNIVERSITY

Founded in 1893, Southern Connecticut State University is located on a 168-acre campus in New Haven, a city renowned for its academic and cultural advantages. During its long history, Southern has grown in diversity and excellence. Today, Southern offers bachelor's and master's degrees and sixth-year diplomas in more than 150 areas of study, providing its students with a challenging variety of academic, professional, and personal opportunities. Southern is part of the Connecticut State University System.

For more information, students should contact:

Sharon Brennan
Director of Admissions and Enrollment Management
Admissions House
Southern Connecticut State University
131 Farnham Avenue
New Haven, Connecticut 06515-1355
Telephone: 203-392-SCSU
888-500-SCSU (toll-free)
World Wide Web:
http://www.Southernct.edu

ACADEMIC PROGRAM

The University operates on a two-semester calendar. The fall semester usually begins the first week in September and ends before Christmas. The spring semester, which includes a one-week spring recess in March, runs from the third week of January to the middle of May. Southern also offers two 5-week sessions during the summer and a three-week intersession program each January. Throughout its history, Southern has held fast to the conviction that the best education stresses the liberal arts and sciences. To ensure all students a chance to acquire such an education, Southern has designed a strong yet flexible program that underscores the basics while encouraging individual choice and self-expression. All baccalaureate degree candidates are required to complete a minimum of 122 hours of credit. Majors consist of at least 30 prescribed hours of credit in one specific, approved field. Degree candidates must also fulfill the All-University Requirements, a common core of courses ranging from 41 to 54 credits in liberal studies. In addition, candidates for the B.A. degree must meet a foreign language requirement and select 28 credits of electives from areas of interest. Candidates for the B.S. degree must also satisfy the foreign language requirement and meet certain distribution requirements. Some of the professional B.S. degree programs enable students to develop a minor or a concentration in addition to the major. Students in these programs are allowed a minimum of 12 credits in electives.

FINANCIAL AID

The Financial Aid Office coordinates a number of programs. These programs, which include grants and scholarships, long-term low-interest loans, and part-time student employment, are based on the demonstrated financial need of students and their families. The University offers the Federal Perkins Loan, the Federal Pell Grant, the Federal Supplemental Educational Opportunity Grant, the Federal Stafford Student Loan, the Federal PLUS loan, and the Federal Work-Study Program. Southern also provides assistance through alumni scholarships. More than 40 percent of Southern's undergraduates receive some form of financial aid. Students interested in applying for assistance must complete the Free Application for Federal Student Aid (FAFSA) and send it to the central processor so that it is received by April 16. The Financial Aid Office also requires students to submit additional forms, including a University financial aid application. All required forms have deadlines and are available at the Financial Aid Office.

APPLICATION AND INFORMATION

Candidates for admission should apply by May of their senior year in high school. The Admissions Office mails its first notice of acceptance on December 1, and early applicants have priority for housing and financial aid. Applicants must submit previous academic records, including a complete transcript of high school grades and rank in class; an admission application; a $40 nonrefundable fee; a written recommendation from the high school principal, a teacher, or a guidance counselor; and an official copy of the SAT I report.

SOUTHWEST TEXAS STATE UNIVERSITY

■ SAN MARCOS, TEXAS

THE UNIVERSITY

Southwest Texas State University (SWT) is a comprehensive public university committed to providing an intellectually stimulating and socially diverse climate for its graduate and undergraduate students. Serving approximately 22,500 students, SWT is the sixth-largest public university in the state. Chartered in 1899, SWT's original mission was to prepare Texas public school teachers. It became renowned for carrying out this mission, but today it does far more. The school has grown to become a multipurpose university offering programs in the Colleges of Applied Arts, Business, Fine Arts and Communication, Health Professions, Education, Liberal Arts, and Science and in the Graduate College. Since living on campus is required for most freshmen and sophomores, SWT students can choose from twenty residence halls (thirteen coed) on campus. Recent improvements to SWT's Residence Halls system include Ethernet-connected rooms, on-site computer labs (eight halls), designated 24-hour quiet floors, and improved food service. SWT is proud of its most famous alumnus, Lyndon Baines Johnson, the thirty-sixth president of the United States. LBJ remains the only U.S. president to have graduated from a Texas college.

For more information, students should contact:

Undergraduate Admissions Center
Southwest Texas State University
429 North Guadalupe
San Marcos, Texas 78666-5709
Telephone: 512-245-2340
E-mail: admissions@swt.edu
World Wide Web:
http://www.swt.edu

ACADEMIC PROGRAM

SWT operates on a two-semester calendar system with the fall semester beginning in late August and the spring semester in mid-January. SWT also offers two 5-week summer sessions. Students may earn college credit hours through the University's credit-by-examination program (AP, CLEP, IB, and departmental exams). The Honors Program offers interdisciplinary courses as part of a five-course requirement, which includes the honors thesis, for graduation in the program. Class size is limited to 17 students. Air Force and Army ROTC programs are also offered. At SWT, all students are required to complete a 52- to 55-hour general studies curriculum that serves as the common foundation for all majors. The requirement for a bachelor's degree is the successful completion of approximately 128 to 136 semester hours, depending on the degree plan.

FINANCIAL AID

Financial aid is provided in the form of grants, loans, work-study, and scholarships. Students should apply early for financial aid. The priority deadline for returning the Free Application for Federal Student Aid (FAFSA) form for the fall semester is April 1. To ensure an early response, students should apply as soon as possible after January 1. For an application or other financial aid materials, students should write to the Office of Student Financial Aid, 601 University Drive, San Marcos, Texas 78666-4602. Scholarships are awarded on a competitive basis and are available at SWT for qualified new and continuing admitted students. They range from $500 to $5000, with a variety of criteria, including academic achievement, proposed major, hometown, economic need, and athletic and performance-based talent. SWT's premier scholarship is the Mitte Foundation Scholarship Program. Each year, 25 entering freshmen are selected as Mitte Scholars and are awarded a $5000 renewable scholarship. To be considered, a prospective freshman must be a Commended Student, a Semifinalist, or a Finalist in the National Merit Competition; a valedictorian or salutatorian of his/her graduating class; or ranked in the top 5 percent of his/her graduating class. The scholarship application is available through the Offices of Admission and Student Financial Aid. The scholarship deadline for freshman candidates is December 1; March 1 for transfer candidates.

APPLICATION AND INFORMATION

To apply for freshman admission (0 to 29 hours completed), students must submit the Texas Common Application (sections A to E), an official high school transcript verifying class rank, an SAT I or ACT test score, a $25 application fee, and one essay of their choosing from section E of the Texas Common Application.

SPRINGFIELD COLLEGE

■ SPRINGFIELD, MASSACHUSETTS

THE COLLEGE

For more information, students should contact:

Office of Admissions
Springfield College
263 Alden Street
Box M
Springfield, Massachusetts 01109
Telephone: 413-748-3136
800-343-1257 (toll-free)
E-mail: admissions@spfldcol.edu
World Wide Web:
http://www.spfldcol.edu (online application available)

Originally founded as a school for training students for service in the YMCA, Springfield College is in its second century of preparing talented young men and women for careers in the human-helping professions. Just a few years after opening its doors to the first eighteen students in 1885, Springfield College could boast an international reputation as a pioneer in teaching and scholarship related to physical education, wellness, and the training of YMCA executives. Today, with a coed undergraduate and graduate body of 3,946, Springfield College is proud of its reputation in these fields and throughout the human helping professions. Springfield's 28,000 alumni work in almost sixty nations. Alumni have served in various capacities, such as a university president in China, initiators of the Olympic movement in Eastern European countries, and educational leaders in Central and South America. Wherever they work or live, Springfield alumni become vital links in a human chain that leads to impressive achievements. On-campus housing is guaranteed for four years, and students have the option of living in either a coeducational or a single-sex dormitory. After the junior year, students may elect to live in off-campus housing.

ACADEMIC PROGRAM

Humanics, the philosophy that has inspired Springfield College from its beginning, calls for educating the whole person—spirit, mind, and body. Undergraduate education at Springfield College is designed to promote an understanding of how these different aspects of ourselves work together in preparation for a life of leadership in service to others. In the classroom, the humanics approach translates to a careful balance of theory and practice—the daily application of an education that connects people to people. The College has a two-semester academic calendar. In order to successfully complete the Springfield College experience, students are required to accumulate a minimum of 130 credits toward graduation. These credits comprise major requirements, elective courses, and the All-College Requirements (which include studies in English, philosophy, social science, health, history, math, and natural science). Qualified students may also earn credit through the Advanced Placement Program and the College-Level Examination Program administered by the College Board.

FINANCIAL AID

Students who feel they do not have sufficient funds to pay for the total cost of their education are encouraged to apply for financial aid in the form of grants, loans, and student employment. All financial aid offered by Springfield College is based on need, intellectual promise, leadership, and character. Students who submit the Free Application for Federal Student Aid (FAFSA) and the College Scholarship Service Financial Aid PROFILE by the following dates are given full consideration for aid: January 30 for early decision candidates, March 15 for first-year students, and May 1 for transfer students. Students not eligible for financial aid may still be considered for institutional employment.

APPLICATION AND INFORMATION

Springfield College's rolling admissions program allows applicants to go into review with the Admissions Committee immediately upon completion of the application process. The deadline for submission of applications for the first-year class is April 1; however, students applying for the programs in physical therapy and athletic training must submit an application prior to December 1. Students applying for the physician assistant program must submit an application prior to January 15. Transfer students must file an application before August 1.

ST. AMBROSE UNIVERSITY

■ DAVENPORT, IOWA

THE UNIVERSITY

St. Ambrose offers all the resources needed for a successful college experience as well as a successful future. The student body of more than 3,000 (57 percent women, 43 percent men) consists of people differing in age and background. Students are encouraged to acquire intellectual awareness for lifelong self-education. St. Ambrose has been providing education of high quality for more than 100 years. Founded in 1882, the University was named for St. Ambrose, the fourth-century saint and bishop of Milan, who was a doctor, scholar, author, orator, and teacher. Classes first met in two rooms of a diocesan school. Today the campus covers nearly fifteen square blocks. There are twenty-six buildings, including historic Ambrose Hall. Extracurricular learning opportunities are available through a student newspaper, a campus radio station, cable TV facilities, athletic programs for men and women, honor societies, professional clubs, and other organizations.

For more information or to arrange a campus visit, students should contact:

Meg Flaherty
Director of Admissions
St. Ambrose University
518 West Locust Street
Davenport, Iowa 52805
Telephone: 319-333-6300
800-383-2627 (toll-free)
E-mail: mflahery@sau.edu
World Wide Web:
http://www.sau.edu

ACADEMIC PROGRAM

St. Ambrose is committed to combining the liberal arts with career preparation. The liberal arts component in each student's program consists of courses in six major divisions: arts, languages and literature, natural sciences, philosophy and theology, physical education, and social sciences and/or economics. Students are required to study history and literature. Individual courses are chosen by the student in consultation with an academic adviser. Students working toward a bachelor's degree in elected studies may develop their own major with the help of a faculty adviser. Courses are scheduled for morning, afternoon, and evening. St. Ambrose has a two-semester calendar. Fall semester examinations are taken before the Christmas break. A special term has been added between semesters for cultural tours of Europe, South America, the Mideast, and Asia, and students also take advantage of summer sessions. To be eligible for graduation, students must maintain an average grade of at least C (2.0) and must complete a minimum of 120 semester credits (usually forty courses) in the Bachelor of Arts, Bachelor of Science (but 135 semester credits for the Bachelor of Science in Industrial Engineering degree program), Bachelor of Arts in Special Studies, and Bachelor of Elected Studies degree programs or 136 semester credits in the Bachelor of Music and Bachelor of Music Education degree programs.

FINANCIAL AID

Federal, state, and University financial aid programs, scholarships, loans, grants, work-study and cooperative programs, and University employment opportunities are available. Federal programs include the Federal Pell Grant, Federal Supplemental Educational Opportunity Grant, Federal Work-Study, and Federal Stafford Loan programs. State programs are the Iowa Scholarship, Iowa PLUS Loan, and Iowa Tuition Grant programs. The priority deadline for financial aid applications is March 15 for the next fall semester. In addition to submitting an application for admission, applicants for financial aid must submit the Free Application for Federal Student Aid (FAFSA). This form is available in the offices of high school counselors or in the St. Ambrose University Financial Aid Office, or online at http://fafsa.ed.gov/.

APPLICATION AND INFORMATION

The completed application for admission, high school transcripts or equivalent credentials, and test scores should be sent to the Director of Admissions. Students also may apply online at http://www.sau.edu/administration/newstudent/admit-form.htm.

ST. FRANCIS COLLEGE

■ BROOKLYN HEIGHTS, NEW YORK

THE COLLEGE

Small, urban, friendly, and caring, St. Francis College was established in 1884 by the Franciscan Brothers of Brooklyn. Today St. Francis is an independent Catholic, Franciscan coeducational college that confers degrees in the arts and sciences and preprofessional disciplines. It is chartered by the Board of Regents of the University of the State of New York and accredited by the Middle States Association of Colleges and Schools. Throughout its long history, the College has offered an education of high quality that reflects its willingness to adapt to a constantly changing society and at the same time retain its tradition of liberal education. St. Francis has an average enrollment of 2,300 students, most of whom come from the Greater New York metropolitan area. The College also takes pride in its sizable international student population; almost eighty nations are represented. Young men and women from a variety of backgrounds feel at home and fit in at St. Francis. It is easy to make friends in the warm, trusting atmosphere that characterizes this college community.

For more information, students should contact:

Office of Admissions
St. Francis College
180 Remsen Street
Brooklyn Heights, New York 11201
Telephone: 718-489-5200
E-mail:
admissions@stfranciscollege.edu
World Wide Web:
http://www.stfranciscollege.edu

ACADEMIC PROGRAM

Each candidate for a bachelor's degree must complete a total of 128 credit hours and achieve a cumulative index of at least 2.0. In keeping with its liberal arts framework, the College requires all students to take a core curriculum of 42 credit hours in the humanities, social sciences, and natural sciences. For each major, each department specifies a number of required courses to give depth, unity, and direction to the course of study. After meeting these College and departmental requirements, students may select the remainder of their courses to suit their own needs and special interests. To enhance its degree programs, the College offers minors in a wide variety of subject areas. St. Francis has an ongoing commitment to increased academic quality and program excellence. The thriving honors program, which has small seminars and personal faculty mentors, has grown by 300 percent in the last two years. Students in the program participate in the annual conference of the National Collegiate Honors Council. Air Force and Army ROTC programs are also available on a cross-registration basis. The Franciscan tradition at St. Francis provides the basis for an atmosphere of personal integrity. Each student is treated as an individual and as an important part of the St. Francis College community. Student development is encouraged on all levels: academically, socially, and spiritually. Each student is given every opportunity to achieve personal and career success.

FINANCIAL AID

More than 80 percent of the students at St. Francis receive some form of financial aid. A comprehensive financial aid program enables the College to offer eligible students financial aid packages that consist of combinations of scholarships, grants, loans, and student employment. A typical student receives more than $7000 in scholarships, grants, and government support. Financial assistance is available from the TAP, Federal Pell Grant, and Federal Supplemental Educational Opportunity Grant Programs. Merit scholarships provided by the College can enhance government funds, and range from $1500 to full tuition. Students seeking assistance for the academic year must file the appropriate College forms by February 15 in order for their financial aid to be processed.

APPLICATION AND INFORMATION

While applications are accepted on a rolling basis, those received before April 1 receive priority of consideration.

ST. MARY'S UNIVERSITY OF SAN ANTONIO

■ SAN ANTONIO, TEXAS

THE UNIVERSITY

St. Mary's University is a private, coeducational institution administered by the Society of Mary (Marianists), a teaching order of Catholic priests and brothers. St. Mary's offers small classes and personalized instruction while integrating a value-centered core curriculum into each student's degree plan. Encompassing course work in the arts, humanities, social sciences, natural sciences, and quantitative disciplines, the core helps develop creativity, analytical skills, and an understanding of the human condition. A St. Mary's education challenges students to academic excellence and personal integrity, preparing them for success in their careers and their lives. Founded in 1852 on the banks of the San Antonio River, the University maintains a 135-acre campus in a residential area of northwest San Antonio. Modern and historic buildings combine to provide students with state-of-the-art learning facilities and comfortable living areas. St. Mary's University is an equal opportunity institution and an Affirmative Action employer.

For application forms and more information, students should contact:

Director of Admissions
St. Mary's University of San Antonio
One Camino Santa Maria
San Antonio, Texas 78228-8503
Telephone: 210-436-3126
800-FOR-STMU (toll-free)
Fax: 210-431-6742
E-mail: uadm@stmarytx.edu
World Wide Web:
http://www.stmarytx.edu

ACADEMIC PROGRAM

For the Bachelor of Arts degree, 128 hours of prescribed courses and electives must be completed. Requirements include English, natural science, mathematics, computer science, social science, theology, philosophy, foreign language, public speaking, and fine arts. Forty-five hours of study in residence are required, 12 of which should be in the major. Students seeking a Bachelor of Science degree are required to complete the same residence and core requirements as those for the Bachelor of Arts program, plus additional hours in their field of study. The Bachelor of Business Administration requires completion of 129 hours (132 hours for accounting); 45 hours must be completed in residence, and 12 of these must be in the major. Requirements include philosophy, English, social science, mathematics, natural science, economics, accounting, speech, fine arts, and theology. In addition to a liberal arts core of 66 hours, requirements for the Bachelor of Business Administration include 36 hours of a common body of business knowledge and 18–24 hours of upper-division course work in the major.

FINANCIAL AID

More than 80 percent of all St. Mary's students receive financial aid funds. A number of academic, music, and athletic scholarships are awarded on a non-need basis. All other financial aid awards are based solely on financial need, as determined by an analysis of the Free Application for Federal Student Aid (FAFSA). Presidential Scholarships may be awarded to incoming freshmen who are in the top 10 percent of their high school class and have an ACT composite score of at least 26 or an SAT I combined score of at least 1150. All students who have applied by March 1 are considered for scholarships. Students should mail the FAFSA by February 1 so that the processed document is on file in the Office of Financial Assistance by April 1, the financial assistance priority deadline.

APPLICATION AND INFORMATION

The application deadline is two weeks prior to registration; however, applicants interested in scholarship consideration must apply by March 1 of the year they intend to enroll. Students applying for financial aid and/or residence hall space on campus are strongly urged to submit all necessary forms and information prior to April 1. When all records are on file, the Admissions Committee will notify the student of its decision.

TEXAS TECH UNIVERSITY

■ LUBBOCK, TEXAS

THE UNIVERSITY

Texas Tech University, founded in 1923, is a residential state university with a population of 25,000 students who come from all fifty states and ninety-nine other countries. Students at Texas Tech have the opportunity to study from more than 300 graduate and undergraduate degree programs. The University is built around eight colleges: Agricultural Sciences and Natural Resources, Architecture, Arts and Sciences, Business Administration, Education, Engineering, Honors, and Human Sciences. A law school, which often boasts the highest number of students passing the bar exam in Texas, is conveniently located on the main campus. Also present is the Texas Tech University Health Sciences Center with its Schools of Medicine, Nursing, Pharmacy, and Allied Health. Academics are the top priority at Texas Tech, and students will find admission standards to be comparable with other state institutions. Texas Tech has become a leader in academic programs ranging from pioneering research with the U.S. Department of Agriculture to improving alternative fuel capabilities for the nation's leading auto makers. Wind engineering research at the University has led to the creation of shelters that withstand the nation's most deadly tornadoes.

For more information, students should contact:

Office of Admissions and School Relations
Texas Tech University
Box 45005
Lubbock, Texas 79409-5005
Telephone: 806-742-1480
Fax: 806-742-0980
E-mail: admissions@ttu.edu
World Wide Web:
http://www.texastech.edu

ACADEMIC PROGRAM

Texas Tech's undergraduate curriculum provides a broad range of courses in more than 150 majors. Recently, students at Texas Tech have seen an increase in competitive scholarships as well as the creation of the University's Honors College. Students accepted into the college will find unparalleled undergraduate research opportunities for students in all major disciplines. As a result, Texas Tech students are consistently awarded the prestigious Barry M. Goldwater Scholarship for science, engineering, and mathematics. In the 1997–98 academic year, Texas Tech led the state's public universities with two Goldwater Scholars; in the 1996–97 year, three students received the honor; and in the 1995–96 academic year, Texas Tech was the only university to have four students receive the Goldwater Scholarship.

FINANCIAL AID

A variety of financial aid is offered in the form of scholarships, grants, and loans. Competitive scholarships are awarded on academic merit, SAT or ACT scores, and class rank. More than 300 Presidential Endowed Scholarships are awarded to students each year. Need-based assistance is also available in the form of scholarships, government and private loans, grants, and work-study. Students' need for assistance is determined from the Free Application for Federal Student Aid (FAFSA). For a guide to scholarships and deadlines, students should contact the Office of Financial Aid (telephone: 806-742-3681).

APPLICATION AND INFORMATION

All students should submit the *State of Texas Common Application*, a high school transcript, SAT I or ACT test scores, and the $40 application fee.

TOWSON UNIVERSITY

■ TOWSON, MARYLAND

THE UNIVERSITY

Established in 1866, Towson University (TU) is a regional comprehensive university that offers degree programs in the liberal arts and sciences and preprofessional and professional areas of study. The University's beautiful 328-acre campus is located in the suburban community of Towson, Maryland, just 8 miles north of downtown Baltimore. Towson is nationally recognized for its programs in business, communications, computer information systems, education, fine arts, health professions, and women's studies. The University offers fifty-seven bachelor's degree programs, thirty master's degree programs, and two applied doctoral programs and emphasizes excellence in teaching and continued scholarly growth by faculty members.

For more information, students should contact:

Office of Admissions
Towson University
8000 York Road
Towson, Maryland 21252-0001
Telephone: 888-4TOWSON (toll-free)
World Wide Web:
http://www.towson.edu

ACADEMIC PROGRAM

The University follows the semester system, with spring and fall semesters, an optional January minimester, three 5-week summer sessions, and one 7-week summer session. The University's goal is to enrich lives by providing a strong liberal arts and sciences education for all students. The General Education Program (46 semester hours) is structured to develop intellectual skills that advance lifelong learning and to help students understand how the chief branches of knowledge investigate, present findings, and form conclusions about human experience and the natural world. The academic majors, whether in the arts and sciences, interdisciplinary fields, or applied and professional practices, are structured to promote liberal learning and explore the continuity and connectedness of experience as well as its factual specificity. In addition, the University takes pride in maintaining in its curriculum a high percentage of small-enrollment sections, which help promote student-centered learning, collaborative exchange, and individualized attention from the instructor. Faculty members offer extensive academic advising both to students in general education and to those enrolled within an academic major. The baccalaureate degree is earned by completing general education and major field requirements and earning a minimum of 120 semester hours of credit. Towson University offers more than 900 courses during the spring and fall semesters and the summer sessions. Students can attend full-time or part-time, and classes are offered during the day, in the evening, and on Saturday.

FINANCIAL AID

Approximately 50 percent of the full-time undergraduates at Towson University receive financial assistance of some kind. Assistance is available to eligible students through loans, grants, scholarships, and on- and off-campus employment. The University participates in major federal and state programs. In addition, the University offers academic and non-need scholarships for qualified students.

APPLICATION AND INFORMATION

Towson offers admission to qualified candidates on a continuous (rolling admissions) basis. Applicants should submit all appropriate application materials and required academic credentials by May 1 for fall admission and by December 1 for spring admission. Priority admission is granted beginning October 1 to those freshman applicants whose secondary school record indicates an overall 3.0 or above average in academic courses from grades 9 to 11 and whose combined SAT I score is at least 1100. It is the applicant's responsibility to forward all required forms and credentials (test scores, transcripts, and recommendations) to the Admissions Office in accordance with established deadlines. Incomplete applications or those improperly filled out are subject to cancellation. A nonrefundable $35 application fee or authorized fee-deferment form is required at the time the application is filed. Application forms are available online at the site listed below or by calling or writing to the Office of Admissions.

TULANE UNIVERSITY

■ NEW ORLEANS, LOUISIANA

THE UNIVERSITY

For more information, students should contact:

Richard Whiteside
Vice President for Enrollment Management and Institutional Research
Tulane University
210 Gibson Hall
6823 St. Charles Avenue
New Orleans, Louisiana 70118-5680
Telephone: 504-865-5731
800-873-9283 (toll-free)
Fax: 504-862-8715
E-mail: undergrad.admission@tulane.edu
World Wide Web: http://www.tulane.edu/Admission

Tulane University in New Orleans is known nationally and internationally for its teaching and research. At Tulane a student can get an international education in a European city without leaving America. One of a handful of national independent universities in the South, Tulane was founded in 1834 as the Medical College of Louisiana and reorganized as Tulane in 1884. The University is comprehensive by nature, with more than 11,000 students enrolled in eleven schools and colleges ranging from the liberal arts and sciences through a full spectrum of professional schools: law, medicine, business, engineering, architecture, social work, and public health and tropical medicine. Tulane's 5,366 full-time undergraduates choose from sixty majors in colleges of liberal arts and sciences, engineering, architecture, and business and may opt for joint-degree programs in Tulane's professional schools to earn undergraduate and graduate degrees in a shorter period of time. Tulane's distinctive arrangement of undergraduate schools gives every student the personal attention and teaching excellence of a small college while providing the interdisciplinary opportunities and research resources of a university that *U.S. News and World Report* ranks in the nation's top quartile. The average class size is 22. Senior faculty members are in the classroom at all levels, and the 12:1 student-teacher ratio ensures individual attention.

ACADEMIC PROGRAM

Tulane has a two-semester calendar, with first-semester exams held before the holiday break. Faculty advisers assist in course selection and in planning major requirements. The Paul Tulane College (for men) and Sophie Newcomb College (for women) offer programs leading to the B.A., B.S., and B.F.A. degrees. The School of Engineering emphasizes design, research, and laboratory experimentation for its Bachelor of Science degree programs in biomedical, chemical, civil, computer, electrical, environmental, and mechanical engineering as well as computer science. The School of Architecture takes advantage of its location in New Orleans, a fascinating living architecture laboratory, where about 300 students are enrolled in the five-year Bachelor/Master of Architecture program. The A. B. Freeman School of Business offers majors in accounting, business, finance, management, and marketing, leading to the Bachelor of Science in Management degree.

FINANCIAL AID

The University operates a comprehensive aid program; more than half of the students receive some form of financial aid. The average financial aid package (through scholarships, federal grants, loans, and work-study jobs) was about $20,000 for 1998–99. Need, determined by family financial information on the Free Application for Federal Student Aid and the PROFILE from the College Scholarship Service, establishes the appropriate amount of assistance. Merit, based on academic record, determines the proportion of Tulane-funded scholarships in the aid package. The University offers assistance to applicants who demonstrate financial need, and 90 percent of freshmen offered aid had their full need met. Deans' Honor Scholarships are offered each year to approximately 100 freshmen and cover tuition for the undergraduate career; other merit scholarships, including those for middle-income students, are also available. Tulane also gives at least thirty National Merit Scholarships to National Merit Finalists who have named Tulane as their first-choice college. Tulane offers creative financing options for families that do not qualify for traditional aid but need assistance in meeting costs.

UNIVERSITY OF MARYLAND, COLLEGE PARK

■ COLLEGE PARK, MARYLAND

THE UNIVERSITY

Throughout its 145-year history, the University of Maryland has served as a premier public research university while dedicating itself to providing the highest quality undergraduate education. Designated as the state's flagship university, Maryland attracts the best students and faculty members from across the nation and around the world. Students enroll at Maryland for the reputation and quality of its academic programs, the outstanding and diverse opportunities both in and outside the classroom, and the success of its alumni. Choosing from among more than 100 academic programs, 21,951 full-time and 2,687 part-time undergraduates are taught by a faculty of more than 1,900. Approximately 8,551 master's- and doctoral-level students are enrolled in the graduate school. About 75 percent of Maryland's undergraduates are state residents, with the remaining quarter coming from all fifty states, the District of Columbia, three territories, and 110 other countries. Maryland's diversity is one of its strongest assets, with 40 percent of students belonging to minority groups.

For application forms and further information about the University of Maryland, students should contact:

Office of Undergraduate Admissions
University of Maryland
College Park, Maryland 20742-5235
Telephone: 301-314-8385
800-422-5867 (toll-free)
301-314-9197 (TTY)
Fax: 301-314-9693
E-mail: um-admit@uga.umd.edu
World Wide Web:
http://www.maryland.edu

ACADEMIC PROGRAM

Undergraduate education at Maryland aims to provide students with a sense of identity and purpose, a concern for others, a sense of responsibility for the quality of life around them, a continuing eagerness for knowledge and understanding, and a foundation for a lifetime of personal enrichment and success. Within a research setting such as Maryland's, undergraduate students take strong, interdisciplinary courses taught by renowned researchers and scholars. Every undergraduate completes at least 120 credit hours to earn a degree, 46 of which are general education or CORE courses. The purpose of CORE is to help students achieve the intellectual integration and awareness they need to meet challenges in their personal, social, political, and professional lives. Although each program is unique, generally 30 to 36 credit hours are earned in the major field. Students may earn a double major, earn a certificate in a second area of study, and use AP and IB credit toward a degree.

FINANCIAL AID

An array of financial aid programs, including scholarships, grants, loans, and student employment opportunities, are available to undergraduates. To be considered for maximum need-based financial aid, students must submit the completed FAFSA to the FAFSA processor in time for receipt and acceptance by the University's February 15 priority financial aid deadline. The University proudly offers several merit scholarships for academically and creatively talented students; approximately $4 million per year is awarded. To be considered for most merit scholarships, an application for admission must be submitted by December 1. Last year, 68 percent of full-time students who applied for financial aid received it and were awarded an average of $7300.

APPLICATION AND INFORMATION

Applications for fall freshman admission are due by February 15. Students are encouraged to apply by Maryland's priority application deadline of December 1 for best consideration for admission, merit-based scholarships, and invitation to University Honors or College Park Scholars. The spring freshman application deadline is December 15. Applications for fall transfer admission are due by July 1; for the spring semester, December 1. International students and students with any foreign academic records have earlier deadlines.

UNIVERSITY OF MASSACHUSETTS DARTMOUTH

■ NORTH DARTMOUTH, MASSACHUSETTS

THE UNIVERSITY

The University of Massachusetts Dartmouth traces its roots to 1895 when the Massachusetts legislature chartered the New Bedford Textile School and the Bradford Durfee Textile School in Fall River. As the region's economic base shifted from textiles to more diverse manufacturing and service industries, the program of the colleges changed. Courses were developed to respond to the needs of new generations of students, stimulated by the clear economic and social advantages of a well-educated citizenry. In 1962 Southeastern Massachusetts Technological Institute (SMTI) was created, and in 1969, out of a need and a clear demand for a comprehensive public university, SMTI became Southeastern Massachusetts University. Then, in 1988, the Swain School of Design was merged with the University's College of Visual and Performing Arts. In 1991, a new University of Massachusetts system was created, which combined the Amherst and Boston campuses with the University of Lowell, Southeastern Massachusetts University, and the Medical Center in Worcester. Today, UMass Dartmouth provides educational programs, research, extension, and continuing education and cyber education in the liberal and creative arts and sciences and in the professions. A broad range of bachelor's and master's degrees and one program leading to a doctorate are offered.

For more information, students should contact:

Office of Admissions
UMass Dartmouth
285 Old Westport Road
North Dartmouth, Massachusetts
02747-2300
Telephone: 508-999-8605
Fax: 508-999-8755
E-mail: admissions@umassd.edu
World Wide Web:
http://explore.umassd.edu/

ACADEMIC PROGRAMS

The University operates on a two-semester calendar with the fall semester beginning the first week of September and concluding in mid-December and the spring semester beginning in late January and concluding in late May. A five-week intersession is offered between semesters. Summer term courses are offered in June, July, and early August. Undergraduate students usually enroll in four or five courses each semester, and a typical course earns 3 credits. An undergraduate degree requires a minimum of 120 credits (there are a few majors which require 135 credits); a student can complete degree requirements for a specified major within a department or an approved interdepartmental major (30 credits). Students must also complete requirements according to the degree being sought. Special learning opportunities include independent study, contract learning, and directed study; study abroad; study at a nearby university through cross-registration; and credit by examination. UMass Dartmouth is a member of SACHEM (Southeastern Association for Cooperation in Higher Education in Massachusetts). Students may also take initiative in finding other programs in addition to the exchange-agreement institutions. The College of Engineering provides majors in any of the engineering fields to gain work experience through cooperative education or internships.

FINANCIAL AID

Nearly all students are eligible for some type of financial aid. UMass Dartmouth awards financial aid based on federal, state, and institutional guidelines; students must submit the Free Application for Federal Student Aid (FAFSA). In determining need, the Financial Aid Services Office considers the total costs of attending the University (tuition, fees, books, room and board, the cost of commuting, and an allowance for living and personal expenses). The difference between total University cost and the estimate of expected family contribution is the amount that the financial aid staff considers to be financial need.

APPLICATION AND INFORMATION

Admissions is rolling except for early decision (freshman). The early decision deadline is November 15, with notification by December 15. All other decisions are made within three weeks of the completion of an application. For application forms and related information, students may call, write, or e-mail the admissions office.

UNIVERSITY OF MINNESOTA, CROOKSTON

■ CROOKSTON, MINNESOTA

THE UNIVERSITY

For more information, students should contact:

Office of Admissions and Financial Aid
170 Owen Hall
University of Minnesota, Crookston
2900 University Avenue
Crookston, Minnesota 56716-5001
Telephone: 218-281-8569
800-862-6466 (toll-free)
World Wide Web:
http://www.crk.umn.edu

Nationally recognized as a leader in information technology education, the University of Minnesota, Crookston (UMC), is part of the world-renowned University of Minnesota System. Founded in the late 1800s as a research station and then as a school of agriculture, UMC became a part of the University of Minnesota in 1965. Today, UMC is a four-year, public coeducational institution of 1,650 full- and part-time students. Its focus on polytechnic education, commitment to technology, and overall high-quality programs have captured national attention. UMC earned a ranking in *U.S. News & World Report*'s 2000 listing of America's Best Colleges and received other national notice in publications such as the *Washington Post* and the *Atlanta Journal-Constitution.* UMC is continuing to evolve to meet the educational demands of Minnesota and the world by developing a technology-rich, interactive living and learning community.

ACADEMIC PROGRAM

Students benefit from a personalized learning approach that centers on practical, real-world direct applications. The curriculum is learner driven, interactive, and supported with technology and involves collaboration among students, faculty members, and prospective employers. Students now enroll in classes at UMC on a semester calendar system. With UMC's emphasis on technology, teaching methods are dramatically different. Students find a classroom environment that is completely connected to technology, allowing students and instructors to gain access to information and exchange information more effectively. That classroom environment also includes the latest in computer- and video-presentation technology that is available to instructors.

FINANCIAL AID

Removing financial barriers to students' enrollment and success is the ultimate goal of UMC's financial aid program. UMC wishes to ensure that any qualified student who desires to pursue an education at UMC can obtain sufficient resources to do so. Accordingly, the University's Office of Admissions and Financial Aid administers a number of financial aid programs. A number of need-based funding sources are available for new, incoming freshman students as well as for transfer students—whether part-time or full-time. UMC also offers a variety of merit-based scholarships. For the need-based funding sources, a formula is used that factors the difference between UMC's estimate of what it will cost to attend UMC and the amount the federal and state governments expect students and their families to contribute to their education, based on information provided on the Free Application for Federal Student Aid (FAFSA). The specialty merit-based scholarships range in awards from $300 to a maximum of full tuition. Many are renewable.

APPLICATION AND INFORMATION

Applying for admission to the University of Minnesota, Crookston, involves some important preliminary steps. Freshman students should send high school transcripts, submit an application fee and a completed application form, and submit results from the ACT. Transfer students must send college transcripts and submit an application fee and completed application form. The application priority deadline is March 1. UMC has developed a helpful application guide called *Getting Started At UMC: Admissions Application Guide,* which is available for free by calling UMC's Office of Admissions and Financial Aid at the toll-free number listed below. Students can also visit UMC on the World Wide Web. Campus tours are available each weekday at 9 a.m., 10 a.m., and 1 p.m. Students are encouraged to call ahead two days before a planned visit.

UNIVERSITY OF THE ARTS Colleges of Art and Design, Performing Arts, and Media and Communication

■ PHILADELPHIA, PENNSYLVANIA

THE UNIVERSITY

The only university in the nation devoted exclusively to education and training in design and the visual, media, and performing arts, the University of the Arts (UArts) is located in the heart of Philadelphia's professional arts community. More than 2,000 students from forty states and thirty countries are enrolled in the undergraduate and graduate programs. Composed of the College of Art and Design, the College of Performing Arts, and the newly formed College of Media and Communication, the University offers intensive concentration within a major field as well as creative challenges in multidisciplinary exploration. Founded in 1876, the Philadelphia College of Art and Design is one of the country's leading art colleges, with nationally renowned design, fine arts, and crafts departments. Since its founding in 1870 as the Philadelphia Musical Academy, the Philadelphia College of Performing Arts has expanded to include a School of Dance, with programs in ballet, modern, jazz, and tap, as well as a School of Theater Arts, with acting and musical theater. In 1996, the University inaugurated the College of Media and Communication to prepare students for new careers in emerging interdisciplinary fields, such as multimedia design, electronic communication, information architecture, computer-generated design, electronic arts and performance, and writing for film/TV.

For additional information, students should contact:

Office of Admission
University of the Arts
320 South Broad Street
Philadelphia, Pennsylvania 19102
Telephone: 215-717-6030
800-616-ARTS (toll-free)

Fax: 215-717-6045
World Wide Web:
http://www.uarts.edu

ACADEMIC PROGRAM

Students are attracted to UArts because of its dynamic, creative atmosphere. Whether majoring in dance, sculpture, graphic design or multimedia, they enjoy interacting with their talented peers in other disciplines. The Freshman Project, the culmination of the required first-year writing course in liberal arts, provides the first opportunity for freshmen to work with students in other majors on a cross-disciplinary creative project. Students are further encouraged, to the extent that their busy schedules allow, to take free elective courses outside their chosen major. All students take a total of 42 credits in liberal arts, which gives them substantial exposure to humanities, social science, and science and provides them with the historical and theoretical framework of their major field.

FINANCIAL AID

More than 85 percent of the University's students received more than $22 million in scholarships and other financial aid in 1999–2000. The University funds presidential scholarships based on artistic potential and academic achievement. Financial aid is also available on the basis of the applicant's demonstrated financial need. Applicants must submit the Free Application for Federal Student Aid (FAFSA). February 15 is the suggested filing date. The University administers the following federal, campus-based student assistance programs: Federal Perkins Loans, Federal Work-Study Program awards, and Federal Supplemental Educational Opportunity Grants. Applicants who wish to be considered for scholarships should complete applications for admission and financial aid prior to March 31. Families from many different income levels can qualify for some type of financial assistance.

APPLICATION AND INFORMATION

In addition to submitting a portfolio or auditioning, applicants should submit their high school transcript, SAT I or ACT scores, one letter of recommendation, and a personal statement of purpose. The placement of transfer students is made after an evaluation of their portfolio or audition and a determination of their approved credits. The University of the Arts follows a system of rolling admission. All students are notified within two weeks of the receipt of all required materials. Students are encouraged to submit applications by March 15 for fall admission and December 1 for spring admission.

UNITED STATES MILITARY ACADEMY

■ WEST POINT, NEW YORK

THE ACADEMY

The United States Military Academy, the nation's oldest service academy, offers young men and women one of the most highly respected, quality education programs in the nation. West Point advocates the "whole person" concept. The Military Academy has, since its founding in 1802, provided the broad college education demanded by the military profession while maintaining a degree of academic specialization comparable to that of civilian universities. West Point's mission is to educate, train, and inspire the Corps of Cadets so that each graduate is a commissioned leader of character committed to the values of duty, honor, and country; professional growth throughout a career as an officer in the United States Army; and a lifetime of selfless service to the nation. The Military Academy provides its graduates with a solid foundation for intellectual and moral/ethical growth that is essential for successfully handling high-level responsibilities in national service. When students enter West Point, they are also beginning a profession. Upon graduation, cadets are commissioned as second lieutenants in the U.S. Army and are normally required to serve on active duty for at least five years. There are approximately 4,000 men and women enrolled at West Point. Cadets compete annually for Rhodes, Olmsted, Marshall, and Daedalian scholarships and for National Science Foundation, Truman, and Hertz graduate fellowships. West Pointers who remain in the Army are normally selected to attend civilian graduate schools in the United States or abroad between their fourth and tenth years of service.

For more information, students should contact:

Director of Admissions
United States Military Academy
606 Thayer Road
West Point, New York 10996-1797
Telephone: 845-938-4041
E-mail: admissions@www.usma.edu
World Wide Web:
http://www.usma.edu/Admissions

ACADEMIC PROGRAM

The academic program at the United States Military Academy provides cadets with a broad background in the arts and sciences and prepares them for future graduate study. The total curriculum is designed to develop essential character, competence, and intellectual ability in an officer. The core curriculum is the foundation of the academic program and provides a background in mathematics, physical science, engineering, humanities, behavioral science, and social science. The core curriculum, consisting of thirty-one courses, represents the essential broad base of knowledge necessary for success as a commissioned officer and supports the subsequent choice of an elected area of academic concentration. Courses are required in chemistry, economics, engineering design, engineering science, English, foreign languages, history, information technology, international relations, literature, mathematics, military history, military leadership, philosophy, physics, political science, and psychology. Classes at West Point are small, averaging 12 to 18 cadets per section. Cadets receive individual attention, and tutorial sessions are available upon request. Advanced and honors courses are available to cadets having exceptional ability. All cadets study military science and receive classroom instruction in the principles of small-unit tactics and leadership during a two-week intersession between the first and second semesters. Concentrated summer field training provides each cadet with the opportunity to learn and practice individual military skills and to apply the principles of tactics and leadership studied in the classroom.

FINANCIAL AID

There are no financial aid programs because expenses are paid by the U.S. government. Scholarship awards may be used by candidates to offset the cost of the initial deposit.

APPLICATION AND INFORMATION

Prospective candidates should write to Admissions, stating their interest in the Military Academy. Each applicant will be sent a Precandidate Questionnaire and prospectus, which outlines the West Point entrance requirements. All applicants are encouraged to start a candidate file at West Point at the end of their junior year or as soon thereafter as possible. This allows for early completion of all candidate file requirements.

VALPARAISO UNIVERSITY

■ VALPARAISO, INDIANA

THE UNIVERSITY

Valparaiso University was founded in 1859 by citizens of Valparaiso, Indiana, but its recent history dates from 1925, when it was purchased by the Lutheran University Association. Valpo is one of the nation's largest Lutheran-affiliated universities, yet it remains independent and is open to individuals of all faiths. The University's 3,700 students represent most states and more than forty countries; 66 percent come from outside of Indiana. Valparaiso University is a residential community in which activities outside the classroom form an important part of campus life; more than 66 percent of its students live on campus. Approximately 100 extracurricular and cocurricular programs are open to all, including the campus radio station, Pre-Medical Society, International Student Association, and various NCAA Division I intercollegiate and intramural sports teams for men and women. Major divisions at Valpo are the Colleges of Arts and Sciences, Business Administration, Engineering, and Nursing; Christ College (the honors college); the School of Law; and the Graduate Division.

For more information, students should contact:

Office of Admissions
Valparaiso University
Valparaiso, Indiana 46383-6493
Telephone: 219-464-5011
888-GO-VALPO (toll-free)
Fax: 219-464-6898
E-mail:
undergrad_admissions@valpo.edu
World Wide Web:
http://www.valpo.edu

ACADEMIC PROGRAM

Valparaiso University has a long tradition of combining professional colleges with a strong commitment to the values and broadening experiences of the liberal arts. The University helps students of varied interests and objectives to clarify their goals and explore new possibilities. Programs are structured to provide a solid base for exploration in various fields, while offering students the freedom to develop depth in a specific interest. This philosophy is extended through the upper division, where students have three options in completing a degree: an individual plan of study involving the major and complementary courses from related fields of study, the election of a second academic major in addition to the first, or a special minor in connection with the major. Career planning is aided through the professional programs and the University's Career Center. Many students also gain professional work experience in their chosen field before graduation by participating in the cooperative education program and internships.

FINANCIAL AID

Eighty-five percent of Valparaiso's students receive financial aid totaling more than $30 million. The University attempts to make up the difference between the cost of attending Valparaiso and the amount a family can afford, as determined by the Free Application for Federal Student Aid (FAFSA). Valpo aid is available in the form of scholarships, grants, loans, and campus employment, and often the aid is a package of these awards. Students are also encouraged to apply for the federal government's Federal Pell Grant, Federal Perkins Loan, and Federal Supplemental Educational Opportunity Grant, state scholarships where applicable, and the various private grants and scholarships that are available. Early application is recommended for Valpo assistance, since the awarding of aid begins in February of the year of enrollment.

APPLICATION AND INFORMATION

An applicant must complete a formal University admission application or the Common Application to be considered for admission. In addition, Valpo requires a high school transcript (complete through the junior year), ACT or SAT I scores, and college transcripts (when applicable). Valpo's nonbinding early action option allows applicants to submit their applications no later than November 1; these applications are reviewed by December 1. Regular admission notification begins on a rolling basis after December 1. For scholarship consideration, January 15 is the deadline for submitting a completed admission application.

VIRGINIA WESLEYAN COLLEGE

■ NORFOLK/VIRGINIA BEACH, VIRGINIA

THE COLLEGE

Virginia Wesleyan College is a community of scholars who strongly believe that education is the key to achieving life's goals and that the environment in which learning takes place makes all the difference in reaching these goals. The expansive 300-acre campus of this coeducational four-year college of liberal arts and sciences is designed to provide every opportunity to live and learn in an energetic, value-centered academic climate. Affiliated with the United Methodist Church and accredited by the Commission on Colleges of the Southern Association of Colleges and Schools, the College maintains a diverse student body and a low student-faculty ratio. Students come to Virginia Wesleyan from more than thirty states and twenty countries and indicate that they are attracted to the College primarily because of its size, the high quality of its academic program, its location, and its friendly atmosphere. Virginia Wesleyan seeks to attract students who can take advantage of the College's commitment to innovation, relevance, and involvement. Students who desire a strong, individualized academic program, who want the opportunity to study matters of concern to them in a key East Coast area, who have the ability to assume responsibility for their education, and who want to be involved with their colleagues and professors in creating a vital educational experience find a receptive environment.

For more information, students should contact:

Office of Admissions and Financial Aid
Virginia Wesleyan College
1584 Wesleyan Drive
Norfolk/Virginia Beach, Virginia 23502-5599
Telephone: 757-455-3208
800-737-8684 (toll-free)
Fax: 757-461-5238
E-mail: admissions@vwc.edu
World Wide Web: http://www.vwc.edu

ACADEMIC PROGRAM

The College offers a liberal arts curriculum that is designed to allow students considerable freedom in planning their own program yet also ensures that they acquire not only the breadth of knowledge traditionally emphasized in a liberal education but also a sound foundation in a specific field. A challenging honors program, in which students compete for full scholarships, is offered each year. The academic calendar is on the 4-1-4 plan, featuring a one-course term in January when students can take special-topic courses, traditional and interdisciplinary courses, and travel-study courses in the United States and abroad. They can also participate in off-campus internships, field study programs, independent study, and senior projects. The College offers study-abroad programs in a number of countries. A personalized faculty and peer advising system is the cornerstone of the College's transition programs. Freshman Seminar assists students in adjusting to college life, and the Senior Integrative Experience helps students progress to life after graduation.

FINANCIAL AID

The College believes that no student who wishes to attend Virginia Wesleyan College should be denied the opportunity because of limited financial resources. The director of financial aid is available to counsel students and their families regarding financial planning. In cases of demonstrated financial need, students may qualify for grants, low-interest loans, and work-study. Financial need is determined by an analysis of the Free Application for Federal Student Aid (FAFSA). March 1 is the mailing deadline for applying for financial assistance. The College also offers merit scholarships, without regard to need, to entering students with outstanding academic records. Scholarships ranging from $4000 to full comprehensive fees (over four years) are awarded to students based on their test scores, academic record, interviews, and essays. Leadership Scholarships from $4000 to $24,000 are available to students with demonstrated leadership abilities as evidenced through community service, extracurricular participation, and volunteerism.

WARREN WILSON COLLEGE

■ ASHEVILLE, NORTH CAROLINA

THE COLLEGE

Since its founding in 1894, Warren Wilson College has educated students with a unique triad of a strong liberal arts program, work for the College, and service to those in need, which makes Warren Wilson unlike any other college. Its 750 students come from forty-two states and twenty-five countries, creating a diverse and vibrant academic community. The academic program features a first-rate faculty that does all of the teaching and frequently participates in research with students. The average class size is small, and discussion is an important part of teaching. Fifteen majors are offered, with a commitment to quality in each program. Art, English, economics and business administration, education, biology, the nationally recognized environmental studies program, and outdoor leadership are the most popular majors. Students at Warren Wilson are integral to the day-to-day operation of the College. Each student works 15 hours a week at a job that is essential to running the school. This experience helps build student confidence (students learn that there is no job they cannot learn to do) and a strong sense of community at the College. Many juniors and seniors have work assignments that coincide with their major. Students receive a work fellowship in the amount of $2472 each year for the work they do. Service is also integral to the College's way of thinking. Warren Wilson is one of only a few colleges in the country that require student participation in community service for graduation. Service is offered to a wide range of individuals and agencies, nationally and abroad. Students must provide at least 20 hours of service each year to someone off campus.

For more information, students should contact:

Office of Admission
Warren Wilson College
701 Warren Wilson Road
Asheville, North Carolina 28815-9000
Telephone: 800-934-3536 (toll-free)
E-mail: admit@warren-wilson.edu
World Wide Web:
http://www.warren-wilson.edu

ACADEMIC PROGRAM

The goal of the degree program at Warren Wilson College is the completion of three well-designed areas of study. First, students are expected to complete a core of required courses based on the theme "ways of knowing." A student earns 4 credits in each of the ten core areas. Second, students must develop a strength in one or more disciplines. A minimum of 128 semester hours is required for the baccalaureate degree, including the core plus major hours. Finally, a student must demonstrate the ability to work effectively with others by participation in a work-and-service program. There is a required freshman seminar designed to provide new students the opportunity to explore various fields. A senior seminar, designed as a capstone experience, is required, as is a senior letter to evaluate the student's college experiences. All Warren Wilson students must demonstrate competence in writing and mathematics either through testing or by completing core courses. Each semester in the academic calendar is broken into two 8-week terms. A student traditionally takes only two courses per term (3 or 4 credit hours per course). There are two honors programs at Warren Wilson. One is in English and the other is in the Division of Natural Sciences, where honors can be earned in biology, chemistry, environmental studies, and mathematics.

FINANCIAL AID

Warren Wilson offers a comprehensive financial aid program that seeks to enroll students from all economic backgrounds. This is accomplished through a combination of work, loans, grants, entitlements, and scholarships to students who complete their file prior to May. Students and their families should file the FAFSA and the Warren Wilson Financial Aid Application to be considered for all possible funds.

WASHINGTON COLLEGE

■ CHESTERTOWN, MARYLAND

THE COLLEGE

Founded in 1782, Washington College is the tenth-oldest college in the United States. George Washington, for whom the College was named, was an early benefactor and member of the College's Board of Visitors and Governors. Today, the College is one of the few nationally recognized selective liberal arts institutions with an enrollment of fewer than 1,200 students. The intimacy of a small-college environment, the tradition of a challenging liberal arts curriculum, and the relaxed informality characteristic of the Chesapeake Bay region continue to exert their influence on the College and all who come to it.

Further information and application forms are available from:

Office of Admissions
Washington College
300 Washington Avenue
Chestertown, Maryland 21620-1197
Telephone: 410-778-7700
800-422-1782 (toll-free)
E-mail: adm.off@washcoll.edu
World Wide Web:
http://www.washcoll.edu

ACADEMIC PROGRAM

The College's four-course plan is intended to broaden and deepen a student's education by providing for the intensive study of a limited number of subjects and by encouraging individual responsibility for learning. General education requirements include two freshman seminars, two sophomore seminars, and eight semester courses chosen from the following categories: social science, natural science, the humanities, and formal studies (mathematics, computer science, music theory, logic, and foreign languages). Candidates for a degree must satisfactorily complete thirty-two semester courses and must fulfill the senior obligation (for example, a comprehensive examination or thesis). Washington College offers a nationally renowned creative writing program and awards the prestigious Sophie Kerr Prize every year to the graduating senior who shows the most promise for a career in literary endeavors. Successful scores (4 or 5) on Advanced Placement examinations can provide exemption from distribution requirements. With the aid of a faculty adviser, students can construct their own major fields of study in some areas or pursue independent study for course credit.

FINANCIAL AID

Washington College offers financial assistance to approximately 80 percent of its student body. Awards are based on need and academic performance. Financial aid includes scholarships, grants, loans, and jobs. The College participates in the Federal Perkins Loan Program, the Federal Stafford Student Loan Program, and the Federal Work-Study program. Federal Pell Grants and Federal Supplemental Educational Opportunity Grants are applicable to Washington College. In addition, financial assistance from the Maryland scholarship program and other state programs can be applied to expenses at the College. Members of the National Honor Society and Cum Laude Society who are admitted to Washington College are awarded $40,000 academic scholarships ($10,000 annually for four years). Other academic scholarships ranging in value from $2500 to $10,000 are offered without regard to financial need. To be eligible for financial assistance, applicants should file the FAFSA by February 15. An application for admission, with all supporting credentials, should be received by February 15 to establish eligibility. Students interested in Federal Pell Grant assistance or in-state scholarship programs must apply directly to the program concerned.

APPLICATION AND INFORMATION

The application, a $40 fee, the high school transcript (and college transcript, for transfer applicants), scores on the SAT I or ACT, and two teacher recommendations are required. Applications for early decision must be received by November 15, and candidates are notified of the admission decision by December 15. For regular admission, forms must be submitted prior to February 15. Regular-decision candidates are notified of the admission decision on a rolling basis between January 15 and April 1. Applicants for financial assistance must complete the procedures outlined under Financial Aid.

WEBBER COLLEGE

■ BABSON PARK, FLORIDA

THE COLLEGE

Webber College was founded in 1927 by Roger Babson, who was an internationally known economist in the early 1900s. The four-year independent coeducational college is located on a beautiful 110-acre campus along the shoreline of Lake Caloosa, 45 minutes from Disney World, Cypress Gardens, and many other attractions. Webber is accredited by the Southern Association of Colleges and Schools. Built on a strong tradition that sets it apart, the College exemplifies integrity, high standards, and achievement. Webber College provides an environment that encourages success through academic excellence and hard work. About 240 men and 200 women are enrolled as undergraduates at Webber. Sixty percent of them are from Florida; the other 40 percent represent seventeen states and thirty-eight different countries.

For application forms, catalogs, and additional information, students should contact:

Director of Admissions
Webber College
1201 North Scenic Highway
P.O. Box 96
Babson Park, Florida 33827-9990

Telephone: 863-638-1431
E-mail: admissions@webber.edu
World Wide Web:
http://www.webber.edu

ACADEMIC PROGRAM

The school operates on the semester system with two 15-week semesters, a six-week Summer Term A, and a six-week Summer Term B. The College requires the completion of 60 credit hours for the Associate of Science degree and 120 credit hours for the Bachelor of Science degree with a minimum grade point average of 2.0. The average course load is 15 hours per semester. Students in the Bachelor of Science degree program are required to complete approximately 30 hours in the major, 36 hours in the business core, 36 hours in the general education core, and 18 hours of tailored electives. Students in the Associate of Science degree program are required to complete 27 hours in the business core, 18 hours in the general education core, and 15 hours in the major and tailored elective. The Bachelor of Science degree in general business studies requires the completion of 45 hours in the general business studies core, 39 hours in the general education core, and 36 hours of tailored electives. All students must complete 30 of the last 33 hours at Webber College to receive a degree.

FINANCIAL AID

The Student Financial Aid Department offers students its counsel and assistance in meeting their educational expenses. Aid is awarded on the basis of an applicant's need, academic performance, and promise. Approximately 70 percent of the students at Webber College receive financial assistance. To demonstrate need, applicants are required to file the Free Application for Federal Student Aid (FAFSA). Various types of aid, such as scholarships, grants, loans, and Federal Work-Study awards, are used to meet student needs. A limited number of no-need scholarships are available; these awards are based on academic performance, on community and college service, or on athletic ability in basketball, tennis, volleyball, golf, soccer, softball, and cross-country. Applicants for aid must reapply each year. Webber College participates in the Federal Perkins Loan, Federal Supplemental Educational Opportunity Grant, and Federal Work-Study programs. All applicants are expected to apply for any entitlement grant for which they are eligible, such as the Federal Pell Grant; Florida residents must apply for a Florida Student Assistance Grant and the Florida Tuition Voucher Program. Federal Stafford Student Loans are also available. Financial aid applicants should submit their requests and forms before April 1 in order to be eligible for certain financial aid programs.

APPLICATION AND INFORMATION

An application is ready for consideration by the Admissions Committee when it has been received with a $35 application fee, the required test scores and references, and transcripts from each school attended. The College uses a system of rolling admissions. It is recommended that applications be submitted as early as possible, since on-campus housing is limited. (Freshmen are required to live in the dormitory unless they reside with a parent, guardian, or spouse.)

WELLS COLLEGE

■ AURORA, NEW YORK

THE COLLEGE

Wells College, founded in 1868, is proud to be the second institution in the country to award the baccalaureate degree to women. Its founder, Henry Wells, who built his fortune with the creation of the Wells Fargo Express, believed that women would play a vital role in the future of America. With an enrollment of 462 students, Wells students do not sit quietly among rows of neatly lined desks; instead, they join their classmates and professors around seminar tables where they are expected to contribute their ideas. Wells faculty members are widely published and respected in their fields, but teaching is their first priority. Academic opportunities include independent and interdisciplinary study, internships, and study-abroad programs. In addition, a campus newspaper, several musical and drama groups, a literary magazine and book arts center, environmental and political organizations, and other organizations provide important opportunities for student involvement. A full program of cultural events, symposia, and lectures enhances the academic and social life of the College. Students interested in athletics may participate on intercollegiate teams in field hockey, lacrosse, soccer, swimming, and tennis.

For more information about Wells College or to schedule a campus visit, students should contact:

Admissions Office
Wells College
Aurora, New York 13026
Telephone: 800-952-9355 (toll-free)

E-mail: admissions@wells.edu
World Wide Web:
http://www.wells.edu

ACADEMIC PROGRAM

The academic philosophy at Wells is firmly rooted in the liberal arts. The College is organized into four academic divisions: the humanities, natural and mathematical sciences, social sciences, and the arts, but faculty members in all divisions work together to produce a curriculum that recognizes connections between subject areas and fits many pieces together, just as they fit together in life. Students take two multidisciplinary courses during their first year that have an emphasis on the scope and breadth of human inquiry and creative synthesis necessary for leadership in a wide range of areas. Wells 101, Approaches to the Liberal Arts, is a shared experience for first-year students in the fall that incorporates a multidisciplinary approach to familiarize students with the liberal arts. Writing, critical thinking, discussion, collaborative learning, respect for diversity, and attendance at campus cultural events are integral to the course. Wells 102, the first-year seminar, consists of various topics that continue to develop writing and other skills that are important to students in their academic careers. Wells students are traditionally required to complete a thesis or project during the senior year. While the core curriculum provides a shared academic experience for students, the senior thesis provides a student with the opportunity to complete a thoughtful, in-depth analysis of a topic of the student's choosing.

FINANCIAL AID

Approximately 85 percent of Wells students receive financial aid packaged in the form of grants, scholarships, and loans.

APPLICATION AND INFORMATION

Applications should be received early in the senior year of high school and not later than March 1 of the year in which entrance is desired. Applications from early decision and early action candidates must be received by December 15. Transfer applications are reviewed on a rolling basis. Transfer students are eligible for merit scholarships and financial aid. A campus visit is highly recommended for prospective students. Typically, the visit includes a guided tour of the Wells College campus and facilities, overnight accommodations in the residence halls, a personal interview, and the option of attending classes. Appointments with faculty members and financial aid representatives are also available.

WENTWORTH INSTITUTE OF TECHNOLOGY

■ BOSTON, MASSACHUSETTS

THE INSTITUTE

Wentworth Institute of Technology was founded in 1904 to provide education in the mechanical arts. Today, it is one of the nation's leading technical institutes, offering study in a variety of disciplines. Wentworth has a current undergraduate day enrollment of approximately 3,000 men and women (2,400 full-time) and graduates more engineering technicians and technologists each year than any other college in the United States. The technical education acquired at Wentworth enables graduates to assume creative and responsible careers in business and industry. Wentworth is located on a 35-acre campus on Huntington Avenue in Boston.

For more information, students should contact:

Admissions Office
Wentworth Institute of Technology
550 Huntington Avenue
Boston, Massachusetts 02115
Telephone: 617-989-4000
800-556-0610 (toll-free)
Fax: 617-989-4010
E-mail: admissions@wit.edu
World Wide Web: http://www.wit.edu

ACADEMIC PROGRAM

At Wentworth Institute of Technology, college-level study in technological fundamentals and principles is combined with appropriate laboratory, field, and studio experience. Students apply theory to practical problems, and they acquire skills and techniques by using, operating, and controlling equipment and instruments particular to their area of specialization. In addition, study in the social sciences and humanities provides a balanced understanding of the world in which graduates work. Wentworth's programs of study are more practical than theoretical in approach, and the Institute's academic requirements demand extensive time and effort. During the first two years of study in a degree program at Wentworth, students lay the foundation for more advanced study in the third and fourth (and fifth, where applicable) years. While nearly all majors allow continuous study from the freshman through the senior year, the architecture major requires a petition for acceptance to the baccalaureate program during the sophomore year. All bachelor's degree programs are conducted as cooperative (co-op) education programs: upon entering their third year, students alternate semesters of academic study at Wentworth with semester-long periods of employment in industry. Two semesters of co-op employment are required; one additional (summer) semester of co-op is optional. Both students and the companies that hire them are enthusiastic about the co-op program and agree that it is a mutually valuable experience.

FINANCIAL AID

Scholarships are available to students who demonstrate need and academic promise. Merit scholarships are also available. Wentworth also provides federal and state financial assistance, such as Federal Pell and Federal Supplemental Educational Opportunity Grants, Federal Perkins Loans, Federal Work-Study awards, Gilbert Matching Grants, and Massachusetts No-Interest Loans to students with financial need in accordance with federal and state guidelines. Wentworth participates in the Federal Direct Lending program. As a result, students are eligible to borrow under the Federal Direct Stafford Loan program and parents may borrow under the Federal Direct PLUS program. Individuals participating in these programs borrow money directly from the federal government rather than through lending institutions. In addition to these need-based programs, Wentworth also participates in the MEFA loan program sponsored by the Massachusetts Educational Financing Authority. Wentworth offers several payment options through payment plans and alternative loan financing. To apply for financial aid, new students should complete the Free Application for Federal Student Aid (FAFSA) by March 1. Applications received after this date will be considered as funds allow.

APPLICATION AND INFORMATION

Students are admitted to Wentworth for September and January enrollment. The priority application deadline for the fall semester is May 1; for the spring, the deadline is December 1. Notification of admission is made on a rolling basis.

WESTERN ILLINOIS UNIVERSITY

■ MACOMB, ILLINOIS

THE UNIVERSITY

The campus of Western Illinois University (WIU) extends over 1,464 acres and includes fifty-two buildings. The residence halls on campus provide for a variety of lifestyles and house more than half of the 13,089 students at the University. Single and double rooms, study floors, nonsmoking rooms, and academic major areas are just a few examples of residence options. The University Union is the center of campus activities and includes a food court, a bookstore, bowling alleys, an ice-cream parlor, meeting rooms, an area for billiards, and lounge areas. More than 250 student organizations offer a variety of cocurricular activities to supplement formal classroom education. Cultural programs reflecting both local and national interests are on the calendar several evenings each week.

For more information, students should contact:

Admissions Office
Sherman Hall 115
Western Illinois University
1 University Circle
Macomb, Illinois 61455-1390
Telephone: 309-298-3157
877-PICKWIU (toll-free)
World Wide Web:
http://www.wiu.edu

ACADEMIC PROGRAM

It is the philosophy of the University that a broad general education should be an integral part of every degree program. Thus, approximately one third of the degree requirements involve study and the development of fundamental skills in the arts and sciences. The remainder of the program is devoted to either a comprehensive major or a major/minor plus general electives. Credit is awarded for acceptable scores on CLEP general and subject examinations and on the College Board's Advanced Placement examinations in English, foreign languages, history, and mathematics. Proficiency examinations are administered on campus through specific departments. Special educational opportunities for students with high aptitude and superior ability are offered in all colleges at WIU through the honors college. Western Illinois University is on the semester system; the fall semester closes before the Christmas holidays and the spring semester closes in mid-May. Two 4-week summer sessions run concurrently with one 8-week summer session from mid-June to early August. Western offers a four-year and a two-year program in the study of military science through Army ROTC. Successful completion of the program and requirements for the baccalaureate degree leads to a commission as a second lieutenant in the Army.

FINANCIAL AID

During the 1999–2000 academic year, 10,604 WIU undergraduate students received financial aid from funds totaling $54 million. Financial aid is available through state and federal programs for full- or part-time WIU students. Students should use the Free Application for Federal Student Aid (FAFSA) to apply for the following state and federal programs: Federal Pell Grant, Federal Supplemental Educational Opportunity Grant, Federal Perkins Loan, Federal Stafford Student Loan, Federal Work-Study Program, and Illinois Monetary Award Program (MAP). Students should begin the process by completing their federal income tax return as early as possible to provide accurate information on the FAFSA and then filing the FAFSA as soon as possible after January 1. Many student jobs are available in areas such as secretarial work, food service, and building and grounds maintenance. WIU also awards talent grants and academic scholarships. Talent grants are offered in men's and women's athletics, music, art, theater, agriculture, student services, and debate. More than 1,000 students annually receive scholarships through the WIU Foundation. The majority of scholarships reward high academic potential and achievement, while others consider hometown, academic interest, or financial need. To receive an application for WIU scholarship opportunities, students should contact the WIU Scholarship Office.

WESTERN MARYLAND COLLEGE

■ WESTMINSTER, MARYLAND

THE COLLEGE

Western Maryland College (WMC) provides an ideal location for learning that brings together students from twenty-three states and nineteen countries. Its picturesque campus, including a nine-hole golf course, is situated on a hilltop in historic Westminster, just a short drive from two of the nation's major metropolitan centers, Baltimore and Washington, D.C. Western Maryland was one of the first coeducational colleges in the nation and has been both innovative and independent since its founding in 1867. The tradition of liberal arts studies rests comfortably at Western Maryland, which has exemplary teaching, both at the undergraduate and graduate levels, as its central mission. Faculty members are engaged in research and professional writing, are involved at the highest levels of their respective professions, and are sought after as consultants in many spheres, but their primary mission is teaching. The enrollment of 1,600 undergraduates enables WMC to care about students in a personal way, to provide individual guidance, and to be responsive to the needs of students. Graduates leave Western Maryland enriched not just because of their classwork but also because of their meaningful interactions with one another. A flexible liberal arts curriculum stresses the ability to think critically and creatively, to act humanely and responsibly, and to be expressive.

For more information, students should contact:

M. Martha O'Connell, Dean of Admissions
Western Maryland College
2 College Hill
Westminster, Maryland 21157-4390
Telephone: 410-857-2230
800-638-5005 (Voice/TDD) (toll-free)
E-mail: admissio@ns1.wmc.car.md.us
World Wide Web: http://www.wmdc.edu

ACADEMIC PROGRAM

WMC's flexible curriculum enables students to acquire a broad base of knowledge in the areas of humanities, natural sciences and mathematics, and social sciences and to pursue in-depth learning in one or more of the sixty fields of study. The program links wide-ranging educational experiences with strong career preparation through an extensive internship program. A total of 128 credit hours is required for graduation. First-year–student seminars provide students with a unique opportunity to become better prepared for many facets of college life. Limited to 15 students, these courses on a variety of topics emphasize important skills—writing, oral presentation, study skills, critical thinking, and time management.

FINANCIAL AID

WMC supports a program of financial aid to eligible students on the basis of both need and merit. Nearly 80 percent of WMC students receive financial assistance. Students who have been accepted by the College and can demonstrate financial need as required by the federal government may be eligible for assistance in the form of scholarships, grants, loans, and opportunities for student employment. Typically an award is a package of these four resources, tailored to the student's needs. Academic scholarships covering partial to full tuition are available for qualified students based on their academic record, SAT I or ACT scores, and extracurricular involvement. First-year students should apply by February 1; transfer scholarships are competitive, and preference is given to students who apply before March 15. The College also offers partial and full ROTC scholarships. To apply, students should file the Free Application for Federal Student Aid (FAFSA) with the federal processor and apply for admission to WMC. Students also must submit a WMC financial aid application, which is available upon request.

APPLICATION AND INFORMATION

Deadlines for receiving completed applications are December 1 for early action, February 1 for academic scholarship consideration, and March 15 for regular admission. Applications from transfer students are accepted through the summer.

WESTERN MICHIGAN UNIVERSITY

■ KALAMAZOO, MICHIGAN

THE UNIVERSITY

Western Michigan University is one of the nation's leading midsized universities, making a difference in the world through a commitment to academic excellence and public service. *U.S. News & World Report* has ranked the University "in the major leagues of American higher education" as one of the country's 100 top national universities. WMU is one of only ninety-one public universities in the nation—and only four in Michigan—to have a chapter of Phi Beta Kappa, the nation's premier honor society. Founded in 1903, WMU has seven degree-granting colleges—Arts and Sciences, Aviation, the Haworth College of Business, Education, Engineering and Applied Sciences, Fine Arts, and Health and Human Services—as well as the Graduate College and Lee Honors College. The University offers 254 academic programs, more than 160 of them at the undergraduate level. Major factors in WMU's success include promotion of out-of-class learning and creation of cutting-edge instructional facilities. More than $320 million has been spent on new buildings and state-of-the-art equipment over the past decade, including $50 million in modern student recreation facilities.

For more information, students should contact:

Office of Admissions and Orientation
Western Michigan University
1903 West Michigan Avenue
Kalamazoo, Michigan 49008–5720
Telephone: 616-387–2000
800-400-4WMU (toll-free)
World Wide Web:
http://www.wmich.edu

ACADEMIC PROGRAM

WMU offers undergraduate students a rich blend of academic majors and minors, as well as its general education program. This program assures that students graduate with proficiencies and perspectives they need to succeed in the next century. The University Curriculum Program is for students who are undecided about a major and wish to explore WMU's academic offerings. Last fall, more than 2,100 students enrolled in the University Curriculum Program, which won a national award for outstanding academic advising. The Lee Honors College provides undergraduates with a unique living/learning environment offering the intimacy of a small college with the resources of a major university.

FINANCIAL AID

Last year, more than 18,000 students received financial assistance totaling nearly $123 million. There are three basic types of financial aid: merit-based programs, need-based programs, and student employment. Merit-based programs include the Medallion Scholarship and the Cultural Diversity Scholarship Programs, the University's two most honored scholarships for entering freshmen. Awards range from $4800 to $32,000 over four years. Other scholarships and awards include the Army ROTC awards, Michigan National Guard awards, the Award for National Merit Scholarships, and many other sponsored and departmental scholarships for new and currently enrolled students. Merit-based scholarships also are available to community college transfer students, ranging in value from $1000 to $6000. Need-based loans, grants, college work-study, and other aid options are provided for students who demonstrate particular financial need. To be considered, students should complete the Free Application for Federal Student Aid. The student employment option reflects research indicating that students who work part-time are more likely to graduate than students who do not work at all. About 40 percent of WMU's students work while in school, and more than 1,200 jobs are offered through the college work-study program. WMU provides a tuition payment plan through Academic Management Services (AMS) and Tuition Management Systems. This allows parents and students to pay college costs in monthly installments. No interest is charged for these services, which may be renewed annually for $45. Students should contact AMS at 800–556–6684 or Tuition Management Systems at 800–722–4867 for more information.

WILLIAM PATERSON UNIVERSITY OF NEW JERSEY

■ WAYNE, NEW JERSEY

THE UNIVERSITY

Since its founding in 1855, William Paterson University has grown into a comprehensive state institution whose programs reflect the area's need for challenging, affordable educational options. Ideally midsized (the total enrollment is 9,945, of whom 8,454 are degree-seeking undergraduates), William Paterson offers a wider variety of academic programs than smaller universities, yet provides students with a more personalized atmosphere than larger institutions. Once the site of the family estate of Garret Hobart, the twenty-fourth vice president of the United States, William Paterson's 370-acre spacious campus, which has wooded areas and waterfalls, offers an environment in which students may develop both intellectually and socially. Although the majority of the University's students come from the New Jersey and New York vicinity, some international and out-of-state students enroll each year. Twenty-seven percent of the undergraduates reside on campus in residence halls or apartment-style facilities, which accommodate 2,267 students. In general, on-campus housing is offered on a first-come, first-served basis.

For more information, students should contact:

Office of Admissions
William Paterson University of New Jersey
Wayne, New Jersey 07470
Telephone: 973-720-2125
877-WPU-EXCEL (toll-free)
World Wide Web:
http://www.wpunj.edu

ACADEMIC PROGRAM

Students must complete a minimum of 128 credits to earn a baccalaureate degree. Degree programs include a 60-credit general education requirement, 30–60 credits in a major, and 20–40 in elective courses. (In specialized degree programs, such as the B.F.A. and the B.M., general education and major course requirements may differ.) Students uncertain of which career path to follow may take advantage of advisement and counseling programs. In addition, the general education requirements enable students to take up to 60 credits before declaring a major, so that they can acquire a basic understanding of all major fields of knowledge before having to choose a specific area. Diagnostic testing and career seminars, provided by the Career Development Office, also ensure that students receive the guidance necessary to make wise course selections and career decisions. William Paterson offers a variety of special programs. Honors programs are designed for those ambitious and well-qualified students who want to add a challenging dimension to their major. Currently, there are seven honors programs—in biopsychology, cognitive sciences, humanities, life science and environmental ethics, music, nursing, and performance studies. Students who have completed the premedical program in the College of Science and Health have consistently been accepted by American medical schools during the last ten years. Students who successfully complete Advanced Placement tests and/or College-Level Examination Program tests may receive credit for acceptable scores. In addition, credit may be awarded for military training and experience. William Paterson University operates on a two-semester and two-summer-session system.

FINANCIAL AID

Financial aid is available through a number of federal and state grant, loan, scholarship, and work-study programs. To apply for need-based aid, students must file the Free Application for Federal Student Aid (FAFSA) with the United States Department of Education by the priority date of April 1. Both the University and the Alumni Association award a number of competitive scholarships, based solely on academic merit, to entering freshmen. They are the Scholarships for Academic Excellence, scholarships for African-American and Hispanic students, and Trustee and Presidential Scholarships. Academic Achievement Scholarships are awarded only on a competitive basis to continuing students.

WOODBURY UNIVERSITY

■ BURBANK, CALIFORNIA

THE UNIVERSITY

Woodbury University offers students practical, applied education; high academic standards; and small classes. The University is an accredited, independent, nonprofit, coeducational, nonsectarian institution. Students attend Woodbury because of its specialization in the areas of architecture, business, computers, professional design, and arts and sciences. Also offered is a Master of Business Administration program. The carefully designed curricula at Woodbury give students hands-on experience in their majors in addition to an effective general education. Woodbury maintains small classes to ensure individual student attention. The University presents a variety of opportunities for all students to join cultural, social, and professional organizations, both on and off campus. The Office of Student Services at Woodbury helps meet students' needs through career planning and job placement workshops; educational, cultural, social, and recreational programs; the sponsorship of various student groups; and special services for international students. The career services office provides Woodbury students and alumni with lifetime employment assistance. Woodbury's 22-acre campus in Burbank provides students with such on-campus amenities as a swimming pool, gymnasium, residence halls, an athletic field, and food services, all situated on beautifully landscaped grounds. Founded in 1884, Woodbury's primary mission is to provide programs requisite for success and leadership and to encourage each person's creativity. The University is accredited by the Senior Commission of the Western Association of Schools and Colleges and is approved by the Postsecondary Commission, California Department of Education.

For more information, students should contact:

Office of Admission
Woodbury University
7500 Glenoaks Boulevard
Burbank, California 91510-7846
Telephone: 818-767-0888, ext. 221
800-784-WOOD (toll-free)
E-mail:
admissions@vaxb.woodbury.edu
World Wide Web:
http://www.woodbury.edu

ACADEMIC PROGRAM

The academic programs at Woodbury are designed to provide students with the higher education necessary for success and leadership in their chosen fields. The principal emphasis is on relevance of subject matter and personalized instruction, complemented by a strong focus on general education. The academic calendar is based on the semester system. The number of elective units varies depending on the major. To encourage the achievement of academic excellence, Woodbury University recognizes students who demonstrate the initiative and sense of responsibility to excel. Such superior performance is recognized with special awards.

FINANCIAL AID

Assisting students who lack adequate financial resources to attend Woodbury is a primary concern of the University. Various sources of financial aid are available to help meet education costs. Eligible students generally are awarded a financial aid package consisting of a combination of available funds. Financial aid for eligible U.S. citizens and permanent residents includes Federal Pell Grants, California Grants A and B for California residents, Federal Family Educational Loans, veterans' educational benefits, Federal Supplemental Educational Opportunity Grants, Federal Work-Study awards, Federal Perkins Loans, local scholarships, and Woodbury grants. The University offers financial aid and counseling, as well as part-time employment and full-time placement services. Classes are scheduled to permit students to work part-time, usually in the area of their major interest, so that they may not only meet financial needs but also gain excellent experience.

APPLICATION AND INFORMATION

Applications are accepted throughout the year for entrance in the fall, spring, and summer terms. Freshman applicants are encouraged to apply before the priority date, March 1. The priority application deadline for transfer students is April 15.

INDEX

of Colleges and Universities

The index lists the colleges and universities in this almanac alphabetically. Page numbers refer to each college's profile; page numbers in **bold-faced** text refer to full-page descriptions.

INDEX OF COLLEGES AND UNIVERSITIES

NOTES

NOTES

NOTES

NOTES